Philosophic Classics, Third Edition

FROM PLATO TO DERRIDA

FORREST E. BAIRD, EDITOR
Whitworth College

WALTER KAUFMANN
Late, of Princeton University

Prentice Hall, Upper Saddle River, New Jersey 07458

Library of Congress Cataloging-in-Publication Data

Philosophic classics : From Plato to Derrida / Forrest E. Baird,
   editor, Walter Kaufmann [editor].—3rd ed.
     p. cm.
   Includes bibliographical references.
   ISBN 0–13–021532–5
    1. Philosophy. I. Baird, Forrest E. II. Kaufmann, Walter
Arnold.
   B72.P45 2000
   100—dc21   98–50173
                                   CIP

Editor-in-chief: Charlyce Jones-Owen
Acquisitions editor: Karita France
Editorial assistant: Jennifer Ackerman
Production liaison: Fran Russello
Editorial/production supervision:
   Bruce Hobart (Pine Tree Composition)
Prepress and manufacturing buyer:
   Tricia Kenny
Cover director: Jayne Conte
Cover photo: Painting—Renaissance—16th c. The School of Athens. One of the murals painted
   by Raffael (Rafaello Santi) (1483–1520) for Pope Julius II. In the center background, Plato
   discourses with Aristotle.
Marketing manager: Ilse Wolfe

This book was set in 10/12 Times Roman by Pine Tree Composition, Inc.,
and was printed and bound by R.R. Donnelley & Sons Company.
The cover was printed by Phoenix Color Corp.

Printed in the United States of America

10 9 8 7 6 5 4 3 2 1

ISBN 0-13-021532-5

Prentice-Hall International (UK) Limited, *London*
Prentice-Hall of Australia Pty. Limited, *Sydney*
Prentice-Hall Canada, Inc., *Toronto*
Prentice-Hall Hispanoamericana, S.A., *Mexico*
Prentice-Hall of India Private Limited, *New Dehli*
Prentice-Hall of Japan, Ltd., *Tokyo*
Pearson Education Asia Pte. Ltd., *Singapore*
Editora Prentice-Hall do Brasil, Ltda., *Rio de Janeiro*

This volume is dedicated to

JACK B. ROGERS

Contents

NINETEENTH-CENTURY PHILOSOPHY   893

MODERN PHILOSOPHY   381

Preface

There is no better introduction to philosophy than to read some of the great philosophers. But few books are more difficult to read than Aristotle's *Metaphysics* or Spinoza's *Ethics*. Even works that are less puzzling are sometimes like snippets of a conversation that you overhear on entering a room: What is said is clear, only you cannot be sure you have got the point because you do not know just what has gone before. A slight point may be crucial to refute some earlier suggestion, and a seemingly pointless remark may contain a barbed allusion. As a result of this difficulty, some students of philosophy cry out for a simple summary of the "central doctrines" of the great philosophers. Yet carving up great books to excerpt essential doctrines is one of the greatest sins against the spirit of philosophy. If the reading of a whole Platonic dialogue leaves one more doubtful and less sure of oneself than the perusal of a brief summary, so much the better. It is part of the point of philosophy to make us a little less sure about things. After all, Socrates himself insisted that what distinguished him from other persons was not that he knew all, or even most, answers but rather that he realized his ignorance.

Still, one need not despair of joining this ongoing conversation. In the first place, you can get in near the beginning of this conversation by starting with Plato and moving on from there. Given that they are over two thousand years old, his early dialogues are surprisingly easy to follow. The later Platonic dialogues, Aristotle, and much which follows will be more difficult, but by that point you will have some idea of what the conversation is about.

Secondly, the structure of this book is designed to make this conversation accessible. There are section introductions and introductions to the individual philosophers. These latter introductions are divided into three sections: (1) biographical (a glimpse of the life), (2) philosophical (a resume of the philosopher's thought), and

(3) bibliographical (suggestions for further reading). To give a sense of the development of ideas, there are short representative passages from some of the less important, but transitional, thinkers. To make all the works more readable, most footnotes treating textual matters (variant readings, etc.) have been omitted and all Greek words have been transliterated and put in angle brackets. My goal throughout this volume is to be unobtrusive and allow you to hear, and perhaps join in, the ongoing conversation that is Western philosophy.

This third edition now includes eight selections from twentieth-century thinkers as well as an introduction to Continental and Anglo-American philosophy. I have also added brief selections from the Renaissance thinker Pico della Mirandola and the early modern Blaise Pascal. To make room for these additional texts, I have made a number of small changes. John Scotus Eriugena, John Duns Scotus, Nicholas Cusanas, and Francis Bacon have been deleted. The partial selections from Plato's *Parmenides,* Leibniz's *Theodicy,* Hegel's *Reason in History,* and Mill's *On Liberty* have also been cut as have small portions of a number of other texts. In several cases, I have substituted texts that seem more representative of the thinker such as more material from the *Summa Theologica* in place of Thomas Aquinas's *The Principles of Nature* and additional sections of Nietzsche's *The Twilight of the Idols* in place of the previous selection from *The Genealogy of Morals.* Throughout the editing of this edition, I have tried to follow the same three principles I used in the individual volumes of the *Philosophic Classics* series: (1) to use complete works or, where more appropriate, complete sections of works (2) in clear translations (3) of texts central to the thinker's philosophy or widely accepted as part of the "canon." Those who use this volume in a one-term introduction to philosophy, history of philosophy, or history of intellectual thought course will find more material here than can easily fit a normal semester. But this embarrassment of riches gives teachers some choice and, for those who offer the same course year after year, an opportunity to change the menu.

*   *   *

I would like to thank the many people who assisted me in this volume, including the library staff of Whitworth College, especially Hans Bynagle, Gail Fielding, and Jeanette Langston; my colleagues, F. Dale Bruner, who made helpful suggestions on all the introductions, Barbara Filo, who helped make selections for the artwork, and Corliss Slack and John Yoder, who provided historical context; Stephen Davis, Claremont McKenna College; Jerry H. Gill, The College of St. Rose; Rex Hollowell, Spokane Falls Community College; Arthur F. Holmes, Wheaton College; Stanley Obitts, Westmont College; Wayne Pomerleau, Gonzaga University; Timothy A. Robinson, The College of St. Benedict; Glenn Ross, Franklin & Marshall College; and Charles Young, The Claremont Graduate School, who each read some of the introductions and gave helpful advice; Edward Beach, University of Wisconsin, Eau Claire, and John Justice, Randolph-Macon Women's College who graciously called my attention to errors in the previous edition; my secretary, Michelle Seefried; my production editor, Bruce Hobart; my acquisitions editor, Karita France of Prentice Hall; and my former acquisitions editors, Angela Stone and Ted Bolen. I would also like to acknowledge the following reviewers: James W. Allard, Montana State University; David Apolloni, Augsburg College; Robert C. Bennett, El Centro College; Herbert L. Carson, Ferris State University; Mary T. Clark, Manhattanville College; Sandra S. Edwards, University of Arkansas; Steven M. Emmanuel, Virginia Wesleyan College; David Griesedieck, University of Missouri, Saint Louis; Helen S. Lang, Trinity College;

Scott MacDonald, University of Iowa; Angel Medina, Georgia State University; Eric Palmer, Allegheny College; Katherine Rogers, University of Delaware; Gregory Schultz, Wisconsin Lutheran College; Stephen Scott, Eastern Washington University; Daniel C. Shartin, Worcester State College; Walter G. Scott, Oklahoma State University; Howard N. Tuttle, University of New Mexico; Richard J. Van Iten, Iowa State University; Donald Phillip Verene, Emory University; Sarah Worth, Allegheny College; and Wilhelm S. Wurzer, Duquesne University.

I am especially thankful to my wife, Joy Lynn Fulton Baird, and to our children, Whitney Jaye, Sydney Tev, and Soren David, who have supported me throughout this enterprise.

Finally, I would like to thank my dear friend and mentor, Jack B. Rogers, to whom this volume is dedicated.

Forrest E. Baird
Professor of Philosophy
Whitworth College
Spokane, WA 99251
fbaird@whitworth.edu

Philosophers in This Volume

400 B.C.	200 B.C.	0	A.D. 200	400	600	800	1000

Plato
Aristotle
Epicurus
Epictetus
Plotinus
Augustine
Boethius
Anselm

Other Important Figures

Socrates
Pyrrho
Alexander the Great
Zeno of Citium
Cleanthes
Julius Caesar
Lucretius
Philo of Alexandria
Jesus
Paul
Justin Martyr
Marcus Aurelius
Ptolemy (astronomer)
Clement of Alexandria
Tertullian
Origen

Sextus Empiricus
Porphyry

Pseudo-Dionysius Areopagite
Mohammed
Charlemagne
Avicenna

A Sampling of Major Events

Death of Socrates
Punic Wars and rise of Roman Empire
Wall of China built
Jerusalem Temple destroyed
Furthest extent of the Roman Empire
Council of Nicea
Roman Empire divided
Fall of Rome
Schools of philosophy in Athens
closed by Justinian
Muslim conquest
of Northern Africa
and Spain
Peak of Mayan
civilization in Central
America

400 B.C.	200 B.C.	0	A.D. 200	400	600	800	1000

1200	1400	1600	1800	2000

Moses Maimonides
Thomas Aquinas
William of Ockham
Pico della Mirandola
Thomas Hobbes
René Descartes
Blaise Pascal
Baruch Spinoza
John Locke
Gottfried Leibniz
George Berkeley
David Hume
Immanuel Kant
G.W.F. Hegel

John Stuart Mill
Søren Kierkegaard
Karl Marx
Friedrich Nietzsche
Edmund Husserl
Bertrand Russell
Martin Heidegger
Ludwig Wittgenstein
Jean-Paul Sartre
Willard Van
Orman Quine
A. J. Ayer
Jacques
Derrida

Peter Abelard
Hildegard of Bingen
Averroës
Zhu Xi (Chu Hsi)
Genghis Khan
Francis of Assisi
Bonaventure
Dante Alighieri
Catherine of Siena
Leonardo da Vinci
Martin Luther
John Calvin
Galileo
Shakespeare
Rembrandt

Louis XIV
Isaac Newton
J. S. Bach
Voltaire
Thomas Reid
J. W. Goethe
Mozart
Mary
Wollstonecraft
Napoleon Bonaparte
Beethoven
Simon Bolivar
Queen Victoria
John Dewey
Henri Bergson
George Santayana

Mahatma Gandhi
G. E. Moore
Martin Buber
Jacques Martin
Adolf Hitler
Gilbert Ryle
Simone
de Beauvoir
Michel Foucault

Paris University founded
Magna Carta
Bubonic Plague
Ming Dynasty in China
Gutenberg invents moveable-
type printing
Columbus sails to America
Luther begins Protestant Reformation
English defeat Spanish Armada
Charles I executed
English "Glorious Revolution"
Declaration
of Independence
French Revolution
Chaka founds Zulu Empire
American Civil War

Wright brothers
invent airplane
World War I
Russian
Revolution
World War II
Korean
War
Vietnam
War
First men
on the
moon

1200	1400	1600	1800	2000

ANCIENT GREEK PHILOSOPHY

———◄○►———

Something unusual happened in Greece and in the Greek colonies of the Aegean Sea some twenty-five hundred years ago. Whereas the previous great cultures of the Mediterranean had used mythological stories of the gods to explain the operations of the world and of the self, some of the Greeks began to discover new ways of explaining these phenomena. Instead of reading their ideas into, or out of, ancient scriptures or poems, they began to use reason, contemplation, and sensory observation to make sense of reality.

The story as we know it began with the Greeks living on the coast of Asia Minor (present-day Turkey). Colonists there, such as Thales, tried to find the one common element in the diversity of nature. Subsequent thinkers, such as Anaximenes, sought not only to find this one common element, but also to find the process by which one form changes into another. Other thinkers, such as Pythagoras, turned to the nature of form itself rather than the basic stuff that takes on a particular form.

With Socrates, the pursuit of knowledge turned inward as he sought not to understand the world, but himself. His call to "know thyself," together with his uncompromising search for truth, inspired generations of thinkers. With the writings of Plato and Aristotle, ancient Greek thought reached its zenith. These giants of human thought developed all-embracing systems that explained both the nature of the universe and the humans who inhabit it.

All these lovers of wisdom, or *philosophers,* came to different conclusions and often spoke disrespectfully of one another. Some held the universe to be one single entity, whereas others insisted that it must be made of many parts. Some believed that human knowledge was capable of understanding virtually everything about the world and the self, whereas others thought that it was not possible to have any knowledge at all. But despite all their differences, there is a thread of continuity, a continuing focus among them: the *human* attempt to understand the world and the self, using *human* reason. This fact distinguishes these philosophers from the great minds that preceded them.

The philosophers of ancient Greece have fascinated thinking persons for centuries, and their writings have been one of the key influences on the development of Western civilization. The works of Plato and Aristotle, especially, have defined the questions and suggested many of the answers for subsequent generations. As the great Greek statesman Pericles sagely predicted, "Future ages will wonder at us, as the present age wonders at us now."

*   *   *

For a comprehensive, yet readable, work on Greek philosophy, see W.K.C. Guthrie's authoritative *The History of Greek Philosophy,* six volumes. (Cambridge: Cambridge University Press, 1962–1981). W.T. Jones, *The Classical Mind* (New York: Harcourt, Brace & World, 1969); Frederick Copleston, *A History of Philosophy: Volume I, Greece & Rome* (Garden City, NY: Doubleday, 1962); Friedo Ricken, *Philosophy of the Ancients,* translated by Eric Watkins (Notre Dame, IN: University of Notre Dame Press, 1991); J.V. Luce, *An Introduction to Greek Philosophy* (New York: Thames and Hudson, 1992); C.C.W. Taylor, ed., *Routledge History of Philosophy, Volume 1: From the Beginning to Plato* (London: Routledge, 1997); and David Furley, ed., *Routledge History of Philosophy, Volume 2: Aristotle to Augustine* (London: Routledge, 1997) provide basic introductions. Julie K. Ward, ed., *Feminism and Ancient Philosophy* (London: Routledge, 1996) provides a feminist critique while Robert S. Brumbaugh, *The Philosophers of Greece* (Albany, NY: SUNY Press, 1981) is an accessible introduction with pictures, charts, and maps.

SOCRATES
470–399 B.C.

PLATO
428/7–348/7 B.C.

Socrates has fascinated and inspired men and women for over two thousand years. All five of the major "schools" of ancient Greece (Academics, Peripatetics, Epicureans, Stoics, and Cynics) were influenced by his thought. Some of the early Christian thinkers, such as Justin Martyr, considered him a "proto-Christian," while others, such as St. Augustine (who rejected this view) still expressed deep admiration for Socrates' ethical life. More recently, existentialists have found in Socrates' admonition "know thyself" an encapsulation of their thought, and opponents of unjust laws have seen in Socrates' trial a blueprint for civil disobedience. In short, Socrates is one of the most admired men who ever lived.

The Athens into which Socrates was born in 470 B.C. was a city still living in the flush of its epic victory over the Persians, and it was bursting with new ideas. The playwrights Euripides and Sophocles were young boys, and Pericles, the great Athenian democrat, was still a young man. The Parthenon's foundation was laid when Socrates was twenty-two, and its construction was completed fifteen years later.

Socrates was the son of Sophroniscus, a sculptor, and of Phaenarete, a midwife. As a boy, Socrates received a classical Greek education in music, gymnastics, and grammar (or the study of language), and he decided early on to become a sculptor like his father. Tradition says he was a gifted artist who fashioned impressively simple statues of the Graces. He married a woman named Xanthippe, and together they had three children. He took an early interest in the developing science of the Milesians, and then he served for a time in the army.

When he was a middle-aged man, Socrates' friend, Chaerephon, asked the oracle at Delphi "if there was anyone wiser than Socrates." For once the mysterious oracle gave an unambiguous answer: "None." When Socrates heard of the incident, he was confused. He knew that he was not a wise man. So he set out to find a wiser man as "an excuse for going back and cross-examining the oracle." Socrates later described the method and results of his mission:

> So I examined this man—there's no need for me to mention his name, let's just say he was a politician—and the result of my examination . . . and of my conversations with him, was this. I decided that although the man seemed to many people, and above all to himself, to be wise, in reality he was not wise. I tried to demonstrate to him that he thought he was wise, but actually was not, and as a result I made an enemy of him, and of many of those present. To myself, as I left him, I reflected, "Here is *one* man less wise than I. In all probability neither of us knows anything worth knowing; but he *thinks* he knows when he doesn't, whereas I, given that I don't in fact know, am at least *aware* I don't know. Apparently, therefore, I am wiser than him in just this one small detail, that when I don't know something, I don't *think* I know it either." From him I went to another man, one of those who seemed wiser than the first. I came to exactly the same conclusion, and made an enemy of him and of many others besides. (*Apology* 21c)

As Socrates continued his mission by interviewing the politicians, poets, and artisans of Athens, young men followed along. They enjoyed seeing the authority figures humiliated by Socrates' intense questioning. Those in authority, however, were not amused. Athens was no longer the powerful, self-confident city of 470 B.C., the year of Socrates' birth. An exhausting succession of wars with Sparta (the Peloponnesian Wars) and an enervating series of political debacles had left the city narrow in vision and suspicious of new ideas and of dissent. In 399 B.C., Meletus and Anytus brought an indictment of "impiety and corrupting the youth" against Socrates. As recorded in the *Apology,* the Athenian assembly found him guilty by a vote of 280 to 220 and sentenced him to death. His noble death is described incomparably in the closing pages of the *Phaedo* by Plato.

Socrates wrote nothing, and our knowledge of his thought comes exclusively from the report of others. The playwright Aristophanes (455–375 B.C.) satirized Socrates in his comedy *The Clouds.* His caricature of Socrates as a cheat and charlatan was apparently so damaging that Socrates felt compelled to offer a rebuttal before the Athenian assembly (see the *Apology,* following). The military general Xenophon (ca. 430–350 B.C.) honored his friend Socrates in his *Apology of Socrates,* his *Symposium,* and, later, in his *Memorabilia* ("Recollections of Socrates"). In an effort to defend his dead friend's memory, Xenophon's writings illumine Socrates' life and character. Though born fifteen years after the death of Socrates, Aristotle (384–322 B.C.) left many fascinating allusions to Socrates in his philosophic works, as did several later Greek philosophers. But the primary source of our knowledge of Socrates comes from one of those young men who followed him: Plato.

*   *   *

Plato was probably born in 428/7 B.C. He had two older brothers, Adeimantus and Glaucon, who appear in Plato's *Republic,* and a sister, Potone. Though he may have known Socrates since childhood, Plato was probably nearer twenty when he came under the intellectual spell of Socrates. The death of Socrates made an enormous impression on Plato and contributed to his call to bear witness to posterity of "the best, . . . the wisest and most just" person that he knew (*Phaedo,* 118). Though Plato was from a distinguished family and might have followed his relatives into politics, he chose philosophy.

Following Socrates' execution, the twenty-eight-year-old Plato left Athens and traveled for a time. He is reported to have visited Egypt and Cyrene—though some scholars doubt this. During this time he wrote his early dialogues on Socrates' life and teachings. He also visited Italy and Sicily, where he became the friend of Dion, a relative of Dionysius, the tyrant of Syracuse, Sicily.

On returning to Athens from Sicily, Plato founded a school, which came to be called the Academy. One might say it was the world's first university, and it endured as a center of higher learning for nearly one thousand years, until the Roman emperor Justinian closed it in A.D. 529. Except for two later trips to Sicily, where he unsuccessfully sought to institute his political theories, Plato spent the rest of his life at the Athenian Academy. Among his students was Aristotle. Plato died at eighty in 348/7 B.C.

Plato's influence was best described by the twentieth-century philosopher Alfred North Whitehead when he said, "The safest general characterization of the European philosophical tradition is that it consists of a series of footnotes to Plato."

*   *   *

It is difficult to separate the ideas of Plato from those of his teacher, Socrates. In virtually all of Plato's dialogues, Socrates is the main character, and it is possible that in the early dialogues Plato is recording his teacher's actual words. But in the later dialogues, "Socrates" gives Plato's views—views that, in some cases, in fact, the historical Socrates denied.

The first four dialogues presented in this text describe the trial and death of Socrates and are arranged in narrative order. The first, the *Euthyphro,* takes place as Socrates has just learned of the indictment against him. He strikes up a conversation with a "theologian" so sure of his piety that he is prosecuting his own father for murder. The dialogue moves on, unsuccessfully, to define piety. Along the way, Socrates asks a question that has vexed philosophers and theologians for centuries: Is something good because the gods say it is, or do the gods say it is good because it is? This dialogue is given in the F.J. Church translation.

The next dialogue, the *Apology,* is generally regarded as one of Plato's first, and as eminently faithful to what Socrates said at his trial on charges of impiety and corruption of youth. The speech was delivered in public and heard by a large audience; Plato has Socrates mention that Plato was present; and there is no need to doubt the historical veracity of the speech, at least in essentials. There are two breaks in the narrative: one after Socrates' defense (during which the Athenians vote "guilty") and one after Socrates proposes an alternative to the death penalty (during which the Athenians decide on death). This dialogue includes Socrates' famous characterization of his mission and purpose in life.

In the *Crito,* Plato has Crito visit Socrates in prison to assure him that his escape from Athens has been well prepared and to persuade him to consent to leave. Socrates argues that one has an obligation to obey the state even when it orders one to suffer wrong. That Socrates, in fact, refused to leave is certain; that he used the arguments Plato ascribes to him is less certain. In any case, anyone who has read the *Apology* will agree that after his speech Socrates could not well escape. For this series, both the *Apology* and the *Crito* are given in translations by Tom Griffith.

The moving account of Socrates' death is given at the end of the *Phaedo,* the last of our group of dialogues. There is common agreement that this dialogue was written much later than the other three and that the earlier part of the dialogue, with its Platonic doctrine of Forms and immortality, uses "Socrates" as a vehicle for Plato's own ideas. Once again, the translation is that of F.J. Church.

Like the *Phaedo,* the *Meno* and the *Republic* were written during Plato's "middle period," when he had returned from Sicily to Athens and had established the Academy. The *Meno* gives a fine and faithful picture of Socrates practicing the art of dialogue; it also marks the point at which Plato moves beyond his master. This dialogue answers the question, "Can virtue be taught?," and treats the issues of knowledge and belief. The *Meno* is given in W.K.C. Guthrie's authoritative translation.

There are few books in Western civilization that have had the impact of Plato's *Republic*—aside from the Bible, perhaps none. Like the Bible, there are also few books whose interpretation and evaluation have differed so widely. Apparently it is a description of Plato's ideal society: a utopian vision of the just state, possible only if philosophers were kings. But some (see the following suggested readings) claim that its purpose is not to give a model of the ideal state, but to show the impossibility of such a state and to convince aspiring philosophers to shun politics. Evaluations of the *Republic* have also varied widely: from the criticisms of Karl Popper, who denounced the *Republic* as totalitarian, to the admiration of more traditional interpreters, such as Gregory Vlastos and Francis MacDonald Cornford (whose translation is used here).

Given the importance of this work and the diversity of opinions concerning its point and value, it was extremely difficult to decide which sections of the *Republic* to include in this series. I chose to include the discussion of justice from Book II, the descriptions of the guardians and of the "noble lie" from Book III, the discussions of the virtues and the soul in Book IV, the presentations of the guardians' qualities and life-styles in Book V, and the key sections on knowledge (including the analogy of the line and the myth of the cave) from the end of Book VI and the beginning of Book VII. I admit that space constraints have forced me to exclude important sections. Ideally, the selections chosen will whet the student's appetite to read the rest of this classic. The marginal page numbers are those of all scholarly editions, Greek, English, German, or French.

*   *   *

For studies of Socrates, see the classic A.E. Taylor, *Socrates: The Man and His Thought* (London: Methuen, 1933); the second half of Volume III of W.K.C. Guthrie, *The History of Greek Philosophy* (Cambridge: Cambridge University Press, 1969); Hugh H. Benson, *Essays on the Philosophy of Socrates* (Oxford: Oxford University Press, 1992); and Thomas C. Brickhouse and Nicholas D. Smith, *Plato's Socrates* (Oxford: Oxford University Press, 1994). For collections of essays, see Gregory Vlastos, ed., *The Philosophy of Socrates* (Garden City, NY: Doubleday, 1971); Hugh H. Benson, ed., *Essays on the Philosophy of Socrates* (Oxford: Oxford University Press, 1992); Terence Irwin, ed., *Socrates and His Contemporaries* (Hamden, CT: Garland Publishing, 1995); and the multi-volume William J. Prior, ed., *Socrates* (Oxford: Routledge, 1996). For discussions of the similarities and differences between the historical Socrates and the "Socrates" of the Platonic dialogues, see Gregory Vlastos, *Socrates: Ironist and Moral Philosopher* (Ithaca, NY: Cornell University Press, 1991), especially Chapters 2 and 3, and Thomas C. Brickhouse and Nicholas D. Smith, *Plato's Socrates* (Oxford: Oxford University Press, 1994).

Books about Plato are legion. Once again the work of W.K.C. Guthrie is sensible, comprehensive, yet readable. See Volumes IV and V of his *The History of Greek Philosophy* (Cambridge: Cambridge University Press, 1975 and 1978). Paul Shorey, *What Plato Said* (Chicago: Chicago University Press, 1933), and G.M.A. Grube, *Plato's Thought* (London: Methuen, 1935) are classic treatments of Plato, while Robert Brumbaugh, *Plato for a Modern Age* (New York: Macmillan, 1964), I.M. Crombie, *An Examination of Plato's Doctrines,* two volumes (New York: Humanities Press, 1963–1969), R.M. Hare, *Plato* (Oxford: Oxford University Press, 1982), and David J. Melling, *Understanding Plato* (Oxford: Oxford University Press, 1987) are more recent studies. For collections of essays, see Gregory Vlastos, ed., *Plato: A Collection of Critical Essays,* two volumes (Garden City, NY: Doubleday, 1971); Richard Kraut, ed., *The Cambridge Companion to Plato* (Cambridge: Cambridge University Press, 1991); Nancy Tuana, ed., *Feminist Interpretations of Plato* (College Park, PA: Pennsylvania State University Press, 1994); Terence Irwin, ed., *Plato's Ethics* and *Plato's Metaphysics and Epistemology* (both Hamden, CT: Garland Publishing, 1995); and Gregory Vlastos, ed., *Studies in Greek Philosophy, Volume II: Socrates, Plato, and Their Tradition* (Princeton, NJ: Princeton University Press, 1995). Jane M. Day, ed., *Plato's Meno in Focus* (Oxford: Routledge, 1994) and Robert G. Turnbull, *The Parmenides and Plato's Late Philosophy* (Toronto: University of Toronto Press, 1998) give insights on their respective dialogues. For further reading on the *Republic,* see Nicholas P. White, *A Companion to Plato's Republic* (Indianapolis, IN: Hackett, 1979); Julia Annas, *An Introduction to Plato's Republic* (Oxford: Clarendon Press, 1981); Nickolas Pappas, *Routledge Guidebook to Plato and the Republic* (Oxford: Routledge, 1995); Daryl Rice, *A Guide to Plato's Republic* (Oxford: Oxford University Press, 1997) and Richard Kraut, ed., *Plato's Republic: Critical Essays* (Lanham, MD: Rowan & Littlefield, 1997). Terence Irwin, *Plato's Ethics* (Oxford: Oxford University Press, 1995) examines several dialogues while thoroughly exploring Plato's ethical thought. Finally, for unusual interpretations of Plato and his work, see Werner Jaeger, *Paideia,* Vols. II and III, translated by Gilbert Highet (New York: Oxford University Press, 1939–1943); Karl R. Popper, *The Open Society and Its Enemies; Volume I: The Spell of Plato* (Princeton, NJ: Princeton University Press, 1962); and Allan Bloom's interpretive essay in Plato, *Republic,* translated by Allan Bloom (New York: Basic Books, 1968).

EUTHYPHRO

Characters
Socrates
Euthyphro
Scene—The Hall of the King*

2   EUTHYPHRO: What in the world are you doing here in the king's hall, Socrates? Why have you left your haunts in the Lyceum? You surely cannot have a suit before him, as I have.

SOCRATES: The Athenians, Euthyphro, call it an indictment, not a suit.

b   EUTHYPHRO: What? Do you mean that someone is prosecuting you? I cannot believe that you are prosecuting anyone yourself.

SOCRATES: Certainly I am not.

EUTHYPHRO: Then is someone prosecuting you?

SOCRATES: Yes.

EUTHYPHRO: Who is he?

SOCRATES: I scarcely know him myself, Euthyphro; I think he must be some unknown young man. His name, however, is Meletus, and his district Pitthis, if you can call to mind any Meletus of that district—a hook-nosed man with lanky hair and rather a scanty beard.

EUTHYPHRO: I don't know him, Socrates. But tell me, what is he prosecuting you for?

c   SOCRATES: What for? Not on trivial grounds, I think. It is no small thing for so young a man to have formed an opinion on such an important matter. For he, he says, knows how the young are corrupted, and who are their corrupters. He must be a wise

d   man who, observing my ignorance, is going to accuse me to the state, as his mother, of corrupting his friends. I think that he is the only one who begins at the right point in his political reforms; for his first care is to make the young men as good as possible, just as a good farmer will take care of his young plants first, and, after he has done that, of the

3   others. And so Meletus, I suppose, is first clearing us away who, as he says, corrupt the young men growing up; and then, when he has done that, of course he will turn his attention to the older men, and so become a very great public benefactor. Indeed, that is only what you would expect when he goes to work in this way.

EUTHYPHRO: I hope it may be so, Socrates, but I fear the opposite. It seems to me that in trying to injure you, he is really setting to work by striking a blow at the foundation of the state. But how, tell me, does he say that you corrupt the youth?

b   SOCRATES: In a way which sounds absurd at first, my friend. He says that I am a maker of gods; and so he is prosecuting me, he says, for inventing new gods and for not believing in the old ones.

EUTHYPHRO: I understand, Socrates. It is because you say that you always have a divine guide. So he is prosecuting you for introducing religious reforms; and he is going into court to arouse prejudice against you, knowing that the multitude are easily

*The anachronistic title "king" was retained by the magistrate who had jurisdiction over crimes affecting the state religion.

Plato, *Euthyphro, Apology, Crito,* translated by F.J. Church (New York: Macmillan/Library of the Liberal Arts, 1963).

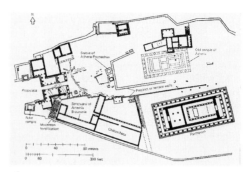

a.

b.

c.   d.

The Acropolis and the Parthenon

a. The *Parthenon*, Athens, built 477–438 B.C. The Parthenon, dedicated to Athena, patron deity of Athens, was at one period rededicated to the Christian Virgin Mary and then later became a Turkish mosque. In 1687 a gunpowder explosion created the ruin we see today. The Doric shell remains as a monument to ancient architectural engineering expertise and to a sense of classical beauty and order. (*Stergios Svaraas/D. A. Harissladis Photographic Agency*)

b. Restored plan of the Acropolis, 400 B.C. The history of the Acropolis is as varied as the style and size of the temples and buildings constructed atop the ancient site. (*Pearson Education/PH College*)

c. This model of the Acropolis of Athens recreates the complexity of fifth century B.C. public space, which included centers for worship, public forum, and entertainment. (*Royal Ontario Museum, Toronto*)

d. Doric, Ionic, and Corinthian columns with their characteristic capitals. (*Library of Congress*)

prejudiced about such matters. Why, they laugh even at me, as if I were out of my mind, when I talk about divine things in the assembly and tell them what is going to happen; and yet I have never foretold anything which has not come true. But they are resentful of all people like us. We must not worry about them; we must meet them boldly.   c

SOCRATES: My dear Euthyphro, their ridicule is not a very serious matter. The Athenians, it seems to me, may think a man to be clever without paying him much attention, so long as they do not think that he teaches his wisdom to others. But as soon as they think that he makes other people clever, they get angry, whether it be from resentment, as you say, or for some other reason.   d

EUTHYPHRO: I am not very anxious to test their attitude toward me in this matter.

SOCRATES: No, perhaps they think that you are reserved, and that you are not anxious to teach your wisdom to others. But I fear that they may think that I am; for my love of men makes me talk to everyone whom I meet quite freely and unreservedly, and without payment. Indeed, if I could I would gladly pay people myself to listen to me. If then, as I said just now, they were only going to laugh at me, as you say they do at you, it would not be at all an unpleasant way of spending the day—to spend it in court, joking and laughing. But if they are going to be in earnest, then only prophets like you can tell where the matter will end.

EUTHYPHRO: Well, Socrates, I dare say that nothing will come of it. Very likely you will be successful in your trial, and I think that I shall be in mine.

SOCRATES: And what is this suit of yours, Euthyphro? Are you suing, or being sued?

EUTHYPHRO: I am suing.

SOCRATES: Whom?

4   EUTHYPHRO: A man whom people think I must be mad to prosecute.

SOCRATES: What? Has he wings to fly away with?

EUTHYPHRO: He is far enough from flying; he is a very old man.

SOCRATES: Who is he?

EUTHYPHRO: He is my father.

SOCRATES: Your father, my good man?

EUTHYPHRO: He is indeed.

SOCRATES: What are you prosecuting him for? What is the accusation?

EUTHYPHRO: Murder, Socrates.

b   SOCRATES: Good heavens, Euthyphro! Surely the multitude are ignorant of what is right. I take it that it is not everyone who could rightly do what you are doing; only a man who was already well advanced in wisdom.

EUTHYPHRO: That is quite true, Socrates.

SOCRATES: Was the man whom your father killed a relative of yours? But, of course, he was. You would never have prosecuted your father for the murder of a stranger?

EUTHYPHRO: You amuse me, Socrates. What difference does it make whether the murdered man were a relative or a stranger? The only question that you have to ask is, did the murderer kill justly or not? If justly, you must let him alone; if unjustly, you

c   must indict him for murder, even though he share your hearth and sit at your table. The pollution is the same if you associate with such a man, knowing what he has done, without purifying yourself, and him too, by bringing him to justice. In the present case the murdered man was a poor laborer of mine, who worked for us on our farm in Naxos. While drunk he got angry with one of our slaves and killed him. My father therefore bound the man hand and foot and threw him into a ditch, while he sent to Athens to ask the priest what he should do. While the messenger was gone, he entirely neglected the man, thinking that he was a murderer, and that it would be no great matter, even if he were to die. And that was exactly what happened; hunger and cold and

d   his bonds killed him before the messenger returned. And now my father and the rest of my family are indignant with me because I am prosecuting my father for the murder of this murderer. They assert that he did not kill the man at all; and they say that, even if he had killed him over and over again, the man himself was a murderer, and that I ought not to concern myself about such a person because it is impious for a son to

e   prosecute his father for murder. So little, Socrates, do they know the divine law of piety and impiety.

SOCRATES: And do you mean to say, Euthyphro, that you think that you understand divine things and piety and impiety so accurately that, in such a case as you have
stated, you can bring your father to justice without fear that you yourself may be doing
something impious?

EUTHYPHRO: If I did not understand all these matters accurately, Socrates, I
should not be worth much—Euthyphro would not be any better than other men.   5

SOCRATES: Then, my dear Euthyphro, I cannot do better than become your pupil
and challenge Meletus on this very point before the trial begins. I should say that I had
always thought it very important to have knowledge about divine things; and that now,
when he says that I offend by speaking carelessly about them, and by introducing reforms, I have become your pupil. And I should say, "Meletus, if you acknowledge Eu-   b
thyphro to be wise in these matters and to hold the correct belief, then think the same
of me and do not put me on trial; but if you do not, then bring a suit, not against me,
but against my master, for corrupting his elders—namely, myself whom he corrupts by
his teaching, and his own father whom he corrupts by admonishing and punishing
him." And if I did not succeed in persuading him to release me from the suit or to indict you in my place, then I could repeat my challenge in court.

EUTHYPHRO: Yes, by Zeus! Socrates, I think I should find out his weak points if
he were to try to indict me. I should have a good deal to say about him in court long   c
before I spoke about myself.

SOCRATES: Yes, my dear friend, and knowing this I am anxious to become your
pupil. I see that Meletus here, and others too, seem not to notice you at all, but he sees
through me without difficulty and at once prosecutes me for impiety. Now, therefore,
please explain to me what you were so confident just now that you knew. Tell me what   d
are righteousness and sacrilege with respect to murder and everything else. I suppose
that piety is the same in all actions, and that impiety is always the opposite of piety,
and retains its identity, and that, as impiety, it always has the same character, which
will be found in whatever is impious.

EUTHYPHRO: Certainly, Socrates, I suppose so.

SOCRATES: Tell me, then, what is piety and what is impiety?

EUTHYPHRO: Well, then, I say that piety means prosecuting the unjust individual
who has committed murder or sacrilege, or any other such crime, as I am doing now,
whether he is your father or your mother or whoever he is; and I say that impiety   e
means not prosecuting him. And observe, Socrates, I will give you a clear proof, which
I have already given to others, that it is so, and that doing right means not letting off
unpunished the sacrilegious man, whosoever he may be. Men hold Zeus to be the best
and the most just of the gods; and they admit that Zeus bound his own father, Cronos,   6
for wrongfully devouring his children; and that Cronos, in his turn, castrated his father
for similar reasons. And yet these same men are incensed with me because I proceed
against my father for doing wrong. So, you see, they say one thing in the case of the
gods and quite another in mine.

SOCRATES: Is not that why I am being prosecuted, Euthyphro? I mean, because I
find it hard to accept such stories people tell about the gods? I expect that I shall be
found at fault because I doubt those stories. Now if you who understand all these matters so well agree in holding all those tales true, then I suppose that I must yield to your   b
authority. What could I say when I admit myself that I know nothing about them? But
tell me, in the name of friendship, do you really believe that these things have actually
happened?

EUTHYPHRO: Yes, and more amazing things, too, Socrates, which the multitude do
not know of.

SOCRATES: Then you really believe that there is war among the gods, and bitter
c   hatreds, and battles, such as the poets tell of, and which the great painters have depicted in our temples, notably in the pictures which cover the robe that is carried up to
the Acropolis at the great Panathenaic festival? Are we to say that these things are true,
Euthyphro?

EUTHYPHRO: Yes, Socrates, and more besides. As I was saying, I will report to
you many other stories about divine matters, if you like, which I am sure will astonish
you when you hear them.

SOCRATES: I dare say. You shall report them to me at your leisure another time.
At present please try to give a more definite answer to the question which I asked you
d   just now. What I asked you, my friend, was, What is piety? and you have not explained
it to me to my satisfaction. You only tell me that what you are doing now, namely,
prosecuting your father for murder, is a pious act.

EUTHYPHRO: Well, that is true, Socrates.

SOCRATES: Very likely. But many other actions are pious, are they not, Euthyphro?

EUTHYPHRO: Certainly.

SOCRATES: Remember, then, I did not ask you to tell me one or two of all the
many pious actions that there are; I want to know what is characteristic of piety which
e   makes all pious actions pious. You said, I think, that there is one characteristic which
makes all pious actions pious, and another characteristic which makes all impious actions impious. Do you not remember?

EUTHYPHRO: I do.

SOCRATES: Well, then, explain to me what is this characteristic, that I may have it
to turn to, and to use as a standard whereby to judge your actions and those of other
men, and be able to say that whatever action resembles it is pious, and whatever does
not, is not pious.

EUTHYPHRO: Yes, I will tell you that if you wish, Socrates.

SOCRATES: Certainly I do.

7   EUTHYPHRO: Well, then, what is pleasing to the gods is pious, and what is not
pleasing to them is impious.

SOCRATES: Fine, Euthyphro. Now you have given me the answer that I wanted.
Whether what you say is true, I do not know yet. But, of course, you will go on to
prove that it is true.

EUTHYPHRO: Certainly.

SOCRATES: Come, then, let us examine our statement. The things and the men that
are pleasing to the gods are pious, and the things and the men that are displeasing to
the gods are impious. But piety and impiety are not the same; they are as opposite as
possible—was not that what we said?

EUTHYPHRO: Certainly.

SOCRATES: And it seems the appropriate statement?

b   EUTHYPHRO: Yes, Socrates, certainly.

SOCRATES: Have we not also said, Euthyphro, that there are quarrels and disagreements and hatreds among the gods?

EUTHYPHRO: We have.

SOCRATES: But what kind of disagreement, my friend, causes hatred and anger?
Let us look at the matter thus. If you and I were to disagree as to whether one number
c   were more than another, would that make us angry and enemies? Should we not settle
such a dispute at once by counting?

EUTHYPHRO: Of course.

SOCRATES: And if we were to disagree as to the relative size of two things, we should measure them and put an end to the disagreement at once, should we not?

EUTHYPHRO: Yes.

SOCRATES: And should we not settle a question about the relative weight of two things by weighing them?

EUTHYPHRO: Of course.

SOCRATES: Then what is the question which would make us angry and enemies if we disagreed about it, and could not come to a settlement? Perhaps you have not an an-   d
swer ready; but listen to mine. Is it not the question of the just and unjust, of the honorable and the dishonorable, of the good and the bad? Is it not questions about these matters which make you and me and everyone else quarrel, when we do quarrel, if we differ about them and can reach no satisfactory agreement?

EUTHYPHRO: Yes, Socrates, it is disagreements about these matters.

SOCRATES: Well, Euthyphro, the gods will quarrel over these things if they quarrel at all, will they not?

EUTHYPHRO: Necessarily.

SOCRATES: Then, my good Euthyphro, you say that some of the gods think one   e
thing just, the others another; and that what some of them hold to be honorable or good, others hold to be dishonorable or evil. For there would not have been quarrels among them if they had not disagreed on these points, would there?

EUTHYPHRO: You are right.

SOCRATES: And each of them loves what he thinks honorable, and good, and just; and hates the opposite, does he not?

EUTHYPHRO: Certainly.

SOCRATES: But you say that the same action is held by some of them to be just, and by others to be unjust; and that then they dispute about it, and so quarrel and fight   8
among themselves. Is it not so?

EUTHYPHRO: Yes.

SOCRATES: Then the same thing is hated by the gods and loved by them; and the same thing will be displeasing and pleasing to them.

EUTHYPHRO: Apparently.

SOCRATES: Then, according to your account, the same thing will be pious and impious.

EUTHYPHRO: So it seems.

SOCRATES: Then, my good friend, you have not answered my question. I did not ask you to tell me what action is both pious and impious; but it seems that whatever is pleasing to the gods is also displeasing to them. And so, Euthyphro, I should not be   b
surprised if what you are doing now in punishing your father is an action well pleasing to Zeus, but hateful to Cronos and Uranus, and acceptable to Hephaestus, but hateful to Hera; and if any of the other gods disagree about it, pleasing to some of them and displeasing to others.

EUTHYPHRO: But on this point, Socrates, I think that there is no difference of opinion among the gods: they all hold that if one man kills another unjustly, he must be punished.

SOCRATES: What, Euthyphro? Among mankind, have you never heard disputes   c
whether a man ought to be punished for killing another man unjustly, or for doing some other unjust deed?

EUTHYPHRO: Indeed, they never cease from these disputes, especially in courts of justice. They do all manner of unjust things; and then there is nothing which they will not do and say to avoid punishment.

SOCRATES: Do they admit that they have done something unjust, and at the same time deny that they ought to be punished, Euthyphro?

EUTHYPHRO: No, indeed, that they do not.

SOCRATES: Then it is not the case that there is nothing which they will not do and say. I take it, they do not dare to say or argue that they must not be punished if they have done something unjust. What they say is that they have not done anything unjust, is it not so?

EUTHYPHRO: That is true.

SOCRATES: Then they do not disagree over the question that the unjust individual must be punished. They disagree over the question, who is unjust, and what was done and when, do they not?

EUTHYPHRO: That is true.

SOCRATES: Well, is not exactly the same thing true of the gods if they quarrel about justice and injustice, as you say they do? Do not some of them say that the others are doing something unjust, while the others deny it? No one, I suppose, my dear friend, whether god or man, dares to say that a person who has done something unjust must not be punished.

EUTHYPHRO: No, Socrates, that is true, by and large.

SOCRATES: I take it, Euthyphro, that the disputants, whether men or gods, if the gods do disagree, disagree over each separate act. When they quarrel about any act, some of them say that it was just, and others that it was unjust. Is it not so?

EUTHYPHRO: Yes.

SOCRATES: Come, then, my dear Euthyphro, please enlighten me on this point. What proof have you that all the gods think that a laborer who has been imprisoned for murder by the master of the man whom he has murdered, and who dies from his imprisonment before the master has had time to learn from the religious authorities what he should do, dies unjustly? How do you know that it is just for a son to indict his father and to prosecute him for the murder of such a man? Come, see if you can make it clear to me that the gods necessarily agree in thinking that this action of yours is just; and if you satisfy me, I will never cease singing your praises for wisdom.

EUTHYPHRO: I could make that clear enough to you, Socrates; but I am afraid that it would be a long business.

SOCRATES: I see you think that I am duller than the judges. To them, of course, you will make it clear that your father has committed an unjust action, and that all the gods agree in hating such actions.

EUTHYPHRO: I will indeed, Socrates, if they will only listen to me.

SOCRATES: They will listen if they think that you are a good speaker. But while you were talking, it occurred to me to ask myself this question: suppose that Euthyphro were to prove to me as clearly as possible that all the gods think such a death unjust, how has he brought me any nearer to understanding what piety and impiety are? This particular act, perhaps, may be displeasing to the gods, but then we have just seen that piety and impiety cannot be defined in that way; for we have seen that what is displeasing to the gods is also pleasing to them. So I will let you off on this point, Euthyphro; and all the gods shall agree in thinking your father's action wrong and in hating it, if you like. But shall we correct our definition and say that whatever all the gods hate is impious, and whatever they all love is pious; while whatever some of them love, and others hate, is either both or neither? Do you wish us now to define piety and impiety in this manner?

EUTHYPHRO: Why not, Socrates?

SOCRATES: There is no reason why I should not, Euthyphro. It is for you to consider whether that definition will help you to teach me what you promised.

EUTHYPHRO: Well, I should say that piety is what all the gods love, and that impi-   e
ety is what they all hate.

SOCRATES: Are we to examine this definition, Euthyphro, and see if it is a good
one? Or are we to be content to accept the bare statements of other men or of ourselves
without asking any questions? Or must we examine the statements?

EUTHYPHRO: We must examine them. But for my part I think that the definition is
right this time.

SOCRATES: We shall know that better in a little while, my good friend. Now consider this question. Do the gods love piety because it is pious, or is it pious because   10
they love it?

EUTHYPHRO: I do not understand you, Socrates.

SOCRATES: I will try to explain myself: we speak of a thing being carried and carrying, and being led and leading, and being seen and seeing; and you understand that
all such expressions mean different things, and what the difference is.

EUTHYPHRO: Yes, I think I understand.

SOCRATES: And we talk of a thing being loved, of a thing loving, and the two are
different?

EUTHYPHRO: Of course.

SOCRATES: Now tell me, is a thing which is being carried in a state of being car-   b
ried because it is carried, or for some other reason?

EUTHYPHRO: No, because it is carried.

SOCRATES: And a thing is in a state of being led because it is led, and of being
seen because it is seen?

EUTHYPHRO: Certainly.

SOCRATES: Then a thing is not seen because it is in a state of being seen: it is in a
state of being seen because it is seen; and a thing is not led because it is in a state of
being led: it is in a state of being led because it is led; and a thing is not carried because
it is in a state of being carried: it is in a state of being carried because it is carried. Is
my meaning clear now, Euthyphro? I mean this: if anything becomes or is affected, it
does not become because it is in a state of becoming: it is in a state of becoming be-   c
cause it becomes; and it is not affected because it is in a state of being affected: it is in
a state of being affected because it is affected. Do you not agree?

EUTHYPHRO: I do.

SOCRATES: Is not that which is being loved in a state either of becoming or of
being affected in some way by something?

EUTHYPHRO: Certainly.

SOCRATES: Then the same is true here as in the former cases. A thing is not loved
by those who love it because it is in a state of being loved; it is in a state of being loved
because they love it.

EUTHYPHRO: Necessarily.

SOCRATES: Well, then, Euthyphro, what do we say about piety? Is it not loved by   d
all the gods, according to your definition?

EUTHYPHRO: Yes.

SOCRATES: Because it is pious, or for some other reason?

EUTHYPHRO: No, because it is pious.

SOCRATES: Then it is loved by the gods because it is pious; it is not pious because
it is loved by them?

EUTHYPHRO: It seems so.

SOCRATES: But, then, what is pleasing to the gods is pleasing to them, and is in a
state of being loved by them, because they love it?

EUTHYPHRO: Of course.

SOCRATES: Then piety is not what is pleasing to the gods, and what is pleasing to the gods is not pious, as you say, Euthyphro. They are different things.

e   EUTHYPHRO: And why, Socrates?

SOCRATES: Because we are agreed that the gods love piety because it is pious, and that it is not pious because they love it. Is not this so?

EUTHYPHRO: Yes.

SOCRATES: And that what is pleasing to the gods because they love it, is pleasing to them by reason of this same love, and that they do not love it because it is pleasing to them.

EUTHYPHRO: True.

SOCRATES: Then, my dear Euthyphro, piety and what is pleasing to the gods are

11   different things. If the gods had loved piety because it is pious, they would also have loved what is pleasing to them because it is pleasing to them; but if what is pleasing to them had been pleasing to them because they loved it, then piety, too, would have been piety because they loved it. But now you see that they are opposite things, and wholly different from each other. For the one is of a sort to be loved because it is loved, while the other is loved because it is of a sort to be loved. My question, Euthyphro, was, What is piety? But it turns out that you have not explained to me the essential character of piety; you have been content to mention an effect which be-

b   longs to it—namely, that all the gods love it. You have not yet told me what its essential character is. Do not, if you please, keep from me what piety is; begin again and tell me that. Never mind whether the gods love it, or whether it has other effects: we shall not differ on that point. Do your best to make clear to me what is piety and what is impiety.

EUTHYPHRO: But, Socrates, I really don't know how to explain to you what is in my mind. Whatever statement we put forward always somehow moves round in a circle, and will not stay where we put it.

SOCRATES: I think that your statements, Euthyphro, are worthy of my ancestor

c   Daedalus.* If they had been mine and I had set them down, I dare say you would have made fun of me, and said that it was the consequence of my descent from Daedalus that the statements which I construct run away, as his statues used to, and will not stay where they are put. But, as it is, the statements are yours, and the joke would have no point. You yourself see that they will not stay still.

EUTHYPHRO: Nay, Socrates, I think that the joke is very much in point. It is not

d   my fault that the statement moves round in a circle and will not stay still. But you are the Daedalus, I think; as far as I am concerned, my statements would have stayed put.

SOCRATES: Then, my friend, I must be a more skillful artist than Daedalus; he only used to make his own works move, while I, you see, can make other people's works move, too. And the beauty of it is that I am wise against my will. I would rather that our statements had remained firm and immovable than have all the wisdom of

e   Daedalus and all the riches of Tantalus to boot. But enough of this. I will do my best to help you to explain to me what piety is, for I think that you are lazy. Don't give in yet. Tell me, do you not think that all piety must be just?

EUTHYPHRO: I do.

12   SOCRATES: Well, then, is all justice pious, too? Or, while all piety is just, is a part only of justice pious, and the rest of it something else?

---

*Daedalus' statues were reputed to have been so lifelike that they came alive.

EUTHYPHRO: I do not follow you, Socrates.

SOCRATES: Yet you have the advantage over me in your youth no less than your wisdom. But, as I say, the wealth of your wisdom makes you complacent. Exert yourself, my good friend: I am not asking you a difficult question. I mean the opposite of what the poet [Stasinus] said, when he wrote:

> "You shall not name Zeus the creator, who made all things: for where there is fear there b
> also is reverence."

Now I disagree with the poet. Shall I tell you why?

EUTHYPHRO: Yes.

SOCRATES: I do not think it true to say that where there is fear, there also is reverence. Many people who fear sickness and poverty and other such evils seem to me to have fear, but no reverence for what they fear. Do you not think so?

EUTHYPHRO: I do.

SOCRATES: But I think that where there is reverence there also is fear. Does any man feel reverence and a sense of shame about anything, without at the same time c dreading and fearing the reputation of wickedness?

EUTHYPHRO: No, certainly not.

SOCRATES: Then, though there is fear wherever there is reverence, it is not correct to say that where there is fear there also is reverence. Reverence does not always accompany fear; for fear, I take it, is wider than reverence. It is a part of fear, just as the odd is a part of number, so that where you have the odd you must also have number, though where you have number you do not necessarily have the odd. Now I think you follow me?

EUTHYPHRO: I do.

SOCRATES: Well, then, this is what I meant by the question which I asked you. Is there always piety where there is justice? Or, though there is always justice where there is piety, yet there is not always piety where there is justice, because piety is only d a part of justice? Shall we say this, or do you differ?

EUTHYPHRO: No, I agree. I think that you are right.

SOCRATES: Now observe the next point. If piety is a part of justice, we must find out, I suppose, what part of justice it is? Now, if you had asked me just now, for instance, what part of number is the odd, and what number is an odd number, I should have said that whatever number is not even is an odd number. Is it not so?

EUTHYPHRO: Yes.

SOCRATES: Then see if you can explain to me what part of justice is piety, that I e may tell Meletus that now that I have been adequately instructed by you as to what actions are righteous and pious, and what are not, he must give up prosecuting me unjustly for impiety.

EUTHYPHRO: Well, then, Socrates, I should say that righteousness and piety are that part of justice which has to do with the careful attention which ought to be paid to the gods; and that what has to do with the careful attention which ought to be paid to men is the remaining part of justice.

SOCRATES: And I think that your answer is a good one, Euthyphro. But there is one little point about which I still want to hear more. I do not yet understand what the 13 careful attention is to which you refer. I suppose you do not mean that the attention which we pay to the gods is like the attention which we pay to other things. We say, for instance, do we not, that not everyone knows how to take care of horses, but only the trainer of horses?

EUTHYPHRO: Certainly.

SOCRATES: For I suppose that the skill that is concerned with horses is the art of taking care of horses.

EUTHYPHRO: Yes.

SOCRATES: And not everyone understands the care of dogs, but only the huntsman.

EUTHYPHRO: True.

b

SOCRATES: For I suppose that the huntsman's skill is the art of taking care of dogs.

EUTHYPHRO: Yes.

SOCRATES: And the herdsman's skill is the art of taking care of cattle.

EUTHYPHRO: Certainly.

SOCRATES: And you say that piety and righteousness are taking care of the gods, Euthyphro?

EUTHYPHRO: I do.

SOCRATES: Well, then, has not all care the same object? Is it not for the good and benefit of that on which it is bestowed? For instance, you see that horses are benefited and improved when they are cared for by the art which is concerned with them. Is it not so?

EUTHYPHRO: Yes, I think so.

c

SOCRATES: And dogs are benefited and improved by the huntsman's art, and cattle by the herdsman's, are they not? And the same is always true. Or do you think care is ever meant to harm that which is cared for?

EUTHYPHRO: No, indeed; certainly not.

SOCRATES: But to benefit it?

EUTHYPHRO: Of course.

SOCRATES: Then is piety, which is our care for the gods, intended to benefit the gods, or to improve them? Should you allow that you make any of the gods better when you do a pious action?

EUTHYPHRO: No indeed; certainly not.

SOCRATES: No, I am quite sure that that is not your meaning, Euthyphro. It was

d

for that reason that I asked you what you meant by the careful attention which ought to be paid to the gods. I thought that you did not mean that.

EUTHYPHRO: You were right, Socrates. I do not mean that.

SOCRATES: Good. Then what sort of attention to the gods will piety be?

EUTHYPHRO: The sort of attention, Socrates, slaves pay to their masters.

SOCRATES: I understand; then it is a kind of service to the gods?

EUTHYPHRO: Certainly.

SOCRATES: Can you tell me what result the art which serves a doctor serves to produce? Is it not health?

EUTHYPHRO: Yes.

e

SOCRATES: And what result does the art which serves a ship-wright serve to produce?

EUTHYPHRO: A ship, of course, Socrates.

SOCRATES: The result of the art which serves a builder is a house, is it not?

EUTHYPHRO: Yes.

SOCRATES: Then tell me, my good friend: What result will the art which serves the gods serve to produce? You must know, seeing that you say that you know more about divine things than any other man.

EUTHYPHRO: Well, that is true, Socrates.

SOCRATES: Then tell me, I beg you, what is that grand result which the gods use our services to produce?

EUTHYPHRO: There are many notable results, Socrates.

SOCRATES: So are those, my friend, which a general produces. Yet it is easy to see   14
that the crowning result of them all is victory in war, is it not?

EUTHYPHRO: Of course.

SOCRATES: And, I take it, the farmer produces many notable results; yet the principal result of them all is that he makes the earth produce food.

EUTHYPHRO: Certainly.

SOCRATES: Well, then, what is the principal result of the many notable results which the gods produce?

EUTHYPHRO: I told you just now, Socrates, that accurate knowledge of all these matters is not easily obtained. However, broadly I say this: if any man knows that his   b
words and actions in prayer and sacrifice are acceptable to the gods, that is what is pious; and it preserves the state, as it does private families. But the opposite of what is acceptable to the gods is sacrilegious, and this it is that undermines and destroys everything.

SOCRATES: Certainly, Euthyphro, if you had wished, you could have answered my main question in far fewer words. But you are evidently not anxious to teach me. Just   c
now, when you were on the very point of telling me what I want to know, you stopped short. If you had gone on then, I should have learned from you clearly enough by this time what piety is. But now I am asking you questions, and must follow wherever you lead me; so tell me, what is it that you mean by piety and impiety? Do you not mean a science of prayer and sacrifice?

EUTHYPHRO: I do.

SOCRATES: To sacrifice is to give to the gods, and to pray is to ask of them, is it not?

EUTHYPHRO: It is, Socrates.

SOCRATES: Then you say that piety is the science of asking of the gods and giving   d
to them?

EUTHYPHRO: You understand my meaning exactly, Socrates.

SOCRATES: Yes, for I am eager to share your wisdom, Euthyphro, and so I am all attention; nothing that you say will fall to the ground. But tell me, what is this service of the gods? You say it is to ask of them, and to give to them?

EUTHYPHRO: I do.

SOCRATES: Then, to ask rightly will be to ask of them what we stand in need of   e
from them, will it not?

EUTHYPHRO: Naturally.

SOCRATES: And to give rightly will be to give back to them what they stand in need of from us? It would not be very skillful to make a present to a man of something that he has no need of.

EUTHYPHRO: True, Socrates.

SOCRATES: Then piety, Euthyphro, will be the art of carrying on business between gods and men?

EUTHYPHRO: Yes, if you like to call it so.

SOCRATES: But I like nothing except what is true. But tell me, how are the gods benefited by the gifts which they receive from us? What they give is plain enough. Every good thing that we have is their gift. But how are they benefited by what we give   15
them? Have we the advantage over them in these business transactions to such an extent that we receive from them all the good things we possess, and give them nothing in return?

EUTHYPHRO: But do you suppose, Socrates, that the gods are benefited by the gifts which they receive from us?

SOCRATES: But what *are* these gifts, Euthyphro, that we give the gods?

EUTHYPHRO: What do you think but honor and praise, and, as I have said, what is acceptable to them.

b   SOCRATES: Then piety, Euthyphro, is acceptable to the gods, but it is not profitable to them nor loved by them?

EUTHYPHRO: I think that nothing is more loved by them.

SOCRATES: Then I see that piety means that which is loved by the gods.

EUTHYPHRO: Most certainly.

SOCRATES: After that, shall you be surprised to find that your statements move about instead of staying where you put them? Shall you accuse me of being the Daedalus that makes them move, when you yourself are far more skillful than Daedalus was, and make them go round in a circle? Do you not see that our statement

c   has come round to where it was before? Surely you remember that we have already seen that piety and what is pleasing to the gods are quite different things. Do you not remember?

EUTHYPHRO: I do.

SOCRATES: And now do you not see that you say that what the gods love is pious? But does not what the gods love come to the same thing as what is pleasing to the gods?

EUTHYPHRO: Certainly.

SOCRATES: Then either our former conclusion was wrong or, if it was right, we are wrong now.

EUTHYPHRO: So it seems.

SOCRATES: Then we must begin again and inquire what piety is. I do not mean to

d   give in until I have found out. Do not regard me as unworthy; give your whole mind to the question, and this time tell me the truth. For if anyone knows it, it is you; and you are a Proteus whom I must not let go until you have told me. It cannot be that you would ever have undertaken to prosecute your aged father for the murder of a laboring man unless you had known exactly what piety and impiety are. You would have feared to risk the anger of the gods, in case you should be doing wrong, and you would have

e   been afraid of what men would say. But now I am sure that you think that you know exactly what is pious and what is not; so tell me, my good Euthyphro, and do not conceal from me what you think.

EUTHYPHRO: Another time, then, Socrates. I am in a hurry now, and it is time for me to be off.

SOCRATES: What are you doing, my friend! Will you go away and destroy all my hopes of learning from you what is pious and what is not, and so of escaping Meletus?

16   I meant to explain to him that now Euthyphro has made me wise about divine things, and that I no longer in my ignorance speak carelessly about them or introduce reforms. And then I was going to promise him to live a better life for the future.

APOLOGY

Well, I don't know what effect the prosecution has had on you, men of Athens. As far   17
as I'm concerned, they made me all but forget the position I am in, they spoke so plausibly. And yet, to all intents and purposes, there was not a word of truth in what they said.

Of their many lies, one in particular filled me with amazement. They said you should be careful to avoid being led astray by my "skill in speaking." They were not in the least embarrassed at the prospect of being immediately proved wrong by my actual performance, when it becomes clear that I am not in the least skilled in speaking. That   b
was what I found the most shameless thing about their behaviour—unless of course they call "skilled in speaking" someone who merely speaks the truth. If *that's* what they mean, then I would agree that I am in a different class from them as an orator.

As I say, they have told you little or nothing that was true, whereas from me you will hear the whole truth—certainly not a piece of polished rhetoric like theirs, men of Athens, with its words and phrases so cleverly arranged. No, the speech you are going   c
to hear from me will use everyday language, arranged in a straightforward way—after all, I have confidence in the justice of what I have to say—so I hope no-one is expecting anything different. And I shall tell the truth, because it wouldn't be appropriate to appear before you at my age making up stories like a schoolboy.

However, there is one important request and concession I am going to ask of you, men of Athens. If you hear me making my defence in the same language I generally use in the city, among people doing business—where many of you have heard me—and elsewhere, do not be surprised on that account, or start interrupting. The reason for it is this. This is the first time I have ever appeared in court, though I am now seventy years of age. The kind of speaking practised here is, quite simply, foreign to   d
me. Imagine I really were a foreigner; you wouldn't hold it against me, presumably, if I spoke in the dialect and manner in which I had been brought up. In the same way   18
now, I make this request—justified, in my view—that you pay no attention to the manner in which I speak, be it inferior or superior. Please consider one point only, and focus your attention on that. Is there any justice in what I have to say, or not? That, after all, is the function of a member of the jury; the speaker's task is to tell the truth.

First of all, then, men of Athens, I am entitled to defend myself against the earliest false accusations made against me, and against my earliest accusers; after that against the more recent falsehoods, and my present accusers. After all, there have been many people, over the years, making accusations about me to you, and speaking not a word of truth. I fear them more than I fear Anytus and his supporters, dangerous   b
though they are as well. But the earlier ones are more dangerous, gentlemen. They took you in hand from childhood, for the most part, and tried to win you over, making accusations every bit as false as these today; they told you there was this man Socrates, an intellectual, a thinker about the heavens, an expert on everything under the earth, a man who could make the weaker argument the stronger.

These people, men of Athens, the ones who have saddled me with this reputation, are my most dangerous accusers, because those who listen to them think that students of these subjects do not recognise the gods. What's more, there are a great many   c of these accusers, and they have been accusing me for a long time now. And thirdly, they were speaking to you at the age when you were most likely to believe them, when many of you were children and adolescents. Quite simply, they were prosecuting in an uncontested case, since there was no-one there to answer their charges.

d   What is particularly unfair is that I cannot even know, or tell you, their names—unless maybe one of them is a writer of comedies. But all those who tried to influence you, out of spite and malice, together with those who were trying to influence others because they were genuinely convinced themselves—all these accusers are very hard to deal with. It is not possible to call any of them as a witness here, or cross-examine them; I just have to make my defence like someone shadow-boxing, and conduct my cross-examination with no-one there to answer.

e   So I hope you will accept my claim that I have two sets of accusers—the ones who have just now brought this case against me, and the ones from way back, the ones I have been telling you about. Please believe also that I must make my defence against this second set first; after all, you heard their accusations at an earlier age, and on many more occasions, than you heard the later ones.

19   Very well. I must make my defence, men of Athens, and try to remove from your minds, in the very brief time available, the prejudice which you have so long held. I hope that is how things will turn out, provided it really *is* the best outcome for you and for me, and that I shall achieve something by my defence. But I think it is difficult, and I am well aware of the magnitude of the task. Still, let it turn out as god wills, I must obey the law, and make my defence.

b   Let us go back to the beginning, then, and see what the accusation is which has created this prejudice against me—the prejudice which Meletus was presumably counting on when he brought this case against me. What exactly did the originators of this prejudice say? We ought really to read out a sworn statement from them, just like the prosecution's. "Socrates is guilty of being a busybody. He enquires into things under the earth and in the heavens, and makes the weaker argument the stronger, and

c   he teaches these same things to other people." That's roughly how it goes. You saw it for yourselves in Aristophanes' comedy; you saw a Socrates there, swinging round and round, claiming he was walking on air, and spouting a whole lot of other drivel on subjects about which I make not the slightest claim to knowledge. Not that I have anything against knowledge of this kind, if anyone is an expert on such subjects; I hope Meletus will never bring enough cases against me to reduce me to that. No, it's just that I myself have no share in such knowledge.

d   Once again, I can call most of you as witnesses. I'm sure you can make the position clear to one another, and explain, those of you who have ever heard me talking—and a lot of you come in that category. Tell one another then, if any of you has ever heard me breathe so much as a word on such topics. That will help you to see that the rest of what is generally said about me has as little foundation.

e   No, there is no truth in these stories. And if anyone has told you that I undertake to educate people, or that I make money out of it, there is equally little truth in that either. Mind you, if anyone *can* educate people—as Gorgias from Leontini can, or Prodicus from Ceos, or Hippias from Elis—then that seems to me to be a fine thing. Any of these men, gentlemen, can go to any city and persuade the young men, who are at liberty to spend their time, free of charge, with whichever of their fellow-citizens they

20   choose, to abandon the company of those fellow-citizens and spend time with him instead—and pay money to do so, *and* be grateful into the bargain.

Come to that, there is even one of them here, a wise man from Paros. I found out he was living in Athens when I ran into Callias, the son of Hipponicus, the man who

has paid more money to these teachers than everyone else put together. I asked him—
you know he has two sons—"Callias," I said, "if your sons were colts or calves, we b
would be able to find and employ someone to look after them, someone who would
turn them into outstanding examples of their particular species; and this person would
be a trainer or farmer of some kind. But they aren't colts or calves; they are men.
Whom do you propose to find to look after them? Who is an expert in this kind of excellence—the excellence of a human being and a citizen? I imagine, since you have
sons, you must have thought about this question. Is there someone," I asked him, "or
not?"

"There certainly is," he said.

"Who is he?" I said. "Where is he from? What does he charge?"

"Evenus," he said. "He is from Paros, Socrates, and he charges 500 drachmas."

I took my hat off to Evenus, if he really did have this ability, and yet taught for
so reasonable a fee. I wouldn't. I'd start giving myself airs, and become extremely c
choosy, if I had this kind of knowledge. But I don't have it, men of Athens.

I can imagine one of you interrupting me, and saying, "That's all very well,
Socrates; but what *do* you do? Where have all these prejudices against you come from?
I take it all this gossip and rumour about you is not the result of your behaving just like
anyone else. You must be doing *something* out of the ordinary. Tell us what it is, so we
can avoid jumping to conclusions about you." This seems to me to be a valid point, so d
I'll try and explain to you what it is that has given me my reputation and created the
prejudice against me. Give me a hearing. It may seem to some of you that I am not
being serious, but I promise you, every word I say will be the truth.

I have gained this reputation, men of Athens, as a direct result of a kind of wisdom. What sort of wisdom? The sort we might perhaps call human wisdom. In fact, if
we are talking about this kind of wisdom, I probably *am* wise. The men I mentioned e
just now may well be wise with some more-than-human wisdom; I don't know how
else to describe it. It's not a wisdom *I* know anything about. Anyone who says I do is
lying, and trying to increase the prejudice against me.

Please do not interrupt me, men of Athens, even if you find what I say a little bit
boastful. The claim I'm about to make is not *my* claim; I shall appeal to a reliable authority. I shall call the god at Delphi to give evidence to you about my wisdom; he can
tell you if I really do possess any, and what it is like.

You remember Chaerephon, I imagine. He was a friend of mine, from an early
age, and a friend of most of you. He shared your recent exile, and returned from exile 21
with you. You know what Chaerephon was like, how impetuous he was when he set
about something. And sure enough, he went to Delphi one day, and went so far as to
put this question to the oracle—I repeat, please do not interrupt, gentlemen—he asked
if there was anyone wiser than me; and the priestess of Apollo replied that there was
no-one wiser. His brother here will give evidence to you about this, since Chaerephon
himself is dead.

Let me remind you of my reason for telling you this. I am trying to show you the b
origin of the prejudice against me. When I heard the priestess's reply, my reaction was
this: "What on earth is the god saying? What is his hidden meaning? I'm well aware
that I have no wisdom, great or small. So what can he mean by saying that I am so
wise? He can't be lying; he's not allowed to." I spent a long time wondering what he
could mean. Finally, with great reluctance, I decided to verify his claim. What I did
was this: I approached one of those who seemed to be wise, thinking that there, if anywhere, I could prove the reply wrong, and say quite clearly to the oracle, "This man is c
wiser than I am, whereas you said that I was the wisest."

So I examined this man—there's no need for me to mention his name, let's just say he was a politician—and the result of my examination, men of Athens, and of my conversations with him, was this. I decided that although the man seemed to many people, and above all to himself, to be wise, in reality he was not wise. I tried to demonstrate to him that he thought he was wise, but actually was not, and as a result I

d   made an enemy of him, and of many of those present. To myself, as I left him, I reflected: "Here is *one* man less wise than I. In all probability neither of us knows anything worth knowing; but he *thinks* he knows when he doesn't, whereas I, given that I don't in fact know, am at least *aware* I don't know. Apparently, therefore, I am wiser than him in just this one small detail, that when I don't know something, I don't *think* I know it either." From him I went to another man, one of those who seemed wiser than

e   the first. I came to exactly the same conclusion, and made an enemy of him and of many others besides.

After that I began approaching people in a systematic way. I could see, with regret and alarm, that I was making enemies, yet I thought it was essential to take the god seriously. So on I had to go, in my enquiry into the meaning of the oracle, to

22   everyone who seemed to have any knowledge. And I swear to you, men of Athens— after all, I am bound to tell you the truth—what I found was this. Those with the highest reputations seemed to me to be pretty nearly the most useless, if I was trying to find out the meaning of what the god had said, whereas others, who appeared of less account, were a much better bet when it came to thinking sensibly.

I can best give an account of my quest by likening it to a set of labours—and all, as it turned out, to satisfy myself of the accuracy of the oracle. After the politicians I

b   went to the writers—writers of plays, and songs, and the rest of them. That would be an open-and-shut case, I thought. I should easily show myself up as less wise than them. So I took to reading their works, the ones which struck me as showing the greatest skill in composition, and asking them what they meant; I hoped to learn from them.

Well, I'm embarrassed to tell you the truth, gentlemen; but I must tell you. Practically anyone present could have given a better account than they did of the works

c   they had themselves written. As a result, I quickly came to a decision about the writers too, in their turn. I realised that their achievements are not the result of wisdom, but of natural talent and inspiration, like fortune-tellers and clairvoyants, who also say many striking things, but have no idea at all of the meaning of what they say. Writers, I felt, were clearly in the same position. Moreover, I could see that their works encouraged them to think that they were the wisest of men in other areas where they were not wise. So I left them too feeling that I had got the better of them, in the same way as I had got the better of the politicians.

Finally I went to the craftsmen. I was well aware that I knew virtually nothing, and confident that I would find much fine knowledge in them. Nor was I disappointed.

d   They *did* know things which I didn't know; in this respect they were wiser than I was. However, our good friends the skilled workmen seemed also to me, men of Athens, to have the same failing as the writers. Each one, because of his skill in practising his

e   craft, thought himself extremely wise in other matters of importance as well; and this presumptuousness of theirs seemed to me to obscure the wisdom they did have. So I asked myself, on behalf of the oracle, whether I should accept being the way I was— without any of their wisdom, or any of their foolishness—or whether I ought to possess both the qualities they possessed. The answer I gave myself and the oracle was that it was best for me to remain as I was.

This survey, men of Athens, has aroused much hostility against me, of the most

23   damaging and serious kind. The result has been a great deal of prejudice, and in partic-

ular, this description of me as being "wise." That is because the people who were present on such occasions think that I am an expert myself on those subjects in which I demolish the claims of others. The truth probably is, gentlemen, that in reality god is wise, and that what he means by his reply to Chaerephon is that human wisdom is of little or no value. When he refers to the man here before you—to Socrates—and goes out of his way to use my name, he is probably using me as an example, as if he were saying "That man is the wisest among you, mortals, who realises, as Socrates does, that he doesn't really amount to much when it comes to wisdom." b

That's why, to this day, I go round investigating and enquiring, as the god would have me do, if I think anyone—Athenian or foreigner—is wise. And when I find he is not, then, in support of the god, I demonstrate that he is not wise. My preoccupation with this task has left me no time worth speaking of to take any part in public life or family life. Instead I live in extreme poverty as a result of my service to the god.

Another problem is that young people follow me—the ones with the most time at their disposal, the sons of the rich—of their own free will; they love listening to people being cross-examined. They often imitate me themselves, and have a go at cross-examining others. Nor do I imagine they have any difficulty in finding people who think they know something, when in fact they know little or nothing. The result is that the victims of their cross-examination are angry with me, rather than themselves; they say Socrates is some sort of criminal, and that he has a bad influence on the young. d When you ask them what I do and what I teach that makes me a criminal, they can't answer; they don't know. But since they don't want to lose face, they come out with the standard accusations made against all philosophers, the stuff about "things in heaven and things under the earth," and "not recognising the gods" and "making the weaker argument stronger." The truth, I think, they would refuse to admit, which is that they have been shown up as pretenders to knowledge who really know nothing. Since, therefore, they are ambitious and energetic, and there are a lot of them, and e since they speak forcibly and persuasively about me, they have been filling your ears for some time now, and most vigorously, with their attacks on me. c

That is what Meletus relied on when he brought this charge against me, with Anytus and Lycon—Meletus feeling offended as one of the poets, Anytus as one of the craftsmen and politicians, Lycon as one of the orators. The result, as I said at the beginning, is that it would surprise me if I were able to remove from your minds, in so short a time, a prejudice which has grown so strong. This is the truth, I assure you, men of 24 Athens. I speak with absolutely no concealment or reservation. I'm pretty sure it's this way of speaking which makes me unpopular. My unpopularity is the proof that I am speaking the truth, that this *is* the prejudice against me, and these *are* the reasons for it. You can enquire into these matters—now or later—and you will find them to be so. b

So much for the accusations made by my first group of accusers. I hope you'll find what I've said a satisfactory defence against them. Now let me try and defend myself against Meletus, that excellent patriot (as he claims) and my more recent accusers. Let's treat them as a separate prosecution, and consider in its turn the charge brought by them. It runs something like this: it says that Socrates is guilty of being a bad influence on the young, and of not recognising the gods whom the state recognises, but practising a new religion of the supernatural.

That's what the charge consists of. Let's examine this charge point by point. He c says I am guilty of having a bad influence on the young. But *I* claim, men of Athens, that Meletus is guilty of playing games with what is deadly serious; he is too quick to bring people to trial, pretending to be serious and care about things to which he has never given a moment's thought. That this is the truth, I will try to prove to you as d well. Come now, Meletus, tell me this. I take it you regard the well-being of the young as of the utmost importance?

MELETUS: I do.

SOCRATES: In that case, please tell these people who it is who is a good influence on the young. Obviously you must know, since you're so concerned about it. You've tracked down, so you say, the man who is a bad influence—me—and are bringing me here before these people and accusing me. So come on, tell them who is a good influence; point out to them who it is.

You see, Meletus? You are silent; you have nothing to say. Don't you think that's a disgrace, and a sufficient proof of what I am saying—that you haven't given it any thought? Tell us, my friend, who is a good influence?

e MELETUS: The laws.

SOCRATES: Brilliant! But that's not what I'm asking. The question is what *man*— who will of course start off with just this knowledge, the laws.

MELETUS: These men, Socrates, the members of the jury.

SOCRATES: Really, Meletus? These men are capable of educating the young and being a good influence on them?

MELETUS: They certainly are.

SOCRATES: All of them? Or are some capable, and others not?

MELETUS: All of them.

25 SOCRATES: How remarkably fortunate—no shortage of benefactors there, then. What about the spectators in court? Do they have a good influence, or not?

MELETUS: Yes, they do, as well.

SOCRATES: What about the members of the council?

MELETUS: Yes, the members of the council also.

SOCRATES: But surely, Meletus, the people in the assembly—the citizens meeting *as* the assembly—surely they don't have a bad influence on the young? Don't they too—all of them—have a good influence?

MELETUS: Yes, they do too.

SOCRATES: Apart from me, then, the entire population of Athens, as it appears, makes the young into upright citizens. I alone am a bad influence. Is that what you mean?

MELETUS: Yes, that's exactly what I mean.

b SOCRATES: That's certainly a great misfortune to charge me with. Answer me this, though: do you think the situation is the same with horses as well? Do the people who are good for them make up the entire population, and is there just one person who has a harmful effect on them? Isn't it the exact opposite? Isn't there just one person, or very few people—trainers—capable of doing them any good? Don't most people, if they spend time with horses, or have anything to do with them, have a harmful effect on them? Isn't that the situation, Meletus, both with horses and with all other living creatures?

It certainly is, whether you and Anytus deny it or admit it. After all, it would be a piece of great good fortune for the young, if only one person has a bad influence on them, and everyone else has a good influence. No, Meletus. You show quite clearly

c that you have never cared in the slightest for the young; you reveal your own lack of interest quite plainly, since you've never given a moment's thought to the things you're prosecuting me for.

Another point. Tell us honestly, Meletus, is it better to live with good fellow-citizens, or with bad? Answer, can't you? It's not a difficult question. Isn't it true that bad citizens do some harm to those who are their neighbours at any particular time, while good citizens do some good?

MELETUS: Yes, of course.

SOCRATES: That being so, does anyone choose to be harmed by those close to him rather than be helped by them? Answer, there's a good fellow. Besides, the law re-   d quires you to answer. Is there anyone who chooses to be harmed?

MELETUS: No, of course not.

SOCRATES: Well, then. You bring me to court for being a bad influence on the young, and making them worse people. Are you saying I do this deliberately, or without realising it?

MELETUS: Deliberately, I'm sure of it.

SOCRATES: Really, Meletus? How odd. Are you, at your age, so much wiser than me at mine? Are *you* aware that bad people generally have a harmful effect on those they come into contact with, and that good people have a good effect? And have *I*   e reached such a height of stupidity as not even to realise that if I make one of my neighbours a worse man, I'm likely to come to some harm at his hands? And is the result that I deliberately do such great damage as you describe? On this point I don't believe you, Meletus; and nor, I think, does anyone else. No. Either I'm not a bad influence on the young, or if I do have a bad influence, I do so without realising it. Either way you are   26 wrong. And if I have a bad influence without realising it, it's not our custom to bring people here to court for errors of this sort, but to take them on one side, and instruct them privately, pointing out their mistakes. Obviously, if I'm taught, I shall stop doing what I don't at the moment realise I *am* doing. But you avoided spending time with me and instructing me; you refused to do it. Instead you bring me here to court, where it is our custom to bring those who need punishment, not those who need to learn.

I needn't go on, men of Athens. It must now be clear, as I've said, that Meletus has never given the slightest thought to these matters. All the same, Meletus, tell us this: *in what way* do you claim I'm a bad influence on the young? Isn't it obvious I do   b it in the way described in the charge you've brought against me—by teaching them not to recognise the gods the city recognises, but to practise this new religion of the supernatural instead? Isn't that your claim, that it's by teaching them these things that I have a bad influence?

MELETUS: Yes, that certainly is exactly what I claim.

SOCRATES: Well then, Meletus, in the name of these gods we are now talking about, make yourself a little clearer, both to me and to these gentlemen here, since *I* at   c least cannot understand you. Do you mean I teach them to accept that there are *some* gods—not the gods the state accepts, but other gods? In that case I myself must also accept that there are gods, so I am not a complete atheist, and am not guilty on that count. Is this what you charge me with, accepting other gods? Or are you saying that I don't myself recognise any gods at all, and that I teach the same beliefs to others?

MELETUS: Yes, that's what I am saying. You don't recognise any gods at all.

SOCRATES: Meletus, you are beyond belief. What can possess you to say that?   d Don't I accept that the sun and moon are gods, in the same way as everyone else does?

MELETUS: Good heavens, no, men of the jury. He says the sun is a stone, and the moon is made of earth.

SOCRATES: Is it Anaxagoras you think you're accusing, my dear Meletus? Do you have such contempt for these men here? Do you think them so illiterate as to be unaware that the works of Anaxagoras of Clazomenae are stuffed full of speculations of that sort? And do the young really learn these things from me, when there are often

books on sale, for a drachma at the very most, in the Orchestra, in the Agora? They can
e   laugh at Socrates if he claims these views as his own—especially such eccentric views.
However, as god is your witness, is that your view of me? Do I not accept the existence of any god at all?

MELETUS: No, in god's name, no god at all.

SOCRATES: What you say is unbelievable, Meletus—even, I think to yourself.
This man here, men of Athens, strikes me as an arrogant lout; his prosecution of me is
prompted entirely by arrogance, loutishness, and youth. It's as if he were setting a trick
27   question, to test me: "Will Socrates the wise realise that I'm playing with words and
contradicting myself, or will I deceive him and the others who hear it?" He certainly
seems to me to contradict himself, in his accusation. He might as well say "Socrates is
guilty of not recognising the gods, but recognising the gods instead." And that is not a
serious proposition.

Please join me, gentlemen, in examining the reasons why I think this is what his
accusation amounts to. You, Meletus, answer us. And you *(to the jurymen),* as I asked
b   you at the beginning, remember not to interrupt me if I construct my argument in my
usual way.

Is there anyone in the world, Meletus, who accepts the existence of human activity, but not of human beings? He must answer, gentlemen. Don't allow him to keep
making all these interruptions. Is there anyone who denies horses, but accepts equine
activity? Or denies the existence of flute-players, but accepts flute-playing? No, my
very good friend, there isn't. If you refuse to answer, then I'll say it—to you and
everyone else present here. But do answer my next question: is there anyone who ac-
c   cepts the activity of the supernatural, but denies supernatural beings?

MELETUS: No, there isn't.

SOCRATES: How kind of you—forced to answer, against your will, by these people here. Very well, then. You claim that I practise and teach a religion of the supernatural—whether of a new or conventional kind—so I do at least, on your own admission,
accept the existence of the supernatural. You even swore to it, on oath, in your indictment. But if I accept the supernatural, it follows, I take it, that I must necessarily admit
the existence of supernatural beings, must I not? I must; I take your silence for agree-
d   ment. And don't we regard supernatural beings as either gods or the children of gods?
Yes or no?

MELETUS: We certainly do.

SOCRATES: In that case, if I accept supernatural beings—as you admit—and if supernatural beings are gods of some sort, then you can see what I mean when I say that
you are setting trick questions, and playing with words, claiming first that I do *not* believe in gods, and then again claiming that I *do* believe in gods, since I do believe in
supernatural beings. If, on the other hand, supernatural beings are some form of illegitimate children of gods—born of nymphs or of some of the other mothers they are said
to be born from—who on earth could believe that there are children of gods, but no
gods? It would be as absurd as saying you believed there were such things as mules,
e   the offspring of horses and donkeys, but didn't believe there were horses and donkeys.

No, Meletus, the only possible explanation for your bringing this accusation
against me is that you wanted to test us—or that you didn't have any genuine offence
to charge me with. There's no conceivable way you could persuade anyone in the
28   world with a grain of intelligence that belief in the supernatural and the divine does not
imply belief in supernatural beings, divine beings and heroes.

So much for that, men of Athens. I don't think it takes much of a defence to
show that in the terms of Meletus' indictment I am not guilty. What I have said so far

should be enough. There remains what I said in the earlier part of my speech, that there is strong and widespread hostility towards me. Be in no doubt that this is true. It is this which will convict me, if it does convict me—not Meletus, not Anytus, but the prejudice and malice of the many. What has convicted many other good men before me will, I think, convict me too. There's no danger of its stopping at me.

That being so, you might ask "Well, Socrates, aren't you ashamed of living a life which has resulted in your now being on trial for your life?" I would answer you, quite justifiably, "You are wrong, sir, if you think that a man who is worth anything at all should take into account the chances of life and death. No, the only thing he should think about, when he acts, is whether he is acting rightly or wrongly, and whether this is the behaviour of a good man or a bad man. After all, if we accept your argument, those of the demigods who died at Troy would have been sorry creatures—and none more so than Achilles, the son of Thetis. Compared with the threat of dishonour, he regarded danger as of no importance at all. When he was eager to kill Hector, his mother, who was a goddess, said something like this to him, I imagine: 'My son, if you avenge the death of your friend Patroclus, and kill Hector, you will yourself be killed, since death awaits you immediately after Hector.' When Achilles heard this, he gave no thought to death or danger; what he feared much more was living as a coward, and not avenging his friends. 'Let me die immediately,' he said, 'after making the wrong-doer pay the penalty, rather than remain here by the curved ships, a laughing-stock, like a clod of earth.' You don't imagine *he* gave any thought to death or danger."

That's the way of things, men of Athens, it really is. Where a man takes up his position—in the belief that it is the best position—or is told to take up a position by his commanding officer, there he should stay, in my view, regardless of danger. He should not take death into account, or anything else apart from dishonour. As for me, when the commanders whom you chose to command me told me to take up position at Potidaea and Amphipolis and Delium, on those occasions I stayed where they posted me, just like anyone else, and risked death. Would it not have been very illogical of me, when *god* deployed me, as I thought and believed, to live my life as a philosopher, examining myself and others, then to be afraid of death—or anything else at all—and abandon my post?

It would indeed be illogical, and in that case you would certainly be completely justified in bringing me to court for not accepting the existence of the gods, since I disobey their oracle, and am afraid of death, and think I am wise when I am not. After all, the fear of death is just that, gentlemen—thinking one is wise when one is not—since it's a claim to know what one doesn't know. For all anyone knows, death may in fact be the best thing in the world that can happen to a man; yet men fear it as if they had certain knowledge that it is the greatest of all evils. This is without doubt the most reprehensible folly—the folly of thinking one knows what one does not know.

As for me, gentlemen, perhaps here too I *am* different from most people, in this one particular; and if I did claim to be in any way wiser than anyone else, it would be in this, that lacking any certain knowledge of what happens after death, I am also aware that I have no knowledge. But that it is evil and shameful to do wrong, and disobey one's superiors, divine or human, that I *do* know. Compared therefore with the evils which I know to be evils, I shall never fear, or try to avoid, what for all I know may turn out to be good.

Suppose you now acquit me, rejecting Anytus' argument that either this case should not have been brought in the first place, or, since it *had* been brought, that it was out of the question not to put me to death. He told you that if I got away with it, your sons would all start putting Socrates' teachings into practice, and be totally overwhelmed by my bad influence. And suppose your response were to say to me: "Socrates, on this occasion we will not do what Anytus wants. We acquit you—on this condition, however, that you give up spending your time in this enquiry, and give up the search for wisdom. If you are caught doing it again, you will be put to death."

d   Even if, then, to repeat, you were to acquit me on these conditions, I would say to you, "Men of Athens, I have the highest regard and affection for you, but I will obey god rather than you. While I have breath and strength, I will not give up the search for wisdom. I will carry on nagging at you, and pointing out your errors to those of you I meet from day to day. I shall say, in my usual way, 'My very good sir, you are a citizen of Athens, a city which is the greatest and most renowned for wisdom and power. Aren't you ashamed to care about money, and how to make as much of it as possible, and about reputation and public recognition, whereas for wisdom and truth, and mak-

e   ing your soul as good as it can possibly be, you do not care, and give no thought to these things at all?' And if any of you objects, and says he does care, I shall not just let him go, or walk away and leave him. No, I shall question him, cross-examine him, try to prove him wrong. And if I find he has not achieved a state of excellence, but still

30   claims he has, then I shall accuse him of undervaluing what is most important, and paying too much attention to what is less important.

"That is what I shall do for anyone I meet, young or old, foreigner or citizen— but especially for my fellow-citizens, since you are more closely related to me. That is what god tells me to do, I promise you, and I believe that this service of mine to god is the most valuable asset you in this city have ever yet possessed. I spend my whole time going round trying to persuade both the young and old among you not to spend your

b   time or energy in caring about your bodies or about money, but rather in making your souls as good as possible. I tell you, 'Money cannot create a good soul, but a good soul can turn money—and everything else in private life and public life—into a good thing for men.' If saying things like this is a bad influence on the young, then things like this must be harmful. But if anyone claims I say anything different from this, he is wrong. With that in mind, Athenians," I would say, "either do what Anytus wants, or don't do it; either acquit me, or don't, knowing that I will not behave differently even if I am to be put to death a thousand times over."

c   Don't interrupt, men of Athens. Please stick to what I asked you to do, which was not to interrupt what I say, but to give me a hearing. It will be in your interest, I think, to hear me. I have some more things to say which you could object to quite violently. Please don't, however.

I have just described the kind of man I am. Take my word for it, if you put me to death, you will harm yourselves more than you will harm me. As for me, no harm can

d   come to me from Meletus or Anytus, who *cannot* injure me, since I do not think god ever allows a better man to be injured by a worse. Yes, I know he might put me to death, possibly, or send me into exile, or deprive me of citizen rights. And perhaps *he* regards these as great evils—as I suppose others may too. However, *I* do not. I regard it as a much greater evil to act as he is acting now, attempting to put a man to death unjustly.

It follows, men of Athens, that in this trial I am not by any means defending myself, as you might think. No, I am defending you. I don't want you to fail to recognise

e   god's gift to you, and find me guilty. If you put me to death, you will not easily find another like me. I have, almost literally, settled on the city at god's command. It's as if the city, to use a slightly absurd simile, were a horse—a large horse, high-mettled, but which because of its size is somewhat sluggish, and needs to be stung into action by some kind of horsefly. I think god has caused me to settle on the city as this horsefly, the sort that never stops, all day long, coming to rest on every part of you, stinging each one of you into action, and persuading and criticising each one of you. 31

Another like me will not easily come your way, gentlemen, so if you take my advice you will spare me. You may very likely get annoyed with me, as people do when they are dozing and somebody wakes them up. And you might then swat me, as Anytus wants you to, and kill me, quite easily. Then you could spend the rest of your lives asleep, unless god cared enough for you to send you someone else.

To convince yourselves that someone like me really is a gift from god to the city, b look at things this way. Behaviour like mine does not seem to be natural. I have completely neglected my own affairs, and allowed my family to be neglected, all these years, while I devoted myself to looking after your interests—approaching each one of you individually, like a father or elder brother, and trying to persuade you to consider the good of your soul.

If I made anything out of it, and charged a fee for this advice, there'd be some sense in my doing it. As it is, you can see for yourselves that although the prosecution accused me, in their unscrupulous way, of everything under the sun, there was one point on which they were not so unscrupulous as to produce any evidence. They didn't c claim that I ever made any money, or asked for any. I can produce convincing evidence, I think, that I am telling the truth—namely my poverty.

It may perhaps seem odd that in my private life I go round giving people advice like this, and interfering, without having the courage, in public life, to come forward before you, the people, and give advice on matters of public interest. The reason for this is what you have often heard me talking about, in all sorts of places, the kind of divine or supernatural sign that comes to me. This must have been what Meletus was d making fun of when he wrote out the charge against me. It started when I was a child, a kind of voice which comes to me, and when it comes, always stops me doing what I'm just about to do; it never tells me what I *should* do. It's this which opposes my taking part in politics, and rightly opposes it, in my opinion. You can be sure, men of Athens, that if I had tried, at any time in the past, to go into politics, I would have been dead long ago, and been no use at all either to you or to myself.

Please don't be annoyed with me for speaking the truth. There is no-one in the e world who can get away with deliberately opposing you—or any other popular assembly—or trying to put a stop to all the unjust and unlawful things which are done in pol- 32 itics; it is essential that the true fighter for justice, if he is to survive even for a short time, should remain a private individual, and not go into public life.

I shall give you compelling evidence for this—not words, but what you value, actions. Listen to things which have actually happened to me, and you will realise that I would never obey anyone if it was wrong to do so, simply through fear of dying. No, I would refuse to obey, even if it meant my death. What I am going to say now is the kind of boasting you often hear in the lawcourts; but it is true, for all that. b

I have never, men of Athens, held any public office in the city, apart from being a member of the Council. It turned out that our tribe, Antiochis, formed the standing committee when you decided, by a resolution of the Council, to put on trial collectively the ten generals who failed to pick up the survivors from the sea battle. This was unconstitutional, as you afterwards all decided. On that occasion I was the only member of the standing committee to argue against you. I told you not to act unconstitutionally, and voted against you. The politicians were all set to bring an immediate action against me, and have me arrested on the spot, and you were encouraging them to do so,

and shouting your approval, but still I thought I ought to take my chance on the side of
law and justice, rather than side with you, through fear of imprisonment or death, when
you were proposing to act unjustly.

That was when the city was still a democracy. When the oligarchy came to
power, the junta in its turn sent for me, with four others, and gave me the task of bringing Leon of Salamis from his home in Salamis to the Council chamber, so he could be
put to death. They often gave orders of this kind, to all sorts of people; they wanted to
implicate as many people as possible in their crimes. Again I demonstrated—by what I
did this time, rather than what I said—that my fear of death was, if you will pardon my
saying so, negligible; what I was afraid of, more than anything, was acting without regard for justice or religion. I was not intimidated by the junta's power—great though it
was—into acting unjustly. When we left the Council chamber, the other four went off
to Salamis and fetched Leon, but I left, and went home. I might perhaps have been put
to death for that, if their power hadn't soon after been brought to an end. Of these
events any number of people will give evidence to you.

Do you think I would have survived all these years if I had taken part in public
life, and played the part a good man should play, supporting what was just, and attaching the highest importance to it, as is right? Don't you believe it, men of Athens. Nor
would anyone else in the world have survived. As for me, it will be clear that, throughout my life, if I have done anything at all in public life, my character is as I have described—and in private life the same. I was never at any time prepared to tolerate injustice in anyone at all—certainly not in any of the people my critics say were my
pupils.

I have never been anyone's teacher. Equally, I never said no to anyone, young or
old, who wanted to listen to me talking and pursuing my quest. Nor do I talk if I am
paid, and not talk if I am not paid. I make myself available to rich and poor alike, so
they can question me and listen, if anyone feels like it, to what I say in reply. And if
any of these people turns out well or badly, I cannot legitimately be held responsible; I
neither promised any knowledge, ever, to any of them, nor did I teach them. If anyone
ever claims to have learnt or heard anything from me privately, beyond what anyone
else learnt or heard, I can assure you he is lying.

Why then do some people like spending so much of their time with me? You
have heard the answer to that, men of Athens; I have told you the whole truth. They
like hearing the cross-examination of those who think they are wise when they are not.
After all, it is quite entertaining. For me, as I say, this is a task imposed by god,
through prophecies and dreams and in every way in which divine destiny has ever imposed any task on a man.

All this is the truth, men of Athens, and easily tested. If I really am a bad influence on some of the young, and have been a bad influence on others in the past, and if
some of them, as they have grown older, have realised that I gave them bad advice at
some point when they were young, they ought to come forward now, I'd have thought,
to accuse me and punish me. And if they weren't prepared to do so themselves, some
of the members of their families—fathers, brothers, or other close relatives—ought
now to remember, if those close to them came to some harm at my hands, and want to
punish me. Certainly I can see plenty of them here today—Crito there, for a start, my
contemporary and fellow-demesman, the father of Critobulus, who's here too. Then
there's Lysanias from the deme of Sphettos, the father of Aeschines here; or indeed
Antiphon over there, from Cephisus, the father of Epigenes.

Then there are the ones whose brothers have spent their time in my company:
Nicostratus the son of Theozotides, the brother of Theodotus—Theodotus of course is

dead, so he couldn't have put any pressure on his brother; and I can see Paralius, the son of Demodocus, whose brother was Theages. Then there's Adeimantus I can see, the son of Ariston, whose brother is Plato here; or Aiantodorus, whose brother Apollodorus is present also.

There are plenty more I could name for you. Ideally, Meletus would have called some of them himself to give evidence during his speech. However, in case he forgot at the time, let him call them now—I give up my place to him—and let him say if he has any evidence of that kind.

It's the exact opposite, gentlemen. You'll find they're all on my side—although I'm a bad influence, although I harm their relatives, as Meletus and Anytus claim. I can   b
see why the actual victims of my influence might have some reason to be on my side; but those who have not been influenced, the older generation, their relatives, what reason do they have for being on my side, other than the correct and valid reason that they know Meletus is lying, and I am telling the truth?

Well, there we are, gentlemen. That, and perhaps a bit more along the same lines, is roughly what I might have to say in my defence. There may possibly be those among   c
you who find it irritating, when you remember your own experience; you may, in a trial less important than this one, have begged and pleaded with the jury, with many tears, bringing your own children, and many others among your family and friends, up here to arouse as much sympathy as possible; whereas I refuse to do any of these things—even though I am, as it probably seems to you, in the greatest danger of all.

Thoughts like this could make some of you feel a little antagonistic towards me.   d
For just this reason, you might get angry, and let anger influence your vote. If any of you does feel like this—I am sure you don't, but if you did—I think I might fairly say to you: "Of course I too have a family, my good friend. I do not come, in Homer's famous words, 'from oak or rock.' No, I was born of men, so I do have a family, and sons, men of Athens, three of them. One is not quite grown-up, the other two still boys. All the same, I am not going to bring any of them up here and beg you to acquit me."

Why will I not do any of these things? Not out of obstinacy, men of Athens, nor   e
out of contempt for you. And whether or not I am untroubled by the thought of death is beside the point. No, it's a question of what is fitting—for me, for you, and for the whole city. I don't think it's right for me to do any of these things, at my age and with the reputation I have. It may be justified or unjustified, but there's a prevailing belief   35
that Socrates is in some way different from other people.

If those of you who seem to be outstanding in wisdom or courage, or any other quality, were to behave like this, it would be deplorable. Yet this is just the way I *have* seen men behaving when they are brought to trial. They may seem to be men of some distinction, but still they act in the most extraordinary way; they seem to think it will be a terrible disaster for them if they are put to death—as if they'd be immortal if you didn't put them to death. I think they bring disgrace on the city. A visitor to our country might imagine that in Athens people of outstanding character, those whom the Athenians themselves single out from among themselves for positions of office and   b
other distinctions—that these men are no better than women.

Such behaviour, men of Athens, is not right for those of you with any kind of reputation at all; and if we who are on trial behave like that, you should not let us get away with it. You should make one thing absolutely clear, which is that you are much more ready to convict a defendant who stages one of these hysterical scenes, and makes our city an object of ridicule, than a defendant who behaves with decorum.

Quite apart from what is fitting, gentlemen, I think there is no justice, either, in begging favours from the jury, or being acquitted by begging; justice requires instruc-   c tion and persuasion. The juryman does not sit there for the purpose of handing out justice as a favour; he sits there to decide what justice is. He has not taken an oath to do a favour to anyone he takes a fancy to, but rather to reach a verdict in accordance with the laws. So *we* should not encourage in you the habit of breaking your oath, nor should *you* allow the habit to develop. If we did, we should neither of us be showing any respect for the gods.

d   Do not ask me, therefore, men of Athens, to conduct myself towards you in a way which I regard as contrary to right, justice and religion—least of all, surely, when I am being accused of impiety by Meletus here. After all, if I did persuade you and coerce you, by my begging, despite your oath, then clearly I *would* be teaching you to deny the existence of the gods; my whole defence would simply amount to accusing myself of not recognising the gods. And that is far from being the case. I do recognise them, men of Athens, as none of my accusers does, and I entrust to you and to god the task of reaching a verdict in my case in whatever way will be best both for me and for you.

*   *   *

e   If I am not upset, men of Athens, at what has just happened—your finding me guilty— there are a number of reasons. In particular, the result was not unexpected; in fact, I'm
36   surprised by the final number of votes on either side. Personally, I was expecting a large margin, not a narrow one; as it is, if only thirty votes had gone the other way, apparently I would have been acquitted. Indeed, on Meletus' charge, as I see it, I *have* been acquitted, even as things are. And not just acquitted; it's clear to anyone that if Anytus had not come forward, with Lycon, to accuse me, Meletus would have incurred
b   a fine of a thousand drachmas for not receiving twenty percent of the votes.

So the man proposes the death penalty for me. Very well. What counter-proposal am I to make to you, men of Athens? What I deserve, obviously. And what is that? What do I deserve to suffer or pay, for . . . for what? For not keeping quiet all through my life, for neglecting the things most people devote their lives to: business, family life, holding office—as general, or as leader of the assembly, or in some other capacity—or the alliances and factions which occur in political life. I thought, quite hon-
c   estly, that my sense of right and wrong would not allow me to survive in politics; so I did not pursue a course in which I should have been no use either to you or to myself, but rather one in which I could give help to each one of you privately—the greatest help possible, as I claim. That is the direction I took. I tried to persuade each of you not to give any thought at all to his own affairs until he had first given some thought to himself, and tried to make himself as good and wise as possible; not to give any thought to the affairs of the city without first giving some thought to the city itself; and to observe the same priorities in other areas as well.

d   What then do I deserve for behaving like this? Something good, men of Athens, if I am really supposed to make a proposal in accordance with what I deserve. And what's more, a good of a kind which is some use to me. What then *is* of use to a poor man, your benefactor, who needs free time in which to advise you? There can't be anything more useful to a man of this sort, men of Athens, than to be given free meals at the public expense; this is much more use to him than it is to any Olympic victor among you, if one of you wins the horse race, or the two-horse or four-horse chariot
e   race. The Olympic winner makes you *seem* to be happy; I make you really happy. He doesn't need the food; I do need it. So if I must propose a penalty based on justice, on
37   what I deserve, then that's what I propose—free meals at the public expense.

Here again, I suppose, in the same sort of way as when I was talking about appeals to pity and pleas for mercy, you may think I speak as I do out of sheer obstinacy. But it's not obstinacy, men of Athens; it's like this. I myself am convinced that I don't knowingly do wrong to anyone in the world, but I can't persuade you of that; we haven't had enough time to talk to one another. Mind you, if it were the custom here, as it is in other places, to decide cases involving the death penalty over several days rather than in one day, I believe you would have been persuaded. As it is, it was not   b
easy in a short time to overcome the strong prejudice against me.

But if I am convinced that I don't do wrong to anyone else, I am certainly not going to do wrong to myself, or speak against myself—saying I deserve something bad, and proposing some such penalty for myself. Why should I? Through fear of undergoing the penalty Meletus proposes, when I claim not to know whether it is good or bad? Should I, in preference to that, choose one of the things I know perfectly well to be bad, and propose that as a penalty?

Imprisonment? What is the point of living in prison, and being the slave of those   c
in the prison service at any particular time? A fine? And be imprisoned until I pay? That's the same as the first suggestion, since I haven't any money to pay a fine. Should I propose exile? I suppose you might accept that. But I'd have to be very devoted to life, men of Athens, to lose the power of rational thought so completely, and not be able to work out what would happen. If you, my fellow-citizens, couldn't stand my talk and my conversation, if you found them too boring and irritating, which is why you   d
now want to be rid of them, will people in some other country find it any easier to put up with them? Don't you believe it, men of Athens.

A fine life I should lead in exile, a man of my age—moving and being driven from city to city. I've no doubt that wherever I go, the young will listen to me, the way they do here. If I tell them to go away, they will send me into exile of their own accord, bringing pressure to bear on their elders; if I don't tell them to go away, their fathers   e
and relatives will exile me, out of concern for them.

I can imagine someone saying, "How about keeping your mouth shut, Socrates, and leading a quiet life? Can't you please go into exile, and live like that?" Of all things, this is the hardest point on which to convince some of you. If I say that it is disobeying god, and that for this reason I can't lead a quiet life, you won't believe me—   38
you'll think I'm using that as an excuse. If on the other hand I say that really the greatest good in a man's life is this, to be each day discussing human excellence and the other subjects you hear me talking about, examining myself and other people, and that the unexamined life isn't worth living—if I say this, you will believe me even less.

All the same, the situation is as I describe it, gentlemen—hard though it is to   b
convince you. Equally, for myself, I can't get used to the idea that I deserve anything bad. If I had any money, I would propose as large a fine as I could afford; that wouldn't do me any harm. As it is, I have no money, unless you are willing to have me propose an amount I *could* afford. I suppose I could pay you something like a hundred drachmas of silver, if you like. So that is the amount I propose.

Plato here, men of Athens—and Crito and Critobulus and Apollodorus—tell me to propose a penalty of three thousand drachmas; they say they guarantee it. I propose that amount, therefore, and they will offer full security to you for the money.

*   *   *

For just a small gain in time, men of Athens, you will now have the reputation and re-   c
sponsibility, among those who want to criticise the city, of having put to death

Despite refuting his accusers (as recorded in the *Apology*), Socrates was found guilty of impiety toward the gods and of corrupting the youth. He was sentenced to die by drinking the poison hemlock. (*Corbis-Bettmann*)

Socrates, that wise man—they will *say* I am wise, the people who want to blame you, even though I am not. If you'd waited a little, you could have had what you wanted without lifting a finger. You can see what age I am—far advanced in years, and close to death.

I say that not to all of you, but to those who voted for the death penalty. And I
d   have something else to say to the same people. You may think, men of Athens, that I have lost my case through inability to make the kind of speech I *could* have used to persuade you, had I thought it right to do and say absolutely anything to secure my acquittal. Far from it. I have lost my case, not for want of a speech, but for want of effrontery and shamelessness, for refusing to make to you the kind of speech you most enjoy listening to. You'd like to have heard me lamenting and bewailing, and doing
e   and saying all sorts of other things which are beneath my dignity, in my opinion—the kind of things you've grown used to hearing from other people.

I did not think it right, when I was speaking, to demean myself through fear of danger, nor do I now regret conducting my defence in the way I did. I had much rather defend myself like this, and be put to death, than behave in the way I have described, and go on living. Neither in the courts, nor in time of war, is it right—either for me or
39   for anyone else—to devote one's efforts simply to avoiding death at all costs.

In battle it is often clear that death can be escaped, by dropping your weapons and throwing yourself on the mercy of your pursuers—and in any kind of danger there are all sorts of other devices for avoiding death, if you can bring yourself not to mind what you do or say. There's no difficulty in *that,* gentlemen, in escaping death. What is much harder is avoiding wickedness, since wickedness runs faster than death. So now, not surprisingly, I, who am old and slow, have been overtaken by the slower of the two. My accusers, being swift and keen, have been overtaken by the faster, by wickedness. Now I am departing, to pay the penalty of death inflicted by you. But they have already incurred the penalty, inflicted by truth, for wickedness and injustice. I accept my sentence, as they do theirs. I suppose that's probably how it was bound to turn out—and I have no complaints.

Having dealt with that, I now wish to make you a prophecy, those of you who voted for my condemnation. I am at that point where people are most inclined to make prophecies—which is when they are just about to die. To you gentlemen who have put me to death, I say that retribution will come to you, directly after my death—retribution far worse, god knows, than the death penalty which you have inflicted on me.

You have acted as you have today in the belief that you will avoid having to submit your lives to examination, but you will find the outcome is just the opposite; that is my prediction. There will be more people now to examine you—the ones I have so far been keeping in check without your realising it. They will be harder to deal with, being so much younger, and you will be more troubled by them. If you think that by putting men to death you can stop people criticising you for not living your lives in the right way, you are miscalculating badly. As a way of escape, this is neither effective nor creditable; the best and simplest way lies not in weeding out other people, but in making oneself as good a person as possible.

That is my prophecy to you who voted for my condemnation, and now I am prepared to let you go. To those who voted for my acquittal I'd like to make a few remarks about what has just happened, while the magistrates get on with the formalities, and it is not yet time for me to go where I must go to die. Please keep me company, gentlemen, for this little time; there's no reason why we shouldn't talk to one another while it is permitted. I regard you as my friends, and so to you I am prepared to explain the significance of today's outcome.

Gentlemen of the jury—since you I properly *can* call jurymen—a remarkable thing has happened to me. The prophetic voice I have got so used to, my supernatural voice, has always in the past been at my elbow, opposing me even in matters of little importance, if I was about to take a false step. You can see for yourselves the situation I'm now in. You might think—and this is how it is generally regarded—it was the ultimate misfortune. Yet the sign from god did not oppose my leaving home this morning, nor my appearance here in court, nor was there any point in my speech when it stopped me saying what I was just about to say.

Often in the past, when I have been talking, the sign has stopped me in full flow; this time it has not opposed me at any stage in the whole proceedings—either in what I have done or in what I have said. What do I take to be the reason for this? I'll tell you. The chances are that what has happened to me here is a good thing, and that it is impossible for those of us who think death is an evil to understand it correctly. I have strong evidence for this. The sign I know so well would unquestionably have opposed me, if things had not been going to turn out all right for me.

There is another reason for being confident that death is a good thing. Look at it like this. Death is one of two things; either it is like the dead person being nothing at all, and having no consciousness of anything at all; or, as we are told, it is actually some sort of change, a journey of the soul from this place to somewhere different. Suppose it is a total absence of consciousness—like sleep, when the sleeper isn't even dreaming. Then death would be a marvellous bonus. At least, I certainly think that if a man had to choose the night on which he slept so soundly that he did not even dream, and if he had to compare all the other nights and days of his life with that night, if he had to think carefully about it, and then say how many days and nights he had spent in his life that were better and more enjoyable than that night—I think that not just a pri-

e   vate individual, but even the great king of Persia could count these dreamless nights on the fingers of one hand compared with the other days and nights. If death is something like that, I call it a bonus. After all, the whole of time, seen in this way, seems no longer than a single night.

If, on the other hand, death is a kind of journey from here to somewhere differ-ent, and what we're told about all the dead being there is true, what greater good could

41   there be than that, gentlemen of the jury? Imagine arriving in the other world, getting away from the people here who claim to be judges, and finding real judges, the ones who are said to decide cases there—Minos, Rhadamanthys, Aeacus, Triptolemus, and others of the demigods who acted with justice in their own lives. Wouldn't that be a worthwhile journey?

Or again, what would any of you give to join Orpheus and Musaeus, Hesiod and Homer? Personally, I am quite prepared to die many times over, if these stories are

b   true. For me at least, time spent there would be wonderful—I'd keep meeting people like Palamedes, or Aias the son of Telamon, or any other of the ancients who died as a result of an unjust verdict; I could compare my own experience with theirs. That would be entertaining, I imagine. Best of all, I could spend my time questioning and examin-ing people there, just as I do people here, to find out which of them is wise, and which thinks he is wise but isn't.

What would you give, men of the jury, to interview the man who led the great

c   expedition to Troy—or Odysseus, or Sisyphus, or thousands of others one could men-tion, men and women? It would be an unimaginable pleasure to talk to them there, to enjoy their company, and question them. They certainly can't put you to death there for asking questions. They are better off than us in many ways—and not least because they are now immune to death for the rest of time, if what we are told is true.

You too, men of the jury, must not be apprehensive about death. You must re-gard one thing at least as certain—that no harm can come to a good man either in his life or after his death; what happens to him is not a matter of indifference to the gods.

d   Nor has my present situation arisen purely by chance; it is clear to me that it was better for me to die now and be released from my task. That's why my sign didn't at any point dissuade me, and why I am not in the least angry with those who voted against me, or with my accusers. Admittedly that wasn't their reason for voting against me, and accusing me; they thought they were doing me some harm. We *can* blame them for that.

However, I do have one request to make. It concerns my sons. When they grow

e   up, gentlemen, get your own back on them, if you think they are more interested in money—or in anything else—than in goodness, by annoying them in exactly the same way as I annoyed you. If they think they amount to something when they don't, then criticise them, as I criticised you. Tell them they are not giving any thought to the things that matter, and that they think they amount to something when they are worth

42   nothing. If you do this, I shall myself have been fairly treated by you—and so will my sons.

I must stop. It is time for us to go—me to my death, you to your lives. Which of us goes to the better fate, only god knows.

CRITO

SOCRATES: What are you doing here at this time, Crito? Isn't it still early?   43

CRITO: Yes, it is.

SOCRATES: How early, exactly?

CRITO: It's not yet started to get light.

SOCRATES: I'm surprised the warder didn't refuse to answer your knock.

CRITO: He's become something of a friend of mine, Socrates, what with my coming here so often. Besides, I've done him a bit of a favour.

SOCRATES: Have you just arrived, or have you been here some time?

CRITO: Quite some time.

SOCRATES: Then why on earth didn't you wake me up? What were you doing just   b
sitting there beside me in silence?

CRITO: I wouldn't have dreamt of it, Socrates. For my part, I wouldn't choose to be in this state of sleeplessness and misery; and for some time now it has astonished me to see how soundly you sleep. I deliberately didn't wake you because I wanted you to enjoy your rest. It has often struck me in the past, throughout my life in fact, how lucky you are in your temperament—and it strikes me much more forcibly in your present misfortune. You bear it so easily and calmly.

SOCRATES: Yes, Crito, I do. It wouldn't make much sense for a man my age to get upset at the prospect of dying.

CRITO: Other people your age, Socrates, find themselves in similar predicaments;   c
their age doesn't stop them getting upset at their misfortune.

SOCRATES: That's true. Anyway, why *have* you come so early?

CRITO: To bring news, Socrates, bad news. Not bad for you, as far as I can see, but for me and all your friends it is bad and hard to bear; and I think I shall find it as hard to bear as anybody.

SOCRATES: What sort of news? Has the boat from Delos arrived—the one my exe-   d
cution has been waiting for?

CRITO: It hasn't actually arrived, but I think it will today, judging by the reports of some people who've just come from Sunium. It was there when they left. It's clear from what they said that it will arrive today, and so tomorrow, Socrates, you will be forced to end your life.

SOCRATES: Well, Crito, if that is how the gods want it, I hope it will all turn out for the best. All the same, I don't think it will come today.

CRITO: What is that based on?   44

SOCRATES: I'll tell you. My death, I assume, is to take place on the day after the ship arrives.

CRITO: Yes. At least, that's what the prison authorities say.

SOCRATES: Then I think it will come tomorrow, not today. That's based on a dream I had last night, just before I woke up. So perhaps it was lucky you didn't wake me.

CRITO: What was the dream?

SOCRATES: I saw a woman, fair and beautiful, in a white cloak. She came up to   b
me, and called my name. "Socrates," she said, "On the third day shall you come to fertile Phthia."

CRITO: A strange dream, Socrates.

SOCRATES: Clear enough, though, I think, Crito.

CRITO: Only too clear, I'm afraid. Now listen, Socrates, it's not too late, even now, to do as I say and escape. For me, if you are put to death, it is a double disaster. Quite apart from losing a friend such as I shall never find again, there will also be

c   many who will think, those who don't know the two of us well, that I had the chance to save you if I'd been prepared to spend some money, and that I wasn't interested in doing so.

Can you think of a worse reputation than being thought to value money more highly than friends? Most people will never believe that it was you yourself who refused to leave here, and that we strongly encouraged you to do so.

SOCRATES: Really, Crito, why should we care so much about what "most people" believe? The best people, who are the ones we should worry about more, will realise that things were done in the way they actually were done.

d   CRITO: Yet you can see that we have no choice, Socrates, but to care about what most people think as well. The present situation is a clear example of how the many can injure us in ways which are not trivial, but just about as great as can be, if they are given the wrong impression about someone.

SOCRATES: If only the many *could* do us the greatest injuries, Crito. That would mean they were capable of doing us the greatest good as well, which would be excellent. As it is, they're incapable of doing either. They have no power to make a man either wise or foolish; nor do they care what effect they have.

e   CRITO: I dare say you are right. But tell me something, Socrates. Are you worried about me and the rest of your friends? Do you think, if you leave here, that we shall get into trouble with the people who make a living out of bringing private prosecutions, be-

45   cause we smuggled you out of here? Do you think we shall be forced to forfeit all our property, or pay a very large fine, and possibly undergo some further penalty in addition?

If something like that is what you are afraid of, don't give it another thought. We are in duty bound to run this risk to save you—that goes without saying—and even greater risks, if need be. Listen to me. Don't say "no."

SOCRATES: It *is* something I worry about, Crito. That, and many other things besides.

CRITO: Well then, do not be afraid on that score. There are people prepared, for not a very large sum of money, to save you and get you out of here. And apart from them, can't you see how easily bought they are, the men who make their living out of

b   prosecutions? It wouldn't need a lot of money to take care of them. You have my resources at your disposal; that should be plenty, I imagine. And if you're worried about me, and feel you shouldn't spend my money, look at the people we've got here who are not Athenians, who are ready to spend theirs. One of them, Simmias the Theban, has actually brought enough money for just this purpose; Cebes too is fully prepared, and so are many others.

So as I say, you should not let these fears stop you saving yourself; and do not let it be an objection, as you claimed in court, that you would not know what to do with yourself if you went into exile. There are lots of places you can go where they'll be

c   glad to see you; if you want to go to Thessaly, for example, my family has friends there who will be delighted to see you, and who will give you sanctuary. Nobody in Thessaly will give you any trouble.

Apart from that, Socrates, it is actually wrong, in my opinion, to sacrifice yourself, as you are proposing to do, when you could escape. You seem to be voluntarily choosing for yourself the kind of fate your enemies would have chosen for you—and *did* choose for you when they were trying to destroy you. Worse still, I think, is the betrayal of your own sons, when there is nothing to stop you bringing them up and educating them—and yet you are going to go away and leave them, and for all you care they can turn out how they will. They will have, in all probability, the kind of life orphans generally have when they lose their parents.

No. Either you shouldn't have children, or you should play your part, and go through with the labour of raising and educating them. You seem to me to be taking the easy way out. What you should do is choose what a decent and courageous man would choose—you who claim to have been concerned with human goodness all your life. Personally, I am ashamed both for you and for those of us who are your friends. I think this whole business of yours will be thought to be the result of some lack of resolution on our part—first of all the fact that the case came to court when it needn't have done, then the actual conduct of the case in court, and now this, as the final absurdity of the whole affair, that we shall be thought to have missed the opportunity—through our own cowardice and lack of resolution, since we didn't save you, nor did you save yourself, though it was possible, and within your power, with even a modest amount of help from us. Don't let all this be a humiliation, Socrates, both for you and for us, in addition to being an evil.

Think it over—or rather, the time for thinking it over is past, you should by now have thought it over—there is only one course of action. The whole thing must be done this coming night. If we wait any longer, it will be impossible; it will not be an option any longer. I cannot urge you too strongly, Socrates. Listen to me. Do as I say.

SOCRATES: My dear Crito, your enthusiasm is most commendable, so long as there is some justification for it. Otherwise, the greater your enthusiasm, the more out of place it is. We'd better look into whether this is the right thing to do or not. It has been my practice, not just now but always, to trust, of all the guides at my disposal, only the principle which on reflection seems most appropriate. I cannot now throw overboard principles which I have put forward in the past, simply because of what has happened to me. They still seem to me very much the same as they always did; I still give pride of place to, and value, the same principles as before. Unless we can find some better principle than these to put forward on this occasion, you can be quite sure I am not going to agree with you, however many bugbears the power of the many produces to scare us with—as if we were children—letting loose on us its imprisonments, its death sentences, and its fines.

What then is the best way of looking into this question? Why don't we start by going back to the argument you put forward based on what people will think? Were we right or wrong, all those times, when we said we should listen to some opinions, but not to others? Or were we right before I was sentenced to death, only for it now to become clear that it was a waste of breath, spoken simply for the sake of having something to say, and that it was really juvenile fantasy? Personally, Crito, I should very much like to carry out a joint enquiry with you, to see whether the principle will seem rather different to me, now that I am in this situation, or whether it will seem the same—and whether we are going to forget about it, or follow it.

The principle so often put forward, I think, by those among us who thought they knew what they were talking about, was the one I referred to just now—that of the opinions held by men, we should regard some as important, and others not. Seriously, Crito, don't you think this is a sound principle? You are, barring accidents, not in the position of having to die tomorrow, so you shouldn't be influenced by the present situation. Examine the question. Don't you think it a sound principle that we should not value all human opinions equally, but should value some highly, and others not? And the same with the people who hold the opinions. We should not value all of them, but should value some, and not others. What do you think? Isn't this a sound principle?

CRITO: Yes, it is.

SOCRATES: We should value the good opinions, but not the bad ones?

CRITO: Yes.

SOCRATES: Aren't good opinions the opinions of the wise, whereas bad opinions are those of the foolish?

CRITO: Obviously.

b   SOCRATES: Well then, what was the kind of analogy we used to employ? If a man is taking physical exercise, and this is what he is interested in, does he listen to the praise and criticism and opinion of just anyone, or only of one person—the person who is in fact a medical expert or a physical training instructor?

CRITO: Only of one person.

SOCRATES: So he should worry about the criticisms, and welcome the praises, of this one person, but not those of the many?

CRITO: Clearly he should.

SOCRATES: In what he does, then—in the exercise he takes, in what he eats and drinks—he should be guided by the one man, the man in charge, the expert, rather than by everyone else.

CRITO: That is so.

c   SOCRATES: All right. If he defies the one man, and doesn't value his opinion and his recommendations, but does value those of the many, those who are not experts, won't he do himself some harm?

CRITO: Of course he will.

SOCRATES: What is this harm? What is its extent? What part of the man who defies the expert does it attack?

CRITO: His body, obviously. That is what it damages.

SOCRATES: Quite right. Well then, is it the same also in other situations, Crito, to save us going through all the examples—and especially with right and wrong, foul and

d   fair, good and bad, the things we are now discussing? Should we follow the opinion of the many, and fear that, or the opinion of the one man, if we can find an expert on the subject? Should we respect and fear this one man more than all the rest put together? And if we don't follow his advice, we shall injure and do violence to that part which we have often agreed improves with justice and is damaged by injustice. Or is this all wrong?

CRITO: No, I think it is right, Socrates.

SOCRATES: Very well. Take that part of us which improves with health, and is damaged by disease. If we ruin it by following advice other than that of the experts, is

e   life worth living once that part is injured? This is the body, of course, isn't it?

CRITO: Yes.

SOCRATES: Is life worth living, then, if our body is in poor condition and injured?

CRITO: Certainly not.

SOCRATES: How about the part of us which is attacked by injustice, and helped by justice? Is life worth living when that is injured? Or do we regard it as less important

48   than the body, this part of us—whichever of our faculties it is—the part to which justice and injustice belong?

CRITO: No, we certainly don't.

SOCRATES: More important, then?

CRITO: Much more important.

SOCRATES: In that case, my dear friend, we should not pay the slightest attention, as you suggested we should, to what most people will say about us. We should listen only to the expert on justice and injustice, to the one man, and to the truth itself. So you were wrong, for a start, in one of your recommendations—when you proposed that we should be concerned about the opinion of the many on the subject of justice, right, good, and their opposites. "Ah!" you might say, "but the many are liable to put us to death."

CRITO: That too is obviously true. You might well say that, Socrates. You are   b quite right.

SOCRATES: All the same, my learned friend, I think the principle we have elaborated still has the same force as it did. And what about this second principle? Tell me, does our belief—that the important thing is not being alive, but living a good life—still hold good, or not?

CRITO: It does still hold good.

SOCRATES: And that when we're talking about a life, good, right, and just are one and the same thing—does that still hold good, or not?

CRITO: It does.

SOCRATES: Well then, in the light of the points we have agreed, we must look into   c the question whether it is right, or not right, for me to attempt to leave here without the permission of the Athenians. If it appears to be right, let us make the attempt; otherwise let us forget about it. As for the considerations you raise—questions of expense, public opinion, the upbringing of children—I suspect that these, Crito, are really the concerns of those who readily put people to death, and would as readily bring them back to life again, if they could—for absolutely no reason. I am, of course, talking about the many.

For us, though, the thing is to follow where the argument leads us, and I rather think the only question we need ask is the one we asked just now: shall we act rightly if we give our money, and our thanks, to those who will arrange my escape from here?   d Shall we ourselves be acting rightly in arranging the escape, and allowing it to be arranged? Or shall we in fact be acting wrongly if we do all these things? If this is clearly the wrong way for us to behave, then I'm pretty sure that compared with the danger of acting wrongly, we should not take into account the certainty either of being put to death if we stay put and accept things quietly, or of suffering anything else at all.

CRITO: I am sure you are right, Socrates. You decide what we should do.

SOCRATES: Let us look into it together, my friend. And if you want to raise an ob-   e jection at any point while I'm talking, then raise it, and I will listen to you. Otherwise, my fine friend, stop repeating the same thing over and over again—that I should leave here in defiance of the wishes of the Athenians. I attach great importance to acting with your agreement, rather than against your wishes.

Now, think about the starting-point of our enquiry. Do you regard it as satisfac-   49 tory? And when you answer the question, mind you say what you really think.

CRITO: I will try.

SOCRATES: Do we agree that we should never deliberately do wrong, or should we sometimes do wrong, and sometimes not? Is wrong-doing absolutely contrary to what is good and fine, as has often been agreed among us in the past? Or have all those things we once agreed on become, in these last few days, so much water under the bridge? Did we, grown men and at the age we were, Crito, discuss things so enthusias-   b tically with one another, without realising we were no better than children? Or is what we said then more true now than ever? Whether "most people" agree or not, and whether we have to undergo hardships more severe even than these—or possibly less severe—isn't wrong-doing in fact, for the person who does it, wholly evil and bad? Is this what we say, or not?

CRITO: It is.

SOCRATES: A man should never do wrong, then.

CRITO: No, he should not.

SOCRATES: So even if he is wronged, he should not do wrong in return, as most people think, since he ought not *ever* to do wrong.

c   CRITO: Apparently not.

SOCRATES: What about harming people, Crito? Should a man do that, or not?

CRITO: I suppose not, Socrates.

SOCRATES: How about harming people in retaliation, if he is injured by them first—which is what most people say he should do? Is that right or wrong?

CRITO: Completely wrong.

SOCRATES: And that, I imagine, is because injuring people is the same thing as doing them wrong.

CRITO: That is right.

SOCRATES: So he should not do wrong to anyone or injure them, in retaliation, no matter how he has been treated by them. And if you say "yes" to that, Crito, make sure

d   you are not saying "yes" against what you really think. I realise not many people accept this view—or ever will accept it. As a result, there is no common ground between those who do accept it and those who do not; each side necessarily regards the opinions of the other side with contempt. So you too must think very hard about it. Are you

e   on our side? Do you agree with us in accepting this view, and shall we base our argument on the premise that it is never legitimate to do wrong to people, nor do them wrong in retaliation, nor, if one is injured, defend oneself by harming them in return? Or do you disagree? Do you reject the original premise? Personally, I have held this view a long time, and I still hold it now. If you have been holding some other view, tell me; instruct me. But if you stand by what we said earlier, then listen to what follows from it.

CRITO: I do stand by it, and I do agree with you. Tell me what follows.

SOCRATES: Very well, I will tell you. Or rather, I'll ask you. If a man makes an agreement—a fair agreement—with someone, should he fulfil his side of the agreement, or should he try to get out of it?

CRITO: He should fulfil it.

50   SOCRATES: Then see what follows from that. If we leave here without persuading the city to change its mind, are we doing harm to anyone or anything—those we have least cause to injure—or not? Are we standing by our agreement—our fair agreement—or not?

CRITO: I can't answer your question, Socrates. I don't understand it.

SOCRATES: Look at it like this. Imagine that, just as we were about to run away, or whatever we are supposed to call it, from here, the laws of Athens and the state of Athens appeared before us, and said: "Tell me, Socrates, what are you trying to do?

b   Aren't you simply trying, by this action you are embarking on, to destroy both us, the laws, and the entire city, as far as lies within your power? Do you think it possible for a city to continue to exist, and not sink without trace, if the verdicts of its courts have no force, if they are rendered invalid, and nullified, by private citizens?"

What shall we say, Crito, to these questions and others like them? There's a lot that could be said, especially by the public advocate, in defence of this law we are trying to do away with—the law which lays down that verdicts arrived at in the courts

should be binding. Shall we say to the laws, "The city wronged us. It did not reach its   c
verdict fairly?" Shall we say that, or what?

CRITO: Yes, we most emphatically should say that, Socrates.

SOCRATES: Suppose then the laws say, "Was *that* what was agreed between us
and you, Socrates? Or was it to abide by the verdicts the city arrives at in its courts?"
And if we expressed surprise at their question, they might add: "Do not be surprised by
our question, Socrates. Answer it. You have had enough practice at question-and-   d
answer. Come on, then. What principle do you appeal to, against us and the city, to
allow you to try and destroy us? Did we not bring you into existence, for a start? Was it
not through us that your father married your mother, and fathered you? Tell us, then,
those of us who are the laws governing marriage, have you some criticism of us? Is
there something wrong with us?"

"I have no criticism," I should have to reply.   e

"All right, then. How about your upbringing and education after you were born?
How about the laws to do with those? Did we not give your father the right instructions—those of us whose job it is to attend to this—when we told him to educate you
by means of the arts and physical training?"

"No, they were the right instructions," I would say.

"Very well. Since you were born, and brought up, and educated, under our protection, you were our offspring and our slave—both you yourself and your parents.
Can you deny that, for a start? And if that is so, do you think that justice gives equivalent rights to you and to us? If we decide to do something to you, do you think you
have the right to do it to us in return?

"There was no equality of rights as between you and your father or your master,
if you had one, entitling you to do to him in retaliation what he did to you—to answer   51
him back if he spoke abusively to you, or beat him in retaliation if he beat you, or anything else like that. Will it then be legitimate for you to retaliate against your country
and its laws? And is the result that if we decide to destroy you, because we think it
right to do so, you in your turn, to the best of your ability, will set about destroying us,
the laws, and your country, in retaliation? Will you claim that in acting like this you
are doing what is right, you who are truly so concerned about human excellence? Are
you so clever that you fail to realise that your country is an object of greater value, an   b
object of greater respect and reverence, and altogether more important, both among
gods and among men, if they have any sense, than your mother and your father and all
the rest of your ancestors put together? That you should revere your country, submit to
it, mollify it when it is angry with you—more than you would your father—and either
persuade it to change its mind, or do what it tells you? That you should quietly accept
whatever treatment it ordains you should receive—beating, perhaps, or imprison-   c
ment—or if it takes you to war, to be wounded or killed, that is what you should do,
and that is what is right? That you should not give way, or retreat, or abandon your position, that in war, in the lawcourts, or anywhere else, you should do what your city
and your country tells you, or else convince it where justice naturally lies? And that the
use of force, against a mother or a father, is against god's law—still more so the use of
force against your country?"

What are we going to say in answer to this, Crito? Shall we say the laws are
right, or not?

CRITO: Well, *I* think they are right.

SOCRATES: "Consider, then, Socrates," the laws might perhaps say, "Are we right
in saying that you are not justified in embarking on the actions against us which you
are now embarking on? We fathered you, brought you up, educated you, gave you and   d

every other citizen a share in every good thing it was in our power to give. And even then, if there is any Athenian who reaches the age of majority, takes a look at his city's constitution, and at us, the laws, and finds we are not to his satisfaction, then by granting him permission we make a public declaration to anyone who wishes that he may take what is his, and go wherever he pleases. If a man chooses to go to one of your colonies, because we and the city are not to his liking, or to leave, emigrate to some other place, and go wherever he wants, with no loss of property, not one of us laws stands in his way, or forbids him.

"To those of you who stay, aware of our way of reaching verdicts in the courts, and of making our other political arrangements, we say that you have now entered into a formal agreement with us, to do what we tell you, and we say that the man who disobeys us is doing wrong in three ways: he is disobeying us who fathered him; he is disobeying those who brought him up; and having made an agreement to obey us, he neither obeys, nor tries to make us change our minds, if we are doing something which is not right. When we make him a fair offer, not harshly demanding that he do whatever we order, but allowing him a straight choice, either to make us change our minds, or to do as we say, he does neither. These are the charges, Socrates, to which we claim that you too will render yourself liable, if you do what you are proposing to do—you in particular, more than any of the Athenians."

If I asked them why me in particular, they might perhaps have a justifiable complaint against me in that I, as much as any of the Athenians, really have entered into this agreement with them. They could say, "Socrates, we have convincing evidence to suggest that we and the city *were* to your liking. You could not possibly have spent more of your time living here in Athens than any other Athenian if the place had not been particularly to your liking; you would not have refused ever to leave the city to see famous places—except Corinth, once—or go anywhere else, unless it was to go somewhere on military service; you never went abroad, as other people do, nor were you seized with a desire to know any other city, or any other laws. No, you were satisfied with us, and with our city. In fact, so strongly did you choose us, and agree to live your life as a citizen under us, that you even produced children in the city. You would not have done that if it had not been to your liking.

"Even at your trial, it was open to you to propose a penalty of exile, if you chose, and do then, with the city's permission, what you are now proposing to do without it. On that occasion you put a brave face on it; you said you didn't mind if you had to die; you preferred, so you said, death to exile. Do not those words now make you feel ashamed? Have you no feeling for us, the laws, as you set about destroying us, and do what the meanest slave might do, trying to run away in breach of the contract and agreement by which you agreed to live your life as a citizen? Answer us this question, for a start: are we right in saying that you have agreed—not just verbally, but by your behaviour—to live your life as a citizen under us? Or are we wrong?"

What are we going to say to this, Crito? Can we do anything but agree?

CRITO: We have no choice, Socrates.

SOCRATES: "Aren't you simply breaking," they might say, "contracts and agreements which you have with us? You did not enter into them under compulsion or false pretences. You were not forced to make up your mind on the spur of the moment, but over a period of seventy years, during which you were at liberty to leave, if we were not to your liking, or if you thought the agreement was unfair. You did not choose Sparta or Crete instead, places which you have always described as well-governed; nor did you choose any other city, inside or outside Greece. Even people who are lame, or blind, or crippled in other ways, spend more time away from Athens than you did. *That* is an indication, quite clearly, of how you, more than any of the Athenians, found the city, and us the laws, to your liking. After all, who could find a city to his liking, and not like its laws? And do you now not stand by what you agreed? You will if you take our advice, Socrates. That way you will avoid making yourself ridiculous by leaving the city.

"Think about it. If you break this agreement, and put yourself in the wrong in   b
this way, what good will you do yourself or your friends? That your friends will probably have to go into exile as well, be cut off from their city, and forfeit their property, is
reasonably clear. And you? Well for a start, if you go to one of the cities nearby, say
Thebes or Megara, both of which have good laws, you will come to them, Socrates, as
an enemy of their constitution; those who care for their city will look at you with suspicion, believing you to be a subverter of the laws. You will also reinforce the opinion of   c
the jury about you. They will decide they did reach the right verdict. After all, there is
a strong presumption that a man who subverts the laws will be a corrupting influence
on people who are young and foolish.

"Will you then keep away from cities with good laws, and the most civilised part
of mankind? If you do, will it be worth your while remaining alive? Or will you spend
your time with them? And will you have the nerve, in your conversations with them—
what sort of conversations, Socrates? The ones you had here, about human excellence   d
and justice being the most valuable things for mankind, together with custom and the
laws? Don't you think the whole idea of Socrates will be clearly seen to be a disgrace?
You certainly should.

"Or will you leave this part of the world and go to Thessaly, to Crito's family
friends? Up there you will find all sorts of anarchy and self-indulgence. I am sure they
would be entertained by the amusing story of your running away from prison in some
costume or other—wearing a leather jerkin, perhaps, or one of the other disguises   e
favoured by people running away—and altering your appearance. That an old man, in
all probability with a small span of life remaining to him, could bring himself to cling
to life in this limpet-like way, by transgressing the most important of the laws—will
there be no-one who will say this? Perhaps not, if you can manage not to annoy anyone. Otherwise, Socrates, you will have to listen to a lot of unflattering comments
about yourself. Are you going to spend your life ingratiating yourself with everyone,
being a slave to them? Oh, yes, you will have a whale of a time up there in Thessaly, as
if you had emigrated out to dinner in Thessaly. But what, please tell us, will become of   54
all those conversations about justice and other forms of human excellence?

"Or do you want to remain alive for your children's sake, so that you can bring
them up and educate them? How do you feel about taking them to Thessaly, and bringing them up and educating them there, turning them into foreigners, so you can give
them that privilege as well? If not, if they are brought up here, will they be any better
brought up and educated because you are alive and separated from them? Your friends
will be looking after them. Will they look after them if you go to Thessaly to live, and
not look after them if you go to the next world? If those who claim to be your friends   b
are any use at all, of course they will not.

"No, Socrates, obey us who brought you up. Do not regard your children, or life,
or anything at all, as more important than justice; you do not want, when you come to
the other world, to have to defend yourself on these charges to the rulers there. Neither
in this world does it seem to be better, or more just or more godfearing, for you or any
of your friends, if you behave like this; nor, when you come to the next world, will it
be better for you there. As it is, you go there, if you do go, as one wronged—not by us,   c
the laws, but by men. If on the other hand you depart, after so shamefully returning

wrong for wrong, and injury for injury, breaking your own agreement and contract with us, and injuring those whom you had least cause to injure—yourself, your friends, your country, and us—then we shall be angry with you while you are alive, and in the

d   next world our brothers, the laws in Hades, will not receive you kindly, since they will know that you tried, to the best of your ability, to destroy us. So do not let Crito persuade you to follow his advice rather than ours."

That, I assure you, Crito, my very dear friend, is what I think I hear them saying, just as those gripped by religious fervour think they hear the pipes; the sound of their words rings in my head, and stops me hearing anything else. Be in no doubt. As far as I can see at the moment, if you disagree with them, you will speak in vain. All the same, though, if you think it will do any good, then speak.

e   CRITO: Socrates, I have nothing to say.

SOCRATES: Then forget about it, Crito. Let us act in the way god points out to us.

PHAEDO (in part)

[Socrates is speaking] . . . My dear Cebes, if all things in which there is any life were to die, and when they were dead were to remain in that form and not come to life again, would not the necessary result be that everything at last would be dead, and

72ᵈ   nothing alive? For if living things were generated from other sources than death, and were to die, the result is inevitable that all things would be consumed by death. Is it not so?

It is indeed, I think, Socrates, said Cebes; I think that what you say is perfectly true.

Yes, Cebes, he said, I think it is certainly so. We are not misled into this conclusion. The dead do come to life again, and the living are generated from them, and the

e   souls of the dead exist; and with the souls of the good it is well, and with the souls of the evil it is evil.

And besides, Socrates, rejoined Cebes, if the doctrine which you are fond of stating, that our learning is only a process of recollection, be true, then I suppose we must have learned at some former time what we recollect now. And that would be impossi-

73   ble unless our souls had existed somewhere before they came into this human form. So that is another reason for believing the soul immortal.

But, Cebes, interrupted Simmias, what are the proofs of that? Recall them to me; I am not very clear about them at present.

One argument, answered Cebes, and the strongest of all, is that if you question men about anything in the right way, they will answer you correctly of themselves. But

b   they would not have been able to do that unless they had had within themselves knowledge and right reason. Again, show them such things as geometrical diagrams, and the proof of the doctrine is complete.*

---

*[For an example of this see Meno 82a–86b (pp. 68ff in this volume).]

Plato, *Phaedo,* translated by F.J. Church (New York: Macmillan/Library of the Liberal Arts, 1951).

And if that does not convince you, Simmias, said Socrates, look at the matter in another way and see if you agree then. You have doubts, I know, how what is called knowledge can be recollection.

Nay, replied Simmias, I do not doubt. But I want to recollect the argument about recollection. What Cebes undertook to explain has nearly brought your theory back to me and convinced me. But I am nonetheless ready to hear you undertake to explain it.

In this way, he returned. We are agreed, I suppose, that if a man remembers any-   c
thing, he must have known it at some previous time.

Certainly, he said.

And are we agreed that when knowledge comes in the following way, it is recol-
lection? When a man has seen or heard anything, or has perceived it by some other sense, and then knows not that thing only, but has also in his mind an impression of some other thing, of which the knowledge is quite different, are we not right in saying   d
that he remembers the thing of which he has an impression in his mind?

What do you mean?

I mean this. The knowledge of a man is different from the knowledge of a lyre, is it not?

Certainly.

And you know that when lovers see a lyre, or a garment, or anything that their favorites are wont to use, they have this feeling. They know the lyre, and in their mind they receive the image of the youth whose the lyre was. That is recollection. For instance, someone seeing Simmias often is reminded of Cebes; and there are endless ex-
amples of the same thing.

Indeed there are, said Simmias.

Is not that a kind of recollection, he said; and more especially when a man has   e
this feeling with reference to things which the lapse of time and inattention have made him forget?

Yes, certainly, he replied.

Well, he went on, is it possible to recollect a man on seeing the picture of a horse, or the picture of a lyre? Or to recall Simmias on seeing a picture of Cebes?

Certainly.

And it is possible to recollect Simmias himself on seeing a picture of Simmias?

No doubt, he said.   74

Then in all these cases there is recollection caused by similar objects, and also by dissimilar objects?

There is.

But when a man has a recollection caused by similar objects, will he not have a further feeling and consider whether the likeness to that which he recollects is defective in any way or not?

He will, he said.

Now see if this is true, he went on. Do we not believe in the existence of equality—not the equality of pieces of wood or of stones, but something beyond that—
equality in the abstract? Shall we say that there is such a thing, or not?

Yes indeed, said Simmias, most emphatically we will.   b

And do we know what this abstract equality is?

Certainly, he replied.

Where did we get the knowledge of it? Was it not from seeing the equal pieces of wood, and stones, and the like, which we were speaking of just now? Did we not form from them the idea of abstract equality, which is different from them? Or do you think that it is not different? Consider the question in this way. Do not equal pieces of wood and stones appear to us sometimes equal and sometimes unequal, though in fact they remain the same all the time?

Certainly they do.

c   But did absolute equals ever seem to you to be unequal, or abstract equality to be inequality?

No, never, Socrates.

Then equal things, he said, are not the same as abstract equality?

No, certainly not, Socrates.

Yet it was from these equal things, he said, which are different from abstract equality, that you have conceived and got your knowledge of abstract equality?

That is quite true, he replied.

And that whether it is like them or unlike them?

Certainly.

d   But that makes no difference, he said. As long as the sight of one thing brings another thing to your mind, there must be recollection, whether or no the two things are like.

That is so.

Well then, said he, do the equal pieces of wood, and other similar equal things, of which we have been speaking, affect us at all this way? Do they seem to us to be equal, in the way that abstract equality is equal? Do they come short of being like abstract equality, or not?

Indeed, they come very short of it, he replied.

Are we agreed about this? A man sees something and thinks to himself, "This

e   thing that I see aims at being like some other thing, but it comes short and cannot be like that other thing; it is inferior"; must not the man who thinks that have known at some previous time that other thing, which he says that it resembles, and to which it is inferior?

He must.

Well, have we ourselves had the same sort of feeling with reference to equal things, and to abstract equality?

Yes, certainly.

75   Then we must have had knowledge of equality before we first saw equal things, and perceived that they all strive to be like equality, and all come short of it.

That is so.

And we are agreed also that we have not, nor could we have, obtained the idea of equality except from sight or touch or some other sense; the same is true of all the senses.

Yes, Socrates, for the purposes of the argument that is so.

b   At any rate, it is by the senses that we must perceive that all sensible objects strive to resemble absolute equality, and are inferior to it. Is not that so?

Yes.

Then before we began to see, and to hear, and to use the other senses, we must have received the knowledge of the nature of abstract and real equality; otherwise we could not have compared equal sensible objects with abstract equality, and seen that the former in all cases strive to be like the latter, though they are always inferior to it?

That is the necessary consequence of what we have been saying, Socrates.

Did we not see, and hear, and possess the other senses as soon as we were born?

Yes, certainly.

c   And we must have received the knowledge of abstract equality before we had these senses?

Yes.

Then, it seems, we must have received that knowledge before we were born?

It does.

Now if we received this knowledge before our birth, and were born with it, we knew, both before and at the moment of our birth, not only the equal, and the greater, and the less, but also everything of the same kind, did we not? Our present reasoning does not refer only to equality. It refers just as much to absolute good, and absolute beauty, and absolute justice, and absolute holiness; in short, I repeat, to everything which we mark with the name of the real, in the questions and answers of our dialectic. So we must have received our knowledge of all realities before we were born.

That is so.

And we must always be born with this knowledge, and must always retain it throughout life, if we have not each time forgotten it, after having received it. For to know means to receive and retain knowledge, and not to have lost it. Do not we mean by forgetting, the loss of knowledge, Simmias?

Yes, certainly, Socrates, he said.

But, I suppose, if it be the case that we lost at birth the knowledge which we received before we were born, and then afterward, by using our senses on the objects of sense, recovered the knowledge which we had previously possessed, then what we call learning is the recovering of knowledge which is already ours. And are we not right in calling that recollection?

Certainly.

For we have found it possible to perceive a thing by sight, or hearing, or any other sense, and thence to form a notion of some other thing, like or unlike, which had been forgotten, but with which this thing was associated. And therefore, I say, one of two things must be true. Either we are all born with this knowledge and retain it all our life; or, after birth, those whom we say are learning are only recollecting, and our knowledge is recollection.

Yes indeed, that is undoubtedly true, Socrates.

Then which do you choose, Simmias? Are we born with knowledge or do we recollect the things of which we have received knowledge before our birth?

I cannot say at present, Socrates.

Well, have you an opinion about this question? Can a man who knows give an account of what he knows, or not? What do you think about that?

Yes, of course he can, Socrates.

And do you think that everyone can give an account of the ideas of which we have been speaking?

I wish I did, indeed, said Simmias, but I am very much afraid that by this time tomorrow there will no longer be any man living able to do so as it should be done.

Then, Simmias, he said, you do not think that all men know these things?

Certainly not.

Then they recollect what they once learned?

Necessarily.

And when did our souls gain this knowledge? It cannot have been after we were born men.

No, certainly not.

Then it was before?

Yes.

Then, Simmias, our souls existed formerly, apart from our bodies, and possessed intelligence before they came into man's shape.

Unless we receive this knowledge at the moment of birth, Socrates. That time still remains.

d

Well, my friend, and at what other time do we lose it? We agreed just now that we are not born with it; do we lose it at the same moment that we gain it, or can you suggest any other time?

I cannot, Socrates. I did not see that I was talking nonsense.

Then, Simmias, he said, is not this the truth? If, as we are forever repeating,

e

beauty, and good, and the other ideas really exist, and if we refer all the objects of sensible perception to these ideas which were formerly ours, and which we find to be ours still, and compare sensible objects with them, then, just as they exist, our souls must have existed before ever we were born. But if they do not exist, then our reasoning will have been thrown away. Is it so? If these ideas exist, does it not at once follow that our souls must have existed before we were born, and if they do not exist, then neither did our souls?

77

Admirably put, Socrates, said Simmias. I think that the necessity is the same for the one as for the other. The reasoning has reached a place of safety in the common proof of the existence of our souls before we were born and of the existence of the ideas of which you spoke. Nothing is so evident to me as that beauty, and good, and the other ideas which you spoke of just now have a very real existence indeed. Your proof is quite sufficient for me.

But what of Cebes? said Socrates. I must convince Cebes too.

I think that he is satisfied, said Simmias, though he is the most skeptical of men in argument. But I think that he is perfectly convinced that our souls existed before we were born.

But I do not think myself, Socrates, he continued, that you have proved that the

b

soul will continue to exist when we are dead. The common fear which Cebes spoke of, that she [the soul] may be scattered to the winds at death, and that death may be the end of her existence, still stands in the way. Assuming that the soul is generated and comes together from some other elements, and exists before she ever enters the human body, why should she not come to an end and be destroyed, after she has entered into the body, when she is released from it?

c

You are right, Simmias, said Cebes. I think that only half the required proof has been given. It has been shown that our souls existed before we were born; but it must also be shown that our souls will continue to exist after we are dead, no less than that they existed before we were born, if the proof is to be complete.

That has been shown already, Simmias and Cebes, said Socrates, if you will

d

combine this reasoning with our previous conclusion, that all life is generated from death. For if the soul exists in a previous state and if, when she comes into life and is born, she can only be born from death, and from a state of death, must she not exist after death too, since she has to be born again? So the point which you speak of has been already proved.

Still I think that you and Simmias would be glad to discuss this question further. Like children, you are afraid that the wind will really blow the soul away and disperse

e

her when she leaves the body, especially if a man happens to die in a storm and not in a calm.

Cebes laughed and said, Try and convince us as if we were afraid, Socrates; or rather, do not think that we are afraid ourselves. Perhaps there is a child within us who has these fears. Let us try and persuade him not to be afraid of death, as if it were a bugbear.

You must charm him every day, until you have charmed him away, said Socrates.

And where shall we find a good charmer, Socrates, he asked, now that you are   78
leaving us?

Hellas is a large country, Cebes, he replied, and good men may doubtless be found in it; and the nations of the Barbarians are many. You must search them all through for such a charmer, sparing neither money nor labor; for there is nothing on which you could spend money more profitably. And you must search for him among yourselves too, for you will hardly find a better charmer than yourselves.

That shall be done, said Cebes. But let us return to the point where we left off, if   b
you will.

Yes, I will: why not?

Very good, he replied.

Well, said Socrates, must we not ask ourselves this question? What kind of thing is liable to suffer dispersion, and for what kind of thing have we to fear dispersion? And then we must see whether the soul belongs to that kind or not, and be confident or afraid about our own souls accordingly.

That is true, he answered.

Now is it not the compound and composite which is naturally liable to be dis-   c
solved in the same way in which it was compounded? And is not what is uncompounded alone not liable to dissolution, if anything is not?

I think that that is so, said Cebes.

And what always remains in the same state and unchanging is most likely to be uncompounded, and what is always changing and never the same is most likely to be compounded, I suppose?

Yes, I think so.

Now let us return to what we were speaking of before in the discussion, he said. Does the being, which in our dialectic we define as meaning absolute existence, remain   d
always in exactly the same state, or does it change? Do absolute equality, absolute beauty, and every other absolute existence, admit of any change at all? Or does absolute existence in each case, being essentially uniform, remain the same and unchanging, and never in any case admit of any sort or kind of change whatsoever?

It must remain the same and unchanging, Socrates, said Cebes.

And what of the many beautiful things, such as men, and horses, and garments, and the like, and of all which bears the names of the ideas, whether equal, or beautiful, or anything else? Do they remain the same or is it exactly the opposite with them? In   e
short, do they never remain the same at all, either in themselves or in their relations?

These things, said Cebes, never remain the same.

You can touch them, and see them, and perceive them with the other senses,   79
while you can grasp the unchanging only by the reasoning of the intellect. These latter are invisible and not seen. Is it not so?

That is perfectly true, he said.

Let us assume then, he said, if you will, that there are two kinds of existence, the one visible, the other invisible.

Yes, he said.

And the invisible is unchanging, while the visible is always changing.

Yes, he said again.

Are not we men made up of body and soul?   b

There is nothing else, he replied.

And which of these kinds of existence should we say that the body is most like, and most akin to?

The visible, he replied; that is quite obvious.

And the soul? Is that visible or invisible?

It is invisible to man, Socrates, he said.

But we mean by visible and invisible, visible and invisible to man; do we not?

Yes; that is what we mean.

Then what do we say of the soul? Is it visible or not visible?

It is not visible.

Then is it invisible?

Yes.

Then the soul is more like the invisible than the body; and the body is like the visible.

c   That is necessarily so, Socrates.

Have we not also said that, when the soul employs the body in any inquiry, and makes use of sight, or hearing, or any other sense—for inquiry with the body means inquiry with the senses—she is dragged away by it to the things which never remain the same, and wanders about blindly, and becomes confused and dizzy, like a drunken man, from dealing with things that are ever changing?

Certainly.

d   But when she investigates any question by herself, she goes away to the pure, and eternal, and immortal, and unchangeable, to which she is akin, and so she comes to be ever with it, as soon as she is by herself, and can be so; and then she rests from her wanderings and dwells with it unchangingly, for she is dealing with what is unchanging. And is not this state of the soul called wisdom?

Indeed, Socrates, you speak well and truly, he replied.

e   Which kind of existence do you think from our former and our present arguments that the soul is more like and more akin to?

I think, Socrates, he replied, that after this inquiry the very dullest man would agree that the soul is infinitely more like the unchangeable than the changeable.

And the body?

That is like the changeable.

Consider the matter in yet another way. When the soul and the body are united, 80   nature ordains the one to be a slave and to be ruled, and the other to be master and to rule. Tell me once again, which do you think is like the divine, and which is like the mortal? Do you not think that the divine naturally rules and has authority, and that the mortal naturally is ruled and is a slave?

I do.

Then which is the soul like?

That is quite plain, Socrates. The soul is like the divine, and the body is like the mortal.

Now tell me, Cebes, is the result of all that we have said that the soul is most like b   the divine, and the immortal, and the intelligible, and the uniform, and the indissoluble, and the unchangeable; while the body is most like the human, and the mortal, and the unintelligible, and the multiform, and the dissoluble, and the changeable? Have we any other argument to show that this is not so, my dear Cebes?

We have not.

Then if this is so, is it not the nature of the body to be dissolved quickly, and of the soul to be wholly or very nearly indissoluble?

c   Certainly.

You observe, he said, that after a man is dead, the visible part of him, his body, which lies in the visible world and which we call the corpse, which is subject to dissolution and decomposition, is not dissolved and decomposed at once? It remains as it was for a considerable time, and even for a long time, if a man dies with his body in good condition and in the vigor of life. And when the body falls in and is embalmed, like the mummies of Egypt, it remains nearly entire for an immense time. And should   d
it decay, yet some parts of it, such as the bones and muscles, may almost be said to be immortal. Is it not so?

Yes.

And shall we believe that the soul, which is invisible, and which goes hence to a place that is like herself, glorious, and pure, and invisible, to Hades, which is rightly called the unseen world, to dwell with the good and wise God, whither, if it be the will of God, my soul too must shortly go—shall we believe that the soul, whose nature is so glorious, and pure, and invisible, is blown away by the winds and perishes   e
as soon as she leaves the body, as the world says? Nay, dear Cebes and Simmias, it is not so. I will tell you what happens to a soul which is pure at her departure, and which in her life has had no intercourse that she could avoid with the body, and so draws after her, when she dies, no taint of the body, but has shunned it, and gathered herself into herself, for such has been her constant study—and that only means that she   81
has loved wisdom rightly, and has truly practiced how to die. Is not this the practice of death?

Yes, certainly.

Does not the soul, then, which is in that state, go away to the invisible that is like herself, and to the divine, and the immortal, and the wise, where she is released from error, and folly, and fear, and fierce passions, and all the other evils that fall to the lot of men, and is happy, and for the rest of time lives in very truth with the gods, as they say that the initiated do? Shall we affirm this, Cebes?

Yes, certainly, said Cebes.

But if she be defiled and impure when she leaves the body, from being ever with   b
it, and serving it and loving it, and from being besotted by it and by its desires and pleasures, so that she thinks nothing true but what is bodily and can be touched, and seen, and eaten, and drunk, and used for men's lusts; if she has learned to hate, and tremble at, and fly from what is dark and invisible to the eye, and intelligible and apprehended   c
by philosophy—do you think that a soul which is in that state will be pure and without alloy at her departure?

No, indeed, he replied.

She is penetrated, I suppose, by the corporeal, which the unceasing intercourse and company and care of the body has made a part of her nature.

Yes.

And, my dear friend, the corporeal must be burdensome, and heavy, and earthy, and visible; and it is by this that such a soul is weighed down and dragged back to the visible world, because she is afraid of the invisible world of Hades, and haunts, it is   d
said, the graves and tombs, where shadowy forms of souls have been seen, which are the phantoms of souls which were impure at their release and still cling to the visible; which is the reason why they are seen.

That is likely enough, Socrates.

That is likely, certainly, Cebes; and these are not the souls of the good, but of the evil, which are compelled to wander in such places as a punishment for the wicked lives that they have lived; and their wanderings continue until, from the desire for the corporeal that clings to them, they are again imprisoned in a body.   e

And, he continued, they are imprisoned, probably, in the bodies of animals with habits similar to the habits which were theirs in their lifetime.

What do you mean by that, Socrates?

I mean that men who have practiced unbridled gluttony, and wantonness, and drunkenness probably enter the bodies of asses and suchlike animals. Do you not think so?

82

Certainly that is very likely.

And those who have chosen injustice, and tyranny, and robbery enter the bodies of wolves, and hawks, and kites. Where else should we say that such souls go?

No doubt, said Cebes, they go into such animals.

In short, it is quite plain, he said, whither each soul goes; each enters an animal with habits like its own.

Certainly, he replied, that is so.

And of these, he said, the happiest, who go to the best place, are those who have practiced the popular and social virtues which are called temperance and justice, and which come from habit and practice, without philosophy or reason.

b

And why are they the happiest?

Because it is probable that they return into a mild and social nature like their own, such as that of bees, or wasps, or ants; or, it may be, into the bodies of men, and that from them are made worthy citizens.

Very likely.

c

But none but the philosopher or the lover of knowledge, who is wholly pure when he goes hence, is permitted to go to the race of the gods; and therefore, my friends, Simmias and Cebes, the true philosopher is temperate and refrains from all the pleasures of the body, and does not give himself up to them. It is not squandering his substance and poverty that he fears, as the multitude and the lovers of wealth do; nor again does he dread the dishonor and disgrace of wickedness, like the lovers of power and honor. It is not for these reasons that he is temperate.

No, it would be unseemly in him if he were, Socrates, said Cebes.

d

Indeed it would, he replied, and therefore all those who have any care for their souls, and who do not spend their lives in forming and molding their bodies, bid farewell to such persons, and do not walk in their ways, thinking that they know not whither they are going. They themselves turn and follow whithersoever philosophy leads them, for they believe that they ought not to resist philosophy, or its deliverance and purification.

How, Socrates?

I will tell you, he replied. The lovers of knowledge know that when philosophy receives the soul, she is fast bound in the body, and fastened to it; she is unable to contemplate what is, by herself, or except through the bars of her prison house, the body; and she is wallowing in utter ignorance. And philosophy sees that the dreadful thing about the imprisonment is that it is caused by lust, and that the captive herself is an accomplice in her own captivity. The lovers of knowledge, I repeat, know that philosophy takes the soul when she is in this condition, and gently encourages her, and strives to release her from her captivity, showing her that the perceptions of the eye, and the ear, and the other senses are full of deceit, and persuading her to stand aloof from the senses and to use them only when she must, and exhorting her to rally and gather herself together, and to trust only to herself and to the real existence which she of her own self apprehends, and to believe that nothing which is subject to change, and which she perceives by other faculties, has any truth, for such things are visible and sensible, while what she herself sees is apprehended by reason and invisible. The soul of the true

e

83

b

philosopher thinks that it would be wrong to resist this deliverance from captivity, and therefore she holds aloof, so far as she can, from pleasure, and desire, and pain, and fear; for she reckons that when a man has vehement pleasure, or fear, or pain, or desire, he suffers from them not merely the evils which might be expected, such as sickness or some loss arising from the indulgence of his desires; he suffers what is the greatest and last of evils, and does not take it into account.

What do you mean, Socrates? asked Cebes.

I mean that when the soul of any man feels vehement pleasure or pain, she is forced at the same time to think that the object, whatever it be, of these sensations is the most distinct and truest, when it is not.

*   *   *

. . . A man should be of good cheer about his soul if in his life he has renounced the pleasures and adornments of the body, because they were nothing to him, and because he thought that they would do him not good but harm; and if he has instead earnestly pursued the pleasures of learning, and adorned his soul with the adornment of temperance, and justice, and courage, and freedom, and truth, which belongs to her and is her own, and so awaits his journey to the other world, in readiness to set forth whenever fate calls him. You, Simmias and Cebes, and the rest will set forth at some future day, each at his own time. But me now, as a tragic poet would say, fate calls at once; and it is time for me to betake myself to the bath. I think that I had better bathe before I drink the poison, and not give the women the trouble of washing my dead body.

When he had finished speaking Crito said, Be it so, Socrates. But have you any commands for your friends or for me about your children, or about other things? How shall we serve you best?

Simply by doing what I always tell you, Crito. Take care of your own selves, and you will serve me and mine and yourselves in all that you do, even though you make no promises now. But if you are careless of your own selves, and will not follow the path of life which we have pointed out in our discussions both today and at other times, all your promises now, however profuse and earnest they are, will be of no avail.

We will do our best, said Crito. But how shall we bury you?

As you please, he answered; only you must catch me first and not let me escape you. And then he looked at us with a smile and said, My friends, I cannot convince Crito that I am the Socrates who has been conversing with you and arranging his arguments in order. He thinks that I am the body which he will presently see a corpse, and he asks how he is to bury me. All the arguments which I have used to prove that I shall not remain with you after I have drunk the poison, but that I shall go away to the happiness of the blessed, with which I tried to comfort you and myself, have been thrown away on him. Do you therefore be my sureties to him, as he was my surety at the trial, but in a different way. He was surety for me then that I would remain; but you must be my sureties to him that I shall go away when I am dead, and not remain with you; then he will feel my death less; and when he sees my body being burned or buried, he will not be grieved because he thinks that I am suffering dreadful things; and at my funeral he will not say that it is Socrates whom he is laying out, or bearing to the grave, or burying. For, dear Crito, he continued, you must know that to use words wrongly is not only a fault in itself, it also creates evil in the soul. You must be of good cheer, and say that you are burying my body; and you may bury it as you please and as you think right.

The Death of Socrates, 1787, by Jacques-Louis David (1748–1825). (*Oil on canvas, 51 ×
77-1/4 inches. The Metropolitan Museum of Art, Wolfe Fund, 1931. Catharine Lorillard
Wolfe Collection. [31.45])*

With these words he rose and went into another room to bathe. Crito went with
him and told us to wait. So we waited, talking of the argument and discussing it, and
then again dwelling on the greatness of the calamity which had fallen upon us: it
b   seemed as if we were going to lose a father and to be orphans for the rest of our lives.
When he had bathed, and his children had been brought to him—he had two sons quite
little, and one grown up—and the women of his family were come, he spoke with them
in Crito's presence, and gave them his last instructions; then he sent the women and
children away and returned to us. By that time it was near the hour of sunset, for he
had been a long while within. When he came back to us from the bath he sat down, but
c   not much was said after that. Presently the servant of the Eleven came and stood before
him and said, "I know that I shall not find you unreasonable like other men, Socrates.
They are angry with me and curse me when I bid them drink the poison because the
authorities make me do it. But I have found you all along the noblest and gentlest and
best man that has ever come here; and now I am sure that you will not be angry with
d   me, but with those who you know are to blame. And so farewell, and try to bear what
must be as lightly as you can; you know why I have come." With that he turned away
weeping, and went out.

Socrates looked up at him and replied, Farewell, I will do as you say. Then he
turned to us and said, How courteous the man is! And the whole time that I have
been here, he has constantly come in to see me, and sometimes he has talked to me,
and has been the best of men; and now, how generously he weeps for me! Come,
Crito, let us obey him; let the poison be brought if it is ready, and if it is not ready,
let it be prepared.

Crito replied: But, Socrates, I think that the sun is still upon the hills; it has not   e
set. Besides, I know that other men take the poison quite late, and eat and drink
heartily, and even enjoy the company of their chosen friends, after the announcement
has been made. So do not hurry; there is still time.

Socrates replied: And those whom you speak of, Crito, naturally do so, for they
think that they will be gainers by so doing. And I naturally shall not do so, for I think
that I should gain nothing by drinking the poison a little later, but my own contempt   117
for so greedily saving a life which is already spent. So do not refuse to do as I say.

Then Crito made a sign to his slave who was standing by; and the slave went out,
and after some delay returned with the man who was to give the poison, carrying it
prepared in a cup. When Socrates saw him, he asked, You understand these things, my
good man, what have I to do?

You have only to drink this, he replied, and to walk about until your legs feel
heavy, and then lie down; and it will act of itself.   b

With that he handed the cup to Socrates, who took it quite cheerfully,
Echecrates, without trembling, and without any change of color or of feature, and
looked up at the man with that fixed glance of his, and asked, What say you to making
a libation from this draught? May I, or not?

We only prepare so much as we think sufficient, Socrates, he answered.   c

I understand, said Socrates. But I suppose that I may, and must, pray to the gods
that my journey hence may be prosperous. That is my prayer; may it be so. With these
words he put the cup to his lips and drank the poison quite calmly and cheerfully.

Till then most of us had been able to control our grief fairly well; but when we
saw him drinking and then the poison finished, we could do so no longer: my tears
came fast in spite of myself, and I covered my face and wept for myself; it was not for
him, but at my own misfortune in losing such a friend. Even before that Crito had been   d
unable to restrain his tears, and had gone away; and Apollodorus, who had never once
ceased weeping the whole time, burst into a loud wail and made us one and all break
down by his sobbing, except Socrates himself.

What are you doing, my friends? he exclaimed. I sent away the women chiefly in   e
order that they might not behave in this way; for I have heard that a man should die in
silence. So calm yourselves and bear up.

When we heard that, we were ashamed, and we ceased from weeping. But he
walked about, until he said that his legs were getting heavy, and then he lay down on
his back, as he was told. And the man who gave the poison began to examine his feet
and legs from time to time. Then he pressed his foot hard and asked if there was any
feeling in it, and Socrates said, No; and then his legs, and so higher and higher, and   118
showed us that he was cold and stiff. And Socrates felt himself and said that when it
came to his heart, he should be gone. He was already growing cold about the groin,
when he uncovered his face, which had been covered, and spoke for the last time.
Crito, he said, I owe a cock to Asclepius; do not forget to pay it.*

It shall be done, replied Crito. Is there anything else that you wish? He made no
answer to this question; but after a short interval there was a movement, and the man
uncovered him, and his eyes were fixed. Then Crito closed his mouth and his eyes.

Such was the end, Echecrates, of our friend, a man, I think, who was the wisest
and justest, and the best man I have ever known.

---

*[Asclepius was the Greek god of healing. When one recovered from an illness it was customary to
offer a cock as a sacrifice, so Socrates' last words imply that death is a kind of healing. See, for instance 66b
ff., 67c.]

MENO

PERSONS OF THE DIALOGUE

> Meno
> A Slave of Meno
> Socrates
> Anytus

70   MENO: Can you tell me Socrates—is virtue something that can be taught? Or does it come by practice? Or is it neither teaching nor practice that gives it to a man but natural aptitude or something else?

b   SOCRATES: Well Meno, in the old days the Thessalians had a great reputation among the Greeks for their wealth and their horsemanship. Now it seems they are philosophers as well—especially the men of Larissa, where your friend Aristippus comes from. It is Gorgias who has done it. He went to that city and captured the hearts of the foremost of the Aleuadae for his wisdom (among them your own admirer Aristippus), not to speak of other leading Thessalians. In particular he got you into the

c   habit of answering any question you might be asked, with the confidence and dignity appropriate to those who know the answers, just as he himself invites questions of every kind from anyone in the Greek world who wishes to ask, and never fails to an-

71   swer them. But here at Athens, my dear Meno, it is just the reverse. There is a dearth of wisdom, and it looks as if it had migrated from our part of the country to yours. At any rate, if you put your question to any of our people, they will all alike laugh and say: "You must think I am singularly fortunate, to know whether virtue can be taught or how it is acquired. The fact is that far from knowing whether it can be taught, I have no idea what virtue itself is."

b   That is my own case. I share the poverty of my fellow-countrymen in this respect, and confess to my shame that I have no knowledge about virtue at all. And how can I know a property of something when I don't even know what it is? Do you suppose that somebody entirely ignorant who Meno is could say whether he is handsome and rich and well-born or the reverse? Is that possible, do you think?

MENO: No. But is this true about yourself, Socrates, that you don't even know

c   what virtue is? Is this the report that we are to take home about you?

SOCRATES: Not only that; you may say also that, to the best of my belief, I have never yet met anyone who did know.

MENO: What! Didn't you meet Gorgias when he was here?

SOCRATES: Yes.

MENO: And you still didn't think he knew?

SOCRATES: I'm a forgetful sort of person, and I can't say just now what I thought at the time. Probably he did know, and I expect you know what he used to say about it.

d   So remind me what it was, or tell me yourself if you will. No doubt you agree with him.

MENO: Yes I do.

From *Protagoras and Meno,* translated with an introduction by W.K.C. Guthrie (Harmondsworth, Middlesex, England: Penguin Classics, 1956). Reprinted by permission of Penguin Books Ltd.

SOCRATES: Then let's leave him out of it, since after all he isn't here. What do you yourself say virtue is? I do ask you in all earnestness not to refuse me, but to speak out. I shall be only too happy to be proved wrong if you and Gorgias turn out to know this, although I said I had never met anyone who did.

MENO: But there is no difficulty about it. First of all, if it is manly virtue you are   e
after, it is easy to see that the virtue of a man consists in managing the city's affairs capably, and so that he will help his friends and injure his foes while taking care to come to no harm himself. Or if you want a woman's virtue, that is easily described. She must be a good housewife, careful with her stores and obedient to her husband. Then there is another virtue for a child, male or female, and another for an old man, free or slave as   72
you like; and a great many more kinds of virtue, so that no one need be at a loss to say what it is. For every act and every time of life, with reference to each separate function, there is a virtue for each one of us, and similarly, I should say, a vice.

SOCRATES: I seem to be in luck. I wanted one virtue and I find that you have a whole swarm of virtues to offer. But seriously, to carry on this metaphor of the swarm, suppose I asked you what a bee is, what is its essential nature, and you replied that bees were of many different kinds; what would you say if I went on to ask: "And is it in being bees that they are many and various and different from one another? Or would   b
you agree that it is not in this respect that they differ, but in something else, some other quality like size or beauty?"

MENO: I should say that in so far as they are bees, they don't differ from one another at all.

SOCRATES: Suppose I then continued: "Well, this is just what I want you to tell me. What is that character in respect of which they don't differ at all, but are all the   c
same?" I presume you would have something to say?

MENO: I should.

SOCRATES: Then do the same with the virtues. Even if they are many and various, yet at least they all have some common character which makes them virtues. That is what ought to be kept in view by anyone who answers the question: "What is virtue?" Do you follow me?   d

MENO: I think I do, but I don't yet really grasp the question as I should wish.

SOCRATES: Well, does this apply in your mind only to virtue, that there is a different one for a man and a woman and the rest? Is it the same with health and size and strength, or has health the same character everywhere, if it is health, whether it be in a   e
man or any other creature?

MENO: I agree that health is the same in a man or in a woman.

SOCRATES: And what about size and strength? If a woman is strong, will it be the same thing, the same strength, that makes her strong? My meaning is that in its character as strength, it is no different, whether it be in a man or in a woman. Or do you think it is?

MENO: No.

SOCRATES: And will virtue differ, in its character as virtue, whether it be in a   73
child or an old man, a woman or a man?

MENO: I somehow feel that this is not on the same level as the other cases.

SOCRATES: Well then, didn't you say that a man's virtue lay in directing the city well, and a woman's in directing her household well?

MENO: Yes.

SOCRATES: And is it possible to direct anything well—city or household or anything else—if not temperately and justly?

MENO: Certainly not.

b   SOCRATES: And that means with temperance and justice?

MENO: Of course.

SOCRATES: Then both man and woman need the same qualities, justice and temperance, if they are going to be good.

MENO: It looks like it.

SOCRATES: And what about your child and old man? Could they be good if they were incontinent and unjust?

c   MENO: Of course not.

SOCRATES: They must be temperate and just?

MENO: Yes.

SOCRATES: So everyone is good in the same way, since they become good by possessing the same qualities.

MENO: So it seems.

SOCRATES: And if they did not share the same virtue, they would not be good in the same way.

MENO: No.

SOCRATES: Seeing then that they all have the same virtue, try to remember and tell me what Gorgias, and you who share his opinion, say it is.

d   MENO: It must be simply the capacity to govern men, if you are looking for one quality to cover all the instances.

SOCRATES: Indeed I am. But does this virtue apply to a child or a slave? Should a slave be capable of governing his master, and if he does, is he still a slave?

MENO: I hardly think so.

SOCRATES: It certainly doesn't sound likely. And here is another point. You speak of "capacity to govern." Shall we not add "justly but not otherwise"?

MENO: I think we should, for justice is virtue.

e   SOCRATES: Virtue, do you say, or *a* virtue?

MENO: What do you mean?

SOCRATES: Something quite general. Take roundness, for instance. I should say that it is a shape, not simply that it is shape, my reason being that there are other shapes as well.

MENO: I see your point, and I agree that there are other virtues besides justice.

74   SOCRATES: Tell me what they are. Just as I could name other shapes if you told me to, in the same way mention some other virtues.

MENO: In my opinion then courage is a virtue and temperance and wisdom and dignity and many other things.

SOCRATES: This puts us back where we were. In a different way we have discovered a number of virtues when we were looking for one only. This single virtue, which permeates each of them, we cannot find.

b   MENO: No, I cannot yet grasp it as you want, a single virtue covering them all, as I do in other instances.

SOCRATES: I'm not surprised, but I shall do my best to get us a bit further if I can. You understand, I expect, that the question applies to everything. If someone took the example I mentioned just now, and asked you: "What is shape?" and you replied that roundness is shape, and he then asked you as I did, "Do you mean it is shape or *a* shape?" you would reply of course that it is *a* shape.

MENO: Certainly.

c   SOCRATES: Your reason being that there are other shapes as well.

MENO: Yes.

SOCRATES: And if he went on to ask you what they were, you would tell him.

MENO: Yes.

SOCRATES: And the same with colour—if he asked you what it is, and on your re-plying "White," took you up with: "Is white colour or *a* colour?" you would say that it is *a* colour, because there are other colours as well.

MENO: I should.

SOCRATES: And if he asked you to, you would mention other colours which are   d
just as much colours as white is.

MENO: Yes.

SOCRATES: Suppose then he pursued the question as I did, and objected: "We al-ways arrive at a plurality, but that is not the kind of answer I want. Seeing that you call these many particulars by one and the same name, and say that every one of them is a shape, even though they are the contrary of each other, tell me what this is which em-braces round as well as straight, and what you mean by shape when you say that   e
straightness is a shape as much as roundness. You do say that?"

MENO: Yes.

SOCRATES: "And in saying it, do you mean that roundness is no more round than straight, and straightness no more straight than round?"

MENO: Of course not.

SOCRATES: "Yet you do say that roundness is no more a shape than straightness, and the other way about."

MENO: Quite true.

SOCRATES: "Then what is this thing which is called 'shape'? Try to tell me." If   75
when asked this question either about shape or colour you said: "But I don't under-stand what you want, or what you mean," your questioner would perhaps be surprised and say: "Don't you see that I am looking for what is the same in all of them?" Would you even so be unable to reply, if the question was: "What is it that is common to roundness and straightness and the other things which you call shapes?"

Do your best to answer, as practice for the question about virtue.

MENO: No, you do it, Socrates.   b

SOCRATES: Do you want me to give in to you?

MENO: Yes.

SOCRATES: And will you in your turn give me an answer about virtue?

MENO: I will.

SOCRATES: In that case I must do my best. It's in a good cause.

MENO: Certainly.

SOCRATES: Well now, let's try to tell you what shape is. See if you accept this definition. Let us define it as the only thing which always accompanies colour. Does that satisfy you, or do you want it in some other way? I should be content if your defin-   c
ition of virtue were on similar lines.

MENO: But that's a naïve sort of definition, Socrates.

SOCRATES: How?

MENO: Shape, if I understand what you say, is what always accompanies colour. Well and good—but if somebody says that he doesn't know what colour is, but is no better off with it than he is with shape, what sort of answer have you given him, do you think?

SOCRATES: A true one; and if my questioner were one of the clever, disputatious and quarrelsome kind, I should say to him: "You have heard my answer. If it is wrong,   d
it is for you to take up the argument and refute it." However, when friendly people, like you and me, want to converse with each other, one's reply must be milder and more conducive to discussion. By that I mean that it must not only be true, but must   e
employ terms with which the questioner admits he is familiar. So I will try to answer you like that. Tell me therefore, whether you recognize the term "end"; I mean limit or

boundary—all these words I use in the same sense. Prodicus might perhaps quarrel with us, but I assume you speak of something being bounded or coming to an end. That is all I mean, nothing subtle.

MENO: I admit the notion, and believe I understand your meaning.

76   SOCRATES: And again, you recognize "surface" and "solid," as they are used in geometry?

MENO: Yes.

SOCRATES: Then with these you should by this time understand my definition of shape. To cover all its instances, I say that shape is that in which a solid terminates, or more briefly, it is the limit of a solid.

MENO: And how do you define colour?

SOCRATES: What a shameless fellow you are, Meno. You keep bothering an old

b   man to answer, but refuse to exercise your memory and tell me what was Gorgias's definition of virtue.

MENO: I will, Socrates, as soon as you tell me this.

SOCRATES: Anyone talking to you could tell blindfolded that you are a handsome man and still have your admirers.

MENO: Why so?

SOCRATES: Because you are forever laying down the law as spoilt boys do, who

c   act the tyrant as long as their youth lasts. No doubt you have discovered that I can never resist good looks. Well, I will give in and let you have your answer.

MENO: Do by all means.

SOCRATES: Would you like an answer *à la* Gorgias, such as you would most readily follow?

MENO: Of course I should.

SOCRATES: You and he believe in Empedocles's theory of effluences, do you not?

MENO: Whole-heartedly.

SOCRATES: And passages to which and through which the effluences make their way?

MENO: Yes.

d   SOCRATES: Some of the effluences fit into some of the passages, whereas others are too coarse or too fine.

MENO: That is right.

SOCRATES: Now you recognize the term "sight"?

MENO: Yes.

SOCRATES: From these notions, then, "grasp what I would tell," as Pindar says. Colour is an effluence from shapes commensurate with sight and perceptible by it.

MENO: That seems to me an excellent answer.

SOCRATES: No doubt it is the sort you are used to. And you probably see that it provides a way to define sound and smell and many similar things.

e   MENO: So it does.

SOCRATES: Yes, it's a high-sounding answer, so you like it better than the one on shape.

MENO: I do.

SOCRATES: Nevertheless, son of Alexidemus, I am convinced that the other is better; and I believe you would agree with me if you had not, as you told me yesterday, to leave before the mysteries, but could stay and be initiated.*

---

*Evidently the Athenians are about to celebrate the famous rites of the Eleusinian Mysteries, but Meno has to return to Thessaly before they fall due. Plato frequently plays upon the analogy between religious initiation, which bestows a revelation of divine secrets, and the insight that comes from initiation into the truths of philosophy.

MENO: I would stay, Socrates, if you gave me more answers like this.

SOCRATES: You may be sure I shan't be lacking in keenness to do so, both for your sake and mine; but I'm afraid I may not be able to do it often. However, now it is your turn to do as you promised, and try to tell me the general nature of virtue. Stop making many out of one, as the humorists say when somebody breaks a plate. Just leave virtue whole and sound and tell me what it is, as in the examples I have given you.

MENO: It seems to me then, Socrates, that virtue is, in the words of the poet, "to rejoice in the fine and have power," and I define it as desiring fine things and being able to acquire them.

SOCRATES: When you speak of a man desiring fine things, do you mean it is good things he desires?

MENO: Certainly.

SOCRATES: Then do you think some men desire evil and others good? Doesn't everyone, in your opinion, desire good things?

MENO: No.

SOCRATES: And would you say that the others suppose evils to be good, or do they still desire them although they recognize them as evil?

MENO: Both, I should say.

SOCRATES: What? Do you really think that anyone who recognizes evils for what they are, nevertheless desires them?

MENO: Yes.

SOCRATES: Desires in what way? To possess them?

MENO: Of course.

SOCRATES: In the belief that evil things bring advantage to their possessor, or harm?

MENO: Some in the first belief, but some also in the second.

SOCRATES: And do you believe that those who suppose evil things bring advantage understand that they are evil?

MENO: No, that I can't really believe.

SOCRATES: Isn't it clear then that this class, who don't recognize evils for what they are, don't desire evil but what they think is good, though in fact it is evil; those who through ignorance mistake bad things for good obviously desire the good.

MENO: For them I suppose that is true.

SOCRATES: Now as for those whom you speak of as desiring evils in the belief that they do harm to their possessor, these presumably know that they will be injured by them?

MENO: They must.

SOCRATES: And don't they believe that whoever is injured is, in so far as he is injured, unhappy?

MENO: That too they must believe.

SOCRATES: And unfortunate?

MENO: Yes.

SOCRATES: Well, does anybody want to be unhappy and unfortunate?

MENO: I suppose not.

SOCRATES: Then if not, nobody desires what is evil; for what else is unhappiness but desiring evil things and getting them?

MENO: It looks as if you are right, Socrates, and nobody desires what is evil.

SOCRATES: Now you have just said that virtue consists in a wish for good things plus the power to acquire them. In this definition the wish is common to everyone, and in that respect no one is better than his neighbour.

MENO: So it appears.

c   SOCRATES: So if one man is better than another, it must evidently be in respect of the power, and virtue, according to your account, is the power of acquiring good things.

MENO: Yes, my opinion is exactly as you now express it.

SOCRATES: Let us see whether you have hit the truth this time. You may well be right. The power of acquiring good things, you say, is virtue?

MENO: Yes.

SOCRATES: And by good do you mean such things as health and wealth?

MENO: I include the gaining both of gold and silver and of high and honourable office in the State.

SOCRATES: Are these the only classes of goods that you recognize?

MENO: Yes, I mean everything of that sort.

d   SOCRATES: Right. In the definition of Meno, hereditary guest-friend of the Great King, the acquisition of gold and silver is virtue. Do you add "just and righteous" to the word "acquisition," or doesn't it make any difference to you? Do you call it virtue all the same even if they are unjustly acquired?

MENO: Certainly not.

SOCRATES: Vice then?

MENO: Most certainly.

SOCRATES: So it seems that justice or temperance or piety, or some other part of

e   virtue, must attach to the acquisition. Otherwise, although it is a means to good things, it will not be virtue.

MENO: No, how could you have virtue without these?

SOCRATES: In fact lack of gold and silver, if it results from failure to acquire it— either for oneself or another—in circumstances which would have made its acquisition unjust, is itself virtue.

MENO: It would seem so.

SOCRATES: Then to have such goods is no more virtue than to lack them. Rather

79   we may say that whatever is accompanied by justice is virtue, whatever is without qualities of that sort is vice.

MENO: I agree that your conclusion seems inescapable.

SOCRATES: But a few minutes ago we called each of these—justice, temperance, and the rest—a part of virtue?

MENO: Yes, we did.

SOCRATES: So it seems you are making a fool of me.

MENO: How so, Socrates?

SOCRATES: I have just asked you not to break virtue up into fragments, and given you models of the type of answer I wanted, but taking no notice of this you tell me that

b   virtue consists in the acquisition of good things with justice; and justice, you agree, is a part of virtue.

MENO: True.

SOCRATES: So it follows from your own statements that to act with a part of virtue is virtue, if you call justice and all the rest parts of virtue. The point I want to make is that whereas I asked you to give me an account of virtue as a whole, far from telling me what it is itself you say that every action is virtue which exhibits a part of

c   virtue, as if you had already told me what the whole is, so that I should recognize it even if you chop it up into bits. It seems to me that we must put the same old question to you, my dear Meno—the question: "What is virtue?"—if every act becomes virtue when combined with a part of virtue. That is, after all, what it means to say that every act performed with justice is virtue. Don't you agree that the same question needs to be put? Does anyone know what a part of virtue is, without knowing the whole?

MENO: I suppose not.

SOCRATES: No, and if you remember, when I replied to you about shape just now,   d
I believe we rejected the type of answer that employs terms which are still in question and not yet agreed upon.

MENO: We did, and rightly.

SOCRATES: Then please do the same. While the nature of virtue as a whole is still under question, don't suppose that you can explain it to anyone in terms of its parts, or by any similar type of explanation. Understand rather that the same question remains   e
to be answered; you say this and that about virtue, but what *is* it? Does this seem nonsense to you?

MENO: No, to me it seems right enough.

SOCRATES: Then go back to the beginning and answer my question. What do you and your friend say that virtue is?

MENO: Socrates, even before I met you they told me that in plain truth you are a perplexed man yourself and reduce others to perplexity. At this moment I feel you are   80
exercising magic and witchcraft upon me and positively laying me under your spell until I am just a mass of helplessness. If I may be flippant, I think that not only in outward appearance but in other respects as well you are exactly like the flat stingray that one meets in the sea. Whenever anyone comes into contact with it, it numbs him, and that is the sort of thing that you seem to be doing to me now. My mind and my lips are   b
literally numb, and I have nothing to reply to you. Yet I have spoken about virtue hundreds of times, held forth often on the subject in front of large audiences, and very well too, or so I thought. Now I can't even say what it is. In my opinion you are well advised not to leave Athens and live abroad. If you behaved like this as a foreigner in another country, you would most likely be arrested as a wizard.

SOCRATES: You're a real rascal, Meno. You nearly took me in.

MENO: Just what do you mean?

SOCRATES: I see why you used a simile about me.   c

MENO: Why, do you think?

SOCRATES: To be compared to something in return. All good-looking people, I know perfectly well, enjoy a game of comparisons. They get the best of it, for naturally handsome folk provoke handsome similes. But I'm not going to oblige you. As for myself, if the stingray paralyses others only through being paralysed itself, then the comparison is just, but not otherwise. It isn't that, knowing the answers myself, I perplex other people. The truth is rather that I infect them also with the perplexity I feel myself. So with virtue now. I don't know what it is. You may have known before you came   d
into contact with me, but now you look as if you don't. Nevertheless I am ready to carry out, together with you, a joint investigation and inquiry into what it is.

MENO: But how will you look for something when you don't in the least know what it is? How on earth are you going to set up something you don't know as the object of your search? To put it another way, even if you come right up against it, how will you know that what you have found is the thing you didn't know?

SOCRATES: I know what you mean. Do you realize that what you are bringing up   e
is the trick argument that a man cannot try to discover either what he knows or what he does not know? He would not seek what he knows, for since he knows it there is no need of the inquiry, nor what he does not know, for in that case he does not even know what he is to look for.

MENO: Well, do you think it a good argument?   81

SOCRATES: No.

MENO: Can you explain how it fails?

SOCRATES: I can. I have heard from men and women who understand the truths of religion—

[Here he presumably pauses to emphasize the solemn change of tone that the dialogue undergoes at this point.]

MENO: What did they say?

SOCRATES: Something true, I thought, and fine.

MENO: What was it, and who were they?

SOCRATES: Those who tell it are priests and priestesses of the sort who make it
b   their business to be able to account for the functions which they perform. Pindar
speaks of it too, and many another of the poets who are divinely inspired. What they
say is this—see whether you think they are speaking the truth. They say that the soul of
man is immortal: At one time it comes to an end—that which is called death—and at
another is born again, but is never finally exterminated. On these grounds a man must
live all his days as righteously as possible. For those from whom

> Persephone receives requital for ancient doom,
> In the ninth year she restores again
> Their souls to the sun above.
> From whom rise noble kings
c   > And the swift in strength and greatest in wisdom;
> And for the rest of time
> They are called heroes and sanctified by men.*

Thus the soul, since it is immortal and has been born many times, and has seen
all things both here and in the other world, has learned everything that is. So we need
not be surprised if it can recall the knowledge of virtue or anything else which, as we
d   see, it once possessed. All nature is akin, and the soul has learned everything, so that
when a man has recalled a single piece of knowledge—*learned* it, in ordinary language—there is no reason why he should not find out all the rest, if he keeps a stout
heart and does not grow weary of the search; for seeking and learning are in fact nothing but recollection.

We ought not then to be led astray by the contentious argument you quoted. It
e   would make us lazy, and is music in the ears of weaklings. The other doctrine produces
energetic seekers after knowledge; and being convinced of its truth, I am ready, with
your help, to inquire into the nature of virtue.

MENO: I see, Socrates. But what do you mean when you say that we don't learn
anything, but that what we call learning is recollection? Can you teach me that it is so?

SOCRATES: I have just said that you're a rascal, and now you ask me if I can teach
82   you, when I say there is no such thing as teaching, only recollection. Evidently you
want to catch me contradicting myself straight away.

MENO: No, honestly, Socrates, I wasn't thinking of that. It was just habit. If you
can in any way make clear to me that what you say is true, please do.

SOCRATES: It isn't an easy thing, but still I should like to do what I can since you
b   ask me. I see you have a large number of retainers here. Call one of them, anyone you
like, and I will use him to demonstrate it to you.

*The quotation is from Pindar.

MENO: Certainly. *(to a slave-boy)* Come here.

SOCRATES: He is a Greek and speaks our language?

MENO: Indeed yes—born and bred in the house.

SOCRATES: Listen carefully then, and see whether it seems to you that he is learning from me or simply being reminded.

MENO: I will.

SOCRATES: Now boy, you know that a square is a figure like this?

[Socrates begins to draw figures in the sand at his feet. He points to the square ABCD.]

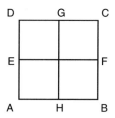

BOY: Yes.

SOCRATES: It has all these four sides equal?   c

BOY: Yes.

SOCRATES: And these lines which go through the middle of it are also equal? (The lines EF *and* GH.)

BOY: Yes.

SOCRATES: Such a figure could be either larger or smaller, could it not?

BOY: Yes.

SOCRATES: Now if this side is two feet long, and this side the same, how many feet will the whole be? Put it this way. If it were two feet in this direction and only one in that, must not the area be two feet taken once?

BOY: Yes.

SOCRATES: But since it is two feet this way also, does it not become twice two feet?   d

BOY: Yes.

SOCRATES: And how many feet is twice two? Work it out and tell me.

BOY: Four.

SOCRATES: Now could one draw another figure double the size of this, but similar, that is, with all its sides equal like this one?

BOY: Yes.

SOCRATES: It is on this line then, according to you, that we shall make the eight-foot square, by taking four of the same length?

BOY: Yes.

SOCRATES: How many feet will its area be?

BOY: Eight.

SOCRATES: Now then, try to tell me how long each of its sides will be. The present figure has a side of two feet. What will be the side of the double-sized one?   e

BOY: It will be double, Socrates, obviously.

SOCRATES: You see, Meno, that I am not teaching him anything, only asking. Now he thinks he knows the length of the side of the eight-foot square.

MENO: Yes.

SOCRATES: But does he?

MENO: Certainly not.

SOCRATES: He thinks it is twice the length of the other.

MENO: Yes.

SOCRATES: Now watch how he recollects things in order—the proper way to recollect.

You say that the side of double length produces the double-sized figure? Like this I mean, not long this way and short that. It must be equal on all sides like the first figure, only twice its size, that is eight feet. Think a moment whether you still expect to get it from doubling the side.

BOY: Yes, I do.

SOCRATES: Well now, shall we have a line double the length of this (AB) if we add another the same length at this end (BJ)?

BOY: Yes.

SOCRATES: It is on this line then, according to you, that we shall make the eight-foot square, by taking four of the same length?

BOY: Yes.

SOCRATES: Let us draw in four equal lines *(that is, counting* AJ, *and adding* JK, KL, *and* LA *made complete by drawing in its second half* LD), using the first as a base. Does this not give us what you call the eight-foot figure?

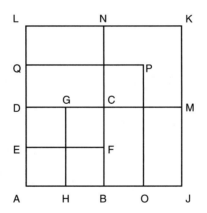

BOY: Certainly.

SOCRATES: But does it contain these four squares, each equal to the original four-foot one?

[Socrates has drawn in the lines CM, CN *to complete the squares that he wishes to point out.]*

BOY: Yes.

SOCRATES: How big is it then? Won't it be four times as big?

BOY: Of course.

SOCRATES: And is four times the same as twice?

BOY: Of course not.

SOCRATES: So doubling the side has given us not a double but a fourfold figure?

BOY: True.

SOCRATES: And four times four are sixteen, are they not?

BOY: Yes.

SOCRATES: Then how big is the side of the eight-foot figure? This one has given us four times the original area, hasn't it?

BOY: Yes.

SOCRATES: And a side half the length gave us a square of four feet?

BOY: Yes.

SOCRATES: Good. And isn't a square of eight feet double this one and half that?

BOY: Yes.

SOCRATES: Will it not have a side greater than this one but less than that?

BOY: I think it will.

d

SOCRATES: Right. Always answer what you think. Now tell me: was not this side two feet long, and this one four?

BOY: Yes.

SOCRATES: Then the side of the eight-foot figure must be longer than two feet but shorter than four?

BOY: It must.

SOCRATES: Try to say how long you think it is.

e

BOY: Three feet.

SOCRATES: If so, shall we add half of this bit (BO, *half of* BJ) and make it three feet? Here are two, and this is one, and on this side similarly we have two plus one; and here is the figure you want.

[Socrates completes the square AOPQ.]

BOY: Yes.

SOCRATES: If it is three feet this way and three that, will the whole area be three times three feet?

BOY: It looks like it.

SOCRATES: And that is how many?

BOY: Nine.

SOCRATES: Whereas the square double our first square had to be how many?

BOY: Eight.

SOCRATES: But we haven't yet got the square of eight feet even from a three-foot side?

BOY: No.

SOCRATES: Then what length will give it? Try to tell us exactly. If you don't want to count it up, just show us on the diagram.

84

BOY: It's no use, Socrates, I just don't know.

SOCRATES: Observe, Meno, the stage he has reached on the path of recollection. At the beginning he did not know the side of the square of eight feet. Nor indeed does he know it now, but then he thought he knew it and answered boldly, as was appropriate—he felt no perplexity. Now however he does feel perplexed. Not only does he not know the answer; he doesn't even think he knows.

MENO: Quite true.

b

SOCRATES: Isn't he in a better position now in relation to what he didn't know?

MENO: I admit that too.

SOCRATES: So in perplexing him and numbing him like the sting-ray, have we done him any harm?

MENO: I think not.

SOCRATES: In fact we have helped him to some extent towards finding out the right answer, for now not only is he ignorant of it but he will be quite glad to look for it. Up to now, he thought he could speak well and fluently, on many occasions and be-fore large audiences, on the subject of a square double the size of a given square, main-

c   taining that it must have a side of double the length.

MENO: No doubt.

SOCRATES: Do you suppose then that he would have attempted to look for, or learn, what he thought he knew (though he did not), before he was thrown into per-plexity, became aware of his ignorance, and felt a desire to know?

MENO: No.

SOCRATES: Then the numbing process was good for him?

MENO: I agree.

SOCRATES: Now notice what, starting from this state of perplexity, he will dis-cover by seeking the truth in company with me, though I simply ask him questions without teaching him. Be ready to catch me if I give him any instruction or explanation

d   instead of simply interrogating him on his own opinions.

[Socrates here rubs out the previous figures and starts again.]

Tell me, boy, is not this our square of four feet? *(ABCD.)* You understand?

BOY: Yes.

SOCRATES: Now we can add another equal to it like this? *(BCEF.)*

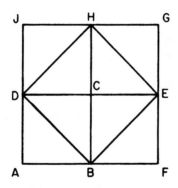

BOY: Yes.

SOCRATES: And a third here, equal to each of the others? *(CEGH.)*

BOY: Yes.

SOCRATES: And then we can fill in this one in the corner? *(DCHJ.)*

BOY: Yes.

SOCRATES: Then here we have four equal squares?

BOY: Yes.

e   SOCRATES: And how many times the size of the first square is the whole?

BOY: Four times.

SOCRATES: And we want one double the size. You remember?

BOY: Yes.

85   SOCRATES: Now does this line going from corner to corner cut each of these squares in half?

BOY: Yes.

SOCRATES: And these are four equal lines enclosing this area? *(BEHD.)*

BOY: They are.

SOCRATES: Now think. How big is this area?

BOY: I don't understand.

SOCRATES: Here are four squares. Has not each line cut off the inner half of each of them?

BOY: Yes.

SOCRATES: And how many such halves are there in this figure? *(BEHD.)*

BOY: Four.

SOCRATES: And how many in this one? *(ABCD.)*

BOY: Two.

SOCRATES: And what is the relation of four to two?   b

BOY: Double.

SOCRATES: How big is this figure then?

BOY: Eight feet.

SOCRATES: On what base?

BOY: This one.

SOCRATES: The line which goes from corner to corner of the square of four feet?

BOY: Yes.

SOCRATES: The technical name for it is "diagonal"; so if we use that name, it is your personal opinion that the square on the diagonal of the original square is double its area.

BOY: That is so, Socrates.

SOCRATES: What do you think, Meno? Has he answered with any opinions that   c were not his own?

MENO: No, they were all his.

SOCRATES: Yet he did not know, as we agreed a few minutes ago.

MENO: True.

SOCRATES: But these opinions were somewhere in him, were they not?

MENO: Yes.

SOCRATES: So a man who does not know has in himself true opinions on a subject without having knowledge.

MENO: It would appear so.

SOCRATES: At present these opinions, being newly aroused, have a dream-like quality. But if the same questions are put to him on many occasions and in different ways, you can see that in the end he will have a knowledge on the subject as accurate   d as anybody's.

MENO: Probably.

SOCRATES: This knowledge will not come from teaching but from questioning. He will recover it for himself.

MENO: Yes.

SOCRATES: And the spontaneous recovery of knowledge that is in him is recollection, isn't it?

MENO: Yes.

SOCRATES: Either then he has at some time acquired the knowledge which he now has, or he has always possessed it. If he always possessed it, he must always have known; if on the other hand he acquired it at some previous time, it cannot have been in this life, unless somebody has taught him geometry. He will behave in the same way   e with all geometrical knowledge, and every other subject. Has anyone taught him all these? You ought to know, especially as he has been brought up in your household.

MENO: Yes, I know that no one ever taught him.

SOCRATES: And has he these opinions, or hasn't he?

MENO: It seems we can't deny it.

86   SOCRATES: Then if he did not acquire them in this life, isn't it immediately clear that he possessed and had learned them during some other period?

MENO: It seems so.

SOCRATES: When he was not in human shape?

MENO: Yes.

SOCRATES: If then there are going to exist in him, both while he is and while he is not a man, true opinions which can be aroused by questioning and turned into knowledge, may we say that his soul has been forever in a state of knowledge? Clearly he always either is or is not a man.

MENO: Clearly.

b   SOCRATES: And if the truth about reality is always in our soul, the soul must be immortal, and one must take courage and try to discover—that is, to recollect—what one doesn't happen to know, or (more correctly) remember, at the moment.

MENO: Somehow or other I believe you are right.

SOCRATES: I think I am. I shouldn't like to take my oath on the whole story, but one thing I am ready to fight for as long as I can, in word and act: that is, that we shall be better, braver, and more active men if we believe it right to look for what we don't

c   know than if we believe there is no point in looking because what we don't know we can never discover.

MENO: There too I am sure you are right.

SOCRATES: Then, since we are agreed that it is right to inquire into something that one does not know, are you ready to face with me the question: what is virtue?

MENO: Quite ready. All the same, I would rather consider the question as I put it at the beginning, and hear your views on it; that is, are we to pursue virtue as some-

d   thing that can be taught, or do men have it as a gift of nature or how?

SOCRATES: If I were your master as well as my own, Meno, we should not have inquired whether or not virtue can be taught until we had first asked the main question—what it is; but not only do you make no attempt to govern your own actions—you prize your freedom, I suppose—but you attempt to govern mine. And you succeed too, so I shall let you have your way. There's nothing else for it, and it seems we must

e   inquire into a single property of something about whose essential nature we are still in the dark. Just grant me one small relaxation of your sway, and allow me, in considering whether or not it can be taught, to make use of a hypothesis—the sort of thing, I mean, that geometers often use in their inquiries. When they are asked, for example,

87   about a given area, whether it is possible for this area to be inscribed as a triangle in a given circle, they will probably reply: "I don't know yet whether it fulfils the conditions, but I think I have a hypothesis which will help us in the matter. It is this. If the area is such that, when one has applied it [e.g., as a rectangle] to the given line [i.e., the diameter] of the circle, it is deficient by another rectangle similar to the one which is applied, then, I should say, one result follows; if not, the result is different. If you ask

b   me, then, about the inscription of the figure in the circle—whether it is possible or not—I am ready to answer you in this hypothetical way."*

*[It is very difficult to understand the geometrical illustration Socrates is giving here.] Sir Thomas Heath in his *History of Greek Mathematics* (1921), Vol. i, p. 298, says that C. Blass, writing in 1861, already knew of thirty different interpretations, and that many more had appeared since then. Fortunately it is not necessary to understand the example in order to grasp the hypothetical method Socrates is expounding.

Let us do the same about virtue. Since we don't know what it is or what it resembles, let us use a hypothesis in investigating whether it is teachable or not. We shall say: "What attribute of the soul must virtue be, if it is to be teachable or otherwise?" Well, in the first place, if it is anything else but knowledge, is there a possibility of anyone teaching it—or, in the language we used just now, reminding someone of it? We needn't worry about which name we are to give to the process, but simply ask: will c it be teachable? Isn't it plain to everyone that a man is not taught anything except knowledge?

MENO: That would be my view.

SOCRATES: If on the other hand virtue is some sort of knowledge, clearly it could be taught.

MENO: Certainly.

SOCRATES: So that question is easily settled; I mean, on what condition virtue would be teachable.

MENO: Yes.

SOCRATES: The next point then, I suppose, is to find out whether virtue is knowl- d edge or something different.

MENO: That is the next question, I agree.

SOCRATES: Well then, do we assert that virtue is something good? Is that assumption a firm one for us?

MENO: Undoubtedly.

SOCRATES: That being so, if there exists any good thing different from, and not associated with, knowledge, virtue will not necessarily be any form of knowledge. If on the other hand knowledge embraces everything that is good, we shall be right to suspect that virtue is knowledge.

MENO: Agreed.

SOCRATES: First then, is it virtue which makes us good?   e

MENO: Yes.

SOCRATES: And if good, then advantageous. All good things are advantageous, are they not?

MENO: Yes.

SOCRATES: So virtue itself must be something advantageous?

MENO: That follows also.

SOCRATES: Now suppose we consider what are the sort of things that profit us. Take them in a list. Health, we may say, and strength and good looks, and wealth— these and their like we call advantageous, you agree?

MENO: Yes.

SOCRATES: Yet we also speak of these things as sometimes doing harm. Would   88 you object to that statement?

MENO: No, it is so.

SOCRATES: Now look here: what is the controlling factor which determines whether each of these is advantageous or harmful? Isn't it right use which makes them advantageous, and lack of it, harmful?

MENO: Certainly.

SOCRATES: We must also take spiritual qualities into consideration. You recognize such things as temperance, justice, courage, quickness of mind, memory, nobility of character and others?

MENO: Yes, of course I do.

SOCRATES: Then take any such qualities which in your view are not knowledge   b but something different. Don't you think they may be harmful as well as advantageous? Courage for instance, if it is something thoughtless, is just a sort of confidence. Isn't it true that to be confident without reason does a man harm, whereas a reasoned confidence profits him?

MENO: Yes.

SOCRATES: Temperance and quickness of mind are no different. Learning and discipline are profitable in conjunction with wisdom, but without it harmful.

c   MENO: That is emphatically true.

SOCRATES: In short, everything that the human spirit undertakes or suffers will lead to happiness when it is guided by wisdom, but to the opposite, when guided by folly.

MENO: A reasonable conclusion.

SOCRATES: If then virtue is an attribute of the spirit, and one which cannot fail to be beneficial, it must be wisdom; for all spiritual qualities in and by themselves are

d   neither advantageous nor harmful, but become advantageous or harmful by the presence with them of wisdom or folly. If we accept this argument, then virtue, to be something advantageous, must be a sort of wisdom.

MENO: I agree.

SOCRATES: To go back to the other class of things, wealth and the like, of which we said just now that they are sometimes good and sometimes harmful, isn't it the same with them? Just as wisdom when it governs our other psychological impulses turns them to advantage, and folly turns them to harm, so the mind by its right use and

e   control of these material assets makes them profitable, and by wrong use renders them harmful.

MENO: Certainly.

SOCRATES: And the right user is the mind of the wise man, the wrong user the mind of the foolish.

MENO: That is so.

SOCRATES: So we may say in general that the goodness of non-spiritual assets depends on our spiritual character, and the goodness of that on wisdom. This argument shows that the advantageous element must be wisdom; and virtue, we agree, is advan-

89   tageous, so that amounts to saying that virtue, either in whole or in part, is wisdom.

MENO: The argument seems to me fair enough.

SOCRATES: If so, good men cannot be good by nature.

MENO: I suppose not.

b   SOCRATES: There is another point. If they were, there would probably be experts among us who could recognize the naturally good at an early stage. They would point them out to us, and we should take them and shut them away safely in the Acropolis, sealing them up more carefully than bullion to protect them from corruption and ensure that when they came to maturity they would be of use to the State.

MENO: It would be likely enough.

c   SOCRATES: Since then goodness does not come by nature, is it got by learning?

MENO: I don't see how we can escape the conclusion. Indeed it is obvious on our assumption that, if virtue is knowledge, it is teachable.

SOCRATES: I suppose so. But I wonder if we were right to bind ourselves to that.

MENO: Well, it seemed all right just now.

SOCRATES: Yes, but to be sound it has got to seem all right not only "just now" but at this moment and in the future.

d   MENO: Of course. But what has occurred to you to make you turn against it and suspect that virtue may not be knowledge?

SOCRATES: I'll tell you. I don't withdraw from the position that if it is knowledge, it must be teachable; but as for its being knowledge, see whether you think my doubts on this point are well founded. If anything—not virtue only—is a possible subject of instruction, must there not be teachers and students of it?

MENO: Surely.

SOCRATES: And what of the converse, that if there are neither teachers nor students of a subject, we may safely infer that it cannot be taught? e

MENO: That is true. But don't you think there are teachers of virtue?

SOCRATES: All I can say is that I have often looked to see if there are any, and in spite of all my efforts I cannot find them, though I have had plenty of fellow-searchers, the kind of men especially whom I believe to have most experience in such matters. But look, Meno, here's a piece of luck. Anytus has just sat down beside us. We couldn't do better than make him a partner in our inquiry. In the first place, he is the 90 son of Anthemion, a man of property and good sense, who didn't get his money out of the blue or as a gift—like Ismenias of Thebes who has just come into the fortune of a Croesus—but earned it by his own brains and hard work. Besides this, he shows himself a decent, modest citizen with no arrogance or bombast or offensiveness about him. Also he brought up his son well and had him properly educated, as the Athenian people appreciate: look how they elect him into the highest offices in the State. This is b certainly the right sort of man with whom to inquire whether there are any teachers of virtue, and if so who they are.

Please help us, Anytus—Meno, who is a friend of your family, and myself—to find out who may be the teachers of this subject. Look at it like this. If we wanted Meno to become a good doctor, shouldn't we send him to the doctors to be taught? c

ANYTUS: Of course.

SOCRATES: And if we wanted him to become a shoemaker, to the shoemakers?

ANYTUS: Yes.

SOCRATES: And so on with other trades?

ANYTUS: Yes.

SOCRATES: Now another relevant question. When we say that to make Meno a doctor we should be right in sending him to the doctors, have we in mind that the sen- d sible thing is to send him to those who profess the subject rather than to those who don't, men who charge a fee as professionals, having announced that they are prepared to teach whoever likes to come and learn?

ANYTUS: Yes.

SOCRATES: The same is surely true of flute-playing and other accomplishments. If you want to make someone a performer on the flute it would be very foolish to refuse e to send him to those who undertake to teach the art and are paid for it, but to go and bother other people instead and have him try to learn from them—people who don't set up to be teachers or take any pupils in the subject which we want our young man to learn. Doesn't that sound very unreasonable?

ANYTUS: Sheer stupidity I should say.

SOCRATES: I agree. And now we can both consult together about our visitor 91 Meno. He has been telling me all this while that he longs to acquire the kind of wisdom and virtue which fits men to manage an estate or govern a city, to look after their parents, and to entertain and send off guests in proper style, both their own countrymen and foreigners. With this in mind, to whom would it be right to send him? What we have just said seems to show that the right people are those who profess to be teachers b of virtue and offer their services freely to any Greek who wishes to learn, charging a fixed fee for their instruction.

ANYTUS: Whom do you mean by that, Socrates?

SOCRATES: Surely you know yourself that they are the men called Sophists.

c   ANYTUS: Good heavens, what a thing to say! I hope no relative of mine or any of my friends, Athenian or foreign, would be so mad as to go and let himself be ruined by those people. That's what they are, the manifest ruin and corruption of anyone who comes into contact with them.

SOCRATES: What, Anytus? Can they be so different from other claimants to useful knowledge that they not only don't do good, like the rest, to the material that one puts in their charge, but on the contrary spoil it—and have the effrontery to take money for doing so? I for one find it difficult to believe you. I know that one of them alone, Pro-
d   tagoras, earned more money from being a Sophist than an outstandingly fine craftsman like Phidias and ten other sculptors put together. A man who mends old shoes or re-stores coats couldn't get away with it for a month if he gave them back in worse condi-tion than he received them; he would soon find himself starving. Surely it is incredible
e   that Protagoras took in the whole of Greece, corrupting his pupils and sending them away worse than when they came to him, for more than forty years. I believe he was nearly seventy when he died, and had been practising for forty years, and all that time—indeed to this very day—his reputation has been consistently high; and there are
92   plenty of others besides Protagoras, some before his time and others still alive. Are we to suppose from your remark that they consciously deceive and ruin young men, or are they unaware of it themselves? Can these remarkably clever men—as some regard them—be mad enough for that?

ANYTUS: Far from it, Socrates. It isn't they who are mad, but rather the young men who hand over their money; and those responsible for them, who let them get into the Sophists' hands, are even worse. Worst of all are the cities who allow them in, or
b   don't expel them, whether it be a foreigner or one of themselves who tries that sort of game.

SOCRATES: Has one of the Sophists done you a personal injury, or why are you so hard on them?

ANYTUS: Heavens, no! I've never in my life had anything to do with a single one of them, nor would I hear of any of my family doing so.

SOCRATES: So you've had no experience of them at all?

ANYTUS: And don't want any either.

c   SOCRATES: You surprise me. How can you know what is good or bad in some-thing when you have no experience of it?

ANYTUS: Quite easily. At any rate I know *their* kind, whether I've had experience or not.

SOCRATES: It must be second sight, I suppose; for how else you know about them, judging from what you tell me yourself, I can't imagine. However, we are not asking
d   whose instruction it is that would ruin Meno's character. Let us say that those are the Sophists if you like, and tell us instead about the ones we want. You can do a good turn to a friend of your father's house if you will let him know to whom in our great city he should apply for proficiency in the kind of virtue I have just described.

ANYTUS: Why not tell him yourself?

SOCRATES: Well, I did mention the men who in my opinion teach these things, but apparently I was talking nonsense. So you say, and you may well be right. Now it is
e   your turn to direct him; mention the name of any Athenian you like.

ANYTUS: But why mention a particular individual? Any decent Athenian gentle-man whom he happens to meet, if he follows his advice, will make him a better man than the Sophists would.

93   SOCRATES: And did these gentlemen get their fine qualities spontaneously—self-taught, as it were, and yet [they are] able to teach this untaught virtue to others?

ANYTUS: I suppose they in their turn learned it from forebears who were gentlemen like themselves. Would you deny that there have been many good men in our city?

SOCRATES: On the contrary, there are plenty of good statesmen here in Athens, and have been as good in the past. The question is, have they also been good teachers of their own virtue? That is the point we are discussing now—not whether or not there are good men in Athens or whether there have been in past times, but whether virtue can be taught. It amounts to the question whether the good men of this and former times have known how to hand on to someone else the goodness that was in themselves, or whether on the contrary it is not something that can be handed over, or that one man can receive from another. That is what Meno and I have long been puzzling over. Look at it from your own point of view. You would say that Themistocles was a good man?

ANYTUS: Yes, none better.

SOCRATES: And that he, if anyone, must have been a good teacher of his own virtue?

ANYTUS: I suppose so, if he wanted to be.

SOCRATES: But don't you think he must have wanted others to become worthy men—above all, surely, his own son? Do you suppose he grudged him this and purposely didn't pass on his own virtue to him? You must have heard that he had his son Cleophantus so well trained in horsemanship that he could stand upright on horseback and throw a javelin from that position; and many other wonderful accomplishments the young man had, for his father had him taught and made expert in every skill that a good instructor could impart. You must have heard this from older people?

ANYTUS: Yes.

SOCRATES: No one, then, could say that there was anything wrong with the boy's natural powers?

ANYTUS: Perhaps not.

SOCRATES: But have you ever heard anyone, young or old, say that Cleophantus the son of Themistocles was a good and wise man in the way that his father was?

ANYTUS: Certainly not.

SOCRATES: Must we conclude then that Themistocles' aim was to educate his son in other accomplishments, but not to make him any better than his neighbours in his own type of wisdom—that is, supposing that virtue could be taught?

ANYTUS: I hardly think we can.

SOCRATES: So much then for Themistocles as a teacher of virtue, whom you yourself agree to have been one of the best men of former times. Take another example, Aristides, son of Lysimachus. You accept him as a good man?

ANYTUS: Surely.

SOCRATES: He too gave his son Lysimachus the best education in Athens, in all subjects where a teacher could help; but did he make him a better man than his neighbour? You know him, I think, and can say what he is like. Or again there is Pericles, that great and wise man. He brought up two sons, Paralus and Xanthippus, and had them taught riding, music, athletics, and all the other skilled pursuits till they were as good as any in Athens. Did he then not want to make them good men? Yes, he wanted that, no doubt, but I am afraid it is something that cannot be done by teaching. And in case you should think that only very few, and those the most insignificant, lacked this power, consider that Thucydides also had two sons, Melesias and Stephanus, to whom he gave an excellent education. Among other things they were the best wrestlers in Athens, for he gave one to Xanthias to train and the other to Eudoxus—the two who, I understand, were considered the finest wrestlers of their time. You remember?

ANYTUS: I have heard of them.

d   SOCRATES: Surely then he would never have had his children taught these expensive pursuits and yet refused to teach them to be good men—which would have cost nothing at all—if virtue could have been taught? You are not going to tell me that Thucydides was a man of no account, or that he had not plenty of friends both at Athens and among the allies? He came of an influential family and was a great power both here and in the rest of Greece. If virtue could have been taught, he would have found the man to make his sons good, either among our own citizens or abroad, supposing his political duties left him no time to do it himself. No, my dear Anytus, it looks as if it cannot be taught.

e

ANYTUS: You seem to me, Socrates, to be too ready to run people down. My advice to you, if you will listen to it, is to be careful. I dare say that in all cities it is easier to do a man harm than good, and it is certainly so here, as I expect you know yourself.

95

SOCRATES: Anytus seems angry, Meno, and I am not surprised. He thinks I am slandering our statesmen, and moreover he believes himself to be one of them. He doesn't know what slander really is: if he ever finds out he will forgive me.

However, tell me this yourself: are there not similar fine characters in your country?

MENO: Yes, certainly.

b   SOCRATES: Do they come forward of their own accord to teach the young? Do they agree that they are teachers and that virtue can be taught?

MENO: No indeed, they don't agree on it at all. Sometimes you will hear them say that it can be taught, sometimes that it cannot.

SOCRATES: Ought we then to class as teachers of it men who are not even agreed that it can be taught?

MENO: Hardly, I think.

SOCRATES: And what about the Sophists, the only people who profess to teach it? Do you think they do?

c   MENO: The thing I particularly admire about Gorgias, Socrates, is that you will never hear him make this claim; indeed he laughs at the others when he hears them do so. In his view his job is to make clever speakers.

SOCRATES: So you too don't think the Sophists are teachers?

MENO: I really can't say. Like most people I waver—sometimes I think they are and sometimes I think they are not.

SOCRATES: Has it ever occurred to you that you and our statesmen are not alone in

d   this? The poet Theognis likewise says in one place that virtue is teachable and in another that it is not.

MENO: Really? Where?

SOCRATES: In the elegiacs in which he writes:

Eat, drink, and sit with men of power and weight,
Nor scorn to gain the favour of the great.
For fine men's teaching to fine ways will win thee:
Low company destroys what wit is in thee.

e   There he speaks as if virtue can be taught, doesn't he?

MENO: Clearly.

SOCRATES: But elsewhere he changes his ground a little:

Were mind by art created and instilled
Immense rewards had soon the pockets filled

of the people who could do this. Moreover

No good man's son would ever worthless be,
Taught by wise counsel. But no teacher's skill
Can turn to good what is created ill.   96

Do you see how he contradicts himself?

MENO: Plainly.

SOCRATES: Can you name any other subject, in which the professed teachers are not only not recognized as teachers of others, but are thought to have no understanding of it themselves, and to be no good at the very subject they profess to teach; whereas those who are acknowledged to be the best at it are in two minds whether it can be   b taught or not? When people are so confused about a subject, can you say that they are in a true sense teachers?

MENO: Certainly not.

SOCRATES: Well, if neither the Sophists nor those who display fine qualities themselves are teachers of virtue, I am sure no one else can be, and if there are no teachers, there can be no students either.   c

MENO: I quite agree.

SOCRATES: And we have also agreed that a subject of which there were neither teachers nor students was not one which could be taught.

MENO: That is so.

SOCRATES: Now there turn out to be neither teachers nor students of virtue, so it would appear that virtue cannot be taught.

MENO: So it seems, if we have made no mistake; and it makes me wonder,   d Socrates, whether there are in fact no good men at all, or how they are produced when they do appear.

SOCRATES: I have a suspicion, Meno, that you and I are not much good. Our masters Gorgias and Prodicus have not trained us properly. We must certainly take ourselves in hand, and try to find someone who will improve us by hook or by crook. I say this with our recent discussion in mind, for absurdly enough we failed to perceive that   e it is not only under the guidance of knowledge that human action is well and rightly conducted. I believe that may be what prevents us from seeing how it is that men are made good.

MENO: What do you mean?

SOCRATES: This: We were correct, were we not, in agreeing that good men must be profitable or useful? It cannot be otherwise, can it?

MENO: No.

SOCRATES: And again that they will be of some use if they conduct our affairs aright—that also was correct?   97

MENO: Yes.

SOCRATES: But in insisting that knowledge was a *sine qua non* [indispensable condition] for right leadership, we look like being mistaken.

MENO: How so?

SOCRATES: Let me explain. If someone knows the way to Larissa, or anywhere else you like, then when he goes there and takes others with him he will be a good and capable guide, you would agree?

MENO: Of course.

b   SOCRATES: But if a man judges correctly which is the road, though he has never been there and doesn't know it, will he not also guide others aright?

MENO: Yes, he will.

SOCRATES: And as long as he has a correct opinion on the points about which the other has knowledge, he will be just as good a guide, believing the truth but not knowing it.

MENO: Just as good.

SOCRATES: Therefore true opinion is as good a guide as knowledge for the purpose of acting rightly. That is what we left out just now in our discussion of the nature

c   of virtue, when we said that knowledge is the only guide to right action. There was also, it seems, true opinion.

MENO: It seems so.

SOCRATES: So right opinion is something no less useful than knowledge.

MENO: Except that the man with knowledge will always be successful, and the man with right opinion only sometimes.

SOCRATES: What? Will he not always be successful so long as he has the right opinion?

MENO: That must be so, I suppose. In that case, I wonder why knowledge should

d   be so much more prized than right opinion, and indeed how there is any difference between them.

SOCRATES: Shall I tell you the reason for your surprise, or do you know it?

MENO: No, tell me.

SOCRATES: It is because you have not observed the statues of Daedalus. Perhaps you don't have them in your country.

MENO: What makes you say that?

SOCRATES: They too, if no one ties them down, run away and escape. If tied, they

e   stay where they are put.

MENO: What of it?

SOCRATES: If you have one of his works untethered, it is not worth much: it gives you the slip like a runaway slave. But a tethered specimen is very valuable, for they are magnificent creations. And that, I may say, has a bearing on the matter of true opinions. True opinions are a fine thing and do all sorts of good so long as they stay in their

98   place; but they will not stay long. They run away from a man's mind, so they are not worth much until you tether them by working out the reason. That process, my dear Meno, is recollection, as we agreed earlier. Once they are tied down, they become knowledge, and are stable. That is why knowledge is something more valuable than right opinion. What distinguishes one from the other is the tether.

MENO: It does seem something like that, certainly.

b   SOCRATES: Well of course, I have only been using an analogy myself, not knowledge. But it is not, I am sure, a mere guess to say that right opinion and knowledge are different. There are few things that I should claim to know, but that at least is among them, whatever else is.

MENO: You are quite right.

SOCRATES: And is this right too, that true opinion when it governs any course of action produces as good a result as knowledge?

MENO: Yes, that too is right, I think.

c   SOCRATES: So that for practical purposes right opinion is no less useful than knowledge, and the man who has it is no less useful than the one who knows.

MENO: That is so.

SOCRATES: Now we have agreed that the good man is useful.

MENO: Yes.

SOCRATES: To recapitulate then: assuming that there are men good and useful to the community, it is not only knowledge that makes them so, but also right opinion, and neither of these comes by nature but both are acquired—or do you think either of   d them *is* natural?

MENO: No.

SOCRATES: So if both are acquired, good men themselves are not good by nature.

MENO: No.

SOCRATES: That being so, the next thing we inquired was whether their goodness was a matter of teaching, and we decided that it would be, if virtue were knowledge, and conversely, that if it could be taught, it would be knowledge.

MENO: Yes.

SOCRATES: Next, that if there were teachers of it, it could be taught, but not if   e there were none.

MENO: That was so.

SOCRATES: But we have agreed that there are no teachers of it, and so that it cannot be taught and is not knowledge.

MENO: We did.

SOCRATES: At the same time we agreed that it is something good, and that to be useful and good consists in giving right guidance.

MENO: Yes.

SOCRATES: And that these two, true opinion and knowledge, are the only things   99 which direct us aright and the possession of which makes a man a true guide. We may except chance, because what turns out right by chance is not due to human direction, and say that where human control leads to right ends, these two principles are directive, true opinion and knowledge.

MENO: Yes, I agree.

SOCRATES: Now since virtue cannot be taught, we can no longer believe it to be knowledge, so that one of our two good and useful principles is excluded, and knowl-   b edge is not the guide in public life.

MENO: No.

SOCRATES: It is not then by the possession of any wisdom that such men as Themistocles, and the others whom Anytus mentioned just now, became leaders in their cities. This fact, that they do not owe their eminence to knowledge, will explain why they are unable to make others like themselves.

MENO: No doubt it is as you say.

SOCRATES: That leaves us with the other alternative, that it is well-aimed conjecture which statesmen employ in upholding their countries' welfare. Their position in relation   c to knowledge is no different from that of prophets and tellers of oracles, who under divine inspiration utter many truths, but have no knowledge of what they are saying.

MENO: It must be something like that.

SOCRATES: And ought we not to reckon those men divine who with no conscious thought are repeatedly and outstandingly successful in what they do or say?

MENO: Certainly.

SOCRATES: We are right therefore to give this title to the oracular priests and the prophets that I mentioned, and to poets of every description. Statesmen too, when by their speeches they get great things done yet know nothing of what they are saying, are to be considered as acting no less under divine influence, inspired and possessed by the   d divinity.

MENO: Certainly.

SOCRATES: Women, you know, Meno, do call good men "divine," and the Spartans too, when they are singing a good man's praises, say "He is divine."

MENO: And it looks as if they are right—though our friend Anytus may be annoyed with you for saying so.

SOCRATES: I can't help that. We will talk to him some other time. If all we have said in this discussion, and the questions we have asked, have been right, virtue will be acquired neither by nature nor by teaching. Whoever has it gets it by divine dispensation without taking thought, unless he be the kind of statesman who can create another like himself. Should there be such a man, he would be among the living practically what Homer said Tiresias was among the dead, when he described him as the only one in the underworld who kept his wits—"the others are mere flitting shades." Where virtue is concerned such a man would be just like that, a solid reality among shadows.

MENO: That is finely put, Socrates.

SOCRATES: On our present reasoning then, whoever has virtue gets it by divine dispensation. But we shall not understand the truth of the matter until, before asking how men get virtue, we try to discover what virtue is in and by itself. Now it is time for me to go; and my request to you is that you will allay the anger of your friend Anytus by convincing him that what you now believe is true. If you succeed, the Athenians may have cause to thank you.

REPUBLIC (in part)

BOOK II

*   *   *

[Socrates is speaking]: Glaucon and the others begged me to step into the breach and carry through our inquiry into the real nature of justice and injustice, and the truth about their respective advantages. So I told them what I thought. This is a very obscure question, I said, and we shall need keen sight to see our way. Now, as we are not remarkably clever, I will make a suggestion as to how we should proceed. Imagine a rather short-sighted person told to read an inscription in small letters from some way off. He would think it a godsend if someone pointed out that the same inscription was written up elsewhere on a bigger scale, so that he could first read the larger characters and then make out whether the smaller ones were the same.

No doubt, said Adeimantus; but what analogy do you see in that to our inquiry?

I will tell you. We think of justice as a quality that may exist in a whole community as well as in an individual, and the community is the bigger of the two. Possibly, then, we may find justice there in larger proportions, easier to make out. So I suggest

The Republic of Plato (Book II, 368c–376e; Book III, 412c–417b; Book IV, 427c–445e; Book V, complete: 448e–480a; Books VI–VII, 502c–521b), translated by Francis MacDonald Cornford (Oxford: Oxford University Press, 1945). Reprinted by permission of Oxford University Press.

that we should begin by inquiring what justice means in a state. Then we can go on to   369
look for its counterpart on a smaller scale in the individual.

That seems a good plan, he agreed.

Well then, I continued, suppose we imagine a state coming into being before our
eyes. We might then be able to watch the growth of justice or of injustice within it.
When that is done, we may hope it will be easier to find what we are looking for.

Much easier.   b

Shall we try, then, to carry out this scheme? I fancy it will be no light undertaking; so you had better think twice.

No need for that, said Adeimantus. Don't waste any more time.

My notion is, said I, that a state comes into existence because no individual is
self-sufficing; we all have many needs. But perhaps you can suggest some different
origin for the foundation of a community?

No, I agree with you.

So, having all these needs, we call in one another's help to satisfy our various re-   c
quirements; and when we have collected a number of helpers and associates to live together in one place, we call that settlement a state.

Yes.

So if one man gives another what he has to give in exchange for what he can get,
it is because each finds that to do so is for his own advantage.

Certainly.

Very well, said I. Now let us build up our imaginary state from the beginning.
Apparently, it will owe its existence to our needs, the first and greatest need being the   d
provision of food to keep us alive. Next we shall want a house; and thirdly, such things
as clothing.

True.

How will our state be able to supply all these demands? We shall need at least
one man to be a farmer, another a builder, and a third a weaver. Will that do, or shall
we add a shoemaker and one or two more to provide for our personal wants?

By all means.

The minimum state, then, will consist of four or five men.

Apparently.   e

Now here is a further point. Is each one of them to bring the product of his work
into a common stock? Should our one farmer, for example, provide food enough for
four people and spend the whole of his working time in producing corn, so as to share   370
with the rest; or should he take no notice of them and spend only a quarter of his time
on growing just enough corn for himself, and divide the other three-quarters between
building his house, weaving his clothes, and making his shoes, so as to save the trouble
of sharing with others and attend himself to all his own concerns?

The first plan might be the easier, replied Adeimantus.

That may very well be so, said I; for, as you spoke, it occurred to me, for one
thing, that no two people are born exactly alike. There are innate differences which fit   b
them for different occupations.

I agree.

And will a man do better working at many trades, or keeping to one only?

Keeping to one.

And there is another point: obviously work may be ruined, if you let the right
time go by. The workman must wait upon the work; it will not wait upon his leisure
and allow itself to be done in a spare moment. So the conclusion is that more things
will be produced and the work be more easily and better done, when every man is set

c   free from all other occupations to do, at the right time, the one thing for which he is naturally fitted.

That is certainly true.

We shall need more than four citizens, then, to supply all those necessaries we mentioned. You see, Adeimantus, if the farmer is to have a good plough and spade and other tools, he will not make them himself. No more will the builder and weaver and

d   shoemaker make all the many implements they need. So quite a number of carpenters and smiths and other craftsmen must be enlisted. Our miniature state is beginning to grow.

It is.

Still, it will not be very large, even when we have added cowherds and shepherds

e   to provide the farmers with oxen for the plough, and the builders as well as the farmers with draught-animals, and the weavers and shoemakers with wool and leather.

No; but it will not be so very small either.

And yet, again, it will be next to impossible to plant our city in a territory where it will need no imports. So there will have to be still another set of people, to fetch what it needs from other countries.

There will.

371   Moreover, if these agents take with them nothing that those other countries require in exchange, they will return as empty handed as they went. So, besides everything wanted for consumption at home, we must produce enough goods of the right kind for the foreigners whom we depend on to supply us. That will mean increasing the number of farmers and craftsmen.

Yes.

b   And then, there are these agents who are to import and export all kinds of goods—merchants, as we call them. We must have them; and if they are to do business overseas, we shall need quite a number of ship-owners and others who know about that branch of trading.

We shall.

Again, in the city itself how are the various sets of producers to exchange their products? That was our object, you will remember, in forming a community and so laying the foundation of our state.

Obviously, they must buy and sell.

c   That will mean having a market-place, and a currency to serve as a token for purposes of exchange.

Certainly.

Now suppose a farmer, or an artisan, brings some of his produce to market at a time when no one is there who wants to exchange with him. Is he to sit there idle, when he might be at work?

No, he replied; there are people who have seen an opening here for their services. In well-ordered communities they are generally men not strong enough to be of

d   use in any other occupation. They have to stay where they are in the market-place and take goods for money from those who want to sell, and money for goods from those who want to buy.

That, then, is the reason why our city must include a class of shopkeepers—so we call these people who sit still in the marketplace to buy and sell, in contrast with merchants who travel to other countries.

Quite so.

e   There are also the services of yet another class, who have the physical strength for heavy work, though on intellectual grounds they are hardly worth including in our society—hired labourers, as we call them, because they sell the use of their strength for wages. They will go to make up our population.

Yes.

Well, Adeimantus, has our state now grown to its full size?

Perhaps.

Then, where in it shall we find justice or injustice? If they have come in with one of the elements we have been considering, can you say with which one?

I have no idea, Socrates; unless it be somewhere in their dealings with one another.   372

You may be right, I answered. Anyhow, it is a question which we shall have to face.

Let us begin, then, with a picture of our citizens' manner of life, with the provision we have made for them. They will be producing corn and wine, and making clothes and shoes. When they have built their houses, they will mostly work without their coats or shoes in summer, and in winter be well shod and clothed. For their food, they will prepare flour and barley-meal for kneading and baking, and set out a grand spread of loaves and cakes on rushes or fresh leaves. Then they will lie on beds of myrtle-boughs and bryony [a type of gourd vine] and make merry with their children, drinking their wine after the feast with garlands on their heads and singing the praises of the gods. So they will live pleasantly together; and a prudent fear of poverty or war will keep them from begetting children beyond their means.   c

Here Glaucon interrupted me: You seem to expect your citizens to feast on dry bread.

True, I said; I forgot that they will have something to give it a relish, salt, no doubt, and olives, and cheese, and country stews of roots and vegetables. And for dessert we will give them figs and peas and beans; and they shall roast myrtle-berries and acorns at the fire, while they sip their wine. Leading such a healthy life in peace, they will naturally come to a good old age, and leave their children to live after them in the same manner.   d

That is just the sort of provender you would supply, Socrates, if you were founding a community of pigs.

Well, how are they to live, then, Glaucon?

With the ordinary comforts. Let them lie on couches and dine off tables on such dishes and sweets as we have nowadays.   e

Ah, I see, said I; we are to study the growth, not just of a state, but of a luxurious one. Well, there may be no harm in that; the consideration of luxury may help us to discover how justice and injustice take root in society. The community I have described seems to me the ideal one, in sound health as it were: but if you want to see one suffering from inflammation, there is nothing to hinder us. So some people, it seems, will not be satisfied to live in this simple way; they must have couches and tables and   373 furniture of all sorts; and delicacies too, perfumes, unguents, courtesans, sweetmeats, all in plentiful variety. And besides, we must not limit ourselves now to those bare necessaries of house and clothes and shoes; we shall have to set going the arts of embroidery and painting, and collect rich materials, like gold and ivory.

Yes.   b

Then we must once more enlarge our community. The healthy one will not be big enough now; it must be swollen up with a whole multitude of callings not ministering to any bare necessity: hunters and fishermen, for instance; artists in sculpture, painting, and music; poets with their attendant train of professional reciters, actors,

dancers, producers; and makers of all sorts of household gear, including everything for
women's adornment. And we shall want more servants: children's nurses and attendants, lady's maids, barbers, cooks and confectioners. And then swineherds—there
was no need for them in our original state, but we shall want them now; and a great
quantity of sheep and cattle too, if people are going to live on meat.

Of course.

And with this manner of life physicians will be in much greater request.

No doubt.

The country, too, which was large enough to support the original inhabitants,
will now be too small. If we are to have enough pasture and plough land, we shall have
to cut off a slice of our neighbours' territory; and if they too are not content with necessaries, but give themselves up to getting unlimited wealth, they will want a slice of
ours.

That is inevitable, Socrates.

So the next thing will be, Glaucon, that we shall be at war.

No doubt.

We need not say yet whether war does good or harm, but only that we have discovered its origin in desires which are the most fruitful source of evils both to individuals and to states.

Quite true.

This will mean a considerable addition to our community—a whole army, to go
out to battle with any invader, in defence of all this property and of the citizens we
have been describing.

Why so? Can't they defend themselves?

Not if the principle was right, which we all accepted in framing our society. You
remember we agreed that no one man can practise many trades or arts satisfactorily.

True.

Well, is not the conduct of war an art, quite as important as shoemaking?

Yes.

But we would not allow our shoemaker to try to be also a farmer or weaver or
builder, because we wanted our shoes well made. We gave each man one trade, for
which he was naturally fitted; he would do good work, if he confined himself to that all
his life, never letting the right moment slip by. Now in no form of work is efficiency so
important as in war; and fighting is not so easy a business that a man can follow another trade, such as farming or shoemaking, and also be an efficient soldier. Why, even
a game like draughts or dice must be studied from childhood; no one can become a fine
player in his spare moments. Just taking up a shield or other weapon will not make a
man capable of fighting that very day in any sort of warfare, any more than taking up a
tool or implement of some kind will make a man a craftsman or an athlete, if he does
not understand its use and has never been properly trained to handle it.

No; if that were so, tools would indeed be worth having.

These guardians of our state, then, inasmuch as their work is the most important
of all, will need the most complete freedom from other occupations and the greatest
amount of skill and practice.

I quite agree.

And also a native aptitude for their calling.

Certainly.

So it is our business to define, if we can, the natural gifts that fit men to be
guardians of a commonwealth, and to select them accordingly. It will certainly be a
formidable task; but we must grapple with it to the best of our power. Yes.

Don't you think then, said I, that, for the purpose of keeping guard, a young man   375
should have much the same temperament and qualities as a well-bred watch-dog? I
mean, for instance, that both must have quick senses to detect an enemy, swiftness in
pursuing him, and strength, if they have to fight when they have caught him.

Yes, they will need all those qualities.

And also courage, if they are to fight well.

Of course.

And courage, in dog or horse or any other creature, implies a spirited disposition.
You must have noticed that a high spirit is unconquerable. Every soul possessed of it is   b
fearless and indomitable in the face of any danger.

Yes, I have noticed that.

So now we know what physical qualities our Guardian must have, and also that
he must be of a spirited temper.

Yes.

Then, Glaucon, how are men of that natural disposition to be kept from behaving
pugnaciously to one another and to the rest of their countrymen?

It is not at all easy to see.

And yet they must be gentle to their own people and dangerous only to enemies;   c
otherwise they will destroy themselves without waiting till others destroy them.

True.

What are we to do, then? If gentleness and a high temper are contraries, where   d
shall we find a character to combine them? Both are necessary to make a good
Guardian, but it seems they are incompatible. So we shall never have a good Guardian.

It looks like it.

Here I was perplexed, but on thinking over what we had been saying, I remarked
that we deserved to be puzzled, because we had not followed up the comparison we
had just drawn.

What do you mean? he asked.

We never noticed that, after all, there are natures in which these contraries are
combined. They are to be found in animals, and not least in the kind we compared to   e
our Guardian. Well-bred dogs, as you know, are by instinct perfectly gentle to people
whom they know and are accustomed to, and fierce to strangers. So the combination of
qualities we require for our Guardian is, after all, possible and not against nature.

Evidently.

Do you further agree that, besides this spirited temper, he must have a philosophical element in his nature?

I don't see what you mean.

This is another trait you will see in the dog. It is really remarkable how the crea-   376
ture gets angry at the mere sight of a stranger and welcomes anyone he knows, though
he may never have been treated unkindly by the one or kindly by the other. Did that
never strike you as curious?

I had not thought of it before; but that certainly is how a dog behaves.

Well, but that shows a fine instinct, which is philosophic in the true sense.   b

How so?

Because the only mark by which he distinguishes a friendly and an unfriendly
face is that he knows the one and does not know the other; and if a creature makes that
the test of what it finds congenial or otherwise, how can you deny that it has a passion
for knowledge and understanding?

Of course, I cannot.

And that passion is the same thing as philosophy—the love of wisdom.

Yes.

Shall we boldly say, then, that the same is true of human beings? If a man is to
c   be gentle towards his own people whom he knows, he must have an instinctive love of
wisdom and understanding.

Agreed.

So the nature required to make a really noble Guardian of our commonwealth
will be swift and strong, spirited, and philosophic.

Quite so.

Given those natural qualities, then, how are these Guardians to be brought up
and educated? First, will the answer to that question help the purpose of our whole in-
d   quiry, which is to make out how justice and injustice grow up in a state? We want to be
thorough, but not to draw out this discussion to a needless length.

Glaucon's brother answered: I certainly think it will help.

If so, I said, we must not think of dropping it, though it may be rather a long
business.

I agree.

Come on then. We will take our time and educate our imaginary citizens.
e   Yes, let us do so.

*   *   *

BOOK III

*   *   *

Good, said I; and what is the next point to be settled? Is it not the question, which of
these Guardians are to be rulers and which are to obey?

412ᶜ   No doubt.

Well, it is obvious that the elder must have authority over the young, and that the
rulers must be the best.

Yes.

And as among farmers the best are those with a natural turn for farming, so, if we
want the best among our Guardians, we must take those naturally fitted to watch over a
commonwealth. They must have the right sort of intelligence and ability; and also they
must look upon the commonwealth as their special concern—the sort of concern that is
d   felt for something so closely bound up with oneself that its interests and fortunes, for
good or ill, are held to be identical with one's own.

Exactly.

So the kind of men we must choose from among the Guardians will be those
who, when we look at the whole course of their lives, are found to be full of zeal to do
whatever they believe is for the good of the commonwealth and never willing to act
e   against its interest.

Yes, they will be the men we want.

We must watch them, I think, at every age and see whether they are capable of
preserving this conviction that they must do what is best for the community, never forgetting it or allowing themselves to be either forced or bewitched into throwing it over.

How does this throwing over come about?

I will explain. When a belief passes out of the mind, a man may be willing to part with it, if it is false and he has learnt better, or unwilling, if it is true.   413

I see how he might be willing to let it go; but you must explain how he can be unwilling.

Where is your difficulty? Don't you agree that men are unwilling to be deprived of good, though ready enough to part with evil? Or that to be deceived about the truth is evil, to possess it good? Or don't you think that possessing truth means thinking of things as they really are?

You are right. I do agree that men are unwilling to be robbed of a true belief.

When that happens to them, then, it must be by theft, or violence, or bewitch-   b
ment.

Again I do not understand.

Perhaps my metaphors are too high-flown. I call it theft when one is persuaded out of one's belief or forgets it. Argument in the one case, and time in the other, steal it away without one's knowing what is happening. You understand now?

Yes.

And by violence I mean being driven to change one's mind by pain or suffering.

That too I understand, and you are right.

And bewitchment, as I think you would agree, occurs when a man is beguiled   c
out of his opinion by the allurements of pleasure or scared out of it under the spell of panic.

Yes, all delusions are like a sort of bewitchment.

As I said just now, then, we must find out who are the best guardians of this in-ward conviction that they must always do what they believe to be best for the commonwealth. We shall have to watch them from earliest childhood and set them tasks in which they would be most likely to forget or to be beguiled out of this duty. We shall then choose only those whose memory holds firm and who are proof against delusion.   d

Yes.

We must also subject them to ordeals of toil and pain and watch for the same qualities there. And we must observe them when exposed to the test of yet a third kind of bewitchment. As people lead colts up to alarming noises to see whether they are timid, so these young men must be brought into terrifying situations and then into scenes of pleasure, which will put them to severer proof than gold tried in the furnace.   e
If we find one bearing himself well in all these trials and resisting every enchantment, a true guardian of himself, preserving always that perfect rhythm and harmony of being which he has acquired from his training in music and poetry, such a one will be of the greatest service to the commonwealth as well as to himself. Whenever we find one who has come unscathed through every test in childhood, youth, and manhood, we   414
shall set him as a Ruler to watch over the commonwealth; he will be honoured in life, and after death receive the highest tribute of funeral rites and other memorials. All who do not reach this standard we must reject. And that, I think, my dear Glaucon, may be taken as an outline of the way in which we shall select Guardians to be set in authority as Rulers.

I am very much of your mind.

These, then, may properly be called Guardians in the fullest sense, who will en-   b
sure that neither foes without shall have the power, nor friends within the wish, to do harm. Those young men whom up to now we have been speaking of as Guardians, will be better described as Auxiliaries, who will enforce the decisions of the Rulers.

I agree.

Now, said I, can we devise something in the way of those convenient fictions we
c   spoke of earlier, a single bold flight of invention,* which we may induce the community in general, and if possible the Rulers themselves, to accept?

What kind of fiction?

Nothing new; something like an Eastern tale of what, according to the poets, has
happened before now in more than one part of the world. The poets have been believed; but the thing has not happened in our day, and it would be hard to persuade
anyone that it could ever happen again.

You seem rather shy of telling this story of yours.

With good reason, as you will see when I have told it.

Out with it; don't be afraid.

d   Well, here it is; though I hardly know how to find the courage or the words to express it. I shall try to convince, first the Rulers and the soldiers, and then the whole
community, that all that nurture and education which we gave them was only something they seemed to experience as it were in a dream. In reality they were the whole
time down inside the earth, being moulded and fostered while their arms and all their
equipment were being fashioned also; and at last, when they were complete, the earth
sent them up from her womb into the light of day. So now they must think of the land
e   they dwell in as a mother and nurse, whom they must take thought for and defend
against any attack, and of their fellow citizens as brothers born of the same soil.

You might well be bashful about coming out with your fiction.

415   No doubt; but still you must hear the rest of the story. It is true, we shall tell our
people in this fable, that all of you in this land are brothers; but the god who fashioned
you mixed gold in the composition of those among you who are fit to rule, so that they
are of the most precious quality; and he put silver in the Auxiliaries, and iron and brass
in the farmers and craftsmen. Now, since you are all of one stock, although your chil-
b   dren will generally be like their parents, sometimes a golden parent may have a silver
child or a silver parent a golden one, and so on with all the other combinations. So the
first and chief injunction laid by heaven upon the Rulers is that, among all the things of
which they must show themselves good guardians, there is none that needs to be so
carefully watched as the mixture of metals in the souls of the children. If a child of
c   their own is born with an alloy of iron or brass, they must, without the smallest pity,
assign him the station proper to his nature and thrust him out among the craftsmen or
the farmers. If, on the contrary, these classes produce a child with gold or silver in his
composition, they will promote him, according to his value, to be a Guardian or an
Auxiliary. They will appeal to a prophecy that ruin will come upon the state when it
passes into the keeping of a man of iron or brass. Such is the story; can you think of
any device to make them believe it?

d   Not in the first generation; but their sons and descendants might believe it, and finally the rest of mankind.

Well, said I, even so it might have a good effect in making them care more for
the commonwealth and for one another; for I think I see what you mean.

---

*[What Cornford translates as "bold flight of invention" is usually rendered "noble lie." Cornford
claims this common translation is unfair to "Plato's harmless allegory." Other scholars are not so generous.
For a discussion of the issues, see the bibliography for books on the *Republic*.]

So, I continued, we will leave the success of our story to the care of popular tradition; and now let us arm these sons of Earth and lead them, under the command of
their Rulers, to the site of our city. There let them look round for the best place to fix
their camp, from which they will be able to control any rebellion against the laws from   e
within and to beat off enemies who may come from without like wolves to attack the
fold. When they have pitched their camp and offered sacrifice to the proper divinities,
they must arrange their sleeping quarters; and these must be sufficient to shelter them
from winter cold and summer heat.

Naturally. You mean they are going to live there?

Yes, said I; but live like soldiers, not like men of business.

What is the difference?   416

I will try to explain. It would be very strange if a shepherd were to disgrace himself by keeping, for the protection of his flock, dogs who were so ill-bred and badly
trained that hunger or unruliness or some bad habit or other would set them worrying
the sheep and behaving no better than wolves. We must take every precaution against   b
our Auxiliaries treating the citizens in any such way and, because they are stronger,
turning into savage tyrants instead of friendly allies; and they will have been furnished
with the best of safeguards, if they have really been educated in the right way.

But surely there is nothing wrong with their education.

We must not be too positive about that, my dear Glaucon; but we can be sure of
what we said not long ago, that if they are to have the best chance of being gentle and   c
humane to one another and to their charges, they must have the right education, whatever that may be.

We were certainly right there.

Then besides that education, it is only common sense to say that the dwellings
and other belongings provided for them must be such as will neither make them less
perfect Guardians nor encourage them to maltreat their fellow citizens.   d

True.

With that end in view, let us consider how they should live and be housed. First,
none of them must possess any private property beyond the barest necessaries. Next,
no one is to have any dwelling or store-house that is not open for all to enter at will.
Their food, in the quantities required by men of temperance and courage who are in   e
training for war, they will receive from the other citizens as the wages of their
guardianship, fixed so that there shall be just enough for the year with nothing over;
and they will have meals in common and all live together like soldiers in a camp. Gold
and silver, we shall tell them, they will not need, having the divine counterparts of
those metals always in their souls as a god-given possession, whose purity it is not
lawful to sully by the acquisition of that mortal dross, current among mankind, which   417
has been the occasion of so many unholy deeds. They alone of all the citizens are forbidden to touch and handle silver or gold, or to come under the same roof with them,
or wear them as ornaments, or drink from vessels made of them. This manner of life
will be their salvation and make them the saviours of the commonwealth. If ever they
should come to possess land of their own and houses and money, they will give up
their guardianship for the management of their farms and households and become   b
tyrants at enmity with their fellow citizens instead of allies. And so they will pass all
their lives in hating and being hated, plotting and being plotted against, in much
greater fear of their enemies at home than of any foreign foe, and fast heading for the
destruction that will soon overwhelm their country with themselves. For all these rea-

sons let us say that this is how our Guardians are to be housed and otherwise provided for, and let us make laws accordingly.

By all means, said Glaucon.

BOOK IV

*   *   *

So now at last, son of Ariston, said I, your commonwealth is established. The
427^d next thing is to bring to bear upon it all the light you can get from any quarter, with the help of your brother and Polemarchus and all the rest, in the hope that we may see where justice is to be found in it and where injustice, how they differ, and which of the two will bring happiness to its possessor, no matter whether gods and men see that he has it or not.

e   Nonsense, said Glaucon; you promised to conduct the search yourself, because it would be a sin not to uphold justice by every means in your power.

That is true; I must do as you say, but you must all help.

We will.

I suspect, then, we may find what we are looking for in this way. I take it that our state, having been founded and built up on the right lines, is good in the complete sense of the word.

It must be.

Obviously, then, it is wise, brave, temperate, and just.

Obviously.

Then if we find some of these qualities in it, the remainder will be the one we
428 have not found. It is as if we were looking somewhere for one of any four things: if we detected that one immediately, we should be satisfied; whereas if we recognized the other three first, that would be enough to indicate the thing we wanted; it could only be the remaining one. So here we have four qualities. Had we not better follow that method in looking for the one we want?

Surely.

To begin then: the first quality to come into view in our state seems to be its wis-
b   dom; and there appears to be something odd about this quality.

What is there odd about it?

I think the state we have described really has wisdom; for it will be prudent in counsel, won't it?

Yes.

And prudence in counsel is clearly a form of knowledge; good counsel cannot be due to ignorance and stupidity.

Clearly.

c   But there are many and various kinds of knowledge in our commonwealth. There is the knowledge possessed by the carpenters or the smiths, and the knowledge how to raise crops. Are we to call the state wise and prudent on the strength of these forms of skill?

No; they would only make it good at furniture-making or working in copper or agriculture.

Well then, is there any form of knowledge, possessed by some among the citizens of our new-founded commonwealth, which will enable it to take thought, not for   d
some particular interest, but for the best possible conduct of the state as a whole in its internal and external relations?

Yes, there is.

What is it, and where does it reside?

It is precisely that art of guardianship which resides in those Rulers whom we just now called Guardians in the full sense.

And what would you call the state on the strength of that knowledge?

Prudent and truly wise.   e

And do you think there will be more or fewer of these genuine Guardians in our state than there will be smiths?

Far fewer.

Fewer, in fact, than any of those other groups who are called after the kind of skill they possess?

Much fewer.

So, if a state is constituted on natural principles, the wisdom it possesses as a whole will be due to the knowledge residing in the smallest part, the one which takes the lead and governs the rest. Such knowledge is the only kind that deserves the name   429
of wisdom, and it appears to be ordained by nature that the class privileged to possess it should be the smallest of all.

Quite true.

Here then we have more or less made out one of our four qualities and its seat in the structure of the commonwealth.

To my satisfaction, at any rate.

Next there is courage. It is not hard to discern that quality or the part of the community in which it resides so as to entitle the whole to be called brave.

Why do you say so?

Because anyone who speaks of a state as either brave or cowardly can only be   b
thinking of that part of it which takes the field and fights in its defence; the reason being, I imagine, that the character of the state is not determined by the bravery or cowardice of the other parts.

No.

Courage, then, is another quality which a community owes to a certain part of itself. And its being brave will mean that, in this part, it possesses the power of preserving, in all circumstances, a conviction about the sort of things that it is right to be   c
afraid of—the conviction implanted by the education which the law-giver has established. Is not that what you mean by courage?

I do not quite understand. Will you say it again?

I am saying that courage means preserving something.

Yes, but what?

The conviction, inculcated by lawfully established education, about the sort of things which may rightly be feared. When I added "in all circumstances," I meant preserving it always and never abandoning it, whether under the influence of pain or of pleasure, of desire or of fear. If you like, I will give an illustration.   d

Please do.

You know how dyers who want wool to take a purple dye, first select the white wool from among all the other colours, next treat it very carefully to make it take the dye in its full brilliance, and only then dip it in the vat. Dyed in that way, wool gets a

fast colour, which no washing, even with soap, will rob of its brilliance; whereas if
e   they choose wool of any colour but white, or if they neglect to prepare it, you know
what happens.

Yes, it looks washed-out and ridiculous.

That illustrates the result we were doing our best to achieve when we were
430   choosing our fighting men and training their minds and bodies. Our only purpose was
to contrive influences whereby they might take the colour of our institutions like a dye,
so that, in virtue of having both the right temperament and the right education, their
convictions about what ought to be feared and on all other subjects might be indelibly
fixed, never to be washed out by pleasure and pain, desire and fear, solvents more terri-
b   bly effective than all the soap and fuller's earth in the world. Such a power of constantly preserving, in accordance with our institutions, the right conviction about the
things which ought, or ought not, to be feared, is what I call courage. That is my position, unless you have some objection to make.

None at all, he replied; if the belief were such as might be found in a slave or an
animal—correct, but not produced by education—you would hardly describe it as in
accordance with our institutions, and you would give it some other name than courage.
c   Quite true.

Then I accept your account of courage.

You will do well to accept it, at any rate as applying to the courage of the ordinary
citizen; if you like we will go into it more fully some other time. At present we are in
search of justice, rather than of courage; and for that purpose we have said enough.

I quite agree.
d   Two qualities, I went on, still remain to be made out in our state, temperance
and the object of our whole inquiry, justice. Can we discover justice without troubling
ourselves further about temperance?

I do not know, and I would rather not have justice come to light first, if that
means that we should not go on to consider temperance. So if you want to please me,
take temperance first.
e   Of course I have every wish to please you.

Do go on then.

I will. At first sight, temperance seems more like some sort of concord or harmony than the other qualities did.

How so?

Temperance surely means a kind of orderliness, a control of certain pleasures
and appetites. People use the expression, "master of oneself," whatever that means,
and various other phrases that point the same way.

Quite true.
431   Is not "master of oneself" an absurd expression? A man who was master of himself would presumably be also subject to himself, and the subject would be master; for
all these terms apply to the same person.

No doubt.

I think, however, the phrase means that within the man himself, in his soul, there
is a better part and a worse; and that he is his own master when the part which is better
by nature has the worse under its control. It is certainly a term of praise; whereas it is
considered a disgrace, when, through bad breeding or bad company, the better part is
b   overwhelmed by the worse, like a small force outnumbered by a multitude. A man in
that condition is called a slave to himself and intemperate.

Probably that is what is meant.

Then now look at our newly founded state and you will find one of these two conditions realized there. You will agree that it deserves to be called master of itself, if temperance and self-mastery exist where the better part rules the worse.

Yes, I can see that is true.

It is also true that the great mass of multifarious appetites and pleasures and pains will be found to occur chiefly in children and women and slaves, and, among free men so called, in the inferior multitude; whereas the simple and moderate desires   c
which, with the aid of reason and right belief, are guided by reflection, you will find only in a few, and those with the best inborn dispositions and the best educated.

Yes, certainly.

Do you see that this state of things will exist in your commonwealth, where the desires of the inferior multitude will be controlled by the desires and wisdom of the su-   d
perior few? Hence, if any society can be called master of itself and in control of pleasures and desires, it will be ours.

Quite so.

On all these grounds, then, we may describe it as temperate. Furthermore, in our state, if anywhere, the governors and the governed will share the same conviction on the question of who ought to rule. Don't you think so?   e

I am quite sure of it.

Then, if that is their state of mind, in which of the two classes of citizens will temperance reside—in the governors or in the governed?

In both, I suppose.

So we were not wrong in divining a resemblance between temperance and some kind of harmony. Temperance is not like courage and wisdom, which made the state wise and brave by residing each in one particular part. Temperance works in a different   432
way; it extends throughout the whole gamut of the state, producing a consonance of all its elements from the weakest to the strongest as measured by any standard you like to take—wisdom, bodily strength, numbers, or wealth. So we are entirely justified in identifying with temperance this unanimity or harmonious agreement between the naturally superior and inferior elements on the question which of the two should govern, whether in the state or in the individual.

I fully agree.   b

Good, said I. We have discovered in our commonwealth three out of our four qualities, to the best of our present judgment. What is the remaining one, required to make up its full complement of goodness? For clearly this will be justice.

Clearly.

Now is the moment, then, Glaucon, for us to keep the closest watch, like huntsmen standing round a covert, to make sure that justice does not slip through and vanish undetected. It must certainly be somewhere hereabouts; so keep your eyes open for a   c
view of the quarry, and if you see it first, give me the alert.

I wish I could, he answered; but you will do better to give me a lead and not count on me for more than eyes to see what you show me.

Pray for luck, then, and follow me.

I will, if you will lead on.

The thicket looks rather impenetrable, said I; too dark for it to be easy to start up the game. However, we must push on.   d

Of course we must.

Here I gave the view halloo. Glaucon, I exclaimed, I believe we are on the track and the quarry is not going to escape us altogether.

That is good news.

Really, I said, we have been extremely stupid. All this time the thing has been
e   under our very noses from the start, and we never saw it. We have been as absurd as a
person who hunts for something he has all the time got in his hand. Instead of looking
at the thing, we have been staring into the distance. No doubt that is why it escaped us.

What do you mean?

I believe we have been talking about the thing all this while without ever understanding that we were giving some sort of account of it.

Do come to the point. I am all ears.

433   Listen, then, and judge whether I am right. You remember how, when we first
began to establish our commonwealth and several times since, we have laid down, as a
universal principle, that everyone ought to perform the one function in the community
for which his nature best suited him. Well, I believe that that principle, or some form
of it, is justice.

We certainly laid that down.

Yes, and surely we have often heard people say that justice means minding one's
b   own business and not meddling with other men's concerns; and we have often said so
ourselves.

We have.

Well, my friend, it may be that this minding of one's own business, when it takes a
certain form, is actually the same thing as justice. Do you know what makes me think so?

No, tell me.

I think that this quality which makes it possible for the three we have already
considered, wisdom, courage, and temperance, to take their place in the commonwealth, and so long as it remains present secures their continuance, must be the re-
c   maining one. And we said that, when three of the four were found, the one left over
would be justice.

It must be so.

Well now, if we had to decide which of these qualities will contribute most to the
excellence of our commonwealth, it would be hard to say whether it was the unanimity
of rulers and subjects, or the soldier's fidelity to the established conviction about what
is, or is not, to be feared, or the watchful intelligence of the Rulers; or whether its ex-
d   cellence were not above all due to the observance by everyone, child or woman, slave
or freeman or artisan, ruler or ruled, of this principle that each one should do his own
proper work without interfering with others.

It would be hard to decide, no doubt.

It seems, then, that this principle can at any rate claim to rival wisdom, temperance, and courage as conducive to the excellence of a state. And would you not say
that the only possible competitor of these qualities must be justice?

Yes, undoubtedly.

Here is another thing which points to the same conclusion. The judging of
e   law-suits is a duty that you will lay upon your Rulers, isn't it?

Of course.

And the chief aim of their decisions will be that neither party shall have what belongs to another or be deprived of what is his own.

Yes.

Because that is just?

Yes.

434   So here again justice admittedly means that a man should possess and concern
himself with what properly belongs to him.

True.

Again, do you agree with me that no great harm would be done to the community by a general interchange of most forms of work, the carpenter and the cobbler exchanging their positions and their tools and taking on each other's jobs, or even the same man undertaking both?

Yes, there would not be much harm in that.

But I think you will also agree that another kind of interchange would be disastrous. Suppose, for instance, someone whom nature designed to be an artisan or tradesman should be emboldened by some advantage, such as wealth or command of votes or bodily strength, to try to enter the order of fighting men; or some member of that order should aspire, beyond his merits, to a seat in the council-chamber of the Guardians. Such interference and exchange of social positions and tools, or the attempt to combine all these forms of work in the same person, would be fatal to the commonwealth.

Most certainly.

Where there are three orders, then, any plurality of functions or shifting from one order to another is not merely utterly harmful to the community, but one might fairly call it the extreme of wrongdoing. And you will agree that to do the greatest of wrongs to one's own community is injustice.

Surely.

This, then, is injustice. And, conversely, let us repeat that when each order—tradesman, Auxiliary, Guardian—keeps to its own proper business in the commonwealth and does its own work, that is justice and what makes a just society.

I entirely agree.

We must not be too positive yet, said I. If we find that this same quality when it exists in the individual can equally be identified with justice, then we can at once give our assent; there will be no more to be said; otherwise, we shall have to look further. For the moment, we had better finish the inquiry which we began with the idea that it would be easier to make out the nature of justice in the individual if we first tried to study it in something on a larger scale. That larger thing we took to be a state, and so we set about constructing the best one we could, being sure of finding justice in a state that was good. The discovery we made there must now be applied to the individual. If it is confirmed, all will be well; but if we find that justice in the individual is something different, we must go back to the state and test our new result. Perhaps if we brought the two cases into contact like flint and steel, we might strike out between them the spark of justice, and in its light confirm the conception in our own minds.

A good method. Let us follow it.

Now, I continued, if two things, one large, the other small, are called by the same name, they will be alike in that respect to which the common name applies. Accordingly, in so far as the quality of justice is concerned, there will be no difference between a just man and a just society.

No.

Well, but we decided that a society was just when each of the three types of human character it contained performed its own function; and again, it was temperate and brave and wise by virtue of certain other affections and states of mind of those same types.

True.

Accordingly, my friend, if we are to be justified in attributing those same virtues to the individual, we shall expect to find that the individual soul contains the same three elements and that they are affected in the same way as are the corresponding types in society.

That follows.

Here, then, we have stumbled upon another little problem: Does the soul contain these three elements or not?

Not such a very little one, I think. It may be a true saying, Socrates, that what is worthwhile is seldom easy.

d   Apparently; and let me tell you, Glaucon, it is my belief that we shall never reach the exact truth in this matter by following our present methods of discussion; the road leading to that goal is longer and more laborious. However, perhaps we can find an answer that will be up to the standard we have so far maintained in our speculations.

Is not that enough? I should be satisfied for the moment.

Well, it will more than satisfy me, I replied.

Don't be disheartened, then, but go on.

e   Surely, I began, we must admit that the same elements and characters that appear in the state must exist in every one of us; where else could they have come from? It would be absurd to imagine that among peoples with a reputation for a high-spirited character, like the Thracians and Scythians and northerners generally, the states have not derived that character from their individual members; or that it is otherwise with the love of knowledge, which would be ascribed chiefly to our own part of the world,
436 or with the love of money, which one would specially connect with Phoenicia and Egypt.

Certainly.

So far, then, we have a fact which is easily recognized. But here the difficulty begins. Are we using the same part of ourselves in all these three experiences, or a different part in each? Do we gain knowledge with one part, feel anger with another, and with yet a third desire the pleasures of food, sex, and so on? Or is the whole soul at
b   work in every impulse and in all these forms of behaviour? The difficulty is to answer that question satisfactorily.

I quite agree.

Let us approach the problem whether these elements are distinct or identical in this way. It is clear that the same thing cannot act in two opposite ways or be in two opposite states at the same time, with respect to the same part of itself, and in relation
c   to the same object. So if we find such contradictory actions or states among the elements concerned, we shall know that more than one must have been involved.

Very well.

Consider this proposition of mine, then. Can the same thing, at the same time and with respect to the same part of itself, be at rest and in motion?

Certainly not.

We had better state this principle in still more precise terms, to guard against misunderstanding later on. Suppose a man is standing still, but moving his head and
d   arms. We should not allow anyone to say that the same man was both at rest and in motion at the same time, but only that part of him was at rest, part in motion. Isn't that so?

Yes.

An ingenious objector might refine still further and argue that a peg-top, spinning with its peg fixed at the same spot, or indeed any body that revolves in the same place, is both at rest and in motion as a whole. But we should not agree, because the parts in respect of which such a body is moving and at rest are not the same. It contains
e   an axis and a circumference; and in respect of the axis it is at rest inasmuch as the axis is not inclined in any direction, while in respect of the circumference it revolves; and

if, while it is spinning, the axis does lean out of the perpendicular in all directions, then it is in no way at rest.

That is true.

No objection of that sort, then, will disconcert us or make us believe that the same thing can ever act or be acted upon in two opposite ways, or be two opposite things, at the same time, in respect of the same part of itself, and in relation to the same object.

437

I can answer for myself at any rate.

Well, anyhow, as we do not want to spend time in reviewing all such objections to make sure that they are unsound, let us proceed on this assumption, with the understanding that, if we ever come to think otherwise, all the consequences based upon it will fall to the ground.

Yes, that is a good plan.

Now, would you class such things as assent and dissent, striving after something and refusing it, attraction and repulsion, as pairs of opposite actions or states of mind—no matter which?

b

Yes, they are opposites.

And would you not class all appetites such as hunger and thirst, and again willing and wishing, with the affirmative members of those pairs I have just mentioned? For instance, you would say that the soul of a man who desires something is striving after it, or trying to draw to itself the thing it wishes to possess, or again, in so far as it is willing to have its want satisfied, it is giving its assent to its own longing, as if to an inward question.

c

Yes.

And, on the other hand, disinclination, unwillingness, and dislike, we should class on the negative side with acts of rejection or repulsion.

Of course.

d

That being so, shall we say that appetites form one class, the most conspicuous being those we call thirst and hunger?

Yes.

Thirst being desire for drink, hunger for food?

Yes.

Now, is thirst, just in so far as it is thirst, a desire in the soul for anything more than simply drink? Is it, for instance, thirst for hot drink or for cold, for much drink or for little, or in a word for drink of any particular kind? Is it not rather true that you will have a desire for cold drink only if you are feeling hot as well as thirsty, and for hot drink only if you are feeling cold; and if you want much drink or little, that will be because your thirst is a great thirst or a little one? But, just in itself, thirst or hunger is a desire for nothing more than its natural object, drink or food, pure and simple.

e

Yes, he agreed, each desire, just in itself, is simply for its own natural object. When the object is of such and such a particular kind, the desire will be correspondingly qualified.

We must be careful here, or we might be troubled by the objection that no one desires mere food and drink, but always wholesome food and drink. We shall be told that what we desire is always something that is good; so if thirst is a desire, its object must be, like that of any other desire, something—drink or whatever it may be—that will be good for one.

438

Yes, there might seem to be something in that objection.

But surely, wherever you have two correlative terms, if one is qualified, the other
b   must always be qualified too; whereas if one is unqualified, so is the other.

I don't understand.

Well, "greater" is a relative term; and the greater is greater than the less; if it is
much greater, then the less is much less; if it is greater at some moment, past or future,
then the less is less at that same moment. The same principle applies to all such correl-
c   atives, like "more" and "fewer," "double" and "half"; and again to terms like "heav-
ier" and "lighter," "quicker" and "slower," and to things like hot and cold.

Yes.

Or take the various branches of knowledge: is it not the same there? The object
of knowledge pure and simple is the knowable—if that is the right word—without any
qualification; whereas a particular kind of knowledge has an object of a particular kind.
d   For example, as soon as men learnt how to build houses, their craft was distinguished
from others under the name of architecture, because it had a unique character, which
was itself due to the character of its object; and all other branches of craft and knowledge were distinguished in the same way.

True.

This, then, if you understand me now, is what I meant by saying that, where
e   there are two correlatives, the one is qualified if, and only if, the other is so. I am not
saying that the one must have the same quality as the other—that the science of health
and disease is itself healthy and diseased, or the knowledge of good and evil is itself
good and evil—but only that, as soon as you have a knowledge that is restricted to a
particular kind of object, namely health and disease, the knowledge itself becomes a
particular kind of knowledge. Hence we no longer call it merely knowledge, which
would have for its object whatever can be known, but we add the qualification and call
it medical science.

I understand now and I agree.

439   Now, to go back to thirst: is not that one of these relative terms? It is essentially
thirst for something.

Yes, for drink.

And if the drink desired is of a certain kind, the thirst will be correspondingly
qualified. But thirst which is just simply thirst is not for drink of any particular
sort—much or little, good or bad—but for drink pure and simple.

Quite so.

We conclude, then, that the soul of a thirsty man, just in so far as he is thirsty,
b   has no other wish than to drink. That is the object of its craving, and towards that it is
impelled.

That is clear.

Now if there is ever something which at the same time pulls it the opposite way,
that something must be an element in the soul other than the one which is thirsting and
driving it like a beast to drink; in accordance with our principle that the same thing
cannot behave in two opposite ways at the same time and towards the same object with
the same part of itself. It is like an archer drawing the bow: it is not accurate to say that
his hands are at the same time both pushing and pulling it. One hand does the pushing,
the other the pulling.

c   Exactly.

Now, is it sometimes true that people are thirsty and yet unwilling to drink?

Yes, often.

What, then, can one say of them, if not that their soul contains something which urges them to drink and something which holds them back, and that this latter is a distinct thing and overpowers the other?

I agree.

And is it not true that the intervention of this inhibiting principle in such cases al-   d ways has its origin in reflection; whereas the impulses driving and dragging the soul are engendered by external influences and abnormal conditions?

Evidently.

We shall have good reason, then, to assert that they are two distinct principles. We may call that part of the soul whereby it reflects, rational; and the other, with which it feels hunger and thirst and is distracted by sexual passion and all the other desires, we will call irrational appetite, associated with pleasure in the replenishment of certain wants.

Yes, there is good ground for that view.   e

Let us take it, then, that we have now distinguished two elements in the soul. What of that passionate element which makes us feel angry and indignant? Is that a third, or identical in nature with one of those two?

It might perhaps be identified with appetite.

I am more inclined to put my faith in a story I once heard about Leontius, son of Aglaion. On his way up from the Piraeus outside the north wall, he noticed the bodies of some criminals lying on the ground, with the executioner standing by them. He wanted to go and look at them, but at the same time he was disgusted and tried to turn away. He struggled for some time and covered his eyes, but at last the desire was too much for him. Opening his eyes wide, he ran up to the bodies and cried, "There you   440 are, curse you; feast yourselves on this lovely sight!"

Yes, I have heard that story too.

The point of it surely is that anger is sometimes in conflict with appetite, as if they were two distinct principles. Do we not often find a man whose desires would   b force him to go against his reason, reviling himself and indignant with this part of his nature which is trying to put constraint on him? It is like a struggle between two factions, in which indignation takes the side of reason. But I believe you have never observed, in yourself or anyone else, indignation make common cause with appetite in behaviour which reason decides to be wrong.

No, I am sure I have not.

Again, take a man who feels he is in the wrong. The more generous his nature,   c the less can he be indignant at any suffering, such as hunger and cold, inflicted by the man he has injured. He recognizes such treatment as just, and, as I say, his spirit refuses to be roused against it.

That is true.

But now contrast one who thinks it is he that is being wronged. His spirit boils with resentment and sides with the right as he conceives it. Persevering all the more for   d the hunger and cold and other pains he suffers, it triumphs and will not give in until its gallant struggle has ended in success or death; or until the restraining voice of reason, like a shepherd calling off his dog, makes it relent.

An apt comparison, he said; and in fact it fits the relation of our Auxiliaries to the Rulers: they were to be like watch-dogs obeying the shepherds of the commonwealth.

Yes, you understand very well what I have in mind. But do you see how we have   e changed our view? A moment ago we were supposing this spirited element to be something of the nature of appetite; but now it appears that, when the soul is divided into factions, it is far more ready to be up in arms on the side of reason.

Quite true.

Is it, then, distinct from the rational element or only a particular form of it, so that the soul will contain no more than two elements, reason and appetite? Or is the soul like the state, which had three orders to hold it together, traders, Auxiliaries, and counsellors? Does the spirited element make a third, the natural auxiliary of reason, when not corrupted by bad upbringing?

It must be a third.

Yes, I said, provided it can be shown to be distinct from reason, as we saw it was from appetite.

That is easily proved. You can see that much in children: they are full of passionate feelings from their very birth; but some, I should say, never become rational, and most of them only late in life.

A very sound observation, said I, the truth of which may also be seen in animals. And besides, there is the witness of Homer in that line I quoted before: "He smote his breast and spoke, chiding his heart." The poet is plainly thinking of the two elements as distinct, when he makes the one which has chosen the better course after reflection rebuke the other for its unreasoning passion.

I entirely agree.

And so, after a stormy passage, we have reached the land. We are fairly agreed that the same three elements exist alike in the state and in the individual soul.

That is so.

Does it not follow at once that state and individual will be wise or brave by virtue of the same element in each and in the same way? Both will possess in the same manner any quality that makes for excellence.

That must be true.

Then it applies to justice: we shall conclude that a man is just in the same way that a state was just. And we have surely not forgotten that justice in the state meant that each of the three orders in it was doing its own proper work. So we may henceforth bear in mind that each one of us likewise will be a just person, fulfilling his proper function, only if the several parts of our nature fulfil theirs.

Certainly.

And it will be the business of reason to rule with wisdom and forethought on behalf of the entire soul; while the spirited element ought to act as its subordinate and ally. The two will be brought into accord, as we said earlier, by that combination of mental and bodily training which will tune up one string of the instrument and relax the other, nourishing the reasoning part on the study of noble literature and allaying the other's wildness by harmony and rhythm. When both have been thus nurtured and trained to know their own true functions, they must be set in command over the appetites, which form the greater part of each man's soul and are by nature insatiably covetous. They must keep watch lest this part, by battening on the pleasures that are called bodily, should grow so great and powerful that it will no longer keep to its own work, but will try to enslave the others and usurp a dominion to which it has no right, thus turning the whole of life upside down. At the same time, those two together will be the best of guardians for the entire soul and for the body against all enemies from without: the one will take counsel, while the other will do battle, following its ruler's commands and by its own bravery giving effect to the ruler's designs.

Yes, that is all true.

And so we call an individual brave in virtue of this spirited part of his nature,   c
when, in spite of pain or pleasure, it holds fast to the injunctions of reason about what
he ought or ought not to be afraid of.

True.

And wise in virtue of that small part which rules and issues these injunctions,
possessing as it does the knowledge of what is good for each of the three elements and
for all of them in common.

Certainly.

And, again, temperate by reason of the unanimity and concord of all three, when   d
there is no internal conflict between the ruling element and its two subjects, but all are
agreed that reason should be ruler.

Yes, that is an exact account of temperance, whether in the state or in the individual.

Finally, a man will be just by observing the principle we have so often stated.

Necessarily.

Now is there any indistinctness in our vision of justice, that might make it seem
somehow different from what we found it to be in the state?   e

I don't think so.

Because, if we have any lingering doubt, we might make sure by comparing it
with some commonplace notions. Suppose, for instance, that a sum of money were entrusted to our state or to an individual of corresponding character and training, would   443
anyone imagine that such a person would be specially likely to embezzle it?

No.

And would he not be incapable of sacrilege and theft, or of treachery to friend or
country; never false to an oath or any other compact; the last to be guilty of adultery or
of neglecting parents or the due service of the gods?

Yes.

And the reason for all this is that each part of his nature is exercising its proper   b
function, of ruling or of being ruled.

Yes, exactly.

Are you satisfied, then, that justice is the power which produces states or individuals of whom that is true, or must we look further?

There is no need; I am quite satisfied.

And so our dream has come true—I mean the inkling we had that, by some
happy chance, we had lighted upon a rudimentary form of justice from the very mo-   c
ment when we set about founding our commonwealth. Our principle that the born
shoemaker or carpenter had better stick to his trade turns out to have been an adumbra-
tion of justice; and that is why it has helped us. But in reality justice, though evidently
analogous to this principle, is not a matter of external behaviour, but of the inward self
and of attending to all that is, in the fullest sense, a man's proper concern. The just man   d
does not allow the several elements in his soul to usurp one another's functions; he is
indeed one who sets his house in order, by self-mastery and discipline coming to be at
peace with himself, and bringing into tune those three parts, like the terms in the proportion of a musical scale, the highest and lowest notes and the mean between them,
with all the intermediate intervals. Only when he has linked these parts together in
well-tempered harmony and has made himself one man instead of many, will he be   e
ready to go about whatever he may have to do, whether it be making money and satisfying bodily wants, or business transactions, or the affairs of state. In all these fields
when he speaks of just and honourable conduct, he will mean the behaviour that helps

to produce and to preserve this habit of mind; and by wisdom he will mean the knowledge which presides over such conduct. Any action which tends to break down this habit will be for him unjust; and the notions governing it he will call ignorance and folly.

That is perfectly true, Socrates.

Good, said I. I believe we should not be thought altogether mistaken, if we claimed to have discovered the just man and the just state, and wherein their justice consists.

Indeed we should not.

Shall we make that claim, then?

Yes, we will.

So be it, said I. Next, I suppose, we have to consider injustice.

Evidently.

This must surely be a sort of civil strife among the three elements, whereby they usurp and encroach upon one another's functions and some one part of the soul rises up in rebellion against the whole, claiming a supremacy to which it has no right because its nature fits it only to be the servant of the ruling principle. Such turmoil and aberration we shall, I think, identify with injustice, intemperance, cowardice, ignorance, and in a word with all wickedness.

Exactly.

And now that we know the nature of justice and injustice, we can be equally clear about what is meant by acting justly and again by unjust action and wrongdoing.

How do you mean?

Plainly, they are exactly analogous to those wholesome and unwholesome activities which respectively produce a healthy or unhealthy condition in the body; in the same way just and unjust conduct produce a just or unjust character. Justice is produced in the soul, like health in the body, by establishing the elements concerned in their natural relations of control and subordination, whereas injustice is like disease and means that this natural order is inverted.

Quite so.

It appears, then, that virtue is as it were the health and comeliness and well-being of the soul, as wickedness is disease, deformity, and weakness.

True.

And also that virtue and wickedness are brought about by one's way of life, honourable or disgraceful.

That follows.

So now it only remains to consider which is the more profitable course: to do right and live honourably and be just, whether or not anyone knows what manner of man you are, or to do wrong and be unjust, provided that you can escape the chastisement which might make you a better man.

But really, Socrates, it seems to me ridiculous to ask that question now that the nature of justice and injustice has been brought to light. People think that all the luxury and wealth and power in the world cannot make life worth living when the bodily constitution is going to rack and ruin; and are we to believe that, when the very principle whereby we live is deranged and corrupted, life will be worth living so long as a man can do as he will, and wills to do anything rather than to free himself from vice and wrong doing and to win justice and virtue?

Yes, I replied, it is a ridiculous question.

Nevertheless, I continued, we are now within sight of the clearest possible proof of our conclusions, and we ought not to slacken our efforts.

No, anything rather than that.

If you will take your stand with me, then, on this point of vantage to which we   c
have climbed, you shall see all the forms that evil takes, or at least all that it seems
worthwhile to look at.

Lead the way and tell me what you see.

What I see is that, whereas there is only one form of excellence, imperfection exists in innumerable shapes, of which there are four that specially deserve notice.

What do you mean?

It looks as if there were as many types of character as there are distinct varieties
of political constitution.

How many?

Five of each.   d

Will you define them?

Yes, I said. One form of constitution will be the form we have been describing,
though it may be called by two names: monarchy, when there is one man who stands
out above the rest of the Rulers; aristocracy, when there are more than one.

True.

That, then, I regard as a single form; for, so long as they observe our principles
of upbringing and education, whether the Rulers be one or more, they will not subvert   e
the important institutions in our commonwealth.

Naturally not.

BOOK V

Such, then, is the type of state or constitution that I call good and right, and the corre-   449
sponding type of man. By this standard, the other forms in which a state or an individual character may be organized are depraved and wrong. There are four of these vicious forms.

What are they?

Here I was going on to describe these forms in the order in which, as I thought,
they develop one from another, when Polemarchus, who was sitting a little way from   b
Adeimantus, reached out his hand and took hold of his garment by the shoulder. Lean-
ing forward and drawing Adeimantus towards him, he whispered something in his ear,
of which I only caught the words: What shall we do? Shall we leave it alone?

Certainly not, said Adeimantus, raising his voice.

What is this, I asked, that you are not going to leave alone?

You, he replied.

Why, in particular? I inquired.   c

Because we think you are shirking the discussion of a very important part of the
subject and trying to cheat us out of an explanation. Everyone, you said, must of
course see that the maxim "friends have all things in common" applies to women and
children. You thought we should pass over such a casual remark!

But wasn't that right, Adeimantus? said I.

Yes, he said, but "right" in this case, as in others, needs to be defined. There may
be many ways of having things in common, and you must tell us which you mean. We   d
have been waiting a long time for you to say something about the conditions in which
children are to be born and brought up and your whole plan of having wives and chil-

dren held in common. This seems to us a matter in which right or wrong management will make all the difference to society; and now, instead of going into it thoroughly, you are passing on to some other form of constitution. So we came to the resolution
450   which you overheard, not to let you off discussing it as fully as all the other institutions.

I will vote for your resolution too, said Glaucon.

In fact, Socrates, Thrasymachus added, you may take it as carried unanimously.

You don't know what you are doing, I said, in holding me up like this. You want to start, all over again, on an enormous subject, just as I was rejoicing at the idea that
b   we had done with this form of constitution. I was only too glad that my casual remark should be allowed to pass. And now, when you demand an explanation, you little know what a swarm of questions you are stirring up. I let it alone, because I foresaw no end of trouble.

Well, said Thrasymachus, what do you think we came here for—to play pitch-and-toss or to listen to a discussion?

A discussion, no doubt, I replied; but within limits.

No man of sense, said Glaucon, would think the whole of life too long to spend on questions of this importance. But never mind about us; don't be faint-hearted your-
c   self. Tell us what you think about this question: how our Guardians are to have wives and children in common, and how they will bring up the young in the interval between their birth and education, which is thought to be the most difficult time of all. Do try to explain how all this is to be arranged.

I wish it were as easy as you seem to think, I replied. These arrangements are even more open to doubt than any we have so far discussed. It may be questioned
d   whether the plan is feasible, and even if entirely feasible, whether it would be for the best. So I have some hesitation in touching on what may seem to be an idle dream.

You need not hesitate, he replied. This is not an unsympathetic audience; we are neither incredulous nor hostile.

Thank you, I said; I suppose that remark is meant to be encouraging.

Certainly it is.

Well, I said, it has just the opposite effect. You would do well to encourage me, if I had any faith in my own understanding of these matters. If one knows the truth, there is no risk to be feared in speaking about the things one has most at heart among
e   intelligent friends; but if one is still in the position of a doubting inquirer, as I am now, talking becomes a slippery venture. Not that I am afraid of being laughed at—that would be childish—but I am afraid I may miss my footing just where a false step is
451   most to be dreaded and drag my friends down with me in my fall. I devoutly hope, Glaucon, that no nemesis will overtake me for what I am going to say; for I really believe that to kill a man unintentionally is a lighter offence than to mislead him concerning the goodness and justice of social institutions. Better to run that risk among ene-
b   mies than among friends; so your encouragement is out of place.

Glaucon laughed at this. No, Socrates, he said, if your theory has any untoward effect on us, our blood shall not be on your head; we absolve you of any intention to mislead us. So have no fear.

Well, said I, when a homicide is absolved of all intention, the law holds him clear of guilt; and the same principle may apply to my case.

Yes, so far as that goes, you may speak freely.

We must go back, then, to a subject which ought, perhaps, to have been treated
c   earlier in its proper place; though, after all, it may be suitable that the women should have their turn on the stage when the men have quite finished their performance, espe-

cially since you are so insistent. In my judgement, then, the question under what conditions people born and educated as we have described should possess wives and children, and how they should treat them, can be rightly settled only by keeping to the course on which we started them at the outset. We undertook to put these men in the position of watch-dogs guarding a flock. Suppose we follow up the analogy and imagine them bred and reared in the same sort of way. We can then see if that plan will suit   d
our purpose.

How will that be?

In this way. Which do we think right for watch-dogs: should the females guard the flock and hunt with the males and take a share in all they do, or should they be kept within doors as fit for no more than bearing and feeding their puppies, while all the hard work of looking after the flock is left to the males?

They are expected to take their full share, except that we treat them as not quite   e
so strong.

Can you employ any creature for the same work as another, if you do not give them both the same upbringing and education?

No.

Then, if we are to set women to the same tasks as men, we must teach them the   452
same things. They must have the same two branches of training for mind and body and also be taught the art of war, and they must receive the same treatment.

That seems to follow.

Possibly, if these proposals were carried out, they might be ridiculed as involving a good many breaches of custom.

They might indeed.

The most ridiculous—don't you think?—being the notion of women exercising naked along with the men in the wrestling-schools; some of them elderly women too,   b
like the old men who still have a passion for exercise when they are wrinkled and not very agreeable to look at.

Yes, that would be thought laughable, according to our present notions.

Now we have started on this subject, we must not be frightened of the many witticisms that might be aimed at such a revolution, not only in the matter of bodily exercise but in the training of women's minds, and not least when it comes to their bearing   c
arms and riding on horseback. Having begun upon these rules, we must not draw back from the harsher provisions. The wits may be asked to stop being witty and try to be serious; and we may remind them that it is not so long since the Greeks, like most foreign nations of the present day, thought it ridiculous and shameful for men to be seen naked. When gymnastic exercises were first introduced in Crete and later at Sparta, the humorists had their chance to make fun of them; but when experience had shown that   d
nakedness is better uncovered than muffled up, the laughter died down and a practice which the reason approved ceased to look ridiculous to the eye. This shows how idle it is to think anything ludicrous but what is base. One who tries to raise a laugh at any spectacle save that of baseness and folly will also, in his serious moments, set before   e
himself some other standard than goodness of what deserves to be held in honour.

Most assuredly.

The first thing to be settled, then, is whether these proposals are feasible; and it   453
must be open to anyone, whether a humorist or serious-minded, to raise the question whether, in the case of mankind, the feminine nature is capable of taking part with the other sex in all occupations, or in none at all, or in some only; and in particular under which of these heads this business of military service falls. Well begun is half done, and would not this be the best way to begin?

Yes.

Shall we take the other side in this debate and argue against ourselves? We do not want the adversary's position to be taken by storm for lack of defenders.

b   I have no objection.

Let us state his case for him. "Socrates and Glaucon," he will say, "there is no need for others to dispute your position; you yourselves, at the very outset of founding your commonwealth, agreed that everyone should do the one work for which nature fits him." Yes, of course; I suppose we did. "And isn't there a very great difference in nature between man and woman?" Yes, surely. "Does not that natural difference imply a corresponding difference in the work to be given to each?" Yes. "But if so, surely you must be mistaken now and contradicting yourselves when you say that men and women, having such widely divergent natures, should do the same things? What is your answer to that, my ingenious friend?"

It is not easy to find one at the moment. I can only appeal to you to state the case on our own side, whatever it may be.

d   This, Glaucon, is one of many alarming objections which I foresaw some time ago. That is why I shrank from touching upon these laws concerning the possession of wives and the rearing of children.

It looks like anything but an easy problem.

True, I said; but whether a man tumbles into a swimming-pool or into mid-ocean, he has to swim all the same. So must we, and try if we can reach the shore, hoping for some Arion's dolphin or other miraculous deliverance to bring us safe to land.

e   I suppose so.

Come then, let us see if we can find the way out. We did agree that different natures should have different occupations, and that the natures of man and woman are different; and yet we are now saying that these different natures are to have the same occupations. Is that the charge against us?

Exactly.

454   It is extraordinary, Glaucon, what an effect the practice of debating has upon people.

Why do you say that?

Because they often seem to fall unconsciously into mere disputes which they mistake for reasonable argument, through being unable to draw the distinctions proper to their subject; and so, instead of a philosophical exchange of ideas, they go off in chase of contradictions which are purely verbal.

I know that happens to many people; but does it apply to us at this moment?

b   Absolutely. At least I am afraid we are slipping unconsciously into a dispute about words. We have been strenuously insisting on the letter of our principle that different natures should not have the same occupations, as if we were scoring a point in a debate; but we have altogether neglected to consider what sort of sameness or difference we meant and in what respect these natures and occupations were to be defined as

c   different or the same. Consequently, we might very well be asking one another whether there is not an opposition in nature between bald and long-haired men, and, when that was admitted, forbid one set to be shoemakers, if the other were following that trade.

That would be absurd.

Yes, but only because we never meant any and every sort of sameness or difference in nature, but the sort that was relevant to the occupations in question. We meant, for instance, that a man and a woman have the same nature if both have a talent for medicine; whereas two men have different natures if one is a born physician, the other a born carpenter.   d

Yes, of course.

If, then, we find that either the male sex or the female is specially qualified for any particular form of occupation, then that occupation, we shall say, ought to be assigned to one sex or the other. But if the only difference appears to be that the male begets and the female brings forth, we shall conclude that no difference between man and woman has yet been produced that is relevant to our purpose. We shall continue to think it proper for our Guardians and their wives to share in the same pursuits.   e

And quite rightly.

The next thing will be to ask our opponent to name any profession or occupation in civic life for the purposes of which woman's nature is different from man's.   455

That is a fair question.

He might reply, as you did just now, that it is not easy to find a satisfactory answer on the spur of the moment, but that there would be no difficulty after a little reflection.

Perhaps.

Suppose, then, we invite him to follow us and see if we can convince him that there is no occupation concerned with the management of social affairs that is peculiar to women. We will confront him with a question: When you speak of a man having a natural talent for something, do you mean that he finds it easy to learn, and after a little instruction can find out much more for himself; whereas a man who is not so gifted learns with difficulty and no amount of instruction and practice will make him even remember what he has been taught? Is the talented man one whose bodily powers are readily at the service of his mind, instead of being a hindrance? Are not these the marks by which you distinguish the presence of a natural gift for any pursuit?   b

Yes, precisely.   c

Now do you know of any human occupation in which the male sex is not superior to the female in all these respects? Need I waste time over exceptions like weaving and watching over saucepans and batches of cakes, though women are supposed to be good at such things and get laughed at when a man does them better?   d

It is true, he replied, in almost everything one sex is easily beaten by the other. No doubt many women are better at many things than many men; but taking the sexes as a whole, it is as you say.

To conclude, then, there is no occupation concerned with the management of social affairs which belongs either to woman or to man, as such. Natural gifts are to be found here and there in both creatures alike; and every occupation is open to both, so far as their natures are concerned, though woman is for all purposes the weaker.   e

Certainly.

Is that a reason for making over all occupations to men only?

Of course not.

No, because one woman may have a natural gift for medicine or for music, another may not.

Surely.

Is it not also true that a woman may, or may not, be warlike or athletic?   456

I think so.

And again, one may love knowledge, another hate it; one may be high-spirited, another spiritless?

Steps in Cloth-Making. Black-figure lekythos (oil jug) attributed to the potter Amasis (sixth century B.C.). The women on the left are hand spinning thread; those in the center are weaving wool. Given that Greek women generally remained at home fulfilling such domestic occupations, Plato's suggestions in the *Republic* were quite revolutionary. Though he claims that women are "for all purposes the weaker [sex]," Plato's character, Socrates, concludes, "There is no occupation concerned with the management of social affairs which belongs to woman or to man, as such. Natural gifts are to be found here and there in both . . . alike; and every occupation is open to both. . . ." (*The Metropolitan Museum of Art, Fletcher Fund, 1931*)

True again.

It follows that one woman will be fitted by nature to be a Guardian, another will not; because these were the qualities for which we selected our men Guardians. So for the purpose of keeping watch over the commonwealth, woman has the same nature as man, save in so far as she is weaker.

So it appears.

b   It follows that women of this type must be selected to share the life and duties of Guardians with men of the same type, since they are competent and of a like nature, and the same natures must be allowed the same pursuits.

Yes.

We come round, then, to our former position, that there is nothing contrary to
c   nature in giving our Guardians' wives the same training for mind and body. The practice we proposed to establish was not impossible or visionary, since it was in accordance with nature. Rather, the contrary practice which now prevails turns out to be unnatural.

So it appears.

Well, we set out to inquire whether the plan we proposed was feasible and also the best. That it is feasible is now agreed; we must next settle whether it is the best.

Obviously.

Now, for the purpose of producing a woman fit to be a Guardian, we shall not have one education for men and another for women, precisely because the nature to be   d taken in hand is the same.

True.

What is your opinion on the question of one man being better than another? Do you think there is no such difference?

Certainly I do not.

And in this commonwealth of ours which will prove the better men—the Guardians who have received the education we described, or the shoemakers who have been trained to make shoes?

It is absurd to ask such a question.

Very well. So these Guardians will be the best of all the citizens?   e

By far.

And these women the best of all the women?

Yes.

Can anything be better for a commonwealth than to produce in it men and women of the best possible type?

No.

And that result will be brought about by such a system of mental and bodily   457 training as we have described?

Surely.

We may conclude that the institution we proposed was not only practicable, but also the best for the commonwealth.

Yes.

The wives of our Guardians, then, must strip for exercise, since they will be clothed with virtue, and they must take their share in war and in the other social duties of guardianship. They are to have no other occupation; and in these duties the lighter part must fall to the women, because of the weakness of their sex. The man who laughs   b at naked women, exercising their bodies for the best of reasons, is like one that "gathers fruit unripe," for he does not know what it is that he is laughing at or what he is doing. There will never be a finer saying than the one which declares that whatever does good should be held in honour, and the only shame is in doing harm.

That is perfectly true.

So far, then, in regulating the position of women, we may claim to have come safely through with one hazardous proposal, that male and female Guardians shall   c have all occupations in common. The consistency of the argument is an assurance that the plan is a good one and also feasible. We are like swimmers who have breasted the first wave without being swallowed up.

Not such a small wave either.

You will not call it large when you see the next.

Let me have a look at the next one, then.

Here it is: a law which follows from that principle and all that has gone before,   d namely that, of these Guardians, no one man and one woman are to set up house together privately: wives are to be held in common by all; so too are the children, and no parent is to know his own child, nor any child his parent.

It will be much harder to convince people that that is either a feasible plan or a good one.

As to its being a good plan, I imagine no one would deny the immense advantage of wives and children being held in common, provided it can be done. I should expect dispute to arise chiefly over the question of whether it is possible.

e   There may well be a good deal of dispute over both points.

You mean, I must meet attacks on two fronts. I was hoping to escape one by running away: if you agreed it was a good plan, then I should only have had to inquire whether it was feasible.

No, we have seen through that manoeuvre. You will have to defend both positions.

Well, I must pay the penalty for my cowardice. But grant me one favour. Let me
458   indulge my fancy, like one who entertains himself with idle day-dreams on a solitary walk. Before he has any notion how his desires can be realized, he will set aside that question, to save himself the trouble of reckoning what may or may not be possible. He will assume that his wish has come true, and amuse himself with settling all the details of what he means to do then. So a lazy mind encourages itself to be lazier than ever;
b   and I am giving way to the same weakness myself. I want to put off till later that question, how the thing can be done. For the moment, with your leave, I shall assume it to be possible, and ask how the Rulers will work out the details in practice; and I shall argue that the plan, once carried into effect, would be the best thing in the world for our commonwealth and for its Guardians. That is what I shall now try to make out with your help, if you will allow me to postpone the other question.

Very good; I have no objection.

Well, if our Rulers are worthy of the name, and their Auxiliaries likewise, these
c   latter will be ready to do what they are told, and the Rulers, in giving their commands, will themselves obey our laws and will be faithful to their spirit in any details we leave to their discretion.

No doubt.

It is for you, then, as their lawgiver, who has already selected the men, to select for association with them women who are so far as possible of the same natural capac-
d   ity. Now since none of them will have any private home of his own, but they will share the same dwelling and eat at common tables, the two sexes will be together; and meeting without restriction for exercise and all through their upbringing, they will surely be drawn towards union with one another by a necessity of their nature—necessity is not too strong a word, I think?

Not too strong for the constraint of love, which for the mass of mankind is more persuasive and compelling than even the necessity of mathematical proof.

Exactly. But in the next place, Glaucon, anything like unregulated unions would
e   be a profanation in a state whose citizens lead the good life. The Rulers will not allow such a thing.

No, it would not be right.

Clearly, then, we must have marriages, as sacred as we can make them; and this sanctity will attach to those which yield the best results.

Certainly.
459   How are we to get the best results? You must tell me, Glaucon, because I see you keep sporting dogs and a great many game birds at your house; and there is something about their mating and breeding that you must have noticed.

What is that?

In the first place, though they may all be of good stock, are there not some that turn out to be better than the rest?

There are.

And do you breed from all indiscriminately? Are you not careful to breed from the best so far as you can?

Yes.

And from those in their prime, rather than the very young or the very old?   b
Yes.

Otherwise, the stock of your birds or dogs would deteriorate very much, wouldn't it?

It would.

And the same is true of horses or of any animal?

It would be very strange if it were not.

Dear me, said I; we shall need consummate skill in our Rulers, if it is also true of the human race.

Well, it is true. But why must they be so skilful?   c

Because they will have to administer a large dose of that medicine we spoke of earlier. An ordinary doctor is thought good enough for a patient who will submit to be dieted and can do without medicine; but he must be much more of a man if drugs are required.

True, but how does that apply?

It applies to our Rulers: it seems they will have to give their subjects a considerable dose of imposition and deception for their good. We said, if you remember, that   d
such expedients would be useful as a sort of medicine.

Yes, a very sound principle.

Well, it looks as if this sound principle will play no small part in this matter of marriage and child-bearing.

How so?

It follows from what we have just said that, if we are to keep our flock at the highest pitch of excellence, there should be as many unions of the best of both sexes, and as few of the inferior, as possible, and that only the offspring of the better unions   e
should be kept. And again, no one but the Rulers must know how all this is being effected; otherwise our herd of Guardians may become rebellious.

Quite true.

We must, then, institute certain festivals at which we shall bring together the brides and the bridegrooms. There will be sacrifices, and our poets will write songs be-   460
fitting the occasion. The number of marriages we shall leave to the Rulers' discretion. They will aim at keeping the number of the citizens as constant as possible, having regard to losses caused by war, epidemics, and so on; and they must do their best to see that our state does not become either great or small.

Very good.

I think they will have to invent some ingenious system of drawing lots, so that, at each pairing off, the inferior candidate may blame his luck rather than the Rulers.

Yes, certainly.

Moreover, young men who acquit themselves well in war and other duties,   b
should be given, among other rewards and privileges, more liberal opportunities to sleep with a wife, for the further purpose that, with good excuse, as many as possible of the children may be begotten of such fathers.

Yes.

As soon as children are born, they will be taken in charge by officers appointed for the purpose, who may be men or women or both, since offices are to be shared by both sexes. The children of the better parents they will carry to the creche to be reared   c
in the care of nurses living apart in a certain quarter of the city. Those of the inferior parents and any children of the rest that are born defective will be hidden away, in some appropriate manner that must be kept secret.

They must be, if the breed of our Guardians is to be kept pure.

These officers will also superintend the nursing of the children. They will bring the mothers to the creche when their breasts are full, while taking every precaution that no mother shall know her own child; and if the mothers have not enough milk, they will provide wet-nurses. They will limit the time during which the mothers will suckle their children, and hand over all the hard work and sitting up at night to nurses and attendants.

That will make child-bearing an easy business for the Guardians' wives.

So it should be. To go on with our scheme: we said that children should be born from parents in the prime of life. Do you agree that this lasts about twenty years for a woman, and thirty for a man? A woman should bear children for the commonwealth from her twentieth to her fortieth year; a man should begin to beget them when he has passed "the racer's prime in swiftness," and continue till he is fifty-five.

Those are certainly the years in which both the bodily and the mental powers of man and woman are at their best.

If a man either above or below this age meddles with the begetting of children for the commonwealth, we shall hold it an offence against divine and human law. He will be begetting for his country a child conceived in darkness and dire incontinence, whose birth, if it escape detection, will not have been sanctioned by the sacrifices and prayers offered at each marriage festival, when priests and priestesses join with the whole community in praying that the children to be born may be even better and more useful citizens than their parents.

You are right.

The same law will apply to any man within the prescribed limits who touches a woman also of marriageable age when the Ruler has not paired them. We shall say that he is foisting on the commonwealth a bastard, unsanctioned by law or by religion.

Perfectly right.

As soon, however, as the men and the women have passed the age prescribed for producing children, we shall leave them free to form a connexion with whom they will, except that a man shall not take his daughter or daughter's daughter or mother or mother's mother, nor a woman her son or father or her son's son or father's father; and all this only after we have exhorted them to see that no child, if any be conceived, shall be brought to light, or, if they cannot prevent its birth, to dispose of it on the understanding that no such child can be reared.

That too is reasonable. But how are they to distinguish fathers and daughters and those other relations you mentioned?

They will not, said I. But, reckoning from the day when he becomes a bridegroom, a man will call all children born in the tenth or the seventh month sons and daughters, and they will call him father. Their children again he will call grandchildren, and they will call his group grandfathers and grandmothers; and all who are born within the period during which their mothers and fathers were having children will be called brothers and sisters. This will provide for those restrictions on unions that we mentioned; but the law will allow brothers and sisters to live together, if the lot so falls out and the Delphic oracle also approves.

Very good.

This, then, Glaucon, is the manner in which the Guardians of your commonwealth are to hold their wives and children in common. Must we not next find arguments to establish that it is consistent with our other institutions and also by far the best plan?

Yes, surely.

We had better begin by asking what is the greatest good at which the lawgiver should aim in laying down the constitution of a state, and what is the worst evil. We can then consider whether our proposals are in keeping with that good and irreconcilable with the evil.

By all means.

Does not the worst evil for a state arise from anything that tends to rend it asunder and destroy its unity, while nothing does it more good than whatever tends to bind   b
it together and make it one?

That is true.

And are not citizens bound together by sharing in the same pleasures and pains, all feeling glad or grieved on the same occasions of gain or loss; whereas the bond is broken when such feelings are no longer universal, but any event of public or personal   c
concern fills some with joy and others with distress?

Certainly.

And this disunion comes about when the words "mine" and "not mine," "another's" and "not another's" are not applied to the same things throughout the community. The best ordered state will be the one in which the largest number of persons use these terms in the same sense, and which accordingly most nearly resembles a single person. When one of us hurts his finger, the whole extent of those bodily connexions which are gathered up in the soul and unified by its ruling element is made aware and it   d
all shares as a whole in the pain of the suffering part; hence we say that the man has a pain in his finger. The same thing is true of the pain or pleasure felt when any other part of the person suffers or is relieved.

Yes; I agree that the best organized community comes nearest to that condition.

And so it will recognize as a part of itself the individual citizen to whom good or   e
evil happens, and will share as a whole in his joy or sorrow.

It must, if the constitution is sound.

It is time now to go back to our own commonwealth and see whether these conclusions apply to it more than to any other type of state. In all alike there are rulers and   463
common people, all of whom will call one another fellow citizens.

Yes.

But in other states the people have another name as well for their rulers, haven't they?

Yes; in most they call them masters; in democracies, simply the government.

And in ours?

The people will look upon their rulers as preservers and protectors.   b

And how will our rulers regard the people?

As those who maintain them and pay them wages.

And elsewhere?

As slaves.

And what do rulers elsewhere call one another?

Colleagues.

And ours?

Fellow Guardians.

And in other states may not a ruler regard one colleague as a friend in whom he has an interest, and another as a stranger with whom he has nothing in common?   c

Yes, that often happens.

But that could not be so with your Guardians? None of them could ever treat a fellow Guardian as a stranger.

Certainly not. He must regard everyone whom he meets as brother or sister, father or mother, son or daughter, grandchild or grandparent.

d   Very good; but here is a further point. Will you not require them, not merely to use these family terms, but to behave as a real family? Must they not show towards all whom they call "father" the customary reverence, care, and obedience due to a parent, if they look for any favour from gods or men, since to act otherwise is contrary to divine and human law? Should not all the citizens constantly reiterate in the hearing of the children from their earliest years such traditional maxims of conduct towards those whom they are taught to call father and their other kindred?

e   They should. It would be absurd that terms of kinship should be on their lips without any action to correspond.

In our community, then, above all others, when things go well or ill with any individual everyone will use that word "mine" in the same sense and say that all is going well or ill with him and his.

Quite true.

464   And, as we said, this way of speaking and thinking goes with fellow-feeling; so that our citizens, sharing as they do in a common interest which each will call his own, will have all their feelings of pleasure or pain in common.

Assuredly.

A result that will be due to our institutions, and in particular to our Guardians' holding their wives and children in common.

Very much so.

b   But you will remember how, when we compared a well-ordered community to the body which shares in the pleasures and pains of any member, we saw in this unity the greatest good that a state can enjoy. So the conclusion is that our commonwealth owes to this sharing of wives and children by its protectors its enjoyment of the greatest of all goods.

Yes, that follows.

Moreover, this agrees with our principle that they were not to have houses or lands or any property of their own, but to receive sustenance from the other citizens, as wages for their guardianship, and to consume it in common. Only so will they keep to their true character; and our present proposals will do still more to make them genuine Guardians. They will not rend the community asunder by each applying that word "mine" to different things and dragging off whatever he can get for himself into a private home, where he will have his separate family, forming a centre of exclusive joys and sorrows. Rather they will all, so far as may be, feel together and aim at the same ends, because they are convinced that all their interests are identical.

Quite so.

Again, if a man's person is his only private possession, lawsuits and prosecutions will all but vanish, and they will be free of those quarrels that arise from ownership of property and from having family ties. Nor would they be justified even in bringing actions for assault and outrage; for we shall pronounce it right and honourable for a man to defend himself against an assailant of his own age, and in that way they will be compelled to keep themselves fit.

That would be a sound law.

465   And it would also have the advantage that, if a man's anger can be satisfied in this way, a fit of passion is less likely to grow into a serious quarrel.

True.

But an older man will be given authority over all younger persons and power to correct them; whereas the younger will, naturally, not dare to strike the elder or do him any violence, except by command of a Ruler. He will not show him any sort of disrespect. Two guardian spirits, fear and reverence, will be enough to restrain him—reverence forbidding him to lay hands on a parent, and fear of all those others who as sons or brothers or fathers would come to the rescue.

Yes, that will be the result.

So our laws will secure that these men will live in complete peace with one another; and if they never quarrel among themselves, there is no fear of the rest of the community being divided either against them or against itself.

No.

There are other evils they will escape, so mean and petty that I hardly like to mention them: the poor man's flattery of the rich, and all the embarrassments and vexations of rearing a family and earning just enough to maintain a household; now borrowing and now refusing to repay, and by any and every means scraping together money to be handed over to wife and servants to spend. These sordid troubles are familiar and not worth describing.

Only too familiar.

Rid of all these cares, they will live a more enviable life than the Olympic victor, who is counted happy on the strength of far fewer blessings than our Guardians will enjoy. Their victory is the nobler, since by their success the whole commonwealth is preserved; and their reward of maintenance at the public cost is more complete, since their prize is to have every need of life supplied for themselves and for their children; their country honours them while they live, and when they die they receive a worthy burial.

Yes, they will be nobly rewarded.

Do you remember, then, how someone who shall be nameless reproached us for not making our Guardians happy: they were to possess nothing, though all the wealth of their fellow citizens was within their grasp? We replied, I believe, that we would consider that objection later, if it came in our way: for the moment we were bent on making our Guardians real guardians, and moulding our commonwealth with a view to the greatest happiness, not of one section of it, but of the whole.

Yes, I remember.

Well, it appears now that these protectors of our state will have a life better and more honourable than that of any Olympic victor; and we can hardly rank it on a level with the life of a shoemaker or other artisan or of a farmer.

I should think not.

However, it is right to repeat what I said at the time: if ever a Guardian tries to make himself happy in such a way that he will be a guardian no longer; if, not content with the moderation and security of this way of living which we think the best, he becomes possessed with some silly and childish notion of happiness, impelling him to make his power a means to appropriate all the citizens' wealth, then he will learn the wisdom of Hesiod's saying that the half is more than the whole.

My advice would certainly be that he should keep to his own way of living.

You do agree, then, that women are to take their full share with men in education, in the care of children, and in the guardianship of the other citizens; whether they stay at home or go out to war, they will be like watch-dogs which take their part either in guarding the fold or in hunting and share in every task so far as their strength allows. Such conduct will not be unwomanly, but all for the best and in accordance with the natural partnership of the sexes.

Yes, I agree.

It remains to ask whether such a partnership can be established among human beings, as it can among animals, and if so, how.

I was just going to put that question.

e   So far as fighting is concerned, it is easy to see how they will go out to war.

How?

Men and women will take the field together and moreover bring with them the children who are sturdy enough, to learn this trade, like any other, by watching what they will have to do themselves when they are grown up; and besides looking on, they will fetch and carry for their fathers and mothers and see to all their needs in time of
467   war. You must have noticed how, in the potter's trade for example, the children watch their fathers and wait on them long before they may touch the wheel. Ought our Guardians to be less careful to train theirs by letting them look on and become familiar with their duties?

No, that would be absurd.

b   Moreover, any creature will fight better in the presence of its young.

That is so. But in case of defeat, which may always happen in war, there will be serious danger of their children's lives being lost with their own, so that the country could never recover.

True; but, in the first place, do you think we must make sure that they never run any risk?

No, far from it.

c   Well, if they are ever to take their chance, should it not be on some occasion when, if all goes well, they will be the better for it?

No doubt.

And is it of no importance that men who are to be warriors should see something of war in childhood? Is that not worth some danger?

Yes; it is important.

Granted, then, that the children are to go to war as spectators, all will be well if
d   we can contrive that they shall do so in safety. To begin with, their fathers will not be slow to judge, so far as human foresight can, which expeditions are hazardous and which are safe; and they will be careful not to take the children into danger. Also they will put them in charge of officers qualified by age and experience to lead and take care of them.

Yes, that would be the proper way.

All the same, the unexpected often happens; and to guard against such chances we must see that they have, from their earliest years, wings to fly away with if need be.

e   What do you mean by wings?

Horses, which they must be taught to ride at the earliest possible age; then, when they are taken to see the fighting, their mounts must not be spirited chargers but the swiftest we can find and the easiest to manage. In that way they will get a good view of their future business, and in case of need they will be able to keep up with their older leaders and escape in safety.

That seems an excellent plan.

468   Now, as to the conduct of war and your soldiers' relations to one another and to the enemy: am I right in thinking that anyone guilty of an act of cowardice, such as deserting his post or throwing away his arms, should be reduced to the artisan or farmer class; while if any fall alive into the enemy's hands, we shall make them a present of him, and they may do what they like with their prey?

b   Certainly.

And what shall be done to the hero who has distinguished himself by his valour? First, should he not be crowned on the field by the youths and children each in turn?

Surely.

And they might shake his hand?

Yes.

But you would stop there, no doubt. I am sure you would not approve of his ex-   c changing kisses with them all?

I am all for that; indeed I would add to the law the provision that, so long as they are on the campaign, no one whom he wishes to kiss may refuse. That would make any soldier who chanced to be in love with a youth or a girl all the more eager to win the prize of valour.

Very well. We have already said that the brave man is to be selected for marriage more frequently than the rest, so that as many children as possible may have such a man for their father. But besides that, these valiant youths may well be rewarded in the   d Homeric manner. When Ajax distinguished himself in the war, he was "honoured with slices of the chine's full length," a suitable compliment to a lusty young hero, and one that would at the same time strengthen his muscles.

An excellent idea.

Then here at any rate we will follow Homer. At sacrificial feasts and all such occasions, we shall reward the brave, in proportion to their merit, not only with songs and those privileges we mentioned but "with seats of honour, meat, and cups brimful"; and so   e at once pay tribute to the bravery of these men and women and improve their physique.

Nothing could be better.

Good. And of those who are slain in the field, we shall say that all who fell with honour are of that Golden Race, who, when they die,

> Dwell here on earth, pure spirits, beneficent.   469
> Guardians to shield us mortal men from harm.

Shall we not believe those words of Hesiod?

We shall.

Then we shall ask the Oracle with what special rites these men of more than human mould should be buried, and we shall do as it prescribes. And for all time to   b come we shall reverence their tombs and worship them as demigods. Others, too, who die in the natural course of old age or otherwise shall be honoured in the same way, if they are judged to have led an exceptionally noble life.

That is but fair.

And next, how will our soldiers deal with enemies?

In what respect?

First take slavery. Is it right that Greek states should sell Greeks into slavery? Ought they not rather to do all they can to stop this practice and substitute the custom   c of sparing their own race, for fear of falling into bondage to foreign nations?

That would be better, beyond all comparison.

They must not, then, hold any Greek in slavery themselves, and they should advise the rest of Greece not to do so.

Certainly. Then they would be more likely to keep their hands off one another and turn their energies against foreigners.

Next, is it well to strip the dead, after a victory, of anything but their arms? It only gives cowards an excuse for not facing the living enemy, as if they were usefully   d employed in poking about over a dead body. Many an army has been lost through this pillaging. There is something mean and greedy in plundering a corpse; and a sort of womanish pettiness in treating the body as an enemy, when the spirit, the real enemy, has flown, leaving behind only the instrument with which he fought. It is to behave no better than a dog who growls at the stone that has hit him and leaves alone the man who threw it.

True.

So we will have no stripping of the slain and we shall not prevent their comrades from burying them. Nor shall we dedicate in the temples trophies of their weapons, least of all those of Greeks, if we are concerned to show loyalty towards the rest of Hellas. We shall rather be afraid of desecrating a sanctuary by bringing to it such spoils of our own people, unless indeed the Oracle should pronounce otherwise.

That is very right.

And what of ravaging Greek lands and burning houses? How will your soldiers deal with their enemies in this matter?

I should like to hear your own opinion.

I think they should do neither, but only carry off the year's harvest. Shall I tell you why?

Please do.

It seems to me that war and civil strife differ in nature as they do in name, according to the two spheres in which disputes may arise: at home or abroad, among men of the same race or with foreigners. War means fighting with a foreign enemy; when the enemy is of the same kindred, we call it civil strife.

That is a reasonable distinction.

Is it not also reasonable to assert that Greeks are a single people, all of the same kindred and alien to the outer world of foreigners?

Yes.

Then we shall speak of war when Greeks fight with foreigners, whom we may call their natural enemies. But Greeks are by nature friends of Greeks, and when they fight, it means that Hellas is afflicted by dissension which ought to be called civil strife.

I agree with that view.

Observe, then, that in what is commonly known as civil strife, that is to say, when one of our Greek states is divided against itself, it is thought an abominable outrage for either party to ravage the lands or burn the houses of the other. No lover of his country would dare to mangle the land which gave him birth and nursed him. It is thought fair that the victors should carry off the others' crops, but do no more. They should remember that the war will not last forever; some day they must make friends again.

That is a much more civilized state of mind.

Well then, is not this commonwealth you are founding a Greek state, and its citizens good and civilized people?

Very much so.

And lovers of Greece, who will think of all Hellas as their home, where they share in one common religion with the rest?

Most certainly.

Accordingly, the Greeks being their own people, a quarrel with them will not be called a war. It will only be civil strife, which they will carry on as men who will some day be reconciled. So they will not behave like a foreign enemy seeking to enslave or destroy, but will try to bring their adversaries to reason by well-meant correction. As Greeks they will not devastate the soil of Greece or burn the homesteads; nor will they allow that all the inhabitants of any state, men, women, and children, are their enemies, but only the few who are responsible for the quarrel. The greater number are friends, whose land and houses, on all these accounts, they will not consent to lay waste and b destroy. They will pursue the quarrel only until the guilty are compelled by the innocent sufferers to give satisfaction.

For my part, I agree that our citizens should treat their adversaries in that way, and deal with foreigners as Greeks now deal with one another.

We will make this a law, then, for our Guardians: they are not to ravage lands or c burn houses.

Yes, we will; it is as satisfactory as all our other laws.

But really, Socrates, Glaucon continued, if you are allowed to go on like this, I am afraid you will forget all about the question you thrust aside some time ago: whether a society so constituted can ever come into existence, and if so, how. No doubt, if it did exist, all manner of good things would come about. I can even add some that you have passed over. Men who acknowledged one another as fathers, sons, or d brothers and always used those names among themselves would never desert one another; so they would fight with unequaled bravery. And if their womenfolk went out with them to war, either in the ranks or drawn up in the rear to intimidate the enemy and act as a reserve in case of need, I am sure all this would make them invincible. At home, too, I can see many advantages you have not mentioned. But, since I admit that our commonwealth would have all these merits and any number more, if once it came e into existence, you need not describe it in further detail. All we have now to do is to convince ourselves that it can be brought into being and how.

This is a very sudden onslaught, said I; you have no mercy on my shilly-shally- 472 ing. Perhaps you do not realize that, after I have barely escaped the first two waves, the third, which you are now bringing down upon me, is the most formidable of all. When you have seen what it is like and heard my reply, you will be ready to excuse the very natural fears which made me shrink from putting forward such a paradox for discussion.

The more you talk like that, he said, the less we shall be willing to let you off from telling us how this constitution can come into existence; so you had better waste b no more time.

Well, said I, let me begin by reminding you that what brought us to this point was our inquiry into the nature of justice and injustice.

True; but what of that?

Merely this: suppose we do find out what justice is, are we going to demand that a man who is just shall have a character which exactly corresponds in every respect to the ideal of justice? Or shall we be satisfied if he comes as near to the ideal as possible and has in him a larger measure of that quality than the rest of the world? c

That will satisfy me.

If so, when we set out to discover the essential nature of justice and injustice and what a perfectly just and a perfectly unjust man would be like, supposing them to exist, our purpose was to use them as ideal patterns: we were to observe the degree of happiness or unhappiness that each exhibited, and to draw the necessary inference that our own destiny would be like that of the one we most resembled. We did not set out to show that these ideals could exist in fact. d

That is true.

Then suppose a painter had drawn an ideally beautiful figure complete to the last touch, would you think any the worse of him, if he could not show that a person as beautiful as that could exist?

No, I should not.

e   Well, we have been constructing in discourse the pattern of an ideal state. Is our theory any the worse, if we cannot prove it possible that a state so organized should be actually founded?

Surely not.

That, then, is the truth of the matter. But if, for your satisfaction, I am to do my best to show under what conditions our ideal would have the best chance of being real-
473 ized, I must ask you once more to admit that the same principle applies here. Can theory ever be fully realized in practice? Is it not in the nature of things that action should come less close to truth than thought? People may not think so; but do you agree or not?

I do.

Then you must not insist upon my showing that this construction we have traced in thought could be reproduced in fact down to the last detail. You must admit that we shall have found a way to meet your demand for realization, if we can discover how a
b   state might be constituted in the closest accordance with our description. Will not that content you? It would be enough for me.

And for me too.

Then our next attempt, it seems, must be to point out what defect in the working of existing states prevents them from being so organized, and what is the least change that would effect a transformation into this type of government—a single change if possible, or perhaps two; at any rate let us make the changes as few and insignificant as may be.

c   By all means.

Well, there is one change which, as I believe we can show, would bring about this revolution—not a small change, certainly, nor an easy one, but possible.

What is it?

I have now to confront what we called the third and greatest wave. But I must state my paradox, even though the wave should break in laughter over my head and drown me in ignominy. Now mark what I am going to say.

Go on.

Unless either philosophers become kings in their countries or those who are now called kings and rulers come to be sufficiently inspired with a genuine desire for wis-
d   dom; unless, that is to say, political power and philosophy meet together, while the many natures who now go their several ways in the one or the other direction are
e   forcibly debarred from doing so, there can be no rest from troubles, my dear Glaucon, for states, nor yet, as I believe, for all mankind; nor can this commonwealth which we have imagined ever till then see the light of day and grow to its full stature. This it was that I have so long hung back from saying; I knew what a paradox it would be, because it is hard to see that there is no other way of happiness either for the state or for the individual.

Socrates, exclaimed Glaucon, after delivering yourself of such a pronouncement as that, you must expect a whole multitude of by no means contemptible assailants to fling off their coats, snatch up the handiest weapon, and make a rush at you, breathing
474   fire and slaughter. If you cannot find arguments to beat them off and make your escape, you will learn what it means to be the target of scorn and derision.

Well, it was you who got me into this trouble.

Yes, and a good thing too. However, I will not leave you in the lurch. You shall have my friendly encouragement for what it is worth; and perhaps you may find me

more complaisant than some would be in answering your questions. With such backing   b
you must try to convince the unbelievers.

I will, now that I have such a powerful ally.

Now, I continued, if we are to elude those assailants you have described, we
must, I think, define for them whom we mean by these lovers of wisdom who, we have
dared to assert, ought to be our rulers. Once we have a clear view of their character, we
shall be able to defend our position by pointing to some who are naturally fitted to   c
combine philosophic study with political leadership, while the rest of the world should
accept their guidance and let philosophy alone.

Yes, this is the moment for a definition.

Here, then, is a line of thought which may lead to a satisfactory explanation.
Need I remind you that a man will deserve to be called a lover of this or that, only if it
is clear that he loves that thing as a whole, not merely in parts?

You must remind me, it seems; for I do not see what you mean.   d

That answer would have come better from someone less susceptible to love than
yourself, Glaucon. You ought not to have forgotten that any boy in the bloom of youth
will arouse some sting of passion in a man of your amorous temperament and seem
worthy of his attentions. Is not this your way with your favourites? You will praise a
snub nose as piquant and a hooked one as giving a regal air, while you call a straight   e
nose perfectly proportioned; the swarthy, you say, have a manly look, the fair are children of the gods; and what do you think is that word "honey-pale," if not the eu-
phemism of some lover who had no fault to find with sallowness on the cheek of
youth? In a word, you will carry pretence and extravagance to any length sooner than   475
reject a single one that is in the flower of his prime.

If you insist on taking me as an example of how lovers behave, I will agree for
the sake of argument.

Again, do you not see the same behaviour in people with a passion for wine?
They are glad of any excuse to drink wine of any sort. And there are the men who
covet honour, who, if they cannot lead an army, will command a company, and if they   b
cannot win the respect of important people, are glad to be looked up to by nobodies,
because they must have someone to esteem them.

Quite true.

Do you agree, then, that when we speak of a man as having a passion for a certain kind of thing, we mean that he has an appetite for everything of that kind without
discrimination?

Yes.

So the philosopher, with his passion for wisdom, will be one who desires all wisdom, not only some part of it. If a student is particular about his studies, especially
while he is too young to know which are useful and which are not, we shall say he is   c
no lover of learning or of wisdom; just as, if he were dainty about his food, we should
say he was not hungry or fond of eating, but had a poor appetite. Only the man who
has a taste for every sort of knowledge and throws himself into acquiring it with an insatiable curiosity will deserve to be called a philosopher. Am I not right?

That description, Glaucon replied, would include a large and ill assorted com-   d
pany. It is curiosity, I suppose, and a delight in fresh experience that gives some people
a passion for all that is to be seen and heard at theatrical and musical performances.
But they are a queer set to reckon among philosophers, considering that they would
never go near anything like a philosophical discussion, though they run round at all the
Dionysiac festivals in town or country as if they were under contract to listen to every

company of performers without fail. Will curiosity entitle all these enthusiasts, not to mention amateurs of the minor arts, to be called philosophers?

Certainly not; though they have a certain counterfeit resemblance.

And whom do you mean by the genuine philosophers?

Those whose passion it is to see the truth.

That must be so; but will you explain?

It would not be easy to explain to everyone; but you, I believe, will grant my premise.

Which is—?

That since beauty and ugliness are opposite, they are two things; and consequently each of them is one. The same holds of justice and injustice, good and bad, and all the essential Forms: each in itself is one; but they manifest themselves in a great variety of combinations, with actions, with material things, and with one another, and so each seems to be many.

That is true.

On the strength of this premise, then, I can distinguish your amateurs of the arts and men of action from the philosophers we are concerned with, who are alone worthy of the name.

What is your distinction?

Your lovers of sights and sounds delight in beautiful tones and colours and shapes and in all the works of art into which these enter; but they have not the power of thought to behold and to take delight in the nature of Beauty itself. That power to approach Beauty and behold it as it is in itself, is rare indeed.

Quite true.

Now if a man believes in the existence of beautiful things, but not of Beauty itself, and cannot follow a guide who would lead him to a knowledge of it, is he not living in a dream? Consider: does not dreaming, whether one is awake or asleep, consist in mistaking a semblance for the reality it resembles?

I should certainly call that dreaming.

Contrast with him the man who holds that there is such a thing as Beauty itself and can discern that essence as well as the things that partake of its character, without ever confusing the one with the other—is he a dreamer or living in a waking state?

He is very much awake.

So may we say that he knows, while the other has only a belief in appearances; and might we call their states of mind knowledge and belief?

Certainly.

But this person who, we say, has only belief without knowledge may be aggrieved and challenge our statement. Is there any means of soothing his resentment and converting him gently, without telling him plainly that he is not in his right mind?

We surely ought to try.

Come then, consider what we are to say to him. Or shall we ask him a question, assuring him that, far from grudging him any knowledge he may have, we shall be only too glad to find that there is something he knows? But, we shall say, tell us this: When a man knows, must there not be something that he knows? Will you answer for him, Glaucon?

My answer will be, that there must.

Something real or unreal?

Something real; how could a thing that is unreal ever be known?

Are we satisfied, then, on this point, from however many points of view we might examine it: that the perfectly real is perfectly knowable, and the utterly unreal is entirely unknowable?

Quite satisfied.

Good. Now if there is something so constituted that it both *is* and *is not,* will it not lie between the purely real and the utterly unreal?

It will.

Well then, as knowledge corresponds to the real, and absence of knowledge necessarily to the unreal, so, to correspond to this intermediate thing, we must look for   b
something between ignorance and knowledge, if such a thing there be.

Certainly.

Is there not a thing we call belief?

Surely.

A different power from knowledge, or the same?

Different.

Knowledge and belief, then, must have different objects, answering to their respective powers.

Yes.

And knowledge has for its natural object the real—to know the truth about reality. However, before going further, I think we need a definition. Shall we distinguish   c
under the general name of "faculties" those powers which enable us—or anything else—to do what we can do? Sight and hearing, for instance, are what I call faculties, if that will help you to see the class of things I have in mind.

Yes, I understand.

Then let me tell you what view I take of them. In a faculty I cannot find any of those qualities, such as colour or shape, which, in the case of many other things, enable me to distinguish one thing from another. I can only look to its field of objects and the state of mind it produces, and regard these as sufficient to identify it and to distinguish   d
it from faculties which have different fields and produce different states. Is that how you would go to work?

Yes.

Let us go back, then, to knowledge. Would you class that as a faculty?

Yes; and I should call it the most powerful of all.

And is belief also a faculty?   e

It can be nothing else, since it is what gives us the power of believing.

But a little while ago you agreed that knowledge and belief are not the same thing.

Yes; there could be no sense in identifying the infallible with the fallible.

Good. So we are quite clear that knowledge and belief are different things?   478

They are.

If so, each of them, having a different power, must have a different field of objects.

Necessarily.

The field of knowledge being the real; and its power, the power of knowing the real as it is.

Yes.

Whereas belief, we say, is the power of believing. Is its object the same as that which knowledge knows? Can the same things be possible objects both of knowledge and of belief?

b   Not if we hold to the principles we agreed upon. If it is of the nature of a different faculty to have a different field, and if both knowledge and belief are faculties and, as we assert, different ones, it follows that the same things cannot be possible objects of both.

So if the real is the object of knowledge, the object of belief must be something other than the real.

Yes.

c   Can it be the unreal? Or is that an impossible object even for belief? Consider: if a man has a belief, there must be something before his mind; he cannot be believing nothing, can he?

No.

He is believing something, then; whereas the unreal could only be called nothing at all.

Certainly.

Now we said that ignorance must correspond to the unreal, knowledge to the real. So what he is believing cannot be real nor yet unreal.

True.

Belief, then, cannot be either ignorance or knowledge.

It appears not.

d   Then does it lie outside and beyond these two? Is it either more clear and certain than knowledge or less clear and certain than ignorance?

No, it is neither.

It rather seems to you to be something more obscure than knowledge, but not so dark as ignorance, and so to lie between the two extremes?

Quite so.

Well, we said earlier that if some object could be found such that it both *is* and at the same time *is not,* that object would lie between the perfectly real and the utterly unreal; and that the corresponding faculty would be neither knowledge nor ignorance, but a faculty to be found situated between the two.

Yes.

And now what we have found between the two is the faculty we call belief.

True.

e   It seems, then, that what remains to be discovered is that object which can be said both to be and not to be and cannot properly be called either purely real or purely unreal. If that can be found, we may justly call it the object of belief, and so give the intermediate faculty the intermediate object, while the two extreme objects will fall to the extreme faculties.

Yes.

479   On these assumptions, then, I shall call for an answer from our friend who denies the existence of Beauty itself or of anything that can be called an essential Form of Beauty remaining unchangeably in the same state forever, though he does recognize the existence of beautiful things as a plurality—that lover of things seen who will not listen to anyone who says that Beauty is one, Justice is one, and so on. I shall say to him, Be so good as to tell us: of all these many beautiful things is there one which will not appear ugly? Or of these many just or righteous actions, is there one that will not appear unjust or unrighteous?

b   No, replied Glaucon, they must inevitably appear to be in some way both beautiful and ugly; and so with all the other terms your question refers to.

And again the many things which are doubles are just as much halves as they are doubles. And the things we call large or heavy have just as much right to be called small or light.

Yes; any such thing will always have a claim to both opposite designations.

Then, whatever any one of these many things may be said to be, can you say that it absolutely *is* that, any more than that it *is not* that?

They remind me of those punning riddles people ask at dinner parties, or the child's puzzle about what the eunuch threw at the bat and what the bat was perched on. These c things have the same ambiguous character, and one cannot form any stable conception of them either as being or as not being, or as both being and not being, or as neither.

Can you think of any better way of disposing of them than by placing them between reality and unreality? For I suppose they will not appear more obscure and so less real than unreality, or clearer and so more real than reality. d

Quite true.

It seems, then, we have discovered that the many conventional notions of the mass of mankind about what is beautiful or honourable or just and so on are adrift in a sort of twilight between pure reality and pure unreality.

We have.

And we agreed earlier that, if any such object were discovered, it should be called the object of belief and not of knowledge. Fluctuating in that half-way region, it would be seized upon by the intermediate faculty.

Yes.

So when people have an eye for the multitude of beautiful things or of just actions or whatever it may be, but can neither behold Beauty or Justice itself nor follow a guide who would lead them to it, we shall say that all they have is beliefs, without any real knowledge of the objects of their belief.

That follows.

But what of those who contemplate the realities themselves as they are forever in the same unchanging state? Shall we not say that they have, not mere belief, but knowledge?

That too follows.

And, further, that their affection goes out to the objects of knowledge, whereas the others set their affections on the objects of belief; for it was they, you remember, 480 who had a passion for the spectacle of beautiful colours and sounds, but would not hear of Beauty itself being a real thing.

I remember.

So we may fairly call them lovers of belief rather than of wisdom—not philosophical, in fact, but philodoxical. Will they be seriously annoyed by that description?

Not if they will listen to my advice. No one ought to take offence at the truth.

The name of philosopher, then, will be reserved for those whose affections are set, in every case, on the reality.

By all means.

BOOK VI

*   *   *

One difficulty, then, has been surmounted. It remains to ask how we can make sure of having men who will preserve our constitution. What must they learn, and at 502^d what age should they take up each branch of study?

Yes, that is the next point.

I gained nothing by my cunning in putting off those thorny questions of the possession of wives and children and the appointment of Rulers. I knew that the ideal plan
would give offence and be hard to carry out; none the less I have had to discuss these
matters. We have now disposed of the women and children, but we must start all over
again upon the training of the Rulers. You remember how their love for their country was
to be proved, by the tests of pain and pleasure, to be a faith that no toil or danger, no turn
of fortune could make them abandon. All who failed were to be rejected; only the man
who came out flawless, like gold tried in the fire, was to be made a Ruler with privileges
and rewards in life and after death. So much was said, when our argument turned aside,
as if hoping, with veiled face, to slip past the danger that now lies in our path.

Quite true, I remember.

Yes, I shrank from the bold words which have now been spoken; but now we
have ventured to declare that our Guardians in the fullest sense must be philosophers.
So much being granted, you must reflect how few are likely to be available. The natural gifts we required will rarely grow together into one whole; they tend to split apart.

How do you mean?

Qualities like ready understanding, a good memory, sagacity, quickness, together with a high-spirited, generous temper, are seldom combined with willingness to
live a quiet life of sober constancy. Keen wits are apt to lose all steadiness and to veer
about in every direction. On the other hand, the steady reliable characters, whose im-
passivity is proof against the perils of war, are equally proof against instruction. Confronted with intellectual work, they become comatose and do nothing but yawn.

That is true.

But we insist that no one must be given the highest education or hold office as
Ruler, who has not both sets of qualities in due measure. This combination will be rare.
So, besides testing it by hardship and danger and by the temptations of pleasure, we
may now add that its strength must be tried in many forms of study, to see whether it
has the courage and endurance to pursue the highest kind of knowledge, without
flinching as others flinch under physical trials.

By all means; but what kinds of study do you call the highest?

You remember how we deduced the definitions of justice, temperance, courage,
and wisdom by distinguishing three parts of the soul?

If I had forgotten that, I should not deserve to hear any more.

Do you also remember my warning you beforehand that in order to gain the
clearest possible view of these qualities we should have to go round a longer way, although we could give a more superficial account in keeping with our earlier argument.
You said that would do; and so we went on in a way which seemed to me not sufficiently exact; whether you were satisfied, it is for you to say.

We all thought you gave us a fair measure of truth.

No measure that falls in the least degree short of the whole truth can be quite fair
in so important a matter. What is imperfect can never serve as a measure; though people sometimes think enough has been done and there is no need to look further.

Yes, indolence is common enough.

But the last quality to be desired in the Guardian of a commonwealth and its
laws. So he will have to take the longer way and work as hard at learning as at training
his body; otherwise he will never reach the goal of the highest knowledge, which most
of all concerns him.

Why, are not justice and the other virtues we have discussed the highest? Is there
something still higher to be known?

There is; and of those virtues themselves we have as yet only a rough outline, where nothing short of the finished picture should content us. If we strain every nerve   e
to reach precision and clearness in things of little moment, how absurd not to demand the highest degree of exactness in the things that matter most.

Certainly. But what do you mean by the highest kind of knowledge and with what is it concerned? You cannot hope to escape that question.

I do not; you may ask me yourself. All the same, you have been told many a time; but now either you are not thinking or, as I rather suspect, you mean to put me to   505
some trouble with your insistence. For you have often been told that the highest object of knowledge is the essential nature of the Good, from which everything that is good and right derives its value for us. You must have been expecting me to speak of this now, and to add that we have no sufficient knowledge of it. I need not tell you that, without that knowledge, to know everything else, however well, would be of no value to us, just as it is of no use to possess anything without getting the good of it. What advantage can there be in possessing everything except what is good, or in understanding   b
everything else while of the good and desirable we know nothing?

None whatever.

Well then, you know too that most people identify the Good with pleasure, whereas the more enlightened think it is knowledge.

Yes, of course.

And further that these latter cannot tell us what knowledge they mean, but are reduced at last to saying, "knowledge of the Good."

That is absurd.   c

It is; first they reproach us with not knowing the Good, and then tell us that it is knowledge of the Good, as if we did after all understand the meaning of that word "Good" when they pronounce it.

Quite true.

What of those who define the Good as pleasure? Are they any less confused in their thoughts? They are obliged to admit that there are bad pleasures; from which it follows that the same things are both good and bad.

Quite so.

Evidently, then, this is a matter of much dispute. It is also evident that, although   d
many are content to do what seems just or honourable without really being so, and to possess a mere semblance of these qualities, when it comes to good things, no one is   e
satisfied with possessing what only seems good: here all reject the appearance and demand the reality.

Certainly.

A thing, then, that every soul pursues as the end of all her actions, dimly divining its existence, but perplexed and unable to grasp its nature with the same clearness and assurance as in dealing with other things, and so missing whatever value those other things might have—a thing of such supreme importance is not a matter about which those cho-   506
sen Guardians of the whole fortunes of our commonwealth can be left in the dark.

Most certainly not.

At any rate, institutions or customs which are desirable and right will not, I imagine, find a very efficient guardian in one who does not know in what way they are good. I should rather guess that he will not be able to recognize fully that they are right and desirable.

No doubt.

So the order of our commonwealth will be perfectly regulated only when it is   b
watched over by a Guardian who does possess this knowledge.

That follows. But, Socrates, what is your own account of the Good? Is it knowledge, or pleasure, or something else?

There you are! I exclaimed; I could see all along that you were not going to be content with what other people think.

Well, Socrates, it does not seem fair that you should be ready to repeat other people's opinions but not to state your own, when you have given so much thought to this subject.

c   And do you think it fair of anyone to speak as if he knew what he does not know?

No, not as if he knew, but he might give his opinion for what it is worth.

Why, have you never noticed that opinion without knowledge is always a shabby sort of thing? At the best it is blind. One who holds a true belief without intelligence is just like a blind man who happens to take the right road, isn't he?

No doubt.

d   Well, then, do you want me to produce one of these poor blind cripples, when others could discourse to you with illuminating eloquence?

No, really, Socrates, said Glaucon, you must not give up within sight of the goal. We should be quite content with an account of the Good like the one you gave us of justice and temperance and the other virtues.

So should I be, my dear Glaucon, much more than content! But I am afraid it is beyond my powers; with the best will in the world I should only disgrace myself and

e   be laughed at. No, for the moment let us leave the question of the real meaning of good; to arrive at what I at any rate believe it to be would call for an effort too ambitious for an inquiry like ours. However, I will tell you, though only if you wish it, what I picture to myself as the offspring of the Good and the thing most nearly resembling it.

Well, tell us about the offspring, and you shall remain in our debt for an account of the parent.

507   I only wish it were within my power to offer, and within yours to receive, a settlement of the whole account. But you must be content now with the interest only; and you must see to it that, in describing this offspring of the Good, I do not inadvertently cheat you with false coin.

We will keep a good eye on you. Go on.

First we must come to an understanding. Let me remind you of the distinction we

b   drew earlier and have often drawn on other occasions, between the multiplicity of things that we call good or beautiful or whatever it may be and, on the other hand, Goodness itself or Beauty itself and so on. Corresponding to each of these sets of many things, we postulate a single Form or real essence, as we call it.

Yes, that is so.

Further, the many things, we say, can be seen, but are not objects of rational thought; whereas the Forms are objects of thought, but invisible.

c   Yes, certainly.

And we see things with our eyesight, just as we hear sounds with our ears and, to speak generally, perceive any sensible thing with our sense-faculties.

Of course.

Have you noticed, then, that the artificer who designed the senses has been exceptionally lavish of his materials in making the eyes able to see and their objects visible?

That never occurred to me.

Well, look at it in this way. Hearing and sound do not stand in need of any third

d   thing, without which the ear will not hear nor sound be heard; and I think the same is true of most, not to say all, of the other senses. Can you think of one that does require anything of the sort?

No, I cannot.

But there is this need in the case of sight and its objects. You may have the power of vision in your eyes and try to use it, and colour may be there in the objects; but sight will see nothing and the colours will remain invisible in the absence of a third   e
thing peculiarly constituted to serve this very purpose.

By which you mean—?

Naturally I mean what you call light; and if light is a thing of value, the sense of sight and the power of being visible are linked together by a very precious bond, such   508
as unites no other sense with its object.

No one could say that light is not a precious thing.

And of all the divinities in the skies is there one whose light, above all the rest, is responsible for making our eyes see perfectly and making objects perfectly visible?

There can be no two opinions: of course you mean the Sun.

And how is sight related to this deity? Neither sight nor the eye which contains it is the Sun, but of all the sense-organs it is the most sun-like; and further, the power it   b
possesses is dispensed by the Sun, like a stream flooding the eye. And again, the Sun is not vision, but it is the cause of vision and also is seen by the vision it causes.

Yes.

It was the Sun, then, that I meant when I spoke of that offspring which the Good has created in the visible world, to stand there in the same relation to vision and visible things as that which the Good itself bears in the intelligible world to intelligence and to   c
intelligible objects.

How is that? You must explain further.

You know what happens when the colours of things are no longer irradiated by the daylight, but only by the fainter luminaries of the night: when you look at them, the eyes are dim and seem almost blind, as if there were no unclouded vision in them. But   d
when you look at things on which the Sun is shining, the same eyes see distinctly and it becomes evident that they do contain the power of vision.

Certainly.

Apply this comparison, then, to the soul. When its gaze is fixed upon an object irradiated by truth and reality, the soul gains understanding and knowledge and is manifestly in possession of intelligence. But when it looks towards that twilight world of things that come into existence and pass away, its sight is dim and it has only opinions and beliefs which shift to and fro, and now it seems like a thing that has no intelligence.

That is true.

This, then, which gives to the objects of knowledge their truth and to him who knows them his power of knowing, is the Form or essential nature of Goodness. It is   e
the cause of knowledge and truth; and so, while you may think of it as an object of knowledge, you will do well to regard it as something beyond truth and knowledge and, precious as these both are, of still higher worth. And, just as in our analogy light and vision were to be thought of as like the Sun, but not identical with it, so here both   509
knowledge and truth are to be regarded as like the Good, but to identify either with the Good is wrong. The Good must hold a yet higher place of honour.

You are giving it a position of extraordinary splendour, if it is the source of knowledge and truth and itself surpasses them in worth. You surely cannot mean that it is pleasure.

Heaven forbid, I exclaimed. But I want to follow up our analogy still further.   b
You will agree that the Sun not only makes the things we see visible, but also brings

them into existence and gives them growth and nourishment; yet he is not the same thing as existence. And so with the objects of knowledge: these derive from the Good not only their power of being known, but their very being and reality; and Goodness is not the same thing as being, but even beyond being, surpassing it in dignity and power.

c   Glaucon exclaimed with some amusement at my exalting Goodness in such extravagant terms.

It is your fault, I replied; you forced me to say what I think.

Yes, and you must not stop there. At any rate, complete your comparison with the Sun, if there is any more to be said.

There is a great deal more, I answered.

Let us hear it, then; don't leave anything out.

I am afraid much must be left unspoken. However, I will not, if I can help it, leave out anything that can be said on this occasion.

Please do not.

d   Conceive, then, that there are these two powers I speak of, the Good reigning over the domain of all that is intelligible, the Sun over the visible world—or the heaven as I might call it; only you would think I was showing off my skill in etymology. At any rate you have these two orders of things clearly before your mind: the visible and the intelligible?

I have.

Now take a line divided into two unequal parts, one to represent the visible order, the other the intelligible; and divide each part again in the same proportion,

e   symbolizing degrees of comparative clearness or obscurity. Then (A) one of the two
510   sections in the visible world will stand for images. By images I mean first shadows, and then reflections in water or in close-grained, polished surfaces, and everything of that kind, if you understand.

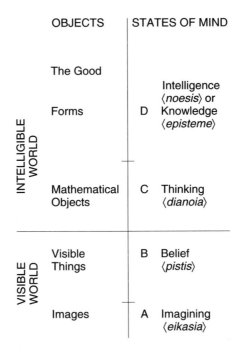

Yes, I understand.

Let the second section (B) stand for the actual things of which the first are likenesses, the living creatures about us and all the works of nature or of human hands.

So be it.

Will you also take the proportion in which the visible world has been divided as corresponding to degrees of reality and truth, so that the likeness shall stand to the original in the same ratio as the sphere of appearances and belief to the sphere of knowledge?

Certainly.   b

Now consider how we are to divide the part which stands for the intelligible world. There are two sections. In the first (C) the mind uses as images those actual things which themselves had images in the visible world; and it is compelled to pursue its inquiry by starting from assumptions and travelling, not up to a principle, but down to a conclusion. In the second (D) the mind moves in the other direction, from an assumption up towards a principle which is not hypothetical; and it makes no use of the images employed in the other section, but only of Forms, and conducts its inquiry solely by their means.

I don't quite understand what you mean.

Then we will try again; what I have just said will help you to understand. (C)   c
You know, of course, how students of subjects like geometry and arithmetic begin by postulating odd and even numbers, or the various figures and the three kinds of angle, and other such data in each subject. These data they take as known; and, having adopted them as assumptions, they do not feel called upon to give any account of them to themselves or to anyone else, but treat them as self-evident. Then, starting from these assumptions, they go on until they arrive, by a series of consistent steps, at all the   d
conclusions they set out to investigate.

Yes, I know that.

You also know how they make use of visible figures and discourse about them, though what they really have in mind is the originals of which these figures are images: they are not reasoning, for instance, about this particular square and diagonal which they have drawn, but about *the* Square and *the* Diagonal; and so in all cases. The diagrams they draw and the models they make are actual things, which may have their   e
shadows or images in water; but now they serve in their turn as images, while the student is seeking to behold those realities which only thought can apprehend.

True.   511

This, then, is the class of things that I spoke of as intelligible, but with two qualifications: first, that the mind, in studying them, is compelled to employ assumptions, and, because it cannot rise above these, does not travel upwards to a first principle; and second, that it uses as images those actual things which have images of their own in the section below them and which, in comparison with those shadows and reflections, are reputed to be more palpable and valued accordingly.

I understand: you mean the subject-matter of geometry and of the kindred arts.   b

(D) Then by the second section of the intelligible world you may understand me to mean all that unaided reasoning apprehends by the power of dialectic, when it treats its assumptions, not as first principles, but as *hypotheses* in the literal sense, things "laid down" like a flight of steps up which it may mount all the way to something that is not hypothetical, the first principle of all; and having grasped this, may turn back and, holding on to the consequences which depend upon it, descend at last to a conclusion, never making use of any sensible object, but only of Forms, moving through   c
Forms from one to another, and ending with Forms.

I understand, he said, though not perfectly; for the procedure you describe sounds like an enormous undertaking. But I see that you mean to distinguish the field of intelligible reality studied by dialectic as having a greater certainty and truth than the subject-matter of the "arts," as they are called, which treat their assumptions as first principles. The students of these arts are, it is true, compelled to exercise thought in contemplating objects which the senses cannot perceive; but because they start from assumptions without going back to a first principle, you do not regard them as gaining true understanding about those objects, although the objects themselves, when connected with a first principle, are intelligible. And I think you would call the state of mind of the students of geometry and other such arts, not intelligence, but thinking, as being something between intelligence and mere acceptance of appearances.

d

You have understood me quite well enough, I replied. And now you may take, as corresponding to the four sections, these four states of mind: *intelligence* for the highest, *thinking* for the second, *belief* for the third, and for the last *imagining*. These you may arrange as the terms in a proportion, assigning to each a degree of clearness and certainty corresponding to the measure in which their objects possess truth and reality.

e

I understand and agree with you. I will arrange them as you say.

Book VII

514   Next, said I, here is a parable to illustrate the degrees in which our nature may be enlightened or unenlightened. Imagine the condition of men living in a sort of cavernous chamber underground, with an entrance open to the light and a long passage all down the cave. Here they have been from childhood, chained by the leg and also by the neck, so that they cannot move and can see only what is in front of them, because the chains will not let them turn their heads. At some distance higher up is the light of a fire burning behind them; and between the prisoners and the fire is a track with a parapet built along it, like the screen at a puppet-show, which hides the performers while they show their puppets over the top.

b

I see, said he.

Now behind this parapet imagine persons carrying along various artificial objects, including figures of men and animals in wood or stone or other materials, which project above the parapet. Naturally, some of these persons will be talking, others silent.

c
515

It is a strange picture, he said, and a strange sort of prisoners.

Like ourselves, I replied; for in the first place prisoners so confined would have seen nothing of themselves or of one another, except the shadows thrown by the fire-light on the wall of the Cave facing them, would they?

b

Not if all their lives they had been prevented from moving their heads.

And they would have seen as little of the objects carried past.

Of course.

Now, if they could talk to one another, would they not suppose that their words referred only to those passing shadows which they saw?

Necessarily.

And suppose their prison had an echo from the wall facing them? When one of the people crossing behind them spoke, they could only suppose that the sound came from the shadow passing before their eyes.

No doubt.

In every way, then, such prisoners would recognize as reality nothing but the   c
shadows of those artificial objects.

Inevitably.

Now consider what would happen if their release from the chains and the healing
of their unwisdom should come about in this way. Suppose one of them were set free
and forced suddenly to stand up, turn his head, and walk with eyes lifted to the light; all
these movements would be painful, and he would be too dazzled to make out the objects
whose shadows he had been used to seeing. What do you think he would say, if someone told him that what he had formerly seen was meaningless illusion, but now, being
somewhat nearer to reality and turned towards more real objects, he was getting a truer   d
view? Suppose further that he were shown the various objects being carried by and were
made to say, in reply to questions, what each of them was. Would he not be perplexed
and believe the objects now shown him to be not so real as what he formerly saw?

Yes, not nearly so real.

And if he were forced to look at the firelight itself, would not his eyes ache, so   e
that he would try to escape and turn back to the things which he could see distinctly,
convinced that they really were clearer than these other objects now being shown to
him?

Yes.

And suppose someone were to drag him away forcibly up the steep and rugged
ascent and not let him go until he had hauled him out into the sunlight, would he not
suffer pain and vexation at such treatment, and, when he had come out into the light,
find his eyes so full of its radiance that he could not see a single one of the things that   516
he was now told were real?

Certainly he would not see them all at once.

He would need, then, to grow accustomed before he could see things in that
upper world. At first it would be easiest to make out shadows, and then the images of
men and things reflected in water, and later on the things themselves. After that, it
would be easier to watch the heavenly bodies and the sky itself by night, looking at the   b
light of the moon and stars rather than the Sun and the Sun's light in the day-time.

Yes, surely.

Last of all, he would be able to look at the Sun and contemplate its nature, not as
it appears when reflected in water or any alien medium, but as it is in itself in its own
domain.

No doubt.

And now he would begin to draw the conclusion that it is the Sun that produces
the seasons and the course of the year and controls everything in the visible world, and
moreover is in a way the cause of all that he and his companions used to see.   c

Clearly he would come at last to that conclusion.

Then if he called to mind his fellow prisoners and what passed for wisdom in his
former dwelling-place, he would surely think himself happy in the change and be sorry
for them. They may have had a practice of honouring and commending one another,
with prizes for the man who had the keenest eye for the passing shadows and the best
memory for the order in which they followed or accompanied one another, so that he   d
could make a good guess as to which was going to come next. Would our released
prisoner be likely to covet those prizes or to envy the men exalted to honour and power
in the Cave? Would he not feel like Homer's Achilles, that he would far sooner "be on
earth as a hired servant in the house of a landless man" or endure anything rather than
go back to his old beliefs and live in the old way?

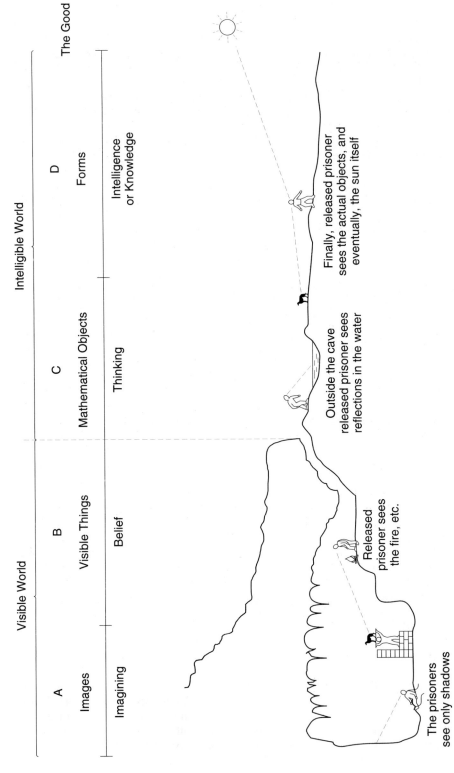

Visible World		Intelligible World	
A	B	C	D
Images	Visible Things	Mathematical Objects	Forms
Imagining	Belief	Thinking	Intelligence or Knowledge

The Good

Finally, released prisoner sees the actual objects, and eventually, the sun itself

Outside the cave released prisoner sees reflections in the water

Released prisoner sees the fire, etc.

The prisoners see only shadows

Adapted from N. Jordan, *Western Philosophy: From Antiquity to the Middle Ages* (New York: Macmillan, 1987), p. 95.

Yes, he would prefer any fate to such a life.

Now imagine what would happen if he went down again to take his former seat in the Cave. Coming suddenly out of the sunlight, his eyes would be filled with darkness. He might be required once more to deliver his opinion on those shadows, in competition with the prisoners who had never been released, while his eyesight was still dim and unsteady; and it might take some time to become used to the darkness. They would laugh at him and say that he had gone up only to come back with his sight ruined; it was worth no one's while even to attempt the ascent. If they could lay hands on the man who was trying to set them free and lead them up, they would kill him.

Yes, they would.

Every feature in this parable, my dear Glaucon, is meant to fit our earlier analysis. The prison dwelling corresponds to the region revealed to us through the sense of sight, and the firelight within it to the power of the Sun. The ascent to see the things in the upper world you may take as standing for the upward journey of the soul into the region of the intelligible; then you will be in possession of what I surmise, since that is what you wish to be told. Heaven knows whether it is true; but this, at any rate, is how it appears to me. In the world of knowledge, the last thing to be perceived and only with great difficulty is the essential Form of Goodness. Once it is perceived, the conclusion must follow that, for all things, this is the cause of whatever is right and good; in the visible world it gives birth to light and to the lord of light, while it is itself sovereign in the intelligible world and the parent of intelligence and truth. Without having had a vision of this Form no one can act with wisdom, either in his own life or in matters of state.

So far as I can understand, I share your belief.

Then you may also agree that it is no wonder if those who have reached this height are reluctant to manage the affairs of men. Their souls long to spend all their time in that upper world—naturally enough, if here once more our parable holds true. Nor, again, is it at all strange that one who comes from the contemplation of divine things to the miseries of human life should appear awkward and ridiculous when, with eyes still dazed and not yet accustomed to the darkness, he is compelled, in a law-court or elsewhere, to dispute about the shadows of justice or the images that cast those shadows, and to wrangle over the notions of what is right in the minds of men who have never beheld Justice itself.

It is not at all strange.

No; a sensible man will remember that the eyes may be confused in two ways—by a change from light to darkness or from darkness to light; and he will recognize that the same thing happens to the soul. When he sees it troubled and unable to discern anything clearly, instead of laughing thoughtlessly, he will ask whether, coming from a brighter existence, its unaccustomed vision is obscured by the darkness, in which case he will think its condition enviable and its life a happy one; or whether, emerging from the depths of ignorance, it is dazzled by excess of light. If so, he will rather feel sorry for it; or, if he were inclined to laugh, that would be less ridiculous than to laugh at the soul which has come down from the light.

That is a fair statement.

If this is true, then, we must conclude that education is not what it is said to be by some, who profess to put knowledge into a soul which does not possess it, as if they could put sight into blind eyes. On the contrary, our own account signifies that the soul of every man does possess the power of learning the truth and the organ to see it with; and that, just as one might have to turn the whole body round in order that the eye should see light instead of darkness, so the entire soul must be turned away from this

changing world, until its eye can bear to contemplate reality and that supreme splen-
d   dour which we have called the Good. Hence there may well be an art whose aim would
be to effect this very thing, the conversion of the soul, in the readiest way; not to put
the power of sight into the soul's eye, which already has it, but to ensure that, instead
of looking in the wrong direction, it is turned the way it ought to be.

Yes, it may well be so.

It looks, then, as though wisdom were different from those ordinary virtues, as
they are called, which are not far removed from bodily qualities, in that they can be
produced by habituation and exercise in a soul which has not possessed them from the
e   first. Wisdom, it seems, is certainly the virtue of some diviner faculty, which never
loses its power, though its use for good or harm depends on the direction towards
519 which it is turned. You must have noticed in dishonest men with a reputation for
sagacity the shrewd glance of a narrow intelligence piercing the objects to which it is
directed. There is nothing wrong with their power of vision, but it has been forced into
the service of evil, so that the keener its sight, the more harm it works.

Quite true.

And yet if the growth of a nature like this had been pruned from earliest child-
b   hood, cleared of those clinging overgrowths which come of gluttony and all luxurious
pleasure and, like leaden weights charged with affinity to this mortal world, hang upon
the soul, bending its vision downwards; if, freed from these, the soul were turned
round towards true reality, then this same power in these very men would see the truth
as keenly as the objects it is turned to now.

Yes, very likely.

Is it not also likely, or indeed certain after what has been said, that a state can
never be properly governed either by the uneducated who know nothing of truth or by
c   men who are allowed to spend all their days in the pursuit of culture? The ignorant
have no single mark before their eyes at which they must aim in all the conduct of their
own lives and of affairs of state; and the others will not engage in action if they can
help it, dreaming that, while still alive, they have been translated to the Islands of the
Blest.

Quite true.

It is for us, then, as founders of a commonwealth, to bring compulsion to bear on
the noblest natures. They must be made to climb the ascent to the vision of Goodness,
d   which we called the highest object of knowledge; and, when they have looked upon it
long enough, they must not be allowed, as they now are, to remain on the heights, refusing to come down again to the prisoners or to take any part in their labours and rewards, however much or little these may be worth.

Shall we not be doing them an injustice, if we force on them a worse life than
they might have?

e   You have forgotten again, my friend, that the law is not concerned to make any
one class specially happy, but to ensure the welfare of the commonwealth as a whole.
520 By persuasion or constraint it will unite the citizens in harmony, making them share
whatever benefits each class can contribute to the common good; and its purpose in
forming men of that spirit was not that each should be left to go his own way, but that
they should be instrumental in binding the community into one.

True, I had forgotten.

You will see, then, Glaucon, that there will be no real injustice in compelling our
philosophers to watch over and care for the other citizens. We can fairly tell them that
b   their compeers in other states may quite reasonably refuse to collaborate: there they
have sprung up, like a self-sown plant, in despite of their country's institutions; no one

has fostered their growth, and they cannot be expected to show gratitude for a care they have never received. "But," we shall say, "it is not so with you. We have brought you into existence for your country's sake as well as for your own, to be like leaders and king-bees in a hive; you have been better and more thoroughly educated than those others and hence you are more capable of playing your part both as men of thought and as men of action. You must go down, then, each in his turn, to live with the rest and let   c your eyes grow accustomed to the darkness. You will then see a thousand times better than those who live there always; you will recognize every image for what it is and know what it represents, because you have seen justice, beauty, and goodness in their reality; and so you and we shall find life in our commonwealth no mere dream, as it is in most existing states, where men live fighting one another about shadows and quar-   d relling for power, as if that were a great prize; whereas in truth government can be at its best and free from dissension only where the destined rulers are least desirous of holding office."

Quite true.

Then will our pupils refuse to listen and to take their turns at sharing in the work of the community, though they may live together for most of their time in a purer air?

No; it is a fair demand, and they are fair-minded men. No doubt, unlike any ruler   e of the present day, they will think of holding power as an unavoidable necessity.

Yes, my friend; for the truth is that you can have a well-governed society only if you can discover for your future rulers a better way of life than being in office; then   521 only will power be in the hands of men who are rich, not in gold, but in the wealth that brings happiness, a good and wise life. All goes wrong when, starved for lack of any-thing good in their own lives, men turn to public affairs hoping to snatch from thence the happiness they hunger for. They set about fighting for power, and this internecine conflict ruins them and their country. The life of true philosophy is the only one that looks down upon offices of state; and access to power must be confined to men who are not in love with it; otherwise rivals will start fighting. So whom else can you com- pel to undertake the guardianship of the commonwealth, if not those who, besides un-   b derstanding best the principles of government, enjoy a nobler life than the politician's and look for rewards of a different kind?

There is indeed no other choice.

ARISTOTLE
384–322 B.C.

Aristotle was born in Stagira, on the border of Macedonia. His mother, Phaestis, was from a family of doctors, and his father, Nicomachus, was the court physician to the king of Macedonia. At seventeen, Aristotle was sent to Athens. There he studied in Plato's Academy for two decades, but, as he later wrote, he loved the truth more than he loved Plato, and so he had no mind to remain a mere disciple. In 347 B.C., after Plato's death, he left Athens and spent the next four years conducting zoological investigations on the islands of Assos and Lesbos.

About 343 B.C., he was called to Macedonia by King Philip to tutor the king's son—the future Alexander the Great. Upon Alexander's ascension to the throne seven years later, Aristotle returned to Athens to set up the Lyceum, a rival to the Academy. Aristotle did much of his teaching walking up and down the colonnades with advanced students. As a result, his school and philosophy came to be called by the Greek word for walking around: *peripatetikos*, from which we get our word "peripatetic." Tradition has it that as Alexander the Great moved east, conquering Persia and moving into India, he would send back biological specimens for Aristotle's school. Although most scholars doubt this popular story, it is nevertheless clear that under Alexander's patronage, the Lyceum flourished.

However, the connection to Alexander proved a liability in the end. On Alexander's death in 323 B.C., Athenians went on a rampage against any and all associated with him. Indicted on charges of impiety, Aristotle fled Athens, "lest," as he put it, "the Athenians sin twice against philosophy" (referring, of course, to the unjust trial and death of Socrates). Aristotle died a year later. A popular but again highly questionable story says he drowned investigating marine life.

There is no doubt that after Plato, Aristotle is the most influential philosopher of all time. In the early Middle Ages, his thought was preserved and commented upon by the great Arab philosophers. He dominated later medieval philosophy to such an extent that St. Thomas Aquinas referred to him simply as *philosophus*, the "philosopher." Logic, as taught until about the time of World War II, was essentially Aristotle's logic. His *Poetics* is still a classic of literary criticism, and his dicta on tragedy are widely accepted even today. Criticism of Aristotle's metaphysical and epistemological views has spread ever since Bacon and Descartes inaugurated modern philosophy; but for all that, the problems Aristotle saw, the distinctions he introduced, and the terms he defined are still central in many, if not most, philosophical discussions. His influence and prestige, like Plato's, are international and beyond all schools.

*   *   *

Aristotle found Plato's theory of Forms unacceptable. Like Plato, he wanted to discover universals, but he did not believe they existed apart from particulars. The form of a chair, for instance, can be thought of apart from the matter out of which the chair is made, but the form does not subsist as a separate invisible entity. The universal of "chairness" exists only in particular chairs—there is no other-worldly "Form of Chairness." Accordingly, Aristotle began his philosophy not with reflection on or dialogue about eternal Forms but with observations of particular objects.

In observing the world, Aristotle saw four "causes" responsible for making an object what it is: the material, formal, efficient, and final. In the case of a chair, for example, the chair's material cause is its wood and cloth, its formal cause is the structure or form given in its plan or blueprint, its efficient cause is the worker who made it, and its final cause is sitting. The material cause, then, is that *out of which* a thing is made, the formal cause is that *into which* a thing is made, the efficient cause is that *by which* a thing is made, and the final cause is that *for which* a thing is made. It is the last of these, the final cause, that Aristotle held to be most important, for it determined the other three. The "goal" or "end" (*telos* in Greek), the final cause, of any given substance is the key to its understanding. This means that all nature is to be understood in terms of final causes or purposes. This is known as a "teleological" explanation of reality.

As Aristotle applied these insights to human beings, he asked what the *telos* of a person could be. By observing what is unique to persons and what they, in fact, do seek, Aristotle came to the conclusion that the highest good or end for humans is *eudaimonia*. While this word is generally translated as "happiness," one must be careful to acknowledge that Aristotle's understanding of "happiness" is rather different from ours. *Eudaimonia* happiness is not a feeling of euphoria—in fact, it is not a feeling at all. It is rather "activity in accordance with virtue." Much of the material from the *Nicomachean Ethics* presented here is devoted both to clarifying the word and to discovering how this kind of "happiness" is to be achieved.

*   *   *

Aristotle's extant works lack the literary grace of Plato's. Like Plato, Aristotle is said to have written popular dialogues—the "exoteric" writings intended for those who were not students at the Lyceum—but they have not survived. What we have instead are the difficult "esoteric" works: lecture notes for classes at school. According to some scholars, these are not even Aristotle's notes, but the notes of students collected by editors. In any case, the writings as we have them contain much overlapping, repetition, and apparent contradiction.

The first five chapters of the *Categories*, with which we begin, help clear up a number of questions about Aristotle's conception of substance. Written as a treatise on language, the *Categories* makes clear why Aristotle rejected Plato's approach to knowledge of the Forms.

The *Physics* deals with some of the main questions of physical science. In Book II, reprinted here (complete), Aristotle makes a distinction between physics and mathematics and discusses the four causes. This work is translated by R.P. Hardie and R.K. Gaye.

The *Metaphysics* probably consists of several independent treatises. Book I (*Alpha*) of this collection develops Aristotle's four causes and reviews the history of philosophy to his time. Book XII (*Lambda*) employs many of the concepts previously introduced, such as substance, actuality, and potency, and then moves to Aristotle's theology of the Unmoved Mover. The work concludes with Aristotle's rejection of Platonic Forms as separate, mathematical entities. Apparently Aristotle was responding to Plato's successors, who emphasized the mathematical nature of the Forms. W.D. Ross is the translator.

The first part of the selection presented from Aristotle's *On the Soul (De Anima)* gives a definition of the soul and distinguishes its faculties. The second part discusses the passive and the active mind. As this selection makes clear, Aristotle rejected Plato's view of a soul separate from the body. The selection is given in the translation by J.A. Smith.

Our final selection, the *Nicomachean Ethics*, is still considered one of the greatest works in ethics. Named for Aristotle's son, Nicomachus, it discusses the nature of the good and of moral and intellectual virtues, as well as investigating specific virtues. The lengthy selection presented here (about one-half of the complete work) reflects this vast range of topics and includes discussions of the subject matter and nature of ethics; of the good for an individual; of moral virtue; of the mean; of the conditions of responsibility for an action; of pride, vanity, humility, and the great-souled man (Aristotle's ideal); of the superiority of loving over being loved; and finally, of human happiness. The translation is Martin Ostwald's.

The marginal page numbers, with their "a" and "b," are those of all scholarly editions—Greek, English, German, French, and others.

* * *

Timothy A. Robinson, *Aristotle in Outline* (Indianapolis, IN: Hackett, 1995) provides an excellent short introduction for the beginning student. W.K.C. Guthrie, *A History of Greek Philosophy, VI: Aristotle: An Encounter* (Cambridge: Cambridge University Press, 1981) and the classic W.D. Ross, *Aristotle* (1923; reprinted in New York: Meridian Books, 1959) are more advanced studies. John Herman Randall, Jr., *Aristotle* (New York: Columbia University Press, 1960); Marjorie Grene, *A Portrait of Aristotle* (Chicago: University of Chicago Press, 1963); J.L. Ackrill, *Aristotle the Philosopher* (Oxford: Oxford University Press, 1981); Jonathan Barnes, *Aristotle* (Oxford: Oxford University Press, 1982); Jonathan Lear, *Aristotle: The Desire to Understand* (Cambridge: Cambridge

University Press, 1988); Terence Irwin, *Aristotle's First Principles* (Oxford: Oxford University Press, 1988); and Jonathan Barnes, ed., *The Cambridge Companion to Aristotle* (Cambridge: Cambridge University Press, 1995) also provide helpful overviews of Aristotle's life and thought. For general collections of essays, see R. Bambrough, ed., *New Essays on Plato and Aristotle* (London: Routledge & Kegan Paul, 1965); J.M.E. Moravcsik, ed., *Aristotle: A Collection of Critical Essays* (New York: Anchor Doubleday, 1967); J. Barnes, M. Schofield, and R. Sorabji, eds., *Articles on Aristotle*, four volumes. (London: Duckworth, 1979); Terence Irwin, ed., *Aristotle's Ethics, Aristotle: Substance, Form, and Matter* and *Aristotle: Metaphysics, Epistemology, Natural Philosophy* (all three, Hamden, CT: Garland Publishing, 1995); and Cynthia A. Freeland, ed., *Feminist Interpretations of Aristotle* (College Park, PA: Pennsylvania State University Press, 1998). For help with specific works (besides the *Nicomachean Ethics*), see Lindsay Judson, ed., *Aristotle's Physics: A Collection of Essays* (Oxford: Oxford University Press, 1991); Helen S. Lang, *Aristotle's Physics and Its Medieval Varieties* (Albany: SUNY Press, 1992); Martha C. Nussbaum and Amelie O. Rorty, eds., *Essays on Aristotle's De Anima* (Oxford: Oxford University Press, 1992); Michael Durrant, ed., *Aristotle's De Anima in Focus* (Oxford: Routledge, 1993); Michael Davis, *The Politics of Philosophy: A Commentary on Aristotle's Politics,* (Lanham, MD: Rowan & Littlefield, 1996); and Helen S. Lang, *The Order of Nature in Aristotle's Physics* (Cambridge: Cambridge University Press, 1998). The *Nichomachean Ethics* has been such an influential book that many commentaries and essays have been written about it. Among these are H.H. Joachim, *Aristotle: The Nicomachean Ethics*, edited by D.A. Rees (Oxford: Clarendon Press, 1951); W.F.R. Hardie, *Aristotle's Ethical Theory*, 2nd edition (Oxford: Oxford University Press, 1980); Amelie O. Rorty, ed., *Essays on Aristotle's Ethics* (Berkeley: University of California Press, 1980); J.O. Urmson, *Aristotle's Ethics* (Oxford: Basil Blackwell, 1988); Sarah Brodie, *Ethics with Aristotle* (Oxford: Oxford University Press, 1991); and Francis Sparshott, *Taking Life Seriously: A Study of the Argument of the Nichomachean Ethics* (Toronto: University of Toronto Press, 1994). Alasdair C. MacIntyre's pair of books, *After Virtue: A Study in Moral Theory* (Notre Dame, IN: University of Notre Dame Press, 1981) and *Whose Justice? Which Rationality?* (Notre Dame, IN: University of Notre Dame Press, 1988) are interesting examples of recent attempts to apply Aristotle's ethics to contemporary moral problems.

CATEGORIES (in part)

1. When things have only a name in common and the definition of being which corresponds to the name is different, they are called *homonymous*. Thus, for example, both a man and a picture are animals. These have only a name in common and the definition

1ᵃ

Aristotle, *Categories*, Chapters 1–5 from *Aristotle's Categories and De Interpretatione*, translated by J.L. Ackrill (Oxford: Oxford University Press, 1963). Reprinted by permission of Oxford University Press.

of being which corresponds to the name is different; for if one is to say what being an
5   animal is for each of them, one will give two distinct definitions.

When things have the name in common and the definition of being which corresponds to the name is the same, they are called *synonymous*. Thus, for example, both a
man and an ox are animals. Each of these is called by a common name, "animal," and
10   the definition of being is also the same; for if one is to give the definition of each—
what being an animal is for each of them—one will give the same definition.

When things get their name from something, with a difference of ending, they
are called *paronymous*. Thus, for example, the grammarian gets his name from gram-
15   mar, the brave get theirs from bravery.

2. Of things that are said, some involve combination while others are said without
combination. Examples of those involving combination are "man runs," "man wins";
and of those without combination "man," "ox," "runs," "wins."
20   Of things there are: (*a*) some are *said of* a subject but are not in any subject. For
example, man is said of a subject, the individual man, but is not in any subject.
(*b*) Some are in a subject but are not said of any subject. (By "in a subject" I mean
what is in something, not as a part, and cannot exist separately from what it is in.) For
25   example, the individual knowledge-of-grammar is in a subject, the soul, but is not
said of any subject; and the individual white is in a subject, the body (for all colour is
in a body), but is not said of any subject. (*c*) Some are both said of a subject and in a
1ᵇ   subject. For example, knowledge is in a subject, the soul, and is also said of a subject,
knowledge-of-grammar. (*d*) Some are neither in a subject nor said of a subject, for ex-
5   ample, the individual man or individual horse—for nothing of this sort is either in a
subject or said of a subject. Things that are individual and numerically one are, without exception, not said of any subject, but there is nothing to prevent some of them
from being in a subject—the individual knowledge-of-grammar is one of the things in
a subject.

10   3. Whenever one thing is predicated of another as of a subject, all things said of what is
predicated will be said of the subject also. For example, man is predicated of the indi-
15   vidual man, and animal of man; so animal will be predicated of the individual man
also—for the individual man is both a man and an animal.

The differentiae of genera which are different and not subordinate one to the
other are themselves different in kind. For example, animal and knowledge: footed,
20   winged, aquatic, two-footed, are differentiae of animal, but none of these is a differentia of knowledge; one sort of knowledge does not differ from another by being two-
footed. However, there is nothing to prevent genera subordinate one to the other from
having the same differentiae. For the higher are predicated of the genera below them,
so that all differentiae of the predicated genus will be differentiae of the subject also.

25   4. Of things said without any combination, each signifies either substance or quantity
or qualification or a relative or where or when or being-in-a-position or having or
doing or being-affected. To give a rough idea, examples of substance are man, horse;
2ᵃ   of quantity: four-foot, five-foot; of qualification: white, grammatical; of a relative:
double, half, larger; of where: in the Lyceum, in the market-place; of when: yesterday,
last-year; of being-in-a-position: is-lying, is-sitting; of having: has-shoes-on, has-
armour-on; of doing: cutting, burning; of being-affected: being-cut, being-burned.
5   None of the above is said just by itself in any affirmation, but by the combination
of these with one another an affirmation is produced. For every affirmation, it seems, is

either true or false; but of things said without any combination none is either true or false (e.g., "man," "white," "runs," "wins"). 10

5. A *substance*—that which is called a substance most strictly, primarily, and most of all—is that which is neither said of a subject nor in a subject, e.g., the individual man 15 or the individual horse. The species in which the things primarily called substances are, are called *secondary substances*, as also are the genera of these species. For example, the individual man belongs in a species, man, and animal is a genus of the species; so these—both man and animal—are called secondary substances.

It is clear from what has been said that if something is said of a subject both its name and its definition are necessarily predicated of the subject. For example, man is 20 said of a subject, the individual man, and the name is of course predicated (since you will be predicating man of the individual man), and also the definition of man will be predicated of the individual man (since the individual man is also a man). Thus both 25 the name and the definition will be predicated of the subject. But as for things which are in a subject, in most cases neither the name nor the definition is predicated of the subject. In some cases there is nothing to prevent the name from being predicated of 30 the subject, but it is impossible for the definition to be predicated. For example, white, which is in a subject (the body), is predicated of the subject; for a body is called white. But the definition of white will never be predicated of the body.

All the other things are either said of the primary substances as subjects or in 35 them as subjects. This is clear from an examination of cases. For example, animal is predicated of man and therefore also of the individual man; for were it predicated of none of the individual men it would not be predicated of man at all. Again, colour is in body and therefore also in an individual body; for were it not in some individual body 2^b it would not be in body at all. Thus all the other things are either said of the primary substances as subjects or in them as subjects. So if the primary substances did not exist 5 it would be impossible for any of the other things to exist.

Of the secondary substances the species is more a substance than the genus, since it is nearer to the primary substance. For if one is to say of the primary substance what it is, it will be more informative and apt to give the species than the genus. For 10 example, it would be more informative to say of the individual man that he is a man than that he is an animal (since the one is more distinctive of the individual man while the other is more general); and more informative to say of the individual tree that it is a tree than that it is a plant. Further, it is because the primary substances are subjects for 15 all the other things and all the other things are predicated of them or are in them, that they are called substances most of all. But as the primary substances stand to the other things, so the species stands to the genus: the species is a subject for the genus (for the 20 genera are predicated of the species but the species are not predicated reciprocally of the genera). Hence for this reason too the species is more a substance than the genus.

But of the species themselves—those which are not genera—one is no more a substance than another: it is no more apt to say of the individual man that he is a man than to say of the individual horse that it is a horse. And similarly of the primary sub- 25 stances one is no more a substance than another: the individual man is no more a substance than the individual ox.

It is reasonable that, after the primary substances, their species and genera should be the only other things called (secondary) substances. For only they, of things predi- 30 cated, reveal the primary substance. For if one is to say of the individual man what he is, it will be in place to give the species or the genus (though more informative to give man than animal); but to give any of the other things would be out of place—for exam-

35   ple, to say "white" or "runs" or anything like that. So it is reasonable that these should be the only other things called substances. Further, it is because the primary substances are subjects for everything else that they are called substances most strictly. But as the

3ᵃ   primary substances stand to everything else, so the species and genera of the primary substances stand to all the rest: all the rest are predicated of these. For if you will call the individual man grammatical it follows that you will call both a man and an animal

5   grammatical; and similarly in other cases.

It is a characteristic common to every substance not to be in a subject. For a pri-

10   mary substance is neither said of a subject nor in a subject. And as for secondary substances, it is obvious at once that they are not in a subject. For man is said of the individual man as subject but is not in a subject: man is not *in* the individual man.

15   Similarly, animal also is said of the individual man as subject but animal is not in the individual man. Further, while there is nothing to prevent the name of what is in a subject from being sometimes predicated of the subject, it is impossible for the definition to be predicated. But the definition of the secondary substances, as well as the name, is

20   predicated of the subject: you will predicate the definition of man of the individual man, and also that of animal. No substance, therefore, is in a subject.

This is not, however, peculiar to substance; the differentia also is not in a subject.

25   For footed and two-footed are said of man as subject but are not in a subject; neither two-footed nor footed is in man. Moreover, the definition of the differentia is predicated of that of which the differentia is said. For example, if footed is said of man the definition of footed will also be predicated of man; for man is footed.

30   We need not be disturbed by any fear that we may be forced to say that the parts of a substance, being in a subject (the whole substance), are not substances. For when we spoke of things *in a subject* we did not mean things belonging in something as *parts*.

It is a characteristic of substances and differentiae that all things called from

35   them are so called synonymously. For all the predicates from them are predicated either of the individuals or of the species. (For from a primary substance there is no predicate, since it is said of no subject; and as for secondary substances, the species is

3ᵇ   predicated of the individual, the genus both of the species and of the individual. Similarly, differentiae too are predicated both of the species and of the individuals.) And the primary substances admit the definition of the species and of the genera, and the

5   species admits that of the genus; for everything said of what is predicated will be said of the subject also. Similarly, both the species and the individuals admit the definition of the differentiae. But synonymous things were precisely those with both the name in common and the same definition. Hence all the things called from substances and differentiae are so called synonymously.

10   Every substance seems to signify a certain "this." As regards the primary substances, it is indisputably true that each of them signifies a certain "this"; for the thing revealed is individual and numerically one. But as regards the secondary substances,

15   though it appears from the form of the name—when one speaks of man or animal— that a secondary substance likewise signifies a certain "this," this is not really true; rather, it signifies a certain qualification, for the subject is not, as the primary substance is, one, but man and animal are said of many things. However, it does not signify sim-

20   ply a certain qualification, as white does. White signifies nothing but a qualification, whereas the species and the genus mark off the qualification of substance—they signify substance of a certain qualification. (One draws a wider boundary with the genus than with the species, for in speaking of animal one takes in more than in speaking of man.)

Another characteristic of substances is that there is nothing contrary to them. For
what would be contrary to a primary substance? For example, there is nothing contrary   25
to an individual man, nor yet is there anything contrary to man or to animal. This, however, is not peculiar to substance but holds of many other things also, for example, of
quantity. For there is nothing contrary to four-foot or to ten or to anything of this
kind—unless someone were to say that many is contrary to few or large to small; but   30
still there is nothing contrary to any *definite* quantity.

Substance, it seems, does not admit of a more and a less. I do not mean that one
substance is not more a substance than another (we have said that it is), but that any   35
given substance is not called more, or less, than that which it is. For example, if this
substance is a man, it will not be more a man or less a man either than itself or than another man. For one man is not more a man than another, as one pale thing is more pale   4ᵃ
than another and one beautiful thing more beautiful than another. Again, a thing is
called more, or less, such-and-such than itself; for example, the body that is pale is
called more pale now than before, and the one that is hot is called more, or less, hot.
Substance, however, is not spoken of thus. For a man is not called more a man now   5
than before, nor is anything else that is a substance. Thus substance does not admit of a
more and a less.

It seems most distinctive of substance that what is numerically one and the same   10
is able to receive contraries. In no other case could one bring forward anything, numerically one, which is able to receive contraries. For example, a colour which is numerically one and the same will not be black and white, nor will numerically one and the
same action be bad and good; and similarly with everything else that is not substance.   15
A substance, however, numerically one and the same, is able to receive contraries. For
example, an individual man—one and the same—becomes pale at one time and dark at
another, and hot and cold, and bad and good.   20

Nothing like this is to be seen in any other case, unless someone might object
and say that statements and beliefs are like this. For the same statement seems to be
both true and false. Suppose, for example, that the statement that somebody is sitting is
true; after he has got up this same statement will be false. Similarly with beliefs. Sup-   25
pose you believe truly that somebody is sitting; after he has got up you will believe
falsely if you hold the same belief about him. However, even if we were to grant this,
there is still a difference in the way contraries are received. For in the case of sub-   30
stances it is by themselves changing that they are able to receive contraries. For what
has become cold instead of hot, or dark instead of pale, or good instead of bad, has
changed (has altered); similarly in other cases too it is by itself undergoing change that
each thing is able to receive contraries. Statements and beliefs, on the other hand,   35
themselves remain completely unchangeable in every way; it is because the actual
thing changes that the contrary comes to belong to them. For the statement that some-   4ᵇ
body is sitting remains the same; it is because of a change in the actual thing that it
comes to be true at one time and false at another. Similarly with beliefs. Hence at least
the way in which it is able to receive contraries— through a change in itself—would be
distinctive of substance, even if we were to grant that beliefs and statements are able to
receive contraries. However, this is not true. For it is not because they themselves re-   5
ceive anything that statements and beliefs are said to be able to receive contraries, but
because of what has happened to something else. For it is because the *actual thing* ex-   10
ists or does not exist that the statement is said to be true or false, not because it is able
itself to receive contraries. No statement, in fact, or belief is changed at all by anything. So, since nothing happens in them, they are not able to receive contraries. A sub-

Diskobolos, by Myron. A Roman copy after a bronze original of ca. 450 B.C. Myron's athlete epitomizes the ideal Olympian goals of godlike perfection and rational beauty. *(Museo del Terme, Rome)*

15   stance, on the other hand, is said to be able to receive contraries because it itself receives contraries. For it receives sickness and health, and paleness and darkness; and because it itself receives the various things of this kind it is said to be able to receive contraries. It is, therefore, distinctive of substance that what is numerically one and the same is able to receive contraries. This brings to an end our discussion of substance.

PHYSICS (in part)

BOOK II

1. Of things that exist, some exist by nature, some from other causes. By nature the an- 192^b imals and their parts exist, and the plants and the simple bodies (earth, fire, air, water)—for we say that these and the like exist by nature.

All the things mentioned plainly differ from things which are not constituted by nature. For each of them has within itself a principle of motion and of stationariness (in respect of place, or of growth and decrease, or by way of alteration). On the other 15 hand, a bed and a coat and anything else of that sort, *qua* receiving these designations—i.e., in so far as they are products of art—have no innate impulse to change. But in so far as they happen to be composed of stone or of earth or of a mixture of the two, 20 they do have such an impulse, and just to that extent—which seems to indicate that nature is a principle or cause of being moved and of being at rest in that to which it belongs primarily, in virtue of itself and not accidentally.

I say "not accidentally," because (for instance) a man who is a doctor might himself be a cause of health to himself. Nevertheless it is not in so far as he is a patient that 25 he possesses the art of medicine: it merely has happened that the same man is doctor and patient—and that is why these attributes are not always found together. So it is with all other artificial products. None of them has in itself the principle of its own production. But while in some cases (for instance houses and the other products of manual 30 labour) that principle is in something else external to the thing, in others—those which may cause a change in themselves accidentally—it lies in the things themselves (but not in virtue of what they are).

Nature then is what has been stated. Things have a nature which have a principle of this kind. Each of them is a substance; for it is a subject, and nature is always in a subject.

The term "according to nature" is applied to all these things and also to the at- 35 tributes which belong to them in virtue of what they are, for instance the property of fire to be carried upwards—which is not a nature nor has a nature but is by nature or 193^a according to nature.

What nature is, then, and the meaning of the terms "by nature" and "according to nature," has been stated. *That* nature exists, it would be absurd to try to prove; for it is obvious that there are many things of this kind, and to prove what is obvious by what is not is the mark of a man who is unable to distinguish what is self-evident from what 5 is not. (This state of mind is clearly possible. A man blind from birth might reason about colours.) Presumably therefore such persons must be talking about words without any thought to correspond.

Some identify the nature or substance of a natural object with that immediate 10 constituent of it which taken by itself is without arrangement, e.g., the wood is the nature of the bed, and the bronze the nature of the statue.

As an indication of this Antiphon points out that if you planted a bed and the rotting wood acquired the power of sending up a shoot, it would not be a bed that would

15   come up, but *wood* which shows that the arrangement in accordance with the rules of the art is merely an accidental attribute, whereas the substance is the other, which, further, persists continuously through the process.

20   But if the material of each of these objects has itself the same relation to something else, say bronze (or gold) to water, bones (or wood) to earth and so on, *that* (they say) would be their nature and substance. Consequently some assert earth, others fire or air or water or some or all of these, to be the nature of the things that are. For whatever any one of them supposed to have this character—whether one thing or more than

25   one thing—this or these he declared to be the whole of substance, all else being its affections, states, or dispositions. Every such thing they held to be eternal (for it could not pass into anything else), but other things to come into being and cease to be times without number.

This then is one account of nature, namely that it is the primary underlying matter of things which have in themselves a principle of motion or change.

30   Another account is that nature is the shape or form which is specified in the definition of the thing.

For the word "nature" is applied to what is according to nature and the natural in the same way as "art" is applied to what is artistic or a work of art. We should not say in the latter case that there is anything artistic about a thing, if it is a bed only poten-

35   tially, not yet having the form of a bed; nor should we call it a work of art. The same is true of natural compounds. What is potentially flesh or bone has not yet its own nature,

193^b   and does not exist by nature, until it receives the form specified in the definition, which we name in defining what flesh or bone is. Thus on the second account of nature, it

5   would be the shape or form (not separable except in statement) of things which have in themselves a principle of motion. (The combination of the two, e.g. man, is not nature but by nature.)

The form indeed is nature rather than the matter; for a thing is more properly said to be what it is when it exists in actuality than when it exists potentially. Again man is born from man but not bed from bed. That is why people say that the shape is not the

10   nature of a bed, but the wood is—if the bed sprouted, not a bed but wood would come up. But even if the shape *is* art, then on the same principle the shape of man is his nature. For man is born from man.

Again, nature in the sense of a coming-to-be proceeds towards nature. For it is not like doctoring, which leads not to the art of doctoring but to health. Doctoring must

15   start from the art, not lead to it. But it is not in this way that nature is related to nature. What grows *qua* growing grows from something into something. Into what then does it grow? Not into that from which it arose but into that to which it tends. The shape then is nature.

Shape and nature are used in two ways. For the privation too is in a way form.

20   But whether in unqualified coming to be there is privation, i.e., a contrary, we must consider later.

2. We have distinguished, then, the different ways in which the term "nature" is used.

The next point to consider is how the mathematician differs from the student of nature; for natural bodies contain surfaces and volumes, lines and points, and these are

25   the subject-matter of mathematics.

Further, is astronomy different from natural science or a department of it? It seems absurd that the student of nature should be supposed to know the nature of sun or moon, but not to know any of their essential attributes, particularly as the writers on nature obvi-

30   ously do discuss their shape and whether the earth and the world are spherical or not.

Now the mathematician, though he too treats of these things, nevertheless does not treat of them as the limits of a natural body; nor does he consider the attributes indicated as the attributes of such bodies. That is why he separates them, for in thought they are separable from motion, and it makes no difference, nor does any falsity result, if they are separated. The holders of the theory of Forms do the same, though they are not aware of it; for they separate the objects of natural science, which are less separable than those of mathematics. This becomes plain if one tries to state in each of the two cases the definitions of the things and of their attributes. Odd and even, straight and curved, and likewise number, line, and figure, do not involve motion; not so flesh and bone and man—*these* are defined like snub nose, not like curved.   35

194ª

5

Similar evidence is supplied by the more natural of the branches of mathematics, such as optics, harmonics, and astronomy. These are in a way the converse of geometry. While geometry investigates natural lines but not *qua* natural, optics investigates mathematical lines, but *qua* natural, not *qua* mathematical.   10

Since two sorts of thing are called nature, the form and the matter, we must investigate its objects as we would the essence of snubness, that is neither independently of matter nor in terms of matter only. Here too indeed one might raise a difficulty. Since there are two natures, with which is the student of nature concerned? Or should he investigate the combination of the two? But if the combination of the two, then also each severally. Does it belong then to the same or to different sciences to know each severally?   15

If we look at the ancients, natural science would seem to be concerned with the *matter*. (It was only very slightly that Empedocles and Democritus touched on form and essence.)   20

But if on the other hand art imitates nature, and it is the part of the same discipline to know the form and the matter up to a point (e.g., the doctor has a knowledge of health and also of bile and phlegm, in which health is realized and the builder both of the form of the house and of the matter, namely that it is bricks and beams, and so forth): if this is so, it would be the part of natural science also to know nature in both its senses.   25

Again, that for the sake of which, or the end, belongs to the same department of knowledge as the means. But the nature is the end or that for the sake of which. For if a thing undergoes a continuous change toward some end, that last stage is actually that for the sake of which. (That is why the poet was carried away into making an absurd statement when he said "he has the end for the sake of which he was born." For not every stage that is last claims to be an end, but only that which is best.)   30

For the arts make their material (some simply make it, others make it serviceable), and we use everything as if it was there for our sake. (We also are in a sense an end. "That for the sake of which" may be taken in two ways, as we said in our work *On Philosophy*.) The arts, therefore, which govern the matter and have knowledge are two, namely the art which uses the product and the art which directs the production of it. That is why the using art also is in a sense directive; but it differs in that it knows the form, whereas the art which is directive as being concerned with production knows the matter. For the helmsman knows and prescribes what sort of form a helm should have, the other from what wood it should be made and by means of what operations. In the products of art, however, we make the material with a view to the function, whereas in the products of nature the matter is there all along.   35

194ᵇ

5

Again, matter is a relative thing—for different forms there is different matter.

How far then must the student of nature know the form or essence? Up to a point, perhaps, as the doctor must know sinew or the smith bronze (i.e., until he understands the purpose of each); and the student of nature is concerned only with things   10

whose forms are separable indeed, but do not exist apart from matter. Man is begotten
15   by man and by the sun as well. The mode of existence and essence of the separable it is
the business of first philosophy to define.

3. Now that we have established these distinctions, we must proceed to consider
causes, their character and number. Knowledge is the object of our inquiry, and men
20   do not think they know a thing till they have grasped the "why" of it (which is to grasp
its primary cause). So clearly we too must do this as regards both coming to be and
passing away and every kind of natural change, in order that, knowing their principles,
we may try to refer to these principles each of our problems.

In one way, then, that out of which a thing comes to be and which persists, is
25   called a cause, e.g., the bronze of the statue, the silver of the bowl, and the genera of
which the bronze and the silver are species.

In another way, the form or the archetype, i.e., the definition of the essence, and
its genera, are called causes (e.g., of the octave the relation of 2:1, and generally number), and the parts in the definition.

30   Again, the primary source of the change or rest; e.g., the man who deliberated is
a cause, the father is cause of the child, and generally what makes of what is made and
what changes of what is changed.

Again, in the sense of end or that for the sake of which a thing is done, e.g.,
health is the cause of walking about. ("Why is he walking about?" We say: "To be
35   healthy," and, having said that, we think we have assigned the cause.) The same is true
also of all the intermediate steps which are brought about through the action of something else as means towards the end, e.g., reduction of flesh, purging, drugs, or surgical
195ª   instruments are means towards health. All these things are for the sake of the end,
though they differ from one another in that some are activities, others instruments.

This then perhaps exhausts the number of ways in which the term "cause" is used.

As things are called causes in many ways, it follows that there are several causes
5   of the same thing (not merely accidentally), e.g., both the art of the sculptor and the
bronze are causes of the statue. These are causes of the statue *qua* statue, not in virtue
of anything else that it may be—only not in the same way, the one being the material
cause, the other the cause whence the motion comes. Some things cause each other
reciprocally, e.g., hard work causes fitness and *vice versa*, but again not in the same
10   way, but the one as end, the other as the principle of motion. Further the same thing is
the cause of contrary results. For that which by its presence brings about one result is
sometimes blamed for bringing about the contrary by its absence. Thus we ascribe the
wreck of a ship to the absence of the pilot whose presence was the cause of its safety.

All the causes now mentioned fall into four familiar divisions. The letters are the
15   causes of syllables, the material of artificial products, fire and the like of bodies, the
parts of the whole, and the premises of the conclusion, in the sense of "that from
which." Of these pairs the one set are causes in the sense of what underlies, e.g., the
20   parts, the other set in the sense of essence—the whole and the combination and the
form. But the seed and the doctor and the deliberator, and generally the maker, are all
sources whence the change or stationariness originates, which the others are causes in
the sense of the end or the good of the rest; for that for the sake of which tends to be
25   what is best and the end of the things that lead up to it. (Whether we call it good or apparently good makes no difference.)

Such then is the number and nature of the kinds of cause.

Now the modes of causation are many, though when brought under heads they
too can be reduced in number. For things are called causes in many ways and even

within the same kind one may be prior to another: e.g., the doctor and the expert are   30
causes of health, the relation 2:1 and number of the octave, and always what is inclusive to what is particular. Another mode of causation is the accidental and its genera,
e.g., in one way Polyclitus, in another a sculptor is the cause of a statue, because being
Polyclitus and a sculptor are accidentally conjoined. Also the classes in which the acci-   35
dental attribute is included; thus a man could be said to be the cause of a statue or, generally, a living creature. An accidental attribute too may be more or less remote, e.g.,   195ᵇ
suppose that a pale man or a musical man were said to be the cause of the statue.

All causes, both proper and accidental, may be spoken of either as potential or as
actual; e.g., the cause of a house being built is either a house-builder or a house-builder   5
building.

Similar distinctions can be made in the things of which the causes are causes,
e.g., of this statue or of a statue or of an image generally, of this bronze or of bronze or
of material generally. So too with the accidental attributes. Again we may use a com-   10
plex expression for either and say, e.g., neither "Polyclitus" nor a "sculptor" but "Polyclitus, the sculptor."

All these various uses, however, come to six in number, under each of which
again the usage is twofold. It is either what is particular or a genus, or an accidental attribute or a genus of that, and these either as a complex or each by itself; and all either   15
as actual or as potential. The difference is this much, that causes which are actually at
work and particular exist and cease to exist simultaneously with their effect, e.g., this
healing person with this being-healed person and that housebuilding man with that
being-built house; but this is not always true of potential causes—the house and the   20
housebuilder do not pass away simultaneously.

In investigating the cause of each thing it is always necessary to seek what is
most precise (as also in other things): thus a man builds because he is a builder, and a
builder builds in virtue of his art of building. This last cause then is prior; and so gener-   25
ally.

Further, generic effects should be assigned to generic causes, particular effects to
particular causes, e.g., statue to sculptor, this statue to this sculptor; and powers are relative to possible effects, actually operating causes to things which are actually being
effected.

This must suffice for our account of the number of causes and the modes of cau-   30
sation.

4. But chance and spontaneity are also reckoned among causes: many things are said
both to be and to come to be as a result of chance and spontaneity. We must inquire
therefore in what manner chance and spontaneity are present among the causes enu-   35
merated, and whether they are the same or different, and generally what chance and
spontaneity are.

Some people even question whether there are such things or not. They say that
nothing happens by chance, but that everything which we ascribe to chance or spon-   196ᵃ
taneity has some definite cause, e.g., coming by chance into the market and finding
there a man whom one wanted but did not expect to meet is due to one's wish to go
and buy in the market. Similarly, in other so-called cases of chance it is always possi-   5
ble, they maintain, to find something which is the cause; but not chance, for if chance
were real, it would seem strange indeed, and the question might be raised, why on
earth none of the wise men of old in speaking of the causes of generation and decay   10
took account of chance; whence it would seem that they too did not believe that anything is by chance. But there is a further circumstance that is surprising. Many things

15 both come to be and are by chance and spontaneity, and although all know that each of them can be ascribed to some cause (as the old argument said which denied chance), nevertheless they all speak of some of these things as happening by chance and others not. For this reason they ought to have at least referred to the matter in some way or other.

Certainly the early physicists found no place for chance among the causes which they recognized—love, strife, mind, fire, or the like. This is strange, whether they supposed that there is no such thing as chance or whether they thought there is but omitted 20 to mention it—and that too when they sometimes used it, as Empedocles does when he says that the air is not always separated into the highest region, but as it may chance. At any rate he says in his cosmogony that "it happened to run that way at that time, but it often ran otherwise." He tells us also that most of the parts of animals came to be by chance.

25 There are some who actually ascribe this heavenly sphere and all the worlds to spontaneity. They say that the vortex arose spontaneously, i.e., the motion that separated and arranged the universe in its present order. This statement might well cause surprise. For they are asserting that chance is not responsible for the existence or gen-30 eration of animals and plants, nature or mind or something of the kind being the cause of them (for it is not any chance thing that comes from a given seed but an olive from one kind and a man from another); and yet at the same time they assert that the heavenly sphere and the divinest of visible things arose spontaneously, having no such 35 cause as is assigned to animals and plants. Yet if this is so, it is a fact which deserves to be dwelt upon, and something might well have been said about it. For besides the other 196ᵇ absurdities of the statement, it is the more absurd that people should make it when they see nothing coming to be spontaneously in the heavens, but much happening by chance among the things which as they say are not due to chance; whereas we should have expected exactly the opposite.

5 Others there are who believe that chance is a cause, but that it is inscrutable to human intelligence, as being a divine thing and full of mystery.

Thus we must inquire what chance and spontaneity are, whether they are the same or different, and how they fit into our division of causes.

10 5. First then we observe that some things always come to pass in the same way, and others for the most part. It is clearly of neither of these that chance, or the result of chance, is said to be the cause—neither of that which is by necessity and always, nor of that which is for the most part. But as there is a third class of events besides these two—events which all say are by chance—it is plain that there is such a thing as 15 chance and spontaneity; for we know that things of this kind are due to chance and that things due to chance are of this kind.

Of things that come to be, some come to be for the sake of something, others not. Again, some of the former class are in accordance with intention, others not, but both are in the class of things which are for the sake of something. Hence it is clear that 20 even among the things which are outside what is necessary and what is for the most part, there are some in connexion with which the phrase "for the sake of something" is applicable. (Things that are for the sake of something include whatever may be done as a result of thought or of nature.) Things of this kind, then, when they come to pass ac-25 cidentally are said to be by chance. For just as a thing is something either in virtue of itself or accidentally, so may it be a cause. For instance, the housebuilding faculty is in virtue of itself a cause of a house, whereas the pale or the musical is an accidental cause. That which is per se cause is determinate, but the accidental cause is indeter-

minable; for the possible attributes of an individual are innumerable. As we said, then, when a thing of this kind comes to pass among events which are for the sake of some- 30
thing, it is said to be spontaneous or by chance. (The distinction between the two must be made later—for the present it is sufficient if it is plain that both are in the sphere of things done for the sake of something.)

Example: A man is engaged in collecting subscriptions for a feast. He would have gone to such and such a place for the purpose of getting the money, if he had known. He actually went there for another purpose, and it was only accidentally that he 35
got his money by going there; and this was not due to the fact that he went there as a rule or necessarily, nor is the end effected (getting the money) a cause present in him- 197ᵃ
self—it belongs to the class of things that are objects of choice and the result of thought. It is when these conditions are satisfied that the man is said to have gone by chance. If he had chosen and gone for the sake of this—if he always or normally went there when he was collecting payments—he would not be said to have gone by chance. 5

It is clear then that chance is an accidental cause in the sphere of those actions for the sake of something which involves choice. Thought, then, and chance are in the same sphere, for choice implies thought.

It is necessary, no doubt, that the causes of what comes to pass by chance be in-definite; and that is why chance is supposed to belong to the class of the indefinite and to be inscrutable to man, and why it might be thought that, in a way, nothing occurs by 10
chance. For all these statements are correct, as might be expected. Things *do*, in a way, occur by chance, for they occur accidentally and chance is an accidental cause. But it is not the cause without qualification of anything; for instance, a housebuilder is the 15
cause of a house; accidentally, a fluteplayer may be so.

And the causes of the man's coming and getting the money (when he did not come for the sake of that) are innumerable. He may have wished to see somebody or been following somebody or avoiding somebody, or may have gone to see a spectacle. Thus to say that chance is unaccountable is correct. For an account is of what holds al-ways or for the most part, whereas chance belongs to a third type of event. Hence, 20
since causes of this kind are indefinite, chance too is indefinite. (Yet in some cases one might raise the question whether *any* chance fact might be the cause of the chance oc-currence, e.g., of health the fresh air or the sun's heat may be the cause, but having had one's hair cut *cannot*; for some accidental causes are more relevant to the effect than others.)

Chance is called good when the result is good, evil when it is evil. The terms 25
"good fortune" and "ill fortune" are used when either result is of considerable magni-tude. Thus one who comes within an ace of some great evil or great good is said to be fortunate or unfortunate. The mind affirms the presence of the attribute, ignoring the hair's breadth of difference. Further, it is with reason that good fortune is regarded as 30
unstable; for chance is unstable, as none of the things which result from it can hold al-ways or for the most part.

Both are then, as I have said, accidental causes—both chance and spontaneity—in the sphere of things which are capable of coming to pass not simply, nor for the most part and with reference to such of these as might come to pass for the sake of 35
something.

6. They differ in that spontaneity is the wider. Every result of chance is from what is spontaneous, but not everything that is from what is spontaneous is from chance.

Chance and what results from chance are appropriate to agents that are capable 197ᵇ
of good fortune and of action generally. Therefore necessarily chance is in the sphere

of actions. This is indicated by the fact that good fortune is thought to be the same, or nearly the same, as happiness, and happiness to be a kind of action, since it is well-doing. Hence what is not capable of action cannot do anything by chance. Thus an inanimate thing or a beast or a child cannot do anything by chance, because it is incapable of choice; nor can good fortune or ill fortune be ascribed to them, except metaphorically, as Protarchus, for example, said that the stones of which altars are made are fortunate because they are held in honour, while their fellows are trodden under foot. Even these things, however, can in a way be affected by chance, when one who is dealing with them does something to them by chance, but not otherwise.

The spontaneous on the other hand is found both in the beasts and in many inanimate objects. We say, for example, that the horse came spontaneously, because, though his coming saved him, he did not come for the sake of safety. Again, the tripod fell spontaneously, because, though it stood on its feet so as to serve for a seat, it did not fall so as to serve for a seat.

Hence it is clear that events which belong to the general class of things that may come to pass for the sake of something, when they come to pass not for the sake of what actually results, and have an external cause, may be described by the phrase "from spontaneity." These spontaneous events are said to be from chance if they have the further characteristics of being the objects of choice and happening to agents capable of choice. This is indicated by the phrase "in vain," which is used when one thing which is for the sake of another, does not result in it. For instance, taking a walk is for the sake of evacuation of the bowels; if this does not follow after walking, we say that we have walked in vain and that the walking was vain. This implies that what is naturally for the sake of an end is in vain, when it does not effect the end for the sake of which it was the natural means—for it would be absurd for a man to say that he had bathed in vain because the sun was not eclipsed, since the one was not done for the sake of the other. Thus the spontaneous is even according to its derivation the case in which the thing itself happens in vain. The stone that struck the man did not fall for the sake of striking him; therefore it fell spontaneously, because it might have fallen by the action of an agent and for the sake of striking. The difference between spontaneity and what results by chance is greatest in things that come to be by nature; for when anything comes to be contrary to nature, we do not say that it came to be by chance, but by spontaneity. Yet strictly this too is different from the spontaneous proper; for the cause of the latter is external, that of the former internal.

We have now explained what chance is and what spontaneity is, and in what they differ from each other. Both belong to the mode of causation "source of change," for either some natural or some intelligent agent is always the cause; but in this sort of causation the number of possible causes is infinite.

Spontaneity and chance are causes of effects which, though they might result from intelligence or nature, have in fact been caused by something accidentally. Now since nothing which is accidental is prior to what is *per se*, it is clear that no accidental cause can be prior to a cause *per se*. Spontaneity and chance, therefore, are posterior to intelligence and nature. Hence, however true it may be that the heavens are due to spontaneity, it will still be true that intelligence and nature will be prior causes of this universe and of many things in it besides.

7. It is clear then that there are causes, and that the number of them is what we have stated. The number is the same as that of the things comprehended under the question "why." The "why" is referred ultimately either, in things which do not involve motion, e.g., in mathematics, to the "what" (to the definition of straight line or commensurable

or the like); or to what initiated a motion, e.g., "why did they go to war?—because there had been a raid"; or we are inquiring "for the sake of what?"—"that they may   20 rule"; or in the case of things that come into being, we are looking for the matter. The causes, therefore, are these and so many in number.

Now, the causes being four, it is the business of the student of nature to know about them all, and if he refers his problems back to all of them, he will assign the "why" in the way proper to his science—the matter, the form, the mover, that for the sake of which. The last three often coincide; for the what and that for the sake of which   25 are one, while the primary source of motion is the same in species as these. For man generates man—and so too, in general, with all things which cause movement by being themselves moved; and such as are not of this kind are no longer inside the province of natural science, for they cause motion not by possessing motion or a source of motion in themselves, but being themselves incapable of motion. Hence there are three branches of study, one of things which are incapable of motion, the second of things in   30 motion, but indestructible, the third of destructible things.

The question "why," then, is answered by reference to the matter, to the form, and to the primary moving cause. For in respect of coming to be it is mostly in this last way that causes are investigated—"what comes to be after what? what was the primary agent or patient?" and so at each step of the series.   35

Now the principles which cause motion in a natural way are two, of which one is not natural, as it has no principle of motion in itself. Of this kind is whatever causes   198^{b} movement, not being itself moved, such as that which is completely unchangeable, the primary reality, and the essence of a thing, i.e., the form; for this is the end or that for the sake of which. Hence since nature is for the sake of something, we must know this cause also. We must explain the "why" in all the senses of the term, namely, that from   5 this that will necessarily result ("from this" either without qualification or for the most part); that this must be so if that is to be so (as the conclusion presupposes the premises); that this was the essence of the thing; and because it is better thus (not without qualification, but with reference to the substance in each case).

8. We must explain then first why nature belongs to the class of causes which act for   10 the sake of something; and then about the necessary and its place in nature, for all writers ascribe things to this cause, arguing that since the hot and the cold and the like are of such and such a kind, therefore certain things *necessarily* are and come to be—and if they mention any other cause (one friendship and strife, another mind), it is only to   15 touch on it, and then good-bye to it.

A difficulty presents itself: why should not nature work, not for the sake of something, nor because it is better so, but just as the sky rains, not in order to make the corn grow, but of necessity? (What is drawn up must cool, and what has been cooled must become water and descend, the result of this being that the corn grows.) Similarly   20 if a man's crop is spoiled on the threshing-floor, the rain did not fall for the sake of this—in order that the crop might be spoiled—but that result just followed. Why then should it not be the same with the parts in nature, e.g., that our teeth should come up of necessity—the front teeth sharp, fitted for tearing, the molars broad and useful for   25 grinding down the food—since they did not arise for this end, but it was merely a coincident result; and so with all other parts in which we suppose that there is purpose? Wherever then all the parts came about just what they would have been if they had come to be for an end, such things survived, being organized spontaneously in a fitting   30 way; whereas those which grew otherwise perished and continue to perish, as Empedocles says his "man-faced ox-progeny" did.

Such are the arguments (and others of the kind) which may cause difficulty on this point. Yet it is impossible that this should be the true view. For teeth and all other
35 natural things either invariably or for the most part come about in a given way; but of not one of the results of chance or spontaneity is this true. We do not ascribe to chance or mere coincidence the frequency of rain in winter, but frequent rain in summer we
199ᵃ do; nor heat in summer but only if we have it in winter. If then, it is agreed that things are either the result of coincidence or for the sake of something, and these cannot be
5 the result of coincidence or spontaneity, it follows that they must be for the sake of something; and that such things are all due to nature even the champions of the theory which is before us would agree. Therefore action for an end is present in things which come to be and are by nature.

Further, where there is an end, all the preceding steps are for the sake of that.
10 Now surely as in action, so in nature; and as in nature, so it is in each action, if nothing interferes. Now action is for the sake of an end; therefore the nature of things also is so. Thus if a house, e.g. had been a thing made by nature, it would have been made in the same way as it is now by art; and if things made by nature were made not only by na-
15 ture but also by art, they would come to be in the same way as by nature. The one, then, is for the sake of the other; and generally art in some cases completes what nature cannot bring to a finish, and in others imitates nature. If, therefore, artificial products are for the sake of an end, so clearly also are natural products. The relation of the later to the earlier items is the same in both.
20 This is most obvious in the animals other than man: they make things neither by art nor after inquiry or deliberation. That is why people wonder whether it is by intelligence or by some other faculty that these creatures work,—spiders, ants, and the like. By gradual advance in this direction we come to see clearly that in plants too that is
25 produced which is conducive to the end—leaves, e.g. grow to provide shade for the fruit. If then it is both by nature and for an end that the swallow makes its nest and the spider its web, and plants grow leaves for the sake of the fruit and send their roots
30 down (not up) for the sake of nourishment, it is plain that this kind of cause is operative in things which come to be and are by nature. And since nature is twofold, the matter and the form, of which the latter is the end, and since all the rest is for the sake of the end, the form must be the cause in the sense of that for the sake of which.

Now mistakes occur even in the operations of art: the literate man makes a mis-
199ᵇ take in writing and the doctor pours out the wrong dose. Hence clearly mistakes are possible in the operations of nature also. If then in art there are cases in which what is rightly produced serves a purpose, and if where mistakes occur there was a purpose in what was attempted, only it was not attained, so must it be also in natural products, and
5 monstrosities will be failures in the purposive effort. Thus in the original combinations the "ox-progeny," if they failed to reach a determinate end must have arisen through the corruption of some principle, as happens now when the seed is defective.

Further, seed must have come into being first, and not straightway the animals: what was "undifferentiated first" was seed.
10 Again, in plants too we find that for the sake of which, though the degree of organization is less. Were there then in plants also olive-headed vine-progeny, like the "man-headed ox-progeny," or not? An absurd suggestion; yet there must have been, if there were such things among animals.

Moreover, among the seeds anything must come to be at random. But the person
15 who asserts this entirely does away with nature and what exists by nature. For those things are natural which, by a continuous movement originated from an internal principle, arrive at some end: the same end is not reached from every principle; nor any

chance end, but always the tendency in each is towards the same end, if there is no impediment.

The end and the means towards it may come about by chance. We say, for instance, that a stranger has come by chance, paid the ransom, and gone away, when he   20
does so as if he had come for that purpose, though it was not for that that he came. This is accidental, for chance is an accidental cause, as I remarked before. But when an event takes place always or for the most part, it is not accidental or by chance. In nat-   25
ural products the sequence is invariable, if there is no impediment.

It is absurd to suppose that purpose is not present because we do not observe the agent deliberating. Art does not deliberate. If the ship-building art were in the wood, it would produce the same results by nature. If, therefore, purpose is present in art, it is present also in nature. The best illustration is a doctor doctoring himself: nature is like   30
that.

It is plain then that nature is a cause, a cause that operates for a purpose.

9. As regards what is of necessity, we must ask whether the necessity is hypothetical,   35
or simple as well. The current view places what is of necessity in the process of production, just as if one were to suppose that the wall of a house necessarily comes to be   200ᵃ
because what is heavy is naturally carried downwards and what is light to the top, so that the stones and foundations take the lowest place, with earth above because it is lighter, and wood at the top of all as being the lightest. Whereas, though the wall does not come to be *without* these, it is not *due* to these, except as its material cause: it comes   5
to be for the sake of sheltering and guarding certain things. Similarly in all other things which involve that for the sake of which: the product cannot come to be without things which have a necessary nature, but it is not due to these (except as its material); it comes to be for an end. For instance, why is a saw such as it is? To effect so-and-so and for the sake of so-and-so. This end, however, cannot be realized unless the saw is made of iron.   10
It is, therefore, necessary for it to be of iron, if we are to have a saw and perform the operation of sawing. What is necessary then, is necessary on a hypothesis, not as an end. Necessity is in the matter, while that for the sake of which is in the definition.

Necessity in mathematics is in a way similar to necessity in things which come   15
to be through the operation of nature. Since a straight line is what it is, it is necessary that the angles of a triangle should equal two right angles. But not conversely; though if the angles are *not* equal to two right angles, then the straight line is not what it is either. But in things which come to be for an end, the reverse is true. If the end is to exist   20
or does exist, that also which precedes it will exist or does exist; otherwise just as there, if the conclusion is not true, the principle will not be true, so here the end or that for the sake of which will not exist. For this too is itself a principle, but of the reasoning, not of the action. (In mathematics the principle is the principle of the reasoning only, as there is no action.) If then there is to be a house, such-and-such things must be   25
made or be there already or exist, or generally the matter relative to the end, bricks and stones if it is a house. But the end is not due to these except as the matter, nor will it come to exist because of them. Yet if they do not exist at all, neither will the house, or the saw—the former in the absence of stones, the latter in the absence of iron—just as in the other case the principles will not be true, if the angles of the triangle are not equal to two right angles.   30

The necessary in nature, then, is plainly what we call by the name of matter, and the changes in it. Both causes must be stated by the student of nature, but especially the end; for that is the cause of the matter, not *vice versa*; and the end is that for the sake of which, and the principle starts from the definition or essence: as in artificial products,   200ᵇ since a house is of such-and-such a kind, certain things must necessarily come to be or be there already, or since health is this, these things must *necessarily* come to be or be there already, so too if man is this, then these; if these, then those. Perhaps the necessary is present also in the definition. For if one defines the operation of sawing as being a certain kind of dividing, then this cannot come about unless the saw has teeth of a certain kind; and these cannot be unless it is of iron. For in the definition too there are some parts that stand as matter.

5

METAPHYSICS (in part)

Book I

980ᵃ   1. All men by nature desire to know. An indication of this is the delight we take in our senses; for even apart from their usefulness they are loved for themselves; and above all others the sense of sight. For not only with a view to action, but even when we are not going to do anything, we prefer sight to almost everything else. The reason is that this, most of all the senses, makes us know and brings to light many differences between things.

25

By nature animals are born with the faculty of sensation, and from sensation memory is produced in some of them, though not in others. And therefore the former are more intelligent and apt at learning than those which cannot remember; those which are incapable of hearing sounds are intelligent though they cannot be taught, e.g., the bee, and any other race of animals that may be like it; and those which besides memory have this sense of hearing, can be taught.

980ᵇ

25

The animals other than man live by appearances and memories, and have but little of connected experience; but the human race lives also by art and reasonings. And from memory experience is produced in men; for many memories of the same thing produce finally the capacity for a single experience. Experience seems to be very similar to science and art, but really science and art come to men *through* experience; for "experience made art," as Polus says, "but inexperience luck." And art arises, when from many notions gained by experience one universal judgement about similar objects is produced. For to have a judgement that when Callias was ill of this disease this did him good, and similarly in the case of Socrates and in many individual cases, is a matter of experience; but to judge that it has done good to all persons of a certain constitution, marked off in one class, when they were ill of this disease, e.g. to phlegmatic or bilious people when burning with fever,—this is a matter of art.

981ᵃ

5

10

With a view to action experience seems in no respect inferior to art, and we even see men of experience succeeding more than those who have theory without experience. The reason is that experience is knowledge of individuals, art of universals, and actions and productions are all concerned with the individual; for the physician does

15

Aristotle, *Metaphysics*, Books I, 1–4, 6, 9, and XII, 6–9, translated by W.D. Ross from *The Works of Aristotle*, translated into English under the editorship of W.D. Ross (Oxford: Clarendon Press, 1908–1952). Reprinted by permission of Oxford University Press.

not cure a man, except in an incidental way, but Callias or Socrates or some other called by some such individual name, who happens to be a man. If, then, a man has 20 theory without experience, and knows the universal but does not know the individual included in this, he will often fail to cure; for it is the individual that is to be cured. But yet we think that *knowledge* and *understanding* belong to art rather than to experience, 25 and we suppose artists to be wiser than men of experience (which implies that wisdom depends in all cases rather on knowledge); and this because the former know the cause, but the latter do not. For men of experience know that the thing is so, but do not know why, while the others know the "why" and the cause. Hence we think that the master- 30 workers in each craft are more honourable and know in a truer sense and are wiser than the manual workers, because they know the causes of the things that are done (we 981^b think the manual workers are like certain lifeless things which act indeed, but act without knowing what they do, as fire burns,—but while the lifeless things perform each of their functions by a natural tendency, the labourers perform them through habit); thus we view them as being wiser not in virtue of being able to act, but of having the theory 5 for themselves and knowing the causes. And in general it is a sign of the man who knows, that he can teach, and therefore we think art more truly knowledge than experience is; for artists can teach, and men of mere experience cannot.

Again, we do not regard any of the senses as wisdom; yet surely these give the 10 most authoritative knowledge of particulars. But they do not tell us the "why" of anything—e.g. why fire is hot; they only say that it is hot.

At first he who invented any art that went beyond the common perceptions of man was naturally admired by men, not only because there was something useful in the 15 inventions, but because he was thought wise and superior to the rest. But as more arts were invented, and some were directed to the necessities of life, others to its recreation, the inventors of the latter were always regarded as wiser than the inventors of the former, because their branches of knowledge did not aim at utility. Hence when all such 20 inventions were already established, the sciences which do not aim at giving pleasure or at the necessities of life were discovered, and first in the places where men first began to have leisure. This is why the mathematical arts were founded in Egypt; for there the priestly caste was allowed to be at leisure.

We have said in the *Ethics* what the difference is between art and science and the 25 other kindred faculties; but the point of our present discussion is this, that all men suppose what is called wisdom to deal with the first causes and the principles of things. This is why, as has been said before, the man of experience is thought to be wiser than 30 the possessors of any perception whatever, the artist wiser than the men of experience, the master-worker than the mechanic, and the theoretical kinds of knowledge to be more of the nature of wisdom than the productive. Clearly then wisdom is knowledge 982^a about certain causes and principles.

2. Since we are seeking this knowledge, we must inquire of what kind are the causes and the principles, the knowledge of which is wisdom. If we were to take the notions 5 we have about the wise man, this might perhaps make the answer more evident. We suppose first, then, that the wise man knows all things, as far as possible, although he has not knowledge of each of them individually; secondly, that he who can learn things 10 that are difficult, and not easy for man to know, is wise (sense-perception is common to all, and therefore easy and no mark of wisdom); again, he who is more exact and more capable of teaching the causes is wiser, in every branch of knowledge; and of the sciences, also, that which is desirable on its own account and for the sake of knowing it 15 is more of the nature of wisdom than that which is desirable on account of its results,

and the superior science is more of the nature of wisdom than the ancillary; for the wise man must not be ordered but must order, and he must not obey another, but the less wise must obey *him*.

20   Such and so many are the notions, then, which we have about wisdom and the wise. Now of these characteristics that of knowing all things must belong to him who has in the highest degree universal knowledge; for he knows in a sense all the subordinate objects. And these things, the most universal, are on the whole the hardest for men

25   to know; for they are furthest from the senses. And the most exact of the sciences are those which deal most with first principles; for those which involve fewer principles are more exact than those which involve additional principles, e.g., arithmetic [is more exact than] than geometry. But the science which investigates causes is also more capable of reaching, for the people who teach are those who tell the causes of each thing.

30   And understanding and knowledge pursued for their own sake are found most in the knowledge of that which is most knowable; for he who chooses to know for the sake of knowing will choose most readily that which is most truly knowledge, and such is

982ᵇ   the knowledge of that which is most knowable; and the first principles and the causes are most knowable; for by reason of these, and from these, all other things are known, but these are not known by means of the things subordinate to them. And the science

5   which knows to what end each thing must be done is the most authoritative of the sciences, and more authoritative than any ancillary science; and this end is the good in each class, and in general the supreme good in the whole of nature. Judged by all the tests we have mentioned, then, the name in question falls to the same science; this must be a science that investigates the first principles and causes; for the good, i.e., that for

10   the sake of which, is one of the causes.

        That it is not a science of production is clear even from the history of the earliest philosophers. For it is owing to their wonder that men both now begin and at first began to philosophize; they wondered originally at the obvious difficulties, then ad-

15   vanced little by little and stated difficulties about the greater matters, e.g., about the phenomena of the moon and those of the sun and the stars, and about the genesis of the universe. And a man who is puzzled and wonders thinks himself ignorant (whence

20   even the lover of myth is in a sense a lover of wisdom, for myth is composed of wonders); therefore since they philosophized in order to escape from ignorance, evidently they were pursuing science in order to know, and not for any utilitarian end. And this is confirmed by the facts; for it was when almost all the necessities of life and the things

25   that make for comfort and recreation were present, that such knowledge began to be sought. Evidently then we do not seek it for the sake of any other advantage; but as the man is free, we say, who exists for himself and not for another, so we pursue this as the only free science, for it alone exists for itself.

        Hence the possession of it might be justly regarded as beyond human power;

30   for in many ways human nature is in bondage, so that according to Simonides "God alone can have this privilege," and it is unfitting that man should not be content to seek the knowledge that is suited to him. If, then, there is something in what the

983ᵃ   poets say, and jealousy is natural to the divine power, it would probably occur in this case above all, and all who excelled in this knowledge would be unfortunate. But the divine power cannot be jealous (indeed, according to the proverb, "bards tell many a

5   lie"), nor should any science be thought more honourable than one of this sort. For the most divine science is also most honourable; and this science alone is, in two ways, most divine. For the science which it would be most meet for God to have is a divine science, and so is any science that deals with divine objects; and this science

alone has both these qualities; for God is thought to be among the causes of all things and to be a first principle, and such a science either God alone can have, or God above all others. All the sciences, indeed, are more necessary than this, but none is better. 10

Yet the acquisition of it must in a sense end in something which is the opposite of our original inquiries. For all men begin, as we said, by wondering that the matter is so (as in the case of automatic marionettes or the solstices or the incommensurability 15 of the diagonal of a square with the side; for it seems wonderful to all men who have not yet perceived the explanation that there is a thing which cannot be measured even by the smallest unit). But we must end in the contrary and, according to the proverb, the better state, as is the case in these instances when men learn the cause; for there is nothing which would surprise a geometer so much as if the diagonal turned out to be 20 commensurable.

We have stated, then, what is the nature of the science we are searching for, and what is the mark which our search and our whole investigation must reach.

3. Evidently we have to acquire knowledge of the original causes (for we say we know each thing only when we think we recognize its first cause), and causes are spoken of 25 in four senses. In one of these we mean the substance, i.e., the essence (for the "why" is referred finally to the formula, and the ultimate "why" is a cause and principle); in another the matter or substratum, in a third the source of the change, and in a fourth the 30 cause opposed to this, that for the sake of which and the good (for this is the end of all generation and change). We have studied these causes sufficiently in our work on nature, but yet let us call to our aid those who have attacked the investigation of being 983^b and philosophized about reality before us. For obviously they too speak of certain principles and causes; to go over their views, then, will be of profit to the present inquiry, for we shall either find another kind of cause, or be more convinced of the correctness 5 of those which we now maintain.

Of the first philosophers, most thought the principles which were of the nature of matter were the only principles of all things; that of which all things that are consist, and from which they first come to be, and into which they are finally resolved (the substance remaining, but changing in its modifications), this they say is the ele- 10 ment and the principle of things, and therefore they think nothing is either generated or destroyed, since this sort of entity is always conserved, as we say Socrates neither comes to be absolutely when he comes to be beautiful or musical, nor ceases to be when he loses these characteristics, because the substratum, Socrates himself, re- 15 mains. So they say nothing else comes to be or ceases to be; for there must be some entity—either one or more than one—from which all other things come to be, it being conserved.

Yet they do not all agree as to the number and the nature of these principles. Thales, the founder of this school of philosophy, says the principle is water (for which 20 reason he declared that the earth rests on water), getting the notion perhaps from seeing that the nutriment of all things is moist, and that heat itself is generated from the moist and kept alive by it (and that from which they come to be is a principle of all things). 25 He got his notion from this fact, and from the fact that the seeds of all things have a moist nature, and that water is the origin of the nature of moist things.

Some think that the ancients who lived long before the present generation, and first framed accounts of the gods, had a similar view of nature; for they made Ocean 30 and Tethys the parents of creation, and described the oath of the gods as being by

984^a water, which they themselves call Styx; for what is oldest is most honourable, and the most honourable thing is that by which one swears. It may perhaps be uncertain whether this opinion about nature is primitive and ancient, but Thales at any rate is said to have declared himself thus about the first cause. Hippo no one would think fit to include among these thinkers, because of the paltriness of his thought.

5   Anaximenes and Diogenes make air prior to water, and the most primary of the simple bodies, while Hippasus of Metapontium and Heraclitus of Ephesus say this of fire, and Empedocles says it of the four elements, adding a fourth—earth—to those which have been named; for these, he says, always remain and do not come to be, ex-
10   cept that they come to be more or fewer, being aggregated into one and segregated out of one.

Anaxagoras of Clazomenae, who, though older than Empedocles, was later in his philosophical activity, says the principles are infinite in number; for he says almost all the things that are homogeneous are generated and destroyed (as water or fire is) only
15   by aggregation and segregation, and are not in any other sense generated or destroyed, but remain eternally.

From these facts one might think that the only cause is the so-called material cause; but as men thus advanced, the very facts showed them the way and joined in forcing them to investigate the subject. However true it may be that all generation
20   and destruction proceed from some one or more elements, why does this happen and what is the cause? For at least the substratum itself does not make itself change; e.g., neither the wood nor the bronze causes the change of either of them, nor does the
25   wood manufacture a bed and the bronze a statue, but something else is the cause of the change. And to seek this is to seek the second cause, as we should say,—that from which comes the beginning of movement. Now those who at the very beginning set themselves to this kind of inquiry, and said the substratum was one, were not at all dissatisfied with themselves; but some at least of those who maintain it to be
30   one—as though defeated by this search for the second cause—say the one and nature as a whole is unchangeable not only in respect of generation and destruction (for this is an ancient belief, and all agreed in it), but also of all other change; and this view is
984^b peculiar to them. Of those who said the universe was one, none succeeded in discovering a cause of this sort, except perhaps Parmenides, and he only insomuch that he supposes that there is not only one but in some sense two causes. But for those who
5   make more elements it is more possible to state the second cause, e.g., for those who make hot and cold, or fire and earth, the elements; for they treat fire as having a nature which fits it to move things, and water and earth and such things they treat in the contrary way.

When these men and the principles of this kind had had their day, as the latter were found inadequate to generate the nature of things, men were again forced by the
10   truth itself, as we said, to inquire into the next kind of cause. For surely it is not likely either that fire or earth or any such element should be the reason why things manifest goodness and beauty both in their being and in their coming to be, or that those thinkers should have supposed it was; nor again could it be right to ascribe so great a
15   matter to spontaneity and luck. When one man said, then, that reason was present—as in animals, so throughout nature—as the cause of the world and of all its order, he seemed like a sober man in contrast with the random talk of his predecessors. We know that Anaxagoras certainly adopted these views, but Hermotimus of Clazomenae
20   is credited with expressing them earlier. Those who thought thus stated that there is a principle of things which is at the same time the cause of beauty, and that sort of cause from which things acquire movement.

4. One might suspect that Hesiod was the first to look for such a thing—or someone else who put love or desire among existing things as a principle, as Parmenides does; for he, in constructing the genesis of the universe, says: 25

> Love first of all the Gods she planned.

And Hesiod says:

> First of all things was chaos made, and then
> Broad-breasted earth, and love that foremost is
> Among all the immortals,

which implies that among existing things there must be a cause which will move things   30
and bring them together. How these thinkers should be arranged with regard to priority of discovery let us be allowed to decide later; but since the contraries of the various forms of good were also perceived to be present in nature—not only order and the beautiful, but also disorder and the ugly, and bad things in greater number than good, and ignoble things than beautiful, therefore another thinker introduced friendship and   985ᵃ
strife, each of the two the cause of one of these two sets of qualities. For if we were to follow out the view of Empedocles, and interpret it according to its meaning and not to its lisping expression, we should find that friendship is the cause of good things, and   5
strife of bad. Therefore, if we said that Empedocles in a sense both mentions, and is the first to mention, the bad and the good as principles, we should perhaps be right, since the cause of all goods is the good itself.   10

These thinkers, as we say, evidently got hold up to a certain point of two of the causes which we distinguished in our work on nature—the matter and the source of the movement,—vaguely, however, and with no clearness, but as untrained men behave in fights; for they go round their opponents and often strike fine blows, but they do not   15
fight on scientific principles, and so these thinkers do not seem to know what they say; for it is evident that, as a rule, they make no use of their causes except to a small extent. For Anaxagoras uses reason as a *deus ex machina* for the making of the world, and when he is at a loss to tell for what cause something necessarily is, then he drags   20
reason in, but in all other cases ascribes events to anything rather than to reason. And Empedocles, though he uses the causes to a greater extent than this, neither does so sufficiently nor attains consistency in their use. At least, in many cases he makes friendship segregate things, and strife aggregate them. For when the universe is dissolved into its elements by strife, fire is aggregated into one, and so is each of the other   25
elements; but when again under the influence of friendship they come together into one, the parts must again be segregated out of each element.

Empedocles, then, in contrast with his predecessors, was the first to introduce this cause in a divided form, not positing one source of movement, but different and   30
contrary sources. Again, he was the first to speak of four material elements; yet he does not use four, but treats them as two only; he treats fire by itself, and its opposites—   985ᵇ
earth, air, and water—as one kind of thing. We may learn this by study of his verses.

This philosopher then, as we say, spoke of the principles in this way, and made them of this number. Leucippus and his associate Democritus say that the full and the   5
empty are the elements, calling the one being and the other non-being—the full and solid being, the empty non-being (that is why they say that what is is no more than what is not, because body no more is than the void); and they make these the material causes of things. And as those who make the underlying substance one generate all   10

other things by its modifications, supposing the rare and the dense to be the sources of the modifications, in the same way these philosophers say the differences in the elements are the causes of all other qualities. These differences, they say, are three—shape and order and position. For they say that what is is differentiated only by "rhythm" and "inter-contact" and "turning"; and of these rhythm is shape, inter-contact is order, and turning is position; for A differs from N in shape, AN from NA in order, Ⅎ from H in position. The question of movement—whence or how it belongs to things—these thinkers, like the others, lazily neglected.

Regarding the two causes, then, as we say, the inquiry seems to have been pushed thus far by the early philosophers.

* * *

987ª   6. After the systems we have named came the philosophy of Plato, which in most respects followed these thinkers, but had peculiarities that distinguished it from the philosophy of the Italians. For, having in his youth first become familiar with Cratylus and with the Heraclitean doctrines (that all sensible things are ever in a state of flux and there is no knowledge about them), these views he held even in later years. Socrates, however, was busying himself about ethical matters and neglecting the world of nature as a whole but seeking the universal in these ethical matters, and fixed thought for the first time on definitions; Plato accepted his teaching, but held that the problem applied not to any sensible thing but to entities of another kind—for this reason, that the common definition could not be a definition of any sensible thing, as they were always changing. Things of this other sort, then, he called Ideas, and sensible things, he said, were apart from these, and were all called after these; for the multitude of things which have the same name as the Form exist by participation in it. Only the name "participation" was new; for the Pythagoreans say that things exist by imitation of numbers, and Plato says they exist by participation, changing the name. But what the participation or the imitation of the Forms could be they left an open question.

Further, besides sensible things and Forms he says there are the objects of mathematics, which occupy an intermediate position, differing from sensible things in being eternal and unchangeable, from Forms in that there are many alike, while the Form itself is in each case unique.

Since the Forms are the causes of all other things, he thought their elements were the elements of all things. As matter, the great and the small were principles; as substance, the One; for from the great and the small, by participation in the One, come the numbers.

But he agreed with the Pythagoreans in saying that the One is substance and not a predicate of something else; and in saying that the numbers are the causes of the substance of other things, he also agreed with them; but positing a dyad and constructing the infinite out of great and small, instead of treating the infinite as one, is peculiar to him; and so is his view that the numbers exist apart from sensible things, while they say that the things themselves are numbers, and do not place the objects of mathematics between Forms and sensible things. His divergence from the Pythagoreans in making the One and the numbers separate from things, and his introduction of the Forms, were due to his inquiries in the region of definitory formulae (for the earlier thinkers had no tincture of dialectic), and his making the other entity besides the One a dyad was due to the belief that the numbers, except those which were prime, could be neatly produced out of the dyad as out of a plastic material.

Yet what happens is the contrary; the theory is not a reasonable one. For they   988ᵃ
make many things out of the matter, and the form generates only once, but what we observe is that one table is made from one matter, while the man who applies the form,
though he is one, makes many tables. And the relation of the male to the female is sim-   5
ilar; for the latter is impregnated by one copulation, but the male impregnates many females; yet these are imitations of those first principles.

Plato, then, declared himself thus on the points in question; it is evident from
what has been said that he has used only two causes, that of the essence and the material cause (for the Forms are the cause of the essence of all other things, and the One is   10
the cause of the essence of the Forms); and it is evident what the underlying matter is,
of which the Forms are predicated in the case of sensible things, and the One in the
case of Forms, viz. that this is a dyad, the great and the small. Further, he has assigned
the cause of good and that of evil to the elements, one to each of the two, as we say   15
some of his predecessors sought to do, e.g. Empedocles and Anaxagoras.

* * *

9. Let us leave the Pythagoreans for the present; for it is enough to have touched on
them as much as we have done. But as for those who posit the Ideas as causes, firstly,
in seeking to grasp the causes of the things around us, they introduced others equal in   990ᵇ
number to these, as if a man who wanted to count things thought he could not do it
while they were few, but tried to count them when he had added to their number. For
the Forms are practically equal to or not fewer than the things, in trying to explain
which these thinkers proceeded from them to the Forms. For to each set of substances   5
there answers a Form which has the same name and exists apart from the substances,
and so also in the case of all other groups in which there is one character common to
many things, whether the things are in this changeable world or are eternal.

Further, of the ways in which we prove that the Forms exist, none is convincing;
for from some no inference necessarily follows, and from some it follows that there are   10
Forms of things of which we think there are no Forms.

For according to the arguments from the existence of the sciences there will be
Forms of all things of which there are sciences, and according to the argument that there
is one attribute common to many things there will be Forms even of negations, and according to the argument that there is an object for thought even when the thing has perished, there will be Forms of perishable things; for we can have an image of these.

Further, of the more accurate arguments, some lead to Ideas of relations, of   15
which we say there is no independent class, and others involve the difficulty of the
"third man."

And in general the arguments for the Forms destroy the things for whose existence we are more anxious than for the existence of the Ideas; for it follows that not the
dyad but number is first, i.e. that the relative is prior to the absolute—besides all the   20
other points on which certain people by following out the opinions held about the Ideas
have come into conflict with the principles of the theory.

Further, according to the assumption on which our belief in the Ideas rests, there
will be Forms not only of substances but also of many other things (for the concept is
single not only in the case of substances but also in the other cases, and there are sci-   25
ences not only of substance but also of other things, and a thousand other such conclusions also follow). But according to the necessities of the case and the opinions held
about the Forms, if they can be shared there must be Ideas of substances only. For they
are not shared incidentally, but a thing must share in its Form as in something not pred-   30

icated of a subject (e.g. if a thing shares in double itself, it shares also in eternal, but incidentally; for eternal happens to be predicable of the double). Therefore the Forms 991ᵃ will be substance; and the same terms indicate substance in this and in the ideal world (or what will be the meaning of saying that there is something apart from the particulars—the one over many?). And if the Ideas and the particulars that share them have the same Form, there will be something common to these; for why should two be one 5 and the same in the perishable 2's or in those which are many but eternal, and not the same in the two itself as in the particular 2? But if they have not the same Form, they must have only the name in common, and it is as if one were to call both Callias and a wooden image a man, without observing any community between them.

Above all one might discuss the question what on earth the Forms contribute to 10 sensible things, either to those that are eternal or to those that come into being and cease to be. For they cause neither movement nor any change in them. But again they help in no way towards the *knowledge* of the other things (for they are not even the substance of these, else they would have been in them), nor towards their being, if they are not in the particulars which share in them; though if they were, they might be thought to be 15 causes, as white causes whiteness in that with which it is mixed. But this argument, which first Anaxagoras and later Eudoxus and certain others used, is too easily upset; for it is not difficult to collect many insuperable objections to such a view.

20 But further all other things cannot come from the Forms in any of the usual senses of "from." And to say that they are patterns and the other things share them is to use empty words and poetical metaphors. For what is it that works, looking to the Ideas? Anything can either be, or become, like another without being copied from it, so 25 that whether Socrates exists or not a man might come to be like Socrates; and evidently this might be so even if Socrates were eternal. And there will be several patterns of the same thing, and therefore several Forms, e.g. animal and two-footed and also man himself will be Forms of man. Again, the Forms are patterns not only of sensible things, 30 but of themselves too, e.g. the Form of genus will be a genus of Forms; therefore the same thing will be pattern and copy.

991ᵇ Again it must be held to be impossible that the substance and that of which it is the substance should exist apart; how, therefore, can the Ideas, being the substances of things, exist apart?

In the Phaedo the case is stated in this way—that the Forms are causes both of being and of becoming; yet when the Forms exist, still the things that share in them do 5 not come into being, unless there is some efficient cause; and many other things come into being (e.g. a house or a ring), of which we say there are no Forms. Clearly, therefore, even the other things can both be and come into being owing to such causes as produce the things just mentioned.

Again, if the forms are numbers, how can they be causes? Is it because existing 10 things are other numbers, e.g. one number is man, another is Socrates, another Callias? Why then are the one set of numbers causes of the other set? It will not make any difference even if the former are eternal and the latter are not. But if it is because things in this sensible world (e.g. harmony) are ratios of numbers, evidently there is some one class of things of which they are ratios. If, then, this—the matter—is some 15 definite thing, evidently the numbers themselves too will be ratios of something to something else. E.g. if Callias is a numerical ratio between fire and earth and water and air, his Idea also will be a number of certain other underlying things; and the Idea of man, whether it is a number in a sense or not, will still be a numerical ratio of certain 20 things and not a number proper, nor will it be a number merely because it is a numerical ratio.

Again, from many numbers one number is produced, but how can one Form come from many Forms? And if the number comes not from the many numbers themselves but from the units in them, e.g. in ten thousand, how is it with the units? If they are specifically alike, numerous absurdities will follow, and also if they are not alike (neither the units in the same number being like one another nor those in different numbers being all like to all); for in what will they differ, as they are without quality? This is not a plausible view, nor can it be consistently thought out. Further, they must set up a second kind of number (with which arithmetic deals), and all the objects which are called intermediate by some thinkers; and how do these exist or from what principles do they proceed? Or why must they be intermediate between the things in this sensible world and the things-in-themselves? Further, the units in two must each come from a prior two; but this is impossible. Further, why is a number, when taken all together, one? Again, besides what has been said, if the units are *diverse* they should have spoken like those who say there are four, or two, elements; for each of these thinkers gives the name of element not to that which is common, e.g. to body, but to fire and earth, whether there is something common to them, viz. body, or not. But in fact they speak as if the One were homogeneous like fire or water; and if this is so, the numbers will not be substances. Evidently, if there is a One-in-itself and this is a first principle, "one" is being used in more than one sense; for otherwise the theory is impossible.

When we wish to refer substances to their principles, we state that lines come from the short and long (i.e. from a kind of small and great), and the plane from the broad and narrow, and the solid from the deep and shallow. Yet how then can the plane contain a line, or the solid a line or a plane? For the broad and narrow is a different class of things from the deep and shallow. Therefore, just as number is not present in these, because the many and few are different from these, evidently no other of the higher classes will be present in the lower. But again the broad is not a genus which includes the deep, for then the solid would have been a species of plane. Further, from what principle will the presence of the points in the line be derived? Plato even used to object to this class of things as being a geometrical fiction. He called the indivisible lines the principle of lines—and he used to lay this down often. Yet these must have a limit; therefore the argument from which the existence of the line follows proves also the existence of the point.

In general, though philosophy seeks the cause of perceptible things, we have given this up (for we say nothing of the cause from which change takes its start), but while we fancy we are stating the substance of perceptible things, we assert the existence of a second class of substances, while our account of the way in which they are the substances of perceptible things is empty talk; for sharing, as we said before, means nothing. Nor have the Forms any connexion with that which we see to be the cause in the case of the sciences, and for whose sake mind and nature produce all that they do produce,—with this cause we assert to be one of the first principles; but mathematics has come to be the whole of philosophy for modern thinkers, though they say that it should be studied for the sake of other things. Further, one might suppose that the substance which according to them underlies as matter is too mathematical, and is a predicate and differentia of the substance, i.e. of the matter, rather than the matter itself; i.e. the great and the small are like the rare and the dense which the natural philosophers speak of, calling these the primary differentiae of the substratum; for these are a kind of excess and defect. And regarding movement, if the great and the small are to be movement, evidently the Forms will be moved; but if they are not, whence did movement come? If we cannot answer this the whole study of nature has been annihilated.

10   And what is thought to be easy—to show that all things are one— is not done; for by "exposition" all things do not come to be one but there comes to be a One-in-itself, if we grant all the assumptions. And not even this follows, if we do not grant that the universal is a class; and this in some cases it cannot be.

    Nor can it be explained either how the lines and planes and solids that come
15   after the numbers exist or can exist, or what meaning they have; for these can neither be Forms (for they are not numbers), nor the intermediates (for those are the objects of mathematics), nor the perishable things. This is evidently a distinct fourth class.

    In general, if we search for the elements of existing things without distinguishing the many senses in which things are said to exist, we cannot succeed, especially if the
20   search for the elements of which things are made is conducted in this manner. For it is surely impossible to discover what acting or being acted on, or the straight, is made of, but if elements can be discovered at all, it is only the elements of substances; therefore to seek the elements of all existing things or to think one has them is incorrect. And how could we *learn* the elements of all things? Evidently we cannot start by knowing
25   something before. For as he who is learning geometry, though he may know other things before, knows none of the things with which the science deals and about which he is to learn, so is it in all other cases. Therefore if there is a science of all things, as
30   some maintain, he who is learning this will know nothing before. Yet all learning is by means of premises which are (either all or some of them) known before,—whether the learning be by demonstration or by definitions; for the elements of the definition must
993ᵃ   be known before and be familiar; and learning by induction proceeds similarly. But again, if the science is innate, it is wonderful that we are unaware of our possession of the greatest of sciences. Again, how is one to *know* what all things are made of, and how is this to be made *evident*? This also affords a difficulty; for there might be a con-
5   flict of opinion, as there is about certain syllables; some say *za* is made out of *s* and *d* and *a*, while others say it is a distinct sound and none of those that are familiar. Further, how could we know the objects of sense without having the sense in question?
10   Yet we should, if the elements of which all things consist, as complex sounds consist of their proper elements, are the same.

*   *   *

Book XII

*   *   *

1071ᵇ   6. Since there were three kinds of substance, two of them natural and one unmovable, regarding the latter we must assert that it is necessary that there should be an eternal
5   unmovable substance. For substances are the first of existing things, and if they are all destructible, all things are destructible. But it is impossible that movement should either come into being or cease to be; for it must always have existed. Nor can time come into being or cease to be; for there could not be a before and an after if time did not exist. Movement also is continuous, then, in the sense in which time is; for time is

either the same thing as movement or an attribute of movement. And there is no con- 10
tinuous movement except movement in place, and of this only that which is circular is
continuous.

But if there is something which is capable of moving things or acting on them,
but is not actually doing so, there will not be movement; for that which has a capacity
need not exercise it. Nothing, then, is gained even if we suppose eternal substances, as
the believers in the Forms do, unless there is to be in them some principle which can 15
cause movement; and even this is not enough, nor is another substance besides the
Forms enough; for if it does not *act*, there will be no movement. Further, even if it acts,
this will not be enough, if its substance is potentiality; for there will not be *eternal*
movement; for that which is potentially may possibly not be. There must, then, be such
a principle, whose very substance is actuality. Further, then, these substances must be 20
without matter; for they must be eternal, at least if anything else is eternal. Therefore
they must be actuality.

Yet there is a difficulty; for it is thought that everything that acts is able to act,
but that not everything that is able to act acts, so that the potentiality is prior. But if
this is so, nothing at all will exist; for it is possible for things to be capable of existing 25
but not yet to exist. Yet if we follow the mythologists who generate the world from
night, or the natural philosophers who say that all things were together, the same impossible result ensues. For how will there be movement, if there is no actual cause?
Matter will surely not move itself—the carpenter's art must act on it; nor will the 30
menstrual fluids nor the earth set themselves in motion, but the seeds and the semen
must act on them.

This is why some suppose eternal actuality—e.g. Leucippus and Plato; for they
say there is always movement. But why and what this movement is they do not say,
nor, if the world moves in this way or that, do they tell us the cause of its doing so.
Now nothing is moved at random, but there must always be something present, e.g. as 35
a matter of fact a thing moves in one way by nature, and in another by force or through
the influence of thought or something else. Further, what sort of movement is primary?
This makes a vast difference. But again Plato, at least, cannot even say what it is that
he sometimes supposes to be the source of movement—that which moves itself; for the 1072ᵃ
soul is later, and simultaneous with the heavens, according to his account. To suppose
potentiality prior to actuality, then, is in a sense right, and in a sense not; and we have
specified these senses.

That actuality is prior is testified by Anaxagoras (for his thought is actuality) and 5
by Empedocles in his doctrine of love and strife, and by those who say that there is always movement, e.g. Leucippus.

Therefore chaos or night did not exist for any infinite time, but the same things
have always existed (either passing through a cycle of changes or in some other way),
since actuality is prior to potentiality. If, then, there is a constant cycle, something
must always remain, acting in the same way. And if there is to be generation and de- 10
struction, there must be something else which is always acting in different ways. This
must, then, act in one way in virtue of itself, and in another in virtue of something
else—either of a third agent, therefore, or of the first. But it must be in virtue of the
first. For otherwise this again causes the motion both of the third agent and of the second. Therefore it is better to say the first. For it was the cause of eternal movement; 15
and something else is the cause of variety, and evidently both together are the cause of
eternal variety. This, accordingly, is the character which the motions actually exhibit.
What need then is there to seek for other principles?

7. Since this is a possible account of the matter, and if it were not true, the world would have proceeded out of night and "all things together" and out of non-being, these difficulties may be taken as solved. There is, then, something which is always moved with an unceasing motion, which is motion in a circle; and this is plain not in theory only but in fact. Therefore the first heavens must be eternal. There is therefore also something which moves them. And since that which is moved and moves is intermediate, there is a mover which moves without being moved, being eternal, substance, and actuality. And the object of desire and the object of thought move in this way; they move without being moved. The primary objects of desire and of thought are the same. For the apparent good is the object of appetite, and the real good is the primary object of wish. But desire is consequent on opinion rather than opinion on desire; for the thinking is the starting-point. And thought is moved by the object of thought, and one side of the list of opposites is in itself the object of thought; and in this, substance is first, and in substance, that which is simple and exists actually. (The one and the simple are not the same; for "one" means a measure, but "simple" means that the thing itself has a certain nature.) But the good, also, and that which is in itself desirable are on this same side of the list; and the first in any class is always best, or analogous to the best.

1072ᵇ   That that for the sake of which is found among the unmovables is shown by making a distinction; for that for the sake of which is both that *for* which and that *towards* which, and of these the one is unmovable and the other is not. Thus it produces motion by being loved, and it moves the other moving things. Now if something is moved it is capable of being otherwise than as it is. Therefore if the actuality of the heavens is primary motion, then in so far as they are in motion, in *this* respect they are capable of being otherwise,—in place, even if not in substance. But since there is something which moves while itself unmoved, existing actually, this can in no way be otherwise than as it is. For motion in space is the first of the kinds of change, and motion in a circle the first kind of spatial motion; and this the first mover *produces*. The first mover, then, of necessity exists; and in so far as it is necessary, it is good, and in this sense a first principle. For the necessary has all these senses—that which is necessary perforce because it is contrary to impulse, that without which the good is impossible, and that which cannot be otherwise but is *absolutely* necessary.

On such a principle, then, depend the heavens and the world of nature. And its life is such as the best which we enjoy, and enjoy for but a short time. For it is ever in this state (which we cannot be), since its actuality is also pleasure. (And therefore waking, perception, and thinking are most pleasant, and hopes and memories are so because of their reference to these.) And thought in itself deals with that which is best in itself, and that which is thought in the fullest sense with that which is best in the fullest sense. And thought thinks itself because it shares the nature of the object of thought; for it becomes an object of thought in coming into contact with and thinking its objects, so that thought and object of thought are the same. For that which is *capable* of receiving the object of thought, i.e. the substance, is thought. And it is active when it *possesses* this object. Therefore the latter rather than the former is the divine element which thought seems to contain, and the act of contemplation is what is most pleasant and best. If, then, God is always in that good state in which we sometimes are, this compels our wonder; and if in a better this compels it yet more. And God *is* in a better state. And life also belongs to God; for the actuality of thought is life, and God is that actuality; and God's essential actuality is life most good and eternal. We say therefore that God is a living being, eternal, most good, so that life and duration continuous and eternal belong to God; for this *is* God.

Those who suppose, as the Pythagoreans and Speusippus do, that supreme beauty and goodness are not present in the beginning, because the beginnings both of plants and of animals are *causes*, but beauty and completeness are in the *effects* of these, are wrong in their opinion. For the seed comes from other individuals which are prior and complete, and the first thing is not seed but the complete being, e.g. we must say that before the seed there is a man,—not the man produced from the seed, but another from whom the seed comes.   1073ª

It is clear then from what has been said that there is a substance which is eternal and unmovable and separate from sensible things. It has been shown also that this substance cannot have any magnitude, but is without parts and indivisible. For it produces movement through infinite time, but nothing finite has infinite power. And, while every magnitude is either infinite or finite, it cannot, for the above reason, have finite magnitude, and it cannot have infinite magnitude because there is no infinite magnitude at all. But it is also clear that it is impassive and unalterable; for all the other changes are posterior to change of place. It is clear, then, why the first mover has these attributes.   5   10

8. We must not ignore the question whether we have to suppose one such substance or more than one, and if the latter, how many; we must also mention, regarding the opinions expressed by others, that they have said nothing that can even be clearly stated about the number of the substances. For the theory of Ideas has no special discussion of the subject; for those who believe in Ideas say the Ideas are numbers, and they speak of numbers now as unlimited, now as limited by the number ten; but as for the reason why there should be just so many numbers, nothing is said with any demonstrative exactness.   15   20

We however must discuss the subject, starting from the presuppositions and distinctions we have mentioned. The first principle or primary being is not movable either in itself or accidentally, but produces the primary eternal and single movement. And since that which is moved must be moved by something, and the first mover must be in itself unmovable, and eternal movement must be produced by something eternal and a single movement by a single thing, and since we see that besides the simple spatial movement of the universe, which we say the first and unmovable substance produces, there are other spatial movements—those of the planets—which are eternal (for the body which moves in a circle is eternal and unresting; we have proved these points in the *Physics*), each of these movements also must be caused by a substance unmovable in itself and eternal. For the nature of the stars is eternal, being a kind of substance, and the mover is eternal and prior to the moved, and that which is prior to a substance must be a substance. Evidently, then, there must be substances which are of the same number as the movements of the stars, and in their nature eternal, and in themselves unmovable, and without magnitude, for the reason before mentioned.   25   30   35   1073ᵇ

That the movers are substances, then, and that one of these is first and another second according to the same order as the movements of the stars, is evident. But in the number of movements we reach a problem which must be treated from the standpoint of that one of the mathematical sciences which is most akin to philosophy—viz. of astronomy; for this science speculates about substance which is perceptible but eternal, but the other mathematical sciences, i.e. arithmetic and geometry, treat of no substance. That the movements are more numerous than the bodies that are moved, is evident to those who have given even moderate attention to the matter; for each of the planets has more than one movement. But as to the actual number of these movements, we now—to give some notion of the subject—quote what some of the mathematicians   5   10

say, that our thought may have some definite number to grasp; but, for the rest, we
must partly investigate for ourselves, partly learn from other investigators, and if those
who study this subject form an opinion contrary to what we have now stated, we must
esteem both parties indeed, but follow the more accurate.

Eudoxus supposed that the motion of the sun or of the moon involves, in either
case, three spheres, of which the first is the sphere of the fixed stars, and the second
moves in the circle which runs along the middle of the zodiac, and the third in the circle which is inclined across the breadth of the zodiac; but the circle in which the moon
moves is inclined at a greater angle than that in which the sun moves. And the motion
of the planets involves, in each case, four spheres, and of these also the first and second
are the same as the first two mentioned above (for the sphere of the fixed stars is that
which moves all the other spheres, and that which is placed beneath this and has its
movement in the circle which bisects the zodiac is common to all), but the *poles* of the
third sphere of each planet are in the circle which bisects the zodiac, and the motion of
the fourth sphere is in the circle which is inclined at an angle to the equator of the third
sphere; and the poles of the third spheres are different for the other planets, but those
of Venus and Mercury are the same.

Callippus made the position of the spheres the same as Eudoxus did, but while
he assigned the same number as Eudoxus did to Jupiter and to Saturn, he thought two
more spheres should be added to the sun and two to the moon, if we were to explain
the phenomena, and one more to each of the other planets.

But it is necessary, if all the spheres combined are to explain the phenomena,
that for each of the planets there should be other spheres (one fewer than those hitherto
assigned) which counteract those already mentioned and bring back to the same position the first sphere of the star which in each case is situated below the star in question;
for only thus can all the forces at work produce the motion of the planets. Since, then,
the spheres by which the planets themselves are moved are eight and twenty-five, and
of these only those by which the lowest-situated planet is moved need not be counter-
acted, the spheres which counteract those of the first two planets will be six in number,
and the spheres which counteract those of the next four planets will be sixteen, and the
number of all the spheres—those which move the planets and those which counteract
these—will be fifty-five. And if one were not to add to the moon and to the sun the
movements we mentioned, all the spheres will be forty-nine in number.

Let this then be taken as the number of the spheres, so that the unmovable substances and principles may reasonably be taken as just so many; the assertion of *necessity* must be left to more powerful thinkers.

If there can be no spatial movement which does not conduce to the moving of a
star, and if further every being and every substance which is immune from change and
in virtue of itself has attained to the best must be considered an end, there can be no
other being apart from these we have named, but this must be the number of the substances. For if there are others, they will cause change as being an end of movement;
but there *cannot* be other movements besides those mentioned. And it is reasonable to
infer this from a consideration of the bodies that are moved; for if everything that
moves is for the sake of that which is moved, and every movement belongs to something that is moved, no movement can be for the sake of itself or of another movement,
but all movements must be for the sake of the stars. For if a movement is to be for the
sake of a movement, this latter also will have to be for the sake of something else; so
that since there cannot be an infinite regress, the end of every movement will be one of
the divine bodies which move through the heaven.

Evidently there is but one heaven. For if there are many heavens as there are many men, the moving principles, of which each heaven will have one, will be one in form but in number many. But all things that are many in number have matter. (For one and the same formula applies to *many* things, e.g. the formula of man; but Socrates is *one*.) But the primary essence has not matter; for it is fulfillment. So the unmovable first mover is one both in formula and in number; therefore also that which is moved always and continuously is one alone; therefore there is one heaven alone. | 35

Our forefathers in the most remote ages have handed down to us their posterity a tradition, in the form of a myth, that these substances are gods and that the divine encloses the whole of nature. The rest of the tradition has been added later in mythical form with a view to the persuasion of the multitude and to its legal and utilitarian expediency; they say these gods are in the form of men or like some of the other animals, and they say other things consequent on and similar to these which we have mentioned. But if we were to separate the first point from these additions and take it alone—that they thought the first substances to be gods—we must regard this as an inspired utterance, and reflect that, while probably each art and science has often been developed as far as possible and has again perished, these opinions have been preserved like relics until the present. Only thus far, then, is the opinion of our ancestors and our earliest predecessors clear to us. | 1074^b, 5, 10

9. The nature of the divine thought involves certain problems; for while thought is held to be the most divine of phenomena, the question what it must be in order to have that character involves difficulties. For if it thinks nothing, what is there here of dignity? It is just like one who sleeps. And if it thinks, but this depends on something else, then (as that which is its substance is not the act of thinking, but a capacity) it cannot be the best substance; for it is through thinking that its value belongs to it. Further, whether its substance is the faculty of thought or the act of thinking, what does it think? Either itself or something else; and if something else, either the same always or something different. Does it matter, then, or not, whether it thinks the good or any chance thing? Are there not some things about which it is incredible that it should think? Evidently, then, it thinks that which is most divine and precious, and it does not change; for change would be change for the worse, and this would be already a movement. First, then, if it is not the act of thinking but a capacity, it would be reasonable to suppose that the continuity of its thinking is wearisome to it. Secondly, there would evidently be something else more precious than thought, viz. that which is thought. For both thinking and the act of thought will belong even to one who has the worst of thoughts. Therefore if this ought to be avoided (and it ought, for there are even some things which it is better not to see than to see), the act of thinking cannot be the best of things. Therefore it must be itself that thought thinks (since it is the most excellent of things), and its thinking is a thinking on thinking. | 15, 20, 25, 30

But evidently knowledge and perception and opinion and understanding have always something else as their object, and themselves only by the way. Further, if thinking and being thought are different, in respect of which does goodness belong to thought? For being an act of thinking and being an object of thought are not the same. We answer that in some cases the knowledge is the object. In the productive sciences (if we abstract from the matter) the substance in the sense of essence, and in the theoretical sciences the formula or the act of thinking, is the object. As, then, thought and the object of thought are not different in the case of things that have not matter, they will be the same, i.e. the thinking will be one with the object of its thought. | 35, 1075^a

5   A further question is left—whether the object of the thought is composite; for if it were, thought would change in passing from part to part of the whole. We answer that everything which has not matter is indivisible. As human thought, or rather the thought of composite objects, is in a certain period of time (for it does not possess the good at this moment or at that, but its best, being something different from it, is at-

10   tained only in a whole period of time), so throughout eternity is the thought which has *itself* for its object.

ON THE SOUL (in part)

Book II

412ᵃ   1. Let the foregoing suffice as our account of the views concerning the soul which have been handed on by our predecessors; let us now make as it were a completely fresh

5   start, endeavouring to answer the question, What is soul? i.e. to formulate the most general possible account of it.

We say that substance is one kind of what is, and that in several senses: in the sense of matter or that which in itself is not a this, and in the sense of form or essence, which is that precisely in virtue of which a thing is called a this, and thirdly in the

10   sense of that which is compounded of both. Now matter is potentiality, form actuality; and actuality is of two kinds, one as e.g. knowledge, the other as e.g. reflecting.

Among substances are by general consent reckoned bodies and especially natural bodies; for they are the principles of all other bodies. Of natural bodies some have life

15   in them, others not; by life we mean self-nutrition and growth and decay. It follows that every natural body which has life in it is a substance in the sense of a composite.

Now given that there are bodies of such and such a kind, viz. having life, the soul cannot be a body; for the body is the subject or matter, not what is attributed to it.

20   Hence the soul must be a substance in the sense of the form of a natural body having life potentially within it. But substance is actuality, and thus soul is the actuality of a body as above characterized. Now there are two kinds of actuality corresponding to knowledge and to reflecting. It is obvious that the soul is an actuality like knowledge; for both sleeping and waking presuppose the existence of soul, and of these waking

25   corresponds to reflecting, sleeping to knowledge possessed but not employed, and knowledge of something is temporally prior.

That is why the soul is an actuality of the first kind of a natural body having life

412ᵇ   potentially in it. The body so described is a body which is organized. The parts of plants in spite of their extreme simplicity are organs; e.g. the leaf serves to shelter the pericarp, the pericarp to shelter the fruit, while the roots of plants are analogous to the mouth of animals, both serving for the absorption of food. If, then, we have to give a general for-

5   mula applicable to all kinds of soul, we must describe it as an actuality of the first kind

Aristotle, *On the Soul*, Book II, 1–3; Book III, 4–5, translated by J.A. Smith from *Complete Works of Aristotle*, edited by Jonathan Barnes. Copyright © 1984 by PUP. Reprinted by permission of Princeton University Press.

of a natural organized body. That is why we can dismiss as unnecessary the question whether the soul and the body are one: it is as though we were to ask whether the wax and its shape are one, or generally the matter of a thing and that of which it is the matter. Unity has many senses (as many as "is" has), but the proper one is that of actuality.

We have now given a general answer to the question, What is soul? It is sub-   10
stance in the sense which corresponds to the account of a thing. That means that it is what it is to be for a body of the character just assigned. Suppose that a tool, e.g. an axe, were a natural body, then being an axe would have been its essence, and so its soul; if this disappeared from it, it would have ceased to be an axe, except in name. As   15
it is, it is an axe; for it is not of a body of that sort that what it is to be, i.e. its account, is a soul, but of a natural body of a particular kind, viz. one having in itself the power of setting itself in movement and arresting itself. Next, apply this doctrine in the case of the parts of the living body. Suppose that the eye were an animal—sight would have been its soul, for sight is the substance of the eye which corresponds to the account, the   20
eye being merely the matter of seeing; when seeing is removed the eye is no longer an eye, except in name—no more than the eye of a statue or of a painted figure. We must now extend our consideration from the parts to the whole living body; for what the part is to the part, that the whole faculty of sense is to the whole sensitive body as such.

We must not understand by that which is potentially capable of living what has   25
lost the soul it had, but only what still retains it; but seeds and fruits are bodies which are potentially of that sort. Consequently, while waking is actuality in a sense corre-sponding to the cutting and the seeing, the soul is actuality in the sense corresponding to sight and the power in the tool; the body corresponds to what is in potentiality; as   413ᵃ
the pupil *plus* the power of sight constitutes the eye, so the soul *plus* the body consti-tutes the animal.

From this it is clear that the soul is inseparable from its body, or at any rate that certain parts of it are (if it has parts)—for the actuality of some of them is the actuality   5
of the parts themselves. Yet some may be separable because they are not the actualities of any body at all. Further, we have no light on the problem whether the soul may not be the actuality of its body in the sense in which the sailor is the actuality of the ship.

This must suffice as our sketch or outline of the nature of soul.   10

2. Since what is clear and more familiar in account emerges from what in itself is con-fused but more observable by us, we must reconsider our results from this point of view. For it is not enough for a definitional account to express as most now do the mere fact; it must include and exhibit the cause also. At present definitions are given in   15
a form analogous to the conclusion of an argument; e.g. What is squaring? The con-struction of an equilateral rectangle equal to a given oblong rectangle. Such a defini-tion is in form equivalent to a conclusion. One that tells us that squaring is the discov-ery of a mean proportional discloses the cause of what is defined.   20

We resume our inquiry from a fresh starting-point by calling attention to the fact that what has soul in it differs from what has not in that the former displays life. Now this word has more than one sense, and provided any one alone of these is found in a thing we say that thing is living—viz. thinking or perception or local movement and rest, or movement in the sense of nutrition, decay and growth. Hence we think of   25
plants also as living, for they are observed to possess in themselves an originative power through which they increase or decrease in all spatial directions; they do not grow up but not down—they grow alike in both, indeed in all, directions; and that holds for everything which is constantly nourished and continues to live, so long as it   30
can absorb nutriment.

This power of self-nutrition can be separated from the other powers mentioned, but not they from it—in mortal beings at least. The fact is obvious in plants; for it is the only psychic power they possess.

413^b   This is the originative power the possession of which leads us to speak of things as *living* at all, but it is the possession of sensation that leads us for the first time to speak of living things as *animals*; for even those beings which possess no power of local movement but do possess the power of sensation we call animals and not merely living things.

The primary form of sense is touch, which belongs to all animals. Just as the 5   power of self-nutrition can be separated from touch and sensation generally, so touch can be separated from all other forms of sense. (By the power of self-nutrition we mean that part of the soul which is common to plants and animals: all animals whatsoever are observed to have the sense of touch.) What the explanation of these two facts 10   is, we must discuss later. At present we must confine ourselves to saying that soul is the source of these phenomena and is characterized by them, viz. by the powers of self-nutrition, sensation, thinking, and movement.

Is each of these a soul or a part of a soul? And if a part, a part merely distinguish-15   able by definition or a part distinct in local situation as well? In the case of certain of these powers, the answers to these questions are easy, in the case of others we are puzzled what to say. Just as in the case of plants which when divided are observed to continue to live though separated from one another (thus showing that in *their* case the soul of each individual plant was actually one, potentially many), so we notice a simi-20   lar result in other varieties of soul, i.e. in insects which have been cut in two; each of the segments possesses both sensation and local movement; and if sensation, necessarily also imagination and appetition; for, where there is sensation, there is also pleasure and pain, and, where these, necessarily also desire.

25   We have no evidence as yet about thought or the power of reflexion; it seems to be a different kind of soul, differing as what is eternal from what is perishable; it alone is capable of being separated. All the other parts of soul, it is evident from what we have said, are, in spite of certain statements to the contrary, incapable of separate existence though, of course, distinguishable by definition. If opining is distinct from per-30   ceiving, to be capable of opining and to be capable of perceiving must be distinct, and so with all the other forms of living above enumerated. Further, some animals possess all these parts of soul, some certain of them only, others one only (this is what enables 414^a   us to classify animals); the cause must be considered later. A similar arrangement is found also within the field of the senses; some classes of animals have all the senses, some only certain of them, others only one, the most indispensable, touch.

Since the expression "that whereby we live and perceive" has two meanings, just 5   like the expression "that whereby we know"—that may mean either knowledge or the soul, for we can speak of knowing *by* either, and similarly that whereby we are in health may be either health or the body or some part of the body; and since of these knowledge or health is a form, essence, or account, or if we so express it an activity of 10   a recipient matter—knowledge of what is capable of knowing, health of what is capable of being made healthy (for the activity of that which is capable of originating change seems to take place in what is changed or altered); further, since it is the soul by which primarily we live, perceive, and think:—it follows that the soul must be an account and essence, not matter or a subject. For, as we said, the word substance has 15   three meanings—form, matter, and the complex of both—and of these matter is potentiality, form actuality. Since then the complex here is the living thing, the body cannot be the actuality of the soul; it is the soul which is the actuality of a certain kind of

body. Hence the rightness of the view that the soul cannot *be* without a body, while it   20
cannot be a body; it is not a body but something relative to a body. That is why it is *in*
a body, and a body of a definite kind. It was a mistake, therefore, to do as former
thinkers did, merely to fit it into a body without adding a definite specification of the
kind or character of that body, although evidently one chance thing will not receive an-   25
other. It comes about as reason requires: the actuality of any given thing can only be
realized in what is already potentially that thing, i.e. in a matter of its own appropriate
to it. From all this it is plain that soul is an actuality or account of something that possesses a potentiality of being such.

3. Of the psychic powers above enumerated some kinds of living things, as we have
said, possess all, some less than all, others one only. Those we have mentioned are the   30
nutritive, the appetitive, the sensory, the locomotive, and the power of thinking. Plants
have none but the first, the nutritive, while another order of living things has this *plus*
the sensory. If any order of living things has the sensory, it must also have the appeti-   414^b
tive; for appetite is the genus of which desire, passion, and wish are the species; now
all animals have one sense at least, viz. touch, and whatever has a sense has the capacity for pleasure and pain and therefore has pleasant and painful objects present to it,
and wherever these are present, there is desire, for desire is appetition of what is pleas-   5
ant. Further, all animals have the sense for food (for touch is the sense for food); the
food of all living things consists of what is dry, moist, hot, cold, and these are the qualities apprehended by touch; all other sensible qualities are apprehended by touch only
indirectly. Sounds, colours, and odours contribute nothing to nutriment; flavours fall   10
within the field of tangible qualities. Hunger and thirst are forms of desire, hunger a
desire for what is dry and hot, thirst a desire for what is cold and moist; flavour is a sort
of seasoning added to both. We must later clear up these points, but at present it may
be enough to say that all animals that possess the sense of touch have also appetition.   15
The case of imagination is obscure; we must examine it later. Certain kinds of animals
possess in addition the power of locomotion, and still others, i.e. man and possibly another order like man or superior to him, the power of thinking and thought. It is now
evident that a single definition can be given of soul only in the same sense as one can   20
be given of figure. For, as in that case there is no figure apart from triangle and those
that follow in order, so here there is no soul apart from the forms of soul just enumerated. It is true that a common definition can be given for figure which will fit all figures
without expressing the peculiar nature of any figure. So here in the case of soul and its
specific forms. Hence it is absurd in this and similar cases to look for a common defini-   25
tion which will not express the peculiar nature of anything that is and will not apply to
the approrate indivisible species, while at the same time omitting to look for an account which will. The cases of figure and soul are exactly parallel; for the particulars
subsumed under the common name in both cases—figures and living beings—consti-   30
tute a series, each successive term of which potentially contains its predecessor, e.g.
the square the triangle, the sensory power the self-nutritive. Hence we must ask in the
case of each order of living things, What is its soul, i.e. What is the soul of plant, man,
beast? Why the terms are related in this serial way must form the subject of examina-   415^a
tion. For the power of perception is never found apart from the power of self-nutrition,
while—in plants—the latter is found isolated from the former. Again, no sense is
found apart from that of touch, while touch *is* found by itself; many animals have neither sight, hearing, nor smell. Again, among living things that possess sense some have   5
the power of locomotion, some not. Lastly, certain living beings—a small minority—
possess calculation and thought, for (among mortal beings) those which possess calcu-

10   lation have all the other powers above mentioned, while the converse does not hold—
indeed some live by imagination alone, while others have not even imagination. Reflective thought presents a different problem.

It is evident that the way to give the most adequate definition of soul is to seek in
the case of *each* of its forms for the most appropriate definition.

*   *   *

Book III

*   *   *

429ᵃ   4. Turning now to the part of the soul with which the soul knows and (whether this is
separable from the others in definition only, or spatially as well) we have to inquire
what differentiates this part, and how thinking can take place.

If thinking is like perceiving, it must be either a process in which the soul is
acted upon by what is capable of being thought, or a process different from but analo-
15   gous to that. The thinking part of the soul must therefore be, while impassible, capable
of receiving the form of an object; that is, must be potentially identical in character
with its object without being the object. Thought must be related to what is thinkable,
as sense is to what is sensible.

Therefore, since everything is a possible object of thought, mind in order, as
Anaxagoras says, to dominate, that is, to know, must be pure from all admixture; for
20   the co-presence of what is alien to its nature is a hindrance and a block: it follows that
it can have no nature of its own, other than that of having a certain capacity. Thus that
in the soul which is called thought (by thought I mean that whereby the soul thinks and
judges) is, before it thinks, not actually any real thing. For this reason it cannot reason-
25   ably be regarded as blended with the body: if so, it would acquire some quality, e.g.
warmth or cold, or even have an organ like the sensitive faculty: as it is, it has none. It
was a good idea to call the soul "the place of forms," though this description holds
only of the thinking soul, and even this is the forms only potentially, not actually.

Observation of the sense-organs and their employment reveals a distinction be-
30   tween the impassibility of the sensitive faculty and that of the faculty of thought. After
strong stimulation of a sense we are less able to exercise it than before, as e.g. in the
429ᵇ   case of a loud sound we cannot hear easily immediately after, or in the case of a bright
colour or a powerful odour we cannot see or smell, but in the case of thought thinking
about an object that is highly thinkable renders it more and not less able afterwards to
think of objects that are less thinkable: the reason is that while the faculty of sensation
5   is dependent upon the body, thought is separable from it.

When thought has become each thing in the way in which a man who actually
knows is said to do so (this happens when he is now able to exercise the power on his
own initiative), its condition is still one of potentiality, but in a different sense from the
potentiality which preceded the acquisition of knowledge by learning or discovery; and
thought is then able to think of itself.

10   Since we can distinguish between a magnitude and what it is to be a magnitude,
and between water and what it is to be water, and so in many other cases (though not in
all; for in certain cases the thing and its form are identical), flesh and what it is to be
flesh are discriminated either by different faculties, or by the same faculty in two different states; for flesh necessarily involves matter and is like what is snub-nosed, a *this*
in a *this*. Now it is by means of the sensitive faculty that we discriminate the hot and

the cold, i.e. the factors which combined in a certain ratio constitute flesh: the essential   15
character of flesh is apprehended by something different either wholly separate from
the sensitive faculty or related to it as a bent line to the same line when it has been
straightened out.

Again in the case of abstract objects what is straight is analogous to what is
snub-nosed; for it necessarily implies a continuum: its constitutive essence is different,
if we may distinguish between straightness and what is straight: let us take it to be two-
ness. It must be apprehended, therefore, by a different power or by the same power in a   20
different state. To sum up, in so far as the realities it knows are capable of being separated from their matter, so it is also with the powers of thought.

The problem might be suggested: if thinking is a passive affection, then if
thought is simple and impassible and has nothing in common with anything else, as
Anaxagoras says, how can it come to think at all? For interaction between two factors   25
is held to require a precedent community of nature between the factors. Again it might
be asked, is thought a possible object of thought to itself? For if thought is thinkable
per se and what is thinkable is in kind one and the same, then either thought will belong to everything, or it will contain some element common to it with all other realities
which makes them all thinkable.

Have not we already disposed of the difficulty about interaction involving a   30
common element, when we said that thought is in a sense potentially whatever is thinkable, though actually it is nothing until it has thought? What it thinks must be in it just
as characters may be said to be on a writing-table on which as yet nothing actually   430ᵃ
stands written: this is exactly what happens with thought.

Thought is itself thinkable in exactly the same way as its objects are. For in the
case of objects which involve no matter, what thinks and what is thought are identical;
for speculative knowledge and its object are identical. (Why thought is not always   5
thinking we must consider later.) In the case of those which contain matter each of the
objects of thought is only potentially present. It follows that while they will not have
thought in them (for thought is a potentiality of them only in so far as they are capable
of being disengaged from matter) thought may yet be thinkable.

5. Since in every class of things, as in nature as a whole, we find two factors involved,   10
a matter which is potentially all the particulars included in the class, a cause which is
productive in the sense that it makes them all (the latter standing to the former, as e.g.
an art to its material), these distinct elements must likewise be found within the soul.

And in fact thought, as we have described it, is what it is by virtue of becoming
all things, while there is another which is what it is by virtue of making all things: this   15
is a sort of positive state like light; for in a sense light makes potential colours into actual colours.

Thought in this sense of it is separable, impassible, unmixed, since it is in its essential nature activity (for always the active is superior to the passive factor, the originating force to the matter).

Actual knowledge is identical with its object: in the individual, potential knowl-   20
edge is in time prior to actual knowledge, but absolutely it is not prior even in time. It
does not sometimes think and sometimes not think. When separated it is alone just
what it is, and this above is immortal and eternal (we do not remember because, while
this is impossible, passive thought is perishable); and without this nothing thinks.

NICHOMACHEAN ETHICS (in part)

BOOK I

1094ª   *1. The Good as the Aim of Action:* Every art or applied science and every systematic investigation, and similarly every action and choice, seem to aim at some good; the good, therefore, has been well defined as that at which all things aim.* But it is clear that there is a difference in the ends at which they aim: in some cases the activ-
5   ity is the end, in others the end is some product beyond the activity. In cases where the end lies beyond the action the product is naturally superior to the activity.

Since there are many activities, arts, and sciences, the number of ends is correspondingly large: of medicine the end is health, of shipbuilding a vessel, of strategy, victory, and of household management, wealth. In many instances several such pur-
10   suits are grouped together under a single capacity: the art of bridle-making, for example, and everything else pertaining to the equipment of a horse are grouped together under horsemanship; horsemanship in turn, along with every other military action, is grouped together under strategy; and other pursuits are grouped together under other capacities. In all these cases the ends of the master sciences are preferable to the ends
15   of the subordinate sciences, since the latter are pursued for the sake of the former. This is true whether the ends of the actions lie in the activities themselves or, as is the case in the disciplines just mentioned, in something beyond the activities.

2. Politics as the Master Science of the Good: Now, if there exists an end in the realm of action which we desire for its own sake, an end which determines all our other desires; if, in other words, we do not make all our choices for the sake of some-
20   thing else—for in this way the process will go on infinitely so that our desire would be futile and pointless—then obviously this end will be the good, that is, the highest good. Will not the knowledge of this good, consequently, be very important to our lives? Would it not better equip us, like archers who have a target to aim at, to hit the proper
25   mark? If so, we must try to comprehend in outline at least what this good is and to which branch of knowledge or to which capacity it belongs.

This good, one should think, belongs to the most sovereign and most comprehensive master science, and politics** clearly fits this description. For it determines which sciences ought to exist in states, what kind of sciences each group of citizens must
1094ᵇ   learn, and what degree of proficiency each must attain. We observe further that the most honored capacities, such as strategy, household management, and oratory, are contained in politics. Since this science uses the rest of the sciences, and since, more-

---

*We do not know who first gave this definition of the good. It is certainly implied in the Platonic dialogues, especially in *Republic,* Book VI; but the most likely candidate for the formulation here is Eudoxus.

**Politike* is the science of the city-state, the *polis,* and its members, not merely in our narrow "political" sense of the word but also in the sense that a civilized human existence is, according to Plato and Aristotle, only possible in the *polis.* Thus *politike* involves not only the science of the state, "politics," but of our concept of "society" as well.

Aristotle, *The Nichomachean Ethics,* Books I–II; Books VI–VII; Book X, 6–8, translated by Martin Ostwald (New York: Macmillan/Library of the Liberal Arts, 1962).

over, it legislates what people are to do and what they are not to do, its end seems to   5
embrace the ends of the other sciences. Thus it follows that the end of politics is the
good for man. For even if the good is the same for the individual and the state, the
good of the state clearly is the greater and more perfect thing to attain and to safeguard.
The attainment of the good for one man alone is, to be sure, a source of satisfaction;   10
yet to secure it for a nation and for states is nobler and more divine. In short, these are
the aims of our investigation, which is in a sense an investigation of social and political
matters.

3. The Limitations of Ethics and Politics: Our discussion will be adequate if it
achieves clarity within the limits of the subject matter. For precision cannot be expected in the treatment of all subjects alike, any more than it can be expected in all
manufactured articles. Problems of what is noble and just, which politics examines,
present so much variety and irregularity that some people believe that they exist only   15
by convention and not by nature. The problem of the good, too, presents a similar kind
of irregularity, because in many cases good things bring harmful results. There are instances of men ruined by wealth, and others by courage. Therefore, in a discussion of
such subjects, which has to start from a basis of this kind, we must be satisfied to indicate the truth with a rough and general sketch: when the subject and the basis of a dis-   20
cussion consist of matters that hold good only as a general rule, but not always, the
conclusions reached must be of the same order. The various points that are made must
be received in the same spirit. For a well-schooled man is one who searches for that
degree of precision in each kind of study which the nature of the subject at hand admits: it is obviously just as foolish to accept arguments of probability from a mathe-   25
matician as to demand strict demonstrations from an orator.

Each man can judge competently the things he knows, and of these he is a good
judge. Accordingly, a good judge in each particular field is one who has been trained in   1095ª
it, and a good judge in general, a man who has received an all-round schooling. For
that reason, a young man is not equipped to be a student of politics; for he has no experience in the actions which life demands of him, and these actions form the basis and
subject matter of the discussion. Moreover, since he follows his emotions, his study
will be pointless and unprofitable, for the end of this kind of study is not knowledge   5
but action. Whether he is young in years or immature in character makes no difference;
for his deficiency is not a matter of time but of living and of pursuing all his interests
under the influence of his emotions. Knowledge brings no benefit to this kind of person, just as it brings none to the morally weak. But those who regulate their desires and   10
actions by a rational principle* will greatly benefit from a knowledge of this subject.
So much by way of a preface about the student, the limitations which have to be accepted, and the objective before us.

4. Happiness Is the Good, But Many Views Are Held About It: To resume the
discussion: since all knowledge and every choice is directed toward some good, let us   15
discuss what is in our view the aim of politics, i.e., the highest good attainable by action. As far as its name is concerned, most people would probably agree: for both the

*The fundamental meaning of *Logos* is "speech," "statement," in the sense of a coherent and rational
arrangement of words; but it can apply to a rational principle underlying many things, and may be translated
in different contexts by "rational account," "explanation," "argument," "treatise," or "discussion." In Chapters 7 and 13 below, *Logos* is used in a normative sense, describing the human faculty which comprehends
and formulates rational principles and thus guides the conduct of a good and reasonable man.

common run of people and cultivated men call it happiness, and understand by "being
happy" the same as "living well" and "doing well." But when it comes to defining
20   what happiness is, they disagree, and the account given by the common run differs
from that of the philosophers. The former say it is some clear and obvious good, such
as pleasure, wealth, or honor; some say it is one thing and others another, and often the
very same person identifies it with different things at different times: when he is sick
he thinks it is health, and when he is poor he says it is wealth; and when people are
25   conscious of their own ignorance, they admire those who talk above their heads in ac-
cents of greatness. Some thinkers used to believe that there exists over and above these
many goods another good, good in itself and by itself, which also is the cause of good
in all these things. An examination of all the different opinions would perhaps be a little pointless, and it is sufficient to concentrate on those which are most in evidence or
30   which seem to make some sort of sense.

Nor must we overlook the fact that arguments which proceed from fundamental principles are different from arguments that lead up to them. Plato, too, rightly
recognized this as a problem and used to ask whether the discussion was proceeding
from or leading up to fundamental principles, just as in a race course there is a dif-
1095ᵇ   ference between running from the judges to the far end of the track and running back
again.* Now, we must start with the known. But this term has two connotations:
"what is known to us" and "what is known" pure and simple. Therefore, we should
5   start perhaps from what is known to us. For that reason, to be a competent student of
what is right and just, and of politics generally, one must first have received a proper
upbringing in moral conduct. The acceptance of a fact as a fact is the starting point,
and if this is sufficiently clear, there will be no further need to ask why it is so. A
man with this kind of background has or can easily acquire the foundations from
which he must start. But if he neither has nor can acquire them, let him lend an ear to
Hesiod's words:

10   That man is all-best who himself works out every problem. . . .
That man, too, is admirable who follows one who speaks well.
He who cannot see the truth for himself, nor, hearing it from others, store it away in his
    mind, that man is utterly useless.

5. Various Views on the Highest Good: But to return to the point from which we
15   digressed. It is not unreasonable that men should derive their concept of the good and
of happiness from the lives which they lead. The common run of people and the most
vulgar identify it with pleasure, and for that reason are satisfied with a life of enjoyment. For the most notable kinds of life are three: the life just mentioned, the political
life, and the contemplative life.

The common run of people, as we saw, betray their utter slavishness in their
20   preference for a life suitable to cattle; but their views seem plausible because many
people in high places share the feelings of Sardanapallus.** Cultivated and active men,
on the other hand, believe the good to be honor, for honor, one might say, is the end of
the political life. But this is clearly too superficial an answer: for honor seems to de-

---

*A Greek race course was U-shaped with the starting line at the open end, which is also where the
judges would have their place. The race was run around a marker set up toward the opposite end of the U,
and back again to the starting line.

**Sardanapallus is the Hellenized name of the Assyrian king Ashurbanipal (669–626 B.C.). Many
stories about his sensual excesses were current in antiquity.

pend on those who confer it rather than on him who receives it, whereas our guess is   25
that the good is a man's own possession which cannot easily be taken away from him.
Furthermore, men seem to pursue honor to assure themselves of their own worth; at
any rate, they seek to be honored by sensible men and by those who know them, and
they want to be honored on the basis of their virtue or excellence [<aretē>].* Obviously, then, excellence, as far as they are concerned, is better than honor. One might   30
perhaps even go so far as to consider excellence rather than honor as the end of political life. However, even excellence proves to be imperfect as an end: for a man might
possibly possess it while asleep or while being inactive all his life, and while, in addi-   1096ᵃ
tion, undergoing the greatest suffering and misfortune. Nobody would call the life of
such a man happy, except for the sake of maintaining an argument. But enough of this:
the subject has been sufficiently treated in our publications addressed to a wider audience. In the third place there is the contemplative life, which we shall examine later on.   5
As for the money-maker, his life is led under some kind of constraint: clearly, wealth is
not the good which we are trying to find, for it is only useful, i.e., it is a means to
something else. Hence one might rather regard the aforementioned objects as ends,
since they are valued for their own sake. But even they prove not to be the good,
though many words have been wasted to show that they are. Accordingly, we may dis-   10
miss them.

   6. Plato's View of the Good: But perhaps we had better examine the universal
good and face the problem of its meaning, although such an inquiry is repugnant, since
those who have introduced the doctrine of Forms** are dear to us. But in the interest of
truth, one should perhaps think a man, especially if he is a philosopher, had better give
up even [theories that once were] his own and in fact must do so. Both are dear to us,   15
but it is our sacred duty to honor truth more highly [than friends].
   The proponents of this theory did not make Forms out of those classes within
which they recognized an order involving priority and posteriority; for that reason they
made no provision, either, for a Form comprising all numbers.*** However, the term
"good" is used in the categories of substance, of quality, and of relatedness alike; but a
thing-as-such, i.e., a substance, is by nature prior to a relation into which it can enter: 20
relatedness is, as it were, an offshoot or logical accident of substance. Consequently,
there cannot be a Form common to the good-as-such and the good as a relation.
   Secondly, the term "good" has as many meanings as the word "is": it is used to
describe substances, e.g., divinity and intelligence are good; qualities, e.g., the virtues   25
are good; quantities, e.g., the proper amount is good; relatedness, e.g., the useful is
good; time, e.g., the right moment is good; place, e.g., a place to live is good; and so
forth. It is clear, therefore, that the good cannot be something universal, common to all

---

   Aretē denotes the functional excellence of any person, animal, or thing—that quality which enables
the possessor to perform his own particular function well. Thus the *aretai* (plural) of man in relation to other
men are his qualities which enable him to function well in society. The translation "virtue" often seems too
narrow, and accordingly "excellence" and "goodness," or a combination of these, will also be used.
   **The reference is of course to Plato's theory of *eide* or *ideai* and especially the Form of the Good,
which is Aristotle's chief target here.
   ***Since for Plato and his followers the Forms are absolute being, in which there is no room for be-
coming or any kind of development, they do not recognize a Form of a developing series, in which each successive member implies the preceding members of the same series. But, as Aristotle proceeds to show, the
term "good" belongs to such a developing series: if we call a certain quality, e.g., blueness, "good," we have
to assume first that there is such a thing as blueness; i.e., we have to predicate it in the category of substance
before we can predicate it in the category of quality.

cases, and single; for if it were, it would not be applicable in all categories but only in one.

30   Thirdly, since the things which are included under one Form are the subject matter of a single science, there should be a single science dealing with all good things. But in actual fact there are many sciences dealing even with the goods that fall into a single category. To take, for example, the right moment: in war it is the proper concern of strategy, whereas in treating a disease it is part of the study of medicine. Or to take the proper amount: in food it is the subject of medicine; in physical training, of gymnastics.

35   One might even [go further and] raise the question what exactly they mean by a
1096ᵇ   "thing-as-such"; for the selfsame definition of "man" applies to both "man-as-such" and a particular man. For inasmuch as they refer to "man," there will be no difference between the two; and if this is true, there will be no difference, either, between "good-as-such" and "good," since both are good. Nor indeed will the "good-as-such" be more of a good because it is everlasting: after all, whiteness which lasts for a long time is no whiter than whiteness which lasts only for a day.

5   The argument of the Pythagoreans on this point seems to be more convincing. They give unity a place in the column of goods; and indeed even Speusippus* seems to follow them. But more about this elsewhere.

An objection might be raised against what we have said on the ground that the [Platonic] doctrine does not refer to every kind of good, and that only things which are
10   pursued and loved for their own sake are called "good" by reference to one single Form. That which produces good or somehow guarantees its permanence, [the Platonists argue,] or that which prevents the opposite of a good from asserting itself is called "good" because it is conducive to the intrinsically good and in a different sense. Now, the term "good" has obviously two different meanings: (1) things which are intrinsically good, and (2) things which are good as being conducive to the intrinsically good.
15   Let us, therefore, separate the intrinsically good things from the useful things and examine whether they are called "good" by reference to a single Form.

What sort of things could be called intrinsically good? Are they the goods that are pursued without regard to additional benefits, such as thought, sight, certain pleasures and honors? For even if we pursue these also for the sake of something else, one would still classify them among things intrinsically good. Or is nothing good except
20   the Form of Good? If that is the case, the Form will be pointless. But if, on the contrary, thought, sight, etc. also belong to the group of intrinsically good things, the same definition of "good" will have to be manifested in all of them, just as, for example, the definition of whiteness is the same in snow and in white paint. But in actual fact, the definitions of "good" as manifested in honor, thought, and pleasure are different and distinct. The good, therefore, is not some element common to all these things as
25   derived from one Form.

What, then, is the meaning of "good" [in these different things]? Surely, it is not that they merely happen to have the same name. Do we call them "good" because they are derived from a single good, or because they all aim at a single good? Or do we rather call them "good" by analogy, e.g., as sight is good in the body, so intelligence is good in the soul, and so other things are good within their respective fields?
30   But perhaps this subject should be dismissed for the present, because a detailed discussion of it belongs more properly to a different branch of philosophy, [namely, first

*Speusippus was Plato's nephew and disciple who succeeded him a head of the Academy from 347–339 B.C.

philosophy]. The same applies to the Form [of the Good]: for, assuming that there is some single good which different things possess in common, or that there exists a good absolutely in itself and by itself, it evidently is something which cannot be realized in action or attained by man. But the good which we are now seeking must be attainable.

Perhaps one may think that the recognition of an absolute good will be advantageous for the purpose of attaining and realizing in action the goods which can be attained and realized. By treating the absolute good as a pattern, [they might argue,] we shall gain a better knowledge of what things are good for us, and once we know that, we can achieve them. This argument has, no doubt, some plausibility; however, it does not tally with the procedure of the sciences. For while all the sciences aim at some good and seek to fulfill it, they leave the knowledge of the absolute good out of consideration. Yet if this knowledge were such a great help, it would make no sense that all the craftsmen are ignorant of it and do not even attempt to seek it. One might also wonder what benefit a weaver or a carpenter might derive in the practice of his own art from a knowledge of the absolute Good, or in what way a physician who has contemplated the Form of the Good will become more of a physician or a general more of a general. For actually, a physician does not even examine health in this fashion; he examines the health of man, or perhaps better, the health of a particular man, for he practices his medicine on particular cases. So much for this.

7. The Good Is Final and Self-Sufficient; Happiness Is Defined: Let us return again to our investigation into the nature of the good which we are seeking. It is evidently something different in different actions and in each art: it is one thing in medicine, another in strategy, and another again in each of the other arts. What, then, is the good of each? Is it not that for the sake of which everything else is done? That means it is health in the case of medicine, victory in the case of strategy, a house in the case of building, a different thing in the case of different arts, and in all actions and choices it is the end. For it is for the sake of the end that all else is done. Thus, if there is some one end for all that we do, this would be the good attainable by action; if there are several ends, they will be the goods attainable by action.

Our argument has gradually progressed to the same point at which we were before, and we must try to clarify it still further. Since there are evidently several ends, and since we choose some of these—e.g., wealth, flutes, and instruments generally—as a means to something else, it is obvious that not all ends are final. The highest good, on the other hand, must be something final. Thus, if there is only one final end, this will be the good we are seeking; if there are several, it will be the most final and perfect of them. We call that which is pursued as an end in itself more final than an end which is pursued for the sake of something else; and what is never chosen as a means to something else we call more final than that which is chosen both as an end in itself and as a means to something else. What is always chosen as an end in itself and never as a means to something else is called final in an unqualified sense. This description seems to apply to happiness above all else: for we always choose happiness as an end in itself and never for the sake of something else. Honor, pleasure, intelligence, and all virtue we choose partly for themselves—for we would choose each of them even if no further advantage would accrue from them—but we also choose them partly for the sake of happiness, because we assume that it is through them that we will be happy. On the other hand, no one chooses happiness for the sake of honor, pleasure, and the like, nor as a means to anything at all.

We arrive at the same conclusion if we approach the question from the standpoint of self-sufficiency. For the final and perfect good seems to be self-sufficient.

35
1097[a]

5

10

15

20

25

30

1097[b]

5

However, we define something as self-sufficient not by reference to the "self" alone. We do not mean a man who lives his life in isolation, but a man who also lives with parents, children, a wife, and friends and fellow citizens generally, since man is by nature a social and political being. But some limit must be set to these relationships; for if they are extended to include ancestors, descendants, and friends of friends, they will go on to infinity. However, this point must be reserved for investigation later. For the present we define as "self-sufficient" that which taken by itself makes life something desirable and deficient in nothing. It is happiness, in our opinion, which fits this description. Moreover, happiness is of all things the one most desirable, and it is not counted as one good thing among many others. But if it were counted as one among many others, it is obvious that the addition of even the least of the goods would make it more desirable; for the addition would produce an extra amount of good, and the greater amount of good is always more desirable than the lesser. We see then that happiness is something final and self-sufficient and the end of our actions.

To call happiness the highest good is perhaps a little trite, and a clearer account of what it is, is still required. Perhaps this is best done by first ascertaining the proper function of man. For just as the goodness and performance of a flute player, a sculptor, or any kind of expert, and generally of anyone who fulfills some function or performs some action, are thought to reside in his proper function, so the goodness and performance of man would seem to reside in whatever is his proper function. Is it then possible that while a carpenter and a shoemaker have their own proper functions and spheres of action, man as man has none, but was left by nature a good-for-nothing without a function? Should we not assume that just as the eye, the hand, the foot, and in general each part of the body clearly has its own proper function, so man too has some function over and above the functions of his parts? What can this function possibly be? Simply living? He shares that even with plants, but we are now looking for something peculiar to man. Accordingly, the life of nutrition and growth must be excluded. Next in line there is a life of sense perception. But this, too, man has in common with the horse, the ox, and every animal. There remains then an active life of the rational element. The rational element has two parts: one is rational in that it obeys the rule of reason, the other in that it possesses and conceives rational rules. Since the expression "life of the rational element" also can be used in two senses, we must make it clear that we mean a life determined by the activity, as opposed to the mere possession, of the rational element. For the activity, it seems, has a greater claim to be the function of man.

The proper function of man, then, consists in an activity of the soul in conformity with a rational principle or, at least, not without it. In speaking of the proper function of a given individual we mean that it is the same in kind as the function of an individual who sets high standards for himself: the proper function of a harpist, for example, is the same as the function of a harpist who has set high standards for himself. The same applies to any and every group of individuals: the full attainment of excellence must be added to the mere function. In other words, the function of the harpist is to play the harp; the function of the harpist who has high standards is to play it well. On these assumptions, if we take the proper function of man to be a certain kind of life, and if this kind of life is an activity of the soul and consists in actions performed in conjunction with the rational element, and if a man of high standards is he who performs these actions well and properly, and if a function is well performed when it is performed in accordance with the excellence appropriate to it; we reach the conclusion that the good of man is an activity of the soul in conformity with excellence or virtue, and if there are several virtues, in conformity with the best and most complete.

But we must add "in a complete life." For one swallow does not make a spring, nor does one sunny day; similarly, one day or a short time does not make a man blessed* and happy.

This will suffice as an outline of the good: for perhaps one ought to make a general sketch first and fill in the details afterwards. Once a good outline has been made, anyone, it seems, is capable of developing and completing it in detail, and time is a good inventor or collaborator in such an effort. Advances in the arts, too, have come about in this way, for anyone can fill in gaps. We must also bear in mind what has been said above, namely that one should not require precision in all pursuits alike, but in each field precision varies with the matter under discussion and should be required only to the extent to which it is appropriate to the investigation. A carpenter and a geometrician both want to find a right angle, but they do not want to find it in the same sense: the former wants to find it to the extent to which it is useful for his work, the latter, wanting to see truth, tries to ascertain what it is and what sort of thing it is. We must, likewise, approach other subjects in the same spirit, in order to prevent minor points from assuming a greater importance than the major tasks. Nor should we demand to know a causal explanation in all matters alike; in some instances, e.g., when dealing with fundamental principles, it is sufficient to point out convincingly that such-and-such is in fact the case. The fact here is the primary thing and the fundamental principle. Some fundamental principles can be apprehended by induction, others by sense perception, others again by some sort of habituation,** and others by still other means. We must try to get at each of them in a way naturally appropriate to it, and must be scrupulous in defining it correctly, because it is of great importance for the subsequent course of the discussion. Surely, a good beginning is more than half the whole, and as it comes to light, it sheds light on many problems.

8. Popular Views About Happiness Confirm Our Position: We must examine the fundamental principle with which we are concerned, [happiness,] not only on the basis of the logical conclusion we have reached and on the basis of the elements which make up its definition, but also on the basis of the views commonly expressed about it. For in a true statement, all the facts are in harmony; in a false statement, truth soon introduces a discordant note.

Good things are commonly divided into three classes: (1) external goods, (2) goods of the soul, and (3) goods of the body. Of these, we call the goods pertaining to the soul goods in the highest and fullest sense. But in speaking of "soul," we refer to our soul's actions and activities. Thus, our definition tallies with this opinion which has been current for a long time and to which philosophers subscribe. We are also right in defining the end as consisting of actions and activities; for in this way the end is included among the goods of the soul and not among external goods.

Also the view that a happy man lives well and fares well fits in with our definition: for we have all but defined happiness as a kind of good life and well-being.

Moreover, the characteristics which one looks for in happiness are all included in our definition. For some people think that happiness is virtue, others that it is practical

---

*The distinction Aristotle seems to observe between *makarios,* "blessed" or "supremely happy," and *eudaimon,* "happy," is that the former describes happiness insofar as it is god-given, while the latter describes happiness as attained by man through his own efforts.

**This, according to Aristotle, is the way in which the fundamental principles of ethics are learned, and for that reason a person must be mature in order to be able to study ethics properly. Aristotle is not trying to persuade his listener of the truth of these principles, but takes it for granted that the listener has learned them at home.

wisdom, others that it is some kind of theoretical wisdom; others again believe it to be all or some of these accompanied by, or not devoid of, pleasure; and some people also include external prosperity in its definition.* Some of these views are expressed by many people and have come down from antiquity, some by a few men of high prestige, and it is not reasonable to assume that both groups are altogether wrong; the presumption is rather that they are right in at least one or even in most respects.

Now, in our definition we are in agreement with those who describe happiness as virtue or as some particular virtue, for our term "activity in conformity with virtue" implies virtue. But it does doubtless make a considerable difference whether we think of the highest good as consisting in the possession or in the practice of virtue, viz., as being a characteristic or an activity. For a characteristic may exist without producing any good result, as for example, in a man who is asleep or incapacitated in some other respect. An activity, on the other hand, must produce a result: [an active person] will necessarily act and act well. Just as the crown at the Olympic Games is not awarded to the most beautiful and the strongest but to the participants in the contests—for it is among them that the victors are found—so the good and noble things in life are won by those who act rightly.

The life of men active in this sense is also pleasant in itself. For the sensation of pleasure belongs to the soul, and each man derives pleasure from what he is said to love: a lover of horses from horses, a lover of the theater from plays, and in the same way a lover of justice from just acts, and a lover of virtue in general from virtuous acts. In most men, pleasant acts conflict with one another because they are not pleasant by nature, but men who love what is noble derive pleasure from what is naturally pleasant. Actions which conform to virtue are naturally pleasant, and, as a result, such actions are not only pleasant for those who love the noble but also pleasant in themselves. The life of such men has no further need of pleasure as an added attraction, but it contains pleasure within itself. We may even go so far as to state that the man who does not enjoy performing noble actions is not a good man at all. Nobody would call a man just who does not enjoy acting justly, nor generous who does not enjoy generous actions, and so on. If this is true, actions performed in conformity with virtue are in themselves pleasant.

Of course it goes without saying that such actions are good as well as noble, and they are both in the highest degree, if the man of high moral standards displays any right judgment about them at all; and his judgment corresponds to our description. So we see that happiness is at once the best, noblest, and most pleasant thing, and these qualities are not separate, as the inscription at Delos makes out:

The most just is most noble, but health is the best, and to win what one loves is pleasantest.

For the best activities encompass all these attributes, and it is in these, or in the best one of them, that we maintain happiness consists.

Still, happiness, as we have said, needs external goods as well. For it is impossible or at least not easy to perform noble actions if one lacks the wherewithal. Many

---

*The view that virtue alone constitutes happiness was espoused by Antisthenes and the Cynics (and later by the Stoics); the doctrine that all virtues are forms of *phronesis* or "practical wisdom" is attributed to Socrates; theoretical wisdom as virtue may perhaps be attributed to Anaxagoras and his doctrine of *Nous;* the view that pleasure must be added to virtue and wisdom is that of Plato; and the ancient commentators on this passage identify Xenocrates, Plato's pupil and later head of the Academy, as regarding external goods as essential for the good life.

actions can only be performed with the help of instruments, as it were: friends, wealth, and political power. And there are some external goods the absence of which spoils supreme happiness, e.g., good birth, good children, and beauty: for a man who is very ugly in appearance or ill-born or who lives all by himself and has no children cannot be classified as altogether happy; even less happy perhaps is a man whose children and friends are worthless, or one who has lost good children and friends through death. Thus, as we have said, happiness also requires well-being of this kind, and that is the reason why some classify good fortune with happiness, while others link it to virtue. 1099^b

5

9. How Happiness Is Acquired: This also explains why there is a problem whether happiness is acquired by learning, by discipline, or by some other kind of training, or whether we attain it by reason of some divine dispensation or even by chance. Now, if there is anything at all which comes to men as a gift from the gods, it is reasonable to suppose that happiness above all else is god-given; and of all things human it is the most likely to be god-given, inasmuch as it is the best. But although this subject is perhaps more appropriate to a different field of study, it is clear that happiness is one of the most divine things, even if it is not god-sent but attained through virtue and some kind of learning or training. For the prize and end of excellence and virtue is the best thing of all, and it is something divine and blessed. Moreover, if happiness depends on excellence, it will be shared by many people; for study and effort will make it accessible to anyone whose capacity for virtue is unimpaired. And if it is better that happiness is acquired in this way rather than by chance, it is reasonable to assume that this is the way in which it is acquired. For, in the realm of nature, things are naturally arranged in the best way possible—and the same is also true of the products of art and of any kind of causation, especially the highest. To leave the greatest and noblest of things to chance would hardly be right. 10

15

20

A solution of this question is also suggested by our earlier definition, according to which the good of man, happiness, is some kind of activity of the soul in conformity with virtue. All the other goods are either necessary prerequisites for happiness, or are by nature co-workers with it and useful instruments for attaining it. Our results also tally with what we said at the outset: for we stated that the end of politics is the best of ends; and the main concern of politics is to engender a certain character in the citizens and to make them good and disposed to perform noble actions. 25

30

We are right, then, when we call neither a horse nor an ox nor any other animal happy, for none of them is capable of participating in an activity of this kind. For the same reason, a child is not happy, either; for, because of his age, he cannot yet perform such actions. When we do call a child happy, we do so by reason of the hopes we have for his future. Happiness, as we have said, requires completeness in virtue as well as a complete lifetime. Many changes and all kinds of contingencies befall a man in the course of his life, and it is possible that the most prosperous man will encounter great misfortune in his old age, as the Trojan legends tell about Priam. When a man has met a fate such as his and has come to a wretched end, no one calls him happy. 1100^a

5

10. Can a Man Be Called "Happy" During His Lifetime?: Must we, then, apply the term "happy" to no man at all as long as he is alive? Must we, as Solon would have us do, wait to see his end?* And, on this assumption, is it also true that a man is actu- 10

---

*This is one of the main points made by Solon, Athenian statesman and poet of the early sixth century B.C., in his conversation with the Lydian king, Croesus.

ally happy after he is dead? Is this not simply absurd, especially for us who define happiness as a kind of activity? Suppose we do not call a dead man happy, and interpret Solon's words to mean that only when a man is dead can we safely say that he has been happy, since he is now beyond the reach of evil and misfortune—this view, too, is open to objection. For it seems that to some extent good and evil really exist for a dead man, just as they may exist for a man who lives without being conscious of them, for example, honors and disgraces, and generally the successes and failures of his children and descendants. This presents a further problem. A man who has lived happily to his old age and has died as happily as he lived may have many vicissitudes befall his descendants: some of them may be good and may be granted the kind of life which they deserve, and others may not. It is, further, obvious that the descendants may conceivably be removed from their ancestors by various degrees. Under such circumstances, it would be odd if the dead man would share in the vicissitudes of his descendants and be happy at one time and wretched at another. But it would also be odd if the fortunes of their descendants did not affect the ancestors at all, not even for a short time.

But we must return to the problem raised earlier, for through it our present problem perhaps may be solved. If one must look to the end and praise a man not as being happy but as having been happy in the past, is it not paradoxical that at a time when a man actually is happy this attribute, though true, cannot be applied to him? We are unwilling to call the living happy because changes may befall them and because we believe that happiness has permanence and is not amenable to changes under any circumstances, whereas fortunes revolve many times in one person's lifetime. For obviously, if we are to keep pace with a man's fortune, we shall frequently have to call the same man happy at one time and wretched at another and demonstrate that the happy man is a kind of chameleon, and that the foundations [of his life] are unsure. Or is it quite wrong to make our judgment depend on fortune? Yes, it is wrong, for fortune does not determine whether we fare well or ill, but is, as we said, merely an accessory to human life; activities in conformity with virtue constitute happiness, and the opposite activities constitute its opposite.

The question which we have just discussed further confirms our definition. For no function of man possesses as much stability as do activities in conformity with virtue: these seem to be even more durable than scientific knowledge. And the higher the virtuous activities, the more durable they are, because men who are supremely happy spend their lives in these activities most intensely and most continuously, and this seems to be the reason why such activities cannot be forgotten.

The happy man will have the attribute of permanence which we are discussing, and he will remain happy throughout his life. For he will always or to the highest degree both do and contemplate what is in conformity with virtue; he will bear the vicissitudes of fortune most nobly and with perfect decorum under all circumstances, inasmuch as he is truly good and "four-square beyond reproach."

But fortune brings many things to pass, some great and some small. Minor instances of good and likewise of bad luck obviously do not decisively tip the scales of life, but a number of major successes will make life more perfectly happy; for, in the first place, by their very nature they help to make life attractive, and secondly, they afford the opportunity for noble and good actions. On the other hand, frequent reverses can crush and mar supreme happiness in that they inflict pain and thwart many activities. Still, nobility shines through even in such circumstances, when a man bears many great misfortunes with good grace not because he is insensitive to pain but because he is noble and high-minded.

If, as we said, the activities determine a man's life, no supremely happy man can ever become miserable, for he will never do what is hateful and base. For in our opinion, the man who is truly good and wise will bear with dignity whatever fortune may bring, and will always act as nobly as circumstances permit, just as a good general makes the most strategic use of the troops at his disposal, and a good shoemaker makes the best shoe he can from the leather available, and so on with experts in all other fields. If this is true, a happy man will never become miserable; but even so, supreme happiness will not be his if a fate such as Priam's befalls him. And yet, he will not be fickle and changeable; he will not be dislodged from his happiness easily by any misfortune that comes along, but only by great and numerous disasters such as will make it impossible for him to become happy again in a short time; if he recovers his happiness at all, it will be only after a long period of time, in which he has won great distinctions. 35 1101ᵃ 5 10

Is there anything to prevent us, then, from defining the happy man as one whose activities are an expression of complete virtue, and who is sufficiently equipped with external goods, not simply at a given moment but to the end of his life? Or should we add that he must die as well as live in the manner which we have defined? For we cannot foresee the future, and happiness, we maintain, is an end which is absolutely final and complete in every respect. If this be granted, we shall define as "supremely happy" those living men who fulfill and continue to fulfill these requirements, but blissful only as human beings. So much for this question. 15 20

11. Do the Fortunes of the Living Affect the Dead?: That the fortunes of his descendants and of all those near and dear to him do not affect the happiness of a dead man at all, seems too unfeeling a view and contrary to the prevailing opinions. Many and different in kind are the accidents that can befall us, and some hit home more closely than others. It would, therefore, seem to be a long and endless task to make detailed distinctions, and perhaps a general outline will be sufficient. Just as one's own misfortunes are sometimes momentous and decisive for one's life and sometimes seem comparatively less important, so the misfortunes of our various friends affect us to varying degrees. In each case it makes a considerable difference whether those who are affected by an event are living or dead; much more so than it matters in a tragedy whether the crimes and horrors have been perpetrated before the opening of the play or are part of the plot. This difference, too, must be taken into account and perhaps still more the problem whether the dead participate in any good or evil. These considerations suggest that even if any good or evil reaches them at all, it must be something weak and negligible (either intrinsically or in relation to them), or at least something too small and insignificant to make the unhappy happy or to deprive the happy of their bliss. The good as well as the bad fortunes of their friends seem, then, to have some effect upon the dead, but the nature and magnitude of the effect is such as not to make the happy unhappy or to produce any similar changes. 25 30 35 1101ᵇ 5

12. The Praise Accorded to Happiness: Now that we have settled these questions, let us consider whether happiness is to be classified among the things which we praise or rather among those which we honor; for it is clear that it is not a potential [but an actual good]. 10

The grounds on which we bestow praise on anything evidently are its quality and the relation in which it stands to other things. In other words, we praise a just man, a courageous man, and in general any good man, and also his virtue or excellence, on the basis of his actions and achievements; moreover, we praise a strong man, a swift 15

runner, and so forth, because he possesses a certain natural quality and stands in a certain relation to something good and worth while. Our feelings about praising the gods provide a further illustration of this point. For it is ridiculous to refer the gods to our
20   standards; but this is precisely what praising them amounts to, since praise, as we said, entails a reference to something else. But if praise is appropriate only for relative things, it is clear that the best things do not call for praise but for something greater and better, as indeed is generally recognized: for we call the gods "blessed" and "happy"
25   and use these terms also for the most godlike man. The same is true of good things: no one praises happiness in the same sense in which he praises justice, but he exalts its bliss as something better and more nearly divine.

Eudoxus, too, seems to have used the right method for advocating that pleasure is the most excellent, for he took the fact that pleasure, though a good, is not praised as
30   an indication of its superiority to the things that are praised, as god and the good are, for they are the standards to which we refer everything else.

Praise is proper to virtue or excellence, because it is excellence that makes men capable of performing noble deeds. Eulogies, on the other hand, are appropriate for achievements of the body as well as of the mind. However, a detailed analysis of this subject is perhaps rather the business of those who have made a study of eulogies. For
35   our present purposes, we may draw the conclusion from the preceding argument that
1102ᵃ   happiness is one of the goods that are worthy of honor and are final. This again seems to be due to the fact that it is a starting point or fundamental principle, since for its sake all of us do everything else. And the source and cause of all good things we consider as something worthy of honor and as divine.

5   *13. The Psychological Foundations of the Virtues:* Since happiness is a certain activity of the soul in conformity with perfect virtue, we must now examine what virtue or excellence is. For such an inquiry will perhaps better enable us to discover the nature of happiness. Moreover, the man who is truly concerned about politics seems to devote special attention to excellence, since it is his aim to make the citizens good and
10   law-abiding. We have an example of this in the lawgivers of Crete and Sparta and in other great legislators. If an examination of virtue is part of politics, this question clearly fits into the pattern of our original plan.

There can be no doubt that the virtue which we have to study is human virtue.
15   For the good which we have been seeking is a human good and the happiness a human happiness. By human virtue we do not mean the excellence of the body, but that of the soul, and we define happiness as an activity of the soul. If this is true, the student of politics must obviously have some knowledge of the workings of the soul, just as the
20   man who is to heal eyes must know something about the whole body. In fact, knowledge is all the more important for the former, inasmuch as politics is better and more valuable than medicine, and cultivated physicians devote much time and trouble to gain knowledge about the body. Thus, the student of politics must study the soul, but he must do so with his own aim in view, and only to the extent that the objects of his
25   inquiry demand: to go into it in greater detail would perhaps be more laborious than his purposes require.

Some things that are said about the soul in our less technical discussions are adequate enough to be used here, for instance, that the soul consists of two elements, one
30   irrational and one rational. Whether these two elements are separate, like the parts of the body or any other divisible thing, or whether they are only logically separable

though in reality indivisible, as convex and concave are in the circumference of a circle, is irrelevant for our present purposes.

Of the irrational element, again, one part seems to be common to all living things and vegetative in nature: I mean that part which is responsible for nurture and growth. We must assume that some such capacity of the soul exists in everything that takes nourishment, in the embryonic stage as well as when the organism is fully developed; for this makes more sense than to assume the existence of some different capacity at the latter stage. The excellence of this part of the soul is, therefore, shown to be common to all living things and is not exclusively human. This very part and this capacity seem to be most active in sleep. For in sleep the difference between a good man and a bad is least apparent—whence the saying that for half their lives the happy are no better off than the wretched. This is just what we would expect, for sleep is an inactivity of the soul in that it ceases to do things which cause it to be called good or bad. However, to a small extent some bodily movements do penetrate to the soul in sleep, and in this sense the dreams of honest men are better than those of average people. But enough of this subject: we may pass by the nutritive part, since it has no natural share in human excellence or virtue.

In addition to this, there seems to be another integral element of the soul which, though irrational, still does partake of reason in some way. In morally strong and morally weak men we praise the reason that guides them and the rational element of the soul, because it exhorts them to follow the right path and to do what is best. Yet we see in them also another natural strain different from the rational, which fights and resists the guidance of reason. The soul behaves in precisely the same manner as do the paralyzed limbs of the body. When we intend to move the limbs to the right, they turn to the left, and similarly, the impulses of morally weak persons turn in the direction opposite to that in which reason leads them. However, while the aberration of the body is visible, that of the soul is not. But perhaps we must accept it as a fact, nevertheless, that there is something in the soul besides the rational element, which opposes and reacts against it. In what way the two are distinct need not concern us here. But, as we have stated, it too seems to partake of reason; at any rate, in a morally strong man it accepts the leadership of reason, and is perhaps more obedient still in a self-controlled and courageous man, since in him everything is in harmony with the voice of reason.

Thus we see that the irrational element of the soul has two parts: the one is vegetative and has no share in reason at all, the other is the seat of the appetites and of desire in general and partakes of reason insofar as it complies with reason and accepts its leadership; it possesses reason in the sense that we say it is "reasonable" to accept the advice of a father and of friends, not in the sense that we have a "rational" understanding of mathematical propositions. That the irrational element can be persuaded by the rational is shown by the fact that admonition and all manner of rebuke and exhortation are possible. If it is correct to say that the appetitive part, too, has reason, it follows that the rational element of the soul has two subdivisions: the one possesses reason in the strict sense, contained within itself, and the other possesses reason in the sense that it listens to reason as one would listen to a father.

Virtue, too, is differentiated in line with this division of the soul. We call some virtues "intellectual" and others "moral": theoretical wisdom, understanding, and practical wisdom are intellectual virtues, generosity and self-control moral virtues. In speaking of a man's character, we do not describe him as wise or understanding, but as gentle or self-controlled; but we praise the wise man, too, for his characteristic, and praiseworthy characteristics are what we call virtues.

1102^b

5

10

15

20

25

30

1103^a

5

10

BOOK II

1. Moral Virtue as the Result of Habits: Virtue, as we have seen, consists of
15   two-kinds, intellectual virtue and moral virtue. Intellectual virtue or excellence owes
its origin and development chiefly to teaching, and for that reason requires experience
and time. Moral virtue, on the other hand, is formed by habit, *ethos,* and its name,
ethike, is therefore derived, by a slight variation, from *ethos.* This shows, too, that none
20   of the moral virtues is implanted in us by nature, for nothing which exists by nature
can be changed by habit. For example, it is impossible for a stone, which has a natural
downward movement, to become habituated to moving upward, even if one should try
ten thousand times to inculcate the habit by throwing it in the air; nor can fire be made
to move downward, nor can the direction of any nature-given tendency be changed by
habituation. Thus, the virtues are implanted in us neither by nature nor contrary to na-
25   ture: we are by nature equipped with the ability to receive them, and habit brings this
ability to completion and fulfillment.

Furthermore, of all the qualities with which we are endowed by nature, we are
provided with the capacity first, and display the activity afterward. That this is true is
shown by the senses: it is not by frequent seeing or frequent hearing that we acquired
our senses, but on the contrary we first possess and then use them; we do not acquire
30   them by use. The virtues, on the other hand, we acquire by first having put them into
action, and the same is also true of the arts. For the things which we have to learn before we can do them we learn by doing: men become builders by building houses, and
harpists by playing the harp. Similarly, we become just by the practice of just actions,
1103^b self-controlled by exercising self-control, and courageous by performing acts of
courage.

This is corroborated by what happens in states. Lawgivers make the citizens
good by inculcating [good] habits in them, and this is the aim of every lawgiver; if he
5   does not succeed in doing that, his legislation is a failure. It is in this that a good constitution differs from a bad one.

Moreover, the same causes and the same means that produce any excellence or
virtue can also destroy it, and this is also true of every art. It is by playing the harp that
men become both good and bad harpists, and correspondingly with builders and all the
10   other craftsmen: a man who builds well will be a good builder, one who builds badly a
bad one. For if this were not so, there would be no need for an instructor, but everybody would be born as a good or a bad craftsman. The same holds true of the virtues:
15   in our transactions with other men it is by action that some become just and others unjust, and it is by acting in the face of danger and by developing the habit of feeling fear
or confidence that some become brave men and others cowards. The same applies to
the appetites and feelings of anger: by reacting in one way or in another to given circumstances some people become self-controlled and gentle, and others self-indulgent
20   and short-tempered. In a word, characteristics develop from corresponding activities.
For that reason, we must see to it that our activities are of a certain kind, since any
variations in them will be reflected in our characteristics. Hence it is no small matter
whether one habit or another is inculcated in us from early childhood; on the contrary,
25   it makes a considerable difference, or, rather, all the difference.

2. Method in the Practical Sciences: The purpose of the present study is not, as
it is in other inquiries, the attainment of theoretical knowledge: we are not conducting
this inquiry in order to know what virtue is, but in order to become good, else there

would be no advantage in studying it. For that reason, it becomes necessary to examine the problem of actions, and to ask how they are to be performed. For, as we have said,   30 the actions determine what kind of characteristics are developed.

That we must act according to right reason is generally conceded and may be assumed as the basis of our discussion. We shall speak about it later and discuss what right reason is and examine its relation to the other virtues. But let us first agree that any discussion on matters of action cannot be more than an outline and is bound to lack 1104^a precision; for as we stated at the outset, one can demand of a discussion only what the subject matter permits, and there are no fixed data in matters concerning action and questions of what is beneficial, any more than there are in matters of health. And if this is true of our general discussion, our treatment of particular problems will be even less   5 precise, since these do not come under the head of any art which can be transmitted by precept, but the agent must consider on each different occasion what the situation demands, just as in medicine and in navigation. But although such is the kind of discussion in which we are engaged, we must do our best.   10

First of all, it must be observed that the nature of moral qualities is such that they are destroyed by defect and by excess. We see the same thing happen in the case of strength and of health, to illustrate, as we must, the invisible by means of visible examples: excess as well as deficiency of physical exercise destroys our strength, and similarly, too much and too little food and drink destroys our health; the proportionate   15 amount, however, produces, increases, and preserves it. The same applies to self-control, courage, and the other virtues: the man who shuns and fears everything and never   20 stands his ground becomes a coward, whereas a man who knows no fear at all and goes to meet every danger becomes reckless. Similarly, a man who revels in every pleasure and abstains from none becomes self-indulgent, while he who avoids every pleasure like a boor becomes what might be called insensitive. Thus we see that self-control and   25 courage are destroyed by excess and by deficiency and are preserved by the mean.

Not only are the same actions which are responsible for and instrumental in the origin and development of the virtues also the causes and means of their destruction, but they will also be manifested in the active exercise of the virtues. We can see the truth of this in the case of other more visible qualities, e.g., strength. Strength is pro-   30 duced by consuming plenty of food and by enduring much hard work, and it is the strong man who is best able to do these things. The same is also true of the virtues: by abstaining from pleasures we become self-controlled, and once we are self-controlled   35 we are best able to abstain from pleasures. So also with courage: by becoming habitu- 1104^b ated to despise and to endure terrors we become courageous, and once we have become courageous we will best be able to endure terror.

3. Pleasure and Pain as the Test of Virtue: An index to our characteristics is provided by the pleasure or pain which follows upon the tasks we have achieved. A   5 man who abstains from bodily pleasures and enjoys doing so is self-controlled; if he finds abstinence troublesome, he is self-indulgent; a man who endures danger with joy, or at least without pain, is courageous; if he endures it with pain, he is a coward. For moral excellence is concerned with pleasure and pain; it is pleasure that makes us do   10 base actions and pain that prevents us from doing noble actions. For that reason, as Plato says, men must be brought up from childhood to feel pleasure and pain at the proper things; for this is correct education.

Furthermore, since the virtues have to do with actions and emotions, and since pleasure and pain are a consequence of every emotion and of every action, it follows   15 from this point of view, too, that virtue has to do with pleasure and pain. This is further

indicated by the fact that punishment is inflicted by means of pain. For punishment is a kind of medical treatment and it is the nature of medical treatments to take effect through the introduction of the opposite of the disease.* Again, as we said just now,
20   every characteristic of the soul shows its true nature in its relation to and its concern with those factors which naturally make it better or worse. But it is through pleasures and pains that men are corrupted, i.e., through pursuing and avoiding pleasures and pains either of the wrong kind or at the wrong time or in the wrong manner, or by going wrong in some other definable respect. For that reason some people define the virtues as states of freedom from emotion and of quietude. However, they make the
25   mistake of using these terms absolutely and without adding such qualifications as "in the right manner," "at the right or wrong time," and so forth. We may, therefore, assume as the basis of our discussion that virtue, being concerned with pleasure and pain in the way we have described, makes us act in the best way in matters revolving pleasure and pain, and that vice does the opposite.

The following considerations may further illustrate that virtue is concerned with
30   pleasure and pain. There are three factors that determine choice and three that determine avoidance: the noble, the beneficial, and the pleasurable, on the one hand, and on the other their opposites: the base, the harmful, and the painful. Now a good man will go right and a bad man will go wrong when any of these, and especially when pleasure
35   is involved. For pleasure is not only common to man and the animals, but also accom-
1105ᵃ   panies all objects of choice: in fact, the noble and the beneficial seem pleasant to us. Moreover, a love of pleasure has grown up with all of us from infancy. Therefore, this emotion has come to be ingrained in our lives and is difficult to erase. Even in our ac-
5   tions we use, to a greater or smaller extent, pleasure and pain as a criterion. For this reason, this entire study is necessarily concerned with pleasure and pain; for it is not unimportant for our actions whether we feel joy and pain in the right or the wrong way. Again, it is harder to fight against pleasure than against anger, as Heraclitus says; and both virtue and art are always concerned with what is harder, for success is better when
10   it is hard to achieve. Thus, for this reason also, every study both of virtue and of politics must deal with pleasures and pains, for if a man has the right attitude to them, he will be good; if the wrong attitude, he will be bad.

We have now established that virtue or excellence is concerned with pleasures
15   and pains; that the actions which produce it also develop it and, if differently performed, destroy it; and that it actualizes itself fully in those activities to which it owes its origin.

4. Virtuous Action and Virtue: However, the question may be raised what we mean by saying that men become just by performing just actions and self-controlled by practicing self-control. For if they perform just actions and exercise self-control, they
20   are already just and self-controlled, in the same way as they are literate and musical if they write correctly and practice music.

But is this objection really valid, even as regards the arts? No, for it is possible for a man to write a piece correctly by chance or at the prompting of another: but he will be literate only if he produces a piece of writing in a literate way, and that
25   means doing it in accordance with the skill of literate composition which he has in himself.

*The idea here evidently is that the pleasure of wrongdoing must be cured by applying its opposite, i.e., pain.

Moreover, the factors involved in the arts and in the virtues are not the same. In the arts, excellence lies in the result itself, so that it is sufficient if it is of a certain kind. But in the case of the virtues an act is not performed justly or with self-control if the act itself is of a certain kind, but only if in addition the agent has certain characteristics   30
as he performs it: first of all, he must know what he is doing; secondly, he must choose to act the way he does, and he must choose it for its own sake; and in the third place, the act must spring from a firm and unchangeable character. With the exception of knowing what one is about, these considerations do not enter into the mastery of the   1105^b
arts; for the mastery of the virtues, however, knowledge is of little or no importance, whereas the other two conditions count not for a little but are all-decisive, since re- peated acts of justice and self-control result in the possession of these virtues. In other words, acts are called just and self-controlled when they are the kind of acts which a   5
just or self-controlled man would perform; but the just and self-controlled man is not he who performs these acts, but he who also performs them in the way just and self- controlled men do.

Thus our assertion that a man becomes just by performing just acts and self- controlled by performing acts of self-control is correct; without performing them, no-   10
body could even be on the way to becoming good. Yet most men do not perform such acts, but by taking refuge in argument they think that they are engaged in philosophy and that they will become good in this way. In so doing, they act like sick men who lis-   15
ten attentively to what the doctor says, but fail to do any of the things he prescribes. That kind of philosophical activity will not bring health to the soul any more than this sort of treatment will produce a healthy body.

5. Virtue Defined: The Genus: The next point to consider is the definition of virtue or excellence. As there are three kinds of things found in the soul: (1) emotions,   20
(2) capacities, and (3) characteristics, virtue must be one of these. By "emotions" I mean appetite, anger, fear, confidence, envy, joy, affection, hatred, longing, emulation, pity, and in general anything that is followed by pleasure or pain; by "capacities" I mean that by virtue of which we are said to be affected by these emotions, for example, the capacity which enables us to feel anger, pain, or pity; and by "characteristics" I   25
mean the condition, either good or bad, in which we are, in relation to the emotions: for example, our condition in relation to anger is bad, if our anger is too violent or not violent enough, but if it is moderate, our condition is good; and similarly with our con- dition in relation to the other emotions.

Now the virtues and vices cannot be emotions, because we are not called good or bad on the basis of our emotions, but on the basis of our virtues and vices. Also, we are   30
neither praised nor blamed for our emotions: a man does not receive praise for being frightened or angry, nor blame for being angry pure and simple, but for being angry in a certain way. Yet we are praised or blamed for our virtues and vices. Furthermore, no   1106^a
choice is involved when we experience anger or fear, while the virtues are some kind of choice or at least involve choice. Moreover, with regard to our emotions we are said to be "moved," but with regard to our virtues and vices we are not said to be "moved"   5
but to be "disposed" in a certain way.

For the same reason, the virtues cannot be capacities, either, for we are neither called good or bad nor praised or blamed simply because we are capable of being af- fected. Further, our capacities have been given to us by nature, but we do not by nature develop into good or bad men. We have discussed this subject before. Thus, if the   10
virtues are neither emotions nor capacities, the only remaining alternative is that they are characteristics. So much for the genus of virtue.

6. Virtue Defined: The Differentia: It is not sufficient, however, merely to define virtue in general terms as a characteristic: we must also specify what kind of characteristic it is. It must, then, be remarked that every virtue or excellence (1) renders good the thing itself of which it is the excellence, and (2) causes it to perform its function well. For example, the excellence of the eye makes both the eye and its function good, for good sight is due to the excellence of the eye. Likewise, the excellence of a horse makes it both good as a horse and good at running, at carrying its rider, and at facing the enemy. Now, if this is true of all things, the virtue or excellence of man, too, will be a characteristic which makes him a good man, and which causes him to perform his own function well. To some extent we have already stated how this will be true; the rest will become clear if we study what the nature of virtue is.

Of every continuous entity that is divisible into parts it is possible to take the larger, the smaller, or an equal part, and these parts may be larger, smaller, or equal either in relation to the entity itself, or in relation to us. The "equal" part is something median between excess and deficiency. By the median of an entity I understand a point equidistant from both extremes, and this point is one and the same for everybody. By the median relative to us I understand an amount neither too large nor too small, and this is neither one nor the same for everybody. To take an example: if ten is many and two is few, six is taken as the median in relation to the entity, for it exceeds and is exceeded by the same amount, and is thus the median in terms of arithmetical proportion. But the median relative to us cannot be determined in this manner: if ten pounds of food is much for a man to eat and two pounds little, it does not follow that the trainer will prescribe six pounds, for this may in turn be much or little for him to eat; it may be little for Milo* and much for someone who has just begun to take up athletics. The same applies to running and wrestling. Thus we see that an expert in any field avoids excess and deficiency, but seeks the median and chooses it—not the median of the object but the median relative to us.

If this, then, is the way in which every science perfects its work, by looking to the median and by bringing its work up to that point—and this is the reason why it is usually said of a successful piece of work that it is impossible to detract from it or to add to it, the implication being that excess and deficiency destroy success while the mean safeguards it (good craftsmen, we say, look toward this standard in the performance of their work)—and if virtue, like nature, is more precise and better than any art, we must conclude that virtue aims at the median. I am referring to moral virtue: for it is moral virtue that is concerned with emotions and actions, and it is in emotions and actions that excess, deficiency, and the median are found. Thus we can experience fear, confidence, desire, anger, pity, and generally any kind of pleasure and pain either too much or too little, and in either case not properly. But to experience all this at the right time, toward the right objects, toward the right people, for the right reason, and in the right manner—that is the median and the best course, the course that is a mark of virtue.

Similarly, excess, deficiency, and the median can also be found in actions. Now virtue is concerned with emotions and actions; and in emotions and actions excess and deficiency miss the mark, whereas the median is praised and constitutes success. But both praise and success are signs of virtue or excellence. Consequently, virtue is a mean in the sense that it aims at the median. This is corroborated by the fact that there are many ways of going wrong, but only one way which is right—for evil belongs to

*Milo of Croton, said to have lived in the second half of the sixth century B.C., was a wrestler famous for his remarkable strength.

the indeterminate, as the Pythagoreans imagined, but good to the determinate. This, by the way, is also the reason why the one is easy and the other hard: it is easy to miss the target but hard to hit it. Here, then, is an additional proof that excess and deficiency characterize vice, while the mean characterizes virtue: for "bad men have many ways, good men but one." 30

35

We may thus conclude that virtue or excellence is a characteristic involving choice, and that it consists in observing the mean relative to us, a mean which is defined by a rational principle, such as a man of practical wisdom would use to determine it. It is the mean by reference to two vices: the one of excess and the other of deficiency. It is, moreover, a mean because some vices exceed and others fall short of what is required in emotion and in action, whereas virtue finds and chooses the median. Hence, in respect of its essence and the definition of its essential nature virtue is a mean, but in regard to goodness and excellence it is an extreme. 1107ᵃ

5

Not every action nor every emotion admits of a mean. There are some actions and emotions whose very names connote baseness, e.g., spite, shamelessness, envy; and among actions, adultery, theft, and murder. These and similar emotions and actions imply by their very names that they are bad; it is not their excess nor their deficiency which is called bad. It is, therefore, impossible ever to do right in performing them: to perform them is always to do wrong. In cases of this sort, let us say adultery, rightness and wrongness do not depend on committing it with the right woman at the right time and in the right manner, but the mere fact of committing such action at all is to do wrong. It would be just as absurd to suppose that there is a mean, an excess, and a deficiency in an unjust or a cowardly or a self-indulgent act. For if there were, we would have a mean of excess and a mean of deficiency, and an excess of excess and a deficiency of deficiency. Just as there cannot be an excess and a deficiency of self-control 10

15

20

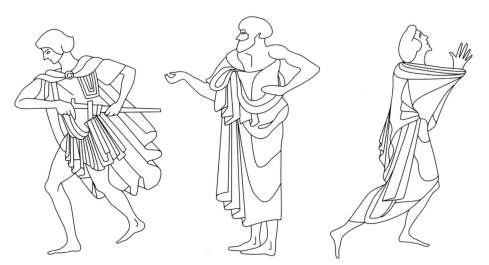

According to Aristotle, virtue or excellence "is the mean by reference to two vices: the one of excess and the other of deficiency." For example, in this drawing the person on the left has an excess of confidence and hence is reckless. The person on the right is deficient in confidence and so is cowardly. In terms of fear, the person on the left has a defect and the person on the right has an excess. In both these cases we should seek to rationally choose the "Golden Mean" of the person in the middle: courage.

and courage—because the intermediate is, in a sense, an extreme—so there cannot be a mean, excess, and deficiency in their respective opposites: their opposites are wrong regardless of how they are performed; for, in general, there is no such thing as the mean of an excess or a deficiency, or the excess and deficiency of a mean.

7. Examples of the Mean in Particular Virtues: However, this general statement is not enough; we must also show that it fits particular instances. For in a discussion of moral actions, although general statements have a wider range of application, statements on particular points have more truth in them: actions are concerned with particulars and our statements must harmonize with them. Let us now take particular virtues and vices from the following table.

In feelings of fear and confidence courage is the mean. As for the excesses, there is no name that describes a man who exceeds in fearlessness—many virtues and vices have no name; but a man who exceeds in confidence is reckless, and a man who exceeds in fear and is deficient in confidence is cowardly.

In regard to pleasures and pains—not all of them and to a lesser degree in the case of pains—the mean is self-control and the excess self-indulgence. Men deficient in regard to pleasure are not often found, and there is therefore no name for them, but let us call them "insensitive."

In giving and taking money, the mean is generosity, the excess and deficiency are extravagance and stinginess. In these vices excess and deficiency work in opposite ways: an extravagant man exceeds in spending and is deficient in taking, while a stingy man exceeds in taking and is deficient in spending. For our present purposes, we may rest content with an outline and a summary, but we shall later define these qualities more precisely.

There are also some other dispositions in regard to money: magnificence is a mean (for there is a difference between a magnificent and a generous man in that the former operates on a large scale, the latter on a small); gaudiness and vulgarity are excesses, and niggardliness a deficiency. These vices differ from the vices opposed to generosity. But we shall postpone until later a discussion of the way in which they differ.

As regards honor and dishonor, the mean is high-mindedness, the excess is what we might call vanity, and the deficiency small-mindedness. The same relation which, as we said, exists between magnificence and generosity, the one being distinguished from the other in that it operates on a small scale, exists also between high-mindedness and another virtue: as the former deals with great, so the latter deals with small honors. For it is possible to desire honor as one should or more than one should or less than one should: a man who exceeds in his desires is called ambitious, a man who is deficient unambitious, but there is no name to describe the man in the middle. There are likewise no names for the corresponding dispositions except for the disposition of an ambitious man which is called ambition. As a result, the men who occupy the extremes lay claim to the middle position. We ourselves, in fact, sometimes call the middle person ambitious and sometimes unambitious; sometimes we praise an ambitious and at other times an unambitious man. The reason why we do that will be discussed in the sequel; for the present, let us discuss the rest of the virtues and vices along the lines we have indicated.

In regard to anger also there exists an excess, a deficiency, and a mean. Although there really are no names for them, we might call the mean gentleness, since we call a man who occupies the middle position gentle. Of the extremes, let the man who exceeds be called short-tempered and his vice a short temper, and the deficient man apathetic and his vice apathy.

There are, further, three other means which have a certain similarity with one another, but differ nonetheless one from the other. They are all concerned with human re-   10
lations in speech and action, but they differ in that one of them is concerned with truth in speech and action and the other two with pleasantness: *(a)* pleasantness in amusement and *(b)* pleasantness in all our daily life. We must include these, too, in our discussion, in order to see more clearly that the mean is to be praised in all things and that   15
the extremes are neither praiseworthy nor right, but worthy of blame. Here, too, most of the virtues and vices have no name, but for the sake of clarity and easier comprehension we must try to coin names for them, as we did in earlier instances.

To come to the point; in regard to truth, let us call the man in the middle position truthful and the mean truthfulness. Pretense in the form of exaggeration is boast-   20
fulness and its possessor boastful, while pretense in the form of understatement is self-depreciation and its possessor a self-depreciator.

Concerning pleasantness in amusement, the man in the middle position is witty and his disposition wittiness; the excess is called buffoonery and its possessor a buf-   25
foon; and the deficient man a kind of boor and the corresponding characteristic boorishness.

As far as the other kind of pleasantness is concerned, pleasantness in our daily life, a man who is as pleasant as he should be is friendly and the mean is friendliness. A man who exceeds is called obsequious if he has no particular purpose in being pleasant, but if he is acting for his own material advantage, he is a flatterer. And a man who is deficient and unpleasant in every respect is a quarrelsome and grouchy kind of per-   30
son.

A mean can also be found in our emotional experiences and in our emotions. Thus, while a sense of shame is not a virtue, a bashful or modest man is praised. For even in these matters we speak of one kind of person as intermediate and of another as exceeding if he is terror-stricken and abashed at everything. On the other hand, a man who is deficient in shame or has none at all is called shameless, whereas the intermedi-   35
ate man is bashful or modest.

Righteous indignation is the mean between envy and spite, all of these being   1108^b
concerned with the pain and pleasure which we feel in regard to the fortunes of our neighbors. The righteously indignant man feels pain when someone prospers undeservedly; an envious man exceeds him in that he is pained when he sees anyone prosper; and a spiteful man is so deficient in feeling pain that he even rejoices [when some-   5
one suffers undeservedly].

But we shall have an opportunity to deal with these matters again elsewhere. After that, we shall discuss justice; since it has more than one meaning, we shall distinguish the two kinds of justice and show in what way each is a mean.   10

8. The Relation Between the Mean and Its Extremes: There are, then, three kinds of disposition: two are vices (one marked by excess and one by deficiency), and one, virtue, the mean. Now, each of these dispositions is, in a sense, opposed to both the others: the extremes are opposites to the middle as well as to one another, and the middle is opposed to the extremes. Just as an equal amount is larger in relation to a smaller and smaller in relation to a larger amount, so, in the case both of emotions and of ac-   15
tions, the middle characteristics exceed in relation to the deficiencies and are deficient in relation to the excesses. For example, a brave man seems reckless in relation to a coward, but in relation to a reckless man he seems cowardly. Similarly, a self-controlled   20
man seems self-indulgent in relation to an insensitive man and insensitive in relation to a self-indulgent man, and a generous man extravagant in relation to a stingy man and

stingy in relation to an extravagant man. This is the reason why people at the extremes each push the man in the middle over to the other extreme: a coward calls a brave man reckless and a reckless man calls a brave man a coward, and similarly with the other qualities.

However, while these three dispositions are thus opposed to one another, the extremes are more opposed to one another than each is to the median; for they are further apart from one another than each is from the median, just as the large is further removed from the small and the small from the large than either one is from the equal. Moreover, there appears to be a certain similarity between some extremes and their median, e.g., recklessness resembles courage and extravagance generosity; but there is a very great dissimilarity between the extremes. But things that are furthest removed from one another are defined as opposites, and that means that the further things are removed from one another the more opposite they are.

In some cases it is the deficiency and in others the excess that is more opposed to the median. For example, it is not the excess, recklessness, which is more opposed to courage, but the deficiency, cowardice; while in the case of self-control it is not the defect, insensitivity, but the excess, self-indulgence which is more opposite. There are two causes for this. One arises from the nature of the thing itself: when one of the extremes is closer and more similar to the median, we do not treat it but rather the other extreme as the opposite of the median. For instance, since recklessness is believed to be more similar and closer to courage, and cowardice less similar, it is cowardice rather than recklessness which we treat as the opposite of courage. For what is further removed from the middle is regarded as being more opposite. So much for the first cause which arises from the thing itself. The second reason is found in ourselves: the more we are naturally attracted to anything, the more opposed to the median does this thing appear to be. For example, since we are naturally more attracted to pleasure we incline more easily to self-indulgence than to a disciplined kind of life. We describe as more opposed to the mean those things toward which our tendency is stronger; and for that reason the excess, self-indulgence, is more opposed to self-control than is its corresponding deficiency.

9. How to Attain the Mean: Our discussion has sufficiently established (1) that moral virtue is a mean and in what sense it is a mean; (2) that it is a mean between two vices, one of which is marked by excess and the other by deficiency; and (3) that it is a mean in the sense that it aims at the median in the emotions and in actions. That is why it is a hard task to be good; in every case it is a task to find the median: for instance, not everyone can find the middle of a circle, but only a man who has the proper knowledge. Similarly, anyone can get angry—that is easy—or can give away money or spend it; but to do all this to the right person, to the right extent, at the right time, for the right reason, and in the right way is no longer something easy that anyone can do. It is for this reason that good conduct is rare, praiseworthy, and noble.

The first concern of a man who aims at the median should, therefore, be to avoid the extreme which is more opposed to it, as Calypso advises: "Keep clear your ship of yonder spray and surf." For one of the two extremes is more in error than the other, and since it is extremely difficult to hit the mean, we must, as the saying has it, sail in the second best way and take the lesser evil; and we can best do that in the manner we have described.

Moreover, we must watch the errors which have the greatest attraction for us personally. For the natural inclination of one man differs from that of another, and we each come to recognize our own by observing the pleasure and pain produced in us [by the different extremes]. We must then draw ourselves away in the opposite direction, for by pulling away from error we shall reach the middle, as men do when they straighten warped timber. In every case we must be especially on our guard against pleasure and what is pleasant, for when it comes to pleasure we cannot act as unbiased judges. Our attitude toward pleasure should be the same as that of the Trojan elders was toward Helen, and we should repeat on every occasion the words they addressed to her. For if we dismiss pleasure as they dismissed her, we shall make fewer mistakes.

In summary, then, it is by acting in this way that we shall best be able to hit the median. But this is no doubt difficult, especially when particular cases are concerned. For it is not easy to determine in what manner, with what person, on what occasion, and for how long a time one ought to be angry. There are times when we praise those who are deficient in anger and call them gentle, and other times when we praise violently angry persons and call them manly. However, we do not blame a man for slightly deviating from the course of goodness, whether he strays toward excess or toward deficiency, but we do blame him if his deviation is great and cannot pass unnoticed. It is not easy to determine by a formula at what point and for how great a divergence a man deserves blame; but this difficulty is, after all, true of all objects of sense perception: determinations of this kind depend upon particular circumstances, and the decision rests with our [moral] sense.

This much, at any rate, is clear: that the median characteristic is in all fields the one that deserves praise, and that it is sometimes necessary to incline toward the excess and sometimes toward the deficiency. For it is in this way that we will most easily hit upon the median, which is the point of excellence.

*　*　*

Book VI

1. Moral and Intellectual Excellence; the Psychological Foundations of Intellectual Excellence: We stated earlier that we must choose the median, and not excess or deficiency, and that the median is what right reason dictates. Let us now analyze this second point.

In all the characteristics we have discussed, as in all others, there is some target on which a rational man keeps his eye as he bends and relaxes his efforts to attain it. There is also a standard that determines the several means which, as we claim, lie between excess and deficiency, and which are fixed by right reason. But this statement, true though it is, lacks clarity. In all other fields of endeavor in which scientific knowledge is possible, it is indeed true to say that we must exert ourselves or relax neither too much nor too little, but to an intermediate extent and as right reason demands. But if this is the only thing a person knows, he will be none the wiser: he will, for example, not know what kind of medicines to apply to his body, if he is merely told to apply whatever medical science prescribes and in a manner in which a medical expert applies them. Accordingly, in discussing the characteristics of the soul, too, it is not enough that the statement we have made be true. We must also have a definition of what right reason is and what standard determines it.

In analyzing the virtues of the soul we said that some are virtues of character and others excellence of thought or understanding. We have now discussed the moral virtues, [i.e., the virtues of character]. In what follows, we will deal with the others, [i.e., the intellectual virtues,] beginning with some prefatory remarks about the soul.

5 We said in our earlier discussion that the soul consists of two parts, one rational and one irrational. We must now make a similar distinction in regard to the rational part. Let it be assumed that there are two rational elements: with one of these we apprehend the realities whose fundamental principles do not admit of being other than they are, and with the other we apprehend things which do admit of being other. For if we grant 10 that knowledge presupposes a certain likeness and kinship of subject and object, there will be a generically different part of the soul naturally corresponding to each of two different kinds of object. Let us call one the scientific and the other the calculative element. Deliberating and calculating are the same thing, and no one deliberates about objects that cannot be other than they are. This means that the calculative constitutes one 15 element of the rational part of the soul. Accordingly, we must now take up the question which is the best characteristic of each element, since that constitutes the excellence or virtue of each. But the virtue of a thing is relative to its proper function.

2. The Two Kinds of Intellectual Excellence and Their Objects: Now, there are three elements in the soul which control action and truth: sense perception, intelligence, and desire. Of these sense perception does not initiate any action. We can see 20 this from the fact that animals have sense perception but have no share in action.* What affirmation and negation are in the realm of thought, pursuit and avoidance are in the realm of desire. Therefore, since moral virtue is a characteristic involving choice, and since choice is a deliberate desire, it follows that, if the choice is to be good, the 25 reasoning must be true and the desire correct; that is, reasoning must affirm what desire pursues. This then is the kind of thought and the kind of truth that is practical and concerned with action. On the other hand, in the kind of thought involved in theoretical knowledge and not in action or production, the good and the bad state are, respectively, truth and falsehood; in fact, the attainment of truth is the function of the intellectual faculty as a whole. But in intellectual activity concerned with action, the good state is 30 truth in harmony with correct desire.

Choice is the starting point of action: it is the source of motion but not the end for the sake of which we act, i.e., the final cause. The starting point of choice, however, is desire and reasoning directed toward some end. That is why there cannot be choice either without intelligence and thought or without some moral characteristic; for good 35 and bad action in human conduct are not possible without thought and character. Now thought alone moves nothing; only thought which is directed to some end and con-
1139^b cerned with action can do so. And it is this kind of thought also which initiates production. For whoever produces something produces it for an end. The product he makes is not an end in an unqualified sense, but an end only in a particular relation and of a particular operation. Only the goal of action is an end in the unqualified sense: for the good life is an end, and desire is directed toward this. Therefore, choice is either intelligence motivated by desire or desire operating through thought, and it is as a combina-
5 tion of these two that man is a starting point of action.

(No object of choice belongs to the past: no one chooses to have sacked Troy. For deliberation does not refer to the past but only to the future and to what is possible; and it is not possible that what is past should not have happened. Therefore, Agathon is 10 right when he says:

*Throughout the *Ethics,* Aristotle uses *praxis* ("action") as equivalent to "moral action," "conduct," and assumes animals are not capable of this.

One thing alone is denied even to god:
to make undone the deeds which have been done.*)

As we have seen, truth is the function of both intellectual parts [of the soul]. Therefore, those characteristics which permit each part to be as truthful as possible will be the virtues of the two parts.

3. The Qualities by Which Truth Is Attained: (a) Pure Science or Knowledge: So let us make a fresh beginning and discuss these characteristics once again. Let us take for granted that the faculties by which the soul expresses truth by way of affirmation or   15
denial are five in number: art, science, practical wisdom, theoretical wisdom, and intelligence. Conviction and opinion do not belong here, for they may be false.

What pure science or scientific knowledge is—in the precise sense of the word and not in any of its wider uses based on mere similarity—will become clear in the following. We are all convinced that what we *know* scientifically cannot be otherwise   20
than it is; but of facts which can possibly be other than they are we do not know whether or not they continue to be true when removed from our observation. Therefore, an object of scientific knowledge exists of necessity, and is, consequently, eternal. For everything that exists of necessity in an unqualified sense is eternal, and what is eternal is ungenerated and imperishable [and hence cannot be otherwise].

Moreover, all scientific knowledge is held to be teachable, and what is scientifi-   25
cally knowable is capable of being learned. All teaching is based on what is already known, as we have stated in the *Analytics;* some teaching proceeds by induction and some by syllogism. Now, induction is the starting point [for knowledge] of the universal as well [as the particular], while syllogism proceeds *from* universals. Consequently, there are starting points or principles from which a syllogism proceeds and which are   30
themselves not arrived at by a syllogism. It is, therefore, induction that attains them. Accordingly, scientific knowledge is a capacity for demonstration and has, in addition, all the other qualities which we have specified in the *Analytics.* When a man believes something in the way there specified, and when the starting points or principles on which his beliefs rest are known to him, then he has scientific knowledge; unless he knows the starting points or principles better than the conclusion, he will have scientific knowledge only incidentally. So much for our definition of scientific knowledge   35
or pure science.

4. (b) Art or Applied Science: Things which admit of being other than they are   1140ᵃ
include both things made and things done. Production is different from action—for that point we can rely even on our less technical discussions. Hence, the characteristic of acting rationally is different from the characteristic of producing rationally. It also   5
follows that one does not include the other, for action is not production nor production action. Now, building is an art or applied science, and it is essentially a characteristic or trained ability of rationally producing. In fact, there is no art that is not a characteristic or trained ability of rationally producing, nor is there a characteristic of rationally producing that is not an art. It follows that art is identical with the characteristic of   10
producing under the guidance of true reason. All art is concerned with the realm of coming-to-be, i.e., with contriving and studying how something which is capable both of being and of not being may come into existence, a thing whose starting point or

*Agathon was a tragic poet who flourished in the last quarter of the fifth century B.C. Plato's *Symposium* is set in his house.

source is in the producer and not in the thing produced. For art is concerned neither with things which exist or come into being by necessity, nor with things produced by nature: these have their source of motion within themselves.

Since production and action are different, it follows that art deals with production and not with action. In a certain sense, fortune and art are concerned with the same things, as Agathon says: "Fortune loves art and art fortune." So, as we have said, art is a characteristic of producing under the guidance of true reason, and lack of art, on the contrary, is a characteristic of producing under the guidance of false reason; and both of them deal with what admits of being other than it is.

5. (c) Practical Wisdom: We may approach the subject of practical wisdom by studying the persons to whom we attribute it. Now, the capacity of deliberating well about what is good and advantageous for oneself is regarded as typical of a man of practical wisdom—not deliberating well about what is good and advantageous in a partial sense, for example, what contributes to health or strength, but what sort of thing contributes to the good life in general. This is shown by the fact that we speak of men as having practical wisdom in a particular respect, i.e., not in an unqualified sense, when they calculate well with respect to some worthwhile end, one that cannot be attained by an applied science or art. It follows that, in general, a man of practical wisdom is he who has the ability to deliberate.

Now no one deliberates about things that cannot be other than they are or about actions that he cannot possibly perform. Since, as we saw, pure science involves demonstration, while things whose starting points or first causes can be other than they are do not admit of demonstration—for such things too and not merely their first causes can all be other than they are—and since it is impossible to deliberate about what exists by necessity, we may conclude that practical wisdom is neither a pure science nor an art. It is not a pure science, because matters of action admit of being other than they are, and it is not an applied science or art, because action and production are generically different.

What remains, then, is that it is a truthful characteristic of acting rationally in matters good and bad for man. For production has an end other than itself, but action does not: good action is itself an end. That is why we think that Pericles* and men like him have practical wisdom. They have the capacity of seeing what is good for themselves and for mankind, and these are, we believe, the qualities of men capable of managing households and states.

This also explains why we call "self-control" *sophrosyne:* it "preserves" our "practical wisdom." What it preserves is the kind of conviction we have described. For the pleasant and the painful do not destroy and pervert every conviction we hold—not, for example, our conviction that a triangle has or does not have the sum of its angles equal to two right angles—but only the convictions we hold concerning how we should act. In matters of action, the principles or initiating motives are the ends at which our actions are aimed. But as soon as a man becomes corrupted by pleasure or pain, the goal no longer appears to him as a motivating principle: he no longer sees that he should choose and act in every case for the sake of and because of this end. For vice tends to destroy the principle or initiating motive of action.

Necessarily, then, practical wisdom is a truthful rational characteristic of acting in matters involving what is good for man. Furthermore, whereas there exists such a

*The name of Pericles (ca. 495–429 B.C.) is almost synonymous with the Athenian democracy.

thing as excellence in art, it does not exist in practical wisdom.* Also, in art a man who makes a mistake voluntarily is preferable to one who makes it involuntarily; but in practical wisdom, as in every virtue or excellence, such a man is less desirable. Thus it is clear that practical wisdom is an excellence or virtue and not an art. Since there are two parts of the soul that contain a rational element, it must be the virtue of one of them, namely of the part that forms opinions.** For opinion as well as practical wisdom deals with things that can be other than they are. However, it is not merely a rational characteristic or trained ability. An indication that it is something more may be seen in the fact that a trained ability of that kind can be forgotten, whereas practical wisdom cannot.

6. (d) Intelligence: Since pure science or scientific knowledge is a basic conviction concerning universal and necessary truths, and since everything demonstrable and all pure science begins from fundamental principles (for science proceeds rationally), the fundamental principle or starting point for scientific knowledge cannot itself be the object either of science, of art, or of practical wisdom. For what is known scientifically is demonstrable, whereas art and practical wisdom are concerned with things that can be other than they are. Nor are these fundamental principles the objects of theoretical wisdom: for it is the task of a man of theoretical wisdom to have a demonstration for certain truths.*** Now, if scientific knowledge, practical wisdom, theoretical wisdom, and intelligence are the faculties by which we attain truth and by which we are never deceived both in matters which can and in those matters which cannot be other than they are; and if three of these—I am referring to practical wisdom, scientific knowledge, and theoretical wisdom—cannot be the faculty in question, we are left with the conclusion that it is intelligence that apprehends fundamental principles.

7. (e) Theoretical Wisdom: We attribute "wisdom" in the arts to the most precise and perfect masters of their skills: we attribute it to Phidias as a sculptor in marble and to Polycletus as a sculptor in bronze. In this sense we signify by "wisdom" nothing but excellence of art or craftsmanship. However, we regard some men as being wise in general, not in any partial sense or in some other particular respect, as Homer says in the *Margites:*

The gods let him not be a digger or a ploughman nor wise at anything.

It is, therefore, clear, that wisdom must be the most precise and perfect form of knowledge. Consequently, a wise man must not only know what follows from fundamental principles, but he must also have true knowledge of the fundamental principles themselves. Accordingly, theoretical wisdom must comprise both intelligence and scientific knowledge. It is science in its consummation, as it were, the science of the things that are valued most highly.

For it would be strange to regard politics or practical wisdom as the highest kind of knowledge, when in fact man is not the best thing in the universe. Surely, if

25

30

35

1141ᵃ

5

10

15

20

---

*Because practical wisdom is itself a complete virtue or excellence, while the excellence of art depends on the goodness or badness of its product.

**"Opinion" here corresponds to the "calculative element" in Chapter 1: both are defined by reference to contingent facts, those which may be otherwise than they are.

***In other words, the undemonstrable first or fundamental principles cannot be the proper and complete object of theoretical wisdom: as the next chapter shows, they are included within its sphere.

"healthy" and "good" mean one thing for men and another for fishes, whereas "white" and "straight" always mean the same, "wise" must mean the same for everyone, but "practically wise" will be different. For each particular being ascribes practical wisdom in matters relating to itself to that thing which observes its interests well, and it will entrust itself to that thing. That is the reason why people attribute practical wisdom even to some animals—to all those which display a capacity of forethought in matters relating to their own life.

It is also evident that theoretical wisdom is not the same as politics. If we are to call "theoretical wisdom" the knowledge of what is helpful to us, there will be many kinds of wisdom. There is no single science that deals with what is good for all living things any more than there is a single art of medicine dealing with everything that is, but a different science deals with each particular good. The argument that man is the best of living things makes no difference. There are other things whose nature is much more divine than man's: to take the most visible example only, the constituent parts of the universe.

Our discussion has shown that theoretical wisdom comprises both scientific knowledge and [apprehension by the] intelligence of things which by their nature are valued most highly. That is why it is said that men like Anaxagoras and Thales have theoretical but not practical wisdom: when we see that they do not know what is advantageous to them, we admit that they know extraordinary, wonderful, difficult, and superhuman things, but call their knowledge useless because the good they are seeking is not human.

Practical wisdom, on the other hand, is concerned with human affairs and with matters about which deliberation is possible. As we have said, the most characteristic function of a man of practical wisdom is to deliberate well: no one deliberates about things that cannot be other than they are, nor about things that are not directed to some end, an end that is a good attainable by action. In an unqualified sense, that man is good at deliberating who, by reasoning, can aim at and hit the best thing attainable to man by action.

Nor does practical wisdom deal only with universals. It must also be familiar with particulars, since it is concerned with action and action has to do with particulars. This explains why some men who have no scientific knowledge are more adept in practical matters, especially if they have experience, than those who do have scientific knowledge. For if a person were to know that light meat is easily digested, and hence wholesome, but did not know what sort of meat is light, he will not produce health, whereas someone who knows that poultry is light and wholesome is more likely to produce health.*

Now, practical wisdom is concerned with action. That means that a person should have both [knowledge of universals and knowledge of particulars] or knowledge of particulars rather [than knowledge of universals]. But here, too, it seems, there is a supreme and comprehensive science involved, [i.e., politics].

8. Practical Wisdom and Politics: Political wisdom and practical wisdom are both the same characteristic, but their essential aspect is not the same. There are two kinds of wisdom concerning the state: the one, which acts as practical wisdom supreme and comprehensive, is the art of legislation; the other, which is practical wisdom as dealing with particular facts, bears the name which, [in everyday speech,] is common

*The point here is that, in practical matters, a man who knows by experience that poultry is wholesome is likely to be more successful than a man who only has the scientific knowledge that light meat is digestible and therefore wholesome, without knowing the particular fact that poultry is light meat.

to both kinds, politics, and it is concerned with action and deliberation. For a decree, [unlike a law, which lays down general principles,] is a matter for action, inasmuch as it is the last step [in the deliberative process]. That is why only those who make decrees are said to engage in politics, for they alone, like workmen, "do" things.*

It is also commonly held that practical wisdom is primarily concerned with one's own person, i.e., with the individual, and it is this kind that bears the name "practical wisdom," which properly belongs to others as well. The other kinds are called household management, legislation, and politics, the last of which is subdivided into deliberative and judicial.**

Now, knowing what is good for oneself is, to be sure, one kind of knowledge; but it is very different from the other kinds. A man who knows and concerns himself with his own interests is regarded as a man of practical wisdom, while men whose concern is politics are looked upon as busybodies. Euripides' words are in this vein:

> How can I be called "wise," who might have filled a common soldier's place, free from all care, sharing an equal lot . . . ? For those who reach too high and are too active. . . .

For people seek their own good and think that this is what they should do. This opinion has given rise to the view that it is such men who have practical wisdom. And yet, surely one's own good cannot exist without household management nor without a political system. Moreover, the problem of how to manage one's own affairs properly needs clarification and remains to be examined.

An indication that what we have said is correct is the following common observation. While young men do indeed become good geometricians and mathematicians and attain theoretical wisdom in such matters, they apparently do not attain practical wisdom. The reason is that practical wisdom is concerned with particulars as well [as with universals], and knowledge of particulars comes from experience. But a young man has no experience, for experience is the product of a long time. In fact, one might also raise the question why it is that a boy may become a mathematician but not a philosopher or a natural scientist. The answer may be that the objects of mathematics are the result of abstraction, whereas the fundamental principles of philosophy and natural science come from experience. Young men can assert philosophical and scientific principles but can have no genuine convictions about them, whereas there is no obscurity about the essential definitions in mathematics.

Moreover, in our deliberations error is possible as regards either the universal principle or the particular fact: we may be unaware either that all heavy water is bad, or that the particular water we are faced with is heavy.

That practical wisdom is not scientific knowledge is [therefore] evident. As we stated, it is concerned with ultimate particulars, since the actions to be performed are ultimate particulars. This means that it is at the opposite pole from intelligence. For the intelligence grasps limiting terms and definitions that cannot be attained by reasoning, while practical wisdom has as its object the ultimate particular fact, of which there is perception but no scientific knowledge. This perception is not the kind with which

30

1142ᵃ

5

10

15

20

25

*I.e., lawgivers and other men who are concerned with political wisdom in the supreme and comprehensive sense are not generally regarded as being engaged in politics. The analogy to workmen represents of course not Aristotle's view, which vigorously distinguishes action from production, but rather reflects a widespread attitude toward politics.

**In Athens, "deliberative" politics referred to matters debated in the Council and the Popular Assembly, and "judicial" politics to matters argued in the lawcourts.

[each of our five senses apprehends] its proper object, but the kind with which we perceive that in mathematics the triangle is the ultimate figure. For in this direction, too, we shall have to reach a stop. But this [type of mathematical cognition] is more truly
30   perception than practical wisdom, and it is different in kind from the other [type of perception which deals with the objects proper to the various senses].

9. Practical Wisdom and Excellence in Deliberation: There is a difference between investigating and deliberating: to deliberate is to investigate a particular kind of object. We must also try to grasp what excellence in deliberation is: whether it is some sort of scientific knowledge, opinion, shrewd guessing, or something generically different from any of these.

Now, scientific knowledge it is certainly not:* people do not investigate matters
1142ᵇ   they already know. But good deliberation is a kind of deliberation, and when a person deliberates he is engaged in investigating and calculating [things not yet decided]. Nor yet is it shrewd guessing. For shrewd guessing involves no reasoning and proceeds quickly, whereas deliberation takes a long time. As the saying goes, the action which follows deliberation should be quick, but deliberation itself should be slow. Furthermore, quickness of mind is not the same as excellence in deliberation: quickness of
5   mind is a kind of shrewd guessing. Nor again is excellence in deliberation any form of opinion at all. But since a person who deliberates badly makes mistakes, while he who deliberates well deliberates correctly, it clearly follows that excellence in deliberation is some kind of correctness. But it is correctness neither of scientific knowledge nor of
10   opinion. There cannot be correctness of scientific knowledge any more than there can be error of scientific knowledge; and correctness of opinion is truth. Moreover, anything that is an object of opinion is already fixed and determined, while deliberation deals with objects which remain to be determined. Still, excellence in deliberation does involve reasoning, and we are, consequently, left with the alternative that it is correctness of a process of thought; for thinking is not yet an affirmation. For while opinion is no longer a process of investigation but has reached the point of affirmation, a person
15   who deliberates, whether he does so well or badly, is still engaged in investigating and calculating something [not yet determined].

Good deliberation is a kind of correctness of deliberation. We must, therefore, first investigate what deliberation is and with what objects it is concerned. Since the term "correctness" is used in several different senses, it is clear that not every kind of correctness in deliberation [is excellence in deliberation]. For (1) a morally weak or a bad man will, as a result of calculation, attain the goal which he has proposed to himself as the right goal to attain. He will, therefore, have deliberated correctly, but what
20   he will get out of it will be a very bad thing. But the result of good deliberation is generally regarded as a good thing. It is this kind of correctness of deliberation which is good deliberation, a correctness that attains what is good.

But (2) it is also possible to attain something good by a false syllogism, i.e., to arrive at the right action, but to arrive at it by the wrong means when the middle term is false. Accordingly, this process, which makes us attain the right goal but not by the
25   right means, is still not good deliberation.

Moreover, (3) it is possible that one man attains his goal by deliberating for a long time, while another does so quickly. Now, long deliberation, too, is not as such

---

*Here, as in most of the following paragraph, Aristotle seems to be taking issue with Plato, who had identified the two, e.g., in *Republic,* Book IV, 428b.

good deliberation: excellence in deliberation is correctness in assessing what is beneficial, i.e., correctness in assessing the goal, the manner, and the time.

Again, (4) it is possible for a person to have deliberated well either in general, in an unqualified sense, or in relation to some particular end. Good deliberation in the unqualified sense of course brings success in relation to what is, in an unqualified sense, 30 the end, [i.e., in relation to the good life]. Excellence in deliberation as directed toward some particular end, however, brings success in the attainment of some particular end.

Thus we may conclude that, since it is a mark of men of practical wisdom to have deliberated well, excellence in deliberation will be correctness in assessing what is conducive to the end, concerning which practical wisdom gives a true conviction.

10. Practical Wisdom and Understanding: Understanding, i.e., excellence in understanding, the quality which makes us call certain people "men of understanding"   1143[a]
and "men of good understanding," is in general not identical with scientific knowledge or with opinion. For [if it were opinion,] everyone would be a man of understanding, [since everyone forms opinions]. Nor is it one of the particular branches of science, in the sense in which medicine, for example, is the science of matters pertaining to health, or geometry the science which deals with magnitudes. For understanding is concerned neither with eternal and unchangeable truth nor with anything and everything that comes into being [and passes away again]. It deals with matters concerning which   5
doubt and deliberation are possible. Accordingly, though its sphere is the same as that of practical wisdom, understanding and practical wisdom are not the same. Practical wisdom issues commands: its end is to tell us what we ought to do and what we ought not to do. Understanding, on the other hand, only passes judgment. [There is no difference between understanding and excellence in understanding:] for excellence in understanding is the same as understanding, and men of understanding are men of good un-   10
derstanding.

Thus understanding is neither possession nor acquisition of practical wisdom. Just as learning is called "understanding" when a man makes use of his faculty of knowledge, so [we speak of "understanding"] when it implies the use of one's faculty of opinion in judging statements made by another person about matters which belong to the realm of practical wisdom—and in judging such statements rightly, for *good* un-   15
derstanding means that the judgment is right. It is from this act of learning or understanding [what someone else says] that the term "understanding" as predicated of "men of good understanding" is derived. For we frequently use the words "learning" and "understanding" synonymously.

11. Practical Wisdom and Good Sense: As for what is called "good sense," the quality which makes us say of a person that he has the sense to forgive others, [i.e., sympathetic understanding], and that he has good sense, this is a correct judgment of   20
what is fair or equitable. This is indicated by the fact that we attribute to an equitable man especially sympathetic understanding and that we say that it is fair, in certain cases, to have the sense to forgive. Sympathetic understanding is a correct critical sense or judgment of what is fair; and a correct judgment is a true one.

All these characteristics, as one would expect, tend toward the same goal. We at-   25
tribute good sense, understanding, practical wisdom, and intelligence to the same persons, and in saying that they have good sense, we imply at the same time that they have a mature intelligence and that they are men of practical wisdom and understanding. For what these capacities [have in common is that they are] all concerned with ultimate particular facts. To say that a person has good judgment in matters of practical   30

wisdom implies that he is understanding and has good sense or that he has sympathetic understanding; for equitable acts are common to all good men in their relation with someone else. Now, all matters of action are in the sphere of the particulars and ultimates. Not only must a man of practical wisdom take cognizance of particulars, but understanding and good sense, too, deal with matters of action, and matters of action are ultimates. As for intelligence, it deals with ultimates at both ends of the scale. It is intelligence, not reasoning, that has as its objects primary terms and definitions as well as ultimate particulars. Intelligence grasps, on the one hand, the unchangeable, primary terms and concepts for demonstrations; on the other hand, in questions of action, it grasps the ultimate, contingent fact and the minor premise. For it is particular facts that form the starting points or principles for [our knowledge of] the goal of action: universals arise out of particulars. Hence one must have perception of particular facts, and this perception is intelligence.* Intelligence is, therefore, both starting point and end; for demonstrations start with ultimate terms and have ultimate facts as their objects.

That is why these characteristics are regarded as natural endowments and, although no one is provided with theoretical wisdom by nature, we do think that men have good sense, understanding, and intelligence by nature. An indication of this is that we think of these characteristics as depending on different stages of life, and that at a given stage of life a person acquires intelligence and good sense: the implication is that [human] nature is the cause. Therefore, we ought to pay as much attention to the sayings and opinions, undemonstrated though they are, of wise and experienced older men as we do to demonstrated truths. For experience has given such men an eye with which they can see correctly.**

We have now completed our discussion of what practical and theoretical wisdom are; we have described the sphere in which each operates, and we have shown that each is the excellence of a different part of the soul.

12. The Use of Theoretical and Practical Wisdom: One might raise some questions about the usefulness of these two virtues. Theoretical wisdom, [as we have described it,] will study none of the things that make a man happy, for it is not at all concerned with the sphere of coming-to-be [but only with unchanging realities]. Practical wisdom, on the other hand, *is* concerned with this sphere, but for what purpose do we need it? (1) It is true that practical wisdom deals with what is just, noble, and good for man; and it is doing such things that characterizes a man as good. But our ability to perform such actions is in no way enhanced by knowing them, since the virtues are characteristics, [that is to say, fixed capacities for action, acquired by habit]. The same also applies, after all, to matters of health and well-being (not in the sense of "producing health and well-being" but in the sense of "being healthy and well" as the manifestation of a physical condition or a characteristic): our ability to perform actions [which show that we are healthy and well] is in no way enhanced by a mastery of the science of medicine or of physical training.

(2) But if we are to say that the purpose of practical wisdom is not to *know* what is just, noble, and good, but to *become* just, noble, and good, it would be of no use at all to a man who is already good. Moreover, it is of no use to those who do not have

*I.e., we can attain the end—happiness—only by discovering the general rules of moral conduct, and these, in turn, rest on the immediate apprehension by intelligence of particular moral facts.

**The "eye given by experience" is of course *nous,* "intelligence."

virtue, for it makes no difference whether they have practical wisdom themselves or   30
listen to others who have it. It is quite sufficient to take the same attitude as we take toward health: we want to be healthy, yet we do not study medicine.

(3) In addition, it would seem strange if practical wisdom, though [intrinsically]
inferior to theoretical wisdom, should surpass it in authority, because that which produces a thing rules and directs it.   35

These, then, are the questions we must discuss: so far we have only stated them
as problems.

First of all, then, we should insist that both theoretical and practical wisdom are   1144ᵃ
necessarily desirable in themselves, even if neither of them produces anything. For
each one of them is the virtue of a different part of the soul.

Secondly, they do in fact produce something: theoretical wisdom produces happiness, not as medicine produces health, but as health itself makes a person healthy.
For since theoretical wisdom is one portion of virtue in its entirety, possessing and ac-   5
tualizing it makes a man happy. [For happiness, as we have seen (Book I, 7) consists in
the activity of virtue.]

In the third place, a man fulfills his proper function only by way of practical wisdom and moral excellence or virtue: virtue makes us aim at the right target, and practical wisdom makes us use the right means. The fourth part of the soul, the nutritive,   10
does not have a virtue [which makes man fulfill his proper function,] since it does not
play any role in the decision to act or not to act.

Finally, the argument has to be met that our ability to perform noble and just
acts is in no way enhanced by practical wisdom. We have to begin a little further
back and take the following as our starting point. It is our contention that people may
perform just acts without actually being just men, as in the case of people who do
what has been laid down by the laws but do so either involuntarily or through igno-   15
rance or for an ulterior motive, and not for the sake of performing just acts. [Such
persons are not just men] despite the fact that they act the way they should, and perform all the actions which a morally good man ought to perform. On the other hand,
it seems that it is possible for a man to be of such a character that he performs each
particular act in such a way as to make him a good man—I mean that his acts are due
to choice and are performed for the sake of the acts themselves. Now, it is virtue   20
which makes our choice right. It is not virtue, however, but a different capacity,
which determines the steps which, in the nature of the case, must be taken to implement this choice.

We must stop for a moment to make this point clearer. There exists a capacity
called "cleverness," which is the power to perform those steps which are conducive to   25
a goal we have set for ourselves and to attain that goal. If the goal is noble, cleverness
deserves praise; if the goal is base, cleverness is knavery. That is why men of practical
wisdom are often described as "clever" and "knavish." But in fact this capacity [alone]
is not practical wisdom, although practical wisdom does not exist without it. Without
virtue or excellence, this eye of the soul, [intelligence,] does not acquire the character-   30
istic of practical wisdom: that is what we have just stated and it is obvious. For the syllogisms which express the principles initiating action run: "Since the end, or the highest good, is such-and-such . . ."—whatever it may be; what it really is does not matter
for our present argument. But whatever the true end may be, only a good man can
judge it correctly. For wickedness distorts and causes us to be completely mistaken   35
about the fundamental principles of action. Hence it is clear that a man cannot have
practical wisdom unless he is good.

1144ᵇ   *13. Practical Wisdom and Moral Virtue:* Accordingly, we must also re-examine virtue or excellence. Virtue offers a close analogy to the relation that exists between practical wisdom and cleverness. Just as these two qualities are not identical but similar, so we find the same relation between natural virtue and virtue in the full sense. It seems that the various kinds of character inhere in all of us, somehow or other, by na-
5   ture. We tend to be just, capable of self-control, and to show all our other character traits from the time of our birth. Yet we still seek something more, the good in a fuller sense, and the possession of these traits in another way. For it is true that children and beasts are endowed with natural qualities or characteristics, but it is evident that without intelligence these are harmful. This much, to be sure, we do seem to notice: as in
10   the case of a mighty body which, when it moves without vision, comes down with a mighty fall because it cannot see, so it is in the matter under discussion. If a man acts blindly, i.e., using his natural virtue alone, he will fail; but once he acquires intelligence, it makes a great difference in his action. At that point, the natural characteristic will become that virtue in the full sense which it previously resembled.

        Consequently, just as there exist two kinds of quality, cleverness and practical
15   wisdom, in that part of us which forms opinions, [i.e., in the calculative element,] so also there are two kinds of quality in the moral part of us, natural virtue and virtue in the full sense. Now virtue in the full sense cannot be attained without practical wisdom. That is why some people maintain that all the virtues are forms of practical wisdom, and why Socrates' approach to the subject was partly right and partly wrong. He
20   was wrong in believing that all the virtues are forms of wisdom, but right in saying that there is no virtue without wisdom. This is indicated by the fact that all the current definitions of virtue,* after naming the characteristic and its objects, add that it is a characteristic "guided by right reason." Now right reason is that which is determined by practical wisdom. So we see that these thinkers all have some inkling that virtue is a
25   characteristic of this kind, namely, a characteristic guided by practical wisdom.

        But we must go a little beyond that. Virtue or excellence is not only a characteristic which is guided by right reason, but also a characteristic which is united with right reason; and right reason in moral matters is practical wisdom.** In other words, while Socrates believed that the virtues *are* rational principles—he said that all of them are
30   forms of knowledge—we, on the other hand, think that they are *united with* a rational principle.

        Our discussion, then, has made it clear that it is impossible to be good in the full sense of the word without practical wisdom or to be a man of practical wisdom without moral excellence or virtue. Moreover, in this way we can also refute the dialectical argument which might be used to prove that the virtues exist independently of one another. The same individual, it might be argued, is not equally well-endowed by nature
35   for all the virtues, with the result that at a given point he will have acquired one virtue but not yet another. In the case of the natural virtues this may be true, but it cannot
1145ᵃ   happen in the case of those virtues which entitle a man to be called good in an unqualified sense. For in the latter case, as soon as he possesses this single virtue of practical wisdom, he will also possess all the rest.

        It is now clear that we should still need practical wisdom, even if it had no bearing on action, because it is the virtue of a part of our soul. But it is also clear that [it does have an important bearing on action, since] no choice will be right without practi-

---

*The reference is to the doctrines of Plato's successors in the Academy.
**I.e., right reason is not only an external standard of action, but it also lives in us and makes us virtuous.

Lapith and Centaur, Metope from Parthenon, 477–438 B.C. According to a Greek myth, the Lapiths invited the Centaurs to the wedding feast of their king, Peirthon, as a gesture of goodwill. Upon seeing the beauty of the Lapiety bride, the Centaurs succumbed to their animal instincts of lust and drunkenness and turned the feast into an abduction attempt and brawl. The Lapith warriors, under the cool wisdom of Apollo, brought a sense of calm to the chaos. The image is a symbolic lesson in its appeal for human reason and order over the lower animal instinct of passion—a lesson also taught by Aristotle in the *Nichomachean Ethics. (British Museum, London, Great Britain)*

cal wisdom and virtue. For virtue determines the end, and practical wisdom makes us   5
do what is conducive to the end.

Still, practical wisdom has no authority over theoretical wisdom or the better part of our soul* any more than the art of medicine has authority over health. [Just as medicine does not use health but makes the provisions to secure it, so] practical wisdom does not use theoretical wisdom but makes the provisions to secure it. It issues commands to attain it, but it does not issue them to wisdom itself. To say the contrary   10

*That is, the scientific or cognitive part in the soul, the rational element which grasps necessary and permanent truths.

would be like asserting that politics governs the gods, because it issues commands about everything in the state, [including public worship].

BOOK VII

1. Moral Strength and Moral Weakness: Their Relation to Virtue and Vice and
15   *Current Beliefs About Them:* We have to make a fresh start now by pointing out that the qualities of character to be avoided are three in kind: vice, moral weakness, and brutishness. The opposites of two of these are obvious: one is called virtue or excellence and the other moral strength. The most fitting description of the opposite of brutishness would be to say that it is superhuman virtue, a kind of heroic and divine excellence; just
20   as Homer has Priam say about Hector that he was of surpassing excellence:

> for he did not seem like one who was child of a mortal man, but of god.

Therefore, if, as is said, an excess of virtue can change a man into a god, the character-
25   istic opposed to brutishness must evidently be something of this sort. For just as vice and virtue do not exist in brute beasts, no more can they exist in a god. The quality of gods is something more worthy of honor than [human] virtue or excellence, and the quality of a brute is generically different from [human] vice.

If it is rare to find a man who is divine—as the Spartans, for example, customar-ily use the attribute "divine man" to express an exceptionally high degree of admira-
30   tion for a person—it is just as rare that a brute is found among men. It does happen, particularly among barbarians, but in some cases disease and physical disability can make a man brutish. "Brutishness" is also used as a term of opprobrium for those who exceed all other men in vice.

But we must defer until later some mention of this kind of disposition, and vice
35   has already been discussed. We must now discuss moral weakness, softness, and ef-feminacy, also moral strength and tenacity. We will do so on the assumption that each
1145ᵇ   of these two sets of characteristics is neither identical with virtue or with wickedness nor generically different from it, but different species respectively of the covering gen-era, [namely, qualities to be sought and qualities to be avoided].

The proper procedure will be the one we have followed in our treatment of other subjects: we must present phenomena, [that is, the observed facts of moral life and the current beliefs about them,] and, after first stating the problems inherent in these, we
5   must, if possible, demonstrate the validity of all the beliefs about these matters,* and, if not, the validity of most of them or of the most authoritative. For if the difficulties are resolved and current beliefs are left intact, we shall have proved their validity suffi-ciently.

Now the current beliefs are as follows: (1) Moral strength and tenacity are quali-ties of great moral value and deserve praise, while moral weakness and softness are
10   base and deserve blame. (2) A man who is morally strong tends to abide by the results

---

*"Matters" here translates the Greek word *pathos,* which we usually render as "emotion" or "affect." Here, however, it is used in a loose and general sense to include the whole class of moral phenomena. In other words, Aristotle does not mean to deny here that the qualities enumerated above are lasting characteristics.

of his calculation, and a morally weak man tends to abandon them. (3) A morally weak man does, on the basis of emotion, what he knows to be base, whereas a morally strong man, knowing that certain appetites are base, refuses to follow them and accepts the guidance of reason. (4) Though a self-controlled man is called morally strong and tenacious, some people affirm and others deny [the converse, namely,] that a morally   15 strong person is self-controlled in every respect; likewise, some people call a self-indulgent person "morally weak" and a morally weak person "self-indulgent" without discriminating between the two, while others say that they are different. (5) Sometimes it is said that a man of practical wisdom cannot possibly be morally weak, and sometimes people who have practical wisdom and who are clever are said to be morally weak. (6) Finally, it is said that moral weakness is shown even in anger and in the pursuit of honor and profit. These, then, are the opinions commonly heard.   20

2. Problems in the Current Beliefs About Moral Strength and Moral Weakness: The problems we might raise are these. [As to (3):] how can a man be morally weak in his actions, when his basic assumption is correct [as to what he should do]? Some people claim that it is impossible for him to be morally weak if he has knowledge [of what he ought to do]. Socrates, for example, believed that it would be strange if, when a man possesses knowledge, something else should overpower it and drag it about like a   25 slave. In fact, Socrates was completely opposed to the view [that a man may know what is right but do what is wrong], and did not believe that moral weakness exists. He claimed that no one acts contrary to what is best in the conviction [that what he is doing is bad], but through [ignorance of the fact that it is bad].

Now this theory is plainly at variance with the observed facts, and one ought to investigate the emotion [involved in the acts of a morally weak man]: if it comes about through ignorance, what manner of ignorance is it? For evidently a man who is morally weak in his actions does not think [that he ought to act the way he does] before he is in the grip of emotion.   30

There are some people* who accept only certain points of Socrates' theory, but reject others. They agree that nothing is better or more powerful than *knowledge,* but they do not agree that no one acts contrary to what he *thought* was the better thing to do. Therefore, they say, a [morally weak person] does not have knowledge but opinion when he is overpowered by pleasures.   35

However, if it really is opinion and not knowledge, if, in other words, the basic conviction which resists [the emotion] is not strong but weak, as it is when people are   1146ᵃ in doubt, we can forgive a man for not sticking to his opinions in the face of strong appetites. But we do not forgive wickedness or anything else that deserves blame [as moral weakness does. Hence it must be something stronger than opinion which is overpowered]. But does that mean that it is practical wisdom** which resists [the appetite]? This, after all, is the strongest [kind of conviction]. But that would be absurd: for it would mean that the same man will have practical wisdom and be morally weak   5 at the same time, and there is no one who would assert that it is the mark of a man of practical wisdom to perform voluntarily the basest actions. In addition, it has been shown before that a man of practical wisdom is a man of action he is concerned with ultimate particulars that he possesses the other virtues.

*I.e., Plato's followers in the Academy.

**The point is this: if the kind of conviction a morally weak man has is neither knowledge nor a weak conviction, it must be a strong conviction, and practical wisdom is such a conviction.

Furthermore, [as regards (4)]: if being a morally strong person involves having
10   strong and base appetites, a self-controlled man will not be morally strong nor a
morally strong man self-controlled. It is out of character for a self-controlled person to
have excessive or base appetites. Yet a morally strong man certainly must have such
appetites: for if the appetites are good, the characteristic which prevents him from following them is bad, and that would mean that moral strength is not always morally
15   good. If, on the other hand, our appetites are weak and not base, there is nothing extraordinary in resisting them, nor is it a great achievement if they are base and weak.

Again, [to take (1) and (2),] if moral strength makes a person abide by any and
every opinion, it is a bad thing; for example, if it makes him persist in a false opinion.
And if moral weakness makes a man abandon any and every opinion, moral weakness
will occasionally be morally good, as, for example, in the case of Neoptolemus in
20   Sophocles' *Philoctetes*. Neoptolemus deserves praise when he does not abide by the
resolution which Odysseus had persuaded him to adopt, because it gives him pain to
tell a lie.

Further, [concerning (1) and (3),] the sophistic argument presents a problem. The
Sophists want to refute their opponents by leading them to conclusions which contradict generally accepted facts. Their purpose is to have success bring them the reputation of being clever, and the syllogism which results only becomes a problem or
25   quandary [for their opponents]. For the mind is in chains when, because it is dissatisfied with the conclusion it has reached, it wishes not to stand still, while on the other
hand its inability to resolve the argument makes forward movement impossible. Now,
they have one argument which leads to the conclusion that folly combined with moral
weakness is virtue. This is the way it runs: [if a man is both foolish and morally weak,]
he acts contrary to his conviction because of his moral weakness; but [because of his
30   folly,] his conviction is that good things are bad and that he ought not to do them.
Therefore, [acting contrary to his conviction,] he will do what is good and not what is
bad.

A further problem [arises from (2) and (4)]. A person who, in his actions, pursues, and prefers what is pleasant, convinced or persuaded [that it is good],* would
seem to be better than one who acts the same way not on the basis of calculation, but
because of moral weakness. For since he may be persuaded to change his mind, he can
be cured more easily. To a morally weak man, on the other hand, applies the proverb,
35   "When water chokes you, what can you wash it down with?" For if he had been per-
1146ᵇ   suaded to act the way he does, he would have stopped acting that way when persuaded
to change his mind. But as it is, though persuaded that he ought to do one thing, he
nevertheless does another.

Finally, if everything is the province of moral weakness and moral strength, who
would be morally weak in the unqualified sense of the word? No one has every form of
5   moral weakness, but we do say of some people that they are morally weak in an unqualified sense.

These are the sort of problems that arise. Some of the conflicting opinions must
be removed and others must be left intact. For the solution of a problem is the discovery [of truth].

3. Some Problems Solved: Moral Weakness and Knowledge: Our first step is,
then, to examine (1) whether morally weak people act knowingly or not, and, if knowingly, in what sense. Secondly, (2) we must establish the kind of questions with which

---

*I.e., a self-indulgent person.

a morally weak and a morally strong man are concerned. I mean, are they concerned   10
with all pleasure and pain or only with certain distinct kinds of them? Is a morally
strong person the same as a tenacious person or are they different? Similar questions
must also be asked about all other matters germane to this study.

The starting point of our investigation is the question *(a)* whether the morally
strong man and the morally weak man have their distinguishing features in the situa-   15
tions with which they are concerned or in their manner [of reacting to the situation].
What I mean is this: does a morally weak person owe his character to certain situations
to [which he reacts], or to the manner [in which he reacts], or to both? Our second
question *(b)* is whether or not moral weakness and moral strength are concerned with
all [situations and feelings. The answer to both these questions is that] a man who is
morally weak in the unqualified sense is not [so described because of his reaction] to   20
every situation, but only to those situations in which also a self-indulgent man may get
involved. Nor is he morally weak because of the mere fact of his relationship to these
situations, [namely, that he yields to temptation]. In that case moral weakness would
be the same as self-indulgence. Instead, his moral weakness is defined by the manner
[in which he yields]. For a self-indulgent person is led on by his own choice, since he
believes that he should always pursue the pleasure of the moment. A morally weak
man, on the other hand, does not think he should, but pursues it, nonetheless.

(1) The contention that it is true opinion rather than knowledge which a morally
weak man violates in his actions has no bearing on our argument. For some people   25
have no doubts when they hold an opinion, and think they have exact knowledge. Accordingly, if we are going to say that the weakness of their belief is the reason why
those who hold opinion will be more liable to act against their conviction than those
who have knowledge, we shall find that there is no difference between knowledge and
opinion. For some people are no less firmly convinced of what they believe than others   30
are of what they know: Heraclitus is a case in point.* *(a)* But the verb "to know" has
two meanings: a man is said to "know" both when he does not use the knowledge he
has and when he does use it. Accordingly, when a man does wrong it will make a difference whether he is not exercising the knowledge he has, [viz., that it is wrong to do
what he is doing,] or whether he is exercising it. In the latter case, we would be baffled,
but not if he acted without exercising his knowledge.   35

Moreover, *(b)* since there are two kinds of premise,** [namely, universal and
particular,] it may well happen that a man knows both [major and minor premise of a   1147ᵃ
practical syllogism] and yet acts against his knowledge, because the [minor] premise
which he uses is universal rather than particular. [In that case, he cannot apply his
knowledge to his action,] for the actions to be performed are particulars. Also, there

---

*The reference is not to any specific utterance of Heraclitus, but to the tone of intense conviction
with which he asserted all his doctrines, some of which Aristotle finds patently false, and hence examples of
opinion rather than knowledge.

**What is involved in this paragraph is the practical syllogism which was briefly explained in the
footnote on p. 389. However, a refinement is added here, which requires further explanation. A major
premise, Aristotle says, may contain two kinds of universal, e.g., the premise that "dry food is good for all
men" makes a universal statement about *(i)* men and *(ii)* about dry food. Accordingly, two kinds of syllogism can be developed from this major premise. The first: "dry food is good for all men"; "I am a man";
therefore, "dry food is good for me" is here neglected by Aristotle, because the agent is obviously always
aware of being a person. But the second possible syllogism: "dry food is good for all men"; "this kind of
food is dry"; therefore, "this kind of food is good for me," leaves the agent only with the general knowledge
that, for example, cereals are good, but the individual will not yet know whether this barley is a cereal.
"Knowledge" of this sort will obviously not serve to check a healthy appetite faced with an attractive bowl
of porridge.

5   are two kinds of universal term to be distinguished: one applies to *(i)* the agent, and the other *(ii)* to the thing. For example, when a person knows that dry food is good for all men, [he may also know] *(i)* that he is a man, or *(ii)* that this kind of food is dry. But whether the particular food before him is of this kind is something of which a morally weak man either does not have the knowledge or does not exercise it. So we see that there will be a tremendous difference between these two ways of knowing. We do not regard it as at all strange that a morally weak person "knows" in the latter sense [with one term nonspecific], but it would be surprising if he "knew" in the other sense, [namely with both terms apprehended as concrete particulars].

10   There is *(c)* another way besides those we have so far described, in which it is possible for men to have knowledge. When a person has knowledge but does not use it, we see that "having" a characteristic has different meanings. There is a sense in which a person both has and does not have knowledge, for example, when he is asleep, mad,
15   or drunk. But this is precisely the condition of people who are in the grip of the emotions. Fits of passion, sexual appetites, and some other such passions actually cause palpable changes in the body, and in some cases even produce madness. Now it is clear that we must attribute to the morally weak a condition similar to that of men who are asleep, mad, or drunk. That the words they utter spring from knowledge [as to what is good] is no evidence to the contrary. People can repeat geometrical demonstrations
20   and verses of Empedocles even when affected by sleep, madness, and drink; and beginning students can reel off the words they have heard, but they do not yet know the subject. The subject must grow to be part of them, and that takes time. We must, therefore, assume that a man who displays moral weakness repeats the formulae [of moral knowledge] in the same way as an actor speaks his lines.

Further, *(d)* we may also look at the cause [of moral weakness] from the viewpoint of the science of human nature, in the following way. [In the practical syllogism,]
25   one of the premises, the universal, is a current belief, while the other involves particular facts which fall within the domain of sense perception. When two premises are combined into one, [i.e., when the universal rule is realized in a particular case,] the soul is thereupon bound to affirm the conclusion, and if the premises involve action, the soul is bound to perform this act at once. For example, if [the premises are]:
30   "Everything sweet ought to be tasted" and "This thing before me is sweet" ("this thing" perceived as an individual particular object), a man who is able [to taste] and is not prevented is bound to act accordingly at once.

Now, suppose that there is within us one universal opinion forbidding us to taste [things of this kind], and another [universal] opinion which tells us that everything sweet is pleasant, and also [a concrete perception], determining our activity, that the particular thing before us is sweet; and suppose further that the appetite [for pleasure] happens to be present. [The result is that] one opinion tells us to avoid that thing, while
35   appetite, capable as it is of setting in motion each part of our body, drives us to it. [This is the case we have been looking for, the defeat of reason in moral weakness.] Thus it turns out that a morally weak man acts under the influence of some kind of reasoning
1147ᵇ   and opinion, an opinion which is not intrinsically but only incidentally opposed to right reason; for it is not opinion but appetite that is opposed to right reason.* And this ex-

---

*The point is this: there is a kind of reasoning involved in the actions of a morally weak person: such a person starts out with the opinion that everything sweet is pleasant, finds a particular sweet thing, and knows that the thing is pleasant. But this person also has right reason, which warns not to taste everything sweet. However, the appetite for pleasure, taking hold of the opinion that everything sweet is pleasant, transforms this opinion into the action of tasting. What is contrary to right reason (i.e., contrary to the knowledge that not everything sweet should be tasted) is not the person's opinion (that sweet things are pleasant) but rather the person's appetite for pleasure.

plains why animals cannot be morally weak: they do not have conceptions of universals, but have only the power to form mental images and memory of particulars.   5

How is the [temporary] ignorance of a morally weak person dispelled and how does he regain his [active] knowledge [of what is good]? The explanation is the same as it is for drunkenness and sleep, and it is not peculiar to the affect of moral weakness. To get it we have to go to the students of natural science.

The final premise, consisting as it does in an opinion about an object perceived   10
by the senses, determines our action. When in the grip of emotion, a morally weak man either does not have this premise, or he has it not in the sense of knowing it, but in the sense of uttering it as a drunken man may utter verses of Empedocles. [Because he is not in active possession of this premise,] and because the final [concrete] term of his reasoning is not a universal and does not seem to be an object of scientific knowledge in the same way that a universal is, [for both these reasons] we seem to be led to the conclusion which Socrates sought to establish. Moral weakness does not occur in the   15
presence of knowledge in the strict sense, and it is sensory knowledge, not science, which is dragged about by emotion.

This completes our discussion of the question whether a morally weak person acts with knowledge or without knowledge, and in what sense it is possible for him to act knowingly.

4. More Problems Solved: The Sphere in Which Moral Weakness Operates: (2)
The next point we have to discuss is whether it is possible for a man to be morally   20
weak in the unqualified sense, or whether the moral weakness of all who have it is concerned with particular situations. If the former is the case, we shall have to see with what kind of situations he is concerned.

Now, it is clearly in their attitude to pleasures and pains that men are morally strong and tenacious and morally weak and soft. There are two sources of pleasure: some are necessary, and others are desirable in themselves but admit of excess. The necessary kind are those concerned with the body: I mean sources of pleasure such as   25
food and drink and sexual intercourse, in short, the kind of bodily pleasures which we assigned to the sphere of self-indulgence and self-control.* By sources of pleasure which are not necessary but desirable in themselves, I mean, for example, victory,   30
honor, wealth, and similar good and pleasant things. Now, *(a)* those who violate the right reason that they possess by excessive indulgence in the second type of pleasures, are not called morally weak in the unqualified sense, but only with a qualification: we call them "morally weak in regard to material goods," or profit, or honor, or anger, but not "morally weak" pure and simple. They are different from the morally weak in the unqualified sense and share the same name only by analogy, as in our example of the   35
man called Man, who won an Olympic victory. In his case there is not much difference   1148ᵃ
between the general definition of man and the definition proper to him alone, and yet there was a difference. [That there is similarly a difference between the two senses of morally weak] is shown by the fact that we blame moral weakness—regardless of whether it is moral weakness in the unqualified sense or moral weakness concerning some particular bodily pleasure—not only as an error, but also as a kind of vice. But   5
we do not blame as vicious those [who are morally weak in matters of material goods, profit, ambition, anger, and so forth].

(b) We now come to those bodily enjoyments which, we say, are the sphere of the self-controlled and the self-indulgent. Here a man who pursues the excesses of

*I.e., the sensual pleasures of taste and touch.

things pleasant and avoids excesses of things painful (of hunger, thirst, heat, cold, and of anything we feel by touch or taste), and does so not by choice but against his choice and thinking, is called "morally weak" without the addition of "in regard to such-and-such," e.g., "in regard to feelings of anger," but simply morally weak without qualification. The truth of this is proved by the fact that persons who indulge in bodily pleasures are called "soft," but not persons who indulge in feelings of anger and so forth. For this reason, we class the morally weak man with the self-indulgent, and the morally strong with the self-controlled. But we do not include [in the same category] those who indulge in feelings of anger, because moral weakness and self-indulgence are, in a way, concerned with the same pleasures and pains. That is, they are concerned with the same pleasures and pains but not in the same way. Self-indulgent men pursue the excess by choice, but the morally weak do not exercise choice.

That is why we are probably more justified in calling a person self-indulgent who shows little or no appetite in pursuing an excess of pleasures and in avoiding moderate pains, than a person who is driven by strong appetite [to pursue pleasure and to avoid pain]. For what would the former do, if, in addition, he had the vigorous appetite of youth and felt strong pain at lacking the objects necessary for his pleasure?

Some appetites and desires are generically noble and worth while—[let us remember] our earlier distinction of pleasant things into those which are by nature desirable, the opposite of these, and those which are intermediate between the two—for example, material goods, profit, victory, and honor. Now, people are not blamed for being affected by all these and similar objects of pleasure and by those of the intermediate kind, nor are they blamed for having an appetite or a liking for them; they are blamed only for the manner in which they do so, if they do so to excess. This, by the way, is why [we do not regard as wicked] all those who, contrary to right reason, are overpowered by something that is noble and good by nature, or who pursue it—those, for example, who devote themselves to the pursuit of honor or to their children and parents more than they should. All these things are good, and those who devote themselves to them are praised. And yet even here there is an element of excess, if, like Niobe, one were to fight against the gods [for the sake of one's children], or if one showed the same excessively foolish devotion to his father as did Satyros, nicknamed "the filial."* So we see that there cannot be any wickedness in this area, because, as we stated, each of these things is in itself naturally desirable. But excess in one's attachment to them is base and must be avoided.

Similarly, there cannot be moral weakness in this area [of things naturally desirable]. Moral weakness is not only something to be avoided, but it is also something that deserves blame. Still, because there is a similarity in the affect, people do call it "moral weakness," but they add "in regard to [such-and-such]," in the same way as they speak of a "bad" doctor or a "bad" actor without meaning to imply that the person is bad in the unqualified sense. So just as in the case of the doctor and the actor [we do not speak of "badness" in the unqualified sense], because their badness is not vice but only something similar to vice by analogy, so it is clear that, in the other case, we must understand by "moral weakness" and "moral strength" only that which operates in the

*Niobe boasted that, with her six (or in some versions, seven) sons and an equal number of daughters, she was at least equal to the goddess Leto, who only had two children, the twins Apollo and Artemis. Apollo and Artemis thereupon killed all her children, and Niobe was turned into stone. Who exactly Satyros was, we do not know. Ancient commentators tell us that he committed suicide when his father died, or that he called his father a god.

same sphere as self-control and self-indulgence. When we use these terms of anger, we do so only in an analogous sense. Therefore, we add a qualification and say "morally weak in regard to anger," just as we say "morally weak in regard to honor or profit."

5. Moral Weakness and Brutishness: (1) Some things are pleasant by nature, partly *(a)* without qualification, and partly *(b)* pleasant for different classes of animals and humans. Then (2) there are things which are not pleasant by nature, but which come to be pleasant *(a)* through physical disability, *(b)* through habit, or *(c)* through an [innate] depravity of nature. We can observe characteristics corresponding to each of the latter group (2), just as [we did in discussing (1), things pleasant by nature]. I mean (2c) characteristics of brutishness, for instance, the female who is said to rip open pregnant women and devour the infants; or what is related about some of the savage tribes near the Black Sea, that they delight in eating raw meat or human flesh, and that some of them lend each other their children for a feast; or the story told about Phalaris.*

These are characteristics of brutishness. Another set of characteristics (2a) develops through disease and occasionally through insanity, as, for example, in the case of the man who offered his mother as a sacrifice to the gods and ate of her, or the case of the slave who ate the liver of his fellow slave. Other characteristics are the result of disease or (2b) of habit, e.g., plucking out one's hair, gnawing one's fingernails, or even chewing coal or earth, and also sexual relations between males. These practices are, in some cases, due to nature, but in other cases they are the result of habit, when, for example, someone has been sexually abused from childhood.

When nature is responsible, no one would call the persons affected morally weak any more than one would call women morally weak, because they are passive and not active in sexual intercourse. Nor would we apply the term to persons in a morbid condition as a result of habit. To have one of these characteristics means to be outside the limits of vice, just as brutishness, too, lies outside the limits of vice. To have such characteristics and to master them or be mastered by them does not constitute moral [strength or] weakness in an unqualified sense but only by analogy, just as a person is not to be called morally weak without qualification when he cannot master his anger, but only morally weak in regard to the emotion involved.

For all excessive folly, cowardice, self-indulgence, and ill-temper is either brutish or morbid. When someone is by nature the kind of person who fears everything, even the rustling of a mouse, his cowardice is brutish, while the man's fear of the weasel was due to disease. In the case of folly, those who are irrational by nature and live only by their senses, as do some distant barbarian tribes, are brutish, whereas those whose irrationality is due to a disease, such as epilepsy, or to insanity, are morbid.

Sometimes it happens that a person merely possesses one of these characteristics without being mastered by it—I mean, for example, if a Phalaris had restrained his appetite so as not to eat the flesh of a child or so as not to indulge in some perverse form of sexual pleasure. But it also happens that a man not only has the characteristic but is mastered by it. Thus, just as the term "wickedness" refers in its unqualified sense to man alone, while in another sense it is qualified by the addition of "brutish" or "morbid," in precisely the same way it is plain that there is a brutish and a morbid kind of

15

20

25

30

1149ᵃ

5

10

15

---

*Phalaris, tyrant of Acragas in the second quarter of the sixth century B.C., was said to have built a hollow brazen bull, in which he roasted his victims alive, presumably to eat them afterwards. There were several other stories current in antiquity about his brutality.

moral weakness [i.e., being mastered by brutishness or disease], but in its unqualified
20   sense the term "moral weakness" refers only to human self-indulgence.

It is, accordingly, clear that moral weakness and moral strength operate only in the same sphere as do self-indulgence and self-control, and that the moral weakness which operates in any other sphere is different in kind, and is called "moral weakness" only by extension, not in an unqualified sense.

25   *6. Moral Weakness in Anger:* At this point we may observe that moral weakness in anger is less base than moral weakness in regard to the appetites. For (1) in a way, anger seems to listen to reason, but to hear wrong, like hasty servants, who run off before they have heard everything their master tells them, and fail to do what they were
30   ordered, or like dogs, which bark as soon as there is a knock without waiting to see if the visitor is a friend. In the same way, the heat and swiftness of its nature make anger hear but not listen to an order, before rushing off to take revenge. For reason and imagination indicate that an insult or a slight has been received, and anger, drawing the conclusion, as it were, that it must fight against this sort of tiring, simply flares up at once.
35   Appetite, on the other hand, is no sooner told by reason and perception that something
1149ᵇ   is pleasant than it rushes off to enjoy it. Consequently, while anger somehow follows reason, appetite does not. Hence appetite is baser [than anger]. For when a person is morally weak in anger, he is in a sense overcome by reason, but the other is not overcome by reason but by appetite.

Further, (2) it is more excusable to follow one's natural desires, inasmuch as we
5   are also more inclined to pardon such appetites as are common to all men and to the extent that they are common to all. Now anger and ill temper are more natural than are the appetites which make us strive for excess and for what is not necessary. Take the example of the man who was defending himself against the charge of beating his father with the words: "Yes, I did it: my father, too, used to beat his father, and he beat his,
10   and"—pointing to his little boy—"he will beat me when he grows up to be a man. It runs in the family." And the story goes that the man who was being dragged out of the house by his son asked him to stop at the door, on the grounds that he himself had not dragged his father any further than that.

Moreover, (3) the more underhanded a person is, the more unjust he is. Now, a
15   hot-tempered man is not underhanded; nor is anger: it is open. But appetite has the same attribute as Aphrodite, who is called "weaver of guile on Cyprus born," and as her "pattern-pierced zone," of which Homer says: "endearment that steals the heart away even from the thoughtful." Therefore, since moral weakness of this type [which involves the appetite] is more unjust and baser than moral weakness concerning anger, it is this type which constitutes moral weakness in the unqualified sense and is even a kind of vice.*

20   Again, (4) no one feels pain when insulting another without provocation, whereas everyone who acts in a fit of anger acts with pain. On the contrary, whoever unprovoked insults another, feels pleasure. If, then, acts which justify outbursts of anger are more unjust than others, it follows that moral weakness caused by appetite [is more unjust than moral weakness caused by anger], for anger does not involve unprovoked insult.

It is now clear that moral weakness in regard to the appetites is more disgraceful than moral weakness displayed in anger, and also that moral strength and weakness op-

*But it is not vice in the unqualified sense, for that would involve choice.

erate in the sphere of the bodily appetites and pleasures. But we must still grasp the   25
distinctions to be made within bodily appetites and pleasures. For, as we stated at the
beginning, some pleasures are human, i.e., natural in kind as well as in degree, while
others are brutish, and others again are due to physical disability and disease. It is only
with the first group of these, [i.e., the human pleasures,] that self-control and self-   30
indulgence are concerned. For that reason, we do not call beasts either self-controlled
or self-indulgent; if we do so, we do it only metaphorically, in cases where a general
distinction can be drawn between one class of animals and another on the basis of wantonness, destructiveness, and indiscriminate voracity. [This use is only metaphorical]
because beasts are incapable of choice and calculation, but [animals of this type] stand
outside the pale of their nature, just as madmen do among humans.   35

Brutishness is a lesser evil than vice, but it is more horrifying. For [in a beast]   1150ᵃ
the better element cannot be perverted, as it can be in man, since it is lacking. [To compare a brute beast and a brutish man] is like comparing an inanimate with an animate
being to see which is more evil. For the depravity of a being which does not possess
the source that initiates its own motion is always less destructive [than the depravity of
a being that possesses this source], and intelligence is such a source. A similar compar-   5
ison can be made between injustice [as such] and an unjust man: each is in some sense
worse than the other, for a bad man can do ten thousand times as much harm as a beast.

7. Moral Strength and Moral Weakness: Tenacity and Softness: As regards the
pleasures, pains, appetites, and aversions that come to us through touch and taste, and
which we defined earlier as the sphere of self-indulgence and self-control, it is possible   10
to be the kind of person who is overcome even by those which most people master; but
it is also possible to master those by which most people are overcome. Those who are
overcome by pleasure or master it are, respectively, morally weak and morally strong;
and in the case of pain, they are, respectively, soft and tenacious. The disposition
which characterizes the majority of men lies between these two, although they tend   15
more to the inferior characteristics.

Some pleasures are necessary, up to a certain point, and others are not, whereas
neither excesses nor deficiencies of pleasure are necessary. The same is also true of appetites and pains. From all this it follows that a man is self-indulgent when he pursues
excesses of pleasant things, or when he [pursues necessary pleasures] to excess, by   20
choice, for their own sakes, and not for an ulterior result. A man of this kind inevitably
feels no regret, and is as a result incorrigible. For a person who feels no regret is incorrigible. A person deficient [in his pursuit of the necessary pleasures] is the opposite [of
self-indulgent], and the man who occupies the middle position is self-controlled. In the
same way, a man who avoids bodily pain [is self-indulgent], provided he does so by
choice and not because he is overcome by them.

A choice is not exercised either by a person who is driven by pleasure, or by a   25
person who is avoiding the pain of [unsatisfied] appetite. There is, accordingly, a difference between indulging by choice and not by choice. Everyone would think worse
of a man who would perform some disgraceful act actuated only slightly or not at all
by appetite, than of a person who was actuated by a strong appetite. And we would regard as worse a man who feels no anger as he beats another man, than someone who
does so in anger. For what would he do, if he were in the grip of emotion when acting?   30
Hence a self-indulgent man is worse than one who is morally weak.

So we see that one of the characteristics described, [viz., the deliberate avoidance of pain,] constitutes rather a kind of softness, while a person possessing the other,
[viz., the deliberate pursuit of excessive pleasures,] is self-indulgent.

A morally strong is opposed to a morally weak man, and a tenacious to a soft man. For being tenacious consists in offering resistance, while moral strength consists in mastering. Resistance and mastery are two different things, just as not being defeated differs from winning a victory. Hence, moral strength is more desirable than tenacity. A man who is deficient [in his resistance to pains] which most people withstand successfully is soft and effeminate. For effeminacy is a form of softness. A man of this kind lets his cloak trail, in order to save himself the pain of lifting it up, and plays the invalid without believing himself to be involved in the misery which a true invalid suffers.

The situation is similar in the case of moral strength and moral weakness. If a person is overcome by powerful and excessive pleasures or pains, we are not surprised. In fact, we find it pardonable if he is overcome while offering resistance, as, for example, Theodectes' Philoctetes* does when bitten by the snake, or as Cercyon in Carcinus' *Alope*,** or as people who try to restrain their laughter burst out in one great guffaw, as actually happened to Xenophantus.*** But we are surprised if a man is overcome by and unable to withstand those [pleasures and pains] which most people resist successfully, unless his disposition is congenital or caused by disease, as among the kings of Scythia, for example, in whom softness is congenital,† and as softness distinguishes the female from the male.

A man who loves amusement is also commonly regarded as being self-indulgent, but he is actually soft. For amusement is relaxation, inasmuch as it is respite from work, and a lover of amusement is a person who goes in for relaxation to excess.

One kind of moral weakness is impetuosity and another is a lack of strength. People of the latter kind deliberate but do not abide by the results of their deliberation, because they are overcome by emotion, while the impetuous are driven on by emotion, because they do not deliberate. [If they deliberated, they would not be driven on so easily,] for as those who have just been tickled are immune to being tickled again, so some people are not overcome by emotion, whether pleasant or painful, when they feel and see it coming and have roused themselves and their power of reasoning in good time. Keen and excitable persons are the most prone to the impetuous kind of moral weakness. Swiftness prevents the keen and vehemence the excitable from waiting for reason to guide them, since they tend to be led by their imagination.

8. Moral Weakness and Self-Indulgence: A self-indulgent man, as we stated, is one who feels no regret, since he abides by the choice he has made. A morally weak person, on the other hand, always feels regret. Therefore, the formulation of the prob-

---

*Theodectes (ca. 375–334 B.C.) spent most of his life at Athens. He studied under Plato, Isocrates, and Aristotle, and in addition to writing tragedies, won a considerable reputation as an orator. An ancient note on this passage tells us that, in Theodectes' tragedy, Philoctetes, after repressing his pain for a long time, finally bursts out: "Cut off my hand!"

**Carcinus was a fourth-century B.C. Athenian tragic poet. According to an ancient commentator, "Cercyon had a daughter Alope. Upon learning that his daughter Alope had committed adultery, he asked her who had perpetrated the deed, and said: 'If you tell me, I will not be grieved at all.' When Alope told him who the adulterer was, Cercyon was so overcome with grief that he could no longer stand life and renounced living."

***The occasion is not known. Xenophantus is said to have been a musician at the court of Alexander the Great (356–323 B.C.). Seneca tells us that when Xenophantus sang, Alexander was so stirred that he seized his weapons in his hands.

†According to the Hippocratic treatise *On Airs, Waters, and Places* 22, horseback riding caused softness among the Scythian aristocracy.

lem, as we posed it above, does not correspond to the facts: it is a self-indulgent man who cannot be cured, but a morally weak man is curable. For wickedness is like a disease such as dropsy or consumption, while moral weakness resembles epilepsy: the former is chronic, the latter intermittent. All in all, moral weakness and vice are generically different from each other. A vicious man is not aware of his vice, but a morally weak man knows his weakness.   35

Among the morally weak, those who lose themselves in [emotion, i.e., the impetuous,] are better than those who have a rational principle but do not abide by it, [i.e., those who lack strength]. For they are overcome by a lesser emotion and do not yield without previous deliberation, as the impetuous do. A man who has this kind of moral weakness resembles those who get drunk quickly and on little wine, or on less wine than most people do.   1151[a]

That moral weakness is not a vice [in the strict sense] is now evident, though in a certain sense it is perhaps one. For moral weakness violates choice, whereas vice is in accordance with choice. Nevertheless, they are similar in the actions to which they lead, just as Demodocus said of the Milesians: 5

The Milesians are no stupid crew, except that they do what the stupid do.*

Similarly, the morally weak are not unjust, but they will act like unjust men.   10

A morally weak man is the kind of person who pursues bodily pleasures to excess and contrary to right reason, though he is not persuaded [that he ought to do so]; the self-indulgent, on the other hand, is persuaded to pursue them because he is the kind of man who does so. This means that it is the former who is easily persuaded to change his mind, but the latter is not. For virtue or excellence preserves and wickedness destroys the initiating motive or first cause [of action], and in actions the initiating motive or first cause is the end at which we aim, as the hypotheses are in mathematics. For neither in mathematics nor in moral matters does reasoning teach us the principles or starting points; it is virtue, whether natural or habitual, that inculcates right opinion about the principle or first premise. A man who has this right opinion is self-controlled, and his opposite is self-indulgent.   15   20

But there exists a kind of person who loses himself under the impact of emotion and violates right reason, a person whom emotion so overpowers that he does not act according to the dictates of right reason, but not sufficiently to make him the kind of man who is persuaded that he must abandon himself completely to the pursuit of such pleasures. This is the morally weak man: he is better than the self-indulgent, and he is not bad in the unqualified sense of the word. For the best thing in him is saved: the principle or premise [as to how he should act]. Opposed to him is another kind of man, who remains steadfast and does not lose himself, at least not under the impact of emotion. These considerations make it clear that moral strength is a characteristic of great moral worth, while moral weakness is bad.   25

9. Steadfastness in Moral Strength and Moral Weakness: Is a man morally strong when he abides by any and every dictate of reason and choice, or only when he abides by the right choice? And is a man morally weak when he does not abide by every choice and dictate of reason, or only when he fails to abide by the rational dictate which is not false and the choice which is right? This is the problem we stated earlier. Or is it true   30

*Demodocus wrote lampooning epigrams in the sixth century B.C.

35   reason and right choice as such, but any other kind of choice incidentally, to which the one remains steadfast and the other does not? [This seems to be the correct answer,] for

1151^b   if a person chooses and pursues the attainment of *a* by means of *b,* his pursuit and choice are for *a* as such but for *b* incidentally. And by "as such" we mean "in the un-qualified sense." Therefore, there is a sense in which the one abides by and the other abandons any and every kind of opinion, but in the unqualified sense, only true opinion.

5   There are those who remain steadfast to their opinion and are called "obstinate." They are hard to convince and are not easily persuaded to change their mind. They bear a certain resemblance to a morally strong person, just as an extravagant man re-sembles one who is generous, and a reckless man resembles one who is confident. But they are, in fact, different in many respects. The one, the morally strong, will be a per-

10   son who does not change under the influence of emotion and appetite, but on occasion he will be persuaded [by argument]. Obstinate men, on the other hand, are not easily persuaded by rational argument; but to appetites they are amenable, and in many cases are driven on by pleasures. The various kinds of obstinate people are the opinionated, the ignorant, and the boorish. The opinionated let themselves be influenced by pleasure

15   and pain: they feel the joy of victory, when someone fails to persuade them to change their mind, and they feel pain when their views are overruled, like decrees that are de-clared null and void. As a result, they bear a greater resemblance to the morally weak than to the morally strong.

Then there are those who do not abide by their decisions for reasons other than moral weakness, as, for example, Neoptolemus in Sophocles' *Philoctetes.* Granted it was under the influence of pleasure that he did not remain steadfast, but it was a noble pleasure: it was noble in his eyes to be truthful, but he was persuaded by Odysseus to

20   tell a lie. For not anybody who acts under the influence of pleasure is self-indulgent, bad, or morally weak, but only those who do so under the influence of a base pleasure.

There is also a type who feels less joy than he should at the things of the body and, therefore, does not abide by the dictates of reason. The median between this type

25   and the morally weak man is the man of moral strength. For a morally weak person does not abide by the dictates of reason, because he feels more joy than he should [in bodily things], but the man under discussion feels less joy than he should. But a morally strong man remains steadfast and does not change on either account. Since moral strength is good, it follows that both characteristics opposed to it are bad, as they

30   in fact turn out to be. But since one of the two opposites is in evidence only in a few people and on few occasions, moral strength is generally regarded as being the only opposite of moral weakness, just as self-control is thought to be opposed only to self-indulgence.

Since many terms are used in an analogical sense, we have come to speak ana-logically of the "moral strength" of a self-controlled man. [There is a resemblance be-tween the two] since a morally strong man is the kind of person who does nothing con-

35   trary to the dictates of reason under the influence of bodily pleasures, and the same is

1152^a   true of a self-controlled man. But while a morally strong man has base appetites, a self-controlled man does not and is, moreover, a person who finds no pleasure in anything that violates the dictates of reason. A morally strong man, on the other hand, does find pleasure in such things, but he is not driven by them. There is also a similarity between

5   the morally weak and the self-indulgent in that both pursue things pleasant to the body; but they are different in that a self-indulgent man thinks he ought to pursue them, while the morally weak thinks he should not.

10. Moral Weakness and Practical Wisdom: It is not possible for the same per-son to have practical wisdom and be morally weak at the same time, for it has been shown that a man of practical wisdom is *ipso facto* a man of good character. Moreover, to be a man of practical wisdom, one must not only know [what one ought to do], but he must also be able to act accordingly. But a morally weak man is not able so to act. However, there is no reason why a clever man could not be morally weak. That is why   10 occasionally people are regarded as possessing practical wisdom, but as being morally weak at the same time; it is because cleverness differs from practical wisdom in the way we have described in our first discussion of the subject. They are closely related in that both follow the guidance of reason, but they differ in that [practical wisdom alone] involves moral choice.

Furthermore, a morally weak man does not act like a man who has knowledge and exercises it, but like a man asleep or drunk. Also, even though he acts voluntar-   15 ily—for he knows in a sense what he is doing and what end he is aiming at—he is not wicked, because his moral choice is good,* and that makes him only half-wicked. He is not unjust, either, for he is no underhanded plotter. [For plotting implies deliberation,] whereas one type of morally weak man does not abide by the results of his deliberation, while the other, the excitable type, does not even deliberate. So we see that a morally weak person is like a state which enacts all the right decrees and has laws of a   20 high moral standard, but does not apply them, a situation which Anaxandrides made fun of: "Thus wills the state, that cares not for its laws."** A wicked man, on the other hand, resembles a state which does apply its laws, but the laws are bad.

In relation to the characteristics possessed by most people, moral weakness and moral strength lie at the extremes. For a morally strong person remains more steadfast   25 and a morally weak person less steadfast than the capacity of most men permits.

The kind of moral weakness displayed by excitable people is more easily cured than the moral weakness of those who deliberate but do not abide by their decisions; and those who are morally weak through habituation are more curable than those who are morally weak by nature. For it is easier to change habit than to change nature. Even   30 habit is hard to change, precisely because it resembles nature, as Euenus says:

A habit, friend, is of long practice born,
and practice ends in fashioning man's nature.***

We have now completed our definitions of moral strength, moral weakness, tenacity, and softness, and stated how these characteristics are related to one another.   35

11. Pleasure: Some Current Views: It is the role of a political philosopher to   1152ᵇ study pleasure and pain. For he is the supreme craftsman of the end to which we look when we call one particular thing bad and another good in the unqualified sense. Moreover, an examination of this subject is one of the tasks we must logically undertake,   5 since we established that virtue and vice of character are concerned with pains and pleasures, and most people claim that happiness involves pleasure. That is why the word "blessed" is derived from the word "enjoy."

Now, (1) some people believe that no pleasure is good, either in itself or incidentally, since the good and pleasure are not the same thing.† (2) Others hold that, though   10

---

*I.e., his basic moral purpose is good, even though it is eventually vitiated by appetite.
**Anaxandrides (fl. 382–349 B.C.) migrated from his native Rhodes (or Colophon) to Athens, where he gained fame as a poet of the Middle Comedy.
***Euenus of Paros was a famous Sophist, who lived in the late fifth century B.C.
†This view seems to have been propounded by Speusippus, Plato's nephew and disciple, who succeeded him as head of the Academy from 347–339 B.C. A similar view had been espoused by Antisthenes (ca. 455–ca. 360 B.C.), the friend of Socrates and precursor of the Cynic School.

some pleasures are good, most of them are bad.* (3) Then there is a third view, according to which it is impossible for pleasure to be the highest good, even if all pleasures are good.**

[The following arguments are advanced to support (1) the contention that] pleasure is not a good at all: *(a)* All pleasure is a process or coming-to-be leading to the natural state [of the subject] and perceived [by the subject]; but no process is of the same order as its ends, e.g., the building process is not of the same order as a house.
15   Further, *(b)* a self-controlled man avoids pleasures. Again, *(c)* a man of practical wisdom does not pursue the pleasant, but what is free from pain.*** Moreover, *(d)* pleasures are an obstacle to good sense: the greater the joy one feels, e.g., in sexual intercourse, the greater the obstacle; for no one is capable of rational insight while enjoying sexual relations.† Also, *(e)* there is no art of pleasure; yet every good is the result of an art. Finally, *(f)* children and beasts pursue pleasures, whereas they do not know what is good.
20   [The arguments for the view (2) that] not all pleasures are good are: *(a)* Some pleasures are disgraceful and cause for reproach; and *(b)* some pleasures are harmful, for there are pleasant things that may cause disease.

[And the argument in favor of (3), the contention that] pleasure is not the highest good, is that it is not an end but a process or coming-to-be. These are roughly the views put forward.

12. The Views Discussed: (1) Is Pleasure a Good Thing?: But the following
25   considerations will show that the arguments we have enumerated do not lead us to the conclusion that (1) pleasure is not a good, or (3) that it is not the highest good. In the first place, [to answer argument (1*a*) and (3),] we use the word "good" in two senses: a thing may be good in the unqualified sense, or "good" for a particular person. Hence the term has also two meanings when applied to natural states and characteristics [of persons], and consequently also when applied to their motions and processes. This means that motions and processes which are generally held to be bad are partly bad
30   without qualification, but not bad for a particular person, and even desirable for him; and partly not even desirable for a particular person except on occasion and for a short time, though they are not desirable in an unqualified sense. Others again are not even pleasures, but only appear to be, for example, all processes accompanied by pain and undergone for remedial purposes, such as the processes to which the sick are subjected.

Secondly, the good has two aspects: it is both an activity and a characteristic. Now, the processes which restore us to our natural characteristic condition are only in-
35   cidentally pleasant; but the activity which is at work when our appetites [want to see us restored] is the activity of that part of our characteristic condition and natural state which has been left unimpaired. For that matter, there are pleasures which do not in-
1153ᵃ   volve pain and appetite (e.g., the activity of studying) and we experience them when there is nothing deficient in our natural state. [That processes of restoration are only incidentally pleasant] is shown by the fact that the pleasant things which give us joy

---

*This is probably a reference to the view stated by Plato in *Philebus* 13b.

**No particular proponents of this view can be identified, but they are also discussed in Plato's *Philebus* 53c–55c.

***Arguments *(b)* and *(c)* had probably been used by Speusippus and before him perhaps by Antisthenes.

†This argument may come from Archytas, a Pythagorean philosopher, mathematician, ruler of Tarentum, and friend of Plato, in the first half of the fourth century B.C.

while our natural state is being replenished are not the same as those which give us joy once it has been restored. Once restored, we feel joy at what is pleasant in the unqualified sense, but while the replenishment goes on, we enjoy even its opposite: for instance, we enjoy sharp and bitter things, none of which are pleasant either by nature or in the unqualified sense. Consequently, the pleasures [derived from them, too, are not pleasant either by nature or in the unqualified sense], for the difference that exists between various pleasant things is the same as that which is found between the pleasures derived from them.

In the third place, there is no need to believe that there exists something better than pleasure which is different from it, just as, according to some, the end is better than the process which leads to it. For pleasures are not processes, nor do all pleasures involve processes: they are activities and an end, and they result not from the process   10
of development we undergo, but from the use we make of the powers we have. Nor do all pleasures have an end other than themselves; that is only true of the pleasures of those who are being led to the perfection of their natural states. For that reason, it is not correct, either, to say that pleasure is a process perceived [by the subject]: one should rather call it an "activity of our characteristic condition as determined by our natural state," and instead of "perceived" we should call it "unobstructed." (There are some   15
who believe pleasure to be process on the ground that it is good in the true sense of the word, for they think that activity is process, but it is, as a matter of fact, different.)

The argument (2b) that pleasures [are bad, because] some pleasant things may cause disease, is like arguing that wholesome things are bad, because some of them are bad for making money. Both pleasant and wholesome things are bad in the relative senses mentioned, but that does not make them bad in themselves: even studying is occasionally harmful to health.   20

Also, (1d) neither practical wisdom nor any characteristic is obstructed by the pleasure arising from it, but only by alien pleasures extraneous to it. The pleasures arising from study and learning will only intensify study and learning, [but they will never obstruct it].

The argument (1e) that no pleasure is the result of an art makes good sense. For art never produces any activity at all: it produces the capacity for the activity. Never-   25
theless, the arts of perfume-making as well as of cooking are generally regarded as arts of pleasure.

The arguments (1b) that a self-controlled person avoids pleasure, (1c) that a man of practical wisdom pursues a life free from pain, and (1f) that children and beasts pursue pleasure, are all refuted by the same consideration. We have stated in what sense pleasures are good without qualification and in what sense not all pleasures are good.   30
These last mentioned are the pleasures which beasts and children pursue, while a man of practical wisdom wants to be free from the pain which they imply. They are the pleasures that involve appetite and pain, i.e., the bodily pleasures—for they are of this sort—and their excesses, in terms of which a self-indulgent man is self-indulgent. That   35
is why a self-controlled man avoids these pleasures. But there are pleasures even for the self-controlled.

13. The Views Discussed: (3) Is Pleasure the Highest Good?: To continue: there is general agreement that pain is bad and must be avoided. One kind of pain is bad in   1153^b
the unqualified sense, and another kind is bad, because in some way or other it obstructs us. Now, the opposite of a thing to be avoided—in the sense that it must be avoided and is bad—is good. It follows, therefore, necessarily that pleasure is a good. Speusippus tried to solve the question by saying that, just as the greater is opposed   5

both to the less and to the equal, [so pleasure is opposed both to pain and to the good]. But this solution does not come out correctly: surely, he would not say that pleasure is essentially a species of evil.

But (2a) even if some pleasures are bad, it does not mean that the highest good cannot be some sort of pleasure, just as the highest good may be some sort of knowledge, even though some kinds of knowledge are bad. Perhaps we must even draw the necessary conclusion that it is; for since each characteristic has its unobstructed activi-
10   ties, the activity of all characteristics or of one of them—depending on whether the former or the latter constitutes happiness—if unobstructed, must be the most desirable of all. And this activity is pleasure. Therefore, the highest good is some sort of pleasure, despite the fact that most pleasures are bad and, if you like, bad in the unqualified sense of the word. It is for this reason that everyone thinks that the happy life is a
15   pleasant life, and links pleasure with happiness. And it makes good sense this way: for no activity is complete and perfect as long as it is obstructed, and happiness is a complete and perfect thing. This is why a happy man also needs the goods of the body, external goods, and the goods of fortune, in order not to be obstructed by their absence.

But those who assert* that a man is happy even on the rack and even when great
20   misfortunes befall him, provided that he is good, are talking nonsense, whether they know it or not. Since happiness also needs fortune, some people regard good fortune as identical with happiness. But that is not true, for even good fortune, if excessive, can be an obstruction; perhaps we are, in that case, no longer justified in calling it "good fortune," for its definition is determined by its relation to happiness.

Also, the fact that all beasts and all men pursue pleasure is some indication that it is, in a sense, the highest good:

> There is no talk that ever quite dies down,
> if spread by many men. . . .

But since no single nature and no single characteristic condition is, or is regarded, as the
30   best [for all], people do not all pursue the same pleasure, yet all pursue pleasure. Perhaps they do not even pursue the pleasure which they think or would say they pursue, but they all pursue the same [thing], pleasure. For everything has by nature something divine about it. But the bodily pleasures have arrogated the name "pleasure" unto themselves as their own private possession, because everyone tends to follow them and participates in
35   them more frequently than in any others. Accordingly, since these are the only pleasures with which they are familiar, people think they are the only ones that exist.

1154ª   It is also evident that if pleasure, i.e., the activity [of our faculties], is not good, it will be impossible for a happy man to live pleasantly. For to what purpose would he need pleasure, if it were not a good and if it is possible that a happy man's life is one of
5   pain? For if pain is neither good nor bad, pleasure is not, either: so why should he avoid it? Surely, the life of a morally good man is no pleasanter [than that of anyone else], if his activities are not more pleasant.

14. The Views Discussed: (2) Are Most Pleasures Bad?: The subject of the pleasures of the body demands the attention of the proponents of the view that, though some pleasures—for instance, the noble pleasures—are highly desirable, the pleasures
10   of the body—that is, the pleasures which are the concern of the self-indulgent man—

*The Cynics are probably meant.

are not. If that is true, why then are the pains opposed to them bad? For bad has good as its opposite. Is it that the necessary pleasures are good in the sense in which anything not bad is good? Or are they good up to a certain point? For all characteristics and motions which cannot have an excess of good cannot have an excess of pleasure, either; but those which can have an excess of good can also have an excess of pleasure. Now, excess is possible in the case of the goods of the body, and it is the pursuit of excess, but not the pursuit of necessary pleasures, that makes a man bad. For all men get some kind of enjoyment from good food, wine, and sexual relations, but not everyone enjoys these things in the proper way. The reverse is true of pain: a bad person does not avoid an excess of it, but he avoids it altogether. For the opposite of an excess is pain only for the man who pursues the excess.

It is our task not only to say what is true, but also to state what causes error, since that helps carry conviction. For when we can give a reasoned explanation why something which appears to be true is, in fact, not true, it makes us give greater credence to what is true. Accordingly, we must now explain why the pleasures of the body appear to be more desirable.

The first reason, then, is that pleasure drives out pain. When men experience an excess of pain, they pursue excessive pleasure and bodily pleasure in general, in the belief that it will remedy the pain. These remedial [pleasures] become very intense—and that is the very reason why they are pursued—because they are experienced in contrast with their opposite.

As a matter of fact, these two reasons which we have stated also explain why pleasure is not regarded as having any moral value: some pleasures are the actions that spring from a bad natural state—either congenitally bad, as in the case of a beast, or bad by habit, as in the case of a bad man—while other pleasures are remedial and indicate a deficient natural state, and to be in one's natural state is better than to be moving toward it. But since the remedial pleasures only arise in the process of reaching the perfected state, they are morally good only incidentally.

The second reason is that the pleasures of the body are pursued because of their intensity by those incapable of enjoying other pleasures. Take, for example, those who induce themselves to be thirsty. There is no objection to this practice, if the pleasures are harmless; but if they are harmful, it is bad. For many people have nothing else to give them joy, and because of their nature, it is painful for them to feel neither [pleasure nor pain]. Actually, animal nature is under a constant strain, as the students of natural science attest when they say that seeing and hearing are painful, but [we do not feel the pain because,] as they assert, we have become accustomed to it. Similarly, whereas the growing process [we go through] in our youth puts us into the same [exhilarated] state as that of a drunken man, and [makes] youth the age of pleasure, excitable natures, on the other hand, always need remedial action: as a result of [the excess of black bile in their] constitutional blend, their bodies are exposed to constant gnawing sensations, and they are always in a state of vehement desire. Now, since pain is driven out by the pleasure opposed to it or by any strong pleasure at all, excitable people become self-indulgent and bad.

Pleasures unattended by pain do not admit of excess. The objects of these pleasures are what is pleasant by nature and not what is incidentally pleasant. By "things incidentally pleasant" I mean those that act as remedies. For since it is through some action of that part of us which has remained sound that a cure is effected, the remedy is regarded as being pleasant. But [pleasant by nature it is not]: pleasant by nature are those things which produce the action of an unimpaired natural state.

There is no single object that continues to be pleasant forever, because our nature is not simple but contains another natural element, which makes us subject to decay. Consequently, whenever one element does something, it runs counter to the nature of the other; and whenever the two elements are in a state of equilibrium, the act per-
25 formed seems neither painful nor pleasant. If there is a being with a simple nature, the same action will always be the most pleasant to him. That is why the divinity always enjoys one single and simple pleasure: for there is not only an activity of motion but also an activity of immobility, and pleasure consists in rest rather than in motion. But "change in all things is pleasant," as the poet has it, because of some evil in us. For just
30 as a man who changes easily is bad, so also is a nature that needs to change. The reason is that such a nature is not simple and not [entirely] good.

This completes our discussion of moral strength and moral weakness, and of pleasure and pain. We have stated what each of them is and in what sense some of them are good and some bad. It now remains to talk about friendship.

*   *   *

Book X

*   *   *

1176ª   6. *Happiness and Activity:* Now that we have completed our discussion of the
30 virtues, and of the different kinds of friendship and pleasure, it remains to sketch an outline of happiness, since, as we assert, it is the end or goal of human [aspirations]. Our account will be more concise if we recapitulate what we have said so far.

We stated, then, that happiness is not a characteristic; if it were, a person who
35 passes his whole life in sleep, vegetating like a plant, or someone who experiences the greatest misfortunes could possess it. If, then, such a conclusion is unacceptable, we
1176ᵇ   must, in accordance with our earlier discussion, classify happiness as some sort of activity. Now, some activities are necessary and desirable only for the sake of something else, while others are desirable in themselves. Obviously, happiness must be classed as
5 an activity desirable in itself and not for the sake of something else. For happiness lacks nothing and is self-sufficient. Activities desirable in themselves are those from which we seek to derive nothing beyond the actual exercise of the activity. Actions in conformity with virtue evidently constitute such activities; for to perform noble and good deeds is something desirable for its own sake.

Pleasant amusements, too, [are desirable for their own sake]. We do not choose
10 them for the sake of something else, since they lead to harm rather than good when we become neglectful of our bodies and our property. But most of those who are considered happy find an escape in pastimes of this sort, and this is why people who are well versed in such pastimes find favor at the courts of tyrants; they make themselves pleas-
15 ant by providing what the tyrants are after, and what they want is amusement. Accordingly, such amusements are regarded as being conducive to happiness, because men who are in positions of power devote their leisure to them. But perhaps such persons cannot be [regarded as] evidence. For virtue and intelligence, which are the sources of morally good activities, do not consist in wielding power. Also, if these men, who have
20 never tasted pure and generous pleasure, find an escape in the pleasures of the body, this is no sufficient reason for thinking that such pleasures are in fact more desirable. For children, too, think that what they value is actually the best. It is, therefore, not surprising that as children apparently do not attach value to the same things as do adults,

so bad men do not attach value to the same things as do good men. Accordingly, as we have stated repeatedly, what is valuable and pleasant to a morally good man actually is 25 valuable and pleasant. Each individual considers that activity most desirable which corresponds to his own proper characteristic condition, and a morally good man, of course, so considers activity in conformity with virtue.

Consequently, happiness does not consist in amusement. In fact, it would be strange if our end were amusement, and if we were to labor and suffer hardships all our life long merely to amuse ourselves. For, one might say, we choose everything for the 30 sake of something else—except happiness; for happiness is an end. Obviously, it is foolish and all too childish to exert serious efforts and toil for purposes of amusement. Anacharsis* seems to be right when he advises to play in order to be serious; for amusement is a form of rest, and since we cannot work continuously we need rest. Thus rest is not an end, for we take it for the sake of [further] activity. The happy life is 35 regarded as a life in conformity with virtue. It is a life which involves effort and is not 1177ª spent in amusement.

Moreover, we say that what is morally good is better than what is ridiculous and brings amusement, and the better the organ or man—whichever may be involved in a particular case—the greater the moral value of the activity. But the activity of the bet- 5 ter organ or the better man is in itself superior and more conducive to happiness.

Furthermore, any person at all, even a slave, can enjoy bodily pleasures no less than the best of men. But no one would grant that a slave has a share in happiness any more than that he lives a life of his own. For happiness does not consist in pastimes of this sort, but in activities that conform with virtue, as we have stated earlier. 10

7. Happiness, Intelligence, and the Contemplative Life: Now, if happiness is activity in conformity with virtue, it is to be expected that it should conform with the highest virtue, and that is the virtue of the best part of us. Whether this is intelligence or something else which, it is thought, by its very nature rules and guides us and which gives us our notions of what is noble and divine; whether it is itself divine or the most 15 divine thing in us; it is the activity of this part [when operating] in conformity with the excellence or virtue proper to it that will be complete happiness. That it is an activity concerned with theoretical knowledge or contemplation has already been stated.

This would seem to be consistent with our earlier statements as well as the truth. For this activity is not only the highest—for intelligence is the highest possession we 20 have in us, and the objects which are the concern of intelligence are the highest objects of knowledge—but also the most continuous: we are able to study continuously more easily than to perform any kind of action. Furthermore, we think of pleasure as a necessary ingredient in happiness. Now everyone agrees that of all the activities that conform with virtue activity in conformity with theoretical wisdom is the most pleasant. At any rate, it seems that [the pursuit of wisdom or] philosophy holds pleasures mar- 25 velous in purity and certainty, and it is not surprising that time spent in knowledge is more pleasant than time spent in research. Moreover, what is usually called "self-sufficiency" will be found in the highest degree in the activity which is concerned with theoretical knowledge. Like a just man and any other virtuous man, a wise man requires the necessities of life; once these have been adequately provided, a just man still 30

*Anacharsis, who is said to have lived early in the sixth century B.C., was a Scythian whose travels all over the Greek world brought him a reputation for wisdom. He allegedly met Solon at Athens and was numbered in some ancient traditions among the Seven Wise Men.

needs people toward whom and in company with whom to act justly, and the same is true of a self-controlled man, a courageous man, and all the rest. But a wise man is able to study even by himself, and the wiser he is the more is he able to do it. Perhaps he could do it better if he had colleagues to work with him, but he still is the most self-1177^b sufficient of all. Again, study seems to be the only activity which is loved for its own sake. For while we derive a greater or a smaller advantage from practical pursuits beyond the action itself, from study we derive nothing beyond the activity of studying. 5   Also, we regard happiness as depending on leisure; for our purpose in being busy is to have leisure, and we wage war in order to have peace. Now, the practical virtues are activated in political and military pursuits, but the actions involved in these pursuits 10   seem to be unleisurely. This is completely true of military pursuits, since no one chooses to wage war or foments war for the sake of war; he would have to be utterly bloodthirsty if he were to make enemies of his friends simply in order to have battle and slaughter. But the activity of the statesman, too, has no leisure. It attempts to gain advantages beyond political action, advantages such as political power, prestige, or at least happiness for the statesman himself and his fellow citizens, and that is something 15   other than political activity: after all, the very fact that we investigate politics shows that it is not the same [as happiness]. Therefore, if we take as established (1) that political and military actions surpass all other actions that conform with virtue in nobility and grandeur; (2) that they are unleisurely, aim at an end, and are not chosen for their own sake; (3) that the activity of our intelligence, inasmuch as it is an activity con-20   cerned with theoretical knowledge, is thought to be of greater value than the others, aims at no end beyond itself, and has a pleasure proper to itself—and pleasure increases activity; and (4) that the qualities of this activity evidently are self-sufficiency, leisure, as much freedom from fatigue as a human being can have, and whatever else falls to the lot of a supremely happy man; it follows that the activity of our intelligence 25   constitutes the complete happiness of man, provided that it encompasses a complete span of life; for nothing connected with happiness must be incomplete.

However, such a life would be more than human. A man who would live it would do so not insofar as he is human, but because there is a divine element within him. This divine element is as far above our composite nature* as its activity is above the active exercise of the other, [i.e., practical,] kind of virtue. So if it is true that intel-30   ligence is divine in comparison with man, then a life guided by intelligence is divine in comparison with human life. We must not follow those who advise us to have human thoughts, since we are [only] men, and mortal thoughts, as mortals should; on the contrary, we should try to become immortal as far as that is possible and do our utmost to 1178^a live in accordance with what is highest in us. For though this is a small portion [of our nature], it far surpasses everything else in power and value. One might even regard it as each man's true self, since it is the controlling and better part. It would, therefore, be strange if a man chose not to live his own life but someone else's.

Moreover, what we stated before will apply here, too: what is by nature proper to 5   each thing will be at once the best and the most pleasant for it. In other words, a life guided by intelligence is the best and most pleasant for man, inasmuch as intelligence, above all else, is man. Consequently, this kind of life is the happiest.

8. The Advantages of the Contemplative Life: A life guided by the other kind of virtue, [the practical,] is happy in a secondary sense, since its active exercise is con-

---

*Human beings, consisting of soul and body, i.e., of form and matter, are composite beings, whereas the divine, being all intelligence, is not.

fined to man. It is in our dealings with one another that we perform just, courageous, and other virtuous acts, when we observe the proper kind of behavior toward each man   10
in private transactions, in meeting his needs, in all manner of actions, and in our emotions, and all of these are, as we see, peculiarly human. Moreover, some moral acts seem to be determined by our bodily condition, and virtue or excellence of character seems in many ways closely related to the emotions. There is also a close mutual connection between practical wisdom and excellence of character, since the fundamental   15
principles of practical wisdom are determined by the virtues of character, while practical wisdom determines the right standard for the moral virtues. The fact that these virtues are also bound up with the emotions indicates that they belong to our composite nature, and the virtues of our composite nature are human virtues; consequently, a life   20
guided by these virtues and the happiness [that goes with it are likewise human]. The happiness of the intelligence, however, is quite separate [from that kind of happiness]. That is all we shall say about it here, for a more detailed treatment lies beyond the scope of our present task.

It also seems that such happiness has little need of external trimmings, or less need than moral virtue has. Even if we grant that both stand in equal need of the necessities of life, and even if the labors of a statesman are more concerned with the needs   25
of our body and things of that sort—in that respect the difference between them may be small—yet, in what they need for the exercise of their activities, their difference will be great. A generous man will need money to perform generous acts, and a just man will need it to meet his obligations. For the mere wish to perform such acts is inscrutable, and even an unjust man can pretend that he wishes to act justly. And a courageous man will need strength if he is to accomplish an act that conforms with his   30
virtue, and a man of self-control the possibility of indulgence. How else can he or any other virtuous man make manifest his excellence? Also, it is debatable whether the   35
moral purpose or the action is the more decisive element in virtue, since virtue depends on both. It is clear of course that completeness depends on both. But many things are   1178^{b}
needed for the performance of actions, and the greater and nobler the actions the more is needed. But a man engaged in study has no need of any of these things, at least not for the active exercise of studying; in fact one might even go so far as to say that they are a hindrance to study. But insofar as he is human and lives in the society of his fel-   5
low men, he chooses to act as virtue demands, and accordingly, he will need externals for living as a human being.

A further indication that complete happiness consists in some kind of contemplative activity is this. We assume that the gods are in the highest degree blessed and happy. But what kind of actions are we to attribute to them? Acts of justice? Will they   10
not look ridiculous making contracts with one another, returning deposits, and so forth? Perhaps acts of courage—withstanding terror and taking risks, because it is noble to do so? Or generous actions? But to whom will they give? It would be strange to think that they actually have currency or something of the sort. Acts of self-control?   15
What would they be? Surely, it would be in poor taste to praise them for not having bad appetites. If we went through the whole list we would see that a concern with actions is petty and unworthy of the gods. Nevertheless, we all assume that the gods exist and, consequently, that they are active; for surely we do not assume them to be always asleep like Endymion.* Now, if we take away action from a living being, to say noth-   20

*Supposedly the most beautiful of men, Endymion was loved by the Moon, who cast him into a perpetual sleep that she might descend and embrace him each night.

ing of production, what is left except contemplation? Therefore, the activity of the divinity which surpasses all others in bliss must be a contemplative activity, and the human activity which is most closely akin to it is, therefore, most conducive to happiness.

25   This is further shown by the fact that no other living being has a share in happiness, since they all are completely denied this kind of activity. The gods enjoy a life blessed in its entirety; men enjoy it to the extent that they attain something resembling the divine activity; but none of the other living beings can be happy, because they have no share at all in contemplation or study. So happiness is coextensive with study, and

30   the greater the opportunity for studying, the greater the happiness, not as an incidental effect but as inherent in study; for study is in itself worthy of honor. Consequently, happiness is some kind of study or contemplation.

But we shall also need external well-being, since we are only human. Our nature

35   is not self-sufficient for engaging in study: our body must be healthy and we must have food and generally be cared for. Nevertheless, if it is not possible for a man to be supremely happy without external goods, we must not think that his needs will be great

1179ᵃ   and many in order to be happy; for self-sufficiency and moral action do not consist in an excess [of possessions]. It is possible to perform noble actions even without being

5   ruler of land and sea; a man's actions can be guided by virtue also if his means are moderate. That this is so can be clearly seen in the fact that private individuals evidently do not act less honorably but even more honorably than powerful rulers. It is enough to have moderate means at one's disposal, for the life of a man whose activity is guided by virtue will be happy.

10   Solon certainly gave a good description of a happy man, when he said that he is a man moderately supplied with external goods, who had performed what he, Solon, thought were the noblest actions, and who had lived with self-control. For it is possible to do what one should even with moderate possessions. Also Anaxagoras, it seems, did not assume that a happy man had to be rich and powerful. He said that he would not be

15   surprised if a happy man would strike the common run of people as strange, since they judge by externals and perceive nothing but externals. So it seems that our account is in harmony with the opinion of the wise.

Now, though such considerations carry some conviction, in the field of moral action truth is judged by the actual facts of life, for it is in them that the decisive element

20   lies. So we must examine the conclusions we have reached so far by applying them to the actual facts of life: if they are in harmony with the facts we must accept them, and if they clash we must assume that they are mere words.

A man whose activity is guided by intelligence, who cultivates his intelligence and keeps it in the best condition, seems to be most beloved by the gods. For if the

25   gods have any concern for human affairs—and they seem to have—it is to be expected that they rejoice in what is best and most akin to them, and that is our intelligence; it is also to be expected that they requite with good those who most love and honor intelligence, as being men who care for what is dear to the gods and who act rightly and nobly. That a wise man, more than any other, has all these qualities is perfectly clear.

30   Consequently, he is the most beloved by the gods, and as such he is, presumably, also the happiest. Therefore, we have here a further indication that a wise man attains a higher degree of happiness than anyone.

HELLENISTIC PHILOSOPHY

◀〇▶

Following the death of Alexander the Great in 323 B.C., three of his generals, Ptolemy, Seleucus, and Antigonus, carved up the empire he had created. For the next three centuries, descendants of these three men ruled the eastern Mediterranean world. By 30 B.C., with the Roman Emperor Octavian's defeat of Anthony and Cleopatra and the annexation of Egypt, the period of Greek rule (known as the "Hellenistic" period from the word ⟨*hellen*⟩, meaning "Greek") was over. Real power in the area had shifted westward to emerging Rome.

This shift from Greek to Roman authority did not happen without social and political turmoil, and the philosophies that developed during this period reflect that turmoil. The emphasis now was not on complete systems of thought, such as those proposed by Plato and Aristotle. In their place were theories focusing on the practical questions of the good life for individuals. In a world that seemed more and more chaotic and uncontrollable, philosophers began to seek personal salvation more than comprehensive theories. Even the Platonic Academy and the Aristotelian Lyceum, which continued for centuries, moved from the constructive doctrines of their founders to more narrowly defined critical issues.

Reviewing the development of Greek philosophy from Socrates to the Stoics and Epicureans, one is struck by the overwhelming concern in the later schools with peace of mind. There is, as a consequence, one quality that classical Greeks possessed preeminently and that Stoics and Epicureans preeminently lacked: enthusiasm.

The last great movement of Greek philosophy was Neoplatonism. The leader of this return to Platonic concepts, Plotinus (A.D. 204–270), did not lack enthusiasm, but he was, nevertheless, more remote from classical Greek attitudes than

Laocoön, second century B.C., by Hagesandros, Polydoros, and Athenodoros, all of Rhodes. The Trojan priest Laocoön protested against bringing the Greeks' wooden horse into the city. According to one version of the legend, he was punished for his interference when Apollo sent two serpents to kill him and his sons. The Hellenistic philosophers sought relief from tortured emotions such as this work depicts. (*Hirmer Fotoarchiv*)

were the Hellenistic philosophers. He extolled the spirit to the point of saying he was ashamed to have a body; his fervor was entirely mystical, and he longed, to cite his famous words, to attain "the flight of the Alone to the Alone." Thus he perfected the less classical tendencies of Plato's thought, merging those tendencies with Neopythagoreanism and with Oriental notions such as the emanations from the One.

In A.D. 529, Plato's Academy was closed by Emperor Justinian, bringing to an end a millennium of Greek philosophy.

*   *   *

For clear, concise introductions to the Hellenistic and Roman philosophers, see Frederick Copleston, "Post-Aristotelian Philosophy," in his *A History of Philosophy: Volume I, Greece & Rome, Part II* (Garden City, NY: Image Books, 1962); D.W. Hamlyn, "Greek Philosophy after Aristotle," in D.J. O'Connor, ed., *A Critical History of Western Philosophy* (New York: The Free Press, 1964); John Dillon, *The Middle Platonists, 80 B.C. to A.D. 220* (Ithaca, NY: Cornell University Press, 1996); and David Furley, *Routledge History of Philosophy, Volume II: From Aristotle to Augustine* (New York: Routledge, 1999). Eduard Zeller, *The Stoics, Epicureans, and Sceptics,* translated by Oswald J. Reichel (New York: Russell & Russell, 1962); Émile Bréhier, *The Hellenistic and Roman Age,* translated by Wade Baskin (Chicago: University of Chicago Press, 1965); A.A. Long, *Hellenistic Philosophy: Stoics, Epicureans, Sceptics* (New York: Scribners, 1974); and R.W. Sharples, *Stoics, Epicureans and Sceptics* (Oxford: Routledge, 1996), are all solid histories of the period. A.A. Long and

D.N. Sedley, eds., *The Hellenistic Philosophers,* two volumes. (Cambridge: Cambridge University Press, 1987), provide source material and discussions, while Jacques Brunschwig, *Papers in Hellenistic Philosophy,* translated by Janet Lloyd (Cambridge: Cambridge University Press, 1994) and Terence Irwin, ed., *Hellenistic Philosophy* (Hamden, CT: Garland Publishing, 1995) give technical expositions of a number of important issues. For primary sources and helpful introductions, see Whitney J. Oates, ed., *The Stoic and Epicurean Philosophers: The Complete Extant Writings of Epicurus, Epictetus, Lucretius, Marcus Aurelius* (New York: Random House, 1940).

EPICURUS
341–270 B.C.

Epicurus was born on the Greek island of Samos. At eighteen he went to Athens for a year, then joined his father in Colophon, the city where Xenophanes had been born. He studied the writings of Democritus and eventually set up his own school on the island of Lesbos. From there he moved to the Hellespont and, finally, to Athens in 307 B.C. As he moved from place to place, many of his students followed him. In Athens he established a community known as the "Garden," where he spent the rest of his life teaching and writing.

Epicurus's community welcomed people of all classes and of both sexes. The school required no fee from students, accepting what each individual was able and willing to pay. Epicurus himself was almost worshiped by his disciples, and members of his group had to swear an oath: "I will be faithful to Epicurus in accordance with whom I have made it my choice to live."* Among the later followers of Epicurus's thought, the Roman poet Lucretius (98–55 B.C.) considered him to be a god. Yet Epicurus was not overbearing or authoritarian. According to all accounts, he was kind and generous, treating his followers as friends, not subordinates. While dying in agony from a urinary obstruction, Epicurus wrote a letter that illustrates his gracious spirit. The extant portion includes these words to his friend Idomeneus: "I have a bulwark against all this pain from the joy in my soul at the memory of our conversations together."**

Epicurus wrote over three hundred volumes, but all that has survived are some fragments, three complete letters, and a short treatise summarizing his

---

*Reported in J.V. Luce, *Introduction to Greek Philosophy* (New York: Thames and Hudson, 1992), p. 140.
**Ibid.

views. These surviving works provide an understanding of Epicurus's physics and ethics and give some sense of his psychology and theory of knowledge. Epicurus's first letter, *To Herodotus,* explains his atomistic theory. Like Democritus, Epicurus asserts that reality is composed of atoms and the void. But unlike Democritus, whose atomism is deterministic, Epicurus broaches the notion that atoms sometimes inexplicably "swerve." As atoms "fell downward" through the void, some of them swerved from their paths and collided with other atoms, setting off a chain reaction that eventually led to the world as we know it. Epicurus goes on to explore the implications of this theory for perception and knowledge.

The second letter, *To Pythocles,* on astronomy and meteorology, is of questionable origin and adds little to our understanding of Epicurus's thought. But the third letter, *To Menoeceus,* together with the short work *Principle Doctrines* explains his central ethical theory. Epicurus declares that pleasure is the highest good, though some pleasures are unnatural and unnecessary. In contrast to the modern understanding of the word "epicurean," Epicurus opposed exotic meals and profuse consumption. Such indulgences never bring permanent pleasure and frequently lead to its opposite: pain. Instead Epicurus advocates enjoying only the "natural" pleasures—those most likely to lead to contentment and repose. Epicurus's ethical works are reprinted here, complete, in the Russel M. Geer translations.

*   *   *

The classic secondary work on Epicurus is Cyril Bailey, *The Greek Atomists and Epicurus* (Oxford: Clarendon Press, 1928). Norman Wentworth De Witt, *Epicurus and His Philosophy* (Minneapolis: University of Minnesota Press, 1954), provides an interesting interpretation—one which John M. Rist, *Epicurus: An Introduction* (Cambridge: Cambridge University Press, 1972), contests. A.E. Taylor, *Epicurus* (1911; reprinted New York: Books for Libraries Press, 1969); G.K. Stradach, *The Philosophy of Epicurus* (Evanston, IL: Northwestern University Press, 1963); and Diskin Clay, *Lucretius and Epicurus* (Ithaca, NY: Cornell University Press, 1983), give helpful overviews. A.J. Festugière, *Epicurus and His Gods,* translated by C.W. Chilton (1955; reprinted London: Russell, 1969), and James H. Nichols, Jr., *Epicurean Political Philosophy* (Ithaca, NY: Cornell University Press, 1976), deal with specific topics.

LETTER TO MENOECEUS

I. INTRODUCTION

Epicurus to Menoeceus, greeting.

Let no young man delay the study of philosophy, and let no old man become weary of it; for it is never too early nor too late to care for the well-being of the soul. The man who says that the season for this study has not yet come or is already past is like the man who says it is too early or too late for happiness. Therefore, both the young and the old should study philosophy, the former so that as he grows old he may still retain the happiness of youth in his pleasant memories of the past, the latter so that although he is old he may at the same time be young by virtue of his fearlessness of the future. We must therefore study the means of securing happiness, since if we have it we have everything, but if we lack it we do everything in order to gain it.

II. BASIC TEACHINGS

A. THE GODS

The gods exist; but it is impious to accept the common beliefs about them. They have no concern with men.

Practice and study without ceasing that which I was always teaching you, being assured that these are the first principles of the good life. After accepting god as the immortal and blessed being depicted by popular opinion, do not ascribe to him anything in addition that is alien to immortality or foreign to blessedness, but rather believe about him whatever can uphold his blessed immortality. The gods do indeed exist, for our perception of them is clear; but they are not such as the crowd imagines them to be, for most men do not retain the picture of the gods that they first receive. It is not the man who destroys the gods of popular belief who is impious, but he who describes the gods in the terms accepted by the many. For the opinions of the many about the gods are not perceptions but false suppositions. According to these popular suppositions, the gods send great evils to the wicked, great blessings to the righteous, for they, being always well disposed to their own virtues, approve those who are like themselves, regarding as foreign all that is different.*

B. DEATH

Philosophy, showing that death is the end of all consciousness, relieves us of all fear of death. A life that is happy is better than one that is merely long.

*The ambiguous rendition of the last part of this sentence is intentional. "They" may be the gods, who approve men like themselves, or men, who approve gods.

Epicurus, *Letters, Principal Doctrines, and Vatican Sayings,* translated by Russel M. Geer (New York: Macmillan/Library of the Liberal Arts, 1964).

Accustom yourself to the belief that death is of no concern to us, since all good and evil lie in sensation and sensation ends with death. Therefore the true belief that death is nothing to us makes a mortal life happy, not by adding to it an infinite time, but by taking away the desire for immortality. For there is no reason why the man who is thoroughly assured that there is nothing to fear in death should find anything to fear in life. So, too, he is foolish who says that he fears death, not because it will be painful when it comes, but because the anticipation of it is painful; for that which is no burden when it is present gives pain to no purpose when it is anticipated. Death, the most dreaded of evils, is therefore of no concern to us; for while we exist death is not present, and when death is present we no longer exist. It is therefore nothing either to the living or to the dead since it is not present to the living, and the dead no longer are.

But men in general sometimes flee death as the greatest of evils, sometimes long for it as a relief from the evils of life.

The wise man neither renounces life nor fears its end; for living does not offend him, nor does he suppose that not to live is in any way an evil. As he does not choose the food that is most in quantity but that which is most pleasant, so he does not seek the enjoyment of the longest life but of the happiest.

He who advises the young man to live well, the old man to die well, is foolish, not only because life is desirable, but also because the art of living well and the art of dying well are one. Yet much worse is he who says that it is well not to have been born, but once born, be swift to pass through Hades' gates.

If a man says this and really believes it, why does he not depart from life? Certainly the means are at hand for doing so if this really be his firm conviction. If he says it in mockery, he is regarded as a fool among those who do not accept his teaching.

Remember that the future is neither ours nor wholly not ours, so that we may neither count on it as sure to come nor abandon hope of it as certain not to be.

III. THE MORAL THEORY

A. PLEASURE AS THE MOTIVE

The necessary desires are for health of body and peace of mind; if these are satisfied, that is enough for the happy life.

You must consider that of the desires some are natural, some are vain, and of those that are natural, some are necessary, others only natural. Of the necessary desires, some are necessary for happiness, some for the ease of the body, some for life itself. The man who has a perfect knowledge of this will know how to make his every choice or rejection tend toward gaining health of body and peace of mind, since this is the final end of the blessed life. For to gain this end, namely freedom from pain and fear, we do everything. When once this condition is reached, all the storm of the soul is stilled, since the creature need make no move in search of anything that is lacking, nor seek after anything else to make complete the welfare of the soul and the body. For we only feel the lack of pleasure when from its absence we suffer pain; but when we do not suffer pain, we no longer are in need of pleasure. For this reason we say that pleasure is the beginning and the end of the blessed life. We recognize pleasure as the first and natural good; starting from pleasure we accept or reject; and we return to this as we judge every good thing, trusting this feeling of pleasure as our guide.

B. Pleasures and Pains

Pleasure is the greatest good; but some pleasures bring pain, and in choosing, we must consider this.

For the very reason that pleasure is the chief and the natural good, we do not choose every pleasure, but there are times when we pass by pleasures if they are out-weighed by the hardships that follow; and many pains we think better than pleasures when a greater pleasure will come to us once we have undergone the long-continued pains. Every pleasure is a good since it has a nature akin to ours; nevertheless, not every pleasure is to be chosen. Just so, every pain is an evil, yet not every pain is of a nature to be avoided on all occasions. By measuring and by looking at advantages and disadvantages, it is proper to decide all these things; for under certain circumstances we treat the good as evil, and again, the evil as good.

C. Self-Sufficiency

The truly wise man is the one who can be happy with a little.

We regard self-sufficiency as a great good, not so that we may enjoy only a few things, but so that, if we do not have many, we may be satisfied with the few, being firmly persuaded that they take the greatest pleasure in luxury who regard it as least needed, and that everything that is natural is easily provided, while vain pleasures are hard to obtain. Indeed, simple sauces bring a pleasure equal to that of lavish banquets if once the pain due to need is removed; and bread and water give the greatest pleasure when one who is in need consumes them. To be accustomed to simple and plain living is conducive to health and makes a man ready for the necessary tasks of life. It also makes us more ready for the enjoyment of luxury if at intervals we chance to meet with it, and it renders us fearless against fortune.

D. True Pleasure

The truest happiness does not come from enjoyment of physical pleasures but from a simple life, free from anxiety, with the normal physical needs satisfied.

When we say that pleasure is the end, we do not mean the pleasure of the profligate or that which depends on physical enjoyment—as some think who do not understand our teachings, disagree with them, or give them an evil interpretation—but by pleasure we mean the state wherein the body is free from pain and the mind from anxiety. Neither continual drinking and dancing, nor sexual love, nor the enjoyment of fish and whatever else the luxurious table offers brings about the pleasant life; rather, it is produced by the reason which is sober, which examines the motive for every choice and rejection, and which drives away all those opinions through which the greatest tumult lays hold of the mind.

E. PRUDENCE

Prudence or practical wisdom should be our guide.

Of all this the beginning and the chief good is prudence. For this reason prudence is more precious than philosophy itself. All the other virtues spring from it. It teaches that it is not possible to live pleasantly without at the same time living prudently, nobly, and justly, nor to live prudently, nobly, and justly without living pleasantly; for the virtues have grown up in close union with the pleasant life, and the pleasant life cannot be separated from the virtues.

IV. CONCLUSION

A. PANEGYRIC* ON THE PRUDENT MAN

Whom then do you believe to be superior to the prudent man: he who has reverent opinions about the gods, who is wholly without fear of death, who has discovered what is the highest good in life and understands that the highest point in what is good is easy to reach and hold and that the extreme of evil is limited either in time or in suffering, and who laughs at that which some have set up as the ruler of all things, Necessity? He thinks that the chief power of decision lies within us, although some things come about by necessity, some by chance, and some by our own wills; for he sees that necessity is irresponsible and chance uncertain, but that our actions are subject to no power. It is for this reason that our actions merit praise or blame. It would be better to accept the myth about the gods than to be a slave to the determinism of the physicists; for the myth hints at a hope for grace through honors paid to the gods, but the necessity of determinism is inescapable. Since the prudent man does not, as do many, regard chance as a god for the gods do nothing in disorderly fashion or as an unstable cause of all things, he believes that chance does not give man good and evil to make his life happy or miserable, but that it does provide opportunities for great good or evil. Finally, he thinks it better to meet misfortune while acting with reason than to happen upon good fortune while acting senselessly; for it is better that what has been well-planned in our actions should fail than that what has been ill-planned should gain success by chance.

B. FINAL WORDS TO MENOECEUS

Meditate on these and like precepts, by day and by night, alone or with a like-minded friend. Then never, either awake or asleep, will you be dismayed; but you will live like a god among men; for life amid immortal blessings is in no way like the life of a mere mortal.

---

*[Formal praise for a festival]

PRINCIPAL DOCTRINES

I. That which is blessed and immortal is not troubled itself, nor does it cause trouble to another. As a result, it is not affected by anger or favor, for these belong to weakness.

II. Death is nothing to us; for what has been dissolved has no sensation, and what has no sensation is nothing to us.

III. The removal of all that causes pain marks the boundary of pleasure. Wherever pleasure is present and as long as it continues, there is neither suffering nor grieving nor both together.

IV. Continuous bodily suffering does not last long. Intense pain is very brief, and even pain that barely outweighs physical pleasure does not last many days. Long illnesses permit physical pleasures that are greater than the pain.

V. It is impossible to live pleasantly without living prudently, well, and justly, and to live prudently, well, and justly without living pleasantly. Even though a man live well and justly, it is not possible for him to live pleasantly if he lacks that from which stems the prudent life.

VI. Any device whatever by which one frees himself from the fear of others is a natural good.

VII. Some, thinking thus to make themselves safe from men, wished to become famous and renowned. They won a natural good if they made their lives secure; but if their lives were not secure, they did not have that for which, following the rule of nature, they first sought.

VIII. No pleasure is evil in itself; but the means by which certain pleasures are gained bring pains many times greater than the pleasures.

IX. If every pleasure were cumulative, and if this were the case both in time and in regard to the whole or the most important parts of our nature, then pleasures would not differ from each other.

X. If the things that produce the pleasures of the dissolute were able to drive away from their minds their fears about what is above them and about death and pain, and to teach them the limit of desires, we would have no reason to find fault with the dissolute; for they would fill themselves with pleasure from every source and would be free from pain and sorrow, which are evil.

XI. If our dread of the phenomena above us, our fear lest death concern us, and our inability to discern the limits of pains and desires were not vexatious to us, we would have no need of the natural sciences.

XII. It is not possible for one to rid himself of his fears about the most important things if he does not understand the nature of the universe but dreads some of the things he has learned in the myths. Therefore, it is not possible to gain unmixed happiness without natural science.

XIII. It is of no avail to prepare security against other men while things above us and beneath the earth and in the whole infinite universe in general are still dreaded.

XIV. When reasonable security from men has been attained, then the security that comes from peace of mind and withdrawal from the crowd is present, sufficient in strength and most unmixed in well-being.

Epicurus, *Letters, Principal Doctrines, and Vatican Sayings,* translated by Russel M. Geer (New York: Macmillan/Library of the Liberal Arts, 1964).

XV. Natural wealth is limited and easily obtained; the wealth defined by vain fancies is always beyond reach.

XVI. Fortune seldom troubles the wise man. Reason has controlled his greatest and most important affairs, controls them throughout his life, and will continue to control them.

XVII. The just man is least disturbed; the unjust man is filled with the greatest turmoil.

XVIII. When once the pain caused by need has been removed, bodily pleasure will not be increased in amount but only varied in quality. The mind attains its utmost pleasure in reflecting on the very things that used to cause the greatest mental fears and on things like them.

XIX. Time that is unlimited and time that is limited afford equal pleasure if one measures pleasure's extent by reason.

XX. The flesh believes that pleasure is limitless and that it requires unlimited time; but the mind, understanding the end and limit of the flesh and ridding itself of fears of the future, secures a complete life and has no longer any need for unlimited time. It does not, however, avoid pleasure; and when circumstances bring on the end of life, it does not depart as if it still lacked any portion of the good life.

XXI. The man who understands the limits of living knows that it is easy to obtain that which removes the pain caused by want and that which perfects the whole life. Therefore, he has no need of things that involve struggle.

XXII. It is necessary to take into account the real purpose of knowledge and all the evidence of that clear perception to which we refer our opinions. If we do not, all will be full of bad judgment and confusion.

XXIII. If you struggle against all your sensations, you will have no standard of comparison by which to measure even the sensations you judge false.

XXIV. If you reject any sensation, and if you fail to distinguish between conjecture based upon that which awaits confirmation and evidence given by the senses, by the feelings, and by the mental examinations of confirmed concepts, you will confuse the other sensations with unfounded conjecture and thus destroy the whole basis for judgment. If among all opinions you accept as equally valid both those that await confirmation and those that have been confirmed, you will not free yourself from error, since you will have preserved all the uncertainty about every judgment of what is true and what is not true.

XXV. If you do not at all times refer each of your actions to the natural end,* but fall short of this and turn aside to something else in choosing and avoiding, your deeds will not agree with your words.

XXVI. Those desires that do not bring pain if they are not satisfied are not necessary; and they are easily thrust aside whenever to satisfy them appears difficult or likely to cause injury.

XXVII. Of the things that wisdom prepares for insuring lifelong happiness, by far the greatest is the possession of friends.

XXVIII. The same wisdom that permits us to be confident that no evil is eternal or even of long duration also recognizes that in our limited state the security that can be most perfectly gained is that of friendship.

XXIX. Of the desires, some are natural and necessary; some are natural but not necessary; and others are neither natural nor necessary but arise from empty opinion.

*That is, to pleasure.

XXX. Among the bodily desires, those rest on empty opinion that are eagerly pursued although if unsatisfied they bring no pain. That they are not got rid of is because of man's empty opinion, not because of their own nature.

XXXI. Natural justice is a compact resulting from expediency by which men seek to prevent one man from injuring others and to protect him from being injured by them.

XXXII. There is no such thing as justice or injustice among those beasts that cannot make agreements not to injure or be injured. This is also true of those tribes that are unable or unwilling to make agreements not to injure or be injured.

XXXIII. There is no such thing as justice in the abstract; it is merely a compact between men in their various relations with each other, in whatever circumstances they may be, that they will neither injure nor be injured.

XXXIV. Injustice is not evil in itself, but only in the fear and apprehension that one will not escape those who have been set up to punish the offense.

XXXV. If a man has secretly violated any of the terms of the mutual compact not to injure or be injured, he cannot feel confident that he will be undetected in the future even if he has escaped ten thousand times in the past; for until his death it will remain uncertain whether he will escape.

XXXVI. In general, justice is the same for all, a thing found useful by men in their relations with each other; but it does not follow that it is the same for all in each individual place and circumstance.

XXXVII. Among the things commonly held just, that which has proved itself useful in men's mutual relationships has the stamp of justice whether or not it be the same for all; if anyone makes a law and it does not prove useful in men's relationships with each other, it is no longer just in its essence. If, however, the law's usefulness in the matter of justice should change and it should meet men's expectations only for a short time, nonetheless during that short time it was just in the eyes of those who look simply at facts and do not confuse themselves with empty words.

XXXVIII. If, although no new circumstances have arisen, those things that were commonly held just in these matters did not in their actual effects correspond with that conception, they were not just. Whenever, as a result of new circumstances, the same things that had been regarded as just were no longer useful, they were just at the time when they were useful for the relations of citizens to each other; but afterwards, when they were no longer useful, they were no longer just.

XXXIX. He who has best controlled his lack of confidence in the face of external forces has, as far as possible, treated these externals as akin to himself or, when that was impossible, at least as not alien. Where he was not able to do even this, he kept to himself and avoided whatever it was best to avoid.

XL. Those who were best able to prepare security for themselves in relation to their neighbors* lived most pleasantly with their neighbors since they had the most perfect assurance; and enjoying the most complete intimacy, they did not lament the death of one who died before his time as if it were an occasion for sorrow.

---

*That is, those who were most self-sufficient and least dependent upon others.

EPICTETUS
ca. A.D. 50–ca. A.D. 130

Epictetus was born a slave in Hierapolis, a small town in Phrygia, Asia Minor (in present-day Turkey). His master was Epaphroditus, a member of Emperor Nero's personal staff in Rome. As was often done at that time, Epaphroditus saw to it that Epictetus had a good education, sending him to study with the Roman Stoic, Rufus. Epictetus gained his freedom sometime after the death of the emperor in A.D. 68 and began to teach philosophy in Rome. In A.D. 89 or 93 Emperor Domitian expelled all philosophers from Rome. Domitian seems to have been especially angry with the Stoics for teaching that sovereignty comes from God and is for the benefit of the people. (Epictetus's reported claim that he had the same regard for the emperor as for his water-pot could not have helped.) Epictetus moved to Nicropolis in Epirus (northwestern Greece), where he established a thriving Stoic school and lived a simple life with few material goods. As an old man, he married so that he could adopt a child who otherwise would have been "exposed," that is, left to die. Those whom he taught described him as a humble, charitable man of great moral and religious devotion.

Epictetus never wrote anything, but one of his admiring students, Arrian, composed eight *Discourses* based on Epictetus's lectures, along with a summary of the great man's thought, the *Encheiridion* (or *Manual*). The *Encheiridion*, given here complete in the W.A. Oldfather translation, builds on the early Stoa's concept of *Logos*. Since the *Logos* or natural law permeates everything, it provides us with moral intuition, so all persons have the capacity for virtue. But in order to live the moral life, one must apply these intuitions to specific cases. Education is necessary if we are to learn how to properly connect moral insights with life. We must begin by recognizing the fact that we cannot change events that happen to us, but we can change our attitude toward those events. To accomplish this and achieve the good life, we must go through three stages. First, we must order our desires and overcome our fears. Next, we must perform our duties—in whatever role fate has given us. Finally, we must think clearly and judge accurately. Only then will we gain inner tranquillity.

Despite Emperor Domitian's condemnation, Stoicism had a special appeal to the Roman mind. The Romans were not much interested in the speculative and theoretical content of Zeno's early Stoa. Instead, in the austere moral emphasis of Epictetus, with his concomitant stress on self-control and superiority to pain, the Romans found an ideal for the wise man, whereas the Stoic description of natural law provided a basis for Roman law. One might say that the pillars of republican Rome tended to be Stoical, even if some Romans had never heard of Stoicism.

* * *

For general introductions to the Stoics, see E. Vernon Arnold, *Roman Stoicism* (1911; reprinted New York: Humanities Press, 1958); L. Edelstein, *The Meaning of Stoicism* (Cambridge, MA: Harvard University Press, 1966); John M. Rist, *Stoic Philosophy* (Cambridge: Cambridge University Press, 1969); F.H. Sandbach, *The Stoics* (New York: Norton, 1975); and Margaret E. Reeser, *The Nature of Man in Early Stoic Philosophy* (New York: St. Martin's Press, 1989). For comparisons between Stoicism and other Hellenistic schools, see R.M. Wenley, *Stoicism and Its Influence* (1924; reprinted New York: Cooper Square, 1963); Edwin R. Bevan, *Stoics and Sceptics* (Oxford: Clarendon Press, 1913); and R.D. Hicks, *Stoic and Epicurean* (1910; reprinted New York: Russell, 1962). For collections of essays consult A.A. Long, ed., *Problems in Stoicism* (London: Athlone Press, 1971); J.M. Rist, ed., *The Stoics* (Berkeley: University of California Press, 1978); and A.A. Long, ed., *Stoic Studies* (Cambridge: Cambridge University Press, 1996).

For a volume specifically on Epictetus, see John Bonforte, *The Philosophy of Epictetus* (New York: Philosophical Library, 1955). Iason Xenakis, *Epictetus: Philosopher-Therapist* (The Hague, Netherlands: Martinus Nijhoff, 1969), makes an interesting application of Epictetus; while W.A. Oldfather, *Contributions Towards a Bibliography of Epictetus* (Urbana: University of Illinois Press, 1927; supplement, 1952), furnishes a bibliography. For a study of Epictetus's star pupil, see Philip A. Stadter, *Arrian of Nicomedia* (Chapel Hill: University of North Carolina Press, 1980).

ENCHEIRIDION (Manual)

1. Some things are under our control, while others are not under our control. Under our control are conception, choice, desire, aversion, and in a word, everything that is our own doing; not under our control are our body, our property, reputation, office and, in a word, everything that is not our own doing. Furthermore, the things under our control are by nature free, unhindered, and unimpeded; while the things not under our control are weak, servile, subject to hindrance, and not our own. Remember, therefore, that if what is naturally slavish you think to be free, and what is not your own to be your own, you will be hampered, will grieve, will be in turmoil, and will blame both gods and men; while if you think only what is your own to be your own, and what is not your own to be, as it really is, not your own, then no one will ever be able to exert compulsion upon you, no one will hinder you, you will blame no one, will find fault with no one, will do absolutely nothing against your will, you will have no personal enemy, no one will harm you, for neither is there any harm that can touch you.

With such high aims, therefore, remember that you must bestir yourself with no slight effort to lay hold of them, but you will have to give up some things entirely, and defer others for the time being. But if you wish for these things also, and at the same time for both office and wealth, it may be that you will not get even these latter, because you aim also at the former, and certainly you will fail to get the former, which alone bring freedom and happiness.

Make it, therefore, your study at the very outset to say to every harsh external impression, "You are an external impression and not at all what you appear to be." After that examine it and test it by these rules which you have, the first and most important of which is this: Whether the impression has to do with the things which are under our control, or with those which are not under our control; and, if it has to do with some one of the things not under our control, have ready to hand the answer, "It is nothing to me."

2. Remember that the promise of desire is the attainment of what you desire, that of aversion is not to fall into what is avoided, and that he who fails in his desire is unfortunate, while he who falls into what he would avoid experiences misfortune. If, then, you avoid only what is unnatural among those things which are under your control, you will fall into none of the things which you avoid; but if you try to avoid disease, or death, or poverty, you will experience misfortune. Withdraw, therefore, your aversion from all the matters that are not under our control, and transfer it to what is unnatural among those which are under our control. But for the time being remove utterly your desire; for if you desire some one of the things that are not under our control you are bound to be unfortunate; and, at the same time, not one of the things that are under our control, which it would be excellent for you to desire, is within your grasp. But employ only choice and refusal, and these too but lightly, and with reservations, and without straining.

3. With everything which entertains you, is useful, or of which you are fond, remember to say to yourself, beginning with the very least things, "What is its nature?" If you are fond of a jug, say, "I am fond of a jug"; for when it is broken you will not be

Reprinted by permission of the publishers and the Loeb Classical Library from Epictetus, *Encheiridion,* translated by W.A. Oldfather (Cambridge, MA: Harvard University Press, 1928). Copyright © 1928 by Harvard University Press.

disturbed. If you kiss your own child or wife, say to yourself that you are kissing a human being; for when it dies you will not be disturbed.

4. When you are on the point of putting your hand to some undertaking, remind yourself what the nature of that undertaking is. If you are going out of the house to bathe, put before your mind what happens at a public bath—those who splash you with water, those who jostle against you, those who vilify you and rob you. And thus you will set about your undertaking more securely if at the outset you say to yourself, "I want to take a bath, and, at the same time, to keep my moral purpose in harmony with nature." And so do in every undertaking. For thus, if anything happens to hinder you in your bathing, you will be ready to say, "Oh, well, this was not the only thing that I wanted, but I wanted also to keep your moral purpose in harmony with nature; and I shall not so keep it if I am vexed at what is going on."

5. It is not the things themselves that disturb men, but their judgements about these things. For example, death is nothing dreadful, or else Socrates too would have thought so, but the judgement that death is dreadful, *this* is the dreadful thing. When, therefore, we are hindered, or disturbed, or grieved, let us never blame anyone but ourselves, that means, our own judgements. It is the part of an uneducated person to blame others where he himself fares ill; to blame himself is the part of one whose education has begun; to blame neither another nor his own self is the part of one whose education is already complete.

6. Be not elated at any excellence which is not your own. If the horse in his elation were to say, "I am beautiful," it could be endured; but when you say in your elation, "I have a beautiful horse," rest assured that you are elated at something good which belongs to a horse. What then, is your own? The use of external impressions. Therefore, when you are in harmony with nature in the use of external impressions, then be elated; for then it will be some good of your own at which you will be elated.

7. Just as on a voyage, when your ship has anchored, if you should go on shore to get fresh water, you may pick up a small shell-fish or little bulb on the way, but you have to keep your attention fixed on the ship, and turn about frequently for fear lest the captain should call; and if he calls, you must give up all these things, if you would escape being thrown on board all tied up like the sheep. So it is also in life: If there be given you, instead of a little bulb and a small shell-fish, a little wife and child, there will be no objection to that; only, if the Captain calls, give up all these things and run to the ship, without even turning around to look back. And if you are an old man, never even get very far away from the ship, for fear that when He calls you may be missing.

8. Do not seek to have everything that happens happen as you wish, but wish for everything to happen as it actually does happen, and your life will be serene.

9. Disease is an impediment to the body, but not to the moral purpose, unless that consents. Lameness is an impediment to the leg, but not to the moral purpose. And say this to yourself at each thing that befalls you; for you will find the thing to be an impediment to something else, but not to yourself.

10. In the case of everything that befalls you, remember to turn to yourself and see what faculty you have to deal with it. If you see a handsome lad or woman, you will find continence the faculty to employ here; if hard labour is laid upon you, you will find endurance; in this fashion, your external impressions will not run away with you.

11. Never say about anything, "I have lost it," but only "I have given it back." Is your child dead? It has been given back. Is your wife dead? She has been given back. "I have had my farm taken away." Very well, this too has been given back. "Yet it was a rascal who took it away." But what concern is it of yours by whose instrumentality

the Giver called for its return? So long as He gives it to you, take care of it as of a thing that is not your own, as travellers treat their inn.

12. If you wish to make progress, dismiss all reasoning of this sort: "If I neglect my affairs, I shall have nothing to live on." "If I do not punish my slave-boy he will turn out bad." For it is better to die of hunger, but in a state of freedom from grief and fear, than to live in plenty, but troubled in mind. And it is better for your slave-boy to be bad than for you to be unhappy. Begin, therefore, with the little things. Your paltry oil gets spilled, your miserable wine stolen; say to yourself, "This is the price paid for a calm spirit, this the price for peace of mind." Nothing is got without a price. And when you call your slave-boy, bear in mind that it is possible he may not heed you, and again, that even if he does heed, he may not do what you want done. But he is not in so happy a condition that your peace of mind depends upon him.

13. If you wish to make progress, then be content to appear senseless and foolish in externals, do not make it your wish to give the appearance of knowing anything; and if some people think you to be an important personage, distrust yourself. For be assured that it is no easy matter to keep your moral purpose in a state of conformity with nature, and, at the same time, to keep externals; but the man who devotes his attention to one of these two things must inevitably neglect the other.

14. If you make it your will that your children and your wife and your friends should live forever, you are silly; for you are making it your will that things not under your control should be under your control, and that what is not your own should be your own. In the same way, too, if you make it your will that your slave-boy be free from faults, you are a fool; for you are making it your will that vice be not vice, but something else. If, however, it is your will not to fail in what you desire, this is in your power. Wherefore, exercise yourself in that which is in your power. Each man's master is the person who has the authority over what the man wishes or does not wish, so as to secure it, or take it away. Whoever, therefore, wants to be free, let him neither wish for anything, nor avoid anything, that is under the control of others; or else he is necessarily a slave.

15. Remember that you ought to behave in life as you would at a banquet. As something is being passed around it comes to you; stretch out your hand and take a portion of it politely. It passes on; do not detain it. Or it has not come to you yet; do not project your desire to meet it, but wait until it comes in front of you. So act toward children, so toward a wife, so toward office, so toward wealth; and then some day you will be worthy of the banquets of the gods. But if you do not take these things even when they are set before you, but despise them, then you will not only share the banquet of the gods, but share also their rule. For it was by so doing that Diogenes and Heracleitus, and men like them, were deservedly divine and deservedly so called.

16. When you see someone weeping in sorrow, either because a child has gone on a journey, or because he has lost his property, beware that you be not carried away by the impression that the man is in the midst of external ills, but straightway keep before you this thought: "It is not what has happened that distresses this man (for it does not distress another), but his judgement about it." Do not, however, hesitate to sympathize with him so far as words go, and, if occasion offers, even to groan with him; but be careful not to groan also in the centre of your being.

17. Remember that you are an actor in a play, the character of which is determined by the Playwright: if He wishes the play to be short, it is short; if long, it is long; if He wishes you to play the part of a beggar, remember to act even this role adroitly; and so if your role be that of a cripple, an official, or a layman. For this is your

Theater at Ephesus, Turkey, built A.D. 41–117. In theaters like this, with a capacity for more than eighteen thousand spectators, Greek playwrights presented all-day festivals of drama on every phase of Greek life from the tragic to the comic. It is not surprising that Epictetus uses the image of the play and the playwright to make his point. *(Gian Berto Vanni/Art Resource)*

business, to play admirably the role assigned you; but the selection of that role is Another's.

18. When a raven croaks inauspiciously, let not the external impression carry you away, but straightway draw a distinction in your own mind, and say, "None of these portents are for me, but either for my paltry body, or my paltry estate, or my paltry opinion, or my children, or my wife. But for me every portent is favourable, if I so wish; for whatever be the outcome, it is within my power to derive benefit from it."

19. You can be invincible if you never enter a contest in which victory is not under your control. Beware lest, when you see some person preferred to you in honour, or possessing great power, or otherwise enjoying high repute, you are ever carried away by the external impression, and deem him happy. For if the true nature of the good is one of the things that are under our control, there is no place for either envy or jealousy; and you yourself will not wish to be a praetor, or a senator, or a consul, but a free man. Now there is but one way that leads to this, and that is to despise the things that are not under our control.

20. Bear in mind that it is not the man who reviles or strikes you that insults you, but it is your judgement that these men are insulting you. Therefore, when someone irritates you, be assured that it is your own opinion which has irritated you. And so make it your first endeavour not to be carried away by the external impression; for if once you gain time and delay, you will more easily become master of yourself.

21. Keep before your eyes day by day death and exile, and everything that seems terrible, but most of all death; and then you will never have any abject thought, nor will you yearn for anything beyond measure.

22. If you yearn for philosophy, prepare at once to be met with ridicule, to have many people jeer at you, and say, "Here he is again, turned philosopher all of a sudden," and "Where do you suppose he got that high brow?" But do you not put on a high brow, and do you so hold fast to the things which to you seem best, as a man who has been assigned by God to this post; and remember that if you abide by the same principles, those who formerly used to laugh at you will later come to admire you, but if you are worsted by them, you will get the laugh on yourself twice.

23. If it should ever happen to you that you turn to externals with a view to pleasing someone, rest assured that you have lost your plan of life. Be content, therefore, in everything to be a philosopher, and if you wish also to be taken for one, show to yourself that you are one, and you will be able to accomplish it.

24. Let not these reflections oppress you: "I shall live without honour, and be nobody anywhere." For, if lack of honour is an evil, you cannot be in evil through the instrumentality of some other person, any more than you can be in shame. It is not your business, is it, to get office, or to be invited to a dinner-party? Certainly not. How, then, can this be any longer a lack of honour? And how is it that you will be "nobody anywhere," when you ought to be somebody only in those things which are under your control, wherein you are privileged to be a man of the very greatest honour? But your friends will be without assistance? What do you mean by being "without assistance"? They will not have paltry coin from you, and you will not make them Roman citizens. Well, who told you that these are some of the matters under our control, and not rather things which others do? And who is able to give another what he does not himself have? "Get money, then," says some friend, "in order that we too may have it." If I can get money and at the same time keep myself self-respecting, and faithful, and high-minded, show me the way and I will get it. But if you require me to lose the good things that belong to me, in order that you may acquire the things that are not good, you can see for yourselves how unfair and inconsiderate you are. And which do you really prefer? Money, or a faithful and self-respecting friend? Help me, therefore, rather to this end, and do not require me to do those things which will make me lose these qualities.

"But my country," says he, "so far as lies in me, will be without assistance." Again I ask, what kind of assistance do you mean? It will not have loggias or baths of your providing. And what does that signify? For neither does it have shoes provided by the blacksmith, nor has it arms provided by the cobbler; but it is sufficient if each man fulfil his own proper function. And if you secured for it another faithful and self-respecting citizen, would you not be doing it any good? "Yes." Very well, and then you also would not be useless to it. "What place, then, shall I have in the State?" says he. Whatever place you can have, and at the same time maintain the man of fidelity and self-respect that is in you. But if, through your desire to help the State, you lose these qualities, of what good would you become to it, when in the end you turned out to be shameless and unfaithful?

25. Has someone been honoured above you at a dinner-party, or in salutation, or in being called in to give advice? Now if these matters are good, you ought to be happy that he got them; but if evil, be not distressed because you did not get them; and bear in mind that, if you do not act the same way that others do, with a view to getting things which are not under our control, you cannot be considered worthy to receive an equal share with others. Why, how is it possible for a person who does not haunt some man's

door, to have equal shares with the man who does? For the man who does not do escort duty, with the man who does? For the man who does not praise, with the man who does? You will be unjust, therefore, and insatiable, if, while refusing to pay the price for which such things are bought, you want to obtain them for nothing. Well, what is the price for heads of lettuce? An obol, perhaps. If, then, somebody gives up his obol and gets his heads of lettuce, while you do not give your obol, and do not get them, do not imagine that you are worse off than the man who gets his lettuce. For as he has his heads of lettuce, so you have your obol which you have not given away.

Now it is the same way also in life. You have not been invited to somebody's dinner-party? Of course not; for you didn't give the host the price at which he sells his dinner. He sells it for praise; he sells it for personal attention. Give him the price, then, for which it is sold, if it is to your interest. But if you wish both not to give up the one and yet to get the other, you are insatiable and a simpleton. Have you, then, nothing in place of the dinner? Indeed you have; you have not had to praise the man you did not want to praise; you have not had to put up with the insolence of his doorkeepers.

26. What the will of nature is may be learned from a consideration of the points in which we do not differ from one another. For example, when some other person's slave-boy breaks his drinking-cup, you are instantly ready to say. "That's one of the things which happen." Rest assured, then, that when your own drinking-cup gets broken, you ought to behave in the same way that you do when the other man's cup is broken. Apply now the same principle to the matters of greater importance. Some other person's child or wife has died; no one but would say, "Such is the fate of man." Yet when a man's own child dies, immediately the cry is, "Alas! Woe is me!" But we ought to remember how we feel when we hear of the same misfortune befalling others.

27. Just as a mark is not set up in order to be missed, so neither does the nature of evil arise in the universe.

28. If someone handed over your body to any person who met you, you would be vexed; but that you hand over your mind to any person that comes along, so that, if he reviles you, it is disturbed and troubled—are you not ashamed of that?

29. In each separate thing that you do, consider the matters which come first and those which follow after, and only then approach the thing itself. Otherwise, at the start you will come to it enthusiastically, because you have never reflected upon any of the subsequent steps, but later on, when some difficulties appear, you will give up disgracefully. Do you wish to win an Olympic victory? So do I, by the gods! for it is a fine thing. But consider the matters which come before that, and those which follow after, and only when you have done that, put your hand to the task. You have to submit to discipline, follow a strict diet, give up sweet cakes, train under compulsion, at a fixed hour, in heat or in cold; you must not drink cold water, nor wine just whenever you feel like it; you must have turned yourself over to your trainer precisely as you would to a physician. Then when the contest comes on, you have to "dig in" beside your opponent, and sometimes dislocate your wrist, sprain your ankle, swallow quantities of sand, sometimes take a scourging, and along with all that get beaten. After you have considered all these points, go on into the games, if you still wish to do so; otherwise, you will be turning back like children. Sometimes they play wrestlers, again gladiators, again they blow trumpets, and then act a play. So you too are now an athlete, now a gladiator, then a rhetorician, then a philosopher, yet with your whole soul nothing; but like an ape you imitate whatever you see, and one thing after another strikes your fancy. For you have never gone out after anything with circumspection, nor after you had examined it all over, but you act haphazard and half-heartedly.

In the same way, when some people have seen a philosopher and have heard someone speaking like Euphrates (though, indeed, who can speak like him?), they wish to be philosophers themselves. Man, consider first the nature of the business, and then learn your own natural ability, if you are able to bear it. Do you wish to be a contender in the pentathlon, or a wrestler? Look to your arms, your thighs, see what your loins are like. For one man has a natural talent for one thing, another for another. Do you suppose that you can eat in the same fashion, drink in the same fashion, give way to impulse and to irritation, just as you do now? You must keep vigils, work hard, abandon your own people, be despised by a paltry slave, be laughed to scorn by those who meet you, in everything get the worst of it, in honour, in office, in court, in every paltry affair. Look these drawbacks over carefully, if you are willing at the price of these things to secure tranquillity, freedom, and calm. Otherwise, do not approach philosophy; don't act like a child—now a philosopher, later on a tax-gatherer, then a rhetorician, then a procurator of Caesar. These things do not go together. You must be one person, either good or bad; you must labour to improve either your own government principle or externals; you must work hard either on the inner man, or on things outside; that is, play either the rôle of a philosopher or else that of a layman.

30. Our duties are in general measured by our social relationships. He is a father. One is called upon to take care of him, to give way to him in all things, to submit when he reviles or strikes you. "But he is a bad father." Did nature, then, bring you into relationship with a *good* father? No, but simply with a father. "My brother does me wrong." Very well, then, maintain the relation that you have toward him; and do not consider what he is doing, but what you will have to do, if your moral purpose is to be in harmony with nature. For no one will harm you without your consent; you will have been harmed only when you think you are harmed. In this way, therefore, you will discover what duty to expect of your neighbour, your citizen, your commanding officer, if you acquire the habit of looking at your social relations with them.

31. In piety towards the gods, I would have you know, the chief element is this, to have right opinions about them—as existing and as administering the universe well and justly—and to have set yourself to obey them and to submit to everything that happens, and to follow it voluntarily, in the belief that it is being fulfilled by the highest intelligence. For if you act in this way, you will never blame the gods, nor find fault with them for neglecting you. But this result cannot be secured in any other way than by withdrawing your idea of the good and the evil from the things which are not under our control, and placing it in those which are under our control, and in those alone. Because, if you think any of those former things to be good or evil, then, when you fail to get what you want and fall into what you do not want, it is altogether inevitable that you will blame and hate those who are responsible for these results. For this is the nature of every living creature, to flee from and to turn aside from the things that appear harmful, and all that produces them, and to pursue after and to admire the things that are helpful, and all that produces them. Therefore, it is impossible for a man who thinks that he is being hurt to take pleasure in that which he thinks is hurting him, just as it is also impossible for him to take pleasure in the hurt itself. Hence it follows that even a father is reviled by a son when he does not give his child some share in the things that seem to be good; and this it was which made Polyneices and Eteocles enemies of one another, the thought that the royal power was a good thing. That is why the farmer reviles the gods, and so also the sailor, and the merchant, and those who have lost their wives and their children. For where a man's interest lies, there is also his piety. Wherefore, whoever is careful to exercise desire and aversion as he should, is at the same time careful also about piety. But it is always appropriate to make libations,

and sacrifices, and to give of the firstfruits after the manner of our fathers, and to do all this with purity, and not in a slovenly or careless fashion, nor, indeed, in a miserly way, nor yet beyond our means.

32. When you have recourse to divination, remember that you do not know what the issue is going to be, but that you have come in order to find this out from the diviner; yet if you are indeed a philosopher, you know, when you arrive, what the nature of it is. For if it is one of the things which are not under our control, it is altogether necessary that what is going to take place is neither good nor evil. Do not, therefore, bring to the diviner desire or aversion, and do not approach him with trembling, but having first made up your mind that every issue is indifferent and nothing to you, but that, whatever it may be, it will be possible for you to turn it to good use, and that no one will prevent this. Go, then, with confidence to the gods as to counsellors; and after that, when some counsel has been given you, remember whom you have taken as counsellors, and whom you will be disregarding if you disobey. But go to divination as Socrates thought that men should go, that is, in cases where the whole inquiry has reference to the outcome, and where neither from reason nor from any other technical art are means vouchsafed for discovering the matter in question. Hence, when it is your duty to share the danger of a friend or of your country, do not ask of the diviner whether you ought to share that danger. For if the diviner forewarns you that the omens of sacrifice have been unfavourable, it is clear that death is portended, or the injury of some member of your body, or exile; yet reason requires that even at this risk you are to stand by your friend, and share the danger with your country. Wherefore, give heed to the greater diviner, the Pythian Apollo, who cast out of his temple the man who had not helped his friend when he was being murdered.

33. Lay down for yourself, at the outset, a certain stamp and type of character for yourself, which you are to maintain whether you are by yourself or are meeting with people. And be silent for the most part, or else make only the most necessary remarks, and express these in few words. But rarely, and when occasion requires you to talk, talk, indeed, but about no ordinary topics. Do not talk about gladiators, or horse-races, or athletes, or things to eat or drink—topics that arise on all occasions; but above all, do not talk about people, either blaming, or praising, or comparing them. If, then, you can, by your own conversation bring over that of your companions to what is seemly. But if you happen to be left alone in the presence of aliens, keep silence.

Do not laugh much, nor at many things, nor boisterously.

Refuse, if you can, to take an oath at all, but if that is impossible, refuse as far as circumstances allow.

Avoid entertainments given by outsiders and by persons ignorant of philosophy; but if an appropriate occasion arises for you to attend, be on the alert to avoid lapsing into the behaviour of such laymen. For you may rest assured, that, if a man's companion be dirty, the person who keeps close company with him must of necessity get a share of his dirt, even though he himself happens to be clean.

In things that pertain to the body take only as much as your bare need requires, I mean such things as food, drink, clothing, shelter, and household slaves; but cut down everything which is for outward show or luxury.

In your sex-life preserve purity, as far as you can, before marriage, and, if you indulge, take only those privileges which are lawful. However, do not make yourself offensive, or censorious, to those who do indulge, and do not make frequent mention of the fact that you do not yourself indulge.

If someone brings you word that So-and-so is speaking ill of you, do not defend yourself against what has been said, but answer, "Yes, indeed, for he did not know the rest of the faults that attach to me; if he had, these would not have been the only ones he mentioned."

It is not necessary, for the most part, to go to the public shows. If, however, a suitable occasion ever arises, show that your principal concern is for none other than yourself, which means, wish only for that to happen which does happen, and for him only to win who does win; for so you will suffer no hindrance. But refrain utterly from shouting, or laughter at anyone, or great excitement. And after you have left, do not talk a great deal about what took place, except in so far as it contributes to your own improvement; for such behaviour indicates that the spectacle has aroused your admiration.

Do not go rashly or readily to people's public reading, but when you do go, maintain your own dignity and gravity, and at the same time be careful not to make yourself disagreeable.

When you are about to meet somebody, in particular when it is one of those men who are held in very high esteem, propose to yourself the question, "What would Socrates or Zeno have done under these circumstances?" and then you will not be at a loss to make proper use of the occasion. When you go to see one of those men who have great power, propose to yourself the thought that you will not find him at home, that you will be shut out, that the door will be slammed in your face, that he will pay no attention to you. And if, despite all this, it is your duty to go, go and take what comes, and never say to yourself, "It was not worth all the trouble." For this is characteristic of the layman, that is, a man who is vexed at externals.

In your conversation avoid making mention at great length and excessively of your own deeds or dangers, because it is not as pleasant for others to hear about your adventures, as it is for you to call to mind your own dangers.

Avoid also raising a laugh, for this is a kind of behaviour that slips easily into vulgarity, and at the same time is calculated to lessen the respect which your neighbours have of you. It is dangerous also to lapse into foul language. When, therefore, anything of the sort occurs, if the occasion be suitable, go even so far as to reprove the person who has made such a lapse; if, however, the occasion does not arise, at all events show by keeping silence, and blushing, and frowning, that you are displeased by what has been said.

34. When you get an external impression of some pleasure, guard yourself, as with impressions in general, against being carried away by it; nay, let the matter wait upon your leisure, and give yourself a little delay. Next think of the two periods of time, first, that in which you will enjoy your pleasure, and second, that in which, after the enjoyment is over, you will later repent and revile your own self; and set over against these two periods of time how much joy and self-satisfaction you will get if you refrain. However, if you feel that a suitable occasion has arisen to do the deed, be careful not to allow its enticement, and sweetness, and attractiveness to overcome you; but set over against all this the thought, how much better is the consciousness of having won a victory over it.

35. When you do a thing which you have made up your mind ought to be done, never try not to be seen doing it, even though most people are likely to think unfavourably about it. If, however, what you are doing is not right, avoid the deed itself altogether; but if it is right, why fear those who are going to rebuke you wrongly?

36. Just as the propositions, "It is day," and "it is night," are full of meaning when separated, but meaningless if united; so also, granted that for you to take the larger share at a dinner is good for your body, still, it is bad for the maintenance of the proper kind of social feeling. When, therefore, you are eating with another person,

remember to regard, not merely the value for your body of what lies before you, but also to maintain your respect for your host.

37. If you undertake a role which is beyond your powers, you both disgrace yourself in that one, and at the same time neglect the role which you might have filled with success.

38. Just as you are careful, in walking about, not to step on a nail or to sprain your ankle, so be careful also not to hurt your governing principle. And if we observe this rule in every action, we shall be more secure in setting about it.

39. Each man's body is a measure for his property, just as the foot is a measure for his shoe. If, then, you abide by this principle, you will maintain the proper measure, but if you go beyond it, you cannot help but fall headlong over a precipice, as it were, in the end. So also in the case of your shoe; if once you go beyond the foot, you get first a gilded shoe, then a purple one, then an embroidered one. For once you go beyond the measure there is no limit.

40. Immediately after they are fourteen, women are called "ladies" by men. And so when they see that they have nothing else but only to be the bedfellows of men, they begin to beautify themselves, and put all their hopes in that. It is worthwhile for us to take pains, therefore, to make them understand that they are honoured for nothing else but only for appearing modest and self-respecting.

41. It is a mark of an ungifted man to spend a great deal of time in what concerns his body, as in much exercise, much eating, much drinking, much evacuating of the bowels, much copulating. But these things are to be done in passing; and let your whole attention be devoted to the mind.

42. When someone treats you ill or speaks ill of you, remember that he acts or speaks thus because he thinks it is incumbent upon him. That being the case, it is impossible for him to follow what appears good to you, but what appears good to himself; whence it follows that, if he gets a wrong view of things, the man that suffers is the man that has been deceived. For if a person thinks a true composite judgement to be false, the composite judgement does not suffer, but the person who has been deceived. If, therefore, you start from this point of view, you will be gentle with the man who reviles you. For you should say on each occasion, "He thought that way about it."

43. Everything has two handles, by one of which it ought to be carried and by the other not. If your brother wrongs you, do not lay hold of the matter by the handle of the wrong that he is doing, because this is the handle by which the matter ought not to be carried; but rather by the other handle—that he is your brother, that you were brought up together, and then you will be laying hold of the matter by the handle by which it ought to be carried.

44. The following statements constitute a *non sequitur:* "I am richer than you are, therefore I am superior to you"; or, "I am more eloquent than you are, therefore I am superior to you." But the following conclusions are better: "I am richer than you are, therefore my property is superior to yours"; or, "I am more eloquent than you are, therefore my elocution is superior to yours." But *you* are neither property nor elocution.

45. Somebody is hasty about bathing; do not say that he bathes badly, but that he is hasty about bathing. Somebody drinks a good deal of wine; do not say that he drinks badly, but that he drinks a good deal. For until you have decided what judgement prompts him, how do you know that what he is doing is bad? And thus the final result will not be that you receive convincing sense-impressions of some things, but give your assent to others.

46. On no occasion call yourself a philosopher, and do not, for the most part, talk among laymen about your philosophic principles, but do what follows from your prin-

ciples. For example, at a banquet do not say how people ought to eat, but eat as a man ought. For remember how Socrates had so completely eliminated the thought of ostentation, that people came to him when they wanted him to introduce them to philosophers, and he used to bring them along. So well did he submit to being overlooked. And if talk about some philosophic principle arises among laymen, keep silence for the most part for there is great danger that you will spew up immediately what you have not digested. So when a man tells you that you know nothing, and you, like Socrates, are not hurt, then rest assured that you are making a beginning with the business you have undertaken. For sheep, too, do not bring their fodder to the shepherds and show how much they have eaten, but they digest their food within them, and on the outside produce wool and milk. And so do you, therefore, make no display to the laymen of your philosophical principles, but let them see the results which come from these principles when digested.

47. When you have become adjusted to simple living in regard to your bodily wants, do not preen yourself about the accomplishment; and so likewise, if you are a water-drinker, do not on every occasion say that you are a water-drinker. And if ever you want to train to develop physical endurance, do it by yourself and not for outsiders to behold; do not throw your arms around statues, but on occasion, when you are very thirsty, take cold water into your mouth, and then spit it out, without telling anybody.

48. This is the position and character of a layman: He never looks for either help or harm from himself, but only from externals. This is the position and character of the philosopher: He looks for all his help or harm from himself.

Signs of one who is making progress are: He censures no one, praises no one, blames no one, finds fault with no one, says nothing about himself as though he were somebody or knew something. When he is hampered or prevented, he blames himself. And if anyone compliments him, he smiles to himself at the person complimenting; while if anyone censures him, he makes no defence. He goes about like an invalid, being careful not to disturb, before it has grown firm, any part which is getting well. He has put away from himself his every desire, and has transferred his aversion to those things only, of what is under our control, which are contrary to nature. He exercises no pronounced choice in regard to anything. If he gives the appearance of being foolish or ignorant he does not care. In a word, he keeps guard against himself as though he were his own enemy lying in wait.

49. When a person gives himself airs because he can understand and interpret the books of Chrysippus, say to yourself, "If Chrysippus had not written obscurely, this man would have nothing about which to give himself airs."

But what is it I want? To learn nature and to follow her. I seek, therefore, someone to interpret her; and having heard that Chrysippus does so, I go to him. But I do not understand what he has written; I seek, therefore, the person who interprets Chrysippus. And down to this point there is nothing to justify pride. But when I find the interpreter, what remains is to put his precepts into practice; this is the only thing to be proud about. If, however, I admire the mere act of interpretation, what have I done but turned into a grammarian instead of a philosopher? The only difference, indeed, is that I interpret Chrysippus instead of Homer. Far from being proud, therefore, when somebody says to me, "Read me Chrysippus," I blush the rather, when I am unable to show him such deeds as match and harmonize with his words.

50. Whatever principles are set before you, stand fast by these like laws, feeling that it would be impiety for you to transgress them. But pay no attention to what somebody says about you, for this is, at length, not under your control.

51. How long will you still wait to think yourself worthy of the best things, and in nothing to transgress against the distinctions set up by the reason? You have

received the philosophical principles which you ought to accept, and you have accepted them. What sort of a teacher, then, do you still wait for, that you should put off reforming yourself until he arrives? You are no longer a lad, but already a full-grown man. If you are now neglectful and easy-going, and always making one delay after another, and fixing first one day and then another, after which you will pay attention to yourself, then without realizing it you will make no progress, but, living and dying, will continue to be a layman throughout. Make up your mind, therefore, before it is too late, that the fitting thing for you to do is to live as a mature man who is making progress, and let everything which seems to you to be best be for you a law that must not be transgressed. And if you meet anything that is laborious, or sweet, or held in high repute, or in no repute, remember that now is the contest, and here before you are the Olympic games, and that it is impossible to delay any longer, and that it depends on a single day and a single action, whether progress is lost or saved. This is the way Socrates became what he was, by paying attention to nothing but his reason in everything that he encountered. And even if you are not yet a Socrates, still you ought to live as one who wishes to be a Socrates.

52. The first and most necessary division in philosophy is that which has to do with the application of the principles, as, for example, Do not lie. The second deals with the demonstrations, as, for example, How comes it that we ought not to lie? The third confirms and discriminates between these processes, as, for example, How does it come that this is a proof? For what is a proof, what is logical consequence, what contradiction, what truth, what falsehood? Therefore, the third division is necessary because of the second, and the second because of the first; while the most necessary of all, and the one in which we ought to rest, is the first. But we do the opposite; for we spend our time in the third division, and all our zeal is devoted to it, while we utterly neglect the first. Wherefore, we lie, indeed, but are ready with the arguments which prove that one ought not to lie.

53. Upon every occasion we ought to have the following thoughts at our command:

> Lead thou me on, O Zeus, and Destiny,
> To that goal long ago to me assigned.
> I'll follow and not falter; if my will
> Prove weak and craven, still I'll follow on.
>
> *Cleanthes*

> Whoso has rightly with necessity complied, We count him wise, and skilled in things divine.
>
> *Euripides*

> Well, O Crito, if so it is pleasing to the gods, so let it be.
>
> *Socrates [Crito, 43D]*

> Anytus and Meletus can kill me, but they cannot hurt me.
>
> *Socrates [Apology, 30C]*

PLOTINUS
ca. A.D. 204–270

The last great school of Greek philosophy was Neoplatonism, and its most famous representative was Plotinus, born in Lykopolis, Egypt, in A.D. 204. In his
late-twenties, Plotinus began to study in Alexandria with Ammonius Saccas, a
shadowy figure who was also the teacher of the theologian Origen. After eleven
years with Ammonius, Plotinus joined an expedition to Persia to learn Persian
and Indian wisdom. The trek proved unsuccessful and Plotinus moved to Rome.
There he established a school of philosophy and a friendship with the emperor
Gallenius. At one point, he sought permission to found a city based on Plato's
Republic, but the plan came to naught. He stayed in Rome, teaching and writing,
until the death of the emperor in 268. He then moved to the home of a friend
where he died in 270, apparently from leprosy.

Developing Plato's dualistic understanding of reality, Plotinus taught that true
reality lies "beyond" the physical world. This "reality beyond reality" has no
limits and so cannot be described by words, since words invariably have limits.
Plotinus, again borrowing from Plato, calls this ultra-reality the "Good" or the
"One." The One/Good has no limits and is so supremely rich that it overflows or
"emanates" to produce "Intellectual-Principle" or "Divine Mind" *<nous>*. This
Intellectual-Principle, in turn, overflows and "Divine-Soul" emanates from it.
This process continues as Divine-Soul generates the material world. The lowest
level of emanation, at the furthest extreme from the One/Good, is the utter form-
lessness and unreality of matter.

The goal of philosophy is to awaken individuals to the reality beyond the material world. But philosophy alone cannot take a person to the highest reality of

the One. Only mystical experience can unite an individual with the One. Plotinus himself claimed to have achieved such a union four times during his life.

Plotinus's writings were edited by one of his pupils, Porphyry, in the form of six groups of nine "Tractates" (treatises), published as the so-called *Enneads* (from the Greek word for "nine"). The selection given here, in the A.H. Armstrong translation, is Plotinus's Treatise on Beauty. This Tractate explains how the ascent of the soul to the One/Good depends on the beauty of soul, a god-like disposition.

*   *   *

Joseph Katz, *Plotinus' Search for the Good* (New York: King's Crown Press, 1950); Émile Bréhier, *The Philosophy of Plotinus,* translated by Joseph Thomas (Chicago: University of Chicago Press, 1958); and Lloyd P. Gerson, *Plotinus* (Oxford: Routledge, 1994) are good introductions to the study of Plotinus. For more advanced studies, see A.H. Armstrong, *The Architecture of the Intelligible Universe in the Philosophy of Plotinus* (Cambridge: Cambridge University Press, 1940); J.M. Rist, *Plotinus: The Road to Reality* (Cambridge: Cambridge University Press, 1967); and Lloyd P. Gerson, ed., *The Cambridge Companion to Plotinus* (Cambridge: Cambridge University Press, 1996). E.R. Dodds, *Select Passages Illustrating Neoplatonism,* translated by E.R. Dodds (New York: Macmillan, 1923), and Dominic J. O'Meara, *Plotinus: An Introduction to the Enneads* (Oxford: Oxford University Press, 1993), provide anthologies of the *Enneads* with discussions of important passages. For discussions of Neoplatonism as a school, see Thomas Whittaker, *The Neo-Platonists* (Cambridge: Cambridge University Press, 1918); Arthur O. Lovejoy's influential book, *The Great Chain of Being* (Cambridge, MA: Harvard University Press, 1936); R.T. Wallis, *Neoplatonism* (London: Duckworth, 1972); and the collection of essays, R. Baine Harris, ed., *The Structure of Being: A Neoplatonic Approach* (Norfolk, VA: International Society for Neoplatonic Studies, 1982). John Dillon, *The Middle Platonists* (Ithaca, NY: Cornell University press, 1996) provides an overview of Platonism in the period leading up to Plotinus.

ENNEADS (in part)

ENNEAD I, TRACTATE 6: BEAUTY

1. Beauty is mostly in sight, but it is to be found too in things we hear, in combinations of words and also in music, and in all music [not only in songs]; for tunes and rhythms are certainly beautiful: and for those who are advancing upwards from sense-perception ways of life and actions and characters and intellectual activities are beautiful, and there is the beauty of virtue. If there is any beauty prior to these, this discussion will reveal it.

Very well then, what is it which makes us imagine that bodies are beautiful and attracts our hearing to sounds because of their beauty? And how are all the things which depend on soul beautiful? Are they all made beautiful by one and the same beauty or is there one beautifulness in bodies and a different one in other things? And what are they, or what is it? Some things, bodies for instance, are not beautiful from the nature of the objects themselves, but by participation, others are beauties themselves, like the nature of virtue. The same bodies appear sometimes beautiful, sometimes not beautiful, so that their being bodies is one thing, their being beautiful another. What is this principle, then, which is present in bodies? We ought to consider this first. What is it that attracts the gaze of those who look at something, and turns and draws them to it and makes them enjoy the sight? If we find this perhaps we can use it as a stepping-stone and get a sight of the rest. Nearly everyone says that it is good proportion of the parts to each other and to the whole, with the addition of good colour, which produces visible beauty, and that with the objects of sight and generally with everything else, being beautiful is being well-proportioned and measured. On this theory nothing single and simple but only a composite thing will have any beauty. It will be the whole which is beautiful, and the parts will not have the property of beauty by themselves, but will contribute to the beauty of the whole. But if the whole is beautiful the parts must be beautiful too; a beautiful whole can certainly not be composed of ugly parts; all the parts must have beauty. For these people, too, beautiful colours, and the light of the sun as well, since they are simple and do not derive their beautifulness from good proportion, will be excluded from beauty. And how do they think gold manages to be beautiful? And what makes lightning in the night and stars beautiful to see? And in sounds in the same way the simple will be banished, though often in a composition which is beautiful as a whole each separate sound is beautiful. And when, though the same good proportion is there all the time, the same face sometimes appears beautiful and sometimes does not, surely we must say that being beautiful is something else over and above good proportion, and good proportion is beautiful because of something else? But if when these people pass on to ways of life and beautiful expressions of thought they allege good proportion as the cause of beauty in these too, what can be meant by good proportion in beautiful ways of life or laws or studies or branches of knowledge? How can speculations be well-proportioned in relation to each other? If it is because they agree, there can be concord and agreement between bad ideas. The statement that "righteousness is a fine sort of silliness" agrees with and is in tune with the saying that "morality is stupidity"; the two fit perfectly. Again, every sort of virtue is a beauty of the soul, a truer beauty than those mentioned before; but how is virtue well-proportioned? Not like magnitudes or a number. We grant that the soul has several parts, but what is the formula for the composition or mixture in the soul of parts or speculations? And what [on this theory], will the beauty of the intellect alone by itself be?

2. So let us go back to the beginning and state what the primary beauty in bodies really is. It is something which we become aware of even at the first glance; the soul speaks of it as if it understood it, recognises and welcomes it and as it were adapts itself to it. But when it encounters the ugly it shrinks back and rejects it and turns away from it and is out of tune and alienated from it. Our explanation of this is that the soul, since it is by nature what it is and is related to the higher kind of reality in the realm of being, when it sees something akin to it or a trace of its kindred reality, is delighted and thrilled and returns to itself and remembers itself and its own possessions. What likeness, then, is there between beautiful things here and There? If there is a likeness, let us agree that they are alike. But how are both the things in that world and the things in this beautiful? We maintain that the things in this world are beautiful by participat-

ing in form; for every shapeless thing which is naturally capable of receiving shape and form is ugly and outside the divine formative power as long as it has no share in formative power and form. This is absolute ugliness. But a thing is also ugly when it is not completely dominated by shape and formative power, since its matter has not submitted to be completely shaped according to the form. The form, then, approaches and composes that which is to come into being from many parts into a single ordered whole; it brings it into a completed unity and makes it one by agreement of its parts; for since it is one itself, that which is shaped by it must also be one as far as a thing can be which is composed of many parts. So beauty rests upon the material thing when it has been brought into unity, and gives itself to parts and wholes alike. When it comes upon something that is one and composed of like parts it gives the same gift to the whole; as sometimes art gives beauty to a whole house with its parts, and sometimes nature gives beauty to a single stone. So then the beautiful body comes into being by sharing in a formative power which comes from the divine forms.

3. The power ordained for the purpose recognises this, and there is nothing more effective for judging its own subject-matter, when the rest of the soul judges along with it; or perhaps the rest of the soul too pronounces the judgement by fitting the beautiful body to the form in itself and using this for judging beauty as we use a ruler for judging straightness. But how does the bodily agree with that which is before body? How does the architect declare the house outside beautiful by fitting it to the form of house within him? The reason is that the house outside, apart from the stones, is the inner form divided by the external mass of matter, without parts but appearing in many parts. When sense-perception, then, sees the form in bodies binding and mastering the nature opposed to it, which is shapeless, and shape riding gloriously upon other shapes, it gathers into one that which appears dispersed and brings it back and takes it in, now without parts, to the soul's interior and presents it to that which is within as something in tune with it and fitting it and dear to it; just as when a good man sees a trace of virtue in the young, which is in tune with his own inner truth, the sight delights him. And the simple beauty of colour comes about by shape and the mastery of the darkness in matter by the presence of light which is incorporeal and formative power and form. This is why fire itself is more beautiful than all other bodies, because it has the rank of form in relation to the other elements; it is above them in place and is the finest and subtlest of all bodies, being close to the incorporeal. It alone does not admit the others; but the others admit it for it warms them but is not cooled itself; it has colour primarily and all other things take the form of colour from it. So it shines and glitters as if it was a form. The inferior thing which becomes faint and dull by the fire's light, is not beautiful any more, as not participating in the whole form of colour. The melodies in sounds, too, the imperceptible ones which make the perceptible ones, make the soul conscious of beauty in the same way, showing the same thing in another medium. It is proper to sensible melodies to be measured by numbers, not according to any and every sort of formula but one which serves for the production of form so that it may dominate. So much, then, for the beauties in the realm of sense, images and shadows which, so to speak, sally out and come into matter and adorn it and excite us when they appear.

4. But about the beauties beyond, which it is no more the part of sense to see, but the soul sees them and speaks of them without instruments—we must go up to them and contemplate them and leave sense to stay down below. Just as in the case of the beauties of sense it is impossible for those who have not seen them or grasped their beauty—those born blind, for instance,—to speak about them, in the same way only those can speak about the beauty of ways of life who have accepted the beauty of ways

of life and kinds of knowledge and everything else of the sort; and people cannot speak about the splendour of virtue who have never even imagined how fair is the face of justice and moral order; "neither the evening nor the morning star are as fair." But there must be those who see this beauty by that with which the soul sees things of this sort, and when they see it they must be delighted and overwhelmed and excited much more than by those beauties we spoke of before, since now it is true beauty they are grasping. These experiences must occur whenever there is contact with any sort of beautiful thing, wonder and a shock of delight and longing and passion and a happy excitement. One can have these experiences by contact with invisible beauties, and souls do have them, practically all, but particularly those who are more passionately in love with the invisible, just as with bodies all see them, but all are not stung as sharply, but some, who are called lovers, are most of all.

5. Then we must ask the lovers of that which is outside sense "What do you feel about beautiful ways of life, as we call them, and beautiful habits and well-ordered characters and in general about virtuous activities and dispositions and the beauty of souls? What do you feel when you see your own inward beauty? How are you stirred to wild exultation, and long to be with yourselves, gathering your selves together away from your bodies?" For this is what true lovers feel. But what is it which makes them feel like this? Not shape or colour or any size, but soul, without colour itself and possessing a moral order without colour and possessing all the other light of the virtues; you feel like this when you see, in yourself or in someone else, greatness of soul, a righteous life, a pure morality, courage with its noble look, and dignity and modesty advancing in a fearless, calm and unperturbed disposition, and the godlike light of intellect shining upon all this. We love and delight in these qualities, but why do we call them beautiful? They exist and appear to us and he who sees them cannot possibly say anything else except that they are what really exists. What does "really exists" mean? That they exist as beauties. But the argument still requires us to explain why real beings make the soul lovable. What is this kind of glorifying light on all the virtues? Would you like to take the opposites, the uglinesses in soul, and contrast them with the beauties? Perhaps a consideration of what ugliness is and why it appears so will help us to find what we are looking for. Suppose, then, an ugly soul, dissolute and unjust, full of all lusts, and all disturbance, sunk in fears by its cowardice and jealousies by its pettiness, thinking mean and mortal thoughts as far as it thinks at all, altogether distorted, loving impure pleasures, living a life which consists of bodily sensations and finding delight in its ugliness. Shall we not say that its ugliness came to it as a "beauty" brought in from outside, injuring it and making it impure and "mixed with a great deal of evil," with its life and perceptions no longer pure, but by the admixture of evil living a dim life and diluted with a great deal of death, no longer seeing what a soul ought to see, no longer left in peace in itself because it keeps on being dragged out, and down, and to the dark? Impure, I think, and dragged in every direction towards the objects of sense, with a great deal of bodily stuff mixed into it, consorting much with matter and receiving a form other than its own it has changed by a mixture which makes it worse; just as if anyone gets into mud or filth he does not show any more the beauty which he had what is seen is what he wiped off on himself from the mud and filth; his ugliness has come from an addition of alien matter, and his business, if he is to be beautiful again, is to wash and clean himself and so be again what he was before. So we shall be right in saying that the soul becomes ugly by mixture and dilution and inclination towards the body and matter. This is the soul's ugliness, not being pure and unmixed, like gold, but full of earthiness; if anyone takes the earthy stuff away the gold is left, and is beautiful, when it is singled out from other things and is alone by itself. In the

same way the soul too, when it is separated from the lusts which it has through the body with which it consorted too much, and freed from its other affections, purged of what it gets from being embodied, when it abides alone has put away all the ugliness which came from the other nature.

6. For, as was said in old times, self-control, and courage and every virtue, is a purification, and so is even wisdom itself. This is why the mysteries are right when they say riddlingly that the man who has not been purified will lie in mud when he goes to Hades, because the impure is fond of mud by reason of its badness; just as pigs, with their unclean bodies, like that sort of thing. For what can true self-control be except not keeping company with bodily pleasures, but avoiding them as impure and belonging to something impure? Courage, too, is not being afraid of death. And death is the separation of body and soul; and a man does not fear this if he welcomes the prospect of being alone. Again, greatness of soul is despising the things here and wisdom is an intellectual activity which turns away from the things below and leads the soul to those above. So the soul when it is purified becomes form and formative power, altogether bodiless and intellectual and entirely belonging to the divine, whence beauty springs and all that is akin to it. Soul, then, when it is raised to the level of intellect increases in beauty. Intellect and the things of intellect are its beauty, its own beauty and not another's, since only then [when it is perfectly conformed to intellect] is it truly soul. For this reason it is right to say that the soul's becoming something good and beautiful is its being made like to God, because from Him come beauty and all else which falls to the lot of real beings. Or rather, beautifulness is reality, and the other kind of thing is the ugly, and this same is the primary evil; so for God the qualities of goodness and beauty are the same, or the realities, the good and the beautiful. So we must follow the same line of enquiry to discover beauty and goodness, and ugliness and evil. And first we must posit beauty which is also the good; from this immediately comes intellect, which is beauty; and soul is given beauty by intellect. Everything else is beautiful by the shaping of soul, the beauties in actions and in ways of life. And soul makes beautiful the bodies which are spoken of as beautiful; for since it is a divine thing and a kind of part of beauty, it makes everything it grasps and masters beautiful, as far as they are capable of participation.

7. So we must ascend again to the good, which every soul desires. Anyone who has seen it knows what I mean when I say that it is beautiful. It is desired as good, and the desire for it is directed to good, and the attainment of it is for those who go up to the higher world and are converted and strip off what we put on in our descent; (just as for those who go up to the celebrations of sacred rites there are purifications, and strippings off of the clothes they wore before, and going up naked) until, passing in the ascent all that is alien to the God, one sees with one's self alone That alone, simple, single and pure, from which all depends and to which all look and are and live and think for it is the cause of life and mind and being. If anyone sees it, what passion will he feel, what longing in his desire to be united with it, what a shock of delight! The man who has not seen it may desire it as good, but he who has seen it glories in its beauty and is full of wonder and delight, enduring a shock which causes no hurt, loving with true passion and piercing longing; he laughs at all other loves and despises what he thought beautiful before; it is like the experience of those who have met appearances of gods or spirits and do not any more appreciate as they did the beauty of other bodies. "What then are we to think, if anyone contemplates the absolute beauty which exists pure by itself, uncontaminated by flesh or body, not in earth or heaven, that it may keep its purity?" All these other things are external additions and mixtures and not primary, but derived from it. If then one sees That which provides for all and remains by itself and gives to all but receives nothing into itself, if he abides in the contemplation

of this kind of beauty and rejoices in being made like it, how can he need any other beauty? For this, since it is beauty most of all, and primary beauty, makes its lovers beautiful and lovable. Here the greatest, the ultimate contest is set before our souls; all our toil and trouble is for this, not to be left without a share in the best of visions. The man who attains this is blessed in seeing that "blessed sight," and he who fails to attain it has failed utterly. A man has not failed if he fails to win beauty of colours or bodies, or power or office or kingship even, but if he fails to win this and only this. For this he should give up the attainment of kingship and of rule over all earth and sea and sky, if only by leaving and overlooking them he can turn to That and see.

8. But how shall we find the way? What method can we devise? How can one see the "inconceivable beauty" which stays within in the holy sanctuary and does not come out where the profane may see it? Let him who can, follow and come within, and leave outside the sight of his eyes and not turn back to the bodily splendours which he saw before. When he sees the beauty in bodies he must not run after them; we must know that they are images, traces, shadows, and hurry away to that which they image. For if a man runs to the image and wants to seize it as if it was the reality (like a beautiful reflection playing on the water, which some story somewhere, I think, said riddlingly a man wanted to catch and sank down into the stream and disappeared) then this man who clings to beautiful bodies and will not let them go, will, like the man in the story, but in soul, not in body, sink down into the dark depths where intellect has no delight, and stay blind in Hades, consorting with shadows there and here. This would be truer advice "Let us fly to our dear country." What then is our way of escape, and how are we to find it? We shall put out to sea, as Odysseus did, from the witch Circe or Calypso—as the poet says (I think with a hidden meaning)—and was not content to stay though he had delights of the eyes and lived among much beauty of sense. Our country from which we came is there, our Father is there. How shall we travel to it, where is our way of escape? We cannot get there on foot; for our feet only carry us everywhere in this world, from one country to another. You must not get ready a carriage, either, or a boat. Let all these things go, and do not look. Shut your eyes, and change to and wake another way of seeing, which everyone has but few use.

9. And what does this inner sight see? When it is just awakened it is not at all able to look at the brilliance before it. So that the soul must be trained, first of all to look at beautiful ways of life then at beautiful works, not those which the arts produce, but the works of men who have a name for goodness: then look at the souls of the people who produce the beautiful works. How then can you see the sort of beauty a good soul has? Go back into yourself and look; and if you do not yet see yourself beautiful, then, just as someone making a statue which has to be beautiful cuts away here and polishes there and makes one part smooth and clears another till he has given his statue a beautiful face, so you too must cut away excess and straighten the crooked and clear the dark and make it bright, and never stop "working on your statue" till the divine glory of virtue shines out on you, till you see "self-mastery enthroned upon its holy seat." If you have become this, and see it, and are at home with yourself in purity, with nothing hindering you from becoming in this way one, with no inward mixture of anything else, but wholly yourself, nothing but true light, not measured by dimensions, or bounded by shape into littleness, or expanded to size by unboundedness, but everywhere unmeasured, because greater than all measure and superior to all quantity; when you see that you have become this, then you have become sight; you can trust yourself then; you have already ascended and need no one to show you; concentrate your gaze and see. This alone is the eye that sees the great beauty. But if anyone comes to the sight bleary-eyed with wickedness, and unpurified, or weak and by his cowardice un-

The School of Plato, Roman Mosaic, n.d. The Platonism of late antiquity (and the Middle Ages) was strongly influenced by Plotinus's development and modification of Plato's thought. (*Art Resource*)

able to look at what is very bright, he sees nothing, even if someone shows him what is there and possible to see. For one must come to the sight with a seeing power made akin and like to what is seen. No eye ever saw the sun without becoming sunlike, nor can a soul see beauty without becoming beautiful. You must become first all godlike and all beautiful if you intend to see God and beauty. First the soul will come in its ascent to intellect and there will know the Forms, all beautiful, and will affirm that these, the Ideas, are beauty; for all things are beautiful by these, by the products and essence of intellect. That which is beyond this we call the nature of the Good, which holds beauty as a screen before it. So in a loose and general way of speaking the Good is the primary beauty; but if one distinguishes the intelligibles [from the Good] one will say that the place of the Forms is the intelligible beauty, but the Good is That which is beyond, the "spring and origin" of beauty; or one will place the Good and the primal beauty on the same level. In any case, however, beauty is in the intelligible world.

CHRISTIANITY AND MEDIEVAL PHILOSOPHY

With only a few exceptions, European medieval thought was deeply imbued with Christian faith. As a result, it is not possible to understand medieval philosophy without at least a rudimentary understanding of Christian beliefs as presented in the Bible. Whether or not today's reader accepts the veracity of the claims put forth in these writings, most medievals did believe them, and that belief formed the foundation of their thought.

Beginning as a Jewish sect, Christianity continued to hold a number of beliefs in common with Judaism, including the following bedrock convictions: that the Hebrew Bible (called the "Old Testament" by Christians) is the revealed Word of God; that God is superior to and distinct from the created world; that the world was created by God at a specific point in time and that the world will come to an end; that God is personal and desires a special relationship with the human race; that humans have sinned against God's Law and need God's forgiveness; that God requires righteousness as a means of a right relationship with God and others; and that God would send the Anointed One ("Messiah" in Hebrew, "Christ" in Greek) to set the people of God free.

But while Christians accepted the foundational beliefs of their Jewish ancestors, they differed on one key point: the identity of the Messiah. Whereas the Jews anticipated a spiritual-political figure to save them from the oppression of their enemies, Christians believed the Christ saved his people mainly from the spiritual oppressors of sin and death. Whereas the Jews believed the Messiah would scrupulously follow the Law, favoring and associating only with those who did likewise, the Christ of the Christians seemed to enjoy a remarkable freedom in relation to several of Israel's most venerable institutions—for example,

Sabbath observances, the Temple, and ritual purity—while associating with the "lowlifes" of society. In short, whereas the Jewish people were (and still are) awaiting the Messiah, Christians believed (and still believe) Jesus of Nazareth was the Messiah.

Christians held that after his death by crucifixion, Jesus rose from the dead (the Resurrection) and taught his followers for forty days before ascending into heaven. As part of that teaching, Jesus promised that he would return again (the Second Coming ⟨parousia⟩) and that in the meantime his followers should spread the Christian faith to all the world.

The basic Christian belief was (and still is) that Jesus is the Son of God who became a human (the Incarnation) to atone for human sin (Redemption). The severed relationship between the Holy God and sinful humanity could be restored only through the sacrifice of one who was consummate righteousness. As the Word (⟨Logos⟩) of God made flesh, Jesus was that righteousness, made that sacrifice, and offered that restoration. Through faith, Christians accept this work done on their behalf (Justification) and receive the power of God's spirit to overcome sin and to serve others (Sanctification).

As Christians spread this message throughout the Roman Empire, they encountered resistance and persecution from both Jewish and Roman authorities. Many Jewish leaders objected to the Christian identification of Jesus with God; Roman authorities objected to the Christians' unwillingness to participate in emperor worship. Jews, too, had refused to participate in state religion and had often been persecuted. But Christians posed a unique threat to the Romans because, unlike the Jews, Christians proclaimed a supranational, supraracial, universal Lord—one very much in competition with Caesar. And Christians indefatigably sought converts to their universal Savior. Accordingly, they were persecuted on and off for three centuries.

Despite persecution, Christianity grew steadily in the centuries after Christ. There have been many explanations for that growth. The eighteenth-century historian Edward Gibbon* listed five causes: (1) Christianity's inheritance of the zeal of the Jews; (2) its connection to the philosophical doctrine of the immortality of the soul; (3) its claim of miracles; (4) the virtue of the early Christians; and (5) the organization of the church. Recent historians have pointed to the moral exclusivity of Christians, who demanded deep commitment; the definite and absolute character of Christian belief in an age of uncertainty; and the social dimensions of Christianity, which made it attractive to women, the poor, and the oppressed.**

As Christianity grew, doctrinal disputes inevitably arose. What was true Christianity? The answers tended to reflect deep convictions about two essential issues: the nature of the person and work of Jesus Christ and the relationship between faith and reason. What was the relationship between Jesus and God? Did Jesus have two distinct natures: one divine and one human? Or were they merged into a single unique nature? Moreover, if there is only one God, how could God also be three (Father, Son, and Holy Spirit)? And how could reason resolve issues of faith?

---

*The Decline and Fall of the Roman Empire, Chapter XV.

**Of course, Christians have always claimed that none of these reasons is entirely adequate and that the most acceptable explanation for the rise of Christianity is a supernatural one.

The first issue, the nature of Christ, was resolved at the Council of Nicea, convened and presided over by the first Christian emperor, Constantine, in A.D. 325. The Council determined that the Son was exactly the same substance, "consubstantial" ⟨*homoousios*⟩, and not just "of like substance" ⟨*homoiousios*⟩, with God the Father. (The single Greek letter "iota," meant a great deal more than "one iota of difference" to the early church.) By the middle of the first millenium, the "Nicene Creed" was confessed by virtually all Christendom as the orthodox answer to the nature-of-Christ question. The Nicene Creed is still authoritative in Orthodox, Catholic, and Protestant churches.

Even though the Christological question was answered at Nicea, the question of the right relation between faith and reason continued to be argued throughout the medieval period. The early Christians had a simple faith in Jesus as Messiah (if they were Jewish Christians) and as Lord (if they were Gentile Christians), and they believed Jesus had lived, taught, died, and risen for them and all others. But almost immediately, that simple faith encountered sophisticated Hellenistic thought throughout the Roman Empire. How much should Christian faith concede to the competence of philosophic reason? What was the relation between sacred writings (i.e., the Bible) and secular writings (e.g., philosophy)? In Acts 17, the Apostle Paul, the early Christian convert, used reason and quoted pagan poets to help him preach the gospel to Epicurean and Stoic philosophers in Athens. Yet later, in Colossians 2:8, he warned, "See to it that no one takes you captive through philosophy and empty deceit. . . ." Some early Church Fathers, such as Justin Martyr, used philosophy to help interpret Christian faith. Other Church Fathers, such as Tertullian, argued that reason could be inimical to faith: "What has Jerusalem to do with Athens?" he asked.

Some in the early church even claimed to have special esoteric knowledge not available to the rabble either in the sacred Scriptures or secular reason. They were known as "Gnostics," from the Greek word for knowledge ⟨*gnosis*⟩. These Gnostics emphasized the Platonic belief in the soul as good and the body as evil, and they sought to free the soul from the body by extreme ascetic practices. Some of the Gnostics taught that Jesus was not *really* a physical person (since the body is evil) and that the Old Testament God, Yahweh, who had created bodies and matter, was really the devil. Manicheaism, which rivaled Christianity in the third and fourth centuries, and for a time claimed Augustine as one of its believers, was based on Gnostic thought.

For the most part, the early medieval philosophers sought to resolve these theological issues within the broad framework of Platonic thought. Augustine (as either the last classical thinker or the first medieval one), Boethius, and Anselm all used Neoplatonic concepts. In the early Middle Ages, most of Aristotle's writings were not available in the West. But in the East, Islamic philosophers, such as Ibn-Sina and Ibn Rushd (or Averroës), and Jewish thinkers, such as Moses Maimonides, read and commented on a wide range of Aristotelian works. These works, along with the Muslim and Jewish commentaries on them, were reintroduced to Western Europe in the late–Middle Ages and became the basis for the monumental work of Thomas Aquinas.

While Thomas lived during a period of relative calm and well-being, the centuries following his death were filled with tumult and upheaval. As a part of the often vicious conflict between church and state, Philip IV of France captured Pope Boniface VIII in 1303 and soon thereafter moved the papal court to Avignon, France—the so-called Babylonian Captivity of the Church. Beginning in

1347, the bubonic plague, or Black Death, struck Western Europe. Responses to the plague ranged from fanatical anti-intellectual apocalypticism to self-indulgent hedonism. Some even blamed the plague on intellectuals such as Thomas Aquinas, saying they provoked divine wrath by explaining God's ways rationally; others simply counselled, "Let us eat, drink, and be merry, for tomorrow we die." Many turned to superstition or to scapegoating Jews. At the same time, England and France were involved in the Hundred Years' War (1337–1453), which brought enormous casualties. Because of the plague and the war, in the years from 1300 to 1450, the population of Western Europe was reduced by half—perhaps by as much as two-thirds. In 1378, the Great Schism divided the Catholic Church as the Italians reinstituted the papacy in Rome, while a second pope reigned in Avignon. For over thirty years, rival popes condemned and excommunicated one another. In 1409, an attempt to end the schism with a compromise pope led only to a third pope and thus a third claimant to St. Peter's universal chair. Finally, in 1417, the church united around one pope ruling in Rome. But by now the power and prestige of the papacy had been severely diminished, and a hundred years later, in the Protestant Reformation, the Western church split decisively.

The philosophy of this later medieval period is commonly viewed in the light of these social upheavals, and, indeed, there does seem to be some connection. Thomas had harmonized philosophy and theology in a systematic way reflective of the relative peacefulness of the thirteenth century. Just as social stability—particularly in the relationship between church and state—deteriorated in the centuries following Thomas, so also the philosophies that developed during this period tended to separate reason and faith. William of Ockham, for example, held that philosophy and theology were separate realms with separate rules. The Renaissance thinker Pico della Mirandola developed a philosophy essentially excluding faith while using reason to draw from sources both within and outside Christendom. In Pico's philosophy, reason and faith were no longer systematically conjoined: Reason stood supremely alone. Clearly the coherent, rational Christian synthesis of Thomas had unraveled.

But as Frederick Copleston has pointed out, there are other ways of understanding this transition. Instead of seeing late-medieval–early-Renaissance philosophy as destructive to a grand synthesis or as reactive to societal chaos, "one can see . . . philosophy being reborn and growing up under the shadow and care of theology, reaching a more or less adult stage and then tending to go its own way and assert its independence" (*A History of Medieval Philosophy*, p. 314). While acknowledging the disintegration of the peculiarly Thomistic approach to synthesis, this view sees the late-medieval period as a natural development of Western European thought.

* * *

For discussions of the interaction between Christianity and its surrounding culture, see A.H. Armstrong and R.A. Markus, *Christian Faith and Greek Philosophy* (New York: Sheed and Ward, 1960); E.R. Dodds, *Pagan and Christian in an Age of Anxiety* (Cambridge: Cambridge University Press, 1965); Jaroslav Pelikan, *The Christian Tradition: A History of the Development of Doctrine*, five volumes (Chicago: University of Chicago Press, 1971–1989); and R.A. Markus, *Christianity in the Roman World* (London: Thames & Hudson, 1974). For a discussion of Christian beliefs in their historical context, see J.N.D. Kelly, *Early Christian Doctrines*, 5th edition (London: Black, 1978). For basic introductions to traditional Christian beliefs, see John R.W. Stott, *Basic Christianity* (Downers Grove, IL: Inter-Varsity Press, 1971), and Hans Küng, *On Being a Christian*, translated by Edward Quinn (Garden City, NY: Doubleday, 1976).

Étienne Gilson's work, *History of Christian Philosophy in the Middle Ages* (New York: Random House, 1955), is the classic study of this time period, while Maurice De Wulf, *History of Mediaeval Philosophy* (New York: Dover, 1952); Armand A. Maurer, *Medieval Philosophy* (New York: Random House, 1962); Michael Haren, *Medieval Thought: The Western Intellectual Tradition from Antiquity to the Thirteenth Century* (New York: St. Martin's Press, 1985); B.B. Price, *Medieval Thought* (Oxford: Blackwell, 1992); and John Marenbon, ed., *Medieval Philosophy* (London: Routledge & Kegan Paul, 1997) are also useful. Frederick Copleston's work on medieval philosophy includes several volumes of his multi-volume set, *A History of Philosophy* (1950; reprinted Garden City, NY: Image Doubleday, 1962–1963), as well as the later single volume, *A History of Medieval Philosophy* (New York: Harper & Row, 1972). Hans-Werner Goetz, *Life in the Middle Ages*, translated by Albert Wimmer (Notre Dame, IN: Notre Dame University Press, 1994) provides historical context.

For books specifically on the early medieval period, see A.H. Armstrong, ed., *The Cambridge History of Later Greek and Early Medieval Philosophy* (Cambridge: Cambridge University Press, 1967); and John Marenbon, *Early Medieval Philosophy (480–1150): An Introduction* (London: Routledge & Kegan Paul, 1983). For books on the later medieval period, see Ray C. Petry, ed., *Late Medieval Mysticism* (Philadelphia: Westminster Press, 1957); Gordon Leff, *The Dissolution of the Medieval Outlook: An Essay on Intellectual and Spiritual Change in the Fourteenth Century* (New York: New York University Press, 1976); Norman Kretzmann et al., eds., *The Cambridge History of Later Medieval Philosophy: From the Rediscovery of Aristotle to the Disintegration of Scholasticism 1100–1600* (Cambridge: Cambridge University Press, 1982); and John Marenbon, *Later Medieval Philosophy (1150–1350): An Introduction* (London: Routledge & Kegan Paul, 1987).

AUGUSTINE

A.D. 354–430

————◀○▶————

Aurelius Augustinus, Saint Augustine, was born of a Christian mother and a pagan father in Thagaste, a small town in what is now Algeria, North Africa. In many ways, his family's mixed religious background represented the crumbling Roman Empire. Even though the influence of Christianity had grown since Emperor Constantine's edict of religious toleration in A.D. 313, there were still many rivals to his mother's faith.

As a boy, Augustine showed intellectual promise, and at seventeen he was sent to Carthage to study rhetoric. While there, Augustine found philosophy, rejected Christianity, took a mistress (who bore him a son), and began to investigate some of the religions of the time. He turned first to the followers of the prophet Mani—the Manichaeans. Mani was a third-century prophet who called himself "the apostle of God." He developed the ancient Persian teaching of Zoroaster (or Zarathustra), which said that there are two great forces in the world, one good and one evil, and that neither can overcome the other. Living a life of sensual indulgence, Augustine took comfort from the idea that God could no more overcome evil in the universe than Augustine could in his own life.

In 375, Augustine returned to Thagaste to begin teaching rhetoric. When his mother, Monica (later sainted for her perseverance in prayer for her son), discovered that he had become a Manichaean, she expelled him from her house. Finding Thagaste boring, and his mother difficult, Augustine returned to Carthage. Over the next seven years, he grew disenchanted with Manichaeism. In 384, he left Carthage for teaching positions in Rome and finally Milan. In Milan, Augustine encountered the writings of Plotinus and was converted to Neoplatonism. At the same time, he came into contact with a group of Christians led by the Bishop of Milan, Ambrose. Under the influence of this group, Augustine was forced to reconsider his earlier rejection of Christianity, yet he was still unwilling to give up his life of self-gratification. In 386, while sitting in a friend's garden, he heard what he thought was a child's voice saying, "Pick it up and read, pick it up and read." Augustine later recounted what happened:

> I returned to the place where Alypius was sitting, for on leaving it I had put down there the book of the apostle's letters. I snatched it up, opened it and read in silence the passsage on which my eyes first lighted: "Not in dissipation and drunkenness, nor in debauchery and lewdness, nor in arguing and jealousy; but put on the Lord Jesus Christ, and make no provision for the flesh or the gratification of your desires." [Rom. 13:13–14] I had no wish to read further, nor was there need. No sooner had I reached the end of the verse than the light of certainty flooded my heart and all dark shades of doubt fled away.*

The following year, Augustine was baptized and returned to Africa to found a monastic community. Within two years he left the cloister, answering the church's call to priesthood. He served as a priest, and later as bishop, in the African town of Hippo for the rest of his life.

*   *   *

While at Hippo, Augustine wrote voluminously on a variety of theological and philosophical topics. Many of his works sought to define exactly what was and was not "Christian." His doctrinal works, such as *The Trinity,* established Christian essentials; whereas his polemical works, directed against "heresies" (positions unacceptable to the church), outlined what was not admissible. Augustine fought two major heresies: the Pelagian and the Donatist. The Pelagians held that sin had affected only Adam, that the will is free from sin, and that God's grace is given on the basis of human merit. The Donatists maintained that the sacraments were effective only when administered by a priest in a state of grace. Augustine argued passionately that both heresies put too much emphasis on human ability and not enough on God's grace.

Augustine's most famous work, the *Confessions,* invented the genre of introspective autobiography. The *Confessions* are full of both psychological and spiritual insight and so can be read as either devotional tract or philosophical essay. Books I through IX are Augustine's life story from the perspective of Christian conversion (detailed in our selection from Book VIII). As Augustine reflects on his life, he sees both his sinfulness and his intellectual aimlessness apart from God's grace. He also gives early glimpses of his mature epistemological position that God must illumine the mind in order for an individual to gain wisdom. Following his conversion, Augustine continued to seek understanding—though now firmly founded on faith. Books X to XII illustrate this "faith seeking understanding," as Augustine examines the questions of memory, time, and creation. Our selection from Book XI explores the nature of time and God's relation to it. Augustine argues that God must be "outside" time in an eternal present. This view of God as timelessly eternal was developed by Boethius and is still influential

---

*Saint Augustine, *Confessions,* Book VIII. See reading on p. 293.

today (see the suggested readings that follow). I am pleased to offer this selection in the outstanding new translation by Maria Boulding.

Of Augustine's many other works, *The City of God* is by far the most influential. During the fourth century, Christianity had become the state religion of the Roman Empire; in 410, Rome fell to the Visigoths, and the eternal city was sacked for the first time. Naturally, many considered the sack of Rome a punishment for the betrayal of the old Roman religion. Augustine wrote *The City of God* to answer this charge and in so doing he developed yet another first: the first Western philosophy of history. Rather than a cycle of repeated events, Augustine described history as being linear—from creation to consummation and final judgment. As history moves from beginning to end, we can observe two cities: the City of God, consisting of those who love God; and the City of Man, those who love self rather than God.

The second selection, from Book XII, explains the origin of evil and of the City of Man. Augustine begins by insisting, against the Manichaeans, that there is no being capable of opposing God: God is all-powerful. But, despite the presence of evil, God is also all-good and everything God created is good. Evil arises when a moral agent (angel or human) wills to love a lesser good (self) rather than the highest good (God). There is no evil "thing" to choose—there is only evil choosing. This leads to the question of what caused the will to choose evilly—a question Augustine says cannot be answered.

Augustine's impact has been enormous. Medieval Catholic philosophers, such as Anselm and Thomas Aquinas, as well as Protestant reformers, such as Martin Luther and John Calvin, wanted to be Augustine's heirs. Many contemporary Christian thinkers still appeal to Augustine's ideas, such as his defense of grace and his explanation of evil. But Augustine's influence has not been limited to theologians and philosophers of religion. Ludwig Wittgenstein began his *Philosophical Investigations* by examining Augustine's theory of language, and Bertrand Russell claimed Augustine's theory of time superior even to that of Kant. Echoes of Augustine's understanding of history as the unfolding of divine purpose can be heard in the writings of Hegel, whereas Augustine's idea that some kind of faith must precede fruitful understanding has been adapted by thinkers in such fields as the sociology of knowledge and philosophy of science.

*   *   *

The best general account of Augustine's philosophy remains Étienne Gilson, *The Christian Philosophy of Saint Augustine,* translated by L.E.M. Lynch (New York: Random House, 1960); Peter Brown, *Augustine of Hippo: A Biography* (Berkeley: University of California Press, 1967), provides an excellent biography. For a brief introduction to Augustine's life and thought, see Henry Chadwick, *Augustine* (Oxford: Oxford University Press, 1986). For more extensive discussions of Augustine's thought, see Robert E. Meagher, *An Introduction to Augustine* (New York: New York University Press, 1978), and Christopher Kirwan, *Augustine* (London: Routledge, 1989). J.N. Figgis, *The Political Aspects of St. Augustine's City of God* (London: Longmans, Green, 1921); Ronald H. Nash, *The Light of the Mind: St. Augustine's Theory of Knowledge* (Lexington: University Press of Kentucky, 1969); R.A. Markus, *Saeculum: History and Society in the Theology of St. Augustine* (Cambridge: Cambridge University Press, 1970); and Brian Stock, *Augustine the Reader* (Cambridge, MA; Harvard University

Press, 1996) deal with the specialized topics indicated by their respective titles. John M. Rist, *Augustine: Ancient Thought Baptized* (Cambridge: Cambridge University Press, 1994) explores the connections between Augustine and Platonic thought. For collections of essays, see M.C. D'Arcy et al., *Saint Augustine* (New York: Meridian, 1957), and R.A. Markus, ed., *Augustine: A Collection of Critical Essays* (Garden City, NY: Anchor, Doubleday, 1972).

CONFESSIONS (in part)

BOOK VIII—CONVERSION

5, 10. . . . It was no iron chain imposed by anyone else that fettered me, but the iron of my own will. The enemy had my power of willing in his clutches, and from it had forged a chain to bind me. The truth is that disordered lust springs from a perverted will; when lust is pandered to, a habit is formed; when habit is not checked, it hardens into compulsion. These were like interlinking rings forming what I have described as a chain, and my harsh servitude used it to keep me under duress.

A new will had begun to emerge in me, the will to worship you disinterestedly and enjoy you, O God, our only sure felicity; but it was not yet capable of surmounting that earlier will strengthened by inveterate custom. And so the two wills fought it out—the old and the new, the one carnal, the other spiritual—and in their struggle tore my soul apart.

*   *   *

8, 19. Within the house of my spirit the violent conflict raged on, the quarrel with my soul that I had so powerfully provoked in our secret dwelling, my heart, and at the height of it I rushed to Alypius with my mental anguish plain upon my face. "What is happening to us?" I exclaimed. "What does this mean? What did you make of it? The untaught are rising up and taking heaven by Storm, while we with all our dreary teachings are still groveling in this world of flesh and blood! Are we ashamed to follow, just because they have taken the lead, yet not ashamed of lacking the courage even to follow?" Some such words as these I spoke, and then my frenzy tore me away from him, while he regarded me in silent bewilderment. Unusual, certainly, was my speech, but my brow, cheeks and eyes, my flushed countenance and the cadences of my voice expressed my mind more fully than the words I uttered.

Adjacent to our lodgings was a small garden. We were free to make use of it as well as of the house, for our host, who owned the house, did not live there. The tumult in my breast had swept me away to this place, where no one would interfere with the blazing dispute I had engaged in with myself until it should be resolved. What the out-

Saint Augustine, *Confessions*, Book VIII (5, 8–12) and XI (14–28), translated by Maria Boulding (New York: New City Press, 1997). ©1997 by the Augustinian Heritage Institute.

come would be you knew, not I. All I knew was that I was going mad, but for the sake of my sanity, and dying that I might live, aware of the evil that I was but unaware of the good I was soon to become. So I went out into the garden and Alypius followed at my heels; my privacy was not infringed by his presence, and, in any case, how could he abandon me in that state? We sat down as far as possible from the house. I was groaning in spirit and shaken by violent anger because I could form no resolve to enter into a covenant with you, though in my bones I knew that this was what I ought to do, and everything in me lauded such a course to the skies. It was a journey not to be undertaken by ship or carriage or on foot, nor need it take me even that short distance I had walked from the house to the place where we were sitting; for to travel—and more, to reach journey's end—was nothing else but to want to go there, but to want it valiantly and with all my heart, not to whirl and toss this way and that a will half crippled by the struggle, as part of it rose up to walk while part sank down.

20. While this vacillation was at its most intense many of my bodily gestures were of the kind that people sometimes want to perform but cannot, either because the requisite limbs are missing, or because they are bound and restricted, or paralyzed through illness, or in some other way impeded. If I tore out my hair, battered my forehead, entwined my fingers and clasped them round my knee, I did so because I wanted to. I might have wanted to but found myself unable, if my limbs had not been mobile enough to obey. So then, there were plenty of actions that I performed where willing was not the same thing as being able; yet I was not doing the one thing that was incomparably more desirable to me, the thing that I would be able to do as soon as I willed, because as soon as I willed—why, then, I would be willing it! For in this sole instance the faculty to act and the will to act precisely coincide, and the willing is already the doing. Yet this was not happening. My body was more ready to obey the slightest whim of my soul in the matter of moving my limbs, than the soul was to obey its own command in carrying out this major volition, which was to be accomplished within the will alone.

9, 21. How did this bizarre situation arise, how develop? May your mercy shed light on my inquiry, so that perhaps an answer may be found in the mysterious punishments meted out to humankind, those utterly baffling pains that afflict the children of Adam. How then did this bizarre situation arise, how develop? The mind commands the body and is instantly obeyed; the mind commands itself, and meets with resistance. When the mind orders the hand to move, so smooth is the compliance that command can scarcely be distinguished from execution; yet the mind is mind, while the hand is body. When the mind issues its command that the mind itself should will something (and the mind so commanded is no other than itself), it fails to do so. How did this bizarre situation arise, how develop? As I say, the mind commands itself to will something: it would not be giving the order if it did not want this thing; yet it does not do what it commands.

Evidently, then, it does not want this thing with the whole of itself, and therefore the command does not proceed from an undivided mind. Inasmuch as it issues the command, it does will it, but inasmuch as the command is not carried out, it does not will it. What the will is ordering is that a certain volition should exist, and this volition is not some alien thing, but its very self. Hence it cannot be giving the order with its whole self. It cannot be identical with that thing which it is commanding to come into existence, for if it were whole and entire it would not command itself to be, since it would be already.

This partial willing and partial non-willing is thus not so bizarre, but a sickness of the mind, which cannot rise with its whole self on the wings of truth because it is heavily burdened by habit. There are two wills, then, and neither is the whole: what one has the other lacks.

10, 22. Some there are who on perceiving two wills engaged in deliberation assert that in us there are two natures, one good, the other evil, each with a mind of its own. Let them perish from your presence, O God, as perish all who talk wildly and lead our minds astray. They are evil themselves as long as they hold these opinions, yet these same people will be good if they embrace true opinions and assent to true teaching, and so merit the apostle's commendation, You were darkness once, but now you are light in the Lord. The trouble is that they want to be light not in the Lord but in themselves, with their notion that the soul is by nature divine, and so they have become denser darkness still, because by their appalling arrogance they have moved further away from you, the true Light, who enlighten everyone who comes into the world. I warn these people, Take stock of what you are saying, and let it shame you; but once draw near to him and be illumined, and your faces will not blush with shame.

When I was making up my mind to serve the Lord my God at last, as I had long since purposed, I was the one who wanted to follow that course, and I was the one who wanted not to. I was the only one involved. I neither wanted it wholeheartedly nor turned from it wholeheartedly. I was at odds with myself, and fragmenting myself. This disintegration was occurring without my consent, but what it indicated was not the presence in me of a mind belonging to some alien nature but the punishment undergone by my own. In this sense, and this sense only, it was not I who brought it about, but the sin that dwelt within me as penalty for that other sin committed with greater freedom;* for I was a son of Adam.

23. Moreover, if we were to take the number of conflicting urges to signify the number of natures present in us, we should have to assume that there are not two, but many. If someone is trying to make up his mind whether to go to a Manichean conventicle or to the theater, the Manichees declare, "There you are, there's the evidence for two natures: the good one is dragging him our way, the bad one is pulling him back in the other direction. How else explain this dithering between contradictory wills?" But I regard both as bad, the one that leads him to them and the one that lures him back to the theater. They, on the contrary, think that an inclination toward them can only be good.

But consider this: suppose one of our people is deliberating, and as two desires clash he is undecided whether to go to the theater or to our church, will not our opponents too be undecided what attitude to take? Either they will have to admit that it is good will that leads a person to our church, just as good as that which leads to theirs the people who are initiated into their sacred rites and trapped there—and this they are unwilling to admit; or they will conclude that two evil natures and two bad minds are pitted against each other within one person, in which case their habitual assertion of one good and one evil nature will be erroneous; or, finally, they will be brought round to the truth and no longer deny that when a person is deliberating there is but one soul, thrown into turmoil by divergent impulses.

24. When, therefore, they observe two conflicting impulses within one person, let them stop saying that two hostile minds are at war, one good, the other evil, and that these derive from two hostile substances and two hostile principles. For you are

---

*[That is, by Adam. Augustine uses the comparative to suggest a relative freedom enjoyed by Adam, superior to our own but short of perfect freedom. He was to spell out the distinction later in *Correction and Grace* XII, 33 between *posse non peccare* (the ability not to sin, Adam's privilege), and *non posse peccare* (the perfection of freedom in heaven)].

true, O God, and so you chide and rebuke them and prove them wrong. The choice may lie between two impulses that are both evil, as when a person is debating whether to murder someone with poison or a dagger; whether to annex this part of another man's property or that, assuming he cannot get both; whether to buy himself pleasure by extravagant spending or hoard his money out of avarice; whether to go to the circus or the theater if both performances are on the same day—and I would even add a third possibility: whether to go and steal from someone else's house while he has the chance, and a fourth as well: whether to commit adultery while he is about it. All these impulses may occur together, at exactly the same time, and all be equally tempting, but they cannot all be acted upon at once. The mind is then rent apart by the plethora of desirable objects as four inclinations, or even more, do battle among themselves; yet the Manichees do not claim that there are as many disparate substances in us as this.

The same holds true for good impulses. I would put these questions to them: Is it good to find delight in a reading from the apostle? To enjoy the serenity of a psalm? To discuss the gospel? To each point they will reply, "Yes, that is good." Where does that leave us? If all these things tug at our will with equal force, and all together at the same time, will not these divergent inclinations put a great strain on the human heart, as we deliberate which to select? All are good, but they compete among themselves until one is chosen, to which the will, hitherto distracted between many options, may move as a united whole. So too when the joys of eternity call us from above, and pleasure in temporal prosperity holds us fast below, our one soul is in no state to embrace either with its entire will. Claimed by truth for the one, to the other clamped by custom, the soul is torn apart in its distress.

11, 25. Such was the sickness in which I agonized, blaming myself more sharply than ever, turning and twisting in my chain as I strove to tear free from it completely, for slender indeed was the bond that still held me. But hold me it did. In my secret heart you stood by me, Lord, redoubling the lashes of fear and shame in the severity of your mercy, lest I give up the struggle and that slender, fragile bond that remained be not broken after all, but thicken again and constrict me more tightly. "Let it be now," I was saying to myself. "Now is the moment, let it be now," and merely by saying this I was moving toward the decision. I would almost achieve it, but then fall just short; yet I did not slip right down to my starting-point, but stood aside to get my breath back. Then I would make a fresh attempt, and now I was almost there, almost there . . . I was touching the goal, grasping it . . . and then I was not there, not touching, not grasping it. I shrank from dying to death and living to life, for ingrained evil was more powerful in me than new-grafted good. The nearer it came, that moment when I would be changed, the more it pierced me with terror. Dismayed, but not quite dislodged, I was left hanging.

26. The frivolity of frivolous aims, the futility of futile pursuits, these things that had been my cronies of long standing, still held me back, plucking softly at my garment of flesh and murmuring in my ear, "Do you mean to get rid of us? Shall we never be your companions again after that moment . . . never . . . never again? From that time onward so-and-so will be forbidden to you, all your life long." And what was it that they were reminding me of by those words, "so-and-so," O my God, what were they bringing to my mind? May your mercy banish such memories far from me! What foul deeds were they not hinting at, what disgraceful exploits! But now their voices were less than half as loud, for they no longer confronted me directly to argue their case, but muttered behind my back and slyly tweaked me as I walked away, trying to make me look back. Yet they did slow me down, for I could not bring myself to

tear free and shake them off and leap across to that place whither I was summoned, while aggressive habit still taunted me: "Do you imagine you will be able to live without these things?"

27. The taunts had begun to sound much less persuasive, however; for a revelation was coming to me from that country toward which I was facing, but into which I trembled to cross. There I beheld the chaste, dignified figure of Continence. Calm and cheerful was her manner, though modest, pure and honorable her charm as she coaxed me to come and hesitate no longer, stretching kindly hands to welcome and embrace me, hands filled with a wealth of heartening examples. A multitude of boys and girls were there, a great concourse of youth and persons of every age, venerable widows and women grown old in their virginity, and in all of them I saw this that this same Continence was by no means sterile, but the fruitful mother of children conceived in joy from you, her Bridegroom. She was smiling at me, but with a challenging smile, as though to say, "Can you not do what these men have done, these women? Could any of them achieve it by their own strength, without the Lord their God? He it was, the Lord their God, who granted me to them. Why try to stand by yourself, only to lose your footing? Cast yourself on him and do not be afraid: he will not step back and let you fall. Cast yourself upon him trustfully; he will support and heal you." And I was bitterly ashamed, because I could still hear the murmurs of those frivolities, and I was still in suspense, still hanging back. Again she appealed to me, as though urging, "Close your ears against those unclean parts of you which belong to the earth and let them be put to death. They tell you titillating tales, but have nothing to do with the law of the Lord your God."

All this argument in my heart raged only between myself and myself. Alypius stood fast at my side, silently awaiting the outcome of my unprecedented agitation.

12, 28. But as this deep meditation dredged all my wretchedness up from the secret profundity of my being and heaped it all together before the eyes of my heart, a huge storm blew up within me and brought on a heavy rain of tears. In order to pour them out unchecked with the sobs that accompanied them I arose and left Alypius, for solitude seemed to me more suitable for the business of weeping. I withdrew far enough to ensure that his presence—even his—would not be burdensome to me. This was my need, and he understood it, for I think I had risen to my feet and blurted out something, my voice already choked with tears. He accordingly remained, in stunned amazement, at the place where we had been sitting. I flung myself down somehow under a fig-tree and gave free rein to the tears that burst from my eyes like rivers, as an acceptable sacrifice to you. Many things I had to say to you, and the gist of them, though not the precise words, was: "O Lord, how long? How long? Will you be angry for ever? Do not remember our age-old sins." For by these I was conscious of being held prisoner. I uttered cries of misery: "Why must I go on saying, 'Tomorrow . . . tomorrow'? Why not now? Why not put an end to my depravity this very hour?"

29. I went on talking like this and weeping in the intense bitterness of my broken heart. Suddenly I heard a voice from a house nearby—perhaps a voice of some boy or girl, I do not know—singing over and over again, "Pick it up and read, pick it up and read." My expression immediately altered and I began to think hard whether children ordinarily repeated a ditty like this in any sort of game, but I could not recall ever having heard it anywhere else. I stemmed the flood of tears and rose to my feet, believing that this could be nothing other than a divine command to open the Book and read the first passage I chanced upon; for I had heard the story of how Antony had been in-

structed by a gospel text. He happened to arrive while the gospel was being read, and took the words to be addressed to himself when he heard, "Go and sell all you possess and give the money to the poor: you will have treasure in heaven. Then come, follow me" [Matt. 19:21]. So he was promptly converted to you by this plainly divine message. Stung into action, I returned to the place where Alypius was sitting, for on leaving it I had put down there the book of the apostle's letters. I snatched it up, opened it and read in silence the passage on which my eyes first lighted: "Not in dissipation and drunkenness, nor in debauchery and lewdness, nor in arguing and jealousy; but put on the Lord Jesus Christ, and make no provision for the flesh or the gratification of your desires" [Rom. 13:13–14]. I had no wish to read further, nor was there need. No sooner had I reached the end of the verse than the light of certainty flooded my heart and all dark shades of doubt fled away.

30. I closed the book, marking the place with a finger between the leaves or by some other means, and told Alypius what had happened. My face was peaceful now. He in return told me what had been happening to him without my knowledge. He asked to see what I had read: I showed him, but he looked further than my reading had taken me. I did not know what followed, but the next verse was, "Make room for the person who is weak in faith." He referred this text to himself and interpreted it to me. Confirmed by this admonition he associated himself with my decision and good purpose without any upheaval or delay, for it was entirely in harmony with his own moral character, which for a long time now had been far, far better than mine.

We went indoors and told my mother, who was overjoyed. When we related to her how it had happened she was filled with triumphant delight and blessed you, who have power to do more than we ask or understand, for she saw that you had granted her much more in my regard than she had been wont to beg of you in her wretched, tearful groaning. Many years earlier you had shown her a vision of me standing on the rule of faith; and now indeed I stood there, no longer seeking a wife or entertaining any worldly hope, for you had converted me to yourself. In so doing you had also converted her grief into a joy far more abundant than she had desired, and much more tender and chaste than she could ever have looked to find in grandchildren from my flesh.

BOOK XI—TIME AND ETERNITY

14, 17. There was therefore never any time when you had not made anything, because you made time itself. And no phases of time are coeternal with you, for you abide, and if they likewise were to abide, they would not be time. For what is time? Who could find any quick or easy answer to that? Who could even grasp it in his thought clearly enough to put the matter into words? Yet is there anything to which we refer in conversation with more familiarity, any matter of more common experience, than time? And we know perfectly well what we mean when we speak of it, and understand just as well when we hear someone else refer to it. What, then, is time? If no one asks me, I know; if I want to explain it to someone who asks me, I do not know. I can state with confidence, however, that this much I do know: if nothing passed away there would be no past time; if there was nothing still on its way there would be no future time; and if nothing existed, there would be no present time.

God in Act of Creation, from a thirteenth-century French Bible. In the *Confessions,* Augustine argues that God created the world *ex nihilo* (out of nothing) and that God is outside of time. *(Corbis-Bettmann)*

Now, what about those two times, past and future: in what sense do they have real being, if the past no longer exists and the future does not exist yet? As for present time, if that were always present and never slipped away into the past, it would not be time at all; it would be eternity. If, therefore, the present's only claim to be called "time" is that it is slipping away into the past, how can we assert that this thing *is*, when its only title to being is that it will soon cease to be? In other words, we cannot really say that time exists, except because it tends to non-being.*

15, 18. Nonetheless we speak of a long time or a short time, and we do so only of time past or time in the future. For example, we call a hundred years ago a long time in the past, and likewise a hundred years hence a long time in the future; but we call—say—ten days ago a short time past, and ten days hence a short time in the future. But on what grounds can something that does not exist be called long or short? The past no longer exists and the future does not exist yet. We ought not, therefore, to say, "That is a long time," but, when speaking of the past, we should say, "That was long," and of the future, "That will be long."

O my Lord, my light, will your truth not deride us humans for speaking so? This long time in the past: was it long when it was already past, or earlier than that, when it was still present? If the latter, yes, then it might have been long, because there was something to be long; but if it was already past it no longer existed, and therefore could not have been long, since it was not in existence at all. We ought not, therefore, to say, "That era in the past was a long one," for we shall not find anything that was long, for since that point at which it became past time it has no longer had any being. Rather, we ought to say, "That era of time was long while present," because while it was present it was long. It had not yet passed away and so passed out of existence, and so there was something there which could be long. But when it passed away it ceased to be long at that very point when it ceased to be at all.

19. Now, human mind, let us consider whether present time can be long, as you seem to think it can, since you have been granted the power to be aware of duration and to measure it. Answer my questions, then. Is the present century a long period of time? Before you say yes, reflect whether a hundred years can be present. If the first of them is running its course, that year is present, but ninety-nine others are future and therefore as yet have no being. If the second year is running its course, one year is already past, another is present, and the remainder are still to come. In the same fashion we may represent any one of the intervening years of the century as present, and always the years that preceded it will be past, and those that follow it future. Evidently, then, a hundred years cannot be present.

Well then, consider whether the one current year at least can be present. If we are in the first month of it, the other months are in the future; if we are in the second, the first month is already past and the rest do not yet exist. Even the current year, then, is not present in its totality, and if it is not present in its totality, the year is not present; for a year consists of twelve months, and while any one of them is current that one is present, but the others are either past or future.

But we must go further, and notice that the current month is not in fact present, because only one day of it is: if we are on the first day, the rest are future; if on the last,

---

*[This is the heart of the matter for Augustine. He pursues the argument relentlessly throughout the rest of this Book XI, revealing time as something elusive that slips the more swiftly through our fingers the more we try to analyze it or justify our habit of measuring it. The inexorable rush of time toward non-being reveals the fragility of time-bound, time-conditioned creatures, whose only refuge from their native nothingness is the eternity of God.]

the others are past; if on any day in the middle, we shall be midway between past and future days.

20. Look where this leaves us. We saw earlier that present time was the only one of the three that might properly be called long, and now this present time has been pared down to the span of a bare day. But let us take the discussion further, because not even a single day is present all at once. It is made up of night hours and day hours, twenty-four in all. From the standpoint of the first hour all the rest are still future; the last hour looks to all those already past; and any one we pick in between has some before it, others to follow. Even a single hour runs its course through fleeing minutes: whatever portion of it has flown is now past, and what remains is future. If we can conceive of a moment in time which cannot be further divided into even the tiniest of minute particles, that alone can be rightly termed the present; yet even this flies by from the future into the past with such haste that it seems to last no time at all. Even if it has some duration, that too is divisible into past and future; hence the present is reduced to vanishing-point.

What kind of time, then, can be referred to as "a long time"? Future time, perhaps? Then we must not say, "That is a long time," because there is as yet nothing to be long; we will have to say, "That will be long." But when will it be so? If at the point of speaking that period is still in the future, it will not be long, because nothing yet exists to be long; if, however, at the moment when we speak it has begun to exist by emerging from the non-existent future, and so has become present, so that there is something in existence to be long, then this present time proclaims itself incapable of being long for the reasons already discussed.

16, 21. All the same, Lord, we are conscious of intervals of time, and we compare them with each other and pronounce some longer, others shorter. We also calculate by how much this period of time is longer or shorter than that other, and we report that the one is twice or three times as long as the other, or that it is the same length. But when we measure periods of time by our awareness of them, what we measure is passing time. Could anyone measure past periods that no longer exist, or future periods that do not yet exist? Only someone who is bold enough to claim that what has no being can be measured. So then, while time is passing it can be felt and measured, but once past it cannot, because it no longer exists.

17, 22. I am asking questions, Father, not making assertions: rule me, O my God, and shepherd me. For who would make so bold as to tell me that there are not really three tenses or times—past, present and future—as we learned as children and as we in our turn have taught our children, but that there is only present, since the other two do not exist? Or is the truth perhaps that they do exist, but that when a future thing becomes present it emerges from some hiding-place, and then retreats into another hiding-place when it moves from the present into the past? Where, otherwise, did soothsayers see future events, if they do not yet exist? What has no being cannot be seen. Nor would people who tell stories about the past be telling true tales if they had no vision of those past events in their minds; and if the events in question were non-existent they could not be seen. The future and the past must exist, then?

18, 23. Allow me, Lord, to press the question further: O my hope, do not let me lose the thread. If future and past things do exist, I want to know where they are. If this is not yet within my compass, I do know at any rate that, wherever they are, they are not there as future or past, but as present. For if in that place too future things are future, they are not there yet; and if there too past things are past, they are there no longer. Clearly, then, wherever they are and whatever they are, they can only be present. Nonetheless, when a true account is given of past events, what is brought forth from the memory is not the events themselves, which have passed away, but words formed from images of those events which as they happened and went on their way left some kind of traces in the mind through the medium of the senses. This is the case with my childhood, which no longer exists: it belongs to past time which exists no longer, but when I recall it and tell the story I contemplate the image of it which is still in my memory.

Whether something similar occurs in the prediction of future events, in that the seer has a presentiment of images which exist already, I confess, O my God, that I do not know. But this I undoubtedly do know, that we often plan our future actions beforehand, and that the plans in our mind are present to us, though the action we are planning has as yet no being, because it is future. When we set about it, and begin to do what we were planning, then the action will have real being, because then it will be not future but present.

24. However the mysterious presentiment of future events may be explained, only what exists can be seen. But what already exists is not future but present. Therefore when it is claimed that future events are seen, it is not that these things are seen in themselves, because they have as yet no existence, being still future. It may be, however, that their causes, or signs of them, are seen, because these already exist; hence they are not future but present to the people who discern them, and from them future events may take shape in the mind and can be foretold. These ideas in the mind also exist already, and can be inwardly contemplated by people who predict the future.

Let me take an example from a wealth of such occurrences. I watch the dawn, and I give advance notice that the sun is about to rise. What I am looking at is present; what I foretell is future. Not that the sun is future, of course—no, that exists already, but its rising is future; it has not yet happened, yet unless I could imagine the sunrise in my mind, as I do now while I speak of it, I would be unable to forecast it. The dawn, which I am watching in the sky, is not the sunrise, but only precedes it; and similarly the picture I have in my mind is not the sunrise either. But these two realities are present and open to observation, so that the future event can be announced before its time.

We must conclude, then, that future events have no being as yet, and if they have no being yet they do not exist, and if they do not exist it is absolutely impossible for anyone to see them. But they can be predicted on the basis of other things which are already present and hence can be seen.

19, 25. You are the king of your creation; tell me, then: how do you instruct people's minds about the future? You did so teach the prophets. What method can you adopt for teaching what is future, when to you nothing is future at all? Would it be better to say that you teach what is present but has a bearing on the future? Yes, because what does not exist obviously cannot be taught. This method of yours is far above the reach of my mind; it is too much for me and of myself I cannot see it, but I will see it with your help, when you grant me this gift, O gracious light of my secret eyes.

20, 26. What is now clear and unmistakable is that neither things past nor things future have any existence, and that it is inaccurate to say, "There are three tenses or times: past, present and future," though it might properly be said, "There are three tenses or times: the present of past things, the present of present things, and the present of future things." These are three realities in the mind, but nowhere else as far as I can see, for the present of past things is memory, the present of present things is attention, and the present of future things is expectation. If we are allowed to put it that way, I do see three tenses or times, and admit that they are three. Very well, then, let the phrase pass: "There are three tenses or times: past, present and future," as common usage improperly has it: let people go on saying this. I do not mind, nor will I put up any opposition or offer correction, provided we understand what we are saying, and do not assert that either the future or the past exists now. There are few things, in fact, which we state accurately; far more we express loosely, but what we mean is understood.

21, 27. I said just now* that we measure periods of time as they pass, so as to declare this interval twice as long as that, or this equal to that, and report anything else about segments of time that our measurements have revealed. It follows, then, that we measure these intervals of time as they are passing by, as I remarked, and if anyone asks me, "How do you know that?" I must be allowed to reply, "I know it because we do in fact measure them; but what does not exist we cannot measure, and past and future do not exist." But how can we measure present time, when it has no extension?** We can only hope to measure it as it passes by, because once it has passed by there will be no measuring; it will not exist to be measured.

But when it is measured, where does it come from, by what path does it pass, and whither go? Where from, if not from the future? By what path, if not the present? Whither, if not into the past? It comes, then, from what is not yet real, travels through what occupies no space, and is bound for what is no longer real. But what are we trying to measure, if not time that does have some extension? We speak of "half as long," "double the time," "three times as long," "equal in length," and make similar statements about time only in reference to extended time, or duration. Where then is this duration which will give us a chance to measure passing time? In the future, whence it has come to pass us by? But we do not measure what does not yet exist. In the present, perhaps, through which it passes on its way? But where there is no extension we cannot measure. In the past, then, to which it has gone? But we cannot measure what no longer exists.

22, 28. My mind is on fire to solve this most intricate enigma. O Lord, my God, my good Father, through Christ I beg you not to shut against me the door to these truths, so familiar yet so mysterious. Do not slam the door in the face of my desire, nor forbid me entrance to that place where I may watch these things grow luminous as your mercy sheds its light upon them, Lord. To whom should I put my questions about them? And to whom should I confess my stupidity with greater profit than to you, who do not weary of my intense, burning interest in your scriptures? Give me what I love; for I love indeed, and this love you have given me. Give this to me, Father, for you truly know how to give good gifts to your children; give me this gift, for I have only just begun to understand, and the labor is too much for me until you open the door. Through Christ I implore you, in the name of that holy of holies, let no noisy person stand in my way. I too have believed, and so I too speak. This is my hope, for this I live: to contemplate the delight of the Lord. See how old you have made my days; they are slipping away and I know not how.

We speak of one time and another time, of this period of time or that; we ask, "How long did that man speak?" or "How long did he take to do it?" We say, "What a long time it is since I saw so-and-so," and "This syllable has twice the length of that short one." We say these things and listen to them, we are understood and we understand. They are perfectly plain and fully familiar, yet at the same time deeply mysterious, and we still need to discover their meaning.

23, 29. I was once told by a certain learned man that the movements of the sun, moon and stars themselves constitute time. I did not agree with him. Why, in that case,

---

*[That is, in XI, 16, 21.]
**[That is, the ideal present is a point, which has position but no magnitude.]

should not the movements of all corporeal things constitute time? Suppose the luminaries of heaven were to halt, but a potter's wheel went on turning, would there not still be time by which we could measure those rotations, and say either that all of them took the same time, or (if the speed of the wheel varied) that some were of longer duration, others shorter? And when we said this, would we too not be speaking within time; and in the words we used, would there not be some long syllables and some short; and why could that be said of them, unless because some of them had taken a longer time to pronounce than others?

Through this small thing, O God, grant our human minds insight into the principles common to small things and great. The stars and the other luminaries in the sky are there to mark our times and days and years. Yes, granted; but as I would not assert that the revolution of that little wooden wheel itself constituted a day, so my learned informant on the other hand had no business to say that its gyrations did not occupy a space of time.

30. I want to know the essence and nature of time, whereby we measure the movement of bodies and say, for instance, that one movement lasts twice as long as another. Now I have a question to ask. Taking the word "day" to apply not only to the period of sunlight on earth—day as opposed to night, that is—but to the sun's whole course from the east and back to the east again, in the sense that we say, "So many days elapsed," meaning to include the nights, and not reckoning the nights as extra time over and above the days; taking it, then, that the movement of the sun in its circular course from the east back to the east completes a day, this is my question: is it the movement itself that constitutes a day? Or the time it takes? Or both? If the movement constitutes a day, then it would still be one day if the sun were to achieve its circuit in an interval of time equivalent to a single hour. If it is the time it takes, there would not be a day if the space between one sunrise and the next were as short as an hour; the sun would have to go round twenty-four times to make up a day. If both were required complete circuit of the sun and the customary duration of this—we could not call it a day if the sun traveled through its whole circuit in the space of an hour, nor could we if the sun stopped and as much time elapsed as it usually takes to run its whole course from morning to morning.

My question now is not, therefore, what is it that we call a day, but what is time itself, the time whereby we would be able to measure the sun's revolution and say that it had been completed in only half the usual time, if the circuit had occupied only that space of time represented by twelve hours? We could compare the two periods in terms of time and say that one was twice the length of the other, and this would still be possible even if the sun sometimes took the single period, and sometimes the double, to circle from the east and back to the east again. Let no one tell me, then, that time is simply the motion of the heavenly bodies. After all, at the prayer of a certain man the sun halted so that he could press home the battle to victory. The sun stood still, but time flowed on its way, and that fight had all the time it needed to be carried through to the finish.

I see, therefore, that time is a kind of strain or tension. But do I really see it? Or only seem to see? You will show me, O Light, O Truth.

24, 31. Are you commanding me to agree with someone who says that time is the motion of a body? You do not so command me. No corporeal object moves except within time: this is what I hear; this is what you tell me. But that a corporeal object's movement is itself time I do not hear; this you do not say. When a body moves, I measure in terms of time how long it is in motion, from the moment when it begins until its motion ceases. If I did not notice when it began, and it continues to move without my seeing when it stops, I cannot measure the time, except perhaps the interval between the moment when I began to watch and that when I ceased to observe it. If my observation is prolonged, I can only say that the process went on for a long time; I cannot say exactly how long, because when we add a definite indication of a length of time we do so by reference to some agreed standard. "This is as long as that," we say; or "This is twice as long as that other," or something similar. If, on the other hand, we have been able to note the position of some corporeal object when it moves (or when parts of it move, if, for example, it is being turned on a lathe), and we have observed its starting-point and its point of arrival, then we are able to state how much time has elapsed while the movement of the object was effected from the one place to the other, or how long it has taken to revolve on its axis.

Therefore if the motion of an object is one thing, and the standard by which we measure its duration another, is it not obvious which of the two has the stronger claim to be called time? Moreover, if the motion is irregular, so that the object is sometimes moving and sometimes stationary, we measure not only its motion but also its static periods in terms of time, and say, "Its stationary periods were equivalent in length to its phases of motion," or "It was stationary for two or three times as long as it was in motion," or whatever else our calculation has ascertained or estimated roughly—more or less, as we customarily say. Clearly, then, time is not the movement of any corporeal object.

25, 32. I confess to you, Lord, that even today I am still ignorant of what time is; but I praise you, Lord, for the fact that I know I am making this avowal within time, and for my realization that within time I am talking about time at such length, and that I know this "length" itself is long only because time has been passing all the while. But how can I know that, when I do not know what time is? Or perhaps I simply do not know how to articulate what I know? Woe is me, for I do not even know what I do not know!

Behold me here before you, O my God; see that I do not lie. As I speak, this is the true state of my heart. You, you alone, will light my lamp, O Lord; O my God, you will illumine my darkness.

26, 33. Am I not making a truthful confession to you when I praise you for my ability to measure time? But this must mean, O my God, that though I can measure it, I do not know what I am measuring! I measure the movement of a body in terms of time, but surely I am by that same calculation measuring time itself? Would it be possible for me to measure a body's motion, to calculate how long it lasts and how long the object takes to travel from here to there, without also measuring the time within which the motion occurs? With what, then, do I measure time itself? Do we measure a longer time by the standard of a shorter, as we use the cubit to measure the span of a cross-beam? That indeed seems to be how we measure the quantity of a long syllable by that of a short syllable, and decide that the former is twice as long. Similarly we measure the length of poems by the length of their lines, and the length of the lines by the length of the feet, and the length of each foot by the length of its syllables, and the length of a long syllable by that of a short syllable. We do not reckon by the number of pages— that would be to impose a spatial, not a temporal standard—but by the pronunciation as voices recite them and die away. We declare, "That is a lengthy poem, for it consists of so many lines; the lines are long, since each is composed of so many feet; the feet are long, since each extends over so many syllables; and a syllable is long, when it is twice the quantity of a short one."

But the mensuration of time by these methods yields no result that is absolute, since it may happen that the sound of a shorter line, spoken with a drawl, actually lasts longer than that of a longer one hurried over. The same holds for the whole poem, a foot, and a syllable.

I have therefore come to the conclusion that time is nothing other than tension: but tension of what, I do not know, and I would be very surprised if it is not tension of consciousness itself. What am I measuring, I beg you to tell me, my God, when I say in imprecise terms, "This is longer than that," or even, precisely, "This is twice that"? That I am measuring time, I know; but I am not measuring future time, because it does not yet exist, not present time, which is a point without extension, nor past time, which exists no more. What, then, am I measuring? Time as it passes by, but not once it has passed? That was what I said earlier.

27, 34. Stick to it, now, my mind, and pay close attention. God is our ally; and he made us, not we ourselves. Mark where truth brightens to the dawn!

Suppose now that a physical voice begins to sound . . . and goes on sounding . . . and is still sounding . . . and now stops. Now there is silence, and that voice is past and is a voice no longer. Before it sounded forth it was a future thing, so it could not be measured because it did not yet exist; neither can it be now, because it exists no more. Perhaps, then, it could be measured while it was sounding forth, because something did then exist that could be measured? But at that time it was not standing still; it was but a fleeting thing that was speeding on its way. Was it therefore any more measurable while sounding than before or after? Only as something transient was it extended over a period of time whereby it might be measured—only as transient, because the present moment has no duration. If it is argued that the sound could, nevertheless, be measured while it lasted, consider this: another voice begins to sound and is still sounding in a continuous, steady tone. Let us measure it, then, while it is sounding, for once it has fallen silent it will be a thing of the past, and nothing measurable will then exist. By all means let us measure it now, and state how long it lasts.

Ah, but it is still sounding, and there is no way of timing it except from its beginning, when the sound originated, to its end, when it ceases. Obviously we measure any interval of time from some inception to some ending. Hence the sound of a voice which has not yet finished cannot be measured in such a way that anyone can say how long or how short it is, nor can it be declared to be of the same length as something else, or half the length, or twice the length, or anything of the kind. But once finished, it will not exist. So by what criteria will it then be subject to measurement?

All the same we do measure periods of time, not periods which as yet have no being, nor those which have ceased to be, nor those which have no duration, nor those which have no terminus. We measure neither future nor past nor present nor passing time. Yet time we do measure.

35. Take the line, *Deus, creator omnium.** This line consists of eight syllables, short and long alternating. The four short ones—the first, third, fifth and seventh—are thus half the length of the four long ones—the second, fourth, sixth and eighth. Each of these latter lasts twice as long as each of the former; I have only to pronounce the line to report that this is the case, insofar as clear sense-perception can verify it. Relying on this unmistakable evidence of my ear I measure each long syllable by the criterion of a short one, and perceive that it is twice the quantity. But the syllables make themselves heard in succession; and if the first is short and the second long, how am I to hold on to the short one, how am I to apply it to the long one as a measuring-rod in order to discover that the long one has twice the quantity, when the long one does not begin to

*[Ambrose's evening hymn: "God, Creator of all."]

sound until the short one has ceased? Am I to measure the long one while it is present? Impossible, because I cannot measure something unfinished. But its completion is its passing away, so what now exists for me to measure? Where is the short syllable I was going to use as a standard? What has become of the long one I want to measure? Both have made their sound, and flown away, and passed by, and exist no more; yet I do my calculation and confidently assert that insofar as the testimony of my trained ear can be trusted, the short is half the long, the long twice the short; and obviously I am speaking about a space of time. I can only do this because the syllables have passed away and are completed. Evidently, then, what I am measuring is not the syllables themselves, which no longer exist, but something in my memory, something fixed and permanent there.

36. In you, my mind, I measure time. Do not interrupt me by clamoring that time has objective existence, nor hinder yourself with the hurly-burly of your impressions. In you, I say, do I measure time. What I measure is the impression which passing phenomena leave in you, which abides after they have passed by: that is what I measure as a present reality, not the things that passed by so that the impression could be formed. The impression itself is what I measure when I measure intervals of time. Hence either time is this impression, or what I measure is not time.

What about when we measure silences, and say that this silent pause lasted as long as that sound? Do we not strain our thought to retain the feeling of a sound's duration, as though it were still audible, so as to be able to estimate the intervals of silence in relation to the whole space of time in question? Without any articulate word or even opening our mouths we go over in our minds poems, their lines, a speech, and we assess their developmental patterns and the time they occupied in relation to one another; and our estimate is no different from what it would have been if we had been reciting them aloud.

Suppose a person wishes to utter a fairly long sound, and has determined beforehand in his own mind how long it is to be. He must have first thought through that period of time in silence and committed the impression of it to memory; then he begins to utter the sound, which continues until it reaches the predetermined end. Or rather, it does not "continue," because the sound is evidently both something already heard and something still to be heard, for the part of it already completed is sound that has been, but the part that remains is sound still to be. Thus it is carried through as our present awareness drags what is future into the past. As the future dwindles the past grows, until the future is used up altogether and the whole thing is past.

28, 37. But how can a future which does not yet exist dwindle or be used up, and how can a past which no longer exists grow? Only because there are three realities in the mind which conducts this operation. The mind expects, and attends, and remembers, so that what it expects passes by way of what it attends to into what it remembers. No one, surely, would deny that the future is as yet non-existent? Yet an expectation of future events does exist in the mind. And would anyone deny that the past has ceased to be? Yet the memory of past events still lives on in the mind. And who would deny that the present has no duration, since it passes in an instant? Yet our attention does endure, and through our attention what is still to be makes its way into the state where it is no more. It is not, therefore, future time which is long, for it does not exist; a long future is simply an expectation of the future which represents it as long. Nor is the past a long period of time, because it does not exist at all; a long past is simply a memory of the past which represents it as long.

38. Suppose I have to recite a poem I know by heart. Before I begin, my expectation is directed to the whole poem, but once I have begun, whatever I have plucked

away from the domain of expectation and tossed behind me to the past becomes the business of my memory, and the vital energy of what I am doing is in tension between the two of them: it strains toward my memory because of the part I have already recited, and to my expectation on account of the part I still have to speak. But my attention is present all the while, for the future is being channeled through it to become the past. As the poem goes on and on, expectation is curtailed and memory prolonged, until expectation is entirely used up, when the whole completed action has passed into memory.

What is true of the poem as a whole is true equally of its individual stanzas and syllables. The same is true of the whole long performance, in which this poem may be a single item. The same thing happens in the entirety of a person's life, of which all his actions are parts; and the same in the entire sweep of human history, the parts of which are individual human lives.

CITY OF GOD (in part)

Book XII

Chapter 1

In the previous book we saw something of the beginning of the two cities, so far as angels are concerned. In the same way, we must now proceed to the creation of men and see the beginning of the cities so far as it concerns the kind of rational creatures who are mortal. First, however, a few remarks about the angels must be made in order to make it as clear as I can how there is no real difficulty or impropriety in speaking of a single society composed of both men and angels; and why, therefore, it is right to say that there are not four cities or societies, namely, two of angels and two of men, but only two, one of them made up of the good—both angels and men—and the other of those who are evil.

There is no reason to doubt that the contrary dispositions which have developed among these good and bad angels are due, not to different natures and origins, for God the Author and Creator of all substances has created them both, but to the dissimilar choices and desires of these angels themselves. Some, remaining faithful to God, the common good of all, have lived in the enjoyment of His eternity, truth, and love, while others, preferring the enjoyment of their own power, as though they were their own good, departed from the higher good and common blessedness for all and turned to goods of their own choosing.

Preferring the pomp of pride to this sublimity of eternity, the craftiness of vanity to the certainty of truth, and the turmoil of dissension to the union of love, they became proud, deceitful, and envious.

St. Augustine, *City of God,* Book VIII, 1–12; Book XII, 1–9; Book XIX, 11–17 from *Fathers of the Church; Writings of Saint Augustine; Saint Augustine: City of God,* translated by Gerald G. Walsh, Daniel J. Honan, and Grace Monahan (Washington, DC: The Catholic University of America Press, 1952, 1954). Reprinted by permission.

Since the happiness of all angels consists in union with God, it follows that their unhappiness must be found in the very contrary, that is, in not adhering to God. To the question: "Why are the good angels happy?" the right answer is: "Because they adhere to God." To the question: "Why are the others unhappy?" the answer is: "Because they do not adhere to God." In fact, there is no other good which can make any rational or intellectual creature happy except God. Not every creature has the potentialities for happiness. Beasts, trees, stones, and such things neither acquire nor have the capacity for this gift. However, every creature which has this capacity receives it, not from itself, since it has been created out of nothing, but from its Creator. To possess Him is to be happy; to lose Him is to be in misery. And, of course, that One whose beatitude depends upon Himself as His own good and not on any other good can never be unhappy since He can never lose Himself.

Thus, there can be no unchangeable good except our one, true, and blessed God. All things which He has made are good because made by Him, but they are subject to change because they were made, not out of Him, but out of nothing. Although they are not supremely good, since God is a greater good than they, these mutable things are, none the less, highly good by reason of their capacity for union with and, therefore, beatitude in the Immutable Good which is so completely their good that, without this good, misery is inevitable.

But it does not follow that other creatures in the universe are better off merely because they are incapable of misery. That would be like saying that other members of the body are better than the eyes because they can never become blind. A sentient nature even in pain is better than a stone that cannot suffer. In the same way, a rational nature even in misery is higher than one which, because it lacks reason or sensation, cannot suffer misery.

This being the case, it is nothing less than a perversion of the nature of the angels if they do not adhere to God. For, remember, their nature is so high in the order of creation that, mutable as it is, it can attain beatitude by adhering to the immutable and supreme Good, which is God, and that, unless it achieves beatitude, this nature fails to satisfy its inmost exigencies, and, finally, that nothing but God can satisfy these needs of the angelic nature.

Now, this perversion, like every imperfection in a nature, harms nature and, therefore, is contrary to the nature. It follows, therefore, that what makes the wicked angels differ from the good ones is not their nature but a perversion or imperfection; and this very blemish is a proof of how highly to be esteemed is the nature itself. Certainly, no blemish in a thing ought to be blamed unless we are praising the thing as a whole, for the whole point of blaming the blemish is that it mars the perfection of something we would like to see praised.

For example, when we say that blindness is a defect of the eyes, we imply that it is the very nature of the eyes to see, and when we say that deafness is a malady of the ears, we are supposing that it is their nature to hear. So, too, when we say that it is a failure in an angel not to attain union with God, we openly proclaim that they were meant by nature to be one with God.

Of course, no one can fully comprehend or properly express the ineffable union of being one with God in His life, in His wisdom, in His joy, and all this without a shadow of death or darkness or disturbance. One thing is certain. The very failure of the bad angels to cling to God—a desertion that damaged their nature like a disease—is itself proof enough that the nature God gave them was good—so good that not to be one with God was for them a disaster.

CHAPTER 2

This explanation just given seemed to me necessary to forestall the objection that the apostate spirits might have received from some principle other than God a nature different from that of the other angels. The malice of this mistake can be more easily and speedily removed the more clearly one grasps what God meant by the words, "I AM WHO AM" (Exod. 3:14), spoken through the medium of an angel at the time when Moses was being sent to the children of Israel.

Since God is supreme being, that is, since He supremely is and, therefore, is immutable, it follows that He gave "being" to all that He created out of nothing; not, however, absolute being. To some things He gave more of being and to others less and, in this way, arranged an order of natures in a hierarchy of being. (This noun, "being," is derived from the verb "to be," just as "wisdom" is from the verb "to be wise." In Latin, *essentia*, "being," is a new word, not used by the ancient writers, recently adopted in order to find an equivalent of the Greek, ⟨*ousía*⟩, of which *essentia* is the exact translation.)

Consequently, no nature—except a non-existent one—can be contrary to the nature which is supreme and which created whatever other natures have being. In other words, nonentity stands in opposition to that which is. Therefore, there is no being opposed to God who is the Supreme Being and Source of all beings without exception.

CHAPTER 3

In Scripture, those who oppose God's rule, not by nature but by sin, are called His enemies. They can do no damage to Him, but only to themselves; their enmity is not a power to harm, but merely an inclination to oppose Him. In any case, God is immutable and completely invulnerable. Hence, the malice by which His so-called enemies oppose God is not a menace to Him, but merely bad for themselves—an evil because what is good in their nature is wounded. It is not their nature, but the wound in their nature, that is opposed to God—as evil is opposed to good.

No one will deny that God is supremely good. Thus, any lack of goodness is opposed to God as evil is opposed to good. At the same time, the nature itself is not less good because the lack of goodness is evil and, therefore, the evil of lacking some goodness is opposed to this good, which is the goodness of the nature. Note that in respect to God the contrast is merely that of evil to good, but in respect to the nature which suffers a lack of something good, the lack is not only evil but also harmful. No evils, of course, can be harmful to God, but only to mutable and corruptible natures—and, even then, the harm done bears witness to the goodness of the natures which suffer, for, unless they were good, they could not suffer the wounds of a lack of goodness.

Just consider the harm done by these wounds—the loss of integrity, of beauty, of health, of virtue, or of any other natural good which can be lost or lessened by sin or sickness. If a nature has nothing of goodness to lose, then there is no harm done by lacking this nothing and, consequently, there is nothing wrong. For, there is no such thing as something wrong that does no harm.

The conclusion is that, although no defect can damage an unchangeable good, no nature can be damaged by a defect unless that nature itself is good—for the simple

St. Matthew, from the Linisfarne Gospels, before A.D. 698. (*The British Library/Superstock*)

reason that a defect exists only where harm is done. To put the matter in another way: a defect can never be found in the highest good, nor ever apart from some kind of good.

Thus, good things without defects can sometimes be found; absolutely bad things, never—for even those natures that were vitiated at the outset by an evil will are only evil in so far as they are defective, while they are good in so far as they are natural. And when a vitiated nature is being punished, in addition to the good of being what it is, it is a good for it not to go unpunished, since this is just and whatever is just is certainly good. No one is punished for natural defects, but only for deliberate faults. And even for a vice to develop, by force of habit and overindulgence, into a strong natural defect, the vice must have begun in the will. But here, of course, I am speaking of the vices of that nature which has a mind illumined by an immaterial light in virtue of which it can distinguish what is just from what is unjust.

CHAPTER 4

Of course, in the case of beasts, trees, and other mutable and mortal creatures which lack not merely an intellect, but even sensation or life itself, it would be ridiculous to condemn in them the defects which destroy their corruptible nature. For, it was by the will of the Creator that they received that measure of being whereby their comings and goings and fleeting existences should contribute to that special, if lowly, loveliness of our earthly seasons which chimes with the harmony of the universe. For, there was never any need for the things of earth either to rival those of heaven or to remain uncreated merely because the latter are better.

It is, in fact, the very law of transitory things that, here on earth where such things are at home, some should be born while others die, the weak should give way to the strong and the victims should nourish the life of the victors. If the beauty of this order fails to delight us, it is because we ourselves, by reason of our mortality, are so enmeshed in this corner of the cosmos that we fail to perceive the beauty of a total pattern in which the particular parts, which seem ugly to us, blend in so harmonious and beautiful a way. That is why, in those situations where it is beyond our power to understand the providence of God, we are rightly commanded to make an act of faith rather than allow the rashness of human vanity to criticize even a minute detail in the masterpiece of our Creator.

Although these defects in the things of earth are involuntary and unpunishable, yet, like voluntary ones, when properly contemplated, they reveal the excellence in the natures themselves, all of which have God for their Author and Creator. For, in both cases, what we dislike is the lack by defect of something which we like in the nature as a whole. Sometimes, of course, natures themselves are displeasing to men because they happen to be harmful. It is a case of regarding only their utility, not the things themselves, as with the plague of frogs and flies which scourged the pride of the Egyptians. But, with such reasoning, fault could be found even with the sun, since criminals and debtors have sometimes been judicially condemned to solar exposure. It is not by our comfort or inconvenience, but by the nature considered in itself, that glory is given to its Creator. So, even the nature of unquenchable fire is, without doubt, worthy of praise, although it is to serve as a punishment for the damned. Is there anything, in fact, more beautiful than a leaping, luminous flame of fire? Or anything more useful, when it warms us, heals us, cooks our food? Yet, nothing is more painful when it burns us. Thus, the same thing applied in one way is harmful, but when properly used is extremely beneficial. It is all but impossible to enumerate all the good uses to which fire is put throughout the world.

We should pay no attention to those who praise fire for its light but condemn its heat—on the principle that a thing should be judged not by its nature, but by our comfort or inconvenience. They like to see it, but hate to be burnt. What they forget is that the same light which they like is injurious and unsuitable for weak eyes, and that the heat which they hate is, for some animals, the proper condition for a healthy life.

CHAPTER 5

All natures, then, are good simply because they exist and, therefore, have each its own measure of being, its own beauty, even, in a way, its own peace. And when each is in the place assigned by the order of nature, it best preserves the full measure of being that was given to it. Beings not made for eternal life, changing for better or for worse according as they promote the good and improvement of things to which, by the law of the Creator, they serve as means, follow the direction of Divine Providence and tend toward the particular end which forms a part of the general plan for governing the universe. This means that the dissolution which brings mutable and mortal things to their death is not so much a process of annihilation as a progress toward something they were designed to become.

The conclusion from all this is that God is never to be blamed for any defects that offend us, but should ever be praised for all the perfection we see in the natures He has made. For God is Absolute Being and, therefore, all other being that is relative was made by Him. No being that was made from nothing could be on a par with God, nor could it even be at all, were it not made by Him.

CHAPTER 6

It follows that the true cause of the good angels' beatitude lies in their union with Absolute Being. And if we seek the cause of the bad angels' misery, we are right in finding it in this, that they abandoned Him whose Being is absolute and turned to themselves whose being is relative—a sin that can have no better name than pride. "For pride is the beginning of all sin" (Eccli. 10:15). They refused to reserve their strength for Him. They might have had more of being if they had adhered to Him whose Being is supreme, but, by preferring themselves to Him, they preferred what was less in the order of being.

Such was the first defect, the first lack, the first perversion of that nature which, being created, could not be absolute, and yet, being created for beatitude, might have rejoiced in Him who is Absolute Being; but which, having turned from Him, was doomed, not to be nothing but to have so much less of being that it was bound to be wretched.

If one seeks for the efficient cause of their evil will, none is to be found. For, what can make the will bad when it is the will itself which makes an action bad? Thus, an evil will is the efficient cause of a bad action, but there is no efficient cause of an evil will. If there is such a cause, it either has or has not a will. If it has, then that will is either good or bad. If good, one would have to be foolish enough to conclude that a good will makes a bad will. In that case, a good will becomes the cause of sin—which is utterly absurd. On the other hand, if the hypothetical cause of a bad will has itself a bad will, I would have to ask what made this will bad, and, to put an end to the inquiry: What made the first bad will bad? Now, the fact is that there was no first bad will that was made bad by any other bad will—it was made bad by itself. For, if it were preceded by a cause that made it evil, that cause came first. But, if I am told that nothing made the will evil but that it always was so, then I ask whether or not it existed in some nature.

If this evil will existed in no nature, then it did not exist at all. If it existed in some nature, then it vitiated, corrupted, injured that nature and, therefore, deprived it of some good. An evil will could not exist in an evil nature but only in a good one, mutable enough to suffer harm from this deprivation. For, if no harm were done, then there was no deprivation and, consequently, no right to call the will evil. But, if harm was done, it was done by destroying or diminishing what was good. Thus, an evil will could not have existed from all eternity in a nature in which a previously existing good had to be eliminated before the evil will could harm the nature. But, if it did not exist from all eternity, who, then, caused this evil will?

The only remaining suggestion is that the cause of the evil will was something which had no will. My next question is whether this "something" was superior, inferior, or equal to the will. If superior, then it was better. So, then, how can it have had no will and not rather a good will? If equal, the case is the same: for, as long as two wills are equally good, one cannot produce an evil will in the other. The supposition remains, then, that it was an inferior thing without a will which produced the evil will of the angelic nature which first sinned.

But that thing itself, whatever it was, even though it was low to the lowest point of earthliness, was, without doubt good since it was a nature and a being having its own character and species in its own genus and order. How, then, can a good thing be the efficient cause of an evil will? How, I ask, can good be the cause of evil? For, when the will, abandoning what is above it, turns itself to something lower, it becomes evil because the very turning itself and not the thing to which it turns is evil. Therefore, an inferior being does not make the will evil but the will itself, because it is a created will, wickedly and inordinately seeks the inferior being.

Take the case of two men whose physical and mental make-up is exactly the same. They are both attracted by the exterior beauty of the same person. While gazing at this loveliness, the will of one man is moved with an illicit desire; the will of the other remains firm in its purity. Why did the will become evil in one case and not in the other? What produced the evil will in the man in whom it began to be evil? The physical beauty of the person could not have been the cause, since that was seen by both in exactly the same way and yet both wills did not become evil. Was the cause the flesh of one of those who looked? Then why not the flesh of the other, also? Or was the cause the mind of one of them? Again, why not the mind of both? For the supposition is that both are equally constituted in mind and body. Must we say, then, that one was tempted by a secret suggestion of the Devil, as if it were not rather by his own will that he consented to this suggestion or enticement or whatever it was?

If so, then what was it in him that was the cause of his consent, of the evil will to follow the evil suggestion? To settle this difficulty, let us suppose that the two men are tempted equally, that one yields and consents to the temptation, that the other remains as he was before. The obvious conclusion is that one was unwilling, the other willing, to fail in chastity. And what else could be the cause of their attitudes but their own wills, since both men have the same constitution and temperament? The beauty which attracted the eyes of both was the same; the secret suggestion by which both were tempted was the same. However carefully they examine the situation, eager to learn what is was that made one of the two evil, no cause is apparent.

For, suppose we say that the man himself made his will evil. Very well, but what was the man himself before he made his will evil? He was a good nature, created by God, the immutable God.

Take a person who says that the one who consents to the temptation and enticement made his own will evil although previously he had been entirely good. Recall the facts. The one consents, while the other does not, to a sinful desire concerning a beautiful person; the beauty was seen by both equally, and before the temptation both men were absolutely alike in mind and body. Now, the person who talks of a man making his own will evil must ask why the man made his will evil, whether because he is a nature or because he is nature made out of nothing? He will learn that the evil arises not from the fact that the man is a nature, but from the fact that the nature was made out of nothing.

For, if a nature is the cause of an evil will, then we are compelled to say that evil springs from good and that good is the cause of evil—since a bad will comes from a good nature. But how can it come about that a good, though mutable, nature, even before its will is evil, can produce something evil, namely, this evil will itself?

CHAPTER 7

No one, therefore, need seek for an efficient cause of an evil will. Since the "effect" is, in fact, a deficiency, the cause should be called "deficient." The fault of an evil will begins when one falls from Supreme Being to some being which is less than absolute. Trying to discover causes of such deficiencies—causes which, as I have said, are not efficient but deficient—is like trying to see darkness or hear silence. True, we have some knowledge of both darkness and silence: of the former only by the eyes; of the latter only by the ears. Nevertheless, we have no sensation but only the privation of sensation.

So there is no point in anyone trying to learn from me what I know I do not know—unless, perhaps, he wants to know how not to know what, as he ought to know, no one can know. For, things we know, not by sensation, but by the absence of sensation, are known—if the word says or means anything—by some kind of "unknowing," so that they are both known and not known at the same time. For example, when the vision of the eye passes from sensation to sensation, it sees darkness only when it begins not to see. So, too, no other sense but the ear can perceive silence, yet silence can only be heard by not being heard.

So, too, it is only the vision of the mind that discerns the species intelligibilis when it understands intelligible realities. But, when the realities are no longer intelligible, the mind, too, knows by "unknowing." For "who can understand sins?" (Ps. 18:13).

CHAPTER 8

This I know, that the nature of God can never and nowhere be deficient in anything, while things made out of nothing can be deficient. In regard to these latter, the more they have of being and the more good things they do or make—for then they are doing or making something positive—the more their causes are efficient; but in so far as they fail or are defective and, in that sense, "do evil"—if a "defect" can be "done"—then their causes are "deficient." I know, further, that when a will "is made" evil, what happens would not have happened if the will had not wanted it to happen. That is why the punishment which follows is just, since the defection was not necessary but voluntary. The will does not fall "into sin"; it falls "sinfully." Defects are not mere relations to natures that are evil; they are evil in themselves because, contrary to the order of natures, there is a defection from Being that is supreme to some lesser being.

Thus, greed is not a defect in the gold that is desired but in the man who loves it perversely by falling from justice which he ought to esteem as incomparably superior to gold; nor is lust a defect in bodies which are beautiful and pleasing: it is a sin in the soul of the one who loves corporal pleasures perversely, that is, by abandoning that temperance which joins us in spiritual and unblemishable union with realities far more beautiful and pleasing; nor is boastfulness a blemish in words of praise: it is a failing in the soul of one who is so perversely in love with other peoples' applause that he despises the voice of his own conscience; nor is pride a vice in the one who delegates power, still less a flaw in the power itself: it is a passion in the soul of the one who loves his own power so perversely as to condemn the authority of one who is still more powerful.

In a word, anyone who loves perversely the good of any nature whatsoever and even, perhaps, acquires this good makes himself bad by gaining something good and sad by losing something better.

CHAPTER 9

There is, then, no natural efficient cause of an evil will or, if I may use the word, no essential cause. The reason for this is that it is the evil will itself that starts that evil in mutable spirits, which is nothing but a weakening and worsening of the good in their nature. What "makes" the will evil is, in reality, an "unmaking," a desertion from God. The very defection is deficient—in the sense of having no cause. However, in saying that there is no efficient cause even of a good will, we must beware of believing that the good will of the good angels was uncreated and co-eternal with God. But, if good angels were created, how can we say that their good will was not created? The fact is, it was created; the only question is whether it was created simultaneously with the creation of the angels or whether they first existed without a good will. If simultaneously, then, undoubtedly, it was created by Him who created the angels, so that, as soon as they were created, they adhered to Him who created them by means of that love with which they were created. Thus, the reason why the bad were separated from the society of good angels was that the good persevered in the same good will, whereas the others changed themselves into bad angels by defection from good will. The only thing that "made" their will bad was that they fell away from a will which was good. Nor would they have fallen away, had they not chosen to fall away.

In the hypothesis, however, that the good angels, existing at first without a good will, produced it in themselves without the help of God, they must have made themselves better than what they were when God created them. This is nonsense. For, without a good will, what could they be but evil? Or, if we may not say evil, since their will was not yet evil—for they could hardly fall away from what they had not yet begun to have—at least, they certainly were not good angels—not as good as they were to become when they came to possess a good will.

So much for the hypothesis. Since they could not make themselves better than God made them—for no one can make anything better than God can—then it follows that, without the co-operation of their Creator, they could never have come into possession of that good will which made them better.

Now, it is true that their good will was not only the cause of their turning and adhering to Him, who is Perfect Being, rather than to themselves, whose being was less than perfect, but also the reason why they had more of being than before and could live wisely and happily in union with God. Nevertheless, this merely shows that any will, however good, would have been destitute and destined to remain in hopeless desire, did not He who had created their good nature out of nothing, and had given it a capacity for union with Himself, first awaken in the will a greater longing for this union and then fill the will with some of His very Being in order to make it better.

This raises another issue. For, if the good angels did something themselves to bring about their good will, did they do this with or without a will? If without, then, of course, they were not the agents. If with a will, was it an evil or a good one? If evil, how could it produce a good will? If good, well, then, they had a good will already. And who made this but God Himself who created them with a good will (that is, with the unblemished love by which they could adhere to Him) and who at the same time created their nature and enriched it with grace?

Thus, we are compelled to believe that the holy angels never existed without a good will, that is, without the love of God. But what of those angels who were created good and became evil by their own bad will for which their good nature is not responsible except in so far as there was a deliberate defection from good—for it is never good, but a defection from good, that is the cause of evil? These angels either received less grace of divine love than those who persevered in grace, or, if both were created equally good, then, while the former were falling by bad will, the latter were increasingly aided to reach that plenitude of beatitude which made them certain that they would never fall—a matter which I discussed in the preceding Book.

Thus with our praise to our Creator, we should all proclaim that, not only of holy men, but also of holy angels, it may be said that "the charity of God is poured forth" in them "by the Holy Spirit who has been given" to them (Rom. 5:5). Nor is it the good only of men, but first and foremost that of angels, which is referred to in the words: "It is good for me to adhere to my God" (Ps. 72:28).

And they who share this common good are in a holy communion both with Him to whom they adhere and one with another, and they form a single community, one City of God, which is also His living sacrifice and His living temple.

This ends the discussion of the origin of this City in so far as it concerns the angels. I must now turn to the rise of that part of the City which is made up of mortal men, created by the same God, who will one day be united to the immortal angels and who, at present, are either sojourning on earth or, if dead, are resting in the hidden sanctuaries where the souls of the departed have their abode.

It was from one man, the first whom God created, that the whole human race took its start. This is the faith revealed in Holy Scripture, a faith that has gained marvelous and merited authority throughout the world and among all peoples—as, along with other truths, Scripture itself divinely predicted would be the case.

BOETHIUS
ca. A.D. 480–ca. A.D. 524

Anicius Manlius Severinus Boethius was the son of a Roman high-government official. Possibly educated in Athens or Alexandria, Boethius had a special interest in the writings of Plato and Aristotle. His intention was to translate all their works into Latin and provide full commentary. He hoped to show the essential unity between Plato and Aristotle, but he finished only Aristotle's logical works. In 510, Boethius became consul and first minister to King Theodoric, the Ostrogothic ruler of Italy. Boethius served the next twelve years in government, wrote commentaries on Porphyry and Cicero, and began his work on Plato and Aristotle. Boethius's sons were named consuls in 522, and Boethius was made the important "master of the offices." But within a year, tragedy struck. Boethius was accused of treason, imprisoned, and executed sometime around 524. The specific charges are not known, but religious differences were probably involved. Theodoric followed the teachings of Arius (ca. A.D. 256–336) that Jesus Christ was neither coeternal with God the Father nor of the same substance. Boethius, as a Catholic, accepted the conclusions of the Council of Nicea (A.D. 325), which condemned Arian theology.

While in prison, Boethius wrote his most famous work, *The Consolation of Philosophy*. Written as a dialogue between Boethius and Lady Philosophy, it begins with Boethius protesting innocence and complaining of God's injustice and fortune's caprice. Using arguments rooted in both Stoic and Platonic thought, Philosophy replies that fortune is indeed fickle, but that the highest Good is found not in circumstances but in God. The selection given here, translated by Richard Green, is from the final book of the *Consolation* and examines how God's foreknowledge is compatible with free will. Boethius asks how one could be free to perform an action if God knew *beforehand* what one would do. Using a conception of time similar to Augustine's in Book XI of the *Confessions,* Lady Philosophy explains that God is completely outside time. This means that God "sees all things in his eternal present as you see some things in your temporal present. . . . This divine foreknowledge does not change the nature and properties of things; it simply sees things present before it as they will later turn out to be in what we regard as the future." For example, just as I know what my son is doing now even though his action is free, so God can know what I will do tomorrow though I act freely—because for God tomorrow *is* now.

It may seem odd that a devout Catholic presented his final thoughts in Neoplatonic and Stoic terms, without any specifically Christian references. Yet Boethius's *magnum opus* was a source of great comfort to Christians in the Middle Ages for, as Étienne Gilson points out, "even when he is speaking only as a philosopher Boethius, thinks as a Christian."

*   *   *

For background work on Boethius, see Howard Rollin Patch, *The Tradition of Boethius: A Study of His Importance in Medieval Culture* (New York: Oxford University Press, 1935) and Helen Marjorie Barrett, *Boethius: Some Aspects of His Times and Work* (Cambridge: Cambridge University Press, 1940). Henry Chadwick, *Boethius: The Consolations of Music, Logic, Theology, and Philosophy* (Oxford: Clarendon Press, 1981) and Edmund Reiss, *Boethius* (Boston: Twayne, 1982) study Boethius's writings, whereas Ralph M. McInerny, *Boethius and Aquinas* (Washington, DC: Catholic University of America Press, 1990) shows his influence on Thomas Aquinas. For collections of essays, see Michael Masi, ed., *Boethius and the Liberal Arts: A Collection of Essays* (Las Vegas, NV: Peter Lang, 1981), and Margaret Gibson, ed., *Boethius, His Life, Thought, and Influence* (Oxford: Blackwell, 1981).

In recent years, there has been renewed interest in the problems posed by Boethius's conception of God's timelessness and foreknowledge. Paul Helm, *Eternal God: A Study of God Without Time* (Oxford: Clarendon Press, 1988), for example, argues in favor of Boethius's position, whereas Richard Swinburne, *The Coherence of Theism* (Oxford: Clarendon Press, 1977) and Stephen T. Davis, *Logic and the Nature of God* (Grand Rapids, MI: Eerdmans, 1983) oppose it. Much of the most interesting work in this area is found only in journals such as the *Journal of Philosophy* and *Faith and Philosophy.*

Theodoric exiles Boethius from Rome to Padua, 1521, woodcut. Boethius was consul and first minister to King Theodoric, the Ostrogothic ruler of Italy. But in 522 Boethius was accused of treason, imprisoned, and executed sometime around 524. The specific charges are not known, but probably involved religious differences between the Catholic Boethius and the Arian Theodoric. *(Library of Congress/Instructional Resources Corp.)*

THE CONSOLATION OF PHILOSOPHY
(in part)

BOOK V

CHAPTER 6: PHILOSOPHY SOLVES THE PROBLEM OF PROVIDENCE AND FREE WILL BY DISTINGUISHING BETWEEN SIMPLE AND CONDITIONAL NECESSITY

"Since, as we have shown, whatever is known is known according to the nature of the knower, and not according to its own nature, let us now consider as far as is lawful the nature of the Divine Being, so that we may discover what its knowledge is. The common judgment of all rational creatures holds that God is eternal. Therefore let us consider what eternity is, for this will reveal both the divine nature and the divine knowledge.

"Eternity is the whole, perfect, and simultaneous possession of endless life. The meaning of this can be made clearer by comparison with temporal things. For whatever

Boethius, *The Consolation of Philosophy,* Book V, Chapters (prose) 2, 3, 6, translated by Richard Green (New York: Macmillan/Library of the Liberal Arts, 1962).

lives in time lives in the present, proceeding from past to future, and nothing is so constituted in time that it can embrace the whole span of its life at once. It has not yet arrived at tomorrow, and it has already lost yesterday; even the life of this day is lived only in each moving, passing moment. Therefore, whatever is subject to the condition of time, even that which—as Aristotle conceived the world to be—has no beginning and will have no end in a life coextensive with the infinity of time, is such that it cannot rightly be thought eternal. For it does not comprehend and include the whole of infinite life all at once, since it does not embrace the future which is yet to come. Therefore, only that which comprehends and possesses the whole plenitude of endless life together, from which no future thing nor any past thing is absent, can justly be called eternal. Moreover, it is necessary that such a being be in full possession of itself, always present to itself, and hold the infinity of moving time present before itself.

"Therefore, they are wrong who, having heard that Plato held that this world did not have a beginning in time and would never come to an end, suppose that the created world is coeternal with its Creator. For it is one thing to live an endless life, which is what Plato ascribed to the world, and another for the whole of unending life to be embraced all at once as present, which is clearly proper to the divine mind. Nor should God be thought of as older than His creation in extent of time, but rather as prior to it by virtue of the simplicity of His nature. For the infinite motion of temporal things imitates the immediate present of His changeless life and, since it cannot reproduce or equal life, it sinks from immobility to motion and declines from the simplicity of the present into the infinite duration of future and past. And, since it cannot possess the whole fullness of its life at once, it seems to imitate to some extent that which it cannot completely express, and it does this by somehow never ceasing to be. It binds itself to a kind of present in this short and transitory period which, because it has a certain likeness to that abiding, unchanging present, gives everything it touches a semblance of existence. But, since this imitation cannot remain still, it hastens along the infinite road of time, and so it extends by movement the life whose completeness it could not achieve by standing still. Therefore, if we wish to call things by their proper names, we should follow Plato in saying that God indeed is eternal, but the world is perpetual.

"Since, then, every judgment comprehends the subjects presented to it according to its own nature, and since God lives in the eternal present, His knowledge transcends all movement of time and abides in the simplicity of its immediate present. It encompasses the infinite sweep of past and future, and regards all things in its simple comprehension as if they were now taking place. Thus, if you will think about the foreknowledge by which God distinguishes all things, you will rightly consider it to be not a foreknowledge of future events, but knowledge of a never changing present. For this reason, divine knowledge is called providence, rather than prevision, because it resides above all inferior things and looks out on all things from their summit.

"Why then do you imagine that things are necessary which are illuminated by this divine light, since even men do not impose necessity on the things they see? Does your vision impose any necessity upon things which you see present before you?"

"Not at all," I answered.

"Then," Philosophy went on, "if we may aptly compare God's present vision with man's, He sees all things in his eternal present as you see some things in your temporal present. Therefore, this divine foreknowledge does not change the nature and properties of things; it simply sees things present before it as they will later turn out to be in what we regard as the future. His judgment is not confused; with a single intuition of his mind He knows all things that are to come, whether necessarily or not. Just as, when you happen to see simultaneously a man walking on the street and the sun shining in the sky, even though you see both at once, you can distinguish between them and realize that one action is voluntary, the other necessary; so the divine mind, looking down on all things, does not disturb the nature of the things which are present before it but are future with respect to time. Therefore, when God knows that something will happen in the future, and at the same time knows that it will not happen through necessity, this is not opinion but knowledge based on truth.

"If you should reply that whatever God foresees as happening cannot help but happen, and that whatever must happen is bound by necessity—if you pin me down to this word 'necessity'—I grant that you state a solid truth, but one which only a profound theologian can grasp. I would answer that the same future event is necessary with respect to God's knowledge of it, but free and undetermined if considered in its own nature. For there are two kinds of necessity: one is simple, as the necessity by which all men are mortals; the other is conditional, as is the case when, if you know that someone is walking, he must necessarily be walking. For whatever is known, must be as it is known to be; but this condition does not involve that other, simple necessity. It is not caused by the peculiar nature of the person in question, but by an added condition. No necessity forces the man who is voluntarily walking to move forward; but as long as he is walking, he is necessarily moving forward. In the same way, if Providence sees anything as present, that thing must necessarily be, even though it may have no necessity by its nature. But God sees as present those future things which result from free will. Therefore, from the standpoint of divine knowledge these things are necessary because of the condition of their being known by God; but, considered only in themselves, they lose nothing of the absolute freedom of their own natures.

"There is no doubt, then, that all things will happen which God knows will happen; but some of them happen as a result of free will. And, although they happen, they do not, by their existence, lose their proper natures by which, before they happened, they were able not to happen. But, you may ask, what does it mean to say that these events are not necessary, since by reason of the condition of divine knowledge they happen just as if they were necessary? The meaning is the same as in the example I used a while ago of the sun rising and the man walking. At the time they are happening, they must necessarily be happening; but the sun's rising is governed by necessity even before it happens, while the man's walking is not. Similarly, all the things God sees as present will undoubtedly come to pass; but some will happen by the necessity of their natures, others by the power of those who make them happen. Therefore, we quite properly said that these things are necessary if viewed from the standpoint of divine knowledge, but if they are considered in themselves, they are free of the bonds of necessity. In somewhat the same way, whatever is known by the senses is singular in itself, but universal as far as the reason is concerned.

"But, you may say, if I can change my mind about doing something, I can frustrate Providence, since by chance I may change something which Providence foresaw. My answer is this: you can indeed alter what you propose to do, but, because the present truth of Providence sees that you can, and whether or not you will, you cannot frustrate the divine knowledge any more than you can escape the eye of someone who is present and watching you, even though you may, by your free will, vary your actions. You may still wonder, however, whether God's knowledge is changed by your decisions, so that when you wish now one thing, now another, the divine knowledge undergoes corresponding changes. This is not the case. For divine Providence anticipates every future action and converts it to its own present knowledge. It does not change, as you imagine, foreknowing this or that in succession, but in a single instant, without being changed itself, anticipates and grasps your changes.

God has this present comprehension and immediate vision of all things not from the outcome of future events, but from the simplicity of his own nature. In this way, the problem you raised a moment ago is settled. You observed that it would be unworthy of God if our future acts were said to be the cause of divine knowledge. Now you see that this power of divine knowledge, comprehending all things as present before it, itself constitutes the measure of all things and is in no way dependent on things that happen later.

"Since this is true, the freedom of the human will remains inviolate, and laws are just since they provide rewards and punishments to human wills which are not controlled by necessity. God looks down from above, knowing all things, and the eternal present of his vision concurs with the future character of our actions, distributing rewards to the good and punishments to the evil. Our hopes and prayers are not directed to God in vain, for if they are just they cannot fail. Therefore, stand firm against vice and cultivate virtue. Lift up your soul to worthy hopes, and offer humble prayers to heaven. If you will face it, the necessity of virtuous action imposed upon you is very great, since all your actions are done in the sight of a Judge who sees all things."

ANSELM (AND GAUNILO)
1033–1109

Saint Anselm was born to a noble family in Aosta, in what is now Italy. Following a youth of travel and learning, Anselm joined the Benedictine monastery in the town of Bec, Normandy (in modern France). He remained in this monastery for the next thirty-three years, the last fifteen as abbot. During this time, he wrote a number of books on theological and philosophical topics. In 1093, Anselm was coerced into leaving the monastery to become Archbishop of Canterbury. Most of his sixteen years in Canterbury were spent skirmishing with the king of England for control of the church (a pattern that continued for five centuries until Henry VIII severed the English church from Rome entirely in 1534). Anselm died in 1109 and was canonized in 1494.

Anselm's thought can be summed up in the Augustinian phrase, "faith seeking understanding." Anselm was a deeply devoted Christian who began his thinking with the assumption that the doctrines of Christianity are true. And this faith drove him to seek understanding, to find rational explanations for the Christian teachings he already believed. His writings reflected this yearning to understand rationally particular problems in faith; he wrote a number of short treatises on such subjects as the Incarnation and the Trinity. He believed that he could demonstrate the truth of these revealed doctrines.

Anselm's most famous work is his attempt to prove the existence of God in Chapters II to IV of the *Proslogion* (or *Discourse*) known now as the "ontological argument" (from Immanuel Kant's description). The ontological argument attempts to show that if one can conceive of "something-than-which-nothing-greater-can-be-thought," one must also acknowledge that this being exists in reality as well as in the understanding. That is, if God is thought of, then God must exist. Recent scholars have pointed out that there are actually two arguments here: one, in Chapter II, that proves that God exists in reality; and another, in Chapters III to IV, that proves that God's existence is necessary.

Anselm's argument was immediately attacked by a fellow monk named Gaunilo. Anselm's exchange with Gaunilo has been preserved and the key sections are reprinted here, along with the *Proslogion*, Chapters II to IV, in the M.J. Charlesworth translation.

Despite the fact that this argument has fascinated thinkers for over nine hundred years, a student's first response to this passage is often one of confusion or simple denial: "He can't do that!" The student is not alone in being confused; the history of the argument is full of misrepresentations and misinterpretations. To be sure, careful thinkers such as Hume and Kant have attacked this argument. But it is notoriously difficult to say exactly what is wrong with Anselm's logic, and many purported refutations have actually been refutations of arguments quite different from Anselm's.

In recent years, there has been renewed interest in the argument, with Charles Hartshorne, Norman Malcom, and Alvin Plantinga claiming that it is successful. There has also been a tradition, beginning with the medieval thinker Bonaventure and continuing through Karl Barth in this century, that claims the *Proslogion*, Chapters II to IV, is not a philosophical argument at all. These theologians are convinced that Anselm is not "proving" anything, that he is simply showing the implications of God's self-revelation.

While the debate continues to rage, one fact is clear: Anselm raised some of the most basic questions in the history of philosophy. Questions about modes of existence, possible beings, necessity and contingency, as well as a range of issues in logic, all emerge in discussions of this provocative passage.

*   *   *

For a study of the complete *Proslogion*, see M.J. Charlesworth, *St. Anselm's Proslogion* (Oxford: Clarendon Press, 1965). For the rest of Anselm's major works see, Anselm, *Basic Writings*, translated by S.N. Deane (1902; reprinted LaSalle, IL: Open Court, 1962). For a study of Anselm's life and times, see R.W. Southern's books *Saint Anselm and His Biographer* (Cambridge: Cambridge University Press, 1963) and *Saint Anselm: A Portrait in a Landscape* (Cambridge: Cambridge University Press, 1990). Jasper Hopkins, *A Companion to the Study of St. Anselm* (Minneapolis: University of Minnesota Press, 1972), provides a comprehensive discussion of Anselm and his work.

For further reading on the ontological argument, the best source is John Hick and Arthur C. McGill, eds., *The Many-Faced Argument* (New York: Macmillan, 1967). Charles Hartshorne, *Anselm's Discovery: A Re-Examination of the Ontological Argument for God's Existence* (LaSalle, IL: Open Court, 1965); Alvin Plantinga, *The Nature of Necessity* (Oxford: Clarendon Press, 1974)—and his "simplified" version of this difficult work, Alvin Plantinga, *God, Freedom, and Evil* (Grand Rapids, MI: Eerdmans, 1977); and Richard Campbell, *From Belief to Understanding* (Canberra: Australian National University Press, 1976), all defend the argument. For theological interpretations, see Karl Barth, *Anselm: Fides Quaren Intellectum,* translated by Ian W. Robinson (London: SCM Press, 1960) (Key chapters from this work are included in Hick and McGill's *The Many-Faced Argument.*)

PROSLOGION (in part)

CHAPTER 2: THAT GOD TRULY EXISTS

Well then, Lord, You who give understanding to faith, grant me that I may understand, as much as You see fit, that You exist as we believe You to exist, and that You are what we believe You to be. Now we believe that You are something than which nothing greater can be thought. Or can it be that a thing of such a nature does not exist, since "the Fool has said in his heart, there is no God" (Ps. xiii. 1, lii. 1)? But surely, when this same Fool hears what I am speaking about, namely, "something-than-which-nothing-greater-can-be-thought," he understands what he hears, and what he understands is in his mind, even if he does not understand that it actually exists. For it is one thing for an object to exist in the mind, and another thing to understand that an object actually exists. Thus, when a painter plans beforehand what he is going to execute, he has [the picture] in his mind, but he does not yet think that it actually exists because he has not yet executed it. However, when he has actually painted it, then he both has it in his mind and understands that it exists because he has now made it. Even the Fool, then, is forced to agree that something-than-which-nothing-greater-can-be-thought exists in the mind, since he understands this when he hears it, and whatever is understood is in the mind. And surely that-than-which-a-greater-cannot-be-thought cannot exist in the mind alone. For if it exists solely in the mind even, it can be thought to exist in reality also, which is greater. If then that-than-which-a-greater-cannot-be-thought exists in the mind alone, this same that-than-which-a-greater-*cannot*-be-thought is that-than-which-a-greater-*can*-be-thought. But this is obviously impossible. Therefore there is absolutely no doubt that something-than-which-a-greater-cannot-be-thought exists both in the mind and in reality.

CHAPTER 3: THAT GOD CANNOT BE THOUGHT NOT TO EXIST

And certainly this being so truly exists that it cannot be even thought not to exist. For something can be thought to exist that cannot be thought not to exist, and this is greater than that which can be thought not to exist. Hence, if that-than-which-a-greater-cannot-be-thought can be thought not to exist, then that-than-which-a-greater-cannot-be-thought is not the same as that-than-which-a-greater-cannot-be-thought, which is absurd. Something-than-which-a-greater-cannot-be-thought exists so truly then, that it cannot be even thought not to exist. And You, Lord our God, are this being. You exist so truly, Lord my God, that You cannot even be thought not to exist. And this is as it should be, for if some intelligence could think of something better than You, the creature would be above its creator and would judge its creator—and that is completely absurd. In fact, everything else there is, except You alone, can be thought of as not existing. You alone, then, of all things most truly exist and therefore of all things possess existence to the highest degree; for anything else does not exist as truly, and so possesses existence to a lesser degree. Why then did "the Fool say in his heart, there is no

From M.J. Charlesworth, *St. Anselm's Proslogion* (Oxford: Oxford University Press, 1965). Reprinted by permission of Oxford University Press.

God" (Ps. xiii. 1, lii. 1) when it is so evident to any rational mind that You of all things exist to the highest degree? Why indeed, unless because he was stupid and a fool?

CHAPTER 4: HOW "THE FOOL SAID IN HIS HEART" WHAT CANNOT BE THOUGHT

How indeed has he "said in his heart" what he could not think; or how could he not think what he "said in his heart," since to "say in one's heart" and to "think" are the same? But if he really (indeed, since he really) both thought because he "said in his heart" and did not "say in his heart" because he could not think, there is not only one sense in which something is "said in one's heart" or thought. For in one sense a thing is thought when the word signifying it is thought; in another sense when the very object which the thing is is understood. In the first sense, then, God can be thought not to exist, but not at all in the second sense.* No one, indeed, understanding what God is can think that God does not exist, even though he may say these words in his heart either without any [objective] signification or with some peculiar signification. For God is that-than-which-nothing-greater-can-be-thought. Whoever really understands this understands clearly that this same being so exists that not even in thought can it not exist. Thus whoever understands that God exists in such a way cannot think of Him as not existing.

I give thanks, good Lord, I give thanks to You, since what I believed before through Your free gift I now so understand through Your illumination, that if I did not want to *believe* that You existed, I should nevertheless be unable not to *understand* it.

GAUNILO AND ANSELM: DEBATE**

GAUNILO

[5.] That, however, [this nature] necessarily exists in reality is demonstrated to me from the fact that, unless it existed, whatever exists in reality would be greater than it and consequently it would not be that which is greater than everything that undoubtedly had already been proved to exist in the mind. To this I reply as follows: if something that cannot even be thought in the true and real sense must be said to exist in the mind, then I do not deny that this also exists in my mind in the same way. But since from this one cannot in any way conclude that it exists also in reality, I certainly do not yet concede that it actually exists, until this is proved to me by an indubitable argu-

---

*[Later manuscripts insert the following: "For no one who understands what fire and water are can think that the reality of fire is the reality of water. At the level of words, however, this confusion is possible."
**[I have followed the procedure of John Hick, *Classical and Contemporary Readings in the Philosophy of Religion* (Englewood Cliffs, NJ: Prentice Hall, 1964) and put the main points of Gaunilo's critique together with Anselm's replies. The numbers before each section refer to the paragraph numbers of Gaunilo's *A Reply to the Foregoing by a Certain Writer on Behalf of the Fool* (in Arabic numbers) and Anselm's *Reply to the Foregoing by the Author of the Book in Question* (in Roman numerals).]

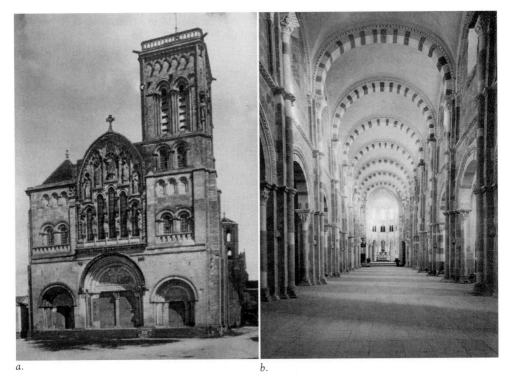

a.   b.

The Romanesque Cathedral
a. Exterior view of the Abbey Church of the Madeleine, Vezelay, France, built in the
twelfth century. This church typifies the Romanesque style that flourished from about
1000 to 1200. The rounded arches above the portals are reminiscent of the arches of
Roman construction. The thickness of the stone walls, together with the relatively simple
facade, gives the structure the impression of solidity and solemnity. *(French Government
Tourist Office)*
b. The nave. The rounded interior arches distribute the weight of the roof outward as well
as downward, necessitating thick stone walls. As a result, only a few small windows are
possible in a Romanesque church—adding to the fortress-like feel of the architecture.
(Caisse Nationale des Monuments Historique)

ment. For he who claims that it actually exists because otherwise it would not be that
which is greater than everything does not consider carefully enough whom he is addressing. For I certainly do not yet admit this greater [than everything] to be any truly
existing thing; indeed I doubt or even deny it. And I do not concede that it exists in a
different way from that—if one ought to speak of "existence" here—when the mind
tries to imagine a completely unknown thing on the basis of the spoken words alone.
How then can it be proved to me on that basis that that which is greater than everything
truly exists in reality (because it is evident that it is greater than all others) if I keep on
denying and also doubting that this is evident and do not admit that this greater [than
everything] is either in my mind or thought, not even in the sense in which many
doubtfully real and unreal things are? It must first of all be proved to me then that this

same greater than everything truly exists in reality somewhere, and then only will the fact that it is greater than everything make it clear that it also subsists in itself.

ANSELM

[II.] I said further that if a thing exists even in the mind alone, it can be thought to exist also in reality, which is greater. If, then, it (namely, "that-than-which-a-greater-cannot-be-thought") exists in the mind alone, it is something than which a greater can be thought. What, I ask you, could be more logical? For if it exists even in the mind alone, cannot it be thought to exist also in reality? And if it can [be so thought], is it not the case that he who thinks this thinks of something greater than it, if it exists in the mind alone? What, then, could follow more logically than that, if "that-than-which-a-greater-*cannot*-be-thought" exists in the mind alone, it is the same as that-than-which-a-greater-*can*-be-thought? But surely "that-than-which-a-greater-*can*-be-thought" is not for any mind [the same as] "that-than-which-a-greater-*cannot*-be-thought." Does it not follow, then, that "that-than-which-a-greater-*cannot*-be-thought," if it exists in anyone's mind, does not exist in the mind alone? For if it exists in the mind alone, it is that-than-which-a-greater-*can*-be-thought, which is absurd.

* * *

[IX.] It is evident, moreover, that in the same way one can think of and understand that which cannot not exist. And one who thinks of this thinks of something greater than one who thinks of what can not exist. When, therefore, one thinks of that-than-which-a-greater-cannot-be-thought, if one thinks of what can not exist, one does not think of that-than-which-a-greater-cannot-be-thought. Now the same thing cannot at the same time be thought of and not thought of. For this reason he who thinks of that-than-which-a-greater-cannot-be-thought does not think of something that can not exist but something that cannot not exist. Therefore what he thinks of exists necessarily, since whatever can not exist is not what he thinks of.

GAUNILO

[6.] They say that there is in the ocean somewhere an island which, because of the difficulty (or rather the impossibility) of finding that which does not exist, some have called the "Lost Island." And the story goes that it is blessed with all manner of priceless riches and delights in abundance, much more even than the Happy Isles, and, having no owner or inhabitant, it is superior everywhere in abundance of riches to all those other lands that men inhabit. Now, if anyone tells me that it is like this, I shall easily understand what is said, since nothing is difficult about it. But if he should then go on to say, as though it were a logical consequence of this: You cannot any more doubt that this island that is more excellent than all other lands truly exists somewhere in reality than you can doubt that it is in your mind; and since it is more excellent to exist not only in the mind alone but also in reality, therefore it must needs be that it exists. For if it did not exist, any other land existing in reality would be more excellent than it, and so this island, already conceived by you to be more excellent than others, will not be more excellent. If, I say, someone wishes thus to persuade me that this island really exists beyond all doubt, I should either think that he was joking, or I should find it hard to decide which of us I ought to judge the bigger fool—I, if I agreed with him, or he, if he thought that he had proved the existence of this island with any certainty, unless he had first convinced me that its very excellence exists in my mind precisely as a thing existing truly and indubitably and not just as something unreal or doubtfully real.

ANSELM

[III.] You claim, however, that this is as though someone asserted that it cannot be doubted that a certain island in the ocean (which is more fertile than all other lands and which, because of the difficulty or even the impossibility of discovering what does not exist, is called the "Lost Island") truly exists in reality since anyone easily understands it when it is described in words. Now, I truly promise that if anyone should discover for me something existing either in reality or in the mind alone—except "that-than-which-a-greater-cannot-be-thought"—to which the logic of my argument would apply, then I shall find that Lost Island and give it, never more to be lost, to that person.

GAUNILO

[7.] If then someone should assert [to the Fool in *Proslogion* III] that this greater [than everything] is such that it cannot be thought not to exist (again without any other proof than that otherwise it would not be greater than everything), then he could make this same reply and say: When have I said that there truly existed some being that is "greater than everything," such that from this it could be proved to me that this same being really existed to such a degree that it could not be thought not to exist? That is why it must first be conclusively proved by argument that there is some higher nature, namely that which is greater and better than all the things that are, so that from this we can also infer everything else which necessarily cannot be wanting to what is greater and better than everything.

ANSELM

[III.] It has already been clearly seen, however, that "that-than-which-a-greater-cannot-be-thought" cannot be thought not to exist, because it exists as a matter of such certain truth. Otherwise it would not exist at all. In short, if anyone says that he thinks that this being does not exist, I reply that, when he thinks of this, either he thinks of something than which a greater cannot be thought, or he does not think of it. If he does not think of it, then he does not think that what he does not think of does not exist. If, however, he does think of it, then indeed he thinks of something which cannot be even thought not to exist. For if it could be thought not to exist, it could be thought to have a begin-ning and an end—but this cannot be. Thus, he who thinks of it thinks of something that cannot be thought not to exist; indeed, he who thinks of this does not think of it as not existing, otherwise he would think what cannot be thought. Therefore "that-than-which-a-greater-cannot-be-thought" cannot be thought not to exist.

GAUNILO

[7.] When, however, it is said that this supreme being cannot be *thought* not to exist, it would perhaps be better to say that it cannot be *understood* not to exist nor even to be able not to exist. For, strictly speaking, unreal things cannot be *understood,* though certainly they can be *thought* of in the same way as the Fool *thought* that God does not exist. I know with complete certainty that I exist, but I also know at the same time nevertheless that I can not-exist. And I *understand* without any doubt that that which exists to the highest degree, namely God, both exists and cannot not exist. I do not know, however, whether I can think of myself as not existing while I know with absolute certainty that I do exist; but if I can, why cannot [I do the same] with regard to anything else I know with the same certainty? If however I cannot, this will not be the distinguishing characteristic of God [namely, to be such that He cannot be thought not to exist].

ANSELM

[IV.] You say, moreover, that when it is said that this supreme reality cannot be *thought* not to exist, it would perhaps be better to say that it cannot be *understood* not to exist or even to be able not to exist. However, it must rather be said that it cannot be *thought.* For if I had said that the thing in question could not be *understood* not to exist, perhaps you yourself (who claim that we cannot understand—if this word is to be taken strictly—things that are unreal) would object that nothing that exists can be understood not to exist. For it is false [to say that] what exists does not exist, so that it is not the distinguishing characteristic of God not to be able to be understood not to exist. But, if any of those things which exist with absolute certainty can be understood not to exist, in the same way other things that certainly exist can be understood not to exist. But, if the matter is carefully considered, this objection cannot be made apropos [the term] "thought." For even if none of those things that exist can be *understood* not to exist, all however can be *thought* as not existing, save that which exists to a supreme degree. For in fact all those things (and they alone) that have a beginning or end or are made up of parts and, as I have already said, all those things that do not exist as a whole in a particular place or at a particular time can be thought as not existing. Only that being in which there is neither beginning nor end nor conjunction of parts, and that thought does not discern save as a whole in every place and at every time, cannot be thought as not existing.

Know then that you can think of yourself as not existing while yet you are absolutely sure that you exist. I am astonished that you have said that you do not know this. For we think of many things that we know to exist, as not existing; and [we think of] many things that we know not to exist, as existing—not judging that it is really as we think but imagining it to be so. We *can,* in fact, think of something as not existing while knowing that it does exist, since we can [think of] the one and know the other at the same time. And we *cannot* think of something as not existing if yet we know that it does exist, since we cannot think of it as existing and not existing at the same time. He, therefore, who distinguishes these two senses of this assertion will understand that [in one sense] nothing can be thought as not existing while yet it is known to exist, and that [in another sense] whatever exists, save that-than-which-a-greater-cannot-be-thought, can be thought of as not existing even when we know that it does exist. Thus it is that, on the one hand, it is the distinguishing characteristic of God that He cannot be thought of as not existing [in the one sense], and that, on the other hand, many things, the while they do exist, cannot be thought of as not existing [in the other sense]. In what sense, however, one can say that God can be thought of as not existing I think I have adequately explained in my tract.

MOSES MAIMONIDES
1135–1204

Moses ben Maimon, or Maimonides (referred to by Jewish scholars as "Rambam" for "Rabbi Moses ben Maimon"), was born at 1:00 P.M. on March 30, 1135, and died on December 13, 1204. The fact that we have such precise dates indicates the esteem with which he was held in his lifetime. As a boy in Córdoba, Spain, he was taught the Torah and the Talmud by his father, along with philosophy and science. At age thirteen, Maimonides and his family were forced to flee Spain after a time of peaceful coexistence between Jews and Muslims came to an end. Following a period of travel, which included a stay in Palestine, Maimonides and his family settled in Cairo, Egypt. There, Maimonides and his brother David became jewel merchants. Within a few years, Maimonides lost both his father and David, the latter killed in a shipwreck in the Indian Ocean during a business trip. Maimonides gave up the jewel business and turned to medicine. His expertise as a doctor eventually led to his appointment as a court physician for the ruler Saladin (the same Saladin who defeated Richard the Lionhearted in the Third Crusade). Maimonides' spiritual insights led to his being named the head of the Egyptian Jewish community. While serving both his religion and the state, he still found time to write extensively. His death in 1204 was mourned by Jews throughout the Mediterranean region, and his remains were taken from Cairo to Tiberias, on the Sea of Galilee, where his tomb is still visited today.

Maimonides' philosophical fame rests squarely on his major work, *The Guide for the Perplexed*. This work was written not for the majority of believers, but for those who knew both Jewish Law and Greek philosophy and were perplexed on how to harmonize the two. Though his religion was different, Maimonides faced questions similar to those of his neighboring Muslims and Christians: how to reconcile faith and reason. In the *Guide,* Maimonides asserts that there can be no conflict between faith and reason. Using Aristotle's philosophy (with some Neoplatonic spin), Maimonides believed he could answer a number of philosophical questions about the nature of God and of God's creation in a way that was consistent with sacred writings. Apparent disagreements between philosophy and theology frequently resulted from either taking figurative passages in Scripture literally or misunderstanding difficult philosophical arguments. Occasionally, philosophy is simply incapable of answering a given question and one must accept "the authority of Prophecy, which can teach things beyond the reach of human speculation." But even in such cases, philosophy can still provide general reasons for believing Scripture. For example, philosophy is inconclusive in determining whether or not the world is eternal. But whichever position we assume, says Maimonides, we can use that assumption to prove that God exists (when using arguments that Maimonides collected).

The selections from the *Guide* given here, in the M. Friedländer translation, present Maimonides' argument for God's existence. This passage greatly influenced Thomas Aquinas, and echoes of Maimonides' thought can be heard throughout Thomas's writings.

*   *   *

For selections from Maimonides' writings, see Jacob Samuel Minkin, *The World of Moses Maimonides,* with Selections From His Writings (New York: T. Yoseloff, 1957), and Moses Maimonides, *Rambam: Readings in the Philosophy of Moses Maimonides,* translated by Lenn Evan Goodman (New York: Viking Press, 1976).

Among the many general introductions to Maimonides' life and thought, more recent helpful studies include Abraham Joshua Heschel, *Maimonides: A Biography*, translated by Joachim Neugroschel (New York: Farrar, Straus & Giroux, 1982), and Oliver Leaman, *Moses Maimonides* (London: Routledge, 1990). For more specialized studies, see Carol Klein, *The Credo of Maimonides: A Synthesis* (New York: Philosophical Library, 1958); Jehuda Melber, *The Universality of Maimonides* (New York: Jonathan David, 1968); Menachem Marc Kellner, *Dogma in Medieval Jewish Thought: From Maimonides to Abravanel* (Oxford: Oxford University Press, 1986); Raymond L. Weiss, *Maimonides' Ethics* (Chicago: University of Chicago Press, 1991); and Howard Kreisel, *Maimonides' Political* Thought (Albany, NY: SUNY Press, 1999). For collections of essays, see Salo Whittmay Baron, ed., *Essays on Maimonides: An Octocennial Volume* (New York: Columbia University Press, 1941); Joseph A. Buijs, ed., Maimonides: *A Collection of Critical Essays* (Notre Dame, IN: University of Notre Dame Press, 1988); and Eric L. Ormsby, ed., *Moses Maimonides and His Time* (Washington, DC: Catholic University of America Press, 1989).

THE GUIDE FOR THE PERPLEXED
(in part)

PART II

INTRODUCTION

Twenty-five of the propositions which are employed in the proof for the existence of God, or in the arguments demonstrating that God is neither corporeal nor a force connected with a material being, or that He is One, have been fully established, and their correctness is beyond doubt. Aristotle and the Peripatetics who followed him have proved each of these propositions. There is, however, one proposition which we do not accept—namely, the proposition which affirms the Eternity of the Universe, but we will admit it for the present, because by doing so we shall be enabled clearly to demonstrate our own theory.

PROPOSITION I: The existence of an infinite magnitude is impossible.

PROPOSITION II: The co-existence of an infinite number of finite magnitudes is impossible.

PROPOSITION III: The existence of an infinite number of causes and effects is impossible, even if these were not magnitudes; if, e.g., one Intelligence were the cause of a second, the second the cause of a third, the third the cause of a fourth, and so on, the series could not be continued ad infinitum.

PROPOSITION IV: Four categories are subject to change:—
　　(a.) *Substance*.—Changes which affect the substance of a thing are called genesis and destruction.
　　(b.) *Quantity*.—Changes in reference to quantity are increase and decrease.
　　(c.) *Quality*.—Changes in the qualities of things are transformations.
　　(d.) *Place*.—Change of place is called motion.

The term "motion" is properly applied to change of place, but is also used in a general sense of all kinds of changes.

PROPOSITION V: Motion implies change and transition from potentiality to actuality.

PROPOSITION VI: The motion of a thing is either essential or accidental; or it is due to an external force, or to the participation of the thing in the motion of another thing. This latter kind of motion is similar to the accidental one. An instance of essential motion may be found in the translation of a thing from one place to another. The accident of a thing, as, e.g., its black color, is said to move when the thing itself changes its place. The upward motion of a stone, owing to a force applied to it in that direction, is an instance of a motion due to an external force. The motion of a nail in a boat may serve to illustrate motion due to the participation of a thing in the motion of another thing; for when the boat moves, the nail is said to move likewise. The same is the case with everything composed of several parts: when the thing itself moves, every part of it is likewise said to move.

PROPOSITION VII: Things which are changeable are, at the same time, divisible. Hence everything that moves is divisible, and consequently corporeal; but that which is indivisible cannot move, and cannot therefore be corporeal.

PROPOSITION VIII: A thing that moves accidentally must come to rest, because it does not move of its own accord; hence accidental motion cannot continue for ever.

PROPOSITION IX: A corporeal thing that sets another corporeal thing in motion can only effect this by setting itself in motion at the time it causes the other thing to move.

PROPOSITION X: A thing which is said to be contained in a corporeal object must satisfy either of the two following conditions: it either exists through that object, as is the case with accidents, or it is the cause of the existence of that object; such is, e.g., its essential property. In both cases it is a force existing in a corporeal object.

PROPOSITION XI: Among the things which exist through a material object, there are some which participate in the division of that object, and are therefore accidentally divisible, as, e.g., its color, and all other qualities that spread throughout its parts. On the other hand, among the things which form the essential elements of an object, there are some which cannot be divided in any way, as, e.g., the soul and the intellect.

PROPOSITION XII: A force which occupies all parts of a corporeal object is finite, that object itself being finite.

PROPOSITION XIII: None of the several kinds of change can be continuous, except motion from place to place, provided it be circular.

PROPOSITION XIV: Locomotion is in the natural order of the several kinds of motion the first and foremost. For genesis and corruption are preceded by transformation, which, in its turn, is preceded by the approach of the transforming agent to the object which is to be transformed. Also, increase and decrease are impossible without previous genesis and corruption.

PROPOSITION XV: Time is an accident that is related and joined to motion in such a manner that the one is never found without the other. Motion is only possible in time, and the idea of time cannot be conceived otherwise than in connection with motion; things which do not move have no relation to time.

PROPOSITION XVI: Incorporeal bodies can only be numbered when they are forces situated in a body; the several forces must then be counted together with substances or objects in which they exist. Hence purely spiritual beings, which are neither corporeal nor forces situated in corporeal objects, cannot be counted, except when considered as causes and effects.

PROPOSITION XVII: When an object moves, there must be some agent that moves it, from without, as, e.g., in the case of a stone set in motion by the hand; or from within, e.g., when the body of a living being moves. Living beings include in themselves, at the same time, the moving agent and the thing moved; when, therefore, a living being dies, and the moving agent, the soul, has left the body, i.e., the thing moved, the body remains for some time in the same condition as before, and yet cannot move in the manner it has moved previously. The moving agent, when included in the thing moved, is hidden from, and imperceptible to, the senses. This circumstance gave rise to the belief that the body of an animal moves without the aid of a moving agent. When we therefore affirm, concerning a thing in motion, that it is its own moving agent, or, as is generally said, that it moves of its own accord, we mean to say that the force which really sets the body in motion exists in that body itself.

PROPOSITION XVIII: Everything that passes over from a state of potentiality to that of actuality, is caused to do so by some external agent; because if that agent existed in the thing itself, and no obstacle prevented the transition, the thing would never be in a state of potentiality, but always in that of actuality. If, on the other hand, while the thing itself contained that agent, some obstacle existed, and at a certain time that obstacle was removed, the same cause which removed the obstacle would undoubtedly be described as the cause of the transition from potentiality to actuality, [and not the force situated within the body]. Note this.

PROPOSITION XIX: A thing which owes its existence to certain causes has in itself merely the possibility of existence; for only if these causes exist, the thing likewise exists. It does not exist if the causes do not exist at all, or if they have ceased to exist, or if there has been a change in the relation which implies the existence of that thing as a necessary consequence of those causes.

PROPOSITION XX: A thing which has in itself the necessity of existence cannot have for its existence any cause whatever.

PROPOSITION XXI: A thing composed of two elements has necessarily their composition as the cause of its present existence. Its existence is therefore not necessitated by its own essence; it depends on the existence of its two component parts and their combination.

PROPOSITION XXII: Material objects are always composed of two elements [at least], and are without exception subject to accidents. The two component elements of all bodies are substance and form. The accidents attributed to material objects are quantity, geometrical form, and position.

PROPOSITION XXIII: Everything that exists potentially, and whose essence includes a certain state of possibility, may at some time be without actual existence.

PROPOSITION XXIV: That which is potentially a certain thing is necessarily material, for the state of possibility is always connected with matter.

PROPOSITION XXV: Each compound substance consists of matter and form, and requires an agent for its existence, viz., a force which sets the substance in motion, and thereby enables it to receive a certain form. The force which thus prepares the substance of a certain individual being, is called the immediate motor. Here the necessity arises of investigating into the properties of motion, the moving agent and the thing moved. But this has already been explained sufficiently; and the opinion of Aristotle may be expressed in the following proposition: Matter does not move of its own accord—an important proposition that led to the investigation of the Prime Motor (the first moving agent).

Of these foregoing twenty-five propositions some may be verified by means of a little reflection and the application of a few propositions capable of proof, or of axioms or theorems of almost the same force, such as have been explained by me. Others require many arguments and propositions, all of which, however, have been established by conclusive proofs partly in the Physics and its commentaries, and partly in the Metaphysics and its commentary. I have already stated that in this work it is not my intention to copy the books of the philosophers or to explain difficult problems, but simply to mention those propositions which are closely connected with our subject, and which we want for our purpose.

To the above propositions one must be added which enunciates that the universe is eternal, and which is held by Aristotle to be true, and even more acceptable than any other theory. For the present we admit it, as a hypothesis, only for the purpose of demonstrating our theory. It is the following proposition:—

PROPOSITION XXVI: Time and motion are eternal, constant, and in actual existence.

In accordance with this proposition, Aristotle is compelled to assume that there exists actually a body with constant motion, viz., the fifth element. He therefore says that the heavens are not subject to genesis or destruction, because motion cannot be generated nor destroyed. He also holds that every motion must necessarily be preceded by another motion, either of the same or of a different kind. The belief that the locomotion of an animal is not preceded by another motion, is not true; for the animal is caused to move, after it had been in rest, by the intention to obtain those very things which bring about that locomotion. A change in its state of health, or some image, or some new idea can produce a desire to seek that which is conducive to its welfare and to avoid that which is contrary. Each of these three causes sets the living being in motion, and each of them is produced by various kinds of motion. Aristotle likewise asserts that everything which is created must, before its actual creation, have existed in potentiâ. By inferences drawn from this assertion he seeks to establish his proposition, viz., the thing that moves is finite, and its path finite; but it repeats the motion in its path an infinite number of times. This can only take place when the motion is circular, as has been stated in Proposition XIII. Hence follows also the existence of an infinite number of things which do not co-exist but follow one after the other.

Aristotle frequently attempts to establish this proposition; but I believe that he did not consider his proofs to be conclusive. It appeared to him to be the most probable and acceptable proposition. His followers, however, and the commentators of his books, contend that it contains not only a probable but a demonstrative proof, and that it has, in fact, been fully established. On the other hand, the Mutakallemim try to prove that the proposition cannot be true, as, according to their opinion, it is impossible to conceive how an infinite number of things could even come into existence successively. They assume this impossibility as an axiom. I, however, think that this proposition is admissible, but neither demonstrative, as the commentators of Aristotle assert, nor, on the other hand, impossible, as the Mutakallemim say. We have no intention to explain here the proofs given by Aristotle, or to show our doubts concerning them, or to set forth our opinions on the creation of the universe. I here simply desire to mention those propositions which we shall require for the proof of the three principles stated above. Having thus quoted and admitted these propositions, I will now proceed to explain what may be inferred from them.

THOMAS AQUINAS
1225–1274

————◄○►————

Saint Thomas Aquinas was indisputably the greatest of the medieval philosophers. He was born in his family's castle of Roccasecca near the town of Aquino, about halfway between Rome and Naples. The seventh son of the Count of Aquino, Landolfo, and his wife Teodora, at the age of five Thomas was sent to the Benedictine monastery of Monte Casino, where his uncle was the abbot. His parents hoped he would get a good education at the monastery and perhaps one day become abbot of Monte Casino. However, political struggles between the pope and the emperor made the monastery unsafe, and at age fourteen Thomas moved to the Imperial University in Naples.

At this university, Thomas came under the influence of the Dominicans, a mendicant, or begging, order of friars. Even though the Dominicans were admired by many for their religious commitment, Thomas's family was appalled when in 1244 he announced his plans to join the order. They considered the Dominicans religious fanatics, virtually a cult, with none of the sophistication, prestige, or power of the long-established Benedictines. At his parents' instigation, Thomas's brothers kidnapped him and held him captive in the family castle. For a year they tried reasoning, shouting, intimidating—even tempting him with a prostitute—but Thomas would not be swayed. He eventually managed to escape and became a Dominican friar.

Thomas went to Paris, where he studied with Albertus Magnus (Albert the Great), an advocate of the newly rediscovered Aristotelian writings, and he even followed his teacher to Cologne to continue his study of Aristotle. As a student, Thomas was so stolid and methodical that many of his peers thought he was dull or downright stupid. Given his deliberate manner and his portly build, his classmates dubbed him "the Dumb Ox." But Albertus saw his potential and turned this cruel epithet into a prophecy, saying, "You call him a Dumb Ox; I tell you the Dumb Ox will bellow so loud his bellowing will fill the world." In 1252, Thomas returned to Paris for graduate studies, eventually receiving the magistrate (doctorate) in theology in 1256.

On concluding his studies, it seemed natural that Thomas would join the faculty of the University of Paris. However, scholars from the mendicant orders were held in suspicion by the regular faculty of the university. Along with the great Franciscan friar Bonaventure, Thomas was not allowed to teach in Paris until the pope himself intervened.

The rest of Thomas's life was spent teaching in France and Italy and writing extensively on philosophical and theological subjects. His complete works in Latin comprise twenty-five volumes. Thomas was also called upon to intervene in several disputes. In addition to defending his Dominican order, he was forced to articulate a middle position between those who rejected Aristotelian philosophy as anti-Christian and those who accepted Aristotle (or, rather, a version of Averroës' interpretation of Aristotle) too uncritically. Throughout his writings, Thomas negotiated a middle path of critical admiration for Aristotle.

Like other Christian thinkers, Thomas was concerned with the relation between reason and faith. Using basically Aristotelian categories, Thomas taught that natural reason could establish some of the truths of religion (such as the existence, unity, and goodness of God), but other truths were accessible only through faith. Contrary to some of the Latin Averroists, Thomas taught that there

The Benedictine Monastery of Monte Casino. At the age of five, St. Thomas Aquinas was sent here to study. His parents hoped that he might someday become abbot of the monastery, but he chose to join the Dominican order instead. (*AP/Wide World Photos*)

was no conflict between the teachings of philosophy and those of theology. To use a later analogy, Thomas believed that "the book of nature" (i.e., the created world) and the "Book of Scripture" were in perfect harmony.

In December 1273, Thomas suddenly stopped writing, apparently the result of a mystical experience. He reported to a friend that "all I have written seems like straw to me." A few months later, he was called to a church council in Lyon, France. On the way there his health forced him to stop at Fossanova (south of Rome) where he died on March 7, 1274, at the age of forty-nine.

Three years after his death, several of Thomas's teachings were condemned by the Bishop of Paris. However, the condemnation did not stand long, and in 1323, Saint Thomas Aquinas was canonized. In 1879, Pope Leo XII commended the study of Aquinas's philosophy in an encyclical, *Aeterni Patris.* This papal proclamation did not launch a revival of Thomism, as is often said, but it did lend an enormous prestige to the study of Thomas and his work. The encyclical praises the saint in the highest terms: "As far as man is concerned, reason can now hardly rise higher than she rose, borne up in the flight of Thomas; and Faith can hardly gain more help from reason than those which Thomas gave her." Despite the encouragement of Leo XII and others, not all Catholic philosophers are by any means Thomists; many twentieth-century Catholic thinkers have shown more interest in existentialism and phenomenology. Today Thomas is studied and admired as much by Protestants and non-Christians as he is by Catholics.

*   *   *

Thomas's most famous work, the *Summa Theologica,* is one of the most comprehensive and systematic works of theology ever written. It has often been likened in its complexity and grandeur to a Gothic cathedral. This monumental classic is divided into four sections that, collectively, include 512 "Questions." Each Question raises a topic or area of investigation and is, in turn, made up of several "Articles" that explore specific concerns. These Articles range from abstract philosophical issues, such as "Whether one can intend two things at the same time," to such minutiae of theology as "Whether one angel can speak to another in such a way that others will not know what he is saying." Each Article is examined in the same manner, beginning with a question, offering an answer that Thomas considers inadequate, then supporting this answer with several "objections." At this point, a quotation or argument that contradicts the position taken thus far is introduced with the words "On the contrary (*sed contra*) . . ." The dramatic tension between two opposing positions is then resolved by the author's concise and straightforward *Respondeo,* or "I answer that . . . ," which introduces his own view. In presenting his answer, Thomas tries to avoid directly denying the preceding objections, seeing them instead as limited truths that his *Respondeo* supersedes. Finally, Thomas moves on to answer, one by one, each of the initial objections. (The reader should keep in mind that the *first* things Thomas says about a subject are the *opposite* of the position he will subsequently defend.)

The selections from the *Summa Theologica* given here include readings from Thomas's "Treatise on God" (including his famous "Five Ways" or five arguments for God's existence); "Treatise on Man" (including a discussion of the nature of the soul); "Treatise on Human Acts" (including his definition of happiness); "Treatise on Law" (describing the kinds of law); and "Treatise on War" (describing his arguments for a just war). The translation is that of the Fathers of the English Dominican Province.

*   *   *

The classic introductions to Thomas Aquinas are F.C. Copleston, *Aquinas* (Baltimore, MD: Penguin Books, 1955), and Étienne Gilson, *The Christian Philosophy of St. Thomas Aquinas* (New York: Random House, 1956). More recent helpful studies include Josef Pieper, *Guide to Thomas Aquinas* (New York: Pantheon, 1962); Ralph McInerny, *St. Thomas Aquinas* (Boston: Twayne, 1977); Anthony Kenny, *Aquinas* (New York: Hill and Wang, 1980); and Brian Davies, *The Thought of Thomas Aquinas* (Oxford: Oxford University Press, 1992). James A. Weisheipl, *Friar Thomas D'Aquino: His Life, Thought, and Works* (Garden City, NY: Doubleday, 1974) offers a biography. G.K. Chesterton's impressionistic study entitled *St. Thomas Aquinas: The "Dumb Ox"* (1933; reprinted New York: Doubleday Image, 1956) is also a good place to become acquainted with Thomas. For collections of general essays, see Anthony Kenny, ed., *Aquinas: A Collection of Critical Essays* (Garden City, NY: Anchor Doubleday, 1969), and Norman Kretzmann and Eleonore Stump, eds., *The Cambridge Companion to Aquinas* (Cambridge: Cambridge University Press, 1993).

There are many studies on aspects of Thomas's thought. For example, a sampling of works on the "Five Ways" includes A.G.N. Flew, *God and Philosophy* (London: Hutchinson, 1966); Anthony Kenny, *The Five Ways: St. Thomas Aquinas' Proofs of God's Existence* (London: Routledge & Kegan Paul, 1969); Richard Swinburne, *The Existence of God* (Oxford: Clarendon Press, 1979); and J.L. Mackie, *The Miracle of Theism: Arguments for and against the Existence of God* (Oxford: Clarendon Press, 1982).

SUMMA THEOLOGICA (in part)

FIRST PART

TREATISE ON GOD

QUESTION 2: THE EXISTENCE OF GOD
(IN THREE ARTICLES)

Because the chief aim of sacred doctrine is to teach the knowledge of God, not only as He is in Himself, but also as He is the beginning of things and their last end, and especially of rational creatures, as is clear from what has been already said, therefore, in our endeavor to expound this science, we shall treat: (1) Of God; (2) Of the rational creature's advance towards God; (3) Of Christ, Who as man, is our way to God.

In treating of God there will be a threefold division:—

For we shall consider (1) Whatever concerns the Divine Essence; (2) Whatever concerns the distinctions of Persons; (3) Whatever concerns the procession of creatures from Him.

Concerning the Divine Essence, we must consider:—

(1) Whether God exists? (2) The manner of His existence, or, rather, what is *not* the manner of His existence; (3) Whatever concerns His operations—namely, His knowledge, will, power.

Concerning the first, there are three points of inquiry:—

(1) Whether the proposition "God exists" is self-evident? (2) Whether it is demonstrable? (3) Whether God exists?

First Article

WHETHER THE EXISTENCE OF GOD IS SELF-EVIDENT?

We Proceed Thus to the First Article:—

Objection 1. It seems that the existence of God is self-evident. Now those things are said to be self-evident to us the knowledge of which is naturally implanted in us, as we can see in regard to first principles. But as Damascene says (*De Fid. Orth.* i. 1, 3), *the knowledge of God is naturally implanted in all.* Therefore the existence of God is self-evident.

Obj. 2. Further, those things are said to be self-evident which are known as soon as the terms are known, which the Philosopher (1 *Poster.* iii) says is true of the first principles of demonstration. Thus, when the nature of a whole and of a part is known, it is at once recognized that every whole is greater than its part. But as soon as the

From St. Thomas Aquinas, *Summa Theologica,* Treatise on God (Part I, Q.2); Treatise on Man (Part I, Q. 75, a. 2; Q. 76, a. 1); Treatise on Human Acts (Part I–II, Q. 2, a. 8; Q. 3, a. 4, 8; Q. 5, a. 5); Treatise on Law (Part I–II, Q. 94, a. 2, 4, 5; Q. 95, a. 1, 2; Q. 96, a. 2); Treatise on War (Part II–II, q. 40, a. 1), translated by the Fathers of the English Dominican Province (New York: Benziger Brothers, 1947). Reprinted by permission.

signification of the word "God" is understood, it is at once seen that God exists. For by this word is signified that thing than which nothing greater can be conceived. But that which exists actually and mentally is greater than that which exists only mentally. Therefore, since as soon as the word "God" is understood it exists mentally, it also follows that it exists actually. Therefore the proposition "God exists" is self-evident.

Obj. 3. Further, the existence of truth is self-evident. For whoever denies the existence of truth grants that truth does not exist: and if truth does not exist, then the proposition "Truth does not exist" is true: and if there is anything true, there must be truth. But God is truth itself: *I am the way, the truth, and the life* (John xiv. 6). Therefore "God exists" is self-evident.

On the contrary, No one can mentally admit the opposite of what is self-evident; as the Philosopher (*Metaph.* iv., lect. vi) states concerning the first principles of demonstration. But the opposite of the proposition "God is" can be mentally admitted: *The fool said in his heart, There is no God* (Ps. lii. 1). Therefore, that God exists is not self-evident.

I answer that, A thing can be self-evident in either of two ways; on the one hand, self-evident in itself, though not to us; on the other, self-evident in itself, and to us. A proposition is self-evident because the predicate is included in the essence of the subject, as "Man is an animal," for animal is contained in the essence of man. If, therefore the essence of the predicate and subject be known to all, the proposition will be self-evident to all; as is clear with regard to the first principles of demonstration, the terms of which are common things that no one is ignorant of, such as being and non-being, whole and part, and such like. If, however, there are some to whom the essence of the predicate and subject is unknown, the proposition will be self-evident in itself, but not to those who do not know the meaning of the predicate and subject of the proposition. Therefore, it happens, as Boethius says (*Hebdom., the title of which is: "Whether all that is, is good"),* "that there are some mental concepts self-evident only to the learned, as that incorporeal substances are not in space." Therefore I say that this proposition, "God exists," of itself is self-evident, for the predicate is the same as the subject; because God is His own existence as will be hereafter shown (Q. 3, A. 4). Now because we do not know the essence of God, the proposition is not self-evident to us; but needs to be demonstrated by things that are more known to us, though less known in their nature—namely, by effects.

Reply Obj. 1. To know that God exists in a general and confused way is implanted in us by nature, inasmuch as God is man's beatitude. For man naturally desires happiness, and what is naturally desired by man must be naturally known to him. This, however, is not to know absolutely that God exists; just as to know that someone is approaching is not the same as to know that Peter is approaching, even though it is Peter who is approaching; for many there are who imagine that man's perfect good which is happiness, consists in riches, and others in pleasures, and others in something else.

Reply Obj. 2. Perhaps not everyone who hears this word "God" understands it to signify something than which nothing greater can be thought, seeing that some have believed God to be a body. Yet, granted that everyone understands that by this word "God" is signified something than which nothing greater can be thought, nevertheless, it does not therefore follow that he understands that what the word signifies exists actually, but only that it exists mentally. Nor can it be argued that it actually exists, unless it be admitted that there actually exists something than which nothing greater can be thought; and this precisely is not admitted by those who hold that God does not exist.

Reply Obj. 3. The existence of truth in general is self-evident but the existence of a Primal Truth is not self-evident to us.

Second Article

WHETHER IT CAN BE DEMONSTRATED THAT GOD EXISTS?

We Proceed Thus to the Second Article:—

Objection 1. It seems that the existence of God cannot be demonstrated. For it is an article of faith that God exists. But what is of faith cannot be demonstrated, because a demonstration produces scientific knowledge; whereas faith is of the unseen (Heb. xi. 1). Therefore it cannot be demonstrated that God exists.

Obj. 2. Further, the essence is the middle term of demonstration. But we cannot know in what God's essence consists, but solely in what it does not consist; as Damascene says (*De Fid. Orth.* i. 4). Therefore we cannot demonstrate that God exists.

Obj. 3. Further, if the existence of God were demonstrated, this could only be from His effects. But His effects are not proportionate to Him, since He is infinite and His effects are finite; and between the finite and infinite there is no proportion. Therefore, since a cause cannot be demonstrated by an effect not proportionate to it, it seems that the existence of God cannot be demonstrated.

On the contrary, The Apostle says: *The invisible things of Him are clearly seen, being understood by the things that are made* (Rom. i. 20). But this would not be unless the existence of God could be demonstrated through the things that are made; for the first thing we must know of anything is, whether it exists.

I answer that, Demonstration can be made in two ways: One is through the cause, and is called *a priori,* and this is to argue from what is prior absolutely. The other is through the effect, and is called a demonstration *a posteriori;* this is to argue from what is prior relatively only to us. When an effect is better known to us than its cause, from the effect we proceed to the knowledge of the cause. And from every effect the existence of its proper cause can be demonstrated, so long as its effects are better known to us; because since every effect depends upon its cause, if the effect exists, the cause must pre-exist. Hence the existence of God, in so far as it is not self-evident to us, can be demonstrated from those of His effects which are known to us.

Reply Obj. 1. The existence of God and other like truths about God, which can be known by natural reason, are not articles of faith, but are preambles to the articles; for faith presupposes natural knowledge, even as grace presupposes nature, and perfection supposes something that can be perfected. Nevertheless, there is nothing to prevent a man, who cannot grasp a proof, accepting, as a matter of faith, something which in itself is capable of being scientifically known and demonstrated.

Reply Obj. 2. When the existence of a cause is demonstrated from an effect, this effect takes the place of the definition of the cause in proof of the cause's existence. This is especially the case in regard to God, because, in order to prove the existence of anything, it is necessary to accept as a middle term the meaning of the word, and not its essence, for the question of its essence follows on the question of its existence. Now the names given to God are derived from His effects; consequently, in demonstrating the existence of God from His effects, we may take for the middle term the meaning of the word "God."

Reply Obj. 3. From effects not proportionate to the cause no perfect knowledge of that cause can be obtained. Yet from every effect the existence of the cause can be clearly demonstrated, and so we can demonstrate the existence of God from His effects; though from them we cannot perfectly know God as He is in His essence.

Third Article

Whether God Exists?

We Proceed Thus to the Third Article:—

Objection 1. It seems that God does not exist; because if one of two contraries be infinite, the other would be altogether destroyed. But the word "God" means that He is infinite goodness. If, therefore, God existed, there would be no evil discoverable; but there is evil in the world. Therefore God does not exist.

Obj. 2. Further, it is superfluous to suppose that what can be accounted for by a few principles has been produced by many. But it seems that everything we see in the world can be accounted for by other principles, supposing God did not exist. For all natural things can be reduced to one principle, which is nature; and all voluntary things can be reduced to one principle, which is human reason, or will. Therefore there is no need to suppose God's existence.

On the contrary, It is said in the person of God: *I am Who am* (Exod. iii. 14).

I answer that, The existence of God can be proved in five ways.

The first and more manifest way is the argument from motion. It is certain, and evident to our senses, that in the world some things are in motion. Now whatever is in motion is put in motion by another, for nothing can be in motion except it is in potentiality to that towards which it is in motion; whereas a thing moves inasmuch as it is in act. For motion is nothing else than the reduction of something from potentiality to actuality. But nothing can be reduced from potentiality to actuality, except by something in a state of actuality. Thus that which is actually hot, as fire, makes wood, which is potentially hot, to be actually hot, and thereby moves and changes it. Now it is not possible that the same thing should be at once in actuality and potentiality in the same respect, but only in different respects. For what is actually hot cannot simultaneously be potentially hot; but it is simultaneously potentially cold. It is therefore impossible that in the same respect and in the same way a thing should be both mover and moved, *i.e.,* that it should move itself. Therefore, whatever is in motion must be put in motion by another. If that by which it is put in motion be itself put in motion, then this also must needs be put in motion by another, and that by another again. But this cannot go on to infinity, because then there would be no first mover, and, consequently, no other mover; seeing that subsequent movers move only inasmuch as they are put in motion by the first mover; as the staff moves only because it is put in motion by the hand. Therefore it is necessary to arrive at a first mover, put in motion by no other; and this everyone understands to be God.

The second way is from the nature of the efficient cause. In the world of sense we find there is an order of efficient causes. There is no case known (neither is it, indeed, possible) in which a thing is found to be the efficient cause of itself; for so it would be prior to itself, which is impossible. Now in efficient causes it is not possible to go on to infinity, because in all efficient causes following in order, the first is the cause of the intermediate cause, and the intermediate is the cause of the ultimate cause, whether the intermediate cause be several, or one only. Now to take away the cause is to take away the effect. Therefore if there be no first cause among efficient causes, there will be no ultimate, nor any intermediate cause. But if in efficient causes it is possible to go on to infinity, there will be no first efficient cause, neither will there be an ultimate effect, nor any intermediate efficient causes; all of which is plainly false.

Therefore it is necessary to admit a first efficient cause, to which everyone gives the name of God.

The third way is taken from possibility and necessity, and runs thus. We find in nature things that are possible to be and not to be, since they are found to be generated, and to corrupt, and consequently, they are possible to be and not to be. But it is impossible for these always to exist, for that which is possible not to be at some time is not. Therefore, if everything is possible not to be, then at one time there could have been nothing in existence. Now if this were true, even now there would be nothing in existence, because that which does not exist only begins to exist by something already existing. Therefore, if at one time nothing was in existence, it would have been impossible for anything to have begun to exist; and thus even now nothing would be in existence—which is absurd. Therefore, not all beings are merely possible, but there must exist something the existence of which is necessary. But every necessary thing either has its necessity caused by another, or not. Now it is impossible to go on to infinity in necessary things which have their necessity caused by another, as has been already proved in regard to efficient causes. Therefore we cannot but postulate the existence of some being having of itself its own necessity, and not receiving it from another, but rather causing in others their necessity. This all men speak of as God.

The fourth way is taken from the gradation to be found in things. Among beings there are some more and some less good, true, noble, and the like. But "more" and "less" are predicated of different things, according as they resemble in their different ways something which is the maximum, as a thing is said to be hotter according as it more nearly resembles that which is hottest; so that there is something which is truest, something best, something noblest, and, consequently, something which is uttermost being; for those things that are greatest in truth are greatest in being, as it is written in *Metaph.* ii. Now the maximum in any genus is the cause of all in that genus; as fire, which is the maximum of heat, is the cause of all hot things. Therefore there must also be something which is to all beings the cause of their being, goodness, and every other perfection; and this we call God.

The fifth way is taken from the governance of the world. We see that things which lack intelligence, such as natural bodies, act for an end, and this is evident from their acting always, or nearly always, in the same way, so as to obtain the best result. Hence it is plain that not fortuitously, but designedly, do they achieve their end. Now whatever lacks intelligence cannot move towards an end, unless it be directed by some being endowed with knowledge and intelligence; as the arrow is shot to its mark by the archer. Therefore some intelligent being exists by whom all natural things are directed to their end; and this being we call God.

Reply Obj. 1. As Augustine says (*Enchir.* xi): *Since God is the highest good, He would not allow any evil to exist in His works, unless His omnipotence and goodness were such as to bring good even out of evil.* This is part of the infinite goodness of God, that He should allow evil to exist, and out of it produce good.

Reply Obj. 2. Since nature works for a determinate end under the direction of a higher agent, whatever is done by nature must needs be traced back to God, as to its first cause. So also whatever is done voluntarily must also be traced back to some higher cause other than human reason or will, since these can change and fail; for all things that are changeable and capable of defect must be traced back to an immovable and self-necessary first principle, as was shown in the body of the *Article.*

* * *

TREATISE ON MAN

QUESTION 75: OF MAN WHO IS COMPOSED OF A SPIRITUAL AND A CORPOREAL SUBSTANCE: AND IN THE FIRST PLACE CONCERNING WHAT BELONGS TO THE ESSENCE OF THE SOUL

*   *   *

Second Article

WHETHER THE HUMAN SOUL IS SOMETHING SUBSISTENT?

We Proceed Thus to the Second Article:—

Objection 1. It would seem that the human soul is not something subsistent. For that which subsists is said to be *this particular thing.* Now *this particular thing* is said not of the soul, but of that which is composed of soul and body. Therefore the soul is not something subsistent.

Obj. 2. Further, everything subsistent operates. But the soul does not operate; for, as the Philosopher says (*De Anima* i. 4), *to say that the soul feels or understands is like saying that the soul weaves or builds.* Therefore the soul is not subsistent.

Obj. 3. Further, if the soul were subsistent, it would have some operation apart from the body. But it has no operation apart from the body, not even that of understanding: for the act of understanding does not take place without a phantasm, which cannot exist apart from the body. Therefore the human soul is not something subsistent.

On the contrary, Augustine says (*de Trin.* x. 7): *Whoever understands that the nature of the soul is that of a substance and not that of a body, will see that those who maintain the corporeal nature of the soul, are led astray through associating with the soul those things without which they are unable to think of any nature—i.e., imaginary pictures of the corporal things.* Therefore the nature of the human intellect is not only incorporeal, but it is also a substance, that is, something subsistent.

I answer that, It must necessarily be allowed that the principle of intellectual operation which we call the soul, is a principle both incorporeal and subsistent. For it is clear that by means of the intellect man can have knowledge of all corporeal things. Now whatever knows certain things cannot have any of them in its own nature; because that which is in it naturally would impede the knowledge of anything else. Thus we observe that a sick man's tongue being vitiated by a feverish and bitter humor, is insensible to anything sweet and everything seems bitter to it. Therefore if the intellectual principle contained the nature of a body it would be unable to know all bodies. Now every body has its own determinate nature. Therefore it is impossible for the intellectual principle to be a body. It is likewise impossible for it to understand by means of a bodily organ; since the determinate nature of that organ would impede knowledge of all bodies; as when a certain determinate color is not only in the pupil of the eye, but also in a glass vase, the liquid in the vase seems to be of that same color.

Therefore the intellectual principle which we call the mind or the intellect has the operation *per se* apart from the body. Now only that which subsists can have an operation *per se*. For nothing can operate but what is actual: wherefore a thing operates according as it is; for which reason we do not say that heat imparts heat, but that what is hot gives heat. We must conclude, therefore, that the human soul, which is called the intellect or the mind, is something incorporeal and subsistent.

Reply Obj. 1. *This particular thing* can be taken in two senses. Firstly, for anything subsistent; secondly, for that which subsists, and is complete in a specific nature. The former sense excludes the inherence of an accident or of a material form; the latter excludes also the imperfection of the part, so that a hand can be called *this particular thing* in the first sense, but not in the second. Therefore as the human soul is a part of human nature, it can indeed be called *this particular thing,* in the first sense, as being something subsistent; but not in the second, for in this sense, what is composed of body and soul is said to be *this particular thing.*

Reply Obj. 2. Aristotle wrote those words as expressing not his own opinion, but the opinion of those who said that to understand is to be moved, as is clear from the context. Or we may reply that to operate *per se* belongs to what exists *per se.* But for a thing to exist *per se,* it suffices sometimes that it be not inherent, as an accident or a material form; even though it be part of something. Nevertheless, that is rightly said to subsist *per se,* which is neither inherent in the above sense nor part of anything else. In this sense, the eye or the hand cannot be said to subsist *per se;* nor can it for that reason be said to operate *per se.* Hence the operation of the parts is through each part attributed to the whole. For we say that the man sees with the eye, and feels with the hand and, and not in the same sense as when we say that what is hot gives heat by its heat; for heat, strictly speaking, does not give heat. We may therefore say that the soul understands, as the eye sees; but it is more correct to say that man understands through the soul.

Reply Obj. 3. The body is necessary for intellect, not as its origin of action, but on the part of the object; for the phantasm is to the intellect what color is to the sight. Neither does such a dependence on the body prove the intellect to be non-subsistent; otherwise it would follow that an animal is not subsistent, since it requires external objects of the senses in order to perform its act of perception.

*   *   *

QUESTION 76: OF THE UNION OF BODY AND SOUL

*   *   *

First Article

WHETHER THE INTELLECTUAL PRINCIPLE IS UNITED TO THE BODY AS ITS FORM?

We Proceed Thus to the First Article:—

Objection 1. It seems that the intellectual principle is not united to the body as its form. For the Philosopher says (*De Anima* iii. 4) that "the intellect is separate," and that it is not the act of any body. Therefore it is not united to the body as its form.

Obj. 2. Further, every form is determined according to the nature of the matter of which it is the form; otherwise no proportion would be required between matter and form. Therefore if the intellect were united to the body as its form since every body has a determinate nature it would follow that the intellect has a determinate nature; and thus, it would not be capable of knowing all things, as is clear from what has been said (Q. 75, A. 2), which is contrary to the notion of intellect. Therefore the intellect is not united to the body as its form.

Obj. 3. Further, whatever receptive power is an act of a body receives a form materially and individually; for what is received must be received according to the mode of the receiver. But the form of the thing understood is not received into the intellect materially and individually, but rather immaterially and universally; otherwise the intellect would not be capable of the knowledge of immaterial and universal objects, but only of individuals, like the senses. Therefore the intellect is not united to the body as its form.

Obj. 4. Further, power and action have the same subject; for the same subject is what can, and does, act. But the intellectual action is not the action of a body, as appears from above (Q. 75, A. 2). Therefore neither is the intellectual power a power of the body. But virtue or power cannot be more abstract or more simple than the essence from which the virtue or power is derived. Therefore neither is the substance of the intellect the form of a body.

Obj. 5. Further, whatever has *per se* being is not united to the body as its form, because a form is that by which a thing is, so that the very being of a form does not belong to the form by itself. But the intellectual principle has *per se* being and is subsistent, as was said above (Q. 75, A. 2). Therefore it is not united to the body as its form.

Obj. 6. Further, whatever exists in a thing by reason of its nature exists in it always. But to be united to matter belongs to the form by reason of its nature. For form is the act of matter not by any accidental quality, but by its own essence; otherwise matter and form would not make a thing substantially one, but only accidentally one. Therefore a form cannot be without its own proper matter. But the intellectual principle, since it is incorruptible, as was shown above (Q. 75, A. 6), remains separate from the body after the dissolution of the body. Therefore the intellectual principle is not united to the body as its form.

On the contrary, According to the Philosopher (*Metaph.* vii. 2), difference is derived from the form. But the difference which constitutes man is *rational* which is applied to man on account of his intellectual principle. Therefore the intellectual principle is the form of man.

I answer that, We must assert that the intellect which is the principle of intellectual operation is the form of the human body. For that whereby primarily anything acts is a form of the thing to which the act is to be attributed; for instance, that whereby a body is primarily healed is health and that whereby the soul knows primarily is knowledge; hence health is a form of the body, and knowledge is a form of the soul. The reason is because nothing acts except so far as it is in act; hence a thing acts by that whereby it is in act. Now it is clear that the first thing by which the body lives is the soul. And as life appears through various operations in different degrees of living things, that whereby we primarily perform each of all these vital actions is the soul. For the soul is the primary principle of our nourishment, sensation, and local movement; and likewise of our understanding. Therefore this principle by which we primarily understand, whether it be called the intellect or the intellectual soul, is the form of the body. This is the demonstration used by Aristotle (*De Anima* ii. 2).

But if anyone say that the intellectual soul is not the form of the body he must first explain how it is that this action of understanding is the action of this particular man; for each one is conscious that it is himself who understands. Now an action may be attributed to anyone in three ways, as is clear from the Philosopher. "For a thing is said to move or act either by virtue of its whole self, for instance, as a physician heals; or by virtue of a part, as a man sees by his eye; or through an accidental quality, as when we say that something that is white build, because it is accidental to the builder to be white" (*Phys.* v. 1) So when we say that Socrates or Plato understands, it is clear that this is not attributed to him accidentally, since it is ascribed to him as man, which is predicated of him essentially. We must therefore say either that Socrates understands by virtue of his whole self, as Plato maintained, holding that man is an intellectual soul, or that the intellect is a part of Socrates. The first cannot stand, as was shown above (Q. 75, A. 4), for this reason, that it is one and the same man who is conscious both that he understands, and that he senses. But one cannot sense without a body; therefore the body must be some part of man. It remains therefore that the intellect by which Socrates understands is a part of Socrates, so that in some way it is united to the body of Socrates.

The Commentator [Averroës] held that this union is through the intelligible species, as having a double subject: in the possible intellect, and in the phantasms which are in the corporeal organs (*De Anima* iii, Comm. 5). Thus through the intelligible species the possible intellect is linked to the body of this or that particular man. But this link or union does not sufficiently explain the fact that the act of the intellect is the act of Socrates. This can be clearly seen from comparison with the sensitive power, from which Aristotle proceeds to consider things relating to the intellect. For the relation of phantasms to the intellect is like the relation of colours to the sense of sight, as he says in the book on the *Soul* (iii. 7). Therefore, as the species of colours are in the sight, so are the species of phantasms in the possible-intellect. Now it is clear that because the colours, the likenesses of which are in the sight, are on a wall, the action of seeing is not attributed to the wall, for

a.

b.

c.   d.

The Gothic Cathedral

a. The Cathedral of Notre Dame de Chartres, Chartres, France, begun in the 1140s. The word "Gothic" was originally a perjorative term coined by Renaissance thinkers who considered this style to be a barbaric break from classical tradition. The two towers shown here, for example, are not symmetrical. Even though the overall design of the cathedral may not be symmetrical, each of its elements was designed to reflect the harmony and beauty of God's creation. (*Lauros-Giraudon/Art Resource*)

b. Interior, Chartres Cathedral. By using pointed arches, it was possible to make soaring open spaces in the nave (main sanctuary) of the Gothic cathedral. The weight was shifted downward instead of outward. (*Bildarchiv Foto Marburg/Art Resource*)

we do not say that the wall sees, but rather that it is seen. Therefore, from the fact that the species of phantasms are in the possible intellect it does not follow that Socrates, in whom are the phantasms, understands, but that he or his phantasms are understood.

Some, however, tried to maintain that the intellect is united to the body as its mover, and hence that the intellect and body form one thing so that the act of the intellect could be attributed to the whole. This is groundless however, for many reasons. First, because the intellect does not move the body except through desire, the movement of which presupposes the operation of the intellect. The reason therefore why Socrates understands is not because he is moved by his intellect, but rather, contrariwise, he is moved by his intellect because he understands. Secondly, because, since Socrates is an individual in a nature of one essence composed of matter and form, if the intellect be not the form, it follows that it must be outside the essence, and then the intellect is to the whole Socrates as a mover to the thing moved. The act of intellect however remains in the agent, and does not pass into something else, as does the action of heating. Therefore the act of understanding cannot be attributed to Socrates for the reason that he is moved by his intellect. Thirdly, because the action of a mover is never attributed to the thing moved, except as to an instrument; as the action of a carpenter to a saw. Therefore if understanding is attributed to Socrates, as the action of what moves him, it follows that it is attributed to him as to an instrument. This is contrary to the teaching of the Philosopher, who holds that understanding is not possible through a corporeal instrument (*De Anima* iii. 4). Fourthly, because, although the action of a part be attributed to the whole, as the action of the eye is attributed to a man, yet it is never attributed to another part, except perhaps accidentally; for we do not say that the hand sees because the eye sees. Therefore if the intellect and Socrates are united in the above manner, the action of the intellect cannot be attributed to Socrates. If, however, Socrates be a whole composed of a union of the intellect with whatever else belongs to Socrates, while nevertheless the intellect is united to those other things only as a mover, it follows that Socrates is not one absolutely, and consequently neither a being absolutely, for a thing is a being according as it is one.

There remains, therefore, no other explanation than that given by Aristotle (*De Anima* ii. 2)—namely, that this particular man understands because the intellectual principle is his form. Thus from the very operation of the intellect it is made clear that the intellectual principle is united to the body as its form.

The same can be clearly shown from the nature of the human species. For the nature of each thing is shown by its operation. Now the proper operation of man as man is to understand, because he thereby surpasses all other animals. From this, too,

---

c. *Flying Buttresses at Reims Cathedral*, ca. 1230–1235, by Villard De Honnecourt. To leave the interior unencumbered, the remaining outward stresses were often buttressed from outside the building. In some cathedrals exterior buttresses could not be built directly along the outside walls because of side aisles. Instead they were built outside the side aisles and connected to the pillars of the nave by stone ribs. These supporting ribs appear to "fly" over the side aisles. (*Villard de Honnecourt/Giraudon, Art Resource*)

d. *The Rose Window*, Notre Dame Cathedral, Paris, thirteenth century. By using pointed arches and flying buttresses, the walls of a cathedral did not have to bear the weight of the roof. Instead they could be used as screens for stained glass ornamentation such as this. (*Giraudon/Art Resource*)

Aristotle concludes (*Ethic.* x. 7) that the ultimate happiness of man must consist in this operation as properly belonging to him. Man must therefore derive his species from that which is the principle of this operation. But the species of anything is derived from its form. It follows therefore that the intellectual principle is the proper form of man.

But we must observe that the nobler a form is, the more it rises above corporeal matter, the less it is merged in matter, and the more it excels matter by its power and its operation; hence we find that the form of a mixed body has another operation not caused by its elemental qualities. And the higher we advance in the nobility of forms, the more we find that the power of the form excels the elementary matter; as the vegetative soul excels the form of the metal, and the sensitive soul excels the vegetative soul. Now the human soul is the highest and noblest of forms. Therefore it excels corporeal matter in its power by the fact that it has an operation and a power in which corporeal matter has no share whatever. This power is called the intellect.

It is well to remark that if anyone holds that the soul is composed of matter and form, it would follow that in no way could the soul be the form of the body. For since the form is an act, and matter is only a being in potency, that which is composed of matter and form cannot be the form of another by virtue of itself as a whole. But if it is a form by virtue of some part of itself, then that part which is the form we call the soul, and that of which it is the form we call the first thing animated, as was said above (Q. 75, A. 5).

Reply Obj. 1. As the Philosopher Says (*Phys.* ii. 2), the ultimate natural form to which the consideration of the natural philosopher is directed, namely, the human soul, is indeed separate; yet it exists in matter. He proves this from the fact that "man and the sun generate man from matter." It is separate indeed according to its intellectual power, because the intellectual power does not belong to a corporeal organ, as the power of seeing is the act of the eye; for understanding is an act which cannot be performed by a corporeal organ, like the act of seeing. But it exists in matter so far as the soul itself, to which this power belongs, is the form of the body, and the term of human generation. And so the Philosopher says (*De Anima* ii. 2) that "the intellect is separate" because it is not the power of a corporeal organ.

From this it is clear how to answer the *Second and Third objections.* For, in order that man may be able to understand all things by means of his intellect, and that his intellect may understand all things immaterial and universal, it is sufficient that the intellectual power be not the act of the body.

Reply Obj. 4. The human soul, by reason of its perfection, is not a form merged in matter, or entirely embraced by matter. Therefore there is nothing to prevent one of its powers not being the act of the body, although the soul is essentially the form of the body.

Reply Obj. 5. The soul communicates that being in which it subsists to the corporeal matter, out of which, combined with the intellectual soul, there results unity of being so that the being of the whole composite is also the being of the soul. This is not the case with other nonsubsistent forms. For this reason the human soul retains its own being after the dissolution of the body, though this is not so with other forms.

Reply Obj. 6. To be united to the body pertains to the soul by reason of itself, as it pertains to a light body by reason of itself to be raised up. And as a light body remains light when removed from its proper place, retaining meanwhile an aptitude and an inclination for its proper place, so the human soul retains its proper being when separated from the body, having an aptitude and a natural inclination to be united to the body.

* * *

FIRST PART OF THE SECOND PART (I–II)

TREATISE ON HUMAN ACTS

* * *

QUESTION 2: OF THOSE THINGS IN WHICH MAN'S HAPPINESS CONSISTS

* * *

Eighth Article

WHETHER ANY CREATED GOOD CONSTITUTES MAN'S HAPPINESS?

We Proceed Thus to the Eighth Article:—

Objection 1. It would seem that some created good constitutes man's happiness. For Dionysius says (*Div. Nom.* vii) that Divine wisdom *unites the ends of first things to the beginnings of second things,* from which we may gather that the summit of a lower nature touches the base of the higher nature. But man's highest good is happiness. Since then the angel is above man in the order of nature, as stated in the First Part (Q. 111, A. 1), it seems that man's happiness consists in man somehow reaching the angel.

Obj. 2. Further, the last end of each thing is that which, in relation to it, is perfect: hence the part is for the whole, as for its end. But the universe of creatures which is called the macrocosm, is compared to man who is called the microcosm (*Phys.* viii. 2), as perfect to imperfect. Therefore man's happiness consists in the whole universe of creatures.

Obj. 3. Further, man is made happy by that which lulls his natural desire. But man's natural desire does not reach out to a good surpassing his capacity. Since then man's capacity does not include that good which surpasses the limits of all creation, it seems that man can be made happy by some created good. Consequently some created good constitutes man's happiness.

On the contrary, Augustine says (*De Civ. Dei* xix. 26): *As the soul is the life of the body, so God is man's life of happiness: of Whom it is written: "Happy is that people whose God is the Lord"* (Ps. cxliii. 15).

I answer that, It is impossible for any created good to constitute man's happiness. For happiness is the perfect good, which lulls the appetite altogether; else it would not be the last end, if something yet remained to be desired. Now the object of the will, *i.e.,* of man's appetite, is the universal good; just as the object of the intellect is the universal true. Hence it is evident that naught can lull man's will, save the universal good. This is to be found, not in any creature, but in God alone; because every creature has goodness by participation. Wherefore God alone can satisfy the will of man, according to the words of Ps. cii. 5: *Who satisfieth thy desire with good things.* Therefore God alone constitutes man's happiness.

Reply Obj. 1. The summit of man does indeed touch the base of the angelic nature, by a kind of likeness; but man does not rest there as in his last end, but reaches out to the universal fount itself of good, which is the common object of happiness of all the blessed, as being the infinite and perfect good.

Reply Obj. 2. If a whole be not the last end, but ordained to a further end, then the last end of a part thereof is not the whole itself, but something else. Now the universe of creatures, to which man is compared as part to whole, is not the last end, but is ordained to God, as to its last end. Therefore the last end of man is not the good of the universe, but God himself.

Reply Obj. 3. Created good is not less than that good of which man is capable, as of something intrinsic and inherent to him: but it is less than the good of which he is capable, as of an object, and which is infinite. And the participated good which is in an angel, and in the whole universe, is a finite and restricted good.

*   *   *

QUESTION 3: WHAT IS HAPPINESS?

*   *   *

Fourth Article

WHETHER, IF HAPPINESS IS IN THE INTELLECTIVE PART, IT IS AN OPERATION OF THE INTELLECT OR OF THE WILL?

We Proceed Thus to the Fourth Article:—

Objection 1. It would seem that happiness consists in an act of the will. For Augustine says (*De Civ. Dei* xix. 10, 11), that man's happiness consists in peace; wherefore it is written (Ps. cxlvii. 3): *Who hath placed peace in thy end.* But peace pertains to the will. Therefore man's happiness is in the will.

Obj. 2. Further, happiness is the supreme good. But good is the object of the will. Therefore happiness consists in an operation of the will.

Obj. 3. Further, the last end corresponds to the first mover: thus the last end of the whole army is victory, which is the end of the general, who moves all the men. But the first mover in regard to operations is the will: because it moves the other powers, as we shall state further on (Q. 9, AA. 1, 3). Therefore happiness regards the will.

Obj. 4. Further, if happiness be an operation, it must needs be man's most excellent operation. But the love of God, which is an act of the will, is a more excellent operation than knowledge, which is an operation of the intellect, as the Apostle declares (1 Cor. xiii). Therefore it seems that happiness consists in an act of the will.

Obj. 5. Further, Augustine says (*De Trin.* xiii. 5) that *happy is he who has whatever he desires, and desires nothing amiss.* And a little further on (6) he adds: *He is almost happy who desires well, whatever he desires: for good things make a man happy, and such a man already possesses some good—i.e., a good will.* Therefore happiness consists in an act of the will.

On the contrary, Our Lord said (Jo. xvii. 3): *This is eternal life: that they may know Thee, the only true God.* Now eternal life is the last end, as stated above (A. 2 *ad* 1). Therefore man's happiness consists in the knowledge of God, which is an act of the intellect.

I answer that, As stated above (Q. 2, A. 6) two things are needed for happiness: one, which is the essence of happiness: the other, that is, as it were, its proper accident, *i.e.,* the delight connected with it. I say, then, that as to the very essence of happiness, it is impossible for it to consist in an act of the will. For it is evident from what has been said (AA. 1, 2; Q. 2, A. 7) that happiness is the attainment of the last end. But the attainment of the end does not consist in the very act of the will. For the will is directed to the end, both absent, when it desires it; and present, when it is delighted by resting therein. Now it is evident that the desire itself of the end is not the attainment of the end, but is a movement towards the end: while delight comes to the will from the end being present; and not conversely, is a thing made present, by the fact that the will delights in it. Therefore, that the end be present to him who desires it, must be due to something else than an act of the will.

This is evidently the case in regard to sensible ends. For if the acquisition of money were through an act of the will, the covetous man would have it from the very moment that he wished for it. But at that moment it is far from him; and he attains it, by grasping it in his hand, or in some like manner; and then he delights in the money got. And so it is with an intelligible end. For at first we desire to attain an intelligible end; we attain it, through its being made present to us by an act of the intellect; and then the delighted will rests in the end when attained.

So, therefore, the essence of happiness consists in an act of the intellect: but the delight that results from happiness pertains to the will. In this sense Augustine says (*Conf.* x. 23) that happiness is *joy in truth,* because, to wit, joy itself is the consummation of happiness.

Reply Obj. 1. Peace pertains to man's last end, not as though it were the very essence of happiness; but because it is antecedent and consequent thereto: antecedent, in so far as all those things are removed which disturb and hinder man in attaining the last end: consequent, inasmuch as, when man has attained his last end, he remains at peace, his desire being at rest.

Reply Obj. 2. The will's first object is not its act: just as neither is the first object of the sight, vision, but a visible thing. Wherefore, from the very fact that happiness belongs to the will, as the will's first object, it follows that it does not belong to it as its act.

Reply Obj. 3. The intellect apprehends the end before the will does: yet motion towards the end begins in the will. And therefore to the will belongs that which last of all follows the attainment of the end, viz., delight or enjoyment.

Reply Obj. 4. Love ranks above knowledge in moving, but knowledge precedes love in attaining: *for naught is loved save what is known,* as Augustine says (*De Trin.* x. 1). Consequently we first attain an intelligible end by an act of the intellect; just as we first attain a sensible end by an act of sense.

Reply Obj. 5. He who has whatever he desires, is happy, because he has what he desires: and this indeed is by something other than the act of his will. But to desire nothing amiss is needed for happiness, as a necessary disposition thereto. And a good will is reckoned among the good things which make a man happy, forasmuch as it is an inclination of the will: just as a movement is reduced to the genus of its terminus, for instance, *alteration* to the genus *quality.*

Eighth Article

We Proceed Thus to the Eighth Article:—

Objection 1. It would seem that man's happiness does not consist in the vision of the Divine Essence. For Dionysius says (*Myst. Theol.* i) that by that which is highest in his intellect, man is united to God as to something altogether unknown. But that which is seen in its essence is not altogether unknown. Therefore the final perfection of the intellect, namely, happiness, does not consist in God being seen in His Essence.

Obj. 2. Further, the higher perfection belongs to the higher nature. But to see His own Essence is the perfection proper to the Divine intellect. Therefore the final perfection of the human intellect does not reach to this, but consists in something less.

On the contrary, It is written (1 Jo. iii. 2): *When He shall appear, we shall be like to Him; and we shall see Him as He is.*

I answer that, Final and perfect happiness can consist in nothing else than the vision of the Divine Essence. To make this clear, two points must be observed. First, that man is not perfectly happy, so long as something remains for him to desire and seek: secondly, that the perfection of any power is determined by the nature of its object. Now the object of the intellect is *what a thing is, i.e.,* the essence of a thing, according to *De Anima* iii. 6. Wherefore the intellect attains perfection, in so far as it knows the essence of a thing. If therefore an intellect know the essence of some effect, whereby it is not possible to know the essence of the cause, *i.e.* to know of the cause *what it is;* that intellect cannot be said to reach that cause simply, although it may be able to gather from the effect the knowledge that the cause is. Consequently, when man knows an effect, and knows that it has a cause, there naturally remains in man the desire to know about that cause, *what it is.* And this desire is one of wonder, and causes inquiry, as is stated in the beginning of the *Metaphysics* (i. 2). For instance, if a man, knowing the eclipse of the sun, consider that it must be due to some cause, and know not what that cause is, he wonders about it, and from wondering proceeds to inquire. Nor does this inquiry cease until he arrive at a knowledge of the essence of the cause.

If therefore the human intellect, knowing the essence of some created effect, knows no more of God than *that He is;* the perfection of that intellect does not yet reach simply the First Cause, but there remains in it the natural desire to seek the cause. Wherefore it is not yet perfectly happy. Consequently, for perfect happiness the intellect needs to reach the very Essence of the First Cause. And thus it will have its perfection through union with God as with that object, in which alone man's happiness consists, as stated above (AA. 1, 7; Q. 2, A. 8).

Reply Obj. 1. Dionysius speaks of the knowledge of wayfarers journeying towards happiness.

Reply Obj. 2. As stated above (Q. 1, A. 8), the end has a twofold acceptation. First, as to the thing itself which is desired: and in this way, the same thing is the end of the higher and of the lower nature, and indeed of all things, as stated above *(ibid.).* Secondly, as to the attainment of this thing; and thus the end of the higher nature is different from that of the lower, according to their respective habitudes to that thing. So then the happiness of God, Who, in understanding his Essence, comprehends It, is higher than that of a man or angel who sees It indeed, but comprehends It not.

* * *

QUESTION 5: OF THE ATTAINMENT OF HAPPINESS

* * *

Fifth Article

WHETHER MAN CAN ATTAIN HAPPINESS BY HIS NATURAL POWERS?

We Proceed Thus to the Fifth Article:—

Objection 1. It would seem that man can attain Happiness by his natural powers. For nature does not fail in necessary things. But nothing is so necessary to man as that by which he attains the last end. Therefore this is not lacking to human nature. Therefore man can attain Happiness by his natural powers.

Obj. 2. Further, since man is more noble than irrational creatures, it seems that he must be better equipped than they. But irrational creatures can attain their end by their natural powers. Much more therefore can man attain Happiness by his natural powers.

Obj. 3. Further, Happiness is a *perfect operation,* according to the Philosopher (*Ethic.* vii. 13). Now the beginning of a thing belongs to the same principle as the perfecting thereof. Since, therefore, the imperfect operation, which is as the beginning in human operations, is subject to man's natural power, whereby he is master of his own actions; it seems that he can attain to perfect operation, *i.e.,* Happiness, by his natural powers.

On the contrary, Man is naturally the principle of his action, by his intellect and will. But final Happiness prepared for the saints, surpasses the intellect and will of man; for the Apostle says (1 Cor. ii. 9): *Eye hath not seen, nor ear heard, neither hath it entered into the heart of man, what things God hath prepared for them that love Him.* Therefore man cannot attain Happiness by his natural powers.

I answer that, Imperfect happiness that can be had in this life, can be acquired by man by his natural powers, in the same way as virtue, in whose operation it consists: on this point we shall speak further on (Q. 63). But man's perfect Happiness, as stated above (Q. 3, A. 8), consists in the vision of the Divine Essence. Now the vision of God's Essence surpasses the nature not only of man, but also of every creature, as was shown in the First Part (Q. 12, A. 4). For the natural knowledge of every creature is in keeping with the mode of his substance: thus it is said of the intelligence (*De Causis;* Prop. viii.) that *it knows things that are above it, and things that are below it, according to the mode of its substance.* But every knowledge that is according to the mode of created substance, falls short of the vision of the Divine Essence, which infinitely surpasses all created substance. Consequently neither man, nor any creature, can attain final Happiness by his natural powers.

Reply Obj. 1. Just as nature does not fail man in necessaries, although it has not provided him with weapons and clothing, as it provided other animals, because it gave him reason and hands, with which he is able to get these things for himself; so neither did it fail man in things necessary, although it gave him not the wherewithal to attain Happiness: since this it could not do. But it did give him freewill, with which he can turn to God, that He may make him happy. *For what we do by means of our friends, is done, in a sense, by ourselves* (*Ethic.* iii. 3).

Reply Obj. 2. The nature that can attain perfect good, although it needs help from without in order to attain it, is of more noble condition than a nature which cannot attain perfect good, but attains some imperfect good, although it need no help from without in order to attain it, as the Philosopher says (*De Cælo* ii. 12). Thus he is better disposed to health who can attain perfect health, albeit by means of medicine, than he who can attain but imperfect health, without the help of medicine. And therefore the rational creature, which can attain the perfect good of happiness, but needs the Divine assistance for the purpose, is more perfect than the irrational creature, which is not capable of attaining this good, but attains some imperfect good by its natural powers.

Reply Obj. 3. When imperfect and perfect are of the same species, they can be caused by the same power. But this does not follow of necessity, if they be of different species: for not everything, that can cause the disposition of matter, can produce the final perfection. Now the imperfect operation, which is subject to man's natural power, is not of the same species as that perfect operation which is man's happiness: since operation takes its species from its object. Consequently the argument does not prove.

*   *   *

TREATISE ON LAW

QUESTION 94: OF THE NATURAL LAW

*   *   *

Second Article

WHETHER THE NATURAL LAW CONTAINS SEVERAL PRECEPTS, OR ONE ONLY?

We Proceed Thus to the Second Article:—

Objection 1. It would seem that the natural law contains, not several precepts, but one only. For law is a kind of precept, as stated above (Q. 92, A. 2). If therefore there were many precepts of the natural law, it would follow that there are also many natural laws.

Obj. 2. Further, the natural law is consequent to human nature. But human nature, as a whole, is one; though, as to its parts, it is manifold. Therefore, either there is but one precept of the law of nature, on account of the unity of nature as a whole; or there are many, by reason of the number of parts of human nature. The result would be that even things relating to the inclination of the concupiscible faculty belong to the natural law.

Obj. 3. Further, law is something pertaining to reason, as stated above (Q. 90, A. 1). Now reason is but one in man. Therefore there is only one precept of the natural law.

On the contrary, The precepts of the natural law in man stand in relation to practical matters, as the first principles to matters of demonstration. But there are several first indemonstrable principles. Therefore there are also several precepts of the natural law.

I answer that, As stated above (Q. 91, A. 3), the precepts of the natural law are to the practical reason, what the first principles of demonstrations are to the speculative reason; because both are self-evident principles. Now a thing is said to be self-evident in two ways: first, in itself; secondly, in relation to us. Any proposition is said to be self-evident in itself, its predicate is contained in the notion of the subject: although, to one who knows not the definition of the subject, it happens that such a proposition is not self-evident. For instance, this proposition, *Man is a rational being,* is, in its very nature, self-evident, since who says *man,* says *a rational being:* and yet to one who knows not what a man is, this proposition is not self-evident. Hence it is that, as Boethius says *(De Hebdom.),* certain axioms or propositions are universally self-evident to all; and such are those propositions whose terms are known to all, as, *Every whole is greater than its part,* and, *Things equal to one and the same are equal to one another.* But some propositions are self-evident only to the wise, who understand the meaning of the terms of such propositions: thus to one who understands that an angel is not a body, it is self-evident that an angel is not circumscriptively in a place: but this is not evident to the unlearned, for they cannot grasp it.

Now a certain order is to be found in those things that are apprehended universally. For that which, before aught else, falls under apprehension, is *being,* the notion of which is included in all things whatsoever a man apprehends. Wherefore the first indemonstrable principle is that *the same thing cannot be affirmed and denied at the same time,* which is based on the notion of being and not-being: and on this principle all others are based, as is stated in *Metaph.* iv, text. 9. Now as being is the first thing that falls under the apprehension simply, so *good* is the first thing that falls under the apprehension of the practical reason, which is directed to action: since every agent acts for an end under the aspect of good. Consequently the first principle in the practical reason is one founded on the notion of good, viz., that *good is that which all things seek after.* Hence this is the first precept of law, that *good is to be done and pursued, and evil is to be avoided.* All other precepts of the natural law are based upon this: so that whatever the practical reason naturally apprehends as man's good (or evil) belongs to the precepts of the natural law as something to be done or avoided.

Since, however, good has the nature of an end, and evil, the nature of a contrary, hence it is that all those things to which man has a natural inclination, are naturally apprehended by reason as being good, and consequently as objects of pursuit, and their contraries as evil, and objects of avoidance. Wherefore according to the order of natural inclinations, is the order of the precepts of the natural law. Because in man there is first of all an inclination to good in accordance with the nature which he has in common with all substances: inasmuch as every substance seeks the preservation of its own being, according to its nature: and by reason of this inclination, whatever is a means of preserving human life, and of warding off its obstacles, belongs to the natural law. Secondly, there is in man an inclination to things that pertain to him more specially, according to that nature which he has in common with other animals: and in virtue of this inclination, those things are said to belong to the natural law, *which nature has taught to all animals,* such as sexual intercourse, education of offspring and so forth. Thirdly, there is in man an inclination to good, according to the nature of his reason, which nature is proper to him: thus man has a natural inclination to know the truth about God, and to live in society: and in this respect, whatever pertains to this inclination belongs to the natural law; for instance, to shun ignorance, to avoid offending those among whom one has to live, and other such things regarding the above inclination.

Reply Obj. 1. All these precepts of the law of nature have the character of one natural law, inasmuch as they flow from one first precept.

Reply Obj. 2. All the inclinations of any parts whatsoever of human nature, *e.g.,* of the concupiscible and irascible parts, in so far as they are ruled by reason, belong to the natural law, and are reduced to one first precept, as stated above: so that the precepts of the natural law are many in themselves, but are based on one common foundation.

Reply Obj. 3. Although reason is one in itself, yet it directs all things regarding man; so that whatever can be ruled by reason, is contained under the law of reason.

*   *   *

Fourth Article

WHETHER THE NATURAL LAW IS THE SAME IN ALL MEN?

We Proceed Thus to the Fourth Article:—

Objection 1. It would seem that the natural law is not the same in all. For it is stated in the Decretals (*Dist.* i) that *the natural law is that which is contained in the*

Law and the Gospel. But this is not common to all men; because, as it is written (Rom. x. 16), *all do not obey the gospel.* Therefore the natural law is not the same in all men.

Obj. 2. Further, *Things which are accordingly to the law are said to be just,* as stated in *Ethic.* v. But it is stated in the same book that nothing is so universally just as not to be subject to change in regard to some men. Therefore even the natural law is not the same in all men.

Obj. 3. Further, as stated above (AA. 2, 3), to the natural law belongs everything to which a man is inclined according to his nature. Now different men are naturally inclined to different things; some to the desire of pleasures, others to the desire of honors, and other men to other things. Therefore there is not one natural law for all.

On the contrary, Isidore says (*Etym.* v. 4): *The natural law is common to all nations.*

I answer that, As stated above (AA. 2, 3), to the natural law belongs those things to which a man is inclined naturally: and among these it is proper to man to be inclined to act according to reason. Now the process of reason is from the common to the proper, as stated in *Phys.* i. The speculative reason, however, is differently situated in this matter, from the practical reason. For, since the speculative reason is busied chiefly with necessary things, which cannot be otherwise than they are, its proper conclusions, like the universal principles, contain the truth without fail. The practical reason, on the other hand, is busied with contingent matters, about which human actions are concerned: and consequently, although there is necessity in the general principles, the more we descend to matters of detail, the more frequently we encounter defects. Accordingly then in speculative matters truth is the same in all men, both as to principles and as to conclusions: although the truth is not known to all as regards the conclusions, but only as regards the principles which are called *common notions.* But in matters of action, truth or practical rectitude is not the same for all, as to matters of detail, but only as to the general principles: and where there is the same rectitude in matters of detail, it is not equally known to all.

It is therefore evident that, as regards the general principles whether of speculative or of practical reason, truth or rectitude is the same for all, and is equally known by all. As to the proper conclusions of the speculative reason, the truth is the same for all, but is not equally known to all: thus it is true for all that the three angles of a triangle are together equal to two right angles, although it is not known to all. But as to the proper conclusions of the practical reason, neither is the truth or rectitude the same for all, nor, where it is the same, is it equally known by all. Thus it is right and true for all to act according to reason: and from this principle it follows as a proper conclusion, that goods entrusted to another should be restored to their owner. Now this is true for the majority of cases: but it may happen in a particular case that it would be injurious, and therefore unreasonable, to restore goods held in trust; for instance if they are claimed for the purpose of fighting against one's country. And this principle will be found to fail the more, according as we descend further into detail, e.g., if one were to say that goods held in trust should be restored with such and such a guarantee, or in such and such a way; because the greater the number of conditions added, the greater the number of ways in which the principle may fail, so that it be not right to restore or not to restore.

Consequently we must say that the natural law, as to general principles, is the same for all, both as to rectitude and as to knowledge. But as to certain matters of detail, which are conclusions, as it were, of those general principles, it is the same for all in the majority of cases, both as to rectitude and as to knowledge; and yet in some few cases it may fail, both as to rectitude, by reason of certain obstacles (just as natures subject to generation and corruption fail in some few cases on account of some obstacle), and as to knowledge, since in some the reason is perverted by passion, or evil habit, or an evil disposition of nature; thus formerly, theft, although it is expressly contrary to the natural law, was not considered wrong among the Germans, as Julius Caesar relates (*De Bello Gall.* vi).

Reply Obj. 1. The meaning of the sentence quoted is not that whatever is contained in the Law and the Gospel belongs to the natural law, since they contain many things that are above nature; but that whatever belongs to the natural law is fully contained in them. Wherefore Gratian, after saying that *the natural law is what is contained in the Law and the Gospel,* adds at once, by way of example, *by which everyone is commanded to do to others as he would be done by.*

Reply Obj. 2. The saying of the Philosopher is to be understood of things that are naturally just, not as general principles, but as conclusions drawn from them, having rectitude in the majority of cases, but failing in a few.

Reply Obj. 3. As, in man, reason rules and commands the other powers, so all the natural inclinations belonging to the other powers must needs be directed according to reason. Wherefore it is universally right for all men, that all their inclinations should be directed according to reason.

Fifth Article

WHETHER THE NATURAL LAW CAN BE CHANGED?

We Proceed Thus to the Fifth Article:—

Objection 1. It would seem that the natural law can be changed. Because on Ecclus. xvii. 9, *He gave them instructions, and the law of life,* the gloss says: *He wished the law of the letter to be written, in order to correct the law of nature.* But that which is corrected is changed. Therefore the natural law can be changed.

Obj. 2. Further, the slaying of the innocent, adultery, and theft are against the natural law. But we find these things changed by God: as when God commanded Abraham to slay his innocent son (Gen. xxii. 2); and when he ordered the Jews to borrow and purloin the vessels of the Egyptians (Exod. xii. 35); and when He commanded Osee to take to himself *a wife of fornications* (Osee i. 2). Therefore the natural law can be changed.

Obj. 3. Further, Isidore says (*Etym.* v. 4) that *the possession of all things in common, and universal freedom, are matters of natural law.* But these things are seen to be changed by human laws. Therefore it seems that the natural law is subject to change.

On the contrary, It is said in the Decretals (*Dist.* v): *The natural law dates from the creation of the rational creature. It does not vary according to time, but remains unchangeable.*

I answer that, A change in the natural law may be understood in two ways. First, by way of addition. In this sense nothing hinders the natural law from being changed: since many things for the benefit of human life have been added over and above the natural law, both by the Divine law and by human laws.

Secondly, a change in the natural law may be understood by way of subtraction, so that what previously was according to the natural law, ceases to be so. In this sense, the natural law is altogether unchangeable in its first principles: but in its secondary principles, which, as we have said (A. 4), are certain detailed proximate conclusions drawn from the first principles, the natural law is not changed so that what it prescribes be not right in most cases. But it may be changed in some particular cases of rare oc-currence, through some special causes hindering the observance of such precepts, as stated above (A. 4).

Reply Obj. 1. The written law is said to be given for the correction of the natural law, either because it supplies what was wanting to the natural law; or because the nat-ural law was perverted in the hearts of some men, as to certain matters, so that they es-teemed those things good which are naturally evil; which perversion stood in need of correction.

Reply Obj. 2. All men alike, both guilty and innocent, die the death of nature: which death of nature is inflicted by the power of God on account of original sin, ac-cording to 1 Kings ii. 6: *The Lord killeth and maketh alive.* Consequently, by the com-mand of God, death can be inflicted on any man, guilty or innocent, without any injus-tice whatever.—In like manner adultery is intercourse with another's wife; who is allotted to him by the law emanating from God. Consequently intercourse with any woman, by the command of God, is neither adultery nor fornication.—The same ap-plies to theft, which is the taking of another's property. For whatever is taken by the command of God, to Whom all things belong, is not taken against the will of its owner, whereas it is in this that theft consists.—Nor is it only in human things, that whatever is commanded by God is right; but also in natural things, whatever is done by God, is, in some way, natural, as stated in the First Part (Q. 105, A. 6 *ad* 1).

Reply Obj. 3. A thing is said to belong to the natural law in two ways. First, be-cause nature inclines thereto: *e.g.,* that one should not do harm to another. Secondly, because nature did not bring in the contrary: thus we might say that for man to be naked is of the natural law, because nature did not give him clothes, but art invented them. In this sense, *the possession of all things in common and universal freedom* are said to be of the natural law, because, to wit, the distinction of possessions and slavery were not brought in by nature, but devised by human reason for the benefit of human life. Accordingly the law of nature was not changed in this respect, except by addition.

* * *

QUESTION 95: OF HUMAN LAW

* * *

First Article

WHETHER IT WAS USEFUL FOR LAWS TO BE FRAMED BY MEN?

We Proceed Thus to the First Article:—

Objection 1. It would seem that it was not useful for laws to be framed by men. Because the purpose of every law is that man be made good thereby, as stated above (Q. 92, A. 1). But men are more to be induced to be good willingly by means of admo-nitions, than against their will, by means of laws. Therefore there was no need to frame laws.

Obj. 2. Further, as the Philosopher says (*Ethic.* v. 4), *men have recourse to a judge as to animate justice.* But animate justice is better than inanimate justice, which is contained in laws. Therefore it would have been better for the execution of justice to be entrusted to the decision of judges, than to frame laws in addition.

Obj. 3. Further, every law is framed for the direction of human actions, as is evident from what has been stated above (Q. 90, AA. 1, 2). But since human actions are about singulars, which are infinite in number, matters pertaining to the direction of human actions cannot be taken into sufficient consideration except by a wise man, who looks into each one of them. Therefore it would have been better for human acts to be directed by the judgment of wise men, than by the framing of laws. Therefore there was no need of human laws.

On the contrary, Isidore says (*Etym.* v. 20): *Laws were made that in fear thereof human audacity might be held in check, that innocence might be safeguarded in the midst of wickedness, and that the dread of punishment might prevent the wicked from doing harm.* But these things are most necessary to mankind. Therefore it was necessary that human laws should be made.

I answer that, As stated above (Q. 63, A. 1; Q. 94, A. 3), man has a natural aptitude for virtue; but the perfection of virtue must be acquired by man by means of some kind of training. Thus we observe that man is helped by industry in his necessities, for instance, in food and clothing. Certain beginnings of these he has from nature, viz., his reason and his hands; but he has not the full complement, as other animals have, to whom nature has given sufficiency of clothing and food. Now it is difficult to see how man could suffice for himself in the matter of this training: since the perfection of virtue consists chiefly in withdrawing man from undue pleasures, to which above all man is inclined, and especially the young, who are more capable of being trained. Consequently a man needs to receive this training from another, whereby to arrive at the perfection of virtue. And as to those young people who are inclined to acts of virtue, by their good natural disposition, or by custom, or rather by the gift of God, paternal training suffices, which is by admonitions. But since some are found to be depraved, and prone to vice, and not easily amenable to words, it was necessary for such to be restrained from evil by force and fear, in order that, at least, they might desist from evil-doing, and leave others in peace, and that they themselves, by being habituated in this way, might be brought to do willingly what hitherto they did from fear, and thus become virtuous. Now this kind of training, which compels through fear of punishment, is the discipline of laws. Therefore, in order that man might have peace and virtue, it was necessary for laws to be framed: for, as the Philosopher says (Polit. i. 2), *as man is the most noble of animals if he be perfect in virtue, so is he the lowest of all, if he be severed from law and righteousness;* because man can use his reason to devise means of satisfying his lusts and evil passions, which other animals are unable to do.

Reply Obj. 1. Men who are well disposed are led willingly to virtue by being admonished better than by coercion: but men who are evilly disposed are not led to virtue unless they are compelled.

Reply Obj. 2. As the Philosopher says (*Rhet.* i. 1), *it is better that all things be regulated by law, than left to be decided by judges: and this for three reasons. First, because it is easier to find a few wise men competent to frame right laws, than to find the many who would be necessary to judge aright of each single case.—Secondly, because those who make laws consider long beforehand* what laws to make; whereas judgment on each single case has to be pronounced as soon as it arises: and it is easier for man to see what is right, by taking many instances into consideration, than by considering one solitary fact.—Thirdly, because lawgivers judge in the abstract and of future events; whereas those who sit in judgment judge of things present, towards which they are affected by love, hatred, or some kind of cupidity; wherefore their judgment is perverted.

Since then the animated justice of the judge is not found in every man, and since it can be deflected, therefore it was necessary, whenever possible, for the law to determine how to judge, and for very few matters to be left to the decision of men.

Reply Obj. 3. Certain individual facts which cannot be covered by the law *have necessarily to be committed to judges,* as the Philosopher says in the same passage: for instance, *concerning something that has happened or not happened,* and the like.

Second Article

WHETHER EVERY HUMAN LAW IS DERIVED FROM THE NATURAL LAW?

We Proceed Thus to the Second Article:—

Objection 1. It would seem that not every human law is derived from the natural law. For the Philosopher says (*Ethic.* v. 7) that *the legal just is that which originally was a matter of indifference.* But those things which arise from the natural law are not matters of indifference. Therefore the enactments of human laws are not all derived from the natural law.

Obj. 2. Further, positive law is contrasted with natural law, as stated by Isidore (*Etym.* v. 4) and the Philosopher (*Ethic.* v, *loc. cit.*). But those things which flow as conclusion from the general principles of the natural law belong to the natural law, as stated above (Q. 94, A. 4). Therefore that which is established by human law does not belong to the natural law.

Obj. 3. Further, the law of nature is the same for all; since the Philosopher says (*Ethic.* v. 7) that *the natural just is that which is equally valid everywhere.* If therefore human laws were derived from the natural law, it would follow that they too are the same for all: which is clearly false.

Obj. 4. Further, it is possible to give a reason for things which are derived from the natural law. But *it is not possible to give the reason for all the legal enactments of the lawgivers,* as the jurist says. Therefore not all human laws are derived from the natural law.

On the contrary, Tully says (*Rhetor.* ii): *Things which emanated from nature and were approved by custom, were sanctioned by fear and reverence for the laws.*

I answer that, As Augustine says (*De Lib. Arb.* i. 5), *that which is not just seems to be no law at all: wherefore the force of a law depends on the extent of its justice. Now in human affairs a thing is said to be just, from being right, according to the rule of reason. But the first rule of reason is the law of nature, as is clear from what has been stated* above (Q. 91, A. 2 *ad* 2). Consequently every human law has just so much of the nature of law, as it is derived from the law of nature. But if in any point it deflects from the law of nature, it is no longer a law but a perversion of law.

But it must be noted that something may be derived from the natural law in two ways: first, as a conclusion from premises, secondly, by way of determination of certain generalities. The first way is like to that by which, in sciences, demonstrated conclusions are drawn from the principles: while the second mode is likened to that whereby, in the arts, general forms are particularized as to details: thus the craftsman needs to determine the general form of a house to some particular shape. Some things are therefore derived from the general principles of the natural law, by way of conclusions; *e.g.*, that *one must not kill* may be derived as a conclusion from the principle that one should do harm to no man: while some are derived therefrom by way of determination; *e.g.*, the law of nature has it that the evil-doer should be punished; but that he be punished in this or that way, is a determination of the law of nature.

Accordingly both modes of derivation are found in the human law. But those things which are derived in the first way, are contained in human law not as emanating therefrom exclusively, but have some force from the natural law also. But those things which are derived in the second way, have no other force than that of human law.

Reply Obj. 1. The Philosopher is speaking of those enactments which are by way of determination or specification of the precepts of the natural law.

Reply Obj. 2. This argument avails for those things that are derived from the natural law, by way of conclusions.

Reply Obj. 3. The general principles of the natural law cannot be applied to all men in the same way on account of the great variety of human affairs: and hence arises the diversity of positive laws among various people.

Reply Obj. 4. These words of the Jurist are to be understood as referring to decisions of rulers in determining particular points of the natural law: on which determinations the judgment of expert and prudent men is based as on its principles; in so far, to wit, as they see at once what is the best thing to decide.

Hence the Philosopher says (*Ethic.* vi. 11) that in such matters, *we ought to pay as much attention to the undemonstrated sayings and opinions of persons who surpass us in experience, age and prudence, as to their demonstrations.*

*   *   *

QUESTION 96: OF THE POWER OF HUMAN LAW

*   *   *

Second Article

WHETHER IT BELONGS TO THE HUMAN LAW TO REPRESS ALL VICES?

We Proceed Thus to the Second Article:—

Objection 1. It would seem that it belongs to human law to repress all vices. For Isidore says (*Etym.* v. 20) that *laws were made in order that, in fear thereof, man's audacity might be held in check.* But it would not be held in check sufficiently, unless all evils were repressed by law. Therefore human law should repress all evils.

Obj. 2. Further, the intention of the lawgiver is to make the citizens virtuous. But a man cannot be virtuous unless he forbear from all kinds of vice. Therefore it belongs to human law to repress all vices.

Obj. 3. Further, human law is derived from the natural law, as stated above (Q. 95, A. 2). But all vices are contrary to the law of nature. Therefore human law should repress all vices.

On the contrary, We read in *De Lib. Arb.* i. 5: *It seems to me that the law which is written for the governing of the people rightly permits these things, and that Divine providence punishes them.* But Divine providence punishes nothing but vices. Therefore human law rightly allows some vices, by not repressing them.

I answer that, As stated above (Q. 90, AA. I, 2), law is framed as a rule or measure of human acts. Now a measure should be homogeneous with that which it measures, as stated in *Metaph.* x, text. 3, 4, since different things are measured by different measures. Wherefore laws imposed on men should also be in keeping with their condition, for, as Isidore says (*Etym.* v. 21), law should be *possible both according to nature, and according to the customs of the country.* Now possibility or faculty of action is due to an interior habit or disposition: since the same thing is not possible to one who has not a virtuous habit, as is possible to one who has. Thus the same is not possible to a child as to a full-grown man: for which reason the law for children is not the same as for adults, since many things are permitted to children, which in an adult are punished by law or at any rate are open to blame. In like manner many things are permissible to men not perfect in virtue, which would be intolerable in a virtuous man.

Now human law is framed for a number of human beings, the majority of whom are not perfect in virtue. Wherefore human laws do not forbid all vices, from which the virtuous abstain, but only the more grievous vices, from which it is possible for the majority to abstain; and chiefly those that are to the hurt of others, without the prohibition of which human society could not be maintained: thus human law prohibits murder, theft and such like.

Reply Obj. 1. Audacity seems to refer to the assailing of others. Consequently it belongs to those sins chiefly whereby one's neighbor is injured: and these sins are forbidden by human law, as stated.

Reply Obj. 2. The purpose of human law is to lead men to virtue, not suddenly, but gradually. Wherefore it does not lay upon the multitude of imperfect men the burdens of those who are already virtuous, viz., that they should abstain from all evil. Otherwise these imperfect ones, being unable to bear such precepts, would break out into yet greater evils: thus it is written (Prov. xxx. 33): *He that violently bloweth his nose, bringeth out blood;* and (Matth. ix. 17) that if *new wine,* i.e., precepts of a perfect life, *is put into old bottles,* i.e., into imperfect men, *the bottles break, and the wine runneth out,* i.e., the precepts are despised, and those men, from contempt, break out into evils worse still.

Reply Obj. 3. The natural law is a participation in us of the eternal law: while human law falls short of the eternal law. Now Augustine says (*De Lib. Arb.* i. 5): *The law which is framed for the government of states, allows and leaves unpunished many things that are punished by Divine providence. Nor, if this law does not attempt to do everything, is this a reason why it should be blamed for what it does.* Wherefore, too, human law does not prohibit everything that is forbidden by the natural law.

* * *

SECOND PART OF THE SECOND PART (II–II)

* * *

QUESTION 40: OF WAR

* * *

First Article

WHETHER IT IS ALWAYS SINFUL TO WAGE WAR?

We Proceed Thus to the First Article:—

Objection 1. It would seem that it is always sinful to wage war. Because punishment is not inflicted except for sin. Now those who wage war are threatened by Our Lord with punishment, according to Matth. xxvi. 52: *All that take the sword shall perish with the sword.* Therefore all wars are unlawful.

Obj. 2. Further, whatever is contrary to a Divine precept is a sin. But war is contrary to a Divine precept, for it is written (Matth. v. 39): *But I say to you not to resist evil;* and (Rom. xii. 19): *Not revenging yourselves, my dearly beloved, but give place unto wrath.* Therefore war is always sinful.

Obj. 3. Further, nothing, except sin, is contrary to an act of virtue. But war is contrary to peace. Therefore war is always a sin.

Obj. 4. Further, the exercise of a lawful thing is itself lawful, as is evident in scientific exercises. But warlike exercises which take place in tournaments are forbidden by the Church, since those who are slain in these trials are deprived of ecclesiastical burial. Therefore it seems that war is a sin in itself.

On the contrary, Augustine says in a sermon on the son of the centurion [*Ep. ad Marcel.,* cxxxviii.]: *If the Christian Religion forbade war altogether, those who sought salutary advice in the Gospel would rather have been counselled to cast aside their arms, and to give up soldiering altogether. On the contrary, they were told: "Do violence to no man; . . . and be content with your pay."* [Luke iii. 14] *If he commanded them to be content with their pay, he did not forbid soldiering.*

I answer that, In order for a war to be just, three things are necessary. First, the authority of the sovereign by whose command the war is to be waged. For it is not the business of a private individual to declare war, because he can seek for redress of his rights from the tribunal of his superior. Moreover it is not the business of a private individual to summon together the people, which has to be done in wartime. And as the care of the common weal is committed to those who are in authority, it is their business to watch over the common weal of the city, kingdom or province subject to them. And just as it is lawful for them to have recourse to the sword in defending that common weal against internal disturbances, when they punish evil-doers, according to the words of the Apostle (Rom. xiii. 4): *He beareth not the sword in vain: for he is God's minister, an avenger to execute wrath upon him that doth evil;* so too, it is their busi-

Three Orders of Society, from *L'image du monde,* Franco-Flemish, late-thirteenth century.
This detail from an illustated manuscript page shows the hierarchy of medieval society
with monk, knight, and peasant. (*British Museum*)

ness to have recourse to the sword of war in defending the common weal against external enemies. Hence it is said to those who are in authority (Ps. lxxxi. 4): *Rescue the
poor: and deliver the needy out of the hand of the sinner;* and for this reason Augustine
says (*Contra Faust.* xxii. 75): *The natural order conducive to peace among mortals
demands that the power to declare and counsel war should be in the hands of those
who hold the supreme authority.*

Secondly, a just cause is required, namely that those who are attacked, should
be attacked because they deserve it on account of some fault. Wherefore Augustine
says (QQ. *in Hept.,* qu. x, *super Jos.*): *A just war is wont to be described as one that
avenges wrongs, when a nation or state has to be punished, for refusing to make
amends for the wrongs inflicted by its subjects, or to restore what it has seized unjustly.*

Thirdly, it is necessary that the belligerents should have a rightful intention, so that they intend the advancement of good, or the avoidance of evil. Hence Augustine says *De Verb. Dom: True religion looks upon as peaceful those wars that are waged not for motives of aggrandizement or cruelty, but with the object of securing peace, of punishing evil-doers, and of uplifting the good.* For it may happen that the war is declared by the legitimate authority, and for a just cause, and yet be rendered unlawful through a wicked intention. Hence Augustine says (*Contra Faust.* xxii. 74): *The passion for inflicting harm, the cruel thirst for vengeance, an unpacific and relentless spirit, the fever of revolt, the lust of power, and such like things, all these are rightly condemned in war.*

Reply Obj. 1. As Augustine says (*Contra Faust.* xxii. 70): *To take the sword is to arm oneself in order to take the life of anyone, without the command or permission of superior or lawful authority.* On the other hand, to have recourse to the sword (as a private person) by the authority of the sovereign or judge, or (as a public person) through zeal for justice, and by the authority, so to speak, of God, is not to *take the sword,* but to use it as commissioned by another, wherefore it does not deserve punishment. And yet even those who make sinful use of the sword are not always slain with the sword, yet they always perish with their own sword, because, unless they repent, they are punished eternally for their sinful use of the sword.

Reply Obj. 2. Such like precepts, as Augustine observes (*De Serm. Dom. in Monte* i. 19), should always be borne in readiness of mind, so that we be ready to obey them, and, if necessary, to refrain from resistance or self-defense. Nevertheless it is necessary sometimes for a man to act otherwise for the common good, or for the good of those with whom he is fighting. Hence Augustine says (*Ep. ad Marcellin.* cxxxviii): *Those whom we have to punish with a kindly severity, it is necessary to handle in many ways against their will. For when we are stripping a man of the lawlessness of sin, it is good for him to be vanquished, since nothing is more hopeless than the happiness of sinners, whence arises a guilty impunity, and an evil will, like an internal enemy.*

Reply Obj. 3. Those who wage war justly aim at peace, and so they are not opposed to peace, except to the evil peace, which Our Lord *came not to send upon earth* (Matth. x. 34). Hence Augustine says (*Ep. ad Bonif.* clxxxix): *We do not seek peace in order to be at war, but we go to war that we may have peace. Be peaceful, therefore, in warring, so that you may vanquish those whom you war against, and bring them to the prosperity of peace.*

Reply Obj. 4. Manly exercises in warlike feats of arms are not all forbidden, but those which are inordinate and perilous, and end in slaying or plundering. In olden times warlike exercises presented no such danger, and hence they were called *exercises of arms* or bloodless wars, as Jerome states in an epistle.

WILLIAM OF OCKHAM
ca. 1285–1349

William was born in Ockham, Surrey, near London, between 1280 and 1290. He joined the Franciscan order as a young man. In 1309 or 1310, he went to Oxford, where his studies included the work of Duns Scotus. Despite his success as a student and, later, as a student lecturer, Ockham was denied a license to teach. The chancellor of the university accused him of heresy, even going to the papal court in Avignon, France, in 1323 to press charges. The following year Ockham was summoned to Avignon by Pope John XXII. The affair dragged on for four years. Meanwhile, Ockham kept writing and came into conflict with the pope again when he joined the general of his Franciscan order in advocating apostolic poverty.

In 1328, Ockham was forced to flee Avignon when the pope was prepared to condemn the Franciscan position on poverty. He eventually found refuge in Munich under the protection of Emperor Ludwig of Bavaria, who was angry with the pope for not recognizing his crown. Ockham reportedly told the emperor, "Defend me with your sword, and I will defend you with my pen."

Over the next twenty years, Ockham did indeed defend the emperor, arguing that imperial power flows from God through the people, not through the pope—a position that anticipated later political theories. Following Ludwig's death in 1347, Ockham sought reconciliation with the pope (now Clement VI), and a document of submission was drawn up. We do not know whether Ockham ever signed the document, for he died in 1349, apparently from the plague.

Ockham's philosophy reflects his times: He is much less optimistic than was Thomas Aquinas about the ability of human reason to understand the things of God. Ockham criticized the proofs for God's existence, arguing that theological truth can be known only by revelation, not reason. In so arguing, he separated

Plague Victim, from *Das Buch der Cirurgia*, 1497, by Hieronymus Brunschwig. Beginning in 1347 the Bubonic Plague, or "Black Death," struck western Europe. Transmitted by flea bite, the disease was characterized by enormous swelling or "buboes" in the groin or armpits. The patient in this woodcut has a large buboe on his armpit—a sure sign that he will be dead within two or three days. Apparently William of Ockham met such a fate in 1349. (*Library of Congress*)

philosophy from theology and reason from faith more completely than had any of his predecessors.

Ockham is probably best known for his "Law of Parsimony," or "Ockham's Razor." This principle has often been formulated as *entia non sunt multiplicanda praeter necessitatem,* "entities are not to be multiplied beyond necessity," though none of Ockham's known works contains that exact phrase.* Essentially this principle holds that we should always seek the simplest explanation, a principle still used by philosophers and scientists. Ockham was not the first to enunciate this principle: It can be found earlier in the writings of Thomas Aquinas,** Duns Scotus, and even, in embryonic form, in Aristotle. But the skill with which Ockham wielded this "razor" ensured its association with his name.

*Ockham's extant writings do include the phrases *pluralitas non est ponenda sine necessitate,* "plurality is not to be posited without necessity," and *frustra fit per plura quod potest fieri per pauciora,* "what can be explained by the assumption of fewer things is vainly explained by the assumption of more things." Perhaps applying his principle to its own formulation, we should say, "Why use many if few will do?"

**See his *Summa Theologica,* Part I, Q. 2, a. 3, obj. 2—page 342 in this volume.

Ockham was especially effective in using his razor on the question of universals. Contrary to the moderate realism dominant in his day, Ockham saw no need to posit universals as real entities beyond individual things. This critique is clear in the selections on universals given here. Following some defining of terms, Ockham argues against the realist position and, with great care, against the position of the "Subtle Doctor," Duns Scotus. Ockham asserts that "in a particular substance there is nothing substantial except the particular form, the particular matter, or the composite of the two"—that is, there is no real universal apart from the particular thing.

In addition, representative passages on being, on knowledge, on God, and on politics are included. The final reading on politics—with its strong, though guarded, antipapal polemic—represents a marked departure from the political theory of John of Salisbury.

*   *   *

Marilyn McCord Adams's *William Ockham,* two volumes (Notre Dame, IN: University of Notre Dame Press, 1987) is the definitive introduction to Ockham, whereas Meyrick Heath Carré, *Realists and Nominalists* (London: Oxford University Press, 1946), and Gordon Leff, *William of Ockham: The Metamorphosis of Scholastic Discourse* (Manchester: Manchester University Press, 1975) provide helpful overviews. Specialized studies include E.A. Moody, *The Logic of William of Ockham* (1935; reprinted New York: Russell and Russell, 1965); Damascene Webering, *The Theory of Demonstration According to William Ockham* (St. Bonaventure, NY: Franciscan Institute, 1953); Herman Shapiro, *Motion, Time and Place According to William Ockham* (St. Bonaventure, NY: Franciscan Institute, 1957); Arthur Stephen McGrade, *The Political Thought of William of Ockham: Personal and Institutional Principles* (London: Cambridge University Press, 1974); and Rega Wood, *Ockham on the Virtues* (West Lafayette, IN: Purdue University Press, 1997). For an important collection of essays, see Philotheus Bohner, ed., *Collected Articles on Ockham* (St. Bonaventure, NY: Franciscan Institute, 1958).

SUMMA LOGICAE (in part)

PART I

CHAPTER 14: ON THE UNIVERSAL

It is not enough for the logician to have a merely general knowledge of terms; he needs a deep understanding of the concept of a term. Therefore, after discussing some general divisions among terms we should examine in detail the various headings under these divisions.

First, we should deal with terms of second intention and afterwards with terms of first intention. I have said that "universal," "genus," and "species" are examples of terms of second intention. We must discuss those terms of second intention which are called the five universals, but first we should consider the common term "universal." It is predicated of every universal and is opposed to the notion of a particular.

First, it should be noted that the term "particular" has two senses. In the first sense a particular is that which is one and not many. Those who hold that a universal is a certain quality residing in the mind which is predicable of many (not suppositing for itself, of course, but for the many of which it is predicated) must grant that, in this sense of the word, every universal is a particular. Just as a word, even if convention makes it common, is a particular, the intention of the soul signifying many is numerically one thing a particular; for although it signifies many things it is nonetheless one thing and not many.

In another sense of the word we use "particular" to mean that which is one and not many and which cannot function as a sign of many. Taking "particular" in this sense no universal is a particular, since every universal is capable of signifying many and of being predicated of many. Thus, if we take the term "universal" to mean that which is not one in number, as many do, then, I want to say that nothing is a universal. One could, of course, abuse the expression and say that a population constitutes a single universal because it is not one but many. But that would be puerile.

Therefore, it ought to be said that every universal is one particular thing and that it is not a universal except in its signification, in its signifying many things. This is what Avicenna means to say in his commentary on the fifth book of the *Metaphysics*. He says, "One form in the intellect is related to many things, and in this respect it is a universal; for it is an intention of the intellect which has an invariant relationship to anything you choose." He then continues, "Although this form is a universal in its relationship to individuals, it is a particular in its relationship to the particular soul in which it resides; for it is just one form among many in the intellect." He means to say that a universal is an intention of a particular soul. Insofar as it can be predicated of many things not for itself but for these many, it is said to be a universal; but insofar as it is a particular form actually existing in the intellect, it is said to be a particular. Thus "particular" is predicated of a universal in the first sense but not in the second. In the same way we say that the sun is a universal cause and, nevertheless, that it is really and truly a particular or individual cause. For the sun is said to be a universal cause because it is the cause of many things (i.e., every object that is generable and corruptible), but it is said to be a particular cause because it is one cause and not many. In the same way the intention of the soul is said to be a universal because it is a sign predicable of many things, but it is said to be a particular because it is one thing and not many.

But it should be noted that there are two kinds of universals. Some things are universal by nature; that is, by nature they are signs predicable of many in the same way that the smoke is by nature a sign of fire; weeping, a sign of grief; and laughter, a sign of internal joy. The intention of the soul, of course, is a universal by nature. Thus, no substance outside the soul, nor any accident outside the soul is a universal of this sort. It is of this kind of universal that I shall speak in the following chapters.

Other things are universals by convention. Thus, a spoken word, which is numerically one quality, is a universal; it is a sign conventionally appointed for the signification of many things. Thus, since the word is said to be common, it can be called a universal. But notice it is not by nature, but only by convention, that this label applies.

CHAPTER 15: THAT THE UNIVERSAL IS NOT
A THING OUTSIDE THE MIND

But it is not enough just to state one's position; one must defend it by philosophical arguments. Therefore, I shall set forth some arguments for my view, and then corroborate it by an appeal to the authorities.

That no universal is a substance existing outside the mind can be proved in a number of ways:

No universal is a particular substance, numerically one; for if this were the case, then it would follow that Socrates is a universal; for there is no good reason why one substance should be a universal rather than another. Therefore no particular substance is a universal; every substance is numerically one and a particular. For every substance is either one thing and not many or it is many things. Now, if a substance is one thing and not many, then it is numerically one; for that is what we mean by "numerically one." But if, on the other hand, some substance is several things, it is either several particular things or several universal things. If the first alternative is chosen, then it follows that some substance would be several particular substances; and consequently that some substance would be several men. But although the universal would be distinguished from a single particular, it would not be distinguished from several particulars. If, however, some substance were to be several universal entities, I take one of those universal entities and ask, "Is it many things or is it one and not many?" If the second is the case then it follows that the thing is particular. If the first is the case then I ask, "Is it several particular things or several universal things?" Thus, either an infinite regress will follow or it will be granted that no substance is a universal in a way that would be incompatible with its also being a particular. From this it follows that no substance is a universal.

Again, if some universal were to be one substance existing in particular substances, yet distinct from them, it would follow that it could exist without them; for everything that is naturally prior to something else can, by God's power, exist without that thing; but the consequence is absurd.

Again, if the view in question were true, no individual would be able to be created. Something of the individual would pre-exist it, for the whole individual would not take its existence from nothing if the universal which is in it were already in something else. For the same reason it would follow that God could not annihilate an individual substance without destroying the other individuals of the same kind. If He were to annihilate some individual, he would destroy the whole which is essentially that individual and, consequently, He would destroy the universal which is in that thing and in others of the same essence. Consequently, other things of the same essence would not remain, for they could not continue to exist without the universal which constitutes a part of them.

Again, such a universal could not be construed as something completely extrinsic to the essence of an individual; therefore, it would belong to the essence of the individual; and, consequently, an individual would be composed of universals, so that the individual would not be any more a particular than a universal.

Again, it follows that something of the essence of Christ would be miserable and damned, since that common nature really existing in Christ would be damned in the damned individual; for surely that essence is also in Judas. But this is absurd.

Many other arguments could be brought forth, but in the interests of brevity, I shall dispense with them. Instead, I shall corroborate my account by an appeal to authorities.

First, in the seventh book of the *Metaphysics,* Aristotle is treating the question of whether a universal is a substance. He shows that no universal is a substance. Thus, he says, "It is impossible that substance be something that can be predicated universally."

Again, in the tenth book of the *Metaphysics,* he says, "Thus, if, as we argued in the discussions on substance and being, no universal can be a substance, it is not possible that a universal be a substance in the sense of a one over and against the many."

From these remarks it is clear that, in Aristotle's view, although universals can supposit for substances, no universal is a substance.

Again, the Commentator in his forty-fourth comment on the seventh book of the *Metaphysics* says, "In the individual, the only substance is the particular form and matter out of which the individual is composed."

Again, in the forty-fifth comment, he says, "Let us say, therefore, that it is impossible that one of those things we call universals be the substance of anything, although they do express the substances of things."

And, again, in the forty-seventh comment, "It is impossible that they (universals) be parts of substances existing of and by themselves."

Again, in the second comment on the eighth book of the *Metaphysics,* he says, "No universal is either a substance or a genus."

Again, in the sixth comment on the tenth book, he says, "Since universals are not substances, it is clear that the common notion of being is not a substance existing outside the mind."

Using these and many other authorities, the general point emerges: no universal is a substance regardless of the viewpoint from which we consider the matter. Thus, the viewpoint from which we consider the matter is irrelevant to the question of whether something is a substance. Nevertheless, the meaning of a term is relevant to the question of whether the expression "substance" can be predicated of the term. Thus, if the term "dog" in the proposition "The dog is an animal" is used to stand for the barking animal, the proposition is true; but if it is used for the celestial body which goes by that name, the proposition is false. But it is impossible that one and the same thing should be a substance from one viewpoint and not a substance from another.

Therefore, it ought to be granted that no universal is a substance regardless of how it is considered. On the contrary, every universal is an intention of the mind which, on the most probable account, is identical with the act of understanding. Thus, it is said that the act of understanding by which I grasp men is a natural sign of men in the same way that weeping is a natural sign of grief. It is a natural sign such that it can stand for men in mental propositions in the same way that a spoken word can stand for things in spoken propositions.

That the universal is an intention of the soul is clearly expressed by Avicenna in the fifth book of the *Metaphysics,* in which he comments, "I say, therefore, that there are three senses of 'universal.' For we say that something is a universal if (like 'man') it is actually predicated of many things; and we also call an intention a universal if it could be predicated of many." Then follows the remark, "An intention is also called a universal if there is nothing inconceivable in its being predicated of many."

From these remarks it is clear that the universal is an intention of the soul capable of being predicated of many. The claim can be corroborated by argument. For every one agrees that a universal is something predicable of many, but only an intention of the soul or a conventional sign is predicated. No substance is ever predicated of anything. Therefore, only an intention of the soul or a conventional sign is a universal; but I am not here using the term "universal" for conventional signs, but only for signs that are universals by nature. That substance is not capable of functioning as predicate is clear; for if it were, it would follow that a proposition would be composed of particular substances; and, consequently, the subject would be in Rome and the predicate in England which is absurd.

Furthermore, propositions occur only in the mind, in speech, or in writing; therefore, their parts can exist only in the mind, in speech, and in writing. Particular substances, however, cannot themselves exist in the mind, in speech, or in writing. Thus, no proposition can be composed of particular substances. Propositions are, however, composed of universals; therefore, universals cannot conceivably be substances.

CHAPTER 16: AGAINST SCOTUS' ACCOUNT OF THE UNIVERSAL

It may be clear to many that a universal is not a substance outside the mind which exists in, but is distinct from, particulars. Nevertheless, some want to claim that the universal is, in some way, outside the soul and in particulars; and while they do not want to say that a universal is really distinct from particulars, they say that it is formally distinct from particulars. Thus, they say that in Socrates there is human nature which is contracted to Socrates by an individual difference which is not really, but only formally, distinct from that nature. Thus, while there are not two things, one is not formally the other.

I do not find this view tenable:

First, in creatures there can never be any distinction outside the mind unless there are distinct things; if, therefore, there is any distinction between the nature and the difference, it is necessary that they really be distinct things. I prove my premise by the following syllogism: the nature is not formally distinct from itself; this individual difference is formally distinct from this nature; therefore, this individual difference is not this nature.

Again, the same entity is not both common and proper, but in their view the individual difference is proper and the universal is common; therefore, no universal is identical with an individual difference.

Again, opposites cannot be attributed to one and the same created thing, but *common* and *proper* are opposites; therefore, the same thing is not both common and proper. Nevertheless, that conclusion would follow if an individual difference and a common nature were the same thing.

Again, if a common nature were the same thing as an individual difference, there would be as many common natures as there are individual differences; and, consequently, none of those natures would be common, but each would be peculiar to the difference with which it is identical.

Again, whenever one thing is distinct from another it is distinguished from that thing either of and by itself or by something intrinsic to itself. Now, the humanity of Socrates is something different from the humanity of Plato; therefore, they are distinguished of and by themselves and not by differences that are added to them.

Again, according to Aristotle things differing in species also differ in number, but the nature of a man and the nature of a donkey differ in species of and by themselves; therefore, they are numerically distinguished of and by themselves; therefore, each of them is numerically one of and by itself.

Again, that which cannot belong to many cannot be predicated of many; but such a nature, if it really is the same thing as the individual difference, cannot belong to many since it cannot belong to any other particular. Thus, it cannot be predicable of many; but, then, it cannot be a universal.

Again, take an individual difference and the nature which it contracts. Either the difference between these two things is greater or less than the difference between two particulars. It is not greater because they do not differ really; particulars, however, do differ really. But neither is it less because then they would admit of one and the same definition, since two particulars, can admit of the same definition. Consequently, if one of them is, by itself, one in number, the other will also be.

Again, either the nature is the individual difference or it is not. If it is the difference I argue as follows: this individual difference is proper and not common; this individual difference is this nature; therefore this nature is proper and not common, but that is what I set out to prove. Likewise, I argue as follows: the individual difference is not formally distinct from the individual difference; the individual difference is the nature; therefore, the nature is not formally distinct from the individual difference. But if it be said that the individual difference is not the nature, my point has been proved; for it follows that if the individual difference is not the nature, the individual difference is not really the nature; for from the opposite of the consequent follows the opposite of the antecedent. Thus, if it is true that the individual difference really is the nature, then the individual difference is the nature. The inference is valid, for from a determinable taken with its determination (where the determination does not detract from or diminish the determinable) one can infer the determinable taken by itself; but "really" does not express a determination that detracts or diminishes. Therefore, it follows that if the individual difference is really the nature, the individual difference is the nature.

Therefore, one should grant that in created things there is no such thing as a formal distinction. All things which are distinct in creatures are really distinct and, therefore, different things. In regard to creatures modes of argument like the following ought never be denied: this is A; this is B; therefore, B is A; and this is not A; this is B; therefore, B is not A. Likewise, one ought never deny that, as regards creatures, there are distinct things where contradictory notions hold. The only exception would be the case where contradictory notions hold true because of some syncategorematic element or similar determination, but in the same present case this is not so.

Therefore, we ought to say with the philosophers that in a particular substance there is nothing substantial except the particular form, the particular matter, or the composite of the two. And, therefore, no one ought to think that in Socrates there is a humanity or a human nature which is distinct from Socrates and to which there is added an individual difference which contracts that nature. The only thing in Socrates which can be construed as substantial is this particular matter, this particular form, or the composite of the two. And, therefore, every essence and quiddity and whatever belongs to substance, if it is really outside the soul, is just matter, form, or the composite of these or, following the doctrine of the Peripatetics, a separated and immaterial substance.

EPILOGUE: GIOVANNI PICO DELLA MIRANDOLA
1463–1494

◀─────◆────▶

In the late-1300s, some Italian thinkers began to talk about a rebirth or "renaissance." They wrote disparagingly of the "Middle" or "Dark Ages," depicting it as a period of barbarian ignorance from which they had just emerged. They saw themselves as awakening to their classical past and continuing the civilizing work of the ancient Greeks and Romans.

Although there are few scholars today who would not modify this self-characterization, there does seem to have been something different about the late-medieval/early-modern period. Whereas the medievals had access to some classical texts, the Renaissance thinkers had a wide, and often contradictory, variety of ancient Greek and Roman works. Whereas the philosophers of the Middle Ages tended to use ancient materials to reinforce their Christian beliefs, the early-modern thinkers found new uses for these ancient texts. But most important, whereas the Middle Ages tended to be vertically oriented, focusing on God and God's Kingdom, the early-modern period became more and more horizontally oriented, examining the created world and celebrating its most important inhabitants, human beings.

The person who most typifies this use of ancient texts to express the importance and "dignity of man" is Count Giovanni Pico della Mirandola. Pico was born in Mirandola, near Ferrara, northern Italy. The son of a minor Italian prince, his education included a variety of subjects and a diversity of institutions. In 1477, he went to the University of Bologna to study canon (church) law. After two years, he moved to study philosophy at the universities of Ferrara and Padua. Finally in 1482, he concluded his studies by examining Hebrew and Arabic thought while in Florence and Paris.

Pico believed it was possible to reconcile the seeming contradictions among the various systems of thought he had studied. Drawing out what he considered the best in each thinker and system he encountered, he developed a philosophy known as "syncretism." Syncretism holds that all schools of philosophy have some truth and so should be examined and defended; but no system of thought has all the truth, and so one must also expose the errors in each scheme.

Applying his philosophy of syncretism, in 1486 Pico drew up a list of nine hundred true theses (or propositions), using various Greek, Arabic, Hebrew, and Roman thinkers who summarized his views. He invited scholars from all over Europe to come to Rome, where he would defend his positions against all challengers. However, the disputation never occurred. Pope Innocent VIII suspended the debate and appointed a commission to investigate the nine hundred theses. Seven of the propositions were subsequently declared unorthodox and six more held to be dangerous. Pico publicly protested the decision by publishing a defense of his positions. This succeeded only in infuriating the pope. The pope condemned all nine hundred propositions, reportedly commenting, "That young man wants someone to burn him." Pico fled to France but was arrested there by papal envoys. Through the intervention of friends in Italy, Pico was released by the French king. He spent the rest of his short life in Florence under the protection of the powerful Medici family.

The *Oration on the Dignity of Man* was intended as an introductory speech for the proposed debate in Rome. In the selection reprinted here, translated by Elizabeth Livermore Forbes, Pico exhibits his syncretistic willingness to draw from many different sources. Quoting from a wide variety of writings, he argues that God has given all creatures besides humans a unique, fixed nature. They have a certain kind of being that they cannot change. But we as human beings do not have a given being—we alone have the freedom to choose what we will become. Even though we can choose to become animals or "couch potatoes" or angelic philosophers, it is the ability to *choose* that gives us dignity.

*   *   *

Pico's life was chronicled by his nephew in the difficult-to-find Giovanni Francesco Pico, *Giovanni Pico della Mirandola: His Life by His Nephew Giovanni Francesco Pico,* translated by Sir Thomas More, edited by J.M. Rigg (London: D. Nutt, 1890). For a general overview of Pico, see William G. Craven, *Giovanni Pico della Mirandola, Symbol of His Age: Modern Interpretations of a Renaissance Philosopher* (Geneve: Droz, 1981).

For collections of primary source readings in Renaissance philosophy, see Ernst Cassirer, Paul O. Kristeller, and John H. Randall, Jr., eds., *The Renaissance Philosophy of Man* (Chicago: University of Chicago Press, 1948), and Arturo B. Fallico and Herman Shapiro, eds., *Renaissance Philosophy,* two volumes (New York: Random House, 1967–1969). For general studies of Renaissance thought, see Ernst Cassirer, *The Individual and Cosmos in Renaissance Philosophy,* translated by Mario Domandi (New York: Harper & Row, 1963); Paul O. Kristeller, *Renaissance Thought and Its Sources* (New York: Columbia University Press, 1979); Charles B. Schmitt, Quentin Skinner, and Eckhard Kessler, eds., *The Cambridge History of Renaissance Philosophy* (Cambridge: Cambridge University Press, 1988); and Brian P. Copenhaver and Charles B. Schmitt, *Renaissance Philosophy,* Vol. 3 of *History of Western Philosophy* (Oxford: Oxford University Press, 1992).

ORATION ON THE DIGNITY OF MAN
(in part)

I have read in the records of the Arabians, reverend Fathers, that Abdala the Saracen [probably the cousin of Mohammed], when questioned as to what on this stage of the world, as it were, could be seen most worthy of wonder, replied: "There is nothing to be seen more wonderful than man." In agreement with this opinion is the saying of Hermes Trismegistus: "A great miracle, Asclepius, is man." But when I weighed the reason for these maxims, the many grounds for the excellence of human nature reported by many men failed to satisfy me—that man is the intermediary between creatures, the intimate of the gods, the king of the lower beings, by the acuteness of his senses, by the discernment of his reason, and by the light of his intelligence the interpreter of nature, the interval between fixed eternity and fleeting time, and (as the Persians say) the bond, nay, rather, the marriage song of the world, on David's testimony but little lower than the angels (Ps. 8:5). Admittedly great though these reasons be, they are not the principal grounds, that is, those which may rightfully claim for themselves the privilege of the highest admiration. For why should we not admire more the angels themselves and the blessed choirs of heaven? At last it seems to me I have come to understand why man is the most fortunate of creatures and consequently worthy of all admiration and what precisely is that rank which is his lot in the universal chain of Being—a rank to be envied not only by brutes but even by the stars and by minds beyond this world. It is a matter past faith and a wondrous one. Why should it not be? For it is on this very account that man is rightly called and judged a great miracle and a wonderful creature indeed.

2. But hear, Fathers, exactly what this rank is and, as friendly auditors, conformably to your kindness, do me this favor. God the Father, the supreme Architect, had already built this cosmic home we behold, the most sacred temple of His godhead, by the laws of His mysterious wisdom. The region above the heavens He had adorned with Intelligences, the heavenly spheres He had quickened with eternal souls, and the excrementary and filthy parts of the lower world He had filled with a multitude of animals of every kind. But, when the work was finished, the Craftsman kept wishing that there were someone to ponder the plan of so great a work, to love its beauty, and to wonder at its vastness. Therefore, when everything was done (as Moses and Timaeus bear witness), He finally took thought concerning the creation of man. But there was not among His archetypes that from which He could fashion a new offspring, nor was there in His treasure-houses anything which He might bestow on His new son as an inheritance, nor was there in the seats of all the world a place where the latter might sit to contemplate the universe. All was now complete; all things had been assigned to the highest, the middle, and the lowest orders. But in its final creation it was not the part of the Father's power to fail as though exhausted. It was not the part of His wisdom to waver in a needful matter through poverty of counsel. It was not the part of His kindly love that he who was to praise God's divine generosity in regard to others should be compelled to condemn it in regard to himself.

Giovanni Pico della Mirandola, *Oration on the Dignity of Man,* 1–7, translated by Elizabeth Livermore Forbes, from *The Renaissance Philosophy of Man,* edited by Ernst Cassirer, Paul Oskar Kristeller, and John Herman Randall, Jr. (Chicago: The University of Chicago Press, 1948). Copyright © 1948 The University of Chicago Press. Reprinted by permission.

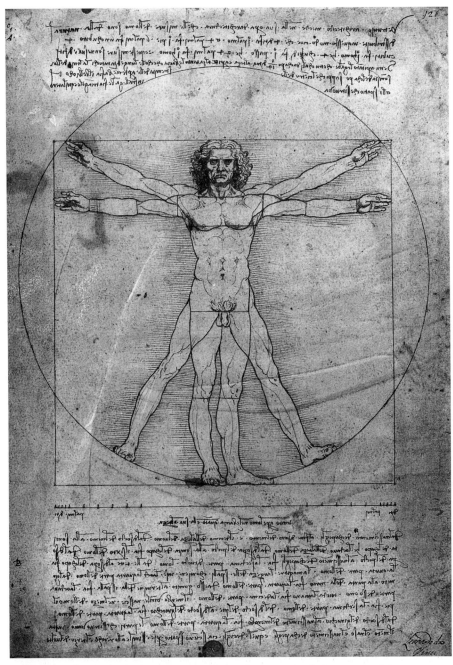

Study of Human Proportions, by Leonardo da Vinci (1452–1519). Like Pico, Leonardo enjoyed the patronage of Lorenzo de Medici; and also like Pico, Leonardo celebrated the "dignity of man" and exuberantly exhibited his own ability. (© *1991 Archivi Alinari/Art Resource*)

3. At last the best of artisans ordained that that creature to whom He had been able to give nothing proper to himself should have joint possession of whatever had been peculiar to each of the different kinds of being. He therefore took man as a creature of indeterminate nature and, assigning him a place in the middle of the world, addressed him thus: "Neither a fixed abode nor a form that is thine alone nor any function peculiar to thyself have we given thee, Adam, to the end that according to thy longing and according to thy judgment thou mayest have and possess what abode, what form, and what functions thou thyself shalt desire. The nature of all other beings is limited and constrained within the bounds of laws prescribed by Us. Thou, constrained by no limits, in accordance with thine own free will, in whose hand We have placed thee, shalt ordain for thyself the limits of thy nature. We have set thee at the world's center that thou mayest from thence more easily observe whatever is in the world. We have made thee neither of heaven nor of earth, neither mortal nor immortal, so that with freedom of choice and with honor, as though the maker and molder of thyself, thou mayest fashion thyself in whatever shape thou shalt prefer. Thou shalt have the power to degenerate into the lower forms of life, which are brutish. Thou shalt have the power, out of thy soul's judgment, to be reborn into the higher forms, which are divine."

4. O supreme generosity of God the Father, O highest and most marvelous felicity of man! To him it is granted to have whatever he chooses, to be whatever he wills. Beasts as soon as they are born (so says Lucilius) bring with them from their mother's womb all they will ever possess. Spiritual beings, either from the beginning or soon thereafter, become what they are to be for ever and ever. On man when he came into life the Father conferred the seeds of all kinds and the germs of every way of life. Whatever seeds each man cultivates will grow to maturity and bear in him their own fruit. If they be vegetative, he will be like a plant. If sensitive, he will become brutish. If rational, he will grow into a heavenly being. If intellectual, he will be an angel and the son of God. And if, happy in the lot of no created thing, he withdraws into the center of his own unity, his spirit, made one with God, in the solitary darkness of God, who is set above all things, shall surpass them all. Who would not admire this our chameleon? Or who could more greatly admire aught else whatever? It is man who Asclepius of Athens, arguing from his mutability of character and from his self-transforming nature, on just grounds says was symbolized by Proteus in the mysteries. Hence those metamorphoses renowned among the Hebrews and the Pythagoreans.

5. For the occult theology of the Hebrews sometimes transforms the holy Enoch into an angel of divinity whom they call "Mal'akh Adonay Shebaoth," and sometimes transforms others into other divinities. The Pythagoreans degrade impious men into brutes and, if one is to believe Empedocles, even into plants. Mohammed, in imitation, often had this saying on his tongue: "They who have deviated from divine law become beasts," and surely he spoke justly. For it is not the bark that makes the plant but its senseless and insentient nature; neither is it the hide that makes the beast of burden but its irrational, sensitive soul; neither is it the orbed form that makes the heavens but their undeviating order; nor is it the sundering from body but his spiritual intelligence that makes the angel. For if you see one abandoned to his appetites crawling on the ground, it is a plant and not a man you see; if you see one blinded by the vain illusions of imagery, as it were of Calypso, and, softened by their gnawing allurement, delivered over to his senses, it is a beast and not a man you see. If you see a philosopher determining all things by means of right reason, him you shall reverence: he is a heavenly being and not of this earth. If you see a pure contemplator, one unaware of the body and confined to the inner reaches of the mind, he is neither an earthly nor a heavenly being; he is a more reverend divinity vested with human flesh.

6. Are there any who would not admire man, who is, in the sacred writings of Moses and the Christians, not without reason described sometimes by the name of "all flesh," sometimes by that of "every creature," inasmuch as he himself molds, fashions, and changes himself into the form of all flesh and into the character of every creature? For this reason the Persian Euanthes, in describing the Chaldaean theology, writes that man has no semblance that is inborn and his very own but many that are external and foreign to him; whence this saying of the Chaldaeans: *Hanorish tharah sharinas,* that is, "Man is a being of varied, manifold, and inconstant nature." But why do we emphasize this? To the end that after we have been born to this condition—that we can become what we will—we should understand that we ought to have especial care to this, that it should never be said against us that, although born to a privileged position, we failed to recognize it and became like unto wild animals and senseless beasts of burden, but that rather the saying of Asaph the prophet should apply: "Ye are all angels and sons of the Most High," and that we may not, by abusing the most indulgent generosity of the Father, make for ourselves that freedom of choice He has given into something harmful instead of salutary. Let a certain holy ambition invade our souls, so that, not content with the mediocre, we shall pant after the highest and (since we may if we wish) toil with all our strength to obtain it.

7. Let us disdain earthly things, despise heavenly things, and, finally, esteeming less whatever is of the world, hasten to that court which is beyond the world and nearest to the Godhead. There, as the sacred mysteries relate, Seraphim, Cherubim and Thrones hold the first places; let us, incapable of yielding to them, and intolerant of a lower place, emulate their dignity and their glory. If we have willed it, we shall be second to them in nothing.

MODERN
PHILOSOPHY

———◆◇◆———

To a large extent, modern philosophy begins with a rejection of tradition. Whereas medieval philosophers such as Thomas Aquinas had taken great pains to incorporate and reconcile ancient writings, early modern philosophers such as René Descartes encouraged their readers to make a clean sweep of the past. Previous thinkers had been deluded by errors in thinking or had relied too heavily on authority. In the modern age, the wisdom of the past was to be discarded as error-prone. As Descartes observed in his *Meditations*,

> Some years ago I was struck by the large number of falsehoods that I had accepted as true in my childhood, and by the highly doubtful nature of the whole edifice that I had subsequently based on them. I realized that it was necessary, once in the course of my life, to demolish everything completely and start again right from the foundations if I wanted to establish anything at all in the sciences that was stable and likely to last.

This quest to establish a stable intellectual foundation on which to build something "likely to last" characterized seventeenth- and eighteenth-century European philosophy. "British Empiricists," such as Thomas Hobbes, John Locke, and David Hume found such a foundation in sensory experience and developed their thought on that basis. On the other hand, the "Continent Rationalists," philosophers such as Descartes, Baruch Spinoza, and Gottfried Leibniz, thought the senses inadequate for such a task. They considered reason superior to experience and sought to establish their philosophies on the basis of more certain principles. The greatest of the modern philosophers, Immanuel Kant, sought to combine these two approaches and in so doing developed a uniquely influential system of philosophy.

Contemporary thinkers in the West are still trying to come to grips with these modern philosophers. For better or for worse, their ideas have influenced virtually all areas of Euro-American civilization. The subtlety and clarity with which these thinkers wrote continues to demand careful study even in this "postmodern" age.

*   *   *

There are a number of fine introductions to modern philosophy. Among the classics in this area are Étienne Gilson, *Modern Philosophy: Descartes to Kant* (New York: Random House, 1963); the appropriate works from Frederick Copleston, *A History of Philosophy, Volume IV: Descartes to Leibniz; Volume V: Hobbes to Hume;* and *Volume VI: Wolff to Kant* (1950; reprinted New York: Image Doubleday, 1959–1960); and W.T. Jones's books, *Hobbes to Hume*, 2nd edition and *Kant and the Nineteenth Century*, 2nd edition, revised (both New York: Harcourt, Brace & World, 1969 and 1975). More recent general surveys include Roger Scruton, *A Short History of Modern Philosophy: From Descartes to Wittgenstein* (London: Routledge, 1984), and Wallace I. Matson, *A New History of Philosophy, Volume II: Modern* (San Diego, CA: Harcourt Brace Jovanovich, 1987). The following volumes from the *Routledge History of Philosophy* series include essays on this period: G.H.R. Parkinson, ed., *Volume 4: The Renaissance and Seventeenth Century Rationalism*; Stuart Brown, ed., *Volume 5: British Empiricism and the Enlightenment*; and Robert Solomon and Kathleen Higgins, eds., *Volume 6: The Age of German Idealism* (all London: Routledge, 1993). A sampling of the many specialized books on specific topics from this era includes Louis E. Loeb, *From Descartes to Hume: Continental Metaphysics and the Development of Modern Philosophy* (Ithaca, NY: Cornell University Press, 1981); Robert C. Solomon, *Continental Philosophy Since 1750: The Rise and Fall of the Self* (Oxford: Oxford University Press, 1988); and Iain Hampshire-Monk, *A History of Modern Political Thought* (Oxford: Blackwell, 1992).

RENÉ DESCARTES
1596–1650

René Descartes was born into the family of a minor noble in the town of La Haye in Touraine, France. At ten, René began a nine-year course of studies at the Royal Jesuit College of La Flèche. There he studied the humanities, theology, and philosophy (which included morals, logic, mathematics, metaphysics, and science). Though he did well in school, he was disillusioned by the uncertainty of his studies and their contradictory conclusions. Like modern students, he felt overwhelmed by the many opinions he encountered. He later wrote in his *Discourse on Method* that upon completing of his course of study, "I found myself embarrassed with so many doubts and errors that it seemed to me that the effort to instruct myself had no effect other than the increasing discovery of my own ignorance."

However, one discipline contained the certainty he was seeking: mathematics. The truths of mathematics were assured regardless of one's metaphysical or epistemological assumptions: $2 + 2 = 4$ whether one is a Platonist or an Aristotelian; $3 \times 3 = 9$ whether one is a Roman Catholic or a Protestant. Given mathematical certainty, Descartes found it odd that on such a firm basis "no loftier edifice had been reared."

Left a modest inheritance by his father, Descartes spent the rest of his life seeking the certainty not found in college. After receiving a law degree at Poitiers in 1616, he served as a gentleman volunteer in the army of Maurice of Nassau. While soldiering, he began to develop the idea of connecting mathematical certainty with philosophy. In 1619, he had a series of dreams convincing him that the "spirit of truth" was leading him and that he had divine approval for his studies. For the next ten years, while traveling and serving in the army, he developed his ideas. In 1628, he had a debate with Chandoux, a scientist who claimed that science could only be founded on probability. Descartes argued eloquently that knowledge must be based on certainty and that he had a system that provided that basis. Encouraged by others to develop his system, he retired to Holland, where he found a greater degree of intellectual freedom and spent the next twenty years writing and publishing his ideas. His major philosophical works include *Rules for the Direction of the Mind* (written 1628, but not published until 1701), *Discourse on Method* (published in 1637 as a preface to the essays *Geometry, Dioptric,* and *Meteors*), and *Meditations on First Philosophy* (1641). Descartes also published seven sets of *Objections to the Meditations* of such thinkers as Hobbes, Arnauld, and Gassendi, accompanied by his *Reply to Objections.* In addition to his work in philosophy, Descartes made major contributions to the fields of optics, anatomy, physiology, and mathematics (especially analytic geometry in which "Cartesian coordinates" are still used).

Descartes chose to write his works in French as well as Latin in order to reach beyond the academics to a wider audience. His writings did, indeed, reach learned people throughout Europe and that fact, unfortunately, led indirectly to his death. In 1649, Queen Christina of Sweden invited Descartes to join a circle of leading thinkers to instruct her in philosophy. Although he initially resisted the invitation, he finally felt compelled to accept. Upon arriving in Sweden, Descartes discovered that Queen Christina had time to see him only at five each morning. Descartes had been used to lying in bed until late in the morning, reflecting and philosophizing. Within a year the rigorous new schedule, together with Sweden's harsh weather, led to his death.

*   *   *

Descartes began his philosophy by sweeping away what he considered the "errors of the past." Using the methods of mathematics, specifically geometry, he began by establishing twenty-one *Rules for the Direction of the Mind.* He would begin by finding knowledge that he could "clearly and evidently intuit, or deduce with certainty." Then he would build from this knowledge deductively, one step at a time. This procedure would parallel the geometrical method of moving with deductive certainty from postulates to axioms. His *Meditations on First Philosophy,* reprinted here (complete) in the Laurence J. Lafleur translation, chronicles this process.

The key was to find the knowledge that he could "clearly and evidently intuit" that could serve as his starting point. Although uncertainty and doubt were the enemies, Descartes hit upon the idea of using doubt as a tool or a weapon. Instead of fighting doubt, he would use it to find certainty. He would use doubt as an acid to pour over every "truth" to see if there was anything that would not be dissolved, any "truth" that could not be doubted. Some of his doubts may seem extreme (such as that the earth may not exist or that I may be dreaming all this), but in order to find 100-percent certainty he had to find a starting point with zero-percent doubt.

After subjecting all his knowledge to the acid of doubt, he concluded that there was one thing he could not doubt: that he was doubting. The one fact the acid of doubt could not dissolve was doubt itself. This meant there had to be an "I" who was doing the doubting. Even if he were deceived about everything else, he had to exist in order to be deceived. This led Descartes to his famous statement, *Cogito ergo sum,* meaning "I think, therefore I am" (although these exact words do not appear in the *Meditations*). Here was the "clearly and evidently intuited" knowledge, the starting point, that Descartes had been seeking.

Having established that there is an "I," a self, a starting point, Descartes began to explore the nature of this "I":

> But what then am I? A thing that thinks. What is that? A thing that doubts, understands, affirms, denies, is willing, is unwilling, and also imagines and has sensory perceptions.

Among the ideas of this "thinking thing" called the "I" is the idea of a perfect God. Descartes went on to argue that nothing less than God could have caused the idea of God. He therefore concluded with a second certainty: God exists.

From here Descartes moved to his third certainty: We have a strong tendency to believe in the existence of a reality beyond our consciousness. If there is no such external world, then we are terribly deceived. But a perfect God would not allow us to be unavoidably deceived, since deceit implies imperfection. Accordingly, we can conclude that we are not misled about those natural beliefs, such as the existence of an external world, so long as they can withstand the scrutiny of reason and are not willfully disregarded.

Descartes had now established a basis for accepting the "obvious" truths he had thrown out earlier by his method of doubt. He had at the same time identified the criterion needed to distinguish the foundational truths upon which his knowl-

The Anatomy Lesson, 1632, by Rembrandt (1606–1669). Members of the Surgeons and Physicians Guild personify the Age of Observation with their intense scientific inquiry into human anatomy. Descartes was also interested in anatomy, making such important discoveries as that muscles work in opposition to each other. (*Mauritshuis, The Hague*)

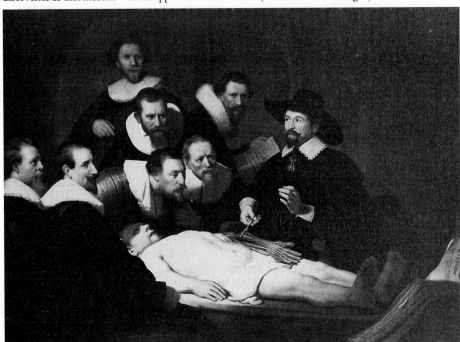

edge rested, namely, the criterion that a truth must be "clearly and distinctly perceived." An example of his rationalistic dependence upon such intuitions is his claim that the essential nature of a material object can only be known intuitively, not through sense perceptions.

One final point needs to be noted. The "I" that Descartes found at the end of his methodological doubting was "entirely distinct from the body." This "I" was an immaterial mind, a "spiritual" thing. The body is an "extended, nonthinking thing." As such, it is part of the material world, subject to the same laws of motion as a billiard ball. The "I," or the mind, on the other hand, is not bound by physical laws. This Cartesian distinction leads to a problem about the relationship between body and mind with which we still struggle today.

*   *   *

For a concise treatment of Descartes' thought in its historical context, see Alexandre Koyré, "Introduction," in E. Anscombe and P.T. Geach, eds., *René Descartes' Philosophical Writings* (Edinburgh: Nelson, 1954). Among the best of several excellent general studies of Descartes are Anthony Kenny, *Descartes: A Study of His Philosophy* (New York: Random House, 1968); Margaret Dauler Wilson, *Descartes* (Oxford: Routledge, 1983); John Cottingham, *Descartes* (Oxford: Basil Blackwell, 1986); and Stephen Gauktoger, *Descartes: An Intellectual Biography* (Oxford: Oxford University Press, 1995). For discussions of Descartes' *Meditations*, see L.J. Beck, *The Metaphysics of Descartes: A Study of the Meditations* (Oxford: Clarendon Press, 1965); E.M. Curley, *Descartes Against the Skeptics* (Cambridge, MA: Harvard University Press, 1978); Stanley Tweyman, ed., *Rene Descartes' Meditations on First Philosophy in Focus* (Oxford: Routledge, 1993); Georges Dicker, *Descartes* (Oxford: Oxford University Press, 1993). Roger Ariew and Marjorie Grene, eds., *Descartes and his Contemporaries: Meditations, Objections, and Replies* (Chicago: University of Chicago Press, 1995 and Vere Chappel, ed., *Descartes's Meditations: Critical Essays* (Lanham, MD: Rowan & Littlefield, 1997) includes the responses of Descartes' contemporaries to the *Meditations*. S. Woolhouse, *Descartes, Spinoza, Leibniz: The Concept of Substance in Seventeenth-Century Metaphysics* (London: Routledge, 1993) provides a comparative study, whereas John Cottingham, *A Descartes Dictionary* (Oxford: Basil Blackwell, 1993) provides a helpful reference work. For collections of essays on Descartes, see Willis Doney, ed., *Descartes: A Collection of Critical Essays* (Garden City, NY: Doubleday, 1967); Michael Hooker, ed., *Descartes: Critical and Interpretive Essays* (Baltimore, MD: Johns Hopkins University Press, 1978); Amelie O. Rorty, ed., *Essays on Descartes' Meditations* (Berkeley: University of California Press, 1986); Georges J.D. Moyal, ed., *René Descartes: Critical Assessments* (London: Routledge, 1991); Vere Chappell, ed., *Essays on Early Modern Philosophers: René Descartes* (Hamden, CT: Garland, 1992); John Cottingham, ed., *The Cambridge Companion to Descartes* (Cambridge: Cambridge University Press, 1992); the multi-volume George J.D. Moyal, *Rene Descartes: Critical Assessments* (Oxford: Routledge, 1992); and Stephen Voss, *Essays on the Philosophy and Science of René Descartes* (Oxford: Oxford University Press, 1993). Gilbert Ryle, *The Concept of Mind* (London: Hutchinson's University Library, 1949) is the classic critique of Descartes' views on body and mind.

MEDITATIONS ON THE FIRST PHILOSOPHY

[Dedicatory letter to the Sorbonne]

To those most learned and most illustrious men, the Dean and Doctors of the Sacred Faculty of Theology of Paris

Gentlemen:

My reason for offering you this work is so logical, and after you have learned its plan you will also, I am sure, have so logical a reason to take it under your protection, that I believe nothing will recommend it to you more than a brief statement of what I herein propose to do.

I have always thought that the two questions, of God and of the soul, were the principal questions among those that should be demonstrated by rational philosophy rather than theology. For although it may suffice us faithful ones to believe by faith that there is a God and that the human soul does not perish with the body, (2) certainly it does not seem possible ever to persuade those without faith to accept any religion, nor even perhaps any moral virtue, unless they can first be shown these two things by means of natural reason. And since in this life one frequently finds greater rewards offered for vice than for virtue, few persons would prefer the just to the useful if they were not restrained either by the fear of God or by the expectation of another life. It is absolutely true, both that we must believe that there is a God because it is so taught in the Holy Scriptures, and, on the other hand, that we must believe the Holy Scriptures because they come from God. The reason for this is that faith is a gift of God, and the very God that gives us the faith to believe other things can also give us the faith to believe that he exists. Nevertheless, we could hardly offer this argument to those without faith, for they might suppose that we were committing the fallacy that logicians call circular reasoning.

And truly I have noticed that you, gentlemen, along with all other theologians, assure us not only that the existence of God can be proved by natural reason, but also that we can infer from the Holy Scriptures that our knowledge of God is much clearer and easier than our knowledge of various created things, so clear in fact, so absolutely easy to attain, that those who do not possess it are blameworthy. This is evidenced in the words of the Book of the Wisdom of Solomon, Chapter XIII, where it is said: "Howbeit they are not to be excused; for if their understanding was so great that they could discern the world and the creatures, why did they not rather find out the Lord thereof?" And in the Epistle to the Romans, Chapter 1, where it is said that they are "without excuse," and again in the same place in these words: "That which may be known of God is manifest in them." It seems that we are being told that all that can be known of God can be demonstrated by reasons that we do not need to seek elsewhere than in ourselves, and that our minds alone are capable of furnishing us. That is why I

René Descartes, *Meditations on First Philosophy,* translated by Laurence J. Lafleur (New York: Macmillan/Library of the Liberal Arts, 1951).

have believed that it would not be inappropriate if I showed here how that can be done, and by what means we can know God more easily and more certainly than we know the things of the world.

And as for the soul, many have believed that it is not easy to understand its nature, (3) and some have even dared to say that human reasoning would convince us that it perishes with the body, and that faith alone can teach us the contrary. Nevertheless, as the Lateran Council, held under Leo X, Session 8, condemns these persons, and expressly orders Christian philosophers to refute their arguments and to employ all their intellectual abilities to make the truth known, I have decided to make the attempt in this work.

Moreover, the principal reason why many outside the Church do not wish to believe that there is a God and that the human soul is distinct from the body is that they claim that no one has so far been able to demonstrate these two things. I do not share their opinion; on the contrary, I hold that almost all of the arguments brought to bear on these two questions by so many illustrious men are valid demonstrations when they are properly understood, and that it is practically impossible to invent new ones. So I believe that there is nothing more useful to be done in philosophy than critically and carefully to seek out, once and for all, the best and most reliable of such arguments, and to give them so clear and exact a presentation that it would thenceforward be evident to everyone that they are valid demonstrations. And finally, several persons have urged me to do this, since they knew that I have been practicing a certain method of solving all sorts of difficulties in the sciences—a method which really is not new, for nothing is older than the truth, but which they knew I was using rather successfully in other matters. I have therefore considered it my duty to see what I could achieve in this field. (4)

I have put in this treatise everything that I was able to discover about this subject. That is not to say that I have collected here all the various arguments which might be adduced as proofs in our subject, for I have never thought that that would be necessary unless no certain proof existed. I have only treated here of the most basic and principal ones in such a way that I can reasonably venture to maintain that they are very evident and very certain demonstrations. And I shall say further that they are such that I do not think there is any way in which the human mind can ever find better ones; for the importance of the subject, and the glory of God, to which all this relates, constrain me to speak somewhat more freely of myself here than I usually do. Nevertheless, whatever certainty and obviousness I find in my own arguments, I cannot convince myself that everyone will be able to understand them. There is a similar situation in geometry, where there are several proofs, left to us by Archimedes, Apollonius, Pappus, and several others, that are accepted by everyone as very certain and evident because they contain nothing but what, considered separately, is very easy to understand, and because there is no place where the consequences do not have an exact connection with and dependence upon their antecedents. Nevertheless, because these proofs are rather long and demand undivided attention, they are comprehended and understood by only a very few persons. In the same way, although I consider that the arguments I use here equal or even surpass in certainty and obviousness the demonstrations of geometry, I nevertheless appreciate that they cannot be sufficiently well understood by many persons, partly because they also are somewhat lengthy and involved, but principally because they require a mind entirely free of all prejudice and one that can readily free itself from its attachment to the senses. And to tell the truth, there are not so many people in the world who are fitted for metaphysical speculations as there are those who are fitted for geometry. (5) There is this further difference, that in geometry everyone is persuaded that nothing should be written for which there is no certain proof. Therefore, those who are not well versed in the field are much more apt to make the mistake of accepting false demonstrations in order to make others believe that they understand them than they are to make the mistake of rejecting good ones. It is different in philosophy, where it is believed that there is nothing about which it is not possible to argue on either side. Thus few people engage in the search for truth, and many, who wish to acquire a reputation as clever thinkers, bend all their efforts to arrogant opposition to the most obvious truths.

That is why, gentlemen, since my arguments belong to philosophy, however strong they may be, I do not suppose that they will have any great effect unless you take them under your protection. But the esteem which everyone has for your Faculty is so great, and the name of the Sorbonne carries such authority, that not only is it more deferred to in matter of faith than any other group except the sacred councils, but even in human philosophy everyone agrees that it is impossible to find anywhere else so much reliability and knowledge, as well as prudence and integrity in the pronouncement of a judgment. Therefore, I do not doubt that if you will deign to give enough attention to this work so as to correct it—for, knowing not only my human fallibility but also my ignorance, I would not dare to affirm that it was free of error—and then to add to it whatever it lacks, to complete whatever is imperfect, and yourselves either to take the trouble to give a more adequate explanation of those points that need it or at least to advise me of them so that I may work on them; and finally, after the reasons by which I prove that there is a God and that the human soul differs from the body have been brought to such a degree of clarity and obviousness, which I am sure is possible, (6) that they should be considered very exact demonstrations, if you then will deign to give them the authority of your approbation and publicly testify to their truth and certitude—I do not doubt, I say, that when this has been done, all the errors and false opinions which have ever been entertained on these two questions will soon be effaced from the minds of men. For the expression of the truth will cause all learned and wise men to subscribe to your judgment, and your authority will cause the atheists, who are ordinarily more arrogant than learned and judicious, to set aside their spirit of contradiction, or perhaps themselves defend the arguments which they see being accepted as demonstrations by all intelligent people, for fear of appearing not to understand them. And finally, everyone else will easily accept the testimony of so many witnesses, and there will no longer be anyone who dares to doubt the existence of God and the real and true distinction between the human soul and the body.

It is for you, who now see the disorders which doubt of these things produces, in your great wisdom to judge the fruit which would grow out of such belief, once it were well established; but it would not be fitting for me further to commend the cause of God and religion to those who have always been the firmest supporters of them and of the Catholic Church. (7)

PREFACE

I have already touched upon these two questions of God and of the human soul in the *Discourse on the Method of Rightly Conducting the Reason and Seeking Truth in the Sciences*, which I published in French in the year 1637. Then I was not concerned to give a complete discussion of the subjects, but only to treat of them in passing, in order to learn from the judgments of the readers in what way I should treat them afterward. For these questions have always seemed to me so important that I judged it appropriate to deal with them more than once. And the road I take to explain them is so little traveled and so far from the ordinary route that I did not think it would be useful to explain it in French in a discourse that might be read by anyone, for fear that those of feeble intellect would think it permissible for them to make the same attempt.

In the *Discourse on Method*, I requested everyone who found in my writings something worthy of criticism to do me the favor of informing me thereof. There were no noteworthy objections concerning these subjects except two, to which I shall here make a short reply before undertaking a more detailed presentation of them later.

The first objection is that it does not follow from the fact that the human mind, reflecting upon its own nature, (8) knows itself solely as a thinking being, that its nature or essence is only to think. The trouble is that this word "only" excludes all those other qualities that might perhaps also pertain to the nature of the mind.

To this objection I reply that it was not my intention at this point to exclude those qualities from the realm of objective reality, with which I was not then concerned, but only from the realm of my thought. My intention was to say that I knew nothing to pertain to my essence except that I was a being which thinks, that is, a being having in itself the faculty of thinking. Nevertheless, I shall show further on how it follows from the fact that I know nothing else which belongs to my essence that nothing else really does belong to it.

The second objection is that it does not follow from the fact that I have in my mind the idea of a thing more perfect than I am that this idea is more perfect than myself, much less that what is represented by this idea exists.

But I reply that in this word "idea" there is here an equivocation. For it can be taken materially, as an operation of my intellect, and in this sense it cannot be said to be more perfect than myself; or it can be taken objectively for the body which is represented by this operation, which, even though it is not supposed to exist outside of my understanding, can nevertheless be more perfect than myself in respect to its essence. In the rest of this treatise I shall show more fully how it follows from the mere fact that I have in my mind an idea of something more perfect than myself that this thing really exists.

In addition, I have seen two other rather long works on this subject which did not so much oppose my reasons as my conclusions, and this by arguments drawn from the commonplaces of the atheists. (9) But since arguments of this type cannot make any impression in the minds of those who fully understand my reasoning, and since the judgment of many persons is so weak and irrational that they much more often let themselves be convinced by the first opinions they hear on a subject, however false and unreasonable they may be, than by a refutation of their opinions which is valid and true but which is heard later, I do not wish to reply to the arguments here, for fear of being obliged first to report them.

I shall only say, in general, that the arguments which atheists use to combat the existence of God always depend either upon the assumption that God has human characteristics, or else upon the assumption that our own minds have so much ability and wisdom that we presume to delimit and comprehend what God can and should do. Thus all that atheists allege will give us no difficulty if only we remind ourselves that we should consider our minds to be finite and limited, and God to be an infinite and incomprehensible Being.

Now, having paid sufficient attention to the opinions of men, I undertake directly to treat of God and of the human mind, and at the same time to lay the foundations of first philosophy. I do this without expecting any praise for it from the vulgar, and without hoping that my book will be read by many. On the contrary, I would not recommend it to any except to those who would want to meditate seriously along with me, and who are capable of freeing the mind from attachment to the senses and clearing it entirely of all sorts of prejudices; and I know only too well that there are very few people of this sort. But as for those who do not care much about the order and connection of my arguments, and who amuse themselves by making clever remarks on the several parts, as (10) some will do—those persons, I say, will not profit much from reading this work. And although they may find opportunities for caviling in many places, they will hardly be able to make any objections which are important or which are worthy of reply.

And since I do not promise others to satisfy them wholly at the first attempt, and since I do not so far presume as to believe that I can foresee all that may entail difficulties for some people, I shall first present in these *Meditations* the same thoughts by which I think I have reached a certain and evident knowledge of the truth, in order to see whether I will be able to persuade others by means of the same reasons that have persuaded me. After that I shall reply to the objections which have been offered to me by people of insight and learning to whom I sent my *Meditations* to be examined before committing them to the press. These have been so numerous and so varied that I feel secure in believing that it would be difficult for anyone else to find an objection of consequence that has not already been treated.

That is why I beg my readers to suspend their judgment upon the *Meditations* until they have taken the trouble of reading all these objections and the replies that I have made to them. (11)

SYNOPSIS OF THE SIX FOLLOWING MEDITATIONS

In the First Meditation, I offer the reasons why we can doubt all things in general, and particularly material objects, at least as long as we do not have other foundations for the sciences than those we have hitherto possessed. And although it is not immediately apparent that so general a doubt can be useful, it is in fact very much so, since it delivers us from all sorts of prejudices and makes available to us an easy method of accustoming our minds to become independent of the senses. Finally, it is useful in making it subsequently impossible to doubt those things which we discover to be true after we have taken doubt into consideration.

In the Second, the mind, which in its intrinsic freedom supposes that everything which is open to the least doubt is nonexistent, recognizes that it is nevertheless absolutely impossible that it does not itself exist. This is also of the highest utility, since by this means the mind can easily distinguish between those qualities which belong to it—that is to say, to its intellectual nature—and those which belong to the body.

But because it might happen that some persons will expect me to offer at this point reasons to prove the immortality of the soul, I think it my duty to warn them now (13) that, since I have tried to write nothing in this treatise for which I did not have very exact demonstrations, I have found myself obliged to follow an order similar to that used by geometricians, which is to present first all those things on which the proposition one is seeking to prove depends, before reaching any conclusions about the proposition itself.

But the first and principal thing required in order to recognize the immortality of the soul is to form the clearest possible conception of it, and one which is entirely distinct from all the conceptions one can have of the body, which has been done in this Second Meditation. It is necessary, in addition, to know that all things which we conceive clearly and distinctly are true in the manner in which we conceive them, and this cannot be proved before the Fourth Meditation. Furthermore, we must have a distinct conception of corporeal nature, which we acquire partly in the Second, and partly in the Fifth and Sixth Meditations. And finally, we must conclude from all this that things which we clearly and distinctly perceive to be diverse substances, as we conceive the mind and the body, are in fact substances which are really distinct from each other; which is what we conclude in the Sixth Meditation. This is confirmed again, in the same Meditation, by the fact that we cannot conceive any body except as divisible, while the mind or soul of man can only be conceived as indivisible. For in reality we cannot conceive of half of any soul, as we can of the smallest possible body, so that we recognize that their natures are not only different but even in some sense contrary. I have not treated this subject further in this treatise, partly because we have already discovered enough to show with sufficient clarity that the corruption of the body does not entail the death of the soul, and so to give men the hope of a second life after death; and partly because the premises from which the immortality of the soul may be concluded depend upon the explanation of the whole of physics. First, (14) we must know that all substances in general—that is to say, all those things which cannot exist without being created by God—are by nature incorruptible and can never cease to be, unless God himself, by denying them his usual support, reduces them to nothingness. And secondly, we must notice that body, taken in general, is a substance, and that it therefore will never perish. But the human body, however much it may differ from other bodies, is only a composite, produced by a certain configuration of members and by other similar accidents, whereas the human soul is not thus dependent upon any accidents, but is a pure substance. For even if all its accidents change—as, for example, if it conceives of certain things, wills others, and receives sense impressions of still others—nevertheless it still remains the same soul. But the human body becomes a different entity from the mere fact that the shape of some of its parts has been changed. From this it follows that the human body may very easily perish, but that the mind or soul of man, between which I find no distinction, is immortal by its very nature.

In the Third Meditation, I have explained at sufficient length, it seems to me, the principal argument I use to prove the existence of God. Nevertheless, I did not want to use at that point any comparisons drawn from physical things, in order that the minds of the readers should be as far as possible withdrawn from the use of and commerce with the senses. There may, therefore, be many obscurities remaining, which I hope will be completely elucidated in my replies to the objections which have since been made to me. One of these obscurities is this: how can the idea of a supremely perfect Being, which we find in ourselves, contain so much objective reality, that is to say, how can it participate by representation in so many degrees of being and of perfection, that it must have come from a supremely perfect cause? This I have explained in these replies by means of a comparison with a very ingenious and artificial machine, the idea of which occurs in the mind of some worker. For as the real cleverness of this idea must have some cause, I conclude it to be either the knowledge of this worker or that of some other from whom he has received this idea. In the same way (15) it is impossible that the idea of God, which is in us, does not have God himself as its cause.

In the Fourth, it is proved that all things which we conceive or perceive very clearly and very distinctly are wholly true. At the same time I explain the nature of error or falsity, which nature we ought to discover, as much to confirm the preceding truths as to understand better those that follow. Nevertheless, it should be noticed that I do not in any way treat here of sin—that is, of error committed in the pursuit of good and evil—but only of that which occurs in the judgment and discernment of the true and the false; and that I do not intend to speak of beliefs which belong to faith or to the conduct of life, but only of those which pertain to speculative truth and which can be known by the aid of the light of nature alone.

In the Fifth Meditation, besides the explanation of corporeal nature in general, the existence of God is again demonstrated by a new argument. There may also be some difficulties in this argument, but the solution will be found in the replies to the objections which have been made to me. In addition, I show how it is true that even the certainty of geometrical demonstrations themselves depends on the knowledge of God.

Finally, in the Sixth, I distinguish the action of the understanding from that of the imagination, and the marks of this distinction are described. Here I show that the mind or soul of man is really distinct from the body, and that nevertheless it is so tightly bound and united with it that it forms with it what is almost a single entity. All the errors which arise from the senses are here exposed, together with the methods of avoiding them. And finally, I here bring out all the arguments from which we may conclude the existence of material things; not because I judge them very useful, in that they prove what (16) they do prove—namely, that there is a world, that men have bodies, and other similar things which have never been doubted by any man of good sense—but because, in considering these arguments more closely, we come to recognize that they are not as firm and as evident as those which lead us to the knowledge of God and of our soul, so that the latter are the most certain and most evident truths which can become known to the human mind. That is all that I had planned to prove in these *Meditations*, which leads me to omit here many other questions with which I have dealt incidentally in this treatise. (17)

First Meditation
Concerning Things That Can be Doubted

There is no novelty to me in the reflection that, from my earliest years, I have accepted many false opinions as true, and that what I have concluded from such badly assured premises could not but be highly doubtful and uncertain. From the time that I first recognized this fact, I have realized that if I wished to have any firm and constant knowledge in the sciences, I would have to undertake, once and for all, to set aside all the opinions which I had previously accepted among my beliefs and start again from the very beginning. But this enterprise appeared to me to be of very great magnitude, and so I waited until I had attained an age so mature that I could not hope for a later time when I would be more fitted to execute the project. Now, however, I have delayed so long that henceforward I should be afraid that I was committing a fault if, in continuing to deliberate, I expended time which should be devoted to action.

The present is opportune for my design; I have freed my mind of all kinds of cares; (18) I feel myself, fortunately, disturbed by no passions; and I have found a serene retreat in peaceful solitude. I will therefore make a serious and unimpeded effort to destroy generally all my former opinions. In order to do this, however, it will not be necessary to show that they are all false, a task which I might never be able to complete; because, since reason already convinces me that I should abstain from the belief in things which are not entirely certain and indubitable no less carefully than from the belief in those which appear to me to be manifestly false, it will be enough to make me reject them all if I can find in each some ground for doubt. And for that it will not be necessary for me to examine each one in particular, which would be an infinite labor; but since the destruction of the foundation necessarily involves the collapse of all the rest of the edifice, I shall first attack the principles upon which all my former opinions were founded.

Everything which I have thus far accepted as entirely true and assured has been acquired from the senses or by means of the senses. But I have learned by experience that these senses sometimes mislead me, and it is prudent never to trust wholly those things which have once deceived us.

But it is possible that, even though the senses occasionally deceive us about things which are barely perceptible and very far away, there are many other things which we cannot reasonably doubt, even though we know them through the senses—as, for example, that I am here, seated by the fire, wearing a winter dressing gown, holding this paper in my hands, and other things of this nature. And how could I deny that these hands and this body are mine, unless I am to compare myself with certain lunatics (19) whose brain is so troubled and befogged by the black vapors of the bile that they continually affirm that they are kings while they are paupers, that they are clothed in gold and purple while they are naked; or imagine that their head is made of clay, or that they are gourds, or that their body is glass? But this is ridiculous; such men are fools, and I would be no less insane than they if I followed their example.

Nevertheless, I must remember that I am a man, and that consequently I am accustomed to sleep and in my dreams to imagine the same things that lunatics imagine when awake, or sometimes things which are even less plausible. How many times has it occurred that the quiet of the night made me dream of my usual habits: that I was here, clothed tin a dressing gown, and sitting by the fire, although I was in fact lying undressed in bed! It seems apparent to me now, that I am not looking at this paper with my eyes closed, that this head that I shake is not drugged with sleep, that it is with design and deliberate intent that I stretch out this hand and perceive it. What happens in sleep seems not at all as clear and as distinct as all this. But I am speaking as though I never recall having been misled, while asleep, by similar illusions. When I consider these matters carefully, I realize so clearly that there are no conclusive indications by which waking life can be distinguished from sleep that I am quite astonished, and my bewilderment is such that it is almost able to convince me that I am sleeping.

So let us suppose now that we are asleep and that all these details, such as opening the eyes, shaking the head, extending the hands, and similar things, are merely illusions; and let us think that perhaps our hands and our whole body are not such as we see them. Nevertheless, we must at least admit that these things which appear to us in sleep are like painted scenes and portraits which can only be formed in imitation of something real and true, and so, at the very least, these types of things—namely, eyes, head, hands, and the whole body—are not imaginary entities, but real and existent. For in truth painters, even when (20) they use the greatest ingenuity in attempting to portray sirens and satyrs in bizarre and extraordinary ways, nevertheless cannot give them wholly new shapes and natures, but only invent some particular mixture composed of parts of various animals; or even if perhaps their imagination is sufficiently extravagant that they invent something so new that nothing like it has ever been seen, and so their work represents something purely imaginary and absolutely false, certainly at the very least the colors of which they are composed must be real.

And for the same reason, even if these types of things—namely, a body, eyes, head, hands, and other similar things—could be imaginary, nevertheless, we are bound to confess that there are some other still more simple and universal concepts which are true and existent], from the mixture of which, neither more nor less than in the case of the mixture of real colors, all these images of things are formed in our minds, whether they are true and real or imaginary and fantastic.

Of this class of entities is corporeal nature in general and its extension, including the shape of extended things, their quantity, or size and number, and also the place where they are, the time that measures their duration, and so forth. That is why we will perhaps not be reasoning badly if we conclude that physics, astronomy, medicine, and all the other sciences which follow from the consideration of composite entities are very dubious and uncertain; whereas arithmetic, geometry, and the other sciences of this nature, which treat only of very simple and general things without concerning themselves as to whether they occur in nature or not, contain some element of certainty and sureness. For whether I am awake or whether I am asleep, two and three together will always make the number five, and the square will never have more than four sides; and it does not seem possible that truths so clear and so apparent can ever be suspected of any falsity for uncertainty. (21)

Nevertheless, I have long held the belief that there is a God who can do anything, by whom I have been created and made what I am. But how can I be sure but that he has brought it to pass that there is no earth, no sky, no extended bodies, no shape, no size, no place, and that nevertheless I have the impressions of all these things and cannot imagine that things might be other than as I now see them? And furthermore, just as I sometimes judge that others are mistaken about those things which they think they know best, how can I be sure but that God has brought it about that I am always mistaken when I add two and three or count the sides of a square, or when I judge of something else even easier, if I can imagine anything easier than that? But perhaps God did not wish me to be deceived in that fashion, since he is said to be supremely good. But if it was repugnant to his goodness to have made me so that I was always mistaken, it would seem also to be inconsistent for him to permit me to be sometimes mistaken, and nevertheless I cannot doubt that he does permit it.

At this point there will perhaps be some persons who would prefer to deny the existence of so powerful a God, rather than to believe that everything else is uncertain. Let us not oppose them for the moment, and let us concede according to their point of view that everything which I have stated here about God is fictitious. Then in whatever way they suppose that I have reached the state of being that I now have, whether they attribute it to some destiny or fate or refer it to chance, or whether they wish to explain it as the result of a continual interplay of events or in any other manner; nevertheless, since to err and be mistaken is a kind of imperfection, to whatever degree less powerful they consider the author to whom they at-tribute my origin, in that degree it will be more probable that I am so imperfect that I am always mistaken. To this reasoning, certainly, I have nothing to reply; and I am at last constrained to admit that there is nothing in what I formerly believed to be true which I cannot somehow doubt, and this not for lack of thought and attention, but for weighty and well-considered reasons. Thus I find that, in the future, I should withhold and suspend my judgment about these matters, and guard myself no less carefully from believing them than I should from believing what is manifestly false (22) if I wish to find any certain and assured knowledge in the sciences.

It is not enough to have made these observations; it is also necessary that I should take care to bear them in mind. For these customary and long-standing beliefs will frequently recur in my thoughts, my long and familiar acquaintance with them giving them the right to occupy my mind against my will and almost to make themselves masters of my beliefs. I will never free myself of the habit of deferring to them and having faith in them as long as I consider that they are what they really are—that is, somewhat doubtful, as I have just shown, even if highly probable—so that there is much more reason to believe than to deny them. That is why I think that I would not do badly if I deliberately took the opposite position and deceived myself in pretending for some time that all these opinions are entirely false and imaginary, until at last I will have so balanced my former and my new prejudices that they cannot incline my mind more to one side than the other, and my judgment will not be mastered and turned by bad habits from the correct perception of things and the straight road leading to the knowledge of the truth. For I feel sure that I cannot overdo this distrust, since it is not now a question of acting, but only of meditating and learning.

I will therefore suppose that, not a true God, who is very good and who is the supreme source of truth, but a certain evil spirit, not less clever and deceitful than powerful, has bent all his efforts to deceiving me. I will suppose that the sky, the air, the earth, colors, shapes, sounds, and all other objective things that we see are nothing but illusions and dreams that he has used to trick my credulity. I will consider (23) myself as having no hands, no eyes, no flesh, no blood, nor any senses, yet falsely believing that I have all these things. I will remain resolutely attached to this hypothesis; and if I cannot attain the knowledge of any truth by this method, at any rate it is in my power to suspend my judgment. That is why I shall take great care not to accept any falsity among my beliefs and shall prepare my mind so well for all the ruses of this great deceiver that, however powerful and artful he may be, he will never be able to mislead me in anything.

But this undertaking is arduous, and a certain laziness leads me insensibly into the normal paths of ordinary life. I am like a slave who, enjoying an imaginary liberty during sleep, begins to suspect that his liberty is only a dream; he fears to wake up and conspires with his pleasant illusions to retain them longer. So insensibly to myself I fall into my former opinions; and I am slow to wake up from this slumber for fear that the labors of waking life which will have to follow the tranquillity of this sleep, instead of leading me into the daylight of the knowledge of the truth, will be insufficient to dispel the darkness of all the difficulties which have just been raised.

Second Meditation
Of the Nature of the Humand Mind, and That it is
more Easily Known Than the Body

Yesterday's Meditation has filled my mind with so many doubts that it is no longer in my power to forget them. Nor do I yet see how I will be able to resolve them; I feel as though (24) I were suddenly thrown into deep water, being so disconcerted that I can neither plant my feet on the bottom nor swim on the surface. I shall nevertheless make every effort to conform precisely to the plan commenced yesterday and put aside every belief in which I could imagine the least doubt, just as though I knew that it was absolutely false. And I shall continue in this manner until I have found something certain, or at least, if I can do nothing else, until I have learned with certainty that there is nothing certain in this world. Archimedes, to move the earth from its orbit and place it in a new position, demanded nothing more than a fixed and immovable fulcrum; in a similar manner I shall have the right to entertain high hopes if I am fortunate enough to find a single truth which is certain and indubitable.

I suppose, accordingly, that everything that I see is false; I convince myself that nothing has ever existed of all that my deceitful memory recalls to me. I think that I have no senses; and I believe that body, shape, extension, motion, and location are merely inventions of my mind. What then could still be thought true? Perhaps nothing else, unless it is that there is nothing certain in the world.

But how do I know that there is not some entity, of a different nature from what I have just judged uncertain, of which there cannot be the least doubt? Is there not some God or some other power who gives me these thoughts? But I need not think this to be true, for possibly I am able to produce them myself. Then, at the very least, am I not an entity myself? But I have already denied that I had any senses or any body. However, at this point I hesitate, for what (25) follows from that? Am I so dependent upon the body and the senses that I could not exist without them? I have just convinced myself that nothing whatsoever existed in the world that there was no sky, no earth, no minds, and no bodies; have I not thereby convinced myself that I did not exist? Not at all; without doubt I existed if I was convinced or even if I thought anything. Even though there may be a deceiver of some sort, very powerful and very tricky, who bends all his efforts to keep me perpetually deceived, there can be no slightest doubt that I exist, since he deceives me; and let him deceive me as much as he will, he can never make me be nothing as long as I think that I am something. Thus, after having thought well on this matter, and after examining all things with care, I must finally conclude and maintain that this proposition: *I am, I exist*, is necessarily true every time that I pronounce it or conceive it in my mind.

But I do not yet know sufficiently clearly what I am, I who am sure that I exist. So I must henceforth take very great care that I do not incautiously mistake some other thing for myself, and so make an error even in that knowledge which I maintain to be more certain and more evident than all other knowledge that I previously had. That is why I shall now consider once more what I thought myself to be before I began these last deliberations. Of my former opinions I shall reject all that are rendered even slightly doubtful by the arguments that I have just now offered, so that there will remain just that part alone which is entirely certain and indubitable.

What then have I previously believed myself to be? Clearly, I believed that I was a man. But what is a man? Shall I say a rational animal? Certainly not, for I would have to determine what an "animal" is and what is meant by "rational"; and so, from a single question, I would find myself gradually enmeshed in an infinity of others more difficult and more inconvenient, and I would not care to waste the little time and leisure remaining to me in disentangling such difficulties. I shall rather pause here to consider the ideas which previously arose naturally and of themselves (26) in my mind whenever I considered what I was. I thought of myself first as having a face, hands, arms, and all this mechanism composed of bone and flesh and members, just as it appears in a corpse, and which I designated by the name of "body." In addition, I thought of the fact that I consumed nourishment, that I walked, that I perceived and thought, and I ascribed all these actions to the soul. But either I did not stop to consider what this soul was or else, if I did, I imagined that it was something very rarefied and subtle, such as a wind, a flame, or a very much expanded air which penetrated into and was infused throughout my grosser components. As for what body was, I did not realize that there could be any doubt about it, for I thought that I recognized its nature very distinctly. If I had wished to explain it according to the notions that I then entertained, I would have described it somewhat in this way: By "body" I understand all that can be bounded by some figure; that can be located in some place and occupy space in such a way that every other body is excluded from it; that can be perceived by touch or sight or hearing or taste or smell; that can be moved in various ways, not by itself but by some other object by which it is touched and from which it receives an impulse. For to possess the power to move itself, and also to feel or to think, I did not believe at all that these are attributes of corporeal nature; on the contrary, rather, I was astonished to see a few bodies possessing such abilities.

But I, what am I, on the basis of the present hypothesis that there is a certain spirit who is extremely powerful and, if I may dare to say so, malicious and tricky, and who uses all his abilities and efforts in order to deceive me? Can I be sure that I possess the smallest fraction of all those characteristics which I have just now said belonged to the nature of body? (27) I pause to consider this attentively. I pass and repass in review in my mind each one of all these things—it is not necessary to pause to take the time to list them—and I do not find any one of them which I can pronounce to be part of me. Let us move on to the attributes of the soul and see if any of these are in me. Is it characteristic of me to consume nourishment and to walk? But if it is true that I do not have a body, these also are nothing but figments of the imagination. To perceive? But once more, I cannot perceive without the body, except in the sense that I have thought I perceived various things during sleep, which I recognized upon waking not to have been really perceived. To think? Here I find the answer. Thought is an attribute that belongs to me; it alone is inseparable from my nature.

I am, I exist—that is certain; but for how long do I exist? For as long as I think; for it might perhaps happen, if I totally ceased thinking, that I would at the same time completely cease to be. I am now admitting nothing except what is necessarily true. I am therefore, to speak precisely, only a thinking being, that is to say, a mind, an understanding, or a reasoning, being, which are terms whose meaning was previously unknown to me.

I am something real and really existing, but what thing am I? I have already given the answer: a thing which thinks. And what more? I will stimulate my imagination to see if I am not something else beyond this. I am not this assemblage of members which is called a human body; I am not a rarefied and penetrating air spread throughout all these members; I am not a wind, a flame, a breath, a vapor, or anything at all that I can imagine and picture to myself—since I have supposed that all that was nothing, and since, without abandoning this supposition, I find that I do not cease to be certain that I am something.

But perhaps it is true that those same things which I suppose not to exist because I do not know them are really no different from the self which I do know. As to that I cannot decide; I am not discussing that question at the moment, since I can pass judgment only upon those things which are known to me: I know that I exist and I am seeking to discover what I am, that "I" that I know to be. Now it is very certain that this notion and knowledge of my being, thus precisely understood, does not depend on things whose existence (28) is not yet known to me; and consequently and even more certainly, it does not depend on any of those things that I can picture in my imagination. And even these terms, "picture" and "imagine," warn me of my error. For I would be imagining falsely indeed were I to picture myself as something; since to imagine is nothing else than to contemplate the shape or image of a bodily entity, and I already know both that I certainly exist and that it is altogether possible that all these images, and everything in general which is involved in the nature of body, are only dreams and illusions. From this I see clearly that there was no more sense in saying that I would stimulate my imagination to learn more distinctly what I am than if I should say: I am now awake, and I see something real and true; but because I do not yet perceive it sufficiently clearly, I will go to sleep on purpose, in order that my dreams will show it to me with more truth and evidence. And thus I know manifestly that nothing of all that I can understand by means of the imagination is pertinent to the knowledge which I have of myself, and that I must remember this and prevent my mind from thinking in this fashion, in order that it may clearly perceive its own nature.

But what then am I? A thinking being. What is a thinking being? It is a being which doubts, which understands, which conceives, which affirms, which denies, which wills, which rejects, which imagines also, and which perceives. It is certainly not a trivial matter if all these things belong to my nature. But why should they not belong to it? Am I not that same person who now doubts almost everything, who nevertheless understands and conceives certain things, who is sure of and affirms the truth of this one thing alone, who denies all the others, who wills and desires to know more about them, who rejects error, who imagines many things, sometimes even against my will, and who also perceives many things, as through the medium of the senses or the organs of the body? Is there anything in all that which is not just as true as it is certain that I am and that I exist, even though I were always asleep (29) and though the one who created me directed all his efforts to deluding me? And is there any one of these attributes which can be distinguished from my thinking or which can be said to be separable from my nature? For it is so obvious that it is I who doubt, understand, and desire, that nothing could be added to make it more evident. And I am also certainly the same one who imagines; for once more, even though it could happen that the things I imagine are not true, nevertheless this power of imagining cannot fail to be real, and it is part of my thinking. Finally I am the same being which perceives—that is, which observes certain objects as though by means of the sense organs, because I do really see light, hear noises, feel heat. Will it be said that these appearances are false and that I am sleeping? Let it be so; yet at the very least it is certain that it seems to me that I see light, hear noises, and feel heat. This much cannot be false, and it is this, properly considered, which in my nature is called perceiving, and that, again speaking precisely, is nothing else but thinking.

As a result of these considerations, I begin to recognize what I am somewhat better and with a little more clarity and distinctness than heretofore. But nevertheless it still seems to me, and I cannot keep myself from believing that corporeal things, images of which are formed by thought and which the senses themselves examine, are much more distinctly known than that indescribable part of myself which cannot be pictured by the imagination. Yet it would truly be very strange to say that I know and comprehend more distinctly things whose existence seems doubtful to me, that are unknown to me and do not belong to me, than those of whose truth I am persuaded, which are known to me, and which belong to my real nature—to say, in a word, that I know them better than myself. But I see well what is the trouble: my mind is a vagabond who likes to wander and is not yet able to stay within the strict bounds of truth. Therefore, let us give it the rein once more and allow it every kind of liberty, (30) permitting it to consider the objects which appear to be external, so that when a little later we come to restrain it gently and at the right time and force it to the consideration of its own nature and of the things that it finds in itself, it will more readily permit itself to be ruled and guided.

Let us now consider the commonest things, which are commonly believed to be the most distinctly known and the easiest of all to know, namely, the bodies which we touch and see. I do not intend to speak of bodies in general, for general notions are usually somewhat more confused; let us rather consider one body in particular. Let us take, for example, this bit of wax which has just been taken from the hive. It has not yet completely lost the sweetness of the honey it contained; it still retains something of the odor of the flowers from which it was collected; its color, shape, and size are apparent; it is hard and cold; it can easily be touched; and, if you knock on it, it will give out some sound. Thus everything which can make a body distinctly known are found in this example.

But now while I am talking I bring it close to the fire. What remains of the taste evaporates; the odor vanishes; its color changes; its shape is lost; its size increases; it becomes liquid; it grows hot; one can hardly touch it; and although it is knocked upon, it will give out no sound. Does the same wax remain after this change? We must admit that it does; no one denies it, no one judges otherwise. What is it then in this bit of wax that we recognize with so much distinctness? Certainly it cannot be anything that I observed by means of the senses, since everything in the field of taste, smell, sight, touch, and hearing are changed, and since the same wax nevertheless remains.

The truth of the matter perhaps, as I now suspect, is that this wax was neither that sweetness of honey, nor that pleasant odor of flowers, nor that whiteness, nor that shape, nor that sound, but only a body which a little while ago appeared to my senses under these forms and which now makes itself felt under others. But what is it, to speak precisely, that I imagine when I conceive it in this fashion? Let us consider it attentively (31) and, rejecting everything that does not belong to the wax, see what remains. Certainly nothing is left but something extended, flexible, and movable. But what is meant by flexible and movable? Does it consist in my picturing that this wax, being round, is capable of becoming square and of passing from the square into a triangular shape? Certainly not; it is not that, since I conceive it capable of undergoing an infinity of similar changes, and I could not compass this infinity in my imagination. Consequently this conception that I have of the wax is not achieved by the faculty of imagination.

Now what is this extension? Is it not also unknown? For it becomes greater in the melting wax, still greater when it is completely melted, and much greater again when the heat increases still more. And I would not conceive clearly and truthfully what wax was if I did not think that even this bit of wax is capable of receiving more variations in extension than I have ever imagined. We must therefore agree that I cannot even conceive what this bit of wax is by means of the imagination, and that there is nothing but my understanding alone which does conceive it. I say this bit of wax in particular, for as to wax in general, it is still more evident. But what is this bit of wax which cannot be comprehended except by the understanding, or by the mind? Certainly it is the same as the one that I see, that I touch, that I imagine; and finally it is the same as I always believed it to be from the beginning. But what is here important to notice is that perception, or the action by which we perceive, is not a vision, a touch, nor an imagination, and has never been that, even though it formerly appeared so; but is solely an inspection by the mind, which can be imperfect and confused as it was formerly, or clear and distinct as it is at present, as I attend more or less to the things which are in it and of which it is composed.

Now I am truly astonished when I consider how weak my mind is and how apt I am to fall into error. For even though I consider all this in my mind without speaking, (32) still words impede me, and I am nearly deceived by the terms of ordinary language. For we say that we see the same wax if it is present, and not that we judge that it is the same from the fact that it has the same color or shape. Thus I might be tempted to conclude that one knows the wax by means of eyesight, and not uniquely by the perception of the mind. So I may by chance look out of a window and notice some men passing in the street, at the sight of whom I do not fail to say that I see men, just as I say that I see wax; and nevertheless what do I see from this window except hats and cloaks which might cover ghosts, or automata which move only by springs? But I judge that they are men, and thus I comprehend, solely by the faculty of judgment which resides in my mind, that which I believed I saw with my eyes.

A person who attempts to improve his understanding beyond the ordinary ought to be ashamed to go out of his way to criticize the forms of speech used by ordinary men. I prefer to pass over this matter and to consider whether I understood what wax was more evidently and more perfectly when I first noticed it and when I thought I knew it by means of the external senses, or at the very least by common sense, as it is called, or the imaginative faculty; or whether I conceive it better at present, after having more carefully examined what it is and how it can be known. Certainly it would be ridiculous to doubt the superiority of the latter method of knowing. For what was there in that first perception which was distinct and evident? What was there which might not occur similarly to the senses of the lowest of the animals? But when I distinguished the real wax from its superficial appearances, and when, just as though I had removed its garments, I consider it all naked, it is certain that although there might still be some

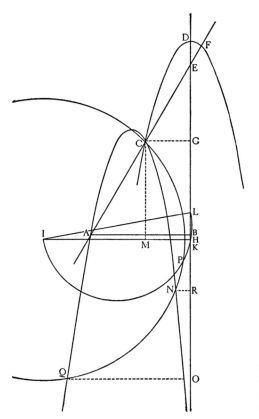

Geometry formula from Descartes' *Geometry* (1637). The X–Y axes in analytic geometry, which Descartes invented, are still called "Cartesian coordinates." (*Library of Congress*)

error in my judgment, I could not conceive it in this fashion without a human mind. (33)

And now what shall I say of the mind, that is to say, of myself? For so far I do not admit in myself anything other than the mind. Can it be that I, who seem to perceive this bit of wax so clearly and distinctly, do not know my own self, not only with much more truth and certainty, but also much more distinctly and evidently? For if I judge that the wax exists because I see it, certainly it follows much more evidently that I exist myself because I see it. For it might happen that what I see is not really wax; it might also happen that I do not even possess eyes to see anything; but it could not happen that, when I see, or what amounts to the same thing, when I think I see, I who think am not something. For a similar reason, if I judge that the wax exists because I touch it, the same conclusion follows once more, namely, that I am. And if I hold to this judgment because my imagination, or whatever other entity it might be, persuades me of it, I will still reach the same conclusion. And what I have said here about the wax can be applied to all other things which are external to me.

Furthermore, if the idea or knowledge of the wax seems clearer and more distinct to me after I have investigated it, not only by sight or touch, but also in many other ways, with how much more evidence, distinctness and clarity must it be admitted that I now know myself; since all the reasons which help me to know and conceive the nature of the wax, or of any other body whatsoever, serve much better to show the nature of my mind! And we also find so many other things in the mind itself which can contribute to the clarification of its nature, that those which depend on the body, such as the ones I have just mentioned, hardly deserve to be taken into account.

And at last here I am, having insensibly returned to where (34) I wished to be; for since it is at present manifest to me that even bodies are not properly known by the senses nor by the faculty of imagination, but by the understanding alone; and since they are not known in so far as they are seen or touched, but only in so far as they are understood by thinking, I see clearly that there is nothing easier for me to understand than my mind. But since it is almost impossible to rid oneself so soon of an opinion of long standing, it would be wise to stop a while at this point, in order that, by the length of my meditation, I may impress this new knowledge more deeply upon my memory.

THIRD MEDITATION
OF GOD: THAT HE EXISTS

Now I shall close my eyes, I shall stop my ears, I shall disregard my senses, I shall even efface from my mind all the images of corporeal things; or at least, since that can hardly be done, I shall consider them vain and false. By thus dealing only with myself and considering what is included in me, I shall try to make myself, little by little, better known and more familiar to myself.

I am a thing which thinks, that is to say, which doubts, which affirms, which denies, which knows a few things, which is ignorant of many, which loves, which hates, which wills, which rejects, which imagines also, and which senses. For as I have previously remarked, although the things which I sense and which I imagine are perhaps nothing at all apart from me and in themselves, I am nevertheless sure that those modes of thought which I call sensations and imaginations, (35) only just as far as they are modes of thought, reside and are found with certainty in myself.

And in this short statement I think I have reported all that I truly know, or at least all that I have so far noticed that I know. Now, in order to try to extend my knowledge further, I shall be circumspect and consider with care if I cannot still discover in myself some other bits of knowledge which I have not yet observed. I am sure that I am a thinking being; but do I not then know what is required to make me sure of something? Certainly, in this first conclusion, there is nothing else which assures me of its truth but the clear and distinct perception of what I affirm. But this would really not be sufficient to assure me that what I affirm is true if it could ever happen that something which I conceived just as clearly and distinctly should prove false. And therefore it seems to me that I can already establish as a general principle that everything which we conceive very clearly and very distinctly is wholly true.

I have, however, previously accepted and admitted several things as very certain and very obvious which I have nevertheless subsequently recognized to be doubtful and uncertain. What, then, were those things? They were the earth, the sky, the stars, and all the other things I perceived through the medium of my senses. But what did I conceive clearly and distinctly in them? Nothing, certainly, unless that the ideas or thoughts of those things were present to my mind. And even now I do not deny the occurrence of these ideas in me. But there was still another thing of which I was sure and which, because of my habit of believing it, I thought I perceived very clearly, although in truth I did not perceive it at all—namely, that there were things outside of myself from which these ideas came and to which they were completely similar. That was the point in which, perhaps, I was mistaken; or at any rate, even if my judgment was in accord with the truth, it was no knowledge of mine which produced the truth of my judgment.

But when I considered something very simple and very easy concerning arithmetic and geometry, (36) as, for example, that two and three joined together produce the number five, and other similar things, did I not conceive them at least sufficiently clearly to guarantee that they were true? Certainly, if I have since judged that these things might be doubted, it was for no other reason than that it occurred to me that some God might perhaps have given me such a nature that I would be mistaken even about those things that seemed most obvious to me. Every time that this idea of the supreme power of a God, as previously conceived, occurs to me, I am constrained to admit that it is easy for him, if he wishes it, to bring it about that I am wrong even in those matters which I believe I perceive with the mind's eye with the greatest possible obviousness. And on the other hand, every time I turn to the things I think I conceive very clearly, I am so convinced by them that I am spontaneously led to proclaim: "Let him deceive me who can; he will never be able to bring it about that I am nothing while I think I am something, or, it being true that I now am, that it will some day be true that I have never been, or that two and three joined together make more or less than five, or similar things in which I recognize a manifest contradiction and which I see clearly could not be otherwise than as I conceive them."

And certainly, since I have no reason to believe that there is a God who is a deceiver, and since I have not yet even considered those reasons that prove that there is a God, the argument for doubting which depends only on this opinion is very tenuous and, so to speak, metaphysical. But in order to remove it altogether I must examine whether there is a God as soon as an opportunity occurs, and if I find that there is one I must also investigate whether he can be a deceiver; for as long as this is unknown, I do not see that I can ever be certain of anything. And now, in order that I shall have an opportunity to examine this question without interrupting the order of thought which I have proposed for myself, which is to pass by degrees from the notions which I discover to be most basic in my mind to those that I can discover afterwards, order seems to demand that I should first classify all (37) my thoughts into certain types and consider in which of these types there is, properly, truth or error.

Among my thoughts some are like images of objects, and it is to these alone that the name of "idea" properly applies, as when I picture to myself a man, or a chimera, or the sky, or an angel, or God himself. Then there are others with different forms, as when I wish, or fear, or affirm, or deny. In these cases I do conceive something as the object of the action of my mind, but I also add something else by this action to the idea which I have of the entity; and of this type of thought, some are called volitions or emotions, and others judgments.

Now as far as ideas are concerned, if we consider them only in themselves and do not relate them to something else, they cannot, properly speaking, be false; for whether I imagine a sage or a satyr, it is no less true that I imagine the one than the other. Similarly, we must not fear to encounter falsity in the emotions or volitions; for even though I may desire bad things, or even things which never existed, nevertheless it is no less true on that account that I desire them. So there is nothing left but judgments alone, in which I must take very great care not to make a mistake. But the principal and most common error which can be encountered here consists in judging that the ideas which are in myself are similar to, or conformable to, things outside of myself; for certainly, if I considered the ideas only as certain modes or aspects of my thought, without intending them to refer to some other exterior object, they could hardly offer me a chance of making a mistake.

Among these ideas, some seem to be born with me, others to be alien to me and to come from without, (38) and the rest to be made and invented by myself. For I have the ability to conceive what is generally called a thing, or a truth, or a thought; and it seems to me that I do not conceive this from anything but my own nature. But if I now hear some noise, if I see the sun, if I feel heat, I have hitherto judged that these feelings proceeded from some things which exist outside of myself; and finally, it seems to me that sirens, hippogriffs, and all other similar chimeras are fictions and inventions of my mind. Perhaps I might persuade myself that all these ideas are of the type of those I call alien and which come from without, or perhaps they are all innate, or perhaps they might all be invented; for I have not yet clearly discovered their true origin. And what I must principally do at this point is to consider, concerning those which seem to me to come from objects outside of me, what evidence obliges me to believe that they resemble those objects.

The first of these reasons is that it seems to me that nature teaches me so, and the second that I have direct experience that these ideas are not dependent upon my will nor upon myself. For often they come to me despite my wishes; just as now, whether I wish it or not, I feel heat, and for that reason I conclude that this sensation, or rather this idea, of heat is produced in me by something different from myself, namely, by the heat of the fire near which I am sitting. And I see nothing which appears more reasonable to me than to judge that this alien entity sends to me and imposes upon me its likeness rather than anything else.

Now I must see whether these reasons are sufficiently strong and convincing. When I say that it seems to me that nature teaches me so, I understand by this word "nature" only a certain inclination which leads me to believe it, and not the light of nature which makes me know that it is true. But these two expressions are very different from each other; for I could not doubt in any way what the light of nature made me see to be true, just as it made me see, a little while ago, that from the fact that I doubted I could conclude that I existed. And there is no way in which this could be doubted, because I have no other faculty or power to distinguish the true from the false which could teach me that what this light of nature shows me as true is not so, and in which I could trust as much as in the light of nature itself. (39) But as for inclinations, which also seem to me to be natural, I have often noticed, when it was a question of choosing between virtues and vices, that they led me to the bad no less than to the good; and for this reason I have not been inclined to follow them even in what concerns the true and the false.

As for the other reason, which is that these ideas must come from elsewhere, since they do not depend upon my will, I do not find this convincing either. For just as the inclinations which we are now considering occur in me, despite the fact that they are not always in accord with my will, so perhaps there is in me some faculty or power adequate to produce these ideas without the aid of any external objects, even though it is not yet known to me; just as it has so far always seemed to me that when I sleep, these ideas are formed in me without the aid of the objects which they represent. And finally, even if I should agree that the ideas are caused by these objects, it does not necessarily follow that they should be similar to them. On the contrary, I have often observed in many instances that there was a great difference between the object and its idea. Thus, for example, I find in myself two completely different ideas of the sun: the one has its origin in the senses, and must be placed in the class of those that, as I said before, came from without, according to which it seems to me extremely small; the other is derived from astronomical considerations that is, from certain innate ideas—or at least is formed by myself in whatever way it may be, according to which it seems to me many times greater than the whole earth. Certainly, these two ideas of the sun cannot both be similar to the same sun existing outside of me, and reason makes me believe that the one which comes directly from its appearance is that which least resembles it.

All this makes me recognize sufficiently well that up to now it has not been by (40) a valid and considered judgment, but only by a blind and rash impulse, that I have believed that there were things outside of myself and different from my own being which, through the organs of my senses or by whatever other method it might be, sent into me their ideas or images and impressed upon me their resemblances.

But there is still another path by which to seek if, among the things of which I possess ideas, there are some which exist outside of myself. If these ideas are considered only in so far as they are particular modes of thought, I do not recognize any difference or inequality among them, and all of them appear to arise from myself in the same fashion. But considering them as images, of which some represent one thing and some another, it is evident that they differ greatly among themselves. For those that represent substances are undoubtedly something more, and contain in themselves, so to speak, more objective reality, or rather, participate by representation in a higher degree of being or perfection, than those that represent only modes or accidents. Furthermore, that by which I conceive a supreme God, eternal, infinite, rimmutable, omniscient, omnipotent, and the universal creator of all things that exist outside of himself—that idea, I say, certainly contains in itself more objective reality than do those by which finite substances are represented.

Now it is obvious, according to the light of nature, that there must be at least as much reality in the total efficient cause as in its effect, for whence can the effect derive its reality, if not from its cause? And how could this cause communicate reality to the effect, unless it possessed it in itself?

And from this it follows, not only that something cannot be derived from nothing, but also that the more perfect—that is to say, that which contains in itself more reality (41)—cannot be a consequence of and dependent upon the less perfect. This truth is not only clear and evident in regard to the effects which have what philosophers call actual or formal reality, but also in regard to the ideas where one considers only what they call objective reality. For example, the stone which has not yet existed cannot now begin to be, unless it is produced by a being that possesses in itself formally or eminently all that enters into the composition of stone—that is, which contains in itself the same things as, or others more excellent than, those which are in stone. Heat cannot be produced in a being that previously lacked it, unless by something which is of an order, a degree, or a type at least as perfect as heat, and so forth. But still, in addition, the idea of heat or of stone cannot be in me, unless it was put there by something which contains in itself at least as much reality as I conceive there is in heat or stone; for even though that cause does not transfer to my idea anything of its actual or formal reality, we must not therefore suppose that such a cause is any less real, nor that the nature of an idea, since it is a work of the mind, is such that it does not require any other formal reality than what it receives and borrows from thought or mind, of which it is only a mode—that is, a way or manner of thinking. In order that an idea should contain one particular objective reality rather than another, it should no doubt obtain it from some cause in which there is at least as much formal reality as the idea contains objective reality. For if we suppose that there is some element in an idea which is not present in its cause, this element must then arise from nothing. However imperfect may be this mode of being, by which a thing exists objectively or is represented by a concept of it in the understanding, certainly we can nevertheless say that this mode and manner of being is not nothing, and consequently the idea cannot derive its origin from nothingness.

Nor must I imagine that, since the reality that I consider to be in my ideas is only objective, the same reality need not (42) be present formally or actually in the causes of these ideas, but that it is sufficient that it should be objectively present in them. For just as this manner of existing objectively belongs to ideas as part of their own nature, so also the manner or fashion of existing formally belongs to the causes of these ideas, or at the very least to their first and principal causes, as part of their own nature. And even though it might happen that one idea gives birth to another idea, that could not continue indefinitely; but we must finally reach a first idea, the cause of which is like an archetype or source, in which is contained formally and in actuality all the reality or perfection that is found only objectively or by representation in the ideas. Thus the light of nature makes me clearly recognize that ideas in me are like paintings or pictures, which can, truly, easily fall short of the perfection of the original from which they have been drawn, but which can never contain anything greater or more perfect. And the longer and the more carefully I consider all these arguments, the more clearly and distinctly I know that they are true.

What, then, shall I conclude from all this evidence? Clearly, that if the objective reality or perfection of some one of my ideas is such that I recognize clearly that this same reality or perfection does not exist in me, either formally or eminently, and consequently that I cannot myself be its cause, it necessarily follows that I am not alone in the world, but that there is also some other entity that exists and is the cause of this idea. On the other hand, if I find no such idea in myself, I will have no argument which can convince me and make me certain of the existence of any entity other than myself; for I have diligently searched for all such arguments and have been thus far unable to find any other.

Among all these ideas which exist in me, besides that which represents myself to myself, concerning which there can be no difficulty here, (43) there is another which represents a God, others corporeal and inanimate things, others angels, others animals, and still others which represent men similar to myself. But as far as the ideas which represent other men, or animals, or angels are concerned, I can easily imagine that they could be formed by the mixture and combination of my other ideas, of myself, of corporeal objects, and of God, even though outside of me there were no other men in the world, nor any animals, nor any angels. And as far as the ideas of corporeal objects are concerned, I recognize nothing in them so great or so excellent that it seems impossible that they could arise from myself. For if I consider them more closely and examine them in the same way that I examined the idea of wax yesterday, I find that there are only a few elements in them which I conceive clearly and distinctly—namely, size, or extension in length, width and depth; shape, which results from the termination and limitation of this extension; location, which the variously shaped objects have with respect to one another; and movement, or the changing of this location. To this one may add substance, duration, and number. As for other elements, such as light, colors, sounds, odors, tastes, heat, cold, and the other qualities involved in the sense of touch, they occur in my thought with so much obscurity and confusion that I do not even know whether they are true or false and only apparent, that is, whether my ideas of these qualities are really ideas of actual bodies or of non-bodies, which are only chimerical and cannot exist. For even though I have previously stated that true and formal falsity can characterize judgments only, there can exist nevertheless a certain material falsity in ideas, as when they represent that which is nothing as though it were something. For example, my ideas of cold and heat are so little clear (44) and distinct that I cannot determine from them whether cold is only the absence of heat or heat the absence of cold, or whether both of them are real qualities, or whether neither is such. Besides, since ideas are like pictures, there can be no ideas which do not seem to us to represent objects; and if it is true to say that cold is nothing but an absence of heat, the idea of cold which represents it as something real and positive could, riot inappropriately, be called false, and so for other similar ideas.

And assuredly, it is not necessary for me to attribute to such ideas any other source than myself. For if they are false—that is, if they represent entities which do not exist—the light of nature lets me know that they proceed from nothingness; that is, that they occur in me only because something is lacking in my nature and that the latter is not altogether perfect. And if these ideas are true, nevertheless, since they show me so little reality that I cannot even clearly distinguish the object represented from the nonexistent, I do not see why they could not be produced by myself and why I could not be their author.

As for my clear and distinct ideas of corporeal things, there are some of them which, it seems to me, might have been derived from my ideas of myself, such as my ideas of substance, duration, number, and other similar things. For I think that stone is a substance, or a thing which is capable of existing by itself, and that I myself am also a substance, even though I understand perfectly that I am a being that thinks and that is not extended, and that stone, on the contrary, is an extended being which does not think. Nevertheless, even though there is a notable difference between these two conceptions, they seem to agree in this fact that both of them represent substances. In the same way, when I think I exist now and remember in addition having existed formerly, or when I conceive various thoughts of which I recognize the number, I acquire (45) the ideas of duration and number which I afterward am able to apply to any other things I wish. As for the other qualities of which the ideas of material entities are composed—namely, extension, shape, location, and movement—it is true that they are not formally in my nature, since I am only a thinking being; but since these are only particular modes of substance, or, as it were, the garments in which corporeal substance appears to us, and since I am myself a substance, it seems that they might be contained in my nature eminently.

Thus there remains only the idea of God, in which we must consider if there is something which could not have come from myself. By the word "God" I mean an infinite substance, eternal, immutable, independent, omniscient, omnipotent, and that by which I myself and all other existent things, if it is true that there are other existent things, have been created and produced. But these attributes are such—they are so great and so eminent—that the more attentively I consider them, the less I can persuade myself that I could have derived them from my own nature. And consequently we must necessarily conclude from all that I have previously said that God exists. For even though the idea of substance exists in me from the very fact that I am a substance, I would nevertheless have no idea of an infinite substance, I who am a finite being, unless the idea had been placed in me by some substance which was in fact infinite.

And I must not imagine that I do not conceive infinity as a real idea, but only through the negation of what is finite in the manner that I comprehend rest and darkness as the negation of movement and light. On the contrary, I see manifestly that there is more reality in infinite substance than in finite substance, and my notion of the infinite is somehow prior to that of the finite, that is, the notion of God is prior to that of myself. For how would it be possible for me to know that I doubt and that I (46) desire—that is, that I lack something and am not all perfect—if I did not have in myself any idea of a being more perfect than my own, by comparison with which I might recognize the defects of my own nature?

And we cannot say that this idea of God might be materially false, and that in consequence I might derive it from nothingness, or, in other words, that it might be in me as a deficiency, as I have just now said about the ideas of heat and cold, and other similar things. For, on the contrary, this idea is very clear and very distinct and contains more objective reality than does any other, so that there is no other which is more true from its very nature, nor which is less open to the suspicion of error and falsity.

This idea, I say, of a supremely perfect and infinite being, is entirely true; for even though one might imagine that such a being does not exist, nevertheless one cannot imagine that the idea of it does not represent anything real, as I have just said of the idea of cold. It is also very clear and very distinct, since everything real and true which my mind conceives clearly and distinctly, and which contains some perfection, is contained and wholly included in this idea. And this will be no less true even though I do not comprehend the infinite and though there is in God an infinity of things which I cannot comprehend, or even perhaps suggest in thought, for it is the nature of infinity that I, who am finite and limited, cannot comprehend it. It is enough that I understand this and that I judge that all qualities which I conceive clearly and in which I know that there is some perfection, and possibly also an infinity of other qualities of which I am ignorant, are in God formally or eminently. Then the idea which I have of God is seen to be the truest, the clearest, and the most distinct of all the ideas which I have in my mind.

But possibly I am something more than I suppose myself to be. Perhaps all the perfections which I attribute to the nature of a God are somehow potentially in me, although they are not yet actualized and do not yet appear (47) and make themselves known by their actions. Experience shows, in fact, that my knowledge increases and improves little by little, and I see nothing to prevent its increasing thus, more and more, to infinity; nor even why, my knowledge having thus been augmented and perfected, I could not thereby acquire all the other perfections of divinity; nor finally, why my potentiality of acquiring these perfections, if it is true that I possess it, should not be sufficient to produce the ideas of them and introduce them into my mind.

Nevertheless, considering the matter more closely, I see that this could not be the case. For, first, even if it were true that my knowledge was always achieving new degrees of perfection and that there were in my nature many potentialities which had not yet been actualized, nevertheless none of these qualities belong to or approach in any way my idea of divinity, in which nothing is merely potential and everything is actual and real. Is it not even a most certain and infallible proof of the imperfection of my knowledge that it can grow little by little and increase by degrees? Furthermore, even if my knowledge increased more and more, I am still unable to conceive how it could ever become actually infinite, since it would never arrive at such a high point of perfection that it would no longer be capable of acquiring some still greater increase. But I conceive God to be actually infinite in such a high degree that nothing could be added to the supreme perfection that he already possesses. And finally, I understand very well that the objective existence of an idea can never be produced by a being that is merely potential and that, properly speaking, is nothing, but only by a formal or actual being.

And certainly there is nothing in all that I have just said which is not easily known by the light of nature to all those who will consider it carefully. But when I relax my attention somewhat, my mind is obscured, as though blinded by the images of sensible objects, and does not easily recall the reason why my idea of a being more perfect than my own must necessarily have been imparted to me by a being that is actually more perfect. (48)

That is why I wish to pass on now to consider whether I myself, who have this idea of God, could exist if there had been no God. And I ask, from what source would I have derived my existence? Possibly from myself, or from my parents, or from some other causes less perfect than God; for we could think of or imagine nothing more perfect, nor even equal to him. But if I were independent of anything else and were the author of my own being, I would doubt nothing, I would experience no desires, and finally I would lack no perfection. For I would have endowed myself with all those perfections of which I had any notion, and thus I would be God himself.

And I must not imagine that what I lack might be more difficult to acquire than what I already possess; for, on the contrary, it is very certain that it was far more difficult for this ego—that is, this being or substance that thinks—to emerge from nothingness than it would be for me to acquire the insight into and knowledge of various matters about which I am ignorant, since this knowledge would only be an accident of this substance. And certainly if I had given myself all the qualities that I have just mentioned and more, that is, if I were myself the author of my birth and of my being, I would at least not have denied to myself those things which could be obtained with greater facility as are an infinity of items of information, of which my nature happens to be deprived. I would not even have denied myself any of the qualities which I see are included in the idea of God, because there is no one of them which seems to me to be more difficult to create or acquire. And if there were one of them which was more difficult, certainly it would have appeared so to me, because, on the assumption that all my other qualities were self-given, I would see in this one quality a limitation of my power since I would not be able to acquire it.

Even if I could suppose that possibly I have always been as I am now, still I could not evade the force of this argument since it would not follow that no author of my existence need then be sought and I would still have to recognize that it is necessary that God is the author of my existence. For the whole duration of my life can be divided into (49) an infinite number of parts, no one of which is in any way dependent upon the others; and so it does not follow from the fact that I have existed a short while before that I should exist now, unless at this very moment some cause produces and creates me, as it were, anew or, more properly, conserves me.

Actually it is quite clear and evident to all who will consider attentively the nature of time that a substance, to be conserved at every moment that it endures, needs the same power and the same action which would be necessary to produce it and create it anew if it did not yet exist. Thus the light of nature makes us see clearly that conservation and creation differ only in regard to our manner of thinking and not in reality.

It is therefore only necessary here for me to question myself and consider my own nature to see whether I possess some power and ability by means of which I can bring it about that I, who exist now, shall still exist a moment later. For since I am nothing but a being which thinks, or at least since we are so far concerned only with that part of me, if such a power resided in me, certainly I should at least be conscious of it and recognize it. But I am aware of no such thing, and from that fact I recognize evidently that I am dependent upon some other being different from myself.

But possibly that being upon whom I am dependent is not God, and I am produced either by my parents or by some other causes less perfect than he. Not at all, that cannot be the case. For, as I have already said, it is very evident that there must be at least as much reality in the cause as in the effect; and since I am a being who thinks and who has some idea of God, whatever turns out to be the cause of my existence must be admitted to be also a being who thinks and which has in itself the idea of all the perfections which I attribute to the divine nature of God. Thus we can in turn inquire whether this cause derives its origin and existence from itself or from something else. For if it is self-caused, it follows, for the reasons that I have previously given, that this cause must be God himself, (50) since, to have the capacity to be or exist by itself, it must also, without doubt, have the power to possess in actuality all the perfections which it can imagine, that is, all those that I conceive to be in God. But if it derives its existence from something else, we ask once more, for the same reason, whether this second cause is caused by itself or by another, until step by step we finally arrive at an ultimate cause which will turn out to be God. And it is very obvious that in this case there cannot be an infinite regress, since it is not so much a question of the cause which produced me in the past as of that which conserves me in the present.

Nor can we pretend that possibly several partial causes have concurred to produce me, and that from one of them I received the idea of one of the perfections which I attribute to God, and from another the idea of some other, so that each of these perfections would actually be found somewhere in the universe, but would nowhere be joined together and assembled in one entity which would be God. For, on the contrary, the unity, simplicity, or inseparability of all the qualities which are in God is one of the principal perfections which I conceive to be in him. And certainly the idea of this unity of all God's perfections could not have been placed in me by any cause from which I had not also received the ideas of all the other perfections. For nothing could have brought it about that I understood these qualities as joined together and inseparable, without having brought it about at the same time that I know what qualities they were and that I knew something about each one of them.

Finally, concerning my parents, from whom it seems that I derive my birth, even if all that I could ever have believed of them should be true, that would still not imply that it is they who conserve me, nor even that they made and produced me in so far as I am a thinking being, there being no relation between the bodily activity by which I have been accustomed to believe I was engendered and the production of a thinking substance. The most that they can have contributed to my birth is that they have produced certain arrangements in the matter within which I have so far believed that the real I, that is, my mind, (51) is enclosed. Thus the existence of my parents is no objection to the argument, and we must necessarily conclude from the mere fact that I exist and that I have an idea of a supremely perfect Being, or God, that the existence of God is very clearly demonstrated.

The only task left is to consider how I received this idea from God; for I did not get it through the senses, nor has it ever appeared to me unexpectedly, as the ideas of sensible objects are wont to do, when these objects are presented or seem to be presented to my external sense organs. Nor is it only a product for fiction of my mind, for it is not in my power to diminish it or to add anything to it. No possibility remains, consequently, except that this idea is born and produced with me from the moment that I was created, just as was the idea of myself.

And truly it must not be thought strange that God, in creating me, put this idea in my nature in much the same way as an artisan imprints his mark on his work. Nor is it necessary that this mark be something different from the work itself. From the very fact that God has created me, it is very credible that he has made me, in some sense, in his own image and similitude, and that I conceive this similitude, in which the idea of God is contained, by the same faculty by which I conceive myself. In other words, when I reflect upon myself, I not only know that I am ran imperfect being, incomplete and dependent upon some other being, and a being which strives and aspires incessantly to become something better and greater than I now am, but also and at the same time I know that the being upon which I depend possesses in itself all these great qualities to which I aspire and the ideas of which I find in myself, and possesses these qualities, not indefinitely and merely potentially, but really, actually, and infinitely, and so that it is God. And the whole force of the argument I have here used to prove the existence of God consists in the fact that I recognize that it would not be possible (52) for my nature to be what it is, possessing the idea of a God, unless God really existed—the same God, I say, the idea of whom I possess, the God who possesses all these high perfections of which my mind can have some slight idea, without however being able fully to comprehend them; who is subject to no defect and who has no part of all those qualities which involve imperfection. And from this it is quite evident that he cannot be a deceiver, since the light of nature teaches us that deception must always be the result of some deficiency.

But before I examine this more carefully and pass on to the consideration of other truths which may follow from this one, it seems proper to pause for a while to contemplate this all-perfect God, to weigh at leisure his marvelous attributes, to consider, admire, and adore the incomparable beauty of this immense magnificence, as far at least as the power of my mind, which is somewhat overwhelmed by it, permits.

For just as faith teaches that the supreme felicity of the next life consists only in this contemplation of divine majesty, so let us try from now on whether a similar contemplation, although incomparably less perfect, will not make us enjoy the greatest happiness that we are capable of experiencing in this life.

FOURTH MEDITATION
OF THE TRUE AND THE FALSE

In these last few days I have become so accustomed to ignoring my senses, and I have so carefully noticed that we know very little (53) with certainty about corporeal things and that we know much more about the human mind, and still more again about God himself, that it is easy for me now to turn my consideration from sensible or picturable things to those which, being wholly dissociated from matter, are purely intelligible. And certainly my idea of the human mind, in so far as it is a thinking being, not extended in length, breadth, and depth, and participating in none of the qualities of body, is incomparably more distinct than my idea of anything corporeal. And when I consider that I doubt, that is to say, that I am an incomplete and dependent being, the idea of a complete and independent being, that is, of God, occurs to my mind with very great distinctness and clearness. And from the very fact that such an idea occurs in me, or that I who possess this idea exist, I so evidently conclude that God exists and that my own existence depends entirely upon him every moment of my life that I am confident that the human mind can know nothing with greater evidence and certainty. And I already seem to have discovered a path that will lead us from this contemplation of the true God, in whom all the treasures of science and wisdom are contained, to the knowledge of all other beings in the universe.

For first, I recognize that it is impossible for God ever to deceive me, since in all fraud and deception there is some kind of imperfection. And although it seems that to be able to deceive is a mark of acumen, subtlety, or power, nevertheless to wish to deceive testifies without question to weakness or malice, which could not be found in God.

Then, I know by my own experience that I have some ability to judge, or to distinguish the true from the false, an ability which I have no doubt received from God just as I have received all the other qualities which are part of me and which I possess. (54) Furthermore, since it is impossible that God wishes to deceive me, it is also certain that he has not given me an ability of such a sort that I could ever go wrong when I use it properly.

And no doubt on this subject would remain, except that we could apparently then draw the conclusion that I can never commit an error. For if everything in me is derived from God, and if he has not given me any ability to make errors, it seems that I should never be mistaken. It is true that when I consider myself only as a creature of God, and when I orient myself completely upon him, I discover in myself no cause of error or falsity. But when, a little later, I think of myself, experience convinces me that I am nevertheless subject to innumerable errors. And when I try to discover the reason for this, I notice that there is present in my thought not only a real and positive idea of God, or rather of a supremely perfect being, but also, so to speak, a certain negative idea of nothingness, or of what is infinitely removed from every kind of perfection. And I see that I am, as it were, a mean between God and nothingness, that is, so placed between the supreme Being and not-being that, in so far as a supreme Being has produced me, there is truly nothing in me which could lead me into error; but if I consider myself as somehow participating in nothingness or not-being, that is, in so far as I am not myself the supreme being and am lacking many things, I find myself exposed to an infinity of defects, so that I should not be astonished if I go wrong.

Thus I clearly recognize that error as such is not something real which depends upon God, but only a deficiency. Thus, in order to err, I do not need a faculty I which God has given to me expressly for the purpose; mistakes on my part occur because the power that God has given me to discriminate between the true and the false is not infinite.

Nevertheless I am not yet altogether satisfied, for error is not (55) a pure negation—that is, it is not a simple deficiency or lack of some perfection which is not my duel, but rather a privation or lack of some knowledge which it seems to me that I should possess. And in considering the nature of God, it does not seem possible that he should have endowed me with any faculty which is not perfect of its kind, or which lacks some perfection which is its due. For if it is true that the more expert the artisan, the more perfect and finished the artifacts produced by his hands, what could we imagine to have been produced by this supreme creator of the universe that is not perfect and entirely complete in all its parts? Certainly there is no doubt but that God could have created me such that I would never be mistaken; it is also certain that he always wills that which is best. Is it therefore a better thing to be able to make a mistake than not to be able to do so?

Considering this question with attention, it occurs to me, to begin with, that I should not be astonished at not being able to understand why God does what he does; and that I must not for this reason doubt his existence, since I may perchance observe in my experience many other beings that exist, even though I cannot understand why or how they were made. For, knowing by now that my nature is extremely weak and limited and that God's, on the contrary, is immense, incomprehensible, and infinite, I no longer have any difficulty in recognizing that there are an infinity of things within his power the causes of which lie beyond the powers of my mind. And this consideration alone is sufficient to persuade me that all causes of the type we are accustomed to call final are useless in physical or natural affairs, for it does not seem possible for me, without presumption, to seek and undertake to discover the impenetrable purposes of God.

Furthermore, it occurs to me that we should not consider a single creation separately when we investigate whether the works of God are perfect, but generally all created objects together. For the same thing which might perhaps, with some sort of justification, appear to be very imperfect if it were alone in the world (56) is seen to be very perfect when considered as constituting a part of this whole universe. And although, since I undertook to doubt everything, I have so far only learned with certainty of my existence and of God's, nevertheless, since I have recognized the infinite power of God, I could not deny that he has produced many other things, or at least that he could produce them, in such a way that I exist and am placed in the world as forming a part of the universality of all beings.

Consequently, when I come to examine myself more closely and to consider what are my errors, which alone testify that there is imperfection in me, I find that they depend upon two joint causes, namely, the faculty of knowing which I possess and the faculty of choice, or rather of free will—that is to say, of my understanding together with my will. For by the understanding alone I neither assert nor deny anything, but I only conceive the ideas of things which I may assert or deny. Nor in considering the understanding thus precisely can we say that any error is ever found in it, provided that we take the word "error" in its proper sense. And even if there might be in the world an infinity of things of which my understanding has no idea, we cannot therefore say that it is deprived of these ideas as of something which is owed to its nature, but only that it does not possess them, because in reality there is no argument which can prove that God ought to have given me a greater and more ample faculty of knowing than what lie has given me; and however adroit and able a worker I consider him to be, I must not therefore think that he ought to have put in each of his works all the perfections which lie is able to bestow upon some. Thus I cannot complain because God has not given me a sufficiently ample and perfect free will or volition, since, as a matter of fact, I experience it to be so ample and extended that there are no limits which restrict it.

And it appears to me to be very remarkable that, of all the other qualities which I possess, there is none (57) so perfect or so great that I do not clearly recognize that it could be even greater or more perfect. Thus for example, if I consider my faculty of conceiving, I immediately recognize that it is of very small extent and greatly limited; and at the same time there occurs to me the idea of another faculty, much more ample, indeed immensely greater and even infinite, and from the very fact that I can imagine this I recognize without difficulty that it belongs to the nature of God. In the same way, if I examine memory, imagination, or any other faculty of mine, I find no one of them which is not quite small and limited and which is not, in God, immense and infinite. There is only volition alone, or the liberty of the free will, which I experience to be so great in myself that I cannot conceive the idea of any other more ample and extended, so that this is what principally indicates to me that I am made in the image and likeness of God. For even though the will may be incomparably greater in God than in myself, either because of the knowledge and the power which are joined with it and which make it surer and more efficacious, or because of its object, since it extends to infinitely more things, nevertheless it does not appear any greater when I consider it formally and precisely by itself. For it consists only in the fact that we can make a choice; we can do a given thing or not do it— that is to say, we can affirm or deny, pursue or avoid. Or more properly, our free will consists only in the fact that in affirming or denying, pursuing or avoiding the things suggested by the understanding, we behave in such a way that we do not feel that any external force has constrained us in our decision.

For in order to be free, it is not necessary for me to be indifferent about the choice of one or the other of the two contraries, but rather, the more I lean to one, either because I see clearly that it contains the preponderance (58) of both goodness and truth or because God so guides my private thoughts, the more freely do I choose and embrace it. And certainly, divine grace and natural understanding, far from diminishing my liberty, rather augment and strengthen it. Moreover, that indifference which I feel when I am not more moved toward one side than the other by the weight of some reason is the lowest degree of liberty, and is rather a defect in the understanding than a perfection of the will. For if I always understood clearly what is true and what is good, I would never need to deliberate about what judgment and what choice I ought to make, and so I would be entirely free without ever being indifferent.

From all this I recognize, on the one hand, that the cause of my errors is not the power of willing considered by itself, which I have received from God, for it is very ample and perfect in its own kind. Nor, on the other hand, is it the power of understanding or conceiving; for since I conceive nothing except by means of this power which God has given me in order to conceive, no doubt everything I conceive I conceive properly, and it is not possible for me to be deceived in that respect.

Whence, then, do my errors arise? Only from the fact that the will is much more ample and far-reaching than the understanding, so that I do not restrain it within the same limits but extend it even to those things which I do not understand. Being by its nature indifferent about such matters, it very easily is turned aside from the true and the good and chooses the false and the evil. And thus it happens that I make mistakes and that I sin.

For example, when I recently examined the question whether anything in the world existed, and I recognized from the very fact that I examined this question that it was very evident that I myself existed, I could not refrain from concluding that what I conceived so clearly was true. Not that I found myself forced to this conclusion by any (59) external cause, but only because the great clarity which was in my understanding produced a great inclination of my will, and I was led to this conviction all the more spontaneously and freely as I experienced in myself less indifference. Now, on the contrary, I know not only that I exist, in so far as I am something that thinks, but there is also present in my mind a certain idea of corporeal nature. In consequence, I wonder whether this nature that thinks, which is in me, or rather which is myself, is different from this corporeal nature, or if both are one and the same. I am supposing, here, that I do not yet know any argument to convince me of one possibility rather than the other, so it follows that I am entirely indifferent as to denying or affirming it, or even as to abstaining from making any judgment.

And this indifference extends not only to those things with which the understanding has no acquaintance, but also to all those generally that it does not comprehend with sufficiently perfect clarity at the moment when the will is deliberating the issue. For however probable may be the conjectures which incline me to a particular judgment, the mere recognition that they are only conjectures and not certain and indubitable reasons is enough to give me grounds for making the contrary judgment. I have had sufficient experience of this in these past few days when I assumed as false all that I had previously held to be very true, merely because I noticed that it was somehow possible to doubt it.

Now, if I abstain from making a judgment upon a topic when I do not conceive it sufficiently clearly and distinctly, it is evident that I do well and am not making a mistake; but if I decide to deny or affirm it, then I am not making a proper use of my free will. And (60) if in this situation I affirm what is not true, it is evident that I am making a mistake; and even when I judge according to the truth, it is only by chance, and I am not for that reason free of blame for misusing my freedom. For the light of nature dictates that the understanding should always know before the will makes a decision.

It is in this improper use of the free will that we find the privation which constitutes the essence of error. Privation, I say, is found in the operation in so far as it proceeds from me, but not in the faculty which I have received from God, nor even in the operation in so far as it depends upon him. For certainly I have no reason to complain because God has not given me a more ample intelligence or a more perfect insight than what he has bestowed upon me, since it is actually the nature of a finite understanding not to comprehend many things, and it is the nature of a created understanding to be finite. On the contrary, far from conceiving such unjust sentiments as to imagine that he has deprived me or unjustly kept from me the other perfections with which he has not endowed me, I have every reason to give him thanks because, never having any obligation to me, he has nevertheless given me those few perfections that I have.

Nor have I any reason to complain because he has given me a volition more ample than my understanding. For as the volition consists of just one body, its subject being apparently indivisible, it seems that its nature is such that nothing could be taken from it without destroying it. And, certainly, the more ample it is, the more reason I have to give thanks for the generosity of the One who has given it to me.

Nor, finally, have I any reason to complain that God concurs with me to perform the acts of this volition, that is, the judgments in which I am mistaken. For those acts are entirely true and absolutely good in so far as they depend upon God, and there is somehow more perfection in my nature because I can perform them than there would be if I could not. As for privation; in which alone is found the formal cause (61) of error and sin, it has no need of any concurrence on the part of God, since it is not a thing of a being and since, if it is referred to God as to its cause, it should not be called privation but only negation according to the significance attached to these words in the schools. For actually it is not an imperfection in God that he has given me the liberty of judging or not judging, or giving or withholding my assent, on certain matters of which he has given me no clear and distinct knowledge. It is, without doubt, an imperfection in myself not to make proper use of this liberty, and rashly to pass judgment on matters which I do not rightly understand and conceive only obscurely and confusedly.

I perceive, nevertheless, that it would have been easy for God to contrive that I would never make mistakes, even though I remained free and with limited knowledge.

He might, for example, have given my understanding a clear and distinct comprehension of all the things about which I should ever deliberate, or he might simply have engraved so deeply in my memory the resolution never to pass judgment on anything without conceiving it clearly and distinctly that I could never forget this rule. And I readily recognize in so far as I possess the comprehension of any whole, that when I consider myself alone, as if I were the only person in the world, I would have been much more perfect than I am if God had so created me that I never made a mistake; nevertheless I cannot therefore deny that the universe may be somehow more perfect because some of its parts are not free from defect while others are, than it would be if all its parts were alike.

And I have no right to complain because God, having put me in the world, has not wished to place me in the ranks of the noblest and most perfect beings. I indeed have reason to rejoice because, even if I do not have the power of avoiding error by the first method which I have just described, which depends upon a clear and evident knowledge of all the things about which I can deliberate, the other method, at least, is within my power. This is, (62) firmly to adhere to the resolution never to pass judgment upon things whose truth is not clearly known to me. For even though I experience in myself the weakness of not being able to keep my mind continuously faithful to a fixed resolution, I can nevertheless, by attentive and frequently repeated meditation, so strongly impress it upon my memory that I will never fail to recollect it whenever there is need, and thus I can acquire the habit of not erring. And since this comprises the greatest and principal perfection of man, I consider that I have benefited not a little by today's meditation, in having discovered the cause of error and falsity.

And certainly, there can be no other cause than the one I have just explained, for whenever I restrict my volition within the bounds of my knowledge, whenever my volition makes no judgment except upon matters clearly and distinctly reported to it by the understanding, it cannot happen that I err. For every clear and distinct conception is without doubt something real and positive, and thus cannot derive its origin from nothingness, but must have God for its author—God, I say, who, being supremely perfect, cannot be the cause of any error—and consequently we must conclude that such a conception or such a judgment is true.

For the rest, I have not only learned today what I must avoid in order not to err, but also what I ought to do to arrive at the knowledge of the truth. For I shall certainly achieve this goal if I hold my attention sufficiently fixed upon all those things which I conceive perfectly and if I distinguish these from the others which I conceive only confusedly and obscurely. And from now on I shall take particular care to act accordingly. (63)

FIFTH MEDITATION
OF THE ESSENCE OF MATERIAL THINGS AND, ONCE MORE,
OF GOD: THAT HE EXISTS

There are many other questions for me to inquire into concerning the attributes of God and concerning my own nature, or the nature of my mind. I may, perhaps, pursue this investigation some other time; for the present, having noticed what must be done or avoided in order to arrive at the knowledge of the truth, my principal task is to attempt to escape from and relieve myself of All the doubts into which I have fallen in these last few days, and to see if we cannot know anything certain about material objects. But before examining whether such objects exist outside of myself, I must consider the concepts of these objects, in so far as they occur in my thought, and see which of them are distinct and which of them are confused.

In the first place, I picture distinctly that quantity which philosophers commonly call the "continuum," or extension in length, width, and depth which exists in this quantity, or rather in the body to which we attribute it. Furthermore, I can distinguish in it various different parts and attribute to each of these parts all sorts of sizes, shapes, positions, and movements; and, finally, I can assign to each of these movements all degrees of duration.

And I not only know these things distinctly when I consider them thus in general, but also, however little I am applying my attention to it, I come to recognize an infinity of details concerning numbers, shapes, movements, and other similar things, the truth of which makes itself so apparent (64) and accords so well with my nature that when I discover them for the first time it does not seem to me as though I were learning anything new, but rather as though I were remembering what I had previously known—that is, that I am perceiving things which were already in my mind, even though I had not yet focussed my attention upon them.

And what I believe to be more important here is that I find in myself an infinity of ideas of certain things which cannot be assumed to be pure nothingness, even though they may perhaps have no existence outside of my thought. These things are not figments of my imagination, even though it is within my power to think of them or not to think of them; on the contrary, they have their own true and immutable natures. Thus, for example, when I imagine a triangle, even though there may perhaps be no such figure anywhere in the world outside of my thought, nor ever have been, nevertheless the figure cannot help having a certain determinate nature, or form, or essence, which is immutable and eternal, which I have not invented and which does not in any way depend upon my mind. This is evidenced by the fact that we can demonstrate various properties of this triangle, namely, that its three angles are equal to two right angles, that the greatest angle subtends the longest side, and other similar properties. Whether I wish it or not, I now recognize very clearly and evidently that these are properties of the triangle, even though I had never previously thought of them in any way when I first imagined one. And therefore it cannot be said that I have imagined or invented them.

Nor can I raise the objection here that possibly this idea of the triangle came to my mind from external things through the medium of my senses, since I have sometimes seen triangularly shaped objects; for I can picture in my mind an infinity of other shapes such that I cannot have the least suspicion that they have ever been present to my senses, and I am still (65) no less able to demonstrate various properties about their nature than I am about that of the triangle. These properties, certainly, must be wholly true, since I conceive them clearly. And thus they are something, and not pure negation, since it is quite evident that everything which is true is something, as truth is the same as being. I have already amply demonstrated that everything that I recognize clearly and distinctly is true; and even if I had not demonstrated this, the nature of my mind is such that I can not help believing things to be true while I am conceiving them clearly and distinctly. And I recollect that even when I was still strongly attached to the objects of sense, I numbered among the most constant truths that which I conceived clearly and distinctly about the shapes, numbers, and other properties which belong to the fields of arithmetic and geometry or, in general, to pure and abstract mathematics.

Now, if from the very fact that I can derive from my thoughts the idea of something, it follows that all that I clearly and distinctly recognize as characteristic of this thing does in reality characterize it, can I not derive from this an argument which will demonstratively prove the existence of God? It is certain that I find in my mind the idea of God, of a supremely perfect Being, no less than that of any shape or number whatsoever; and I recognize that an actual and eternal existence belongs to his nature no less clearly and distinctly than I recognize that all I can demonstrate about some figure or number actually belongs to the nature of that figure or number. Thus, even if everything that I concluded in the preceding Meditations were by chance not true, the existence of God should pass in my mind as at least as certain (66) as I have hitherto considered all the truths of mathematics, which deal only with numbers and figures.

And this is true even though I must admit that it does not at first appear entirely obvious, but seems to have some appearance of sophistry. For since in all other matters I have become accustomed to make a distinction between existence and essence, I am easily convinced that the existence of God can be separated from his essence, and that thus I can conceive of God as not actually existing. Nevertheless, when I consider this with more attention, I find it manifest that we can no more separate the existence of God from his essence than we can separate from the essence of a rectilinear triangle the fact that the size of its three angles equals two right angles, or from the idea of a mountain the idea of a valley. Thus it is no less self-contradictory to conceive of a God, a supremely perfect Being, who lacks existence—that is, who lacks some perfection—than it is to conceive of a mountain for which there is no valley.

But even though in fact I cannot conceive of a God without existence, any more than of a mountain without a valley, nevertheless, just as from the mere fact that I conceive a mountain with a valley, it does not follow that any mountain exists in the world, so likewise, though I conceive of God as existing, it does not seem to follow for this reason that God exists. For my thought does not impose any necessity upon things; and just as I can at my pleasure imagine a winged horse, even though no horse has wings, so I could perhaps attribute existence to God, even though no God existed.

This is far from the truth; it is here that there is sophistry hidden under the guise of a valid objection. For from the fact that I cannot conceive a mountain without a valley it does not follow that there is a mountain or a valley anywhere in the world, but only that the mountain (67) and the valley, whether they exist or not, are inseparable from each other. From the fact alone that I cannot conceive God except as existing, it follows that existence is inseparable from him, and consequently that he does, in truth, exist. Not that my thought can bring about this result or that it imposes any necessity upon things; on the contrary, the necessity which is in the thing itself—that is, the necessity of the existence of God—determines me to have this thought. For it is not in my power to conceive of a God without existence—that is to say, of a supremely perfect Being without a supreme perfection—as it is in my power to imagine a horse either with or without wings.

And it must not be said here that it is only necessary that I admit that God exists after I have supposed that he possesses all sorts of perfections, since existence is one of them, but that my first supposition was not really necessary. Thus it is not necessary to think that all four-sided figures can be inscribed in a circle; but if we suppose that I do have this idea, I am forced to admit that a rhombus can be inscribed in one, since it is a four-sided figure, and by this I will be forced to admit what is clearly false. We must not, I say, argue thus; for even though it is not necessary that I should ever have any thought about God, nevertheless, whenever I do choose to think of a first and supreme being and to derive, so to speak, the idea of God from the treasure house of my mind, it is necessary that I attribute to him all kinds of perfections, even though it does not occur to me to mention them all and to pay attention to each one of them severally. And this necessity is enough to bring it about that afterward, as soon as I come to recognize that existence is a perfection, I conclude very properly that this first and supreme Being truly exists; just as it is not necessary that I should ever imagine any triangle, but every time that I wish to consider a rectilinear figure containing three angles only, it is absolutely necessary that I attribute to it everything that leads (68) to the conclusion that these three angles are not greater than two right angles, even if perhaps I do not then consider this matter in particular. But when I wish to determine what figures can be inscribed in a circle, it is in no way necessary that I think that all four-sided figures are of this number; on the contrary, I cannot even pretend that this is the case as long as I do not wish to accept anything but what I can conceive clearly and distinctly. Consequently, there is a vast difference between false suppositions, such as this one, and the true ideas which are inborn in me, of which the first and chief one is that of God. For actually I have several reasons for recognizing that this idea is not something imaginary or fictitious, depending only on my thought, but that it is the image of a true and immutable nature. The first reason is that I cannot conceive anything but God alone, to whose essence existence belongs with necessity. Another reason is that it is not possible for me to conceive in the same way two or more gods such as he. Again, assuming that there is now a God who exists, I see clearly that he must have existed before from all eternity and that he should be eternally in the future. And a final reason is that I conceive various other qualities in God, of which I can neither diminish nor change a particle.

For the rest, whatever proof or argument I use, I must always come back to this conclusion: that it is only the things that I conceive clearly and distinctly which have the power to convince me completely. And although among the things which I conceive in this way there are, in truth, some which are obviously known to everyone, while others of them only become known to those who consider them more closely and examine them more carefully, nevertheless, after they have once been discovered, none of them can be esteemed less certain than the rest. Thus, for example, in every right-angled triangle, even though it is not so readily apparent (69) that the square of the hypotenuse is equal to the squares of the other two sides as it is that this hypotenuse is opposite the greatest angle, nevertheless, after this fact has once been recognized, we are as much convinced of the truth of the one proposition as of the other. And as for the question of God, certainly, if my mind were not prejudiced and if my thought were not distracted by the constant presence on all sides of images of sensible objects, there would be nothing that I would recognize sooner or more easily than God. For is there anything clearer and more obvious in itself than to think that there is a God, that is to say, a supreme and perfect Being, in whom uniquely necessary for eternal existence is included in essence, and who consequently exists?

And although, in order thoroughly to understand this truth, I have bad to make a great mental effort, nevertheless I find myself at present not only as certain of this as of everything which seems to me most certain, but even beyond that I notice that the certainty of all other things depends upon this so absolutely that, without this knowledge, it is impossible ever to be able to know anything perfectly.

For even though my nature is such that as soon as I understand anything very clearly and very distinctly I cannot help but believe it to be true, nevertheless, because I am also of such a nature that I cannot always confine my attention to one thing and frequently remember having judged a thing to be true when I have ceased considering the reasons which forced me to that conclusion, it can happen at such a time that other reasons occur to me which would easily make me change my mind if I did not know that there was a God. And so I would never have true and certain knowledge concerning anything at all, but only vague and fluctuating opinions.

Thus, for example, when I consider the nature of the rectilinear triangle, I recognize most evidently, I, who am somewhat skilled in geometry, that its three angles are equal to two right angles; nor can I disbelieve this while I am paying attention to (70) its demonstration. But as soon as I turn my attention away from the demonstration, even while I remember having clearly understood it, it can easily happen that I doubt its truth, if I do not know that there is a God. For I can persuade myself that I was so made by nature that I could easily make mistakes, even in those matters which I believe I understand with the greatest evidence and certainty, especially because I remember having often judged many things true and certain, which, later, other reasons constrained me to consider absolutely false.

But after having recognized that there is a God, and having recognized at the same time that all things arc dependent upon him and that he is not a deceiver, I can infer as a consequence that everything which I conceive clearly and distinctly is necessarily true. Therefore, even if I am no longer thinking of the reasons why I have judged something to be true, provided only I remember having understood it clearly and distinctly, there can never be a reason on the other side which can make me consider the matter doubtful. Thus I have a true and certain body of knowledge on this matter. And this same body of knowledge extends also to all the other things which I remember having formerly demonstrated such as the truths of geometry and other similar matters. For what reason can anyone give to make me doubt them? Would it be that my nature is such that I am very likely to be frequently deceived? But I know already that I cannot go wrong in judgments for which I clearly know the reasons. Would it be that I have formerly considered many things true and certain which I later recognized to be false? But I had not clearly or distinctly known any of those things; and not yet knowing this rule by which I am certain of truth, I had been led to believe them by reasons that I have since recognized to be less strong than I had then imagined them. What further objections could be raised? Would it be that possibly I am asleep, as I had myself argued earlier, or that all the thoughts that I now have are no more true than the dreams we imagine when asleep? But even so, nothing would be altered. For (71) even if I were asleep, all that appears evident to my mind is absolutely true.

And thus I recognize very clearly that the certainty and truth of all knowledge depends solely on the knowledge of the true God, so that before I knew him I could not know any other thing perfectly. And now that I know him, I have the means of acquiring clear and certain and perfect knowledge about an infinity of things, not only about God himself and about other intellectual matters, but also about that which pertains to corporeal nature, in so far as it can be the object of pure mathematics—that is, of the demonstrations of geometricians who are not concerned with its existence.

Sixth Meditation
Of the Existence of Corporeal Things and of the Real Distinction Between the Mind and Body of Man

Nothing more is now left for me to do except to examine whether corporeal things exist; and I already know for certain that they can exist at least in so far as they are considered as the objects of pure mathematics, or of the demonstrations of geometry, since I conceive them in this way very clearly and very distinctly. For there is no doubt but that God has the power of producing everything that I am able to conceive with distinctness; and I have never supposed that it was impossible for him to do anything, except only when I found a contradiction in being able to conceive it well. Furthermore, my faculty of imagination, which I find by experience that I use when I apply myself to the consideration of material objects, is capable of persuading me of their existence. For when I consider attentively what the imagination is, (72) I find that it is nothing else than a particular application of the faculty of knowledge to a body which is intimately present to it and which therefore exists.

And to make this very obvious, I take note of the difference between imagination and pure intellection or conception. For example, when I imagine a triangle, not only do I conceive that it is a figure composed of three lines, but along with that I envision these three lines as present, by the force and the internal effort of my mind; and it is just this that I call "imagination." But if I wish to think of a chiliogon, I recognize quite well, indeed, that it is a figure composed of a thousand sides, as easily as I conceive that a triangle is a figure composed of only three sides, but I cannot imagine the thousand sides of a chiliogon as I can the three of a triangle, nor, so to speak, look at them as though they were present to the eyes of my mind. And although, following my habit of always using my imagination when I think of corporeal things, it may happen that in conceiving a chiliogon I confusedly picture some figure to myself, nevertheless it is quite evident that this figure is not a chiliogon, since it is in no way different from what I would picture to myself if I thought of a myriogon or of some other figure of many sides, and that it in no way serves to bring out the properties which constitute the difference between the chiliogon and the other polygons. But if it is a question of considering a pentagon, it is quite true that I can conceive its shape, just as well as that of a chiliogon, without the aid of the imagination; but I can also imagine it by applying my mind attentively to each of its five sides, and at the same time collectively to the area or space that they enclose.

Thus I recognize clearly that I have need of a special (73) mental effort in order to imagine, which I do not require in order to conceive or understand, and this special mental effort clearly shows the difference that exists between imagination and pure intellection or conception. In addition, I notice that this ability to imagine which I possess, in so far as it differs from the power of conceiving, is in no way necessary to my nature or essence, that is to say, to the essence of my mind. For even if I did not possess it, there is no doubt that I would still remain the same person I now am, from which it seems to follow that it depends upon something other than my mind. And I readily conceive that if some body exists with which my mind is so joined and united] that it can consider it whenever it wishes, it could be that by this means it imagines corporeal things. Thus this method of thinking only differs from pure intellection in that the mind, in conceiving, turns somehow toward itself and considers some one of the ideas which it possesses in itself, whereas in imagining it turns toward the body and considers in the latter something conformable to the idea which it has either thought of by itself or perceived through the senses. I easily conceive, I say, that the imagination can work in this fashion, if it is true that there are bodies; and because I cannot find any other way in which this can be explained equally well, I therefore conjecture that bodies probably exist. But this is only a probability; and although I carefully consider all aspects of the question, I nevertheless do not see that from this distinct idea of corporeal nature which I find in my imagination, I can derive any argument which necessarily proves the existence of any body. (74)

But I have become accustomed to imagine many other things besides that corporeal nature which is the object of pure mathematics or geometry, although less distinctly, such as colors, sounds, tastes, pain, and other similar qualities. And inasmuch as I perceive those qualities much better by the senses, through the medium of which, with the help of the memory, they seem to have reached my imagination, I believe that in order to examine them more readily it is appropriate to consider at the same time the nature of the sensation and to see whether, from those ideas which are perceived by the method of thinking which I call "sensation," I will not be able to derive some certain proof of the existence of corporeal things.

First, I shall recall in my memory what are the things which I formerly held to be true because I had received them through the senses, and what were the bases on which my belief was founded. Afterward I shall examine the reasons which since then have obliged me to consider them doubtful, and finally, I shall consider what I ought now to believe about them.

First, then, I felt that I had a head, hands, feet, and all the other members which compose this body which I thought of as a part, or possibly even as the whole, of myself. Furthermore, I felt that this body was one of a world of bodies, from which it was capable of receiving various advantages and disadvantages; and I identified these advantages by a certain feeling of pleasure or enjoyment, and the disadvantages by a feeling of pain. Besides this pleasure and pain, I also experienced hunger, thirst, and other similar appetites, as well as certain bodily tendencies toward gaiety, sadness, anger, and other similar emotions. And externally, in addition to the extension, shapes, and (75) movements of bodies, I observed in them hardness, warmth, and all the other qualities perceived by touch. Furthermore, I noticed in them light, colors, odors, tastes, and sounds, the variety of which enabled me to distinguish the sky, the earth, the sea, and, in general, all other bodies, one from another.

And certainly, considering the ideas of all these qualities which were presented to my mind and which alone I directly sensed, in the true significance of that term, it was not without reason that I believed I had sensory knowledge of things entirely different from my thought—of bodies, namely, from which these ideas came. For I was aware that these ideas occurred without the necessity of my consent, so that I could not perceive any object, however much I wished, unless it was present to one of my sense organs; nor was it in my power not to perceive it when it was present. And because the ideas I received through the senses were much more vivid, more detailed, and even in their own way more distinct than any of those which I could picture to myself with conscious purpose while meditating, or even than those which I found impressed upon my memory, it seemed that they could not be derived from my own mind, and therefore they must have been produced in me by some other things. Of these things I have no knowledge whatsoever, except that derived from the ideas themselves, so nothing else could occur to my mind except that those things were similar to the ideas they caused. And since I remembered that I had used my senses earlier than my reason, and since I recognized that the ideas I formed by myself were not as detailed as those I received through the senses and were most commonly composed. of the latter as parts, I easily became persuaded that I had no idea in my mind which I had not previously acquired through my senses.

It was also not without reason that I believed that this body, which by a certain particular privilege I called mine, (76) belonged to me more properly and strictly than any other. For in fact I could never be separated from it, as I could be from other bodies; I felt in it and for it all my appetites and all my emotions; and finally I experienced the sensations of pain and the thrill of pleasure in its parts, and not in those of other bodies which are separated from it.

But when I inquired why any particular sensation of pain should be followed by unhappiness in the mind and the thrill of pleasure should give rise to happiness, or even why a particular feeling of the stomach, which I call hunger, makes us want to eat, and the dryness of the throat makes us want to drink, and so on, I could give no reason except that nature teaches me so. For there is certainly no affinity and no relationship, or at least none that I can understand, between the feeling in the stomach and the desire to eat, no more than between the perception of the, object which causes pain and the feeling of displeasure produced by it. And in the same way, it seemed to me that I had learned from nature all the other beliefs which I held about the objects of my senses, since I noticed that the judgments I habitually made about these objects took form in my mind before I had the opportunity to weigh and consider any reasons which could oblige me to make them.

Later on, various experiences gradually destroyed all my faith in my senses. For I often observed that towers which, viewed from far away, had appeared round to me, seemed at close range to be square, and that colossal statues placed on the highest summits of these towers appeared small when viewed from below. And similarly in a multitude of other experiences, I encountered errors in judgments based on the external senses. And not only on the external senses, but even on the internal ones, (77) for is there anything more intimate or more internal than pain? Yet I have learned from certain persons whose arms or legs had been amputated that it still seemed to them sometimes that they felt pain in the parts which they no longer possessed. This gives me reason to think that I could not be entirely sure either that there was something wrong with one of my limbs, even though I felt a pain in it.

And to these reasons for doubting I have recently added two other very general ones. The first is that I have never thought I perceived anything when awake that I might not sometimes also think I perceived when I am asleep; and since I do not believe that the things I seem to perceive when asleep proceed from objects outside of myself, I did not see any better reason why I ought to believe this about what I seem to perceive when awake. The other reason was that, not yet knowing, or rather pretending not to know the author of my being, I saw nothing to make it impossible that I was so constructed by nature that I should be mistaken even in the things which seemed to me most true.

And as for the reasons which had previously persuaded me that sensible objects truly existed, I did not find it very difficult to answer them. For as nature seemed to lead me to many conclusions from which reason dissuaded me, I did not believe that I ought to have much faith in the teachings of this nature. And although my sense perceptions do not depend upon my volition, I did not think that I should therefore conclude that they proceeded from things different from myself, since there might perhaps be some faculty in myself even though it has been thus far unknown to me, which could bwe their cause and produce them.

But now that I am beginning to know myself better and to discover more clearly the author of my origin, I do not think in truth that I ought rashly to admit everything which the senses seem to teach us, (78) but on the other hand I do not think that I should doubt them all in general.

First, since I know that all the things I conceive clearly and distinctly can be produced by God exactly as I conceive them, it is sufficient that I can clearly and distinctly conceive one thing apart from another to be certain that the one is distinct or different from the other. For they can be made to exist separately, at least by the omnipotence of God, and we are obliged to consider them different no matter what power produces this separation. From the very fact that I know with certainty that I exist, and that I find that absolutely nothing else belongs necessarily to my nature or essence except that I am a thinking being, I readily conclude that my essence consists solely in being a body which thinks or a substance whose whole essence or nature is only to think. And although perhaps, or rather certainly, as I will soon show, I have a body with which I am very closely united, nevertheless, since on the one hand I have a clear and distinct idea of myself in so far as I am only a thinking and not an extended being, and since on the other hand I have a distinct idea of body in so far as it is only an extended being which does not think, it is certain that this "I"—that is to say, my soul, by virtue of which I am what I am—is entirely and truly distinct from my body and that it can be or exist without it.

Furthermore, I find in myself various faculties of thinking which each have their own particular characteristics and are distinct from myself. For example, I find in myself the faculties of imagination and of perception, without which I might no doubt conceive of myself, clearly and distinctly, as a whole being; but I could not I, conversely, conceive of those faculties without me, that is to say, without an intelligent substance to which they are attached or in which they inhere. For in our notion of them or, to use the scholastic vocabulary, in their formal concept, they embrace some type of intellection. From all this I reach the conception that these faculties are distinct from me as shapes, movements, and other modes or accidents of objects are distinct from the very objects that sustain them.

I also recognize in myself some other faculties, such as the power of changing location, of assuming various postures, and other similar ones; which cannot be conceived without some substance in which they inhere, any more than the preceding ones, (79) and which therefore cannot exist without such a substance. But it is quite evident that these faculties, if it is true that they exist, must inhere in some corporeal or extended substance, and not in an intelligent substance, since their clear and distinct concept does actually involve some sort of extension, but no sort of intelligence whatsoever. Furthermore, I cannot doubt that there is in me a certain passive faculty of perceiving, that is, of receiving and recognizing the ideas of sensible objects; but it would be valueless to me, and I could in no way use it if there were not also in me, or in something else, another active faculty capable of forming and producing these ideas. But this active faculty cannot be in me, in so far as I am a thinking being, since it does not at all presuppose my intelligence and also since those ideas often occur to me without my contributing to them in any way, and even frequently against my will. Thus it must necessarily exist in some substance different from myself, in which all the reality that exists objectively in the ideas produced by this faculty is formally or eminently contained, as I have said before. This substance is either a body—that is, a corporeal nature—in which is formally and actually contained all that which is contained objectively and by representation in these ideas; or else it is God himself, or some other creation more noble than the body, in which all this is eminently contained.

But since God is not a deceiver, it is very manifest that he does not send me these ideas directly by his own agency, nor by the mediation of some creation in which their objective reality does not exist formally but only eminently. For since he has not given me any faculty for recognizing what that creation might be, but on the contrary a very great (80) inclination to believe that these ideas come from corporeal objects, I do not see how we could clear God of the charge of deceit if these ideas did in fact come from some other source or were produced by other causes than corporeal objects. Therefore we must conclude that corporeal objects exist. Nevertheless, they are not perhaps entirely what our senses perceive them to be, for there are many ways in which this sense perception is very obscure and confused; but we must at least admit that everything which I conceive clearly and distinctly as occuring in them—that is to say, everything,

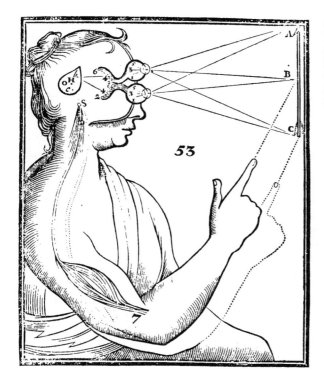

A diagram from Descartes'
Tractatus de Homine (1677)
showing how the pineal gland
(shown here at the back of the head)
connects sensory images from the
eyes to the muscles of the arm.
(*Library of Congress*)

generally speaking, which is discussed in pure mathematics or geometry—does in truth occur in them.

As for the rest, there are other beliefs, which are very doubtful and uncertain, which are either merely particular—as, for example, that the sun is of such a size and such a shape—or else are conceived less clearly and less distinctly—such as light, sound, pain, and other similar things. Nevertheless, from the mere fact that God is not a deceiver, and that in consequence he has not permitted any falsity in my opinions without having given me some faculty capable of correcting it, I think I can conclude with assurance that I have some hope of learning the truth even about these matters and the means of knowing them with certainty.

First, there is no doubt but that all that nature teaches me contains some truth. For by nature, considered in general, I now understand nothing else but God himself, or else the order and! system that God has established for created things; and by my nature in particular I understand nothing else but the arrangement or assemblage of all that God has given me.

Now there is nothing that this nature teaches me more expressly or more obviously than that I have a body which is in poor condition when I feel pain, which needs food or drink when I have the feelings of hunger or thirst, and so on. And therefore I ought to have no doubt that in this there is some truth. (81)

Nature also teaches me by these feelings of pain, hunger, thirst, and so on that I am not only residing in my body, as a pilot in his ship, but furthermore, that I am intimately connected with it, and that the mixture is so blended, as it were, that something like a single whole is produced. For if that were not the case, when my body is wounded I would not therefore feel pain, I, who am only a thinking being; but I would perceive that wound by the understanding alone, as a pilot perceives by sight if something in his vessel is broken. And when my body needs food or drink, I would simply know the fact itself, instead of receiving notice of it by having confused feelings of hunger and thirst. For actually all these feelings of hunger, thirst, pain, and so on are nothing else but certain confused modes of thinking, which have their origin in and depend upon the union and apparent fusion of the mind with the body.

Furthermore, nature teaches me that many other bodies exist in the vicinity of my own, of which I must seek some and avoid others. And certainly, from the fact that I perceive different kinds of colors, odors, tastes, sounds, heat, hardness, and so on, I very readily conclude that in the objects from which these various sense perceptions proceed there are some corresponding variations, although perhaps these variations are not really similar to the perceptions. And from the fact that some of these various sense. perceptions are agreeable to me and others are disagreeable, there is absolutely no doubt that my body, or rather my whole self, in so far as I am composed of body and mind, can in various ways be benefited or harmed by the other objects which surround it. (82)

But there are many other opinions that nature has apparently taught me which, however, I have not truly learned from her, but which were introduced into my mind by my habit of judging things inattentively. Thus it can easily happen that these opinions contain some falsity—as, for example, my opinion that all spaces in which there is nothing which affects and makes an impression on my senses are empty; that in an object which is hot there is some quality similar to my idea of heat; that in a white, or black, or green object there is the same whiteness, or blackness, for greenness that I perceive; that in a bitter or sweet object there is the same taste or the same flavor, and so on for the other senses; and that stars, towers, and all other distant objects are the same shape and size that they appear from afar to our eyes, and so forth.

In order that there should be nothing in this matter that I do not conceive sufficiently distinctly, I should define more precisely what I properly mean when I say that nature teaches me something. For I am here using the word "nature" in a more restricted sense than when I use it to mean a combination or assemblage of everything God has given me, seeing that this assemblage or combination includes many things which pertain to the mind alone, to which I do not intend to refer here when speaking of nature—as for example my knowledge of this truth: that what has once been done can never after not have been done, and all of an infinity of other similar truths known to me by the light of nature without any aid of the body. Such an assemblage also includes many other things which belong to body alone and are not here included under the name of "nature," such as its quality of being heavy and many other similar ones; for I am not concerned with these either, but only with those things which God has presented to me as a being composed of mind and body. This nature effectively teaches me to avoid things which produce in me the feeling of pain and to seek those which make me have some feeling of pleasure and so on. But I do not see that beyond this it teaches me that I should ever conclude anything from these various sense perceptions concerning things outside of ourselves, unless the mind has carefully and maturely examined them. For it seems to me that it is the business of the mind alone, and not of the being composed of mind and body, to decide the truth of such matters. (83)

Thus, although a star makes no more impression on my eye than the flame of a candle, and there is no real or positive inclination or natural faculty in me that leads me to believe that it is larger than this flame, nevertheless I have so judged it from infancy for no adequate reason. And although in approaching the flame I feel heat, and even though in approaching it a little too closely I feel pain, there is still no reason that can convince me that there is some quality in the flame similar to this heat, any more than to this pain. I only have reason to believe there is some quality in it, whatever it may be, which arouses in me these feelings of heat or pain.

Similarly, although there are parts of space in which I find nothing that excites and affects my senses, I ought not therefore to conclude that they contain no objects. Thus I see that both here and in many other similar cases I am accustomed to misunderstand and misconstrue the order of nature, because although these sensations or sense perceptions were given to me only to indicate to my mind which objects are useful or harmful to the composite body of which it is a part, and are for that purpose sufficiently clear and distinct, I nevertheless use them as though they were very certain rules by which I could obtain direct information about the essence and the nature of external objects, about which they can of course give me no information except very obscurely and confusedly.

In the previous discussion I have already explained sufficiently how it happens, despite the supreme goodness of God, that error occurs in my judgments. One further difficulty, though, presents itself here. This concerns objects which I am taught by nature to seek or avoid and also the internal sensations which she has given me. For it seems to me that I have noticed error here and thus that I am sometimes directly deceived by my nature—as, for example, when the pleasant taste of some food in which poison has been mixed can induce me to take the poison, and so misleads me. (84) It is nevertheless true that in this case nature can be excused, for it only leads me to desire the food in which a pleasant taste is found, and not to desire the poison which is unknown to it. Thus I cannot conclude anything from this except that my nature is not entirely and universally cognizant of all things. And at this there is no reason to be surprised, since man, being of a finite nature, is also restricted to a knowledge of a limited perfection.

But we also make mistakes sufficiently frequently even about matters of which we are directly informed by nature, as happens to sick people when they desire to drink or eat things which can later harm them. It might be argued here that the reason that they err is that their nature is corrupted. But this does not remove the difficulty, for a sick man is in truth no less the creation of God than is a man in full health, and therefore it is just as inconsistent with the goodness of God for him as for the other to have a misleading and faulty nature. A clock, composed of wheels and counterweights, is no less exactly obeying all the laws of nature when it is badly made and does not mark the time correctly than when it completely fulfills the intention of its maker; so also, the human body may be considered as a machine, so built and composed of bones, nerves, muscles, veins, blood, and skin that even if there were no mind in it, it would not cease to move in all the ways that it does at present when it is not moved under the direction of the will, nor consequently with the aid of the mind, but only by the condition of its organs I readily recognize that it is quite natural, for example, for this body to suffer dryness in the throat as a result of a dropsical condition, and thus to produce a feeling of thirst in the mind and a consequent disposition on the part of the mind to stimulate the nerves and other parts in the manner requisite for drinking, and so to increase the body's illness and injure itself. It is just as natural, I say, as it is for it to be beneficially influenced to drink by a similar dryness of the throat, when it is not ill at all. (85)

And although in considering the purpose for which a clock has been intended by its designer, I can say that it is false to its nature when it does not correctly indicate the time, and although in considering the mechanism of the human body in the same way as having been formed by God to provide all the customary activities, I have reason to think that it is not functioning according to its nature when its throat is dry and drinking injures its chances of self-preservation, I nevertheless recognize that this last usage of the word "nature" is very different from the other. For the latter is nothing else but an arbitrary appellation which depends entirely on my own idea in comparing a sick man and a poorly made clock, and contrasting them with my idea of a healthy man and a wellmade clock; this appellation refers to nothing which is actually found in the objects of which we are talking. On the contrary, by the other usage of the word "nature," I mean something which is actually found in objects and which therefore is not without some truth.

But certainly, although as far as a dropsical body is concerned, it is only an arbitrary appellation to say that its nature is corrupted when, without needing to drink, it still has a dry and and throat; nevertheless, when we consider the composite body as a whole—that is to say, the mind or soul United with the body—it is not a pure appellation, but truly an actual error on the part of nature that it is thirsty when it is very harmful to it to drink. Therefore we must examine how it is that the goodness of God does not prevent man's nature, so considered, from being faulty and deceptive.

To begin this examination, I first take notice here that there is a great difference between the mind and the body, in that the body, from its nature, is always divisible and the mind is completely (86) indivisible. For in reality, when I consider the mind—that is, when I consider myself in so far as I am only a thinking being—I cannot distinguish any parts, but I recognize and conceive very clearly that I am a thing which is absolutely unitary and entire. And although the whole mind seems to be united with the whole body, nevertheless when a foot or an arm or some other part of the body is amputated, I recognize quite well that nothing has been lost to my mind on that account. Nor can the faculties of willing, perceiving, understanding, and so forth be any more properly called parts of the mind, for it is one and the same mind which as a complete unit wills, perceives, and understands, and so forth. But just the contrary is the case with corporeal or extended objects, for I cannot imagine any, however small they might be, which my mind does not very easily divide into several parts, and I consequently recognize these objects to be divisible. This alone would suffice to show me that the mind or soul. of man is altogether different from the body, if I did not already know it sufficiently well for other reasons.

I also take notice that the mind does not receive impressions from all parts of the body directly, but only from the brain, or perhaps even from one of its smallest parts—the one, namely, where the senses in common have their seat. This makes the mind feel the same thing whenever it is in the same condition, even though the other parts of the body can be differently arranged, as is proved by an infinity of experiments which it is not necessary to describe here.

I furthermore notice that the nature of the body is such that no one of its parts can be moved by another part some little distance away without its being possible for it to be moved in the same way by any one of the intermediate parts, even when the more distant part does not act. For example, in the cord ABCD which is thoroughly stretched, if (87) we pull and move the last part D, the first part A will not be moved in any different manner from that in which it could also be moved if we pulled one of the middle parts B or C, while the last part D remained motionless. And in the same way, when I feel pain in my foot, physics teaches me that this sensation is communicated by means of nerves distributed through the foot. When these nerves are pulled in the foot, being stretched like cords from there to the brain, they likewise pull at the same time the internal part of the brain from which they come and where they terminate, and there produce a certain movement which nature has arranged to make my mind feel pain as though that pain were in my foot. But because these nerves must pass through the leg, the thigh, the loins, the back, and the neck, in order to extend from the foot to the brain, it can happen that even when the nerve endings in the foot are not stimulated, but only some of the lintermediate parts located in the loins or the neck, precisely the same movements are nevertheless produced in the brain that could be produced there by a wound received in the foot, as a result of which it necessarily follows that the mind feels the same pain in the foot as though the foot had been wounded. And we must make the same judgment about all our other sense perceptions.

Finally, I notice that since each one of the movements that occurs in the part of the brain from which the mind receives impressions directly can only produce in the mind a single sensation, we cannot desire or imagine any better arrangement than that this movement should cause the mind to feel that sensation, of all the sensations the movement is capable of causing, which is most effectively and frequently useful for the preservation of the human body when it is in full health. But experience shows us that all the sensations which nature has given us are such as I have just stated, and therefore there is nothing in their nature which does not show the power and the goodness of the God who has produced them.

Thus, for example, (88) when the nerves of the foot are stimulated violently and more than is usual, their movement, passing through the marrow of the backbone up to the interior of the brain, produces there an impression upon the mind which makes the mind feel something—namely, pain as though in the foot—by which the mind is warned and stimulated to do whatever it can to remove the cause, taking it to be very dangerous and harmful to the foot.

It is true that God could establish the nature of man in such a way that this same brain event would make the mind feel something quite different; for example, it might cause the movement to be felt as though it were in the brain, or in the foot, or else in some other intermediate location between the foot and the brain, or finally it might produce any other feeling that can exist; but none of those would have contributed so well to the preservation of the body as that which it does produce.

In the same way, when we need to drink, there results a certain dryness in the throat which affects its nerves and, by means of them, the interior of the brain. This brain event makes the mind feel the sensation of thirst, because under those conditions there is nothing more useful to us than to know that we need to drink for the conservation of our health. And similar reasoning applies to other sensations.

From this it is entirely manifest that, despite the supreme goodness of God, the nature of man, in so far as he is composed of mind and body, cannot escape being sometimes faulty and deceptive. For if there is some cause which produces, not in the foot, but in some other part of the nerve which is stretched from the foot to the brain, or even in the brain itself, the same effect which ordinarily occurs when the foot is injured, we will feel pain as though it were in the foot, and we will naturally be deceived by the sensation. The reason for this is that the same brain event can cause only a single sensation in the mind; and this sensation being much more frequently produced by a cause which wounds the foot than by another acting in a different location, it is much more reasonable (89) that it should always convey to the mind a pain in the foot rather than one in any other part of the body. And if it happens that sometimes the dryness of the throat does not come in the usual manner from the fact that drinking is necessary for the health of the body, but from some quite contrary cause, as in the case of those afflicted with dropsy, nevertheless it is much better that we should be deceived in that instance than if, on the contrary, we were always deceived when the body was in health; and similarly for the other sensations.

And certainly this consideration is very useful to me, not only so that I can recognize all the errors to which my nature is subject, but also so that I may avoid them or correct them more easily. For knowing that each of my senses conveys truth to me more often than falsehood concerning whatever is useful or harmful to the body, and being almost always able to use several of them to examine the same object, and being in addition able to use my memory to bind and join together present information with what is past, and being able to use my understanding, which has already discovered all the causes of my errors, I should no longer fear to encounter falsity in the objects which are most commonly represented to me by my senses.

And I should reject all the doubts of these last few days as exaggerated and ridiculous, particularly that very general uncertainty about sleep, which I could not distinguish from waking life. For now I find in them a very notable difference, in that our memory can never bind and join our dreams together one with another and all with the course of our lives, as it habitually joins together what happens to us when we are awake. And so, in effect, if someone suddenly appeared to me when I was awake and afterward disappeared in the same way, as do images that I see in my sleep, so that I could not determine where he came from or where he went, it would not be without reason that I would consider it a ghost (90) or a phantom produced in my brain and similar to those produced there when I sleep, rather than truly a man.

But when I perceive objects in such a way that I distinctly recognize both the place from which they come and the place where they are, as well as the time when they appear to me; and when, without any hiatus, I can relate my perception of them with all the rest of my life, I am entirely certain that I perceive them wakefully and not in sleep. And I should not in any way doubt the truth of these things if, having made use of all my senses, my memory, and my understanding, to examine them, nothing is reported to me by any of them which is inconsistent with what is reported by the others. For, from the fact that God is not a deceiver, it necesarily follows that in this matter I am not deceived.

But because the exigencies of action frequently oblige us to make decisions and do not always allow us the leisure to examine these things with sufficient care, we must admit that human life is very often subject to error in particular matters; and we must in the end recognize the infirmity and weakness of our nature.

THOMAS HOBBES
1588–1679

Born prematurely when his mother heard of the approach of the Spanish Armada, Thomas Hobbes often quipped that he was born "a twin with fear." Hobbes saw much to fear in his long life. He observed a civil war, the execution of Charles I, and periods of great political and social upheaval. On more than one occasion, he was forced to flee England; and he often feared for his life. It is not surprising, then, that he developed a political philosophy emphasizing fear of death and the need for security.

Hobbes was born in Malmesbury, Whiltshire, England, the son of a disreputable vicar. His father was forced to leave the Whiltshire area after brawling outside his church. Young Thomas was sent to live with a rich uncle. At the age of fourteen, he went to Oxford University. Like Descartes, he found most of his schooling to be a waste of time. He particularly disliked the Aristotelianism of his college, Magdalen Hall. In 1608, he became the tutor to the son of William Cavendish, Earl of Devonshire. For the rest of his life, Hobbes remained a friend of the Cavendish family and a royalist sympathizer.

Hobbes made several extended visits to the Continent—some voluntary, some a result of running for his life. At home and on the Continent, Hobbes met and conversed with such leading thinkers as Descartes, Galileo, and Bacon. Although he, of course, had differences with them, he nevertheless used each thinker's ideas to refine his own philosophy. From Descartes, he learned to value the geometric method. Descartes used geometry to establish epistemological certainty. Hobbes used geometry to develop a political theory. In opposition to the dominant Aristotelian thesis that rest is the natural state of objects, Galileo had proposed that all bodies are naturally in motion. Hobbes took Galileo's postulate and proceeded to argue that all things in the world, including human beings, are bodies in motion. With Bacon, Hobbes agreed that scientific knowledge was primarily useful for improving the human condition.

In 1628, Hobbes published his first literary work: a translation of *Thucydides*, by which he hoped to use history to enlighten the English people. In Thucydides' *Peloponnesian War*, democratic Athens had been defeated by monarchical Sparta. Hobbes wanted to warn his fellow citizens of the creeping democracy threatening England. Hobbes was convinced that democracy led to chaos and that a strong central government was essential for national stability. In 1640, Hobbes was forced to flee England for Paris when the Long Parliament supplanted the king. In Paris, Hobbes wrote the book for which he is famous, *Leviathan, or the Matter, Form, and Power of a Commonwealth, Ecclesiastical and Civil*. The book was published between the execution of Charles I (1649) and the Protectorate of Cromwell (1653), a time ripe for political philosophy.

Cromwell permitted Hobbes to return to England in 1652. Although Hobbes had always been a royalist, his argument for the absolute power of the sovereign was not restricted to kings. Thus Cromwell had no reason to consider Hobbes's doctrine seditious—nor did Charles II, whom Hobbes had tutored in Paris, and who was later restored to the monarchy.

Hobbes's later years were spent writing and arguing for his ideas. Although he continued to have enemies, with the king's friendship he managed to stay out of serious trouble. In his early-eighties, Hobbes wrote a history of the period 1640 to 1660, which he called *Behemoth*. When he was eighty-four, Hobbes published his autobiography in Latin verse; at eighty-six, he produced a verse translation of both the *Iliad* and the *Odyssey* (for lack of anything better to do, he commented). He died in 1679 at the age of 91.

*   *   *

The *Leviathan* is known primarily for its political philosophy, but it touches on a number of other issues including epistemology, metaphysics, ethics, and religion. Hobbes begins with a thoroughgoing version of materialism. Everything in the world, including humans, consists of bodies in motion. Knowledge of the world begins in sensation. Bodies in motion outside of a person cause motion within the person. Memories, imagination, and other "mental" phenomena are the aftershocks of sensations—what Hobbes calls "decaying sense." *Willing* is that "beginning of motion" that leads to action when individuals move and so move other bodies.

Using a mechanistic explanation of "voluntary motions," which he calls "endeavors," Hobbes believes that in human life self-interest and the desire for power are the basic motive powers. According to Hobbes, each person constantly seeks an advantage over everyone else. Yet since all are born equal, there is no inherent reason why one person should give way to another. The result is what Hobbes calls "a war of every man against every man . . . [in which] the notions of right and wrong, justice and injustice, have no place." In such an environment, life is "solitary, poor, nasty, brutish, and short."

To avoid this natural state of anarchy, individuals must enter into a social contract or covenant with all other individuals to give up their power irrevocably to a sovereign: "This is the generation of that great LEVIATHAN, or rather, to speak more reverently, of that 'mortal god,' to which we owe under the 'immortal God,' our peace and defence." This contract is not binding on the sovereign, as the sovereign is not a party to it. Hence there is no legal limitation on the sovereign's power. The sovereign is the essence of the commonwealth, which can be defined as

> one person, of whose acts a great multitude, by mutual covenants one with another, have made themselves every one the author, to the end he may use the strength and means of them all, as he shall think expedient, for their peace and common defence. . . . And he that carries this person, is called SOVEREIGN, and said to have sovereign power; and every one besides, his SUBJECT.

Hobbes believes this sovereign did not have to be a single person—sovereignty could reside in an individual (a monarchy), a small group (an aristocracy), or in the entire population (a democracy)—though he shows a marked preference for monarchy because of its greater stability and efficiency. What matters to Hobbes above all else is that the sovereign has absolute power in order to keep the peace and to guarantee security. To be sure, an absolute sovereign might abuse power, but the only alternative to this possible abuse, Hobbes claims, is an unthinkable anarchy.

*   *   *

Hobbes wrote many books over the course of his long life—the standard Oxford edition of his English works includes eleven volumes with another five volumes of his Latin works—but *Leviathan* (1651) is the basis of his fame. The key sections of this work, from Chapters 1–3, 6, 9, 12, 15, 17–18, and 21, are reprinted here. The spelling has been updated and standardized.

For a general introduction to Hobbes's life and thought, see John Laird, Hobbes (London: Ernest Benn, 1934); Richard Peters, *Hobbes* (Baltimore, MD: Penguin Books, 1956); G.C. Robertson, *Hobbes* (New York: AMS Press, 1968); and Tom Sorell, *Hobbes* (London: Routledge, 1986). For discussions of Hobbes's ethical and political thought as developed in *Leviathan*, see Leo Strauss, *The Political Philosophy of Hobbes* (Chicago: University of Chicago Press, 1952); Howard Warrender, *The Political Philosophy of Hobbes: His Theory of Obligation* (Oxford: Clarendon Press, 1957); David P. Gauthier, *The Logic of Leviathan: The Moral and Political Theory of Thomas Hobbes* (Oxford: Clarendon Press, 1969); and Michael Oakeshott, *Hobbes on Civil Association* (Berkeley: University of California Press, 1975). G.A.J. Rogers, ed., *Leviathan: Contemporary Responses to the Political Theory of Thomas Hobbes* (Bristol, UK: Thoemmes Press, 1995) includes the responses of Hobbes's contemporaries to the *Leviathan*. A.P. Martinish, *A Hobbes Dictionary* (Oxford: Basil Blackwell, 1995) provides a helpful reference work. For collections of essays on Hobbes, see Keith Brown, ed., *Hobbes Studies* (Cambridge, MA: Harvard University Press, 1965); G.A.J. Rogers and Alan Ryan, eds., *Perspectives on Thomas Hobbes* (Oxford: Oxford University Press, 1989); Vere Chappell, ed., *Essays on Early Modern Philosophers: Thomas Hobbes* (Hamden, CT: Garland, 1992); Tom Sorell, ed., *The Cambridge Companion to Hobbes* (Cambridge: Cambridge University Press, 1996); and the multi-volume G.A.J. Rogers, ed., *Critical Responses to Hobbes* (Oxford: Routledge, 1997).

LEVIATHAN OR THE MATTER, FORM, AND POWER OF A COMMONWEALTH, ECCLESIASTICAL AND CIVIL (in part)

PART I—OF MAN

CHAPTER 1. OF SENSE

Concerning the thoughts of man, I will consider them first singly, and afterwards in train, or dependence upon one another. Singly, they are every one a "representation" or "appearance" of some quality, or other accident of a body without us, which is commonly called an "object." Which object works on the eyes, ears, and other parts of a man's body, and, by diversity of working, produces diversity of appearances.

The title page of Hobbes's *Leviathan* (1651). The sovereign in the background, whose body is composed of the people, is supreme. He is shown here holding the symbols of both church and state. (*Library of Congress*)

The original of them all is that which we call "sense," for there is no conception in a man's mind which hath not at first, totally or by parts, been begotten upon the organs of sense. The rest are derived from that original.

To know the natural cause of sense is not very necessary to the business now in hand; and I have elsewhere written of the same at large. Nevertheless, to fill each part of my present method I will briefly deliver the same in this place.

The cause of sense is the external body, or object, which presses the organ proper to each sense, either immediately, as in the taste and touch, or mediately, as in seeing, hearing, and smelling; which pressure, by the mediation of the nerves and other strings and membranes of the body continued inwards to the brain and heart, causes there a resistance, or counter-pressure, or endeavor of the heart to deliver itself, which endeavor, because "outward," seems to be some matter without. And this "seeming" or "fancy" is that which men call "sense" and consists, as to the eye, in a "light" or "color figured"; to the ear, in a "sound"; to the nostril, in an "odor"; to the tongue and palate, in a "savor"; and to the rest of the body, in "heat," "cold," "hardness," "softness," and such other qualities as we discern by "feeling." All which qualities, called "sensible" are in the object that causes them but so many several motions of the matter, by which it presses our organs diversely. Neither in us that are pressed are they anything else but divers motions; for motion produces nothing but motion. But their appearance to us is fancy, the same waking that dreaming. And as pressing, rubbing, or striking the eye, makes us fancy a light, and pressing the ear produces a din, so do the bodies also we see or hear produce the same by their strong, though unobserved, action. For if those colors and sounds were in the bodies, or objects that cause them, they could not be severed from them, as by glasses, and in echoes by reflection, we see they are, where we know the thing we see is in one place, the appearance in another. And though at some certain distance the real and very object seem invested with the fancy it begets in us, yet still the object is one thing, the image or fancy is another. So that sense in all cases is nothing else but original fancy, caused, as I have said, by the pressure, that is by the motion, of external things upon our eyes, ears, and other organs thereunto ordained.

But the philosophy schools through all the universities of Christendom, grounded upon certain texts of Aristotle, teach another doctrine, and say, for the cause of "vision," that the thing seen sends forth on every side a "visible species," in English, a "visible show," "apparition," or "aspect," or "a being seen"; the receiving whereof into the eye is "seeing." And for the cause of "hearing," that the thing heard sends forth an "audible species," that is an "audible aspect," or "audible being seen," which entering at the ear makes "hearing." Nay, for the cause of "understanding" also, they say the thing understood sends forth an "intelligible species," that is, an "intelligible being seen," which, coming into the understanding, makes us understand. I say not this as disproving the use of universities; but, because I am to speak hereafter of their office in a commonwealth. I must let you see on all occasions by the way what things would be amended in them, amongst which the frequency of insignificant speech is one.

CHAPTER 2. OF IMAGINATION

That when a thing lies still, unless somewhat else stir it, it will lie still for ever, is a truth that no man doubts of. But that when a thing is in motion, it will eternally be in motion, unless somewhat else stay it, though the reason be the same, namely that nothing can change itself, is not so easily assented to. For men measure not only other men but all other things, by themselves; and, because they find themselves subject after motion to pain and lassitude, think everything else grows weary of motion, and seeks repose of its own accord; little considering whether it be not some other motion wherein that desire of rest they find in themselves consists. From hence it is that the schools say heavy bodies fall downwards out of an appetite to rest, and to conserve their nature in that place which is most proper for them; ascribing appetite and knowledge of what is good for their conservation, which is more than man has, to things inanimate, absurdly.

When a body is once in motion, it moves, unless something else hinder it, eternally; and whatsoever hinders it cannot in an instant, but in time and by degrees, quite extinguish it; and, as we see in the water though the wind cease the waves give not over rolling for a long time after: so also it happens in that motion which is made in the internal parts of a man, then, when he sees, dreams, etc. For, after the object is removed, or the eye shut, we still retain an image of the thing seen, though more obscure than when we see it. And this is it the Latins call "imagination," from the image made in seeing; and apply the same, though improperly, to all the other senses. But the Greeks call it "fancy," which signifies "appearance," and is as proper to one sense as to another. "Imagination," therefore, is nothing but "decaying sense," and is found in men, and many other living creatures, as well sleeping as waking.

The decay of sense in men waking is not the decay of the motion made in sense, but an obscuring of it in such manner as the light of the sun obscures the light of the stars, which stars do no less exercise their virtue, by which they are visible, in the day than in the night. But because amongst many strokes which our eyes, ears, and other organs, receive from external bodies, the predominant only is sensible; therefore, the light of the sun being predominant, we are not affected with the action of the stars. And any object being removed from our eyes, though the impression it made in us remain, yet other objects more present succeeding and working on us, the imagination of the past is obscured and made weak, as the voice of a man is in the noise of the day. From whence it follows that the longer the time is, after the sight or sense of any object, the weaker is the imagination. For the continual change of man's body destroys in time the parts which in sense were moved; so that distance of time, and of place, hath one and the same effect in us. For as at a great distance of place that which we look at appears dim and without distinction of the smaller parts, and as voices grow weak and inarticulate, so also after great distance of time our imagination of the past is weak; and we lose, for example, of cities we have seen many particular streets, and of actions many particular circumstances. This "decaying sense," when we would express the thing itself, I mean "fancy" itself, we call "imagination," as I said before; but when we would express the decay, and signify that the sense is fading, old, and past, it is called "memory." So that imagination and memory are but one thing, which for divers considerations hath divers names.

Much memory, or memory of many things, is called "experience." Again, imagination being only of those things which have been formerly perceived by sense, either all at once or by parts at several times the former, which is the imagining the whole object as it was presented to the sense, is "simple" imagination, as when one imagines a man, or horse, which he hath seen before. The other is "compounded," as when, from the sight of a man at one time, and of a horse at another, we conceive in our mind a Centaur. So when a man compounds the image of his own person with the image of the actions of another man, as when a man images himself a Hercules or an Alexander, which happens often to them that are much taken with reading of romances, it is a compound imagination, and properly but a fiction of the mind. There be also other imaginations that rise in men, though waking, from the great impression made in sense; as, from gazing upon the sun, the impression leaves an image of the sun before our eyes a long time after; and, from being long and vehemently intent upon geometrical figures, a man shall in the dark, though awake, have the images of lines and angles before his eyes; which kind of fancy hath no particular name, as being a thing that doth not commonly fall into men's discourse.

The imaginations of them that sleep are those we call "dreams." And these also, as also all other imaginations, have been before, either totally or by parcels, in the sense. And, because in sense, the brain and nerves, which are the necessary organs of sense, are so benumbed in sleep as not easily to be moved by the action of external objects, there can happen in sleep no imagination, and therefore no dream, but what proceeds from the agitation of the inward parts of man's body; which inward parts, for the connection they have with the brain and other organs, when they be distempered, do keep the same in motion; whereby the imaginations there formerly made, appear as if a man were waking; saving that the organs of sense being now benumbed, so as there is no new object which can master and obscure them with a more vigorous impression, a dream must needs be more clear in this silence of sense than our waking thoughts. And hence it comes to pass that it is a hard matter, and by many thought impossible, to distinguish exactly between sense and dreaming. For my part, when I consider that in dreams I do not often nor constantly think of the same persons, places, objects, and actions, that I do waking, nor remember so long a train of coherent thoughts, dreaming, as at other times, and because waking I often observe the absurdity of dreams, but never dream of the absurdities of my waking thoughts, I am well satisfied, that, being awake, I know I dream not, though when I dream I think myself awake.

And, seeing dreams are caused by the distemper of some of the inward parts of the body, divers distempers must needs cause different dreams. And hence it is that lying cold breeds dreams of fear, and raises the thought and image of some fearful object, the motion from the brain to the inner parts and from the inner parts to the brain being reciprocal; and that, as anger causes heat in some parts of the body when we are awake, so when we sleep the overheating of the same parts causes anger, and raises up in the brain the imagination of an enemy. In the same manner, as natural kindness, when we are awake, causes desire, and desire makes heat in certain other parts of the body; so also too much heat in those parts, while we sleep, raises in the brain an imagination of some kindness shown. In sum, our dreams are the reverse of our waking imaginations, the motion when we are awake beginning at one end, and when we dream at another.

The most difficult discerning of a man's dream from his waking thoughts is, then, when by some accident we observe not that we have slept: which is easy to happen to a man full of fearful thoughts, and whose conscience is much troubled, and that sleeps without the circumstances of going to bed or putting off his clothes, as one that nods in a chair. For he that takes pains, and industriously lays himself to sleep, in case any uncouth and exorbitant fancy come unto him, cannot easily think it other than a dream. We read of Marcus Brutus (one that had his life given him by Julius Cæsar, and was also his favorite, and notwithstanding murdered him) how at Philippi, the night before he gave battle to Augustus Cæsar, he saw a fearful apparition, which is commonly related by historians as a vision; but, considering the circumstances, one may easily judge to have been but a short dream. For, sitting in his tent, pensive and troubled with the horror of his rash act, it was not hard for him, slumbering in the cold, to dream of that which most frightened him; which fear, as by degrees it made him wake, so also it must needs make the apparition by degrees to vanish; and, having no assurance that he slept, he could have no cause to think it a dream or anything but a vision. And this is no very rare accident; for even they that be perfectly awake, if they be timorous and superstitious, possessed with fearful tales, and alone in the dark, are subject to the like fancies, and believe they see spirits and dead men's ghosts walking in churchyards; whereas it is either their fancy only, or else the knavery of such persons as make use of such superstitious fear to pass disguised in the night to places they would not be known to haunt.

From this ignorance of how to distinguish dreams and other strong fancies from vision and sense, did arise the greatest part of the religion of the Gentiles in time past, that worshipped satyrs, fawns, nymphs, and the like; and now-a-days the opinion that rude people have of fairies, ghosts, and goblins, and of the power of witches. For as for witches, I think not that their witchcraft is any real power; but yet that they are justly punished for the false belief they have that they can do such mischief, joined with their purpose to do it if they can; their trade being nearer to a new religion than to a craft or science. And for fairies and walking ghosts, the opinion of them has, I think, been on purpose either taught, or not confuted, to keep in credit the use of exorcism, of crosses, of holy water, and other such inventions of ghostly men. Nevertheless there is no doubt but God can make unnatural apparitions; but that He does it so often as men need to fear such things more than they fear the stay or change of the course of nature, which He also can stay and change, is no point of Christian faith. But evil men, under pretext that God can do anything, are so bold as to say anything when it serves their turn, though they think it untrue; it is the part of a wise man to believe them no farther than right reason makes that which they say appear credible. If this superstitious fear of spirits were taken away, and with it prognostics from dreams, false prophecies, and many other things depending thereon, by which crafty ambitious persons abuse the simple people, men would be much more fitted than they are for civil obedience.

And this ought to be the work of the schools; but they rather nourish such doctrine. For, not knowing what imagination or the senses are, what they receive they teach; some saying that imaginations rise of themselves and have no cause; others that they rise most commonly from the will, and that good thoughts are blown (inspired) into a man by God, and evil thoughts by the devil; or that good thoughts are poured (infused) into a man by God, and evil ones by the devil. Some say the senses receive the species of things, and deliver them to the common sense, and the common sense delivers them over to the fancy, and the fancy to the memory, and the memory to the judgment, like handling of things from one to another, with many words making nothing understood.

The imagination that is raised in man, or any other creature endowed with the faculty of imagining, by words or other voluntary signs, is that we generally call "understanding," and is common to man and beast. For a dog by custom will understand the call or the rating of his master; and so will many other beasts. That understanding which is peculiar to man, is the understanding not only his will, but his conceptions and thoughts, by the sequel and contexture of the names of things into affirmations, negations, and other forms of speech; and of this kind of understanding I shall speak hereafter.

CHAPTER 3. OF THE CONSEQUENCE OR TRAIN OF IMAGINATIONS

By "consequence," or "train," of thoughts I understand that succession of one thought to another which is called, to distinguish it from discourse in words, "mental discourse."

When a man thinks on anything whatever, his next thought after is not altogether so casual as it seems to be. Not every thought to every thought succeeds indifferently.

But as we have no imagination whereof we have not formerly had sense, in whole or in parts, so we have no transition from one imagination to another whereof we never had the like before in our senses. The reason whereof is this. All fancies are motions within us, relics of those made in the sense, and those motions that immediately succeeded one another in the sense continue also together after sense: in so much as the former coming again to take place, and be predominant, the latter followeth, by coherence of the matter moved, in such manner as water upon a plane table is drawn which way any one part of it is guided by the finger. But because in sense to one and the same thing perceived, sometimes one thing sometimes another, succeeds, it comes to pass in time that in the imagining of anything there is no certainty what we shall imagine next: only this is certain, it shall be something that succeeded the same before, at one time or another.

This train of thoughts, or mental discourse, is of two sorts. The first is "unguided," "without design," and inconstant; wherein there is no passionate thought, to govern and direct those that follow, to itself, as the end and scope of some desire or other passion: in which case the thoughts are said to wander, and seem impertinent one to another as in a dream. Such are commonly the thoughts of men that are not only without company but also without care of anything; though even then their thoughts are as busy as at other times, but without harmony; as the sound which a lute out of tune would yield to any man, or in tune to one that could not play. And yet in this wild ranging of the mind a man may oft-times perceive the way of it, and the dependence of one thought upon another. For in a discourse of our present civil war, what could seem more impertinent than to ask, as one did, what was the value of a Roman penny. Yet the coherence to me was manifest enough. For the thought of the war introduced the thought of the delivering up the king to his enemies, the thought of that brought in the thought of the delivering up of Christ; and that again the thought of the thirty pence, which was the price of that treason; and thence easily followed that malicious question; and all this in a moment of time—for thought is quick.

The second is more constant; as being "regulated" by some desire and design. For the impression made by such things as we desire, or fear, is strong and permanent, or, if it cease for a time, of quick return: so strong it is sometimes as to hinder and break our sleep. From desire arises the thought of some means we have seen produce the like of that which we aim at; and from the thought of that, the thought of means to that mean, and so continually till we come to some beginning within our own power. And because the end, by the greatness of the impression, comes often to mind, in case our thoughts begin to wander, they are quickly again reduced into the way: which observed by one of the Seven Wise Men, made him give men this precept, which is now worn out, *Respice finem;* that is to say, in all your actions look often upon what you would have as the thing that directs all your thoughts in the way to attain it.

The train of regulated thoughts is of two kinds; one, when of an effect imagined we seek the causes or means that produce it; and this is common to man and beast. The other is when imagining anything whatsoever we seek all the possible effects that can by it be produced, that is to say, we imagine what we can do with it when we have it. Of which I have not at any time seen any sign but in man only; for this is a curiosity hardly incident to the nature of any living creature that has no other passion but sensual, such as are hunger, thirst, lust, and anger. In sum, the discourse of the mind, when it is governed by design, is nothing but "seeking," or the faculty of invention, which the Latins called sagacitas, and solertia; a hunting out of the causes, of some effect, present or past; or of the effects, of some present or past cause. Sometimes a man seeks what he hath lost; and from that place and time wherein he misses it his mind runs back, from place to place, and time to time, to find where and when he had it, that is to say, to find some certain and limited time and place in which to begin a method of seeking. Again, from thence his thoughts run over the same places and times to find what action or other occasion might make him lose it. This we call "remembrance," or calling to mind: the Latins call it *reminiscentia*, as it were a "re-conning" of our former actions.

Sometimes a man knows a place determinate, within the compass whereof he is to seek; and then his thoughts run over all the parts thereof, in the same manner as one would sweep a room to find a jewel, or as a spaniel ranges the field till he find a scent, or as a man should run over the alphabet to start a rhyme.

Sometimes a man desires to know the event of an action; and then he thinks of some like action past, and the events thereof one after another, supposing like events will follow like actions. As he that foresees what will become of a criminal recons what he has seen follow on the like crime before, having this order of thoughts, the crime, the officer, the prison, the judge, and the gallows. Which kind of thoughts is called "foresight," and "prudence," or "providence," and sometimes "wisdom," though such conjecture, through the difficulty of observing all circumstances, be very fallacious. But this is certain: by how much one man has more experience of things past than another, by so much also he is more prudent, and his expectations the seldomer fail him. The "present" only has a being in nature; things "past" have a being in the memory only, but things "to come" have no being at all, the "future" being but a fiction of the mind, applying the sequels of actions past to the actions that are present; which with most certainty is done by him that has most experience, but not with certainty enough. And though it be called prudence, when the event answers our expectation, yet, in its own nature, it is but presumption. For the foresight of things to come, which is providence, belongs only to him by whose will they are to come. From him only, and supernaturally, proceeds prophecy. The best prophet naturally is the best guesser; and the best guesser he that is most versed and studied in the matters he guesses at, for he hath most "signs" to guess by.

A "sign" is the event antecedent of the consequent; and, contrarily, the consequent of the antecedent, when the like consequences have been observed before; and the oftener they have been observed, the less uncertain is the sign. And therefore he that has most experience in any kind of business has most signs whereby to guess at the future time, and consequently is the most prudent; and so much more prudent than he that is new in that kind of business as not to be equalled by any advantage of natural and extemporary wit; though perhaps many young men think the contrary.

Nevertheless it is not prudence that distinguishes man from beast. There be beasts that at a year old observe more, and pursue that which is for their good more prudently than a child can do at ten.

As prudence is a "presumption" of the "future" contracted from the "experience" of time "past," so there is a presumption of things past taken from other things, not future, but past also. For he that hath seen by what courses and degrees a flourishing state hath first come into civil war, and then to ruin, upon the sight of the ruins of any other state will guess the like war and the like courses have been there also. But this conjecture has the same uncertainty almost with the conjecture of the future, both being grounded only upon experience.

There is no other act of man's mind that I can remember naturally planted in him, so as to need no other thing to the exercise of it but to be born a man, and live with the use of his five senses. Those other faculties of which I shall speak by and by, and which seem proper to man only, are acquired and increased by study and industry, and of most men learned by instruction and discipline; and proceed all from the invention of words and speech. For besides sense, and thoughts, and the train of thoughts, the mind of man has no other motion, though by the help of speech and method the same faculties may be improved to such a height as to distinguish men from all other living creatures.

Whatsoever we imagine is "finite." Therefore there is no idea or conception of any thing we call "infinite." No man can have in his mind an image of infinite magnitude, nor conceive infinite swiftness, infinite time, or infinite force, or infinite power. When we say anything is infinite, we signify only that we are not able to conceive the ends and bounds of the things named; having no conception of the thing, but of our own inability. And therefore the name of God is used, not to make us conceive Him, for He is incomprehensible, and His greatness and power are inconceivable, but that we may honor Him. Also because, whatsoever, as I said before, we conceive, has been perceived first by sense, either all at once or by parts; a man can have no thought representing anything not subject to sense. No man therefore can conceive anything but he must conceive it in some place, and endowed with some determinate magnitude, and which may be divided into parts; nor that anything is all in this place and all in another place at the same time; nor that two or more things can be in one and the same place at once: for none of these things ever have or can be incident to sense, but are absurd speeches, taken upon credit, without any signification at all, from deceived philosophers, and deceived or deceiving schoolmen.

*   *   *

CHAPTER 6. OF THE INTERIOR BEGINNINGS OF VOLUNTARY MOTIONS; COMMONLY CALLED THE PASSIONS; AND THE SPEECHES BY WHICH THEY ARE EXPRESSED

There be in animals two sorts of "motions" peculiar to them: one called "vital," begun in generation, and continued without interruption through their whole life, such as are the "course" of the "blood," the "pulse," the "breathing," the "concoction, nutrition, excretion," etc., to which motions there needs no help of imagination: the other is "animal motion," otherwise called "voluntary motion," as to "go," to "speak," to "move" any of our limbs in such manner as is first fancied in our minds. That sense is motion in the organs and interior parts of man's body, caused by the action of the things we see, hear, etc.; and that fancy is but the relics of the same motion, remaining after sense, has been already said in the first and second chapters. And, because "going," "speaking," and the like voluntary motions, depend always upon a precedent thought of "whither," "which way," and "what," it is evident that the imagination is the first internal beginning of all voluntary motion. And, although unstudied men do not conceive any motion at all to be there where the thing moved is invisible, or the space it is moved in is, for the shortness of it, insensible, yet that doth not hinder but that such motions are. For, let a space be never so little, that which is moved over a greater space, whereof that little one is part, must first be moved over that. These small beginnings of motion within the body of man before they appear in walking, speaking, striking, and other visible actions, are commonly called "endeavor."

This endeavor, when it is toward something which causes it, is called "appetite," or "desire," the latter being the general name, and the other oftentimes restrained to signify the desire of food, namely "hunger" and "thirst." And, when the endeavor is fromward something, it is generally called "aversion." These words, "appetite" and "aversion," we have from the Latins—and they both of them signify the motions, one of approaching, the other of retiring. So also do the Greek words for the same, which are ⟨*horma*⟩ and ⟨*aphorma*⟩. For Nature itself does often press upon men those truths which afterwards, when they look for somewhat beyond Nature, they stumble at. For the schools find in mere appetite to go, or move, no actual motion at all; but, because some motion they must acknowledge, they call it metaphorical motion, which is but an absurd speech; for though words may be called metaphorical, bodies and motions cannot.

That which men desire they are also said to "love"; and to "hate" those things for which they have aversion. So that desire and love are the same thing, save that by desire we always signify the absence of the object, by love most commonly the presence of the same. So also by aversion we signify the absence, and by hate, the presence of the object.

Of appetites and aversions, some are born with men, as appetite of food, appetite of excretion, and exoneration, which may also and more properly be called aversions from somewhat they feel in their bodies; and some other appetites, not many. The rest, which are appetites of particular things, proceed from experience and trial of their effects upon themselves or other men. For of things we know not at all, or believe not to be, we can have no further desire than to taste and try. But aversion we have for things not only which we know have hurt us, but also that we do not know whether they will hurt us or not.

Those things which we neither desire nor hate we are said to "contemn," "contempt" being nothing else but an immobility or contumacy of the heart in resisting the action of certain things, and proceeding from that the heart is already moved otherwise by other more potent objects, or from want of experience of them.

And, because the constitution of a man's body is in continual mutation, it is impossible that all the same things should always cause in him the same appetites and aversions: much less can all men consent in the desire of almost any one and the same object.

But whatsoever is the object of any man's appetite or desire, that is it which he for his part calls "good"; and the object of his hate and aversion, "evil"; and of his contempt "vile" and "inconsiderable." For these words of good, evil, and contemptible, are ever used with relation to the person that uses them, there being nothing simply and absolutely so; nor any common rule of good and evil, to be taken from the nature of the objects themselves; but from the person of the man, where there is no commonwealth, or, in a commonwealth, from the person that represents it; or from an arbitrator or judge, whom men disagreeing shall by consent set up, and make his sentence the rule thereof.

The Latin tongue has two words whose significations approach to those of good and evil, but are not precisely the same; and those are *pulchrum* and *turpe*. Whereof the former signifies that which by some apparent signs promises good; and the latter that which promises evil. But in our tongue we have not so general names to express them by. But for pulchrum we say in some things "fair," in others, "beautiful," or "handsome," or "gallant," or "honorable," or "comely," or "amiable"; and for *turpe*, "foul," "deformed," "ugly," "base," "nauseous," and the like, as the subject shall require; all which words, in their proper places, signify nothing else but the "mien," or countenance, that promises good and evil. So that of good there be three kinds: good in the promise, that is *pulchrum*; good in effect, as the end desired, which is called *jucundum*, "delightful"; and good as the means which is called *utile*, "profitable"; and as many of evil: for "evil" in promise is that they call *turpe*; evil in effect, and end is molestum, "unpleasant," "troublesome"; and evil in the means, *inutile*, "unprofitable," "hurtful."

As, in sense, that which is really within us is, as I have said before, only motion caused by the action of external objects but in appearance—to the sight, light and color; to the ear, sound; to the nostril, odor, etc.; so, when the action of the same object is continued from the eyes, ears, and other organs to the heart, the real effect there is nothing but motion or endeavor which consists in appetite, or aversion, to or from the object moving. But the appearance, or sense of that motion, is that we either call "delight" or "trouble of mind."

This motion, which is called appetite, and for the appearance of it "delight" and "pleasure," seems to be a corroboration of vital motion, and a help thereunto; and therefore such things as caused delight were not improperly called *jucunda—juvando*, from helping or fortifying; and the contrary *molesta*, "offensive," from hindering and troubling the motion vital.

"Pleasure," therefore, or "delight," is the appearance or sense of good; and "molestation," or "displeasure," the appearance or sense of evil. And consequently all appetite, desire, and love, is accompanied with some delight more or less; and all hatred and aversion with more or less displeasure and offence.

Of pleasures or delights some arise from the sense of an object present; and those may be called "pleasures of sense," the word "sensual," as it is used by those only that condemn them, having no place till there be laws. Of this kind are all onerations and exonerations of the body, as also all that is pleasant in the "sight," "hearing," "smell," "taste," or "touch." Others arise from the expectation that proceeds from foresight of the end or consequence of things, whether those things in the sense please or displease. And these are "pleasures of the mind" of him that draws those consequences, and are generally called "joy." In the like manner, displeasures are some in the sense, and called "pain"; others in the expectation of consequences, and are called "grief."

These simple passions called "appetite," "desire," "love," "aversion," "hate," "joy," and "grief," have their names for divers considerations diversified. As first, when they one succeed another, they are diversely called from the opinion men have of the likelihood of attaining what they desire. Secondly, from the object loved or hated. Thirdly, from the consideration of many of them together. Fourthly, from the alteration or succession itself.

For "appetite" with an opinion of attaining is called "hope."

The same without such opinion, "despair."

"Aversion" with opinion of "hurt" from the object "fear."

The same with hope of avoiding that hurt by resistance, "courage."

Sudden "courage," "anger."

Constant "hope," "confidence" of ourselves.

Constant "despair," "diffidence" of ourselves.

"Anger" for great hurt done to another, when we conceive the same to be done by injury, "indignation."

"Desire" of good to another, "benevolence," "good will," "charity." If to man generally, "good-nature."

"Desire" of riches, "covetousness," a name used always in signification of blame, because men contending for them are displeased with one another attaining them, though the desire in itself be to be blamed, or allowed, according to the means by which those riches are sought.

"Desire" of office, or precedence, "ambition," a name used also in the worse sense, for the reason before mentioned.

"Desire" of things that conduce but a little to our ends, and fear of things that are but of little hindrance, "pusillanimity."

"Contempt" of little helps and hindrances, "magnanimity."

"Magnanimity" in danger of death or wounds, "valor," "fortitude."

"Magnanimity" in the use of riches, "liberality."

"Pusillanimity" in the same, "wretchedness," "miserableness," or "parsimony," as it is liked or disliked.

"Love" of persons for society, "kindness."

"Love" of persons for pleasing the sense only, "natural lust."

"Love" of the same, acquired from rumination, that is imagination of pleasure past, "luxury."

"Love" of one singularly, with desire to be singularly beloved, "the passion of love." The same, with fear that the love is not mutual, "jealousy."

"Desire," by doing hurt to another, to make him condemn some fact of his own, "revengefulness."

"Desire" to know why and how, "curiosity," such as is in no living creature but "man," so that man is distinguished not only by his reason but also by this singular passion from other "animals," in whom the appetite of food, and other pleasures of sense, by predominance take away the care of knowing causes, which is a lust of the mind, that by a perseverance of delight in the continual and indefatigable generation of knowledge exceeds the short vehemence of any carnal pleasure.

"Fear" of power invisible, feigned by the mind or imagined from tales publicly allowed, "religion," not allowed, "superstition." And when the power imagined is truly such as we imagine, "true religion."

"Fear," without the apprehension of why or what, "panic terror," called so from the fables that make Pan the author of them, whereas in truth there is always in him that so fears, first some apprehension of the cause, though the rest run away by example, every one supposing his fellow to know why. And therefore this passion happens to none but in a throng or multitude of people.

"Joy," from apprehension of novelty "admiration," proper to man, because it excites the appetite of knowing the cause.

"Joy," arising from imagination of a man's own power and ability is that exultation of the mind which is called "glorying," which, if grounded upon the experience of his own former actions, is the same as "confidence," but if grounded on the flattery of others or only supposed by himself for delight in the consequences of it, is called "vain-glory," which name is properly given, because a well-grounded "confidence" begets attempt, whereas the supposing of power does not, and is therefore rightly called "vain."

"Grief" from opinion of want of power is called "dejection of mind."

The "vain-glory" which consists in the feigning or supposing of abilities in ourselves which we know are not is most incident to young men, and nourished by the histories or fictions of gallant persons, and is corrected oftentimes by age and employment.

"Sudden glory" is the passion which makes those "grimaces" called "laughter"; and is caused either by some sudden act of their own that pleases them, or by the apprehension of some deformed thing in another by comparison whereof they suddenly applaud themselves. And it is incident most to them that are conscious of the fewest abilities in themselves; who are forced to keep themselves in their own favor by observing the imperfections of other men. And therefore much laughter at the defects of others is a sign of pusillanimity. For of great minds one of the proper works is to help and free others from scorn and compare themselves only with the most able.

On the contrary, "sudden dejection" is the passion that causes "weeping," and is caused by such accidents as suddenly take away some vehement hope or some prop of their power; and they are most subject to it that rely principally on helps external, such as are women and children. Therefore some weep for the loss of friends, others for their unkindness, others for the sudden stop made to their thoughts of revenge by reconciliation. But in all cases, both laughter and weeping, are sudden motions, custom taking them both away. For no man laughs at old jests, or weeps for an old calamity.

"Grief" for the discovery of some defect of ability is "shame," or the passion that discovers itself in "blushing," and consists in the apprehension of something dishonorable; and in young men is a sign of the love of good reputation, and commendable: in old men it is a sign of the same; but, because it comes too late, not commendable.

The "contempt" of good reputation is called "impudence."

"Grief" for the calamity of another is "pity," and arises from the imagination that the like calamity may befall himself; and therefore is called also "compassion," and in the phrase of this present time a "fellow-feeling"; and therefore for calamity arriving from great wickedness the best men have the least pity; and for the same calamity those have least pity that think themselves least obnoxious to the same.

"Contempt," or little sense of the calamity of others, is that which men call "cruelty," proceeding from security of their own fortune. For, that any man should take pleasure in other men's great harms without other end of his own, I do not conceive it possible.

"Grief" for the success of a competitor in wealth, honor, or other good, if it be joined with endeavor to enforce our own abilities to equal or exceed him, is called "emulation"; but joined with endeavor to supplant or hinder a competitor, "envy."

When in the mind of man, appetites and aversions, hopes and fears, concerning one and the same thing, arise alternately, and divers good and evil consequences of the doing or omitting the thing propounded, come successively into our thoughts, so that sometimes we have an appetite to it, sometimes an aversion from it, sometimes hope to be able to do it, sometimes despair or fear to attempt it, the whole sum of desires, aversions, hopes, and fears, continued till the thing be either done or thought impossible, is that we call "deliberation."

Therefore of things past there is no "deliberation," because manifestly impossible to be changed; nor of things known to be impossible, or thought so, because men know, or think, such deliberation vain. But of things impossible which we think possible we may deliberate, not knowing it is in vain. And it is called "deliberation," because it is a putting an end to the "liberty" we had of doing or omitting according to our own appetite or aversion.

This alternate succession of appetites, aversions, hopes, and fears, is no less in other living creatures than in man; and therefore beasts also deliberate.

Every "deliberation" is then said to "end" when that whereof they deliberate is either done or thought impossible because till then we retain the liberty of doing or omitting according to our appetite or aversion.

In "deliberation," the last appetite, or aversion, immediately adhering to the action, or to the omission thereof, is that we call the "will," the act, not the faculty, of "willing." And beasts that have "deliberation" must necessarily also have "will." The definition of the "will" given commonly by the schools, that it is a "rational appetite," is not good. For if it were, then could there be no voluntary act against reason. For a "voluntary act" is that which proceeds from the "will" and no other. But if instead of a rational appetite we shall say an appetite resulting from a precedent deliberation, then the definition is the same that I have given here. Will, therefore, is the last appetite in deliberating. And, though we say in common discourse a man had a will once to do a thing, that nevertheless he forbore to do, yet that is properly but an inclination, which makes no action voluntary; because the action depends not of it, but of the last inclination or appetite. For if the intervenient appetites make any action voluntary, then by the same reason all intervenient aversions should make the same action involuntary; and so one and the same action should be both voluntary and involuntary.

By this it is manifest that not only actions that have their beginning from covetousness, ambition, lust, or other appetites to the thing propounded, but also those that have their beginning from aversion, or fear of those consequences that follow the omission, are "voluntary actions."

The forms of speech by which the passions are expressed are partly the same, and partly different from those by which we express our thoughts. And, first, generally all passions may be expressed "indicatively," as "I love," "I fear," "I joy," "I deliberate," "I will," "I command," but some of them have particular expressions by themselves, which nevertheless are not affirmations, unless it be when they serve to make other inferences besides that of the passion they proceed from. Deliberation is expressed "subjunctively," which is a speech proper to signify suppositions, with their consequences: as, "if this be done, then this will follow," and differs not from the language of reasoning, save that reasoning is in general words—but deliberation for the most part is of particulars. The language of desire, and aversion, is "imperative," as "do this," "forbear that," which when the party is obliged to do, or forbear, is "command"; otherwise "prayer," or else "counsel." The language of vain-glory, of indignation, pity and revengefulness, "optative," but of the desire to know there is a peculiar expression, called "interrogative," as "what is it"? "when shall it"? "how is it done"? and "why so"? Other language of the passions I find none; for cursing, swearing, reviling, and the like, do not signify as speech, but as the actions of a tongue accustomed.

These forms of speech, I say, are expressions, or voluntary significations of our passions—but certain signs they be not, because they may be used arbitrarily, whether they that use them have such passions or not. The best signs of passions present are either in the countenance, motions of the body, actions, and ends, or aims, which we otherwise know the man to have.

And because in deliberation the appetites and aversions are raised by foresight of the good and evil consequences, and sequels of the action whereof we deliberate, the good or evil effect thereof depends on the foresight of a long chain of consequences of which very seldom any man is able to see to the end. But for so far as a man sees, if the good in those consequences be greater than the evil, the whole chain is that which writers call "apparent" or "seeming good." And, contrarily, when the evil exceeds the good, the whole is "apparent" or "seeming evil," so that he who hath by experience, or reason, the greatest and surest prospect of consequences, deliberates best himself, and is able, when he will, to give the best counsel unto others.

"Continual success" in obtaining those things which a man from time to time desires, that is to say continual prospering, is that men call "felicity"; I mean the felicity of this life. For there is no such thing as perpetual tranquility of mind while we live here, because life itself is but motion, and can never be without desire, nor without fear, no more than without sense. What kind of felicity God hath ordained to them that devoutly honor Him a man shall no sooner know than enjoy, being joys that now are as incomprehensible as the word of schoolmen "beatifical vision" is unintelligible.

The form of speech whereby men signify their opinion of the goodness of anything is "praise." That whereby they signify the power and greatness of anything is "magnifying." And that whereby they signify the opinion they have of a man's felicity is by the Greeks called ⟨*makarismos*⟩ for which we have no name in our tongue. And thus much is sufficient for the present purpose, to have been said of the "passions."

*   *   *

CHAPTER 9. OF THE SEVERAL SUBJECTS OF KNOWLEDGE

There are of "knowledge" two kinds, whereof one is "knowledge of fact," the other "knowledge of the consequence of one affirmation to another." The former is nothing else but sense and memory, and is "absolute knowledge," as when we see a fact doing or remember it done; and this is the knowledge required in a witness. The latter is called "science," and is "conditional," as when we know that "if the figure shown be a circle, then any straight line through the center shall divide it into two equal parts." And this is the knowledge required in a philosopher, that is to say of him that pretends to reasoning.

The register of "knowledge of fact" is called "history," whereof there be two sorts: one called "natural history," which is the history of such facts or effects of Nature as have no dependence on man's "will," such as are the histories of "metals," "plants," "animals," "regions," and the like. The other is "civil history," which is the history of the voluntary actions of men in commonwealths.

The registers of science are such "books," as contain the "demonstrations" of consequences of one affirmation to another, and are commonly called "books of philosophy," whereof the sorts are many, according to the diversity of the matter, and may be divided in such manner as I have divided them in the . . . table [see following page].

*   *   *

CHAPTER 12. OF RELIGION

Seeing there are no signs nor fruit of "religion" but in man only, there is no cause to doubt but that the seed of "religion" is also only in man—and consists in some peculiar quality or at least in some eminent degree thereof not to be found in other living creatures.

And, first, it is peculiar to the nature of man to be inquisitive into the causes of the events they see, some more, some less; but all men so much as to be curious in the search of the causes of their own good and evil fortune.

Secondly, upon the sight of anything that hath a beginning to think also it had a cause which determined the same to begin, then when it did, rather than sooner or later.

Thirdly, whereas there is no other felicity of beasts but the enjoying of their quotidian food, ease, and lusts, as having little or no foresight of the time to come, for want of observation and memory of the order, consequence, and dependence of the things they see, man observes how one event hath been produced by another, and remembers in them antecedence and consequence; and, when he cannot assure himself

SCIENCE, that is, Knowledge of Consequences; which is called also PHILOSOPHY

- Consequences from the Accidents of Bodies Natural; which is called NATURAL PHILOSOPHY.
  - Consequences from the Accidents common to all Bodies Natural; which are *Quantity*, and *Motion*.
    - Consequences from Quantity, and Motion determined
      - Consequences from Quantity, and Motion *determined.* — *Mathematics,*
        - By Figure, ... { GEOMETRY.
        - By Number, .. { ARITHMETIC. } PHILOSOPHIA PRIMA.
      - Consequences from the Motion, and Quantity of Bodies in *special*.
        - Consequences from the Motion, and Quantity of the great parts of the World, as the *Earth* and *Stars* — *Cosmography* { ASTRONOMY. GEOGRAPHY.
        - Consequences from the Motion of Special kinds, and Figures of Body, — *Mechanics,* Doctrine of *Weight,* { Science of ENGINEERS. ARCHITECTURE. NAVIGATION. METEOROLOGY. SCIOGRAPHY.
  - PHYSICS, or Consequences from *Qualities.*
    - Consequences from the Qualities of Bodies *Transient*, such as sometimes appear, sometimes vanish, — ASTROLOGY.
    - Consequences from the Qualities of Bodies *Permanent.*
      - Consequences from the Qualities of the *Stars.*
        - Consequences from the *Light* of the Stars. Out of this, and the Motion of the Sun, is made the Science of ......
        - Consequences from the *Influence* of the Stars, ...
      - Consequences of the Qualities from *Liquid* Bodies that fill the space between the Stars; such as are the *Air*, or Substance etherial.
      - Consequences from the Qualities of Bodies *Terrestrial.*
        - Consequences from the parts of the Earth, that are *without Sense.*
          - Consequences from the Qualities of *Minerals,* as *Stones, Metals,* & *etc.*
          - Consequences from the Qualities of *Vegetables.*
        - Consequences from the Qualities of *Animals.*
          - Consequences from the Qualities of Animals in *general.*
            - Consequences from *Vision.* { OPTICS.
            - Consequences from *Sounds.* .. { MUSIC.
            - Consequences from the rest of the *Senses.*
          - Consequences from the Qualities of *Men in special.*
            - Consequences from the *Passions* of Men, ... { ETHICS.
            - Consequences from *Speech,*
              - In *Magnifying, Vilifying,* & etc. { POETRY.
              - In *Persuading,* { RHETORIC.
              - In *Reasoning,* { LOGIC.
              - In *Contracting,* { The *Science* of *Just and Unjust*

- Consequences from the Accidents of Politic Bodies; which is called POLITICS, and CIVIL PHILOSOPHY.
  1. Of Consequences from the *Institution* of COMMONWEALTHS, to the *Rights*, and *Duties* of the *Body Politic,* or *Sovereign.*
  2. Of Consequences from the same to the *Duty,* and *Right of the Subjects.*

of the true causes of things (for the causes of good and evil fortune for the most part are invisible), he supposes causes of them, either such as his own fancy suggests, or trusts the authority of other men, such as he thinks to be his friends and wiser than himself.

The two first make anxiety. For, being assured that there be causes of all things that have arrived hitherto or shall arrive hereafter, it is impossible for a man, who continually endeavors to secure himself against the evil he fears and procure the good he desires, not to be in a perpetual solicitude of the time to come; so that every man, especially those that are over-provident, are in a state like to that of Prometheus. For as Prometheus, which interpreted is "the prudent man," was bound to the hill Caucasus, a place of large prospect, where an eagle feeding on his liver devoured in the day as much as was repaired in the night, so that man, which looks too far before him in the care of future time, hath his heart all the day long gnawed on by fear of death, poverty, or other calamity, and has no repose nor pause of his anxiety but in sleep.

This perpetual fear, always accompanying mankind in the ignorance of causes, as it were in the dark, must needs have for object something. And therefore, when there is nothing to be seen, there is nothing to accuse, either of their good or evil fortune, but some ''power'' or agent "invisible" in which sense perhaps it was that some of the old poets said that the gods were at first created by human fear; which spoken of the gods, that is to say of the many gods of the Gentiles, is very true. But the acknowledging of one God, eternal, infinite, and omnipotent, may more easily be derived, from the desire men have to know the causes of natural bodies and their several virtues and operations, than from the fear of what was to befall them in time to come. For he that from any effect he sees come to pass should reason to the next and immediate cause thereof, and from thence to the cause of that cause, and plunge himself profoundly in the pursuit of causes, shall at last come to this, that there must be, as even the heathen philosophers confessed, one first mover, that is, a first and an eternal cause of all things, which is that which men mean by the name of God, and all this without thought of their fortune; the solicitude whereof both inclines to fear and hinders them from the search of the causes of other things, and thereby gives occasion of feigning of as many gods as there be men that feign them.

And, for the matter or substance of the invisible agents so fancied, they could not by natural cogitation fall upon any other conceit, but that it was the same with that of the soul of man; and that the soul of man was of the same substance with that which appears in a dream to one that sleeps or in a looking-glass to one that is awake, which, men not knowing that such apparitions are nothing else but creatures of the fancy, think to be real and external substances, and therefore call them ghosts; as the Latins called them *imagines* and *umbræ*, and thought them spirits, that is thin aerial bodies, and those invisible agents which they feared, to be like them, save that they appear and vanish when they please. But the opinion that such spirits were incorporeal, or immaterial, could never enter into the mind of any man by nature, because, though men may put together words of contradictory signification, as "spirit" and "incorporeal," yet they can never have the imagination of anything answering to them; and therefore men that by their own meditation arrive to the acknowledgment of one infinite, omnipotent, and eternal God chose rather to confess He is incomprehensible and above their understanding than to define His nature by "spirit incorporeal," and then confess their definition to be unintelligible; or, if they give Him such a title, it is not "dogmatically" with intention to make the divine nature understood, but "piously," to honor Him with attributes of significations as remote as they can from the grossness of bodies visible.

Then for the way by which they think these invisible agents wrought their effects, that is to say, what immediate causes they used in bringing things to pass, men that know not what it is that we call "causing," that is almost all men, have no other rule to guess by but by observing and remembering what they have seen to precede the like effect at some other time or times before, without seeing between the antecedent and subsequent event any dependence or connection at all; and therefore from the like things past they expect the like things to come, and hope for good or evil luck, superstitiously, from things that have no part at all in the causing of it: as the Athenians did for their war at Lepanto, demand another Phormio; the Pompeian faction for their war in Africa, another Scipio, and others have done in divers other occasions since. In like manner they attribute their fortune to a stander-by, to a lucky or unlucky place, to words spoken, especially if the name God be amongst them, as charming and conjuring, the liturgy of witches; inasmuch as to believe they have power to turn a stone into bread, bread into a man, or anything into anything.

Thirdly, for the worship which naturally men exhibit to powers invisible, it can be no other but such expressions of their reverence, as they would use towards men; gifts, petitions, thanks, submission of body, considerate addresses, sober behavior, premeditated words, swearing, that is assuring one another of their promises by invoking them. Beyond that, reason suggests nothing, but leaves them either to rest there, or, for further ceremonies, to rely on those they believe to be wiser than themselves.

Lastly, concerning how these invisible powers declare to men the things which shall hereafter come to pass, especially concerning their good or evil fortune in general or good or ill success in any particular undertaking, men are naturally at a stand, save that, using to conjecture of the time to come by the time past, they are very apt not only to take casual things, after one or two encounters, for prognostics of the like encounter ever after, but also to believe the like prognostics from other men of whom they have once conceived a good opinion.

And, in these four things, opinion of ghosts, ignorance of second causes, devotion towards what men fear, and taking of things casual for prognostics, consists the natural seed of "religion," which, by reason of the different fancies, judgments, and passions of several men, hath grown up into ceremonies so different that those which are used by one man are for the most part ridiculous to another.

For these seeds have received culture from two sorts of men. One sort have been they that have nourished and ordered them according to their own invention. The other have done it by God's commandment and direction; but both sorts have done it with a purpose to make those men that relied on them the more apt to obedience, laws, peace, charity and civil society. So that the religion of the former sort is a part of human politics, and teaches part of the duty which earthly kings require of their subjects. And the religion of the latter sort is divine politics, and contains precepts to those that have yielded themselves subjects in the kingdom of God. Of the former sort were all the founders of commonwealths and the lawgivers of the Gentiles; of the latter sort, were Abraham, Moses, and our blessed Savior, by whom have been derived unto us the laws of the kingdom of God.

* * *

CHAPTER 13. OF THE NATURAL CONDITION OF MANKIND AS CONCERNING THEIR FELICITY AND MISERY

Nature hath made men so equal in the faculties of the body and mind, as that, though there be found one man sometimes manifestly stronger in body or of quicker mind than another, yet when all is reckoned together the difference between man and man is not so considerable as that one man can thereupon claim to himself any benefit to which another may not pretend as well as he. For, as to the strength of body, the weakest has strength enough to kill the strongest, either by secret machination or by confederacy with others that are in the same danger with himself.

And, as to the faculties of the mind, setting aside the arts grounded upon words and especially that skill of proceeding upon general and infallible rules called science, which very few have and but in few things, as being not a native faculty born with us, nor attained, as prudence, while we look after somewhat else, I find yet a greater equality amongst men than that of strength. For prudence is but experience, which equal time equally bestows on all men in those things they equally apply themselves unto. That which may perhaps make such equality incredible is but a vain conceit of one's own wisdom, which almost all men think they have in a greater degree than the vulgar, that is, than all men but themselves, and a few others whom by fame or for concurring with themselves they approve. For such is the nature of men that, howsoever they may acknowledge many others to be more witty or more eloquent or more learned, yet they will hardly believe there be many so wise as themselves, for they see their own wit at hand and other men's at a distance. But this proves rather that men are in that point equal than unequal. For there is not ordinarily a greater sign of the equal distribution of anything than that every man is contented with his share.

From this equality of ability arises equality of hope in the attaining of our ends. And therefore, if any two men desire the same thing which nevertheless they cannot both enjoy, they become enemies—and, in the way to their end, which is principally their own conservation and sometimes their delectation only, endeavor to destroy or subdue one another. And from hence it comes to pass that, where an invader hath no more to fear than another man's single power, if one plant, sow, build, or possess, a convenient seat others may probably be expected to come prepared with forces united to dispossess and deprive him not only of the fruit of his labor but also of his life or liberty. And the invader again is in the like danger of another.

And from this diffidence of one another there is no way for any man to secure himself so reasonable as anticipation, that is, by force or wiles to master the persons of all men he can so long till he see no other power great enough to endanger him; and this is no more than his own conservation requires and is generally allowed. Also, because there be some that, taking pleasure in contemplating their own power in the acts of conquest, which they pursue farther than their security requires, if others, that otherwise would be glad to be at ease within the modest bounds, should not by invasion increase their power, they would not be able for a long time, by standing only on their defence, to subsist. And by consequence, such augmentation of dominion over men being necessary to a man's conservation, it ought to be allowed him.

Again, men have no pleasure, but on the contrary a great deal of grief, in keeping company where there is no power able to overawe them all. For every man looks that his companion should value him at the same rate he sets upon himself, and, upon all signs of contempt or undervaluing, naturally endeavors as far as he dares (which amongst them that have no common power to keep them in quiet, is far enough to make them destroy each other) to extort a greater value from his condemners by damage, and from others by the example.

So that in the nature of man we find three principal causes of quarrel. First, competition; secondly, diffidence; thirdly, glory.

The first makes man invade for gain; the second, for safety; and the third, for reputation. The first use violence, to make themselves masters of other men's persons, wives, children, and cattle; the second, to defend them; the third, for trifles, as a word, a smile, a different opinion, and any other sign of undervalue, either direct in their persons or by reflection in their kindred, their friends, their nation, their profession, or their name.

Hereby it is manifest that, during the time men live without a common power to keep them all in awe, they are in that condition which is called war, and such a war as is of every man against every man. For "war" consists not in battle only or the act of fighting, but in a tract of time wherein the will to contend by battle is sufficiently known, and therefore the notion of "time" is to be considered in the nature of war, as it is in the nature of weather. For as the nature of foul weather lies not in a shower or two of rain but in an inclination thereto of many days together, so the nature of war consists not in actual fighting but in the known disposition thereto during all the time there is no assurance to the contrary. All other time is "peace."

Whatsoever therefore is consequent to a time of war where every man is enemy to every man, the same is consequent to the time wherein men live without other security than what their own strength and their own invention shall furnish them withal. In such condition there is no place for industry, because the fruit thereof is uncertain, and consequently no culture of the earth, no navigation nor use of the commodities that may be imported by sea, no commodious building, no instruments of moving and removing such things as require much force, no knowledge of the face of the earth; no account of time, no arts, no letters, no society, and, which is worst of all, continual fear and danger of violent death, and the life of man solitary, poor, nasty, brutish, and short.

It may seem strange to some man that has not well weighed these things that Nature should thus dissociate and render men apt to invade and destroy one another; and he may therefore, not trusting to this inference made from the passions, desire perhaps to have the same confirmed by experience. Let him therefore consider with himself, when taking a journey, he arms himself and seeks to go well accompanied; when going to sleep, he locks his doors; when even in his house, he locks his chests; and this when he knows there be laws and public officers armed to revenge all injuries shall be done him; what opinion he has of his fellow-subjects, when he rides armed—of his fellow-citizens, when he locks his doors; and of his children and servants, when he locks his chests. Does he not there as much accuse mankind by his actions as I do by my words? But neither of us accuse man's nature in it. The desires and other passions of man are in themselves no sin. No more are the actions that proceed from those passions, till they know a law that forbids them; which, till laws be made, they cannot know, nor can any law be made till they have agreed upon the person that shall make it.

It may peradventure be thought there was never such a time nor condition of war as this; and I believe it was never generally so over all the world, but there are many places where they live so now. For the savage people in many places of America, except the government of small families the concord whereof depends on natural lust, have no government at all, and live at this day in that brutish manner as I said before. Howsoever, it may be perceived what manner of life there would be where there were no common power to fear, by the manner of life which men that have formerly lived under a peaceful government use to degenerate into, in a civil war. But, though there had never been any time wherein particular men were in a condition of war one against another, yet in all times kings and persons of sovereign authority, because of their independence, are in continual jealousies and in the state and posture of gladiators, having their weapons pointing, and their eyes fixed on one another, that is, their forts, garrisons, and guns, upon the frontiers of their kingdoms, and continual spies upon their neighbors: which is a posture of war. But because they uphold thereby the industry of their subjects, there does not follow from it that misery which accompanies the liberty of particular men.

To this war of every man against every man this also is consequent, that nothing can be unjust. The notions of right and wrong, justice and injustice, have there no place. Where there is no common power, there is no law; where no law, no injustice. Force and fraud are in war the two cardinal virtues. Justice and injustice are none of the faculties neither of the body nor mind. If they were, they might be in a man that were alone in the world, as well as his senses and passions. They are qualities that relate to men in society, not in solitude. It is consequent also to the same condition that there be no propriety, no dominion, no "mine" and "thine" distinct, but only that to be every man's that he can get, and for so long as he can keep it. And thus much for the ill condition which man by mere nature is actually placed in, though with a possibility to come out of it, consisting partly in the passions, partly in his reason.

The passions that incline men to peace are fear of death, desire of such things as are necessary to commodious living, and a hope by their industry to obtain them. And reason suggests convenient articles of peace, upon which men may be drawn to agreement. These articles are they which otherwise are called the Laws of Nature, whereof I shall speak more particularly in the two following chapters.

CHAPTER 14. OF THE FIRST AND SECOND NATURAL LAWS,
AND OF CONTRACTS

"The right of Nature," which writers commonly call *jus naturale*, is the liberty each man hath to use his own power as he will himself for the preservation of his own nature, that is to say, of his own life; and consequently of doing anything which in his own judgment and reason he shall conceive to be the aptest means thereunto.

By "liberty" is understood, according to the proper signification of the word, the absence of external impediments which impediments may oft take away part of a man's power to do what he would, but cannot hinder him from using the power left him according as his judgment and reason shall dictate to him.

A "law of Nature," *lex naturalis*, is a precept or general rule found out by reason by which a man is forbidden to do that which is destructive of his life or takes away the means of preserving the same, and to omit that by which he thinks it may be best preserved. For, though they that speak of this subject use to confound *jus* and *lex*, "right" and "law," yet they ought to be distinguished; because "right" consists in liberty to do or to forbear, whereas "law" determines and binds to one of them: so that law and right differ as much as obligation and liberty; which in one and the same matter are inconsistent.

And because the condition of man, as hath been declared in the precedent chapter, is a condition of war of every one against every one, in which case every one is governed by his own reason, and there is nothing he can make use of that may not be a help unto him in preserving his life against his enemies, it follows that in such a condition every man has a right to everything, even to one another's body. And therefore, as long as this natural right of every man to everything endures, there can be no security to any man, how strong or wise soever he be, of living out the time which Nature ordinarily allows men to live. And consequently it is a precept or general rule of reason "that every man ought to endeavor peace as far as he has hope of obtaining it, and, when he cannot obtain it, that he may seek and use all helps and advantages of war." The first branch of which rule contains the first and fundamental law of Nature, which is, "to seek peace, and follow it." The second, the sum of the right of Nature, which is, "by all means we can, to defend ourselves."

From this fundamental law of Nature, by which men are commanded to endeavor peace, is derived this second law, "that a man be willing, when others are so too, as far-forth as for peace and defence of himself he shall think it necessary, to lay down this right to all things, and be contented with so much liberty against other men as he would allow other men against himself." For as long as every man holds this right of doing anything he likes, so long are all men in the condition of war. But if other men will not lay down their right as well as he, then there is no reason for any one to divest himself of his: for that were to expose himself to prey, which no man is bound to, rather than to dispose himself to peace. This is that law of the Gospel: "whatsoever you require that others should do to you, that do ye to them." And that law of all men, *quod tibi fieri non vis, alteri ne feceris.*

To "lay down" a man's "right" to anything is to "divest" himself of the "liberty," of hindering another of the benefit of his own right to the same. For he that renounces or passes away his right gives not to any other man a right which he had not before, because there is nothing to which every man had not right by Nature; but only stands out of his way that he may enjoy his own original right without hindrance from him, not without hindrance from another. So that the effect which redounds to one man, by another man's defect of right, is but so much diminution of impediments to the use of his own right original.

Right is laid aside either by simply renouncing it, or by transferring it to another. By "simply renouncing" when he cares not to whom the benefit thereof redounds. By "transferring," when he intends the benefit thereof to some certain person or persons. And, when a man hath in either manner abandoned or granted away his right, then is he said to be "obliged" or "bound" not to hinder those to whom such right is granted or abandoned from the benefit of it; and that he "ought," and it is his "duty," not to make void that voluntary act of his own; and that such hindrance is "injustice" and "injury" as being sine jure, the right being before renounced or transferred. So that "injury" or "injustice," in the controversies of the world, is somewhat like to that which in the disputations of scholars is called "absurdity." For, as it is there called an absurdity to contradict what one maintained in the beginning, so in the world it is called injustice and injury voluntarily to undo that from the beginning he had voluntarily done. The way by which a man either simply renounces or transfers his right is a declaration or signification, by some voluntary and sufficient sign or signs, that he doth so renounce or transfer, or hath so renounced or transferred, the same, to him that accepts it. And these signs are either words only or actions only, or, as it happens most often, both words and actions. And the same are the "bonds" by which men are bound and obliged: bonds that have their strength not from their own nature, for nothing is more easily broken than a man's word, but from fear of some evil consequence upon the rupture.

Whensoever a man transfers his right or renounces it, it is either in consideration of some right reciprocally transferred to himself, or for some other good he hopes for thereby. For it is a voluntary act: and of the voluntary acts of every man the object is some good "to himself." And therefore there be some rights which no man can be understood by any words or other signs to have abandoned or transferred. As first a man cannot lay down the right of resisting them that assault him by force to take away his life, because he cannot be understood to aim thereby at any good to himself. The same may be said of wounds, and chains, and imprisonment, both because there is no benefit consequent to such patience, as there is to the patience of suffering another to be wounded or imprisoned, as also because a man cannot tell when he sees men proceed against him by violence whether they intend his death or not. And lastly the motive and end for which this renouncing and transferring of right is introduced is nothing else but the security of a man's person in his life and in the means of so preserving life as not to be weary of it. And therefore if a man by words or other signs seem to despoil himself of the end for which those signs were intended, he is not to be understood as if he meant it or that it was his will, but that he was ignorant of how such words and actions were to be interpreted.

The mutual transferring of right is that which men call "contract."

*   *   *

Chapter 15. Other Laws of Nature

From that law of Nature by which we are obliged to transfer to another such rights as, being retained, hinder the peace of mankind, there follows a third, which is this, "that men perform their covenants made"; without which covenants are in vain, and but empty words: and the right of all men to all things remaining, we are still in the condition of war.

And in this law of Nature consists the fountain and original of "justice." For, where no covenant hath preceded, there hath no right been transferred, and every man has right to everything; and consequently, no action can be unjust. But when a covenant is made, then to break it is "unjust"; and the definition of "injustice" is no other than "the not performance of covenant." And whatsoever is not unjust is "just."

But because covenants of mutual trust, where there is a fear of not performance on either part, as hath been said in the former chapter, are invalid, though the original of justice be the making of covenants, yet injustice actually there can be none, till the cause of such fear be taken away, which, while men are in the natural condition of war, cannot be done. Therefore, before the names of just and unjust can have place, there must be some coercive power to compel men equally to the performance of their covenants, by the terror of some punishment greater than the benefit they expect by the breach of their covenant; and to make good that propriety which by mutual contract men acquire in recompense of the universal right they abandon; and such power there is none before the erection of a commonwealth. And this is also to be gathered out of the ordinary definition of justice in the schools; for they say that "justice is the constant will of giving to every man his own." And therefore where there is no "own" there is no propriety, there is no injustice; and where there is no coercive power erected, that is, where there is no commonwealth, there is no propriety, all men having right to all things: therefore, where there is no commonwealth, there nothing is unjust. So that the nature of justice consists in keeping of valid covenants; but the validity of covenants begins not but with the constitution of a civil power sufficient to compel men to keep them; and then it is also that propriety begins.

The fool hath said in his heart there is no such thing as justice, and sometimes also with his tongue, seriously alleging that every man's conservation and contentment, being committed to his own care, there could be no reason why every man might not do what he thought conduced thereunto; and therefore also to make or not make, keep or not keep, covenants was not against reason when it conduced to one's benefit. He does not therein deny that there be covenants, and that they are sometimes broken, sometimes kept, and that such breach of them may be called injustice, and the observance of them justice; but he questions whether injustice taking away the fear of God, for the same fool hath said in his heart there is no God, may not sometimes stand with that reason which dictates to every man his own good; and particularly then when it conduces to such a benefit as shall put a man in a condition to neglect not only the dispraise and revilings, but also the power, of other men. The kingdom of God is gotten by violence; but what if it could be gotten by unjust violence? Were it against reason so to get it, when it is impossible to receive hurt by it? And, if it be not against reason, it is not against justice, or else justice is not to be approved for good. From such reasoning as this, successful wickedness hath obtained the name of virtue, and some that in all other things have disallowed the violation of faith, yet have allowed it when it is for the getting of a kingdom. And the heathen that believed that Saturn was deposed by his son Jupiter believed nevertheless the same Jupiter to be the avenger of injustice somewhat like to a piece of law in Coke's *Commentaries on Littleton*, where he says, if the right heir of the crown be attainted of treason, yet the crown shall descend to him, and *eo instante* the attainder be void; from which instances a man will be very prone to infer that, when the heir apparent of a kingdom shall kill him that is in possession, though his father, you may call it injustice or by what other name you will, yet it can never be against reason seeing all the voluntary actions of men tend to the benefit of themselves; and those actions are most reasonable that conduce most to their ends. This specious reasoning is nevertheless false.

For the question is not of promises mutual, where there is no security of performance on either side, as when there is no civil power erected over the parties promising, for such promises are no covenants, but either where one of the parties has performed already, or where there is a power to make him perform, there is the question whether it be against reason, that is against the benefit of the other to perform or not. And I say it is not against reason. For the manifestation whereof we are to consider, first that when a man doth a thing which notwithstanding anything can be foreseen and reckoned on tends to his own destruction, howsoever some accident which he could not expect, arriving may turn it to his benefit, yet such events do not make it reasonably or wisely done. Secondly, that, in a condition of war, wherein every man to every man, for want of a common power to keep them all in awe, is an enemy, there is no man who can hope by his own strength or wit to defend himself from destruction without the help of confederates; where every one expects the same defence by the confederation that any one else does; and therefore he which declares he thinks it reason to deceive those that help him can in reason expect no other means of safety than what can be had from his own single power. He therefore that breaks his covenant, and consequently declares that he thinks he may with reason do so, cannot be received into any society that unite themselves for peace and defence but by the error of them that receive him; nor, when he is received, be retained in it without seeing the danger of their error; which errors a man cannot reasonably reckon upon as the means of his security; and therefore, if he be left or cast out of society, he perishes; and if he live in society, it is by the errors of other men which he could not foresee nor reckon upon, and consequently against the reason of his preservation; and so, as all men that contribute not to his destruction, forbear him only out of ignorance of what is good for themselves.

As for the instance of gaining the secure and perpetual felicity of heaven by any way, it is frivolous; there being but one way imaginable; and that is not breaking, but keeping of covenant.

And, for the other instance of attaining sovereignty by rebellion, it is manifest that, though the event follow, yet, because it cannot reasonably be expected, but rather the contrary, and because by gaining it so, others are taught to gain the same in like manner, the attempt thereof is against reason. Justice therefore, that is to say keeping of covenant, is a rule of reason by which we are forbidden to do anything destructive to our life; and consequently a law of Nature.

There be some that proceed further, and will not have the law of Nature to be those rules which conduce to the preservation of man's life on earth, but to the attaining of an eternal felicity after death; to which they think the breach of covenant may conduce; and consequently be just and reasonable; such are they that think it a work of merit to kill or depose or rebel against the sovereign power constituted over them by their own consent. But, because there is no natural knowledge of man's estate after death, much less of the reward that is then to be given to breach of faith, but only a belief grounded upon other men's saying that they know it supernaturally, or that they know those that knew them, that knew others, that knew it supernaturally; breach of faith cannot be called a precept of reason or nature.

Others that allow for a law of Nature the keeping of faith do nevertheless make exception of certain persons as heretics and such as use not to perform their covenant to others; and this also is against reason. For if any fault of a man be sufficient to discharge our covenant made, the same ought in reason to have been sufficient to have hindered the making of it.

The names of just and unjust, when they are attributed to men, signify one thing; and when they are attributed to actions, another. When they are attributed to men they signify conformity or inconformity of manners to reason. But, when they are attributed to actions, they signify the conformity or inconformity to reason, not of manners or manner of life but of particular actions. A just man, therefore, is he that takes all the care he can that his actions may be all just, and an unjust man is he that neglects it. And such men are more often in our language styled by the names of righteous and unrighteous than just and unjust, though the meaning be the same. Therefore a righteous man does not lose that title by one or a few unjust actions that proceed from sudden passion or mistake of things or persons; nor does an unrighteous man lose his character for such actions as he does, or forbears to do, for fear, because his will is not framed by the justice but by the apparent benefit of what he is to do. That which gives to human actions the relish of justice is a certain nobleness or gallantness of courage, rarely found, by which a man scorns to be beholden for the contentment of his life to fraud or breach of promise. This justice of the manners is that which is meant where justice is called a virtue, and injustice a vice.

But the justice of actions denominates men not just, "guiltless"; and the injustice of the same, which is also called injury, gives them but the name of "guilty."

Again, the injustice of manners is the disposition or aptitude to do injury, and is injustice before it proceeds to act, and without supposing any individual person injured. But the injustice of an action, that is to say injury, supposes an individual person injured, namely him to whom the covenant was made; and therefore many times the injury is received by one man when the damage redounds to another. As when the master commands his servant to give money to a stranger: if it be not done, the injury is done to the master, whom he had before covenanted to obey; but the damage redounds to the stranger, to whom he had no obligation, and therefore could not injure him. And so also in commonwealths. Private men may remit to one another their debts, but not robberies or other violences whereby they are endamaged, because the detaining of debt is an injury to themselves, but robbery and violence are injuries to the person of the commonwealth.

Whatsoever is done to a man conformable to his own will signified to the doer is no injury to him. For, if he that does it hath not passed away his original right to do what he please by some antecedent covenant, there is no breach of covenant, and therefore no injury done him. And if he have, then his will to have it done being signified is a release of that covenant, and so again there is no injury done him.

Justice of action is by writers divided into "commutative" and "distributive"; and the former they say consists in proportion arithmetical, the latter in proportion geometrical. Commutative, therefore, they place in the equality of value of the things contracted for—and distributive, in the distribution of equal benefit to men of equal merit. As if it were injustice to sell dearer than we buy, or to give more to a man than he merits. The value of all things contracted for is measured by the appetite of the contractors; and therefore the just value is that which they be contented to give. And merit, besides that which is by covenant, where the performance on one part merits the performance of the other part, and falls under justice commutative not distributive, is not due by justice, but is rewarded of grace only. And therefore this distinction, in the sense wherein it uses to be expounded, is not right. To speak properly, commutative justice is the justice of a contractor; that is, a performance of covenant in buying and selling, hiring and letting to hire, lending and borrowing, exchanging, bartering, and other acts of contract.

And distributive justice, the justice of an arbitrator; that is to say, the act of defining what is just. Wherein, being trusted by them that make him arbitrator, if he perform his trust he is said to distribute to every man his own; and this is indeed just distribution, and may be called, though improperly, distributive justice, but more properly equity, which also is a law of Nature, as shall be shown in due place.

As justice depends on antecedent covenant, so does "gratitude" depend on antecedent grace, that is to say, antecedent free gift; and is the fourth law of Nature; which may be conceived in this form, "that a man, which receives benefit from another of mere grace, endeavor that he which gives it have no reasonable cause to repent him of his good will." For no man gives but with intention of good to himself; because gift is voluntary; and of all voluntary acts the object is to every man his own good, of which, if men see they shall be frustrated, there will be no beginning of benevolence, or trust, nor consequently of mutual help, nor of reconciliation of one man to another; and therefore they are to remain still in the condition of "war," which is contrary to the first and fundamental law of Nature, which commands men to "seek peace." The breach of this law is called "ingratitude," and hath the same relation to grace that injustice hath to obligation by covenant.

A fifth law of Nature, is "complaisance," that is to say, "that every man strive to accommodate himself to the rest." For the understanding whereof, we may consider that there is in men's aptness to society, a diversity of nature, rising from their diversity of affections, not unlike to that we see in stones brought together for building of an edifice. For as that stone which by the asperity and irregularity of figure takes more room from others than itself fills, and for the hardness cannot be easily made plain, and thereby hinders the building, is by the builders cast away as unprofitable and troublesome, so also a man that by asperity of nature will strive to retain those things which to himself are superfluous and to others necessary, and for the stubbornness of his passions cannot be corrected, is to be left or cast out of society as cumbersome thereunto.

For seeing every man, not only by right but also by necessity of nature, is supposed to endeavor all he can to obtain that which is necessary for his conversation, he that shall oppose himself against it for things superfluous is guilty of the war that thereupon is to follow; and therefore doth that which is contrary to the fundamental law of Nature, which commands "to seek peace." The observers of this law may be called "sociable"— the Latins call them *commodi;* the contrary, "stubborn," "insociable," "froward," "intractable."

A sixth law of Nature is this, "that, upon caution of the future time, a man ought to pardon the offenses past of them that, repenting, desire it." For "pardon" is nothing but granting of peace, which, though granted to them that persevere in their hostility, be not peace but fear; yet not granted to them that give caution of the future time is sign of an aversion to peace, and therefore contrary to the law of Nature.

A seventh is, "that in revenges," that is, retribution of evil for evil, "men look not at the greatness of the evil past but the greatness of the good to follow." Whereby we are forbidden to inflict punishment with any other design than for correction of the offender or direction of others. For this law is consequent to the next before it, that commands pardon, upon security of the future time. Besides, revenge, without respect to the example and profit to come, is a triumph or glorying in the hurt of another tending to no end; for the end is always somewhat to come; and glorying to no end is vainglory and contrary to reason, and to hurt without reason tends to the introduction of war, which is against the law of Nature, and is commonly by the name of "cruelty."

*   *   *

PART II—OF COMMONWEALTH

Chapter 17. Of the Causes, Generation, and Definition of a Commonwealth

The final cause, end, or design of men, who naturally love liberty, and dominion over others, in the introduction of that restraint upon themselves, in which we see them live in commonwealths, is the foresight of their own preservation, and of a more contented life thereby; that is to say, of getting themselves out from that miserable condition of war, which is necessarily consequent, as hath been shown in Chapter XIII, to the natural passions of men, when there is no visible power to keep them in awe, and tie them by fear of punishment to the performance of their covenants, and observation of those laws of nature set down in the fourteenth and fifteenth chapters.

For the laws of nature, as "justice," "equity," "modesty," "mercy," and, in sum, "doing to others, as we would be done to," of themselves, without the terror of some power, to cause them to be observed, are contrary to our natural passions, that carry us to partiality, pride, revenge, and the like. And covenants, without the sword, are but words, and of no strength to secure a man at all. Therefore notwithstanding the laws of nature (which every one hath then kept, when he has the will to keep them, when he can do it safely) if there be no power erected, or not great enough for our security; every man will, and may lawfully rely on his own strength and art, for caution against all other men. And in all places, where men have lived by small families, to rob and spoil one another, has been a trade, and so far from being reputed against the law of nature, that the greater spoils they gained, the greater was their honor; and men observed no other laws therein, but the laws of honor; that is, to abstain from cruelty, leaving to men their lives, and instruments of husbandry. And as small families did then; so now do cities and kingdoms which are but greater families, for their own security, enlarge their dominions, upon all pretenses of danger, and fear of invasion, or assistance that may be given to invaders, and endeavor as much as they can, to subdue, or weaken their neighbors, by open force, and secret arts, for want of other caution, justly; and are remembered for it in after ages with honor.

Nor is it the joining together of a small number of men, that gives them this security; because in small numbers, small additions on the one side or the other, make the advantage of strength so great, as is sufficient to carry the victory; and therefore gives encouragement to an invasion. The multitude sufficient to confide in for our security, is not determined by any certain number, but by comparison with the enemy we fear; and is then sufficient, when the odds of the enemy is not of so visible and conspicuous moment, to determine the event of war, as to move him to attempt.

And be there never so great a multitude; yet if their actions be directed according to their particular judgments, and particular appetites, they can expect thereby no defence, nor protection, neither against a common enemy, nor against the injuries of one another. For being distracted in opinions concerning the best use and application of

The execution of King Charles I of England, 1649, engraving by Wenceslaus Holler (1607–1677). Hobbes considered this event a horrible example of what happens when the sovereign does not have absolute power. (*Library of Congress*)

their strength, they do not help but hinder one another; and reduce their strength by mutual opposition to nothing: whereby they are easily, not only subdued by a very few that agree together; but also when there is no common enemy, they make war upon each other, for their particular interests. For if we could suppose a great multitude of men to consent in the observation of justice, and other laws of nature, without a common power to keep them all in awe; we might as well suppose all mankind to do the same; and then there neither would be, nor need to be any civil government, or commonwealth at all; because there would be peace without subjection.

Nor is it enough for the security, which men desire should last all the time of their life, that they be governed, and directed by one judgment, for a limited time; as in one battle, or one war. For though they obtain a victory by their unanimous endeavor against a foreign enemy; yet afterwards, when either they have no common enemy, or he that by one part is held for an enemy, is by another part held for a friend, they must needs by the difference of their interests dissolve, and fall again into a war amongst themselves.

It is true that certain living creatures, as bees, and ants, live sociably one with another, which are therefore by Aristotle numbered amongst political creatures; and yet have no other direction, than their particular judgments and appetites; nor speech, whereby one of them can signify to another, what he thinks expedient for the common benefit: and therefore some man may perhaps desire to know, why mankind cannot do the same. To which I answer,

First, that men are continually in competition for honor and dignity, which these creatures are not; and consequently amongst men there arises on that ground, envy and hatred, and finally war; but amongst these not so.

Secondly, that amongst these creatures, the common good differs not from the private; and being by nature inclined to their private, they procure thereby the common benefit. But man, whose joy consists in comparing himself with other men, can relish nothing but what is eminent.

Thirdly, that these creatures, having not, as man, the use of reason, do not see, nor think they see any fault, in the administration of their common business; whereas amongst men, there are very many, that think themselves wiser, and abler to govern the public, better than the rest; and these strive to reform and innovate, one this way, another that way; and thereby bring it into distraction and civil war.

Fourthly, that these creatures, though they have some use of voice, in making known to one another their desires, and other affections; yet they want that art of words, by which some men can represent to others, that which is good, in the likeness of evil; and evil, in the likeness of good; and augment, or diminish the apparent greatness of good and evil; discontenting men, and troubling their peace at their pleasure.

Fifthly, irrational creatures cannot distinguish between "injury," and "damage"; and therefore as long as they be at ease, they are not offended with their fellows: whereas man is then most troublesome, when he is most at ease: for then it is that he loves to shew his wisdom, and control the actions of them that govern the commonwealth.

Lastly, the agreement of these creatures is natural; that of men, is by covenant only, which is artificial: and therefore it is no wonder if there be somewhat else required, besides covenant, to make their agreement constant and lasting; which is a common power, to keep them in awe, and to direct their actions to the common benefit.

The only way to erect such a common power, as may be able to defend them from the invasion of foreigners, and the injuries of one another, and thereby to secure them in such sort, as that by their own industry, and by the fruits of the earth, they may nourish themselves and live contentedly; is, to confer all their power and strength upon one man, or upon one assembly of men, that may reduce all their wills, by plurality of voices, unto one will: which is as much as to say, to appoint one man, or assembly of men, to bear their person; and every one to own, and acknowledge himself to be author of whatsoever he that so bears their person, shall act, or cause to be acted, in those things which concern the common Peace and safety; and therein to submit their wills, every one to his will, and their judgments, to his judgment. This is more than consent, or concord; it is a real unity of them all, in one and the same person, made by covenant of every man with every man, in such manner, as if every man should say to every man, "I authorize and give up my right of governing myself to this man, or to this as- sembly of men, on this condition, that thou give up thy right to him, and authorize all his actions in like manner." This done, the multitude so united in one person, is called a COMMONWEALTH, in Latin *CIVITAS*. This is the generation of that great LEVIATHAN, or rather, to speak more reverently, of that "mortal god," to which we owe under the "immortal God," our peace and defence. For by this authority, given him by every particular man in the commonwealth, he hath the use of so much power and strength conferred on him, that by terror thereof, he is enabled to form the wills of them all, to peace at home, and mutual aid against their enemies abroad. And in him consists the essence of the commonwealth; which, to define it, "is one person, of whose acts a great multitude, by mutual covenants one with another, have made them- selves every one the author, to the end he may use the strength and means of them all, as he shall think expedient, for their peace and common defence."

And he that carries this person, is called SOVEREIGN, and said to have sover- eign power; and every one besides, his SUBJECT.

The attaining to this sovereign power, is by two ways. One, by natural force; as when a man makes his children, to submit themselves, and their children to his govern- ment, as being able to destroy them if they refuse; or by war subdues his enemies to his will, giving them their lives on that condition. The other, is when men agree amongst themselves, to submit to some man, or assembly of men, voluntarily, on confidence to be protected by him against all others. This latter, may be called a political common- wealth, or commonwealth by "institution"; and the former, a commonwealth by "ac- quisition." And first, I shall speak of a commonwealth by institution.

Chapter 18. Of the Rights of Sovereigns by Institution

A "commonwealth" is said to be "instituted," when a "multitude" of men do agree, and "covenant, every one, with every one," that to whatsoever "man," or "assembly of men," shall be given by the major part, the "right" to "present" the person of them all, that is to say, to be their "representative"; every one, as well he that "voted for it," as he that "voted against it," shall "authorize" all the actions and judgments, of that man, or assembly of men, in the same manner, as if they were his own, to the end, to live peaceably amongst themselves, and be protected against other men.

From this institution of a commonwealth are derived all the "rights," and facul- ties of him, or them, on whom the sovereign power is conferred by the consent of the people assembled.

First, because they covenant, it is to be understood, they are not obliged by for- mer covenant to any thing repugnant hereunto. And consequently they that have al- ready instituted a commonwealth, being thereby bound by covenant, to own the actions, and judgments of one, cannot lawfully make a new covenant, amongst themselves, to be obedient to any other, in any thing whatsoever, without his permission. And therefore, they that are subjects to a monarch, cannot without his leave cast off monarchy, and return to the confusion of a disunited multitude; nor transfer their person from him that bears it, to another man, or other assembly of men: for they are bound, every man to every man, to own, and be reputed author of all, that he that already is their sovereign, shall do, and judge fit to be done: so that any one man dissenting, all the rest should break their covenant made to that man, which is injustice: and they have also every man given the sovereignty to him that bears their person; and therefore if they depose him, they take from him that which is his own, and so again it is injustice. Besides, if he that attempts to depose his sovereign, be killed, or punished by him for such attempt, he is author of his own punishment, as being by the institution, author of all his sovereign shall do: and because it is injustice for a man to do any thing, for which he may be punished by his own authority, he is also upon that title, unjust. And whereas some men have pretended for their disobedience to their sovereign, a new covenant, made, not with men, but with God; this also is unjust: for there is no covenant with God, but by mediation of somebody that represents God's person which none doth but God's lieutenant, who hath the sovereignty under God. But this pretence of covenant with God, is so evident a lie, even in the pretenders' own consciences, that it is not only an act of an unjust, but also of a vile, and unmanly disposition.

Secondly, because the right of bearing the person of them all, is given to him they make sovereign, by covenant only of one to another, and not of him to any of them; there can happen no breach of covenant on the part of the sovereign; and consequently none of his subjects, by any pretence of forfeiture, can be freed from his subjection. That he which is made sovereign makes no covenant with his subjects beforehand, is manifest; because either he must make it with the whole multitude, as one party to the covenant; or he must make a several covenant with every man. With the whole, as one party, it is impossible; because as yet they are not one person: and if he make so many several covenants as there be men, those covenants after he hath the sovereignty are void; because what act soever can be pretended by any one of them for breach thereof, is the act both of himself, and of all the rest, because done in the person, and by the right of every one of them in particular. Besides, if any one, or more of them, pretend a breach of the covenant made by the sovereign at his institution; and others, or one other of his subjects, or himself alone, pretend there was no such breach, there is in this case, no judge to decide the controversy; it returns therefore to the sword again; and every man recovers the right of protecting himself by his own strength, contrary to the design they had in the institution. It is therefore in vain to grant sovereignty by way of precedent covenant. The opinion that any monarch receives his power by covenant, that is to say, on condition, proceeds from want of understanding this easy truth, that covenants being but words and breath, have no force to oblige, contain, constrain, or protect any man, but what it has from the public sword; that is, from the untied hands of that man, or assembly of men that hath the sovereignty, and whose actions are avouched by them all, and performed by the strength of them all, in him united. But when an assembly of men is made sovereign; then no man imagines any such covenant to have passed in the institution; for no man is so dull as to say, for example, the people of Rome made a covenant with the Romans, to hold the sovereignty on such or such conditions; which not performed, the Romans might lawfully depose the Roman people. That men see not the reason to be alike in a monarchy, and in a popular government, proceeds from the ambition of some, that are kinder to the government of an assembly, whereof they may hope to participate, than of monarchy, which they despair to enjoy.

Thirdly, because the major part hath by consenting voices declared a sovereign; he that dissented must now consent with the rest—that is, be contented to avow all the actions he shall do, or else justly be destroyed by the rest. For if he voluntarily entered into the congregation of them that were assembled, he sufficiently declared thereby his will, and therefore tacitly covenanted, to stand to what the major part should ordain: and therefore if he refuse to stand thereto, or make protestation against any of their decrees, he does contrary to his covenant, and therefore unjustly. And whether he be of the congregation, or not; and whether his consent be asked, or not, he must either submit to their decrees, or be left in the condition of war he was in before; wherein he might without injustice be destroyed by any man whatsoever.

Fourthly, because every subject is by this institution author of all the actions, and judgments of the sovereign instituted; it follows, that whatsoever he doth, it can be no injury to any of his subjects; nor ought he to be by any of them accused of injustice. For he that doth anything by authority from another, doth therein no injury to him by whose authority he acts: but by this institution of a commonwealth, every particular man is author of all the sovereign doth: and consequently he that complains of injury from his sovereign, complains of that whereof he himself is author, and therefore ought not to accuse any man but himself; no nor himself of injury; because to do injury to one's self, is impossible. It is true that they that have sovereign power may commit iniquity; but not injustice, or injury in the proper signification.

Fifthly, and consequently to that which was said last, no man that hath sovereign power can justly be put to death, or otherwise in any manner by his subject punished. For seeing every subject is author of the actions of his sovereign; he punishes another for the actions committed by himself.

And because the end of this institution, is the peace and defence of them all; and whosoever has right to the end, has right to the means; it belongs of right, to whatsoever man, or assembly that hath the sovereignty, to be judge both of the means of peace and defence, and also of the hindrances, and disturbances of the same; and to do whatsoever he shall think necessary to be done, both beforehand, for the preserving of peace and security, by prevention of discord at home, and hostility from abroad; and, when peace and security are lost, for the recovery of the same. And therefore,

Sixthly, it is annexed to the sovereignty, to be judge of what opinions and doctrines are averse, and what conducing to peace; and consequently, on what occasions, how far, and what men are to be trusted withal, in speaking to multitudes of people; and who shall examine the doctrines of all books before they be published. For the actions of men proceed from their opinions; and in the well-governing of opinions, consists the well-governing of men's actions, in order to their peace, and concord. And though in matter of doctrine, nothing ought to be regarded but the truth; yet this is not repugnant to regulating the same by peace. For doctrine repugnant to peace, can no more be true, than peace and concord can be against the law of nature. It is true, that in a commonwealth, where by the negligence, or unskillfulness of governors, and teachers, false doctrines are by time generally received; the contrary truths may be generally offensive. Yet the most sudden, and rough bustling in of a new truth, that can be, does never break the peace, but only sometimes awake the war. For those men that are so remissly governed, that they dare take up arms to defend, or introduce an opinion, are still in war; and their condition not peace, but only a cessation of arms for fear of one another; and they live, as it were, in the precincts of battle continually. It belongs therefore to him that hath the sovereign power, to be judge, or constitute all judges of opinions and doctrines, as a thing necessary to peace; thereby to prevent discord and civil war.

Seventhly, is annexed to the sovereignty, the whole power of prescribing the rules, whereby every man may know, what goods he may enjoy, and what actions he may do, without being molested by any of his fellow-subjects; and this is it men call "propriety." For before constitution of sovereign power, as hath already been shown, all men had right to all things; which necessarily causes war: and therefore this propriety, being necessary to peace, and depending on sovereign power, is the act of that power, in order to the public peace. These rules of propriety, or *meum* and *tuum*, and of "good," "evil," "lawful," and "unlawful" in the actions of subjects, are the civil laws; that is to say, the laws of each commonwealth in particular; though the name of civil law be now restrained to the ancient civil laws of the city of Rome—which being the head of a great part of the world, her laws at that time were in these parts the civil law.

Eighthly, is annexed to the sovereignty, the right judicature; that is to say, of hearing and deciding all controversies, which may arise concerning law, either civil, or natural; or concerning fact. For without the decision of controversies, there is no protection of one subject, against the injuries of another; the laws concerning *meum* and *tuum* are in vain; and to every man remains, from the natural and necessary appetite of his own conservation, the right of protecting himself by his private strength, which is the condition of war, and contrary to the end for which every commonwealth is instituted.

Ninthly, is annexed to the sovereignty, the right of making war and peace with other nations, and commonwealths; that is to say, of judging when it is for the public good, and how great forces are to be assembled, armed, and paid for that end; and to levy money upon the subjects, to defray the expenses thereof. For the power by which the people are to be defended, consists in their armies; and the strength of an army, in the union of their strength under one command, which command the sovereign instituted, therefore hath; because the command of the "militia," without other institution, makes him that hath it sovereign. And therefore whosoever is made general of an army, he that hath the sovereign power is always generalissimo.

Tenthly, is annexed to the sovereignty, the choosing of all counsellors, ministers, magistrates, and officers, both in peace, and war. For seeing the sovereign is charged with the end, which is the common peace and defence, he is understood to have power to use such means, as he shall think most fit for his discharge.

Eleventhly, to the sovereign is committed the power of rewarding with riches, or honor, and of punishing with corporal or pecuniary punishment, or with ignominy, every subject according to the law he hath formerly made; or if there be no law made, according as he shall judge most to conduce to the encouraging of men to serve the commonwealth, or deterring of them from doing disservice to the same.

Lastly, considering what value men are naturally apt to set upon themselves; what respect they look for from others; and how little they value other men; from whence continually arise amongst them, emulation, quarrels, factions, and at last war, to the destroying of one another, and diminution of their strength against a common enemy; it is necessary that there be laws of honor, and a public rate of the worth of such men as have deserved, or are able to deserve well of the commonwealth; and that there be force in the hands of some or other, to put those laws in execution. But it hath already been shown, that not only the whole "militia," or forces of the commonwealth; but also the judicature of all controversies, is annexed to the sovereignty. To the sovereign therefore it belongs also to give titles of honor; and to appoint what order of place, and dignity, each man shall hold; and what signs of respect, in public or private meetings, they shall give to one another.

These are the rights, which make the essence of sovereignty, and which are the marks, whereby a man may discern in what man, or assembly of men, the sovereign power is placed, and resides. For these are incommunicable, and inseparable. The power to coin money; to dispose of the estate and persons of infant heirs; to have pre-emption in markets; and all other statute prerogatives, may be transferred by the sovereign; and yet the power to protect his subjects be retained. But if he transfer the "militia," he retains the judicature in vain, for want of execution of the laws: or if he grant away the power of raising money; the "militia" is in vain; or if he give away the government of doctrines, men will be frighted into rebellion with the fear of spirits. And so if we consider any one of the said rights, we shall presently see, that the holding of all the rest will produce no effect, in the conservation of peace and justice, the end for which all commonwealths are instituted. And this division is it, whereof it is said, "a kingdom divided in itself cannot stand": for unless this division precede, division into opposite armies can never happen. If there had not first been an opinion received of the greatest part of England, that these powers were divided between the King, and the Lords, and the House of Commons, the people had never been divided and fallen into this civil war; first between those that disagreed in politics; and after between the dissenters about the liberty of religion; which have so instructed men in this point of sovereign right, that there be few now in England that do not see, that these rights are inseparable, and will be so generally acknowledged at the next return of peace; and so continue, till their miseries are forgotten; and no longer, except the vulgar be better taught than they have hitherto been.

And because they are essential and inseparable rights, it follows necessarily, that in whatsoever words any of them seem to be granted away, yet if the sovereign power itself be not in direct terms renounced, and the name of sovereign no more given by the grantees to him that grants them, the grant is void: for when he has granted all he can, if we grant back the sovereignty, all is restored, as inseparably annexed thereunto.

This great authority being indivisible and inseparably annexed to the sovereignty, there is little ground for the opinion of them, that say of sovereign kings, though they be *singulis majores*, of greater power than every one of their subjects, yet they be *universis minores*, of less power than them all together. For if by "all together," they mean not the collective body as one person, then "all together," and "every one," signify the same; and the speech is absurd. But if by "all together," they understand them as one person, which person the sovereign bears, then the power of all together, is the same with the sovereign's power; and so again the speech is absurd: which absurdity they see well enough, when the sovereignty is in an assembly of the people; but in a monarch they see it not; and yet the power of sovereignty is the same in whomsoever it be placed.

And as the power, so also the honor of the sovereign, ought to be greater, than that of any, or all the subjects. For in the sovereignty is the fountain of honor. The dignities of lord, earl, duke, and prince are his creatures. As in the presence of the master, the servants are equal, and without any honor at all; so are the subjects, in the presence of the sovereign. And though they shine some more, some less, when they are out of his sight; yet in his presence, they shine no more than the stars in the presence of the sun.

But a man may here object, that the condition of subjects is very miserable; as being obnoxious to the lusts, and other irregular passions of him, or them that have so unlimited a power in their hands. And commonly they that live under a monarch, think it the fault of monarchy; and they that live under the government of democracy, or other sovereign assembly, attribute all the inconvenience to that form of commonwealth; whereas the power in all forms, if they be perfect enough to protect them, is the same: not considering that the state of man can never be without some incommodity or other; and that the greatest, that in any form of government can possibly happen to the people in general, is scarce sensible in respect of the miseries, and horrible calamities, that accompany a civil war, or that dissolute condition of masterless men, without subjection to laws, and a coercive power to tie their hands from rapine and revenge: nor considering that the greatest pressure of sovereign governors, proceeds not from any delight, or profit they can expect in the damage or weakening of their subjects, in whose vigor, consists their own strength and glory; but in the restiveness of themselves, that unwillingly contributing to their own defence, make it necessary for their governors to draw from them what they can in time of peace, that they may have means on any emergent occasion, or sudden need, to resist, or take advantage on their enemies. For all men are by nature provided of notable multiplying glasses, that is their passions and self-love, through which, every little payment appears a great grievance; but are destitute of those prospective glasses, namely moral and civil science, to see afar off the miseries that hang over them, and cannot without such payments be avoided.

* * *

CHAPTER 21. OF THE LIBERTY OF SUBJECTS

LIBERTY, or FREEDOM, signifies, properly, the absence of opposition; by opposition, I mean external impediments of motion; and may be applied no less to irrational, and inanimate creatures, than to rational. For whatsoever is so tied, or environed, as it cannot move but within a certain space, which space is determined by the opposition of some external body, we say it hath not liberty to go further. And so of all living creatures, whilst they are imprisoned, or restrained, with walls, or chains; and of the water whilst it is kept in by banks, or vessels, that otherwise would spread itself into a larger space, we use to say, they are not at liberty, to move in such manner, as without those external impediments they would. But when the impediment of motion, is in the constitution of the thing itself, we use not to say; it wants the liberty; but the power to move; as when a stone lies still, or a man is fastened to his bed by sickness.

And according to this proper, and generally received meaning of the word, a FREEMAN, is he, that in those things, which by his strength and wit he is able to do, is not hindered to do what he has a will to. But when the words "free," and "liberty," are applied to any thing but "bodies," they are abused; for that which is not subject to motion, is not subject to impediment: and therefore, when it is said, for example, the way is free, no liberty of the way is signified, but of those that walk in it without stop. And when we say a gift is free, there is not meant any liberty of the gift but of the giver, that was not bound by any law or covenant to give it. So when we "speak freely," it is not the liberty of voice, or pronunciation, but of the man, whom no law hath obliged to speak otherwise than he did. Lastly, from the use of the word "freewill," no liberty can be inferred of the will, desire, or inclination, but the liberty of the man; which consists in this, that he finds no stop, in doing what he has the will, desire, or inclination to do.

Fear and liberty are consistent; as when a man throws his goods into the sea for "fear" the ship should sink, he doth it nevertheless very willingly, and may refuse to do it if he will: it is therefore the action of one that was "free"; so a man sometimes pays his debt, only for "fear" of imprisonment, which because nobody hindered him from detaining, was the action of a man at "liberty." And generally all actions which men do in commonwealths, for fear of the law, are actions, which the doers had liberty to omit.

"Liberty," and "necessity" are consistent: as in the water, that hath not only "liberty," but a "necessity" of descending by the channel; so likewise in the actions which men voluntarily do: which, because they proceed from their will, proceed from liberty; and yet, because every act of man's will, and every desire, and inclination proceeds from some cause, and that from another cause, in a continual chain, whose first link is in the hand of God the first of all causes, proceed from "necessity." So that to him that could see the connection of those causes, the necessity of all men's voluntary actions, would appear manifest. And therefore God, that sees, and disposes all things, sees also that the "liberty" of man in doing what he will, is accompanied with the "necessity" of doing that which God will, and no more, nor less. For though men may do many things, which God does not command, nor is therefore author of them; yet they can have no passion, nor appetite to any thing, of which appetite God's will is not the cause. And did not his will assure the "necessity" of man's will, and consequently of all that on man's will depends, the "liberty" of men would be a contradiction, and impediment to the omnipotence and "liberty" of God. And this shall suffice, as to the matter in hand, of that natural "liberty," which only is properly called "liberty."

But as men, for the attaining of peace, and conservation of themselves thereby, have made an artificial man, which we call a commonwealth; so also have they made artificial chains, called "civil laws," which they themselves, by mutual covenants, have fastened at one end, to the lips of that man, or assembly, to whom they have given the sovereign power; and at the other end to their own ears. These bonds, in their own nature but weak, may nevertheless be made to hold, by the danger, though not by the difficulty of breaking them.

In relation to these bonds only it is, that I am to speak now, of the "liberty" of "subjects." For seeing there is no commonwealth in the world, wherein there be rules enough set down, for the regulating of all the actions, and words of men; as being a thing impossible: it follows necessarily, that in all kinds of actions by the laws pretermitted, men have the liberty, of doing what their own reasons shall suggest, for the most profitable to themselves. For if we take liberty in the proper sense, for corporal liberty; that is to say, freedom from chains and prison; it were very absurd for men to clamor as they do, for the liberty they so manifestly enjoy. Again, if we take liberty, for an exemption from laws, it is no less absurd, for men to demand as they do, that liberty, by which all other men may be masters of their lives. And yet, as absurd as it is, this is it they demand; not knowing that the laws are of no power to protect them, without a sword in the hands of a man, or men, to cause those laws to be put in execution. The liberty of a subject, lies therefore only in those things, which in regulating their actions, the sovereign hath pretermitted: such as is the liberty to buy, and sell, and otherwise contract with one another; to choose their own abode, their own diet, their own trade of life, and institute their children as they themselves think fit; and the like.

Nevertheless we are not to understand, that by such liberty, the sovereign power of life and death, is either abolished, or limited. For it has been already shown, that nothing the sovereign representative can do to a subject, on what pretence soever, can properly be called injustice, or injury; because every subject is author of every act the sovereign doth; so that he never wants right to any thing, otherwise, than as he himself is the subject of God, and bound thereby to observe the laws of nature. And therefore it may, and doth often happen in commonwealths, that a subject may be put to death, by the command of the sovereign power; and yet neither do the other wrong: as when

Jephtha caused his daughter to be sacrificed: in which, and the like cases, he that so dies, had liberty to do the action, for which he is nevertheless, without injury put to death. And the same holds also in a sovereign prince, that puts to death an innocent subject. For though the action be against the law of nature, as being contrary to equity, as was the killing of Uriah, by David; yet it was not an injury to Uriah, but to God. Not to Uriah, because the right to do what he pleased was given him by Uriah himself: and yet to God, because David was God's subject, and prohibited all iniquity by the law of nature: which distinction, David himself, when he repented the fact, evidently confirmed, saying, "To thee only have I sinned." In the same manner, the people of Athens, when they banished the most potent of their commonwealth for ten years, thought they committed no injustice; and yet they never questioned what crime he had done; but what hurt he would do: nay they commanded the banishment of they knew not whom; and every citizen bringing his oystershell into the market place, written with the name of him he desired should be banished, without actually accusing him, sometimes banished an Aristides, for his reputation of justice; and sometimes a scurrilous jester, as Hyperbolus, to make a jest of it. And yet a man cannot say, the sovereign people of Athens wanted right to banish them; or an Athenian the liberty to jest, or to be just.

The liberty, whereof there is so frequent and honorable mention, in the histories, and philosophy of the ancient Greeks, and Romans, and in the writings, and discourse of those that from them have received all their learning in the politics, is not the liberty of particular men; but the liberty of the commonwealth: which is the same with that which every man then should have, if there were no civil laws, nor commonwealth at all. And the effects of it also be the same. For as amongst masterless men, there is perpetual war, of every man against his neighbor; no inheritance, to transmit to the son, nor to expect from the father; no propriety of goods, or lands; no security; but a full and absolute liberty in every particular man: so in states, and commonwealths not dependent on one another, every commonwealth, not every man, has an absolute liberty, to do what it shall judge, that is to say, what that man, or assembly that represents it, shall judge most conducing to their benefit. But withal, they live in the condition of a perpetual war, and upon the confines of battle, with their frontiers armed, and cannons planted against their neighbors round about. The Athenians, and Romans were free; that is, free commonwealths: not that any particular men had the liberty to resist their own representative; but that their representative had the liberty to resist, or invade other people. There is written on the turrets of the city of Lucca in great characters at this day, the word LIBERTAS; yet no man can thence infer, that a particular man has more liberty, or immunity from the service of the commonwealth there, than in Constantinople. Whether a commonwealth be monarchical, or popular, the freedom is still the same.

But it is an easy thing, for men to be deceived, by the specious name of liberty; and for want of judgment to distinguish, mistake that for their private inheritance, and birth-right, which is the right of the public only. And when the same error is confirmed by the authority of men in reputation for their writings on this subject, it is no wonder if it produce sedition, and change of government. In these western parts of the world, we are made to receive our opinions concerning the institution, and rights of commonwealths, from Aristotle, Cicero, and other men, Greeks and Romans, that living under popular states, derived those rights, not from the principles of nature, but transcribed them into their books, out of the practice of their own commonwealths, which were popular; as the grammarians describe the rules of language, out of the practice of the time; or the rules of poetry, out of the poems of Homer and Virgil. And because the Athenians were taught, to keep them from desire of changing their government, that they were freemen, and all that lived under monarchy were slaves; therefore Aristotle puts it down in his Politics (lib. 6. cap. ii.): "In democracy, LIBERTY is to be supposed: for it is commonly held, that no man is FREE in any other government." And as Aristotle; so Cicero, and other writers have grounded their civil doctrine, on the opinions of the Romans, who were taught to hate monarchy, at first, by them that having deposed their sovereign, shared amongst them the sovereignty of Rome; and afterwards by their successors. And by reading of these Greek, and Latin authors, men from their childhood have gotten a habit, under a false show of liberty, of favoring tumults, and of licentious controlling the actions of their sovereigns, and again of controlling those controllers; with the effusion of so much blood, as I think I may truly say, there was never any thing so dearly bought, as these western parts have bought the learning of the Greek and Latin tongues.

To come now to the particulars of the true liberty of a subject; that is to say, what are the things, which though commanded by the sovereign, he may nevertheless, without injustice, refuse to do; we are to consider, what rights we pass away, when we make a commonwealth; or, which is all one, what liberty we deny ourselves, by owning all the actions, without exception, of the man, or assembly we make our sovereign. For in the act of our "submission," consists both our "obligation," and our "liberty"; which must therefore be inferred by arguments taken from thence; there being no obligation on any man, which arises not from some act of his own; for all men equally, are by nature free. And because such arguments, must either be drawn from the express words, I "authorize all his actions," or from the intention of him that submits himself to his power, which intention is to be understood by the end for which he so submits; the obligation, and liberty of the subject, is to be derived, either from those words, or others equivalent; or else from the end of the institution of sovereignty, namely, the peace of the subjects within themselves, and their defence against a common enemy.

First therefore, seeing sovereignty by institution, is by covenant of every one to every one; and sovereignty by acquisition, by covenants of the vanquished to the victor, or child to the parent; it is manifest, that every subject has liberty in all those things, the right whereof cannot by covenant be transferred. I have shown before in the 14th chapter, that covenants, not to defend a man's own body, are void. Therefore,

If the sovereign command a man, though justly condemned, to kill, wound, or maim himself; or not to resist those that assault him; or to abstain from the use of food, air, medicine, or any other thing, without which he cannot live; yet hath that man the liberty to disobey.

If a man be interrogated by the sovereign, or his authority, concerning a crime done by himself, he is not bound, without assurance of pardon, to confess it; because no man, as I have shown in the same chapter, can be obliged by covenant to accuse himself.

Again, the consent of a subject to sovereign power, is contained in these words, "I authorize, or take upon me, all his actions"; in which there is no restriction at all, of his own former natural liberty: for by allowing him to "kill me," I am not bound to kill myself when he commands me. It is one thing to say, "kill me, or my fellow, if you please"; another thing to say, "I will kill myself, or my fellow." It follows therefore, that

No man is bound by the words themselves, either to kill himself, or any other man; and consequently, that the obligation a man may sometimes have, upon the command of the sovereign to execute any dangerous, or dishonorable office, depends not on the words of our submission; but on the intention, which is to be understood by the end thereof. When therefore our refusal to obey, frustrates the end for which the sovereignty was ordained; then there is no liberty to refuse: otherwise there is.

Upon this ground, a man that is commanded as a soldier to fight against the enemy, though his sovereign have right enough to punish his refusal with death, may nevertheless in many cases refuse, without injustice; as when he substitutes a sufficient soldier in his place: for in this case he deserts not the service of the commonwealth. And there is allowance to be made for natural timorousness; not only to women, of whom no such dangerous duty is expected, but also to men of feminine courage. When armies fight, there is on one side, or both, a running away; yet when they do it not out of treachery, but fear, they are not esteemed to do it unjustly, but dishonorably. For the same reason, to avoid battle, is not injustice, but cowardice. But he that enrolls himself a soldier, or takes imprest money, takes away the excuse of a timorous nature; and is obliged, not only to go to the battle, but also not to run from it, without his captain's leave. And when the defence of the commonwealth, requires at once the help of all that are able to bear arms, every one is obliged; because otherwise the institution of the commonwealth, which they have not the purpose, or courage to preserve, was in vain.

To resist the sword of the commonwealth, in defence of another man, guilty, or innocent, no man hath liberty; because such liberty, takes away from the sovereign, the means of protecting us; and is therefore destructive of the very essence of government. But in case a great many men together, have already resisted the sovereign power unjustly, or committed some capital crime, for which every one of them expects death, whether have they not the liberty then to join together, and assist, and defend one another? Certainly they have: for they but defend their lives, which the guilty man may as well do, as the innocent. There was indeed injustice in the first breach of their duty; their bearing of arms subsequent to it, though it be to maintain what they have done, is no new unjust act. And if it be only to defend their persons, it is not unjust at all. But the offer of pardon takes from them, to whom it is offered, the plea of self-defence, and makes their perseverance in assisting, or defending the rest, unlawful.

As for other liberties, they depend on the silence of the law. In cases where the sovereign has prescribed no rule, there the subject hath the liberty to do, or forbear, according to his own discretion. And therefore such liberty is in some places more, and in some less; and in some times more, in other times less, according as they that have the sovereignty shall think most convenient. As for example, there was a time, when in England a man might enter into his own land, and dispossess such as wrongfully possessed it, by force. But in aftertimes, that liberty of forcible entry, was taken away by a statute made, by the king, in parliament. And in some places of the world, men have the liberty of many wives: in other places, such liberty is not allowed.

If a subject have a controversy with his sovereign, of debt, or of right of possession of lands or goods, or concerning any service required at his hands, or concerning any penalty, corporal, or pecuniary, grounded on a precedent law; he hath the same liberty to sue for his right, as if it were against a subject; and before such judges, as are appointed by the sovereign. For seeing the sovereign demands by force of a former law, and not by virtue of his power; he declares thereby, that he requires no more, than shall appear to be due by that law. The suit therefore is not contrary to the will of the sovereign; and consequently the subject hath the liberty to demand the hearing of his cause; and sentence, according to that law. But if he demand, or take any thing by pretence of his power; there lies, in that case, no action of law; for all that is done by him in virtue of his power, is done by the authority of every subject, and consequently he that brings an action against the sovereign, brings it against himself.

If a monarch, or sovereign assembly, grant a liberty to all, or any of his subjects, which grant standing, he is disabled to provide for their safety, the grant is void; unless he directly renounce, or transfer the sovereignty to another. For in that he might openly, if it had been his will, and in plain terms, have renounced, or transferred it, and did not; it is to be understood it was not his will, but that the grant proceeded from ignorance of the repugnancy between such a liberty and the sovereign power; and therefore the sovereignty is still retained; and consequently all those powers, which are necessary to the exercising thereof; such as are the power of war, and peace, of judicature, of appointing officers, and councilors, of levying money, and the rest named in the eighteenth chapter.

The obligation of subjects to the sovereign, is understood to last as long, and no longer, than the power lasts, by which he is able to protect them. For the right men have by nature to protect themselves, when none else can protect them, can by no covenant be relinquished. The sovereignty is the soul of the commonwealth which once departed from the body, the members do no more receive their motion from it. The end of obedience is protection; which, wheresoever a man sees it, either in his own, or in another's sword, nature applies his obedience to it, and his endeavor to maintain it. And though sovereignty, in the intention of them that make it, be immortal; yet is it in its own nature, not only subject to violent death, by foreign war; but also through the ignorance, and passions of men, it hath in it, from the very institution, many seeds of a natural mortality, by intestine discord.

If a subject be taken prisoner in war; or his person, or his means of life be within the guards of the enemy, and hath his life and corporal liberty given him, on condition to be subject to the victor, he hath liberty to accept the condition; and having accepted it, is the subject of him that took him; because he had no other way to preserve himself. The case is the same, if he be detained on the same terms, in a foreign country. But if a man be held in prison, or bonds, or is not trusted with the liberty of his body; he cannot be understood to be bound by covenant to subjection; and therefore may, if he can, make his escape by any means whatsoever.

If a monarch shall relinquish the sovereignty, both for himself, and his heirs; his subjects return to the absolute liberty of nature; because, though nature may declare who are his sons, and who are the nearest of his kin; yet it depends on his own will, as hath been said in the precedent chapter, who shall be his heir. If therefore he will have no heir, there is no sovereignty, nor subjection. The case is the same, if he die without known kindred, and without declaration of his heir. For then there can no heir be known, and consequently no subjection be due.

If the sovereign banish his subject; during the banishment, he is not subject. But he that is sent on a message, or hath leave to travel, is still subject; but it is, by contract between sovereigns, not by virtue of the covenant of subjection. For whosoever enters into another's dominion, is subject to all the laws thereof; unless he have a privilege by the amity of the sovereigns, or by special license.

If a monarch subdued by war, render himself subject to the victor; his subjects are delivered from their former obligation, and become obliged to the victor. But if he be held prisoner, or have not the liberty of his own body; he is not understood to have given away the right of sovereignty; and therefore his subjects are obliged to yield obedience to the magistrates formerly placed, governing not in their own name, but in his. For, his right remaining, the question is only of the administration; that is to say, of the magistrates and officers; which, if he have not means to name, he is supposed to approve those, which he himself had formerly appointed.

BLAISE PASCAL
1623–1662

Blaise Pascal was the middle child of an upper-class magistrate in Clermont-Ferrand, France. His mother died when he was three years old, and five years later Pascal's father moved the family to Paris. His father, Etienne, an excellent amateur mathematician, educated young Blaise at home. Etienne first taught young Blaise Latin and Greek, deciding to wait on his own love, mathematics, until his son was older. By the age of twelve, however, Blaise had figured out many of the principles of Euclidian geometry on his own. His father finally relented and bought Blaise a copy of Euclid, which he devoured. Over the next several years, father and son attended weekly mathematical lectures and were regular guests at important intellectual salons in Paris. In 1638, the family underwent another trauma when Etienne Pascal was forced by a conflict with the powerful Cardinal Richelieu to flee Paris. However, Blaise Pascal's younger sister, Jacqueline, performed so well in a children's play for the Cardinal that their father was given a pardon and installed as tax commissioner for Rouen.

At Rouen Blaise Pascal began to concentrate on mathematics. While still a teenager, he wrote his first book (on conic sections in geometry) and developed a plan for a calculating machine to help his father with his tax work. In 1644, he built the first of the machine's several working models—no small feat given the state of metalworking at the time. Pascal's contributions to mathematics and computing machines were so important that a major contemporary programming language is named in his honor. Pascal also experimented on the nature of a vacuum showing that, contrary to Artistotle's belief, "Nature has no abhorrence of a vacuum."

In 1647 Pascal became seriously ill and returned to Paris with his younger sister to recover. Following his father's death in 1651, his sister entered a convent, leaving Pascal alone. Over the next several years Pascal seemed to drift: he outwardly enjoying the social life of Paris as a successful mathematician and eligible bachelor, but he was inwardly dissatisfied. Although he had undergone a conversion in 1646 under the influence of the Jansenists, a group of devout Catholics, Pascal still found himself without direction. On the night of November 23, 1654, Pascal had a remarkable second conversion experience, the description of which he sewed inside his coat:

> . . . From about half past ten in the evening until about half past midnight.
> Fire.
> God of Abraham, God of Isaac, God of Jacob, not of philosophers and scholars.
> Certainty, joy, certainty, emotion, sight, joy
> God of Jesus Christ. . . .
> Oblivious to the world and to everything except GOD. . . .
> This is life eternal, that they might know you,
> the only true God, and him whom you sent,
> Jesus Christ
> Jesus Christ
> I have cut myself off from him for ever. I have fled from him, denied
> him, crucified him.
> Let me never be cut off from him.
> He can only be kept by the ways taught in the Gospel.
> Sweet and total renunciation.
> Total submission to Jesus Christ and my director.
> Everlasting joy for one day's tribulation on earth.
> *I will not forget thy word.* Amen.*

Pascal committed himself to living out his faith by doing good works. He wrote a remarkable series of *Provincial Letters* defending the Jansenists against the Jesuits. Pascal also worked on one of the first regularly-scheduled public transit services, with profits for the poor; the line became operational shortly before Pascal's death in 1662. But Pascal's most important mature work was his *Apology for the Christian Religion,* the completed portion of which is now known as the *Pensées* (*Thoughts*).

*   *   *

Collected and published after Pascal's death at age thirty-nine, the *Pensées* is considered a French classic—despite its fragmentary character. Touching on numerous areas of religious and philosophical thought, the *Pensées* portray humanity "engulfed in the infinite immensity" of the universe. Unlike Descartes, Pascal claims that reason is insufficient to find certainty. While the *cogito* ("I think") is indeed one of God's greatest gift to humanity and "all our dignity consists . . . in thought," there is nevertheless something more important than thought and reason: the heart. As Pascal put it, "The heart has its reasons, which reason does not know."

---

*"The Memorial," Blaise Pascal, *Pensées and Other Writings,* translated by Honor Levi (Oxford: Oxford University Press, 1995), p. 178.

As for knowledge of God, Pascal claims that reason is utterly insufficient for the enterprise. Against Descartes, St. Thomas Aquinas, and others, proofs for God's existence and the Christian truth "are not of such a nature that they can be said to be absolutely convincing." There is always "both evidence and obscurity [enough] to enlighten some and [to] confuse others." Given that one can never *know* if there is a God, how can one *live* one's life? According to Pascal, one can never have true knowledge of *anything* until one has submitted to it—and so there can be no true knowledge of God until one has submitted to God as revealed in Jesus Christ. Is there, then, no rational basis for making the Christian commitment? In the selection given here, Pascal appeals to the *bon vivants* of Paris by asking them to consider faith as a wager. If you bet your life on God and you turn out to be right, you have gained eternity. If you are wrong and there is no God, what have you lost—except the possibility of "those poisonous pleasures, glory and luxury?" But, if you bet your life against the reality of God, you gain little if correct, but lose eternally if wrong.

Some critics have argued that Pascal's Wager hardly seems like faith at all—that it is a "calculating and self-regarding attitude" and is "profoundly irreligious."* Others have claimed that the wager leads not to Christianity, but to any religion with a great reward for belief and a great penalty for disbelief. Still others argue that the most reasonable choice is to avoid wagering at all until the evidence is clear. (See the suggested readings below.) However, to be fair, Pascal never claimed the wager was the *way* to faith or that it provided the *means* for proving Christian truth. His two goals were to show that while being *supra*rational, belief is not *ir*rational and one *must* decide. As Pascal put it,

> Do not then reprove for error those who have made a choice; for you know nothing about it. "No, but I blame them for having made, not this choice, but a choice . . . The true course is not to wager at all."
>
> Yes; but you must wager. It is not optional. You are embarked. Which will you choose then?

* * *

There is little consistency in the numbering of different editions of the *Pensées.* The system used here is from W.F. Trotter's translation.

The best general introduction to Pascal remains J.H. Broome, *Pascal* (London: E. Arnold, 1972). Other general studies include Émile Cailliet, *Pascal: The Emergence of Genius,* 2nd edition (New York: Harper, 1961); Morris Bishop, *Pascal: The Life of a Genius* (1936; reprint Westport, CO: Greenwood Press, 1968); Jean Mesnard, *Pascal,* translated by Claude and Marcia Abraham (University, AL: University of Alabama Press, 1969); Alban Krailsheimer, *Pascal,* Past Masters Series (Oxford: Oxford University Press, 1980); and Hugh M. Davidson, *Blaise Pascal* (Boston: Twayne, 1983). More specialized studies include F.T.H. Fletcher, *Pascal and the Mystical Tradition* (Oxford: Basil Blackwell, 1954); Jan Miel, *Pascal and Theology* (Baltimore, MD: Johns Hopkins University Press, 1969); Robert James Nelson, *Pascal: Adversary and Advocate* (Cambridge, MA: Harvard University Press, 1981); Sara E. Melzer, *Discourses of the Fall: A Study of Pascal's Pensées* (Berkeley, CA: University of California

---

*John Hick, *Philosophy of Religion,* 4th edition (Englewood Cliffs, NJ: Prentice Hall, 1990), p. 59.

Press, 1986); and Nicholas Hammond, *Playing with Truth: Language and the Human Condition in Pascal's 'Pensées'* (Oxford: Oxford University Press, 1994). For discussions of Pascal's wager, see Nicholas Rescher, *Pascal's Wager: A Study of Practical Reasoning in Philosophical Theology* (Notre Dame, IN: University of Notre Dame Press, 1985) and Jeff Jordan, ed., *Gambling on God: Essays on Pascal's Wager* (Lanham, MD: Rowman & Littlefield, 1994).

PENSÉES (in part)

185. The conduct of God, who disposes all things kindly, is to put religion into the mind by reason, and into the heart by grace. But to will to put it into the mind and heart by force and threats is not to put religion there, but terror. . . .

187. Order.—Men despise religion; they hate it, and fear it is true. To remedy this, we must begin by showing that religion is not contrary to reason; that it is venerable, to inspire respect for it; then we must make it lovable, to make good men hope it is true; finally, we must prove it is true.

194. . . . Let them at least learn what is the religion they attack, before attacking it. If this religion boasted of having a clear view of God, and of possessing it open and unveiled, it would be attacking it to say that we see nothing in the world which shows it with this clearness. But since, on the contrary, it says that men are in darkness and estranged from God, that He has hidden Himself from their knowledge, that this is in fact the name which He gives Himself in the Scriptures, *Deus absconditus* [hidden God]; and finally, if it endeavors equally to establish these two things: that God has set up in the Church visible signs to make Himself known to those who should seek Him sincerely, and that He has nevertheless so disguised them that He will only be perceived by those who seek Him with all their heart; . . .

We do not require great education of the mind to understand that here is no real and lasting satisfaction; that our pleasures are only vanity; that our evils are infinite; and, lastly, that death, which threatens us every moment, must infallibly place us within a few years under the dreadful necessity of being for ever either annihilated or unhappy.

There is nothing more real than this, nothing more terrible. Be we as heroic as we like, that is the end which awaits the noblest life in the world. Let us reflect on this, and then say whether it is not beyond doubt that there is no good in this life but in the hope of another; that we are happy only in proportion as we draw near it; and that, as there are no more woes for those who have complete assurance of eternity, so there is no more happiness for those who have no insight into it.

199. Let us imagine a number of men in chains, and all condemned to death, where some are killed each day in the sight of the others, and those who remain see their own fate in that of their fellows, and wait their turn, looking at each other sorrowfully and without hope. It is an image of the condition of men.

205. When I consider the short duration of my life, swallowed up in the eternity before and after, the little space which I fill, and even can see, engulfed in the infinite immensity of spaces of which I am ignorant, and which know me not, I am frightened, and am astonished at being here rather than there; for there is no reason why here rather than there, why now rather than then. Who has put me here? By whose order and direction have this place and time been allotted to me? . . .

206. The eternal silence of these infinite spaces frightens me.

210. The last act is tragic, however happy all the rest of the play is; at the last a little earth is thrown upon our head, and that is the end for ever.

229. . . . If I saw nothing there which revealed a Divinity, I would come to a negative conclusion; if I saw everywhere the signs of a Creator, I would remain peacefully in faith. But, seeing too much to deny and too little to be sure, I am in a state to be pitied; wherefore I have a hundred times wished that if a God maintains nature, she should testify to Him unequivocally, and that, if the signs she gives are deceptive, she should suppress them altogether; that she should say everything or nothing, that I might see which cause I ought to follow. Whereas in my present state, ignorant of what I am or of what I ought to do, I know neither my condition nor my duty. My heart inclines wholly to know where is the true good, in order to follow it; nothing would be too dear to me for eternity.

I envy those whom I see living in the faith with such carelessness, and who make such a bad use of a gift of which it seems to me I would make such a different use.

230. It is incomprehensible that God should exist, and it is incomprehensible that He should not exist; that the soul should be joined to the body, and that we should have no soul; that the world should be created, and that it should not be created, etc., that original sin should be, and that it should not be.

233. [*The Wager*] . . . Let us then examine this point, and say, "God is, or He is not."

But to which side shall we incline? Reason can decide nothing here. There is an infinite chaos which separated us. A game is being played at the extremity of this infinite distance where heads or tails will turn up. What will you wager? According to reason, you can do neither the one thing nor the other; according to reason, you can defend neither of the propositions.

Do not then reprove for error those who have made a choice; for you know nothing about it. "No, but I blame them for having made, not this choice, but a choice; for again both he who chooses heads and he who chooses tails are equally at fault, they are both in the wrong. The true course is not to wager at all."

Yes; but you must wager. It is not optional. You are embarked. Which will you choose then? Let us see. Since you must choose, let us see which interests you least. You have two things to lose, the true and the good; and two things to stake, your reason and your will, your knowledge and your happiness; and your nature has two things to shun, error and misery. Your reason is no more shocked in choosing one rather than the other, since you must of necessity choose. This is one point settled. But your happiness? Let us weight the gain and the loss in wagering that God is. Let us estimate these two chances. If you gain, you gain all; if you lose, you lose nothing. Wager, then, without hesitation that He is.— "That is very fine. Yes, I must wager; but I may perhaps wager too much."—Let us see. Since there is an equal risk of gain and of loss, but if you had only to gain two lives, instead of one, you might still wager. But if there were three lives to gain, you would have to play (since you are under the necessity of playing), and you would be imprudent, when you are forced to play, not chance your life to gain three at a game where there is an equal risk of loss and gain. But there is an eternity of life and happiness. And this being so, if there were an infinity of chances, of which one only would be for you, you would still be right in wagering one to win two, and you would act stupidly, being obliged to play, by refusing to stake one life against three at a game in which out of an infinity of chances there is one for you, if there were an infinity of an infinitely happy life to gain. But there is here an infinity of an infinitely happy life to gain, a chance to gain against a finite number of chances to lose, and what you stake is finite. . . .

And so our proposition is of infinite force, when there is the finite to stake in a game where there are equal risks of gain and of loss, and the infinite to gain. This is demonstrable: and if men are capable of any truths, this is one.

"I confess it, I admit it. But, still, is there no means of seeing the faces of the cards?"—Yes, Scripture and the rest, etc. "Yes, but I have my hands tied and my mouth closed; I am forced to wager, and am not free. I am not released, and am so made that I cannot believe. What, then, would you have me do?"

True. But at least learn your inability to believe, since reason brings you to this, and yet you cannot believe. Endeavour then to convince yourself, not by increase of proofs of God, but by the abatement of your passions. You would like to attain faith, and do not know the way; you would like to cure yourself of unbelief, and ask the remedy for it. Learn of those who have been bound like you, and who now stake all their possessions. These are people who know the way which you would follow, and who are cured of an ill of which you would be cured. Follow the way by which they began; by acting as if they believed, taking the holy water, having masses said, etc. Even this will naturally make you believe, and deaden your acuteness.—"But this is what I am afraid of."—And why? What have you to lose? . . .

The end of this discourse.—Now, what harm will befall you in taking this side? You will be faithful, honest, humble, grateful, generous, a sincere friend, truthful. Certainly you will not have those poisonous pleasures, glory and luxury; but will you not have other? I will tell you that you will thereby gain in this life, and that, at each step you take on this road, you will see so great certainty of gain, so much nothingness in what you risk, that you will at last recognize that you have wagered for something certain and infinite, for which you have given nothing.

"Ah! This discourse transports me, charms me," etc.

If this discourse pleases you and seems impressive, know that it is made by a man who has knelt, both before and after it, in prayer to that Being, infinite and without parts, before whom he lays all he has, for you also to lay before Him all you have for your own good and for His glory, so that strength may be given to lowliness.

240. "I would soon have renounced pleasure," say they, "had I faith."

For my part I tell you, "You would soon have faith, if you renounced pleasure." Now, it is for you to begin. . . .

242. I admire the boldness with which these persons undertake to speak of God. In addressing their argument to infidels, their first chapter is to prove Divinity from the works of nature. I should not be astonished at their enterprise, if they were addressing their argument to the faithful; for it is certain that those who have the living faith in their heart see at once that all existence is none other than the work of the God whom

they adore. But for those in whom this light is extinguished, and in whom we purpose to rekindle it, persons destitute of faith and grace, who, seeking with all their light, whatever they see in nature that can bring them to this knowledge, find only obscurity and darkness; to tell them that they have only to look at the smallest things which surround them, and they will see God openly, to give them, as a complete proof of this great and important matter, the course of the moon and planets, and to claim to have concluded the proof with such an argument, is to give them ground for believing that the proofs of our religion are very weak. And I see by reason and experience that nothing is more calculated to arouse their contempt.

It is not after this manner that Scripture speaks, which has a better knowledge of the things that are of God. It says, on the contrary, that God is a hidden God, and that, since the corruption of nature, He has left men in a darkness from which they can escape only through Jesus Christ, without whom all communion with God is cut off. . . .

253. Two extremes: to exclude reason, to admit reason only.

277. The heart has its reasons, which reason does not know. We feel it in a thousand things. I say that the heart naturally loves the Universal Being, and also itself naturally, according as it gives itself to them; and it hardens itself against one or the other at its will. You have rejected the one, and kept the other at its will. You have rejected the one, and kept the other. Is it by reason that you love yourself?

278. It is the heart which experiences God, and not the reason. This, then, is faith: God felt by the heart, not by the reason.

Faith is a gift of God; do not believe that we said it was a gift of reasoning. Other religions do not say this of their faith. They only give reasoning in order to arrive at it, and yet it does not bring them to it.

280. The knowledge of God is very far from the love of Him.

282. We know truth, not only by the reason, but also by the heart, and it is in this last way that we know first principles; and reason, which has no part in it, tries in vain to impugn them. The skeptics, who have only this for their object, labor to no purpose. We know that we do not dream, and however impossible it is for us to prove it by reason, this inability demonstrates only the weakness of our reason, but not, as they affirm, the uncertainty of all our knowledge. For the knowledge of first principles, as space, time, motion, number, is as sure as any of those which we get from reasoning. And reason must trust these intuitions of the heart, and must base on them every argument. (We have intuitive knowledge of the tri-dimensional nature of space, and of the infinity of number, and reason then shows that there are no two square numbers one of which is double of the other. Principles are intuited, propositions are inferred, all with certainty, though in different ways.) And it is as useless and absurd for reason to demand from the heart proofs of her first principles, before admitting them, as it would be for the heart to demand from reason an intuition of all demonstrated propositions before accepting them.

This inability ought, then, to serve only to humble reason, which would judge all, but not to impugn our certainty, as if only reason were capable of instructing us. Would to God, on the contrary, that we had never need of it, and that we knew everything by instinct and intuition! But nature has refused us this boon. On the contrary, she has given us but very little knowledge of this kind; and all the rest can be acquired only by reasoning.

Therefore, those to whom God has imparted religion by intuition are very fortunate, and justly convinced. But to those who do not have it, we can give it only by reasoning, waiting for God to give them spiritual insight, without which faith is only human, and useless for salvation.

347. Man is but a reed, the most feeble thing in nature; but he is a thinking reed. The entire universe need not arm itself to crush him. A vapor, a drop of water suffices to kill him. But, if the universe were to crush him, man would still be more noble than that which killed him, because he knows that he dies and the advantage which the universe has over him; the universe knows nothing of this.

All our dignity consists, then, in thought. By it we must elevate ourselves, and not by space and time which we cannot fill. Let us endeavour, then, to think well; this is the principle of morality.

365. Thought.—All the dignity of man consists in thought. Thought is therefore by its nature a wonderful and incomparable thing. It must have strange defects to be contemptible. But it has such, so that nothing is more ridiculous. How great it is in its nature! How vile it is in its defects!

But what is this thought? How foolish it is!

409. The greatness of man.—The greatness of man is so evident, that it is even proved by his wretchedness. For what in animals is nature we call in man wretchedness; by which we recognize that, his nature being now like that of animals, he has fallen from a better nature which once was his.

For who is unhappy at not being a king, except a deposed king? Was Paulus Aemilius unhappy at being no longer consul? On the contrary, everybody thought him happy in having been consul, because the office could only be held for a time. But men thought Perseus so unhappy in being no longer king, because the condition of kingship implied his being always king, that they thought it strange that he endured life. Who is unhappy at having only one eye? Probably no man ever ventured to mourn at not having three eyes. But any one is inconsolable at having none.

430. The greatness and the wretchedness of man are so evident that the true religion must necessarily teach us both that there is in man some great source of greatness, and a great source of wretchedness. It must then give us a reason for these astonishing contradictions. . . .

434. . . . Again, no person is certain, apart from faith, whether he is awake or sleeps, seeing that during sleep we believe that we are awake as firmly as we do when we are awake; we believe that we see space, figure, and motion; we are aware of the passage of time, we measure it; and in fact we act as if we were awake. So that half of our life being passed in sleep, we have on our own admission no idea of truth, whatever we may imagine. As all our intuitions are then illusions, who knows whether the other half of our life, in which we think we are awake, is not another sleep a little different from the former, from which we awake when we suppose ourselves asleep? . . .

What then shall man do in this state? Shall he doubt everything? Shall he doubt whether he is awake, whether he is being pinched, or whether he is being burned? Shall he doubt whether he doubts? Shall he doubt whether he exists? We cannot go so far as that; and I lay it down as a fact that there never has been a real complete skeptic. Nature sustains our feeble reason, and prevents it raving to this extent.

Shall he then say, on the contrary, that he certainly possesses truth—he who, when pressed ever so little, can show no title to it, and is forced to let go his hold?

What a chimera then is man! What a novelty! What a monster, what a chaos, what a contradiction, what a prodigy! Judge of all things, imbecile worm of the earth; depositary of truth, a sink of uncertainty and error; the pride and refuse of the universe!

Who will unravel this tangle? Nature confutes the skeptics, and reason confutes the dogmatists. What then will you become, O men! who try to find out by your natural reason what is your true condition? You cannot avoid one of these sects, nor adhere to one of them.

Know then, proud man, what a paradox you are to yourself. Humble yourself, weak reason; be silent, foolish nature; learn that man infinitely transcends man, and learn from your Master your true condition, of which you are ignorant. Hear God. . . .

555. . . . The Christian religion, then, teaches men these two truths; that there is a God whom men can know, and that there is a corruption in their nature which renders them unworthy of Him. It is equally important to men to know both these points; and it is equally dangerous for man to know God without knowing his own wretchedness, and to know his own wretchedness without knowing the Redeemer who can free him from it. The knowledge of only one of these points gives rise either to the pride of philosophers, who have known God, and not their own wretchedness, or to the despair of atheists, who know their own wretchedness, but not the Redeemer.

And, as it is alike necessary to man to know these two points, so is it alike merciful to God to have made us know them. The Christian religion does this; it is in this that it consists.

Let us herein examine the order of the world, and see if all things do not tend to establish these two chief points of this religion: Jesus Christ is the end of all, and the center to which all tends. Whoever knows Him knows the reason of everything.

Those who fall into error err only through failure to see one of these two things. We can then have an excellent knowledge of God without that of our own wretchedness, and of our own wretchedness without that of God. But we cannot know Jesus Christ without knowing at the same time both God and our own wretchedness. . . .

The God of Christians is not a God who is simply the author of mathematical truths, or of the order of the elements; that is the view of heathens and Epicureans. He is not merely a God who exercises His providence over the life and fortunes of men, to bestow on those who worship Him a long and happy life. That was the portion of the Jews. But the God of Abraham, the God of Isaac, and God of Jacob, and God of Christians, is a God of love and of comfort, a God who fills the soul and heart of those whom He possesses, a God who makes them conscious of their inward wretchedness, and His infinite mercy, who unites Himself to their inmost soul, who fills it with humility and joy, with confidence and love, who renders them incapable of any other end than Himself.

All who seek God without Jesus Christ, and who rest in nature, either find no light to satisfy them, or come to form for themselves a means of knowing God and serving Him without a mediator. Thereby they fall either into atheism, or into deism, two things which the Christian religion abhors almost equally. . . .

563. The prophecies, the very miracles and proofs of our religion, are not of such a nature that they can be said to be absolutely convincing. But they are also of such a kind

that it cannot be said that it is unreasonable to believe them. Thus there is both evidence and obscurity to enlighten some and confuse others. But the evidence is such that it surpasses, or at least equals, the evidence to the contrary; so that it is not reason which can determine men not to follow it, and thus it can only be lust or malice of heart. And by this means there is sufficient evidence to condemn, and insufficient to convince; so that it appears in those who follow it, that it is grace, and not reason, which makes them follow it; and in those who shun it, that it is lust, not reason, which makes them shun it.

BARUCH SPINOZA
1632–1677

Except for Socrates himself, it would be difficult to find a philosopher who was a more highly regarded person than Benedict (Baruch) Spinoza. Like Socrates, he was not interested in power or wealth. Like Socrates, he was accused of atheism and was hounded for his unorthodox beliefs. Like Socrates, he was interested in philosophy as a way of life, not as a professional discipline.

Spinoza was born in Amsterdam the son of Jewish refugees who had fled from Portugal to escape persecution. As a young man, he was trained in Jewish tradition under a celebrated Talmudist, Saul Levi Morteira. He later studied with Manasseh ben Israel, the man who persuaded Cromwell to allow Jews to return to England, and with a Dutch physician, Franz van der Ende.

As a Jew, Spinoza was an outsider in Holland—not even entitled to citizenship because of his faith. As an original thinker, Spinoza soon became an outsider within the Jewish community as well. He was accused of heresy by the synagogue of Amsterdam and required to disavow his teachings. Spinoza refused and was officially excommunicated in 1656, when he was twenty-three years old. (In the twentieth century, the new state of Israel formally revoked the ban.)

With no wish to join any other religious community, Spinoza left Amsterdam and eventually settled in The Hague. He lived very simply, supporting himself by grinding and polishing lenses, a craft he had adopted out of respect for the Jewish tradition, which required scholars to learn a trade.

Spinoza published only two works during his lifetime. His first work was *Principles of Descartes' Philosophy* (1663), which critically examined the presuppositions and structure of Descartes' system. Using what later came to be called "higher criticism," his second book, *Theological-Political Treatise* (1670), subjected Scripture to rational analysis. He concluded that the Bible does not aim at truth but at pious and obedient behavior. Writing soon after the Thirty Years War (1618–1648), he proposed that religion and truth be separated altogether. This separation, he believed, would be the best safeguard against fanaticism. And pious conduct flourishes best in an atmosphere of free speech.

His *Theological-Political Treatise* attracted a great deal of criticism. It also brought an invitation to the chair of philosophy at the University of Heidelberg, Germany. Although the invitation included a guarantee of academic freedom, Spinoza rejected it out of his passion for freedom to speak and write as he saw fit.

The rigor of his simple life, with the glass dust of his trade, hastened his death from consumption at the age of forty-four, two years before Hobbes died at ninety-one. Immediately following his death, Spinoza's other works, including *Political Treatise* (which supports individual liberty, religious tolerance, and democracy), *On the Improvement of the Intellect*, and his masterpiece, *Ethics*, were published.

*   *   *

Whereas Descartes and Hobbes used the geometrical *method*, Spinoza used geometrical *form* as well. The *Ethics* is presented as a geometrical system, developing propositions from axioms and definitions.

In Books I and II of his *Ethics,* reprinted here in the E. Curley translation, Spinoza explores God and the nature and origin of mind. He begins by accepting Descartes' idea that "infinite substance" is completely independent and necessary. But he claims that Descartes had contradicted himself by allowing for "finite substances" as well. Instead, Spinoza claims that there could only be one substance: God. God exists necessarily and as God is the only substance, what we call "Nature" is also God. This also means that whatever happens is necessary (though individuals are often confused and do not understand the connections).

Although God is the only substance, God has infinite attributes. The only two divine attributes we can know are thought (of which minds are modifications) and extension (of which bodies are modifications). To Spinoza, Descartes was wrong to present mind and body as two separate substances (with all the concomitant problems of interaction). Instead, says Spinoza, body and mind are both attributes of the One substance. Thinking substance and extended substance are really the same substance.

In Books III to V of the *Ethics*, Spinoza argues that we must free ourselves from the tyranny of the passions. The key to this freedom is an understanding of God that allows us to see the necessary, rational structure of reality: "The more this knowledge, that things are necessary, is applied to particular things . . . the greater is the power of the mind over the emotions." The final goal of this knowledge is "blessedness," which consists of intellectual love towards God. This program of overcoming the passions by reason may be difficult, but Spinoza concludes that "all things excellent are as difficult as they are rare" (an apt description of Spinoza's classic).

*   *   *

For a general introduction to Spinoza's life and thought, see Stuart Hampshire, *Spinoza* (Baltimore, MD: Penguin Books, 1952); Henry E. Allison, *Benedict De Spinoza*, rev. ed. (New Haven, CT: Yale University Press, 1987); Alan Donagan, *Spinoza* (Chicago: University of Chicago Press, 1988); and Herman De Dijn, *Spinoza:*

The Way to Wisdom (West Lafayette, IN: Purdue University Press, 1996). For an interesting study of Spinoza's thought in relation to the other Continental rationalists, see John Cottingham, *The Rationalists* (Oxford: Oxford University Press, 1988). The generally accepted "classic" commentary on the *Ethics* remains Harry Austryn Wolfson, *The Philosophy of Spinoza: Unfolding the Latent Processes of His Reasoning* (1934; reprint New York: Schocken, 1969). For more recent discussions of Spinoza's *Ethics,* see Jonathan Bennett, *A Study of Spinoza's Ethics* (Indianapolis, IN: Hackett, 1984); Edwin Curley, *Behind the Geometrical Method: A Reading of Spinoza's Ethics* (Princeton, NJ: Princeton University Press, 1988); and Genevieve Lloyd, *Spinoza and the Ethics* (Oxford: Routledge, 1996). For collections of essays on Spinoza, see S. Paul Kashap, ed., *Studies in Spinoza* (Berkeley: University of California Press, 1972); Robert W. Shahan and J.I. Biro, eds., *Spinoza: New Perspectives* (Norman, OK: University of Oklahoma Press, 1978); Richard Kennington, ed., *The Philosophy of Baruch Spinoza* (Washington, DC: Catholic University of America Press, 1980); Vere Chappell, ed., *Essays on Early Modern Philosophers: Baruch De Spinoza* (Hamden, CT: Garland, 1992); Graeme Hunter, ed., *Spinoza: The Enduring Questions* (Toronto: University of Toronto Press, 1994); and Don Garrett, ed., *The Cambridge Companion to Spinoza* (Cambridge: Cambridge University Press, 1995); and Warren Montag and Ted Stolze, eds., *The New Spinoza* (Minneapolis, MN: University of Minnesota Press, 1998). Richard Mason, *The God of Spinoza: A Philosophical Study* (Cambridge: Cambridge University Press, 1997) is a study of Spinoza's philosophy of religion while the Jewish character of Spinoza's thought is discussed in Yirmiyahu Yovel's pair of books, *The Marrano of Reason* and *The Adventures of Immanence* (both Princeton, NJ: Princeton University Press, 1991) and Steven Smith, *Spinoza, Liberalism, and the Question of Jewish Identity* (New Haven, CT: Yale University Press, 1997).

ETHICS (in part)

FIRST PART OF THE ETHICS

ON GOD

Definitions

D1: By cause of itself I understand that whose essence involves existence, or that whose nature cannot be conceived except as existing.

D2: That thing is said to be finite in its own kind that can be limited by another of the same nature.

Baruch Spinoza, *Ethics* from *Collected Works of Spinoza,* Vol. 1, edited and translated by Edwin Curley (Princeton, NJ: Princeton University Press, 1985). © 1985 by Princeton University Press. Reprinted by permission of Princeton University Press. [Material within square brackets is from *De Nagelate Schriften van B.D.S.*, a later edition of the *Ethics,* and is included by Curley in the primary text.]

For example, a body is called finite because we always conceive another that is greater. Thus a thought is limited by another thought. But a body is not limited by a thought nor a thought by a body.

D3: By substance I understand what is in itself and is conceived through itself, i.e., that whose concept does not require the concept of another thing, from which it must be formed.

D4: By attribute I understand what the intellect perceives of a substance, as constituting its essence.

D5: By mode I understand the affections of a substance, or that which is in another through which it is also conceived.

D6: By God I understand a being absolutely infinite, i.e., a substance consisting of an infinity of attributes, of which each one expresses an eternal and infinite essence.
Exp.: I say absolutely infinite, not infinite in its own kind; for if something is only infinite in its own kind, we can deny infinite attributes of it [(i.e., we can conceive infinite attributes which do not pertain to its nature)]; but if something is absolutely infinite, whatever expresses essence and involves no negation pertains to its essence.

D7: That thing is called free which exists from the necessity of its nature alone, and is determined to act by itself alone. But a thing is called necessary, or rather compelled, which is determined by another to exist and to produce an effect in a certain and determinate manner.

D8: By eternity I understand existence itself, insofar as it is conceived to follow necessarily from the definition alone of the eternal thing.
Exp.: For such existence, like the essence of a thing, is conceived as an eternal truth, and on that account cannot be explained by duration or time, even if the duration is conceived to be without beginning or end.

Axioms

A1: Whatever is, is either in itself or in another.

A2: What cannot be conceived through another, must be conceived through itself.

A3: From a given determinate cause the effect follows necessarily; and conversely, if there is no determinate cause, it is impossible for an effect to follow.

A4: The knowledge of an effect depends on, and involves, the knowledge of its cause.

A5: Things that have nothing in common with one another also cannot be understood through one another, or the concept of the one does not involve the concept of the other.

A6: A true idea must agree with its object.

A7: If a thing can be conceived as not existing, its essence does not involve existence.

P1: *A substance is prior in nature to its affections.*
    Dem.: This is evident from D3 and D5.

P2: *Two substances having different attributes have nothing in common with one another.*
    Dem.: This is also evident from D3. For each must be in itself and be conceived through itself, *or* the concept of the one does not involve the concept of the other.

P3: *If things have nothing in common with one another, one of them cannot be the cause of the other.*
    Dem.: If they have nothing in common with one another, then (by A5) they cannot be understood through one another, and so (by A4) one cannot be the cause of the other, q.e.d.*

P4: *Two or more distinct things are distinguished from one another, either by a difference in the attributes of the substances or by a difference in their affections.*
    Dem.: Whatever is, is either in itself or in another (by A1), i.e. (by D3 and D5), outside the intellect there is nothing except substances and their affections. Therefore, there is nothing outside the intellect through which a number of things can be distinguished from one another except substances, or what is the same (by D4), their attributes, and their affections, q.e.d.

P5: *In nature there cannot be two or more substances of the same nature or attribute.*
    Dem.: If there were two or more distinct substances, they would have to be distinguished from one another either by a difference in their attributes, or by a difference in their affections (by P4). If only by a difference in their attributes, then it will be conceded that there is only one of the same attribute. But if by a difference in their affections, then since a substance is prior in nature to its affections (by P1), if the affections are put to one side and [the substance] is considered in itself, i.e. (by D3 and A6), considered truly, one cannot be conceived to be distinguished from another, i.e. (by P4), there cannot be many, but only one [of the same nature or attribute], q.e.d.

P6: *One substance cannot be produced by another substance.*
    Dem.: In nature there cannot be two substances of the same attribute (by P5), i.e. (by P2), which have something in common with each other. Therefore (by P3) one cannot be the cause of the other, or cannot be produced by the other, q.e.d.
    Cor.: From this it follows that a substance cannot be produced by anything else. For in nature there is nothing except substances and their affections, as is evident from A1, D3, and D5. But it cannot be produced by a substance (by P6). Therefore, substance absolutely cannot be produced by anything else, q.e.d.
    Alternatively: This is demonstrated even more easily from the absurdity of its contradictory. For if a substance could be produced by something else, the knowledge of it would have to depend on the knowledge of its cause (by A4). And so (by D3) it would not be a substance.

*[*quod erat demonstandum*—"which was to be demonstrated"]

P7: *It pertains to the nature of a substance to exist.*

Dem.: A substance cannot be produced by anything else (by P6C); therefore it will be the cause of itself, i.e. (by D1), its essence necessarily involves existence, or it pertains to its nature to exist, q.e.d.

P8: *Every substance is necessarily infinite.*

Dem.: A substance of one attribute does not exist unless it is unique (P5), and it pertains to its nature to exist (P7). Of its nature, therefore, it will exist either as finite or as infinite. But not as finite. For then (by D2) it would have to be limited by something else of the same nature, which would also have to exist necessarily (by P7), and so there would be two substances of the same attribute, which is absurd (by P5). There-fore, it exists as infinite, q.e.d.

Schol. 1: Since being finite is really, in part, a negation, and being infinite is an absolute affirmation of the existence of some nature, it follows from P7 alone that every substance must be infinite. [For if we assumed a finite substance, we would, in part, deny existence to its nature, which (by P7) is absurd.]

Schol. 2: I do not doubt that the demonstration of P7 will be difficult to conceive for all who judge things confusedly, and have not been accustomed to know things through their first causes—because they do not distinguish between the modifications of substances and the substances themselves, nor do they know how things are pro-duced. So it happens that they fictitiously ascribe to substances the beginning which they see that natural things have; for those who do not know the true causes of things confuse everything and without any conflict of mind feign that both trees and men speak, imagine that men are formed both from stones and from seed, and that any form whatever is changed into any other. So also, those who confuse the divine nature with the human easily ascribe human affects to God, particularly so long as they are also ig-norant of how those affects are produced in the mind.

But if men would attend to the nature of substance, they would have no doubt at all of the truth of P7. Indeed, this proposition would be an axiom for everyone, and would be numbered among the common notions. For by substance they would under-stand what is in itself and is conceived through itself, i.e., that the knowledge of which does not require the knowledge of any other thing. But by modifications they would understand what is in another, those things whose concept is formed from the concept of the thing in which they are.

This is how we can have true ideas of modifications which do not exist; for though they do not actually exist outside the intellect, nevertheless their essences are comprehended in another in such a way that they can be conceived through it. But the truth of substances is not outside the intellect unless it is in them themselves, because they are conceived through themselves.

Hence, if someone were to say that he had a clear and distinct, i.e., true, idea of a substance, and nevertheless doubted whether such a substance existed, that would in-deed be the same as if he were to say that he had a true idea, and nevertheless doubted whether it was false (as is evident to anyone who is sufficiently attentive). Or if some-one maintains that a substance is created, he maintains at the same time that a false idea has become true. Of course nothing more absurd can be conceived. So it must be confessed that the existence of a substance, like its essence, is an eternal truth.

And from this we can infer in another way that there is only one [substance] of the same nature, which I have considered it worth the trouble of showing here. But to do this in order, it must be noted,

    I. that the true definition of each thing neither involves nor expresses anything except the nature of the thing defined.

From which it follows,

    II. that no definition involves or expresses any certain number of individuals,

since it expresses nothing other than the nature of the thing defined. E.g., the definition of the triangle expresses nothing but the simple nature of the triangle, but not any certain number of triangles. It is to be noted,

    III. that there must be, for each existing thing, a certain cause on account of which it exists.

Finally, it is to be noted,

    IV. that this cause, on account of which a thing exists, either must be contained in the very nature and definition of the existing thing (viz. that it pertains to its nature to exist) or must be outside it.

From these propositions it follows that if, in nature, a certain number of individuals exists, there must be a cause why those individuals, and why neither more nor fewer, exist.

For example, if 20 men exist in nature (to make the matter clearer, I assume that they exist at the same time, and that no others previously existed in nature), it will not be enough (i.e., to give a reason why 20 men exist) to show the cause of human nature in general; but it will be necessary in addition to show the cause why not more and not fewer than 20 exist. For (by III) there must necessarily be a cause why each [particular man] exists. But this cause (by II and III) cannot be contained in human nature itself, since the true definition of man does not involve the number 20. So (by IV) the cause why these 20 men exist, and consequently, why each of them exists, must necessarily be outside each of them.

For that reason it is to be inferred absolutely that whatever is of such a nature that there can be many individuals [of that nature] must, to exist, have an external cause to exist. Now since it pertains to the nature of a substance to exist (by what we have already shown in this Scholium), its definition must involve necessary existence, and consequently its existence must be inferred from its definition alone. But from its definition (as we have shown from II and III) the existence of a number of substances cannot follow. Therefore it follows necessarily from this, that there exists only one of the same nature, as was proposed.

P9: *The more reality or being each thing has, the more attributes belong to it.*
    Dem.: This is evident from D4.

P10: *Each attribute of a substance must be conceived through itself.*
    Dem.: For an attribute is what the intellect perceives concerning a substance, as constituting its essence (by D4); so (by D3) it must be conceived through itself, q.e.d.
    Schol.: From these propositions it is evident that although two attributes may be conceived to be really distinct (i.e., one may be conceived without the aid of the other),

we still cannot infer from that that they constitute two beings, *or* two different substances. For it is of the nature of a substance that each of its attributes is conceived through itself, since all the attributes it has have always been in it together, and one could not be produced by another, but each expresses the reality, *or* being of substance.

So it is far from absurd to attribute many attributes to one substance. Indeed, nothing in nature is clearer than that each being must be conceived under some attribute, and the more reality, or being it has, the more it has attributes which express necessity, *or* eternity, and infinity. And consequently there is also nothing clearer than that a being absolutely infinite must be defined (as we taught in D6) as a being that consists of infinite attributes, each of which expresses a certain eternal and infinite essence.

But if someone now asks by what sign we shall be able to distinguish the diversity of substances, let him read the following propositions, which show that in Nature there exists only one substance, and that it is absolutely infinite. So that sign would be sought in vain.

P11: *God, or a substance consisting of infinite attributes, each of which expresses eternal and infinite essence, necessarily exists.*

Dem.: If you deny this, conceive, if you can, that God does not exist. Therefore (by A7) his essence does not involve existence. But this (by P7) is absurd. Therefore God necessarily exists, q.e.d.

Alternatively: For each thing there must be assigned a cause, or reason, as much for its existence as for its nonexistence. For example, if a triangle exists, there must be a reason *or* cause why it exists; but if it does not exist, there must also be a reason or cause which prevents it from existing, *or* which takes its existence away.

But this reason, *or* cause, must either be contained in the nature of the thing, or be outside it. E.g., the very nature of a square circle indicates the reason why it does not exist, viz. because it involves a contradiction. On the other hand, the reason why a substance exists also follows from its nature alone, because it involves existence (see P7). But the reason why a circle or triangle exists, or why it does not exist, does not follow from the nature of these things, but from the order of the whole of corporeal Nature. For from this [order] it must follow either that the triangle necessarily exists now or that it is impossible for it to exist now.

These things are evident through themselves, but from them it follows that a thing necessarily exists if there is no reason or cause which prevents it from existing. Therefore, if there is no reason or cause which prevents God from existing, or which takes his existence away, it must certainly be inferred that he necessarily exists.

But if there were such a reason, *or* cause, it would have to be either in God's very nature or outside it, i.e., in another substance of another nature. For if it were of the same nature, that very supposition would concede that God exists. But a substance which was of another nature [than the divine] would have nothing in common with God (by P2), and therefore could neither give him existence nor take it away.

Since, then, there can be, outside the divine nature, no reason, or cause, which takes away the divine existence, the reason will necessarily have to be in his nature itself, if indeed he does not exist. That is, his nature would involve a contradiction [as in our second Example]. But it is absurd to affirm this of a Being absolutely infinite and supremely perfect. Therefore, there is no cause, or reason, either in God or outside God, which takes his existence away. And therefore, God necessarily exists, q.e.d.

Alternatively: To be able not to exist is to lack power, and conversely, to be able to exist is to have power (as is known through itself). So, if what now necessarily exists are only finite beings, then finite beings are more powerful than an absolutely infinite Being. But this, as is known through itself, is absurd. So, either nothing exists or an absolutely infinite Being also exists. But we exist, either in ourselves, or in something else, which necessarily exists (see A1 and P7). Therefore an absolutely infinite Being—i.e. (by D6), God—necessarily exists, q.e.d.

Schol.: In this last demonstration I wanted to show God's existence a posteriori, so that the demonstration would be perceived more easily—but not because God's existence does not follow a priori from the same foundation. For since being able to exist is power, it follows that the more reality belongs to the nature of a thing, the more powers it has, of itself, to exist. Therefore, an absolutely infinite Being, or God, has, of himself, an absolutely infinite power of existing. For that reason, he exists absolutely.

Still, there may be many who will not easily be able to see how evident this demonstration is, because they have been accustomed to contemplate only those things that flow from external causes. And of these, they see that those which quickly come to be, i.e., which easily exist, also easily perish. And conversely, they judge that those things to which they conceive more things to pertain are more difficult to do, i.e., that they do not exist so easily. But to free them from these prejudices, I have no need to show here in what manner this proposition—*what quickly comes to be, quickly perishes*—is true, nor whether or not all things are equally easy in respect to the whole of Nature. It is sufficient to note only this, that I am not here speaking of things that come to be from external causes, but only of substances that (by P6) can be produced by no external cause.

For things that come to be from external causes—whether they consist of many parts or of few—owe all the perfection or reality they have to the power of the external cause; and therefore their existence arises only from the perfection of their external cause, and not from their own perfection. On the other hand, whatever perfection substance has is not owed to any external cause. So its existence must follow from its nature alone; hence its existence is nothing but its essence.

Perfection, therefore, does not take away the existence of a thing, but on the contrary asserts it. But imperfection takes it away. So there is nothing of whose existence we can be more certain than we are of the existence of an absolutely infinite, or perfect, Being—i.e., God. For since his essence excludes all imperfection, and involves absolute perfection, by that very fact it takes away every cause of doubting his existence, and gives the greatest certainty concerning it. I believe this will be clear even to those who are only moderately attentive.

P12: *No attribute of a substance can be truly conceived from which it follows that the substance can be divided.*

Dem.: For the parts into which a substance so conceived would be divided either will retain the nature of the substance or will not. If the first [viz. they retain the nature of the substance], then (by P8) each part will have to be infinite, and (by P7) its own cause, and (by P5) each part will have to consist of a different attribute. And so many substances will be able to be formed from one, which is absurd (by P6). Furthermore, the parts (by P2) would have nothing in common with their whole, and the whole (by D4 and P10) could both be and be conceived without its parts, which is absurd, as no one will be able to doubt.

But if the second is asserted, viz. that the parts will not retain the nature of substance, then since the whole substance would be divided into equal parts, it would lose the nature of substance, and would cease to be, which (by P7) is absurd.

P13:   *A substance which is absolutely infinite is indivisible.*

Dem.: For if it were divisible, the parts into which it would be divided will either retain the nature of an absolutely infinite substance or they will not. If the first, then there will be a number of substances of the same nature, which (by P5) is absurd. But if the second is asserted, then (as above [P12]), an absolutely infinite substance will be able to cease to be, which (by P11) is also absurd.

Cor.: From these [propositions] it follows that no substance, and consequently no corporeal substance, insofar as it is a substance, is divisible.

Schol.: That substance is indivisible, is understood more simply merely from this, that the nature of substance cannot be conceived unless as infinite, and that by a part of substance nothing can be understood except a finite substance, which (by P8) implies a plain contradiction.

P14:   *Except God, no substance can be or be conceived.*

Dem.: Since God is an absolutely infinite being, of whom no attribute which expresses an essence of substance can be denied (by D6), and he necessarily exists (by P11), if there were any substance except God, it would have to be explained through some attribute of God, and so two substances of the same attribute would exist, which (by P5) is absurd. And so except God, no substance can be or, consequently, be conceived. For if it could be conceived, it would have to be conceived as existing. But this (by the first part of this demonstration) is absurd. Therefore, except for God no substance can be or be conceived, q.e.d.

Cor. 1: From this it follows most clearly, first, that God is unique, i.e. (by D6), that in Nature there is only one substance, and that it is absolutely infinite (as we indicated in P10S).

Cor. 2: It follows, second, that an extended thing and a thinking thing are either attributes of God, or (by A1) affections of God's attributes.

P15:   *Whatever is, is in God, and nothing can be or be conceived without God.*

Dem.: Except for God, there neither is, nor can be conceived, any substance (by P14), i.e. (by D3), thing that is in itself and is conceived through itself. But modes (by D5) can neither be nor be conceived without substance. So they can be in the divine nature alone, and can be conceived through it alone. But except for substances and modes there is nothing (by A1). Therefore, [everything is in God and] nothing can be or be conceived without God, q.e.d.

Schol.: [I.] There are those who feign a God, like man, consisting of a body and a mind, and subject to passions. But how far they wander from the true knowledge of God, is sufficiently established by what has already been demonstrated. Them I dismiss. For everyone who has to any extent contemplated the divine nature denies that God is corporeal. They prove this best from the fact that by body we understand any quantity, with length, breadth, and depth, limited by some certain figure. Nothing more absurd than this can be said of God, viz. of a being absolutely infinite.

But meanwhile, by the other arguments by which they strive to demonstrate this same conclusion they clearly show that they entirely remove corporeal, *or* extended, substance itself from the divine nature. And they maintain that it has been created by God. But by what divine power could it be created? They are completely ignorant of that. And this shows clearly that they do not understand what they themselves say.

At any rate, I have demonstrated clearly enough—in my judgment, at least—that no substance can be produced or created by any other (see P6C and P8S2). Next, we have shown (P14) that except for God, no substance can either be or be conceived, and hence [in P14C2] we have concluded that extended substance is one of God's infinite attributes. But to provide a fuller explanation, I shall refute my opponents' arguments, which all reduce to these.

[II.] *First*, they think that corporeal substance, insofar as it is substance, consists of parts. And therefore they deny that it can be infinite, and consequently, that it can pertain to God. They explain this by many examples, of which I shall mention one or two.

[i] If corporeal substance is infinite, they say, let us conceive it to be divided in two parts. Each part will be either finite or infinite. If the former, then an infinite is composed of two finite parts, which is absurd. If the latter [i.e., if each part is infinite], then there is one infinite twice as large as another, which is also absurd. [ii] Again, if an infinite quantity is measured by parts [each] equal to a foot, it will consist of infinitely many such parts, as it will also, if it is measured by parts [each] equal to an inch. And therefore, one infinite number will be twelve times greater than another [which is no less absurd]. [iii] Finally, if we conceive that from one point of a certain infinite quantity two lines, say AB and AC, are extended to infinity, it is certain that, although in the beginning they are a certain, determinate distance apart, the distance between B and C is continuously increased, and at last, from being determinate, it will become indeterminable.

Since these absurdities follow—so they think—from the fact that an infinite quantity is supposed, they infer that corporeal substance must be finite, and consequently cannot pertain to God's essence.

[III.] Their *second* argument is also drawn from God's supreme perfection. For God, they say, since he is a supremely perfect being, cannot be acted on. But corporeal substance, since it is divisible, can be acted on. It follows, therefore, that it does not pertain to God's essence.

[IV.] These are the arguments which I find authors using, to try to show that corporeal substance is unworthy of the divine nature, and cannot pertain to it. But anyone who is properly attentive will find that I have already replied to them, since these arguments are founded only on their supposition that corporeal substance is composed of parts, which I have already (P12 and P13C) shown to be absurd. And then anyone who wishes to consider the matter rightly will see that all those absurdities (*if indeed they are all absurd, which I am not now disputing*), from which they wish to infer that extended substance is finite, do not follow at all from the fact that an infinite quantity is supposed, but from the fact that they suppose an infinite quantity to be measurable and composed of finite parts. So from the absurdities which follow from that they can infer only that infinite quantity is not measurable, and that it is not composed of finite parts. This is the same thing we have already demonstrated above (P12, etc.). So the weapon they aim at us, they really turn against themselves.

If, therefore, they still wish to infer from this absurdity of theirs that extended substance must be finite, they are indeed doing nothing more than if someone feigned that a circle has the properties of a square, and inferred from that the circle has no center, from which all lines drawn to the circumference are equal. For corporeal substance, which cannot be conceived except as infinite, unique, and indivisible (see P8, 5 and 12), they conceive to be composed of finite parts, to be many, and to be divisible, in order to infer that it is finite.

So also others, after they feign that a line is composed of points, know how to invent many arguments, by which they show that a line cannot be divided to infinity. And indeed it is no less absurd to assert that corporeal substance is composed of bodies, or parts, than that a body is composed of surfaces, the surfaces of lines, and the lines, finally, of points.

All those who know that clear reason is infallible must confess this—particularly those who deny that there is a vacuum. For if corporeal substance could be so divided that its parts were really distinct, why, then, could one part not be annihilated, the rest remaining connected with one another as before? And why must they all be so fitted together that there is no vacuum? Truly, of things which are really distinct from one another, one can be, and remain in its condition, without the other. Since, therefore, there is no vacuum in nature (a subject I discuss elsewhere), but all its parts must so concur that there is no vacuum, it follows also that they cannot be really distinguished, i.e., that corporeal substance, insofar as it is a substance, cannot be divided.

[V.] If someone should now ask why we are, by nature, so inclined to divide quantity, I shall answer that we conceive quantity in two ways: abstractly, or superficially, as we [commonly] imagine it, *or* as substance, which is done by the intellect alone [without the help of the imagination]. So if we attend to quantity as it is in the imagination, which we do often and more easily, it will be found to be finite, divisible, and composed of parts; but if we attend to it as it is in the intellect, and conceive it insofar as it is a substance, which happens [seldom and] with great difficulty, then (as we have already sufficiently demonstrated) it will be found to be infinite, unique, and indivisible.

This will be sufficiently plain to everyone who knows how to distinguish between the intellect and the imagination—particularly if it is also noted that matter is everywhere the same, and that parts are distinguished in it only insofar as we conceive matter to be affected in different ways, so that its parts are distinguished only modally, but not really.

For example, we conceive that water is divided and its parts separated from one another—insofar as it is water, but not insofar as it is corporeal substance. For insofar as it is substance, it is neither separated nor divided. Again, water, insofar as it is water, is generated and corrupted, but insofar as it is substance, it is neither generated nor corrupted.

[VI.] And with this I think I have replied to the second argument also, since it is based on the supposition that matter, insofar as it is substance, is divisible, and composed of parts. Even if this [reply] were not [sufficient], I do not know why [divisibility] would be unworthy of the divine nature. For (by P14) apart from God there can be no substance by which [the divine nature] would be acted on. All things, I say, are in God, and all things that happen, happen only through the laws of God's infinite nature and follow (as I shall show) from the necessity of his essence. So it cannot be said in any way that God is acted on by another, or that extended substance is unworthy of the divine nature, even if it is supposed to be divisible, so long as it is granted to be eternal and infinite. But enough of this for the present.

P16: *From the necessity of the divine nature there must follow infinitely many things in infinitely many modes (i.e., everything which can fall under an infinite intellect).*

Dem.: This Proposition must be plain to anyone, provided he attends to the fact that the intellect infers from the given definition of any thing a number of properties that really do follow necessarily from it (i.e., from the very essence of the thing); and that it infers more properties the more the definition of the thing expresses reality, i.e., the more reality the essence of the defined thing involves. But since the divine nature has absolutely infinite attributes (by D6), each of which also expresses an essence infinite in its own kind, from its necessity there must follow infinitely many things in infinite modes (i.e., everything which can fall under an infinite intellect), q.e.d.

Cor. 1: From this it follows that God is the efficient cause of all things which can fall under an infinite intellect.

Cor. 2: It follows, secondly, that God is a cause through himself and not an accidental cause.

Cor. 3: It follows, thirdly, that God is absolutely the first cause.

P17: *God acts from the laws of his nature alone, and is compelled by no one.*

Dem.: We have just shown (P16) that from the necessity of the divine nature alone, or (what is the same thing) from the laws of his nature alone, absolutely infinite things follow, and in P15 we have demonstrated that nothing can be or be conceived without God, but that all things are in God. So there can be nothing outside him by which he is determined or compelled to act. Therefore, God acts from the laws of his nature alone, and is compelled by no one, q.e.d.

Cor. 1: From this it follows, first, that there is no cause, either extrinsically or intrinsically, which prompts God to action, except the perfection of his nature.

Cor. 2: It follows, secondly, that God alone is a free cause. For God alone exists only from the necessity of his nature (by P11 and P14C1), and acts from the necessity of his nature (by P17). Therefore (by D7) God alone is a free cause, q.e.d.

Schol.: [I.] Others think that God is a free cause because he can (so they think) bring it about that the things which we have said follow from his nature (i.e., which are in his power) do not happen or are not produced by him. But this is the same as if they were to say that God can bring it about that it would not follow from the nature of a triangle that its three angles are equal to two right angles; or that from a given cause the effect would not follow—which is absurd.

Further, I shall show later, without the aid of this Proposition, that neither intellect nor will pertain to God's nature. Of course I know there are many who think they can demonstrate that a supreme intellect and a free will pertain to God's nature. For they say they know nothing they can ascribe to God more perfect than what is the highest perfection in us.

Moreover, even if they conceive God to actually understand in the highest degree, they still do not believe that he can bring it about that all the things he actually understands exist. For they think that in that way they would destroy God's power. If he had created all the things in his intellect (they say), then he would have been able to create nothing more, which they believe to be incompatible with God's omnipotence. So they preferred to maintain that God is indifferent to all things, not creating anything except what he has decreed to create by some absolute will.

But I think I have shown clearly enough (see P16) that from God's supreme power, *or* infinite nature, infinitely many things in infinitely many modes, i.e., all things, have necessarily flowed, or always follow, by the same necessity and in the same way as from the nature of a triangle it follows, from eternity and to eternity, that its three angles are equal to two right angles. So God's omnipotence has been actual from eternity and will remain in the same actuality to eternity. And in this way, at least in my opinion, God's omnipotence is maintained far more perfectly.

Indeed—to speak openly—my opponents seem to deny God's omnipotence. For they are forced to confess that God understands infinitely many creatable things, which nevertheless he will never be able to create. For otherwise, if he created everything he understood [to be creatable] he would (according to them) exhaust his omnipotence and render himself imperfect. Therefore to maintain that God is perfect, they are driven to maintain at the same time that he cannot bring about everything to which his power extends. I do not see what could be feigned which would be more absurd than this or more contrary to God's omnipotence.

[II.] Further—to say something here also about the intellect and will which we commonly attribute to God—if will and intellect do pertain to the eternal essence of God, we must of course understand by each of these attributes something different from what men commonly understand. For the intellect and will which would constitute God's essence would have to differ entirely from our intellect and will, and could not agree with them in anything except the name. They would not agree with one another any more than do the dog that is a heavenly constellation and the dog that is a barking animal. I shall demonstrate this.

If intellect pertains to the divine nature, it will not be able to be (like our intellect) by nature either posterior to (as most would have it), or simultaneous with, the things understood, since God is prior in causality to all things (by P16C1). On the contrary, the truth and formal essence of things is what it is because it exists objectively in that way in God's intellect. So God's intellect, insofar as it is conceived to constitute God's essence, is really the cause both of the essence and of the existence of things. This seems also to have been noticed by those who asserted that God's intellect, will and power are one and the same.

Therefore, since God's intellect is the only cause of things (viz. as we have shown, both of their essence and of their existence), he must necessarily differ from them both as to his essence and as to his existence. For what is caused differs from its cause precisely in what it has from the cause [for that reason it is called the effect of such a cause]. E.g., a man is the cause of the existence of another man, but not of his essence, for the latter is an eternal truth. Hence, they can agree entirely according to their essence. But in existing they must differ. And for that reason, if the existence of one perishes, the other's existence will not thereby perish. But if the essence of one could be destroyed, and become false, the other's essence would also be destroyed [and become false].

So the thing that is the cause both of the essence and of the existence of some effect, must differ from such an effect, both as to its essence and as to its existence. But God's intellect is the cause both of the essence and of the existence of our intellect. Therefore, God's intellect, insofar as it is conceived to constitute the divine essence, differs from our intellect both as to its essence and as to its existence, and cannot agree with it in anything except in name, as we supposed. The proof proceeds in the same way concerning the will, as anyone can easily see.

P18: *God is the immanent, not the transitive, cause of all things.*

Dem.: Everything that is, is in God, and must be conceived through God (by P15), and so (by P16C1) God is the cause of [all] things, which are in him. That is the first [thing to be proven]. And then outside God there can be no substance (by P14), i.e. (by D3), thing which is in itself outside God. That was the second. God, therefore, is the immanent, not the transitive cause of all things, q.e.d.

P19: *God is eternal, or all God's attributes are eternal.*

Dem.: For God (by D6) is substance, which (by P11) necessarily exists, i.e. (by P7), to whose nature it pertains to exist, or (what is the same) from whose definition it follows that he exists; and therefore (by D8), he is eternal.

Next, by God's attributes are to be understood what (by D4) expresses an essence of the Divine substance, i.e., what pertains to substance. The attributes themselves, I say, must involve it itself. But eternity pertains to the nature of substance (as I have already demonstrated from P7). Therefore each of the attributes must involve eternity, and so, they are all eternal, q.e.d.

Schol.: This Proposition is also as clear as possible from the way I have demonstrated God's existence (P11). For from that demonstration, I say, it is established that God's existence, like his essence, is an eternal truth. And then I have also demonstrated God's eternity in another way (Descartes' *Principles* IP19), and there is no need to repeat it here.

P20: *God's existence and his essence are one and the same.*

Dem.: God (by P19) and all of his attributes are eternal, i.e. (by D8), each of his attributes expresses existence. Therefore, the same attributes of God which (by D4) explain God's eternal essence at the same time explain his eternal existence, i.e., that itself which constitutes God's essence at the same time constitutes his existence. So his existence and his essence are one and the same, q.e.d.

Cor. 1: From this it follows, first, that God's existence, like his essence, is an eternal truth.

Cor. 2: It follows, secondly, that God, or all of God's attributes, are immutable. For if they changed as to their existence, they would also (by P20) change as to their essence, i.e. (as is known through itself), from being true become false, which is absurd.

P21: *All the things which follow from the absolute nature of any of God's attributes have always had to exist and be infinite, or are, through the same attribute, eternal and infinite.*

Dem.: If you deny this, then conceive (if you can) that in some attribute of God there follows from its absolute nature something that is finite and has a determinate existence, or duration, e.g., God's idea in thought. Now since thought is supposed to be an attribute of God, it is necessarily (by P11) infinite by its nature. But insofar as it has God's idea, [thought] is supposed to be finite. But (by D2) [thought] cannot be conceived to be finite unless it is determined through thought itself. But [thought can] not [be determined] through thought itself, insofar as it constitutes God's idea, for to that extent [thought] is supposed to be finite. Therefore, [thought must be determined] through thought insofar as it does not constitute God's idea, which [thought] nevertheless (by P11) must necessarily exist. Therefore, there is thought which does not constitute God's idea, and on that account God's idea does not follow necessarily from the nature [of this thought] insofar as it is absolute thought (for [thought] is conceived both as constituting God's idea and as not constituting it). [That God's idea does not follow from thought, insofar as it is absolute thought] is contrary to the hypothesis. So if God's idea in thought, or anything else in any attribute of God (for it does not matter what example is taken, since the demonstration is universal), follows from the necessity of the absolute nature of the attribute itself, it must necessarily be infinite. This was the first thing to be proven.

Next, what follows in this way from the necessity of the nature of any attribute cannot have a determinate [existence, or] duration. For if you deny this, then suppose there is, in some attribute of God, a thing which follows from the necessity of the nature of that attribute—e.g., God's idea in thought—and suppose that at some time [this idea] did not exist or will not exist. But since thought is supposed to be an attribute of God, it must exist necessarily and be immutable (by P11 and P20C2). So beyond the limits of the duration of God's idea (for it is supposed that at some time [this idea] did not exist or will not exist) thought will have to exist without God's idea. But this is contrary to the hypothesis, for it is supposed that God's idea follows necessarily from the given thought. Therefore, God's idea in thought, or anything else which follows necessarily from the absolute nature of some attribute of God, cannot have a determinate duration, but through the same attribute is eternal. This was the second thing [to be proven]. Note that the same is to be affirmed of any thing which, in some attribute of God, follows necessarily from God's absolute nature.

P22: *Whatever follows from some attribute of God insofar as it is modified by a modification which, through the same attribute, exists necessarily and is infinite, must also exist necessarily and be infinite.*

Dem.: The demonstration of this proposition proceeds in the same way as the demonstration of the preceding one.

P23: *Every mode which exists necessarily and is infinite has necessarily had to follow either from the absolute nature of some attribute of God, or from some attribute, modified by a modification which exists necessarily and is infinite.*

Dem.: For a mode is in another, through which it must be conceived (by D5), i.e. (by P15), it is in God alone, and can be conceived through God alone. So if a mode is conceived to exist necessarily and be infinite, [its necessary existence and infinitude] must necessarily be inferred, or perceived through some attribute of God, insofar as that attribute is conceived to express infinity and necessity of existence, or (what is the same, by D8) eternity, i.e. (by D6 and P19), insofar as it is considered absolutely. Therefore, the mode, which exists necessarily and is infinite, has had to follow from the absolute nature of some attribute of God—either immediately (see P21) or by some mediating modification, which follows from its absolute nature, i.e. (by P22), which exists necessarily and is infinite, q.e.d.

P24: *The essence of things produced by God does not involve existence.*

Dem.: This is evident from D1. For that whose nature involves existence (considered in itself), is its own cause, and exists only from the necessity of its nature.

Cor.: From this it follows that God is not only the cause of things' beginning to exist, but also of their persevering in existing, or (to use a Scholastic term) God is the cause of the being of things. For—whether the things [produced] exist or not—so long as we attend to their essence, we shall find that it involves neither existence nor duration. So their essence can be the cause neither of their existence nor of their duration, but only God, to whose nature alone it pertains to exist [can be the cause] (by P14C1).

P25: *God is the efficient cause, not only of the existence of things, but also of their essence.*

Dem.: If you deny this, then God is not the cause of the essence of things; and so (by A4) the essence of things can be conceived without God. But (by P15) this is absurd. Therefore God is also the cause of the essence of things, q.e.d.

Schol.: This Proposition follows more clearly from P16. For from that it follows that from the given divine nature both the essence of things and their existence must necessarily be inferred; and in a word, God must be called the cause of all things in the same sense in which he is called the cause of himself. This will be established still more clearly from the following corollary.

Cor.: Particular things are nothing but affections of God's attributes, or modes by which God's attributes are expressed in a certain and determinate way. The demonstration is evident from P15 and D5.

P26: *A thing which has been determined to produce an effect has necessarily been determined in this way by God; and one which has not been determined by God cannot determine itself to produce an effect.*

Dem.: That through which things are said to be determined to produce an effect must be something positive (as is known through itself). And so, God, from the necessity of his nature, is the efficient cause both of its essence and of its existence (by P15 and 16); this was the first thing. And from it the second thing asserted also follows very clearly. For if a thing which has not been determined by God could determine itself, the first part of this [proposition] would be false, which is absurd, as we have shown.

P27: *A thing which has been determined by God to produce an effect, cannot render itself undetermined.*

Dem.: This proposition is evident from A3.

The Synagogue, Amsterdam, n.d., by Rembrandt (1606–1669). Spinoza was a member of the Amsterdam Synagogue until he was excommunicated in 1656. (*Musée de la Ville de Paris, Musée du Petit-Palais/Art Resource*)

P28: *Every singular thing, or any thing which is finite and has a determinate existence, can neither exist nor be determined to produce an effect unless it is determined to exist and produce an effect by another cause, which is also finite and has a determinate existence; and again, this cause also can neither exist nor be determined to produce an effect unless it is determined to exist and produce an effect by another, which is also finite and has a determinate existence, and so on, to infinity.*

Dem.: Whatever has been determined to exist and produce an effect has been so determined by God (by P16 and P24C). But what is finite and has a determinate existence could not have been produced by the absolute nature of an attribute of God; for whatever follows from the absolute nature of an attribute of God is eternal and infinite (by P21). It had, therefore, to follow either from God or from an attribute of God insofar as it is considered to be affected by some mode. For there is nothing except substance and its modes (by A1, D3, and D5) and modes (by P25C) are nothing but affections of God's attributes. But it also could not follow from God, or from an attribute of God, insofar as it is affected by a modification which is eternal and infinite (by P22). It had, therefore, to follow from, or be determined to exist and produce an effect by God or an attribute of God insofar as it is modified by a modification which is finite and has a determinate existence. This was the first thing to be proven.

And in turn, this cause, or this mode (by the same reasoning by which we have already demonstrated the first part of this proposition) had also to be determined by another, which is also finite and has a determinate existence; and again, this last (by the same reasoning) by another, and so always (by the same reasoning) to infinity, q.e.d.

Schol.: Since certain things had to be produced by God immediately, viz. those which follow necessarily from his absolute nature, and others (which nevertheless can neither be nor be conceived without God) had to be produced by the mediation of these first things, it follows:

I. That God is absolutely the proximate cause of the things produced immediately by him, and not [a proximate cause] in his own kind, as they say. For God's effects can neither be nor be conceived without their cause (by P15 and P24C).

II. That God cannot properly be called the remote cause of singular things, except perhaps so that we may distinguish them from those things that he has produced immediately, or rather, that follow from his absolute nature. For by a remote cause we understand one which is not conjoined in any way with its effect. But all things that are, are in God, and so depend on God that they can neither be nor be conceived without him.

P29: *In nature there is nothing contingent, but all things have been determined from the necessity of the divine nature to exist and produce an effect in a certain way.*

Dem.: Whatever is, is in God (by P15); but God cannot be called a contingent thing. For (by P11) he exists necessarily, not contingently. Next, the modes of the divine nature have also followed from it necessarily and not contingently (by P16)—either insofar as the divine nature is considered absolutely (by P21) or insofar as it is considered to be determined to act in a certain way (by P18). Further, God is the cause of these modes not only insofar as they simply exist (by P24C), but also (by P16) insofar as they are considered to be determined to produce an effect. For if they have not been determined by God, then (by P16) it is impossible, not contingent, that they should determine themselves. Conversely (by P17) if they have been determined by God, it is not contingent, but impossible, that they should render themselves undetermined. So all things have been determined from the necessity of the divine nature, not only to exist, but to exist in a certain way, and to produce effects in a certain way. There is nothing contingent, q.e.d.

Schol.: Before I proceed further, I wish to explain here—or rather to advise [the reader]—what we must understand by *Natura naturans* and *Natura naturata*. For from the preceding I think it is already established that by *Natura naturans* we must understand what is in itself and is conceived through itself, or such attributes of substance as express an eternal and infinite essence, i.e. (by P14C1 and P17C2), God, insofar as he is considered as a free cause.

But by *Natura naturata* I understand whatever follows from the necessity of God's nature, or from any of God's attributes, i.e., all the modes of God's attributes in-sofar as they are considered as things which are in God, and can neither be nor be con-ceived without God.

P30: *An actual intellect, whether finite or infinite, must comprehend God's attributes and God's affections, and nothing else.*

Dem.: A true idea must agree with its object (by A6), i.e. (as is known through itself), what is contained objectively in the intellect must necessarily be in nature. But in nature (by P14C1) there is only one substance, viz. God, and there are no affections other than those which are in God (by P15) and which can neither be nor be conceived without God (by P15). Therefore, an actual intellect, whether finite or infinite, must comprehend God's attributes and God's affections, and nothing else, q.e.d.

P31: *The actual intellect, whether finite or infinite, like will, desire, love, etc., must be referred to* Natura naturata, *not to* Natura naturans.

Dem.: By intellect (as is known through itself) we understand not absolute thought, but only a certain mode of thinking, which mode differs from the others, such as desire, love, etc., and so (by D5) must be conceived through absolute thought, i.e. (by P15 and D6), it must be so conceived through an attribute of God, which expresses the eternal and infinite essence of thought, that can neither be nor be conceived without [that attribute]; and so (by P29S), like the other modes of thinking, it must be referred to *Natura naturata,* not to *Natura naturans,* q.e.d.

Schol.: The reason why I speak here of actual intellect is not because I concede that there is any potential intellect, but because, wishing to avoid all confusion, I wanted to speak only of what we perceive as clearly as possible, i.e., of the intellection itself. We perceive nothing more clearly than that. For we can understand nothing that does not lead to more perfect knowledge of the intellection.

P32: *The will cannot be called a free cause, but only a necessary one.*

Dem.: The will, like the intellect, is only a certain mode of thinking. And so (by P18) each volition can neither exist nor be determined to produce an effect unless it is determined by another cause, and this cause again by another, and so on, to infinity. Even if the will be supposed to be infinite, it must still be determined to exist and pro-duce an effect by God, not insofar as he is an absolutely infinite substance, but insofar as he has an attribute that expresses the infinite and eternal essence of thought (by P13). So in whatever way it is conceived, whether as finite or as infinite, it requires a cause by which it is determined to exist and produce an effect. And so (by D7) it can-not be called a free cause, but only a necessary or compelled one, q.e.d.

Cor. 1: From this it follows, first, that God does not produce any effect by free-dom of the will.

Cor. 2: It follows, secondly, that will and intellect are related to God's nature as motion and rest are, and as are absolutely all natural things, which (by P29) must be determined by God to exist and produce an effect in a certain way. For the will, like all other things, requires a cause by which it is determined to exist and produce an effect in a certain way. And although from a given will, *or* intellect infinitely many things may follow, God still cannot be said, on that account, to act from freedom of the will, any more than he can be said to act from freedom of motion and rest on account of those things that follow from motion and rest (for infinitely many things also follow from motion and rest). So will does not pertain to God's nature any more than do the other natural things, but is related to him in the same way as motion and rest, and all the other things which, as we have shown, follow from the necessity of the divine nature and are determined by it to exist and produce an effect in a certain way.

P33: *Things could have been produced by God in no other way, and in no other order than they have been produced.*

Dem.: For all things have necessarily followed from God's given nature (by P16), and have been determined from the necessity of God's nature to exist and produce an effect in a certain way (by P29). Therefore, if things could have been of another nature, or could have been determined to produce an effect in another way, so that the order of Nature was different, then God's nature could also have been other than it is now, and therefore (by P11) that [other nature] would also have had to exist, and consequently, there could have been two or more Gods, which is absurd (by P14C1). So things could have been produced in no other way and no other order, etc., q.e.d.

Schol. 1: Since by these propositions I have shown more clearly than the noon light that there is absolutely nothing in things on account of which they can be called contingent, I wish now to explain briefly what we must understand by contingent—but first, what [we must understand] by necessary and impossible.

A thing is called necessary either by reason of its essence or by reason of its cause. For a thing's existence follows necessarily either from its essence and definition or from a given efficient cause. And a thing is also called impossible from these same causes—viz. either because its essence, or definition, involves a contradiction, or because there is no external cause which has been determined to produce such a thing.

But a thing is called contingent only because of a defect of our knowledge. For if we do not know that the thing's essence involves a contradiction, or if we do know very well that its essence does not involve a contradiction, and nevertheless can affirm nothing certainly about its existence, because the order of causes is hidden from us, it can never seem to us either necessary or impossible. So we call it contingent or possible.

Schol. 2: From the preceding it clearly follows that things have been produced by God with the highest perfection, since they have followed necessarily from a given most perfect nature. Nor does this convict God of any imperfection, for his perfection compels us to affirm this. Indeed, from the opposite, it would clearly follow (as I have just shown), that God is not supremely perfect; because if things had been produced by God in another way, we would have to attribute to God another nature, different from that which we have been compelled to attribute to him from the consideration of the most perfect Being.

Of course, I have no doubt that many will reject this opinion as absurd, without even being willing to examine it—for no other reason than because they have been accustomed to attribute another freedom to God, far different from that we have taught

(D7), viz. an absolute will. But I also have no doubt that, if they are willing to reflect on the matter, and consider properly the chain of our demonstrations, in the end they will utterly reject the freedom they now attribute to God, not only as futile, but as a great obstacle to science. Nor is it necessary for me to repeat here what I said in P17S.

Nevertheless, to please them, I shall show that even if it is conceded that will pertains to God's essence, it still follows from his perfection that things could have been created by God in no other way or order. It will be easy to show this if we consider, first, what they themselves concede, viz. that it depends on God's decree and will alone that each thing is what it is. For otherwise God would not be the cause of all things. Next, that all God's decrees have been established by God himself from eternity. For otherwise he would be convicted of imperfection and inconstancy. But since, in eternity, there is neither when, nor *before*, nor *after*, it follows, from God's perfection alone, that he can never decree anything different, and never could have, or that God was not before his decrees, and cannot be without them.

But they will say that even if it were supposed that God had made another nature of things, or that from eternity he had decreed something else concerning nature and its order, no imperfection in God would follow from that.

Still, if they say this, they will concede at the same time that God can change his decrees. For if God had decreed, concerning nature and its order, something other than what he did decree, i.e., had willed and conceived something else concerning nature, he would necessarily have had an intellect other than he now has, and a will other than he now has. And if it is permitted to attribute to God another intellect and another will, without any change of his essence and of his perfection, why can he not now change his decrees concerning created things, and nevertheless remain equally perfect? For his intellect and will concerning created things and their order are the same in respect to his essence and his perfection, however his will and intellect may be conceived.

Further, all the Philosophers I have seen concede that in God there is no potential intellect, but only an actual one. But since his intellect and his will are not distinguished from his essence, as they all also concede, it follows that if God had had another actual intellect, and another will, his essence would also necessarily be other. And therefore (as I inferred at the beginning) if things had been produced by God otherwise than they now are, God's intellect and his will, i.e. (as is conceded), his essence, would have to be different [from what it now is]. And this is absurd.

Therefore, since things could have been produced by God in no other way, and no other order, and since it follows from God's supreme perfection that this is true, no truly sound reason can persuade us to believe that God did not will to create all the things that are in his intellect, with that same perfection with which he understands them.

But they will say that there is no perfection or imperfection in things; what is in them, on account of which they are perfect or imperfect, and are called good or bad, depends only on God's will. And so, if God had willed, he could have brought it about that what is now perfection would have been the greatest imperfection, and conversely [that what is now an imperfection in things would have been the most perfect]. How would this be different from saying openly that God, who necessarily understands what he wills, can bring it about by his will that he understands things in another way than he does understand them? As I have just shown, this is a great absurdity.

So I can turn the argument against them in the following way. All things depend on God's power. So in order for things to be able to be different, God's will would necessarily also have to be different. But God's will cannot be different (as we have just shown most evidently from God's perfection). So things also cannot be different.

I confess that this opinion, which subjects all things to a certain indifferent will of God, and makes all things depend on his good pleasure, is nearer the truth than that of those who maintain that God does all things for the sake of the good. For they seem to place something outside God, which does not depend on God, to which God attends, as a model, in what he does, and at which he aims, as at a certain goal. This is simply to subject God to fate. Nothing more absurd can be maintained about God, whom we have shown to be the first and only free cause, both of the essence of all things, and of their existence. So I shall waste no time in refuting this absurdity.

P34: *God's power is his essence itself.*

Dem.: For from the necessity alone of God's essence it follows that God is the cause of himself (by P11) and (by P16 and P16C) of all things. Therefore, God's power, by which he and all things are and act, is his essence itself, q.e.d.

P35: *Whatever we conceive to be in God's power, necessarily exists.*

Dem.: For whatever is in God's power must (by P34) be so comprehended by his essence that it necessarily follows from it, and therefore necessarily exists, q.e.d.

P36: *Nothing exists from whose nature some effect does not follow.*

Dem.: Whatever exists expresses the nature, or essence of God in a certain and determinate way (by P25C), i.e. (by P34), whatever exists expresses in a certain and determinate way the power of God, which is the cause of all things. So (by P16), from [everything that exists] some effect must follow, q.e.d.

Appendix

With these [demonstrations] I have explained God's nature and properties: that he exists necessarily; that he is unique; that he is and acts from the necessity alone of his nature; that (and how) he is the free cause of all things; that all things are in God and so depend on him that without him they can neither be nor be conceived; and finally, that all things have been predetermined by God, not from freedom of the will *or* absolute good pleasure, but from God's absolute nature, or infinite power.

Further, I have taken care, whenever the occasion arose, to remove prejudices that could prevent my demonstrations from being perceived. But because many prejudices remain that could, and can, be a great obstacle to men's understanding the connection of things in the way I have explained it, I considered it worthwhile to submit them here to the scrutiny of reason. All the prejudices I here undertake to expose depend on this one: that men commonly suppose that all natural things act, as men do, on account of an end; indeed, they maintain as certain that God himself directs all things to some certain end, for they say that God has made all things for man, and man that he might worship God.

So I shall begin by considering this one prejudice, asking *first* [I] why most people are satisfied that it is true, and why all are so inclined by nature to embrace it. Then [II] I shall show its falsity, and finally [III] how, from this, prejudices have arisen concerning *good* and *evil*, *merit* and *sin*, *praise* and *blame*, *order* and *confusion*, *beauty* and *ugliness*, and other things of this kind.

[I.] Of course this is not the place to deduce these things from the nature of the human mind. It will be sufficient here if I take as a foundation what everyone must acknowledge: that all men are born ignorant of the causes of things, and that they all want to seek their own advantage, and are conscious of this appetite.

From these [assumptions] it follows, *first*, that men think themselves free, because they are conscious of their volitions and their appetite, and do not think, even in their dreams, of the causes by which they are disposed to wanting and willing, because they are ignorant of [those causes]. It follows, *secondly*, that men act always on account of an end, viz. on account of their advantage, which they want. Hence they seek to know only the final causes of what has been done, and when they have heard them, they are satisfied, because they have no reason to doubt further. But if they cannot hear them from another, nothing remains for them but to turn toward themselves, and reflect on the ends by which they are usually determined to do such things; so they necessarily judge the temperament of other men from their own temperament.

Furthermore, they find—both in themselves and outside themselves—many means that are very helpful in seeking their own advantage, e.g., eyes for seeing, teeth for chewing, plants and animals for food, the sun for light, the sea for supporting fish [and so with almost all other things whose natural causes they have no reason to doubt]. Hence, they consider all natural things as means to their own advantage. And knowing that they had found these means, not provided them for themselves, they had reason to believe that there was someone else who had prepared those means for their use. For after they considered things as means, they could not believe that the things had made themselves; but from the means they were accustomed to prepare for themselves, they had to infer that there was a ruler, or a number of rulers of nature, endowed with human freedom, who had taken care of all things for them, and made all things for their use.

And since they had never heard anything about the temperament of these rulers, they had to judge it from their own. Hence, they maintained that the Gods direct all things for the use of men in order to bind men to them and be held by men in the highest honor. So it has happened that each of them has thought up from his own temperament different ways of worshipping God, so that God might love them above all the rest, and direct the whole of Nature according to the needs of their blind desire and insatiable greed. Thus this prejudice was changed into superstition, and struck deep roots in their minds. This was why each of them strove with great diligence to understand and explain the final causes of all things.

But while they sought to show that nature does nothing in vain (i.e., nothing which is not of use to men), they seem to have shown only that nature and the Gods are as mad as men. See, I ask you, how the matter has turned out in the end! Among so many conveniences in nature they had to find many inconveniences: storms, earthquakes, diseases, etc. These, they maintain, happen because the Gods [(whom they judge to be of the same nature as themselves)] are angry on account of wrongs done to them by men, or on account of sins committed in their worship. And though their daily experience contradicted this, and though infinitely many examples showed that conveniences and inconveniences happen indiscriminately to the pious and the impious alike, they did not on that account give up their longstanding prejudice. It was easier for them to put this among the other unknown things, whose use they were ignorant of, and so remain in the state of ignorance in which they had been born, than to destroy that whole construction, and think up a new one.

So they maintained it as certain that the judgments of the Gods far surpass man's grasp. This alone, of course, would have caused the truth to be hidden from the human race to eternity, if Mathematics, which is concerned not with ends, but only with the essences and properties of figures, had not shown men another standard of truth. And besides Mathematics, we can assign other causes also (which it is unnecessary to enumerate here), which were able to bring it about that men [—but very few, in relation to the whole human race—] would notice these common prejudices and be led to the true knowledge of things.

[II.] With this I have sufficiently explained what I promised in the first place [viz. why men are so inclined to believe that all things act for an end]. Not many words will be required now to show that Nature has no end set before it, and that all final causes are nothing but human fictions. For I believe I have already sufficiently established it, both by the foundations and causes from which I have shown this prejudice to have had its origin, and also by P16, P32C1 and C2, and all those [propositions] by which I have shown that all things proceed by a certain eternal necessity of nature, and with the greatest perfection.

I shall, however, add this: this doctrine concerning the end turns nature completely upside down. For what is really a cause, it considers as an effect, and conversely [what is an effect it considers as a cause]. What is by nature prior, it makes posterior. And finally, what is supreme and most perfect, it makes imperfect.

For—to pass over the first two, since they are manifest through themselves—as has been established in PP21–23, that effect is most perfect which is produced immediately by God, and the more something requires intermediate causes to produce it, the more imperfect it is. But if the things which have been produced immediately by God had been made so that God would achieve his end, then the last things, for the sake of which the first would have been made, would be the most excellent of all.

Again, this doctrine takes away God's perfection. For if God acts for the sake of an end, he necessarily wants something which he lacks. And though the Theologians and Metaphysicians distinguish between an end of need and an end of assimilation, they nevertheless confess that God did all things for his own sake, not for the sake of the things to be created. For before creation they can assign nothing except God for whose sake God would act. And so they are necessarily compelled to confess that God lacked those things for the sake of which he willed to prepare means, and that he desired them. This is clear through itself.

Nor ought we here to pass over the fact that the Followers of this doctrine, who have wanted to show off their cleverness in assigning the ends of things, have introduced—to prove this doctrine of theirs—a new way of arguing: by reducing things, not to the impossible, but to ignorance. This shows that no other way of defending their doctrine was open to them.

For example, if a stone has fallen from a roof onto someone's head and killed him, they will show, in the following way, that the stone fell in order to kill the man. For if it did not fall to that end, God willing it, how could so many circumstances have concurred by chance (for often many circumstances do concur at once)? Perhaps you will answer that it happened because the wind was blowing hard and the man was walking that way. But they will persist: why was the wind blowing hard at that time? why was the man walking that way at that same time? If you answer again that the wind arose then because on the preceding day, while the weather was still calm, the sea began to toss, and that the man had been invited by a friend, they will press on—for there is no end to the questions which can be asked: but why was the sea tossing? why was the man invited at just that time? And so they will not stop asking for the causes of causes until you take refuge in the will of God, i.e., the sanctuary of ignorance.

Similarly, when they see the structure of the human body, they are struck by a foolish wonder, and because they do not know the causes of so great an art, they infer that it is constructed, not by mechanical, but by divine, or supernatural art, and constituted in such a way that one part does not injure another.

Hence it happens that one who seeks the true causes of miracles, and is eager, like an educated man, to understand natural things, not to wonder at them, like a fool, is generally considered and denounced as an impious heretic by those whom the people honor as interpreters of nature and the Gods. For they know that if ignorance is taken away, then foolish wonder, the only means they have of arguing and defending their authority, is also taken away. But I leave these things, and pass on to what I have decided to treat here in the third place.

[III.] After men persuaded themselves that everything that happens, happens on their account, they had to judge that what is most important in each thing is what is most useful to them, and to rate as most excellent all those things by which they were most pleased. Hence, they had to form these notions, by which they explained natural things: *good*, *evil*, *order*, *confusion*, *warm*, *cold*, *beauty*, *ugliness*. And because they think themselves free, those notions have arisen: *praise* and *blame*, *sin* and *merit*. The latter I shall explain after I have treated human nature; but the former I shall briefly explain here.

Whatever conduces to health and the worship of God, they have called *good*; but what is contrary to these, *evil*.

And because those who do not understand the nature of things, but only imagine them, affirm nothing concerning things, and take the imagination for the intellect, they firmly believe, in their ignorance of things and of their own nature, that there is an order in things. For when things are so disposed that, when they are presented to us through the senses, we can easily imagine them, and so can easily remember them, we say that they are wellordered; but if the opposite is true, we say that they are badly ordered, or confused.

And since those things we can easily imagine are especially pleasing to us, men prefer order to confusion, as if order were anything in nature more than a relation to our imagination. They also say that God has created all things in order, and so, unknowingly attribute imagination to God—unless, perhaps, they mean that God, to provide for human imagination, has disposed all things so that men can very easily imagine them. Nor will it, perhaps, give them pause that infinitely many things are found which far surpass our imagination, and a great many which confuse it on account of its weakness. But enough of this.

The other notions are also nothing but modes of imagining, by which the imagination is variously affected; and yet the ignorant consider them the chief attributes of things, because, as we have already said, they believe all things have been made for their sake, and call the nature of a thing good or evil, sound or rotten and corrupt, as they are affected by it. For example, if the motion the nerves receive from objects presented through the eyes is conducive to health, the objects by which it is caused are called beautiful; those which cause a contrary motion are called ugly. Those which move the sense through the nose, they call pleasant-smelling or stinking; through the tongue, sweet or bitter, tasty or tasteless; through touch, hard or soft, rough or smooth, etc.; and finally, those which move the ears are said to produce noise, sound or harmony. Men have been so mad as to believe that God is pleased by harmony. Indeed there are Philosophers who have persuaded themselves that the motions of the heavens produce a harmony.

All of these things show sufficiently that each one has judged things according to the disposition of his brain; or rather, has accepted affections of the imagination as things. So it is no wonder (to note this, too, in passing) that we find so many controversies to have arisen among men, and that they have finally given rise to Skepticism. For although human bodies agree in many things, they still differ in very many. And for that reason what seems good to one, seems bad to another; what seems ordered to one, seems confused to another; what seems pleasing to one, seems displeasing to another, and so on.

I pass over the [other notions] here, both because this is not the place to treat them at length, and because everyone has experienced this [variability] sufficiently for himself. That is why we have such sayings as "So many heads, so many attitudes," "everyone finds his own judgment more than enough," and "there are as many differences of brains as of palates." These proverbs show sufficiently that men judge things according to the disposition of their brain, and imagine, rather than understand them. For if men had understood them, the things would at least convince them all, even if they did not attract them all, as the example of mathematics shows.

We see, therefore, that all the notions by which ordinary people are accustomed to explain nature are only modes of imagining, and do not indicate the nature of anything, only the constitution of the imagination. And because they have names, as if they were [notions] of beings existing outside the imagination, I call them beings, not of reason, but of imagination. So all the arguments in which people try to use such notions against us can easily be warded off.

For many are accustomed to arguing in this way: if all things have followed from the necessity of God's most perfect nature, why are there so many imperfections in nature? why are things corrupt to the point where they stink? so ugly that they produce nausea? why is there confusion, evil, and sin?

As I have just said, those who argue in this way are easily answered. For the perfection of things is to be judged solely from their nature and power; things are not more or less perfect because they please or offend men's senses, or because they are of use to, or are incompatible with, human nature.

But to those who ask "why God did not create all men so that they would be governed by the command of reason?" I answer only "because he did not lack material to create all things, from the highest degree of perfection to the lowest"; or, to speak more properly, "because the laws of his nature have been so ample that they sufficed for producing all things which can be conceived by an infinite intellect" (as I have demonstrated in P16).

These are the prejudices I undertook to note here. If any of this kind still remain, they can be corrected by anyone with only a little meditation. [And so I find no reason to devote more time to these matters, etc.]

SECOND PART OF THE ETHICS

ON THE NATURE AND ORIGIN OF THE MIND

I pass now to explaining those things which must necessarily follow from the essence of God, or the infinite and eternal Being—not, indeed, all of them, for we have demonstrated (IP16) that infinitely many things must follow from it in infinitely many modes, but only those that can lead us, by the hand, as it were, to the knowledge of the human Mind and its highest blessedness.

Definitions

D1: By body I understand a mode that in a certain and determinate way expresses God's essence insofar as he is considered as an extended thing (see IP25C).

D2: I say that to the essence of any thing belongs that which, being given, the thing is [also] necessarily posited and which, being taken away, the thing is necessarily [also] taken away; or that without which the thing can neither be nor be conceived, and which can neither be nor be conceived without the thing.

D3: By idea I understand a concept of the Mind that the Mind forms because it is a thinking thing.
    Exp.: *I say concept rather than perception, because the word perception seems to indicate that the Mind is acted on by the object. But concept seems to express an action of the Mind.*

D4: By adequate idea I understand an idea which, insofar as it is considered in itself, without relation to an object, has all the properties, or intrinsic denominations of a true idea.

Exp.: *I say intrinsic to exclude what is extrinsic, viz. the agreement of the idea with its object.*

D5: Duration is an indefinite continuation of existing.

Exp.: *I say indefinite because it cannot be determined at all through the very nature of the existing thing, nor even by the efficient cause, which necessarily posits the existence of the thing, and does not take it away.*

D6: By reality and perfection I understand the same thing.

D7: By singular things I understand things that are finite and have a determinate existence. And if a number of Individuals so concur in one action that together they are all the cause of one effect, I consider them all, to that extent, as one singular thing.

Axioms

A1: The essence of man does not involve necessary existence, i.e., from the order of nature it can happen equally that this or that man does exist, or that he does not exist.

A2: Man thinks.

A3: There are no modes of thinking, such as love, desire, or whatever is designated by the word affects of the mind, unless there is in the same Individual the idea of the thing loved, desired, etc. But there can be an idea, even though there is no other mode of thinking.

A4: We feel that a certain body is affected in many ways.

A5: We neither feel nor perceive any singular things [or anything of *natura naturata*], except bodies and modes of thinking.

    See the postulates after P13.

P1: *Thought is an attribute of God, or God is a thinking thing.*

    Dem.: Singular thoughts, or this or that thought, are modes that express God's nature in a certain and determinate way (by IP25C). Therefore (by ID5) there belongs to God an attribute whose concept all singular thoughts involve, and through which they are also conceived. Therefore, Thought is one of God's infinite attributes, which expresses an eternal and infinite essence of God (see ID6), *or* God is a thinking thing, q.e.d.

    Schol.: This Proposition is also evident from the fact that we can conceive an infinite thinking being. For the more things a thinking being can think, the more reality, or perfection, we conceive it to contain. Therefore, a being that can think infinitely many things in infinitely many ways is necessarily infinite in its power of thinking. So since we can conceive an infinite Being by attending to thought alone, Thought (by ID4 and D6) is necessarily one of God's infinite attributes, as we maintained.

P2: *Extension is an attribute of God, or God is an extended thing.*

    Dem.: The demonstration of this proceeds in the same way as that of the preceding Proposition.

P3: *In God there is necessarily an idea, both of his essence and of everything that necessarily follows from his essence.*

    Dem.: For God (by P1) can think infinitely many things in infinitely many modes, *or* (what is the same, by IP16) can form the idea of his essence and of all the things which necessarily follow from it. But whatever is in God's power necessarily exists (by IP35); therefore, there is necessarily such an idea, and (by IP15) it is only in God, q.e.d.

    Schol.: By God's power ordinary people understand God's free will and his right over all things which are, things which on that account are commonly considered to be contingent. For they say that God has the power of destroying all things and reducing them to nothing. Further, they very often compare God's power with the power of Kings.

    But we have refuted this in IP32C1 and C2, and we have shown in IP16 that God acts with the same necessity by which he understands himself, i.e., just as it follows from the necessity of the divine nature (as everyone maintains unanimously) that God understands himself, with the same necessity it also follows that God does infinitely many things in infinitely many modes. And then we have shown in IP34 that God's power is nothing except God's active essence. And so it is as impossible for us to conceive that God does not act as it is to conceive that he does not exist.

    Again, if it were agreeable to pursue these matters further, I could also show here that that power which ordinary people fictitiously ascribe to God is not only human (which shows that ordinary people conceive God as a man, or as like a man), but also involves lack of power. But I do not wish to speak so often about the same topic. I only ask the reader to reflect repeatedly on what is said concerning this matter in Part I, from P16 to the end. For no one will be able to perceive rightly the things I maintain unless he takes great care not to confuse God's power with the human power or right of Kings.

P4: *God's idea, from which infinitely many things follow in infinitely many modes, must be unique.*

Dem.: An infinite intellect comprehends nothing except God's attributes and his affections (by IP30). But God is unique (by IP14C1). Therefore God's idea, from which infinitely many things follow in infinitely many modes, must be unique, q.e.d.

P5: *The formal being of ideas admits God as a cause only insofar as he is considered as a thinking thing, and not insofar as he is explained by any other attribute. I.e., ideas, both of God's attributes and of singular things, admit not the objects themselves, or the things perceived, as their efficient cause, but God himself, insofar as he is a thinking thing.*

Dem.: This is evident from P3. For there we inferred that God can form the idea of his essence, and of all the things that follow necessarily from it, solely from the fact that God is a thinking thing, and not from the fact that he is the object of his own idea. So the formal being of ideas admits God as its cause insofar as he is a thinking thing.

But another way of demonstrating this is the following. The formal being of ideas is a mode of thinking (as is known through itself), i.e. (by IP25C), a mode that expresses, in a certain way, God's nature insofar as he is a thinking thing. And so (by IP10) it involves the concept of no other attribute of God, and consequently (by IA4) is the effect of no other attribute than thought. And so the formal being of ideas admits God as its cause insofar as he is considered only as a thinking thing, etc., q.e.d.

P6: *The modes of each attribute have God for their cause only insofar as he is considered under the attribute of which they are modes, and not insofar as he is considered under any other attribute.*

Dem.: For each attribute is conceived through itself without any other (by IP10). So the modes of each attribute involve the concept of their own attribute, but not of another one; and so (by IA4) they have God for their cause only insofar as he is considered under the attribute of which they are modes, and not insofar as he is considered under any other, q.e.d.

Cor.: From this it follows that the formal being of things which are not modes of thinking does not follow from the divine nature because [God] has first known the things; rather the objects of ideas follow and are inferred from their attributes in the same way and by the same necessity as that with which we have shown ideas to follow from the attribute of Thought.

P7: *The order and connection of ideas is the same as the order and connection of things.*

Dem.: This is clear from IA4. For the idea of each thing caused depends on the knowledge of the cause of which it is the effect.

Cor.: From this it follows that God's [actual] power of thinking is equal to his actual power of acting. I.e., whatever follows formally from God's infinite nature follows objectively in God from his idea in the same order and with the same connection.

Schol.: Before we proceed further, we must recall here what we showed [in the First Part], viz. that whatever can be perceived by an infinite intellect as constituting an essence of substance pertains to one substance only, and consequently that the thinking substance and the extended substance are one and the same substance, which is now comprehended under this attribute, now under that. So also a mode of extension and the idea of that mode are one and the same thing, but expressed in two ways. Some of the Hebrews seem to have seen this, as if through a cloud, when they maintained that God, God's intellect, and the things understood by him are one and the same.

For example, a circle existing in nature and the idea of the existing circle, which is also in God, are one and the same thing, which is explained through different attributes. Therefore, whether we conceive nature under the attribute of Extension, or under the attribute of Thought, or under any other attribute, we shall find one and the same order, or one and the same connection of causes, i.e., that the same things follow one another.

When I said [before] that God is the cause of the idea, say of a circle, only insofar as he is a thinking thing, and [the cause] of the circle, only insofar as he is an extended thing, this was for no other reason than because the formal being of the idea of the circle can be perceived only through another mode of thinking, as its proximate cause, and that mode again through another, and so on, to infinity. Hence, so long as things are considered as modes of thinking, we must explain the order of the whole of nature, *or* the connection of causes, through the attribute of Thought alone. And insofar as they are considered as modes of Extension, the order of the whole of nature must be explained through the attribute of Extension alone. I understand the same concerning the other attributes.

So of things as they are in themselves, God is really the cause insofar as he consists of infinite attributes. For the present, I cannot explain these matters more clearly.

P8: *The ideas of singular things, or of modes, that do not exist must be comprehended in God's infinite idea in the same way as the formal essences of the singular things, or modes, are contained in God's attributes.*

Dem.: This Proposition is evident from the preceding one, but is understood more clearly from the preceding scholium.

Cor.: From this it follows that so long as singular things do not exist, except insofar as they are comprehended in God's attributes, their objective being, *or* ideas, do not exist except insofar as God's infinite idea exists. And when singular things are said to exist, not only insofar as they are comprehended in God's attributes, but insofar also as they are said to have duration, their ideas also involve the existence through which they are said to have duration.

Schol.: If anyone wishes me to explain this further by an example, I will, of course, not be able to give one which adequately explains what I speak of here, since it is unique. Still I shall try as far as possible to illustrate the matter: the circle is of such a nature that the rectangles formed from the segments of all the straight lines intersecting in it are equal to one another. So in a circle there are contained infinitely many rectangles that are equal to one another. Nevertheless, none of them can be said to exist except insofar as the circle exists, nor also can the idea of any of these rectangles be said to exist except insofar as it is comprehended in the idea of the circle. Now of these infinitely many [rectangles] let two only, viz. [those formed from the segments of lines] D and E, exist.

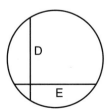

Of course their ideas also exist now, not only insofar as they are only comprehended in the idea of the circle, but also insofar as they involve the existence of those rectangles. By this they are distinguished from the other ideas of the other rectangles.

P9: *The idea of a singular thing which actually exists has God for a cause not insofar as he is infinite, but insofar as he is considered to be affected by another idea of a singular thing which actually exists; and of this [idea] God is also the cause, insofar as he is affected by another third [idea], and so on, to infinity.*

Dem.: The idea of a singular thing which actually exists is a singular mode of thinking, and distinct from the others (by P8C and S), and so (by P6) has God for a cause only insofar as he is a thinking thing. But not (by IP28) insofar as he is a thing thinking absolutely; rather insofar as he is considered to be affected by another [determinate] mode of thinking. And God is also the cause of this mode, insofar as he is affected by another [determinate mode of thinking], and so on, to infinity. But the order and connection of ideas (by P7) is the same as the order and connection of causes. Therefore, the cause of one singular idea is another idea, or God, insofar as he is considered to be affected by another idea; and of this also [God is the cause], insofar as he is affected by another, and so on, to infinity, q.e.d.

Cor.: Whatever happens in the singular object of any idea, there is knowledge of it in God, only insofar as he has the idea of the same object.

Dem.: Whatever happens in the object of any idea, there is an idea of it in God (by P3), not insofar as he is infinite, but insofar as he is considered to be affected by another idea of [an existing] singular thing (by P9); but the order and connection of ideas (by P7) is the same as the order and connection of things; therefore, knowledge of what happens in a singular object will be in God only insofar as he has the idea of the same object, q.e.d.

P10: *The being of substance does not pertain to the essence of man, or substance does not constitute the form of man.*

Dem.: For the being of substance involves necessary existence (by IP7). Therefore, if the being of substance pertained to the essence of man, then substance being given, man would necessarily be given (by D2), and consequently man would exist necessarily, which (by A1) is absurd, q.e.d.

Schol.: This proposition is also demonstrated from IP5, viz. that there are not two substances of the same nature. Since a number of men can exist, what constitutes the form of man is not the being of substance. Further, this proposition is evident from the other properties of substance, viz. that substance is, by its nature, infinite, immutable, indivisible, etc., as anyone can easily see.

Cor.: From this it follows that the essence of man is constituted by certain modifications of God's attributes.

Dem.: For the being of substance does not pertain to the essence of man (by P10). Therefore, it is something (by IP15) which is in God, and which can neither be nor be conceived without God, *or* (by IP25C) an affection, *or* mode, which expresses God's nature in a certain and determinate way.

Schol.: Everyone, of course, must concede that nothing can either be or be conceived without God. For all confess that God is the only cause of all things, both of their essence and of their existence. I.e., God is not only the cause of the coming to be of things, as they say, but also of their being.

But in the meantime many say that anything without which a thing can neither be nor be conceived pertains to the nature of the thing. And so they believe either that the nature of God pertains to the essence of created things, or that created things can be or be conceived without God—or what is more certain, they are not sufficiently consistent.

The cause of this, I believe, was that they did not observe the [proper] order of Philosophizing. For they believed that the divine nature, which they should have contemplated before all else (because it is prior both in knowledge and in nature) is last in the order of knowledge, and that the things that are called objects of the senses are prior to all. That is why, when they contemplated natural things, they thought of nothing less than they did of the divine nature; and when afterwards they directed their minds to contemplating the divine nature, they could think of nothing less than of their first fictions, on which they had built the knowledge of natural things, because these could not assist knowledge of the divine nature. So it is no wonder that they have generally contradicted themselves.

But I pass over this. For my intent here was only to give a reason why I did not say that anything without which a thing can neither be nor be conceived pertains to its nature—viz. because singular things can neither be nor be conceived without God, and nevertheless, God does not pertain to their essence. But I have said that what necessarily constitutes the essence of a thing is that which, if it is given, the thing is posited, and if it is taken away, the thing is taken away, i.e., the essence is what the thing can neither be nor be conceived without, and vice versa, what can neither be nor be conceived without the thing.

P11: *The first thing that constitutes the actual being of a human Mind is nothing but the idea of a singular thing which actually exists.*

Dem.: The essence of man (by P10C) is constituted by certain modes of God's attributes, viz. (by A2) by modes of thinking, of all of which (by A3) the idea is prior in nature, and when it is given, the other modes (to which the idea is prior in nature) must be in the same individual (by A3). And therefore an idea is the first thing that constitutes the being of a human Mind. But not the idea of a thing which does not exist. For then (by P8C) the idea itself could not be said to exist. Therefore, it will be the idea of a thing which actually exists. But not of an infinite thing. For an infinite thing (by IP21 and 22) must always exist necessarily. But (by A1) it is absurd [that this idea should be of a necessarily existing object]. Therefore, the first thing that constitutes the actual being of a human Mind is the idea of a singular thing which actually exists, q.e.d.

Cor.: From this it follows that the human Mind is a part of the infinite intellect of God. Therefore, when we say that the human Mind perceives this or that, we are saying nothing but that God, not insofar as he is infinite, but insofar as he is explained through the nature of the human Mind, *or* insofar as he constitutes the essence of the human Mind, has this or that idea; and when we say that God has this or that idea, not only insofar as he constitutes the nature of the human Mind, but insofar as he also has the idea of another thing together with the human Mind, then we say that the human Mind perceives the thing only partially, *or* inadequately.

Schol.: Here, no doubt, my readers will come to a halt, and think of many things which will give them pause. For this reason I ask them to continue on with me slowly, step by step, and to make no judgment on these matters until they have read through them all.

P12: *Whatever happens in the object of the idea constituting the human Mind must be perceived by the human Mind, or there will necessarily be an idea of that thing in the*

Mind; i.e., if the object of the idea constituting a human Mind is a body, nothing can happen in that body which is not perceived by the Mind.

Dem.: For whatever happens in the object of any idea, the knowledge of that thing is necessarily in God (by P9C), insofar as he is considered to be affected by the idea of the same object, i.e. (by P11), insofar as he constitutes the mind of some thing. Therefore, whatever happens in the object of the idea constituting the human Mind, the knowledge of it is necessarily in God insofar as he constitutes the nature of the human Mind, i.e. (by P11C), knowledge of this thing will necessarily be in the Mind, or the Mind will perceive it, q.e.d.

Schol.: This Proposition is also evident, and more clearly understood from P7S, which you should consult.

P13: *The object of the idea constituting the human Mind is the Body, or a certain mode of Extension which actually exists, and nothing else.*

Dem.: For if the object of the human Mind were not the Body, the ideas of the affections of the Body would not be in God (by P9C) insofar as he constituted our Mind, but insofar as he constituted the mind of another thing, i.e. (by P11C), the ideas of the affections of the Body would not be in our Mind; but (by A4) we have ideas of the affections of the body. Therefore, the object of the idea that constitutes the human Mind is the Body, and it (by P11) actually exists.

Next, if the object of the Mind were something else also, in addition to the Body, then since (by IP36) nothing exists from which there does not follow some effect, there would necessarily (by P12) be an idea in our Mind of some effect of it. But (by A5) there is no idea of it. Therefore, the object of our Mind is the existing Body and nothing else, q.e.d.

Cor.: From this it follows that man consists of a Mind and a Body, and that the human Body exists, as we are aware of it.

Schol.: From these [propositions] we understand not only that the human Mind is united to the Body, but also what should be understood by the union of Mind and Body. But no one will be able to understand it adequately, or distinctly, unless he first knows adequately the nature of our Body. For the things we have shown so far are completely general and do not pertain more to man than to other Individuals, all of which, though in different degrees, are nevertheless animate. For of each thing there is necessarily an idea in God, of which God is the cause in the same way as he is of the idea of the human Body. And so, whatever we have said of the idea of the human Body must also be said of the idea of any thing.

However, we also cannot deny that ideas differ among themselves, as the objects themselves do, and that one is more excellent than the other, and contains more reality, just as the object of the one is more excellent than the object of the other and contains more reality. And so to determine what is the difference between the human Mind and the others, and how it surpasses them, it is necessary for us, as we have said, to know the nature of its object, i.e., of the human Body. I cannot explain this here, nor is that necessary for the things I wish to demonstrate. Nevertheless, I say this in general, that in proportion as a Body is more capable than others of doing many things at once, or being acted on in many ways at once, so its Mind is more capable than others of perceiving many things at once. And in proportion as the actions of a body depend more on itself alone, and as other bodies concur with it less in acting, so its mind is more capable of understanding distinctly. And from these [truths] we can know the excellence of one mind over the others, and also see the cause why we have only a completely confused knowledge of our Body, and many other things which I shall deduce from them in the following [propositions]. For this reason I have thought it worthwhile to explain and demonstrate these things more accurately. To do this it is necessary to premise a few things concerning the nature of bodies.

A1′: All bodies either move or are at rest.

A2′: Each body moves now more slowly, now more quickly.

L1: *Bodies are distinguished from one another by reason of motion and rest, speed and slowness, and not by reason of substance.*

Dem.: I suppose that the first part of this is known through itself. But that bodies are not distinguished by reason of substance is evident both from IP5 and from IP8. But it is more clearly evident from those things which are said in IP15S.

L2: *All bodies agree in certain things.*

Dem.: For all bodies agree in that they involve the concept of one and the same attribute (by D1), and in that they can move now more slowly, now more quickly, and absolutely, that now they move, now they are at rest.

L3: *A body which moves or is at rest must be determined to motion or rest by another body, which has also been determined to motion or rest by another, and that again by another, and so on, to infinity.*

Dem.: Bodies (by D1) are singular things which (by L1) are distinguished from one another by reason of motion and rest; and so (by IP28), each must be determined necessarily to motion or rest by another singular thing, viz. (by P6) by another body, which (by A19) either moves or is at rest. But this body also (by the same reasoning) could not move or be at rest if it had not been determined by another to motion or rest, and this again (by the same reasoning) by another, and so on, to infinity, q.e.d.

Cor.: From this it follows that a body in motion moves until it is determined by another body to rest; and that a body at rest also remains at rest until it is determined to motion by another.

This is also known through itself. For when I suppose that body A, say, is at rest, and do not attend to any other body in motion, I can say nothing about body A except that it is at rest. If afterwards it happens that body A moves, that of course could not have come about from the fact that it was at rest. For from that nothing else could follow but that body A would be at rest.

If, on the other hand, A is supposed to move, then as often as we attend only to A, we shall be able to affirm nothing concerning it except that it moves. If afterwards it happens that A is at rest, that of course also could not have come about from the motion it had. For from the motion nothing else could follow but that A would move. Therefore, it happens by a thing which was not in A, viz. by an external cause, by which [the Body in motion, A] has been determined to rest.

A1″: All modes by which a body is affected by another body follow both from the nature of the body affected and at the same time from the nature of the affecting body, so that one and the same body may be moved differently according to differences in the nature of the bodies moving it. And conversely, different bodies may be moved differently by one and the same body.

A2″: When a body in motion strikes against another which is at rest and cannot give way, then it is reflected, so that it continues to move, and the angle of the line of the reflected motion with the surface of the body at rest which it struck against will be equal to the angle which the line of the incident motion makes with the same surface.

This will be sufficient concerning the simplest bodies, which are distinguished from one another only by motion and rest, speed and slowness. Now let us move up to composite bodies.

Definition: *When a number of bodies, whether of the same or of different size, are so constrained by other bodies that they lie upon one another, or if they so move, whether with the same degree or different degrees of speed, that they communicate their motions to each other in a certain fixed manner, we shall say that those bodies are united with one another and that they all together compose one body or Individual, which is distinguished from the others by this union of bodies.*

A3″: As the parts of an Individual, or composite body, lie upon one another over a larger or smaller surface, so they can be forced to change their position with more or less difficulty; and consequently the more or less will be the difficulty of bringing it about that the Individual changes its shape. And therefore the bodies whose parts lie upon one another over a large surface, I shall call *hard;* those whose parts lie upon one another over a small surface, I shall call *soft;* and finally those whose parts are in motion, I shall call *fluid.*

L4: *If, of a body, or of an Individual, which is composed of a number of bodies, some are removed, and at the same time as many others of the same nature take their place, the [body, or the] Individual will retain its nature, as before, without any change of its form.*

Dem.: For (by L1) bodies are not distinguished in respect to substance; what constitutes the form of the Individual consists [only] in the union of the bodies (by the preceding definition). But this [union] (by hypothesis) is retained even if a continual change of bodies occurs. Therefore, the Individual will retain its nature, as before, both in respect to substance, and in respect to mode, q.e.d.

L5: *If the parts composing an Individual become greater or less, but in such a proportion that they all keep the same ratio of motion and rest to each other as before, then the Individual will likewise retain its nature, as before, without any change of form.*

Dem.: The demonstration of this is the same as that of the preceding Lemma.

L6: *If certain bodies composing an Individual are compelled to alter the motion they have from one direction to another, but so that they can continue their motions and communicate them to each other in the same ratio as before, the Individual will likewise retain its nature, without any change of form.*

Dem.: This is evident through itself. For it is supposed that it retains everything which, in its definition, we said constitutes its form. [See the Definition before L4.]

L7: *Furthermore, the Individual so composed retains its nature, whether it, as a whole, moves or is at rest, or whether it moves in this or that direction, so long as each part retains its motion, and communicates it, as before, to the others.*

Dem.: This [also] is evident from the definition preceding L4.

Schol.: By this, then, we see how a composite Individual can be affected in many ways, and still preserve its nature. So far we have conceived an Individual which is composed only of bodies which are distinguished from one another only by motion and rest, speed and slowness, i.e., which is composed of the simplest bodies. But if we should now conceive of another, composed of a number of Individuals of a different nature, we shall find that it can be affected in a great many other ways, and still preserve its nature. For since each part of it is composed of a number of bodies, each part will therefore (by L7) be able, without any change of its nature, to move now more slowly, now more quickly, and consequently communicate its motion more quickly or more slowly to the others.

But if we should further conceive a third kind of Individual, composed [of many individuals] of this second kind, we shall find that it can be affected in many other ways, without any change of its form. And if we proceed in this way to infinity, we shall easily conceive that the whole of nature is one Individual, whose parts, i.e., all bodies, vary in infinite ways, without any change of the whole Individual.

If it had been my intention to deal expressly with body, I ought to have explained and demonstrated these things more fully. But I have already said that I intended something else, and brought these things forward only because I can easily deduce from them the things I have decided to demonstrate.

Postulates

I. The human Body is composed of a great many individuals of different natures, each of which is highly composite.

II. Some of the individuals of which the human Body is composed are fluid, some soft, and others, finally are hard.

III. The individuals composing the human Body, and consequently, the human Body itself, are affected by external bodies in very many ways.

IV. The human Body, to be preserved, requires a great many other bodies, by which it is, as it were, continually regenerated.

V. When a fluid part of the human Body is determined by an external body so that it frequently thrusts against a soft part [of the Body], it changes its surface and, as it were, impresses on [the soft part] certain traces of the external body striking against [the fluid part].

VI. The human Body can move and dispose external bodies in a great many ways.

P14: *The human Mind is capable of perceiving a great many things, and is the more capable, the more its body can be disposed in a great many ways.*

Dem.: For the human Body (by Post. 3 and 6) is affected in a great many ways by external bodies, and is disposed to affect external bodies in a great many ways. But the human Mind must perceive everything which happens in the human body (by P12). Therefore, the human Mind is capable of perceiving a great many things, and is the more capable [as the human Body is more capable], q.e.d.

P15: *The idea that constitutes the formal being [esse] of the human Mind is not simple, but composed of a great many ideas.*

Dem.: The idea that constitutes the formal being of the human Mind is the idea of a body (by P13), which (by Post. 1) is composed of a great many highly composite Individuals. But of each Individual composing the body, there is necessarily (by P8C) an idea in God. Therefore (by P7), the idea of the human Body is composed of these many ideas of the parts composing the Body, q.e.d.

P16: *The idea of any mode in which the human Body is affected by external bodies must involve the nature of the human Body and at the same time the nature of the external body.*

Dem.: For all the modes in which a body is affected follow from the nature of the affected body, and at the same time from the nature of the affecting body (by A10 [II/99]). So the idea of them (by IA4) will necessarily involve the nature of each body. And so the idea of each mode in which the human Body is affected by an external body involves the nature of the human Body and of the external body, q.e.d.

Cor. 1: From this it follows, first, that the human Mind perceives the nature of a great many bodies together with the nature of its own body.

Cor. 2: It follows, second, that the ideas which we have of external bodies indicate the condition of our own body more than the nature of the external bodies. I have explained this by many examples in the Appendix of Part I.

P17: *If the human Body is affected with a mode that involves the nature of an external body, the human Mind will regard the same external body as actually existing, or as present to it, until the Body is affected by an affect that excludes the existence or presence of that body.*

Dem.: This is evident. For so long as the human Body is so affected, the human Mind (by P12) will regard this affection of the body, i.e. (by P16), it will have the idea of a mode that actually exists, an idea that involves the nature of the external body, i.e., an idea that does not exclude, but posits, the existence or presence of the nature of the external body. And so the Mind (by P16C1) will regard the external body as actually existing, or as present, until it is affected, etc., q.e.d.

Cor.: Although the external bodies by which the human body has once been affected neither exist nor are present, the mind will still be able to regard them as if they were present.

Dem.: While external bodies so determine the fluid parts of the human body that they often thrust against the softer parts, they change (by Post. 5) their surfaces with the result (see A20 after L3) that they are reflected from it in another way than they used to be before, and still later, when the fluid parts, by their spontaneous motion, encounter those new surfaces, they are reflected in the same way as when they were driven against those surfaces by the external bodies. Consequently, while, thus reflected, they continue to move, they will affect the human Body with the same mode, concerning which the Mind (by P12) will think again, i.e. (by P17), the Mind will again regard the external body as present; this will happen as often as the fluid parts of the human body encounter the same surfaces by their spontaneous motion. So although the external bodies by which the human Body has once been affected do not exist, the

Mind will still regard them as present, as often as this action of the body is repeated, q.e.d.

Schol.: We see, therefore, how it can happen (as it often does) that we regard as present things that do not exist. This can happen from other causes also, but it is suffi-cient for me here to have shown one through which I can explain it as if I had shown it through its true cause; still, I do not believe that I wander far from the true [cause] since all those postulates which I have assumed contain hardly anything that is not es-tablished by experience which we cannot doubt, after we have shown that the human Body exists as we are aware of it (see P13C).

Furthermore (from P17C and P16C2), we clearly understand what is the differ-ence between the idea of, say, Peter, which constitutes the essence of Peter's mind, and the idea of Peter which is in another man, say in Paul. For the former directly explains the essence of Peter's body, and does not involve existence, except so long as Peter ex-ists; but the latter indicates the condition of Paul's body more than Peter's nature [see P16C2], and therefore, while that condition of Paul's body lasts, Paul's Mind will still regard Peter as present to itself, even though Peter does not exist.

Next, to retain the customary words, the affections of the human Body whose ideas present external bodies as present to us, we shall call images of things, even if they do not reproduce the [external] figures of things. And when the Mind regards bod-ies in this way, we shall say that it imagines.

And here, in order to begin to indicate what error is, I should like you to note that the imaginations of the Mind, considered in themselves contain no error, or that the Mind does not err from the fact that it imagines, but only insofar as it is considered to lack an idea that excludes the existence of those things that it imagines to be present to it. For if the Mind, while it imagined nonexistent things as present to it, at the same time knew that those things did not exist, it would, of course, attribute this power of imagining to a virtue of its nature, not to a vice—especially if this faculty of imagining depended only on its own nature, i.e. (by ID7), if the Mind's faculty of imagining were free.

P18: *If the human Body has once been affected by two or more bodies at the same time, then when the Mind subsequently imagines one of them, it will immediately recol-lect the others also.*

Dem.: The Mind (by P17C) imagines a body because the human Body is affected and disposed as it was affected when certain of its parts were struck by the external body itself. But (by hypothesis) the Body was then so disposed that the Mind imagined two [or more] bodies at once; therefore it will now also imagine two [or more] at once, and when the Mind imagines one, it will immediately recollect the other also, q.e.d.

Schol.: From this we clearly understand what Memory is. For it is nothing other than a certain connection of ideas involving the nature of things which are outside the human Body—a connection that is in the Mind according to the order and connection of the affections of the human Body.

I say, *first,* that the connection is only of those ideas that involve the nature of things which are outside the human Body, but not of the ideas that explain the nature of the same things. For they are really (by P16) ideas of affections of the human Body which involve both its nature and that of external bodies.

I say, *second,* that this connection happens according to the order and connection of the affections of the human Body in order to distinguish it from the connection of ideas which happens according to the order of the intellect, by which the Mind per-ceives things through their first causes, and which is the same in all men.

And from this we clearly understand why the Mind, from the thought of one thing, immediately passes to the thought of another, which has no likeness to the first: as, for example, from the thought of the word *pomum* a Roman will immediately pass to the thought of the fruit [viz. an apple], which has no similarity to that articulate sound and nothing in common with it except that the Body of the same man has often been affected by these two [at the same time], i.e., that the man often heard the word pomum while he saw the fruit.

And in this way each of us will pass from one thought to another, as each one's association has ordered the images of things in the body. For example, a soldier, having seen traces of a horse in the sand, will immediately pass from the thought of a horse to the thought of a horseman, and from that to the thought of war, etc. But a Farmer will pass from the thought of a horse to the thought of a plow, and then to that of a field, etc. And so each one, according as he has been accustomed to join and connect the images of things in this or that way, will pass from one thought to another.

P19: *The human Mind does not know the human Body itself, nor does it know that it exists, except through ideas of affections by which the Body is affected.*

Dem.: For the human Mind is the idea itself, or knowledge of the human Body (by P13), which (by P9) is indeed in God insofar as he is considered to be affected by another idea of a singular thing, or because (by Post. 4) the human Body requires a great many bodies by which it is, as it were, continually regenerated; and [because] the order and connection of ideas is (by P7) the same as the order and connection of causes, this idea will be in God insofar as he is considered to be affected by the ideas of a great many singular things. Therefore, God has the idea of the human Body, or knows the human Body, insofar as he is affected by a great many other ideas, and not insofar as he constitutes the nature of the human Mind, i.e. (by P11C), the human Mind does not know the human Body.

But the ideas of affections of the Body are in God insofar as he constitutes the nature of the human Mind, or the human Mind perceives the same affections (by P12), and consequently (by P16) the human Body itself, as actually existing (by P17).

Therefore to that extent only, the human Mind perceives the human Body itself, q.e.d.

P20: *There is also in God an idea, or knowledge, of the human Mind, which follows in God in the same way and is related to God in the same way as the idea, or knowledge, of the human Body.*

Dem.: Thought is an attribute of God (by P1), and so (by P3) there must necessarily be in God an idea both of [thought] and of all of its affections, and consequently (by P11), of the human Mind also. Next, this idea, or knowledge, of the Mind does not follow in God insofar as he is infinite, but insofar as he is affected by another idea of a singular thing (by P9). But the order and connection of ideas is the same as the order and connection of causes (by P7). Therefore, this idea, *or* knowledge, of the Mind follows in God and is related to God in the same way as the idea, *or* knowledge, of the Body, q.e.d.

P21: *This idea of the Mind is united to the Mind in the same way as the Mind is united to the Body.*

Dem.: We have shown that the Mind is united to the Body from the fact that the Body is the object of the Mind (see P12 and 13); and so by the same reasoning the idea of the Mind must be united with its own object, i.e., with the Mind itself, in the same way as the Mind is united with the Body, q.e.d.

Schol.: This proposition is understood far more clearly from what is said in P7S; for there we have shown that the idea of the Body and the Body, i.e. (by P13), the Mind and the Body, are one and the same Individual, which is conceived now under the attribute of Thought, now under the attribute of Extension. So the idea of the Mind and the Mind itself are one and the same thing, which is conceived under one and the same attribute, viz. Thought. The idea of the Mind, I say, and the Mind itself follow in God from the same power of thinking and by the same necessity. For the idea of the Mind, i.e., the idea of the idea, is nothing but the form of the idea insofar as this is considered as a mode of thinking without relation to the object. For as soon as someone knows something, he thereby knows that he knows it, and at the same time knows that he knows that he knows, and so on, to infinity. But more on these matters later.

P22: *The human Mind perceives not only the affections of the Body, but also the ideas of these affections.*

Dem.: The ideas of the ideas of the affections follow in God in the same way and are related to God in the same way as the ideas themselves of the affections (this is demonstrated in the same way as P20). But the ideas of the affections of the Body are in the human Mind (by P12), i.e. (by P11C), in God, insofar as he constitutes the essence of the human Mind. Therefore, the ideas of these ideas will be in God insofar as he has the knowledge, *or* idea, of the human Mind, i.e. (by P21), they will be in the human Mind itself, which for that reason perceives not only the affections of the Body, but also their ideas, q.e.d.

P23: *The Mind does not know itself, except insofar as it perceives the ideas of the affections of the Body.*

Dem.: The idea, *or* knowledge, of the Mind (by P20) follows in God in the same way, and is related to God in the same way as the idea, *or* knowledge, of the body. But since (by P19) the human Mind does not know the human Body itself, i.e. (by P11C), since the knowledge of the human Body is not related to God insofar as he constitutes the nature of the human Mind, the knowledge of the Mind is also not related to God insofar as he constitutes the essence of the human Mind. And so (again by P11C) to that extent the human Mind does not know itself.

Next, the ideas of the affections by which the Body is affected involve the nature of the human Body itself (by P16), i.e. (by P13), agree with the nature of the Mind. So knowledge of these ideas will necessarily involve knowledge of the Mind. But (by P22) knowledge of these ideas is in the human Mind itself. Therefore, the human Mind, to that extent only, knows itself, q.e.d.

P24: *The human Mind does not involve adequate knowledge of the parts composing the human Body.*

Dem.: The parts composing the human Body pertain to the essence of the Body itself only insofar as they communicate their motions to one another in a certain fixed manner (see the Definition after L3C), and not insofar as they can be considered as Individuals, without relation to the human Body. For (by Post. 1) the parts of the human Body are highly composite Individuals, whose parts (by L4) can be separated from the human Body and communicate their motions (see A10 after L3) to other bodies in another manner, while the human Body completely preserves its nature and form. And so the idea, or knowledge, of each part will be in God (by P3), insofar as he is considered to be affected by another idea of a singular thing (by P9), a singular thing which is prior, in the order of nature, to the part itself (by P7). The same must also be said of each part of the Individual composing the human Body. And so, the knowledge of each part composing the human Body is in God insofar as he is affected with a great many ideas of things, and not insofar as he has only the idea of the human Body, i.e. (by P13), the idea that constitutes the nature of the human Mind. And so, (by P11C) the human Mind does not involve adequate knowledge of the parts composing the human Body, q.e.d.

P25: *The idea of any affection of the human Body does not involve adequate knowledge of an external body.*
    Dem.: We have shown (P16) that the idea of an affection of the human Body involves the nature of an external body insofar as the external body determines the human Body in a certain fixed way. But insofar as the external body is an Individual that is not related to the human Body, the idea, *or* knowledge, of it is in God (by P9) insofar as God is considered to be affected with the idea of another thing which (by P7) is prior in nature to the external body itself. So adequate knowledge of the external body is not in God insofar as he has the idea of an affection of the human Body, *or* the idea of an affection of the human Body does not involve adequate knowledge of the external body, q.e.d.

P26: *The human Mind does not perceive any external body as actually existing, except through the ideas of the affections of its own Body.*
    Dem.: If the human Body is not affected by an external body in any way, then (by P7) the idea of the human Body, i.e. (by P13), the human Mind, is also not affected in any way by the idea of the existence of that body, *or* it does not perceive the existence of that external body in any way. But insofar as the human Body is affected by an external body in some way, to that extent [the human Mind] (by P16 and P16C1) perceives the external body, q.e.d.
    Cor.: Insofar as the human Mind imagines an external body, it does not have adequate knowledge of it.
    Dem.: When the human Mind regards external bodies through ideas of the affections of its own Body, then we say that it imagines (see P17S); and the Mind cannot in any other way (by P16) imagine external bodies as actually existing. And so (by P15), insofar as the Mind imagines external bodies, it does not have adequate knowledge of them, q.e.d.

P27: *The idea of any affection of the human Body does not involve adequate knowledge of the human body itself.*
    Dem.: Any idea of any affection of the human Body involves the nature of the human Body insofar as the human Body itself is considered to be affected with a certain definite mode (see P16). But insofar as the human Body is an Individual, which can be affected with many other modes, the idea of this [affection] etc. (See P25D.)

P28: *The ideas of the affections of the human Body, insofar as they are related only to the human Mind, are not clear and distinct, but confused.*
    Dem.: For the ideas of the affections of the human Body involve the nature of external bodies as much as that of the human Body (by P16), and must involve the nature not only of the human Body [as a whole], but also of its parts; for the affections are modes (by Post. 3), with which the parts of the human Body, and consequently the

whole Body, are affected. But (by P14 and P15) adequate knowledge of external bodies and of the parts composing the human Body is in God, not insofar as he is considered to be affected with the human Mind, but insofar as he is considered to be affected with other ideas. Therefore, these ideas of the affections, insofar as they are related only to the human Mind, are like conclusions without premises, i.e. (as is known through itself), they are confused ideas, q.e.d.

Schol.: In the same way we can demonstrate that the idea that constitutes the nature of the human Mind is not, considered in itself alone, clear and distinct; we can also demonstrate the same of the idea of the human Mind and the ideas of the ideas of the human Body's affections [viz. that are confused], insofar as they are referred to the Mind alone. Anyone can easily see this.

P29: *The idea of the idea of any affection of the human Body does not involve adequate knowledge of the human Mind.*

Dem.: For the idea of an affection of the human Body (by P17) does not involve adequate knowledge of the Body itself, *or* does not express its nature adequately, i.e. (by P13), does not agree adequately with the nature of the Mind; and so (by IA6) the idea of this idea does not express the nature of the human mind adequately, or does not involve adequate knowledge of it, q.e.d.

Cor.: From this it follows that so long as the human Mind perceives things from the common order of nature, it does not have an adequate, but only a confused and mutilated knowledge of itself, of its own Body, and of external bodies. For the Mind does not know itself except insofar as it perceives ideas of the affections of the body (by P13). But it does not perceive its own Body (by P19) except through the very ideas themselves of the affections [of the body], and it is also through them alone that it perceives external bodies (by P16). And so, insofar as it has these [ideas], then neither of itself (by P29), nor of its own Body (by P17), nor of external bodies (by P15) does it have an adequate knowledge, but only (by P18 and P28S) a mutilated and confused knowledge, q.e.d.

Schol.: I say expressly that the Mind has, not an adequate, but only a confused [and mutilated] knowledge, of itself, of its own Body, and of external bodies, so long as it perceives things from the common order of nature, i.e., so long as it is determined externally, from fortuitous encounters with things, to regard this or that, and not so long as it is determined internally, from the fact that it regards a number of things at once, to understand their agreements, differences, and oppositions. For so often as it is disposed internally, in this or another way, then it regards things clearly and distinctly, as I shall show below.

P30: *We can have only an entirely inadequate knowledge of the duration of our Body.*

Dem.: Our body's duration depends neither on its essence (by A1), nor even on God's absolute nature (by IP21). But (by IP28) it is determined to exist and produce an effect from such [other] causes as are also determined by others to exist and produce an effect in a certain and determinate manner, and these again by others, and so to infinity. Therefore, the duration of our Body depends on the common order of nature and the constitution of things. But adequate knowledge of how things are constituted is in God, insofar as he has the ideas of all of them, and not insofar as he has only the idea of the human Body (by P9C). So the knowledge of the duration of our Body is quite inadequate in God, insofar as he is considered to constitute only the nature of the human Mind, i.e. (by P11C), this knowledge is quite inadequate in our Mind, q.e.d.

P31: *We can have only an entirely inadequate knowledge of the duration of the singular things which are outside us.*

Dem.: For each singular thing, like the human Body, must be determined by another singular thing to exist and produce effects in a certain and determinate way, and this again by another, and so to infinity (by IP28). But since (in P30) we have demonstrated from this common property of singular things that we have only a very inadequate knowledge of the duration of our Body, we shall have to draw the same conclusion concerning the duration of singular things [outside us], viz. that we can have only a very inadequate knowledge of their duration, q.e.d.

Cor.: From this it follows that all particular things are contingent and corruptible. For we can have no adequate knowledge of their duration (by P31), and that is what we must understand by the contingency of things and the possibility of their corruption (see IP33S1). For (by IP29) beyond that there is no contingency.

P32: *All ideas, insofar as they are related to God, are true.*

Dem.: For all ideas which are in God agree entirely with their objects (by P7C), and so (by IA6) they are all true, q.e.d.

P33: *There is nothing positive in ideas on account of which they are called false.*

Dem.: If you deny this, conceive (if possible) a positive mode of thinking which constitutes the form of error, or falsity. This mode of thinking cannot be in God (by P32). But it also can neither be nor be conceived outside God (by IP15). And so there can be nothing positive in ideas on account of which they are called false, q.e.d.

P34: *Every idea that in us is absolute, or adequate and perfect, is true.*

Dem.: When we say that there is in us an adequate and perfect idea, we are saying nothing but that (by P11C) there is an adequate and perfect idea in God insofar as he constitutes the essence of our Mind, and consequently (by P32) we are saying nothing but that such an idea is true, q.e.d.

P35: *Falsity consists in the privation of knowledge which inadequate, or mutilated and confused, ideas involve.*

Dem.: There is nothing positive in ideas that constitutes the form of falsity (by P33); but falsity cannot consist in an absolute privation (for it is Minds, not Bodies, which are said to err, or be deceived), nor also in absolute ignorance. For to be ignorant and to err are different. So it consists in the privation of knowledge that inadequate knowledge of things, *or* inadequate and confused ideas, involve, q.e.d.

Schol.: In P17S I explained how error consists in the privation of knowledge. But to explain the matter more fully, I shall give [one or two examples]: men are deceived in that they think themselves free [i.e., they think that, of their own free will, they can either do a thing or forbear doing it], an opinion which consists only in this, that they are conscious of their actions and ignorant of the causes by which they are determined. This, then, is their idea of freedom—that they do not know any cause of their actions. They say, of course, that human actions depend on the will, but these are only words for which they have no idea. For all are ignorant of what the will is, and how it moves the Body; those who boast of something else, who feign seats and dwelling places of the soul, usually provoke either ridicule or disgust.

Similarly, when we look at the sun, we imagine it as about 200 feet away from us, an error that does not consist simply in this imagining, but in the fact that while we imagine it in this way, we are ignorant of its true distance and of the cause of this imagining. For even if we later come to know that it is more than 600 diameters of the earth away from us, we nevertheless imagine it as near. For we imagine the sun so near not because we do not know its true distance, but because an affection of our body involves the essence of the sun insofar as our body is affected by the sun.

P36: *Inadequate and confused ideas follow with the same necessity as adequate, or clear and distinct ideas.*

Dem.: All ideas are in God (by IP15); and, insofar as they are related to God, are true (by P32), and (by P7C) adequate. And so there are no inadequate or confused ideas except insofar as they are related to the singular Mind of someone (see P14 and P18). And so all ideas—both the adequate and the inadequate—follow with the same necessity (by P6C), q.e.d.

P37: *What is common to all things (on this see L2, above) and is equally in the part and in the whole, does not constitute the essence of any singular thing.*

Dem.: If you deny this, conceive (if possible) that it does constitute the essence of some singular thing, say the essence of B. Then (by D2) it can neither be nor be conceived without B. But this is contrary to the hypothesis. Therefore, it does not pertain to the essence of B, nor does it constitute the essence of any other singular thing, q.e.d.

P38: *Those things which are common to all, and which are equally in the part and in the whole, can only be conceived adequately.*

Dem.: Let A be something which is common to all bodies, and which is equally in the part of each body and in the whole. I say that A can only be conceived adequately. For its idea (by P7C) will necessarily be adequate in God, both insofar as he has the idea of the human Body and insofar as he has ideas of its affections, which (by P16, P15, and P17) involve in part both the nature of the human Body and that of external bodies. That is (by P12 and P13), this idea will necessarily be adequate in God insofar as he constitutes the human Mind, *or* insofar as he has ideas that are in the human Mind. The Mind therefore (by P11C) necessarily perceives A adequately, and does so both insofar as it perceives itself and insofar as it perceives its own or any external body. Nor can A be conceived in another way, q.e.d.

Cor.: From this it follows that there are certain ideas, or notions, common to all men. For (by L2) all bodies agree in certain things, which (by P38) must be perceived adequately, or clearly and distinctly, by all.

P39: *If something is common to, and peculiar to, the human Body and certain external bodies by which the human Body is usually affected, and is equally in the part and in the whole of each of them, its idea will also be adequate in the Mind.*

Dem.: Let A be that which is common to, and peculiar to, the human Body and certain external bodies, which is equally in the human Body and in the same external bodies, and finally, which is equally in the part of each external body and in the whole. There will be an adequate idea of A in God (by P7C), both insofar as he has the idea of the human Body, and insofar as he has ideas of the posited external bodies. Let it be posited now that the human Body is affected by an external body through what it has in common with it, i.e., by A; the idea of this affection will involve property A (by P16), and so (by P7C) the idea of this affection, insofar as it involves property A, will be adequate in God insofar as he is affected with the idea of the human Body, i.e. (by P13), insofar as he constitutes the nature of the human Mind. And so (by P11C), this idea is also adequate in the human Mind, q.e.d.

Cor.: From this it follows that the Mind is the more capable of perceiving many things adequately as its Body has many things in common with other bodies.

P40: *Whatever ideas follow in the Mind from ideas that are adequate in the mind are also adequate.*

Dem.: This is evident. For when we say that an idea in the human Mind follows from ideas that are adequate in it, we are saying nothing but that (by P11C) in the Divine intellect there is an idea of which God is the cause, not insofar as he is infinite, nor insofar as he is affected with the ideas of a great many singular things, but insofar as he constitutes only the essence of the human Mind [and therefore, it must be adequate].

Schol. 1: With this I have explained the cause of those notions which are called *common*, and which are the foundations of our reasoning.

But some axioms, or notions, result from other causes which it would be helpful to explain by this method of ours. For from these [explanations] it would be established which notions are more useful than the others, and which are of hardly any use; and then, which are common, which are clear and distinct only to those who have no prejudices, and finally, which are ill-founded. Moreover, we would establish what is the origin of those notions they call *Second*, and consequently of the axioms founded on them, and other things I have thought about, from time to time, concerning these matters. But since I have set these aside for another Treatise, and do not wish to give rise to disgust by too long a discussion, I have decided to pass over them here.

But not to omit anything it is necessary to know, I shall briefly add something about the causes from which the terms called *Transcendental* have had their origin—I

Interior of a House, ca. 1660, by Pieter De Hooch (1629–1684). This Dutch Baroque painting provides a visual metaphor for the precise geometry of Spinoza's *Ethics.* (*Wallace Collection, London,* © *Archivi Alinari, 1990/Art Resource*)

mean terms like Being, Thing and something. These terms arise from the fact that the human Body, being limited, is capable of forming distinctly only a certain number of images at the same time (I have explained what an image is in P17S). If that number is exceeded, the images will begin to be confused, and if the number of images the Body is capable of forming distinctly in itself at once is greatly exceeded, they will all be completely confused with one another.

Since this is so, it is evident from P17C and P18, that the human Mind will be able to imagine distinctly, at the same time, as many bodies as there can be images formed at the same time in its body. But when the images in the body are completely confused, the Mind also will imagine all the bodies confusedly, without any distinction, and comprehend them as if under one attribute, viz. under the attribute of Being, Thing, etc. This can also be deduced from the fact that images are not always equally vigorous and from other causes like these, which it is not necessary to explain here. For our purpose it is sufficient to consider only one. For they all reduce to this: these terms signify ideas that are confused in the highest degree.

Those notions they call *Universal*, like Man, Horse, Dog, etc., have arisen from similar causes, viz. because so many images (e.g., of men) are formed at one time in the human Body that they surpass the power of imagining—not entirely, of course, but still to the point where the Mind can imagine neither slight differences of the singular [men] (such as the color and size of each one, etc.) nor their determinate number, and imagines distinctly only what they all agree in, insofar as they affect the body. For the body has been affected most [forcefully] by [what is common], since each singular has affected it [by this property]. And [the mind] expresses this by the word *man*, and predicates it of infinitely many singulars. For as we have said, it cannot imagine a determinate number of singulars.

But it should be noted that these notions are not formed by all [men] in the same way, but vary from one to another, in accordance with what the body has more often been affected by, and what the Mind imagines or recollects more easily. For example, those who have more often regarded men's stature with wonder will understand by the word *man* an animal of erect stature. But those who have been accustomed to consider something else, will form another common image of men—e.g., that man is an animal capable of laughter, or a featherless biped, or a rational animal.

And similarly concerning the others—each will form universal images of things according to the disposition of his body. Hence it is not surprising that so many controversies have arisen among the philosophers, who have wished to explain natural things by mere images of things.

Schol. 2: From what has been said above, it is clear that we perceive many things and form universal notions:

I. from singular things which have been represented to us through the senses in a way that is mutilated, confused, and without order for the intellect (see P29C); for that reason I have been accustomed to call such perceptions knowledge from random experience;

II. from signs, e.g., from the fact that, having heard or read certain words, we recollect things, and form certain ideas of them, which are like them, and through which we imagine the things (P18S). These two ways of regarding things I shall henceforth call knowledge of the first kind, opinion or imagination.

III. Finally, from the fact that we have common notions and adequate ideas of the properties of things (see P38C, P39, P39C, and P40). This I shall call reason and the second kind of knowledge.

[IV]. In addition to these two kinds of knowledge, there is (as I shall show in what follows) another, third kind, which we shall call intuitive knowledge. And this kind of knowing proceeds from an adequate idea of the formal essence of certain attributes of God to the adequate knowledge of the [formal] essence of things.

I shall explain all these with one example. Suppose there are three numbers, and the problem is to find a fourth which is to the third as the second is to the first. Merchants do not hesitate to multiply the second by the third, and divide the product by the first, because they have not yet forgotten what they heard from their teacher without any demonstration, or because they have often found this in the simplest numbers, or from the force of the Demonstration of P7 in Bk. VII of Euclid, viz. from the common property of proportionals. But in the simplest numbers none of this is necessary. Given the numbers 1, 2, and 3, no one fails to see that the fourth proportional number is 6— and we see this much more clearly because we infer the fourth number from the ratio which, in one glance, we see the first number to have the second.

P41: *Knowledge of the first kind is the only cause of falsity, whereas knowledge of the second and of the third kind is necessarily true.*
Dem.: We have said in the preceding scholium that to knowledge of the first kind pertain all those ideas which are inadequate and confused; and so (by P35) this knowledge is the only cause of falsity. Next, we have said that to knowledge of the second and third kinds pertain those which are adequate; and so (by P34) this knowledge is necessarily true.

P42: *Knowledge of the second and third kinds, and not of the first kind, teaches us to distinguish the true from the false.*
Dem.: This Proposition is evident through itself. For he who knows how to distinguish between the true and the false must have an adequate idea of the true and of the false, i.e. (P40S2), must know the true and the false by the second or third kind of knowledge.

P43: *He who has a true idea at the same time knows that he has a true idea, and cannot doubt the truth of the thing.*
Dem.: An idea true in us is that which is adequate in God insofar as he is explained through the nature of the human Mind (by P11C). Let us posit, therefore, that there is in God, insofar as he is explained through the nature of the human Mind, an adequate idea, A. Of this idea there must necessarily also be in God an idea which is related to God in the same way as idea A (by P20, whose demonstration is universal [and can be applied to all ideas]). But idea A is supposed to be related to God insofar as he is explained through the nature of the human Mind; therefore the idea of idea A must also be related to God in the same way, i.e. (by the same P11C), this adequate idea of idea A will be in the Mind itself which has the adequate idea A. And so he who has an adequate idea, *or* (by P34) who knows a thing truly, must at the same time have an adequate idea, *or* true knowledge, of his own knowledge. I.e. (as is manifest through itself), he must at the same time be certain, q.e.d.
Schol.: In P21S I have explained what an idea of an idea is. But it should be noted that the preceding proposition is sufficiently manifest through itself. For no one who has a true idea is unaware that a true idea involves the highest certainty. For to have a true idea means nothing other than knowing a thing perfectly, *or* in the best way. And of course no one can doubt this unless he thinks that an idea is something

mute, like a picture on a tablet, and not a mode of thinking, viz. the very [act of] understanding. And I ask, who can know that he understands some thing unless he first understands it? I.e., who can know that he is certain about some thing unless he is first certain about it? What can there be which is clearer and more certain than a true idea, to serve as a standard of truth? As the light makes both itself and the darkness plain, so truth is the standard both of itself and of the false.

By this I think we have replied to these questions: if a true idea is distinguished from a false one, [not insofar as it is said to be a mode of thinking, but] only insofar as it is said to agree with its object, then a true idea has no more reality or perfection than a false one (since they are distinguished only through the extrinsic denomination [and not through the intrinsic denomination])—and so, does the man who has true ideas [have any more reality or perfection] than him who has only false ideas? Again, why do men have false ideas? And finally, how can someone know certainly that he has ideas which agree with their objects?

To these questions, I say, I think I have already replied. For as far as the difference between a true and a false idea is concerned, it is established from P35 that the true is related to the false as being is to nonbeing. And the causes of falsity I have shown most clearly from P19 to P35S. From this it is also clear what is the difference between the man who has true ideas and the man who has only false ideas. Finally, as to the last, viz. how a man can know that he has an idea that agrees with its object? I have just shown, more than sufficiently, that this arises solely from his having an idea that does agree with its object—or that truth is its own standard. Add to this that our Mind, insofar as it perceives things truly, is part of the infinite intellect of God (by P11C); hence, it is as necessary that the mind's clear and distinct ideas are true as that God's ideas are.

P44: *It is of the nature of Reason to regard things as necessary, not as contingent.*

Dem.: It is of the nature of reason to perceive things truly (by P41), viz. (by IA6) as they are in themselves, i.e. (by IP29), not as contingent but as necessary, q.e.d.

Cor. 1: From this it follows that it depends only on the imagination that we regard things as contingent, both in respect to the past and in respect to the future.

Schol.: I shall explain briefly how this happens. We have shown above (by P17 and P17C) that even though things do not exist, the Mind still imagines them always as present to itself, unless causes occur which exclude their present existence. Next, we have shown (P18) that if the human Body has once been affected by two external bodies at the same time, then afterwards, when the Mind imagines one of them, it will immediately recollect the other also, i.e., it will regard both as present to itself unless causes occur which exclude their present existence. Moreover, no one doubts but what we also imagine time, viz. from the fact that we imagine some bodies to move more slowly, or more quickly, or with the same speed.

Let us suppose, then, a child, who saw Peter for the first time yesterday, in the morning, but saw Paul at noon, and Simon in the evening, and today again saw Peter in the morning. It is clear from P18 that as soon as he sees the morning light, he will immediately imagine the sun taking the same course through the sky as he saw on the preceding day, or he will imagine the whole day, and Peter together with the morning, Paul with noon, and Simon with the evening. That is, he will imagine the existence of Paul and of Simon with a relation to future time. On the other hand, if he sees Simon in the evening, he will relate Paul and Peter to the time past, by imagining them together with past time. And he will do this more uniformly, the more often he has seen them in this same order.

But if it should happen at some time that on some other evening he sees James instead of Simon, then on the following morning he will imagine now Simon, now James, together with the evening time, but not both at once. For it is supposed that he has seen one or the other of them in the evening, but not both at once. His imagination, therefore, will vacillate and he will imagine now this one, now that one, with the future evening time, i.e., he will regard neither of them as certainly future, but both of them as contingently future.

And this vacillation of the imagination will be the same if the imagination is of things we regard in the same way with relation to past time or to present time. Consequently we shall imagine things as contingent in relation to present time as well as to past and future time.

Cor. 2: It is of the nature of Reason to perceive things under a certain species of eternity.

Dem.: It is of the nature of Reason to regard things as necessary and not as contingent (by P44). And it perceives this necessity of things truly (by P41), i.e. (by IA6), as it is in itself. But (by IP16) this necessity of things is the very necessity of God's eternal nature. Therefore, it is of the nature of Reason to regard things under this species of eternity.

Add to this that the foundations of Reason are notions (by P38) which explain those things that are common to all, and which (by P37) do not explain the essence of any singular thing. On that account, they must be conceived without any relation to time, but under a certain species of eternity, q.e.d.

P45: *Each idea of each body, or of each singular thing which actually exists, necessarily involves an eternal and infinite essence of God.*

Dem.: The idea of a singular thing which actually exists necessarily involves both the essence of the thing and its existence (by P8C). But singular things (by IP15) cannot be conceived without God—on the contrary, because (by P6) they have God for a cause insofar as he is considered under the attribute of which the things are modes, their ideas must involve the concept of their attribute (by IA4), i.e. (by ID6), must involve an eternal and infinite essence of God, q.e.d.

Schol.: By existence here I do not understand duration, i.e., existence insofar as it is conceived abstractly, and as a certain species of quantity. For I am speaking of the very nature of existence, which is attributed to singular things because infinitely many things follow from the eternal necessity of God's nature in infinitely many modes (see IP16). I am speaking, I say, of the very existence of singular things insofar as they are in God. For even if each one is determined by another singular thing to exist in a certain way, still the force by which each one perseveres in existing follows from the eternal necessity of God's nature. Concerning this, see IP24C.

P46: *The knowledge of God's eternal and infinite essence which each idea involves is adequate and perfect.*

Dem.: The demonstration of the preceding Proposition is Universal, and whether the thing is considered as a part or as a whole, its idea, whether of the whole or a part (by P45), will involve God's eternal and infinite essence. So what gives knowledge of an eternal and infinite essence of God is common to all, and is equally in the part and in the whole. And so (by P38) this knowledge will be adequate, q.e.d.

P47: *The human Mind has an adequate knowledge of God's eternal and infinite essence.*

Dem.: The human Mind has ideas (by P22) from which it perceives (by P13) itself, (by P19) its own Body, and (by P16C1 and P17) external bodies as actually existing. And so (by P45 and P46) it has an adequate knowledge of God's eternal and infinite essence, q.e.d.

Schol.: From this we see that God's infinite essence and his eternity are known to all. And since all things are in God and are conceived through God, it follows that we can deduce from this knowledge a great many things which we know adequately, and so can form that third kind of knowledge of which we spoke in P40S2 and of whose excellence and utility we shall speak in Part V.

But that men do not have so clear a knowledge of God as they do of the common notions comes from the fact that they cannot imagine God, as they can bodies, and that they have joined the name *God* to the images of things which they are used to seeing. Men can hardly avoid this, because they are continually affected by bodies.

And indeed, most errors consist only in our not rightly applying names to things. For when someone says that the lines which are drawn from the center of a circle to its circumference are unequal, he surely understands (then at least) by a circle something different from what Mathematicians understand. Similarly, when men err in calculating, they have certain numbers in their mind and different ones on the paper. So if you consider what they have in Mind, they really do not err, though they seem to err because we think they have in their mind the numbers which are on the paper. If this were not so, we would not believe that they were erring, just as I did not believe that he was erring whom I recently heard cry out that his courtyard had flown into his neighbor's hen [although his words were absurd], because what he had in mind seemed sufficiently clear to me [viz. that his hen had flown into his neighbor's courtyard].

And most controversies have arisen from this, that men do not rightly explain their own mind, or interpret the mind of the other man badly. For really, when they contradict one another most vehemently, they either have the same thoughts, or they are thinking of different things, so that what they think are errors and absurdities in the other are not.

P48: *In the Mind there is no absolute, or free, will, but the Mind is determined to will this or that by a cause which is also determined by another, and this again by another, and so to infinity.*

Dem.: The Mind is a certain and determinate mode of thinking (by P11), and so (by IP17C2) cannot be a free cause of its own actions, or cannot have an absolute faculty of willing and not willing. Rather, it must be determined to willing this or that (by IP28) by a cause which is also determined by another, and this cause again by another, etc., q.e.d.

Schol.: In this same way it is also demonstrated that there is in the Mind no absolute faculty of understanding, desiring, loving, etc. From this it follows that these and similar faculties are either complete fictions *or* nothing but Metaphysical beings, or universals, which we are used to forming from particulars. So intellect and will are to this or that idea, or to this or that volition as "stone-ness" is to this or that stone, or man to Peter or Paul.

We have explained the cause of men's thinking themselves free in the Appendix of Part I. But before I proceed further, it should be noted here that by will I understand a faculty of affirming and denying, and not desire. I say that I understand the faculty by which the Mind affirms or denies something true or something false, and not the desire by which the Mind wants a thing or avoids it.

But after we have demonstrated that these faculties are universal notions which are not distinguished from the singulars from which we form them, we must now investigate whether the volitions themselves are anything beyond the very ideas of things. We must investigate, I say, whether there is any other affirmation or negation in the Mind except that which the idea involves, insofar as it is an idea—on this see the following Proposition and also D3—so that our thought does not fall into pictures. For by ideas I understand, not the images that are formed at the back of the eye (and, if you like, in the middle of the brain), but concepts of Thought [or the objective Being of a thing insofar as it consists only in Thought].

P49: *In the Mind there is no volition, or affirmation and negation, except that which the idea involves insofar as it is an idea.*

Dem.: In the Mind (by P48) there is no absolute faculty of willing and not willing, but only singular volitions, viz. this and that affirmation, and this and that negation. Let us conceive, therefore, some singular volition, say a mode of thinking by which the Mind affirms that the three angles of a triangle are equal to two right angles.

This affirmation involves the concept, *or* idea, of the triangle, i.e., it cannot be conceived without the idea of the triangle. For to say that A must involve the concept of B is the same as to say that A cannot be conceived without B. Further, this affirmation (by A3) also cannot be without the idea of the triangle. Therefore, this affirmation can neither be nor be conceived without the idea of the triangle.

Next, this idea of the triangle must involve this same affirmation, viz. that its three angles equal two right angles. So conversely, this idea of the triangle also can neither be nor be conceived without this affirmation.

So (by D2) this affirmation pertains to the essence of the idea of the triangle, and is nothing beyond it. And what we have said concerning this volition (since we have selected it at random), must also be said concerning any volition, viz. that it is nothing apart from the idea, q.e.d.

Cor.: The will and the intellect are one and the same.

Dem.: The will and the intellect are nothing apart from the singular volitions and ideas themselves (by P48 and P48S). But the singular volitions and ideas are one and the same (by P49). Therefore the will and the intellect are one and the same, q.e.d.

Schol.: [I.] By this we have removed what is commonly maintained to be the cause of error. Moreover, we have shown above that falsity consists only in the privation that mutilated and confused ideas involve. So a false idea, insofar as it is false, does not involve certainty. When we say that a man rests in false ideas, and does not doubt them, we do not, on that account, say that he is certain, but only that he does not doubt, or that he rests in false ideas because there are no causes to bring it about that his imagination wavers [or to cause him to doubt them]. On this, see P44S.

Therefore, however stubbornly a man may cling to something false [so that we cannot in any way make him doubt it], we shall still never say that he is certain of it. For by certainty we understand something positive (see P43 and P43S), not the privation of doubt. But by the privation of certainty, we understand falsity.

However, to explain the preceding Proposition more fully, there remain certain things I must warn you of. And then I must reply to the objections that can be made against this doctrine of ours. And finally, to remove every uneasiness, I thought it worthwhile to indicate some of the advantages of this doctrine. Some, I say—for the most important ones will be better understood from what we shall say in Part V.

[II.] I begin, therefore, by warning my Readers, first, to distinguish accurately between an idea, *or* concept, of the Mind, and the images of things that we imagine. And then it is necessary to distinguish between ideas and the words by which we signify things. For because many people either completely confuse these three—ideas, images, and words—or do not distinguish them accurately enough, or carefully enough, they have been completely ignorant of this doctrine concerning the will. But it is quite necessary to know it, both for the sake of speculation and in order to arrange one's life wisely.

Indeed, those who think that ideas consist in images which are formed in us from encounters with [external] bodies, are convinced that those ideas of things [which can make no trace in our brains, or] of which we can form no similar image [in our brain] are not ideas, but only fictions which we feign from a free choice of the will. They look on ideas, therefore, as mute pictures on a panel and preoccupied with this prejudice, do not see that an idea, insofar as it is an idea, involves an affirmation or negation.

And then, those who confuse words with the idea, or with the very affirmation that the idea involves, think that they can will something contrary to what they are aware of, when they only affirm or deny with words something contrary to what they are aware of. But these prejudices can easily be put aside by anyone who attends to the nature of thought, which does not at all involve the concept of extension. He will then understand clearly that an idea (since it is a mode of thinking) consists neither in the image of anything, nor in words. For the essence of words and of images is constituted only by corporeal motions, which do not at all involve the concept of thought.

It should suffice to have issued these few words of warning on this matter, so I pass to objections mentioned above.

[III.A.(i)] The first of these is that they think it clear that the will extends more widely than the intellect, and so is different from the intellect. The reason why they think the will extends more widely than the intellect is that they say they know by experience that they do not require a greater faculty of assenting, or affirming, and denying, than we already have, in order to assent to infinitely many other things which we do not perceive—but they do require a greater faculty of understanding. The will, therefore, is distinguished from the intellect because the intellect is finite and the will is infinite.

[III.A.(ii)] Secondly, it can be objected to us that experience seems to teach nothing more clearly than that we can suspend our judgment so as not to assent to things we perceive. This also seems to be confirmed from the fact that no one is said to be deceived insofar as he perceives something, but only insofar as he assents or dissents. E.g., someone who feigns a winged horse does not on that account grant that there is a winged horse, i.e., he is not on that account deceived unless at the same time he grants that there is a winged horse. Therefore, experience seems to teach nothing more clearly than that the will, or faculty of assenting, is free, and different from the faculty of understanding.

[III.A.(iii)] Thirdly, it can be objected that one affirmation does not seem to contain more reality than another, i.e., we do not seem to require a greater power to affirm that what is true, is true, than to affirm that something false is true. But [with ideas it is different, for] we perceive that one idea has more reality, *or* perfection, than another. As some objects are more excellent than others, so also some ideas of objects are more perfect than others. This also seems to establish a difference between the will and the intellect.

[III.A.(iv)] Fourth, it can be objected that if man does not act from freedom of the will, what will happen if he is in a state of equilibrium, like Buridan's ass? Will he perish of hunger and of thirst? If I concede that he will, I would seem to conceive an ass, or a statue of a man, not a man. But if I deny that he will, then he will determine himself, and consequently have the faculty of going where he wills and doing what he wills.

Perhaps other things in addition to these can be objected. But because I am not bound to force on you what anyone can dream, I shall only take the trouble to reply to these objections—and that as briefly as I can.

[III.B.(i)] To the first I say that I grant that the will extends more widely than the intellect, if by intellect they understand only clear and distinct ideas. But I deny that the will extends more widely than perceptions, *or* the faculty of conceiving. And indeed, I do not see why the faculty of willing should be called infinite, when the faculty of sensing is not. For just as we can affirm infinitely many things by the same faculty of willing (but one after another, for we cannot affirm infinitely many things at once), so also we can sense, *or* perceive, infinitely many bodies by the same faculty of sensing (viz. one after another [and not at once]).

If they say that there are infinitely many things which we cannot perceive, I reply that we cannot reach them by any thought, and consequently, not by any faculty of willing. But, they say, if God willed to bring it about that we should perceive them also, he would have to give us a greater faculty of perceiving, but not a greater faculty of willing than he has given us. This is the same as if they said that, if God should will to bring it about that we understood infinitely many other beings, it would indeed be necessary for him to give us a greater intellect, but not a more universal idea of being, in order for us to embrace the same infinity of beings. For we have shown that the will is a universal being, *or* idea, by which we explain all the singular volitions, i.e., it is what is common to them all.

Therefore, since they believe that this common or universal idea of all volitions is a faculty, it is not at all surprising if they say that this faculty extends beyond the limits of the intellect to infinity. For the universal is said equally of one, a great many, or infinitely many individuals.

[III.B.(ii)] To the second objection I reply by denying that we have a free power of suspending judgment. For when we say that someone suspends judgment, we are saying nothing but that he sees that he does not perceive the thing adequately. Suspension of judgment, therefore, is really a perception, not [an act of] free will.

To understand this clearly, let us conceive a child imagining a winged horse, and not perceiving anything else. Since this imagination involves the existence of the horse (by P17C), and the child does not perceive anything else that excludes the existence of the horse, he will necessarily regard the horse as present. Nor will he be able to doubt its existence, though he will not be certain of it.

We find this daily in our dreams, and I do not believe there is anyone who thinks that while he is dreaming he has a free power of suspending judgment concerning the things he dreams, and of bringing it about that he does not dream the things he dreams he sees. Nevertheless, it happens that even in dreams we suspend judgment, viz. when we dream that we dream.

Next, I grant that no one is deceived insofar as he perceives, i.e., I grant that the imaginations of the Mind, considered in themselves, involve no error. But I deny that a man affirms nothing insofar as he perceives. For what is perceiving a winged horse other than affirming wings of the horse? For if the Mind perceived nothing else except the winged horse, it would regard it as present to itself, and would not have any cause of doubting its existence, or any faculty of dissenting, unless either the imagination of the winged horse were joined to an idea which excluded the existence of the same horse, or the Mind perceived that its idea of a winged horse was inadequate. And then either it will necessarily deny the horse's existence, or it will necessarily doubt it.

[III.B.(iii)] As for the third objection, I think what has been said will be an answer to it too: viz. that the will is something universal, which is predicated of all ideas, and which signifies only what is common to all ideas, viz. the affirmation, whose adequate essence, therefore, insofar as it is thus conceived abstractly, must be in each idea, and in this way only must be the same in all, but not insofar as it is considered to constitute the idea's essence; for in that regard the singular affirmations differ from one another as much as the ideas themselves do. For example, the affirmation that the idea of a circle involves differs from that which the idea of a triangle involves as much as the idea of the circle differs from the idea of the triangle.

Next, I deny absolutely that we require an equal power of thinking, to affirm that what is true is true, as to affirm that what is false is true. For if you consider the mind, they are related to one another as being to not-being. For there is nothing positive in ideas which constitutes the form of falsity (see P35, P35S, and P47S). So the thing to note here, above all, is how easily we are deceived when we confuse universals with singulars, and beings of reason and abstractions with real beings.

[III.B.(iv)] Finally, as far as the fourth objection is concerned, I say that I grant entirely that a man placed in such an equilibrium (viz. who perceives nothing but thirst and hunger, and such food and drink as are equally distant from him) will perish of hunger and thirst. If they ask me whether such a man should not be thought an ass, rather than a man, I say that I do not know—just as I also do not know how highly we should esteem one who hangs himself, or children, fools, and madmen, etc.

[IV.] It remains now to indicate how much knowledge of this doctrine is to our advantage in life. We shall see this easily from the following considerations:

[A.] Insofar as it teaches that we act only from God's command, that we share in the divine nature, and that we do this the more, the more perfect our actions are, and the more and more we understand God. This doctrine, then, in addition to giving us complete peace of mind, also teaches us wherein our greatest happiness, *or* blessedness, consists: viz. in the knowledge of God alone, by which we are led to do only those things which love and morality advise. From this we clearly understand how far they stray from the true valuation of virtue, who expect to be honored by God with the greatest rewards for their virtue and best actions, as for the greatest bondage—as if virtue itself, and the service of God, were not happiness itself, and the greatest freedom.

[B.] Insofar as it teaches us how we must bear ourselves concerning matters of fortune, or things which are not in our power, i.e., concerning things which do not follow from our nature—that we must expect and bear calmly both good fortune and bad. For all things follow from God's eternal decree with the same necessity as from the essence of a triangle it follows that its three angles are equal to two right angles.

[C.] This doctrine contributes to social life, insofar as it teaches us to hate no one, to disesteem no one, to mock no one, to be angry at no one, to envy no one; and also insofar as it teaches that each of us should be content with his own things, and should be helpful to his neighbor, not from unmanly compassion, partiality, or superstition, but from the guidance of reason, as the time and occasion demand. I shall show this in the Fourth Part.

[D.] Finally, this doctrine also contributes, to no small extent, to the common society insofar as it teaches how citizens are to be governed and led, not so that they may be slaves, but that they may do freely the things that are best.

And with this I have finished what I had decided to treat in this scholium, and put an end to this our Second Part. In it I think that I have explained the nature and properties of the human Mind in sufficient detail, and as clearly as the difficulty of the subject allows, and that I have set out doctrines from which we can infer many excellent things, which are highly useful and necessary to know.

JOHN LOCKE
1632–1704

John Locke was born in Wrington, Somerset, the son of a Puritan lawyer. His father fought on the side of the Parliament against Charles I, and Locke himself was a lifelong defender of the parliamentary system.

As a teenager, Locke attended Westminster School, studying classics under the harsh discipline of the time. He later condemned the English educational system for its brutality and one-sided emphasis on the past. In 1652, he entered Christ Church, Oxford, where he received his B.A. in 1656 and an M.A. in 1658. Again, he found his Oxford education obsessed with the past—in particular the Scholasticism of the late Middle Ages. Hence, he sought knowledge in the emerging sciences. In 1659, he was named a Senior Student at Oxford—a position he held until he lost it for political reasons in 1684.

In 1662, Locke met Lord Ashley, the Earl of Shaftesbury. Locke and Shaftesbury became close friends and in 1667 Locke went to live with Shaftesbury as his personal physician, securing his medical degree and license in 1674. Locke also helped Shaftesbury with several projects, including writing a constitution for the colony of Carolina. As a member of Shaftesbury's entourage, Locke traveled extensively and met many of the leading thinkers of his day.

When Shaftesbury became the leader of the parliamentary opposition to the king, Locke's friendship became a liability. Shaftesbury was tried for treason in 1681; and although he was acquitted, he fled to Holland where he died in 1683. Without the backing of his powerful patron, Locke also fled to Holland where he became an advisor to William and Mary of Orange. Following the Glorious Revolution of 1688, which removed Locke's enemy, James II, from the throne,

Locke returned home in the company of William and Mary—now king and queen of England.

Following his return to England, Locke published his two most important works, *Essay Concerning Human Understanding* (1690) and *Two Treatises of Government* (1690). Locke spent the rest of his life writing and serving the new government as Commissioner of Appeals and, later, as Commissioner of Trade and Plantations. He died quietly at the home of a friend in 1704.

*   *   *

Locke begins his first major work, *Essays Concerning Human Understanding*, with several arguments against the Cartesian notion of innate ideas. He claims that the mind is a *tabula rasa*, a blank tablet or "white paper, void of all characters, without any ideas." All ideas come from one source: experience. Experience, in turn, is of two types: sensation or reflection. Sensations are derived from our sensory perceptions of the external world. Reflection, on the other hand, provides ideas by the mind "reflecting on its own operations within itself."

Having explained the *origin* of ideas, Locke then explains the *nature* of ideas. All ideas are either simple or complex. Simple ideas are uncompounded; that is, they cannot be broken down further, such as the ideas of "sweetness" or "redness." Complex ideas are composed of two or more simple ideas, such as the idea of a red, sweet apple. Locke then classifies simple and complex ideas by sources (sensation, reflection, or both).

Having explained the sources of ideas, Locke next asks if the ideas that come from sensation actually resemble the qualities of the external objects that gave rise to them. He answers first by dividing qualities into primary and secondary. Primary qualities are "utterly inseparable" from external objects regardless of their state—such qualities include solidity, extension, figure, motion, rest, and number. On the other hand, secondary qualities are "nothing in the objects themselves, but powers to produce various sensations in us by their primary qualities." These secondary qualities would include such things as colors, sounds, tastes, and the like. So, for example, the primary qualities of an apple (a solid, being extended in space, etc.) have the power to produce the secondary quality of a sweet taste and a red color. This analysis means that the world *as we experience it* is only a representation of the way the world actually is. The blooming, buzzing, colorful world of our experience is not the real world.

Finally, Locke asks what these primary and secondary qualities are qualities *of*. He argues that there must be "some *substratum* wherein [ideas] do subsist, and from which they do result, which therefore we call *substance*." Although we cannot have any idea of substance, nor can we explain the concept, we must posit substance as a "supporter" of qualities—a "something I know not what," Locke said.

Locke spent twenty years preparing his *Essay Concerning Human Understanding* for publication in 1690. The *Essay* went through several editions while Locke was still living, including an abridgment with his consent. The following selection is an abridgment by Walter Kaufmann, which I have modified. This abridgment owes much to John Wynne's (1695) editing and to the modern work of A.S. Pringle-Pattison.

In addition to this work, Locke wrote *Two Treatises of Government* (1690), *The Reasonableness of Christianity as Delivered in the Scriptures* (1695), *Vindications of the Reasonableness of Christianity* (1695 and 1697), and several "Letters" concerning toleration.

* * *

The best commentary on Locke's thought in general and on the *Essay* in particular is Richard I. Aaron, *John Locke* (Oxford: Clarendon Press, 1971). Also useful as a general overview are D.J. O'Connor, *John Locke* (Harmondsworth, Middlesex: Penguin Books, 1952); John W. Yolton, *Locke and the Way of Ideas* (Oxford: Clarendon Press, 1968); R.S. Woolhouse, *Locke* (Minneapolis: University of Minnesota Press, 1983); John Dunn, *Locke* (New York: Oxford University Press, 1984)—part of the "Past Masters" series, now reprinted in the combined volume of John Dunn et al., eds., *The British Empiricists* (Oxford: Oxford University Press, 1992); and Michael Ayers, *Locke* (Oxford: Routledge, 1994). For help with Locke's *Essay*, see John W. Yolton, *Locke and the Compass of Human Understanding: A Selective Commentary on the "Essay"* (London: Cambridge University Press, 1970), and John L. Mackie, *Problems from Locke* (Oxford: Oxford University Press, 1976). Nicholas Wolterstorff, *John Locke and the Ethics of Belief* (Cambridge: Cambridge University Press, 1996) provides guidance to the last section of the *Essay*. For guides to Locke's political thought, see John Dunn, *The Political Thought of John Locke* (Cambridge: Cambridge University Press, 1969), and J.W. Gough, *John Locke's Political Philosophy* (Oxford: Clarendon Press, 1973). John Yolton, *A Locke Dictionary* (Oxford: Basil Blackwell, 1993) provides a useful reference work. For collections of essays on Locke's thought, see C.B. Martin and D.M. Armstrong, eds., *Locke and Berkeley: A Collection of Critical Essays* (Notre Dame, IN: Notre Dame University Press, 1968); John W. Yolton, ed., *John Locke: Problems and Perspectives: A Collection of New Essays* (Cambridge: Cambridge University Press, 1969); Vere Chappell's trio of books, *Essays on Early Modern Philosophers: John Locke—Theory of Knowledge, John Locke—Political Philosophy* (both Hamden, CT: Garland Press, 1992); and *The Cambridge Companion to Locke* (Cambridge: Cambridge University Press, 1994). For an interesting, if unusual, analysis of Locke's political thought, see Leo Strauss, *Natural Right and History* (Chicago: University of Chicago Press, 1952).

AN ESSAY CONCERNING HUMAN UNDERSTANDING (in part)

Introduction

1. *An enquiry into the understanding, pleasant and useful.*—Since it is the *understanding* that sets man above the rest of sensible beings, and gives him all the advantage and dominion which he has over them, it is certainly a subject, even for its nobleness, worth our labour to enquire into. The understanding, like the eye, whilst it makes us see and perceive all other things, takes no notice of itself; and it requires art and pains to set it at a distance, and make it its own object. But whatever be the difficulties that lie in the way of this enquiry; whatever it be that keeps us so much in the dark to ourselves; sure I am that all the light we can let in upon our own minds, all the acquaintance we can make with our own understandings, will not only be very pleasant, but bring us great advantage in directing our thoughts in the search of other things.

2. *Design.*—This, therefore, being my purpose, to enquire into the original, certainty, and extent of *human knowledge*, together with the grounds and degrees of *belief*, *opinion*, and *assent*, I shall not at present meddle with the physical consideration of the mind, or trouble myself to examine wherein its essence consists, or by what motions of our spirits, or alterations of our bodies, we come to have any *sensation* by our organs, or any *ideas* in our understandings; and whether those ideas do, in their formation, any or all of them, depend on matter or no. These are speculations which, however curious and entertaining, I shall decline, as lying out of my way in the design I am now upon. It shall suffice to my present purpose, to consider the discerning faculties of a man as they are employed about the objects which they have to do with: and I shall imagine I have not wholly misemployed myself in the thoughts I shall have on this occasion, if, in this historical, plain method, I can give any account of the ways whereby our understandings come to attain those notions of things we have, and can set down any measures of the certainty of our knowledge, or the grounds of those persuasions which are to be found amongst men, so various, different, and wholly contradictory; and yet asserted somewhere or other with such assurance, and confidence, that he that shall take a view of the opinions of mankind, observe their opposition, and at the same time consider the fondness and devotion wherewith they are embraced, the resolution and eagerness wherewith they are maintained, may perhaps have reason to suspect that either there is no such thing as truth at all, or that mankind hath no sufficient means to attain a certain knowledge of it.

3. *Method.*—It is therefore worth while to search out the bounds between opinion and knowledge, and examine by what measures, in things whereof we have no certain knowledge, we ought to regulate our assent, and moderate our persuasions. In order whereunto, I shall pursue this following method:—

First, I shall enquire into the original of those *ideas*, notions, or whatever else you please to call them, which a man observes, and is conscious to himself he has in his mind; and the ways whereby the understanding comes to be furnished with them.

Secondly, I shall endeavour to show what *knowledge* the understanding hath by those ideas, and the certainty, evidence, and extent of it.

Thirdly, I shall make some enquiry into the nature and grounds of *faith* or *opinion*: whereby I mean that assent which we give to any proposition as true, of whose truth yet we have no certain knowledge. And here we shall have occasion to examine the reasons and degrees of assent.

4. *Useful to know the extent of our comprehension.*—If by this enquiry into the nature of the understanding, I can discover the powers thereof, how far they reach, to what things they are in any degree proportionate, and where they fail us, I suppose it may be of use, to prevail with the busy mind of man to be more cautious in meddling with things exceeding its comprehension, to stop when it is at the utmost extent of its tether, and to sit down in a quiet ignorance of those things which, upon examination, are found to be beyond the reach of our capacities. We should not then perhaps be so forward, out of an affection of an universal knowledge, to raise questions, and perplex ourselves and others with disputes about things to which our understandings are not suited, and of which we cannot frame in our minds any clear or distinct perceptions, or whereof (as it has, perhaps, too often happened) we have not any notions at all. If we can find out how far the understanding can extend its view, how far it has faculties to attain certainty, and in what cases it can only judge and guess, we may learn to content ourselves with what is attainable by us in this state.

*   *   *

8. *What "idea" stands for.*—Thus much I thought necessary to say concerning the occasion of this enquiry into human understanding. But, before I proceed on to what I have thought on this subject, I must here, in the entrance, beg pardon of my reader for the frequent use of the word *idea* which he will find in the following treatise. It being that term which, I think, serves best to stand for whatsoever is the object of the understanding when a man thinks, I have used it to express whatever is meant by *phantasm, notion, species, or whatever it is which the mind can be employed about in thinking*; and I could not avoid frequently using it.

I presume it will be easily granted me, that there are such *ideas* in men's minds; every one is conscious of them in himself, and men's words and actions will satisfy him that they are in others.

Our first enquiry then shall be,—how they come into the mind.

BOOK I. NEITHER PRINCIPLES NOR IDEAS ARE INNATE

CHAPTER 1. NO INNATE PRINCIPLES IN THE MIND

1. *The way shown how we come by any knowledge, sufficient to prove it not innate.*—It is an established opinion amongst some men, that there are in the understanding certain innate principles; some primary notions, ⟨*koinai ennoiai*⟩, characters, as it were stamped upon the mind of man, which the soul receives in its very first being, and brings into the world with it. It would be sufficient to convince unprejudiced readers of the falseness of this supposition, if I should only show (as I hope I shall in the following parts of this discourse) how men, barely by the use of their natural faculties, may attain to all the knowledge they have, without the help of any innate impressions; and may arrive at certainty, without any such original notions or principles. For I imagine any one will easily grant, that it would be impertinent to suppose the ideas of colours innate in a creature to whom God hath given sight, and a power to receive them by the

St. Paul's Cathedral, London, facade, built 1675–1710. Like Locke,
Sir Christopher Wren (1632–1723) was interested in science and
combining reason and religion. The left turret of the facade he
designed for St. Paul's conceals an observatory (opposite the clock in
the right turret). (*The British Tourist Authority*)

eyes from external objects: and no less unreasonable would it be to attribute several
truths to the impressions of nature and innate characters, when we may observe in ourselves faculties fit to attain as easy and certain knowledge of them as if they were originally imprinted on the mind.

But because a man is not permitted without censure to follow his own thoughts
in the search of truth, when they lead him ever so little out of the common road, I shall
set down the reasons that made me doubt of the truth of that opinion, as an excuse for
my mistake, if I be in one; which I leave to be considered by those who, with me, dispose themselves to embrace truth wherever they find it.

2. *General assent the great argument.*—There is nothing more commonly taken
for granted, than that there are certain principles, both *speculative* and *practical* (for
they speak of both), universally agreed upon by all mankind; which therefore, they
argue, must needs be the constant impressions which the souls of men receive in their
first beings and which they bring into the world with them, as necessarily and really as
they do any of their inherent faculties.

3. *Universal consent proves nothing innate.*—This argument, drawn from universal consent, has this misfortune in it, that if it were true in matter of fact, that there
were certain truths wherein all mankind agreed, it would not prove them innate, if
there can be any other way shown, how men may come to that universal agreement in
the things they do consent in; which I presume may be done.

4. *"What is, is,"* and *"It is impossible for the same Thing to be and not to be,"* *not universally assented to.*—But, which is worse, this argument of universal consent which is made use of to prove innate principles, seems to me a demonstration that there are none such: because there are none to which all mankind give an universal assent. I shall begin with the speculative, and instance in those magnified principles of demonstration, "Whatsoever is, is," and "It is impossible for the same thing to be and not to be"; which, of all others, I think have the most allowed title to innate. These have so settled a reputation of maxims universally received, that it will no doubt be thought strange if any one should seem to question it. But yet I take liberty to say, that these propositions are so far from having an universal assent, that there are a great part of mankind to whom they are not so much as known.

5. *Not on the mind naturally imprinted, because not known to children, idiots, etc.*—For, first, it is evident, that all children and idiots have not the least apprehension or thought of them. And the want of that is enough to destroy that universal assent, which must needs be the necessary concomitant of all innate truths: it seeming to me near a contradiction to say, that there are truths imprinted on the soul which it perceives or understands not; imprinting, if it signify anything, being nothing else but the making certain truths to be perceived. . . . No proposition can be said to be in the mind which it never yet knew, which it was never yet conscious of. For if any one may, then, by the same reason, all propositions that are true, and the mind is *capable* ever of assenting to, may be said to be in the mind, and to be imprinted; since if any one can be said to be in the mind, which it never yet knew, it must be only because it is capable of knowing it; and so the mind is of all truths it ever shall know. Nay, thus truths may be imprinted on the mind which it never did, nor ever shall know: for a man may live long, and die at last in ignorance of many truths which his mind was capable of knowing, and that with certainty. So that if the capacity of knowing be the natural impression contended for, all the truths a man ever comes to know will, by this account, be every one of them innate: and this great point will amount to no more, but only to a very high improper way of speaking. But then, to what end such contest for certain innate maxims? If truths can be imprinted on the understanding without being perceived, I can see no difference there can be between any truths the mind is capable of knowing in respect of their original: they must all be innate, or all adventitious; in vain shall a man go about to distinguish them. He therefore that talks of innate notions in the understanding, cannot (if he intend thereby any distinct sort of truths) mean such truths to be in the understanding as it never perceived, and is yet wholly ignorant of. For if these words "to be in the understanding" have any propriety, they signify to be understood. If therefore these two propositions: "Whatsoever is, is," and, "It is impossible for the same thing to be, and not to be," are by nature imprinted, children cannot be ignorant of them; infants, and all that have souls, must necessarily have them in their understandings, know the truth of them, and assent to it.

*   *   *

CHAPTER 2. NO INNATE PRACTICAL PRINCIPLES

1. *No moral principles so clear and so generally received as the forementioned speculative maxims.*—If those speculative maxims whereof we discoursed in the foregoing chapter have not an actual universal assent from all mankind, as we there

proved, it is much more visible concerning practical principles, that they come short of an universal reception. . . .

2. *Faith and justice not owned as principles by all men.*—Whether there be any such moral principles wherein all men do agree, I appeal to any who have been but moderately conversant in the history of mankind, and looked abroad beyond the smoke of their own chimneys. Where is that practical truth that is universally received without doubt or question, as it must be if innate? *Justice*, and keeping of contracts, is that which most men seem to agree in. This is a principle which is thought to extend itself to the dens of thieves, and the confederacies of the greatest villains; and they who have gone farthest towards the putting off of humanity itself, keep faith and rules of justice one with another. I grant that outlaws themselves do this one amongst another; but it is without receiving these as the innate laws of nature. They practice them as rules of convenience within their own communities: but it is impossible to conceive that he embraces justice as a practical principle who acts fairly with his fellow-highwayman, and at the same plunders or kills the next honest man he meets with.

*   *   *

CHAPTER 3. CONSIDERATIONS ON INNATE PRINCIPLES

8. *Idea of God not innate.*—If any idea can be imagined innate, the idea of God may, of all others, for many reasons, be thought so; since it is hard to conceive how there should be innate moral principles without an innate idea of a Deity: without a notion of a lawmaker, it is impossible to have a notion of a law, and an obligation to observe it. Besides the atheists taken notice of amongst the ancients, and left branded upon the records of history, hath not navigation discovered, in these latter ages, whole nations, at the Bay of Soldania, in Brazil, in Boranday, and the Caribbee Islands, etc., amongst whom there was to be found no notion of a God, no religion? . . . Perhaps, if we should with attention mind the lives and discourses of people not so far off, we should have too much reason to fear that many, in more civilized countries, have no very strong and clear impressions of a Deity upon their minds; and that the complaints of atheism made from the pulpit are not without reason. . . .

9. *The name of God not universal or obscure in meaning.*—But had all mankind everywhere a notion of a God (whereof yet history tells us the contrary), it would not from thence follow that the idea of him was innate, . . . especially if it be such an idea as is agreeable to the common light of reason, and naturally deducible from every part of our knowledge, as that of a God is. For the visible marks of extraordinary wisdom and power appear so plainly in all the work of the creation, that a rational creature who will but seriously reflect on them, cannot miss the discovery of a Deity; and the influence that the discovery of such a Being must necessarily have on the minds of all that have but once heard of it, is so great, and carries such a weight of thought and communication with it, that it seems stranger to me that a whole nation of men should be anywhere found so brutish as to want the notion of a God, than that they should be without any notion of numbers, or fire.

*   *   *

BOOK II. OF IDEAS

CHAPTER 1. OF IDEAS IN GENERAL AND THEIR ORIGINAL

1. *Idea is the object of thinking.*—Every man being conscious to himself that he thinks, and that which his mind is applied about whilst thinking being the ideas that are there, it is past doubt that men have in their minds several ideas, such as are those expressed by the words *whiteness, hardness, sweetness, thinking, motion, man, elephant, army, drunkenness,* and others. It is in the first place then to be enquired, How he comes by them?

I know it is a received doctrine, that men have native ideas and original characters stamped upon their minds in their very first being. This opinion I have at large examined already; and, I suppose, what I have said in the foregoing Book will be much more easily admitted, when I have shown whence the understanding may get all the ideas it has, and by what ways and degrees they may come into the mind; for which I shall appeal to every one's own observation and experience.

2. *All ideas come from sensation or reflection.*—Let us then suppose the mind to be, as we say, white paper, void of all characters, without any ideas; how comes it to be furnished? Whence comes it by that vast store, which the busy and boundless fancy of man has painted on it with an almost endless variety? Whence has it all the *materials* of reason and knowledge? To this I answer, in one word, from EXPERIENCE; in that all our knowledge is founded, and from that it ultimately derives itself. Our observation, employed either about external sensible objects, or about the internal operations of our minds, perceived and reflected on by ourselves, is that which supplies our understandings with all the materials of thinking. These two are the fountains of knowledge, from whence all the ideas we have or can naturally have, do spring.

3. *The objects of sensation one source of ideas.*—First, our senses, conversant about particular sensible objects, do convey into the mind several distinct perceptions of things, according to those various ways wherein those objects do affect them; and thus we come by those *ideas* we have of *yellow, white, heat, cold, soft, hard, bitter, sweet,* and all those which we call sensible qualities; which when I say the senses convey into the mind, I mean, they from external objects convey into the mind what produces there those perceptions. This great source of most of the ideas we have, depending wholly upon our senses, and derived by them to the understanding, I call, SENSATION.

4. *The operations of our minds the other source of them.*—Secondly, the other fountain, from which experience furnishes the understanding with ideas, is the perception of the operations of our mind within us, as it is employed about the ideas it has got; which operations, when the soul comes to reflect on and consider, do furnish the understanding with another set of ideas which could not be had from things without: and such are *perception, thinking, doubting, believing, reasoning, knowing, willing,* and all the different actings of our own minds; which we being conscious of, and observing in ourselves, do from these receive into our understanding as distinct ideas, as we do from bodies affecting our senses. This source of ideas every man has wholly in himself: and though it be not sense, as having nothing to do with external objects, yet it is very like it, and might properly enough be called *internal sense*. But as I call the other SENSATION, so I call this REFLECTION, the ideas it affords being such only as the mind gets by reflecting on its own operations within itself. By Reflection, then,

in the following part of this discourse, I would be understood to mean that notice which the mind takes of its own operations, and the manner of them, by reason whereof there come to be ideas of these operations in the understanding. These two, I say, viz., external material things as the objects of SENSATION, and the operations of our own minds within as the objects of REFLECTION are, to me, the only originals from whence all our ideas take their beginnings. The term *operations* here, I use in a large sense, as comprehending not barely the actions of the mind about its ideas, but some sort of passions arising sometimes from them, such as is the satisfaction or uneasiness arising from any thought.

5. *All our ideas are of the one or the other of these.*—The understanding seems to me not to have the least glimmering of any ideas which it doth not receive from one of these two. *External objects* furnish the mind with the ideas of sensible qualities, which are all those different perceptions they produce in us; and *the mind* furnishes the understanding with ideas of its own operations. These, when we have taken a full survey of them, and their several modes, combinations, and relations, we shall find to contain all our whole stock of ideas; and that we have nothing in our minds which did not come in one of these two ways. Let any one examine his own thoughts, and thoroughly search into his understanding, and then let him tell me, whether all the original ideas he has there, are any other than of the objects of his senses, or of the operations of his mind considered as objects of his reflection; and how great a mass of knowledge soever he imagines to be lodged there, he will, upon taking a strict view, see that he has not any idea in his mind but what one of these two have imprinted, though perhaps with infinite variety compounded and enlarged by the understanding, as we shall see hereafter.

6. *Observable in children.*—He that attentively considers the state of a child at his first coming into the world, will have little reason to think him stored with plenty of ideas that are to be the matter of his future knowledge. It is *by degrees* he comes to be furnished with them: and though the ideas of obvious and familiar qualities themselves before the memory begins to keep a register of time and order, yet it is often so late before some unusual qualities come in the way, that there are few men that cannot recollect the beginning of their acquaintance with them: and if it were worth while, no doubt a child might be so ordered as to have but a very few even of the ordinary ideas till he were grown up to a man. But all that are born into the world being surrounded with bodies that perpetually and diversely affect them, variety of ideas, whether care be taken about it or no, are imprinted on the minds of children. Light and colours are busy and at hand everywhere when the eye is but open; sounds and some tangible qualities fail not to solicit their proper senses, and force an entrance to the mind; but yet I think it will be granted easily, that if a child were kept in a place where he never saw any other but black and white till he were a man, he would have no more ideas of scarlet or green, than he that from his childhood never tasted an oyster or a pineapple has of those particular relishes.

7. *Men are differently furnished with these according to the different objects they converse with.*—Men then come to be furnished with fewer or more simple ideas from without, according as the objects they converse with afford greater or less variety; and from the operations of their minds within, according as they more or less reflect on them. For, though he that contemplates the operations of his mind cannot but have plain and clear ideas of them; yet, unless he turn his thoughts that way, and considers them *attentively*, he will no more have clear and distinct ideas of all the operations of his mind, and all that may be observed therein, than he will have all the particular ideas of any landscape, or of the parts and motions of a clock, who will not turn his eyes to

it, and with attention heed all the parts of it. The picture or clock may be so placed, that they may come in his way every day; but yet he will have but a confused idea of all the parts they are made up of, till he applies himself with attention to consider them each in particular.

8. *Ideas of reflection later, because they need attention.*—And hence we see the reason why it is pretty late before most children get ideas of the operations of their own minds; and some have not any very clear or perfect ideas of the greatest part of them all their lives. Because, though they pass there continually, yet, like floating visions, they make not deep impressions enough to leave in the mind clear, distinct, lasting ideas, till the understanding turns inward upon itself, reflects on its own operations, and makes them the object of its own contemplation. Children, when they come first into it, are surrounded with a world of new things, which, by a constant solicitation of their senses, draw the mind constantly to them, forward to take notice of new, and apt to be delighted with the variety of changing objects. Thus the first years are usually employed and diverted in looking abroad. Men's business in them is to acquaint themselves with what is to be found without; and so, growing up in a constant attention to outward sensations, seldom make any considerable reflection on what passes within them till they come to be of riper years; and some scarce ever at all.

9. *The soul begins to have ideas when it begins to perceive.*—To ask, at what time a man has first any ideas, is to ask when he begins to perceive; having ideas, and perception, being the same thing. I know it is an opinion, that the soul always thinks; and that it has the actual perception of ideas in itself constantly, as long as it exists; and that actual thinking is as inseparable from the soul, as actual extension is from the body: which if true, to enquire after the beginning of a man's ideas is the same as to enquire after the beginning of his soul. For by this account, soul and its ideas, as body and its extension, will begin to exist both at the same time.

* * *

CHAPTER 2. OF SIMPLE IDEAS

1. *Uncompounded appearances.*—The better to understand the nature, manner, and extent of our knowledge, one thing is carefully to be observed concerning the ideas we have; and that is, that some of them are *simple*, and some *complex*.

Though the qualities that affect our senses are, in the things themselves, so united and blended that there is no separation, no distance between them; yet it is plain the ideas they produce in the mind enter by the senses simple and unmixed. For though the sight and touch often take in from the same object at the same time different ideas; as a man sees at once motion and colour, the hand feels softness and warmth in the same piece of wax; yet the simple ideas thus united in the same subject are as perfectly distinct as those that come in by different senses. The coldness and hardness which a man feels in a piece of ice being as distinct ideas in the mind as the smell and whiteness of a lily, or as the taste of sugar and smell of a rose: and there is nothing can be plainer to a man than the clear and distinct perception he has of those simple ideas; which, being each in itself uncompounded, contains in it nothing but *one uniform appearance or conception in the mind*, and is not distinguishable into different ideas.

2. *The mind can neither make nor destroy them.*—These simple ideas, the materials of all our knowledge, are suggested and furnished to the mind only by those two

ways above mentioned, viz., sensation and reflection. When the understanding is once stored with these simple ideas, it has the power to repeat, compare, and unite them, even to an almost infinite variety, and so can make at pleasure new complex ideas. But it is not in the power of the most exalted wit or enlarged understanding, by any quickness or variety of thought, to *invent* or *frame* one new simple idea in the mind, not taken in by the ways before mentioned; nor can any force of the understanding *destroy* those that are there. The dominion of man in this little world of his own understanding, being much-what the same as it is in the great world of visible things, wherein his power, however managed by art and skill, reaches no farther than to compound and divide the materials that are made to his hand, but can do nothing towards the making the least particle of new matter, or destroying one atom of what is already in being. The same inability will every one find in himself, who shall go about to fashion in his understanding any simple idea not received in by his senses from external objects, or by reflection from the operations of his own mind about them. I would have any one try to fancy any taste which had never affected his palate, or frame the idea of a scent he had never smelt; and when he can do this, I will also conclude, that a blind man hath ideas of colours, and a deaf man true distinct notions of sounds.

3. *Only the qualities that affect the sense are imaginable.*—This is the reason why, though we cannot believe it impossible to God to make a creature with other organs, and more ways to convey into the understanding the notice of corporeal things than those five, as they are usually counted, which he has given to man—yet I think it is *not possible* for any one to imagine any other qualities in bodies, howsoever constituted, whereby they can be taken notice of, besides sounds, tastes, smells, visible and tangible qualities. And had mankind been made with but four senses, the qualities then which are the object of the fifth sense, had been as far from our notice, imagination, and conception, as now any belonging to a sixth, seventh, or eighth sense, can possibly be: which, whether yet some other creatures, in some other parts of this vast and stupendous universe, may not have, will be a great presumption to deny. He that will not set himself proudly at the top of all things, but will consider the immensity of this fabric, and the great variety that is to be found in this little and inconsiderable part of it which he has to do with, may be apt to think, that in other mansions of it there may be other and different intelligible beings, of whose faculties he has as little knowledge or apprehension, as a worm shut up in one drawer of a cabinet hath of the senses or understanding of a man; such variety and excellency being suitable to the wisdom and power of the Maker. I have here followed the common opinion of man's having but five senses, though perhaps there may be justly counted more, but either supposition serves equally to my present purpose.

CHAPTER 3. OF IDEAS OF ONE SENSE

1. *Division of simple ideas.*—The better to conceive the ideas we receive from sensation, it may not be amiss for us to consider them in reference to the different ways whereby they make their approaches to our minds, and make themselves perceivable by us.

First, then, There are some which come into our minds *by one sense only*.

Secondly. There are others that convey themselves into the mind *by more senses than one*.

Thirdly. Others that are from *reflection only*.

Fourthly. There are some that make themselves way, and are suggested to the mind *by all the ways of sensation and reflection.*

We shall consider them apart under these several heads.

Ideas of one sense. There are some ideas which have admittance only through one sense, which is peculiarly adapted to receive them. Thus light and colours, as white, red, yellow, blue, with their several degrees or shades and mixtures, as green, scarlet, purple, sea-green, and the rest come in only by the eyes; all kinds of noises, sounds, and tones, only by the ears; the several tastes and smells, by the nose and palate. And if these organs, or the nerves which are the conduits to convey them from without to their audience in the brain, the mind's presence-room (as I may so call it), are, any of them, so disordered as not to perform their functions, they have no postern to be admitted by, no other way to bring themselves into view, and be perceived by the understanding.

The most considerable of those belonging to the touch are heat, and cold, and so-lidity; all the rest, consisting almost wholly in the sensible configuration, as smooth and rough; or else, more or less firm adhesion of the parts, as hard and soft, tough and brittle, are obvious enough.

2. *Few simple ideas have names.*—I think it will be needless to enumerate all the particular simple ideas belonging to each sense. Nor indeed is it possible if we would, there being a great many more of them belonging to most of the senses than we have names for. The variety of smells, which are as many almost, if not more than species of bodies in the world, do most of them want names. Sweet and stinking commonly serve our turn for these ideas, which in effect is little more than to call them pleasing or dis-pleasing; though the smell of a rose and violet, both sweet, are certainly very distinct ideas. Nor are the different tastes that by our palates we receive ideas of, much better provided with names. Sweet, bitter, sour, harsh, and salt, are almost all the epithets we have to denominate that numberless variety of relishes which are to be found distinct, not only in almost every sort of creatures, but in the different parts of the same plant, fruit, or animal. The same may be said of colours and sounds. I shall therefore, in the account of simple ideas I am here giving, content myself to set down only such as are most material to our present purpose, or are in themselves less apt to be taken notice of, though they are very frequently the ingredients of our complex ideas; amongst which, I think, I may well account solidity, which therefore I shall treat of in the next chapter.

CHAPTER 4. OF SOLIDITY

1. *We receive this idea from touch.*—The idea of solidity we receive by our touch; and it arises from the resistance which we find in body to the entrance of any other body into the place it possesses, till it has left it. There is no idea which we re-ceive more constantly from sensation than solidity. Whether we move or rest, in what posture soever we are, we always feel something under us that supports us, and hinders our farther sinking downwards; and the bodies which we daily handle make us per-ceive that whilst they remain between them, they do, by an insurmountable force, hin-der the approach of the parts of our hands that press them. *That which thus hinders the approach of two bodies, when they are moving one towards another, I call solidity.* I will not dispute whether this acceptation of the word solid be nearer to its original sig-nification than that which mathematicians use it in: it suffices that, I think, the common notion of solidity will allow, if not justify, this use of it; but if any one think it better to

call it *impenetrability*, he has my consent. Only I have thought the term solidity the more proper to express this idea, not only because of its vulgar use in that sense, but also because it carries something more of positive in it than impenetrability, which is negative, and is, perhaps, more a consequence of solidity than solidity itself. This, of all other, seems the idea most intimately connected with and essential to body, so as nowhere else to be found or imagined, but only in matter; and though our senses take no notice of it, but in masses of matter, of a bulk sufficient to cause a sensation in us; yet the mind, having once got this idea from such grosser sensible bodies, traces it farther, and considers it, as well as figure, in the minutest particle of matter that can exist, and finds it inseparably inherent in body, wherever or however modified.

2. *Solidity fills space.*—This is the idea which belongs to body, whereby we conceive it to fill space. The idea of which filling of space is,—that where we imagine any space taken up by a solid substance, we conceive it so to possess it, that it excludes all other solid substances; and will for ever hinder any other two bodies, that move towards one another in a straight line, from coming to touch one another, unless it removes from between them in a line not parallel to that which they move in. This idea of it, the bodies which we ordinarily handle sufficiently furnish us with.

*   *   *

6. *What solidity is.*—If any one asks me, *what this solidity is*, I send him to his senses to inform him: let him put a flint or a football between his hands, and then endeavour to join them, and he will know. If he thinks this is not a sufficient explanation of solidity, what it is, and wherein it consists, I promise to tell him what it is, and wherein it consists, when he tells me what thinking is, or wherein it consists; or explains to me what extension or motion is, which perhaps seems much easier. The simple ideas we have are such as experience teaches them to us; but if, beyond that, we endeavour by words to make them clearer in the mind, we shall succeed no better than if we went about to clear up the darkness of a blind man's mind by talking, and to discourse into him the ideas of light and colours. The reason of this I shall show in another place.

CHAPTER 5. OF SIMPLE IDEAS OF DIVERS SENSES

Ideas received both by seeing and touching.—The ideas we get by more than one sense are of space or extension, figure, rest and motion: for these make perceivable impressions both on the eyes and touch; and we can receive and convey into our minds the ideas of the extension, figure, motion, and rest of bodies, both by seeing and feeling. But having occasion to speak more at large of these in another place, I here only enumerate them.

CHAPTER 6. OF SIMPLE IDEAS OF REFLECTION

1. *Simple ideas are the operations of the mind about its other ideas.*—The mind, receiving the ideas mentioned in the foregoing chapters from without, when it turns its view inward upon itself, and observes its own actions about those ideas it has, takes from thence other ideas, which are as capable to be the objects of its contemplation as any of those it received from foreign things.

2. *The idea of perception, and idea of willing, we have from reflection.*—The two great and principal actions of the mind, which are most frequently considered, and which are so frequent that every one that pleases may take notice of them in himself, are these two:—*Perception* or *Thinking*, and *Volition* or *Willing*. The power of thinking is called the *Understanding* and the power of volition is called the *Will*; and these two powers of abilities in the mind are denominated *faculties*. Of some of the *modes* of these simple ideas of reflection, such as are *remembrance, discerning, reasoning, judging, knowledge, faith, etc.*, I shall have occasion to speak hereafter.

CHAPTER 7. OF SIMPLE IDEAS OF BOTH SENSATION AND REFLECTION

1. *Ideas of pleasure and pain.*—There be other simple ideas which convey themselves into the mind by all the ways of sensation and reflection; viz., *pleasure* or *delight*, and its opposite, *pain* or *uneasiness*; *power*; *existence*; *unity*.

2. *Mix with almost all our other ideas.*—Delight or uneasiness, one or other of them, join themselves to almost all our ideas both of sensation and reflection; and there is scarce any affection of our senses from without, any retired thought of our mind within, which is not able to produce in us pleasure or pain. By pleasure and pain, I would be understood to signify whatsoever delights or molests us; whether it arises from the thoughts of our minds, or anything operating on our bodies. For whether we call it satisfaction, delight, pleasure, happiness, etc., on the one side, or uneasiness, trouble, pain, torment, anguish, misery, etc., on the other, they are still but different degrees of the same thing, and belong to the ideas of pleasure and pain, delight or uneasiness; which are the names I shall most commonly use for those two sorts of ideas.

* * *

7. *Ideas of existence and unity.*—Existence and unity are two other ideas that are suggested to the understanding by every object without, and every idea within. When ideas are in our minds, we consider them as being actually there, as well as we consider things to be actually without us: which is, that they exist, or have existence. And whatever we can consider as one thing, whether a real being or idea, suggests to the understanding the idea of unity.

8. *Idea of power.*—Power also is another of those ideas which we receive from sensation and reflection. For, observing in ourselves that we do and can think, and that we can at pleasure move several parts of our bodies which were at rest, the effects also that natural bodies are able to produce in one another occurring every moment to our senses, we both these ways get the idea of power.

9. *Idea of succession.*—Besides these there is another idea, which though suggested by our senses yet is more constantly offered us by what passes in our own minds; and that is the idea of succession. For if we look immediately into ourselves, and reflect on what is observable there, we shall find our ideas always, whilst we are awake or have any thought, passing in train, one going and another coming without intermission.

10. *Simple ideas the materials of all our knowledge.*—These, if they are not all, are at least (as I think) the most considerable of those simple ideas which the mind has, and out of which is made all its other knowledge: all of which it receives only by the two forementioned ways of sensation and reflection.

Nor let any one think these too narrow bounds for the capacious mind of man to expatiate in, which takes its flight farther than the stars, and cannot be confined by the limits of the world. I grant all this, but desire any one to assign any *simple idea* which is not received from one of those inlets before mentioned, or any *complex idea* not made out of those simple ones.

Nor will it be so strange to think these few simple ideas sufficient to employ the quickest thought or largest capacity, and to furnish the materials of all that various knowledge and more various fancies and opinions of all mankind, if we consider how many words may be made out of the various composition of twenty-four letters; or if, going one step farther, we will but reflect on the variety of combinations may be made with barely one of the above-mentioned ideas, viz., number, whose stock is inexhaustible and truly infinite: and what a large and immense field doth extension alone afford the mathematicians?

CHAPTER 8. SOME FURTHER CONSIDERATIONS CONCERNING OUR SIMPLE IDEAS OF SENSATION

7. *Ideas in the mind, qualities in bodies.*—To discover the nature of our ideas the better, and to discourse of them intelligibly, it will be convenient to distinguish them *as they are ideas or perceptions in our minds, and as they are modifications of matter in the bodies that cause such perceptions in us:* that so we may not think (as perhaps usually is done) that they are exactly the images and resemblances of something inherent in the subject; most of those of sensation being in the mind no more the likeness of something existing without us than the names that stand for them are the likeness of our ideas, which yet upon hearing they are apt to excite in us.

8. *Our ideas and the qualities of bodies.*—Whatsoever the mind perceives *in itself*, or is the immediate object of perception, thought, or understanding, that I call *idea*; and the power to produce any idea in our mind, I call *quality* of the subject wherein that power is. Thus a snowball having the power to produce in us the ideas of white, cold, and round, the powers to produce those ideas in us as they are in the snowball, I call qualities; and as they are sensations or perceptions in our understandings, I call them ideas; which *ideas*, if I speak of them sometimes as in the things themselves, I would be understood to mean those qualities in the objects which produce them in us.

9. *Primary qualities of bodies.*—Qualities thus considered in bodies are, *First*, such as are utterly inseparable from the body, in what estate soever it be; such as, in all the alterations and changes it suffers, all the force can be used upon it, it constantly keeps; and such as sense constantly finds in every particle of matter which has bulk enough to be perceived, and the mind finds inseparable from every particle of matter, though less than to make itself singly be perceived by our senses: v.g., take a grain of wheat, divide it into two parts, each part has still solidity, extension, figure, and mobility; divide it again, and it retains still the same qualities: and so divide it on, till the parts become insensible; they must retain still each of them all those qualities. . . . These I call *original* or *primary qualities* of body, which I think we may observe to produce simple ideas in us, viz., solidity, extension, figure, motion or rest, and number.

10. *Secondary qualities of bodies.*—Secondly, such qualities, which in truth are nothing in the objects themselves, but powers to produce various sensations in us by their primary qualities, i.e., by the bulk, figure, texture, and motion of their insensible parts, as colours, sounds, tastes, etc., these I call *secondary qualities*. To these might be added a third sort, which are allowed to be barely powers, though they are as much real

qualities in the subject as those which I, to comply with the common way of speaking, call qualities, but, for distinction, secondary qualities. For the power in fire to produce a new colour or consistence in *wax* or *clay* by its primary qualities, is as much a quality in fire as the power it has to produce in me a new idea or sensation of warmth or burning, which I felt not before, by the same primary qualities, viz., the bulk, texture, and motion of its insensible parts.

11. *How bodies produce ideas in us.*—The next thing to be considered is, how bodies produce ideas in us; and that is manifestly by impulse, the only way which we can conceive bodies operate in.

12. *By motions, external, and in our organism.*—If, then, external objects be not united to our minds when they produce ideas in it, and yet we perceive these original qualities in such of them as singly fall under senses, it is evident that some motion must be thence continued by our nerves or animal spirits, by some parts of our bodies, to the brains or the seat of sensation, there to produce in our minds the particular ideas we have of them. And since the extension, figure, number, and motion of bodies of an observable bigness, may be perceived at a distance by the sight, it is evident some singly imperceptible bodies must come from them to the eyes, and thereby convey to the brain some motion which produces these ideas which we have of them in us.

13. *How secondary qualities produce their ideas.*—After the same manner that the ideas of these original qualities are produced in us, we may conceive that the ideas of *secondary* qualities are also produced, viz., by the operation of insensible particles on our senses. . . . The different motions and figures, bulk and number of such particles, affecting the several organs of our senses, produce in us those different sensations which we have from the colours and smells of bodies; v.g., that a violet, by the impulse of such insensible particle, of matter of peculiar figures and bulks, and in different degrees and modifications of their motions, causes the ideas of the blue colour and sweet scent of that flower to be produced in our minds. It being no more impossible to conceive that God should annex such ideas to such motions with which they have no similitude, than that he should annex the idea of pain to the motion of a piece of steel dividing our flesh, with which that idea hath no resemblance.

14. *They depend on the primary qualities.*—What I have said concerning colours and smells may be understood also of tastes and sounds, and other the like sensible qualities; which, whatever reality we by mistake attribute to them, are in truth nothing in the objects themselves, but powers to produce various sensations in us, and depend on those primary qualities, viz., bulk, figure, texture, and motion of parts, as I have said.

15. *Ideas of primary qualities are resemblances; of secondary, not.*—From whence I think it is easy to draw this observation, that the ideas of primary qualities of bodies are resemblances of them, and their patterns do really exist in the bodies themselves; but the ideas produced in us by these secondary qualities have no resemblance of them at all. There is nothing like our ideas existing in the bodies themselves. They are, in the bodies we denominate from them, only a power to produce those sensations in us: and what is sweet, blue, or warm in idea, is but the certain bulk, figure, and motion of the insensible parts in the bodies themselves, which we call so.

16. *Examples.*—Flame is denominated hot and light; snow, white and cold; and manna, white and sweet, from the ideas they produce in us. Which qualities are commonly thought to be the same in those bodies that those ideas are in us, the one the perfect resemblance of the other, as they are in a mirror; and it would by most men be judged very extravagant, if one should say otherwise. And yet he that will consider that the same fire that at one distance produces in us the sensation of warmth, does at a nearer approach produce in us the far different sensation of pain, ought to bethink

himself what reason he has to say, that his idea of warmth which was produced in him by the fire, is *actually in the fire*; and his idea of pain which the same fire produced in him the same way is not in the fire. Why is whiteness and coldness in snow, and pain not, when it produces the one and the other idea in us, and can do neither, but by the bulk, figure, number, and motion of its solid parts?

17. *The ideas of the primary alone really exist.*—The particular bulk, number, figure, and motion of the parts of fire or snow are really in them, whether any one's senses perceive them or no; and therefore they may be called *real* qualities, because they really exist in those bodies. But light, heat, whiteness, or coldness, are no more really in them than sickness or pain is in manna. Take away the sensation of them; let not the eyes see light or colours, nor the ears hear sounds; let the palate not taste, nor the nose smell; and all colours, tastes, odours, and sounds, *as they are such particular ideas*, vanish and cease, and are reduced to their causes, i.e., bulk, figure, and motion of parts.

18. *Secondary exist only as modes of the primary.*—A piece of manna of a sensible bulk is able to produce in us the idea of a round or square figure; and, by being removed from one place to another, the idea of motion. This idea of motion represents it as it really is in the manna moving; a circle or square are the same, whether in idea or existence, in the mind or in the manna; and this, both motion and figure are really in the manna, whether we take notice of them or no: this everybody is ready to agree to. Besides, manna, by the bulk, figure, texture, and motion of its parts, has a power to produce the sensations of sickness, and sometimes of acute pains or gripings, in us. That these ideas of sickness and pain are not in the manna, but effects of its operations on us, and are nowhere when we feel them not: this also every one readily agrees to. And yet men are hardly to be brought to think that sweetness and whiteness are not really in manna, which are but the effects of the operations of manna by the motion, size, and figure of its particles on the eyes and palate: as the pain and sickness caused by manna are confessedly nothing but the effects of its operations on the stomach. . . . Why the pain and sickness, ideas that are the effects of manna, should be thought to be nowhere when they are not felt; and yet the sweetness and whiteness, effects of the same manna on other parts of the body, by ways equally as unknown, should be thought to exist in the manna, when they are not seen nor tasted, would need some reason to explain.

19. *Examples.*—Let us consider the red and white colours in porphyry: hinder light but from striking on it, and its colours vanish; it no longer produces any such ideas in us. Upon the return of light, it produces these appearances on us again. Can any one think any real alterations are made in the porphyry by the presence or absence of light, and that those ideas of whiteness and redness are really in porphyry in the light, when it is plain *it has no colour in the dark?* It has indeed such a configuration of particles, both night and day, as are apt, by the rays of light rebounding from some parts of that hard stone, to produce in us the idea of redness, and from others the idea of whiteness: but whiteness or redness are not in it at any time, but such a texture that hath the power to produce such a sensation in us.

*   *   *

22. *Excursion into natural philosophy.*—I have, in what just goes before, been engaged in physical enquiries a little farther than perhaps I intended. But it being necessary to make the nature of sensation a little understood, and to make the difference between the *qualities* in bodies and the *ideas* produced by them in the mind to be distinctly conceived, without which it were impossible to discourse intelligibly of them, I

hope I shall be pardoned this little excursion into natural philosophy, it being necessary in our present enquiry to distinguish the *primary* and *real* qualities of bodies, which are always in them (viz., solidity, extension, figure, number, and motion or rest, and are sometimes perceived by us, viz., when the bodies they are in are big enough singly to be discerned), from those *secondary* and *imputed* qualities, which are but the powers of several combinations of those primary ones, when they operate without being distinctly discerned: whereby we also may come to know what ideas are, and what are not, resemblances of something really existing in the bodies we denominate from them.

23. *Three sorts of qualities in bodies.*—The qualities then that are in bodies, rightly considered, are of three sorts:

First, the bulk, figure, number, situation, and motion or rest of their solid parts. Those are in them, whether we perceive them or no; and when they are of that size that we can discover them, we have by these an idea of the thing as it is in itself, as is plain in artificial things. These I call *primary qualities*.

Secondly, the power that is in any body, by reason of its insensible primary qualities, to operate after a peculiar manner on any of our senses, and thereby produce in us the different ideas of several colours, sounds, smells, tastes, etc. These are usually called *sensible qualities*.

Thirdly, the power that is in any body, by reason of the particular constitution of its primary qualities, to make such a change in the bulk, figure, texture, and motion of *another body*, as to make it operate on our senses differently from what it did before. Thus the sun has a power to make wax white, and fire, to make lead fluid. These are usually called *powers*.

The first of these, as has been said, I think may be properly called real, original, or primary qualities, because they are in the things themselves, whether they are perceived or no: and upon their different modifications it is that the secondary qualities depend.

The other two are only powers to act differently upon other things, which powers result from the different modifications of those primary qualities.

24. *The first are resemblances; the second thought to be resemblances, but are not; the third neither are, nor are thought so.*—But though these two latter sorts of qualities are powers barely, and nothing but powers, relating to several other bodies, and resulting from the different modifications of the original qualities, yet they are generally otherwise thought of. . . . V.g., the idea of heat or light which we receive by our eyes or touch from the sun, are commonly thought real qualities existing in the sun, and something more than mere powers in it. But when we consider the sun in reference to wax, which it melts or blanches, we look upon the whiteness and softness produced in the wax, not as qualities in the sun, but effects produced by powers in it: whereas, if rightly considered, these qualities of light and warmth, which are perceptions in me when I am warmed or enlightened by the sun, are no otherwise in the sun than the changes made in the wax, when it is blanched or melted, are in the sun. They are all of them equally powers in the sun, depending on its primary qualities. . . .

25. *Why the secondary are ordinarily taken for real qualities, and not for bare powers.*—The reason why the one are ordinarily taken for real qualities, and the other only for bare powers, seems to be because the ideas we have of distinct colours, sounds, etc., containing nothing at all in them of bulk, figure, or motion, we are not apt to think them the effects of these primary qualities which appear not to our senses to operate in their production, and with which they have not any apparent congruity, or conceivable connexion. Hence it is that we are so forward to imagine that those ideas

are the resemblances of something really existing in the objects themselves. . . . But, in the other case, in the operations of bodies changing the qualities one of another, we plainly discover that the quality produced hath commonly no resemblance with anything in the thing producing it; wherefore we look on it as a bare effect of power. . . .

*   *   *

CHAPTER 9. OF PERCEPTION

1. *Perception the first simple idea of reflection.*—PERCEPTION, as it is the first faculty of the mind exercised about our ideas; so it is the first and simplest idea we have from reflection, and is by some called thinking in general. Though thinking, in the propriety of the English tongue, signifies that sort of operation in the mind about its ideas, wherein the mind is active; where it, with some degree of voluntary attention, considers anything. For in bare naked perception, the mind is, for the most part, only passive; and what it perceives, it cannot avoid perceiving.

2. *Reflection alone can give us the idea of what, perception is.*—What perception is, every one will know better by reflecting on what he does himself, when he sees, hears, feels, etc., or thinks, than by any discourse of mine. Whoever reflects on what passes in his own mind cannot miss it. And if he does not reflect, all the words in the world cannot make him have any notion of it.

3. *Arises in sensation only when the mind notices the organic impression.*—This is certain, that whatever alterations are made in the body, if they reach not the mind; whatever impressions are made on the outward parts, if they are not taken notice of within, there is no perception. Fire may burn our bodies with no other effect than it does a billet, unless the motion be continued to the brain, and there the sense of heat, or idea of pain, produced in the mind; wherein consists actual perception.

4. *Impulse on the organ insufficient.*—How often may a man observe in himself, that whilst his mind is intently employed in the contemplation of some objects, and curiously surveying some ideas that are there, it takes no notice of impressions of sounding bodies made upon the organ of hearing, with the same alteration that uses to be for the producing the idea of sound? A sufficient impulse there may be on the organ; but it not reaching the observation of the mind, there follows no perception: and though the motion that uses to produce the idea of sound be made in the ear, yet no sound is heard. Want of sensation, in this case, is not through any defect in the organ, or that the man's ears are less affected than at other times when he does hear: but that which uses to produce the idea, though conveyed in by the usual organ, not being taken notice of in the understanding, and so imprinting no idea in the mind, there follows no sensation. So that wherever there is sense or perception, there some idea is actually produced, and present in the understanding.

*   *   *

8. *Sensations often changed by the judgment.*—We are further to consider concerning perception, that the ideas we receive by sensation are often, in grown people, altered by the judgment, without our taking notice of it. When we set before our eyes a round globe of any uniform colour, v.g., gold, alabaster, or jet, it is certain that the idea thereby imprinted on our mind is of a flat circle, variously shadowed, with several de-

grees of light and brightness coming to our eyes. But we having, by use, been accustomed to perceive what kind of appearance convex bodies are wont to make in us; what alterations are made in the reflections of light by the difference of the sensible figures of bodies;—the judgment presently, by an habitual custom, alters the appearances into their causes. So that from that which is truly variety of shadow or colour, collecting the figure, it makes it pass for a mark of figure, and frames to itself the perception of a convex figure and an uniform colour; when the idea we receive from thence is only a plane variously coloured, as is evident in painting. To which purpose I shall here insert a problem of that very ingenious and studious promoter of real knowledge, the learned and worthy Mr. Molyneux, which he was pleased to send me in a letter some months since; and it is this:—"Suppose a man born blind, and now adult, and taught by his touch to distinguish between a cube and a sphere of the same metal, and nighly of the same bigness, so as to tell, when he felt one and the other, which is the cube, which the sphere. Suppose then the cube and sphere placed on a table, and the blind man be made to see: *quære* whether *by his sight, before he touched them*, he could now distinguish and tell which is the globe, which the cube?" To which the acute and judicious proposer answers, "Not. For, though he has obtained the experience of how a globe, how a cube affects his touch, yet he has not yet obtained the experience, that what affects his touch so or so, must affect his sight so or so; or that a protuberant angle in the cube, that pressed his hand unequally, shall appear to his eye as it does in the cube."—I agree with this thinking gentleman, whom I am proud to call my friend, in his answer to this problem; and am of opinion that the blind man, at first sight, would not be able with certainty to say which was the globe, which the cube, whilst he only saw them; though he could unerringly name them by his touch, and certainly distinguish them by the difference of their figures felt. This I have set down, and leave with my reader, as an occasion for him to consider how much he may be beholden to experience, improvement, and acquired notions, where he thinks he had not the least use of, or help from them. And the rather, because this observing gentleman further adds, that "having, upon the occasion of my book, proposed this to divers very ingenious men, he hardly ever met with one that at first gave the answer to it which he thinks true, till by hearing his reasons they were convinced."

*   *   *

CHAPTER 12. OF COMPLEX IDEAS

1. *Made by the mind out of simple ones.*—We have hitherto considered those ideas, in the reception whereof the mind is only passive, which are those simple ones received from sensation and reflection before mentioned, whereof the mind cannot make one to itself, nor have any idea which does not wholly consist of them. [But as the mind is wholly passive in the reception of all its simple ideas, so it exerts several acts of its own, whereby out of its simple ideas, as the materials and foundations of the rest, the other are framed. The acts of the mind wherein it exerts its power over its simple ideas are chiefly these three: (1) Combining several simple ideas into one compound one; and thus all *complex ideas* are made. (2) The second is bringing two ideas, whether simple or complex, together, and setting them by one another, so as to take a view of them at once, without uniting them into one; by which it gets all its *ideas of relations*. (3) The third is separating them from all other ideas that accompany them in

their real existence; this is called abstraction: and thus all its *general ideas* are made. This shows man's power and its way of operation to be much the same in the material and intellectual world. For, the materials in both being such as he has no power over, either to make or destroy, all that man can do is either to unite them together, or to set them by one another, or wholly separate them. I shall here begin with the first of these in the consideration of complex ideas, and come to the other two in their due places.] As simple ideas are observed to exist in several combinations united together, so the mind has a power to consider several of them united together as one idea; and that not only as they are united in external objects, but as itself has joined them. Ideas thus made up of several simple ones put together I call *complex*; such as are beauty, gratitude, a man, an army, the universe; which, though complicated of various simple ideas or complex ideas made up of simple ones, yet are, when the mind pleases, considered each by itself as one entire thing, and signified by one name.

2. *Made voluntarily.*—In this faculty of repeating and joining together its ideas, the mind has great power in varying and multiplying the objects of its thoughts infinitely beyond what sensation or reflection furnished it with: but all this still confined to those simple ideas which it received from those two sources, and which are the ultimate materials of all its compositions. For simple ideas are all from things themselves; and of these the mind can have no more nor other than what are suggested to it. It can have no other ideas of sensible qualities than what come from without by the senses, nor any ideas of other kind of operations of a thinking substance than what it finds in itself: but when it has once got these simple ideas, it is not confined barely to observation, and what offers itself from without; it can, by its own power, put together those ideas it has, and make new complex ones which it never received so united.

3. *Complex ideas are either modes, substances, or relations.*—COMPLEX IDEAS, however compounded and decompounded, though their number be infinite, and the variety endless wherewith they fill and entertain the thoughts of men, yet I think they may be all reduced under these three heads: 1. *Modes.* 2. *Substances.* 3. *Relations.*

4. *Ideas of modes.*—First, *Modes* I call such complex ideas which, however compounded, contain not in them the supposition of subsisting by themselves, but are considered as dependences on, or affections of substances; such as are the ideas signified by the words triangle, gratitude, murder, etc. And if in this I use the word mode in somewhat a different sense from its ordinary signification, I beg pardon; it being unavoidable in discourses differing from the ordinary received notions, either to make new words, or to use old words in somewhat a new signification: the latter whereof, in our present case, is perhaps the more tolerable of the two.

5. *Simple and mixed modes of simple ideas.*—Of these modes there are two sorts which deserve distinct consideration. First, there are some which are only variations or different combinations of the same simple idea, without the mixture of any other, as a dozen, or score; which are nothing but the ideas of so many distinct units added together: and these I call *simple modes*, as being contained within the bounds of one simple idea. Secondly, there are others compounded of simple ideas of several kinds, put together to make one complex one; v.g., beauty, consisting of a certain composition of colour and figure, causing delight in the beholder; theft, which, being the concealed change of the possession of anything, without the consent of the proprietor, contains, as is visible, a combination of several ideas of several kinds: and these I call *mixed modes*.

6. *Ideas of substances, single or collective.*—Secondly, the ideas of *Substances* are such combinations of simple ideas as are taken to represent distinct particular

things subsisting by themselves, in which the supposed or confused idea of substance, such as it is, is always the first and chief. Thus, if to substance be joined the simple idea of a certain dull whitish colour, with certain degrees of weight, hardness, ductility, and fusibility, we have the idea of lead; and a combination of the ideas of a certain sort of figure, with the powers of motion, thought, and reasoning, joined to substance, make the ordinary idea of a man. Now of substances also there are two sorts of ideas, one of single substances, as they exist separately, as of a man or a sheep; the other of several of those put together, as an army of men, or flock of sheep; which *collective* ideas of several substances thus put together, are as much each of them one single idea as that of a man or an unit.

7. *Ideas of relation.*—Thirdly, the last sort of complex ideas is that we call Relation, which consists in the consideration and comparing one idea with another. Of these several kinds we shall treat in their order.

8. *The abstrusest ideas we can have are all from two sources.*—If we will trace the progress of our minds, and with attention observe how it repeats, adds together, and unites its simple ideas received from sensation or reflection, it will lead us farther than at first perhaps we should have imagined. And I believe we shall find, if we warily observe the originals of our notions, that *even the most abstruse ideas*, how remote soever they may seem from sense, or from any operation of our own minds, are yet only such as the understanding frames to itself, by repeating and joining together ideas that it had either from objects of sense, or from its own operations about them: so that those even large and abstract ideas are *derived from sensation or reflection*, being no other than what the mind, by the ordinary use of its own faculties, employed about ideas received from objects of sense, or from the operations it observes in itself about them, may and does attain unto. This I shall endeavour to show in the ideas we have of space, time, and infinity, and some few other, that seem the most remote from those originals.

* * *

CHAPTER 21. OF POWER

1. *This idea how got.*—The mind being every day informed, by the senses, of the alteration of those simple ideas it observes in things without; and taking notice how one comes to an end and ceases to be, and another begins to exist which was not before; reflecting also, on what passes within itself, and observing a constant change of its ideas, sometimes by the impression of outward objects on the senses, and sometimes by the determination of its own choice; and concluding from what it has so constantly observed to have been, that the like changes will for the future be made in the same things by like agents, and by the like ways; considers in one thing the possibility of having any of its simple ideas changed, and in another the possibility of making that change; and so comes by that idea which we call *power*. Thus we say, fire has a power to melt gold, i.e., to destroy the consistency of its insensible parts, and consequently its hardness, and make it fluid; and gold has a power to be melted: that the sun has a power to blanch wax; and wax a power to be blanched by the sun, whereby the yellowness is destroyed, and whiteness made to exist in its room. In which and the like cases, the power we consider is in reference to the change of perceivable ideas. For we cannot observe any alteration to be made in, or operation upon, anything, but by the observ-

able change of its sensible ideas: nor conceive any alteration to be made, but by conceiving a change of some of its ideas.

2. *Power, active and passive.*—Power thus considered is twofold, viz., as able to make, or able to receive, any change: the one may be called *active*, and the other passive, power. Whether matter be not wholly destitute of active power, as its author, God, is truly above all passive power; and whether the intermediate state of created spirits be not that alone which is capable of both active and passive power, may be worth consideration. I shall not now enter into that enquiry: my present business being not to search into the original of power, but how we come by the *idea* of it. But since active powers make so great a part of our complex ideas of natural substances (as we shall see hereafter), yet they being not, perhaps, so truly active powers as our hasty thoughts are apt to represent them, I judge it not amiss, by this intimation, to direct our minds to the consideration of God and spirits, for the clearest idea of *active* power.

3. *Power includes relation.*—I confess power includes in it some kind of relation (a relation to action or change), as indeed, which of our ideas, of what kind soever, when attentively considered, does not? For our ideas of extension, duration, and number, do they not all contain in them a secret relation of the parts? Figure and motion have something relative in them much more visibly: and sensible qualities, as colours and smells, etc., what are they but the powers of different bodies in relation to our perception? And if considered in the things themselves, do they not depend on the bulk, figure, texture, and motion of the parts? All which include some kind of relation in them. Our idea therefore of power, I think, may well have a place amongst other *simple ideas*, and be considered as one of them, being one of those that make a principal ingredient in our complex ideas of substances, as we shall hereafter have occasion to observe.

4. *The clearest idea of active power had from spirit.*—We are abundantly furnished with the idea of passive power, by almost all sorts of sensible things. In most of them we cannot avoid observing their sensible qualities, nay, their very substances, to be in a continual flux: and therefore with reason we look on them as liable still to the same change. Nor have we of *active* power (which is the more proper signification of the word power) fewer instances. Since whatever change is observed, the mind must collect a power somewhere, able to make that change, as well as a possibility in the thing itself to receive it. But yet, if we will consider it attentively, bodies by our senses do not afford us so clear and distinct an idea of active power as we have from reflection on the operations of our minds. For all power relating to action, and there being but two sorts of action whereof we have any idea, viz., thinking and motion, let us consider whence we have the clearest ideas of the powers which produce these actions. (1) Of thinking, body affords us no idea at all: it is only from reflection that we have that. (2) Neither have we from body any idea of the beginning of motion. A body at rest affords us no idea of any active power to move; and when it is set in motion itself, that motion is rather a passion than an action in it. For when the ball obeys the stroke of a billiard-stick, it is not any action of the ball, but bare passion. Also when by impulse it sets another ball in motion that lay in its way, it only communicates the motion it had received from another, and loses in itself so much as the other received: which gives us but a very obscure idea of an *active* power of moving in body, whilst we observe it only to *transfer*, but not *produce* any motion. . . . The idea of the *beginning* of motion we have only from reflection on what passes in ourselves, where we find by experience, that, barely by willing it, barely by a thought of the mind, we can move the parts of our bodies which were before at rest. So that it seems to me, we have, from the observation of the operation of bodies by our senses, but a very imperfect, obscure idea

The Funeral of Phocion, 1648, by Nicholas Poussin (1594–1665). In this classical-style painting, nature is depicted in geometrical terms that imply a sense of permanence. Locke believed that the complex ideas we have about such scenes are built up out of "a great number of the simple ideas conveyed in by the senses." (*Louvre / Paris*)

of *active* power, since they afford us not any idea in themselves of the power to begin any action, either motion or thought. But if, from the impulse bodies are observed to make one upon another, any one thinks he has a clear idea of power, it serves as well to my purpose, sensation being one of those ways whereby the mind comes by its ideas: only I thought it worth while to consider here by the way, whether the mind doth not receive its idea of active power clearer from reflection on its own operations, than it doth from any external sensation.

*   *   *

Chapter 23. Of Our Complex Ideas of Substances

1. *Ideas of particular substances, how made.*—The mind being, as I have declared, furnished with a great number of the simple ideas conveyed in by the senses, as they are found in exterior things, or by reflection on its own operations, takes notice also, that a certain number of these simple ideas go constantly together; which being presumed to belong to one thing, and words being suited to common apprehensions, and made use of for quick dispatch, are called, so united in one subject, by one name; which, by inadvertency, we are apt afterward to talk of and consider as one simple

idea, which indeed is a complication of many ideas together: because, as I have said, not imagining how these simple ideas can subsist by themselves, we accustom ourselves to suppose some *substratum* wherein they do subsist, and from which they do result, which therefore we call *substance*.

2. *Our obscure idea of substance in general.*—So that if any one will examine himself concerning his notion of pure substance in general, he will find he has no other idea of it at all, but only a supposition of he knows not what of such qualities which are capable of producing simple ideas in us; which qualities are commonly called accidents. If any one should be asked, what is the subject wherein colour or weight inheres, he would have nothing to say, but the solid extended parts: and if he were demanded, what is it that that solidity and extension inhere in, he would not be in a much better case than the Indian before mentioned, who saying that the world was supported by a great elephant, was asked, what the elephant rested on; to which his answer was, a great tortoise: but being again pressed to know what gave support to the broad-backed tortoise, replied, *something, he knew not what.* And thus here, as in all other cases where we use words without having clear and distinct ideas, we talk like children; who being questioned what such a thing is which they know not, readily give this satisfactory answer, that it is *something*; which in truth signifies no more, when so used, either by children or men, but that they know not what; and that the thing they pretend to know, and talk of, is what they have no distinct idea of at all, and so are perfectly ignorant of it, and in the dark. The idea, then, we have, to which we give the general name substance, being nothing but the supposed, but unknown, support of those qualities we find existing, which we imagine cannot subsist *sine re substante*, without something to support them, we call that support *substantia*; which, according to the true import of the word, is, in plain English, standing under, or upholding.

3. *Of the sorts of substances.*—An obscure and relative idea of *substance in general* being thus made, we come to have the ideas of *particular sorts of substances*, by collecting *such* combinations of simple ideas as are, by experience and observation of men's senses, taken notice of to exist together, and are therefore supposed to flow from the particular internal constitution or unknown essence of that substance. Thus we come to have the ideas of a man, horse, gold, water, etc., of which substances, whether any one has any other *clear* idea, farther than of certain simple ideas coexisting together, I appeal to every one's own experience. It is the ordinary qualities observable in iron or a diamond, put together, that make the true complex idea of those substances, which a smith or a jeweller commonly knows better than a philosopher; who, whatever *substantial forms* he may talk of, has no other idea of those substances than what is framed by a collection of those simple ideas which are to be found in them. Only we must take notice, that our complex ideas of substances, besides all these simple ideas they are made up of, have always the confused idea of something to which they belong and in which they subsist. And therefore, when we speak of any sort of substance, we say it is a thing having such or such qualities; as body is a thing that is extended, figured, and capable of motion; a spirit, a thing capable of thinking; and so hardness, friability, and power to draw iron, we say, are qualities to be found in a loadstone. These and the like fashions of speaking intimate that the substance is supposed always *something besides* the ex-tension, figure, solidity, motion, thinking, or other observable ideas, though we know not what it is.

4. *No clear or distinct idea of substance in general.*—Hence, when we talk or think of any particular sort of corporeal substances, as horse, stone, etc., though the idea we have of either of them be but the complication or collection of those several simple ideas of sensible qualities which we use to find united in the thing called horse

or stone; yet *because we cannot conceive how they should subsist alone, nor one in another*, we suppose them existing in, and supported by, some common subject; which support we denote by the name substance, though it be certain we have no clear or distinct idea of that thing we suppose a support.

5. *As clear an idea of spiritual substance as of corporeal substance.*—The same happens concerning the operations of the mind, viz., thinking, reasoning, fearing, etc., which we concluding not to subsist of themselves, nor apprehending how they can belong to body, or be produced by it, we are apt to think these the actions of some other *substance*, which we call *spirit*; whereby yet it is evident, that having no other idea or notion of matter, but something wherein those many sensible qualities which affect our senses do subsist; by supposing a substance wherein thinking, knowing, doubting, and a power of moving, etc., do subsist; we have as clear a notion of the substance of spirit as we have of body; the one being supposed to be (without knowing what it is) the *substratum* to those simple ideas we have from without; and the other supposed (with a like ignorance of what it is) to be the *substratum* to those operations which we experiment in ourselves within. It is plain, then, that the idea of *corporeal substance* in matter is as remote from our conceptions and apprehensions as that of *spiritual substance* or spirit; and therefore, from our not having any notion of the substance of spirit, we can no more conclude its nonexistence than we can, for the same reason, deny the existence of body: it being as rational to affirm there is no body, because we have no clear and distinct idea of the substance of matter, as to say there is no spirit, because we have no clear and distinct idea of the substance of a spirit.

6. *Our ideas of particular sorts of substances.*—Whatever therefore be the secret and abstract nature of substance in general, all the ideas we have of particular distinct sorts of substances are nothing but several combinations of simple ideas coexisting in such, though unknown, cause of their union, as makes the whole subsist of itself. It is by such combinations of simple ideas, and nothing else, that we represent particular sorts of substances to ourselves. Such are the ideas we have of their several species in our minds; and such only do we, by their specific names, signify to others, v.g., man, horse, sun, water, iron; upon hearing which words, every one who understands the language frames in his mind a combination of those several simple ideas which he has usually observed or fancied to exist together under that denomination; all which he supposes to rest in, and be, as it were, adherent to, that unknown common subject, which inheres not in anything else. Though in the meantime it be manifest, and every one upon enquiry into his own thoughts will find, that he has no other idea of any substance but what he has barely of those sensible qualities, which he supposes to inhere, with a supposition of such a *substratum*, as gives, as it were, a support to those qualities or simple ideas, which he has observed to exist united together. Thus the idea of the sun, what is it but an aggregate of those several simple ideas, bright, hot, roundish, having a constant regular motion, at a certain distance from us, and perhaps some other? As he who thinks and discourses of the sun, has been more or less accurate in observing those sensible qualities, ideas, or properties, which are in that thing which he calls the sun.

7. *Their active and passive powers a great part of our complex ideas of substances.*—For he has the perfectest idea of any of the particular sorts of substances who has gathered and put together most of those simple ideas which do exist in it, among which are to be reckoned its active powers and passive capacities; which, though not simple ideas, yet in this respect, for brevity's sake, may conveniently enough be reckoned amongst them; . . . We immediately by our senses perceive in fire its heat and colour; which are, if rightly considered, nothing but powers in it to produce

those ideas in us: we also by our senses perceive the colour and brittleness of charcoal, whereby we come by the knowledge of another power in fire, which it has to change the colour and consistency of *wood*. By the former, fire immediately, by the latter, it mediately discovers to us these several powers; which therefore we look upon to be a part of the qualities of fire, and so make them a part of the complex idea of it. For all those powers that we take cognizance of, terminating only in the alteration of some sensible qualities in those subjects on which they operate, and so making them exhibit to us new sensible ideas; therefore it is that I have reckoned these powers amongst the simple ideas which make the complex ones of the sorts of substances; though these powers, considered in themselves, are truly complex ideas. . . .

8. *And why.*—Nor are we to wonder that powers make a great part of our complex ideas of substances, since their secondary qualities are those which, in most of them, serve principally to distinguish substances one from another and commonly make a considerable part of the complex idea of the several sorts of them. For our senses failing us in the discovery of the bulk, texture, and figure of the minute parts of bodies, on which their real constitutions and differences depend, we are fain to make use of their secondary qualities as the characteristical notes and marks whereby to frame ideas of them in our minds, and distinguish them one from another. All which secondary qualities, as has been shown, are nothing but bare powers. For the colour and taste of opium are, as well as its soporific or anodyne virtues, mere powers depending on its primary qualities, whereby it is fitted to produce different operations on different parts of our bodies.

9. *Three sorts of ideas make our complex ones of corporeal substances.*—The ideas that make our complex ones of corporeal substances are of these three sorts. First, the ideas of the primary qualities of things which are discovered by our senses, and are in them even when we perceive them not: such are the bulk, figure, number, situation, and motion of the parts of bodies, which are really in them, whether we take notice of them or no. Secondly, the sensible secondary qualities which, depending on these, are nothing but the powers those substances have to produce several ideas in us by our senses; which ideas are not in the things themselves otherwise than as anything is in its cause. Thirdly, the aptness we consider in any substance to give or receive such alterations of primary qualities as that the substance so altered should produce in us different ideas from what it did before; these are called active and passive powers: all which powers, as far as we have any notice or notion of them, terminate only in sensible simple ideas. For whatever alteration a loadstone has the power to make in the minute particles of iron, we should have no notion of any power it had at all to operate on iron, did not its sensible motion discover it; and I doubt not but there are a thousand changes that bodies we daily handle have a power to cause in one another, which we never suspect, because they never appear in sensible effects.

10. *Powers thus make a great part of our complex ideas of particular substances.*—Powers therefore justly make a great part of our complex ideas of substances. He that will examine his complex idea of gold, will find several of its ideas that make it up to be only powers: as the power of being melted, but of not spending itself in the fire, of being dissolved in *aqua regia*, are ideas as necessary to make up our complex idea of gold, as its colour and weight: which, if duly considered, are also nothing but different powers. For to speak truly, yellowness is not actually in gold, but is a power in gold to produce that idea in us by our eyes when placed in a due light: and the heat which we cannot leave out of our idea of the sun, is no more really in the sun than the white colour it introduces into wax. . . .

11. *The now secondary qualities of bodies would disappear, if we could discover the primary ones of their minute parts.*—Had we senses acute enough to discern the minute particles of bodies, and the real constitution on which their sensible qualities depend, I doubt not but they would produce quite different ideas in us, and that which is now the yellow colour of gold would then disappear, and instead of it we should see an admirable texture of parts of a certain size and figure. This microscopes plainly discover to us; for what to our naked eyes produces a certain colour is, by thus augmenting the acuteness of our senses, discovered to be quite a different thing; and the thus altering, as it were, the proportion of the bulk of the minute parts of a coloured object to our usual sight, produces different ideas from what it did before. Thus sand, or pounded glass, which is opaque and white to the naked eye, is pellucid in a microscope: . . . blood to the naked eye appears all red; but by a good microscope, wherein its lesser parts appear, shows only some few globules of red, swimming in a pellucid liquor; and how these red globules would appear, if glasses could be found that yet could magnify them one thousand or ten thousand times more, is uncertain.

*　*　*

30. *Our idea of spirit and our idea of body compared.*—So that, in short, the idea we have of spirit, compared with the idea we have of body, stands thus: The substance of spirit is unknown to us; and so is the substance of body equally unknown to us. Two primary qualities or properties of body, viz., solid coherent parts and impulse, we have distinct clear ideas of: so likewise we know and have distinct clear ideas of two primary qualities or properties of spirit, viz., thinking, and a power of action; i.e., a power of beginning or stopping several thoughts or motions. We have also the ideas of several qualities inherent in bodies, and have the clear distinct ideas of them: which qualities are but the various modifications of the extension of cohering solid parts and their motion. We have likewise the ideas of the several modes of thinking, viz., believing, doubting, intending, fearing, hoping; all which are but the several modes of thinking. We have also the ideas of willing, and moving the body consequent to it, and with the body itself too; for, as has been showed, spirit is capable of motion.

*　*　*

33. *Our complex idea of God.*—For if we examine the idea we have of the incomprehensible Supreme Being, we shall find, that we come by it the same way; and that the complex ideas we have both of God and separate spirits are made up of the simple ideas we receive from reflection: v.g., having, from what we experiment in ourselves, got the ideas of existence and duration, of knowledge and power, of pleasure and happiness, and of several other qualities and powers which it is better to have than to be without; when we would frame an idea the most suitable we can to the Supreme Being, we enlarge every one of these with our idea of infinity; and so, putting them together, make our complex idea of God. For that the mind has such a power of enlarging some of its ideas, received from sensation and reflection, has been already showed.

*　*　*

35. *God in his own essence incognisable.*—It is infinity which, joined to our ideas of existence, power, knowledge, etc., makes that complex idea whereby we

represent to ourselves, the best we can, the Supreme Being. For though in his own essence (which certainly we do not know, not knowing the real essence of a pebble, or a fly, or of our own selves) God be simple and uncompounded; yet, I think, I may say we have no other idea of him but a complex one of existence, knowledge, power, happiness, etc., infinite and eternal: which are all distinct ideas, and some of them being relative are again compounded of others; all which being, as has been shown, originally got from sensation and reflection, go to make up the idea or notion we have of God.

*   *   *

37. *Recapitulation.*—And thus we have seen what kind of ideas we have of *substances of all kinds*, wherein they consist, and how we come by them. From whence, I think, it is very evident,

First, That all our ideas of the several *sorts* of substances are nothing but collections of simple ideas, with a supposition of *something* to which they belong, and in which they subsist; though of this supposed something we have no clear distinct idea at all.

Secondly, That all the simple ideas that, thus united in one common *substratum*, make up our complex ideas of several *sorts* of substances, are no other but such as we have received from sensation or reflection. . . .

Thirdly, That most of the simple ideas that make up our complex ideas of substances, when truly considered, are only *powers*, however we are apt to take them for positive qualities: v.g., the greatest part of the ideas that make our complex idea of *gold* are yellowness, great weight, ductility, fusibility, and solubility in *aqua regia*, etc., all united together in an unknown *substratum*; all which ideas are nothing else but so many relations to other substances, and are not really in the gold considered barely in itself, though they depend on those real and primary qualities of its internal constitution, whereby it has a fitness differently to operate and be operated on by several other substances.

*   *   *

CHAPTER 27. OF IDENTITY AND DIVERSITY

1. *Wherein identity consists.*—Another occasion the mind often takes of comparing, is the very being of things, when, considering *anything as existing at any determined time and place*, we compare it with *itself existing at another time*, and thereon form the ideas of *identity* and *diversity*. When we see anything to be in any place in any instant of time, we are sure (be it what it will) that it is that very thing, and not another which at that same time exists in another place, how like and undistinguishable soever it may be in all other respects: and in this consists *identity*, when the ideas it is attributed to vary not at all from what they were that moment wherein we consider their former existence, and to which we compare the present. For we never finding, nor conceiving it possible, that two things of the same kind should exist in the same place at the same time, we rightly conclude, that, whatever exists anywhere at any time, excludes all of the same kind, and is there itself alone. When therefore we demand whether anything be the *same* or no, it refers always to something that existed such a time in such a place, which it was certain, at that instant, was the same with itself, and

no other. From whence it follows, that one thing cannot have two beginnings of existence, nor two things one beginning; it being impossible for two things of the same kind to be or exist in the same instant, in the very same place; or one and the same thing in different places. That, therefore, that had one beginning, is the same thing; and that which had a different beginning in time and place from that, is not the same, but diverse. That which has made the difficulty about this relation has been the little care and attention used in having precise notions of the things to which it is attributed.

2. *Identity of substances.*—We have the ideas but of three sorts of substances: 1. *God.* 2. *Finite intelligences.* 3. *Bodies.*

First, *God* is without beginning, eternal, unalterable, and everywhere, and therefore concerning his identity there can be no doubt.

Secondly, *finite spirits* having had each its determinate time and place of beginning to exist, the relation to that time and place will always determine to each of them its identity, as long as it exists.

Thirdly, The same will hold of every *particle of matter*, to which no addition or subtraction of matter being made, it is the same. For, though these three sorts of substances, as we term them, do not exclude one another out of the same place, yet we cannot conceive but that they must necessarily each of them exclude any of the same kind out of the same place: or else the notions and names of identity and diversity would be in vain, and there could be no such distinctions of substances, or anything else one from another. For example: could two bodies be in the same place at the same time; then those two parcels of matter must be one and the same, take them great or little; nay, all bodies must be one and the same. For, by the same reason that two particles of matter may be in one place, all bodies may be in one place: which, when it can be supposed, takes away the distinction of identity and diversity of one and more, and renders it ridiculous. But it being a contradiction that two or more should be one, identity and diversity are relations and ways of comparing well founded, and of use to the understanding.

Identity of modes and relations.—All other things being but modes or relations ultimately terminated in substances, the identity and diversity of each particular existence of them too will be by the same way determined: only as to things whose existence is in succession, such as are the actions of finite beings, v.g., *motion* and *thought*, both which consist in a continued train of succession, concerning *their* diversity there can be no question: because each perishing the moment it begins, they cannot exist in different times, or in different places, as permanent beings can at different times exist in distant places; and therefore no motion or thought, considered as at different times, can be the same, each part thereof having a different beginning of existence.

3. *Principium individuationis.*—From what has been said, it is easy to discover what is so much inquired after, the *principium individuationis*; and that, it is plain, is existence itself; which determines a being of any sort to a particular time and place, incommunicable to two beings of the same kind. This, though it seems easier to conceive in simple substances or modes; yet, when reflected on, is not more difficult in compound ones, if care be taken to what it is applied: v.g., let us suppose an atom, i.e., a continued body under one immutable superficies, existing in a determined time and place; it is evident, that, considered in any instant of its existence, it is in that instant the same with itself. For, being at that instant what it is, and nothing else, it is the same, and so must continue as long as its existence is continued; for so long it will be the same, and no other. In like manner, if two or more atoms be joined together into the same mass, every one of those atoms will be the same, by the foregoing rule: and whilst they exist united together, the mass, consisting of the same atoms, must be the

same mass, or the same body, let the parts be ever so differently jumbled. But if one of these atoms be taken away, or one new one added, it is no longer the same mass or the same body. In the state of living creatures, their identity depends not on a mass of the same particles, but on something else. For in them the variation of great parcels of matter alters not the identity: an oak growing from a plant to a great tree, and then lopped, is still the same oak; and a colt grown up to a horse, sometimes fat, sometimes lean, is all the while the same horse: though, in both these cases, there may be a manifest change of the parts; so that truly they are not either of them the same masses of matter, though they be truly one of them the same oak, and the other the same horse. The reason whereof is, that, in these two cases—a *mass of matter* and a *living body*—identity is not applied to the same thing.

4. *Identity of vegetables.*—We must therefore consider wherein an oak differs from a mass of matter, and that seems to me to be in this, that the one is only the cohesion of particles of matter any how united, the other such a disposition of them as constitutes the parts of an oak; and such an organization of those parts as is fit to receive and distribute nourishment, so as to continue and frame the wood, bark, and leaves, etc., of an oak, in which consists the vegetable life. That being then one plant which has such an organization of parts in one coherent body, partaking of one common life, it continues to be the same plant as long as it partakes of the same life, though that life be communicated to new particles of matter vitally united to the living plant, in a like continued organization conformable to that sort of plants. For this organization, being at any one instant in any one collection of matter, is in that particular concrete distinguished from all other, and is that individual life, which existing constantly from that moment both forwards and backwards, in the same continuity of insensibly succeeding parts united to the living body of the plant, it has that identity which makes the same plant, and all the parts of it, parts of the same plant, during all the time that they exist united in that continued organization, which is fit to convey that common life to all the parts so united.

5. *Identity of animals.*—The case is not so much different in brutes but that any one may hence see what makes an animal and continues it the same. Something we have like this in machines, and may serve to illustrate it. For example, what is a watch? It is plain it is nothing but a fit organization or construction of parts to a certain end, which, when a sufficient force is added to it, it is capable to attain. If we would suppose this machine one continued body, all whose organized parts were repaired, increased, or diminished by a constant addition or separation of insensible parts, with one common life, we should have something very much like the body of an animal; with this difference, That, in an animal the fitness of the organization, and the motion wherein life consists, begin together, the motion coming from within; but in machines the force coming sensibly from without, is often away when the organ is in order, and well fitted to receive it.

6. *The identity of man.*—This also shows wherein the identity of the same *man* consists; viz., in nothing but a participation of the same continued life, by constantly fleeting particles of matter, in succession vitally united to the same organized body. He that shall place the identity of man in anything else, but, like that of other animals, in one fitly organized body, taken in any one instant, and from thence continued, under one organization of life, in several successively fleeting particles of matter united to it, will find it hard to make an embryo, one of years, mad and sober, the *same* man, by any supposition, that will not make it possible for Seth, Ismael, Socrates, Pilate, St. Austin, and Caesar Borgia, to be the same man. For if the identity of *soul alone* makes the same *man*; and there be nothing in the nature of matter why the same individual

spirit may not be united to different bodies, it will be possible that those men, living in distant ages, and of different tempers, may have been the same man: which way of speaking must be from a very strange use of the word man, applied to an idea out of which body and shape are excluded. And that way of speaking would agree yet worse with the notions of those philosophers who allow of transmigration, and are of opinion that the souls of men may, for their miscarriages, be detruded into the bodies of beasts, as fit habitations, with organs suited to the satisfaction of their brutal inclinations. But yet I think nobody, could he be sure that the *soul* of Heliogabalus were in one of his hogs, would yet say that hog were a *man* or Heliogabalus.

7. *Idea of identity suited to the idea it is applied to.*—It is not therefore unity of substance that comprehends all sorts of identity, or will determine it in every case; but to conceive and judge of it aright, we must consider what idea the word it is applied to stands for: it being one thing to be the same substance, another the same man, and a third the same person, it person, man, and substance, are three names standing for three different ideas;—for such as is the idea belonging to that name, such must be the identity; which, if it had been a little more carefully attended to, would possibly have prevented a great deal of that confusion which often occurs about this matter, with no small seeming difficulties, especially concerning personal identity, which therefore we shall in the next place a little consider.

*   *   *

9. *Personal identity.*—This being premised, to find wherein personal identity consists, we must consider what *person* stands for;—which, I think, is a thinking intelligent being, that has reason and reflection, and can consider itself as itself, the same thinking thing, in different times and places; which it does only by that consciousness which is inseparable from thinking, and, as it seems to me, essential to it: it being impossible for any one to perceive without *perceiving* that he does perceive. When we see, hear, smell, taste, feel, meditate, or will anything, we know that we do so. Thus it is always as to our present sensations and perceptions: and by this every one is to himself that which he calls *self*:—it not being considered, in this case, whether the same self be continued in the same or divers substances. For, since consciousness always accompanies thinking, and it is that which makes every one to be what he calls self, and thereby distinguishes himself from all other thinking things, in this alone consists personal identity, i.e., the sameness of a rational being: and as far as this consciousness can be extended backwards to any past action or thought, so far reaches the identity of that person; it is the same self now it was then; and it is by the same self with this present one that now reflects on it, that that action was done.

10. *Consciousness makes personal identity.*—But it is further inquired, whether it be the same identical substance. This few would think they had reason to doubt of, if these perceptions, with their consciousness, always remained present in the mind, whereby the same thinking thing would be always consciously present, and, as would be thought, evidently the same to itself. But that which seems to make the difficulty is this, that this consciousness being interrupted always by forgetfulness, there being no moment of our lives wherein we have the whole train of all our past actions before our eyes in one view, but even the best memories losing the sight of one part whilst they are viewing another; and we sometimes, and that the greatest part of our lives, not reflecting on our past selves, being intent on our present thoughts, and in sound sleep having no thoughts at all, or at least none with that consciousness which remarks our waking thoughts,—I say, in all these cases, our consciousness being interrupted, and

we losing the sight of our past selves, doubts are raised whether we are the same thinking thing, i.e., the same *substance* or no. Which, however reasonable or unreasonable, concerns not *personal* identity at all. The question being what makes the same person, and not whether it be the same identical substance, which always thinks in the same person, which, in this case, matters not at all: different substances, by the same consciousness (where they do partake in it) being united into one person, as well as different bodies by the same life are united into one animal, whose identity is preserved in that change of substances by the unity of one continued life. For, it being the same consciousness that makes a man be himself to himself, personal identity depends on that only, whether it be annexed solely to one individual substance, or can be continued in a succession of several substances. For as far as any intelligent being *can* repeat the idea of any past action with the same consciousness it had of it at first, and with the same consciousness it has of any present action; so far it is the same personal self. For it is by the consciousness it has of its present thoughts and actions, that it is *self* to *itself* now, and so will be the same self, as far as the same consciousness can extend to actions past or to come; and would be by distance of time, or change of substance, no more two persons, than a man be two men by wearing other clothes today than he did yesterday, with a long or a short sleep between: the same consciousness uniting those distant actions into the same person, whatever substances contributed to their production.

*   *   *

16. *Consciousness alone unites actions into the same person.*—But though the same immaterial substance or soul does not alone, wherever it be, and in whatsoever state, make the same *man*; yet it is plain, consciousness, as far as ever it can be extended—should it be to ages past—unites existences and actions very remote in time into the same *person*, as well as it does the existences and actions of the immediately preceding moment: so that whatever has the consciousness of present and past actions, is the same person to whom they both belong. Had I the same consciousness that I saw the ark and Noah's flood, as that I saw an overflowing of the Thames last winter, or as that I write now, I could no more doubt that I who write this now, that saw the Thames overflowed last winter, and that viewed the flood at the general deluge, was the same *self*,—place that self in what *substance* you please—than that I who write this am the same myself now whilst I write (whether I consist of all the same substance, material or immaterial, or no) that I was yesterday. For as to this point of being the same self, it matters not whether this present self be made up of the same or other substances—I being as much concerned, and as justly accountable for any action that was done a thousand years since, appropriated to me now by this self consciousness, as I am for what I did the last moment.

17. *Self depends on consciousness, not on substance.*—Self is that conscious thinking thing,—whatever substance made up of, (whether spiritual or material, simple or compounded, it matters not)—which is sensible or conscious of pleasure and pain, capable of happiness or misery, and so is concerned for itself, as far as that consciousness extends. Thus every one finds that, whilst comprehended under that consciousness, the little finger is as much a part of himself as what is most so. Upon separation of this little finger, should this consciousness go along with the little finger, and leave the rest of the body, it is evident the little finger would be the person, the same person; and self then would have nothing to do with the rest of the body. As in this case it is the consciousness that goes along with the substance, when one part is separate from

another, which makes the same person, and constitutes this inseparable self: so it is in reference to substances remote in time. That with which the consciousness of this present thinking thing *can* join itself, makes the same person, and is one self with it, and with nothing else; and so attributes to itself, and owns all the actions of that thing, as its own, as far as that consciousness reaches, and no further; as every one who reflects will perceive.

18. *Persons, not substances, the objects of reward and punishment.*—In this personal identity is founded all the right and justice of reward and punishment; happiness and misery being that for which every one is concerned for *himself*, and not mattering what becomes of any *substance*, not joined to, or affected with that consciousness. For, as it is evident in the instance I gave but now, if the consciousness went along with the little finger when it was cut off, that would be the same self which was concerned for the whole body yesterday, as making part of itself, whose actions then it cannot but admit as its own now. Though, if the same body should still live, and immediately from the separation of the little finger have its own peculiar consciousness, whereof the little finger knew nothing, it would not at all be concerned for it, as a part of itself, or could own any of its actions, or have any of them imputed to him.

19. *Which shows wherein personal identity consists.*—This may show us wherein personal identity consists: not in the identity of substance, but, as I have said, in the identity of consciousness, wherein if Socrates and the present mayor of Queinborough agree, they are the same person: if the same Socrates waking and sleeping do not partake of the same consciousness, Socrates waking and sleeping are not the same person. And to punish Socrates waking for what Socrates sleeping thought, and waking Socrates was never conscious of, would be no more of right, than to punish one twin for what his brother-twin did, whereof he knew nothing, because their outsides were so alike, that they could not be distinguished; for such twins have been seen.

20. *Absolute oblivion separates what is thus forgotten from the person, but not from the man.*—But yet possibly it will still be objected,—Suppose I wholly lose the memory of some parts of my life, beyond a possibility of retrieving them, so that perhaps I shall never be conscious of them again; yet am I not the same person that did those actions, had those thoughts that I once was conscious of, though I have now forgot them? To which I answer, that we must here take notice what the word *I* is applied to; which, in this case, is the *man* only. And the same man being presumed to be the same person, I is easily here supposed to stand also for the same person. But if it be possible for the same man to have distinct incommunicable consciousness at different times, it is past doubt the same man would at different times make different persons; which, we see, is the sense of mankind in the solemnest declaration of their opinions, human laws not punishing the mad man for the sober man's actions, nor the sober man for what the mad man did,—thereby making them two persons: which is somewhat explained by our way of speaking in English when we say such an one is "not himself," or is "beside himself"; in which phrases it is insinuated, as if those who now, or at least first used them, thought that self was changed; the self-same person was no longer in that man.

* * *

22. *Is not a man drunk and sober the same person?*—Why else is he punished for the fact he commits when drunk, though he be never afterwards conscious of it? Just as much the same person as a man that walks, and does other things in his sleep, is the same person, and is answerable for any mischief he shall do in it. Human laws

punish both, with a justice suitable to *their* way of knowledge;—because, in these cases, they cannot distinguish certainly what is real, what counterfeit: and so the ignorance in drunkenness or sleep is not admitted as a plea. For, though punishment be annexed to personality, and personality to consciousness, and the drunkard perhaps be not conscious of what he did, yet human judicatures justly punish him; because the fact is proved against him, but want of consciousness cannot be proved for him. But in the Great Day, wherein the secrets of all hearts shall be laid open, it may be reasonable to think, no one shall be made to answer for what he knows nothing of; but shall receive his doom, his conscience accusing or excusing him.

*   *   *

25. *Consciousness unites substances, material or spiritual, with the same personality.*—I agree, that more probable opinion is, that this consciousness is annexed to, and the affection of, one individual immaterial substance.

But let men, according to their diverse hypotheses, resolve of that as they please. This every intelligent being, sensible of happiness or misery, must grant—that there is something that is *himself*, that he is concerned for, and would have happy; that this self has existed in a continued duration more than one instant, and therefore it is possible may exist, as it has done, months and years to come, without any certain bounds to be set to its duration; and may be the same self, by the same consciousness continued on for the future. And thus, by this consciousness he finds himself to be the same self which did such and such an action some years since, by which he comes to be happy or miserable now. In all which account of self, the same numerical substance is not considered as making the same self; but the same continued *consciousness*, in which several substances may have been united, and again separated from it, which, whilst they continued in a vital union with that wherein this consciousness then resided, made a part of that same self. Thus any part of our bodies, vitally united to that which is conscious in us, makes a part of ourselves: but upon separation from the vital union by which that consciousness is communicated, that which a moment since was part of ourselves, is now no more so than a part of another man's self is a part of me: and it is not impossible but in a little time may become a real part of another person. And so we have the same numerical substance become a part of two different persons; and the same person preserved under the change of various substances. Could we suppose any spirit wholly stripped of all its memory or consciousness of past actions, as we find our minds always are of a great part of ours, and sometimes of them all; the union or separation of such a spiritual substance would make no variation of personal identity, any more than that of any particle of matter does. Any substance vitally united to the present thinking being is a part of that very same self which now is; anything united to it by a consciousness of former actions, makes also a part of the same self, which is the same both then and now.

*   *   *

BOOK III. OF WORDS

CHAPTER 3. OF GENERAL TERMS

*   *   *

6. *How general words are made.*—The next thing to be considered is,—How general words come to be made. For, since all things that exist are only particulars, how come we by general terms; or where find we those general natures they are supposed to stand for? Words become general by being made the signs of general ideas: and ideas become general, by separating from them the circumstances of time and place, and any other ideas that may determine them to this or that particular existence. By this way of abstraction they are made capable of representing more individuals than one; each of which having in it a conformity to that abstract idea, is (as we call it) of that sort.

7. *Shown by the way we enlarge our complex ideas from infancy.*—But, to deduce this a little more distinctly, it will not perhaps be amiss to trace our notions and names from their beginning, and observe by what degrees we proceed, and by what steps we enlarge our ideas from our first infancy. There is nothing more evident, than that the ideas of the persons children converse with (to instance in them alone) are like the persons themselves, only particular. The ideas of the nurse and the mother are well framed in their minds; and, like pictures of them there, represent only those individuals. The names they first gave to them are confined to these individuals; and the names of *nurse* and *mamma*, the child uses, determine themselves to those persons. Afterwards, when time and a larger acquaintance have made them observe that there are a great many other things in the world, that in some common agreements of shape, and several other qualities, resemble their father and mother, and those persons they have been used to, they frame an idea, which they find those many particulars do partake in; and to that they give, with others, the name *man*, for example. And thus they come to have a general name, and a general idea. Wherein they make nothing new; but only leave out of the complex idea they had of Peter and James, Mary and Jane, that which is peculiar to each, and retain only what is common to them all.

8. *And further enlarge our complex ideas, by still leaving out properties contained in them.*—By the same way that they come by the general name and idea of man, they easily advance to more general names and notions. For, observing that several things that differ from their idea of man, and cannot therefore be comprehended under that name, have yet certain qualities wherein they agree with man, by retaining only those qualities, and uniting them into one idea, they have again another and more general idea; to which having given a name they make a term of a more comprehensive extension: which new idea is made, not by any new addition, but only as before, by leaving out the shape, and some other properties signified by the name man, and retaining only a body, with life, sense, and spontaneous motion, comprehended under the name animal.

9. *General natures are nothing but abstract end partial ideas of more complex ones.*—That this is the way whereby men first formed general ideas, and general names to them, I think is so evident, that there needs no other proof of it but the considering of a man's self, or others, and the ordinary proceedings of their minds in knowledge. And he that thinks *general natures* or *notions* are anything else but such abstract and partial ideas of more complex ones, taken at first from particular existences, will, I

fear, be at a loss where to find them. For let any one effect, and then tell me, wherein does his idea of *man* differ from that of *Peter* and *Paul*, or his idea of horse from that of *Bucephalus*, but in the leaving out something that is peculiar to each individual, and retaining so much of those particular complex ideas of several particular existences as they are found to agree in? Of the complex ideas signified by the names *man* and *horse*, leaving out but those particulars wherein they differ, and retaining only those wherein they agree, and of those making a new distinct complex idea, and giving the name *animal* to it, one has a more general term, that comprehends with man several other creatures. Leave out of the idea of *animal*, sense and spontaneous motion, and the remaining complex idea, made up of the remaining simple ones of body, life, and nourishment, becomes a more general one, under the more comprehensive term, *vivens*. And, not to dwell longer upon this particular, so evident in itself; by the same way the mind proceeds to *body*, *substance*, and at last to *being*, *thing*, and such universal terms, which stand for any of our ideas whatsoever. To conclude: this whole mystery of genera and species, which make such a noise in the schools, and are with justice so little regarded out of them, is nothing else but *abstract ideas*, more or less comprehensive, with names annexed to them. In all which this is constant and unvariable, that every more general term stands for such an idea, and is but a part of any of those contained under it.

10. *Why the genus is ordinarily made use of in definitions.*—This may show us the reason why, in the defining of words, which is nothing but declaring their signification, we make use of the *genus*, or next general word that comprehends it. Which is not out of necessity, but only to save the labour of enumerating the several simple ideas which the next general word or genus stands for; or, perhaps, sometimes the shame of not being able to do it. But though defining by *genus* and *differentia* (I crave leave to use these terms of art, though originally Latin, since they most properly suit those notions they are applied to), I say, though defining by the *genus* be the shortest way, yet I think it may be doubted whether it be the best. This I am sure, it is not the only, and so not absolutely necessary. For, definition being nothing but making another understand by words what idea the term defined stands for, a definition is best made by enumerating those simple ideas that are combined in the signification of the term defined: and, if, instead of such an enumeration, men have accustomed themselves to use the next general term, it has not been out of necessity, or for greater clearness, but for quickness and dispatch sake. For I think that, to one who desired to know what idea the word man stood for; if it should be said, that man was a solid extended substance, having life, sense, spontaneous motion, and the faculty of reasoning, I doubt not but the meaning of the term man would be as well understood, and the idea it stands for be at least as clearly made known, as when it is defined to be a rational animal: which, by the several definitions of *animal*, *vivens*, and *corpus*, resolves itself into those enumerated ideas. I have, in explaining the term man, followed here the ordinary definition of the schools; which, though perhaps not the most exact, yet serves well enough to my present purpose. And one may, in this instance, see what gave occasion to the rule, that a definition must consist of *genus* and *differentia*; and it suffices to show us the little necessity there is of such a rule, or advantage in the strict observing of it. For, definitions, as has been said, being only the explaining of one word by several others, so that the meaning or idea it stands for may be certainly known; languages are not always so made according to the rules of logic, that every term can have its signification exactly and clearly expressed by two others. Experience sufficiently satisfies us to the contrary; or else those who have made this rule have done ill, that they have given us so few definitions conformable to it. But of definitions more in the next chapter.

11. *General and universal are creatures of the understanding, and belong not to the real existence of things.*—To return to general words: it is plain, by what has been said, that *general* and *universal* belong not to the real existence of things; but are the inventions and creatures of the understanding, made by it for its own use, and concern only signs, whether words or ideas. Words are general, as has been said, when used for signs of general ideas, and so are applicable indifferently to many particular things; and ideas are general when they are set up as the representatives of many particular things: but universality belongs not to things themselves, which are all of them particular in their existence, even those words and ideas which in their signification are general. When therefore we quit particulars, the generals that rest are only creatures of our own making; their general nature being nothing but the capacity they are put into, by the understanding, of signifying or representing many particulars. For the signification they have is nothing but a relation that, by the mind of man, is added to them.

12. *Abstract ideas are the essences of genera and species.*—The next thing therefore to be considered is, What kind of signification it is that general words have. For, as it is evident that they do not signify barely one particular thing; for then they would not be general terms, but proper names, so, on the other side, it is as evident they do not signify a plurality; for *man* and *men* would then signify the same; and the distinction of numbers (as the grammarians call them) would be superfluous and useless. That then which general words signify is a *sort* of things; and each of them does that, by being a sign of an abstract idea in the mind; to which idea, as things existing are found to agree, so they come to be ranked under that name, or, which is all one, be of that sort. Whereby it is evident that the *essences* of the sorts, or, if the Latin word pleases better, *species* of things, are nothing else but these abstract ideas. For the having the essence of any species, being that which makes anything to be of that species; and the conformity to the idea to which the name is annexed being that which gives a right to that name; the having the essence, and the having that conformity, must needs be the same thing: since to be of any species, and to have a right to the name of that species, is all one. As, for example, to be a *man*, or of the *species* man, and to have right to the *name* man, is the same thing. Again, to be a man, or of the species man, and have the *essence* of a man, is the same thing. Now, since nothing can be a man, or have a right to the name man, but what has a conformity to the abstract idea the name man stands for, nor anything be a man, or have a right to the species man, but what has the essence of that species; it follows, that the abstract idea for which the name stands, and the essence of the species, is one and the same. From whence it is easy to observe, that the essences of the sorts of things, and, consequently, the sorting of things, is the workmanship of the understanding that abstracts and makes those general ideas.

13. *They are the workmanship of the understanding, but have their foundation in the similitude of things.*—I would not here be thought to forget, much less to deny, that Nature, in the production of things, makes several of them alike: there is nothing more obvious, especially in the races of animals, and all things propagated by seed. But yet I think we may say, *the sorting of them under names is the workmanship of the understanding, taking occasion, from the similitude it observes amongst them, to make abstract general ideas*, and set them up in the mind, with names annexed to them, as patterns or forms (for, in that sense, the word *form* has a very proper signification) to which as particular things existing are found to agree, so they come to be of that species, have that denomination, or are put into that *classis*. For when we say this is a man, that a horse; this justice, that cruelty; this a watch, that a jack; what do we else but rank things under different specific names, as agreeing to those abstract ideas, of which we have made those names the signs? And what are the essences of those

species set out and marked by names, but those abstract ideas in the mind; which are, as it were, the bonds between particular things that exist, and the names they are to be ranked under? And when general names have any connexion with particular beings, these abstract ideas are the medium that unites them: so that the essences of species, as distinguished and denominated by us, neither are nor can be anything but those precise abstract ideas we have in our minds. And therefore the supposed real essences of substances, if different from our abstract ideas, cannot be the essences of the species we rank things into. For two species may be one, as rationally as two different essences be the essence of one species: and I demand what are the alterations [which] may, or may not be made in a *horse* or *lead*, without making either of them to be of another species? In determining the species of things by *our* abstract ideas, this is easy to resolve, but if any one will regulate himself herein by supposed *real* essences, he will, I suppose, be at a loss: and he will never be able to know when anything precisely ceases to be of the species of a *horse* or *lead*.

14. *Each distinct abstract idea is a distinct essence.*—Nor will any one wonder that I say these essences, or abstract ideas (which are the measures of name, and the boundaries of species) are the workmanship of the understanding, who considers that at least the complex ones are often, in several men, different collections of simple ideas; and therefore that is *covetousness* to one man, which is not so to another. Nay, even in substances, where their abstract ideas seem to be taken from the things themselves, they are not constantly the same; no, not in that species which is most familiar to us, and with which we have the most intimate acquaintance: it having been more than once doubted, whether the *fetus* born of a woman were a *man*, even so far as that it hath been debated, whether it were or were not to be nourished and baptized: which could not be, if the abstract idea or essence to which the name man belonged were of nature's making; and were not the uncertain and various collection of simple ideas, which the understanding put together, and then, abstracting it, affixed a name to it. So that, in truth, every distinct abstract idea is a distinct essence; and the names that stand for such distinct ideas are the names of things essentially different. Thus a circle is as essentially different from an oval as a sheep from a goat; and rain is as essentially different from snow as water from earth: that abstract idea which is the essence of one being impossible to be communicated to the other. And thus any two abstract ideas, that in any part vary one from another, with two distinct names annexed to them, constitute two distinct sorts, or, if you please, species, as essentially different as any two of the most remote or opposite in the world.

15. *Several significations of the word "essence."*—But since the essences of things are thought by some (and not without reason) to be wholly unknown, it may not be amiss to consider the several significations of the word essence.

Real essence.—First, Essence may be taken for the very being of anything, whereby it is what it is. And thus the real internal, but generally (in substances) unknown constitution of things, whereon their discoverable qualities depend, may be called their essence. This is the proper original signification of the word, as is evident from the formation of it; *essentia*, in its primary notation, signifying properly, being. And in this sense it is still used, when we speak of the essence of *particular* things, without giving them any name.

Nominal essences.—Secondly, The learning and disputes of the schools having been much busied about *genus* and *species*, the word *essence* has almost lost its primary signification: and, instead of the real constitution of things, has been almost wholly applied to the artificial constitution of *genus* and *species*. It is true, there is ordinarily supposed a real constitution of the sorts of things; and it is past doubt there must be some real constitution, on which any collection of simple ideas co-existing must depend. But, it being evident that things are ranked under names into sorts or species, only as they agree to certain abstract ideas, to which we have annexed those names, the essence of each *genus*, or sort, comes to be nothing but that abstract idea which the general, or sortal (if I may have leave so to call it from sort, as I do general from genus) name stands for. And this we shall find to be that which the word essence imports in its most familiar use.

These two sorts of essences, I suppose, may not unfitly be termed, the one the *real*, the other *nominal essence*.

*   *   *

BOOK IV. OF KNOWLEDGE AND PROBABILITY

CHAPTER 1. OF KNOWLEDGE IN GENERAL

1. *Our knowledge conversant about our ideas only.*—Since the mind, in all its thoughts and reasonings, hath no other immediate object but its own ideas, which it alone does or can contemplate, it is evident that our knowledge is only conversant about them.

2. *Knowledge is the perception of the agreement or disagreement of two ideas.*— *Knowledge* then seems to me to be nothing but the *perception of the connexion and agreement, or disagreement and repugnancy, of any of our ideas*. In this alone it consists. Where this perception is, there is knowledge; and where it is not, there, though we may fancy, guess, or believe, yet we always come short of knowledge. For when we know that white is not black, what do we else but perceive that these two ideas do not agree? When we possess ourselves with the utmost security of the demonstration that the three angles of a triangle are equal to two right ones, what do we more but perceive, that equality to two right ones does necessarily agree to, and is inseparable from, the three angles of a triangle?

3. *This agreement or disagreement may be any of four sorts.*—But to understand a little more distinctly wherein this agreement or disagreement consists, I think we may reduce it all to these four sorts: (1) *Identity,* or *diversity.* (2) *Relation.* (3) *Coexistence*, or *necessary connexion.* (4) *Real existence.*

4. *Of identity, or diversity in ideas.*—First, As to the first sort of agreement or disagreement, viz., *identity*, or *diversity*. It is the first act of the mind, when it has any sentiments or ideas at all, to perceive its ideas, and, so far as it perceives them, to know each what it is, and thereby also to perceive their difference, and that one is not another. This is so absolutely necessary, that without it there could be no knowledge, no reasoning, no imagination, no distinct thoughts at all. By this the mind clearly and infallibly perceives each idea to agree with itself, and to be what it is; and all distinct ideas to disagree, i.e., the one not to be the other: and this it does without pains, labour, or deduction; but at first view, by its natural power of perception and distinction. And though men of art have reduced this into those general rules, *What is, is*; and, *It is impossible for the same thing to be and not to be*, for ready application in all cases wherein there may be occasion to reflect on it; yet it is certain that the first exercise of this faculty is about particular ideas. A man infallibly knows, as soon as ever he has

them in his mind, that the ideas he calls *white* and *round* are the very ideas they are, and that they are not other ideas which he calls *red* or *square*. Nor can any maxim or proposition in the world make him know it clearer or surer than he did before, and without any such general rule. This then is the first agreement or disagreement which the mind perceives in its ideas; which it always perceives at first sight; and if there ever happen any doubt about it, it will always be found to be about the names, and not the ideas themselves, whose identity and diversity will always be perceived as soon and as clearly as the ideas themselves are, nor can it possibly be otherwise.

5. *Of abstract relations between ideas.—Secondly*, The next sort of agreement or disagreement the mind perceives in any of its ideas may, I think, be called *relative*, and is nothing but the perception of the *relation* between any two ideas, of what kind soever, whether substances, modes, or any other. For, since all distinct ideas must eternally be known not to be the same, and so be universally and constantly denied one of another, there could be no room for any positive knowledge at all, if we could not perceive any relation between our ideas, and find out the agreement or disagreement they have one with another, in several ways the mind takes of comparing them.

6. *Of their necessary coexistence in substances.—Thirdly*, The third sort of agreement or disagreement to be found in our ideas, which the perception of the mind is employed about, is *coexistence*, or *non-coexistence* in the *same subject*; and this belongs particularly to substances. Thus when we pronounce concerning gold that it is fixed, our knowledge of this truth amounts to no more but this, that fixedness, or a power to remain in the fire unconsumed, is an idea that always accompanies and is joined with that particular sort of yellowness, weight, fusibility, malleableness, and solubility in aqua regia, which make our complex idea, signified by the word gold.

7. *Of real existence agreeing to any idea.—Fourthly*, The fourth and last sort is that of *actual real existence* agreeing to any idea. Within these four sorts of agreement or disagreement is, I suppose, contained all the knowledge we have or are capable of; for all the enquiries that we can make concerning any of our ideas, all that we know or can affirm concerning any of them, is, that it is or is not the same with some other; that it does or does not always coexist with some other idea in the same subject; that it has this or that relation to some other idea; or that it has a real existence without the mind. Thus, "Blue is not yellow," is of identity. "Two triangles upon equal bases between two parallels are equal," is of relation. "Iron is susceptible of magnetical impressions," is of coexistence. "God is," is of real existence. Though identity and coexistence are truly nothing but relations, yet they are so peculiar ways of agreement or disagreement of our ideas, that they deserve well to be considered as distinct heads, and not under relation in general: since they are so different grounds of affirmation and negation, as will easily appear to any one who will but reflect on what is said in several places of this Essay. I should now proceed to examine the several degrees of our knowledge, but that it is necessary first to consider the different acceptations of the word knowledge.

8. *Knowledge is either actual or habitual.*—There are several ways wherein the mind is possessed of truth, each of which is called knowledge.

(1) There is *actual knowledge*, which is the present view the mind has of the agreement or disagreement of any of its ideas, or of the relation they have one to another.

(2) A man is said to know any proposition which having been once laid before his thoughts, he evidently perceived the agreement or disagreement of the ideas whereof it consists; and so lodged it in his memory, that whenever that proposition comes again to be reflected on, he, without doubt or hesitation, embraces the right side, assents to and is certain of the truth of it. This, I think, one may call *habitual knowl-*

edge. . . . For our finite understandings being able to think clearly and distinctly but on one thing at once, if men had no knowledge of any more than what they actually thought on, they would all be very ignorant; and he that knew most would know but one truth, that being all he was able to think on at one time.

9. *Habitual knowledge is of two degrees.*—Of habitual knowledge there are also, vulgarly speaking, two degrees:——

First, The one of such truths laid up in the memory as, whenever they occur to the mind, it *actually perceives the relation is between those ideas.* And this is in all those truths whereof we have an intuitive knowledge, where the ideas themselves, by an immediate view, discover their agreement or disagreement one with another.

Secondly, The other is of such truths, whereof the mind having been convinced, it retains *the memory of the conviction without the proofs.* Thus a man that remembers certainly that he once perceived the demonstration that the three angles of a triangle are equal to two right ones, is certain that he knows it, because he cannot doubt of the truth of it. In his adherence to a truth where the demonstration by which it was at first known is forgot, though a man may be thought rather to believe his memory than really to know, and this way of entertaining a truth seemed formerly to me like something between opinion and knowledge, a sort of assurance which exceeds bare belief, for that relies on the testimony of another; yet, upon a due examination, I find it comes not short of perfect certainty, and is, in effect, true knowledge. That which is apt to mislead our first thoughts into a mistake in this matter is, that the agreement or disagreement of the ideas in this case is not perceived, as it was at first, by an actual view of all the intermediate ideas whereby the agreement or disagreement of those in the proposition was at first perceived; but by other intermediate ideas, that show the agreement or disagreement of the ideas contained in the proposition whose certainty we remember. For example: in this proposition, that "the three angles of a triangle are equal to two right ones," one who has seen and clearly perceived the demonstration of this truth knows it to be true, when that demonstration is gone out of his mind, so that at present it is not actually in view, and possibly cannot be recollected; but he knows it in a different way from what he did before. The agreement of the two ideas joined in that proposition is perceived; but it is by the intervention of other ideas than those which at first produced that perception. He remembers, i.e., he knows (for remembrance is but the reviving of some past knowledge) that he was once certain of the truth of this proposition, that "the three angles of a triangle are equal to two right ones." The immutability of the same relations between the same immutable things is now the idea that shows him, that if the three angles of a triangle were once equal to two right ones, they will always be equal to two right ones. And hence he comes to be certain, that what was once true in the case is always true; what ideas once agreed will always agree: and consequently, what he once knew to be true he will always know to be true, as long as he can remember that he once knew it. Upon this ground it is that particular demonstrations in mathematics afford general knowledge. If then the perception that the same ideas will eternally have the same habitudes and relations be not a sufficient ground of knowledge, there could be no knowledge of general propositions in mathematics; for no mathematical demonstration would be any other than particular and when a man had demonstrated any proposition concerning one triangle or circle, his knowledge would not reach beyond that particular diagram. If he would extend it farther, he must renew his demonstration in another instance, before he could know it to be true in another like triangle, and so on by which means one could never come to the knowledge of any general propositions. Nobody, I think, can deny that Mr. Newton certainly knows any proposition that he now at any time reads in his book to be true, though he has not in actual view that admirable chain of intermediate ideas whereby he at first discovered it to be true. Such a memory as that, able to retain such a train of particulars, may be well thought beyond the reach of human faculties, when the very discovery, perception, and laying together that wonderful connexion of ideas is found to surpass most readers' comprehension. But yet it is evident the author himself knows the proposition to be true, remembering he once saw the connexion of those ideas, as certainly as he knows such a man wounded another, remembering that he saw him run him through. But because the memory is not always so clear as actual perception, and does in all men more or less decay in length of time, this amongst other differences, is one which shows that *demonstrative* knowledge is much more imperfect than *intuitive*, as we shall see in the following chapter.

CHAPTER 2. OF THE DEGREES OF OUR KNOWLEDGE

1. *Of the degree, or differences in clearness, of our knowledge*: I. *Intuitive*—All our knowledge consisting, as I have said, in the view the mind has of its own ideas, which is the utmost light and greatest certainty we, with our faculties and in our way of knowledge, are capable of, it may not be amiss to consider a little the degrees of its evidence. The different clearness of our knowledge seems to me to lie in the different way of perception the mind has of the agreement or disagreement of any of its ideas. For if we will reflect on our own ways of thinking, we shall find that sometimes the mind perceives the agreement or disagreement of two ideas *immediately by themselves*, without the intervention of any other and this, I think, we may call *intuitive knowledge*. For in this the mind is at no pains of proving or examining, but perceives the truth, as the eye doth light, only by being directed towards it. Thus the mind perceives that *white* is not black, that a *circle* is not a *triangle*, that *three* are more than *two*, and equal to *one and two*. Such kind of truths the mind perceives at the first sight of the ideas together, by bare intuition, without the intervention of any other idea; and this kind of knowledge is the clearest and most certain that human frailty is capable of. This part of knowledge is irresistible, and like bright sunshine, forces itself immediately to be perceived as soon as ever the mind turns its view that way; and leaves no room for hesitation, doubt, or examination, but the mind is presently filled with the clear light of it. *It is on this intuition that depends all the certainty and evidence of all our knowledge*; which certainty every one finds to be so great, that he cannot imagine, and therefore not require, a greater for a man cannot conceive himself capable of a greater certainty, than to know that any idea in his mind is such as he perceives it to be; and that two ideas wherein he perceives a difference, are different, and not precisely the same. He that demands a greater certainty that this demands he knows not what, and shows only that he has a mind to be a skeptic without being able to be so. Certainty depends so wholly on this intuition, that in the next degree of knowledge, which I call demonstrative, this intuition is necessary in all the connexions of the intermediate ideas, without which we cannot attain knowledge and certainty.

2. II. *Demonstrative.*—The next degree of knowledge is, where the mind perceives the agreement or disagreement of any ideas, but not immediately. . . . In this case, when the mind cannot so bring its ideas together as, by their immediate comparison and, as it were, juxtaposition or application one to another, to perceive their agreement or disagreement, it is fain, by the intervention of other ideas (one or more, as it happens), to discover the agreement or disagreement which it searches; and this is that which we call *reasoning*. Thus the mind, being willing to know the agreement or dis-

agreement in bigness between the three angles of a triangle and two right ones, cannot, by an immediate view and comparing them, do it: because the three angles of a triangle cannot be brought at once, and be compared with any other one or two angles; and so of this the mind has no immediate, no intuitive knowledge. In this case the mind is fain to find out some other angles, to which the three angles of a triangle have an equality; and finding those equal to two right ones, comes to know their equality to two right ones.

3. *Demonstration depends on clearly perceived proofs.*—Those intervening ideas which serve to show the agreement of any two others, are called *proofs*; and where the agreement or disagreement is by this means plainly and clearly perceived, it is called *demonstration*, it being *shown* to the understanding, and the mind made to see that it is so. A quickness in the mind to find out these intermediate ideas (that shall discover the agreement or disagreement of any other), and to apply them right, is, I suppose, that which is called *sagacity*.

4. *As certain, but not so easy and ready as intuitive knowledge.*—This knowledge by intervening proofs, though it be certain, yet the evidence of it is not altogether so clear and bright, nor the assent so ready, as in intuitive knowledge. For though in demonstration the mind does at last perceive the agreement or disagreement of the ideas it considers, yet it is not without pains and attention: there must be more than one transient view to find it. A steady application and pursuit is required to this discovery: and there must be a progression by steps and degrees before the mind can in this way arrive at certainty. . . .

5. *The demonstrated conclusion not without doubt, precedent to the demonstration.*—Another difference between intuitive and demonstrative knowledge is, that though in the latter all doubt be removed, when by the intervention of the intermediate ideas the agreement or disagreement is perceived; yet before the demonstration there was a doubt; which in intuitive knowledge cannot happen to the mind that has its faculty of perception left to a degree capable of distinct ideas, no more than it can be a doubt to the eye (that can distinctly see white and black), whether this ink and this paper be all of a colour. . . .

6. *Not so clear as intuitive knowledge.*—It is true, the perception produced by demonstration is also very clear; yet it is often with a great abatement of that evident lustre and full assurance that always accompany that which I call intuitive; like a face reflected by several mirrors one to another, where, as long as it retains the similitude and agreement with the object, it produces a knowledge; but it is still, in every successive reflection, with a lessening of that perfect clearness and distinctness which is in the first, till at last, after many removes, it has a great mixture of dimness, and is not at first sight so knowable, especially to weak eyes. Thus it is with knowledge made out by a long train of proofs.

7. *Each step in demonstrated knowledge must have intuitive evidence.*—Now, in every step reason makes in demonstrative knowledge, there is an intuitive knowledge of that agreement or disagreement it seeks with the next intermediate idea, which it uses as a proof: for it were not so, that yet would need a proof; since without the perception of such agreement or disagreement there is no knowledge produced. . . . This intuitive perception of the agreement or disagreement of the intermediate ideas, in each step and progression of the demonstration, must also be carried exactly in the mind, and a man must be sure that no part is left out: which, because in long deductions, and the use of many proofs, the memory does not always so readily and exactly retain; therefore it comes to pass, that this is more imperfect than intuitive knowledge, and men embrace often falsehood for demonstrations.

8. *Hence the mistake, ex præcognitis et præconcessis.*—The necessity of this intuitive knowledge, in each step of scientifical or demonstrative reasoning, gave occasion, I imagine, to that mistaken axiom, that all reasoning was *ex præcognitis et præconcessis*; which how far it is mistaken, I shall have occasion to show more at large where I come to consider propositions, and particularly those propositions which are called "maxims"; and to show that it is by a mistake that they are supposed to be the foundations of all our knowledge and reasonings.

9. *Demonstration not limited to ideas of mathematical quantity.*—It has been generally taken for granted, that mathematics alone are capable of demonstrative certainty: but to have such an agreement or disagreement as may intuitively be perceived being, as I imagine, not the privilege of the ideas of number, extension, and figure alone, it may possibly be the want of due method and application in us, and not of sufficient evidence in things, that demonstration has been thought to have so little to do in other parts of knowledge, and been scarce so much as aimed at by any but mathematicians. . . .

10. *Why it has been thought to be so limited.*—The reason why it has been generally sought for and supposed to be only in those, I imagine, has been not only the general usefulness of those sciences, but because, in comparing their equality or excess, the modes of numbers have every the least difference very clear and perceivable: and though in extension every the least excess is not so perceptible, yet the mind has found out ways to examine and discover demonstratively the just equality of two angles, or extensions, or figures. . . .

11. *Modes of qualities not demonstrable like modes of quantity.*—But in other simple ideas, whose modes and differences are made and counted by degrees, and not quantity, we have not so nice and accurate a distinction of their differences as to perceive or find ways to measure their just equality or the least differences. For those other simple ideas, being appearances or sensations produced in us by the size, figure, number, and motion of minute corpuscles singly insensible, their different degrees also depend upon the variation of some or all of those causes; which since it cannot be observed by us in particles of matter whereof each is too subtle to be perceived, it is impossible for us to have any exact measures of the different degrees of these simple ideas. . . .

*   *   *

13. *The secondary qualities of things not discovered by demonstration.*—Not knowing what number of particles, nor what motion of them, is fit to produce any precise degree of whiteness, we cannot demonstrate the certain equality of any two degrees of whiteness; because we have no certain standard to measure them by, nor means to distinguish every the least real difference; the only help we have being from our senses, which in this point fail us. But where the difference is so great as to produce in the mind clearly distinct ideas, whose differences can be perfectly retained, there these ideas of colours, as we see in different kinds, as blue and red, are as capable of demonstration as ideas of number and extension. What I have here said of whiteness and colours, I think, holds true in all secondary qualities, and their modes.

14. *Sensitive knowledge of the particular existence of finite beings without us.*—These two, viz., intuition and demonstration, are the degrees of our *knowledge*; whatever comes short of one of these, with what assurance soever embraced, is but *faith* or *opinion*, but not knowledge, at least in all general truths. There is, indeed,

another perception of the mind employed about *the particular existence of finite beings without us*, which, going beyond bare probability, and yet not reaching perfectly to either of the foregoing degrees of certainty, passes under the name of *knowledge*. There can be nothing more certain, than that the idea we receive from an external object is in our minds; this is intuitive knowledge. But whether there be anything more than barely that idea in our minds, whether we can thence certainly infer the existence of anything without us which corresponds to that idea, is that whereof some men think there may be a question made; because men may have such ideas in their minds when no such thing exists, no such object affects their senses. But yet here, I think, we are provided with an evidence that puts us past doubting; for I ask any one, whether he be not invincibly conscious to himself of a different perception when he looks on the sun by day, and thinks on it by night; when he actually tastes wormwood, or smells a rose, or only thinks on that savour or odour? We as plainly find the difference there is between any idea revived in our minds by our own memory, and actually coming into our minds by our senses, as we do between any two distinct ideas. If any one say, a dream may do the same thing, and all these ideas may be produced in us without any external objects; he may please to dream that I make him this answer: (1) That it is no great matter whether I remove his scruple or no: where all is but dream, reasoning and arguments are of no use, truth and knowledge nothing. (2) That I believe he will allow a very manifest difference between dreaming of being in the fire, and being actually in it. But yet if he be resolved to appear so skeptical as to maintain, that what I call being actually in the fire is nothing but a dream; and that we cannot thereby certainly know that any such thing as fire actually exists without us; I answer, that we certainly finding that pleasure or pain follows upon the application of certain objects to us, whose existence we perceive, or dream that we perceive, by our senses; this certainly is as great as our happiness or misery, beyond which we have no concernment to know or to be. So that, I think, we may add to the two former sorts of knowledge this also, of the existence of particular external objects by that perception and consciousness we have of the actual entrance of ideas from them, and allow these three degrees of knowledge, viz., *intuitive*, *demonstrative*, and *sensitive*: in each of which there are different degrees and ways of evidence and certainty.

*   *   *

CHAPTER 3. OF THE EXTENT OF HUMAN KNOWLEDGE

1. *Extent of our knowledge.*—KNOWLEDGE, as has been said, lying in the perception of the agreement or disagreement of any of our ideas, it follows from hence that,

It extends no farther than we have ideas.—First, We can have knowledge no farther than we have ideas.

2. *It extends no farther than we can perceive their agreement or disagreement.*—Secondly, That we can have no knowledge farther than we can have perception of that agreement or disagreement: which perception being, (1) Either by *intuition*, or the immediate comparing any two ideas; or, (2) By *reason*, examining the agreement or disagreement of two ideas by the intervention of some others; or (3) By *sensation*, perceiving the existence of particular things; hence it also follows,

3. *Intuitive knowledge extends itself not to all the relations of all our ideas.*—Thirdly, that we cannot have an *intuitive knowledge* that shall extend itself to all our ideas, and all that we would know about them; because we cannot examine and perceive all the relations they have one to another by juxtaposition, or an immediate comparison one with another. Thus having the ideas of an obtuse and an acute angled triangle, both drawn from equal bases, and between parallels, I can by intuitive knowledge perceive the one not to be the other; but cannot that way know whether they be equal or no: because their agreement or disagreement in equality can never be perceived by an immediate comparing them; the difference of figure makes their parts incapable of an exact immediate application; and therefore there is need of some intervening quantities to measure them by, which is demonstration or rational knowledge.

4. *Nor does demonstrative knowledge.*—Fourthly, It follows also, from what is above observed, that our *rational knowledge* cannot reach to the whole extent of our ideas. Because between two different ideas we would examine, we cannot always find such mediums as we can connect one to another with an intuitive knowledge, in all the parts of the deduction; and wherever that fails, we come short of knowledge and demonstration.

5. *Sensitive knowledge narrower than either.*—Fifthly, *Sensitive knowledge*, reaching no farther than the existence of things actually present to our senses, is yet much narrower than either of the former.

* * *

CHAPTER 9. OF OUR THREEFOLD KNOWLEDGE OF EXISTENCE

1. *General propositions that are certain concern not existence.*—Hitherto we have only considered the essences of things; which being only abstract ideas, and thereby removed in our thoughts from particular existence, (that being the proper operation of the mind, in abstraction, to consider an idea under no other existence but what it has in the understanding,) gives us no knowledge of real existence at all. Where, by the way, we may take notice, that universal propositions of whose truth or falsehood we can have certain knowledge concern not existence: and further, that all particular affirmations or negations that would not be certain if they were made general, are only concerning existence; they declaring only the accidental union or separation of ideas in things existing, which, in their abstract natures, have no known necessary union or repugnancy.

2. *A threefold knowledge of existence.*—But, leaving the nature of propositions, and different ways of predication to be considered more at large in another place, let us proceed now to inquire concerning our knowledge of the *existence of things*, and how we come by it. I say, then, that we have the knowledge of *our own* existence by intuition; of the existence of *God* by demonstration; and of *other things* by sensation.

3. *Our knowledge of our own existence is intuitive.*—As for our own existence, we perceive it so plainly and so certainly, that it neither needs nor is capable of any proof. For nothing can be more evident to us than our own existence. I think, I reason, I feel pleasure and pain: can any of these be more evident to me than my own existence? If I doubt of all other things, that very doubt makes me perceive my own existence, and will not suffer me to doubt of that. For if I know I feel pain, it is evident I have as certain perception of my own existence, as of the existence of the pain I feel:

or if I know I doubt, I have as certain perception of the existence of the thing doubting, as of that thought which I *call doubt*. Experience then convinces us, that we have an *intuitive knowledge* of our own existence, and an internal infallible perception that we are. In every act of sensation, reasoning, or thinking, we are conscious to ourselves of our own being; and, in this matter, come not short of the highest degree of certainty.

Chapter 10. Of Our Knowledge of the Existence of a God

1. *We are capable of knowing certainly that there is a God.*—Though God has given us no innate ideas of himself; though he has stamped no original characters on our minds, wherein we may read his being; yet having furnished us with those faculties our minds are endowed with, he hath not left himself without witness: since we have sense, perception, and reason, and cannot want a clear proof of him, as long as we carry *ourselves* about us. Nor can we justly complain of our ignorance in this great point; since he has so plentifully provided us with the means to discover and know him; so far as is necessary to the end of our being, and the great concernment of our happiness. But, though this be the most obvious truth that reason discovers, and though its evidence be (if I mistake not) equal to mathematical certainty: yet it requires thought and attention; and the mind must apply itself to a regular deduction of it from some part of our intuitive knowledge, or else we shall be as uncertain and ignorant of this as of other propositions, which are in themselves capable of clear demonstration. To show, therefore, that we are capable of *knowing*, i.e., *being certain* that there is a God, and *how we may come by* this certainty, I think we need go no further than *ourselves*, and that undoubted knowledge we have of our own existence.

2. *For man knows that he himself exists.*—I think it is beyond question, that man has a clear idea of his own being; he knows certainly he exists, and that he is something. He that can doubt—whether he be anything or no, I speak not to; no more than I would argue with pure nothing, or endeavour to convince nonentity that it were something. If any one pretends to be so sceptical as to deny his own existence, (for really to doubt of it is manifestly impossible,) let him for me enjoy his beloved happiness of being nothing, until hunger or some other pain convince him of the contrary. This, then, I think I may take for a truth, which every one's certain knowledge assures him of, beyond the liberty of doubting, viz., that he is something that actually exists.

3. *He knows also that nothing cannot produce a being; therefore something must have existed from eternity.*—In the next place, man knows, by an intuitive certainty, that bare *nothing can no more produce any real being, than it can be equal to two right angles*. If a man knows not that nonentity, or the absence of all being, cannot be equal to two right angles, it is impossible he should know any demonstration in Euclid. If, therefore, we know there is some real being, and that nonentity cannot produce any real being, it is an evident demonstration, that *from eternity there has been something*; since what was not from eternity had a beginning; and what had a beginning must be produced by something else.

4. *And that eternal Being must be most powerful.*—Next, it is evident, that what had its being and beginning from another, must also have all that which is in and belongs to its being from another too. All the powers it has must be owing to and received from the same source. This eternal source, then, of all being must also be the source and original of all power; and so *this eternal Being must be also the most powerful.*

5. *And most knowing.*—Again, a man finds in *himself* perception and knowledge. We have then got one step further; and we are certain now that there is not only some being, but some knowing, intelligent being in the world. There was a time, then, when there was no knowing being and when knowledge began to be; or else there has been also a *knowing being from eternity*. If it be said, there was a time when no being had any knowledge, when that eternal being was void of all understanding; I reply, that then it was impossible there should ever have been any knowledge: it being as impossible that things wholly void of knowledge, and operating blindly, and without any perception, should produce a knowing being, as it is impossible that a triangle should make itself three angles bigger than two right ones. For it is as repugnant to the idea of senseless matter, that it should put into itself sense, perception, and knowledge, as it is repugnant to the idea of a triangle, that it should put into itself greater angles than two right ones.

6. *And therefore God.*—Thus, from the consideration of ourselves, and what we infallibly find in our own constitutions, our reason leads us to the knowledge of this certain and evident truth,—*That there is an eternal, most powerful, and most knowing Being*; which whether any one will please to call God, it matters not. The thing is evident, and from this idea duly considered, will easily be deduced all those other attributes, which we ought to ascribe to this eternal Being. If, nevertheless, any one should be found so senselessly arrogant, as to suppose man alone knowing and wise, but yet the product of mere ignorance and chance; and that all the rest of the universe acted only by that blind haphazard; I shall leave with him that very rational and emphatical rebuke of Tully, to be considered at his leisure: "What can be more sillily arrogant and misbecoming, than for a man to think that he has a mind and understanding in him, but yet in all the universe beside there is no such thing? Or that those things, which with the utmost stretch of his reason he can scarce comprehend, should be moved and managed without any reason at all?" . . .

From what has been said, it is plain to me we have a more certain knowledge of the existence of a God, than of anything our senses have not immediately discovered to us. Nay, I presume I may say, that we more certainly know that there is a God, than that there is anything else without us. When I say we *know*, I mean there is such a knowledge within our reach which we cannot miss, if we will but apply our minds to that, as we do to several other inquiries.

* * *

CHAPTER 11. OF OUR KNOWLEDGE OF THE EXISTENCE
OF OTHER THINGS

1. *Knowledge of the existence of other finite beings is to be had only by actual sensation.*—The knowledge of our own being we have by intuition. The existence of a God, reason clearly makes known to us, as has been shown.

The knowledge of the existence of *any other thing* we can have only by sensation: for there being no necessary connexion of real existence with any idea a man hath in his memory; nor of any other existence but that of God with the existence of any particular man: no particular man can know the existence of any other being, but only when, by actual operating upon him, it makes itself perceived by him. For, the having the idea of anything in our mind, no more proves the existence of that thing, than the picture of a man evidences his being in the world, or the visions of a dream make thereby a true history.

2. *Instance: whiteness of this paper.*—It is therefore the *actual receiving* of ideas from without that gives us notice of the existence of other things, and makes us know, that something doth exist at that time without us, which causes that idea in us; though perhaps we neither know nor consider how it does it. For it takes not from the certainty of our senses, and the ideas we receive by them, that we know not the manner wherein they are produced: v.g., whilst I write this, I have, by the paper affecting my eyes, that idea produced in my mind, which, whatever object causes, I call *white*; by which I know that that quality or accident (i.e., whose appearance before my eyes always causes that idea) doth really exist, and hath a being without me. And of this, the greatest assurance I can possibly have, and to which my faculties can attain, is the testimony of my eyes, which are the proper and sole judges of this thing; whose testimony I have reason to rely on as so certain, that I can no more doubt, whilst I write this, that I see white and black, and that something really exists that causes that sensation in me, than that I write or move my hand; which is a certainty as great as human nature is capable of, concerning the existence of anything, but a man's self alone, and of God.

3. *This notice by our senses, though not so certain as demonstration, yet may be called knowledge, and proves the existence of things without us.*—The notice we have by our senses of the existing of things without us, though it be not altogether so certain as our intuitive knowledge, or the deductions of our reason employed about the clear abstract ideas of our own minds; yet it is an assurance that deserves the name of *knowledge*. If we persuade ourselves that our faculties act and inform us right concerning the existence of those objects that affect them, it cannot pass for an ill-grounded confidence: for I think nobody can, in earnest, be so sceptical as to be uncertain of the existence of those things which he sees and feels. At least, he that can doubt so far, (whatever he may have with his own thoughts,) will never have any controversy with me; since he can never be sure I say anything contrary to his own opinion. As to myself, I think God has given me assurance enough of the existence of things without me: since, by their different application, I can produce in myself both pleasure and pain, which is one great concernment of my present state. This is certain: the confidence that our faculties do not herein deceive us, is the greatest assurance we are capable of concerning the existence of material beings. For we cannot act anything but by our faculties; nor talk of knowledge itself, but by the help of those faculties which are fitted to apprehend even what knowledge is.

But besides the assurance we have from our senses themselves, that they do not err in the information they give us of the existence of things without us, when they are affected by them, we are further confirmed in this assurance by other concurrent reasons:—

4. I. *Confirmed by concurrent reasons:—First, because we cannot have ideas of sensation but by the inlet of the senses.*—It is plain those perceptions are produced in us by exterior causes affecting our senses: because those that want the organs of any sense, never can have the ideas belonging to that sense produced in their minds. This is too evident to be doubted: and therefore we cannot but be assured that they come in by the organs of that sense, and no other way. The organs themselves, it is plain, do not produce them: for then the eyes of a man in the dark would produce colours, and his nose smell roses in the winter: but we see nobody gets the relish of a pineapple, till he goes to the Indies, where it is, and tastes it.

5. II. *Secondly, Because we find that an idea from actual sensation, and another from memory, are very distinct perceptions.*—Because sometimes I find that *I cannot*

avoid the having those ideas produced in my mind. For though, when my eyes are shut, or windows fast, I can at pleasure recall to my mind the ideas of light, or the sun, which former sensations had lodged in my memory; so I can at pleasure lay by *that* idea, and take into my view that of the smell of a rose, or taste of sugar. But, if I turn my eyes at noon towards the sun, I cannot avoid the ideas which the light or sun then produces in me. So that there is a manifest difference between the ideas laid up in my memory, (over which, if they were there only, I should have constantly the same power to dispose of them, and lay them by at pleasure,) and those which force themselves upon me, and I cannot avoid having. And therefore it must needs be some exterior cause, and the brisk acting of some objects without me, whose efficacy I cannot resist, that produces those ideas in my mind, whether I will or no. Besides, there is nobody who doth not perceive the difference in himself between contemplating the sun, as he hath the idea of it in his memory, and actually looking upon it: of which two, his perception is so distinct, that few of his ideas are more distinguishable one from another. And therefore he hath certain knowledge that they are not *both* memory, or the actions of his mind, and fancies only within him; but that actual seeing hath a cause without.

6. III. *Thirdly, because pleasure or pain, which accompanies actual sensation, accompanies not the returning of those ideas without the external objects.*—Add to this, that many of those ideas are *produced in us with pain*, which afterwards we remember without the least offence. Thus, the pain of heat or cold, when the idea of it is revived in our minds, gives us no disturbance; which, when felt, was very troublesome; and is again, when actually repeated: which is occasioned by the disorder the external object causes in our bodies when applied to them: and we remember the pains of hunger, thirst, or the headache, without any pain at all; which would either never disturb us, or else constantly do it, as often as we thought of it, were there nothing more but ideas floating in our minds, and appearances entertaining our fancies, without the real existence of things affecting us from abroad. The same may be said of *pleasure,* accompanying several actual sensations. And though mathematical demonstration depends not upon sense, yet the examining them by diagrams gives great credit to the evidence of our sight, and seems to give it a certainty approaching to that of demonstration itself. For, it would be very strange, that a man should allow it for an undeniable truth, that two angles of a figure, which he measures by lines and angles of a diagram, should be bigger one than the other, and yet doubt of the existence of those lines and angles, which by looking on he makes use of to measure that by.

7. IV. *Fourthly, because our senses assist one Another's testimony of the existence of outward things, and enable us to predict.*—Our senses in many cases *bear witness to the truth of each other's report,* concerning the existence of sensible things without us. He that sees a fire, may, if he doubt whether it be anything more than a bare fancy, *feel* it too; and be convinced, by putting his hand in it. Which certainly could never be put into such exquisite pain by a bare idea or phantom, unless that the pain be a fancy too: which yet he cannot, when the burn is well, by raising the idea of it, bring upon himself again.

Thus I see, whilst I write this, I can change the appearance of the paper; and by designing the letters, tell *beforehand* what new idea it shall exhibit the very next moment, by barely drawing my pen over it: which will neither appear (let me fancy as much as I will) if my hands stand still; or though I move my pen, if my eyes be shut: nor, when those characters are once made on the paper, can I choose afterwards but see them as they are; that is, have the ideas of such letters as I have made. Whence it is manifest, that they are not barely the sport and play of my own imagination, when I find that the characters that were made at the pleasure of my own thoughts, do not obey them; nor yet cease to be, whenever I shall fancy it, but continue to affect my senses constantly and regularly, according to the figures I made them. To which if we will add, that the sight of those shall, from another man, draw such sounds as I beforehand design they shall stand for, there will be little reason left to doubt that those words I write do really exist without me, when they cause a long series of regular sounds to affect my ears, which could not be the effect of my imagination, nor could my memory retain them in that order.

8. *This certainty is as great as our condition needs.*—But yet, if after all this any one will be so sceptical as to distrust his senses, and to affirm that all we see and hear, feel and taste, think and do, during our whole being, is but the series and deluding appearances of a long dream, whereof there is no reality; and therefore will question the existence of all things, or our knowledge of anything: I must desire him to consider, that, if all be a dream, then he doth but dream that he makes the question, and so it is not much matter that a waking man should answer him. But yet, if he pleases, he may dream that I make him this answer, That the certainty of things existing in *rerum natura* when we have the testimony of our senses for it is not only as great as our frame can attain to, but as our condition needs. For, our faculties being suited not to the full extent of being, nor to a perfect, clear, comprehensive knowledge of things free from all doubt and scruple; but to the preservation of us, in whom they are; and accommodated to the use of life: they serve to our purpose well enough, if they will but give us certain notice of those things, which are convenient or inconvenient to us. For he that sees a candle burning, and hath experimented the force of its flame by putting his finger in it, will little doubt that this is something existing without him, which does him harm, and puts him to great pain: which is assurance enough, when no man requires greater certainty to govern his actions by than what is as certain as his actions themselves. And if our dreamer pleases to try whether the glowing heat of a glass furnace be barely a wandering imagination in a drowsy man's fancy, by putting his hand into it, he may perhaps be wakened into a certainty greater than he could wish, that it is something more than bare imagination. So that this evidence is as great as we can desire, being as certain to us as our pleasure or pain, i.e., happiness or misery; beyond which we have no concernment, either of knowing or being. Such an assurance of the existence of things without us is sufficient to direct us in the attaining the good and avoiding the evil which is caused by them, which is the important concernment we have of being made acquainted with them.

9. *But reaches no further than actual sensation.*—In fine, then, when our senses do actually convey into our understandings any idea, we cannot but be satisfied that there doth something *at that time* really exist without us, which doth affect our senses, and by them give notice of itself to our apprehensive faculties, and actually produce that idea which we then perceive: and we cannot so far distrust their testimony, as to doubt that such *collections* of simple ideas as we have observed by our senses to be united together, do really exist together. But this knowledge extends as far as the present testimony of our senses, employed about particular objects that do then affect them, and no further. For if I saw such a collection of simple ideas as is wont to be called *man*, existing together one minute since, and am now alone, I cannot be certain that the same man exists now, since there is no *necessary connexion* of his existence a minute since with his existence now: by a thousand ways he may cease to be, since I had the testimony of my senses for his existence. And if I cannot be certain that the man I saw last today is now in being, I can less be certain that he is so who hath been longer removed from my senses, and I have not seen since yesterday, or since the last year: and

much less can I be certain of the existence of men that I never saw. And, therefore, though it be highly probable that millions of men do now exist, yet, whilst I am alone, writing this, I have not that certainty of it which we strictly call knowledge; though the great likelihood of it puts me past doubt, and it be reasonable for me to do several things upon the confidence that there are men (and men also of my acquaintance, with whom I have to do) now in the world: but this is but probability, not knowledge.

10. *Folly to expect demonstration in everything.*—Whereby yet we may observe how foolish and vain a thing it is for a man of a narrow knowledge, who having reason given him to judge of the different evidence and probability of things, and to be swayed accordingly; how vain, I say, it is to expect demonstration and certainty in things not capable of it—and refuse assent to very rational propositions, and act contrary to very plain and clear truths, because they cannot be made out so evident, as to surmount every the least (I will not say reason, but) pretence of doubting. He that, in the ordinary affairs of life, would admit of nothing but direct plain demonstration would be sure of nothing in this world but of perishing quickly. The wholesomeness of his meat or drink would not give him reason to venture on it: and I would fain know what it is he could do upon such grounds as are capable of no doubt, no objection.

GOTTFRIED LEIBNIZ
1646–1716

Gottfried Wilhelm Von Leibniz was born and raised in academe. His father was a professor of moral philosophy at the University of Leipzig and his mother was the daughter of a law professor at the same institution. His advance was prodigious: At fifteen, he began his study of the history of philosophy at the university; at seventeen, after defending his thesis, he proceeded to the University of Jena where he studied mathematics and law; at eighteen, he published his treatise on law; and at twenty, he was ready to present himself as a candidate for the doctor of law degree, but he was declared too young. So he moved to the University of Altdorf, where he not only received his doctoral degree but was offered a professorship. He declined this invitation and settled into a position with Johann Philipp von Schönborn, elector of Mainz.

While in the service of the Mainz court, he lived for a time in Paris, where he made the acquaintance of leading thinkers of his day, such as the physicist Christian Huygens and the philosophers Antoine Arnauld and Nicolas Malebranche. As part of his mission in Paris, Leibniz prepared a plan for invading Egypt for Louis XIV (hoping to deflect Louis from military action in Europe). Though Louis never acted on the plan, many scholars believe that Napoleon used the scheme 120 years later.

In addition to diplomatic initiatives, Leibniz worked extensively on mathematics while he was in Paris. He invented a calculating machine that could add, subtract, multiply, divide, and extract square roots. When he demonstrated his machine in London, he was made a member of the Royal Society (1673). He also discovered differential and integral calculus—though years later there was an unpleasant dispute over whether Leibniz or Newton should get the credit for it.

Did one of these great men steal the idea from the other? The Royal Society officially belittled Leibniz's achievement (quite unjustly according to the verdict of subsequent scholarship). It has been said that the dispute "redounded to the discredit of all concerned." It may be best to credit both men with the discovery. Interestingly, Leibniz's notation proved the more convenient and is the system currently used.

In 1676, Leibniz went into the service of the Duke of Brunswick in Hanover, where he remained the rest of his life. He traveled extensively and met such notable people as Spinoza and the chemist Robert Boyle. In 1700, he was elected a foreign member of the French Academy. In the same year, by his inspiration, the *Akademie der Wissenschaften* was founded in Berlin and he was elected its first president. He was a close friend of Sophie Charlotte, the wife of the Elector of Brandenburg (subsequently the first king of Prussia). The only large systematic philosophic work he published, *Theodicy* (1710), grew out of his discussions with Sophie Charlotte.

Despite his accomplishments, Leibniz was not well liked. As Bertrand Russell later commented, "Leibniz was one of the supreme intellects of all time, but he was not admirable." Leibniz's death in 1716 was ignored not only by the Royal Society in London but also by the *Akademie* in Berlin and by the court at Hanover. His secretary is said to have been his only mourner, and an eyewitness reports in his memoirs that Leibniz "was buried more like a robber than what he really was, the ornament of his country."

At his death, he left an enormous number of unpublished letters and manuscripts. One major work was published in 1765: his detailed critique of Locke's *Essay,* entitled *Nouveaux essais sur L'entendement humain.* Leibniz had completed the book in 1704 but withheld it from publication when Locke died the same year. The book greatly stimulated Immanuel Kant, particularly his *Critique of Pure Reason.* In the twentieth century, thinkers such as Bertrand Russell and Ernst Cassirer have focused attention on Leibniz's work in logic. The neglect of Leibniz in his lifetime has given way to great admiration for the scope and originality of his thought.

*   *   *

Leibniz's philosophy begins by rejecting the notion that extension is a substance (as Descartes claimed) or an attribute of substance (as Spinoza thought). Instead of understanding nature as a collection of discrete extended entities, such as atoms, Leibniz says that the basic substance is a "Monad," or a unit of psychic force. Such Monads are without parts (i.e., simple) and have no interaction with one another. As Leibniz puts it, they have "no windows through which anything may come in or go out." Each Monad has within itself an internal principle of "appetition" that causes it to change. Although there is no causal interaction between Monads, they may *appear* to influence one another. This connection is merely a reflection of the "pre-established harmony" by which God created each of the Monads to "mirror" the others. A Monad's entire past and present are contained within it so that whatever it does, it does so by necessity. If we could know the entire past of a given Monad, we could predict its entire future.

Monads all differ qualitatively and occupy different points of view. This means that each Monad "mirrors" the world in a slightly different way and with different levels of clarity. Rocks and dirt are made of colonies of "low level"

Monads that have only dull and confused perceptions as they mirror the world. It might seem odd to talk about rocks as having perceptions at all, but according to Leibniz, every Monad has some sort of psychic life: Each Monad has an "internal state [by which it] represent[s] external things." Those Monads whose perceptions are "more distinct and are accompanied by memory" are on a higher level. The dominant Monad of an animal, for example, has distinct perceptions and memory of those perceptions: "If you show a stick to a dog, for instance, it remembers the pain caused by it and howls or runs away." This dominant Monad Leibniz calls a "soul" to distinguish it from lower level or "naked" Monads. Human beings are Monad aggregates of yet a higher degree. Whereas human bodies are colonies of lower Monads, the dominant Monad in a person is a "spirit," because it is capable of performing "reflective acts." Spirits are also capable of knowing the universe and of entering into a relationship with the chief Monad, God.

Leibniz's metaphysics seems to exclude the possibility of freedom. If each Monad has its entire future within it, and if it thus unfolds that future by necessity, how can we, as colonies of a dominant "spirit" Monad and lower "body" Monads, be free? Leibniz's answer to this question turns on his definition of "freedom." To be "free," claims Leibniz, does not mean "liberty of indifference." Instead we are "free" in that our actions flow from our wills and there is no logical contradiction in our willing other than we do. As Leibniz put it, "there is always a prevailing reason which prompts the will to its choice, and for the maintenance of freedom for the will it suffices that this reason should incline without necessitating." Of course, he also claims that our wills are created by God and that God foreknows what we will will ourselves to do. But the action of our wills is not necessary in the sense that willing something else involves a logical contradiction; hence, our wills can be said to be "free."

* * *

Leibniz never wrote a *magnum opus* that clearly defined his position on philosophical issues. *The Discourse on Metaphysics* (1686), reprinted here (complete) in the Martin and Brown translation, gives his early ideas on metaphysics. The *Monadology* (1714), also reprinted here (complete) in the Paul Schrecker and Anne Martin Schrecker translation, presents his mature position on metaphysics.

For general introductions to Leibniz's philosophy, see Herbert Wildon Carr, *Leibniz* (Boston: Little, Brown, 1929); Ruth Lydia Saw, *Leibniz* (Baltimore, MD: Penguin Books, 1954); Nicholas Rescher, *The Philosophy of Leibniz* (Englewood Cliffs, NJ: Prentice Hall, 1967); C.D. Broad, *Leibniz: An Introduction*, edited by C. Lewy (Cambridge: Cambridge University Press, 1975); Stuart Brown, *Leibniz* (Minneapolis: University of Minnesota Press, 1984); and Robert Merrihew Adams, *Leibniz: Determinist, Theist, Idealist* (Oxford: Oxford University Press, 1994). For a discussion of the logic and metaphysics of Leibniz, Bertrand Russell, *A Critical Exposition of the Philosophy of Leibniz* (London: George Allen & Unwin, 1900), is still a valuable source. For more recent treatments of these issues, see Hidé Ishiguro, *Leibniz's Philosophy of Logic and Language* (Ithaca, NY: Cornell University Press, 1972); Robert McRae, *Leibniz: Perception, Apperception, and Thought* (Toronto: University of Toronto Press, 1976); Benson Mates, *The Philosophy of Leibniz: Metaphysics and Language*

(Oxford: Oxford University Press, 1986); and Reginald Osburn Savage, *Real Alternatives: Leibniz's Metaphysics of Choice* (Norwell, MA: Kluwer, 1998). For a commentary on *The Monadology*, see Herbert Wildon Carr, *The Monadology of Leibniz* (Los Angeles: University of Southern California Press, 1930). For collections of essays, see Harry G. Frankfurt, ed., *Leibniz: A Collection of Critical Essays* (Garden City, NY: Doubleday, 1972); R.S. Woolhouse, ed., *Leibniz: Metaphysics and Philosophy of Science* (Oxford: Oxford University Press, 1981); Michael Hooker, *Leibniz: Critical and Interpretive Essays* (Minneapolis: University of Minnesota Press, 1984); Vere Chappell, ed., *Essays on Early Modern Philosophers: Gottfried Wilhelm Leibniz* (Hamden, CT: Garland Press, 1992); and Nicholas Jolley, ed., *The Cambridge Companion to Leibniz* (Cambridge: Cambridge University Press, 1995).

DISCOURSE ON METAPHYSICS

1. ON THE DIVINE PERFECTION: GOD DOES EVERYTHING IN THE MOST DESIRABLE WAY.

The most commonly accepted notion of God we have, and the one most full of meaning, is well enough expressed in these terms: God is an absolutely perfect being. Not enough thought, however, is given to its consequences. If we are to make progress, it is relevant to note that in nature there are several entirely different perfections, that God possesses them all together, and that each belongs to Him to the highest degree.

We also need to understand what a perfection is. A sure enough mark of one is that forms or natures not admitting of an ultimate degree are not perfections, as for example the nature of numbers or of shape. For the greatest of all numbers (or rather the number of all numbers), and the greatest of all shapes imply contradictions while omniscience and omnipotence involve no impossibility. Consequently, power and knowledge are perfections, and to the extent that they belong to God, they have no limits.

Hence it follows that since God possesses supreme and infinite wisdom, He acts in the most perfect manner, not only in the metaphysical sense, but also morally speaking. From our point of view we can express ourselves thus: the more we are enlightened and informed about the works of God, the more we shall be disposed to find that they are excellent and satisfactory in every way we could hope.

Gottfried Liebniz, *Discourse on Metaphysics and Related Writings*, edited and translated by R.N.D. Martin and Stuart Brown (Manchester and New York: Manchester University Press, 1988). Reprinted by permission of Manchester University Press.

[Liebniz made minor additions, deletions, and/or changes to virtually every paragraph of this work. I have chosen to reproduce Liebniz's text minus all material deleted by Liebniz.]

2. Against Those Who Maintain that There Is No Goodness in the Works of God, or that the Rules of Goodness and Beauty Are Arbitrary.

Thus I am far removed from the opinion of those who maintain that there are no rules of goodness or perfection in the nature of things or in the ideas God has of them, and that the works of God are good only for the formal reason that God made them. For if that were so, since God knew He was their author, He had only to look at them after making them to find them good, in accordance with the testimony of Holy Scripture. But Scripture seems to have made use of this anthropomorphic way of speaking only to make us realise that we recognise the excellence of God's works by considering them by themselves, even when we disregard the purely extrinsic denomination that refers them to their cause. This is all the more true in that it is by considering the works that we can discover the Worker, so that the works must carry His marks in themselves. I confess that the contrary opinion seems to me extremely dangerous, and very close to the way the Spinozists think of goodness and harmony. Their opinion is that the beauty of the universe and the goodness we attribute to the works of God are no more than the chimeras of men who conceive God according to their own way of thinking. Also, if we say that things are good by no rule of goodness beyond the will of God alone, we thoughtlessly destroy, I feel, all the love and glory of God. For why praise Him for what He had done if He would be equally praiseworthy for doing the opposite? Where will His justice and His wisdom be, if all that remains of Him is some kind of a despotic power, if His will takes the place of reason, and if, by the very definition of tyranny, what pleases the Almighty is *ipso facto* just? Besides, it seems that every act of willing presupposes some reason for willing, and that reason is naturally prior to will. That is why I still find altogether strange the expression of Descartes who says that even the eternal truths of metaphysics and geometry, and consequently also the rules of goodness, justice and perfection are no more than the effects of God's will. It seems to me, rather, that they are no more than the consequences of His understanding, which certainly does not depend on His will, any more His essence does.

3. Against Those Who Think God Could Have Done Better.

Neither can I approve the opinion of some scholastics who maintain boldly that what God has done is not absolutely perfect, and that He could have done much better. For it seems to me that the consequences of this opinion are altogether contrary to the glory of God. "Just as the lesser evil contains a proportion of good, so the lesser good contains a proportion of evil." To act with less perfection than one could have done is to act imperfectly. To show that an architect could have done better is to find fault with his work. It also runs counter to the assurance of the goodness of God's works in Holy Scripture. For, since perfections decrease to infinity, however God did his work, it would always be good in comparison with the less perfect, if that were enough. But a thing is not very praiseworthy if it is only so in that way. I also think that a very large number of passages favouring my opinion could be found in the divine Scriptures and the holy Fathers, with scarcely any favouring that of those new scholastics a view unknown, in my opinion, to the whole of antiquity. It is based on our insufficient knowledge of the general harmony of the universe and of the hidden reasons for God's conduct which lead us to the rash judgement that many things could have been done better. Besides, these moderns insist on some subtleties that are not very sound, for they imagine that nothing is so perfect but that there is something that is more perfect, which is a mistake. There is an infinity of regular figures, but one is the most perfect, namely the circle. If a triangle had to be made and there was no further specification of the kind of triangle, God would assuredly make an equilateral triangle because, absolutely speaking, that is the most perfect.

They also think that in this way they are providing for the liberty of God, as if it were not the highest liberty to act in accordance with sovereign reason. For, apart from its apparent impossibility, the belief that God acts in some matter without any reason for His act of will is hardly consistent with His glory. Suppose, for example, that God chooses between A and B, and that He takes A without any reason for preferring it to B; I say that that action of God would at the least not be praiseworthy. For every praise must be based on some reason and here *ex hypothesi* there is none. On the contrary, I hold that God does nothing for which He does not merit being glorified.

4. LOVING GOD DEMANDS COMPLETE SATISFACTION WITH AND ACQUIESCENCE IN WHAT HE DOES, BUT WE DO NOT, ON THAT ACCOUNT, HAVE TO BE QUIETISTS.

The general recognition of this great truth—that God always acts in the most perfect and desirable manner possible—is to my mind the basis of the love we owe to God concerning all things. For he who loves seeks his satisfaction in the happiness or perfection of the loved one and his actions. "True friendship is to want the same and to reject the same." And I think that it is difficult to love God well when not disposed to will what He wills, if changing that were in our power. Indeed those who are not satisfied with what He does seem to me like discontented subjects of a king or of a republic whose intentions are little different from those of rebels.

Hence, in accordance with these principles, I hold that to act in conformity with the love of God it is not enough to be patient under duress. We must be truly satisfied with all that happens to us in consequence of His will. I mean this acquiescence to apply to the past. As far as the future is concerned, we must not be quietists nor wait ridiculously with arms folded for what God will do, in accordance with the sophism the Ancients called ⟨*logon aegon*⟩ lazy reason. On the contrary, we must act in accordance with the presumptive will of God, as far as we can judge it, trying with all our ability to contribute to the general good, especially to the adornment and perfection of what concerns us or is near us, or, so to speak, within our range. For when the outcome shows that God may perhaps not want our good will to have its effect for the present, it does not follow that He does not want us to do what we have done. On the contrary, since He is the best of all masters, He never asks for more than the right intentions, and it is for Him to know the hour and the place for bringing good plans to fruition.

5. WHAT ARE THE RULES OF PERFECTION OF GOD'S CONDUCT; AND THAT THE SIMPLICITY OF MEANS IS BALANCED BY THE RICHNESS OF EFFECTS.

Hence it is enough to have this confidence in God, that He does everything for the best and that nothing can harm those who love him. But to know in detail the reasons that could have moved Him to choose this order of the universe, to allow sins, or to dispense His saving grace in a particular way, is beyond the power of a finite mind, particularly of a finite mind that has not yet attained enjoyment of the sight of God.

Nevertheless, some general remarks can be made on the conduct of Providence in the government of things. Thus it can be said that whatever encloses more reality in less volume is more perfect, that he who acts perfectly is like an excellent geometer who knows how to find the best constructions for a problem; like a good architect who arranges his site and the funds intended for the building in the most advantageous manner, so as to leave nothing that jars or lacks the beauty of which it is capable; like a good householder who uses his property so that nothing is left uncultivated or barren; like a skilled engineer who achieves his result by the least complicated way that could be chosen; like an experienced author who includes as much reality as he is able in the least space. Now the most perfect of all beings, occupying the least volume, in other words, those which hinder the least, are minds, and their perfections are the virtues. That is why we must not doubt that the happiness of minds is the principal objective of God and that He pursues it as much as the general harmony allows. More will be said of this presently.

As for the simplicity of God's ways, that applies properly in respect of means whereas the variety, richness or abundance applies to aims or effects. The one has to be in balance with the other, like the expenses of a building with the size and beauty expected of it. It is true that nothing costs God anything, much less than it costs a philosopher to make hypotheses for the construction of his imaginary world, since God has only to make decrees to bring a real world to birth; but in relation to wisdom, in so far as they are mutually independent, decrees or hypotheses take the place of expenditure, for reason demands that we avoid a multiplicity of hypotheses or principles; in almost the same way the simplest system is always preferred in astronomy.

6. GOD DOES NOTHING OUT OF ORDER AND IT IS NOT EVEN POSSIBLE TO IMAGINE EVENTS THAT ARE NOT REGULAR.

The decisions or actions of God are commonly divided into ordinary and extraordinary. But it is well to bear in mind that God does nothing out of order. So, whatever passes for extraordinary is only so in relation to some particular order established among creatures. For, in relation to the universal order, everything conforms to it. So true is this, that not only does nothing happen in the world that is absolutely irregular, but such a thing cannot even be imagined. Suppose, for example, that someone puts a number of points on paper completely at random like those who practise the ridiculous art of geomancy, then I say that it is possible to find a geometric line whose notion is constant and uniform according to some rule, so that this line passes through all these points and does so in the same order as they were made by the hand.

And if someone were to draw in one movement a line that was sometimes straight, sometimes circular, and sometimes of some other kind, it is possible to find a notion, a rule, or an equation common to all the points in that line and in virtue of which these same changes had to occur. For example there is no face whose contour is not part of a geometric line and cannot be drawn all in one movement by some rule-governed motion. But when a rule is very complicated, what conforms to it is taken to be irregular.

Thus it can be said that however God might have created the world, it would always have been regular and within some general order. But God chose that world that is the most perfect, i.e. the one that is simultaneously the simplest in hypotheses and richest in phenomena, just as a geometric line might be if its construction was easy but its properties most admirable and extensive. I make use of these comparisons to sketch some kind of imperfect resemblance to the divine wisdom and to say something that could at least raise our minds to conceive in some way what cannot be adequately expressed. But by this I do not claim to explain the great mystery on which the whole universe depends.

7. MIRACLES CONFORM TO THE GENERAL ORDER ALTHOUGH THEY ARE CONTRARY TO SUBALTERN NORMS. WHAT GOD WISHES OR PERMITS BY A GENERAL OR PARTICULAR WILL.

Now, since nothing can take place that is not within the order, it can be said that miracles are just as much within the order as natural operations, are so called because they conform to certain subaltern norms we call the nature of things. For it can be said that this "nature" is no more than a custom of God from which He can exempt Himself in virtue of a stronger reason than the one that moved Him to make use of these norms.

As for the general and particular wills, depending on how we take the matter, it can be said that God does everything in accordance with His most general will, the one in conformity with the most perfect order He chose. But it can also be said that He has particular wills, which are exceptions to the subaltern norms mentioned above; for the most general of the laws of God, by means of which He regulates the whole universe, are without exception.

It can also be said that God wills everything that is an object of His particular will. But as for the objects of His general will, such as the actions of other creatures, particularly of those that are rational, and with which, (i.e. the *actions*) God wishes to concur, we must draw a distinction: if the action is good in itself, it can be said that God wills it and sometimes commands it, even when it does not happen; but if it is evil in itself, and only becomes good by accident, it has to be said that God permits it and not that He wills it, though He concurs in it through the laws of nature established by Him, and because he is able to draw from it greater good. This comes about because the sequence of things, particularly punishment and recompense, corrects its evil nature, and compensates for the evil with interest, so that in the end there is more perfection in all that follows than if none of the evil had happened.

8. IN ORDER TO DISTINGUISH THE ACTIONS OF GOD FROM THOSE OF CREATURES, AN EXPLANATION IS GIVEN OF THE NOTION OF AN INDIVIDUAL SUBSTANCE.

It is rather difficult to distinguish the actions of God from those of creatures as well as the actions and passions of these same creatures. For there are those who think that God does everything, while others imagine that He does no more than conserve the force He has given to creatures. What follows will show how far either of these can be said. Now since, properly speaking, actions belong to individual substances ("actions belong to supposita"), it will be necessary to explain just what such a substance is.

It seems to me that when several predications are attributed to the same subject and this subject is not attributed to any other, this subject is called an individual substance. But that is not enough and such an explanation is merely nominal, so we need to consider what it is to be truly attributed to a particular subject.

Now it is acknowledged that all true predication has some basis in the nature of things, and when a proposition is not an identity, that is, when the predicate is not expressly included in the subject, it must be so included virtually. That is what the Philosophers call *inesse*, when they say that the predicate is in the subject. Thus the subject term must always include that of the predicate, so that whoever understood the notion of the subject perfectly would also judge that the predicate belongs to it.

That being so, we can say that the nature of an individual substance or complete being is to have such a complete notion as to include and entail all the predicates of the subject that notion is attributed to. In contrast, an accident is a being whose notion does not include all that can be attributed to the subject it is attributed to. Thus* the quality of being king that belongs to Alexander the Great, taken in abstraction from the subject, is not sufficiently determinate for one individual, and does not include the other qualities of the same subject, nor everything that the notion of this prince includes, whereas God who sees the individual notion or *haecceity*** of Alexander sees in it at the same time the foundation and reason for all the predicates that can truly be ascribed to him, such as that he would defeat Darius and Porus even to the point of knowing *a priori* (and not by experience) whether he died naturally or by poison, something we can only know historically. Also, when we consider well the connection of things, we can say that there is in the soul of Alexander for all time traces of everything that happened to him, and marks of everything that will happen to him, and even traces of everything happening in the universe, though to recognise them all belongs to God alone.

9. EACH UNIQUE SUBSTANCE EXPRESSES THE WHOLE UNIVERSE IN ITS OWN WAY, AND INCLUDED IN ITS NOTION ARE ALL THE EVENTS THAT HAPPEN TO IT WITH ALL THEIR CIRCUMSTANCES, AND THE WHOLE SEQUENCE OF EXTERNAL THINGS.

Among several paradoxical conclusions following from this, is that it is not true that two substances are completely alike, differing only numerically, and what St Thomas has to say on this point about angels and intelligences ("in these cases every individual is a lowest species") is true of all substances provided that the specific difference is taken in the way geometers take it in relation to their figures. Likewise, if bodies are substances, their natures cannot possibly consist solely in size, figure and motion: something else is needed. Likewise, a substance can begin only by creation and perish only by annihilation; a substance cannot be divided into two, nor can two substances become one, and so the number of substances does not naturally increase or diminish, though they are frequently transformed.

Moreover every substance is as it were an entire world and a mirror of God, or rather of the whole universe, expressing it in its own way, somewhat as the same town is variously represented according to the different positions of an observer. It can even be said that every substance bears in some way the mark of the infinite wisdom and omnipotence of God, imitating Him as far as it is capable. For it expresses, if only con-

---

*The first edition of the text used the following example: "Thus the circular figure of the ring of Gyges, does not contain everything that makes up the individual notion of this ring. Whereas God sees in it at the same time the foundation and cause for all the predicates that can truly be applied to it, such as that it would be swallowed by a fish and nevertheless returned to its master. I speak here as if this ring were a substance."

**Literally "thisness," an allusion to the theory of what makes something an individual substance produced by Duns Scotus and in which Leibniz had taken an interest when writing a student dissertation. Every individual has its own *haecceity*, according to Duns Scotus, though (like Leibniz) he believed it was only known to God.

fusedly, all that happens in the universe, past, present and future, and this has some resemblance to an infinite perception or knowledge. And since all other substances in turn express it and are accommodated to it, it can be said to extend its power over all the others in imitation of the omnipotence of the Creator.

10. THERE IS SOME SOUNDNESS TO THE BELIEF IN SUBSTANTIAL FORMS, BUT THESE MAKE NO DIFFERENCE TO THE PHENOMENA, AND SHOULD NOT BE USED TO EXPLAIN PARTICULAR EFFECTS.

It seems that the ancients in distinguishing an *ens per se* from an *ens per accidens* and in introducing substantial forms, as well as the many able people who were accustomed to profound meditations and who taught theology and philosophy centuries ago, many of them praiseworthy for their sanctity, had some knowledge of what we have just said. This is what led them to introduce and uphold the substantial forms so much in disfavour today. But they are neither so far from the truth nor as ridiculous as the common run of our modern philosophers imagine.

I agree that the knowledge of forms is of no use in the details of physics and should not be used for explaining the particulars of phenomena. That is where our scholastics went wrong, and with them the physicians of the past who followed their example, in thinking to account for the properties of bodies by mentioning forms and qualities without taking the trouble to examine their manner of operation. It is as if we were to content ourselves with saying that a clock has the horodictic [time-telling] quality deriving from its form without considering what that consists in. That indeed might be enough for whoever buys the clock, provided he left its maintenance to someone else.

But this shortcoming and misuse of forms should not make us reject something whose knowledge is so necessary in metaphysics that without it, I hold, the first principles cannot be well understood, nor the mind sufficiently raised to the knowledge of incorporeal natures and the wonders of God.

Nevertheless, a geometer has no need to trouble his mind with the famous labyrinth of the composition of the continuum, and neither has any moral philosopher, and still less any legal expert or politician, any need to trouble himself with the great difficulties involved in reconciling the freedom of the will with the providence of God. For the geometer can complete all his demonstrations and the politician conclude all his deliberations without entering into these discussions, important as they are in philosophy and theology. In the same way, a physicist can account for experiments, sometimes by means of simpler experiments carried out before, and sometimes by means of geometrical and mechanical demonstrations, without the need of forms and other general considerations belonging to another sphere. If he employs the extraordinary concurrence of God, or some soul, *arché* or other thing of that nature, he is wandering as far off course as he who tries to introduce the nature of destiny and our liberty into a deliberation about an important practical matter. Men often make this mistake without thinking when they trouble their minds by considering fate, and sometimes they are even diverted from some good resolution or necessary care as a result.

11. THE MEDITATIONS OF THE THEOLOGIANS AND PHILOSOPHERS CALLED "SCHOLASTICS" ARE NOT TO BE DESPISED ENTIRELY.

I know that in claiming in some way to rehabilitate the old philosophy and restore the all but banished substantial forms to which not enough justice has been done to life, I am proposing a big paradox. But I only do this on the supposition that it is possible to speak of bodies as substances. But perhaps I shall not be lightly condemned if it is known that I have long meditated on modern philosophy, and spent much time on physical experiments and geometrical demonstrations, and that I was long persuaded of the vanity of such beings. But I was eventually obliged to take them up again against my will and as if by force. It was as a result of carrying out my own researches that I was made to recognise that our moderns do not do full justice to St. Thomas and other great men of those times, and that the opinions of scholastic philosophers and theologians are much more sound than is imagined, as long as they are used appropriately and in their place. I am even convinced that if some exact and reflecting mind took the trouble to clarify and digest their thoughts in the manner of analytical geometry, he would find a treasure store of very important truths which could be demonstrated completely.

12. NOTIONS DEFINED BY EXTENSION INVOLVE SOMETHING IMAGINARY AND CANNOT CONSTITUTE THE ESSENCE OF BODIES.

But, to take up again the thread of our considerations, I believe that any one who meditates on the nature of substance as I have explained it above will find that either bodies are not substances in strict metaphysical rigour (the view indeed of the Platonists), or that the whole nature of body does not consist solely in extension, i.e. in size, shape and motion. On the contrary, something related to souls which is commonly called a "substantial form" has necessarily to be recognised in them, though that makes no more difference to the phenomena than the souls of animals, if they have any. It can even be demonstrated that the notions of size, shape and motion are not so distinct as is imagined and that they involve something imaginary and relative to our perceptions, just as colour, heat and other similar qualities also do, (to an even greater extent)—we may doubt that these are truly in the nature of external things. That is why qualities of these kinds could not constitute any substance. And if there were no other principle of identity in body than the one just considered, no body would ever last more than a moment.

　　Nevertheless, souls and substantial forms of other bodies are very different from intelligent souls, who alone know what they do, and which not only do not naturally perish but even for ever retain the basis of the knowledge of what they are. This makes them liable to punishment and reward, and makes them citizens of the republic of the universe whose monarch is God. It also follows that all other creatures ought to serve them, something we shall discuss more fully presently.

13. SINCE THE INDIVIDUAL NOTION OF EVERY PERSON INCLUDES ONCE FOR ALL EVERYTHING THAT WILL EVER HAPPEN TO HIM, IN IT ARE TO BE SEEN THE A PRIORI PROOFS OF EACH EVENT, OR RATHER WHY ONE HAPPENED RATHER THAN THE OTHER. BUT ALTHOUGH THESE TRUTHS ARE ASSURED, THEY DO NOT CEASE TO BE CONTINGENT, SINCE THEY ARE BASED ON THE FREE WILL OF GOD OR OF CREATURES. THERE ARE ALWAYS REASONS FOR THEIR CHOICES BUT THESE INCLINE WITHOUT NECESSITATING.

But a great difficulty can arise from the foundations laid above, and before proceeding further, we must try to deal with it. We said that the notion of an individual substance includes once for all everything that can ever happen to it, and that by considering this notion, we can see in it everything that can truly be stated about it, just as we can see in the nature of the circle all the properties that can be derived from it. But from that it seems that all events will become fatally necessary that the difference between necessary and contingent truths will be destroyed, that all the fate of the Stoics will take the place of liberty, there will no longer be any room for human liberty, and absolute fate will reign over all our actions as well as over all other events in the world. My reply is: we must distinguish between what is certain and what is necessary. Everyone agrees that future contingents are assured since God foresees them, but it is not for all that admitted that they are necessary. But (it will be said) if some conclusion can be infallibly deduced from a definition or notion, it will be necessary. Now in fact we do maintain that everything that is to happen to a person is already included virtually in his nature or notion, just as the properties of a circle are included in its definition. So the difficulty remains. In order to give a sound answer, I claim that connection or derivation is of two kinds: one is absolutely necessary (its contrary implies a contradiction) and occurs with eternal truths like those of geometry; the other is necessary only *ex hypothesi*, by accident, so to speak, but in itself it is contingent, since its contrary does not imply a contradiction. This connection is based, not on the absolutely pure ideas and God's bare understanding alone, but also on His free decrees and the connection of the universe.

Let us take an example. Since Peter will deny our Lord, that action is included in his notion, for we are supposing it to be in the nature of such a perfect notion to include everything, so that the predicate should be included in it, *ut possit inesse subjecto*. We could say that it is not in virtue of this notion or idea or nature that he must sin, since that only applies to him because God knows everything. But, it will be insisted, his nature or form corresponds to his notion. I reply that it is indeed true and since God imposed this personality on him he must henceforth conform to it. I could reply with the objection of future contingents, for these have as yet no reality outside the understanding and the will, and since God gave them this form in advance, they will have to conform to it all the same.

But I prefer to deal with difficulties than make excuses for them with examples of some other similar difficulties, and what I am going to say will help clarify both. Thus it is here that we must apply the distinction between the kinds of connection. I say that what happens in accordance with these prior conditions is assured, but that it is not necessary; and if he did the opposite, he would be doing nothing impossible in itself though it would be *ex hypothesi* impossible that this should happen. For if someone were capable of completing the whole of the demonstration by virtue of which he proved the connection between the subject Peter and the predicate (namely, his denial), he would show that this fact had its basis in his notion or nature, and that it was reasonable and consequently assured that it should come about; but he would not show that it was necessary in itself, nor that its contrary implied a contradiction. In almost the same way, it is reasonable and assured that God will always do the best, although what is less perfect involves no contradiction in itself.

For it would be found that this demonstration of this predicate of Peter is not as absolute as those of numbers and geometry, but that it supposes the sequence of things freely chosen by God and founded on the first free decree of God, which always leads him to do what is most perfect, as well as on the decree God made (in consequence of the first) concerning human nature, which is that man will always (although freely) do what seems best. Now every truth founded on decrees of this kind is contingent, although certain, since those decrees make no difference to the possibility of things and, as I have already said, although God assuredly always chooses the best, that does not prevent what is less perfect remaining possible in itself, though it does not happen. It is not its impossibility but its imperfection that causes it to be rejected. Nothing is necessary if its contrary is possible.

Hence, we are in a position to meet such difficulties, great as they may appear to be (and indeed they are no less pressing for all others who have ever dealt with this matter,) provided it is fully realised that contingent propositions have reasons for being that way rather than otherwise, or (what comes to the same thing) that there are *a priori* proofs of their truth which make them certain and show that the subject-predicate connection in these propositions has its basis in the nature of each. But these are not necessary demonstrations, since these reasons are only based on the principle of the contingency or of the existence of things, i.e. on what is or seems to be the best of several equally possible things; whereas necessary truths are founded on the principle of contradiction and on the possibility or impossibility of the essences themselves, without regard to the free will of God or of creatures.

14. God Produces Different Substances According
to the Different Views He Has of the Universe.
The Distinctive Nature of Each Substance Ensures,
by the (Mediation) of God, that what Happens
to Each Corresponds to what Happens to All the Others,
Without Them Acting Directly on Each Other.

Having after a fashion come to know what the nature of created substances consists in, we must try to explain their mutual dependence and their actions and passions. Now, in the first place, it is altogether obvious that created substances depend on God who conserves them—and even continually produces them by a kind of emanation, as we do our thoughts. For as God, so to speak, turns on all its sides and in all ways the general system of phenomena which He finds it good to produce to manifest His glory, and as He looks at all the faces of the world in all possible ways—because there is no relation that escapes His omniscience—the result of each view of the universe as if seen from a particular place is a substance expressing the universe in conformity with that view, if God finds it good to make His thought effective and produce this substance. And since the view of God is always true, our perceptions are so too; it is those of our judgements that derive from us that deceive us.

Now we have said above, and it follows from what we have just said, that each substance is like a world on its own, independent of everything else apart from God. Hence all our phenomena, that is, all that can ever happen to us, are consequences of our natures and, since we are free substances, of our wills. Since these phenomena preserve a particular order conforming to our nature or, so to speak, the world within us, so that we are able (to make observations useful for regulating our conduct which are justified by the favourable outcome of future phenomena) and to judge the future by the past without error, this enables us to say that these phenomena are true, without worrying whether they are outside us or whether others perceive them as well. Nevertheless, it is very true that the perceptions or qualities of all substances correspond with each other, so that each, carefully following the particular reasons or laws it has observed, fits in with the other in doing the same, just as when several people agree with each other to be at a particular place at a prearranged day, they can in fact do so if they wish. Now although all express the same phenomena, it does not follow from this that their expressions should be perfectly similar: it is enough that they are proportionate to each other. In the same way several spectators think they have seen the same thing and indeed agree with each other, although each sees and speaks according to his point of view.

Now it is God from whom all substances emanate continually and He sees the universe, not only as they see it, but quite differently from them all as well. He is the only cause of this correspondence between their phenomena, and He alone makes what is peculiar to one public to all, otherwise there would be no connection between them. Hence it can be said in a manner of speaking and in a sense that is good, though remote from ordinary usage that a particular substance never acts on another particular substance and is not acted upon by another either. This follows if we remember that what happens to each is only a consequence of its idea or complete notion alone, since that idea already includes all the predicates or events, and expresses the whole universe. Indeed, nothing can happen to us but thoughts and perceptions, and all our thoughts and our future perceptions are no more than consequences, albeit contingent, of our previous thoughts and perceptions. Hence, if I were capable of considering distinctly everything happening or appearing to me at the present time, I would be able to see therein everything that would ever happen or appear to me. This would not fail, but would happen in any case, if everything outside me were destroyed and only God and myself remained. But as we attribute to other things, as if to causes acting on us, what we perceive in some way in other things, we have to consider the basis of this judgement, and what truth there is in it.

It is above all agreed that if we desire some phenomenon to happen at a certain time and it occurs in the ordinary course of things, we say that we acted and that we were the cause of it, as when I want to, as we say, "move my hand." Also, when it seems to me that by my will something happens to what I call another substance (and that this is the way it would happen as I judge from frequent observation) although it was not willed by it, I judge that this substance is acted upon. I admit this of myself when something happens to me in accordance with the will of another substance. Also, when we will something to happen, and something else follows from it that we did not want, we still say that we did it, provided that we understood how it followed. There are also some phenomena of extension that we attribute to ourselves more particularly and which have their basis *a parte rei* in what is called our body. As everything of importance happening to it (i.e. all the notable changes appearing to us in it) make themselves strongly felt in it, ordinarily at least, we attribute all the passions to this body to ourselves. We do so with very good reason, for even if we did not perceive them at the time, we do not fail to become well aware of the consequences, just as if we had been transported from one place to another while asleep. We also attribute to ourselves the actions of this body, as when we run, hit or fall, and when our body, continuing the motion once begun, has some effect. But I do not attribute to myself what happens to other bodies, because I realise that great changes can happen that I cannot perceive, unless my body is exposed to them in a way I conceive appropriate to that assumption.

So it is quite clear that although all the bodies of the universe belong to us in some way and harmonise with ours, we do not attribute to ourselves what happens to them. For when my body is pushed, I say that I myself have been pushed, but if someone else is pushed, I do not say that I have been pushed, even though I may perceive it and some passion in me may arise from it, since I measure where I am by the place my body is in. And this language is highly reasonable because it is appropriate for clear expression in everyday practice. As for the mind, it can be said briefly that our acts of will and judgements or reasonings are actions while our perceptions or sensations are passions. As for the body, we say that a change that happens to it is an action when it follows from a previous change, but otherwise it is a passion.

In general, to give our terms a meaning that reconciles metaphysics with practice, it can be said that when several powers are affected by the same change the one that passes to a higher degree of perfection or continues in the same acts, while the one that immediately becomes more limited thereby, so that its expressions become more confused, is acted upon.

15. The Action of One Finite Substance on Another Consists Solely in the Increase in the Degree of Its Expression Together With the Diminution of that of the Other, in so Far as God Has Made Them Conform to Each Other.

But without getting involved in a long discussion, it is enough for the present to reconcile the language of metaphysics with that of practice by noting that we attribute to ourselves our more clear and distinct perceptions and that we can in general attribute to a substance its more clear and distinct expression and, with reason, the phenomena we express more perfectly, while we attribute to other substances what each best expresses. Thus a substance of infinite extension, in so far as it expresses everything, becomes limited by its more or less perfect manner of expression. Thus in this way it is possible to conceive that substances mutually hinder or limit each other and, consequently, in this sense, to say that they act on each other and, so to speak, are obliged to conform to each other. For it can happen that a change which increases the expression of the one diminishes that of the other. Now, the virtue of a particular substance is to express well the glory of God, and it is there that it is least limited, and everything that exerts its virtue or power, that is when it acts, changes for the better and is extended in so far as it acts. Thus when a change affects several substances (since indeed every change touches all of them), I think that it can be said that the one that thereby passes to a higher degree of perfection or to a more perfect expression exerts its power and acts, while the other one that passes to a lesser degree shows its weakness and is acted upon. So I hold that every action of a substance possessing perception implies some pleasure and every passion some pain, and vice versa. This notwithstanding that it can easily happen that a present advantage is destroyed in what follows. Hence it follows that it is possible to sin by acting or exerting one's power and finding pleasure therein.

16. The Extraordinary Concurrence of God Is Included in the Expression of our Essence Because It Applies to Everything, but It Transcends the Powers of Our Nature of Distinct Expression (Which Is Finite and Follows Particular Subaltern Norms).

All that remains for the present is to explain how it is sometimes possible for God to have influence on men or other substances through an extraordinary or miraculous concurrence, since it seems that everything that has to happen to them is natural in so far as it is a consequence of their substance. But what we said above about miracles in the universe must be remembered: they always conform to the universal laws of the general order, even though these transcend the subordinate norms. And, to the extent that every person or substance is like a little world expressing the great one, it can even be said that this extraordinary concurrence of God is included in the general order of the universe in so far as that is expressed by the nature of this person, but it does not cease to be miraculous and to be beyond the norms. That is why, if everything it expresses is included in our nature, nothing is supernatural with respect to it, for it extends to everything, since an effect always expresses its cause and God is the true cause of substances. But since what our nature expresses more perfectly particularly belongs to it, that is what its power consists in—and since, as I have just explained, it is limited, there are many things that surpass the powers of our natures, and even those of every limited nature. Consequently, to speak more clearly, I say that miracles and the extraordinary acts of God's concurrence have the particular character that they could not be foreseen by the reasoning of any created mind, however enlightened it might be, since the comprehension of the general order surpasses them all, while everything called natural depends on the less general norms creatures can understand. Hence, in order to say nothing of these norms or laws of nature that might cause offence, it would be good to link particular ways of speaking with particular thoughts: whatever includes everything we express could then be called our essence or idea, and since it expresses our union with God, it has no limits and nothing exceeds it. But what is limited in us could be called our nature or power, and in this respect what exceeds the natures of all created substances is supernatural.

17. EXAMPLE OF A SUBALTERN NORM OR LAW OF NATURE; IN WHICH IT IS SHOWN THAT GOD ALWAYS PRESERVES THE SAME FORCE, BUT NOT THE SAME QUANTITY OF MOTION . . . AGAINST THE CARTESIANS AND SOME OTHERS.

I have often mentioned subaltern maxims or laws of nature already, and it would be good to give an example. Our new philosophers commonly make use of that famous rule advanced by Descartes that God always preserves the same quantity of motion in the world. It seems highly plausible indeed, and in the past I held it to be indubitable. But I have since come to recognise wherein lay its error. It is that Descartes and many other able mathematicians thought that the quantity of motion (i.e. the speed times the size of the mobile) was the same thing as the force, or at least expressed it perfectly, or geometrically speaking, that the forces are in compound proportion of the speeds and the bodies. Now it is obvious indeed that the same force should always be preserved in the universe. So, when we attend to the phenomena with care, we see clearly that mechanical perpetual motion does not occur, because then the force of a machine, which is continually being slightly diminished by friction, and must consequently soon cease, would be replaced and so would increase of itself without any new impulsion from outside. We also note that the force of a body is diminished solely to the extent that it gives some of it to neighbouring bodies or to its own parts in so far as these have independent motions.

Thus they thought that what can be said of force could also be said of quantity of motion. But, to show the difference, I suppose that a body falling from a particular height acquires the force needed to climb up again, if its direction of travel should take it that way, unless there are hindrances. For example, a pendulum would rise right back again to the height it had fallen from if the resistance of the air and other small obstacles did not somehow diminish the force acquired.

I *suppose* also that as much force is needed to raise a body A of one pound a height CD of four fathoms as to raise a body B of four pounds a height EF of one fathom. All this is accepted by our new philosophers.

Hence, it is manifest that body (A), after falling from the height CD has acquired as much force precisely as body (B) after falling from the height EF. For when body (B) has arrived at F and has the force to climb back to E (by the first supposition), it has in consequence the force to carry a body of four pounds, that is its own body, to the height EF of one fathom, and similarly, when body (A) has reached D and has the force to climb back to C, it has the force to carry a body of one pound, that is its own body, to the height CD of four fathoms. Hence (by the second supposition), the forces of the two bodies are equal.

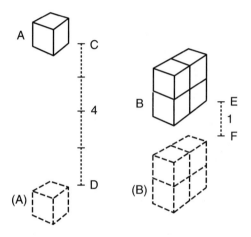

Now let us see whether the quantity of motion is also the same in both cases: but it is here that there will be surprise at finding a very great difference. For it has been demonstrated by Galileo that the speed acquired in the fall CD is twice that acquired in the fall EF, though the height is quadruple. If then, we multiply the body (A), in the proportion 1, by the speed, in the proportion 2, the product or quantity of motion will be as 2, and if on the other hand, we multiply the body (B), which is as 4, by its speed, which is as 1, then the product or quantity of motion will be as 4. Hence the quantity of motion of body (A) at point D is half the quantity of motion of body (B) at point F, though their forces are equal. Hence there is a great difference between the quantity of motion and the force, as was to be proved.

From this it is seen that the force must be measured by the quantity of the effect it can produce, e.g. by the height to which a heavy body of a particular size and kind can be raised, something very different from the speed that can be given it, and that to give it twice the speed more than twice the force is needed.

Nothing is simpler than this proof. Descartes only fell into error here because he trusted too much in his thoughts before they had matured enough with a confidence based on the happy success of some of his thoughts and on his experience of the penetration of his mind, which rendered him rather too rash in the end. But I am astonished that his followers have not recognised this error since, and I fear that little by little they begin to imitate the Peripatetics they so make fun of, and that like them they grow accustomed to consulting the books of their master rather than reason and nature.

18. IMPORTANCE OF THE DISTINCTION BETWEEN FORCE
AND QUANTITY OF MOTION INTER ALIA IN DECIDING THAT WE
MUST HAVE RECOURSE TO METAPHYSICAL CONSIDERATIONS
DISTINCT FROM EXTENSION TO EXPLAIN THE NATURE OF BODIES.

This consideration of the distinction of force from quantity of motion is important enough, not only in physics and mechanics in the discovery of the true laws of nature and rules of motions, and even in the correction of several practical errors that have slipped into the writings of some able mathematicians, but also in metaphysics, in the better understanding of the principles of things. For motion, if its precise formal content only—i.e. change of place—is considered, is not a completely real thing, and when several bodies mutually exchange their places, it is impossible to determine from these changes alone which of them ought to have motion or rest attributed to it, as I could show geometrically if I wanted to dwell on this point now.

But the force or direct cause of these changes is something more real, and there is some basis for attributing it to one body rather than to another, and it is only thereby that we can know which one the motion is best attributed to. Now, this force is something different from size and motion, and it can be concluded from this that what is conceived in bodies does not consist solely in extension and its modifications, contrary to the conviction of our moderns. Hence, too, we are obliged to re-establish some of the beings or forms banished by them. And although all the particular phenomena of corporeal nature can be explained mathematically or mechanically by those who understand them, it nevertheless appears more and more that the general principles of corporeal mechanical nature itself are metaphysical rather than geometrical, belonging to forms or indivisible natures functioning as causes of the matter or extension rather than to corporeal or extended mass—a reflection capable of reconciling the mechanical philosophy of the moderns with the circumspection of some intelligent well-intentioned people who fear quite reasonably that we are moving too far from immaterial beings to the disadvantage of piety.

19. USEFULNESS OF FINAL CAUSES IN PHYSICS.

As I do not like to judge people's intentions, or only do so favourably if I can, I am not accusing our new philosophers of impiety when they claim to banish final causes in physics. Nevertheless I am obliged to admit that I do not recognise their usual intelligence and prudence therein and that the consequences of this opinion seem dangerous to me, particularly when it is connected with that refuted by me at the beginning of this discourse, which seems to lead to their removal altogether, as if God never had any aim, whether good or active, or as if the good were not the object of His will. . . . For my part, I hold on the contrary that it is just there that we have to seek the principle of all existences and even of the laws of nature, since God always intends what is best and most perfect.

I am happy to admit that we are liable to error when we want to determine the aims and counsels of God, but that is only when we try to restrict them to a particular plan, in the belief that He has only one single thing in view, whereas in fact He considers everything at once. Thus, when we think that God made the world for us alone, we are greatly mistaken, although it is true that He made it in its totality for us and that there is nothing in the world that does not affect us and does not also conform to His concerns for us, in accordance with the above principles. Thus, when we see some good effect or perfection happening or resulting from the works of God, we can certainly say that God intended it, for He does nothing by chance and unlike us does not sometimes fail to do well. That is why, far from being in an error here, akin to that of the overly political who attribute excessive refinement to the designs of princes, or to that of commentators who search for too much erudition in their authors, we cannot attribute too many reflections to this infinite Wisdom, and there is no matter in which there is less danger of error as long as we only affirm and avoid negative propositions here that limit the plans of God.

Everyone who sees the admirable structure of animals is led to recognise the wisdom of the Author of things, and I advise those with any feeling of piety or even of true Philosophy to avoid the expression of some would-be tough minds who say that we see because we happen to have eyes, without noting that the eyes were made to see. If we are seriously involved in these opinions that assign everything to the necessity of matter or to a particular chance (although both must seem ridiculous to those who understand what we have explained above), we will inevitably fail to recognise an intelligent Author of nature. For it is ridiculous to introduce a Sovereign Intelligence as the Ordainer of things and not use His wisdom to account for phenomena. As if, in accounting for the conquest of a great prince in capturing an important position, a historian tried to say that it was because the particles of the gunpowder liberated by lighting the fuse escaped at a speed capable of pushing a hard heavy body against the walls of the position, while the branches of the particles composing the copper of the cannon were sufficiently intertwined not to be separated by this speed, instead of showing how the foresight of the victor caused him to choose the appropriate time and means, and how his power overcame all the obstacles.

20. Remarkable Passage of Socrates in Plato Against Excessively Materialistic Philosophers.

This point reminds me of a fine passage of Socrates in Plato's *Phaedo*. In marvellous agreement with my thoughts on this point, it seems to be written expressly against our excessively materialistic philosophers. So this account made me want to translate it, and though it is rather long, perhaps this sample will give one of us the occasion to share many other fine sound thoughts from the writings of the great man.

"One day," he said, "I heard someone read a book of Anaxagoras, where there were these words 'that an Intelligent Being was the cause of all things, and that He arranged and adorned them.' I was extremely pleased with that, for I thought that if the world was the result of an Intelligence, everything would have been made in the most perfect way possible. That is why I thought that he who wanted to explain why things came to be, perished or subsisted had to search for what suited the perfection of each. Thus man would only have to consider in himself or in some other thing, what was best or most perfect, alone. For he who knew the most perfect would easily decide thereby what was imperfect, since there is only one true knowledge of both.

"In view of all this, I rejoiced to have found a master able to teach the reason of things: whether, for example, the earth was round or flat, and why it was best that way rather than otherwise. . . . Moreover, I expected that when he said that the earth was or was not at the centre of the universe, he would explain to me why that was the most suitable. And when he said the same of the sun, the moon, the stars and their motions.

. . . And finally, after showing what was suitable to each thing individually, he would show me what was best in general.

"Full of this hope, I took and skimmed through the books of Anaxagoras with great eagerness, but I was far from my expectation, for I was surprised to see that he made no use of this governing Intelligence, set out in advance, that he spoke no more of the adornment and the perfection of things, and introduced some rather implausible ethereal matters.

"In this he was rather like the man who said that Socrates did things intelligently, but when he came to explaining in particular the causes of his actions, thereupon said that he was sitting here because he had a body composed of bone, flesh and nerves, that the bones were solid, but had gaps and joints, that the nerves could be tensed or relaxed, and that was why the body was flexible and I was sitting. Or if he wanted to explain the present speech, he had recourse to the air, to vocal and aural organs and like things, while forgetting the true causes, that is that the Athenians thought it better to condemn than to acquit me, and I for my part thought it better to sit here than to take flight. For, by my faith, these nerves and these bones would long since be with the Boeotians and the Megarans, if I had not found it more just and more honest for me to suffer the penalty the fatherland wants to impose on me than live elsewhere a wanderer in exile. That is why it is unreasonable to call these bones and nerves and their motions causes.

"It is true that whoever said that I could not do all this without bones and nerves would be right, but the true cause is something else . . . and that is no more than a condition without which the cause could not be the cause. . . .

"People who say no more than, for example, that the motions of the bodies surrounding the earth support the earth where it is, forget that the divine power arranges everything in the finest way, and do not understand that it is the good and the beautiful that join, form and preserve the world. . . ." Thus far Socrates, for the things about ideas or forms that follow in Plato are not less excellent but a bit more difficult.

21. IF THE RULES OF MECHANICS DEPENDED ON GEOMETRY ALONE WITHOUT METAPHYSICS, THE PHENOMENA WOULD BE QUITE DIFFERENT.

Now, since the wisdom of God has always been recognised in the details of the mechanical structures of particular bodies, it is very necessary that it should also be shown in the general set-up of the world and the constitution of the laws of nature. This is so true that the counsels of this Wisdom are observed in the laws of motion in general. For if there were nothing else to bodies but an extended mass and nothing to motion but change of place, and if everything had to and could be deduced from these definitions alone by geometrical necessity, it would follow, as I have shown elsewhere, that the least body would give the same speed as its own to the largest resting body it met without losing any of its own, and many other rules of this sort would have to be accepted, such as are altogether contrary to the construction of a system. But the decree of the divine wisdom to preserve always the same total force and direction has provided for this.

I even find that many natural effects can be demonstrated doubly, i.e. through the efficient cause and separately through the final cause as well, by using for example the decree of God to produce His effect by the simplest and most determinate ways, as I have shown elsewhere in my account of the rules of catoptrics and dioptrics, and I shall say more of it below.

22. RECONCILIATION OF THE TWO WAYS BY FINAL AND EFFICIENT CAUSES IN DEFENCE OF BOTH THOSE WHO EXPLAIN NATURE MECHANICALLY AND THOSE WHO HAVE RECOURSE TO INCORPOREAL NATURES.

It is good to note this point to reconcile those who hope to explain mechanically the formation of the first tissues of an animal and the complete machine of its parts with those who account for the same structure by final causes. Both are good and both can be useful, not only for admiring the artifice of the great Workman, but also in discovering something useful in physics and medicine. Authors who follow these different routes should not be hard on each other.

For I see that those who concentrate on explaining the beauty of divine Anatomy laugh at others who imagine that an apparently fortuitous motion of particular fluids can make such a beautiful variety of members, and call such people rash and profane, while on the other hand the latter call the former simple and superstitious like the ancients who took it that the physicists were impious when they held that it was not Jupiter that thundered but some matter in the clouds. The best thing would be to unite both considerations, for, to use a vulgar comparison, the skill of a workman is recognised and praised not only by showing what designs he had when he made the parts of his machine, but also by explaining the tools he used to make each part, particularly when these tools are simple and ingeniously contrived. *God is skilful enough an artisan* to produce a machine a thousand times still more ingenious than that of our body if that were possible, using only a few simple enough fluids expressly formed so that only the ordinary laws of nature are needed to sort them out as necessary to produce such an admirable effect, but it is also true that this would not happen if God were not the Author of nature.

I find, nevertheless, that the way of efficient causes is while indeed more profound and in one way more direct and *a priori*, on the other hand rather difficult when we get down to details and I think that our Philosophers are most often still rather far from that. In contrast, the way of final causes is easier and is moreover often helpful in guessing important and useful truths that would have been a long time in the searching by the former more physical route, and of this Anatomy can furnish important examples. I also hold that Snell, the first discoverer of the rules of refraction, would have taken a long time to find them if he had tried to find out first how light was formed. But he seems to have followed the method the ancients used in catoptrics, that of final causes in fact. For, in the search for the easiest way of conducting a ray from one given point to another by reflection at a given plane (supposing that this is nature's design), they discovered the equality of the angles of incidence and reflection, as can be seen in a little treatise of Heliodorus of Larissa and elsewhere. That is what in my opinion Snell, and after him (though without knowing anything about him) Fermat, applied more ingeniously to refraction. For when in the same media the rays observe the same proportion of sines which is also that of the resistances of the media, it turns out to be the easiest, or at least the most determinate way of passing from a given point in one medium to a given point in the other. The demonstration Descartes tried to give of this same theorem by the way of efficient causes is far from being as good. At least there are grounds for suspecting that he would never have found it that way if he had not heard something of Snell's discovery in Holland.

23. RETURNING TO IMMATERIAL SUBSTANCES; THE EXPLANATION OF HOW GOD ACTS ON THE UNDERSTANDING OF MINDS AND OF WHETHER WE ALWAYS HAVE AN IDEA OF WHAT WE THINK.

I have found it relevant to insist somewhat on these considerations concerning final causes, incorporeal natures and an Intelligent Cause in relation to bodies, to make known their use even in physics and mathematics. On the one hand, this is to purge the mechanical philosophy of the profanity imputed to it. On the other hand it is to raise the minds of our philosophers from mere material considerations to more noble meditations. It is now time to return from bodies to immaterial natures, to minds in particular, and to say something of the ways God uses to illumine them and act on them, for we must not doubt that here too there are laws of nature, a point I could discuss more fully elsewhere. For now, it is enough to touch a little on ideas, on whether we see all things in God, and on how God is our light.

Now, it is relevant to note that several errors are occasioned by the misuse of ideas. For when we reason on something we imagine we have an idea of it, and on that foundation some recent authors have built a demonstration of God that is, rigorously speaking, very imperfect. For, they say, I must have an idea of God or of a perfect being, since I am thinking of Him, and it is impossible to think without an idea. Now the idea of this Being includes all the perfections and existence is one of these, so that consequently He exists. But as we often think of impossible chimerae, such as the ultimate degree of speed or the greatest number or the meeting of the conchoid [a plane curve in geometry] with its base or rule, this reasoning is not enough. Hence in this sense a person can say he has true or false ideas according as the thing in question is possible or not, and it is only when we are assured of its possibility that we can boast of having an idea of the thing. Thus the above argument proves at least that God necessarily exists if He is possible. This is indeed an excellent privilege of the divine nature: to need only its possibility or essence to exist in fact, just what is called an *Ens a se*.

24. JUST WHAT IS CLEAR OR OBSCURE, DISTINCT OR CONFUSED, ADEQUATE AND INTUITIVE OR SUPPOSITIVE KNOWLEDGE, AND WHAT ARE NOMINAL, REAL, CAUSAL AND ESSENTIAL DEFINITIONS.

The better to understand the nature of ideas, we have to touch a little on the varieties of knowledge. When I know only through experience that something is possible, because everything that exists is possible, my knowledge is confused. It is in this way that we know bodies and their qualities. But when I can prove *a priori* that something is possible, this knowledge is distinct. When I can recognise one thing among others without being able to say in what its *differentiae* or properties consist, my knowledge is confused. Thus it is that we sometimes know *clearly* without being in any doubt at all whether a poem or picture is well or badly made, because there is an I don't know what that satisfies or shocks us. But only when I can explain the marks available to me is my knowledge called *distinct*. Such is the knowledge of the assayer who discerns the true and the false by particular tests or marks comprising the definition of gold.

But there are degrees of distinct knowledge, for the notions that enter the definition would ordinarily themselves need definition and are only confusedly known. But when every thing that enters a definition or distinct item of knowledge is distinctly known right back to the primitive notions, I call this knowledge *adequate*, and when my mind understands all the primitive ingredients of a notion all at once and distinctly, then it has an intuitive knowledge of it, something very rare since most human knowledge is confused or even *suppositive*.

It is also good to distinguish nominal definitions from real ones. I refer to a nominal definition when it is still possible to doubt that the notion defined is possible. Thus, for example, when I say that an endless screw is a solid line whose parts are congruent or can coincide with each other, whoever did not otherwise know what an endless screw was could doubt the possibility of such a line, though indeed it was a reciprocal property of an endless screw, since the other lines whose parts are congruent are planar (the circumference of the circle and the straight line only), that is they can be drawn *in a plane*. This shows that every reciprocal property can be used in a nominal definition, whereas when the property makes known the possibility of the thing, it makes the definition real. As long as we have a mere nominal definition, we could never be sure of the consequences drawn from it, for if it concealed some contradiction or impossibility, contrary conclusions could be drawn from it. That is why truths do not depend on names and are not arbitrary as held by some new philosophers.

25. IN WHAT CASE OUR KNOWLEDGE IS JOINED TO THE CONTEMPLATION OF THE IDEA.

Now it is obvious that we have no idea of a notion when it is impossible. And when our knowledge is merely *suppositive*, when we have the idea we do not contemplate it, for such a notion is known only in the same way as those that are occultly impossible, and if it is possible it is not learned by that method of knowing. For example, when I think of a thousand, or of chiliagon [a group of one thousand things], I often do so without contemplating the idea, as when I say that a thousand is ten times a hundred without putting myself to the trouble of thinking what ten and a hundred are. That is because I *suppose* I know it and see no need for the present to pause to conceive it. Thus it can easily happen, as indeed it does often enough, that I am in error with respect to a notion I suppose or believe I understand, although in truth it is impossible, or at least incompatible with the others I join it to. Whether or not I am in error, this suppositive way of conceiving remains the same. Hence, it is only when our knowledge of confused things is *clear* or our knowledge of distinct things intuitive, that we contemplate the complete idea of them.

26. WE HAVE ALL IDEAS IN US; PLATO'S NOTION OF REMINISCENCE.

If we are to conceive properly what an idea is, we must avoid an ambiguity. For there are some who take the idea to be the form or way of distinguishing our thoughts. On this view we have the idea in our minds only to the extent that we think of it, and whenever we think of it again, we have ideas of the same thing different from though similar to the previous ones. But it seems that others take the idea to be an immediate object of thought, or some permanent form remaining when we do not contemplate it. Indeed, there is always in our souls the capacity to conceive any nature or form whatever, when the opportunity of thinking of it presents itself. I think that this capacity of our souls, to the extent that it expresses some nature, form or essence, is properly speaking the idea of the thing, in us and always in us, whether we think of it or not. For our soul expresses God and the universe, and all essences as well as all existences.

This follows from my principles, for nothing enters our minds naturally from outside, and it is a bad habit of ours to think as if our souls received some messenger—species or had gates and windows. We have all the forms in our minds, for all time even, because the mind always expresses all its future thoughts, and already thinks confusedly everything it will ever think distinctly. Nothing could be taught us whose idea was not already present in our minds as the matter from which this thought was formed.

That is what Plato understood so well when he put forward his doctrine of reminiscence, which is very sound provided we take it the right way and purge it of the error of pre-existence, and do not imagine that the soul has to have once known and distinctly thought what it is now learning and thinking. He also confirmed his opinion by a beautiful experiment. He introduced a little boy in his dialogue called *Meno* whom he led insensibly into the most difficult geometrical truths concerning incommensurables, without teaching him anything, merely putting relevant questions in order. This shows that our souls have virtual knowledge of everything. They need only attention to know the truths, and consequently have at least the truths on which these truths depend. It can even be said, if the latter are taken for the relations of ideas, that they already possess these truths.

27. IN WHAT SENSE OUR SOULS MAY BE COMPARED TO EMPTY TABLETS, AND HOW OUR NOTIONS COME FROM THE SENSES.

Aristotle preferred to compare our souls to tablets that were still bare with space for writing on, and he claimed that nothing was in our understanding that did not come from the senses. As is the way with Aristotle, this is more in conformity with popular notions, whereas Plato goes deeper. Nevertheless, such everyday expressions or practical sayings are liable to pass into common usage, almost as with the followers of Copernicus who continue to say that the sun rises and sets. I often find, even, that a good sense can be given to them in accordance with which there is nothing wrong with them. Just as I have already remarked on the way it is possible to say truly that particular substances act on each other, in this same sense it can be said that we receive some knowledge from outside by the ministry of the senses, because some external things contain, or more particularly express, the reasons determining our souls to particular thoughts. But when we are concerned with the accuracy of metaphysical truths, it is important to recognise the extent and independence of our souls. This goes infinitely further than is vulgarly supposed, although in the ordinary course of life only what is more certainly perceived and belongs to us in a particular way is attributed to it, since there is no purpose in going further.

Nevertheless, it would be good to choose special terms for both senses to avoid ambiguity. Hence, expressions in our souls, whether conceived or not, can be called ideas, while those we conceive or form can be called *notions* or *concepts*. But however we take it, it is always false to say that all our notions come from the senses called external, since the one I have of myself, and of my thoughts, and consequently of being, substance, action, identity and many others, comes from internal experience.

28. GOD ALONE IS THE IMMEDIATE OBJECT OF OUR PERCEPTIONS EXISTING OUTSIDE US, FOR HE ALONE IS OUR LIGHT.

Now, in the rigour of metaphysical truth, there is no external cause acting on us but God alone, and He alone communicates himself to us directly in virtue of our continual dependence. It follows from this that there is no other external object touching our souls and exciting our perceptions directly. So it is only in virtue of the continual action of God on us that we have in our souls the ideas of everything, i.e. because every effect expresses its cause and hence the essence of our souls is a particular expression, imitation, or image of the essence, thought and will of God and of all the ideas included in Him. Hence, it can be said that God alone is our immediate object outside us, and that it is in Him that we see all things. For example, when we see the sun and the stars, it is God who gave us them and preserves their ideas in us, and in fact determines us to think of them at the time at which our senses are disposed in a particular way, through His ordinary concurrence and in accordance with the laws established by Him. God is the sun and light of souls, "the light enlightening every man born into the world." It is not just today that people are of this opinion. After Holy Scripture and the Fathers—always more for Plato than for Aristotle—I recall noticing once that in the time of the Scholastics some believed that God was the light of the soul and, in their way of speaking, "the active intellect of the rational soul." The Averroists gave this a bad meaning, but others such as, I think, William of St. Amour, doctor of the Sorbonne, and several mystical theologians, took it in a manner worthy of God and capable of raising the soul to the knowledge of its good.

29. Nevertheless We Think Directly by Our Own Ideas and Not by Those of God.

Nevertheless I am not of the opinion of some able philosophers who seem to maintain that our very ideas are in God, and not at all in us. In my opinion, this comes about because they have still not pondered enough what we have just explained concerning substances, nor the entire extent and independence of our souls (which means that they include everything happening to them and express the essence of God, and with Him all possible and actual beings, like an effect its cause). Also, it is inconceivable that I should think by means of the thoughts of someone else. It is very necessary that an effect should express its cause and it is also very necessary that the soul should be actually affected in a particular way when it thinks of something and that it should have in advance, not only the passive power of being affected in this way, something already determined, but also an active power, in virtue of which there has always been in its nature the marks of the future production of that thought and dispositions to produce it when the time came. All this already includes the idea contained in that thought.

30. How God Inclines Without Necessitating; We Have No Right to Complain, and We Must Not Ask Why Judas Sins Since this Free Action Is Included in His Notion, Only Why Judas the Sinner Is Admitted to Existence in Preference to Other Possible Persons. The Origin of Evil Comes From this, the Original Imperfection Before Sin, and the Degrees of Grace.

Concerning the action of God on the human will, there are many rather difficult questions that would take time to pursue here. Nevertheless, in outline, this is what can be said. When God concurs in our actions, He ordinarily does no more than follow the laws of nature He has established, i.e. He preserves and continually produces our nature, so that the thoughts spontaneously and naturally or freely happen to us in the order carried by the notion of our individual substance, within which they could have been foreseen from all eternity. Moreover, in virtue of the decree that the will should always tend towards the apparent good, and so express or imitate God's will in certain particular respects in respect of which this apparent good always has something of the true, He determines our will to choose what seems the best without nonetheless necessitating it. For, absolutely speaking, in so far as it may be opposed to necessity, our will is indifferent and has the power to do otherwise or to suspend its action altogether, since both are and remain possible.

Hence it falls to the soul to take precautions against the appearances taking it by surprise by means of a firm resolve to reflect and to refuse to act or judge on particular occasions without thorough deliberation. Nevertheless it is true and even certain from all eternity that a particular soul will not use this power on one such occasion. But who could do anything about it or do other than complain about himself? For all complaints after the fact are unjust when they would have been unjust before. Now would this soul, shortly before sinning, be in the right to complain of God, who has not determined him to flee from the sin as if He had determined him to sin? Since God's determinations in these matters are unforeseeable, how does he know himself to be determined to sin, unless in fact he is already actually sinning? It is only a matter of not willing, and God could propose no easier or juster condition. Moreover, any judge stops only to consider how far a man's will is bad without searching for the reasons disposing him to have a bad will. But perhaps it is certain from all eternity that I will sin? Answer yourself: perhaps not. Do not think about what you cannot know and cannot enlighten you, but act in accordance with the duty you know.

But, someone else will ask, whence comes it that that man will certainly do this sin? The answer is easy: otherwise he would not be that man. For God sees for all time that there will be a certain Judas whose notion, or idea God has of him, contains this future free action. Hence the only question that remains is why such a Judas, the traitor, who is merely a possible in the idea of God actually exists. But to that question there is no answer to be expected here below, unless that in general we must say that since God thought it good for him to exist, despite the sin he foresaw this evil must be repaid with interest in the universe, that God will obtain a greater good from it; and that in all He will find this sequence of things including the existence of this sinner the most perfect of all the other possible ones. But to explain in all cases the admirable economy of this choice is not possible while we are travellers in this vale of tears in this world. It is enough to know without understanding it. It is time here to recognise "the height of the riches," the width and depth of the divine wisdom, without seeking a detail involving these infinite considerations.

Nevertheless, it is clear that God is not the cause of evil. For not only did original sin take hold of the soul after the loss of innocence but before then there was a limitation or original imperfection common to the natures of all creatures making them capable of sin or liable to fail. Thus there is no more difficulty with regard to the supralapsarians* than with the others. In my opinion, it is to this that the opinion of St. Augustine and other authors that the root of evil is in nothingness should be reduced, i.e. in the privation or the limitation of creatures that God graciously remedies by giving them the degree of perfection it pleases Him to give. Whether ordinary or extraordinary, this grace of God has its degrees and measures, always in itself efficacious in

---

*[Calvinists who believe that election to heaven or hell was a part of God's original plan.]

producing a proportionate effect. Moreover it is always sufficient, not only to guarantee us against sin, but to produce salvation, if the man joins himself to it with his will, though it is not always sufficient to surmount human inclinations, otherwise it would depend on nothing more, and that is reserved to the absolutely efficacious grace alone that is always victorious whether by itself or by the congruity of circumstances.

31. The Foreknowledge of Merit, the Dispensing of Grace, the Motives of Election, the Middle Knowledge, the Absolute Decree; that Everything Reduces to the Reason Why God Chose a Particular Possible Person for Existence, Whose Notion Includes that Particular Sequence of Graces and Free Actions, so that All the Difficulties Are Removed at Once.

In the end, the graces of God are graces pure and simple over which creatures have no claim. However, just as when we are giving an account of the action of God in dispensing these graces it is not enough to have recourse to His fore-sight, whether absolute or conditional, of the future actions of men, so we must not imagine absolute decrees with no reasonable motive. As regards God's fore-sight of faith and good works, it is very true that God has elected only those whose faith and charity He foresaw, "those He foreknew He would give faith to," but the same question returns: why God will give the grace of faith and good works to some rather than to others. As for this middle knowledge of God's, the fore-sight, not of good works, but of their matter and predisposition, or of what the man would contribute from his side (since it is true that there is diversity on the human side wherever there is on the side of grace, and since indeed, although man needs to be excited towards the good and converted, it is very necessary that he should also play his part here after the fact) some people think that it could be said that since God sees what man would do without grace or extraordinary assistance, or at least what he will have on his side apart from grace, He could resolve to give grace to those whose natural disposition was the best or at any rate the least imperfect or least evil. But if that was the case, it could be said that these natural dispositions, in so far as they are good, are still the effect of an act of grace, even if an ordinary one, since God has advantaged some more than others. And since He well knows that these natural advantages He gives will provide the motive for grace or extraordinary assistance, does it not follow from the doctrine that truly everything in the end reduces to His mercy?

Hence, I believe (since we do not know how much or how God takes account of natural dispositions in dispensing grace) that the most accurate and certain thing to say is, as already noted and in conformity with our principles, that among the possible beings there should be the person of Peter or John whose notion or idea contains the whole sequence of ordinary and extraordinary graces and all the other events along with their circumstances, and that it pleased God to choose him from among an infinity of other equally possible persons for actual existence. After that it seems that there is no more to ask and that all the difficulties disappear.

For, considering this single great question, why it pleased God to choose one from so many other possible persons, we would have to be unreasonable indeed not to be satisfied with the general reasons given, for which the detail is beyond our reach. So, we should not have recourse to an absolute decree, which is unreasonable since there is no reason for it, or to reasons that do not succeed in resolving the difficulty. Instead the best will be to say with St. Paul that there are certain grand reasons for this unknown to mortals and founded in the general order whose aim is the greatest perfection of the universe, and that God has observed these. It is to this that the motives of the glory of God and the manifestation of His justice reduce, as well as His mercy and His perfections generally, and finally that immense depth of His riches Paul's soul was enchanted with.

32. USEFULNESS OF THESE PRINCIPLES IN MATTERS OF PIETY AND RELIGION.

For the rest, it seems that the thoughts we have just explained, particularly the grand principle of the perfection of the operations of God and the notion of the substance including all the events with all their circumstances, far from harming religion, serve to confirm it, removing very great difficulties, inflaming souls with a divine love and raising minds to the knowledge of incorporeal substances to a much greater extent than the hypotheses we have seen up to now. For it is clear that just as thoughts depend on our substance, all other substances depend on God, that God is all in all, and that He is intimately united with all creatures (though to the extent of their perfection), and that He alone determines them externally by His influence. And if to act is to determine directly, it can be said in this sense, in the language of metaphysics, that God operates on me and is alone able to do me good or ill, while other substances are nothing but occasional causes, for the reason that as God considers all of them, He distributes His acts of goodness and obliges them to conform to each other. Also, God alone makes the connection and communication of substances, and it is by Him that phenomena of any given substance meet and fit with those of the others, and consequently that there is reality in our perceptions. But in practice action is attributed to particular occasional causes in the sense explained above, because it is not always necessary to mention the universal cause in particular cases.

It is seen also that every substance has a perfect spontaneity (which in intelligent substances becomes liberty): that everything that happens to it is a consequence of its ideas or being, and that it is determined by nothing but God alone. That is why a person of noble mind whose sanctity is greatly revered used to say that the soul must often think as if there were only God and it in the world.

Now nothing makes immortality more completely comprehensible than this independence and extent of the soul. It protects it absolutely from all external things, since it alone constitutes the whole world and, with God, suffices to itself. It is also impossible for it to perish other than by annihilation, and impossible for the world (of which it is a living and perpetual expression) to destroy itself. Hence, it is not possible for the changes in that extended mass called our body to do anything to our soul, or for the disappearance of that body to destroy what is indivisible.

33. EXPLANATION OF THE UNION OF SOUL AND BODY SOMETHING ONCE THOUGHT INEXPLICABLE OR MIRACULOUS, AND THE ORIGIN OF CONFUSED PERCEPTIONS.

Also clear is the unexpected solution of that great mystery of the union of soul and body, i.e. how it happens that the actions and passions of the one are accompanied by the actions and passions, or rather appropriate phenomena, of the other. For there is no way of conceiving any influence of the one on the other, and it is unreasonable simply to have recourse to the extraordinary operation of the universal cause in something ordinary and particular. But here is the true reason. We have said that everything happening to the soul and to every substance is a consequence of its notion. Hence the very idea or essence of the soul makes all its appearances or perceptions arise spontaneously out of its own nature, and just so, that they answer of themselves to what happens in the whole universe, though particularly in the body assigned to it, because in a way and for a time, it is in accordance with the relation of other bodies to its own that the soul expresses the state of the universe. This shows yet again how our bodies belong to us without nevertheless being attached to our essences. I believe that persons able to meditate will see advantage in our principles in just this, that it is easy to see in what exactly the connection between soul and body—apparently inexplicable by any other means—consists.

It can also be seen that the perceptions of our senses, even when they are clear, must necessarily contain some confused sensations. For as all the bodies in the universe are in sympathy, ours receive the impressions of all the others. Although our senses relate to everything, it is not possible for our souls to attend to all individually, and that is why our confused sensations are the result of a variety, altogether infinite, of perceptions. It is almost like the confused murmur heard by those approaching the shores of the sea that arises from the accumulation of the reverberations of innumerable waves. Now if of several perceptions (not coming together to become a single one) none stands out above the others, and if they make almost equally strong impressions, or are equally capable of determining the attention of the soul, it can only register them confusedly.

34. THE EXCELLENCE OF MINDS COMPARED WITH OTHER
SUBSTANCES OR SUBSTANTIAL FORMS. THE IMMORTALITY CALLED
FOR IMPLIES MEMORY.

One thing I do not propose to decide is whether in metaphysical rigour bodies are substances or are no more than *true* phenomena like the rainbow, nor consequently whether there are substances, souls or substantial forms that are not intelligent. But if we suppose that bodies like man that constitute unities in themselves are substances and have substantial forms, we are obliged to admit that these souls and substantial forms could no more entirely perish than atoms if there are any or ultimate particles of matter can, in the opinion of other philosophers. For though it may become quite different, no substance perishes. Although more imperfectly than minds, they too express the whole universe. But the principal difference is that they do not know what they are nor what they are doing. Consequently, since they have no power of reflection, they are unable to discover necessary and universal truths. It is also for want of reflection on themselves that they have no moral qualities, so that, when we consider how a caterpillar changes into a butterfly through almost a thousand transformations, it comes to the same for morals and practice as saying that they perish, as can indeed be said physically (as we say of bodies that they perish by corruption). But the intelligent soul that knows what it is, and is capable of pronouncing this me which says so much, not only remains the same metaphysically to a greater extent than the others, but it also remains morally the same and constitutes the same personality. For it is the memory and knowledge of this me that makes it liable to punishment and reward. Also, the immortality called for both in morality and religion does not consist merely in that perpetual subsistence proper to all substances. For without the memory of what has been, there would be nothing desirable about it. Let us suppose that some poor wretch suddenly became King of China, but only on condition that he forgot what he had been, as if he had just been reborn: does that not come to the same in practice, or in the effects that could be registered, as if he had to be annihilated and a King of China created at the same instant and at the same place? Something this individual has no reason to desire.

35. THE EXCELLENCE OF MINDS. GOD CONSIDERS THEM IN PREFERENCE TO OTHER CREATURES. MINDS EXPRESS GOD RATHER THAN THE WORLD, BUT OTHER SUBSTANCES EXPRESS THE WORLD RATHER THAN GOD.

But to show by natural reasons that God always will preserve not only our substance but also our personality, that is memory and knowledge of what we are although distinct knowledge of that may sometimes be suspended when asleep or unconscious, morality must be joined to Metaphysics. That is, God has not only to be considered as the principle and cause of all substances and all beings, but also as the chief of all persons or intelligent substances and the absolute monarch of the most perfect city or republic, like that of the universe composed of all minds together, since God himself is the most accomplished of all Minds as well as the greatest of all Beings. For assuredly, minds are either the only substances existing in the world if bodies are no more than true phenomena, or else they are at least the most perfect ones. And since the whole nature, end, virtue and function of substances is merely to express God and the universe, as has been sufficiently explained, there are no grounds for doubting that substances expressing Him in the knowledge of what they are doing, and capable of knowing great truths regarding God and the universe, express Him incomparably better than those natures that are either animal and incapable of knowing truths, or altogether destitute of sense and knowledge; and the difference between intelligent substances and those that are not is as great as that between the mirror and he who sees.

And since God Himself is the greatest and wisest of minds, it is easy to conclude that beings with whom He can so to speak enter into conversation or even into fellowship, communicating His thoughts and intentions individually, so that they can know and love their Benefactor, must concern Him infinitely more than all other beings, able only to pass for the tools of minds, just as we can see wise persons taking infinitely more account of a man than of some other thing, however precious that may be. It seems that the greatest satisfaction an otherwise contented soul can have is to see himself loved by others although in respect of God there is this difference that His glory and our worship can add nothing to His satisfaction, since the knowledge of creatures is no more than a consequence of His sovereign and perfect happiness and very far from contributing to the latter or being part of the cause thereof. Nevertheless, what is good and reasonable in finite minds is supremely so in Him and just as we would praise a king who preferred to preserve the life of a man before the most precious and rare of animals, we should not doubt that the most enlightened and just of all Monarchs is of the same opinion.

36. GOD IS THE MONARCH OF THAT MOST PERFECT REPUBLIC THAT CONSISTS OF ALL MINDS, AND THE HAPPINESS OF THIS CITY OF GOD IS HIS PRINCIPAL DESIGN.

In fact, minds are the most perfectible of all substances and their perfections have this characteristic that they hinder each other the least, or rather that they assist each other, for only the most virtuous can be the most perfect friends. Hence it manifestly follows that God who always looks to the greatest perfection in general, will have the most care of minds, and will give them, not only generally but to each individually, the greatest perfection the universal harmony can permit.

It can even be said that God, in so far as He is a mind, is the origin of existent things—if there were no will to choose best there would be no reason for one possible thing to exist in preference to others. Hence God's quality of being Himself a mind precedes all other considerations He may have with respect to creatures. Minds only are made in His image, and it is as if they are of His race and children of His house, since they alone can serve Him freely and act consciously in imitation of the divine nature. One mind is worth an entire world, since it does not only express it, but knows it, and governs itself there in the manner of God. So much so that it seems that while every substance expresses the whole universe, other substances express the world rather than God while minds express God rather than the world. And this natural nobility of minds, which brings them as near to the divine as is possible for mere creatures, means that God receives from them infinitely more glory than from other beings, or rather other beings merely give minds matter for glorifying Him.

That is why this moral quality of God that makes Him the Lord and Monarch of Minds, affects Him so to speak personally in a quite special manner. It is in this that He becomes human and is willing to allow human ways of speaking about Him, and enters into fellowship with us like a Prince with his subjects. This consideration is so dear to Him that the happy and flourishing state of His empire, that consists in the greatest possible happiness of the inhabitants, becomes the supreme subaltern law of His conduct. For happiness is to persons what perfection is to beings, and if the first principle of existence of the physical world is the decree giving it the greatest possible perfection, the first principle of existence of the moral world or City of God, the most noble part of the universe, must be to spread as much happiness as possible in it.

Hence it must not be doubted that God so ordained (not only that minds could live forever, which is inevitable, but also that they should conserve forever their moral nature) so that this city should lose no person just as the world loses no substance. And consequently, they will always know what they are, otherwise they would not be liable to reward or punishment, which however is the essence of any republic, above all of one that is the most perfect, in which nothing can be neglected.

Finally, since God is at once the most just and the most good-natured of monarchs, and asks only for good will, provided that it is sincere and serious, His subjects could not hope for better conditions: to make them perfectly happy, He wants only that they love Him.

37. Jesus Christ Has Revealed to Men the Mystery and Admirable Laws of the Kingdom of Heaven and the Greatness of the Supreme Happiness God Prepares for Those Who Love Him.

The ancient philosophers had very little knowledge of these important truths. Jesus Christ alone expressed them divinely well and in such a clear and familiar way, that the most crude minds came to understand them. So His gospel changed the entire face of human affairs. He brought us knowledge of the Kingdom of Heaven or this perfect republic of minds that merits the title "City of God" whose admirable laws he revealed to us, and he alone shows us how much God loves us; the exactness with which He has provided for all that concerns us; that since He cares for sparrows, He will not neglect the reasonable creatures who are infinitely more dear to Him; that all the hairs in our heads are counted; that heaven and earth will pass away before the Word of God and everything belonging to the pattern of our salvation is changed; God has more concern with the least of intelligent souls than with the whole machine of the world; that we must not fear those who can destroy the body but are unable to harm souls, since God alone can make them happy or unhappy; that the just are in His hand protected from all the revolutions of the universe, since nothing can act on them but God alone; that none of our actions is forgotten; that everything is taken into account, right down to unguarded words, and a spoonful of water well used; and finally that all things must result in the greatest good for those that are good; that the just are like suns and that neither our senses nor our minds have ever tasted anything approaching the happiness God prepares for those who love Him.

THE MONADOLOGY

1. The object of this discourse, the *monad*, is nothing else than a simple substance, which enters into the composites; *simple* meaning, which has no parts.

2. And there must be simple substances, since there are composites; for the composite is nothing else than an accumulation or aggregate of the simples.

3. But where there are no parts, neither extension, nor figure, nor divisibility is possible. Thus, these monads are the veritable atoms of nature, and, in one word, the elements of all things.

4. Hence no dissolution is to be feared for them, and a simple substance cannot perish naturally in any conceivable manner.

5. For the same reason, no simple substance can come into being naturally, since it cannot be formed by composition.

6. Thus it may be maintained that monads cannot begin or end otherwise than instantaneously, that is, they can begin only by creation, and end only by annihilation; while what is complete begins and ends through and in its parts.

7. It is impossible also to explain how a monad can be altered, that is, internally changed, by any other creature. For there is nothing in it which might be transposed, nor can there be conceived in it any internal movement which could be excited, directed, or diminished. In composites this is possible, since the parts can interchange place. The monads have no windows through which anything could come in or go out.

8. Nevertheless, the monads must have some qualities, otherwise they would not even be beings. And if the simple substances did not differ through their qualities, there would be no means at all of perceiving any change in things. For what is in the composites can come only from the ingredient simples. So the monads, if they were without qualities, would be indistinguishable the one from the other, since they do not differ in quantity either. The plenum being presupposed, no space, consequently, could ever receive through movement anything but the equivalent of what has been in it, and one state of things would be indiscernible from another.

Gottfried Wilhelm Von Leibniz, *Monadology and Other Philosophical Essays*, translated by Paul Schrecker and Anne Martin Schrecker (New York: Macmillan/Library of the Liberal Arts, 1965).

9. Each monad must even be different from every other. For in nature there are never two beings which are perfectly like one another, and between which it would not be possible to find an internal difference, that is, a difference founded on an intrinsic denomination.

10. I take it also for granted that all created beings, consequently the created monads as well, are subject to change, and that this change is even continual in each one.

11. In consequence of what has been said, the natural changes of the monads must result from an *internal principle*, since no external cause could influence their interior.

12. But besides the principle of change, there must be a *particular trait of what is changing*, which produces, so to speak, the specification and variety of the simple substances.

13. This particular must comprehend a multiplicity in the unity, that is, in the simple. For since all natural change proceeds by degrees, something changes and something remains. Consequently, there must be in the simple substance a plurality of affections and relations, though it has no parts.

14. The passing state which comprehends and represents a multiplicity in the unity or simple substance is nothing but what is called *perception*; it must be clearly distinguished from apperception or consciousness, as will become clear later on. On this point the Cartesian doctrine has been very defective, since it has entirely neglected those perceptions which are not apperceived; the same failure to distinguish has made the Cartesians believe that only spirits are monads, and that there are neither animal souls nor other entelechies. Therefore, they, like the unlearned, have confused a long swoon with death, strictly speaking, and yielded to the scholastic prejudice that there are entirely separated souls. The same error has even confirmed unsound minds in the opinion that souls are mortal.

15. The action of the internal principle which produces change, that is, the passage from one perception to another, may be called *appetition*. It is true that appetition may not always entirely attain the whole perception toward which it tends, but it always obtains something and arrives at new perceptions.

16. We ourselves experience a multiplicity in the simple substance, when we observe that the least thought which we apperceive in ourselves comprehends a variety in its object. Thus, all those who recognize that the soul is a simple substance must recognize this multiplicity in the monad. Pierre Bayle should not have found a difficulty in this theory, as he indeed did in the article "Rorarius" of his *Dictionary*.

17. Moreover, it must be avowed that *perception* and what depends upon it *cannot possibly be explained by mechanical reasons*, that is, by figure and movement. Suppose that there be a machine, the structure of which produces thinking, feeling, and perceiving; imagine this machine enlarged but preserving the same proportions, so that you could enter it as if it were a mill. This being supposed, you might visit its inside; but what would you observe there? Nothing but parts which push and move each other, and never anything that could explain perception. This explanation must therefore be sought in the simple substance, not in the composite, that is, in the machine. However, there is nothing else to be found in the simple substance but perceptions and their changes. In this alone can consist all the *internal actions* of simple substances.

18. The name *entelechies* would fit all the simple substances or created monads. For they have in themselves a certain perfection *[echousi to enteles]*, and they are endowed with a selfsufficiency *[autarkeia]* which makes them the sources of their own actions and, so to speak, incorporeal automata.

19. If we want to call *soul* all that has perception and appetition, in the general sense explained above, we might give the name soul to all simple substances or created monads. But since sensation is something more than a simple perception, I agree that the general name monad or entelechy may suffice for those simple substances which have nothing but perception and appetition; the name souls may then be reserved for those having perception that is more distinct and is accompanied by memory.

20. Indeed, we experience in ourselves a state in which we remember nothing and have no distinct perception at all, e.g., when we faint or are overcome by a deep and dreamless sleep. In this state the soul is not noticeably different from a simple monad. However, since this state does not last, the soul being able to pull itself out of it, the soul is more than a simple monad.

21. Besides, it does not follow at all that in such a state the simple substance entirely lacks perception. For the reasons propounded a while ago, this lack is not possible; for the monad cannot perish, nor can it subsist without some affection, which is nothing but its perception. But when there is a great multitude of minute perceptions lacking distinctness, one becomes dizzy: for example, when you turn around several consecutive times, you get a vertigo which may make you faint and leave you without any distinct perception. Death may throw animals into such a state for a time.

22. The present state of a simple substance is the natural result of its precedent state, so much so that the present is pregnant with the future.

23. Therefore, since on awakening from such a swoon, you apperceive your perceptions, it follows that you must have had some perceptions immediately before, though you did not apperceive them. For a perception cannot come naturally except from another perception, just as movement cannot come naturally except from another movement.

24. Hence it is evident that if in our perceptions there were nothing distinct nor anything, so to speak, in relief and of a more marked taste, we would always be in a swoon. And that is the state of the mere naked monads.

25. We see indeed that nature has given distinct perceptions to the animals, for care has been taken to provide them with organs which collect several light rays or several air waves, to unite them and thereby give them greater effect. Something similar occurs in scent, taste, and touch, and perhaps in many other senses unknown to us. I shall explain soon how what occurs in the soul represents what occurs in the sense organs.

26. Memory provides the souls with a sort of *consistency* which imitates reason but has to be distinguished from it. For we see that animals, perceiving something which impresses them and of which they have previously had a resembling perception, are brought by the representation of their memory to expect what has been associated with this perception in the past and are moved to feelings similar to those they had then. If you show a stick to a dog, for instance, it remembers the pain caused by it and howls or runs away.

27. The vividness of the imagination which strikes and moves animals comes from either the strength or the frequency of preceding perceptions. For often one strong impression produces at once the effect of a long *habit* or of many reiterated impressions of minor strength.

28. Men act like animals in so far as the succession of their perceptions is brought about by the principle of memory. In this they resemble medical empiricists whose practice is not backed by theory. In fact, we are mere empiricists in three quarters of all our actions. If you expect, for instance, that the sun will rise tomorrow be-

cause up to now it has always happened, you act as an empiricist. The astronomer alone judges by reason.

29. Knowledge of necessary and eternal truths, however, distinguishes us from mere animals and grants us *reason* and the sciences, elevating us to the knowledge of ourselves and of God. This possession is what is called our reasonable soul or *spirit*.

30. By this knowledge of necessary truths and by the abstractions made possible through them, we also are raised to *acts of reflection* which enable us to think of the so-called *self* and to consider this or that to be in us. Thinking thus about ourselves, we think of being, substance, the simple and the composite, the immaterial, and even of God, conceiving what is limited in us as without limit in him. These acts of reflection furnish the principal objects of our reasoning.

31. Our reasoning is founded on two great principles: The first is the principle of *contradiction*, by virtue of which we consider as false what implies a contradiction and as true what is the opposite of the contradictory or false.

32. The second is the principle of *sufficient reason*, by virtue of which we hold that no fact can be true or existing and no statement truthful without a sufficient reason for its being so and not different; albeit these reasons most frequently must remain unknown to us.

33. There are also two kinds of *truths*: those of *reason*, which are necessary and of which the opposite is impossible, and those of *fact*, which are contingent and of which the opposite is possible. When a truth is necessary, the reasons for it can be found through analysis, that is, by resolving it into simpler ideas and truths until one comes to primitives.

34. Thus the mathematicians, using the analytical method, reduce the speculative theorems and the practical canons to *definitions*, *axioms*, and *postulates*.

35. In the end, there are simple ideas of which no definition can be given. Moreover, there are axioms and postulates, in short, *primitive principles*, which cannot be demonstrated and do not need demonstration. They are *identical propositions*, the opposite of which contains an express contradiction.

36. A *sufficient reason*, however, must also exist for *contingent truths* or *truths of fact*, that is, for the series of things comprehended in the universe of creatures. Here the resolution into particular reasons could be continued without limit; for the variety of natural things is immense, and bodies are infinitely divided. There is an infinity of figures and movements, past and present, which contribute to the efficient cause of my presently writing this. And there is an infinity of minute inclinations and dispositions of my soul, which contribute to the final cause of my writing.

37. Now, all of this detail implies previous or more particular contingents, each of which again stands in need of a similar analysis to be accounted for, so that nothing is gained by such an analysis. The sufficient or ultimate reason must therefore exist outside the succession or series of contingent particulars, infinite though this series may be.

38. Consequently, the ultimate reason of all things must subsist in a necessary substance, in which all particular changes may exist only virtually as in its source: this substance is what we call *God*.

39. Now, this substance is the sufficient reason for all this particular existence which is, moreover, interconnected throughout. Hence, there is but one God, and this God suffices.

40. This Supreme Substance is unique, universal, and necessary. There is nothing existing apart from it which would be independent of it, and the existence of this

being is a simple consequence of its possibility. It follows that this substance does not admit of any limitation and must contain as much reality as is possible.

41. God, therefore, is absolutely perfect, *perfection* meaning the quantity of positive reality. In things which have limits, that is, in finite things, this perfection has to be strictly interpreted, namely as the quantity of positive reality within their given limits. But where there are no limits, namely in God, perfection is absolutely infinite.

42. It follows that creatures owe their perfections to the divine influence, but their imperfections to their proper nature, which is incapable of being without limits. For it is in this that they are distinguished from God. The created things' *original imperfection* manifests itself through the *natural inertia* of all bodies.

43. Moreover, it is true that in God is the source not only of all existence, but also of all essence endowed with reality, that is, the source of what is real in the possibles. For the divine understanding is the region of the eternal truths and of the ideas on which they depend, and without him there would not be anything real in the possibles; that is, without him there would not only be nothing existing, but even nothing possible.

44. Indeed, if there is to be any reality in the essences or possibles, that is, in the necessary truths, this reality must be founded on the existence of the necessary being whose essence implies its existence, that is, to which it suffices to be possible in order to be actual.

45. Thus God alone (or the necessary being) has the privilege of existing necessarily, provided only he be possible. Now, since nothing can hinder the possibility of the substance which contains no limits, no negation, and hence no contradiction, this provides a sufficient reason for the knowledge *a priori* of God's existence. Besides, we have proved it by the reality of the eternal truths. In addition, we also have proved this existence *a posteriori* by the existence of contingent beings. For the sufficient and ultimate reason of these can lie only in the necessary being which has in itself the reason of its existence.

46. It must not be imagined, however, as certain authors have imagined, that since the eternal truths depend upon God, they are arbitrary and depend upon his will. Descartes seems to have thought so, and after him Poiret. This is true only of the contingent truths which are based on the principle of fitness, that is, the choice of the best possible; while the necessary truths depend only on his understanding, of which they are the internal object.

47. Thus God is the only primitive unit or the only original simple substance, of which all the created or derivative monads are the products, born, so to speak, every moment by continual fulgurations from the divinity, and limited by the capacities of creatures, to which limitation is essential.

48. In God there are his *power* which is the source of everything, his *knowledge* which contains the particulars of the ideas, and finally his *will* which is the source of change or production and acts according to the principle of the best possible. Corresponding to these divine attributes, there is in the created monads the subject or basis, namely, the faculty of perception and the faculty of appetition. In God, however, these attributes are absolutely infinite and perfect, whereas in the created monads or *entelechies* (Hermolaus Barbarus translated this word into Latin by *perfectihabies*) these attributes are only likenesses, possessed by the monads in proportion to their perfections.

49. Creatures are said to act outwardly in so far as they have perfection, and to *suffer* from other creatures in so far as they are imperfect. Thus *activity* has to be attrib-

uted to the monad in so far as it has distinct perceptions, and passivity in so far as it has confused perceptions.

50. One creature is more perfect than another, in so far as there is found in the former a reason to account *a priori* for what is happening in the latter; this is why one says that the former acts upon the latter.

51. But in the simple substances this influence of one monad upon the other is but *ideal* and can take effect only through the intervention of God; in the ideas of God, indeed, any monad reasonably requires that in his ruling of all others, God, from the beginning, take that monad into consideration. For since no created monad can exercise a physical influence upon the interior of any other, this is the only means by which the one can depend upon the other.

52. By this means actions and passions among creatures are mutual. For when God compares two simple substances, he finds in either one reasons which oblige him to adjust the other to it. What appears as active in certain respects, consequently appears as passive from another point of view: it appears as *active* in so far as what is distinctly known in one monad serves to account for what happens in another; it appears as passive in so far as the reason for what happens in it is to be found in what is distinctly known in another.

53. Now, since in the divine ideas there is an infinity of possible universes of which only one can exist, the choice made by God must have a sufficient reason which determines him to the one rather than to another.

54. This reason can be found only in fitness, that is, in the degree of perfection contained in these worlds. For each possible has a right to claim existence in proportion to the perfection it involves. Thus nothing is entirely arbitrary.

55. This is the cause for the existence of the best, which is disclosed to him by his wisdom, determines his choice by his goodness, and is produced by his power.

56. This *connection* of all created things with every single one of them and their adaptation to every single one, as well as the connection and adaptation of every single thing to all others, has the result that every single substance stands in relations which express all the others. Whence every single substance is a perpetual living mirror of the universe.

57. Just as the same city regarded from different sides offers quite different aspects, and thus appears multiplied *by the perspective*, so it also happens that the infinite multitude of simple substances creates the appearance of as many different universes. Yet they are but perspectives of a single universe, varied according to the *points of view*, which differ in each monad.

58. This is the means of obtaining the greatest possible variety, together with the greatest possible order; in other words, it is the means of obtaining as much perfection as possible.

59. Only by this hypothesis (which I dare to call demonstrated) can the greatness of God be exalted as it ought to be. Pierre Bayle has recognized this when he objected to the hypothesis in the article "Rorarius" of his *Dictionary*. In that passage he was inclined to believe that I attributed to God too much, and even more than is possible. But he was unable to adduce any reason why this universal harmony, due to which every substance exactly expresses all the others through the relations it has with them, should be impossible.

60. In what I have just stated, there can also be discerned reasons *a priori* why things could not be different. For God, legislating the whole, has considered every part and particularly every monad. And since the nature of every monad is representative,

there is nothing which could limit it to representing only a part of all things. It is true, however, that this representation is but confused concerning the particulars of the whole universe and can be distinct concerning only a small part of all things, namely those which are either the nearest or the largest in respect to each of the monads. For otherwise every monad would be a deity. It is not in the objects of their knowledge, but in the modes of this knowledge that the monads are limited. All of them have a confused knowledge of the infinite, that is, of the whole; but they are limited and distinguished by the degrees of distinct perception.

61. The composite substances are in this respect symbols of the simples. For since all is a plenum, all matter is connected and all movement in the plenum produces some effect on the distant bodies, in proportion to the distance. Hence every body is affected not only by those with which it is in contact, and thus feels in some way everything that happens to them; but through them it also feels those that touch the ones with which it is in immediate contact. Hence it follows that this communication extends over any distance whatever. Consequently, every body experiences everything that goes on in the universe, so much so that he who sees everything might read in any body what is happening anywhere, and even what has happened or will happen. He would be able to observe in the present what is remote in both time and space: [*sumpnoia panta*], as Hippocrates stated. A soul, however, can read in itself only what is distinctly represented in it; it is unable to unfold all at once all its folds; for these go on into infinity.

62. Thus, every created monad represents the whole universe; nevertheless, it represents more distinctly the body which is particularly attached to it and of which it is the entelechy. And since this body expresses the whole universe through the interconnection of all the matter in the plenum, the soul, too, represents the whole universe by representing this body which in a particular manner belongs to it.

63. The body belonging to a monad which is its entelechy or its soul constitutes, together with this entelechy, what may be called a *living unit*, and together with this soul what may be called an *animal*. This body of a living being or of an animal is always an organism. For since every monad is, in its way, a mirror of the universe, and since the universe is ruled in a perfect order, there must also be an order in the representing, that is, in the perceptions of the soul, and consequently in the body. The representation of the universe in the body evinces this order.

64. Thus every body of a living being is a sort of divine machine or natural automaton, which infinitely surpasses all artificial automata. For a machine made by human art is not a machine in all its parts. The cog on a brass wheel, for instance, has parts or fragments which for us are no longer artificial things, and are no longer proper to the machine with respect to the purpose for which the wheel was designed. The machines of nature (namely, the living bodies) are, on the contrary, machines even in their smallest parts without any limit. Herein lies the difference between nature and art, that is, between divine and human art.

65. The author of nature, indeed, has been able to practice this divine and infinitely marvellous art because any portion of matter is not only infinitely divisible, as the ancients recognized, but also actually subdivided *ad infinitum*: every part having parts each of which has its own particular movement. For otherwise it would be impossible for every portion of matter to express the whole universe.

66. Hence it can be seen that in the smallest portion of matter there is a world of creatures, living beings, animals, entelechies, and souls.

67. Thus every portion of matter can be conceived as a garden full of plants or as a pond full of fish. But every branch of the plant, every limb of the animal, every drop of its humors, is again such a garden or such a pond.

68. And though the soil and the air in the intervals between the plants of the garden is not a plant, nor the water between the fishes a fish, yet these intervals contain again plants or fishes. But these living beings most frequently are so minute that they remain imperceptible to us.

69. Thus there is nothing uncultured, sterile or dead in the universe, no chaos, no disorder, though this may be what appears. It would be about the same with a pond seen from a distance: you would perceive a confused movement, a squirming of fishes, if I may say so, without discerning the single fish.

70. Hence it becomes clear that every living body has a dominant entelechy which in an animal is its soul. But the limbs of this living body are full of other living beings, plants or animals, each of which again has its entelechy or its dominant soul.

71. But you must not imagine—like some authors who have misinterpreted my thought—that each soul has a mass or portion of matter forever belonging or attached to it and that, consequently, it owns other living, though inferior, beings forever destined to serve it. For all bodies are, like rivers, in a perpetual flux; small parts enter and leave them continually.

72. Thus the soul changes its body bit by bit, and by degrees, so that it never is deprived all at once of all its organs; in animals there is frequently metamorphosis. Never, however, is there metempsychosis nor transmigration of souls. Nor are there any totally separate *souls*, nor *genii* without body. God alone is entirely bodiless.

73. This also proves that, strictly speaking, there never is either complete generation or perfect death, which would consist in the separation of the soul. What we call *generation* consists in developments and growths, just as what we call *death* consists in involutions and diminutions.

74. Philosophers formerly have been very perplexed concerning the origin of forms, entelechies, or souls. Today, however, it has been discovered through precise observations made on plants, insects, and animals that the organized bodies of nature are never produced out of a chaos or putrefaction, but always out of seeds, in which doubtless there has been some *preformation*. Hence it has been concluded, not only that the organized body was already in the seed before conception, but also that there was a soul in this body, and, in short, the animal itself. Through the conception, furthermore, the animal has only been disposed to a great transformation, namely to become an animal of a different species. Something similar can even be observed outside generation, as, for instance, when worms become flies, or caterpillars butterflies.

75. Those animals among which some are elevated by means of the conception to the grade of larger animals, may be called *spermatic*; while those among them which remain within their species, that is, the majority, are born, multiply, and are destroyed like the large animals. Only a small number of elect pass on to a greater stage.

76. This, so far, has been but half the truth. Therefore I have concluded that if it be true that the animal never begins naturally, it will not end naturally either, and that consequently there will be, strictly speaking, neither generation nor entire destruction, that is, death. These arguments made a posteriori and drawn from experience agree perfectly with my principles deduced *a priori* a while ago.

77. Thus it may be said that not only the soul (mirror of an indestructible universe) is indestructible, but also that the animal itself is indestructible, albeit its machine often partly perishes, and casts off or takes on organic accretions.

78. These principles have enabled me to propose a natural explanation for the union or conformity of the soul and the organized body. The soul follows its own laws, and so does the body. They meet by virtue of the *pre-established harmony* prevailing among all substances, since they all are representations of one and the same universe.

79. The souls act according to the laws of final causes, through appetitions, ends, and means. The bodies act according to the laws of efficient causes, that is, of motion. And the two realms, that of efficient causes and that of final causes, are in mutual harmony.

80. Descartes has recognized that souls cannot impart force to bodies, because there is always the same quantity of force in matter. He believed, however, that the soul was able to change the directions of bodies. For at his time it was unknown yet that there is a law of nature according to which the total direction of matter is equally conserved. If he had been aware of this, he would have hit upon my system of pre-established harmony.

81. This system maintains that bodies act as though there were no souls (assuming the impossible); and that souls act as though there were no bodies; and that both act as though the one influenced the other.

82. As to *spirits* or reasonable souls, I find that essentially all the living beings and animals have the same nature, as I have said before, namely that the animal and the soul begin with the world and end no more than the world. Nevertheless, the reasonable souls have this in particular, that their little spermatic animals have only ordinary or sensitive souls, as long as they remain undeveloped. As soon, however, as those who, so to speak, are elected attain human nature through an actual conception, their sensitive souls are promoted to the rank of human nature and to the prerogative of spirits.

83. Among other differences existing between ordinary souls and spirits, some of which I have already pointed out, there is also this one, that souls in general are living mirrors or images of the created universe, while the spirits are in addition the images of the Deity itself or of the author of nature himself. They are capable of knowing the system of the universe and of imitating some of it by architectonic specimens, each spirit being like a small deity in his field.

84. This is the reason why the spirits are capable of entering a kind of society with God, and why with respect to them he is not only as an inventor is to his machine (this being the relation of God to the other creatures), but also as a prince to his subjects and even as a father to his children.

85. Hence it may easily be concluded that the assemblage of all the spirits must compose the City of God, that is, the most perfect city possible, under the most perfect monarch possible.

86. This City of God, this truly universal monarchy, is a moral world within the natural world; it is among the works of God the most exalted and the most divine. In it consists veritably the glory of God: for he would be without glory unless his greatness and goodness were recognized and admired by the spirits. Properly speaking, his goodness is directed toward this divine City, while his wisdom and power manifest themselves everywhere.

87. We have established above the perfect harmony between two natural realms, that of efficient causes and the other of final causes. To this we must add here still another harmony, namely, between the physical realm of nature and the moral realm of grace, that is, between God considered as the architect of the machine of the universe, and God considered as the monarch of the divine city of the spirits.

88. This harmony has the result that events lead to grace through the very processes of nature, and that our globe, for instance, must be destroyed and repaired through natural processes at the moments when the government of the spirits so demands, to chastise some and to reward others.

89. One may add that God as the architect satisfies in all respects God as the legislator. Thus sin must entail punishment according to the order of nature and as the

very result of the mechanical structure of the universe; and, analogously, good actions will attract their rewards through machinelike corporeal processes. Of course, these results cannot be and ought not always to be obtained as an immediate consequence.

90. Finally, under this perfect government, no good action will remain without its reward, no evil action without its punishment. All events in this city conspire to the advantage of the good people, that is, of those who are not discontented in this great State; who, once they have fulfilled their duties, trust in providence and duly love and imitate the author of all good; who enjoy the contemplation of his perfections as required by the nature of the true *pure love*, which consists in taking pleasure in the felicity of the beloved. This pure love makes the wise and virtuous people work at everything that seems conformable to the divine will, presumed or antecedent, and yet renders them contented with any event that God actually brings about through his secret, consequent, and decisive will. They realize that, could we only understand sufficiently the order of the universe, we should find that this order surpasses all the wishes of the wisest and that it is impossible to improve it; that it is the best not only for the whole in general, but also for ourselves in particular. For ourselves, that is, provided we are duly attached to the author of all things, not only as to the architect and efficient cause of our being, but also as to the master and to the final cause who ought to provide the sole goal of our will and who alone can give us happiness.

GEORGE BERKELEY
1685–1753

George Berkeley was born near Kilkenny, Ireland, and, although an Anglican of English descent, he emphatically considered himself Irish. He studied at Kilkenny College and in 1700 went on to Trinity College, Dublin. There he read Descartes, Newton, and Locke. In 1707, he became a Fellow of the College and was ordained in the Anglican church. The next six years were the most philosophically productive in his life. In 1709, he published his *New Theory of Vision,* and in the following year his most important philosophic work, *A Treatise Concerning the Principles of Human Knowledge*. In 1711, he wrote *Discourse on Passive Obedience*. Two years later, he published a more popular exposition of the doctrine of his *Principles* in the form of *Three Dialogues Between Hylas and Philonous*.

For the next eleven years, Berkeley traveled widely, visiting with many of the great thinkers of his day. He became Dean of Derry in 1724, though most of his energy at this time seems to have been given to the founding of a college in the Bermudas. With promises of financial support, he sailed for Rhode Island in 1728 to establish farms for supplying his future college with food. Berkeley spent two and a half years in Rhode Island with his new wife and friends, waiting for the twenty-thousand pounds the government had promised. When the funds never arrived, he finally gave up and returned to London.

In 1733, he published *Alciphron, or The Minute Philosopher*, against the freethinkers (agnostics), and in the following year *The Analyst*, a criticism of Newton. That same year, he was made Bishop of Cloyne. For the next eighteen years, he energetically served his remote, poor diocese. Among the works he wrote during this period are *The Querist* (1737), which used questions to propose public works and education as remedies to the crushing poverty he observed, and *Siris* (1744), an unusual work dealing with the medicinal value of tar water. In 1751, he lost his eldest son, and the next year he moved to Oxford, where another son was beginning his studies. On January 14, 1753, Berkeley died suddenly; he was buried at Christ Church, Oxford.

*   *   *

Like Locke before him, Berkeley accepted the empiricist doctrine that all we can know are ideas and that ideas come from perception or reflection. But Berkeley saw a problem in Locke's assertion of an external world of material "substances" giving rise to perceptions. If all we can know are ideas, how can we know there is a world "out there" giving rise to our ideas? Locke had said that the primary qualities of an "external object" (such as extension and solidity) are "utterly inseparable" from the objects themselves, whereas this is not the case with secondary qualities (such as color, taste, etc.). But again, asked Berkeley, how can Locke know this? He cannot get "outside himself" to see which of his perceptions are actually a part of objects "out there." Berkeley concluded that Locke's philosophy will lead to skepticism, whereby we must admit that we cannot really know anything about the world "out there."

To avoid this skepticism, Berkeley made the radical claim that there is no "out there," or, more precisely, there is no *matter*. Berkeley's position, which is called "idealism," can be summed up in his famous phrase "*esse* is *percipi*": to be is to be perceived. What we call "bodies," or physical objects, are simply stable collections of perceptions to which we give names such as "apples," "trees," and so on. These collections of perceptions have no existence apart from a perceiving mind. The answer to the famous conundrum "If a tree falls in the forest and no one hears it, does it make a sound?" is that if no one is perceiving it, it not only does not make a sound, the tree does not even exist!

Does this mean that trees go out of existence when no one is left in the forest to perceive them and that they come back into existence when someone enters the forest to perceive them again? It would seem that Berkeley must accept this odd conclusion were it not for one important point: God never leaves the forest, and God is *always* perceiving the trees. By always holding all collections of perceptions in the divine mind, God ensures their continued existence and the perceived regularity in what we call "nature." This point has been classically formulated in the following limericks:

> There was a young man who said, "God,
> Must think it exceedingly odd
> If he finds that this tree
> Continues to be
> When there's no one about in the Quad."

> REPLY:
> "Dear Sir: Your astonishment's odd:
> I am always about in the Quad.
> And that's why the tree
> Continues to be,
> Since observed by, Yours faithfully, God."

Berkeley saw his philosophy as a commonsense attack on the metaphysical excesses of medieval Scholastics, Continental Rationalists, and even fellow empiricists such as Hobbes and Locke. Although Berkeley understood his philosophy to be common sense, his readers drew different conclusions. One prominent physician of his day claimed Berkeley was insane. The great Dr. Samuel Johnson dismissed Berkeley's ideas with his famous "I refute Berkeley *thus*" and then he kicked a rock. Of course, this did not refute Berkeley at all. It only proved Johnson had not understood Berkeley's point. Berkeley did not claim the non-existence of stones or that kicking a stone will not produce sensation. He claimed the rock did not exist apart from the perception of its solidity or the perception of pain when struck, and so on. An oft-repeated epitaph summarizes the general reaction to Berkeley: "His arguments produce no conviction, though they cannot be refuted."

*   *   *

In Berkeley's *Three Dialogues between Hylas and Philonous*, reprinted here complete, Hylas argues for materialism, whereas Philonous presents Berkeley's own position. The dialogue form allows Berkeley to expound his own philosophy while meeting various anticiated objections.

For general introductions to Berkeley, see G.J. Warnock, *Berkeley* (Harmondsworth, Middlesex: Penguin Books, 1953); Harry M. Bracken, *Berkeley* (New York: St. Martin's Press, 1974); J.O. Urmson, *Berkeley* (Oxford: Oxford University Press, 1982)—part of the Past Masters series, now reprinted in the combined volume John Dunn et al., eds., *The British Empiricists* (Oxford: Oxford University Press, 1992); and David Berman, *George Berkeley: Idealism and the Man* (Oxford: Oxford University Press, 1994). For interesting but difficult discussions of Berkeley's arguments, see George Pitcher, *Berkeley* (London: Routledge, 1977) or Kenneth Winkler, *Berkeley: An Interpretation* (Oxford: Oxford University Press, 1989). For collections of essays, see Gale W. Engle and Gabriele Taylor, eds., *Berkeley's Principles of Human Knowledge* (Belmont, CA: Wadsworth, 1968); Colin M. Turbayne, ed., *Berkeley: Critical and Interpretive Essays* (Minneapolis: University of Minnesota Press, 1982); John Foster and Howard Robinson, eds., *Essays on Berkeley: A Tercentennial Celebration* (Oxford: Oxford University Press, 1985); and D.M. Armstrong and C.B. Martin, *Berkeley: A Collection of Critical Essays* (Hamden, CT: Garland, 1992)—a reprint of the second half of *Locke and Berkeley: A Collection of Critical Essays* (Garden City, NY: Doubleday, 1968).

THREE DIALOGUES BETWEEN HYLAS AND PHILONOUS, IN OPPOSITION TO SCEPTICS AND ATHEISTS

THE FIRST DIALOGUE

PHILONOUS: Good morrow, Hylas: I did not expect to find you abroad so early.

HYLAS: It is indeed something unusual; but my thoughts were so taken up with a subject I was discoursing of last night, that finding I could not sleep, I resolved to rise and take a turn in the garden.

PHILONOUS: It happened well, to let you see what innocent and agreeable pleasures you lose every morning. Can there be a pleasanter time of the day, or a more delightful season of the year? That purple sky, those wild but sweet notes of birds, the fragrant bloom upon the trees and flowers, the gentle influence of the rising sun, these

Fruits and Dishes on the Table, by Jan Davids de Heem (1606–1683). The underlying theme of *Vanitas* in Dutch still life presents a dual message in the arrangement of fine and rare objects. On the one hand, the objects represent the joy of possessions and the good life, yet the half-eaten pie and the peeled fruit cause reflection on the brevity of human existence and the fleeting nature of material objects. Berkeley takes this a step further by denying material substance and claiming that such objects do not exist apart from a perceiving mind. (*Lauros-Giraudon/Art Resource*)

and a thousand nameless beauties of nature inspire the soul with secret transports; its faculties too being at this time fresh and lively, are fit for those meditations, which the solitude of a garden and tranquillity of the morning naturally dispose us to. But I am afraid I interrupt your thoughts: for you seemed very intent on something.

HYLAS: It is true, I was, and shall be obliged to you if you will permit me to go on in the same vein; not that I would by any means deprive myself of your company, for my thoughts always flow more easily in conversation with a friend, than when I am alone: but my request is, that you would suffer me to impart my reflexions to you.

PHILONOUS: With all my heart, it is what I should have requested myself if you had not prevented me.

HYLAS: I was considering the odd fate of those men who have in all ages, through an affectation of being distinguished from the vulgar, or some unaccountable turn of thought, pretended either to believe nothing at all, or to believe the most extravagant things in the world. This however might be borne, if their paradoxes and scepticism did not draw after them some consequences of general disadvantage to mankind. But the mischief lies here; that when men of less leisure see them who are supposed to have spent their whole time in the pursuits of knowledge professing an entire ignorance of all things, or advancing such notions as are repugnant to plain and commonly received principles, they will be tempted to entertain suspicions concerning the most important truths, which they had hitherto held sacred and unquestionable.

PHILONOUS: I entirely agree with you, as to the ill tendency of the affected doubts of some philosophers, and fantastical conceits of others. I am even so far gone of late in this way of thinking, that I have quitted several of the sublime notions I had got in their schools for vulgar opinions. And I give it you on my word; since this revolt from metaphysical notions to the plain dictates of nature and common sense, I find my understanding strangely enlightened, so that I can now easily comprehend a great many things which before were all mystery and riddle.

HYLAS: I am glad to find there was nothing in the accounts I heard of you.

PHILONOUS: Pray, what were those?

HYLAS: You were represented, in last night's conversation, as one who maintained the most extravagant opinion that ever entered into the mind of man, to wit, that there is no such thing as *material substance* in the world.

PHILONOUS: That there is no such thing as what philosophers call *material substance,* I am seriously persuaded: but, if I were made to see anything absurd or sceptical in this, I should then have the same reason to renounce this that I imagine I have now to reject the contrary opinion.

HYLAS: What! Can anything be more fantastical, more repugnant to common sense, or a more manifest piece of scepticism, than to believe there is no such thing as *matter?*

PHILONOUS: Softly, good Hylas. What if it should prove that you, who hold there is, are, by virtue of that opinion, a greater *sceptic,* and maintain more paradoxes and repugnances to common sense, than I who believe no such thing?

HYLAS: You may as soon persuade me, the part is greater than the whole, as that, in order to avoid absurdity and scepticism, I should ever be obliged to give up my opinion in this point

PHILONOUS: Well then, are you content to admit that opinion for true, which upon examination shall appear most agreeable to common sense, and remote from scepticism?

HYLAS: With all my heart. Since you are for raising disputes about the plainest things in nature, I am content for once to hear what you have to say.

PHILONOUS: Pray, Hylas, what do you mean by a *sceptic?*

HYLAS: I mean what all men mean—one that doubts of everything.

PHILONOUS: He then who entertains no doubts concerning some particular point, with regard to that point cannot be thought a *sceptic.*

HYLAS: I agree with you.

PHILONOUS: Whether does doubting consist in embracing the affirmative or negative side of a question?

HYLAS: In neither; for whoever understands English cannot but know that doubting signifies a suspense between both.

PHILONOUS: He then that denies any point, can no more be said to doubt of it, than he who affirms it with the same degree of assurance.

HYLAS: True.

PHILONOUS: And, consequently, for such his denial is no more to be esteemed a *sceptic* than the other.

HYLAS: I acknowledge it.

PHILONOUS: How comes it to pass then, Hylas, that you pronounce me a *sceptic,* because I deny what you affirm, to wit the existence of matter? Since, for aught you can tell I am as peremptory in my denial, as you in your affirmation.

HYLAS: Hold, Philonous, I have been a little out in my definition; but every false step a man makes in discourse is not to be insisted on. I said indeed that a sceptic was one who doubted of everything; but I should have added, or who denies the reality and truth of things.

PHILONOUS: What things? Do you mean the principles and theorems of sciences? But these you know are universal intellectual notions, and consequently independent of matter. The denial therefore of this does not imply the denying them.

HYLAS: I grant it. But are there no other things? What think you of distrusting the senses, of denying the real existence of sensible things, or pretending to know nothing of them. Is not this sufficient to denominate a man a *sceptic?*

PHILONOUS: Shall we therefore examine which of us it is that denies the reality of sensible things, or professes the greatest ignorance of them; since, if I take you rightly, he is to be esteemed the greatest *sceptic?*

HYLAS: That is what I desire.

PHILONOUS: What mean you by Sensible Things?

HYLAS: Those things which are perceived by the senses. Can you imagine that I mean anything else?

PHILONOUS: Pardon me, Hylas, if I am desirous clearly to apprehend your notions, since this may much shorten our inquiry. Suffer me then to ask you this farther question. Are those things only perceived by the senses which are perceived immediately? Or, may those things properly be said to be *sensible* which are perceived mediately, or not without the intervention of others?

HYLAS: I do not sufficiently understand you.

PHILONOUS: In reading a book, what I immediately perceive are the letters; but mediately, or by means of these, are suggested to my mind the notions of God, virtue, truth, &c. Now, that the letters are truly sensible things, or perceived by sense, there is no doubt: but I would know whether you take the things suggested by them to be so too.

HYLAS: No, certainly: it were absurd to think *God* or *virtue* sensible things; though they may be signified and suggested to the mind by sensible marks, with which they have an arbitrary connexion.

PHILONOUS: It seems then, that by *sensible things* you mean those only which can be perceived immediately by sense?

HYLAS: Right.

PHILONOUS: Does it not follow from this, that though I see one part of the sky red, and another blue, and that my reason does thence evidently conclude there must be some cause of that diversity of colours, yet that cause cannot be said to be a sensible thing, or perceived by the sense of seeing?

HYLAS: It does.

PHILONOUS: In like manner, though I hear variety of sounds, yet I cannot be said to hear the causes of those sounds?

HYLAS: You cannot.

PHILONOUS: And when by my touch I perceive a thing to be hot and heavy, I cannot say, with any truth or propriety, that I feel the cause of its heat or weight?

HYLAS: To prevent any more questions of this kind, I tell you once for all, that by *sensible things* I mean those only which are perceived by sense; and that in truth the senses perceive nothing which they do not perceive immediately: for they make no inferences. The deducing therefore of causes or occasions from effects and appearances, which alone are perceived by sense, entirely relates to reason.

PHILONOUS: This point then is agreed between us—That *sensible things are those only which are immediately perceived by sense.* You will farther inform me, whether we immediately perceive by sight anything beside light, and colours, and figures; or by hearing, anything but sounds; by the palate, anything beside tastes; by the smell, beside odours; or by the touch, more than tangible qualities.

HYLAS: We do not.

PHILONOUS: It seems, therefore, that if you take away all sensible qualities, there remains nothing sensible?

HYLAS: I grant it.

PHILONOUS: Sensible things therefore are nothing else but so many sensible qualities, or combinations of sensible qualities?

HYLAS: Nothing else.

PHILONOUS: Heat then is a sensible thing?

HYLAS: Certainly.

PHILONOUS: Does the reality of sensible things consist in being perceived? Or, is it something distinct from their being perceived, and that bears no relation to the mind?

HYLAS: To *exist* is one thing, and to be *perceived* is another.

PHILONOUS: I speak with regard to sensible things only. And of these I ask, whether by their real existence you mean a subsistence exterior to the mind, and distinct from their being perceived?

HYLAS: I mean a real absolute being, distinct from, and without any relation to, their being perceived.

PHILONOUS: Heat therefore, if it be allowed a real being, must exist without the mind?

HYLAS: It must.

PHILONOUS: Tell me, Hylas, is this real existence equally compatible to all degrees of heat, which we perceive; or is there any reason why we should attribute it to some, and deny it to others? And if there be, pray let me know that reason.

HYLAS: Whatever degree of heat we perceive by sense, we may be sure the same exists in the object that occasions it.

PHILONOUS: What! The greatest as well as the least?

HYLAS: I tell you, the reason is plainly the same in respect of both. They are both perceived by sense; nay, the greater degree of heat is more sensibly perceived, and consequently, if there is any difference, we are more certain of its real existence than we can be of the reality of a lesser degree.

PHILONOUS: But is not the most vehement and intense degree of heat a very great pain?

HYLAS: No one can deny it.

PHILONOUS: And is any unperceiving thing capable of pain or pleasure?

HYLAS: No, certainly.

PHILONOUS: Is your material substance a senseless being, or a being endowed with sense and perception?

HYLAS: It is senseless without doubt.

PHILONOUS: It cannot therefore be the subject of pain?

HYLAS: By no means.

PHILONOUS: Nor consequently of the greatest heat perceived by sense, since you acknowledge this to be no small pain?

HYLAS: I grant it.

PHILONOUS: What shall we say then of your external object; is it a material substance, or no?

HYLAS: It is a material substance with the sensible qualities inhering in it.

PHILONOUS: How then can a great heat exist in it, since you own it cannot in a material substance? I desire you would clear this point.

HYLAS: Hold, Philonous, I fear I was out in yielding intense heat to be a pain. It should seem rather, that pain is something distinct from heat, and the consequence or effect of it.

PHILONOUS: Upon putting your hand near the fire, do you perceive one simple uniform sensation, or two distinct sensations?

HYLAS: But one simple sensation.

PHILONOUS: Is not the heat immediately perceived?

HYLAS: It is.

PHILONOUS: And the pain?

HYLAS: True.

PHILONOUS: Seeing therefore they are both immediately perceived at the same time, and the fire affects you only with one simple or uncompounded idea, it follows that this same simple idea is both the intense heat immediately perceived, and the pain; and, consequently, that the intense heat immediately perceived is nothing distinct from a particular sort of pain.

HYLAS: It seems so.

PHILONOUS: Again, try in your thoughts, Hylas, if you can conceive a vehement sensation to be without pain or pleasure.

HYLAS: I cannot.

PHILONOUS: Or can you frame to yourself an idea of sensible pain or pleasure in general, abstracted from every particular idea of heat, cold, tastes, smells? &c.

HYLAS: I do not find that I can.

PHILONOUS: Does it not therefore follow, that sensible pain is nothing distinct from those sensations or ideas, in an intense degree?

HYLAS: It is undeniable; and, to speak the truth, I begin to suspect a very great heat cannot exist but in a mind perceiving it.

PHILONOUS: What! Are you then in that *sceptical* state of suspense, between affirming and denying?

HYLAS: I think I may be positive in the point. A very violent and painful heat cannot exist without the mind.

PHILONOUS: It hath not therefore, according to you, any real being?

HYLAS: I own it.

PHILONOUS: Is it therefore certain, that there is no body in nature really hot?

HYLAS: I have not denied there is any real heat in bodies. I only say, there is no such thing as an intense real heat.

PHILONOUS: But, did you not say before that all degrees of heat were equally real; or, if there was any difference, that the greater were more undoubtedly real than the lesser?

HYLAS: True: but it was because I did not then consider the ground there is for distinguishing between them, which I now plainly see. And it is this: because intense heat is nothing else but a particular kind of painful sensation; and pain cannot exist but in a perceiving being; it follows that no intense heat can really exist in an unperceiving corporeal substance. But this is no reason why we should deny heat in an inferior degree to exist in such a substance.

PHILONOUS: But how shall we be able to discern those degrees of heat which exist only in the mind from those which exist without it?

HYLAS: That is no difficult matter. You know the least pain cannot exist unperceived; whatever, therefore, degree of heat is a pain exists only in the mind. But, as for all other degrees of heat, nothing obliges us to think the same of them.

PHILONOUS: I think you granted before that no unperceiving being was capable of pleasure, any more than of pain.

HYLAS: I did.

PHILONOUS: And is not warmth, or a more gentle degree of heat than what causes uneasiness, a pleasure?

HYLAS: What then?

PHILONOUS: Consequently, it cannot exist without the mind in an unperceiving substance, or body.

HYLAS: So it seems.

PHILONOUS: Since, therefore, as well those degrees of heat that are not painful, as those that are, can exist only in a thinking substance; may we not conclude that external bodies are absolutely incapable of any degree of heat whatsoever?

HYLAS: On second thoughts, I do not think it so evident that warmth is a pleasure as that a great degree of heat is a pain.

PHILONOUS: I do not pretend that warmth is as great a pleasure as heat is a pain. But, if you grant it to be even a small pleasure, it serves to make good my conclusion.

HYLAS: I could rather call it an *indolence*. It seems to be nothing more than a privation of both pain and pleasure. And that such a quality or state as this may agree to an unthinking substance, I hope you will not deny.

PHILONOUS: If you are resolved to maintain that warmth, or a gentle degree of heat, is no pleasure, I know not how to convince you otherwise than by appealing to your own sense. But what think you of cold?

HYLAS: The same that I do of heat. An intense degree of cold is a pain; for to feel a very great cold, is to perceive a great uneasiness: it cannot therefore exist without the mind; but a lesser degree of cold may, as well as a lesser degree of heat.

PHILONOUS: Those bodies, therefore, upon whose application to our own, we perceive a moderate degree of heat, must be concluded to have a moderate degree of heat or warmth in them—and those, upon whose application we feel a like degree of cold, must be thought to have cold in them.

HYLAS: They must.

PHILONOUS: Can any doctrine be true that necessarily leads a man into an absurdity?

HYLAS: Without doubt it cannot.

PHILONOUS: Is it not an absurdity to think that the same thing should be at the same time both cold and warm?

HYLAS: It is.

PHILONOUS: Suppose now one of your hands hot, and the other cold, and that they are both at once put into the same vessel of water, in an intermediate state; will not the water seem cold to one hand, and warm to the other?

HYLAS: It will.

PHILONOUS: Ought we not therefore, by your principles, to conclude it is really both cold and warm at the same time, that is, according to your own concession, to believe an absurdity?

HYLAS: I confess it seems so.

PHILONOUS: Consequently, the principles themselves are false, since you have granted that no true principle leads to an absurdity.

HYLAS: But, after all, can anything be more absurd than to say, *there is no heat in the fire?*

PHILONOUS: To make the point still clearer; tell me whether, in two cases exactly alike, we ought not to make the same judgment?

HYLAS: We ought.

PHILONOUS: When a pin pricks your finger, does it not rend and divide the fibres of your flesh?

HYLAS: It does.

PHILONOUS: And when a coal burns your finger, does it any more?

HYLAS: It does not.

PHILONOUS: Since, therefore, you neither judge the sensation itself occasioned by the pin, nor anything like it to be in the pin; you should not, conformably to what you have now granted, judge the sensation occasioned by the fire, or anything like it, to be in the fire.

HYLAS: Well, since it must be so, I am content to yield this point, and acknowledge that heat and cold are only sensations existing in our minds. But there still remain qualities enough to secure the reality of external things.

PHILONOUS: But what will you say, Hylas, if it shall appear that the case is the same with regard to all other sensible qualities, and that they can no more be supposed to exist without the mind, than heat and cold?

HYLAS: Then indeed you will have done something to the purpose; but that is what I despair of seeing proved.

PHILONOUS: Let us examine them in order. What think you of tastes—do they exist without the mind, or no?

HYLAS: Can any man in his senses doubt whether sugar is sweet, or wormwood bitter?

PHILONOUS: Inform me, Hylas. Is a sweet taste a particular kind of pleasure or pleasant sensation, or is it not?

HYLAS: It is.

PHILONOUS: And is not bitterness some kind of uneasiness or pain?

HYLAS: I grant it.

PHILONOUS: If therefore sugar and wormwood are unthinking corporeal substances existing without the mind, how can sweetness and bitterness, that is, pleasure and pain, agree to them?

HYLAS: Hold, Philonous, I now see what it was deluded me all this time. You asked whether heat and cold, sweetness and bitterness, were not particular sorts of pleasure and pain; to which I answered simply, that they were. Whereas I should have thus distinguished:—those qualities, as perceived by us, are pleasures or pains; but not as existing in the external objects. We must not therefore conclude absolutely, that there is no heat in the fire, or sweetness in the sugar, but only that heat or sweetness, as perceived by us, are not in the fire or sugar. What say you to this?

PHILONOUS: I say it is nothing to the purpose. Our discourse proceeded altogether concerning sensible things, which you defined to be, the things we *immediately perceive by our senses.* Whatever other qualities, therefore, you speak of as distinct from these, I know nothing of them, neither do they at all belong to the point in dispute. You may, indeed, pretend to have discovered certain qualities which you do not perceive, and assert those insensible qualities exist in fire and sugar. But what use can be made of this to your present purpose, I am at a loss to conceive. Tell me then once more, do you acknowledge that heat and cold, sweetness and bitterness (meaning those qualities which are perceived by the senses), do not exist without the mind?

HYLAS: I see it is to no purpose to hold out, so I give up the cause as to those mentioned qualities. Though I profess it sounds oddly, to say that sugar is not sweet.

PHILONOUS: But, for your farther satisfaction, take this along with you: that which at other times seems sweet, shall, to a distempered palate, appear bitter. And, nothing can be plainer than that divers persons perceive different tastes in the same food; since that which one man delights in, another abhors. And how could this be, if the taste was something really inherent in the food?

HYLAS: I acknowledge I know not how.

PHILONOUS: In the next place, *odours* are to be considered. And, with regard to these, I would fain know whether what hath been said of tastes does not exactly agree to them? Are they not so many pleasing or displeasing sensations?

HYLAS: They are.

PHILONOUS: Can you then conceive it possible that they should exist in an unperceiving thing?

HYLAS: I cannot.

PHILONOUS: Or, can you imagine that filth and ordure affect those brute animals that feed on them out of choice, with the same smells which we perceive in them?

HYLAS: By no means.

PHILONOUS: May we not therefore conclude of smells, as of the other forementioned qualities, that they cannot exist in any but a perceiving substance or mind?

HYLAS: I think so.

PHILONOUS: Then as to *sounds,* what must we think of them: are they accidents really inherent in external bodies, or not?

HYLAS: That they inhere not in the sonorous bodies is plain from hence: because a bell struck in the exhausted receiver of an air- pump sends forth no sound. The air, therefore, must be thought the subject of sound.

PHILONOUS: What reason is there for that, Hylas?

HYLAS: Because, when any motion is raised in the air, we perceive a sound greater or lesser, according to the air's motion; but without some motion in the air, we never hear any sound at all.

PHILONOUS: And granting that we never hear a sound but when some motion is produced in the air, yet I do not see how you can infer from thence, that the sound itself is in the air.

HYLAS: It is this very motion in the external air that produces in the mind the sensation of *sound.* For, striking on the drum of the ear, it causes a vibration, which by the auditory nerves being communicated to the brain, the soul is thereupon affected with the sensation called *sound.*

PHILONOUS: What! Is sound then a sensation?

HYLAS: I tell you, as perceived by us, it is a particular sensation in the mind.

PHILONOUS: And can any sensation exist without the mind?

HYLAS: No, certainly.

PHILONOUS: How then can sound, being a sensation, exist in the air, if by the *air* you mean a senseless substance existing without the mind?

HYLAS: You must distinguish, Philonous, between sound as it is perceived by us, and as it is in itself; or (which is the same thing) between the sound we immediately perceive, and that which exists without us. The former, indeed, is a particular kind of sensation, but the latter is merely a vibrative or undulatory motion in the air.

PHILONOUS: I thought I had already obviated that distinction, by the answer I gave when you were applying it in a like case before. But, to say no more of that, are you sure then that sound is really nothing but motion?

HYLAS: I am.

PHILONOUS: Whatever therefore agrees to real sound, may with truth be attributed to motion?

HYLAS: It may.

PHILONOUS: It is then good sense to speak of *motion* as of a thing that is *loud, sweet, acute,* or *grave.*

HYLAS: I see you are resolved not to understand me. Is it not evident those accidents or modes belong only to sensible sound, or *sound* in the common acceptation of the word, but not to *sound* in the real and philosophic sense; which, as I just now told you, is nothing but a certain motion of the air?

PHILONOUS: It seems then there are two sorts of sound—the one vulgar, or that which is heard, the other philosophical and real?

HYLAS: Even so.

PHILONOUS: And the latter consists in motion?

HYLAS: I told you so before.

PHILONOUS: Tell me, Hylas, to which of the senses, think you, the idea of motion belongs? To the hearing?

HYLAS: No, certainly; but to the sight and touch.

PHILONOUS: It should follow then, that, according to you, real sounds may possibly be *seen* or *felt,* but never *heard.*

HYLAS: Look you, Philonous, you may, if you please, make a jest of my opinion, but that will not alter the truth of things. I own, indeed, the inferences you draw me into sound something oddly, but common language, you know, is framed by, and for the use of the vulgar: we must not therefore wonder if expressions adapted to exact philosophic notions seem uncouth and out of the way.

PHILONOUS: Is it come to that? I assure you, I imagine myself to have gained no small point, since you make so light of departing from common phrases and opinions; it being a main part of our inquiry, to examine whose notions are widest of the common road, and most repugnant to the general sense of the world. But, can you think it no more than a philosophical paradox, to say that *real sounds are never heard,* and that the idea of them is obtained by some other sense? And is there nothing in this contrary to nature and the truth of things?

HYLAS: To deal ingenuously, I do not like it. And, after the concessions already made, I had as well grant that sounds too have no real being without the mind.

PHILONOUS: And I hope you will make no difficulty to acknowledge the same of colours.

HYLAS: Pardon me: the case of colours is very different. Can anything be plainer than that we see them on the objects?

PHILONOUS: The objects you speak of are I suppose, corporeal substances existing without the mind?

HYLAS: They are.

PHILONOUS: And have true and real colours inhering in them?

HYLAS: Each visible object hath that colour which we see in it.

PHILONOUS: How! Is there anything visible but what we perceive by sight?

HYLAS: There is not.

PHILONOUS: And, do we perceive anything by sense which we do not perceive immediately?

HYLAS: How often must I be obliged to repeat the same thing? I tell you, we do not.

PHILONOUS: Have patience, good Hylas; and tell me once more, whether there is anything immediately perceived by the senses, except sensible qualities. I know you asserted there was not; but I would now be informed, whether you still persist in the same opinion.

HYLAS: I do.

PHILONOUS: Pray, is your corporeal substance either a sensible quality, or made up of sensible qualities?

HYLAS: What a question that is! Who ever thought it was?

PHILONOUS: My reason for asking was, because in saying, *each visible object hath that colour which we see in it,* you make visible objects to be corporeal substances; which implies either that corporeal substances are sensible qualities, or else that there is something besides sensible qualities perceived by sight: but, as this point was formerly agreed between us, and is still maintained by you, it is a clear consequence, that your corporeal substance is nothing distinct from sensible qualities.

HYLAS: You may draw as many absurd consequences as you please, and endeavour to perplex the plainest things; but you shall never persuade me out of my senses. I clearly understand my own meaning.

PHILONOUS: I wish you would make me understand it too. But, since you are unwilling to have your notion of corporeal substance examined, I shall urge that point no farther. Only be pleased to let me know, whether the same colours which we see exist in external bodies, or some other.

HYLAS: The very same.

PHILONOUS: What! Are then the beautiful red and purple we see on yonder clouds really in them? Or do you imagine, they have in themselves any other form than that of a dark mist or vapour?

HYLAS: I must own, Philonous, those colours are not really in the clouds as they seem to be at this distance. They are only apparent colours.

PHILONOUS: *Apparent* call you them? How shall we distinguish these apparent colours from real?

HYLAS: Very easily. Those are to be thought apparent which, appearing only at a distance, vanish upon a nearer approach.

PHILONOUS: And those, I suppose, are to be thought real which are discovered by the most near and exact survey.

HYLAS: Right.

PHILONOUS: Is the nearest and exactest survey made by the help of a microscope, or by the naked eye?

HYLAS: By a microscope, doubtless.

PHILONOUS: But a microscope often discovers colours in an object different from those perceived by the unassisted sight. And, in case we had microscopes magnifying to any assigned degree, it is certain that no object whatsoever, viewed through them, would appear in the same colour which it exhibits to the naked eye.

HYLAS: And what will you conclude from all this? You cannot argue that there are really and naturally no colours on objects: because by artificial managements they may be altered, or made to vanish.

PHILONOUS: I think it may evidently be concluded from your own concessions, that all the colours we see with our naked eyes are only apparent as those on the clouds, since they vanish upon a more close and accurate inspection which is afforded us by a microscope. Then, as to what you say by way of prevention: I ask you whether the real and natural state of an object is better discovered by a very sharp and piercing sight, or by one which is less sharp?

HYLAS: By the former without doubt.

PHILONOUS: Is it not plain from *Dioptrics* that microscopes make the sight more penetrating, and represent objects as they would appear to the eye in case it were naturally endowed with a most exquisite sharpness?

HYLAS: It is.

PHILONOUS: Consequently the microscopical representation is to be thought that which best sets forth the real nature of the thing, or what it is in itself. The colours, therefore, by it perceived are more genuine and real than those perceived otherwise.

HYLAS: I confess there is something in what you say.

PHILONOUS: Besides, it is not only possible but manifest, that there actually are animals whose eyes are by nature framed to perceive those things which by reason of their minuteness escape our sight. What think you of those inconceivably small animals perceived by glasses? Must we suppose they are all stark blind? Or, in case they see, can it be imagined their sight hath not the same use in preserving their bodies from injuries, which appears in that of all other animals? And if it hath, is it not evident they must see particles less than their own bodies; which will present them with a far different view in each object from that which strikes our senses? Even our own eyes do not always represent objects to us after the same manner. In the jaundice every one knows that all things seem yellow. Is it not therefore highly probable those animals in whose eyes we discern a very different texture from that of ours, and whose bodies abound with different humors, do not see the same colours in every object that we do? From all which, should it not seem to follow that all colours are equally apparent, and that none of those which we perceive are really inherent in any outward object?

HYLAS: It should.

PHILONOUS: The point will be past all doubt, if you consider that, in case colours were real properties or affections inherent in external bodies, they could admit of no alteration without some change wrought in the very bodies themselves: but, is it not evident from what hath been said that, upon the use of microscopes, upon a change happening in the humors of the eye, or a variation of distance, without any manner of real alteration in the thing itself, the colours of any object are either changed, or totally disappear? Nay, all other circumstances remaining the same, change but the situation of some objects, and they shall present different colours to the eye. The same thing happens upon viewing an object in various degrees of light. And what is more known than that the same bodies appear differently colored by candle-light from what they do in the open day? Add to these the experiment of a prism which, separating the heterogeneous rays of light, alters the colour of any object, and will cause the whitest to appear of a deep blue or red to the naked eye. And now tell me whether you are still of opinion that every body hath its true real colour inhering in it; and, if you think it hath, I would fain know farther from you, what certain distance and position of the object, what peculiar texture and formation of the eye, what degree or kind of light is necessary for ascertaining that true colour, and distinguishing it from apparent ones.

Hylas: I own myself entirely satisfied, that they are all equally apparent, and that there is no such thing as colour really inhering in external bodies, but that it is altogether in the light. And what confirms me in this opinion is, that in proportion to the light colours are still more or less vivid; and if there be no light, then are there no colours perceived. Besides, allowing there are colours on external objects, yet, how is it possible for us to perceive them? For no external body affects the mind, unless it acts first on our organs of sense. But the only action of bodies is motion; and motion cannot be communicated otherwise than by impulse. A distant object therefore cannot act on the eye, nor consequently make itself or its properties perceivable to the soul. Whence it plainly follows that it is immediately some contiguous substance, which, operating on the eye, occasions a perception of colours: and such is light.

Philonous: How! Is light then a substance?

Hylas: I tell you, Philonous, external light is nothing but a thin fluid substance, whose minute particles being agitated with a brisk motion, and in various manners reflected from the different surfaces of outward objects to the eyes, communicate different motions to the optic nerves; which, being propagated to the brain, cause therein various impressions; and these are attended with the sensations of red, blue, yellow, &c.

Philonous: It seems then the light does no more than shake the optic nerves.

Hylas: Nothing else.

Philonous: And consequent to each particular motion of the nerves, the mind is affected with a sensation, which is some particular colour.

Hylas: Right.

Philonous: And these sensations have no existence without the mind.

Hylas: They have not.

Philonous: How then do you affirm that colours are in the light; since by light you understand a corporeal substance external to the mind?

Hylas: Light and colours, as immediately perceived by us, I grant cannot exist without the mind. But in themselves they are only the motions and configurations of certain insensible particles of matter.

Philonous: Colours then, in the vulgar sense, or taken for the immediate objects of sight, cannot agree to any but a perceiving substance.

Hylas: That is what I say.

Philonous: Well then, since you give up the point as to those sensible qualities which are alone thought colours by all mankind beside, you may hold what you please with regard to those invisible ones of the philosophers. It is not my business to dispute about them; only I would advise you to bethink yourself, whether, considering the inquiry we are upon, it be prudent for you to affirm—*the red and blue which we see are not real colours, but certain unknown motions and figures which no man ever did or can see are truly so.* Are not these shocking notions, and are not they subject to as many ridiculous inferences, as those you were obliged to renounce before in the case of sounds?

Hylas: I frankly own, Philonous, that it is in vain to stand out any longer. Colours, sounds, tastes, in a word all those termed *secondary qualities,* have certainly no existence without the mind. But by this acknowledgment I must not be supposed to derogate anything from the reality of matter, or external objects; seeing it is no more than several philosophers maintain, who nevertheless are the farthest imaginable from denying matter. For the clearer understanding of this, you must know sensible qualities are by philosophers divided into *primary* and *secondary*. The former are extension, figure, solidity, gravity, motion, and rest; and these they hold exist really in bodies. The latter are those above enumerated; or, briefly, all sensible qualities beside the primary; which they assert are only so many sensations or ideas existing nowhere but in the mind. But all this, I doubt not, you are apprised of. For my part, I have been a long time sensible there was such an opinion current among philosophers, but was never thoroughly convinced of its truth until now.

PHILONOUS: You are still then of opinion that extension and figures are inherent in external unthinking substances?

HYLAS: I am.

PHILONOUS: But what if the same arguments which are brought against secondary qualities will hold good against these also?

HYLAS: Why then I shall be obliged to think, they too exist only in the mind.

PHILONOUS: Is it your opinion the very figure and extension which you perceive by sense exist in the outward object or material substance?

HYLAS: It is.

PHILONOUS: Have all other animals as good grounds to think the same of the figure and extension which they see and feel?

HYLAS: Without doubt, if they have any thought at all.

PHILONOUS: Answer me, Hylas. Think you the senses were bestowed upon all animals for their preservation and well-being in life? Or were they given to men alone for this end?

HYLAS: I make no question but they have the same use in all other animals.

PHILONOUS: If so, is it not necessary they should be enabled by them to perceive their own limbs, and those bodies which are capable of harming them?

HYLAS: Certainly.

PHILONOUS: A mite therefore must be supposed to see his own foot, and things equal or even less than it, as bodies of some considerable dimension, though at the same time they appear to you scarce discernible, or at best as so many visible points?

HYLAS: I cannot deny it.

PHILONOUS: And to creatures less than the mite they will seem yet larger?

HYLAS: They will.

PHILONOUS: Insomuch that what you can hardly discern will to another extremely minute animal appear as some huge mountain?

HYLAS: All this I grant.

PHILONOUS: Can one and the same thing be at the same time in itself of different dimensions?

HYLAS: That were absurd to imagine.

PHILONOUS: But, from what you have laid down it follows that both the extension by you perceived, and that perceived by the mite itself, as likewise all those perceived by lesser animals, are each of them the true extension of the mite's foot; that is to say, by your own principles you are led into an absurdity.

HYLAS: There seems to be some difficulty in the point.

PHILONOUS: Again, have you not acknowledged that no real inherent property of any object can be changed without some change in the thing itself?

HYLAS: I have.

PHILONOUS: But, as we approach to or recede from an object, the visible extension varies, being at one distance ten or a hundred times greater than another. Does it not therefore follow from hence likewise that it is not really inherent in the object?

HYLAS: I own I am at a loss what to think.

PHILONOUS: Your judgment will soon be determined, if you will venture to think as freely concerning this quality as you have done concerning the rest. Was it not admitted as a good argument, that neither heat nor cold was in the water, because it seemed warm to one hand and cold to the other?

HYLAS: It was.

PHILONOUS: Is it not the very same reasoning to conclude, there is no extension or figure in an object, because to one eye it shall seem little, smooth, and round, when at the same time it appears to the other, great, uneven, and regular?

HYLAS: The very same. But does this latter fact ever happen?

PHILONOUS: You may at any time make the experiment, by looking with one eye bare, and with the other through a microscope.

HYLAS: I know not how to maintain it; and yet I am loath to give up *extension,* I see so many odd consequences following upon such a concession.

PHILONOUS: Odd, say you? After the concessions already made, I hope you will stick at nothing for its oddness. But, on the other hand, should it not seem very odd, if the general reasoning which includes all other sensible qualities did not also include extension? If it be allowed that no idea, nor anything like an idea, can exist in an unperceiving substance, then surely it follows that no figure, or mode of extension, which we can either perceive, or imagine, or have any idea of, can be really inherent in matter; not to mention the peculiar difficulty there must be in conceiving a material substance, prior to and distinct from extension to be the *substratum* of extension. Be the sensible quality what it will—figure, or sound, or colour, it seems alike impossible it should subsist in that which does not perceive it.

HYLAS: I give up the point for the present, reserving still a right to retract my opinion, in case I shall hereafter discover any false step in my progress to it.

PHILONOUS: That is a right you cannot be denied. Figures and extension being dispatched, we proceed next to *motion.* Can a real motion in any external body be at the same time very swift and very slow?

HYLAS: It cannot.

PHILONOUS: Is not the motion of a body swift in a reciprocal proportion to the time it takes up in describing any given space? Thus a body that describes a mile in an hour moves three times faster than it would in case it described only a mile in three hours.

HYLAS: I agree with you.

PHILONOUS: And is not time measured by the succession of ideas in our minds?

HYLAS: It is.

PHILONOUS: And is it not possible ideas should succeed one another twice as fast in your mind as they do in mine, or in that of some spirit of another kind?

HYLAS: I own it.

PHILONOUS: Consequently the same body may to another seem to perform its motion over any space in half the time that it does to you. And the same reasoning will hold as to any other proportion: that is to say, according to your principles (since the motions perceived are both really in the object) it is possible one and the same body shall be really moved the same way at once, both very swift and very slow. How is this consistent either with common sense, or with what you just now granted?

HYLAS: I have nothing to say to it.

PHILONOUS: Then as for *solidity;* either you do not mean any sensible quality by that word, and so it is beside our inquiry: or if you do, it must be either hardness or resistance. But both the one and the other are plainly relative to our senses: it being evident that what seems hard to one animal may appear soft to another, who hath greater force and firmness of limbs. Nor is it less plain that the resistance I feel is not in the body.

HYLAS: I own the very sensation of resistance, which is all you immediately perceive, is not in the *body;* but the cause of that sensation is.

PHILONOUS: But the causes of our sensations are not things immediately perceived, and therefore are not sensible. This point I thought had been already determined.

HYLAS: I own it was; but you will pardon me if I seem a little embarrassed: I know not how to quit my old notions.

PHILONOUS: To help you out, do but consider that if extension be once acknowledged to have no existence without the mind, the same must necessarily be granted of motion, solidity, and gravity; since they all evidently suppose extension. It is therefore superfluous to inquire particularly concerning each of them. In denying extension, you have denied them all to have any real existence.

HYLAS: I wonder, Philonous, if what you say be true, why those philosophers who deny the secondary qualities any real existence should yet attribute it to the primary. If there is no difference between them, how can this be accounted for?

PHILONOUS: It is not my business to account for every opinion of the philosophers. But, among other reasons which may be assigned for this, it seems probable that pleasure and pain being rather annexed to the former than the latter may be one. Heat and cold, tastes and smells, have something more vividly pleasing or disagreeable than the ideas of extension, figure, and motion affect us with. And, it being too visibly absurd to hold that pain or pleasure can be in an unperceiving substance, men are more easily weaned from believing the external existence of the secondary than the primary qualities. You will be satisfied there is something in this, if you recollect the difference you made between an intense and more moderate degree of heat; allowing the one a real existence, while you denied it to the other. But, after all, there is no rational ground for that distinction; for, surely an indifferent sensation is as truly a *sensation* as one more pleasing or painful; and consequently should not any more than they be supposed to exist in an unthinking subject.

HYLAS: It is just come into my head, Philonous, that I have somewhere heard of a distinction between absolute and sensible extension. Now, though it be acknowledged that *great* and *small,* consisting merely in the relation which other extended beings have to the parts of our own bodies, do not really inhere in the substances themselves; yet nothing obliges us to hold the same with regard to *absolute extension,* which is something abstracted from *great* and *small,* from this or that particular magnitude or figure. So likewise as to motion; *swift* and *slow* are altogether relative to the succession of ideas in our own minds. But, it does not follow, because those modifications of motion exist not without the mind, that therefore absolute motion abstracted from them does not.

PHILONOUS: Pray what is it that distinguishes one motion, or one part of extension, from another? Is it not something sensible, as some degree of swiftness or slowness, some certain magnitude or figure peculiar to each?

HYLAS: I think so.

PHILONOUS: These qualities, therefore, stripped of all sensible properties, are without all specific and numerical differences, as the schools call them.

HYLAS: They are.

PHILONOUS: That is to say, they are extension in general, and motion in general.

HYLAS: Let it be so.

PHILONOUS: But it is a universally received maxim that *Everything which exists is particular.* How then can motion in general, or extension in general, exist in any corporeal substance?

HYLAS: I will take time to solve your difficulty.

PHILONOUS: But I think the point may be speedily decided. Without doubt you can tell whether you are able to frame this or that idea. Now I am content to put our dispute on this issue. If you can frame in your thoughts a distinct abstract idea of motion or extension, divested of all those sensible modes, as swift and slow, great and small, round and square, and the like, which are acknowledged to exist only in the mind, I will then yield the point you contend for. But if you cannot, it will be unreasonable on your side to insist any longer upon what you have no notion of.

HYLAS: To confess ingenuously, I cannot.

PHILONOUS: Can you even separate the ideas of extension and motion from the ideas of all those qualities which they who make the distinction term *secondary?*

HYLAS: What! Is it not an easy matter to consider extension and motion by themselves, abstracted from all other sensible qualities? Pray how do the mathematicians treat of them?

PHILONOUS: I acknowledge, Hylas, it is not difficult to form general propositions and reasonings about those qualities, without mentioning any other; and, in this sense, to consider or treat of them abstractedly. But, how does it follow that, because I can pronounce the word *motion* by itself, I can form the idea of it in my mind exclusive of body? Or, because theorems may be made of extension and figures, without any mention of *great* or *small,* or any other sensible mode or quality, that therefore it is possible such an abstract idea of extension, without any particular size or figure, or sensible quality, should be distinctly formed, and apprehended by the mind? Mathematicians treat of quantity, without regarding what other sensible qualities it is attended with, as being altogether indifferent to their demonstrations. But, when laying aside the words, they contemplate the bare ideas, I believe you will find, they are not the pure abstracted ideas of extension.

HYLAS: But what say you to *pure intellect?* May not abstracted ideas be framed by that faculty?

PHILONOUS: Since I cannot frame abstract ideas at all, it is plain I cannot frame them by the help of *pure intellect;* whatsoever faculty you understand by those words. Besides, not to inquire into the nature of pure intellect and its spiritual objects, as *virtue, reason, God,* or the like, thus much seems manifest—that sensible things are only to be perceived by sense, or represented by the imagination. Figures, therefore, and extension, being originally perceived by sense, do not belong to pure intellect: but, for your farther satisfaction, try if you can frame the idea of any figure, abstracted from all particularities of size, or even from other sensible qualities.

HYLAS: Let me think a little—I do not find that I can.

PHILONOUS: And can you think it possible that should really exist in nature which implies a repugnancy in its conception?

HYLAS: By no means.

PHILONOUS: Since therefore it is impossible even for the mind to disunite the ideas of extension and motion from all other sensible qualities, does it not follow, that where the one exist there necessarily the other exist likewise?

HYLAS: It should seem so.

PHILONOUS: Consequently, the very same arguments which you admitted as conclusive against the secondary qualities are, without any farther application of force, against the primary too. Besides, if you will trust your senses, is it not plain all sensible qualities coexist, or to them appear as being in the same place? Do they ever represent a motion, or figure, as being divested of all other visible and tangible qualities?

HYLAS: You need say no more on this head. I am free to own, if there be no secret error or oversight in our proceedings hitherto, that all sensible qualities are alike to be denied existence without the mind. But, my fear is that I have been too liberal in my former concessions, or overlooked some fallacy or other. In short, I did not take time to think.

PHILONOUS: For that matter, Hylas, you may take what time you please in reviewing the progress of our inquiry. You are at liberty to recover any slips you might have made, or offer whatever you have omitted which makes for your first opinion.

HYLAS: One great oversight I take to be this—that I did not sufficiently distinguish the *object* from the *sensation*. Now though this latter may not exist without the mind, yet it will not thence follow that the former cannot.

PHILONOUS: What object do you mean? The object of the senses?

HYLAS: The same.

PHILONOUS: It is then immediately perceived?

HYLAS: Right.

PHILONOUS: Make me to understand the difference between what is immediately perceived and a sensation.

HYLAS: The sensation I take to be an act of the mind perceiving; besides which, there is something perceived, and this I call the *object*. For example, there is red and yellow on that tulip. But then the act of perceiving those colours is in me only, and not in the tulip.

PHILONOUS: What tulip do you speak of? Is it that which you see?

HYLAS: The same.

PHILONOUS: And what do you see beside colour, figure, and extension?

HYLAS: Nothing.

PHILONOUS: What you would say then is that the red and yellow are coexistent with the extension; is it not?

HYLAS: That is not all; I would say they have a real existence without the mind, in some unthinking substance.

PHILONOUS: That the colours are really in the tulip which I see is manifest. Neither can it be denied that this tulip may exist independent of your mind or mine; but, that any immediate object of the senses—that is, any idea, or combination of ideas—should exist in an unthinking substance, or exterior to all minds, is in itself an evident contradiction. Nor can I imagine how this follows from what you said just now, to wit, that the red and yellow were on the tulip *you saw,* since you do not pretend to see that unthinking substance.

HYLAS: You have an artful way, Philonous, of diverting our inquiry from the subject.

PHILONOUS: I see you have no mind to be pressed that way. To return then to your distinction between *sensation* and *object;* if I take you right, you distinguish in every perception two things, the one an action of the mind, the other not.

HYLAS: True.

PHILONOUS: And this action cannot exist in, or belong to, any unthinking thing; but, whatever beside is implied in a perception may?

HYLAS: That is my meaning.

PHILONOUS: So that if there was a perception without any act of the mind, it were possible such a perception should exist in an unthinking substance?

HYLAS: I grant it. But it is impossible there should be such a perception.

PHILONOUS: When is the mind said to be active?

HYLAS: When it produces, puts an end to, or changes, anything.

PHILONOUS: Can the mind produce, discontinue, or change anything, but by an act of the will?

HYLAS: It cannot.

PHILONOUS: The mind therefore is to be accounted active in its perceptions so far forth as volition is included in them?

HYLAS: It is.

PHILONOUS: In plucking this flower I am *active;* because I do it by the motion of my hand, which was consequent upon my *volition;* so likewise in applying it to my nose. But is either of these smelling?

HYLAS: No.

PHILONOUS: I act too in drawing the air through my nose; because my breathing so rather than otherwise is the effect of my volition. But neither can this be called *smelling:* for, if it were, I should smell every time I breathed in that manner?

HYLAS: True.

PHILONOUS: Smelling then is somewhat consequent to all this?

HYLAS: It is.

PHILONOUS: But I do not find my will concerned any farther. Whatever more there is—as that I perceive such a particular smell, or any smell at all—this is independent of my will, and therein I am altogether passive. Do you find it otherwise with you, Hylas?

HYLAS: No, the very same.

PHILONOUS: Then, as to seeing, is it not in your power to open your eyes, or keep them shut; to turn them this or that way?

HYLAS: Without doubt.

PHILONOUS: But does it in like manner depend on your will that in looking on this flower you perceive *white* rather any other colour? Or, directing your open eyes towards yonder part of the heaven, can you avoid seeing the sun? Or is light or darkness the effect of your volition?

HYLAS: No, certainly.

PHILONOUS: You are then in these respects altogether passive?

HYLAS: I am.

PHILONOUS: Tell me now, whether *seeing* consists in perceiving light and colours, or in opening and turning the eyes?

HYLAS: Without doubt, in the former.

PHILONOUS: Since therefore you are in the very perception of light and colours altogether passive, what is become of that action you were speaking of as an ingredient in every sensation? And, does it not follow from your own concessions, that the perception of light and colours, including no action in it, may exist in an unperceiving substance? And is not this a plain contradiction?

HYLAS: I know not what to think of it.

PHILONOUS: Besides, since you distinguish the *active* and *passive* in every perception, you must do it in that of pain. But how is it possible that pain, be it as little active as you please, should exist in an unperceiving substance? In short, do but consider the point, and then confess ingenuously, whether light and colours, tastes, sounds, &c. are not all equally passions or sensations in the soul. You may indeed call them *external objects,* and give them in words what subsistence you please. But, examine your own thoughts, and then tell me whether it be not as I say?

HYLAS: I acknowledge, Philonous, that, upon a fair observation of what passes in my mind I can discover nothing else but that I am a thinking being, affected with variety of sensations; neither is it possible to conceive how a sensation should exist in an unperceiving substance.—But then, on the other hand, when I look on sensible things in a different view, considering them as so many modes and qualities, I find it necessary to suppose a *material* substratum, without which they cannot be conceived to exist.

PHILONOUS: *Material substratum* call you it? Pray, by which of your senses came you acquainted with that being?

HYLAS: It is not itself sensible; its modes and qualities only being perceived by the senses.

PHILONOUS: I presume then it was by reflexion and reason you obtained the idea of it?

HYLAS: I do not pretend to any proper positive idea of it. However, I conclude it exists, because qualities cannot be conceived to exist without a support.

PHILONOUS: It seems then you have only a relative notion of it, or that you conceive it not otherwise than by conceiving the relation it bears to sensible qualities?

HYLAS: Right.

PHILONOUS: Be pleased therefore to let me know wherein that relation consists.

HYLAS: Is it not sufficiently expressed in the term *substratum,* or *substance?*

PHILONOUS: If so, the word *substratum* should import that it is spread under the sensible qualities or accidents?

HYLAS: True.

PHILONOUS: And consequently under extension?

HYLAS: I own it.

PHILONOUS: It is therefore somewhat in its own nature entirely distinct from extension?

HYLAS: I tell you, extension is only a mode, and matter is something that supports modes. And is it not evident the thing supported is different from the thing supporting?

PHILONOUS: So that something distinct from, and exclusive of, extension is supposed to be the substratum of extension?

HYLAS: Just so.

PHILONOUS: Answer me, Hylas. Can a thing be spread without extension? or is not the idea of extension necessarily included in *spreading?*

HYLAS: It is.

PHILONOUS: Whatsoever therefore you suppose spread under anything must have in itself an extension distinct from the extension of that thing under which it is spread?

HYLAS: It must.

PHILONOUS: Consequently, every corporeal substance, being the *substratum* of extension, must have in itself another extension, by which it is qualified to be a *substratum:* and so on to infinity. And I ask whether this be not absurd in itself, and repugnant to what you granted just now, to wit, that the *substratum* was something distinct from and exclusive of extension?

HYLAS: Aye but, Philonous, you take me wrong. I do not mean that matter is *spread* in a gross literal sense under extension. The word *substratum* is used only to express in general the same thing with *substance.*

PHILONOUS: Well then, let us examine the relation implied in the term *substance.* Is it not that it stands under accidents?

HYLAS: The very same.

PHILONOUS: But, that one thing may stand under or support another, must it not be extended?

HYLAS: It must.

PHILONOUS: Is not therefore this supposition liable to the same absurdity with the former?

HYLAS: You still take things in a strict literal sense. That is not fair, Philonous.

PHILONOUS: I am not for imposing any sense on your words: you are at liberty to explain them as you please. Only, I beseech you, make me understand something by them. You tell me matter supports or stands under accidents. How! is it as your legs support your body?

HYLAS: No; that is the literal sense.

PHILONOUS: Pray let me know any sense, literal or not literal, that you understand it in.—How long must I wait for an answer, Hylas?

HYLAS: I declare I know not what to say. I once thought I understood well enough what was meant by matter's supporting accidents. But now, the more I think on it the less can I comprehend it: in short I find that I know nothing of it.

PHILONOUS: It seems then you have no idea at all, neither relative nor positive, of matter; you know neither what it is in itself, nor what relation it bears to accidents?

HYLAS: I acknowledge it.

PHILONOUS: And yet you asserted that you could not conceive how qualities or accidents should really exist, without conceiving at the same time a material support of them?

HYLAS: I did.

PHILONOUS: That is to say, when you conceive the real existence of qualities, you do withal conceive something which you cannot conceive?

HYLAS: It was wrong, I own. But still I fear there is some fallacy or other. Pray what think you of this? It is just come into my head that the ground of all our mistake lies in your treating of each quality by itself. Now, I grant that each quality cannot singly subsist without the mind. Colour cannot without extension, neither can figure without some other sensible quality. But, as the several qualities united or blended together form entire sensible things, nothing hinders why such things may not be supposed to exist without the mind.

PHILONOUS: Either, Hylas, you are jesting, or have a very bad memory. Though indeed we went through all the qualities by name one after another, yet my arguments or rather your concessions, nowhere tended to prove that the secondary qualities did not subsist each alone by itself; but, that they were not *at all* without the mind. Indeed, in treating of figure and motion we concluded they could not exist without the mind, because it was impossible even in thought to separate them from all secondary qualities, so as to conceive them existing by themselves. But then this was not the only argument made use of upon that occasion. But (to pass by all that hath been hitherto said, and reckon it for nothing, if you will have it so) I am content to put the whole upon this issue. If you can conceive it possible for any mixture or combination of qualities, or any sensible object whatever, to exist without the mind, then I will grant it actually to be so.

HYLAS: If it comes to that the point will soon be decided. What more easy than to conceive a tree or house existing by itself, independent of, and unperceived by, any mind whatsoever? I do at this present time conceive them existing after that manner.

PHILONOUS: How say you, Hylas, can you see a thing which is at the same time unseen?

HYLAS: No, that were a contradiction.

PHILONOUS: Is it not as great a contradiction to talk of *conceiving* a thing which is *unconceived?*

HYLAS: It is.

PHILONOUS: The tree or house therefore which you think of is conceived by you?

HYLAS: How should it be otherwise?

PHILONOUS: And what is conceived is surely in the mind?

HYLAS: Without question, that which is conceived is in the mind.

PHILONOUS: How then came you to say, you conceived a house or tree existing independent and out of all minds whatsoever?

HYLAS: That was I own an oversight; but stay, let me consider what led me into it.— It is a pleasant mistake enough. As I was thinking of a tree in a solitary place, where no one was present to see it, methought that was to conceive a tree as existing unperceived or unthought of; not considering that I myself conceived it all the while. But now I plainly see that all I can do is to frame ideas in my own mind. I may indeed conceive in my own thoughts the idea of a tree, or a house, or a mountain, but that is all. And this is far from proving that I can conceive them *existing out of the minds of all spirits.*

PHILONOUS: You acknowledge then that you cannot possibly conceive how any one corporeal sensible thing should exist otherwise than in the mind?

HYLAS: I do.

PHILONOUS: And yet you will earnestly contend for the truth of that which you cannot so much as conceive?

HYLAS I profess I know not what to think, but still there are some scruples remain with me. Is it not certain I *see* things at a distance? Do we not perceive the stars and moon, for example, to be a great way off? Is not this, say, manifest to the senses?

PHILONOUS: Do you not in a dream too perceive those or the like objects?

HYLAS: I do.

PHILONOUS: And have they not then the same appearance of being distant?

HYLAS: They have.

PHILONOUS: But you do not thence conclude the apparitions in a dream to be without the mind?

HYLAS: By no means.

PHILONOUS: You ought not therefore to conclude that sensible objects are without the mind, from their appearance, or manner wherein they are perceived.

HYLAS: I acknowledge it. But does not my sense deceive me in those cases?

PHILONOUS: By no means. The idea or thing which you immediately perceive, neither sense nor reason informs you that it actually exists without the mind. By sense you only know that you are affected with such certain sensations of light and colours, &c. And these you will not say are without the mind.

HYLAS: True: but, beside all that, do you not think the sight suggests something of *outness* or *distance?*

PHILONOUS: Upon approaching a distant object, do the visible size and figure change perpetually, or do they appear the same at all distances?

HYLAS: They are in a continual change.

PHILONOUS: Sight therefore does not suggest, or any way inform you, that the visible object you immediately perceive exists at a distance, or will be perceived when you advance farther onward; there being a continued series of visible objects succeeding each other during the whole time of your approach.

HYLAS: It does not; but still I know, upon seeing an object, what object I shall perceive after having passed over a certain distance: no matter whether it be exactly the same or no: there is still something of distance suggested in the case.

PHILONOUS: Good Hylas, do but reflect a little on the point, and then tell me whether there be any more in it than this: from the ideas you actually perceive by sight, you have by experience learned to collect what other ideas you will (according to the standing order of nature) be affected with, after such a certain succession of time and motion.

HYLAS: Upon the whole, I take it to be nothing else.

PHILONOUS: Now, is it not plain that if we suppose a man born blind was on a sudden made to see, he could at first have no experience of what may be suggested by sight?

HYLAS: It is.

PHILONOUS: He would not then, according to you, have any notion of distance annexed to the things he saw; but would take them for a new set of sensations, existing only in his mind?

HYLAS: It is undeniable.

PHILONOUS: But, to make it still more plain: is not *distance* a line turned endwise to the eye?

HYLAS: It is.

PHILONOUS: And can a line so situated be perceived by sight?

HYLAS: It cannot.

PHILONOUS: Does it not therefore follow that distance is not properly and immediately perceived by sight?

HYLAS: It should seem so.

PHILONOUS: Again, is it your opinion that colours are at a distance?

HYLAS: It must be acknowledged they are only in the mind.

PHILONOUS: But do not colours appear to the eye as coexisting in the same place with extension and figures?

HYLAS: They do.

PHILONOUS: How can you then conclude from sight that figures exist without, when you acknowledge colours do not; the sensible appearance being the very same with regard to both?

HYLAS: I know not what to answer.

PHILONOUS: But, allowing that distance was truly and immediately perceived by the mind, yet it would not thence follow it existed out of the mind. For, whatever is immediately perceived is an idea: and can any *idea* exist out of the mind?

HYLAS: To suppose that were absurd: but, inform me, Philonous, can we perceive or know nothing beside our ideas?

PHILONOUS: As for the rational deducing of causes from effects, that is beside our inquiry. And, by the senses you can best tell whether you perceive anything which is not immediately perceived. And I ask you, whether the things immediately perceived are other than your own sensations or ideas? You have indeed more than once, in the course of this conversation, declared yourself on those points; but you seem, by this last question, to have departed from what you then thought.

HYLAS: To speak the truth, Philonous, I think there are two kinds of objects:—the one perceived immediately, which are likewise called *ideas;* the other are real things or external objects, perceived by the mediation of ideas, which are their images and representations. Now, I own ideas do not exist without the mind; but the latter sort of objects do. I am sorry I did not think of this distinction sooner; it would probably have cut short your discourse.

PHILONOUS: Are those external objects perceived by sense or by some other faculty?

HYLAS: They are perceived by sense.

PHILONOUS: How! Is there any thing perceived by sense which is not immediately perceived?

HYLAS: Yes, Philonous, in some sort there is. For example when I look on a picture or statue of Julius Caesar, I may be said after a manner to perceive him (though not immediately) by my senses.

PHILONOUS: It seems then you will have our ideas, which alone are immediately perceived, to be pictures of external things: and that these also are perceived by sense, inasmuch as they have a conformity or resemblance to our ideas?

HYLAS: That is my meaning.

PHILONOUS: And, in the same way that Julius Caesar, in himself invisible, is nevertheless perceived by sight; real things, in themselves imperceptible, are perceived by sense.

HYLAS: In the very same.

PHILONOUS: Tell me, Hylas, when you behold the picture of Julius Caesar, do you see with your eyes any more than some colours and figures, with a certain symmetry and composition of the whole?

HYLAS: Nothing else.

PHILONOUS: And would not a man who had never known anything of Julius Caesar see as much?

HYLAS: He would.

PHILONOUS: Consequently he hath his sight, and the use of it, in as perfect a degree as you?

HYLAS: I agree with you.

PHILONOUS: Whence comes it then that your thoughts are directed to the Roman emperor, and his are not? This cannot proceed from the sensations or ideas of sense by you then perceived; since you acknowledge you have no advantage over him in that respect. It should seem therefore to proceed from reason and memory: should it not?

HYLAS: It should.

PHILONOUS: Consequently, it will not follow from that instance that anything is perceived by sense which is not immediately perceived. Though I grant we may, in one acceptation, be said to perceive sensible things mediately by sense: that is, when, from a frequently perceived connexion, the immediate perception of ideas by one sense suggests to the mind others, perhaps belonging to another sense, which are wont to be connected with them. For instance, when I hear a coach drive along the streets, immediately I perceive only the sound; but, from the experience I have had that such a sound is connected with a coach, I am said to hear the coach. It is nevertheless evident that, in truth and strictness, nothing can be *heard* but *sound;* and the coach is not then properly perceived by sense, but suggested from experience. So likewise when we are said to see a red-hot bar of iron; the solidity and heat of the iron are not the objects of sight, but suggested to the imagination by the colour and figure which are properly perceived by that sense. In short, those things alone are actually and strictly perceived by any sense, which would have been perceived in case that same sense had then been first conferred on us. As for other things, it is plain they are only suggested to the mind by experience, grounded on former perceptions. But, to return to your comparison of Caesar's picture, it is plain, if you keep to that, you must hold the real things, or archetypes of our ideas, are not perceived by sense, but by some internal faculty of the soul, as reason or memory. I would therefore fain know what arguments you can draw from reason for the existence of what you call real *things* or *material objects*. Or, whether you remember to have seen them formerly as they are in themselves; or, if you have heard or read of any one that did.

HYLAS: I see, Philonous, you are disposed to raillery; but that will never convince me.

PHILONOUS: My aim is only to learn from you the way to come at the knowledge of *material beings.* Whatever we perceive is perceived immediately or mediately: by sense, or by reason and reflexion. But, as you have excluded sense, pray show me what reason you have to believe their existence; or what *medium* you can possibly make use of to prove it, either to mine or your own understanding.

HYLAS: To deal ingenuously, Philonous, now I consider the point, I do not find I can give you any good reason for it. But, thus much seems pretty plain, that it is at least possible such things may really exist. And, as long as there is no absurdity in supposing them, I am resolved to believe as I did, till you bring good reasons to the contrary.

PHILONOUS: What! Is it come to this, that you only believe the existence of material objects, and that your belief is founded barely on the possibility of its being true? Then you will have me bring reasons against it: though another would think it reasonable the proof should lie on him who holds the affirmative. And, after all, this very point which you are now resolved to maintain, without any reason, is in effect what you have more than once during this discourse seen good reason to give up. But, to pass over all this; if I understand you rightly, you say our ideas do not exist without the mind, but that they are copies, images, or representations, of certain originals that do?

HYLAS: You take me right.

PHILONOUS: They are then like external things?

HYLAS: They are.

PHILONOUS: Have those things a stable and permanent nature, independent of our senses; or are they in a perpetual change, upon our producing any motions in our bodies—suspending, exerting, or altering, our faculties or organs of sense?

HYLAS: Real things, it is plain, have a fixed and real nature, which remains the same notwithstanding any change in our senses, or in the posture and motion of our bodies; which indeed may affect the ideas in our minds, but it were absurd to think they had the same effect on things existing without the mind.

PHILONOUS: How then is it possible that things perpetually fleeting and variable as our ideas should be copies or images of anything fixed and constant? Or, in other words, since all sensible qualities, as size, figure, colour, &c., that is, our ideas, are continually changing, upon every alteration in the distance, medium, or instruments of sensation; how can any determinate material objects be properly represented or painted forth by several distinct things, each of which is so different from and unlike the rest? Or, if you say it resembles some one only of our ideas, how shall we be able to distinguish the true copy from all the false ones?

HYLAS: I profess, Philonous, I am at a loss. I know not what to say to this.

PHILONOUS: But neither is this all. Which are material objects in themselves—perceptible or imperceptible?

HYLAS: Properly and immediately nothing can be perceived but ideas. All material things, therefore, are in themselves insensible, and to be perceived only by our ideas.

PHILONOUS: Ideas then are sensible, and their archetypes or originals insensible?

HYLAS: Right.

PHILONOUS: But how can that which is sensible be like that which is insensible? Can a real thing, in itself *invisible,* be like a *colour;* or a real thing, which is not *audible,* be like a *sound?* In a word, can anything be like a sensation or idea, but another sensation or idea?

HYLAS: I must own, I think not.

PHILONOUS: Is it possible there should be any doubt on the point? Do you not perfectly know your own ideas?

HYLAS: I know them perfectly; since what I do not perceive or know can be no part of my idea.

PHILONOUS: Consider, therefore, and examine them, and then tell me if there be anything in them which can exist without the mind: or if you can conceive anything like them existing without the mind.

HYLAS: Upon inquiry, I find it is impossible for me to conceive or understand how anything but an idea can be like an idea. And it is most evident that *no idea can exist without the mind.*

PHILONOUS: You are therefore, by your principles, forced to deny the reality of sensible things; since you made it to consist in an absolute existence exterior to the mind. That is to say, you are a downright *sceptic.* So I have gained my point, which was to show your principles led to scepticism.

HYLAS: For the present I am, if not entirely convinced, at least silenced.

PHILONOUS: I would fain know what more you would require in order to a perfect conviction. Have you not had the liberty of explaining yourself all manner of ways? Were any little slips in discourse laid hold and insisted on? Or were you not allowed to retract or reinforce anything you had offered, as best served your purpose? Hath not everything you could say been heard and examined with all the fairness imaginable? In a word, have you not in every point been convinced out of your own mouth? And, if you can at present discover any flaw in any of your former concessions, or think of any remaining subterfuge, any new distinction, colour, or comment whatsoever, why do you not produce it?

HYLAS: A little patience, Philonous. I am at present so amazed to see myself ensnared, and as it were imprisoned in the labyrinths you have drawn me into, that on the sudden it cannot be expected I should find my way out. You must give me time to look about me and recollect myself.

PHILONOUS: Hark; is not this the college bell?

HYLAS: It rings for prayers.

PHILONOUS: We will go in then, if you please, and meet here again tomorrow morning. In the meantime, you may employ your thoughts on this morning's discourse, and try if you can find any fallacy in it, or invent any new means to extricate yourself.

HYLAS: Agreed.

THE SECOND DIALOGUE

HYLAS: I beg your pardon, Philonous, for not meeting you sooner. All this morning my head was so filled with our late conversation that I had not leisure to think of the time of the day, or indeed of anything else.

PHILONOUS: I am glad you were so intent upon it, in hopes if there were any mistakes in your concessions, or fallacies in my reasonings from them, you will now discover them to me.

HYLAS: I assure you I have done nothing ever since I saw you but search after mistakes and fallacies, and, with that view, have minutely examined the whole series of yesterday's discourse: but all in vain, for the notions it led me into, upon review, appear still more clear and evident; and, the more I consider them, the more irresistibly do they force my assent.

PHILONOUS: And is not this, think you, a sign that they are genuine, that they proceed from nature, and are conformable to right reason? Truth and beauty are in this alike, that the strictest survey sets them both off to advantage; while the false lustre of error and disguise cannot endure being reviewed, or too nearly inspected.

HYLAS: I own there is a great deal in what you say. Nor can any one be more entirely satisfied of the truth of those odd consequences, so long as I have in view the reasonings that lead to them. But, when these are out of my thoughts, there seems, on the other hand, something so satisfactory, so natural and intelligible, in the modern way of explaining things that, I profess, I know not how to reject it.

PHILONOUS: I know not what way you mean.

HYLAS: I mean the way of accounting for our sensations or ideas.

PHILONOUS: How is that?

HYLAS: It is supposed the soul makes her residence in some part of the brain, from which the nerves take their rise, and are thence extended to all parts of the body; and that outward objects, by the different impressions they make on the organs of sense, communicate certain vibrative motions to the nerves; and these being filled with spirits propagate them to the brain or seat of the soul, which, according to the various impressions or traces thereby made in the brain, is variously affected with ideas.

PHILONOUS: And call you this an explication of the manner whereby we are affected with ideas?

HYLAS: Why not, Philonous? Have you anything to object against it?

PHILONOUS: I would first know whether I rightly understand your hypothesis. You make certain traces in the brain to be the causes or occasions of our ideas. Pray tell me whether by the brain you mean any sensible thing.

HYLAS: What else think you I could mean?

PHILONOUS: Sensible things are all immediately perceivable; and those things which are immediately perceivable are ideas; and these exist only in the mind. Thus much you have, if I mistake not, long since agreed to.

HYLAS: I do not deny it.

PHILONOUS: The brain therefore you speak of, being a sensible thing, exists only in the mind. Now, I would fain know whether you think it reasonable to suppose that one idea or thing existing in the mind occasions all other ideas. And, if you think so, pray how do you account for the origin of that primary idea or brain itself?

HYLAS: I do not explain the origin of our ideas by that brain which is perceivable to sense—this being itself only a combination of sensible ideas—but by another which I imagine.

PHILONOUS: But are not things imagined as truly *in the mind as* things perceived?

HYLAS: I must confess they are.

PHILONOUS: It comes therefore, to the same thing; and you have been all this while accounting for ideas by certain motions or impressions of the brain; that is, by some alterations in an idea, whether sensible or imaginable it matters not.

HYLAS: I begin to suspect my hypothesis.

PHILONOUS: Besides spirits, all that we know or conceive are our own ideas. When, therefore, you say all ideas are occasioned by impressions in the brain, do you conceive this brain or no? If you do, then you talk of ideas imprinted in an idea causing that same idea, which is absurd. If you do not conceive it, you talk unintelligibly, instead of forming a reasonable hypothesis.

HYLAS: I now clearly see it was a mere dream. There is nothing in it.

PHILONOUS: You need not be much concerned at it; for after all, this way of explaining things, as you called it, could never have satisfied any reasonable man. What connexion is there between a motion in the nerves, and the sensations of sound or colour in the mind? Or how is it possible these should be the effect of that?

HYLAS: But I could never think it had so little in it as now it seems to have.

PHILONOUS: Well then, are you at length satisfied that no sensible things have a real existence; and that you are in truth an arrant *sceptic?*

HYLAS: It is too plain to be denied.

PHILONOUS: Look! Are not the fields covered with a delightful verdure? Is there not something in the woods and groves, in the rivers and clear springs, that soothes, that delights, that transports the soul? At the prospect of the wide and deep ocean, or some huge mountain whose top is lost in the clouds, or of an old gloomy forest, are not our minds filled with a pleasing horror? Even in rocks and deserts is there not an agreeable wildness? How sincere a pleasure is it to behold the natural beauties of the earth! To preserve and renew our relish for them, is not the veil of night alternately drawn over her face, and does she not change her dress with the seasons? How aptly are the elements disposed! What variety and use in the meanest productions of nature! What delicacy, what beauty, what contrivance, in animal and vegetable bodies! How exquisitely are all things suited, as well to their particular ends, as to constitute opposite parts of the whole! And, while they mutually aid and support, do they not also set off and illustrate each other? Raise now your thoughts from this ball of earth to all those glorious luminaries that adorn the high arch of heaven. The motion and situation of the planets, are they not admirable for use and order? Were those (miscalled *erratic*) globes once known to stray, in their repeated journeys through the pathless void? Do they not measure areas round the sun ever proportioned to the times? So fixed, so immutable are the laws by which the unseen author of nature actuates the universe. How vivid and radiant is the lustre of the fixed stars! How magnificent and rich that negligent profusion with which they appear to be scattered throughout the whole azure vault! Yet, if you take the telescope, it brings into your sight a new host of stars that escape the naked eye. Here they seem contiguous and minute, but to a nearer view immense orbs of light at various distances, far sunk in the abyss of space. Now you must call imagination to your aid. The feeble narrow sense cannot descry innumerable worlds revolving round the central fires and in those worlds the energy of an all-perfect mind displayed in endless forms. But, neither sense nor imagination are big enough to comprehend the boundless extent, with all its glittering furniture. Though the labouring mind exert and strain each power to its utmost reach, there still stands out ungrasped a surplusage immeasurable. Yet all the vast bodies that compose this mighty frame, how distant and remote soever, are by some secret mechanism, some divine art and force, linked in a mutual dependence and intercourse with each other; even with this earth, which was almost slipt from my thoughts and lost in the crowd of worlds. Is not the whole system immense, beautiful, glorious beyond expression and beyond thought! What treatment, then, do those philosophers deserve, who would deprive these noble and delightful scenes of all reality? How should those principles be entertained that lead us to think all the visible beauty of the creation a false imaginary glare? To be plain, can you expect this scepticism of yours will not be thought extravagantly absurd by all men of sense?

HYLAS: Other men may think as they please; but for your part you have nothing to reproach me with. My comfort is, you are as much a *sceptic* as I am.

PHILONOUS: There, Hylas, I must beg leave to differ from you.

HYLAS: What! Have you all along agreed to the premises, and do you now deny the conclusion, and leave me to maintain those paradoxes by myself which you led me into? This surely is not fair.

PHILONOUS: I deny that I agreed with you in those notions that led to scepticism. You indeed said the *reality* of sensible things consisted in an *absolute existence* out of the minds of spirits, or distinct from their being perceived. And pursuant to this notion of reality, you are obliged to deny sensible things any real existence: that is, according to your own definition, you profess yourself a *sceptic*. But I neither said nor thought the reality of sensible things was to be defined after that manner. To me it is evident for the reasons you allow of, that sensible things cannot exist otherwise than in a mind or spirit. Whence I conclude, not that they have no real existence, but that, seeing they depend not on my thought, and have an existence distinct from being perceived by me, *there must be some other mind wherein they exist.* As sure, therefore, as the sensible world really exists, so sure is there an infinite omnipresent spirit who contains and supports it.

HYLAS: What! This is no more than I and all Christians hold; nay, and all others too who believe there is a God, and that he knows and comprehends all things.

PHILONOUS: Aye, but here lies the difference. Men commonly believe that all things are known or perceived by God, because they believe the being of a God; whereas I, on the other side, immediately and necessarily conclude the being of a God, because all sensible things must be perceived by him.

HYLAS: But, so long as we all believe the same thing, what matter is it how we come by that belief?

PHILONOUS: But neither do we agree in the same opinion. For philosophers, though they acknowledge all corporeal beings to be perceived by God, yet they attribute to them an absolute subsistence distinct from their being perceived by any mind whatever; which I do not. Besides, is there no difference between saying, *There is a God, therefore he perceives all things;* and saying, *Sensible things do really exist; and, if they really exist, they are necessarily perceived by an infinite mind: therefore there is an infinite mind or God?* This furnishes you with a direct and immediate demonstration, from a most evident principle, of the *being of a God.* Divines and philosophers had proved beyond all controversy, from the beauty and usefulness of the several parts of the creation, that it was the workmanship of God. But that—setting aside all help of astronomy and natural philosophy, all contemplation of the contrivance, order, and adjustment of things—an infinite mind should be necessarily inferred from the bare *existence* of the sensible world, is an advantage to them only who have made this easy reflexion: that the sensible world is that which we perceive by our several senses; and that nothing is perceived by the senses beside ideas; and that no idea or archetype of an idea can exist otherwise than in a mind. You may now, without any laborious search into the sciences, without any subtlety of reason, or tedious length of discourse, oppose and baffle the most strenuous advocate for Atheism. Those miserable refuges, whether in an eternal succession of unthinking causes and effects, or in a fortuitous concourse of atoms; those wild imaginations of Vanini, Hobbes, and Spinoza: in a word, the whole system of Atheism, is it not entirely overthrown, by this single reflexion on the repugnancy included in supposing the whole, or any part, even the most rude and shapeless, of the visible world, to exist without a mind? Let any one of those abettors of impiety but look into his own thoughts, and there try if he can conceive how so much as a rock, a desert, a chaos, or confused jumble of atoms; how anything at all, either sensible or imaginable, can exist independent of a mind, and he need go no farther to be convinced of his folly. Can anything be fairer than to put a dispute on such an issue, and leave it to a man himself to see if he can conceive, even in thought, what he holds to be true in fact, and from a notional to allow it a real existence?

HYLAS: It cannot be denied there is something highly serviceable to religion in what you advance. But do you not think it looks very like a notion entertained by some eminent moderns, of *seeing all things in God?*

PHILONOUS: I would gladly know that opinion: pray explain it to me.

HYLAS: They conceive that the soul, being immaterial, is incapable of being united with material things, so as to perceive them in themselves; but that she perceives them by her union with the substance of God, which, being spiritual, is therefore purely intelligible, or capable of being the immediate object of a spirit's thought. Besides the divine essence contains in it perfections correspondent to each created being; and which are, for that reason, proper to exhibit or represent them to the mind.

PHILONOUS: I do not understand how our ideas, which are things altogether passive and inert, can be the essence, or any part (or like any part) of the essence or substance of God, who is an impassive, indivisible, pure, active being. Many more difficulties and objections there are which occur at first view against this hypothesis; but I shall only add that it is liable to all the absurdities of the common hypothesis, in making a created world exist otherwise than in the mind of a spirit. Besides all which it hath this peculiar to itself; that it makes that material world serve to no purpose. And, if it pass for a good argument against other hypotheses in the sciences, that they suppose nature, or the divine wisdom, to make something in vain, or do that by tedious roundabout methods which might have been performed in a much more easy and compendious way, what shall we think of that hypothesis which supposes the whole world made in vain?

HYLAS: But what say you? Are not you too of opinion that we see all things in God? If I mistake not, what you advance comes near it.

PHILONOUS: Few men think; yet all have opinions. Hence men's opinions are superficial and confused. It is nothing strange that tenets which in themselves are ever so different, should nevertheless be confounded with each other, by those who do not consider them attentively. I shall not therefore be surprised if some men imagine that I run into the enthusiasm of Malebranche; though in truth I am very remote from it. He builds on the most abstract general ideas, which I entirely disclaim. He asserts an absolute external world, which I deny. He maintains that we are deceived by our senses, and know not the real natures or the true forms and figures of extended beings; of all which I hold the direct contrary. So that upon the whole there are no principles more fundamentally opposite than his and mine. It must be owned that I entirely agree with what the holy Scripture says, "That in God we live and move and have our being" [Acts 17:28]. But that we see things in His essence, after the manner above set forth, I am far from believing. Take here in brief my meaning:—It is evident that the things I perceive are my own ideas, and that no idea can exist unless it be in a mind: nor is it less plain that these ideas or things by me perceived, either themselves or their archetypes, exist independently of my mind, since I know myself not to be their author, it being out of my power to determine at pleasure what particular ideas I shall be affected with upon opening my eyes or ears: they must therefore exist in some other mind, whose will it is they should be exhibited to me. The things, I say, immediately perceived are ideas or sensations, call them which you will. But how can any idea or sensation exist in, or be produced by, anything but a mind or spirit? This indeed is inconceivable. And to assert that which is inconceivable is to talk nonsense: is it not?

HYLAS: Without doubt.

PHILONOUS: But, on the other hand, it is very conceivable that they should exist in and be produced by a spirit; since this is no more than I daily experience in myself, inasmuch as I perceive numberless ideas; and, by an act of my will, can form a great variety of them, and raise them up in my imagination: though, it must be confessed, these creatures of the fancy are not altogether so distinct, so strong, vivid, and permanent, as those perceived by my senses—which latter are called *real things*. From all which I conclude, *there is a mind which affects me every moment with all the sensible impressions I perceive*. And, from the variety, order, and manner of these, I conclude the author of them to be *wise, powerful, and good, beyond comprehension*. Mark it well; I do not say, I see things by perceiving that which represents them in the intelligible substance of God. This I do not understand; but I say, the things by me perceived are known by the understanding, and produced by the will of an infinite spirit. And is not all this most plain and evident? Is there any more in it than what a little observation in our own minds, and that which passes in them, not only enables us to conceive, but also obliges us to acknowledge.

HYLAS: I think I understand you very clearly; and own the proof you give of a deity seems no less evident than it is surprising. But, allowing that God is the supreme and universal cause of all things, yet, may there not be still a third nature besides spirits and ideas? May we not admit a subordinate and limited cause of our ideas? In a word, may there not for all that be *matter?*

PHILONOUS: How often must I inculcate the same thing? You allow the things immediately perceived by sense to exist nowhere without the mind; but there is nothing perceived by sense which is not perceived immediately: therefore there is nothing sensible that exists without the mind. The matter, therefore, which you still insist on is something intelligible, I suppose; something that may be discovered by reason, and not by sense.

HYLAS: You are in the right.

PHILONOUS: Pray let me know what reasoning your belief of matter is grounded on; and what this matter is, in your present sense of it.

HYLAS: I find myself affected with various ideas, whereof I know I am not the cause; neither are they the cause of themselves, or of one another, or capable of subsisting by themselves, as being altogether inactive, fleeting, dependent beings. They have therefore some cause distinct from me and them: of which I pretend to know no more than that it is *the cause of my ideas*. And this thing, whatever it be, I call matter.

PHILONOUS: Tell me, Hylas, hath every one a liberty to change the current proper signification attached to a common name in any language? For example, suppose a traveler should tell you that in a certain country men pass unhurt through the fire; and, upon explaining himself, you found he meant by the word *fire* that which others call *water*. Or, if he should assert that there are trees that walk upon two legs, meaning men by the term *trees*. Would you think this reasonable?

HYLAS: No; I should think it very absurd. Common custom is the standard of propriety in language. And for any man to affect speaking improperly is to pervert the use of speech, and can never serve to a better purpose than to protract and multiply disputes where there is no difference in opinion.

PHILONOUS: And does not *matter,* in the common current acceptation of the word, signify an extended, solid, moveable, unthinking, inactive substance?

HYLAS: It does.

PHILONOUS: And, has it not been made evident that no such substance can possibly exist? And, though it should be allowed to exist, yet how can that which is *inactive* be a cause; or that which is *unthinking* be a *cause of thought?* You may, indeed, if you please, annex to the word *matter* a contrary meaning to what is vulgarly received; and tell me you understand by it, an unextended, thinking, active being, which is the cause of our ideas. But what else is this than to play with words, and run into that very fault you just now condemned with so much reason? I do by no means find fault with your reasoning, in that you collect a cause from the *phenomena:* but I deny that the cause deducible by reason can properly be termed matter.

HYLAS: There is indeed something in what you say. But I am afraid you do not thoroughly comprehend my meaning. I would by no means be thought to deny that God, or an infinite spirit, is the supreme cause of all things. All I contend for is, that, subordinate to the supreme agent, there is a cause of a limited and inferior nature, which concurs in the production of our ideas, not by any act of will, or spiritual efficiency, but by that kind of action which belongs to matter, *viz.* motion.

PHILONOUS: I find you are at every turn relapsing into your old exploded conceit, of a moveable, and consequently an extended, substance, existing without the mind. What! Have you already forgotten you were convinced; or are you willing I should repeat what has been said on that head? In truth this is not fair dealing in you, still to suppose the being of that which you have so often acknowledged to have no being. But, not to insist farther on what has been so largely handled, I ask whether all your ideas are not perfectly passive and inert, including nothing of action in them.

HYLAS: They are.

PHILONOUS: And are sensible qualities anything else but ideas?

HYLAS: How often have I acknowledged that they are not.

PHILONOUS: But is not motion a sensible quality?

HYLAS: It is.

PHILONOUS: Consequently it is no action?

HYLAS: I agree with you. And indeed it is very plain that when I stir my finger, it remains passive; but my will which produced the motion is active.

PHILONOUS: Now, I desire to know, in the first place, whether motion being allowed to be no action, you can conceive any action besides volition: and, in the second place, whether to say something and conceive nothing be not to talk nonsense: and, lastly, whether, having considered the premises, you do not perceive that to suppose any efficient or active cause of our ideas, other than *spirit,* is highly absurd and unreasonable?

HYLAS: I give up the point entirely. But, though matter may not be a cause, yet what hinders its being an *instrument,* subservient to the supreme agent in the production of our ideas?

PHILONOUS: An instrument say you; pray what may be the figure, springs, wheels, and motions, of that instrument?

HYLAS: Those I pretend to determine nothing of, both the substance and its qualities being entirely unknown to me.

PHILONOUS: What? You are then of opinion it is made up of unknown parts, that it hath unknown motions, and an unknown shape?

HYLAS: I do not believe that it hath any figure or motion at all, being already convinced, that no sensible qualities can exist in an unperceiving substance.

PHILONOUS: But what notion is it possible to frame of an instrument void of all sensible qualities, even extension itself?

HYLAS: I do not pretend to have any notion of it.

PHILONOUS: And what reason have you to think this unknown, this inconceivable somewhat does exist? Is it that you imagine God cannot act as well without it; or that you find by experience the use of some such thing, when you form ideas in your own mind?

HYLAS: You are always teasing me for reasons of my belief. Pray what reasons have you not to believe it?

PHILONOUS: It is to me a sufficient reason not to believe the existence of anything, if I see no reason for believing it. But, not to insist on reasons for believing, you will not so much as let me know what it is you would have me believe; since you say you have no manner of notion of it. After all, let me entreat you to consider whether it be like a philosopher, or even like a man of common sense, to pretend to believe you know not what, and you know not why.

HYLAS: Hold, Philonous. When I tell you matter is an *instrument,* I do not mean altogether nothing. It is true I know not the particular kind of instrument; but, however, I have some notion of *instrument in general,* which I apply to it.

PHILONOUS: But what if it should prove that there is something, even in the most general notion of *instrument,* as taken in a distinct sense from *cause,* which makes the use of it inconsistent with the divine attributes?

HYLAS: Make that appear and I shall give up the point.

PHILONOUS: What mean you by the general nature or notion of instrument?

HYLAS: That which is common to all particular instruments composes the general notion.

PHILONOUS: Is it not common to all instruments, that they are applied to the doing those things only which cannot be performed by the mere act of our wills? Thus, for instance, I never use an instrument to move my finger, because it is done by a volition. But I should use one if I were to remove part of a rock, or tear up a tree by the roots. Are you of the same mind? Or, can you show any example where an instrument is made use of in producing an effect immediately depending on the will of the agent?

HYLAS: I own I cannot.

PHILONOUS: How therefore can you suppose that an all-perfect spirit, on whose will all things have an absolute and immediate dependence, should need an instrument in his operations, or, not needing it, make use of it? Thus it seems to me that you are obliged to own the use of a lifeless inactive instrument to be incompatible with the infinite perfection of God; that is, by your own confession, to give up the point.

HYLAS: It does not readily occur what I can answer you.

PHILONOUS: But, methinks you should be ready to own the truth, when it has been fairly proved to you. We indeed, who are beings of finite powers, are forced to make use of instruments. And the use of an instrument shows the agent to be limited by rules of another's prescription, and that he cannot obtain his end but in such a way, and by such conditions. Whence it seems a clear consequence, that the supreme unlimited agent uses no tool or instrument at all. The will of an omnipotent spirit is no sooner exerted than executed, without the application of means; which, if they are employed by inferior agents, it is not upon account of any real efficacy that is in them, or necessary aptitude to produce any effect, but merely in compliance with the laws of nature, or those conditions prescribed to them by the first cause, who is himself above all limitation or prescription whatsoever.

HYLAS: I will no longer maintain that matter is an instrument. However, I would not be understood to give up its existence neither; since, notwithstanding what hath been said, it may still be an *occasion.*

PHILONOUS: How many shapes is your matter to take? Or, how often must it be proved not to exist, before you are content to part with it? But, to say no more of this (though by all the laws of disputation I may justly blame you for so frequently changing the signification of the principal term)—I would fain know what you mean by affirming that matter is an occasion, having already denied it to be a cause. And, when you have shown in what sense you understand *occasion,* pray, in the next place be pleased to show me what reason induces you to believe there is such an occasion of our ideas?

HYLAS: As to the first point: by *occasion* I mean an inactive unthinking being, at the presence whereof God excites ideas in our minds.

PHILONOUS: And what may be the nature of that inactive unthinking being?

HYLAS: I know nothing of its nature.

PHILONOUS: Proceed then to the second point, and assign some reason why we should allow an existence to this inactive, unthinking, unknown thing.

HYLAS: When we see ideas produced in our minds, after an orderly and constant manner, it is natural to think they have some fixed and regular occasions, at the presence of which they are excited.

PHILONOUS: You acknowledge then God alone to be the cause of our ideas, and that he causes them at the presence of those occasions.

HYLAS: That is my opinion.

PHILONOUS: Those things which you say are present to God, without doubt he perceives.

HYLAS: Certainly; otherwise they could not be to him an occasion of acting.

PHILONOUS: Not to insist now on your making sense of this hypothesis, or answering all the puzzling questions and difficulties it is liable to: I only ask whether the order and regularity observable in the series of our ideas, or the course of nature, be not sufficiently accounted for by the wisdom and power of God; and whether it does not derogate from those attributes, to suppose he is influenced, directed, or put in mind, when and what he is to act, by an unthinking substance? And, lastly, whether, in case I granted all you contend for, it would make anything to your purpose; it not being easy to conceive how the external or absolute existence of an unthinking substance, distinct from its being perceived, can be inferred from my allowing that there are certain things perceived by the mind of God, which are to him the occasion of producing ideas in us?

HYLAS: I am perfectly at a loss what to think, this notion of occasion seeming now altogether as groundless as the rest.

PHILONOUS: Do you not at length perceive that in all these different acceptations of *matter,* you have been only supposing you know not what, for no manner of reason, and to no kind of use?

HYLAS: I freely own myself less fond of my notions since they have been so accurately examined. But still, methinks, I have some confused perception that there is such a thing as *matter.*

PHILONOUS: Either you perceive the being of matter immediately or mediately. If immediately, pray inform me by which of the senses you perceive it. If mediately, let me know by what reasoning it is inferred from those things which you perceive immediately. So much for the perception. Then for the matter itself, I ask whether it is object, *substratum,* cause, instrument, or occasion? You have already pleaded for each of these, shifting your notions, and making matter to appear sometimes in one shape, then in another. And what you have offered hath been disapproved and rejected by yourself. If you have anything new to advance I would gladly hear it.

HYLAS: I think I have already offered all I had to say on those heads. I am at a loss what more to urge.

PHILONOUS: And yet you are loath to part with your old prejudice. But, to make you quit it more easily, I desire that, beside what has been hitherto suggested, you will farther consider whether, upon supposition that matter exists, you can possibly conceive how you should be affected by it. Or, supposing it did not exist, whether it be not evident you might for all that be affected with the same ideas you now are, and consequently have the very same reasons to believe its existence that you now can have.

HYLAS: I acknowledge it is possible we might perceive all things just as we do now, though there was no matter in the world; neither can I conceive, if there be matter, how it should produce any idea in our minds. And, I do farther grant you have entirely satisfied me that it is impossible there should be such a thing as matter in any of the foregoing acceptations. But still I cannot help supposing that there is *matter* in some sense or other. What that is I do not indeed pretend to determine.

PHILONOUS: I do not expect you should define exactly the nature of that unknown being. Only be pleased to tell me whether it is a substance; and if so, whether you can suppose a substance without accidents; or, in case you suppose it to have accidents or qualities, I desire you will let me know what those qualities are, at least what is meant by matter's supporting them?

HYLAS: We have already argued on those points. I have no more to say to them. But, to prevent any farther questions, let me tell you I at present understand by *matter* neither substance nor accident, thinking nor extended being, neither cause, instrument, nor occasion, but something entirely unknown, distinct from all these.

PHILONOUS: It seems then you include in your present notion of matter nothing but the general abstract idea of *entity.*

HYLAS: Nothing else; save only that I superadd to this general idea the negation of all those particular things, qualities, or ideas, that I perceive, imagine, or in anywise apprehend.

PHILONOUS: Pray where do you suppose this unknown matter to exist?

HYLAS: Oh Philonous! Now you think you have entangled me, for, if I say it exists in place, then you will infer that it exists in the mind, since it is agreed that place or extension exists only in the mind. But I am not ashamed to own my ignorance. I know not where it exists; only I am sure it exists not in place. There is a negative answer for you. And you must expect no other to all the questions you put for the future about matter.

PHILONOUS: Since you will not tell me where it exists, be pleased to inform me after what manner you suppose it to exist, or what you mean by its *existence?*

HYLAS: It neither thinks nor acts, neither perceives nor is perceived.

PHILONOUS: But what is there positive in your abstracted notion of its existence?

HYLAS: Upon a nice observation, I do not find I have any positive notion or meaning at all. I tell you again, I am not ashamed to own my ignorance. I know not what is meant by its *existence,* or how it exists.

PHILONOUS: Continue, good Hylas, to act the same ingenuous part, and tell me sincerely whether you can frame a distinct idea of Entity in general, prescinded from and exclusive of all thinking and corporeal beings, all particular things whatsoever.

HYLAS: Hold, let me think a little—I profess, Philonous I do not find that I can. At first glance, methought I had some dilute and airy notion of pure entity in abstract; but, upon closer attention, it hath quite vanished out of sight. The more I think on it, the more am I confirmed in my prudent resolution of giving none but negative answers, and not pretending to the least degree of any positive knowledge or conception of matter, its *where,* its *how,* its *entity,* or anything belonging to it.

PHILONOUS: When, therefore, you speak of the existence of matter, you have not any notion in your mind?

HYLAS: None at all.

PHILONOUS: Pray tell me if the case stands not thus: At first, from a belief of material substance, you would have it that the immediate objects existed without the mind;

then that they are archetypes; then causes; next instruments; then occasions: lastly *something in general,* which being interpreted proves *nothing.* So matter comes to nothing. What think you, Hylas, is not this a fair summary of your whole proceeding?

HYLAS: Be that as it will, yet I still insist upon it, that our not being able to conceive a thing is no argument against its existence.

PHILONOUS: That from a cause, effect, operation, sign, or other circumstance, there may reasonably be inferred the existence of a thing not immediately perceived; and that it were absurd for any man to argue against the existence of that thing, from his having no direct and positive notion of it, I freely own. But, where there is nothing of all this; where neither reason nor revelation induces us to believe the existence of a thing; where we have not even a relative notion of it; where an abstraction is made from perceiving and being perceived, from spirit and idea: lastly, where there is not so much as the most inadequate or faint idea pretended to—I will not indeed thence conclude against the reality of any notion, or existence of anything; but my inference shall be, that you mean nothing at all; that you employ words to no manner of purpose, without any design or signification whatsoever. And I leave it to you to consider how mere jargon should be treated.

HYLAS: To deal frankly with you, Philonous, your arguments seem in themselves unanswerable; but they have not so great an effect on me as to produce that entire conviction, that hearty acquiescence, which attends demonstration. I find myself relapsing into an obscure surmise of I know not what, *matter.*

PHILONOUS: But, are you not sensible, Hylas, that two things must concur to take away all scruple, and work a plenary assent in the mind? Let a visible object be set in never so clear a light, yet, if there is any imperfection in the sight, or if the eye is not directed towards it, it will not be distinctly seen. And though a demonstration be never so well grounded and fairly proposed, yet, if there is withal a stain of prejudice, or a wrong bias on the understanding, can it be expected on a sudden to perceive clearly, and adhere firmly to the truth? No; there is need of time and pains: the attention must be awakened and detained by a frequent repetition of the same thing placed oft in the same, oft in different lights. I have said it already, and find I must still repeat and inculcate, that it is an unaccountable licence you take, in pretending to maintain you know not what, for you know not what reason, to you know not what purpose. Can this be paralleled in any art or science, any sect or profession of men? Or is there anything so barefacedly groundless and unreasonable to be met with even in the lowest of common conversation? But, perhaps you will still say, matter may exist; though at the same time you neither know what is meant by *matter,* or by its *existence.* This indeed is surprising, and the more so because it is altogether voluntary, you not being led to it by any one reason; for I challenge you to show me that thing in nature which needs matter to explain or account for it.

HYLAS: The reality of things cannot be maintained without supposing the existence of matter. And is not this, think you, a good reason why I should be earnest in its defence?

PHILONOUS: The reality of things! What things, sensible or intelligible?

HYLAS: Sensible things.

PHILONOUS: My glove for example?

HYLAS: That, or any other thing perceived by the senses.

PHILONOUS: But to fix on some particular thing. Is it not a sufficient evidence to me of the existence of this *glove,* that I see it, and feel it, and wear it? Or, if this will not do, how is it possible I should be assured of the reality of this thing, which I actually see in this place, by supposing that some unknown thing, which I never did or can see, exists after an unknown manner, in an unknown place, or in no place at all? How can the supposed reality of that which is intangible be a proof that anything tangible really exists? Or, of that which is invisible, that any visible thing, or, in general of anything which is imperceptible, that a perceptible exists? Do but explain this and I shall think nothing too hard for you.

HYLAS: Upon the whole, I am content to own the existence of matter is highly improbable, but the direct and absolute impossibility of it does not appear to me.

PHILONOUS: But granting matter to be possible, yet, upon that account merely, it can have no more claim to existence than a golden mountain, or a centaur.

HYLAS: I acknowledge it; but still you do not deny it is possible; and that which is possible, for aught you know, may actually exist.

PHILONOUS: I deny it to be possible; and have, if I mistake not, evidently proved, from your own concessions, that it is not. In the common sense of the word *matter,* is there any more implied than an extended, solid, figured, movable substance, existing without the mind? And have not you acknowledged, over and over, that you have seen evident reason for denying the possibility of such a substance?

HYLAS: True, but that is only one sense of the term matter.

PHILONOUS: But is it not the only proper genuine received sense? And, if matter, in such a sense, be proved impossible, may it not be thought with good grounds absolutely impossible? Else how could anything be proved impossible? Or, indeed, how could there be any proof at all one way or other, to a man who takes the liberty to unsettle and change the common signification of words?

HYLAS: I thought philosophers might be allowed to speak more accurately than the vulgar, and were not always confined to the common acceptation of a term.

PHILONOUS: But this now mentioned is the common received sense among philosophers themselves. But, not to insist on that, have you not been allowed to take matter in what sense you pleased? And have you not used this privilege in the utmost extent; sometimes entirely changing, at others leaving out, or putting into the definition of it whatever, for the present, best served your design, contrary to all the known rules of reason and logic? And hath not this shifting, unfair method of yours spun out our dispute to an unnecessary length; matter having been particularly examined, and by your own confession refuted in each of those senses? And can any more be required to prove the absolute impossibility of a thing, than the proving it impossible in every particular sense that either you or any one else understands it in?

HYLAS: But I am not so thoroughly satisfied that you have proved the impossibility of matter, in the last most obscure abstracted and indefinite sense.

PHILONOUS: When is a thing shown to be impossible?

HYLAS: When a repugnancy is demonstrated between the ideas comprehended in its definition

PHILONOUS: But where there are no ideas, there no repugnancy can be demonstrated between ideas?

HYLAS: I agree with you.

PHILONOUS: Now, in that which you call the obscure indefinite sense of the word matter, it is plain, by your own confession, there was included no idea at all, no sense except an unknown sense; which is the same thing as none. You are not, therefore, to expect I should prove a repugnancy between ideas, where there are no ideas; or the impossibility of matter taken in an *unknown* sense, that is, no sense at all. My business was only to show you meant *nothing;* and this you were brought to own. So that, in all your various senses, you have been showed either to mean nothing at all, or, if anything, an absurdity. And if this be not sufficient to prove the impossibility of a thing, I desire you will let me know what is.

HYLAS: I acknowledge you have proved that matter is impossible; nor do I see what more can be said in defence of it. But, at the same time that I give up this, I suspect all my other notions. For surely none could be more seemingly evident than this once was: and yet it now seems as false and absurd as ever it did true before. But I think we have discussed the point sufficiently for the present. The remaining part of the day I would willingly spend in running over in my thoughts the several heads of this morning's conversation, and tomorrow shall be glad to meet you here again about the same time.

PHILONOUS: I will not fail to attend you.

THE THIRD DIALOGUE

PHILONOUS: Tell me, Hylas, what are the fruits of yesterday's meditation? Has it confirmed you in the same mind you were in at parting? or have you since seen cause to change your opinion?

HYLAS: Truly my opinion is that all our opinions are alike vain and uncertain. What we approve today, we condemn tomorrow. We keep a stir about knowledge, and spend our lives in the pursuit of it, when, alas! we know nothing all the while: nor do I think it possible for us ever to know anything in this life. Our faculties are too narrow and too few. Nature certainly never intended us for speculation.

PHILONOUS: What! Say you we can know nothing, Hylas?

HYLAS: There is not that single thing in the world whereof we can know the real nature, or what it is in itself.

PHILONOUS: Will you tell me I do not really know what fire or water is?

HYLAS: You may indeed know that fire appears hot, and water fluid; but this is no more than knowing what sensations are produced in your own mind, upon the application of fire and water to your organs of sense. Their internal constitution, their true and real nature, you are utterly in the dark as to *that*.

PHILONOUS: Do I not know this to be a real stone that I stand on, and that which I see before my eyes to be a real tree?

HYLAS: Know? No, it is impossible you or any man alive should know it. All you know is, that you have such a certain idea or appearance in your own mind. But what is this to the real tree or stone? I tell you that colour, figure, and hardness, which you perceive, are not the real natures of those things, or in the least like them. The same may be said of all other real things, or corporeal substances, which compose the world. They have none of them anything of themselves, like those sensible qualities by us perceived. We should not therefore pretend to affirm or know anything of them, as they are in their own nature.

PHILONOUS: But surely, Hylas, I can distinguish gold, for example, from iron: and how could this be, if I knew not what either truly was?

HYLAS: Believe me, Philonous, you can only distinguish between your own ideas. That yellowness, that weight, and other sensible qualities, think you they are really in the gold? They are only relative to the senses, and have no absolute existence in nature. And in pretending to distinguish the species of real things, by the appearances in your mind, you may perhaps act as wisely as he that should conclude two men were of a different species, because their clothes were not of the same colour.

PHILONOUS: It seems, then, we are altogether put off with the appearances of things, and those false ones too. The very meat I eat, and the cloth I wear, have nothing in them like what I see and feel.

HYLAS: Even so.

PHILONOUS: But is it not strange the whole world should be thus imposed on, and so foolish as to believe their senses? And yet I know not how it is, but men eat, and drink, and sleep, and perform all the offices of life, as comfortably and conveniently as if they really knew the things they are conversant about.

HYLAS: They do so: but you know ordinary practice does not require a nicety of speculative knowledge. Hence the vulgar retain their mistakes, and for all that make a shift to bustle through the affairs of life. But philosophers know better things.

PHILONOUS: You mean, they know that they *know nothing*.

HYLAS: That is the very top and perfection of human knowledge.

PHILONOUS: But are you all this while in earnest, Hylas; and are you seriously persuaded that you know nothing real in the world? Suppose you are going to write, would you not call for pen, ink, and paper, like another man; and do you not know what it is you call for?

HYLAS: How often must I tell you, that I know not the real nature of any one thing in the universe? I may indeed upon occasion make use of pen, ink, and paper. But what any one of them is in its own true nature, I declare positively I know not. And the same is true with regard to every other corporeal thing. And, what is more, we are not only ignorant of the true and real nature of things, but even of their existence. It cannot be denied that we perceive such certain appearances or ideas; but it cannot be concluded from thence that bodies really exist. Nay, now I think on it, I must, agreeably to my former concessions, farther declare that it is impossible any real corporeal thing should exist in nature.

PHILONOUS: You amaze me. Was ever anything more wild and extravagant than the notions you now maintain: and is it not evident you are led into all these extravagances by the belief of *material substance?* This makes you dream of those unknown natures in everything. It is this occasions your distinguishing between the reality and sensible appearances of things. It is to this you are indebted for being ignorant of what everybody else knows perfectly well. Nor is this all: you are not only ignorant of the true nature of everything, but you know not whether anything really exists, or whether there are any true natures at all; forasmuch as you attribute to your material beings an absolute or external existence, wherein you suppose their reality consists. And, as you are forced in the end to acknowledge such an existence means either a direct repugnancy, or nothing at all, it follows that you are obliged to pull down your own hypothesis of material substance, and positively to deny the real existence of any part of the universe. And so you are plunged into the deepest and most deplorable *scepticism* that ever man was. Tell me, Hylas, is it not as I say?

HYLAS: I agree with you. *Material substance* was no more than an hypothesis; and a false and groundless one too. I will no longer spend my breath in defence of it. But whatever hypothesis you advance, or whatsoever scheme of things you introduce in its stead, I doubt not it will appear every whit as false: let me but be allowed to question you upon it. That is, suffer me to serve you in your own kind, and I warrant it shall conduct you through as many perplexities and contradictions, to the very same state of scepticism that I myself am in at present.

PHILONOUS: I assure you, Hylas, I do not pretend to frame any hypothesis at all. I am of a vulgar cast, simple enough to believe my senses, and leave things as I find them. To be plain, it is my opinion that the real things are those very things I see, and feel, and perceive by my senses. These I know; and, finding they answer all the necessities and purposes of life, have no reason to be solicitous about any other unknown beings. A piece of sensible bread, for instance, would stay my stomach better than ten thousand times as much of that insensible, unintelligible, real bread you speak of. It is likewise my opinion that colours and other sensible qualities are on the objects. I cannot for my life help thinking that snow is white, and fire hot. You indeed, who by *snow* and *fire* mean certain external, unperceived, unperceiving substances, are in the right to deny whiteness or heat to be affections inherent in them. But I, who understand by those words the things I see and feel, am obliged to think like other folks. And, as I am no sceptic with regard to the nature of things, so neither am I as to their existence. That a thing should be really perceived by my senses, and at the same time not really exist, is to me a plain contradiction; since I cannot prescind or abstract, even in thought, the existence of a sensible thing from its being perceived. Wood, stones, fire, water, flesh, iron, and the like things, which I name and discourse of, are things that I know. And I should not have known them but that I perceived them by my senses; and things perceived by the senses are immediately perceived; and things immediately perceived are ideas; and ideas cannot exist without the mind, their existence therefore consists in being perceived; when, therefore, they are actually perceived there can be no doubt of their existence. Away then with all that scepticism, all those ridiculous philosophical doubts. What a jest is it for a philosopher to question the existence of sensible things, till he hath it proved to him from the veracity of God; or to pretend our knowledge in this point falls short of intuition or demonstration! I might as well doubt of my own being, as of the being of those things I actually see and feel.

HYLAS: Not so fast, PHILONOUS: you say you cannot conceive how sensible things should exist without the mind. Do you not?

PHILONOUS: I do.

HYLAS: Supposing you were annihilated, cannot you conceive it possible that things perceivable by sense may still exist?

PHILONOUS: I can, but then it must be in another mind. When I deny sensible things an existence out of the mind, I do not mean my mind in particular, but all minds. Now, it is plain they have an existence exterior to my mind, since I find them by experience to be independent of it. There is therefore some other mind wherein they exist, during the intervals between the times of my perceiving them: as likewise they did before my birth, and would do after my supposed annihilation. And, as the same is true with regard to all other finite created spirits, it necessarily follows there is an *omnipresent eternal mind,* which knows and comprehends all things, and exhibits them to our view in such a manner, and according to such rules, as he himself hath ordained, and are by us termed the *laws of nature.*

HYLAS: Answer me, Philonous. Are all our ideas perfectly inert beings? Or have they any agency included in them?

PHILONOUS: They are altogether passive and inert.

HYLAS: And is not God an agent, a being purely active?

PHILONOUS: I acknowledge it.

HYLAS: No idea therefore can be like unto, or represent the nature of God?

PHILONOUS: It cannot.

HYLAS: Since therefore you have no idea of the mind of God, how can you conceive it possible that things should exist in His mind? Or, if you can conceive the mind of God, without having an idea of it, why may not I be allowed to conceive the existence of matter, notwithstanding I have no idea of it?

PHILONOUS: As to your first question: I own I have properly no idea, either of God or any other spirit; for these being active, cannot be represented by things perfectly inert, as our ideas are. I do nevertheless know that I, who am a spirit or thinking substance, exist as certainly as I know my ideas exist. Farther, I know what I mean by the terms *I* and *myself;* and I know this immediately or intuitively, though I do not perceive it as I perceive a triangle, a colour, or a sound. The mind, spirit, or soul is that indivisible unextended thing which thinks, acts, and perceives. I say *indivisible,* because *unextended;* and unextended, because extended, figured, movable things are ideas; and that which perceives ideas, which thinks and wills, is plainly itself no idea, nor like an idea. Ideas are things inactive, and perceived. And spirits a sort of beings altogether different from them. I do not therefore say my soul is an idea, or like an idea. However, taking the word *idea* in a large sense, my soul may be said to furnish me with an idea, that is, an image or likeness of God—though indeed extremely inadequate. For, all the notion I have of God is obtained by reflecting on my own soul, heightening its powers, and removing its imperfections. I have, therefore, though not an inactive idea, yet in *myself* some sort of an active thinking image of the Deity. And, though I perceive him not by sense, yet I have a notion of him, or know him by reflexion and reasoning. My own mind and my own ideas I have an immediate knowledge of; and, by the help of these, do mediately apprehend the possibility of the existence of other spirits and ideas. Farther, from my own being, and from the dependency I find in myself and my ideas, I do, by an act of reason, necessarily infer the existence of a God, and of all created things in the mind of God. So much for your first question. For the second: I suppose by this time you can answer it yourself. For you neither perceive matter objectively, as you do an inactive being or idea; nor know it, as you do yourself, by a reflex act, neither do you mediately apprehend it by similitude of the one or the other; nor yet collect it by reasoning from that which you know immediately. All which makes the case of *matter* widely different from that of the *Deity.*

HYLAS: You say your own soul supplies you with some sort of an idea or image of God. But, at the same time, you acknowledge you have, properly speaking, no idea of your own soul. You even affirm that spirits are a sort of beings altogether different from ideas. Consequently that no idea can be like a spirit. We have therefore no idea of any spirit. You admit nevertheless that there is spiritual substance, although you have no idea of it; while you deny there can be such a thing as material substance, because you have no notion or idea of it. Is this fair dealing? To act consistently, you must either admit matter or reject spirit. What say you to this?

PHILONOUS: I say, in the first place, that I do not deny the existence of material substance, merely because I have no notion of it, but because the notion of it is inconsistent; or, in other words, because it is repugnant that there should be a notion of it. Many things, for aught I know, may exist, whereof neither I nor any other man hath or can have any idea or notion whatsoever. But then those things must be possible, that is, nothing inconsistent must be included in their definition. I say, secondly, that, although we believe things to exist which we do not perceive, yet we may not believe that any particular thing exists, without some reason for such belief: but I have no reason for believing the existence of matter. I have no immediate intuition thereof: neither can I immediately from my sensations, ideas, notions, actions, or passions, infer an unthinking, unperceiving, inactive substance—either by probable deduction, or necessary consequence. Whereas the being of my Self, that is, my own soul, mind, or thinking principle, I evidently know by reflexion. You will forgive me if I repeat the same things in answer to the same objections. In the very notion or definition of *material substance,* there is included a manifest repugnance and inconsistency. But this cannot be said of the notion of spirit. That ideas should exist in what does not perceive or be produced by what does not act, is repugnant. But, it is no repugnancy to say that a perceiving thing should be the subject of ideas, or an active thing the cause of them. It is granted we have neither an immediate evidence nor a demonstrative knowledge of the existence of other finite spirits; but it will not thence follow that such spirits are on a foot with material substances: if to suppose the one be inconsistent, and it be not inconsistent to suppose the other; if the one can be inferred by no argument, and there is a probability for the other; if we see signs and effects indicating distinct finite agents like ourselves, and see no sign or symptom whatever that leads to a rational belief of matter. I say, lastly, that I have a notion of spirit, though I have not, strictly speaking, an idea of it. I do not perceive it as an idea, or by means of an idea, but know it by reflexion.

HYLAS: Notwithstanding all you have said, to me it seems that, according to your own way of thinking, and in consequence of your own principles, it should follow that you are only a system of floating ideas, without any substance to support them. Words are not to be used without a meaning. And, as there is no more meaning in *spiritual substance* than in *material substance,* the one is to be exploded as well as the other.

PHILONOUS: How often must I repeat, that I know or am conscious of my own being; and that *I myself* am not my ideas, but somewhat else, a thinking, active principle that perceives, knows, wills, and operates about ideas I know that I, one and the same self, perceive both colours and sounds: that a colour cannot perceive a sound, nor a sound a colour: that I am therefore one individual principle, distinct from colour and sound, and, for the same reason, from all other sensible things and inert ideas. But, I am not in like manner conscious either of the existence or essence of matter. On the contrary, I know that nothing inconsistent can exist, and that the existence of matter implies an inconsistency. Farther, I know what I mean when I affirm that there is a spiritual substance or support of ideas, that is, that a spirit knows and perceives ideas. But, I do not know what is meant when it is said that an unperceiving substance hath inherent in it and supports either ideas or the archetypes of ideas. There is therefore upon the whole no parity of case between spirit and matter.

HYLAS: I own myself satisfied in this point. But, do you in earnest think the real existence of sensible things consists in their being actually perceived? If so; how comes it that all mankind distinguish between them? Ask the first man you meet, and he shall tell you, *to be perceived* is one thing, and *to exist* is another.

PHILONOUS: I am content, Hylas, to appeal to the common sense of the world for the truth of my notion. Ask the gardener why he thinks yonder cherry-tree exists in the garden, and he shall tell you, because he sees and feels it; in a word, because he perceives it by his senses. Ask him why he thinks an orange-tree not to be there, and he shall tell you, because he does not perceive it. What he perceives by sense, that he terms a real being, and says it *is* or *exists;* but, that which is not perceivable, the same, he says, has no being.

HYLAS: Yes, Philonous, I grant the existence of a sensible thing consists in being perceivable, but not in being actually perceived.

PHILONOUS: And what is perceivable but an idea? And can an idea exist without being actually perceived? These are points long since agreed between us.

HYLAS: But, be your opinion never so true, yet surely you will not deny it is shocking, and contrary to the common sense of men. Ask the fellow whether yonder tree hath an existence out of his mind: what answer think you he would make?

PHILONOUS: The same that I should myself, to wit, that it does exist out of his mind. But then to a Christian it cannot surely be shocking to say, the real tree, existing without his mind, is truly known and comprehended by (that is *exists in*) the infinite mind of God. Probably he may not at first glance be aware of the direct and immediate proof there is of this; inasmuch as the very being of a tree, or any other sensible thing, implies a mind wherein it is. But the point itself he cannot deny. The question between the materialists and me is not, whether things have a real existence out of the mind of this or that person, but whether they have an absolute existence, distinct from being perceived by God, and exterior to all minds. This indeed some heathens and philosophers have affirmed, but whoever entertains notions of the Deity suitable to the Holy Scriptures will be of another opinion.

HYLAS: But, according to your notions, what difference is there between real things, and chimeras formed by the imagination, or the visions of a dream—since they are all equally in the mind?

PHILONOUS: The ideas formed by the imagination are faint and indistinct; they have, besides, an entire dependence on the will. But the ideas perceived by sense, that is, real things, are more vivid and clear; and, being imprinted on the mind by a spirit distinct from us, have not the like dependence on our will. There is therefore no danger of confounding these with the foregoing; and there is as little of confounding them with the visions of a dream, which are dim, irregular, and confused. And, though they should happen to be never so lively and natural, yet, by their not being connected, and of a piece with the preceding and subsequent transactions of our lives, they might easily be distinguished from realities. In short, by whatever method you distinguish *things* from *chimeras* on your scheme, the same, it is evident, will hold also upon mine. For, it must be, I presume, by some perceived difference; and I am not for depriving you of any one thing that you perceive.

HYLAS: But still, Philonous, you hold, there is nothing in the world but spirits and ideas. And this, you must needs acknowledge, sounds very oddly.

PHILONOUS: I own the word *idea,* not being commonly used for *thing,* sounds something out of the way. My reason for using it was, because a necessary relation to the mind is understood to be implied by that term; and it is now commonly used by philosophers to denote the immediate objects of the understanding. But, however oddly the proposition may sound in words, yet it includes nothing so very strange or shocking in its sense, which in effect amounts to no more than this, to wit, that there are only things perceiving, and things perceived; or that every unthinking being is necessarily, and from the very nature of its existence, perceived by some mind; if not by a finite created mind, yet certainly by the infinite mind of God, in whom "we live, and move, and have our being." Is this as strange as to say, the sensible qualities are not on the objects: or that we cannot be sure of the existence of things, or know any thing of their real natures—though we both see and feel them, and perceive them by all our senses?

HYLAS: And, in consequence of this, must we not think there are no such things as physical or corporeal causes; but that a spirit is the immediate cause of all the phenomena in nature? Can there be anything more extravagant than this?

PHILONOUS: Yes, it is infinitely more extravagant to say—a thing which is inert operates on the mind, and which is unperceiving is the cause of our perceptions, without any regard either to consistency, or the old known axiom: *Nothing can give to another that which it hath not itself.* Besides, that which to you, I know not for what reason, seems so extravagant is no more than the Holy Scriptures assert in a hundred places. In them God is represented as the sole and immediate author of all those effects which some heathens and philosophers are wont to ascribe to nature, matter, fate, or the like unthinking principle. This is so much the constant language of Scripture that it were needless to confirm it by citations.

HYLAS: You are not aware Philonous, that in making God the immediate author of all the motions in nature, you make him the author of murder, sacrilege, adultery, and the like heinous sins.

PHILONOUS: In answer to that, I observe, first, that the imputation of guilt is the same, whether a person commits an action with or without an instrument. In case therefore you suppose God to act by the mediation of an instrument or occasion, called *matter,* you as truly make him the author of sin as I, who think him the immediate agent in all those operations vulgarly ascribed to nature. I farther observe that sin or moral turpitude does not consist in the outward physical action or motion, but in the internal deviation of the will from the laws of reason and religion. This is plain, in that the killing an enemy in a battle, or putting a criminal legally to death, is not thought sinful; though the outward act be the very same with that in the case of murder. Since therefore, sin does not consist in the physical action, the making God an immediate cause of all such actions is not making him the author of sin. Lastly, I have nowhere said that God is the only agent who produces all the motions in bodies. It is true I have denied there are any other agents besides spirits, but this is very consistent with allowing to thinking rational beings, in the production of motions, the use of limited powers, ultimately indeed derived from God, but immediately under the direction of their own wills which is sufficient to entitle them to all the guilt of their actions.

HYLAS: But the denying matter, Philonous, or corporeal substance; there is the point. You can never persuade me that this is not repugnant to the universal sense of mankind. Were our dispute to be determined by most voices, I am confident you would give up the point, without gathering the votes.

PHILONOUS: I wish both our opinions were fairly stated and submitted to the judgment of men who had plain common sense, without the prejudices of a learned education. Let me be represented as one who trusts his senses, who thinks he knows the things he sees and feels, and entertains no doubts of their existence, and you fairly set forth with all your doubts, your paradoxes, and your scepticism about you, and I shall willingly acquiesce in the determination of any indifferent person. That there is no substance wherein ideas can exist beside spirit is to me evident. And that the objects immediately perceived are ideas, is on all hands agreed. And that sensible qualities are objects immediately perceived no one can deny. It is therefore evident there can be no *substratum* of those qualities but spirit; in which they exist, not by way of mode or property, but as a thing perceived in that which perceives it. I deny therefore that there is any unthinking *substratum* of the objects of sense, and in that acceptation that there is any material substance. But if by *material substance* is meant only sensible body— that which is seen and felt (and the unphilosophical part of the world, I dare say, mean no more)—then I am more certain of matter's existence than you or any other philosopher pretend to be. If there be anything which makes the generality of mankind averse from the notions I espouse: it is a misapprehension that I deny the reality of sensible things. But, as it is you who are guilty of that, and not I, it follows that in truth their aversion is against your notions and not mine. I do therefore assert that I am as certain as of my own being, that there are bodies or corporeal substances (meaning the things I perceive by my senses); and that, granting this, the bulk of mankind will take no thought about, nor think themselves at all concerned in the fate of those unknown natures, and philosophical quiddities, which some men are so fond of.

HYLAS: What say you to this? Since, according to you, men judge of the reality of things by their senses, how can a man be mistaken in thinking the moon a plain lucid surface, about a foot in diameter; or a square tower, seen at a distance, round; or an oar, with one end in the water, crooked?

PHILONOUS: He is not mistaken with regard to the ideas he actually perceives, but in the inference he makes from his present perceptions. Thus, in the case of the oar, what he immediately perceives by sight is certainly crooked; and so far he is in the right. But if he thence conclude that upon taking the oar out of the water he shall perceive the same crookedness; or that it would affect his touch as crooked things are wont to do: in that he is mistaken. In like manner, if he shall conclude from what he perceives in one station, that, in case he advances towards the moon or tower, he should still be affected with the like ideas, he is mistaken. But his mistake lies not in what he perceives immediately, and at present, (it being a manifest contradiction to suppose he should err in respect of that) but in the wrong judgment he makes concerning the ideas he apprehends to be connected with those immediately perceived: or, concerning the ideas that, from what he perceives at present, he imagines would be perceived in other circumstances. The case is the same with regard to the Copernican system. We do not here perceive any motion of the earth: but it were erroneous thence to conclude, that, in case we were placed at as great a distance from that as we are now from the other planets, we should not then perceive its motion.

HYLAS: I understand you; and must needs own you say things plausible enough. But, give me leave to put you in mind of one thing. Pray, Philonous, were you not formerly as positive that matter existed, as you are now that it does not?

PHILONOUS: I was. But here lies the difference. Before, my positiveness was founded, without examination, upon prejudice; but now, after inquiry, upon evidence.

HYLAS: After all, it seems our dispute is rather about words than things. We agree in the thing, but differ in the name. That we are affected with ideas from without is evident, and it is no less evident that there must be (I will not say archetypes, but) Powers without the mind, corresponding to those ideas. And, as these Powers cannot subsist by themselves, there is some subject of them necessarily to be admitted; which I call *matter,* and you call *spirit.* This is all the difference.

PHILONOUS: Pray, Hylas, is that powerful being, or subject of powers, extended?

HYLAS: It hath not extension; but it hath the power to raise in you the idea of extension.

PHILONOUS: It is therefore itself unextended?

HYLAS: I grant it.

PHILONOUS: Is it not also active?

HYLAS: Without doubt. Otherwise, how could we attribute powers to it?

PHILONOUS: Now let me ask you two questions: *First,* whether it be agreeable to the usage either of philosophers or others to give the name *matter* to an unextended active being? And, *secondly,* whether it be not ridiculously absurd to misapply names contrary to the common use of language?

HYLAS: Well then, let it not be called matter, since you will have it so, but some *third nature* distinct from matter and spirit. For what reason is there why you should call it spirit? Does not the notion of spirit imply that it is thinking, as well as active and unextended?

PHILONOUS: My reason is this: because I have a mind to have some notion of meaning in what I say: but I have no notion of any action distinct from volition, neither can I conceive volition to be anywhere but in a spirit: therefore, when I speak of an active being, I am obliged to mean a spirit. Beside, what can be plainer than that a thing which hath no ideas in itself cannot impart them to me, and, if it hath ideas, surely it must be a spirit. To make you comprehend the point still more clearly if it be possible,

I assert as well as you that, since we are affected from without, we must allow powers to be without, in a being distinct from ourselves. So far we are agreed. But then we differ as to the kind of this powerful being. I will have it to be spirit, you matter, or I know not what (I may add too, you know not what) third nature. Thus, I prove it to be spirit. From the effects I see produced, I conclude there are actions; and, because actions, volitions; and, because there are volitions, there must be a will. Again, the things I perceive must have an existence, they or their archetypes, out of my mind: but, being ideas, neither they nor their archetypes can exist otherwise than in an understanding, there is therefore an understanding. But will and understanding constitute in the strictest sense a mind or spirit. The powerful cause, therefore, of my ideas is in strict propriety of speech a *spirit*.

HYLAS: And now I warrant you think you have made the point very clear, little suspecting that what you advance leads directly to a contradiction. Is it not an absurdity to imagine any imperfection in God?

PHILONOUS: Without a doubt.

HYLAS: To suffer pain is an imperfection?

PHILONOUS: It is.

HYLAS: Are we not sometimes affected with pain and uneasiness by some other being?

PHILONOUS: We are.

HYLAS: And have you not said that being is a spirit, and is not that spirit God?

PHILONOUS: I grant it.

HYLAS: But you have asserted that whatever ideas we perceive from without are in the mind which affects us. The ideas, therefore, of pain and uneasiness are in God; or, in other words, God suffers pain: that is to say, there is an imperfection in the divine nature: which, you acknowledged, was absurd. So you are caught in a plain contradiction.

PHILONOUS: That God knows or understands all things, and that he knows, among other things, what pain is, even every sort of painful sensation, and what it is for His creatures to suffer pain, I make no question. But, that God, though he knows and sometimes causes painful sensations in us, can himself suffer pain, I positively deny. We, who are limited and dependent spirits, are liable to impressions of sense, the effects of an external agent, which, being produced against our wills, are sometimes painful and uneasy. But God, whom no external being can affect, who perceives nothing by sense as we do; whose will is absolute and independent, causing all things, and liable to be thwarted or resisted by nothing: it is evident, such a being as this can suffer nothing, nor be affected with any painful sensation, or indeed any sensation at all. We are chained to a body: that is to say, our perceptions are connected with corporeal motions. By the law of our nature, we are affected upon every alteration in the nervous parts of our sensible body; which sensible body, rightly considered, is nothing but a complexion of such qualities or ideas as have no existence distinct from being perceived by a mind. So that this connexion of sensations with corporeal motions means no more than a correspondence in the order of nature, between two sets of ideas, or things immediately perceivable. But God is a pure spirit, disengaged from all such sympathy, or natural ties. No corporeal motions are attended with the sensations of pain or pleasure in His mind. To know everything knowable, is certainly a perfection; but to endure or suffer, or feel anything by sense, is an imperfection. The former, I say, agrees to God, but not the latter. God knows, or hath ideas; but His ideas are not conveyed to him by sense, as ours are. Your not distinguishing, where there is so manifest a difference, makes you fancy you see an absurdity where there is none.

Hylas: But, all this while you have not considered that the quantity of matter has been demonstrated to be proportioned to the gravity of bodies. And what can withstand demonstration?

Philonous: Let me see how you demonstrate that point.

Hylas: I lay it down for a principle, that the moments or quantities of motion in bodies are in a direct compounded reason of the velocities and quantities of matter contained in them. Hence, where the velocities are equal, it follows the moments are directly as the quantity of matter in each. But it is found by experience that all bodies (bating the small inequalities, arising from the resistance of the air) descend with an equal velocity; the motion therefore of descending bodies, and consequently their gravity, which is the cause or principle of that motion, is proportional to the quantity of matter; which was to be demonstrated.

Philonous: You lay it down as a self-evident principle that the quantity of motion in any body is proportional to the velocity and *matter* taken together: and this is made use of to prove a proposition from whence the existence of *matter* is inferred. Pray is not this arguing in a circle?

Hylas: In the premise I only mean that the motion is proportional to the velocity, jointly with the extension and solidity.

Philonous: But, allowing this to be true, yet it will not thence follow that gravity is proportional to *matter,* in your philosophic sense of the word, except you take it for granted that unknown *substratum,* or whatever else you call it, is proportional to those sensible qualities; which to suppose is plainly begging the question. That there is magnitude and solidity, or resistance, perceived by sense, I readily grant, as likewise, that gravity may be proportional to those qualities I will not dispute. But that either these qualities as perceived by us, or the powers producing them, do exist in a *material substratum;* this is what I deny, and you indeed affirm, but, notwithstanding your demonstration, have not yet proved.

Hylas: I shall insist no longer on that point. Do you think, however, you shall persuade me the natural philosophers have been dreaming all this while? Pray what becomes of all their hypotheses and explications of the *phenomena,* which suppose the existence of matter?

Philonous: What mean you, Hylas, by the *phenomena?*

Hylas: I mean the appearances which I perceive by my senses.

Philonous: And the appearances perceived by sense, are they not ideas?

Hylas: I have told you so a hundred times.

Philonous: Therefore, to explain the phenomena, is, to show how we come to be affected with ideas, in that manner and order wherein they are imprinted on our senses. Is it not?

Hylas: It is.

Philonous: Now, if you can prove that any philosopher has explained the production of any one idea in our minds by the help of *matter,* I shall for ever acquiesce, and look on all that hath been said against it as nothing; but, if you cannot, it is vain to urge the explication of *phenomena.* That a being endowed with knowledge and will should produce or exhibit ideas is easily understood. But that a being which is utterly destitute of these faculties should be able to produce ideas, or in any sort to affect an intelligence, this I can never understand. This I say, though we had some positive conception of matter, though we knew its qualities, and could comprehend its existence, would yet be so far from explaining things, that it is itself the most inexplicable thing in the world. And yet, for all this, it will not follow that philosophers have been doing nothing; for, by observing and reasoning upon the connexion of ideas, they discover the laws and methods of nature, which is a part of knowledge both useful and entertaining.

HYLAS: After all, can it be supposed God would deceive all mankind? Do you imagine he would have induced the whole world to believe the being of matter, if there was no such thing?

PHILONOUS: That every epidemical opinion, arising from prejudice, or passion, or thoughtlessness, may be imputed to God, as the author of it, I believe you will not affirm. Whatsoever opinion we father on him, it must be either because he has discovered it to us by supernatural revelation; or because it is so evident to our natural faculties, which were framed and given us by God, that it is impossible we should withhold our assent from it. But where is the revelation? Or where is the evidence that extorts the belief of matter? Nay, how does it appear, that matter, taken for something distinct from what we perceive by our senses, is thought to exist by all mankind; or indeed, by any except a few philosophers, who do not know what they would be at? Your question supposes these points are clear; and, when you have cleared them, I shall think myself obliged to give you another answer. In the meantime, let it suffice. That I tell you, I do not suppose God has deceived mankind at all.

HYLAS: But the novelty, Philonous, the novelty! There lies the danger. New notions should always be discountenanced; they unsettle men's minds, and nobody knows where they will end.

PHILONOUS: Why the rejecting a notion that has no foundation, either in sense, or in reason, or in divine authority, should be thought to unsettle the belief of such opinions as are grounded on all or any of these, I cannot imagine. That innovations in government and religion are dangerous, and ought to be discountenanced, I freely own. But is there the like reason why they should be discouraged in philosophy? The making anything known which was unknown before is an innovation in knowledge: and, if all such innovations had been forbidden, men would have made a notable progress in the arts and sciences. But it is none of my business to plead for novelties and paradoxes. That the qualities we perceive are not on the objects: that we must not believe our senses: that we know nothing of the real nature of things, and can never be assured even of their existence: that real colours and sounds are nothing but certain unknown figures and motions: that motions are in themselves neither swift nor slow: that there are in bodies absolute extensions, without any particular magnitude or figure: that a thing stupid, thoughtless, and inactive, operates on a spirit: that the least particle of a body contains innumerable extended parts:—these are the novelties, these are the strange notions which shock the genuine uncorrupted judgment of all mankind; and being once admitted, embarrass the mind with endless doubts and difficulties. And it is against these and the like innovations I endeavour to vindicate common sense. It is true, in doing this, I may perhaps be obliged to use some *ambages,* and ways of speech not common. But, if my notions are once thoroughly understood, that which is most singular in them will, in effect, be found to amount to no more than this:—that it is absolutely impossible, and a plain contradiction, to suppose any unthinking being should exist without being perceived by a mind. And, if this notion be singular, it is a shame it should be so, at this time of day, and in a Christian country.

HYLAS: As for the difficulties other opinions may be liable to, those are out of the question. It is your business to defend your own opinion. Can anything be plainer than that you are for changing all things into ideas? You, I say, who are not ashamed to charge me with *scepticism.* This is so plain, there is no denying it.

PHILONOUS: You mistake me. I am not for changing things into ideas, but rather ideas into things; since those immediate objects of perception, which, according to you, are only appearances of things, I take to be the real things themselves.

HYLAS: Things! You may pretend what you please; but it is certain you leave us nothing but the empty forms of things, the outside only which strikes the senses.

PHILONOUS: What you call the empty forms and outside of things seem to me the very things themselves. Nor are they empty or incomplete, otherwise than upon your supposition—that matter is an essential part of all corporeal things. We both, therefore, agree in this, that we perceive only sensible forms: but herein we differ—you will have them to be empty appearances, I real beings. In short, you do not trust your senses, I do.

HYLAS: You say you believe your senses; and seem to applaud yourself that in this you agree with the vulgar. According to you, therefore, the true nature of a thing is discovered by the senses. If so, whence comes that disagreement? Why is not the same figure, and other sensible qualities, perceived all manner of ways? And why should we use a microscope the better to discover the true nature of a body, if it were discoverable to the naked eye?

PHILONOUS: Strictly speaking, Hylas, we do not see the same object that we feel; neither is the same object perceived by the microscope which was by the naked eye. But, in case every variation was thought sufficient to constitute a new kind of individual, the endless number of confusion of names would render language impracticable. Therefore, to avoid this, as well as other inconveniences which are obvious upon a little thought, men combine together several ideas, apprehended by divers senses, or by the same sense at different times, or in different circumstances, but observed, however, to have some connexion in nature, either with respect to co-existence or succession; all which they refer to one name, and consider as one thing. Hence it follows that when I examine, by my other senses, a thing I have seen, it is not in order to understand better the same object which I had perceived by sight, the object of one sense not being perceived by the other senses. And, when I look through a microscope, it is not that I may perceive more clearly what I perceived already with my bare eyes; the object perceived by the glass being quite different from the former. But, in both cases, my aim is only to know what ideas are connected together; and the more a man knows of the connexion of ideas, the more he is said to know of the nature of things. What, therefore, if our ideas are variable; what if our senses are not in all circumstances affected with the same appearances. It will not thence follow they are not to be trusted; or that they are inconsistent either with themselves or anything else: except it be with your preconceived notion of (I know not what) one single, unchanged, unperceivable, real nature, marked by each name. Which prejudice seems to have taken its rise from not rightly understanding the common language of men, speaking of several distinct ideas as united into one thing by the mind. And, indeed, there is cause to suspect several erroneous conceits of the philosophers are owing to the same original: while they began to build their schemes not so much on notions as on words, which were framed by the vulgar, merely for conveniency and dispatch in the common actions of life, without any regard to speculation.

HYLAS: Methinks I apprehend your meaning.

PHILONOUS: It is your opinion the ideas we perceive by our senses are not real things, but images or copies of them. Our knowledge, therefore, is no farther real than as our ideas are the true representations of those originals. But, as these supposed originals are in themselves unknown, it is impossible to know how far our ideas resemble them; or whether they resemble them at all. We cannot, therefore, be sure we have any real knowledge. Farther, as our ideas are perpetually varied, without any change in the supposed real things, it necessarily follows they cannot all be true copies of them: or, if some are and others are not, it is impossible to distinguish the former from the latter. And this plunges us yet deeper in uncertainty. Again, when we consider the point, we cannot conceive how any idea, or anything like an idea, should have an absolute existence out of a mind: nor consequently, according to you, how there should be any real thing in nature. The result of all which is that we are thrown into the most hopeless and abandoned *scepticism.* Now, give me leave to ask you, *first,* whether your referring ideas to certain absolutely existing unperceived substances, as their originals, be not the source of all this *scepticism? Secondly,* whether you are informed, either by sense or reason, of the existence of those unknown originals? And, in case you are not, whether it be not absurd to suppose them? *Thirdly,* whether, upon inquiry, you find there is anything distinctly conceived or meant by the *absolute or external existence of unperceiving substances? Lastly,* whether, the premises considered, it be not the wisest way to follow nature, trust your senses, and, laying aside all anxious thought about unknown natures or substances, admit with the vulgar those for real things which are perceived by the senses?

HYLAS: For the present, I have no inclination to the answering part. I would much rather see how you can get over what follows. Pray are not the objects perceived by the senses of one, likewise perceivable to others present? If there were a hundred more here, they would all see the garden, the trees, and flowers, as I see them. But they are not in the same manner affected with the ideas I frame in my imagination. Does not this make a difference between the former sort of objects and the latter?

PHILONOUS: I grant it does. Nor have I ever denied a difference between the objects of sense and those of imagination. But what would you infer from thence? You cannot say that sensible objects exist unperceived, because they are perceived by many.

HYLAS: I own I can make nothing of that objection: but it hath led me into another. Is it not your opinion that by our senses we perceive only the ideas existing in our minds?

PHILONOUS: It is.

HYLAS: But the same idea which is in my mind cannot be in yours, or in any other mind. Does it not therefore follow, from your principles, that no two can see the same thing? And is not this highly absurd?

PHILONOUS: If the term *same* be taken in the vulgar acceptation, it is certain (and not at all repugnant to the principles I maintain) that different persons may perceive the same thing; or the same thing or idea exist in different minds. Words are of arbitrary imposition, and since men are used to apply the word *same* where no distinction or variety is perceived, and I do not pretend to alter their perceptions, it follows that, as men have said before, *several saw the same thing,* so they may, upon like occasions, still continue to use the same phrase, without any deviation either from propriety of language, or the truth of things. But, if the term *same* be used in the acceptation of philosophers, who pretend to an abstracted notion of identity, then, according to their sundry definitions of this notion (for it is not yet agreed wherein that philosophic identity consists), it may or may not be possible for divers persons to perceive the same thing. But whether philosophers shall think fit to call a thing the *same* or no, is, I conceive, of small importance. Let us suppose several men together, all endued with the same faculties, and consequently affected in like sort by their senses, and who had yet never known the use of language; they would, without question, agree in their perceptions. Though perhaps, when they came to the use of speech, some regarding the uniformness of what was perceived, might call it the *same* thing: others, especially regarding the diversity of persons who perceived, might choose the denomination of *different* things. But who sees not that all the dispute is about a word? To wit, whether what is perceived by different persons may yet have the term *same* applied to it? Or, suppose a house, whose walls or outward shell remaining unaltered, the chambers are all pulled down, and new ones built in their place; and that you should call this the *same,* and I should say it was not the *same* house:—would we not, for all this, perfectly agree in our thoughts of the house, considered in itself? And would not all the difference consist in a sound? If you should say, We differed in our notions; for that you superadded to your idea of the house the simple abstracted idea of identity, whereas I did not; I would tell you, I know not what you mean by the *abstracted idea of identity;* and should desire you to look into your own thoughts, and be sure you understood yourself.—Why so silent, Hylas? Are you not yet satisfied men may dispute about identity and diversity, without any real difference in their thoughts and opinions, abstracted from names? Take this farther reflexion with you—that whether matter be allowed to exist or no, the case is exactly the same as to the point in hand. For the materialists themselves acknowledge what we immediately perceive by our senses to be our own ideas. Your difficulty, therefore, that no two see the same thing, makes equally against the materialists and me.

HYLAS: But they suppose an external archetype, to which referring their several ideas they may truly be said to perceive the same thing.

PHILONOUS: And (not to mention your having discarded those archetypes) so may you suppose an external archetype on my principles; *external,* I mean, to your own mind: though indeed it must be supposed to exist in that mind which comprehends all things; but then, this serves all the ends of identity, as well as if it existed out of a mind. And I am sure you yourself will not say it is less intelligible.

HYLAS: You have indeed clearly satisfied me—either that there is no difficulty at bottom in this point; or, if there be, that it makes equally against both opinions.

PHILONOUS: But that which makes equally against two contradictory opinions can be a proof against neither.

HYLAS: I acknowledge it. But, after all, Philonous, when I consider the substance of what you advance against *scepticism,* it amounts to no more than this:—We are sure that we really see, hear, feel; in a word, that we are affected with sensible impressions.

PHILONOUS: And how are we concerned any farther? I see this *cherry,* I feel it, I taste it: and I am sure *nothing* cannot be seen, or felt, or tasted: it is therefore *real.* Take away the sensations of softness, moisture, redness, tartness, and you take away the *cherry,* since it is not a being distinct from sensations. A *cherry,* I say, is nothing but a congeries of sensible impressions, or ideas perceived by various senses: which ideas are united into one thing (or have one name given them) by the mind, because they are observed to attend each other. Thus, when the palate is affected with such a particular taste, the sight is affected with a red colour, the touch with roundness, softness, &c. Hence, when I see, and feel, and taste, in such sundry certain manners, I am sure the *cherry* exists, or is real; its reality being in my opinion nothing abstracted from those sensations. But if by the word *cherry* you mean an unknown nature, distinct from all those sensible qualities, and by its existence something distinct from its being perceived; then, indeed, I own, neither you nor I, nor any one else, can be sure it exists.

HYLAS: But, what would you say, Philonous, if I should bring the very same reasons against the existence of sensible things in a mind, which you have offered against their existing in a material *substratum?*

PHILONOUS: When I see your reasons, you shall hear what I have to say to them.

HYLAS: Is the mind extended or unextended?

PHILONOUS: Unextended, without doubt.

HYLAS: Do you say the things you perceive are in your mind?

PHILONOUS: They are.

HYLAS: Again, have I not heard you speak of sensible impressions?

PHILONOUS: I believe you may.

HYLAS: Explain to me now, O Philonous! how it is possible there should be room for all those trees and houses to exist in your mind. Can extended things be contained in that which is unextended? Or, are we to imagine impressions made on a thing void of all solidity? You cannot say objects are in your mind, as books in your study: or that things are imprinted on it, as the figure of a seal upon wax. In what sense, therefore, are we to understand those expressions? Explain me this if you can: and I shall then be able to answer all those queries you formerly put to me about my *substratum.*

PHILONOUS: Look you, Hylas, when I speak of objects as existing in the mind, or imprinted on the senses, I would not be understood in the gross literal sense, as when bodies are said to exist in a place, or a seal to make an impression upon wax. My meaning is only that the mind comprehends or perceives them; and that it is affected from without, or by some being distinct from itself. This is my explication of your difficulty; and how it can serve to make your tenet of an unperceiving material substratum intelligible, I would fain know.

HYLAS: Nay, if that be all, I confess I do not see what use can be made of it. But are you not guilty of some abuse of language in this?

PHILONOUS: None at all. It is no more than common custom, which you know is the rule of language, hath authorised: nothing being more usual, than for philosophers to speak of the immediate objects of the understanding as things existing in the mind. Nor is there anything in this but what is conformable to the general analogy of language; most part of the mental operations being signified by words borrowed from sensible things; as is plain in the terms *comprehend, reflect, discourse,* &c., which, being applied to the mind, must not be taken in their gross, original sense.

HYLAS: You have, I own, satisfied me in this point. But there still remains one great difficulty, which I know not how you will get over. And, indeed, it is of such importance that if you could solve all others, without being able to find a solution for this, you must never expect to make me a proselyte to your principles.

PHILONOUS: Let me know this mighty difficulty.

HYLAS: The Scripture account of the creation is what appears to me utterly irreconcilable with your notions. Moses tells us of a creation: a creation of what? Of ideas? No, certainly, but of things, of real things, solid corporeal substances. Bring your principles to agree with this, and I shall perhaps agree with you.

PHILONOUS: Moses mentions the sun, moon, and stars, earth and sea, plants and animals. That all these do really exist, and were in the beginning created by God, I make no question. If by *ideas* you mean fictions and fancies of the mind, then these are no ideas. If by *ideas* you mean immediate objects of the understanding, or sensible things, which cannot exist unperceived, or out of a mind, then these things are ideas. But whether you do or do not call them *ideas,* it matters little. The difference is only about a name. And, whether that name be retained or rejected, the sense, the truth, and reality of things continues the same. In common talk, the objects of our senses are not termed *ideas,* but *things.* Call them so still: provided you do not attribute to them any absolute external existence, and I shall never quarrel with you for a word. The creation, therefore, I allow to have been a creation of things, of *real* things. Neither is this in the least inconsistent with my principles, as is evident from what I have now said; and would have been evident to you without this, if you had not forgotten what had been so often said before. But as for solid corporeal substances, I desire you to show where Moses makes any mention of them; and, if they should be mentioned by him, or any other inspired writer, it would still be incumbent on you to show those words were not taken in the vulgar acceptation, for things falling under our senses, but in the philosophic acceptation, for matter, or an unknown quiddity, with an absolute existence. When you have proved these points, then (and not till then) may you bring the authority of Moses into our dispute.

HYLAS: It is in vain to dispute about a point so clear. I am content to refer it to your own conscience. Are you not satisfied there is some peculiar repugnancy between the Mosaic account of the creation and your notions?

PHILONOUS: If all possible sense which can be put on the first chapter of Genesis may be conceived as consistently with my principles as any other, then it has no peculiar repugnancy with them. But there is no sense you may not as well conceive, believing as I do. Since, besides spirits, all you conceive are ideas; and the existence of these I do not deny. Neither do you pretend they exist without the mind.

HYLAS: Pray let me see any sense you can understand it in.

PHILONOUS: Why, I imagine that if I had been present at the creation, I should have seen things produced into being—that is become perceptible—in the order prescribed by the sacred historian. I never before believed the Mosaic account of the creation, and now find no alteration in my manner of believing it. When things are said to begin or end their existence, we do not mean this with regard to God, but His creatures. All objects are eternally known by God, or, which is the same thing, have an eternal existence in His mind: but when things, before imperceptible to creatures, are, by a decree of God, perceptible to them, then are they said to begin a relative existence, with respect to created minds. Upon reading therefore the Mosaic account of the creation, I understand that the several parts of the world became gradually perceivable to finite spirits, endowed with proper faculties; so that, whoever such were present, they were in truth perceived by them. This is the literal obvious sense suggested to me by the words of the Holy Scripture: in which is included no mention, or no thought, either of *substratum,* instrument, occasion, or absolute existence. And, upon inquiry, I doubt not it will be found that most plain honest men, who believe the creation, never think of those things any more than I. What metaphysical sense you may understand it in, you only can tell.

HYLAS: But, Philonous, you do not seem to be aware that you allow created things, in the beginning, only a relative, and consequently hypothetical being: that is to say, upon supposition there were men to perceive them; without which they have no actuality of absolute existence, wherein creation might terminate. Is it not, therefore, according to you, plainly impossible the creation of any inanimate creatures should precede that of man? And is not this directly contrary to the Mosaic account?

PHILONOUS: In answer to that, I say, *first,* created beings might begin to exist in the mind of other created intelligences, beside men. You will not therefore be able to prove any contradiction between Moses and my notions, unless you first show there was no other order of finite created spirits in being, before man. I say farther, in case we conceive the creation, as we should at this time, a parcel of plants or vegetables of all sorts produced, by an invisible Power, in a desert where nobody was present—that this way of explaining or conceiving it is consistent with my principles, since they deprive you of nothing, either sensible or imaginable; that it exactly suits with the common, natural, and undebauched notions of mankind; that it manifests the dependence of all things on God; and consequently hath all the good effect or influence, which it is possible that important article of our faith should have in making men humble, thankful, and resigned to their great creator. I say, moreover, that, in this naked conception of things, divested of words, there will not be found any notion of what you call the *actuality of absolute existence.* You may indeed raise a dust with those terms, and so lengthen our dispute to no purpose. But I entreat you calmly to look into your own thoughts, and then tell me if they are not a useless and unintelligible jargon.

HYLAS: I own I have no very clear notion annexed to them. But what say you to this? Do you not make the existence of sensible things consist in their being in a mind? And were not all things eternally in the mind of God? Did they not therefore exist from all eternity, according to you? And how could that which was eternal be created in time? Can anything be clearer or better connected than this?

PHILONOUS: And are not you too of opinion, that God knew all things from eternity?

HYLAS: I am.

PHILONOUS: Consequently they always had a being in the divine intellect.

HYLAS: This I acknowledge.

PHILONOUS: By your own confession, therefore, nothing is new, or begins to be, in respect of the mind of God. So we are agreed in that point.

HYLAS: What shall we make then of the creation?

PHILONOUS: May we not understand it to have been entirely in respect of finite spirits; so that things, with regard to us, may properly be said to begin their existence, or be created, when God decreed they should become perceptible to intelligent creatures, in that order and manner which he then established, and we now call the laws of nature? You may call this a *relative,* or *hypothetical existence* if you please. But, so long as it supplies us with the most natural, obvious, and literal sense of the Mosaic history of the creation; so long as it answers all the religious ends of that great article; in a word, so long as you can assign no other sense or meaning in its stead; why should we reject this? Is it to comply with a ridiculous sceptical humour of making everything nonsense and unintelligible? I am sure you cannot say it is for the glory of God. For, allowing it to be a thing possible and conceivable that the corporeal world should have an absolute existence extrinsical to the mind of God, as well as to the minds of all created spirits; yet how could this set forth either the immensity or omniscience of the Deity, or the necessary and immediate dependence of all things on him? Nay, would it not rather seem to derogate from those attributes?

HYLAS: Well, but as to this decree of God's, for making things perceptible, what say you, Philonous? Is it not plain, God did either execute that decree from all eternity or at some certain time began to will what he had not actually willed before, but only designed to will? If the former, then there could be no creation, or beginning of existence, in finite things. If the latter, then we must acknowledge something new to befall the Deity; which implies a sort of change: and all change argues imperfection.

PHILONOUS: Pray consider what you are doing. Is it not evident this objection concludes equally against a creation in any sense; nay, against every other act of the Deity, discoverable by the light of nature? None of which can we conceive, otherwise than as performed in time, and having a beginning. God is a being of transcendent and unlimited perfections: His nature, therefore, is incomprehensible to finite spirits. It is not, therefore, to be expected that any man, whether *materialist* or *immaterialist,* should have exactly just notions of the Deity, His attributes, and ways of operation. If then you would infer anything against me, your difficulty must not be drawn from the inadequateness of our conceptions of the divine nature, which is unavoidable on any scheme; but from the denial of matter, of which there is not one word, directly or indirectly, in what you have now objected.

HYLAS: I must acknowledge the difficulties you are concerned to clear are such only as arise from the non-existence of matter, and are peculiar to that notion. So far you are in the right. But I cannot by any means bring myself to think there is no such peculiar repugnancy between the creation and your opinion; though indeed where to fix it, I do not distinctly know.

PHILONOUS: What would you have? Do I not acknowledge a twofold state of things—the one ectypal or natural, the other archetypal and eternal? The former was created in time; the latter existed from everlasting in the mind of God. Is not this agreeable to the common notions of divines? or, is any more than this necessary in order to conceive the creation? But you suspect some peculiar repugnancy, though you know not where it lies. To take away all possibility of scruple in the case, do but consider this one point. Either you are not able to conceive the creation on any hypothesis whatsoever; and, if so, there is no ground for dislike or complaint against any particular opinion on that score: or you are able to conceive it; and, if so, why not on my principles, since thereby nothing conceivable is taken away? You have all along been allowed the full scope of sense, imagination, and reason. Whatever, therefore, you could before apprehend, either immediately or mediately by your senses, or by ratiocination from your senses; whatever you could perceive, imagine, or understand, remains still with you. If, therefore, the notion you have of the creation by other principles be intelligible, you have it still upon mine; if it be not intelligible, I conceive it to be no notion at all; and so there is no loss of it. And indeed it seems to me very plain that the supposition of matter, that is a thing perfectly unknown and inconceivable, cannot serve to make us conceive anything. And, I hope it need not be proved to you that if the existence of matter does not make the creation conceivable, the creation's being without it inconceivable can be no objection against its non-existence.

HYLAS: I confess, Philonous, you have almost satisfied me in this point of the creation.

PHILONOUS: I would fain know why you are not quite satisfied. You tell me indeed of a repugnancy between the Mosaic history and immaterialism: but you know not where it lies. Is this reasonable, Hylas? Can you expect I should solve a difficulty without knowing what it is? But, to pass by all that, would not a man think you were assured there is no repugnancy between the received notions of materialists and the inspired writings?

HYLAS: And so I am.

PHILONOUS: Ought the historical part of Scripture to be understood in a plain obvious sense, or in a sense which is metaphysical and out of the way?

HYLAS: In the plain sense, doubtless.

PHILONOUS: When Moses speaks of herbs, earth, water, &c. as having been created by God; think you not the sensible things commonly signified by those words are suggested to every unphilosophical reader?

HYLAS: I cannot help thinking so.

PHILONOUS: And are not all ideas, or things perceived by sense, to be denied a real existence by the doctrine of the materialist?

HYLAS: This I have already acknowledged.

PHILONOUS: The creation, therefore, according to them, was not the creation of things sensible, which have only a relative being, but of certain unknown natures, which have an absolute being, wherein creation might terminate?

HYLAS: True.

PHILONOUS: Is it not therefore evident the assertors of matter destroy the plain obvious sense of Moses, with which their notions are utterly inconsistent; and instead of it obtrude on us I know not what; something equally unintelligible to themselves and me?

HYLAS: I cannot contradict you.

PHILONOUS: Moses tells us of a creation. A creation of what? of unknown quiddities, of occasions, or *substratum?* No, certainly; but of things obvious to the senses. You must first reconcile this with your notions, if you expect I should be reconciled to them.

HYLAS: I see you can assault me with my own weapons.

PHILONOUS: Then as to *absolute existence;* was there ever known a more jejune notion than that? Something it is so abstracted and unintelligible that you have frankly owned you could not conceive it, much less explain anything by it. But allowing matter to exist, and the notion of absolute existence to be clear as light; yet, was this ever known to make the creation more credible? Nay, hath it not furnished the atheists and infidels of all ages with the most plausible arguments against a creation? That a corporeal substance, which hath an absolute existence without the minds of spirits, should be produced out of nothing, by the mere will of a spirit, hath been looked upon as a thing so contrary to all reason, so impossible and absurd, that not only the most celebrated among the ancients, but even divers modern and Christian philosophers have thought matter co-eternal with the Deity. Lay these things together, and then judge you whether materialism disposes men to believe the creation of things.

HYLAS: I own, Philonous, I think it does not. This of the *creation* is the last objection I can think of; and I must needs own it hath been sufficiently answered as well as the rest. Nothing now remains to be overcome but a sort of unaccountable backwardness that I find in myself towards your notions.

PHILONOUS: When a man is swayed, he knows not why, to one side of the question, can this, think you, be anything else but the effect of prejudice, which never fails to attend old and rooted notions? And indeed in this respect I cannot deny the belief of matter to have very much the advantage over the contrary opinion, with men of a learned education.

HYLAS: I confess it seems to be as you say.

PHILONOUS: As a balance, therefore, to this weight of prejudice, let us throw into the scale the great advantages that arise from the belief of immaterialism, both in regard to religion and human learning. The being of a God, and incorruptibility of the soul, those great articles of religion, are they not proved with the clearest and most immediate evidence? When I say the being of a *God,* I do not mean an obscure general cause of things, whereof we have no conception, but *God,* in the strict and proper sense of the word. A being whose spirituality, omnipresence, providence, omniscience, infinite power and goodness, are as conspicuous as the existence of sensible things, of which (nothwithstanding the fallacious pretences and affected scruples of *sceptics*) there is no more reason to doubt than of our own being. Then, with relation to human sciences. In natural philosophy, what intricacies, what obscurities, what contradictions hath the belief of matter led men into! To say nothing of the numberless disputes about its extent, continuity, homogeneity, gravity, divisibility, &c.—do they not pretend to explain all things by bodies operating on bodies, according to the laws of motion? And yet, are they able to comprehend how one body should move another? Nay, admitting there was no difficulty in reconciling the notion of an inert being with a cause, or in conceiving how an accident might pass from one body to another; yet, by all their strained thoughts and extravagant suppositions, have they been able to reach the mechanical production of any one animal or vegetable body? Can they account, by the laws of motion, for sounds, tastes, smells, or colours; or for the regular course of things? Have they accounted, by physical principles, for the aptitude and contrivance even of the most inconsiderable parts of the universe? But, laying aside matter and corporeal causes, and admitting only the efficiency of an all-perfect mind, are not all the effects of nature easy and intelligible? If the *phenomena* are nothing else but *ideas;* God is a *spirit,* but matter an unintelligent, unperceiving being. If they demonstrate an unlimited power in their cause; God is active and omnipotent, but matter an inert mass. If the order regularity, and usefulness of them can never be sufficiently admired; God is infinitely wise and provident, but matter destitute of all contrivance and design. These surely are great advantages in *physics.* Not to mention that the apprehension of a distant Deity naturally disposes men to a negligence in their *moral* actions; which they would be more cautious of, in case they thought him immediately present, and acting on their minds, without the interposition of matter, or unthinking second causes. Then in *metaphysics:* what difficulties concerning entity in abstract, substantial forms, hylarchic principles, plastic natures, substance and accident, principle of individuation, possibility of matter's thinking, origin of ideas, the manner how two independent substances so widely different as *spirit* and *matter,* should mutually operate on each other? What difficulties, I say, and endless disquisitions, concerning these and innumerable other the like points, do we escape, by supposing only spirits and ideas? Even the *mathematics* themselves, if we take away the absolute existence of extended things, become much more clear and easy; the most shocking paradoxes and intricate speculations in those sciences depending on the infinite divisibility of finite extension; which depends on that supposition. But what need is there to insist on the particular sciences? Is not that opposition to all science whatsoever, that frenzy of the ancient and modern *sceptics,* built on the same foundation? Or can you produce so much as one argument against the reality of corporeal things, or in behalf of that avowed utter ignorance of their natures, which does not suppose their reality to consist in an external absolute existence? Upon this supposition, indeed, the objections from the change of colours in a pigeon's neck, or the appearance of the broken oar in the water, must be allowed to have weight. But these and the like objections vanish, if we do not maintain the being of absolute external originals, but place the reality of things in ideas, fleeting indeed, and changeable; however, not changed at random, but according to the fixed order of nature. For, herein consists that constancy and truth of things which secures all the concerns of life, and distinguishes that which is *real* from the irregular visions of the fancy.

HYLAS: I agree to all you have now said, and must own that nothing can incline me to embrace your opinion more than the advantages I see it is attended with. I am by nature lazy; and this would be a mighty abridgment in knowledge. What doubts, what hypotheses, what labyrinths of amusement, what fields of disputation, what an ocean of false learning, may be avoided by that single notion of *immaterialism!*

PHILONOUS: After all, is there anything farther remaining to be done? You may remember you promised to embrace that opinion which upon examination should appear most agreeable to common sense and remote from *scepticism.* This, by your own confession, is that which denies matter, or the absolute existence of corporeal things. Nor is this all; the same notion has been proved several ways, viewed in different lights, pursued in its consequences, and all objections against it cleared. Can there be a greater evidence of its truth? Or is it possible it should have all the marks of a true opinion and yet be false?

HYLAS: I own myself entirely satisfied for the present in all respects. But, what security can I have that I shall still continue the same full assent to your opinion, and that no unthought-of objection or difficulty will occur hereafter?

PHILONOUS: Pray, Hylas, do you in other cases, when a point is once evidently proved, withhold your consent on account of objections or difficulties it may be liable to? Are the difficulties that attend the doctrine of incommensurable quantities, of the angle of contact, of the asymptotes to curves, or the like, sufficient to make you hold out against mathematical demonstration? Or will you disbelieve the Providence of God, because there may be some particular things which you know not how to reconcile with it? If there are difficulties attending *immaterialism,* there are at the same time direct and evident proofs of it. But for the existence of matter there is not one proof, and far more numerous and insurmountable objections lie against it. But where are those mighty difficulties you insist on? Alas! you know not where or what they are; something which may possibly occur hereafter. If this be a sufficient pretence for withholding your full assent, you should never yield it to any proposition, how free soever from exceptions, how clearly and solidly soever demonstrated.

HYLAS: You have satisfied me, Philonous.

PHILONOUS: But, to arm you against all future objections, do but consider: That which bears equally hard on two contradictory opinions can be proof against neither. Whenever, therefore, any difficulty occurs, try if you can find a solution for it on the hypothesis of the *materialists.* Be not deceived by words; but sound your own thoughts. And in case you cannot conceive it easier by the help of *materialism,* it is plain it can be no objection against *immaterialism.* Had you proceeded all along by this rule, you would probably have spared yourself abundance of trouble in objecting; since of all your difficulties I challenge you to show one that is explained by matter: nay, which is not more unintelligible with than without that supposition; and consequently makes rather *against* than *for* it. You should consider, in each particular, whether the difficulty arises from the *non-existence of matter.* If it does not, you might as well argue from the infinite divisibility of extension against the divine prescience, as from such a difficulty against *immaterialism.* And yet, upon recollection, I believe you will find this to have been often, if not always, the case. You should likewise take heed not to argue on a *petitio principii.* One is apt to say, the unknown substances ought to be esteemed real things, rather than the ideas in our minds: and who can tell but the unthinking external substance may concur, as a cause or instrument, in the productions of our ideas? But is not this proceeding on a supposition that there are such external substances? And to suppose this is it not begging the question? But, above all things, you should beware of imposing on yourself by that vulgar sophism which is called *ignoratio elenchi.* You talked often as if you thought I maintained the non-existence of Sensible Things. Whereas in truth no one can be more thoroughly assured of their existence than I am. And it is you who doubt; I should have said, positively deny it. Everything that is seen, felt, heard, or any way perceived by the senses, is, on the principles I embrace, a real being; but not on yours. Remember, the matter you contend for is an unknown somewhat (if indeed it may be termed *somewhat*), which is quite stripped of all sensible qualities, and can neither be perceived by sense, nor apprehended by the mind. Remember I say, that it is not any object which is hard or soft, hot or cold, blue or white, round or square, &c. For all these things I affirm do exist. Though indeed I deny they have an existence distinct from being perceived; or that they exist out of all minds whatsoever. Think on these points; let them be attentively considered and still kept in view. Otherwise you will not comprehend the state of the question; without which your objections will always be wide of the mark, and, instead of mine, may possibly be directed (as more than once they have been) against your own notions.

HYLAS: I must needs own, Philonous, nothing seems to have kept me from agreeing with you more than this same *mistaking the question.* In denying matter, at first glimpse I am tempted to imagine you deny the things we see and feel: but, upon reflexion, find there is no ground for it. What think you, therefore, of retaining the name *matter,* and applying it to sensible things? This may be done without any change in your sentiments: and, believe me, it would be a means of reconciling them to some persons who may be more shocked at an innovation in words than in opinion.

PHILONOUS: With all my heart: retain the word *matter,* and apply it to the objects of sense, if you please; provided you do not attribute to them any subsistence distinct from their being perceived. I shall never quarrel with you for an expression. *Matter,* or *material substance,* are terms introduced by philosophers; and, as used by them, imply a sort of independency, or a subsistence distinct from being perceived by a mind: but are never used by common people; or, if ever, it is to signify the immediate objects of sense. One would think, therefore, so long as the names of all particular things, with the terms *sensible, substance, body, stuff,* and the like, are retained, the word *matter* should be never missed in common talk. And in philosophical discourses it seems the best way to leave it quite out: since there is not, perhaps, any one thing that hath more favoured and strengthened the depraved bent of the mind towards Atheism than the use of that general confused term.

HYLAS: Well but, Philonous, since I am content to give up the notion of an unthinking substance exterior to the mind, I think you ought not to deny me the privilege of using the word *matter* as I please, and annexing it to a collection of sensible qualities subsisting only in the mind. I freely own there is no other substance, in a strict sense, than *spirit.* But I have been so long accustomed to the term *matter* that I know not how to part with it: to say, there is no matter in the world, is still shocking to me. Whereas to say, there is no *matter,* if by that term be meant an unthinking substance existing without the mind; but if by matter is meant some sensible thing, whose existence consists in being perceived, then there is matter: this distinction gives it quite another turn; and men will come into your notions with small difficulty, when they are proposed in that manner. For, after all, the controversy about *matter* in the strict acceptation of it, lies altogether between you and the philosophers: whose principles, I acknowledge, are not near so natural, or so agreeable to the common sense of mankind, and Holy Scripture, as yours. There is nothing we either desire or shun but as it makes, or is apprehended to make, some part of our happiness or misery. But what has happiness or misery, joy or grief, pleasure or pain, to do with absolute existence; or with unknown entities, abstracted from all relation to us? It is evident, things regard us only as they are pleasing or displeasing: and they can please or displease only so far forth as they are perceived. Farther, therefore, we are not concerned, and thus far you leave things as you found them. Yet still there is something new in this doctrine. It is plain, I do not now think with the philosophers; nor yet altogether with the vulgar. I would know how the case stands in that respect; precisely, what you have added to, or altered in my former notions.

PHILONOUS: I do not pretend to be a setter-up of new notions. My endeavours tend only to unite, and place in a clearer light, that truth which was before shared between the vulgar and the philosophers:—the former being of opinion, that *those things they immediately perceive are the real things;* and the latter, that *the things immediately perceived are ideas, which exist only in the mind.* Which two notions put together, do, in effect, constitute the substance of what I advance.

HYLAS: I have been a long time distrusting my senses: methought I saw things by a dim light and through false glasses. Now the glasses are removed and a new light breaks in upon my understanding. I am clearly convinced that I see things in their native forms, and am no longer in pain about their *unknown natures* or *absolute existence*. This is the state I find myself in at present; though, indeed, the course that brought me to it I do not yet thoroughly comprehend. You set out upon the same principles that Academics, Cartesians, and the like sects usually do; and for a long time it looked as if you were advancing their philosophical *scepticism:* but, in the end, your conclusions are directly opposite to theirs.

PHILONOUS: You see, Hylas, the water of yonder fountain, how it is forced upwards, in a round column, to a certain height; at which it breaks, and falls back into the basin from whence it rose: its ascent, as well as descent, proceeding from the same uniform law or principle of *gravitation.* Just so, the same principles which, at first view, lead to *scepticism,* pursued to a certain point, bring men back to common sense.

DAVID HUME
1711–1776

David Hume was born in Edinburgh, Scotland, in 1711. His father, a lawyer, died before David was two years old. He was raised by his mother, a deeply religious woman, on a pleasant, but modest, family estate at Ninewells, near Berwick in southern Scotland. Young David was very religious as a boy, often making lists of his sins so that he could seek forgiveness. But shortly after beginning his studies at the University of Edinburgh, at age twelve, he seems to have lost his faith.

Although the family was not poor, there was not enough wealth to provide a comfortable life of study for David, the youngest child. His family decided, therefore, that Hume should follow his father into law. This was not to be, however, for as Hume later wrote, "I found an unsurmountable aversion to everything but the pursuit of philosophy and general learning."

In 1729, when he was only eighteen, Hume had a breakthrough, discovering what he called "a new Science of Thought." He gave up all pretense of becoming a lawyer and applied his energies to his new insight. To conserve his limited finances, he moved to a small town in France, La Flèche, where Descartes had studied. There he completed his first work, *A Treatise of Human Nature, Being an Attempt to Introduce the Experimental Method of Reasoning into Moral Subjects*, published in 1739 and 1740. Hume hoped this work would give him his "love of literary fame"—while putting him in a more comfortable financial situation. But, as he later said, the work "fell dead-born from the press, without reaching such distinction as even to excite a murmur among the zealots."

For the next thirteen years, Hume held a variety of positions, including tutor to a mad marquess and secretary to a general. During this time, Hume wrote and published his *Essays, Moral and Political* (1741–1742). The success of this work led him to rewrite Book I of his earlier *Treatise*, this time titled as *An Enquiry Concerning Human Understanding* (1748). He added chapters on miracles, free will, and the argument from design, which he had left out of the earlier work, and he omitted many of his psychological speculations. This book enjoyed some success, though its antireligious nature may have contributed to Hume's rejected applications for two different chairs of philosophy. In 1751, he also recast Book III of the earlier *Treatise*, under the title *Enquiry Concerning the Principles of Morals*.

Hume was appointed Librarian to the Faculty of Advocates in Edinburgh in 1752. In this post, he wrote a multivolume history of England. He also managed to infuriate the library curators with his selections, and in 1757 he was forced to resign when he refused to remove books the curators considered obscene. In the same year, he published *Four Dissertations*, including "The Natural History of Religion," "Of the Passions" (a truncated version of Book II of the *Treatise*), "Of Tragedy," and "Of the Standard of Taste." By now Hume's works had become well known on the Continent, and when he returned to France in 1763 as part of the British ambassador's staff, he was lionized by French intellectual society. Hume was a favorite at French soirées: Sociable and witty, he was called "le bon David" by his French friends.

When Hume returned to England in 1766, he found that his works had finally brought him the literary fame at home that he had so long desired. In 1767, he took another government post, but two years later he resigned and retired to Edinburgh. There he spent his last years quietly, until his death, probably from cancer, in 1776. His *Dialogues Concerning Natural Religion*, written in the 1750s, was published posthumously in 1779.

*   *   *

Hume's philosophy, as developed in the *Enquiry*, begins with a rejection of the "abstruse speculations" and "superstitions" of contemporary thought. With Locke, Hume agrees that there are no such things as innate ideas; all knowledge comes through sensory experience. Yet as he worked out the implications of these convictions, he came to conclusions quite different from those of his predecessor.

According to Hume, all the perceptions of the mind may be divided into "impressions" and "ideas." Using an empirical distinction, Hume believes impressions to be "more lively" than ideas. These impressions and ideas are then divided into simple and complex, impressions of sensation and impressions of reflection, and so on. The source of impressions cannot be known empirically, so Hume does not address this question. Simple ideas, on the other hand, must come from impressions. In fact, for an idea to have any meaning whatever, it must be derived from an impression or from a combination of impressions. If I have the idea of a gold mountain, for instance, it is because I have previously had impressions that gave rise to the ideas of "gold" and "mountain" that I am now associating. Using this empirical criterion of meaning, it becomes clear that ideas such as "substance," "God," or even "the self" are without a clear meaning. So according to Hume, Locke's idea of an eternal world of "substances" and Berkeley's idea of an all-perceiving God are without meaning.

Hume then considers the association between ideas and argues that there are "only three principles of connexion among ideas, namely, *Resemblance, Contiguity* in time or place, and *Cause* or *Effect*." These associations of ideas are really nothing more than habit or "custom" and so do not necessarily reflect the "real world." Take causality, for example. One could imagine Pavlov's dogs hearing the bell, getting the food, hearing the bell, getting the food, hearing the bell . . . and after a period of time concluding, "bells cause food." But there is obviously no necessary relation between cause and effect in this case. There is no logical reason why the bell might not sound and yet no food appear. Hume argues that all supposed instances of cause and effect are of this kind. We get so used to seeing two events joined that we conclude that one caused the other. Thus, according to Hume, Locke's claim that the "external world" causes sensations and the Thomistic First-Cause argument for God's existence are without empirical foundation. It also means that the "laws of nature" are founded only on past experience and that we have no *a priori* evidence that tomorrow will be the same as today.

The remainder of the *Enquiry* develops the implications of Hume's radical empiricism and deals with the skepticism arising from it. He acknowledges that his own practice does not always reflect his philosophical position. Hume recognizes that despite his causal skepticism, it would not be wise to "throw himself out at the window." As he wrote early on in this work, we must "be modest in our pretensions; and even to discover the difficulty ourselves before it is objected to us. By this means, we may make a kind of merit of our very ignorance."

*   *   *

Philosophers differ in their appraisals of Hume's two greatest works, the *Treatise* and its reworking, the *Enquiry*. Many consider the *Enquiry* more mature; others think the *Treatise* more brilliant. Hume himself said that the *Enquiry*, not the *Treatise*, contained his "philosophical sentiments and principles." The *Enquiry* is reprinted here complete.

For a comprehensive biography of Hume, including interesting material from his letters, see Ernest Campbell Mossner, *The Life of David Hume* (Oxford: Clarendon Press, 1954, 1980). The classic studies of Hume's thought are Charles William Hendel, *Studies in the Philosophy of David Hume* (Princeton, NJ: Princeton University Press, 1925); and, especially, Norman Kemp Smith, *The Philosophy of David Hume* (London: Macmillan, 1941). A short, clear overview of his thought is A.J. Ayer, *Hume* (New York: Oxford University Press, 1981)— part of the "Past Masters" series, now reprinted in a combined volume, John Dunn et al., eds., *The British Empiricists* (Oxford: Oxford University Press, 1992). Barry Stroud, *Hume* (Oxford: Routledge, 1981) and Terence Penelhum, *David Hume: An Introduction to His Philosophical System* (West Lafayette, IN: Purdue University Press, 1995) are also useful. For studies in specific areas of Hume's thought, see Tom L. Beauchamp, *Hume and the Problem of Causation* (New York: Oxford University Press, 1981); Robert J. Fogelin, *Hume's Skepticism in the Treatise of Human Nature* (London: Routledge, 1985); and David Pears, *Hume's System* (Oxford: Oxford University Press, 1991), George Dicker, *Hume's Epistemology and Metaphysics* (London: Routledge, 1998); H.O. Mounce, *Hume's Naturalism* (London: Routledge, 1999), for epistemology and philosophy of mind; Jonathan Harrison, *Hume's Moral Epistemology* (Oxford: Clarendon Press, 1976), and J.L. Mackie, *Hume's Moral Theory* (London: Routledge & Kegan Paul, 1980), for ethics; and Antony Flew, *Hume's Philosophy of Belief* (London: Routledge & Kegan Paul; New York: Humanities Press, 1961); J.C.A. Gaskin, *Hume's Philosophy of Religion* (New York: Barnes & Noble,

1978); and Keith E. Yandell, *Hume's "Inexplicable Mystery": His Views on Religion* (Philadelphia: Temple University Press, 1990); Stanley Tweyman, ed., *David Hume—Dialogues Concerning Natural Religion in Focus* (Oxford: Routledge, 1991), for philosophy of religion. For collections of essays, see David Pears, ed., *David Hume: A Symposium* (London: St. Martin's Press, 1963); A. Sesonke and N. Fleming, eds., *Human Understanding: Studies in the Philosophy of David Hume* (Belmont, CA: Wadsworth, 1965); and the excellent V.C. Chappell, ed., *Hume: A Collection of Critical Essays* (Notre Dame, IN: Notre Dame University Press, 1968); and Stanley Tweyman, ed., *David Hume: Critical Assessments,* six volumes (London: Routledge, 1996).

AN ENQUIRY CONCERNING HUMAN UNDERSTANDING

Section I. Of the Different Species of Philosophy

Moral philosophy, or the science of human nature, may be treated after two different manners; each of which has its peculiar merit, and may contribute to the entertainment, instruction, and reformation of mankind. The one considers man chiefly as born for action; and as influenced in his measures by taste and sentiment; pursuing one object, and avoiding another, according to the value which these objects seem to possess, and according to the light in which they present themselves. As virtue, of all objects, is allowed to be the most valuable, this species of philosophers paint her in the most amiable colours; borrowing all helps from poetry and eloquence, and treating their subject in an easy and obvious manner, and such as is best fitted to please the imagination, and engage the affections. They select the most striking observations and instances from common life; place opposite characters in a proper contrast; and alluring us into the paths of virtue by the views of glory and happiness, direct our steps in these paths by the soundest precepts and most illustrious examples. They make us *feel* the difference between vice and virtue; they excite and regulate our sentiments; and so they can but bend our hearts to the love of probity and true honour, they think, that they have fully attained the end of all their labours.

The other species of philosophers consider man in the light of a reasonable rather than an active being, and endeavour to form his understanding more than cultivate his manners. They regard human nature as a subject of speculation; and with a narrow scrutiny examine it, in order to find those principles, which regulate our understanding, excite our sentiments, and make us to approve or blame any particular object, action, or behaviour. They think it a reproach to all literature, that philosophy should not yet have fixed, beyond controversy, the foundation of morals, reasoning, and criticism; and should for ever talk of truth and falsehood, vice and virtue, beauty and deformity, without being able to determine the source of these distinctions. While they attempt this arduous task, they are deterred by no difficulties; but proceeding from particular instances to general principles, they still push on their enquiries to principles more general, and rest not satisfied till they arrive at those original principles, by which, in every science, all human curiosity must be bounded. Though their speculations seem abstract, and even unintelligible to common readers, they aim at the approbation of the learned and the wise; and think themselves sufficiently compensated for the labour of their whole lives, if they can discover some hidden truths, which may contribute to the instruction of posterity.

It is certain that the easy and obvious philosophy will always, with the generality of mankind, have the preference above the accurate and abstruse; and by many will be recommended, not only as more agreeable, but more useful than the other. It enters more into common life; moulds the heart and affections; and, by touching those principles which actuate men, reforms their conduct, and brings them nearer to that model of perfection which it describes. On the contrary, the abstruse philosophy, being founded on a turn of mind, which cannot enter into business and action, vanishes when the philosopher leaves the shade, and comes into open day; nor can its principles easily retain any influence over our conduct and behaviour. The feelings of our heart, the agitation of our passions, the vehemence of our affections, dissipate all its conclusions, and reduce the profound philosopher to a mere plebeian.

This also must be confessed, that the most durable, as well as justest fame, has been acquired by the easy philosophy, and that abstract reasoners seem hitherto to have enjoyed only a momentary reputation, from the caprice or ignorance of their own age, but have not been able to support their renown with more equitable posterity. It is easy for a profound philosopher to commit a mistake in his subtile reasonings; and one mistake is the necessary parent of another, while he pushes on his consequences, and is not deterred from embracing any conclusion, by its unusual appearance, or its contradiction to popular opinion. But a philosopher, who purposes only to represent the common sense of mankind in more beautiful and more engaging colours, if by accident he falls into error, goes not farther; but renewing his appeal to common sense, and the natural sentiments of the mind, returns into the right path, and secures himself from any dangerous illusions. The fame of Cicero flourishes at present; but that of Aristotle is utterly decayed. La Bruyere passes the seas, and still maintains his reputation: But the glory of Malebranche is confined to his own nation, and to his own age. And Addison, perhaps, will be read with pleasure, when Locke shall be entirely forgotten.

The mere philosopher is a character, which is commonly but little acceptable in the world, as being supposed to contribute nothing either to the advantage or pleasure of society; while he lives remote from communication with mankind, and is wrapped up in principles and notions equally remote from their comprehension. On the other hand, the mere ignorant is still more despised; nor is any thing deemed a surer sign of an illiberal genius in an age and nation where the sciences flourish, than to be entirely destitute of all relish for those noble entertainments. The most perfect character is supposed to lie between those extremes; retaining an equal ability and taste for books, company, and business; preserving in conversation that discernment and delicacy which arise from polite letters; and in business, that probity and accuracy which are the natural result of a just philosophy. In order to diffuse and cultivate so accomplished a character, nothing can be more useful than compositions of the easy style and manner, which draw not too much from life, require no deep application or retreat to be comprehended, and send back the student among mankind full of noble sentiments and wise precepts, applicable to every exigence of human life. By means of such compositions, virtue becomes amiable, science agreeable, company instructive, and retirement entertaining.

Man is a reasonable being; and as such, receives from science his proper food and nourishment: But so narrow are the bounds of human understanding, that little satisfaction can be hoped for in this particular, either from the extent or security of his acquisitions. Man is a sociable, no less than a reasonable being: But neither can he always enjoy company agreeable and amusing, or preserve the proper relish for them. Man is also an active being; and from that disposition, as well as from the various necessities of human life, must submit to business and occupation: But the mind requires some relaxation, and cannot always support its bent to care and industry. It seems, then, that nature has pointed out a mixed kind of life as most suitable to the human race, and secretly admonished them to allow none of these biases to draw too much, so as to incapacitate them for other occupations and entertainments. Indulge your passion for science, says she, but let your science be human, and such as may have a direct reference to action and society. Abstruse thought and profound researches I prohibit, and will severely punish, by the pensive melancholy which they introduce, by the endless uncertainty in which they involve you, and by the cold reception which your pretended discoveries shall meet with, when communicated. Be a philosopher; but, amidst all your philosophy, be still a man.

Were the generality of mankind contented to prefer the easy philosophy to the abstract and profound, without throwing any blame or contempt on the latter, it might not be improper, perhaps, to comply with this general opinion, and allow every man to enjoy, without opposition, his own taste and sentiment. But as the matter is often carried farther, even to the absolute rejecting of all profound reasonings, or what is commonly called *metaphysics*, we shall now proceed to consider what can reasonably be pleaded in their behalf.

We may begin with observing, that one considerable advantage, which results from the accurate and abstract philosophy, is, its subserviency to the easy and humane, which, without the former, can never attain a sufficient degree of exactness in its sentiments, precepts, or reasonings. All polite letters are nothing but pictures of human life in various attitudes and situations; and inspire us with different sentiments, of praise or blame, admiration or ridicule, according to the qualities of the object, which they set before us. An artist must be better qualified to succeed in this undertaking, who, besides a delicate taste and a quick apprehension, possesses an accurate knowledge of the internal fabric, the operations of the understanding, the workings of the passions, and the various species of sentiment which discriminate vice and virtue. How painful soever this inward search or enquiry may appear, it becomes, in some measure, requisite to those, who would describe with success the obvious and outward appearances of life and manners. The anatomist presents to the eye the most hideous and disagreeable objects; but his science is useful to the painter in delineating even a Venus or an Helen. While the latter employs all the richest colours of his art, and gives his figures the most graceful and engaging airs; he must still carry his attention to the inward structure of the human body, the position of the muscles, the fabric of the bones, and the use and figure of every part or organ. Accuracy is, in every case, advantageous to beauty and just reasoning to delicate sentiment. In vain would we exalt the one by depreciating the other.

Besides, we may observe, in every art or profession, even those which most concern life or action, that a spirit of accuracy, however acquired, carries all of them nearer their perfection, and renders them more subservient to the interests of society. And though a philosopher may live remote from business, the genius of philosophy, if carefully cultivated by several, must gradually diffuse itself throughout the whole

An Experiment on a Bird in the Air Pump, ca. 1767–1768, by Joseph Wright of Derby (1734–1797). The artist is showing the interplay between rational analysis and human emotion, between reason and feeling. The scientist in the center is demonstrating that a bird cannot fly in a vacuum. In doing so he is also killing the bird—a fact not lost on the little girls to the right. (*Tate Gallery, London*)

society, and bestow a similar correctness on every art and calling. The politician will acquire greater foresight and subtlety, in the subdividing and balancing of power; the lawyer more method and finer principles in his reasonings; and the general more regularity in his discipline, and more caution in his plans and operations. The stability of modern governments above the ancient, and the accuracy of modern philosophy, have improved, and probably will still improve, by similar gradations.

Were there no advantage to be reaped from these studies, beyond the gratification of an innocent curiosity, yet ought not even this to be despised; as being one accession to those few safe and harmless pleasures, which are bestowed on the human race. The sweetest and most inoffensive path of life leads through the avenues of science and learning; and whoever can either remove any obstructions in this way, or open up any new prospect, ought so far to be esteemed a benefactor to mankind. And though these researches may appear painful and fatiguing, it is with some minds as with some bodies, which being endowed with vigorous and florid health, require severe exercise, and reap a pleasure from what, to the generality of mankind, may seem burdensome and laborious. Obscurity, indeed, is painful to the mind as well as to the eye; but to bring light from obscurity, by whatever labour, must needs be delightful and rejoicing.

But this obscurity in the profound and abstract philosophy, is objected to, not only as painful and fatiguing, but as the inevitable source of uncertainty and error. Here indeed lies the justest and most plausible objection against a considerable part of metaphysics, that they are not properly a science; but arise either from the fruitless efforts of human vanity, which would penetrate into subjects utterly inaccessible to the understanding, or from the craft of popular superstitions, which, being unable to defend themselves on fair ground, raise these entangling brambles to cover and protect their weakness. Chased from the open country, these robbers fly into the forest, and lie in wait to break in upon every unguarded avenue of the mind, and overwhelm it with religious fears and prejudices. The stoutest antagonist, if he remit his watch a moment, is oppressed. And many, through cowardice and folly, open the gates to the enemies, and willingly receive them with reverence and submission, as their legal sovereigns.

But is this a sufficient reason, why philosophers should desist from such researches, and leave superstition still in possession of her retreat? Is it not proper to draw an opposite conclusion, and perceive the necessity of carrying the war into the most secret recesses of the enemy? In vain do we hope, that men, from frequent disappointment, will at last abandon such airy sciences, and discover the proper province of human reason. For, besides, that many persons find too sensible an interest in perpetually recalling such topics; besides this, I say, the motive of blind despair can never reasonably have place in the sciences; since, however unsuccessful former attempts may have proved, there is still room to hope, that the industry, good fortune, or improved sagacity of succeeding generations may reach discoveries unknown to former ages. Each adventurous genius will leap at the arduous prize, and find himself stimulated, rather than discouraged, by the failures of his predecessors; while he hopes that the glory of achieving so hard an adventure is reserved for him alone. The only method of freeing learning, at once, from these abstruse questions, is to enquire seriously into the nature of human understanding, and show, from an exact analysis of its powers and capacity, that it is by no means fitted for such remote and abstruse subjects. We must submit to this fatigue, in order to live at ease ever after: And must cultivate true metaphysics with some care, in order to destroy the false and adulterate. Indolence, which, to some persons, affords a safeguard against this deceitful philosophy, is, with others, overbalanced by curiosity; and despair, which, at some moments, prevails, may give place afterwards to sanguine hopes and expectations. Accurate and just reasoning is the only catholic remedy, fitted for all persons and all dispositions; and is alone able to subvert that abstruse philosophy and metaphysical jargon, which, being mixed up with popular superstition, renders it in a manner impenetrable to careless reasoners, and gives it the air of science and wisdom.

Besides this advantage of rejecting, after deliberate enquiry, the most uncertain and disagreeable part of learning, there are many positive advantages, which result from an accurate scrutiny into the powers and faculties of human nature. It is remarkable concerning the operations of the mind, that, though most intimately present to us, yet, whenever they become the object of reflection, they seem involved in obscurity; nor can the eye readily find those lines and boundaries, which discriminate and distinguish them. The objects are too fine to remain long in the same aspect or situation; and must be apprehended in an instant, by a superior penetration, derived from nature, and improved by habit and reflection. It becomes, therefore, no inconsiderable part of science barely to know the different operations of the mind, to separate them from each other, to class them under their proper heads, and to correct all that seeming disorder, in which they lie involved, when made the object of reflection and enquiry. This talk of ordering and distinguishing, which has no merit, when performed with regard to external bodies, the objects of our senses, rises in its value, when directed towards the operations of the mind, in proportion to the difficulty and labour, which we meet with in performing it. And if we can go no farther than this mental geography, or delineation of the distinct parts and powers of the mind, it is at least a satisfaction to go so far; and the more obvious this science may appear (and it is by no means obvious) the more contemptible still must the ignorance of it be esteemed, in all pretenders to learning and philosophy.

Nor can there remain any suspicion, that this science is uncertain and chimerical; unless we should entertain such a scepticism as is entirely subversive of all speculation, and even action. It cannot be doubted, that the mind is endowed with several powers and faculties, that these powers are distinct from each other, that what is really distinct to the immediate perception may be distinguished by reflection; and consequently, that there is a truth and falsehood in all propositions on this subject, and a truth and falsehood, which lie not beyond the compass of human understanding. There are many obvious distinctions of this kind, such as those between the will and understanding, the imagination and passions, which fall within the comprehension of every human creature; and the finer and more philosophical distinctions are no less real and certain, though more difficult to be comprehended. Some instances, especially late ones, of success in these enquiries, may give us a juster notion of the certainty and solidity of this branch of learning. And shall we esteem it worthy the labour of a philosopher to give us a true system of the planets, and adjust the position and order of those remote bodies; while we affect to overlook those, who, with so much success, delineate the parts of the mind, in which we are so intimately concerned?

But may we not hope, that philosophy, if cultivated with care, and encouraged by the attention of the public, may carry its researches still farther, and discover, at least in some degree, the secret springs and principles, by which the human mind is actuated in its operations? Astronomers had long contented themselves with proving, from the phenomena, the true motions, order, and magnitude of the heavenly bodies: Till a philosopher, at last, arose, who seems, from the happiest reasoning, to have also determined the laws and forces, by which the revolutions of the planets are governed and directed. The like has been performed with regard to other parts of nature. And there is no reason to despair of equal success in our enquiries concerning the mental powers and economy, if prosecuted with equal capacity and caution. It is probable, that one operation and principle of the mind depends on another; which, again, may be resolved into one more general and universal: And how far these researches may possibly be carried, it will be difficult for us, before, or even after, a careful trial, exactly to determine. This is certain, that attempts of this kind are every day made even by those who philosophize the most negligently: And nothing can be more requisite than to enter upon the enterprize with thorough care and attention; that, if it lie within the compass of human understanding, it may at last be happily achieved; if not, it may, however, be rejected with some confidence and security. This last conclusion, surely, is not desirable; nor ought it to be embraced too rashly. For how much must we diminish from the beauty and value of this species of philosophy, upon such a supposition? Moralists have hitherto been accustomed, when they considered the vast multitude and diversity of those actions that excite our approbation or dislike, to search for some common principle, on which this variety of sentiments might depend. And though they have sometimes carried the matter too far, by their passion for some one general principle; it must, however, be confessed, that they are excusable in expecting to find some general principles, into which all the vices and virtues were justly to be resolved. The like has been the endeavour of critics, logicians, and even politicians: Nor have their attempts been wholly unsuccessful; though perhaps longer time, greater accuracy, and more ardent application may bring these sciences still nearer their perfection. To throw up at once all pretensions of this kind may justly be deemed more rash, precipitate, and dogmatical, than even the boldest and most affirmative philosophy, that has ever attempted to impose its crude dictates and principles on mankind.

What though these reasonings concerning human nature seem abstract, and of difficult comprehension? This affords no presumption of their falsehood. On the contrary, it seems impossible, that what has hitherto escaped so many wise and profound philosophers can be very obvious and easy. And whatever pains these researches may cost us, we may think ourselves sufficiently rewarded, not only in point of profit but of pleasure, if, by that means, we can make any addition to our stock of knowledge, in subjects of such unspeakable importance.

But as, after all, the abstractedness of these speculations is no recommendation, but rather a disadvantage to them, and as this difficulty may perhaps be surmounted by care and art, and the avoiding of all unnecessary detail, we have, in the following enquiry, attempted to throw some light upon subjects, from which uncertainty has hitherto deterred the wise, and obscurity the ignorant. Happy, if we can unite the boundaries of the different species of philosophy, by reconciling profound enquiry with clearness, and truth with novelty! And still more happy, if reasoning in this easy manner, we can undermine the foundations of an abstruse philosophy, which seems to have hitherto served only as a shelter to superstition, and a cover to absurdity and error!

Section II. Of the Origin of Ideas

Every one will readily allow, that there is a considerable difference between the perceptions of the mind, when a man feels the pain of excessive heat, or the pleasure of moderate warmth, and when he afterwards recalls to his memory this sensation, or anticipates it by his imagination. These faculties may mimic or copy the perceptions of the senses; but they never can entirely reach the force and vivacity of the original sentiment. The utmost we say of them, even when they operate with greatest vigour, is, that they represent their object in so lively a manner, that we could almost say we feel or see it: But, except the mind be disordered by disease or madness, they never can arrive at such a pitch of vivacity, as to render these perceptions altogether undistinguishable. All the colours of poetry, however splendid, can never paint natural objects in such a manner as to make the description be taken for a real landscape. The most lively thought is still inferior to the dullest sensation.

We may observe a like distinction to run through all the other perceptions of the mind. A man in a fit of anger, is actuated in a very different manner from one who only thinks of that emotion. If you tell me, that any person is in love, I easily understand your meaning, and form a just conception of his situation; but never can mistake that conception for the real disorders and agitations of the passion. When we reflect on our past sentiments and affections, our thought is a faithful mirror, and copies its objects truly; but the colours which it employs are faint and dull, in comparison of those in which our original perceptions were clothed. It requires no nice discernment or metaphysical head to mark the distinction between them.

Here therefore we may divide all the perceptions of the mind into two classes or species, which are distinguished by their different degrees of force and vivacity. The less forcible and lively are commonly denominated *Thoughts* or *Ideas*. The other species want a name in our language, and in most others; I suppose, because it was not requisite for any, but philosophical purposes, to rank them under a general term or appellation. Let us, therefore, use a little freedom, and call them *Impressions*; employing that word in a sense somewhat different from the usual. By the term impression, then, I mean all our more lively perceptions, when we hear, or see, or feel, or love, or hate, or desire, or will. And *impressions* are distinguished from ideas which are the less lively perceptions, of which we are conscious, when we reflect on any of those sensations or movements above mentioned.

Nothing, at first view, may seem more unbounded than the thought of man, which not only escapes all human power and authority, but is not even restrained within the limits of nature and reality. To form monsters, and join incongruous shapes and appearances, costs the imagination no more trouble than to conceive the most natural and familiar objects. And while the body is confined to one planet, along which it creeps with pain and difficulty; the thought can in an instant transport us into the most distant regions of the universe; or even beyond the universe, into the unbounded chaos, where nature is supposed to lie in total confusion. What never was seen, or heard of, may yet be conceived; nor is any thing beyond the power of thought, except what implies an absolute contradiction.

But though our thought seems to possess this unbounded liberty, we shall find, upon a nearer examination, that it is really confined within very narrow limits, and that all this creative power of the mind amounts to no more than the faculty of compounding, transposing, augmenting, or diminishing the materials afforded us by the senses and experience. When we think of a golden mountain, we only join two consistent ideas, *gold* and *mountain*, with which we were formerly acquainted. A virtuous horse we can conceive; because, from our own feeling, we can conceive virtue; and this we may unite to the figure and shape of a horse, which is an animal familiar to us. In short, all the materials of thinking are derived either from our outward or inward sentiment: the mixture and composition of these belongs alone to the mind and will. Or, to express myself in philosophical language, all our ideas or more feeble perceptions are copies of our impressions or more lively ones.

To prove this, the two following arguments will, I hope, be sufficient. First, when we analyze our thoughts or ideas, however compounded or sublime, we always find that they resolve themselves into such simple ideas as were copied from a precedent feeling or sentiment. Even those ideas, which, at first view, seem the most wide of this origin, are found, upon a nearer scrutiny, to be derived from it. The idea of God, as meaning an infinitely intelligent, wise, and good Being, arises from reflecting on the operations of our own mind, and augmenting, without limit, those qualities of goodness and wisdom. We may prosecute this enquiry to what length we please; where we shall always find, that every idea which we examine is copied from a similar impression. Those who would assert that this position is not universally true nor without exception, have only one, and that an easy method of refuting it; by producing that idea, which, in their opinion, is not derived from this source. It will then be incumbent on us, if we would maintain our doctrine, to produce the impression, or lively perception, which corresponds to it.

Secondly. If it happens, from a defect of the organ, that a man is not susceptible of any species of sensation, we always find that he is as little susceptible of the correspondent ideas. A blind man can form no notion of colours; a deaf man of sounds. Restore either of them that sense in which he is deficient; by opening this new inlet for his sensations, you also open an inlet for the ideas; and he finds no difficulty in conceiving these objects. The case is the same, if the object, proper for exciting any sensation, has never been applied to the organ. A Laplander or Negro has no notion of the relish of wine. And though there are few or no instances of a like deficiency in the mind, where a person has never felt or is wholly incapable of a sentiment or passion that belongs to his species; yet we find the same observation to take place in a less degree. A man of mild manners can form no idea of inveterate revenge or cruelty; nor can a selfish heart easily conceive the heights of friendship and generosity. It is readily allowed, that other beings may possess many senses of which we can have no conception, because the ideas of them have never been introduced to us in the only manner by which an idea can have access to the mind, to wit, by the actual feeling and sensation.

There is, however, one contradictory phenomenon, which may prove that it is not absolutely impossible for ideas to arise, independent of their correspondent impressions. I believe it will readily be allowed, that the several distinct ideas of colour, which enter by the eye, or those of sound, which are conveyed by the ear, are really different from each other; though, at the same time, resembling. Now if this be true of different colours, it must be no less so of the different shades of the same colour; and each shade produces a distinct idea, independent of the rest. For if this should be denied, it is possible, by the continual gradation of shades, to run a colour insensibly into what is most remote from it; and if you will not allow any of the means to be different, you cannot, without absurdity, deny the extremes to be the same. Suppose, therefore, a person to have enjoyed his sight for thirty years, and to have become perfectly acquainted with colours of all kinds except one particular shade of blue, for instance, which it never has been his fortune to meet with. Let all the different shades of that colour, except that single one, be placed before him, descending gradually from the deepest to lightest; it is plain that he will perceive a blank, where that shade is wanting, and will be sensible that there is a greater distance in that place between the contiguous colours than in any other. Now I ask, whether it be possible for him, from his own imagination, to supply this deficiency, and raise up to himself the idea of that particular shade, though it had never been conveyed to him by his senses? I believe there are few but will be of opinion that he can: and this may serve as a proof that the simple ideas are not always, in every instance, derived from the correspondent impressions; though this instance is so singular, that it is scarcely worth our observing, and does not merit that for it alone we should alter our general maxim.

Here, therefore, is a proposition, which not only seems, in itself, simple and intelligible; but, if a proper use were made of it, might render every dispute equally intelligible, and banish all that jargon, which has so long taken possession of metaphysical reasonings, and drawn disgrace upon them. All ideas, especially abstract ones, are naturally faint and obscure: the mind has but a slender hold of them: they are apt to be confounded with other resembling ideas; and when we have often employed any term, though without a distinct meaning, we are apt to imagine it has a determinate idea annexed to it. On the contrary, all impressions, that is, all sensations, either outward or inward, are strong and vivid: the limits between them are more exactly determined: nor is it easy to fall into any error or mistake with regard to them. When we entertain, therefore, any suspicion that a philosophical term is employed without any meaning or idea (as is but too frequent), we need but enquire, *from what impressions is that supposed idea derived*? And if it be impossible to assign any, this will serve to confirm our suspicion.* By bringing ideas into so clear a light we may reasonably hope to remove all dispute, which may arise, concerning their nature and reality.

Section III. Of the Association of Ideas

It is evident that there is a principle of connexion between the different thoughts or ideas of the mind, and that, in their appearance to the memory or imagination, they introduce each other with a certain degree of method and regularity. In our more serious thinking or discourse this is so observable that any particular thought, which breaks in upon the regular tract or chain of ideas, is immediately remarked and rejected. And even in our wildest and most wandering reveries, nay in our very dreams, we shall find, if we reflect, that the imagination ran not altogether at adventures, but that there was still a connexion upheld among the different ideas, which succeeded each other. Were the loosest and freest conversation to be transcribed, there would immediately be observed something which connected it in all its transitions. Or where this is wanting, the person who broke the thread of discourse might still inform you, that there had secretly revolved in his mind a succession of thought, which had gradually led him from the subject of conversation. Among different languages, even where we cannot suspect the least connexion or communication, it is found, that the words, expressive of ideas, the most compounded, do yet nearly correspond to each other: a certain proof that the simple ideas, comprehended in the compound ones, were bound together by some universal principle, which had an equal influence on all mankind.

Though it be too obvious to escape observation, that different ideas are connected together; I do not find that any philosopher has attempted to enumerate or class all the principles of association; a subject, however, that seems worthy of curiosity. To me, there appear to be only three principles of connexion among ideas, namely, *Resemblance*, *Contiguity* in time or place, and *Cause* or *Effect*.

---

*It is probable that no more was meant by those, who denied innate ideas, than that all ideas were copies of our impressions; though it must be confessed, that the terms, which they employed, were not chosen with such caution, nor so exactly defined, as to prevent all mistakes about their doctrine. For what is meant by *innate*? If innate be equivalent to natural, then all the perceptions and ideas of the mind must be allowed to be innate or natural, in whatever sense we take the latter word, whether in opposition to what is uncommon, artificial, or miraculous. If by innate be meant, contemporary to our birth, the dispute seems to be frivolous; nor is it worth while to enquire at what time thinking begins, whether before, at, or after our birth. Again, the word idea, seems to be commonly taken in a very loose sense, by LOCKE and others; as standing for any of our perceptions, our sensations and passions, as well as thoughts. Now in this sense, I should desire to know, what can be meant by asserting, that self-love, or resentment of injuries, or the passion between the sexes is not innate?

But admitting these terms, *impressions* and *ideas*, in the sense above explained, and understanding by *innate*, what is original or copied from no precedent perception, then may we assert that all our impressions are innate and our ideas not innate.

To be ingenuous, I must own it to be my opinion, that LOCKE was betrayed into this question by the schoolmen, who, making use of undefined terms, draw out their disputes to a tedious length, without ever touching the point in question. A like ambiguity and circumlocution seem to run through that philosopher's reasonings on this as well as most other subjects.

That these principles serve to connect ideas will not, I believe, be much doubted. A picture naturally leads our thoughts to the original:* the mention of one apartment in a building naturally introduces an enquiry or discourse concerning the others:** and if we think of a wound, we can scarcely forbear reflecting on the pain which follows it.*** But that this enumeration is complete, and that there are no other principles of association except these, may be difficult to prove to the satisfaction of the reader, or even to a man's own satisfaction. All we can do, in such cases, is to run over several instances, and examine carefully the principle which binds the different thoughts to each other, never stopping till we render the principle as general as possible.† The more instances we examine, and the more care we employ, the more assurance shall we acquire, that the enumeration, which we form from the whole, is complete and entire.

SECTION IV. SCEPTICAL DOUBTS CONCERNING THE OPERATIONS OF THE UNDERSTANDING

PART I

All the objects of human reason or enquiry may naturally be divided into two kinds, to wit, *Relations of Ideas*, and *Matters of Fact*. Of the first kind are the sciences of Geometry, Algebra, and Arithmetic; and in short, every affirmation which is either intuitively or demonstratively certain. *That the square of the hypothenuse is equal to the squares of the two sides*, is a proposition which expresses a relation between these figures. *That three times five is equal to the half of thirty*, expresses a relation between these numbers. Propositions of this kind are discoverable by the mere operation of thought, without dependence on what is anywhere existent in the universe. Though there never were a circle or triangle in nature, the truths demonstrated by Euclid would for ever retain their certainty and evidence.

Matters of fact, which are the second objects of human reason, are not ascertained in the same manner; nor is our evidence of their truth however great, of a like nature with the foregoing. The contrary of every matter of fact is still possible; because it can never imply a contradiction, and is conceived by the mind with the same facility and distinctness, as if ever so conformable to reality. *That the sun will not rise tomorrow* is no less intelligible a proposition, and implies no more contradiction than the affirmation, *that it will rise*. We should in vain, therefore, attempt to demonstrate its falsehood. Were it demonstratively false, it would imply a contradiction, and could never be distinctly conceived by the mind.

It may, therefore, be a subject worthy of curiosity, to enquire what is the nature of that evidence which assures us of any real existence and matter of fact, beyond the

---

*Resemblance.
**Contiguity.
***Cause and effect.
†For instance, Contrast or Contrariety is also a connexion among Ideas but it may, perhaps, be considered as a mixture of *Causation* and *Resemblance*. Where two objects are contrary, the one destroys the other; that is, the cause of its annihilation, and the idea of the annihilation of an object implies the idea of its former existence.

present testimony of our senses, or the records of our memory. This part of philosophy, it is observable, has been little cultivated, either by the ancients or moderns; and therefore our doubts and errors, in the prosecution of so important an enquiry, may be the more excusable; while we march through such difficult paths without any guide or direction. They may even prove useful, by exciting curiosity, and destroying that implicit faith and security, which is the bane of all reasoning and free enquiry. The discovery of defects in the common philosophy, if any such there be, will not, I presume, be a discouragement, but rather an incitement, as is usual, to attempt something more full and satisfactory than has yet been proposed to the public.

All reasonings concerning matter of fact seem to be founded on the relation of *Cause* and *Effect*. By means of that relation alone we can go beyond the evidence of our memory and senses. If you were to ask a man, why he believes any matter of fact, which is absent; for instance, that his friend is in the country, or in France; he would give you a reason; and this reason would be some other fact; as a letter received from him, or the knowledge of his former resolutions and promises. A man finding a watch or any other machine in a desert island, would conclude that there had once been men in that island. All our reasonings concerning fact are of the same nature. And here it is constantly supposed that there is a connexion between the present fact and that which is inferred from it. Were there nothing to bind them together, the inference would be entirely precarious. The hearing of an articulate voice and rational discourse in the dark assures us of the presence of some person: Why? because these are the effects of the human make and fabric, and closely connected with it. If we anatomize all the other reasonings of this nature, we shall find that they are founded on the relation of cause and effect, and that this relation is either near or remote, direct or collateral. Heat and light are collateral effects of fire, and the one effect may justly be inferred from the other.

If we would satisfy ourselves, therefore, concerning the nature of that evidence, which assures us of matters of fact, we must enquire how we arrive at the knowledge of cause and effect.

I shall venture to affirm, as a general proposition, which admits of no exception, that the knowledge of this relation is not, in any instance, attained by reasonings *a priori;* but arises entirely from experience, when we find that any particular objects are constantly conjoined with each other. Let an object be presented to a man of ever so strong natural reason and abilities; if that object be entirely new to him, he will not be able, by the most accurate examination of its sensible qualities, to discover any of its causes or effects. Adam, though his rational faculties be supposed, at the very first, entirely perfect, could not have inferred from the fluidity and transparency of water that it would suffocate him, or from the light and warmth of fire that it would consume him. No object ever discovers, by the qualities which appear to the senses, either the causes which produced it, or the effects which will arise from it; nor can our reason, unassisted by experience, ever draw any inference concerning real existence and matter of fact.

This proposition, *that causes and effects are discoverable, not by reason but by experience*, will readily be admitted with regard to such objects, as we remember to have once been altogether unknown to us; since we must be conscious of the utter inability, which we then lay under, of foretelling what would arise from them. Present two smooth pieces of marble to a man who has no tincture of natural philosophy; he will never discover that they will adhere together in such a manner as to require great force to separate them in a direct line, while they make so small a resistance to a lateral pressure. Such events, as bear little analogy to the common course of nature, are also readily confessed to be known only by experience; nor does any man imagine that the explosion of gunpowder, or the attraction of a loadstone, could ever be discovered by arguments *a priori*. In like manner, when an effect is supposed to depend upon an intricate machinery or secret structure of parts, we make no difficulty in attributing all our knowledge of it to experience. Who will assert that he can give the ultimate reason, why milk or bread is proper nourishment for a man, not for a lion or a tiger?

But the same truth may not appear, at first sight, to have the same evidence with regard to events, which have become familiar to us from our first appearance in the world, which bear a close analogy to the whole course of nature, and which are supposed to depend on the simple qualities of objects, without any secret structure of parts. We are apt to imagine that we could discover these effects by the mere operation of our reason, without experience. We fancy, that were we brought on a sudden into this world, we could at first have inferred that one Billiard-ball would communicate motion to another upon impulse; and that we needed not to have waited for the event, in order to pronounce with certainty concerning it. Such is the influence of custom, that, where it is strongest, it not only covers our natural ignorance, but even conceals itself, and seems not to take place, merely because it is found in the highest degree.

But to convince us that all the laws of nature, and all the operations of bodies without exception, are known only by experience, the following reflections may, perhaps, suffice. Were any object presented to us, and were we required to pronounce concerning the effect, which will result from it, without consulting past observation; after what manner, I beseech you, must the mind proceed in this operation? It must invent or imagine some event, which it ascribes to the object as its effect; and it is plain that this invention must be entirely arbitrary. The mind can never possibly find the effect in the supposed cause, by the most accurate scrutiny and examination. For the effect is totally different from the cause, and consequently can never be discovered in it. Motion in the second Billiard-ball is a quite distinct event from motion in the first: nor is there anything in the one to suggest the smallest hint of the other. A stone or piece of metal raised into the air, and left without any support, immediately falls: but to consider the matter *a priori*, is there anything we discover in this situation which can beget the idea of a downward, rather than an upward, or any other motion, in the stone or metal?

And as the first imagination or invention of a particular effect, in all natural operations, is arbitrary, where we consult not experience; so must we also esteem the supposed tie or connexion between the cause and effect, which binds them together, and renders it impossible that any other effect could result from the operation of that cause. When I see, for instance, a Billiard-ball moving in a straight line towards another; even suppose motion in the second ball should by accident be suggested to me, as the result of their contact or impulse; may I not conceive, that a hundred different events might as well follow from that cause? May not both these balls remain at absolute rest? May not the first ball return in a straight line, or leap off from the second in any line or direction? All these suppositions are consistent and conceivable. Why then should we give the preference to one, which is no more consistent or conceivable than the rest? All our reasonings *a priori* will never be able to show us any foundation for this preference.

In a word, then, every effect is a distinct event from its cause. It could not, therefore, be discovered in the cause, and the first invention or conception of it, *a priori*, must be entirely arbitrary. And even after it is suggested, the conjunction of it with the cause must appear equally arbitrary; since there are always many other effects, which, to reason, must seem fully as consistent and natural. In vain, therefore, should we pretend to determine any single event, or infer any cause or effect, without the assistance of observation and experience.

Hence we may discover the reason why no philosopher, who is rational and modest, has ever pretended to assign the ultimate cause of any natural operation, or to show distinctly the action of that power, which produces any single effect in the universe. It is confessed, that the utmost effort of human reason is to reduce the principles, productive of natural phenomena, to a greater simplicity, and to resolve the many particular effects into a few general causes, by means of reasonings from analogy, experience, and observation. But as to the causes of these general causes, we should in vain attempt their discovery; nor shall we ever be able to satisfy ourselves, by any particular explication of them. These ultimate springs and principles are totally shut up from human curiosity and enquiry. Elasticity, gravity, cohesion of parts, communication of motion by impulse; these are probably the ultimate causes and principles which we ever discover in nature; and we may esteem ourselves sufficiently happy, if, by accurate inquiry and reasoning, we can trace up the particular phenomena to, or near to, these general principles. The most perfect philosophy of the natural kind only staves off our ignorance a little longer: as perhaps the most perfect philosophy of the moral or metaphysical kind serves only to discover larger portions of it. Thus the observation of human blindness and weakness is the result of all philosophy, and meets us at every turn, in spite of our endeavours to elude or avoid it.

Nor is geometry, when taken into the assistance of natural philosophy, ever able to remedy this defect, or lead us into the knowledge of ultimate causes, by all that accuracy of reasoning for which it is so justly celebrated. Every part of mixed mathematics proceeds upon the supposition that certain laws are established by nature in her operations; and abstract reasonings are employed, either to assist experience in the discovery of these laws, or to determine their influence in particular instances, where it depends upon any precise degree of distance and quantity. Thus, it is a law of motion, discovered by experience, that the movement or force of any body in motion is in the compound ratio or proportion of its solid contents and its velocity; and consequently, that a small force may remove the greatest obstacle or raise the greatest weight, if, by any contrivance or machinery, we can increase the velocity of that force, so as to make it an overmatch for its antagonist. Geometry assists us in the application of this law, by giving us the just dimensions of all the parts and figures which can enter into any species of machines; but still the discovery of the law itself is owing merely to experience, and all the abstract reasonings in the world could never lead us one step towards the knowledge of it. When we reason *a priori*, and consider merely any object or cause, as it appears to the mind, independent of all observation, it never could suggest to us the notion of any distinct object, such as its effect; much less, show us the inseparable and inviolable connexion between them. A man must be very sagacious who could discover by reasoning that crystal is the effect of heat, and ice of cold, without being previously acquainted with the operation of these qualities.

PART II

But we have not yet attained any tolerable satisfaction with regard to the question first proposed. Each solution still gives rise to a new question as difficult as the foregoing, and leads us on to farther enquiries. When it is asked, *What is the nature of all our reasonings concerning matter of fact?* the proper answer seems to be, that they are founded on the relation of cause and effect. When again it is asked, *What is the founda-*

tion of all our reasonings and conclusions concerning that relation? it may be replied in one word, Experience. But if we still carry on our sifting humour, and ask, *What is the foundation of all conclusions from experience?* this implies a new question, which may be of more difficult solution and explication. Philosophers, that give themselves airs of superior wisdom and sufficiency, have a hard task when they encounter persons of inquisitive dispositions, who push them from every corner to which they retreat, and who are sure at last to bring them to some dangerous dilemma. The best expedient to prevent this confusion, is to be modest in our pretensions; and even to discover the difficulty ourselves before it is objected to us. By this means, we may make a kind of merit of our very ignorance.

I shall content myself, in this section, with an easy task, and shall pretend only to give a negative answer to the question here proposed. I say then, that, even after we have experience of the operations of cause and effect, our conclusions from that experience are not founded on reasoning, or any process of the understanding. This answer we must endeavour both to explain and to defend.

It must certainly be allowed, that nature has kept us at a great distance from all her secrets, and has afforded us only the knowledge of a few superficial qualities of objects; while she conceals from us those powers and principles on which the influence of those objects entirely depends. Our senses inform us of the colour, weight, and consistence of bread; but neither sense nor reason can ever inform us of those qualities which fit it for the nourishment and support of a human body. Sight or feeling conveys an idea of the actual motion of bodies; but as to that wonderful force or power, which would carry on a moving body for ever in a continued change of place, and which bodies never lose but by communicating it to others; of this we cannot form the most distant conception. But notwithstanding this ignorance of natural powers* and principles, we always presume, when we see like sensible qualities, that they have like secret powers, and expect that effects, similar to those which we have experienced, will follow from them. If a body of like colour and consistence with that bread, which we have formerly eat, be presented to us, we make no scruple of repeating the experiment, and foresee, with certainty, like nourishment and support. Now this is a process of the mind or thought, of which I would willingly know the foundation. It is allowed on all hands that there is no known connexion between the sensible qualities and the secret powers; and consequently, that the mind is not led to form such a conclusion concerning their constant and regular conjunction, by anything which it knows of their nature. As to past Experience, it can be allowed to give direct and certain information of those precise objects only, and that precise period of time, which fell under its cognizance: but why this experience should be extended to future times, and to other objects, which, for aught we know, may be only in appearance similar; this is the main question on which I would insist. The bread, which I formerly eat, nourished me; that is, a body of such sensible qualities was, at that time, endued with such secret powers: but does it follow, that other bread must also nourish me at another time, and that like sensible qualities must always be attended with like secret powers? The consequence seems nowise necessary. At least, it must be acknowledged that there is here a consequence drawn by the mind; that there is a certain step taken; a process of thought, and an inference, which wants to be explained. These two propositions are far from being the same, *I have found that such an object has always been attended with such an effect, and I foresee, that other objects, which are, in appearance, similar, will be attended*

---

*The word, Power, is here used in a loose and popular sense. The most accurate explication of it would give additional evidence to this argument. See Sec. 7.

with similar effects. I shall allow, if you please, that the one proposition may justly be inferred from the other; I know, in fact, that it always is inferred. But if you insist that the inference is made by a chain of reasoning, I desire you to produce that reasoning. The connexion between these propositions is not intuitive. There is required a medium, which may enable the mind to draw such an inference, if indeed it be drawn by reasoning and argument. What that medium is, I must confess, passes my comprehension; and it is incumbent on those to produce it, who assert that it really exists, and is the origin of all our conclusions concerning matter of fact.

This negative argument must certainly, in process of time, become altogether convincing, if many penetrating and able philosophers shall turn their enquiries this way and no one be ever able to discover any connecting proposition or intermediate step, which supports the understanding in this conclusion. But as the question is yet new, every reader may not trust so far to his own penetration, as to conclude, because an argument escapes his enquiry, that therefore it does not really exist. For this reason it may be requisite to venture upon a more difficult task; and enumerating all the branches of human knowledge, endeavour to show that none of them can afford such an argument.

All reasonings may be divided into two kinds, namely, demonstrative reasoning, or that concerning relations of ideas, and moral reasoning, or that concerning matter of fact and existence. That there are no demonstrative arguments in the case seems evident; since it implies no contradiction that the course of nature may change, and that an object, seemingly like those which we have experienced, may be attended with different or contrary effects. May I not clearly and distinctly conceive that a body, falling from the clouds, and which, in all other respects, resembles snow, has yet the taste of salt or feeling of fire? Is there any more intelligible proposition than to affirm, that all the trees will flourish in December and January, and decay in May and June? Now whatever is intelligible, and can be distinctly conceived, implies no contradiction, and can never be proved false by any demonstrative argument or abstract reasoning *a priori.*

If we be, therefore, engaged by arguments to put trust in past experience, and make it the standard of our future judgement, these arguments must be probable only, or such as regard matter of fact and real existence, according to the division above mentioned. But that there is no argument of this kind, must appear, if our explication of that species of reasoning be admitted as solid and satisfactory. We have said that all arguments concerning existence are founded on the relation of cause and effect; that our knowledge of that relation is derived entirely from experience; and that all our experimental conclusions proceed upon the supposition that the future will be conformable to the past. To endeavour, therefore, the proof of this last supposition by probable arguments, or arguments regarding existence, must be evidently going in a circle, and taking that for granted, which is the very point in question.

In reality, all arguments from experience are founded on the similarity which we discover among natural objects, and by which we are induced to expect effects similar to those which we have found to follow from such objects. And though none but a fool or madman will ever pretend to dispute the authority of experience, or to reject that great guide of human life, it may surely be allowed a philosopher to have so much curiosity at least as to examine the principle of human nature, which gives this mighty authority to experience, and makes us draw advantage from that similarity which nature has placed among different objects. From causes which appear similar we expect similar effects. This is the sum of all our experimental conclusions. Now it seems evident that, if this conclusion were formed by reason, it would be as perfect at first, and upon one instance, as after ever so long a course of experience. But the case is far otherwise. Nothing so like as eggs; yet no one, on account of this appearing similarity, expects the same taste and relish in all of them. It is only after a long course of uniform experiments in any kind, that we attain a firm reliance and security with regard to a particular event. Now where is that process of reasoning which, from one instance, draws a conclusion, so different from that which it infers from a hundred instances that are nowise different from that single one? This question I propose as much for the sake of information, as with an intention of raising difficulties. I cannot find, I cannot imagine any such reasoning. But I keep my mind still open to instruction, if any one will vouchsafe to bestow it on me.

Should it be said that, from a number of uniform experiments, we *infer* a connexion between the sensible qualities and the secret powers; this, I must confess, seems the same difficulty, couched in different terms. The question still recurs, on what process of argument this *inference* is founded? Where is the medium, the interposing ideas, which join propositions so very wide of each other? It is confessed that the colour, consistence, and other sensible qualities of bread appear not, of themselves, to have any connexion with the secret powers of nourishment and support. For otherwise we could infer these secret powers from the first appearance of these sensible qualities, without the aid of experience; contrary to the sentiment of all philosophers, and contrary to plain matter of fact. Here, then, is our natural state of ignorance with regard to the powers and influence of all objects. How is this remedied by experience? It only shows us a number of uniform effects, resulting from certain objects, and teaches us that those particular objects, at that particular time, were endowed with such powers and forces. When a new object, endowed with similar sensible qualities, is produced, we expect similar powers and forces, and look for a like effect. From a body of like colour and consistence with bread we expect like nourishment and support. But this surely is a step or progress of the mind, which wants to be explained. When a man says, *I have found, in all past instances, such sensible qualities conjoined with such secret powers*: And when he says, *Similar sensible qualities will always be conjoined with similar secret powers*, he is not guilty of a tautology, nor are these propositions in any respect the same. You say that the one proposition is an inference from the other. But you must confess that the inference is not intuitive; neither is it demonstrative: Of what nature is it, then? To say it is experimental, is begging the question. For all inferences from experience suppose, as their foundation, that the future will resemble the past, and that similar powers will be conjoined with similar sensible qualities. If there be any suspicion that the course of nature may change, and that the past may be no rule for the future, all experience becomes useless, and can give rise to no inference or conclusion. It is impossible, therefore, that any arguments from experience can prove this resemblance of the past to the future: since all these arguments are founded on the supposition of that resemblance. Let the course of things be allowed hitherto ever so regular; that alone, without some new argument or inference, proves not that, for the future, it will continue so. In vain do you pretend to have learned the nature of bodies from your past experience. Their secret nature, and consequently all their effects and influence, may change, without any change in their sensible qualities. This happens sometimes, and with regard to some objects: Why may it not happen always, and with regard to all objects? What logic, what process of argument secures you against this supposition? My practice, you say, refutes my doubts. But you mistake the purport of my question. As an agent, I am quite satisfied in the point; but as a philosopher, who has some share of curiosity, I will not say scepticism, I want to learn the foundation of this inference. No reading, no enquiry has yet been able to remove my difficulty, or give me satisfaction in a matter of such importance. Can I do better than propose the difficulty to the public, even though, perhaps, I have small hopes of obtaining a solution? We shall, at least, by this means, be sensible of our ignorance, if we do not augment our knowledge.

I must confess that a man is guilty of unpardonable arrogance who concludes, because an argument has escaped his own investigation, that therefore it does not really exist. I must also confess that, though all the learned, for several ages, should have employed themselves in fruitless search upon any subject, it may still, perhaps, be rash to conclude positively that the subject must, therefore, pass all human comprehension. Even though we examine all the sources of our knowledge, and conclude them unfit for such a subject, there may still remain a suspicion, that the enumeration is not complete, or the examination not accurate. But with regard to the present subject, there are some considerations which seem to remove all this accusation of arrogance or suspicion of mistake.

It is certain that the most ignorant and stupid peasants—nay infants, nay even brute beasts—improve by experience, and learn the qualities of natural objects, by observing the effects which result from them. When a child has felt the sensation of pain from touching the flame of a candle, he will be careful not to put his hand near any candle; but will expect a similar effect from a cause which is similar in its sensible qualities and appearance. If you assert, therefore, that the understanding of the child is led into this conclusion by any process of argument or ratiocination, I may justly require you to produce that argument; nor have you any pretense to refuse so equitable a demand. You cannot say that the argument is abstruse, and may possibly escape your enquiry; since you confess that it is obvious to the capacity of a mere infant. If you hesitate, therefore, a moment, or if, after reflection, you produce any intricate or profound argument, you, in a manner, give up the question, and confess that it is not reasoning which engages us to suppose the past resembling the future, and to expect similar effects from causes which are, to appearance, similar. This is the proposition which I intended to enforce in the present section. If I be right, I pretend not to have made any mighty discovery. And if I be wrong, I must acknowledge myself to be indeed a very backward scholar; since I cannot now discover an argument which, it seems, was perfectly familiar to me long before I was out of my cradle.

SECTION V. SCEPTICAL SOLUTION OF THESE DOUBTS

PART I

The passion for philosophy, like that for religion, seems liable to this inconvenience, that, though it aims at the correction of our manners, and extirpation of our vices, it may only serve, by imprudent management, to foster a predominant inclination, and push the mind, with more determined resolution, towards that side which already *draws* too much, by the bias and propensity of the natural temper. It is certain that, while we aspire to the magnanimous firmness of the philosophic sage, and endeavour to confine our pleasures altogether within our own minds, we may, at last, render our philosophy like that of Epictetus, and other *Stoics*, only a more refined system of selfishness, and reason ourselves out of all virtue as well as social enjoyment. While we study with attention the vanity of human life, and turn all our thoughts towards the empty and transitory nature of riches and honours, we are, perhaps, all the while flattering our natural indolence, which, hating the bustle of the world, and drudgery of business, seeks a pretence of reason to give itself a full and uncontrolled indulgence. There is, however, one species of philosophy which seems little liable to this inconvenience, and that because it strikes in with no disorderly passion of the human mind, nor can mingle itself with any natural affection or propensity; and that is the Academic or Sceptical philosophy. The academics always talk of doubt and suspense of judgement, of danger in hasty determinations, of confining to very narrow bounds the enquiries of the understanding, and of renouncing all speculations which lie not within the limits of common life and practice. Nothing, therefore, can be more contrary than such a philosophy to the supine indolence of the mind, its rash arrogance, its lofty pretensions, and its superstitious credulity. Every passion is mortified by it, except the love of truth; and that passion never is, nor can be, carried to too high a degree. It is surprising, therefore, that this philosophy, which, in almost every instance, must be harmless and innocent, should be the subject of so much groundless reproach and obloquy. But, perhaps, the very circumstance which renders it so innocent is what chiefly exposes it to the public hatred and resentment. By flattering no irregular passion, it gains few partizans: By opposing so many vices and follies, it raises to itself abundance of enemies, who stigmatize it as libertine, profane, and irreligious.

Nor need we fear that this philosophy, while it endeavours to limit our enquiries to common life, should ever undermine the reasonings of common life, and carry its doubts so far as to destroy all action, as well as speculation. Nature will always maintain her rights, and prevail in the end over any abstract reasoning whatsoever. Though we should conclude, for instance, as in the foregoing section, that, in all reasonings from experience, there is a step taken by the mind which is not supported by any argument or process of the understanding; there is no danger that these reasonings, on which almost all knowledge depends, will ever be affected by such a discovery. If the mind be not engaged by argument to make this step, it must be induced by some other principle of equal weight and authority; and that principle will preserve its influence as long as human nature remains the same. What that principle is may well be worth the pains of enquiry.

Suppose a person, though endowed with the strongest faculties of reason and reflection, to be brought on a sudden into this world; he would, indeed, immediately observe a continual succession of objects, and one event following another; but he would not be able to discover anything farther. He would not, at first, by any reasoning, be able to reach the idea of cause and effect; since the particular powers, by which all natural operations are performed, never appear to the senses; nor is it reasonable to conclude, merely because one event, in one instance, precedes another, that therefore the one is the cause, the other the effect. Their conjunction may be arbitrary and casual. There may be no reason to infer the existence of one from the appearance of the other. And in a word, such a person, without more experience, could never employ his conjecture or reasoning concerning any matter of fact, or be assured of anything beyond what was immediately present to his memory and senses.

Suppose, again, that he has acquired more experience, and has lived so long in the world as to have observed familiar objects or events to be constantly conjoined together; what is the consequence of this experience? He immediately infers the existence of one object from the appearance of the other. Yet he has not, by all his experience, acquired any idea or knowledge of the secret power by which the one object produces the other; nor is it, by any process of reasoning, he is engaged to draw this inference. But still he finds himself determined to draw it: And though he should be convinced that his understanding has no part in the operation, he would nevertheless continue in the same course of thinking. There is some other principle which determines him to form such a conclusion.

This principle is Custom or Habit. For wherever the repetition of any particular act or operation produces a propensity to renew the same act or operation, without being impelled by any reasoning or process of the understanding, we always say, that this propensity is the effect of *Custom*. By employing that word, we pretend not to have given the ultimate reason of such a propensity. We only point out a principle of human nature, which is universally acknowledged, and which is well known by its effects. Perhaps we can push our enquiries no farther, or pretend to give the cause of this cause; but must rest contented with it as the ultimate principle, which we can assign, of all our conclusions from experience. It is sufficient satisfaction, that we can go so far, without repining at the narrowness of our faculties because they will carry us no farther. And it is certain we here advance a very intelligible proposition at least, if not a true one, when we assert that, after the constant conjunction of two objects—heat and flame, for instance, weight and solidity—we are determined by custom alone to expect the one from the appearance of the other. This hypothesis seems even the only one which explains the difficulty, why we draw, from a thousand instances, an inference which we are not able to draw from one instance, that is, in no respect, different from them. Reason is incapable of any such variation. The conclusions which it draws from considering one circle are the same which it would form upon surveying all the circles in the universe. But no man, having seen only one body move after being impelled by another, could infer that every other body will move after a like impulse. All inferences from experience, therefore, are effects of custom, not of reasoning.*

---

*Nothing is more useful than for writers, even, on *moral*, *political*, or *physical* subjects to distinguish between *reason* and *experience*, and to suppose, that these species of argumentation are entirely different from each other. The former are taken for the mere result of our intellectual faculties, which, by considering *a priori* the nature of things, and examining the effects that must follow from their operation, establish particular principles of science and philosophy. The latter are supposed to be derived entirely from sense and observation, by which we learn what has actually resulted from the operation of particular objects, and are thence able to infer, what will, for the future, result from them. Thus, for instance, the limitations and restraints of civil government, and a legal constitution, may be defended, either from *reason*, which reflecting on the great frailty and corruption of human nature, teaches, that no man can safely be trusted with unlimited authority; or from *experience* and history which inform us of the enormous abuses, that ambition, in every age and country, has been found to make of so imprudent a confidence.

The same distribution between reason and experience is maintained in all our deliberations concerning the conduct of life; while the experienced statesman, general, physician, or merchant is trusted and followed; and the unpractised novice, with whatever natural talents endowed, neglected and despised. Though it be allowed, that reason may form very plausible conjectures with regard to the consequences of such a particular conduct in such the assistance of experience, which is alone able to give stability and certainty to the maxims, derived from study and reflection.

But notwithstanding that this distinction be thus universally received, both in the active speculative scenes of life, I shall not scruple to pronounce, that it is, at bottom, erroneous, at least, superficial.

If we examine those arguments, which, in any of the sciences above mentioned, are supposed to be the mere effects of reasoning and reflection, they will be found to terminate at last, in some general principle or conclusion, for which we can assign no reason but observation and experience. The only difference between them and those maxims, which are vulgarly esteemed the result of pure experience, is, that the former cannot be established without some process of thought, and some reflection on what we have observed, in order to distinguish its circumstances, and trace its consequences: Whereas in the latter, the experienced event is exactly and fully familiar to that which we infer as the result of any particular situation. The history of a Tiberius or a Nero makes us dread a like tyranny, were our monarchs freed from the restraints of laws and senates. But the observation of any fraud or cruelty in private life is sufficient, with the aid of a little

Custom, then, is the great guide of human life. It is that principle alone which renders our experience useful to us, and makes us expect, for the future, a similar train of events with those which have appeared in the past. Without the influence of custom, we should be entirely ignorant of every matter of fact beyond what is immediately present to the memory and senses. We should never know to adjust means to ends, or to employ our natural powers in the production of any effect. There would be an end at once of all action, as well as of the chief part of speculation.

But here it may be proper to remark, that though our conclusions from experience carry us beyond our memory and senses, and assure us of matters of fact which happened in the most distant places and most remote ages, yet some fact must always be present to the senses or memory, from which we may first proceed in drawing these conclusions. A man, who should find in a desert country the remains of pompous buildings, would conclude that the country had, in ancient times, been cultivated by civilized inhabitants; but did nothing of this nature occur to him, he could never form such an inference. We learn the events of former ages from history; but then we must peruse the volumes in which this instruction is contained, and thence carry up our inferences from one testimony to another, till we arrive at the eyewitnesses and spectators of these distant events. In a word, if we proceed not upon some fact, present to the memory or senses, our reasonings would be merely hypothetical; and however the particular links might be connected with each other, the whole chain of inferences would have nothing to support it, nor could we ever, by its means, arrive at the knowledge of any real existence. If I ask why you believe any particular matter of fact, which you relate, you must tell me some reason; and this reason will be some other fact, connected with it. But as you cannot proceed after this manner, *in infinitum*, you must at last terminate in some fact, which is present to your memory or senses; or must allow that your belief is entirely without foundation.

What, then, is the conclusion of the whole matter? A simple one; though, it must be confessed, pretty remote from the common theories of philosophy. All belief of matter of fact or real existence is derived merely from some object, present to the memory or senses, and a customary conjunction between that and some other object. Or in other words; having found in many instances, that any two kinds of objects— flame and heat, snow and cold—have always been conjoined together; if flame or snow be presented anew to the senses, the mind is carried by custom to expect heat or cold, and to *believe* that such a quality does exist, and will discover itself upon a nearer approach. This belief is the necessary result of placing the mind in such circumstances. It

---

thought, to give us the same apprehension; while it serves as an instance of the general corruption of human nature, and shows us the danger which we must incur by reposing an entire confidence in mankind. In both cases, it is experience which is ultimately the foundation of our inference and conclusion.

There is no man so young and experienced, as not to have formed, from observation, many general and just maxims concerning human affairs and the conduct of life; but it must be confessed, that, when a man comes to put these in practice, he will be extremely liable to error, till time and farther experience both enlarge these maxims, and teach him their proper use and application. In every situation or incident, there are many particular and seemingly minute circumstances, which the man of greatest talent is, at first, apt to overlook, though on them the justness of his conclusions, and consequently the prudence of his conduct, entirely depend. Not to mention, that, to a young beginner, the general observations and maxims occur not always on the proper occasions, nor can be immediately applied with due calmness and distinction. The truth is, an unexperienced reasoner could be no reasoner at all, were he absolutely unexperienced; and when we assign that character to any one, we mean it only in a comparative sense, and suppose him possessed of experience, in a smaller and more imperfect degree.

is an operation of the soul, when we are so situated, as unavoidable as to feel the passion of love, when we receive benefits; or hatred, when we meet with injuries. All these operations are a species of natural instincts, which no reasoning or process of the thought and understanding is able either to produce or to prevent.

At this point, it would be very allowable for us to stop our philosophical researches. In most questions we can never make a single step farther; and in all questions we must terminate here at last, after our most restless and curious enquiries. But still our curiosity will be pardonable, perhaps commendable, if it carry us on to still farther researches, and make us examine more accurately the nature of this belief, and of the *customary conjunction*, whence it is derived. By this means we may meet with some explications and analogies that will give satisfaction; at least to such as love the abstract sciences, and can be entertained with speculations, which, however accurate, may still retain a degree of doubt and uncertainty. As to readers of a different taste; the remaining part of this section is not calculated for them, and the following enquiries may well be understood, though it be neglected.

PART II

Nothing is more free than the imagination of man; and though it cannot exceed that original stock of ideas furnished by the internal and external senses, it has unlimited power of mixing, compounding, separating, and dividing these ideas, in all the varieties of fiction and vision. It can feign a train of events, with all the appearance of reality, ascribe to them a particular time and place, conceive them as existent, and paint them out to itself with every circumstance, that belongs to any historical fact, which it believes with the greatest certainty. Wherein, therefore, consists the difference between such a *fiction* and *belief*? It lies not merely in any peculiar idea, which is annexed to such a conception as commands our assent, and which is wanting to every known fiction. For as the mind has authority over all its ideas, it could voluntarily annex this particular idea to any fiction, and consequently be able to believe whatever it pleases; contrary to what we find by daily experience. We can, in our conception, join the head of a man to the body of a horse; but it is not in our power to believe that such an animal has ever really existed.

It follows, therefore, that the difference between fiction and belief lies in some sentiment or feeling, which is annexed to the latter, not to the former, and which depends not on the will, nor can be commanded at pleasure. It must be excited by nature, like all other sentiments; and must arise from the particular situation, in which the mind is placed at any particular juncture. Whenever any object is presented to the memory or senses, it immediately, by the force of custom, carries the imagination to conceive that object, which is usually conjoined to it; and this conception is attended with a feeling or sentiment, different from the loose reveries of the fancy. In this consists the whole nature of belief. For as there is no matter of fact which we believe so firmly that we cannot conceive the contrary, there would be no difference between the conception assented to and that which is rejected, were it not for some sentiment which distinguishes the one from the other. If I see a Billiard-ball moving towards another, on a smooth table, I can easily conceive it to stop upon contact. This conception implies no contradiction; but still it feels very differently from that conception by which I represent to myself the impulse and the communication of motion from one ball to another.

Were we to attempt a *definition* of this sentiment, we should, perhaps, find it a very difficult, if not an impossible task; in the same manner as if we should endeavour to define the feeling of cold or passion of anger, to a creature who never had any experience of these sentiments. Belief is the true and proper name of this feeling; and no one is ever at a loss to know the meaning of that term; because every man is every moment conscious of the sentiment represented by it. It may not, however, be improper to attempt a *description* of this sentiment; in hopes we may, by that means, arrive at some analogies, which may afford a more perfect explication of it. I say, then, that belief is nothing but a more vivid, lively, forcible, firm, steady conception of an object, than what the imagination alone is ever able to attain. This variety of terms, which may seem so unphilosophical, is intended only to express that act of the mind, which renders realities, or what is taken for such, more present to us than fictions, causes them to weigh more in the thought, and gives them a superior influence on the passions and imagination. Provided we agree about the thing, it is needless to dispute about the terms. The imagination has the command over all its ideas, and can join and mix and vary them, in all the ways possible. It may conceive fictitious objects with all the circumstances of place and time. It may set them, in a manner, before our eyes, in their true colours, just as they might have existed. But as it is impossible that this faculty of imagination can ever, of itself, reach belief, it is evident that belief consists not in the peculiar nature or order of ideas, but in the *manner* of their conception, and in their *feeling* to the mind. I confess, that it is impossible perfectly to explain this feeling or manner of conception. We may make use of words which express something near it. But its true and proper name, as we observed before, is *belief;* which is a term that every one sufficiently understands in common life. And in philosophy, we can go no farther than assert, that *belief* is something felt by the mind, which distinguishes the ideas of the judgement from the fictions of the imagination. It gives them more weight and influence; makes them appear of greater importance; enforces them in the mind; and renders them the governing principle of our actions. I hear at present, for instance, a person's voice, with whom I am acquainted; and the sound comes as from the next room. This impression of my senses immediately conveys my thought to the person, together with all the surrounding objects. I paint them out to myself as existing at present, with the same qualities and relations, of which I formerly knew them possessed. These ideas take faster hold of my mind than ideas of an enchanted castle. They are very different to the feeling, and have a much greater influence of every kind, either to give pleasure or pain, joy or sorrow.

Let us, then, take in the whole compass of this doctrine, and allow, that the sentiment of belief is nothing but a conception more intense and steady than what attends the mere fictions of the imagination, and that this manner of conception arises from a customary conjunction of the object with something present to the memory or senses: I believe that it will not be difficult, upon these suppositions, to find other operations of the mind analogous to it, and to trace up these phenomena to principles still more general.

We have already observed that nature has established connexions among particular ideas, and that no sooner one idea occurs to our thoughts than it introduces its correlative, and carries our attention towards it, by a gentle and insensible movement. These principles of connexion or association we have reduced to three, namely, *Resemblance, Contiguity* and *Causation;* which are the only bonds that unite our thoughts together, and beget that regular train of reflection or discourse, which, in a greater or less degree, takes place among mankind. Now here arises a question, on which the solution of the present difficulty will depend. Does it happen, in all these relations, that, when one of the objects is presented to the senses or memory the mind is not only carried to the conception of the correlative, but reaches a steadier and stronger conception of it than what otherwise it would have been able to attain? This seems to be the case with that belief which arises from the relation of cause and effect. And if the case be the same with the other relations or principles of associations, this may be established as a general law, which takes place in all the operations of the mind.

We may, therefore, observe, as the first experiment to our present purpose, that, upon the appearance of the picture of an absent friend, our idea of him is evidently enlivened by the *resemblance*, and that every passion, which that idea occasions, whether of joy or sorrow, acquires new force and vigour. In producing this effect, there concur both a relation and a present impression. Where the picture bears him no resemblance, at least was not intended for him, it never so much as conveys our thought to him: And where it is absent, as well as the person, though the mind may pass from the thought of the one to that of the other, it feels its idea to be rather weakened than enlivened by that transition. We take a pleasure in viewing the picture of a friend, when it is set before us; but when it is removed, rather choose to consider him directly than by reflection in an image, which is equally distant and obscure.

The ceremonies of the Roman Catholic religion may be considered as instances of the same nature. The devotees of that superstition usually plead in excuse for the mummeries, with which they were upbraided, that they feel the good effect of those external motions, and postures, and actions, in enlivening their devotion and quickening their fervour, which otherwise would decay, if directed entirely to distant and immaterial objects. We shadow out the objects of our faith, say they, in sensible types and images, and render them more present to us by the immediate presence of these types, than it is possible for us to do merely by an intellectual view and contemplation. Sensible objects have always a greater influence on the fancy than any other; and this influence they readily convey to those ideas to which they are related, and which they resemble. I shall only infer from these practices, and reasoning, that the effect of resemblance in enlivening the ideas is very common; and as in every case a resemblance and a present impression must concur, we are abundantly supplied with experiments to prove the reality of the foregoing principle.

We may add force to these experiments by others of a different kind, in considering the effects of *contiguity* as well as of *resemblance*. It is certain that distance diminishes the force of every idea, and that, upon our approach to any object; though it does not discover itself to our senses; it operates upon the mind with an influence, which imitates an immediate impression. The thinking on any object readily transports the mind to what is contiguous; but it is only the actual presence of an object, that transports it with a superior vivacity. When I am a few miles from home, whatever relates to it touches me more nearly than when I am two hundred leagues distant; though even at that distance the reflecting on any thing in the neighbourhood of my friends or family naturally produces an idea of them. But as in this latter case, both the objects of the mind are ideas; notwithstanding there is an easy transition between them; that transition alone is not able to give a superior vivacity to any of the ideas, for want of some immediate impression.* No one can doubt but causation has the same influence as the other two relations of resemblance and contiguity. Superstitious people are fond of the relics of saints and holy men, for the same reason, that they seek after types or images,

---

*"Should I call it our nature or some error that leads us to feel more deeply moved upon seeing places where memorable men are said to have spent much time than we feel when hearing of their deeds or reading their writings? Thus I feel deeply moved now. For Plato comes to my mind, who is said to have been the first philosopher to have made a practice of holding discussions here; and his little garden nearby not only stirs memories but makes me all but see him in the flesh. Here is Speusippus, here Xenocrates, here his student Polemo; it was his seat that we see before us. Even looking at our senate building—that of Hostilius, not the new building which looks smaller to me since it was made larger—made me think of Scipio, Cato, Laelius, and above all my grandfather. Such power of stirring recollection resides in places: no wonder that the training of the memory is based on them." Cicero, *De Finibus*, Book V. [Hume's footnote is in Latin, translation by W.K.]

in order to enliven their devotion, and give them a more intimate and strong conception of those exemplary lives, which they desire to imitate. Now it is evident, that one of the best relics, which a devotee could procure, would be the handywork of a saint; and if his clothes and furniture are ever to be considered in this light, it is because they were once at his disposal, and were moved and affected by him; in which respect they are to be considered as imperfect effects, and as connected with him by a shorter chain of consequences than any of those, by which we learn the reality of his existence.

Suppose, that the son of a friend, who had been long dead or absent, were presented to us; it is evident, that this object would instantly revive its correlative idea, and recall to our thoughts all past intimacies and familiarities, in more lively colours than they would otherwise have appeared to us. This is another phenomenon, which seems to prove the principle above mentioned.

We may observe, that, in these phenomena, the belief of the correlative object is always presupposed; without which the relation could have no effect. The influence of the picture supposes, that we *believe* our friend to have once existed. Contiguity to home can never excite our ideas of home, unless we *believe* that it really exists. Now I assert, that this belief, where it reaches beyond the memory or senses, is of a similar nature, and arises from similar causes, with the transition of thought and vivacity of conception here explained. When I throw a piece of dry wood into a fire, my mind is immediately carried to conceive, that it augments, not extinguishes the flame. This transition of thought from the cause to the effect proceeds not from reason. It derives its origin altogether from custom and experience. And as it first begins from an object, present to the senses, it renders the idea or conception of flame more strong and lively than any loose, floating reverie of the imagination. That idea arises immediately. The thought moves instantly towards it, and conveys to it all that force of conception, which is derived from the impression present to the senses. When a sword is levelled at my breast, does not the idea of wound and pain strike me more strongly, than when a glass of wine is presented to me, even though by accident this idea should occur after the appearance of the latter object? But what is there in this whole matter to cause such a strong conception, except only a present object and a customary transition to the idea of another object, which we have been accustomed to conjoin with the former? This is the whole operation of the mind, in all our conclusions concerning matter of fact and existence; and it is a satisfaction to find some analogies, by which it may be explained. The transition from a present object does in all cases give strength and solidity to the related idea.

Here, then, is a kind of pre-established harmony between the course of nature and the succession of our ideas; and though the powers and forces, by which the former is governed, be wholly unknown to us; yet our thoughts and conceptions have still, we find, gone on in the same train with the other work of nature. Custom is that principle, by which this correspondence has been effected; so necessary to the subsistence of our species, and the regulation of our conduct, in every circumstance and occurrence of human life. Had not the presence of an object, instantly excited the idea of those objects, commonly conjoined with it, all our knowledge must have been limited to the narrow sphere of our memory and senses; and we should never have been able to adjust means to ends, or employ our natural powers, either to the producing of good, or avoiding of evil. Those, who delight in the discovery and contemplation of *final causes*, have here ample subject to employ their wonder and admiration.

I shall add, for a further confirmation of the foregoing theory, that, as this operation of the mind, by which we infer like effects from like causes, and *vice versa*, is so essential to the subsistence of all human creatures, it is not probable, that it could be trusted to the fallacious deductions of our reason, which is slow in its operations; appears not, in any degree, during the first years of infancy; and at best is, in every age and period of human life, extremely liable to error and mistake. It is more conformable to the ordinary wisdom of nature to secure so necessary an act of the mind, by some instinct or mechanical tendency, which may be infallible in its operations, may discover itself at the first appearance of life and thought, and may be independent of all the laboured deductions of the understanding. As nature has taught us the use of our limbs, without giving us the knowledge of the muscles and nerves, by which they are actuated; so has she implanted in us an instinct, which carries forward the thought in a correspondent course to that which she has established among external objects; though we are ignorant of those powers and forces, on which this regular course and succession of objects totally depends.

Section VI. Of Probability[*]

Though there be no such thing as *Chance* in the world; our ignorance of the real cause of any event has the same influence on the understanding, and begets a like species of belief or opinion.

There is certainly a probability, which arises from a superiority of chances on any side; and according as this superiority increases, and surpasses the opposite chances, the probability receives a proportionable increase, and begets still a higher degree of belief or assent to that side, in which we discover the superiority. If a dye were marked with one figure or number of spots on four sides, and with another figure or number of spots on the two remaining sides, it would be more probable, that the former would turn up than the latter; though, if it had a thousand sides marked in the same manner, and only one side different, the probability would be much higher, and our belief or expectation of the event more steady and secure. This process of the thought or reasoning may seem trivial and obvious; but to those who consider it more narrowly, it may, perhaps, afford matter for curious speculation.

It seems evident, that, when the mind looks forward to discover the event, which may result from the throw of such a dye, it considers the turning up of each particular side as alike probable; and this is the very nature of chance, to render all the particular events, comprehended in it, entirely equal. But finding a greater number of sides concur in the one event than in the other, the mind is carried more frequently to that event, and meets it oftener, in revolving the various possibilities or chances, on which the ultimate result depends. This concurrence of several views in one particular event begets immediately, by an inexplicable contrivance of nature, the sentiment of belief, and gives that event the advantage over its antagonist, which is supported by a smaller number of views, and recurs less frequently to the mind. If we allow, that belief is nothing but a firmer and stronger conception of an object than what attends the mere fictions of the imagination, this operation may, perhaps, in some measure, be accounted for. The concurrence of these several views or glimpses imprints the idea more strongly on the imagination; gives it superior force and vigour; renders its influ-

---

*Mr. Locke divides all arguments into demonstrative and probable. In this view, we must say, that it is only probable all men must die, or that the sun will rise tomorrow. But to conform our language more to common use, we ought to divide arguments into *demonstrations*, *proofs*, and *probabilities*. By proofs meaning such arguments from experience as leave no room for doubt or opposition.

ence on the passions and affections more sensible; and in a word, begets that reliance or security, which constitutes the nature of belief and opinion.

The case is the same with the probability of causes, as with that of chance. There are some causes, which are entirely uniform and constant in producing a particular effect; and no instance has ever yet been found of any failure or irregularity in their operation. Fire has always burned, and water suffocated every human creature: The production of motion by impulse and gravity is an universal law, which has hitherto admitted of no exception. But there are other causes which have been found more irregular and uncertain; nor has rhubarb always proved a purge, or opium a soporific to every one, who has taken these medicines. It is true, when any cause fails of producing its usual effect, philosophers ascribe not this to any irregularity in nature; but suppose, that some secret causes, in the particular structure of parts, have prevented the operation. Our reasonings, however, and conclusions concerning the event are the same as if this principle had no place. Being determined by custom to transfer the past to the future, in all our inferences; where the past has been entirely regular and uniform, we expect the event with the greatest assurance, and leave no room for any contrary supposition. But where different effects have been found to follow from causes, which are to *appearance* exactly similar, all these various effects must occur to the mind in transferring the past to the future, and enter into our consideration, when we determine the probability of the event. Though we give the preference to that which has been found most usual, and believe that this effect will exist, we must not overlook the other effects, but must assign to each of them a particular weight and authority, in proportion as we have found it to be more or less frequent. It is more probable, in almost every country of Europe, that there will be frost sometime in January, than that the weather will continue open throughout the whole month; though this probability varies according to the different climates, and approaches to a certainty in the more northern kingdoms. Here then it seems evident, that, when we transfer the past to the future, in order to determine the effect, which will result from any cause, we transfer all the different events, in the same proportion as they have appeared in the past, and conceive one to have existed a hundred times, for instance, another ten times, and another once. As a great number of views do here concur in one event, they fortify and confirm it to the imagination, beget that sentiment which we call *belief*, and give its object the preference above the contrary event, which is not supported by an equal number of experiments, and recurs not so frequently to the thought in transferring the past to the future. Let any one try to account for this operation of the mind upon any of the received systems of philosophy, and he will be sensible of the difficulty. For my part, I shall think it sufficient, if the present hints excite the curiosity of philosophers, and make them sensible how defective all common theories are in treating of such curious and such sublime subjects.

SECTION VII. OF THE IDEA OF NECESSARY CONNEXION

PART I

The great advantage of the mathematical sciences above the moral consists in this, that the ideas of the former, being sensible, are always clear and determinate, the smallest distinction between them is immediately perceptible, and the same terms are still expressive of the same ideas, without ambiguity or variation. An oval is never mistaken for a circle, nor an hyperbola for an ellipsis. The isosceles and scalenum are distinguished by boundaries more exact than vice and virtue, right and wrong. If any term be defined in geometry, the mind readily, of itself, substitutes, on all occasions, the definition for the term defined: Or even when no definition is employed, the object itself may be presented to the senses, and by that means be steadily and clearly apprehended. But the finer sentiments of the mind, the operations of the understanding, the various agitations of the passions, though really in themselves distinct, easily escape us, when surveyed by reflection; nor is it in our power to recall the original object, as often as we have occasion to contemplate it. Ambiguity, by this means, is gradually introduced into our reasonings: Similar objects are readily taken to be the same: And the conclusion becomes at last very wide of the premises.

One may safely, however, affirm, that, if we consider these sciences in a proper light, their advantages and disadvantages nearly compensate each other, and reduce both of them to a state of equality. If the mind, with greater facility, retains the ideas of geometry clear and determinate, it must carry on a much longer and more intricate chain of reasoning, and compare ideas much wider of each other, in order to reach the abstruser truths of that science. And if moral ideas are apt, without extreme care, to fall into obscurity and confusion, the inferences are always much shorter in these disquisitions, and the intermediate steps, which lead to the conclusion, much fewer than in the sciences which treat of quantity and number. In reality, there is scarcely a proposition in Euclid so simple, as not to consist of more parts, than are to be found in any moral reasoning which runs not into chimera and conceit. Where we trace the principles of the human mind through a few steps, we may be very well satisfied with our progress; considering how soon nature throws a bar to all our enquiries concerning causes, and reduces us to an acknowledgment of our ignorance. The chief obstacle, therefore, to our improvement in the moral or metaphysical sciences is the obscurity of the ideas, and ambiguity of the terms. The principal difficulty in the mathematics is the length of inferences and compass of thought, requisite to the forming of any conclusion. And, perhaps, our progress in natural philosophy is chiefly retarded by the want of proper experiments and phenomena, which are often discovered by chance, and cannot always be found, when requisite, even by the most diligent and prudent enquiry. As moral philosophy seems hitherto to have received less improvement than either geometry or physics, we may conclude, that, if there be any difference in this respect among these sciences, the difficulties, which obstruct the progress of the former, require superior care and capacity to be surmounted.

There are no ideas, which occur in metaphysics, more obscure and uncertain, than those of *power*, *force*, *energy* or *necessary connexion*, of which it is every moment necessary for us to treat in all our disquisitions. We shall, therefore, endeavour, in this section, to fix, if possible, the precise meaning of these terms, and thereby remove some part of that obscurity, which is so much complained of in this species of philosophy.

It seems a proposition, which will not admit of much dispute, that all our ideas are nothing but copies of our impressions, or, in other words, that it is impossible for us to *think* of any thing, which we have not antecedently *felt*, either by our external or internal senses. I have endeavoured* to explain and prove this proposition, and have expressed my hopes, that, by a proper application of it, men may reach a greater clearness and precision in philosophical reasonings, than what they have hitherto been able

---

*Section II.

to attain. Complex ideas may, perhaps, be well known by definition, which is nothing but an enumeration of those parts or simple ideas, that compose them. But when we have pushed up definitions to the most simple ideas, and find still some ambiguity and obscurity; what resource are we then possessed of? By what invention can we throw light upon these ideas, and render them altogether precise and determinate to our intellectual view? Produce the impressions or original sentiments, from which the ideas are copied. These impressions are all strong and sensible. They admit not of ambiguity. They are not only placed in a full light themselves, but may throw light on their correspondent ideas, which lie in obscurity. And by this means, we may, perhaps, attain a new microscope or species of optics, by which, in the moral sciences, the most minute, and most simple ideas may be so enlarged as to fall readily under our apprehension, and be equally known with the grossest and most sensible ideas, that can be the object of our enquiry.

To be fully acquainted, therefore, with the idea of power or necessary connexion, let us examine its impression; and in order to find the impression with greater certainty, let us search for it in all the sources, from which it may possibly be derived.

When we look about us towards external objects, and consider the operation of causes, we are never able, in a single instance, to discover any power or necessary connexion; and quality, which binds the effect to the cause, and renders the one an infallible consequence of the other. We only find, that the one does actually, in fact, follow the other. The impulse of one Billiard-ball is attended with motion in the second. This is the whole that appears to the *outward senses*. The mind feels no sentiment or *inward* impression from this succession of objects: Consequently there is not, in any single, particular instance of cause and effect, any thing which can suggest the idea of power or necessary connexion.

From the first appearance of an object, we never can conjecture what effect will result from it. But were the power or energy of any cause discoverable by the mind, we could foresee the effect, even without experience; and might, at first, pronounce with certainty concerning it, by mere dint of thought and reasoning.

In reality, there is no part of matter, that does ever, by its sensible qualities, discover any power or energy, or give us ground to imagine, that it could produce any thing, or be followed by any other object, which we could denominate its effect. Solidity, extension, motion; these qualities are all complete in themselves, and never point out any other event which may result from them. The scenes of the universe are continually shifting, and one object follows another in an uninterrupted succession; but the power of force, which actuates the whole machine, is entirely concealed from us, and never discovers itself in any of the sensible qualities of body. We know, that, in fact, heat is a constant attendant of flame; but what is the connexion between them, we have no room so much as to conjecture or imagine. It is impossible, therefore, that the idea of power can be derived from the contemplation of bodies, in single instances of their operation; because no bodies ever discover any power, which can be the original of this idea.*

Since, therefore, external objects as they appear to the senses, give us no idea of power or necessary connexion, by their operation in particular instances, let us see, whether this idea be derived from reflection on the operations of our own minds, and

---

*Mr. Locke, in his chapter of power, says, that, finding from experience, that there are several new productions in matter, and concluding that there must somewhere be a power capable of producing them, we arrive at last by this reasoning at the idea of power. But no reasoning can ever give us a new, original, simple idea; as this philosopher himself confesses. This, therefore, can never be the origin of that idea.

be copied from any internal impression. It may be said, that we are every moment conscious of internal power; while we feel, that, by the simple command of our will, we can move the organs of our body, or direct the faculties of our mind. An act of volition produces motion in our limbs, or raises a new idea in our imagination. This influence of the will we know by consciousness. Hence we acquire the idea of power or energy; and are certain, that we ourselves and all other intelligent beings are possessed of power. This idea, then, is an idea of reflection, since it arises from reflecting on the operations of our own mind, and on the command which is exercised by will, both over the organs of the body and faculties of the soul.

We shall proceed to examine this pretension; and first with regard to the influence of volition over the organs of the body. This influence, we may observe, is a fact, which, like all other natural events, can be known only by experience, and can never be foreseen from any apparent energy or power in the cause, which connects it with the effect, and renders the one an infallible consequence of the other. The motion of our body follows upon the command of our will. Of this we are every moment conscious. But the means, by which this is effected; the energy, by which the will performs so extraordinary an operation; of this we are so far from being immediately conscious, that it must for ever escape our most diligent enquiry.

For *first;* is there any principle in all nature more mysterious than the union of soul with body; by which a supposed spiritual substance acquires such an influence over a material one, that the most refined thought is able to actuate the grossest matter? Were we empowered, by a secret wish, to remove mountains, or control the planets in their orbit; this extensive authority would not be more extraordinary, nor more beyond our comprehension. But if by consciousness we perceived any power or energy in the will, we must know this power; we must know its connexion with the effect; we must know the secret union of soul and body, and the nature of both these substances; by which the one is able to operate, in so many instances, upon the other.

Secondly, We are not able to move all the organs of the body with a like authority; though we cannot assign any reason besides experience, for so remarkable a difference between one and the other. Why has the will an influence over the tongue and fingers, not over the heart and liver? This question would never embarrass us, were we conscious of a power in the former case, not in the latter. We should then perceive, independent of experience, why the authority of will over the organs of the body is circumscribed within such particular limits. Being in that case fully acquainted with the power or force, by which it operates, we should also know, why its influence reaches precisely to such boundaries, and no farther.

A man, suddenly struck with palsy in the leg or arm, or who had newly lost those members, frequently endeavours, at first to move them, and employ them in their usual offices. Here he is as much conscious of power to command such limbs, as a man in perfect health is conscious of power to actuate any member which remains in its natural state and condition. But consciousness never deceives. Consequently, neither in the one case nor in the other, are we ever conscious of any power. We learn the influence of our will from experience alone. And experience only teaches us, how one event constantly follows another; without instructing us in the secret connexion, which binds them together, and renders them inseparable.

Thirdly, We learn from anatomy, that the immediate object of power in voluntary motion, is not the member itself which is moved, but certain muscles, and nerves, and animal spirits, and, perhaps, something still more minute and more unknown, through which the motion is successfully propagated, ere it reach the member itself whose motion is the immediate object of volition. Can there be a more certain proof that the power, by which this whole operation is performed, so far from being directly and fully known by an inward sentiment or consciousness, is, to the last degree, mysterious and unintelligible? Here the mind wills a certain event: Immediately another event, unknown to ourselves, and totally different from the one intended, is produced: This event produces another, equally unknown: Till at last, through a long succession, the desired event is produced. But if the original power were felt, it must be known: Were it known, its effect also must be known; since all power is relative to its effect. And *vice versa,* if the effect be not known, the power cannot be known nor felt. How indeed can we be conscious of a power to move our limbs, when we have no such power; but only that to move certain animal spirits, which, though they produce at last the motion of our limbs, yet operate in such a manner as is wholly beyond our comprehension?

We may, therefore, conclude from the whole, I hope, without any temerity, though with assurance; that our idea of power is not copied from any sentiment or consciousness of power within ourselves, when we give rise to animal motion, or apply our limbs, to their proper use and office. That their motion follows the command of the will is a matter of common experience, like other natural events: But the power or energy by which this is effected, like that in other natural events, is unknown and inconceivable.*

Shall we then assert, that we are conscious of a power or energy in our own minds, when, by an act or command of our will, we raise up a new idea, fix the mind to the contemplation of it, turn it on all sides, and at last dismiss it for some other idea, when we think that we have surveyed it with sufficient accuracy? I believe the same arguments will prove, that even this command of the will gives us no real idea of force or energy.

First, It must be allowed, that, when we know a power, we know that very circumstance in the cause, by which it is enabled to produce the effect: For these are supposed to be synonymous. We must, therefore, know both the cause and effect, and the relation between them. But do we pretend to be acquainted with the nature of the human soul and the nature of an idea, or the aptitude of the one to produce the other? This is a real creation; a production of something out of nothing: Which implies a power so great, that it may seem, at first sight, beyond the reach of any being, less than infinite. At least it must be owned, that such a power is not felt, nor known, nor even conceivable by the mind. We only feel the event, namely, the existence of an idea, consequent to a command of the will: But the manner, in which this operation is performed, the power by which it is produced, is entirely beyond our comprehension.

Secondly, The command of the mind over itself is limited, as well as its command over the body; and these limits are not known by reason, or any acquaintance with the nature of cause and effect, but only by experience and observation, as in all other natural events and in the operation of external objects. Our authority over our

---

*It may be pretended, that the resistance which we meet with in bodies, obliging us frequently to exert our force, and call up all our power, this gives us the idea of force and power. It is this nisus, or strong endeavour, of which we are conscious, that is the original impression from which this idea is copied. But, *first,* we attribute power to a vast number of objects, where we never can suppose this resistance or exertion of force to take place, to the Supreme Being, who never meets with any resistance; to the mind in its command over its ideas and limbs, in common thinking and motion, where the effect follows immediately upon the will, without any exertion or summoning up of force, to inanimate matter, which is not capable of this sentiment. *Secondly,* This sentiment of an endeavour to overcome resistance has no known connexion with any event: What follows it we know by experience; but could not know it *a priori.* It must, however, be confessed that the animal nisus, which we experience though it can afford no accurate precise idea of power, enters very much into that vulgar, inaccurate idea, which is formed of it.

sentiments and passions is much weaker than that over our ideas; and even the latter authority is circumscribed within very narrow boundaries, or show why the power is deficient in one case, not in another.

Thirdly, This self-command is very different at different times. A man in health possesses more of it than one languishing with sickness. We are more master of our thoughts in the morning than in the evening: Fasting, than after a full meal. Can we give any reason for these variations, except experience? Where then is the power, of which we pretend to be conscious? Is there not here, either in a spiritual or material substance, or both, some secret mechanism or structure of parts, upon which the effect depends, and which, being entirely unknown to us, renders the power or energy of the will equally unknown and incomprehensible?

Volition is surely an act of the mind, with which we are sufficiently acquainted. Reflect upon it. Consider it on all sides. Do you find anything in it like this creative power, by which it raises from nothing a new idea, and with a kind of *Fiat*, imitates the omnipotence of its Maker, if I may be allowed so to speak, who called forth into existence all the various scenes of nature? So far from being conscious of this energy in the will, it requires as certain experience as that of which we are possessed, to convince us that such extraordinary effects do ever result from a simple act of volition.

The generality of mankind never find any difficulty in accounting for the more common and familiar operations of nature—such as the descent of heavy bodies, the growth of plants, the generation of animals, or the nourishment of bodies by food: But suppose that, in all these cases, they perceive the very force or energy of the cause, by which it is connected with its effect, and is for ever infallible in its operation. They acquire, by long habit, such a turn of mind, that, upon the appearance of the cause, they immediately expect with assurance its usual attendant, and hardly conceive it possible that any other event could result from it. It is only on the discovery of extraordinary phenomena, such as earthquakes, pestilence, and prodigies of any kind, that they find themselves at a loss to assign a proper cause, and to explain the manner in which the effect is produced by it. It is usual for men, in such difficulties, to have recourse to some invisible intelligent principle as the Immediate cause of that event which surprises them, and which, they think, cannot be accounted for from the common powers of nature. But philosophers, who carry their scrutiny a little farther, immediately perceive that, even in the most familiar events, the energy of the cause is as unintelligible as in the most unusual, and that we only learn by experience the frequent *Conjunction* of objects, without being ever able to comprehend anything like *Connexion* between them. Here, then, many philosophers think themselves obliged by reason to have recourse, on all occasions, to the same principle, which the vulgar never appeal to but in cases that appear miraculous and supernatural. They acknowledge mind and intelligence to be, not only the ultimate and original cause of all things, but the immediate and sole cause of every event which appears in nature. They pretend that those objects which are commonly denominated *causes*, are in reality nothing but *occasions*; and that the true and direct principle of every effect is not any power or force in nature, but a volition of the Supreme Being, who wills that such particular objects should for ever be conjoined with each other. Instead of saying that one Billiard-ball moves another by a force which it has derived from the author of nature, it is the Deity himself, they say, who, by a particular volition, moves the second ball, being determined to this operation by the impulse of the first ball, in consequence of those general laws which he has laid down to himself in the government of the universe. But philosophers advancing still in their inquiries, discover that, as we are totally ignorant of the power on which depends the mutual operation of bodies, we are no less ignorant of that power on which depends the operation of mind on body, or of body on mind; nor are we able, either from our sense or consciousness, to assign the ultimate principle in one case more than in the other. The same ignorance, therefore, reduces them to the same conclusion. They assert that the Deity is the immediate cause of the union between soul and body; and that they are not the organs of sense, which, being agitated by external objects, produce sensations in the mind; but that it is a particular volition of our omnipotent Maker, which excites such a sensation, in consequence of such a motion in the organ. In like manner, it is not any energy in the will that produces local motion in our members: It is God himself, who is pleased to second our will, in itself important, and to command that motion which we erroneously attribute to our own power and efficacy. Nor do philosophers stop at this conclusion. They sometimes extend the same inference to the mind itself, in its internal operations. Our mental vision or conception of ideas is nothing but a revelation made to us by our Maker. When we voluntarily turn our thoughts to any object, and raise up its image in the fancy, it is not the will which creates that idea: It is the universal Creator, who discovers it to the mind, and renders it present to us.

Thus, according to these philosophers, every thing is full of God. Not content with the principle, that nothing exists but by his will, that nothing possesses any power but by his concession: They rob nature, and all created beings, of every power, in order to render their dependence on the Deity still more sensible and immediate. They consider not that, by this theory, they diminish, instead of magnifying, the grandeur of those attributes, which they affect so much to celebrate. It argues surely more power in the Deity to delegate a certain degree of power to inferior creatures, than to produce every thing by his own immediate volition. It argues more wisdom to contrive at first the fabric of the world with such perfect foresight that, of itself, and by its proper operation, it may serve all the purposes of providence, than if the great Creator were obliged every moment to adjust its parts, and animate by his breath all the wheels of that stupendous machine.

But if we would have a more philosophical confutation of this theory, perhaps the two following reflections may suffice.

First, It seems to me that this theory of the universal energy and operation of the Supreme Being is too bold ever to carry conviction with it to a man, sufficiently apprized of the weakness of human reason, and the narrow limits to which it is confined in all its operations. Though the chain of arguments which conduct to it were ever so logical, there must arise a strong suspicion, if not an absolute assurance, that it has carried us quite beyond the reach of our faculties, when it leads to conclusions so extraordinary, and so remote from common life and experience. We are got into fairy land, long ere we have reached the last steps of our theory; and *there* we have no reason to trust our common methods of argument, or to think that our usual analogies and probabilities have any authority. Our line is too short to fathom such immense abysses. And however we may flatter ourselves that we are guided, in every step which we take, by a kind of verisimilitude and experience, we may be assured that this fancied experience has no authority when we thus apply it to subjects that lie entirely out of the sphere of experience. But on this we shall have occasion to touch afterwards.*

Secondly, I cannot perceive any force in the arguments on which this theory is founded. We are ignorant, it is true, of the manner in which bodies operate on each other: Their force or energy is entirely incomprehensible: But are we not equally ignorant of the manner of force by which a mind, even the supreme mind, operates either on itself or on body? Whence, I beseech you, do we acquire any idea of it? We have no

*Section XII.

sentiment or consciousness of this power in ourselves. We have no idea of the Supreme Being but what we learn from reflection on our own faculties. Were our ignorance, therefore, a good reason for rejecting any thing, we should be led into that principle of denying all energy in the Supreme Being as much as in the grossest matter. We surely comprehend as little the operations of one as of the other. Is it more difficult to conceive that motion may arise from impulse than that it may arise from volition? All we know is our profound ignorance in both cases.*

Part II

But to hasten to a conclusion of this argument, which is already drawn out to too great a length: We have sought in vain for an idea of power or necessary connexion in all the sources from which we could suppose it to be derived. It appears that, in single instances of the operation of bodies, we never can, by our utmost scrutiny, discover any thing but one event following another, without being able to comprehend any force or power by which the cause operates, or any connexion between it and its supposed effect. The same difficulty occurs in contemplating the operations of mind on body—where we observe the motion of the latter to follow upon the volition of the former, but are not able to observe or conceive the tie which binds together the motion and volition, or the energy by which the mind produces this effect. The authority of the will over its own faculties and ideas is not a whit more comprehensible: So that, upon the whole, there appears not, throughout all nature, any one instance of connexion which is conceivable by us. All events seem entirely loose and separate. One event follows another; but we never can observe any tie between them. They seem *conjoined,* but never connected. And as we can have no idea of any thing which never appeared to our outward sense or inward sentiment, the necessary conclusion *seems* to be that we have no idea of connexion or power at all, and that these words are absolutely without any meaning, when employed either in philosophical reasonings or common life.

But there still remains one method of avoiding this conclusion, and one source which we have not yet examined. When any natural object or event is presented, it is impossible for us, by any sagacity or penetration, to discover, or even conjecture, without experience, what event will result from it, or to carry our foresight beyond that object which is immediately present to the memory and senses. Even after one instance or experiment where we have observed a particular event to follow upon another, we are not entitled to form a general rule, or foretell what will happen in like cases; it being

---

*I need not examine at length the *vis inertiae* [force of inertia] which is so much talked of in the new philosophy, and which is ascribed to matter. We find by experience, that a body at rest or in motion continues for ever in its present state, till put from it by some new cause; and that a body impelled takes as much motion from the impelling body as it acquires itself. These are facts. When we call this a *vis inertiae,* we only mark these facts, without pretending to have any idea of the inert power; in the same manner as, when we talk of gravity, we mean certain effects without comprehending that active power. It was never the meaning of SIR ISAAC NEWTON to rob second causes of all forces of energy though some of his followers have endeavoured to establish that theory upon his authority. On the contrary, that great philosopher had recourse to an etherial active fluid to explain his universal attraction; though he was so cautious and modest as to allow that it was a mere hypothesis, not to be insisted on, without more experiments. I must confess, that there is something in the fate of opinions a little extraordinary. DESCARTES insinuated that doctrine of the universal and sole efficacy of the Deity, without insisting on it. MALEBRANCHE and other CARTESIANS made it the foundation of all their philosophy. It had, however, no authority in England. LOCKE, CLARKE, and CUDWORTH, never so much as take notice of it, but suppose all along, that matter has a real, though subordinate and derived power. By what means has it become so prevalent among our modern metaphysicians?

justly esteemed an unpardonable temerity to judge of the whole course of nature from one single experiment, however accurate or certain. But when one particular species of event has always, in all instances, been conjoined with another, we make no longer any scruple of foretelling one upon the appearance of the other, and of employing that reasoning which can alone assure us of any matter of fact or existence. We then call the one object, *Cause*; the other, *Effect*. We suppose that there is some connexion between them; some power in the one, by which it infallibly produces the other, and operates with the greatest certainty and strongest necessity.

It appears, then, that this idea of a necessary connexion among events arises from a number of similar instances which occur of the constant conjunction of these events; nor can that idea ever be suggested by any one of these instances, surveyed in all possible lights and positions. But there is nothing in a number of instances, different from every single instance, which is supposed to be exactly similar; except only, that after a repetition of similar instances, the mind is carried by habit, upon the appearance of one event, to expect its usual attendant, and to believe that it will exist. This connexion, therefore, which we *feel* in the mind, this customary transition of the imagination from one object to its usual attendant, is the sentiment or impression from which we form the idea of power or necessary connexion. Nothing farther is in the case. Contemplate the subject on all sides; you will never find any other origin of that idea. This is the sole difference between one instance, from which we can never receive the idea of connexion, and a number of similar instances, by which it is suggested. The first time a man saw the communication of motion by impulse, as by the shock of two Billiard-balls, he could not pronounce that the one event was *connected*: but only that it was *conjoined* with the other. After he has observed several instances of this nature, he then pronounces them to be *connected*. What alteration has happened to give rise to this new idea of connexion? Nothing but that he now *feels* these events to be *connected* in his imagination, and can readily foretell the existence of one from the appearance of the other. When we say, therefore, that one object is connected with another, we mean only that they have acquired a connexion in our thought, and give rise to this inference, by which they become proofs of each other's existence: A conclusion which is somewhat extraordinary, but which seems founded on sufficient evidence. Nor will its evidence be weakened by any general diffidence of the understanding, or sceptical suspicion concerning every conclusion which is new and extraordinary. No conclusions can be more agreeable to scepticism than such as make discoveries concerning the weakness and narrow limits of human reason and capacity.

And what stronger instance can be produced of the surprising ignorance and weakness of the understanding than the present? For surely, if there be any relation among objects which it imports to us to know perfectly, it is that of cause and effect. On this are founded all our reasonings concerning matter of fact or existence. By means of it alone we attain any assurance concerning objects which are removed from the present testimony of our memory and senses. The only immediate utility of all sciences, is to teach us, how to control and regulate future events by their causes. Our thoughts and enquiries are, therefore, every moment, employed about this relation: Yet so imperfect are the ideas which we form concerning it, that it is impossible to give any just definition of cause, except what is drawn from something extraneous and foreign to it. Similar objects are always conjoined with similar. Of this we have experience. Suitably to this experience, therefore, we may define a cause to be *an object, followed by another, and where all the objects similar to the first are followed by objects similar to the second. Or in other words where, if the first object had not been, the second never had existed.* The appearance of a cause always conveys the mind, by a customary transition, to the idea of the effect. Of this also we have experience. We may, therefore, suitably to this experience, form another definition of cause, and call it, *an object followed by another and whose appearance always conveys the thought to that other*. But though both these definitions be drawn from circumstances foreign to the cause, we cannot remedy this inconvenience, or attain any more perfect definition, which may point out that circumstance in the cause, which gives it a connexion with its effect. We have no idea of this connexion, nor even any distinct notion what it is we desire to know, when we endeavour at a conception of it. We say, for instance, that the vibration of this string is the cause of this particular sound. But what do we mean by that affirmation? We either mean *that this vibration is followed by this sound, and that all similar vibrations have been followed by similar sounds*: Or, that this vibration is followed by this sound, and that upon the appearance of one the mind anticipates the senses, and forms immediately an idea of the other. We may consider the relation of cause and effect in either of these two lights; but beyond these, we have no idea of it.*

To recapitulate, therefore, the reasonings of this section: Every idea is copied from some preceding impression or sentiment; and where we cannot find any impression, we may be certain that there is no idea. In all single instances of the operation of bodies or minds, there is nothing that produces any impression, nor consequently can suggest any idea of power or necessary connexion. But when many uniform instances appear, and the same object is always followed by the same event; we then begin to entertain the notion of cause and connexion. We then *feel* a new sentiment or impression, to wit, a customary connexion in the thought or imagination between one object and its usual attendant; and this sentiment is the original of that idea which we seek for. For as this idea arises from a number of similar instances, and not from any single instance, it must arise from that circumstance, in which the number of instances differ from every individual instance. But this customary connexion or transition of the imagination is the only circumstance in which they differ. In every other particular they are alike. The first instance which we saw of motion communicated by the shock of two Billiard-balls (to return to this obvious illustration) is exactly similar to any instance that may, at present, occur to us; except only, that we could not, at first, *infer* one event from the other; which we are enabled to do at present, after so long a course of uniform experience. I know not whether the reader will readily apprehend this reasoning. I am afraid that, should I multiply words about it, or throw it into a greater variety of lights, it would

---

*According to these explanations and definitions, the idea of *power* is relative as much as that of cause; and both have a reference to an effect, or some other event constantly conjoined with the former. When we consider the *unknown* circumstance of an object, by which the degree of quantity of its effect is fixed and determined, we call that its power: And accordingly, it is allowed by all philosophers, that the effect is the measure of the power. But if they had any idea of power, as it is in itself, why could not they measure it in itself? The dispute whether the force of a body in motion be as its velocity, or the square of its velocity; this dispute, I say, need not be decided by comparing its effects in equal or unequal times; but by a direct mensuration and comparison.

As to the frequent use of the words, Force, Power, Energy, etc., which every where occur in common conversation, as well as in philosophy; that is no proof, that we are acquainted, in any instance, with the connecting principle between cause and effect or can account ultimately for the production of one thing to another. These words, as commonly used, have very loose meanings annexed to them; and their ideas in motion without the sentiment of a *nisus* or endeavour; and every animal has a sentiment or feeling from the stroke or blow of an external object, that is in motion. These sensations, which are merely animal, and from which we can *a priori* draw no inference, we are apt to transfer to inanimate objects, and to suppose, that they have some such feelings, whenever they transfer or receive motion. With regard to energies, which are exerted, without our annexing to them any idea of communicated motion, we consider only the constant experienced conjunction of the events; and as we *feel* a customary connexion between the ideas, we transfer that feeling to the objects; as nothing is more usual than to apply to external bodies every internal sensation which they occasion.

only become more obscure and intricate. In all abstract reasonings there is one point of view which, if we can happily hit, we shall go farther towards illustrating the subject than by all the eloquence in the world. This point of view we should endeavour to reach, and reserve the flowers of rhetoric for subjects which are more adapted to them.

Section VIII. Of Liberty and Necessity

Part I

It might reasonably be expected in questions which have been canvassed and disputed with great eagerness, since the first origin of science and philosophy, that the meaning of all the terms, at least, should have been agreed upon among the disputants; and our enquiries, in the course of two thousand years, been able to pass from words to the true and real subject of the controversy. For how easy may it seem to give exact definitions of the terms employed in reasoning, and make these definitions, not the mere sound of words, the object of future scrutiny and examination? But if we consider the matter more narrowly, we shall be apt to draw a quite opposite conclusion. From this circumstance alone, that a controversy has been long kept on foot, and remains still undecided, we may presume that there is some ambiguity in the expression, and that the disputants affix different ideas to the terms employed in the controversy. For as the faculties of the mind are supposed to be naturally alike in every individual; otherwise nothing could be more fruitless than to reason or dispute together; it were impossible, if men affix the same ideas to their terms, that they could so long form different opinions of the same subject; especially when they communicate their views, and each party turn themselves on all sides, in search of arguments which may give them the victory over their antagonists. It is true, if men attempt the discussion of questions which lie entirely beyond the reach of human capacity, such as those concerning the origin of worlds, or the economy of the intellectual system or region of spirits, they may long beat the air in their fruitless contests, and never arrive at any determinate conclusion. But if the question regard any subject of common life and experience, nothing, one would think, could preserve the dispute so long undecided but some ambiguous expressions, which keep the antagonists still at a distance, and hinder them from grappling with each other.

This has been the case in the long disputed question concerning liberty and necessity; and to so remarkable a degree that, if I be not much mistaken, we shall find, that all mankind, both learned and ignorant, have always been of the same opinion with regard to this subject, and that a few intelligible definitions would immediately have put an end to the whole controversy. I own that this dispute has been so much canvassed on all hands, and has led philosophers into such a labyrinth of obscure sophistry, that it is no wonder, if a sensible reader indulge his ease so far as to turn a deaf ear to the proposal of such a question, from which he can expect neither instruction nor entertainment. But the state of the argument here proposed may, perhaps, serve to renew his attention; as it has more novelty, promises at least some decision of the controversy, and will not much disturb his ease by any intricate or obscure reasoning.

I hope, therefore, to make it appear that all men have ever agreed in the doctrine both of necessity and of liberty, according to any reasonable sense, which can be put on these terms; and that the whole controversy has hitherto turned merely upon words. We shall begin with examining the doctrine of necessity.

It is universally allowed that matter, in all its operations, is actuated by a necessary force, and that every natural effect is so precisely determined by the energy of its cause that no other effect, in such particular circumstances, could possibly have resulted from it. The degree and direction of every motion is, by the laws of nature, prescribed with such exactness that a living creature may as soon arise from the shock of two bodies as motion in any other degree or direction than what is actually produced by it. Would we, therefore, form a just and precise idea of *necessity* we must consider whence that idea arises when we apply it to the operation of bodies.

It seems evident that, if all the scenes of nature were continually shifted in such a manner that no two events bore any resemblance to each other, but every object was entirely new, without any similitude to whatever had been seen before, we should never, in that case, have attained the least idea of necessity, or of a connexion among these objects. We might say, upon such a supposition, that one object or event has followed another; not that one was produced by the other. The relation of cause and effect must be utterly unknown to mankind. Inference and reasoning concerning the operations of nature would, from that moment, be at an end; and the memory and senses remain the only canals, by which the knowledge of any real existence could possibly have access to the mind. Our idea, therefore, of necessity and causation arises entirely from the uniformity observable in the operations of nature, where similar objects are constantly conjoined together, and the mind is determined by custom to infer the one from the appearance of the other. These two circumstances form the whole of that necessity, which we ascribe to matter. Beyond the constant conjunction of similar objects, and the consequent *inference* from one to the other, we have no notion of any necessity or connexion.

If it appear, therefore, that all mankind have ever allowed, without any doubt or hesitation, that these two circumstances take place in the voluntary actions of men, and in the operations of mind; it must follow, that all mankind have ever agreed in the doctrine of necessity, and that they have hitherto disputed, merely for not understanding each other.

As to the first circumstance, the constant and regular conjunction of similar events, we may possibly satisfy ourselves by the following considerations. It is universally acknowledged that there is a great uniformity among the actions of men, in all nations and ages, and that human nature remains still the same, in its principles and operations. The same motives always produce the same actions: The same events follow from the same causes. Ambition, avarice, self-love, vanity, friendship, generosity, public spirit: these passions, mixed in various degrees, and distributed through society, have been, from the beginning of the world, and still are, the source of all the actions and enterprises, which have ever been observed among mankind. Would you know the sentiments, inclinations, and course of life of the Greeks and Romans? Study well the temper and actions of the French and English: You cannot be much mistaken in transferring to the former *most* of the observations which you have made with regard to the latter. Mankind are so much the same, in all times and places, that history informs us of nothing new or strange in this particular. Its chief use is only to discover the constant and universal principles of human nature, by showing men in all varieties of circumstances and situations, and furnishing us with materials from which we may form our observations and become acquainted with the regular springs of human action and behaviour. These records of wars, intrigues, factions, and revolutions, are so many collections of experiments, by which the politician or moral philosopher fixes the principles of his science, in the same manner as the physician or natural philosopher becomes acquainted with the nature of plants, minerals, and other external objects, by the experiments which he forms concerning them. Nor are the earth, water, and other elements, examined by Aristotle, and Hippocrates, more like to those which at present lie under our observation than the men described by Polybius and Tacitus are to those who now govern the world.

Should a traveller, returning from a far country, bring us an account of men, wholly different from any with whom we were ever acquainted; men, who were entirely divested of avarice, ambition, or revenge; who knew no pleasure but friendship, generosity, and public spirit; we should immediately, from these circumstances, detect the falsehood, and prove him a liar, with the same certainty as if he had stuffed his narration with stories of centaurs and dragons, miracles and prodigies. And if we would explode any forgery in history, we cannot make use of a more convincing argument, than to prove, that the actions ascribed to any person are directly contrary to the course of nature, and that no human motives, in such circumstances, could ever induce him to such a conduct. The veracity of Quintus Curtius is as much to be suspected, when he describes the supernatural courage of Alexander, by which he was hurried on singly to attack multitudes, as when he describes his supernatural force and activity, by which he was able to resist them. So readily and universally do we acknowledge a uniformity in human motives and actions as well as in the operations of body.

Hence likewise the benefit of that experience, acquired by long life and a variety of business and company, in order to instruct us in the principles of human nature, and regulate our future conduct, as well as speculation. By means of this guide, we mount up to the knowledge of men's inclinations and motives, from their actions, expressions, and even gestures; and again descend to the interpretation of their actions from our knowledge of their motives and inclinations. The general observations treasured up by a course of experience, give us the clue of human nature, and teach us to unravel all its intricacies. Pretexts and appearances no longer deceive us. Public declarations pass for the specious colouring of a cause. And though virtue and honour be allowed their proper weight and authority, that perfect disinterestedness, so often pretended to, is never expected in multitudes and parties; seldom in their leaders; and scarcely even in individuals of any rank or station. But were there no uniformity in human actions, and were every experiment which we could form of this kind irregular and anomalous, it were impossible to collect any general observations concerning mankind; and no experience, however accurately digested by reflection, would ever serve to any purpose. Why is the aged husbandman more skilful in his calling than the young beginner but because there is a certain uniformity in the operation of the sun, rain, and earth towards the production of vegetables; and experience teaches the old practitioner the rules by which this operation is governed and directed.

We must not, however, expect that this uniformity of human actions should be carried to such a length as that all men, in the same circumstances, will always act precisely in the same manner, without making any allowance for the diversity of characters, prejudices, and opinions. Such a uniformity in every particular, is found in no part of nature. On the contrary, from observing the variety of conduct in different men, we are enabled to form a greater variety of maxims, which still suppose a degree of uniformity and regularity.

Are the manners of men different in different ages and countries? We learn thence the great force of custom and education, which mould the human mind from its infancy and form it into a fixed and established character. Is the behaviour and conduct of the one sex very unlike that of the other? Is it thence we become acquainted with the different characters which nature has impressed upon the sexes, and which she preserves with constancy and regularity? Are the actions of the same person much diversified in the different periods of his life, from infancy to old age? This affords room for many general observations concerning the gradual change of our sentiments and inclinations, and the different maxims which prevail in the different ages of human creatures. Even the characters, which are peculiar to each individual, have a uniformity in their influence; otherwise our acquaintance with the persons and our observation of their conduct could never teach us their dispositions, or serve to direct our behaviour with regard to them.

I grant it possible to find some actions, which seem to have no regular connexion with any known motives, and are exceptions to all the measures of conduct which have ever been established for the government of men. But if we would willingly know what judgement should be formed of such irregular and extraordinary actions, we may consider the sentiments commonly entertained with regard to those irregular events which appear in the course of nature, and the operations of external objects. All causes are not conjoined to their usual effects with like uniformity. An artificer, who handles only dead matter, may be disappointed of his aim, as well as the politician, who directs the conduct of sensible and intelligent agents.

The vulgar, who take things according to their first appearance, attribute the uncertainty of events to such an uncertainty in the causes as makes the latter often fail of their usual influence; though they meet with no impediment in their operation. But philosophers, observing that, almost in every part of nature, there is contained a vast variety of springs and principles, which are hid, by reason of their minuteness or remoteness, find, that it is at least possible the contrariety of events may not proceed from any contingency in the cause, but from the secret operation of contrary causes. This possibility is converted into certainty by farther observation, when they remark that, upon an exact scrutiny, a contrariety of effects always betrays a contrariety of causes, and proceeds from their mutual opposition. A peasant can give no better reason for the stopping of any clock or watch than to say that it does not commonly go right: But an artist easily perceives that the same force in the spring or pendulum has always the same influence on the wheels; but fails of its usual effect, perhaps by reason of a grain of dust, which puts a stop to the whole movement. From the observation of several parallel instances, philosophers form a maxim that the connexion between all causes and effects is equally necessary, and that its seeming uncertainty in some instances proceeds from the secret opposition of contrary causes.

Thus, for instance, in the human body, when the usual symptoms of health or sickness disappoint our expectation; when medicines operate not with their wonted powers; when irregular events follow from any particular cause; the philosopher and physician are not surprised at the matter, nor are ever tempted to deny, in general, the necessity and uniformity of those principles by which the animal economy is conducted. They know that a human body is a mighty complicated machine: That many secret powers lurk in it, which are altogether beyond our comprehension: That to us it must often appear very uncertain in its operations: And that therefore the irregular events, which outwardly discover themselves, can be no proof that the laws of nature are not observed with the greatest regularity in its internal operations and government.

The philosopher, if he be consistent, must apply the same reasoning to the actions and volitions of intelligent agents. The most irregular and unexpected resolutions of men may frequently be accounted for by those who know every particular circumstance of their character and situation. A person of an obliging disposition gives a peevish answer: But he has the toothache, or has not dined. A stupid fellow discovers an uncommon alacrity in his carriage: But he has met with a sudden piece of good fortune. Or even when an action, as sometimes happens, cannot be particularly accounted for, either by the person himself or by others; we know, in general, that the characters of men are, to a certain degree, inconstant and irregular. This is, in a manner, the constant character of human nature; though it be applicable, in a more particular manner, to some persons who have no fixed rule for their conduct, but proceed in a continued course of caprice and inconstancy. The internal principles and motives may operate in a uniform manner, notwithstanding these seeming irregularities; in the same manner as the winds, rain, clouds, and other variations of the weather are supposed to be governed by steady principles; though not easily discoverable by human sagacity and enquiry.

Thus it appears, not only that the conjunction between motives and voluntary actions is as regular and uniform as that between the cause and effect in any part of nature; but also that this regular conjunction has been universally acknowledged among mankind, and has never been the subject of dispute, either in philosophy or common life. Now, as it is from past experience that we draw all inferences concerning the future, and as we conclude that objects will always be conjoined together which we find to have always been conjoined; it may seem superfluous to prove that this experienced uniformity in human actions is a source whence we draw *inferences* concerning them. But in order to throw the argument into a greater variety of lights we shall also insist, though briefly, on this latter topic.

The mutual dependence of men is so great in all societies that scarce any human action is entirely complete in itself, or is performed without some reference to the actions of others, which are requisite to make it answer fully the intention of the agent. The poorest artificer, who labours alone, expects at least the protection of the magistrate, to ensure him the enjoyment of the fruits of his labour. He also expects that, when he carries his goods to market, and offers them at a reasonable price, he shall find purchasers, and shall be able, by the money he acquires, to engage others to supply him with those commodities which are requisite for his subsistence. In proportion as men extend their dealings, and render their intercourse with others more complicated, they always comprehend, in their schemes of life, a greater variety of voluntary actions, which they expect, from the proper motives, to co-operate with their own. In all these conclusions they take their measures from past experience, in the same manner as in their reasonings concerning external objects; and firmly believe that men, as well as all the elements, are to continue, in their operations, the same that they have ever found them. A manufacturer reckons upon the labour of his servants for the execution of any work as much as upon the tools which he employs, and would be equally surprised were his expectations disappointed. In short, this experimental inference and reasoning concerning the actions of others enters so much into human life, that no man, while awake, is ever a moment without employing it. Have we not reason, therefore, to affirm that all mankind have always agreed in the doctrine of necessity according to the foregoing definition and explication of it?

Nor have philosophers ever entertained a different opinion from the people in this particular. For, not to mention that almost every action of their life supposes that opinion, there are even few of the speculative parts of learning to which it is not essential. What would become of *history*, had we not a dependence on the veracity of the historian according to the experience which we have had of mankind? How could *politics* be a science, if laws and forms of government had not a uniform influence upon society? Where would be the foundation of *morals*, if particular characters had no certain or determinate power to produce particular sentiments, and if these sentiments had no constant operation on actions? And with what pretence could we employ our *criticism* upon any poet or polite author, if we could not pronounce the conduct and sentiments of his actors either natural or unnatural to such characters, and in such circumstances? It seems almost impossible, therefore, to engage either in science or action of any kind without acknowledging the doctrine of necessity, and this *inference* from motive to voluntary actions, from characters to conduct.

And indeed, when we consider how aptly *natural* and *moral* evidence link together, and form only one chain of argument, we shall make no scruple to allow that they are of the same nature, and derived from the same principles. A prisoner who has neither money nor interest, discovers the impossibility of his escape, as well when he considers the obstinacy of the gaoler, as the walls and bars with which he is surrounded; and, in all attempts for his freedom, chooses rather to work upon the stone and iron of the one, than upon the inflexible nature of the other. The same prisoner, when conducted to the scaffold, foresees his death as certainly from the constancy and fidelity of his guards, as from the operation of the axe or wheel. His mind runs along a certain train of ideas: The refusal of the soldiers to consent to his escape; the action of the executioner; the separation of the head and body; bleeding, convulsive motions, and death. Here is a connected chain of natural causes and voluntary actions; but the mind feels no difference between them in passing from one link to another: Nor is less certain of the future event than if it were connected with the objects present to the memory or senses, by a train of causes, cemented together by what we are pleased to call a *physical* necessity. The same experienced union has the same effect on the mind, whether the united objects be motives, volition, and actions; or figure and motion. We may change the name of things; but their nature and their operation on the understanding never change.

Were a man, whom I know to be honest and opulent, and with whom I live in intimate friendship, to come into my house, where I am surrounded with my servants, I rest assured that he is not to stab me before he leaves it in order to rob me of my silver standish; and I no more suspect this event than the falling of the house itself, which is new, and solidly built and founded.—*But he may have been seized with a sudden and unknown frenzy.*—So may a sudden earthquake arise, and shake and tumble my house about my ears. I shall therefore change the suppositions. I shall say that I know with certainty that he is not to put his hand into the fire and hold it there till it be consumed: And this event I think I can foretell with the same assurance, as that, if he throw himself out at the window, and meet with no obstruction, he will not remain a moment suspended in the air. No suspicion of an unknown frenzy can give the least possibility to the former event, which is so contrary to all the known principles of human nature. A man who at noon leaves his purse full of gold on the pavement at Charing-Cross, may as well expect that it will fly away like a feather, as that he will find it untouched an hour after. Above one half of human reasonings contain inferences of a similar nature, attended with more or less degrees of certainty proportioned to our experience of the usual conduct of mankind in such particular situations.

I have frequently considered, what could possibly be the reason why all mankind, though they have ever, without hesitation, acknowledged the doctrine of necessity in their whole practice and reasoning, have yet not discovered such a reluctance to acknowledge it in words, and have rather shown a propensity, in all ages, to profess the contrary opinion. The matter, I think, may be accounted for after the following manner. If we examine the operations of body, and the production of effects from their causes, we shall find that all our faculties can never carry us farther in our knowledge of this relation than barely to observe that particular objects are *constantly conjoined* together, and that the mind is carried, by a *customary transition*, from the appearance of one to the belief of the other. But though this conclusion concerning human ignorance be the result of the strictest scrutiny of this subject, men still entertain a strong propensity to believe that they penetrate farther into the powers of nature, and perceive something like a necessary connexion between the cause and the effect. When again they turn their reflections towards the operations of their own minds, and *feel* no such connexion of the motive and the action; they are thence apt to suppose, that there is a difference between the effects which result from material force, and those which arise from thought and intelligence. But being once convinced that we know nothing farther of causation of any kind than merely the *constant conjunction* of objects, and the consequent *inference* of the mind from one to another, and finding that these two circumstances are universally allowed to have place in voluntary actions; we may be more easily led to own the same necessity common to all causes. And though this reasoning may contradict the systems of many philosophers, in ascribing necessity to the determinations of the will, we shall find, upon reflection, that they dissent from it in words only, not in their real sentiment. Necessity, according to the sense in which it is here taken, has never yet been rejected, nor can ever, I think, be rejected by any philosopher. It may only, perhaps, be pretended that the mind can perceive, in the operations of matter, some farther connexion between the cause and effect; and connexion that has no place in voluntary actions of intelligent beings. Now whether it be so or not, can only appear upon examination; and it is incumbent on these philosophers to make good their assertion, by defining or describing that necessity, and pointing it out to us in the operations of material causes.

It would seem, indeed, that men begin at the wrong end of this question concerning liberty and necessity, when they enter upon it by examining the faculties of the soul, the influence of the understanding, and the operations of the will. Let them first discuss a more simple question, namely, the operations of body and of brute unintelligent matter; and try whether they can there form any idea of causation and necessity, except that of a constant conjunction of objects, and subsequent inference of the mind from one to another. If these circumstances form, in reality, the whole of that necessity, which we conceive in matter, and if these circumstances be also universally acknowledged to take place in the operations of the mind, the dispute is at an end; at least, must be owned to be thenceforth merely verbal. But as long as we will rashly suppose, that we have some farther idea of necessity and causation in the operations of external objects; at the same time, that we can find nothing farther in the voluntary actions of the mind; there is no possibility of bringing the question to any determinate issue, while we proceed upon so erroneous a supposition. The only method of undeceiving us is to mount up higher; to examine the narrow extent of science when applied to material causes; and to convince ourselves that all we know of them is the constant conjunction and inference above mentioned. We may, perhaps, find that it is with difficulty we are induced to fix such narrow limits to human understanding: But we can afterwards find no difficulty when we come to apply this doctrine to the actions of the will. For as it is evident that these have a regular conjunction with motives and circumstances and characters, and as we always draw inferences from one to the other, we must be obliged to acknowledge in words that necessity, which we have already avowed, in every deliberation of our lives, and in every step of our conduct and behaviour.*

---

*The prevalence of the doctrine of liberty may be accounted for, from another cause viz. a false sensation or seeming experience which we have, or may have, of liberty or indifference, in many of our actions. The necessity of any action, whether of matter or of mind, is not, properly speaking, a quality in the agent, but in any thinking or intelligent being, who may consider the action; and it consists chiefly in the determination of his thoughts to infer the existence of that action from some preceding objects; as liberty, when opposed to necessity, is nothing but the want of that determination, and a certain looseness or indifference, which we feel, in passing or not passing, from the idea of one object to that of any succeeding one. Now we may observe, that, though, in *reflecting* on human actions, we seldom feel such a looseness, or indifference, but are commonly able to infer them with considerable certainty from their motives, and from the dispositions of the agent; yet it frequently happens, that, in *performing* the actions themselves, we are sensible of something like it: And as all resembling objects are readily taken for each other, this has been employed as a demonstrative and even intuitive proof of human liberty. We feel, that our actions are subject to our will, on most occasions; and imagine we feel, that the will itself is subject to nothing, because, when by a denial of it we are provoked to try, we feel, that it moves easily every way, and produces an image of itself (or a

But to proceed in this reconciling project with regard to the question of liberty and necessity; the most contentious question of metaphysics, the most contentious science; it will not require many words to prove, that all mankind have ever agreed in the doctrine of liberty as well as in that of necessity, and that the whole dispute, in this respect also, has been hitherto merely verbal. For what is meant by liberty, when applied to voluntary actions? We cannot surely mean that actions have so little connexion with motives, inclinations, and circumstances, that one does not follow with a certain degree of uniformity from the other, and that one affords no inference by which we can conclude the existence of the other. For these are plain and acknowledged matters of fact. By liberty, then, we can only mean *a power of acting or not acting, according to the determinations of the will;* that is, if we choose to remain at rest, we may; if we choose to move, we also may. Now this hypothetical liberty is universally allowed to belong to every one who is not a prisoner and in chains. Here, then, is no subject of dispute.

Whatever definition we may give of liberty, we should be careful to observe two requisite circumstances; *first*, that it be consistent with plain matter of fact; *secondly*, that it be consistent with itself. If we observe these circumstances, and render our definition intelligible, I am persuaded that all mankind will be found of one opinion with regard to it.

It is universally allowed that nothing exists without a cause of its existence, and that chance, when strictly examined, is a mere negative word, and means not any real power which has anywhere a being in nature. But it is pretended that some causes are necessary, some not necessary. Here then is the advantage of definitions. Let any one *define* a cause, without comprehending, as a part of the definition, a *necessary connexion* with its effect; and let him show distinctly the origin of the idea, expressed by the definition; and I shall readily give up the whole controversy. But if the foregoing explication of the matter be received, this must be absolutely impracticable. Had not objects a regular conjunction with each other, we should never have entertained any notion of cause and effect; and this regular conjunction produces that inference of the understanding, which is the only connexion, that we can have any comprehension of. Whoever attempts a definition of cause, exclusive of these circumstances, will be obliged either to employ unintelligible terms or such as are synonymous to the term which he endeavours to define.* And if the definition above mentioned be admitted; liberty, when opposed to necessity, not to constraint, is the same thing with chance; which is universally allowed to have no existence.

Velleïty, as it is called in the schools) even on that side, on which it did not settle. This image, or faint motion, we persuade ourselves, could, at that time, have been completed into the thing itself; because, should that be denied, we find, upon a second trial, that, at present it can. We consider not that the fantastical desire of showing liberty, is here the motive of our actions. And it seems certain, that, however, we may imagine we feel a liberty within ourselves, a spectator can commonly infer our actions from our motives and character, and even where he cannot, he concludes in general, that he might, were he perfectly acquainted with every circumstance of our situation and temper, and the most secret springs of our complexion and disposition. Now this is the very essence of necessity, according to the foregoing doctrine.

*Thus, if a cause be defined, *that which produces any thing;* it is easy to observe, that *producing* is synonymous to *causing*. In like manner, if a cause be defined, *that by which any thing exists;* this is liable to the same objection. For what is meant by these words, *by which?* Had it been said, that a cause is *that* after which *any thing constantly exists;* we should have understood the terms. For this is, indeed, all we know of the matter. And this constancy forms the very essence of necessity, nor have we any other idea of it.

PART II

There is no method of reasoning more common, and yet none more blameable, than, in philosophical disputes, to endeavour the refutation of any hypothesis, by a pretence of its dangerous consequences to religion and morality. When any opinion leads to absurdities, it is certainly false; but it is not certain that an opinion is false, because it is of dangerous consequence. Such topics, therefore, ought entirely to be forborne; as serving nothing to the discovery of truth, but only to make the person of an antagonist odious. This I observe in general, without pretending to draw any advantage from it. I frankly submit to an examination of this kind, and shall venture to affirm that the doctrines, both of necessity and of liberty, as above explained, are not only consistent with morality, but are absolutely essential to its support.

Necessity may be defined two ways, conformably to the two definitions of *cause,* of which it makes an essential part. It consists either in the constant conjunction of like objects, or in the inference of the understanding from one object to another. Now necessity, in both these senses, (which, indeed, are at bottom the same) has universally, though tacitly, in the schools, in the pulpit, and in common life, been allowed to belong to the will of man; and no one has ever pretended to deny that we can draw inferences concerning human actions, and that those inferences are founded on the experienced union of like actions, with like motives, inclinations, and circumstances. The only particular in which any one can differ, is, that either, perhaps, he will refuse to give the name of necessity to this property of human actions: But as long as the meaning is understood, I hope the word can do no harm: Or that he will maintain it possible to discover something farther in the operations of matter. But this, it must be acknowledged, can be of no consequence to morality or religion, whatever it may be to natural philosophy or metaphysics. We may here be mistaken in asserting that there is no idea of any other necessity or connexion in the actions of body: But surely we ascribe nothing to the actions of the mind, but what everyone does, and must readily allow of. We change no circumstance in the received orthodox system with regard to the will, but only in that with regard to material objects and causes. Nothing, therefore, can be more innocent, at least, than this doctrine.

All laws being founded on rewards and punishments, it is supposed as a fundamental principle, that these motives have a regular and uniform influence on the mind, and both produce the good and prevent the evil actions. We may give to this influence what name we please; but, as it is usually conjoined with the action, it must be esteemed a *cause,* and be looked upon as an instance of that necessity, which we would here establish.

The only proper object of hatred or vengeance is a person or creature, endowed with thought and consciousness; and when any criminal or injurious actions excite that passion, it is only by their relation to the person, or connexion with him. Actions are, by their very nature, temporary and perishing; and where they proceed not from some cause in the character and disposition of the person who performed them, they can neither redound to his honour, if good; nor infamy, if evil. The actions themselves may be blameable; they may be contrary to all the rules of morality and religion: But the person is not answerable for them; and as they proceeded from nothing in him that is durable and constant, and leave nothing of that nature behind them, it is impossible he can, upon their account, become the object of punishment or vengeance. According to the principle, therefore, which denies necessity, and consequently causes, a man is as pure and untainted, after having committed the most horrid crime, as at the first moment of his birth, nor is his character anywise concerned in his actions, since they are not derived from it, and the wickedness of the one can never be used as a proof of the depravity of the other.

Men are not blamed for such actions as they perform ignorantly and casually, whatever may be the consequences. Why? but because the principles of these actions are only momentary, and terminate in them alone. Men are less blamed for such actions as they perform hastily and unpremeditately than for such as proceed from deliberation. For what reason? but because a hasty temper, though a constant cause or principle in the mind, operates only by intervals, and infects not the whole character. Again, repentance wipes off every crime, if attended with a reformation of life and manners. How is this to be accounted for? but by asserting that actions render a person criminal merely as they are proofs of criminal principles in the mind; and when, by an alteration of these principles, they cease to be just proofs, they likewise cease to be criminal. But, except upon the doctrine of necessity, they never were just proofs, and consequently never were criminal.

It will be equally easy to prove, and from the same arguments, that *liberty*, according to that definition above mentioned, in which all men agree, is also essential to morality, and that no human actions, where it is wanting, are susceptible of any moral qualities, or can be the objects either of approbation or dislike. For as actions are objects of our moral sentiment, so far only as they are indications of the internal character, passions, and affections; it is impossible that they can give rise either to praise or blame, where they proceed not from these principles, but are derived altogether from external violence.

I pretend not to have obviated or removed all objections to this theory, with regard to necessity and liberty. I can foresee other objections, derived from topics which have not here been treated of. It may be said, for instance, that, if voluntary actions be subjected to the same laws of necessity with the operations of matter, there is a continued chain of necessary causes, pre-ordained and pre-determined, reaching from the original cause of all to every single volition of every human creature. No contingency anywhere in the universe; no indifference; no liberty. While we act, we are, at the same time, acted upon. The ultimate Author of all our volitions is the Creator of the world, who first bestowed motion on this immense machine, and placed all beings in that particular position, whence every subsequent event, by an inevitable necessity, must result. Human actions, therefore, either can have no moral turpitude at all, as proceeding from so good a cause; or if they have any turpitude, they must involve our Creator in the same guilt, while he is acknowledged to be their ultimate cause and author. For as a man, who fired a mine, is answerable for all the consequences whether the train he employed be long or short; so wherever a continued chain of necessary causes is fixed, that Being, either finite or infinite, who produces the first, is likewise the author of all the rest, and must both bear the blame and acquire the praise which belong to them. Our clear and unalterable ideas of morality establish this rule, upon unquestionable reasons, when we examine the consequences of any human action; and these reasons must still have greater force when applied to the volitions and intentions of a Being infinitely wise and powerful. Ignorance or impotence may be pleaded for so limited a creature as man; but those imperfections have no place in our Creator. He foresaw, he ordained, he intended all those actions of men, which we so rashly pronounce criminal. And we must therefore conclude, either that they are not criminal, or that the Deity, not man, is accountable for them. But as either of these positions is absurd and impious, it follows, that the doctrine from which they are deduced cannot possibly be true, as being liable to all the same objections. An absurd consequence, if necessary, proves the original doctrine to be absurd in the same manner as criminal actions render criminal the original cause, if the connexion between them be necessary and inevitable.

This objection consists of two parts, which we shall examine separately; *First*, that, if human actions can be traced up, by a necessary chain, to the Deity, they can never be criminal; on account of the infinite perfection of that Being from whom they are derived, and who can intend nothing but what is altogether good and laudable. Or, *Secondly*, if they be criminal, we must retract the attribute of perfection, which we ascribe to the Deity, and must acknowledge him to be the ultimate author of guilt and moral turpitude in all his creatures.

The answer to the first objection seems obvious and convincing. There are many philosophers who, after an exact scrutiny of all the phenomena of nature, conclude, that the WHOLE, considered as one system is, in every period of its existence, ordered with perfect benevolence; and that the utmost possible happiness will, in the end, result to all created beings, without any mixture of positive or absolute ill or misery. Every physical ill, say they, makes an essential part of this benevolent system, and could not possibly be removed, even by the Deity himself, considered as a wise agent, without giving entrance to greater ill, or excluding greater good, which will result from it. From this theory, some philosophers, and the ancient *Stoics* among the rest, derived a topic of consolation under all afflictions, while they taught their pupils that those ills under which they laboured were, in reality, goods to the universe; and that to an enlarged view, which could comprehend the whole system of nature, every event became an object of joy and exultation. But though this topic be specious and sublime, it was soon found in practice weak and ineffectual. You would surely more irritate than appease a man lying under the racking pains of the gout by preaching up to him the rectitude of those general laws, which produced the malignant humours in his body, and led them through the proper canals, to the sinews and nerves, where they now excite such acute torments. These enlarged views may, for a moment, please the imagination of a speculative man, who is placed in ease and security; but neither can they dwell with constancy on his mind, even though undisturbed by the emotions of pain or passion; much less can they maintain their ground when attacked by such powerful antagonists. The affections take a narrower and more natural survey of their object; and by an economy, more suitable to the infirmity of human minds, regard alone the beings around us, and are actuated by such events as appear good or ill to the private system.

The case is the same with *moral* as with *physical* ill. It cannot reasonably be supposed, that those remote considerations, which are found of so little efficacy with regard to one, will have a more powerful influence with regard to the other. The mind of man is so formed by nature that, upon the appearance of certain characters, dispositions, and actions, it immediately feels the sentiment of approbation or blame; nor are there any emotions more essential to its frame and constitution. The characters which engage our approbation are chiefly such as contribute to the peace and security of human society; as the characters which excite blame are chiefly such as tend to public detriment and disturbance: Whence it may reasonably be presumed, that the moral sentiments arise, either mediately or immediately, from a reflection of these opposite interests. What though philosophical meditations establish a different opinion or conjecture; that everything is right with regard to the WHOLE, and that the qualities, which disturb society, are, in the main, as beneficial, and are as suitable to the primary intention of nature as those which more directly promote its happiness and welfare? Are such remote and uncertain speculations able to counterbalance the sentiments which arise from the natural and immediate view of the objects? A man who is robbed of a considerable sum; does

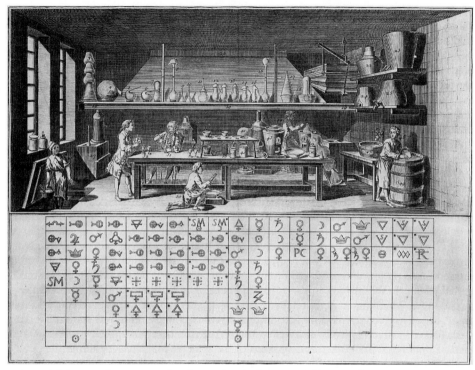

A chemist's laboratory from Denis Diderot's *Encyclopedia* (1751–1772) illustrates the state of empirical science during Hume's lifetime. The symbols below are an early periodic table of elements. (*The Bettmann Archive*)

he find his vexation for the loss anywise diminished by these sublime reflections? Why then should his moral resentment against the crime be supposed incompatible with them? Or why should not the acknowledgment of a real distinction between vice and virtue be reconcileable to all speculative systems of philosophy, as well as that of a real distinction between personal beauty and deformity? Both these distinctions are founded in the natural sentiments of the human mind: And these sentiments are not to be controlled or altered by any philosophical theory or speculation whatsoever.

The *second* objection admits not of so easy and satisfactory an answer; nor is it possible to explain distinctly, how the Deity can be the mediate cause of all the actions of men, without being the author of sin and moral turpitude. These are mysteries, which mere natural and unassisted reason is very unfit to handle; and whatever system she embraces, she must find herself involved in inextricable difficulties, and even contradictions, at every step which she takes with regard to such subjects. To reconcile the indifference and contingency of human actions with prescience; or to defend absolute decrees, and yet free the Deity from being the author of sin, has been found hitherto to exceed all the power of philosophy. Happy, if she be thence sensible of her temerity, when she pries into these sublime mysteries; and leaving a scene so full of obscurities and perplexities, return, with suitable modesty, to her true and proper province, the examination of common life; where she will find difficulties enough to employ her enquiries, without launching into so boundless an ocean of doubt, uncertainty, and contradiction!

Section IX. Of the Reason of Animals

All our reasonings concerning matter of fact are founded on a species of Analogy, which leads us to expect from any cause the same events, which we have observed to result from similar causes. Where the causes are entirely similar, the analogy is perfect, and the inference, drawn from it, is regarded as certain and conclusive: nor does any man ever entertain a doubt, when he sees a piece of iron, that it will have weight and cohesion of parts; as in all other instances, which have ever fallen under his observation. But where the objects have not so exact a similarity, the analogy is less perfect, and the inference is less conclusive; though still it has some force, in proportion to the degree of similarity and resemblance. The anatomical observations, formed upon one animal, are, by this species of reasoning, extended to all animals; and it is certain, that when the circulation of the blood for instance, is clearly proved to have place in one creature, as a frog, or fish, it forms a strong presumption, that the same principle has place in all. These analogical observations may be carried farther, even to this science, of which we are now treating; and any theory, by which we explain the operations of the understanding, or the origin and connexion of the passions in man, will acquire additional authority, if we find, that the same theory is requisite to explain the same phenomena in all other animals. We shall make trial of this, with regard to the hypothesis, by which we have, in the foregoing discourse, endeavoured to account for all experimental reasonings; and it is hoped, that this new point of view will serve to confirm all our former observations.

First, It seems evident, that animals as well as men learn many things from experience, and infer, that the same events will always follow from the same causes. By this principle they become acquainted with the more obvious properties of external objects, and gradually, from their birth, treasure up a knowledge of the nature of fire, water, earth, stones, heights, depths, etc., and of the effects which result from their operation. The ignorance and inexperience of the young are here plainly distinguishable from the cunning and sagacity of the old, who have learned, by long observation, to avoid what hurt them, and to pursue what gave ease or pleasure. A horse, that has been accustomed to the field, becomes acquainted with the proper height which he can leap, and will never attempt what exceeds his force and ability. An old greyhound will trust the more fatiguing part of the chase to the younger, and will place himself so as to meet the hare in her doubles; nor are the conjectures, which he forms on this occasion, founded in any thing but his observation and experience.

This is still more evident from the effects of discipline and education on animals, who, by the proper application of rewards and punishments, may be taught any course of action, and most contrary to their natural instincts and propensities. Is it not experience, which renders a dog apprehensive of pain, when you menace him, or lift up the whip to beat him? Is it not even experience, which makes him answer to his name, and infer, from such an arbitrary sound, that you mean him rather than any of his fellows, and intend to call him, when you pronounce it in a certain manner, and with a certain tone and accent?

In all these cases, we may observe, that the animal infers some fact beyond what immediately strikes his senses; and that this inference is altogether founded on past experience, while the creature expects from the present object the same consequences, which it has always found in its observation to result from similar objects.

Secondly, It is impossible, that this inference of the animal can be founded on any process of argument or reasoning, by which he concludes, that like events must follow like objects, and that the course of nature will always be regular in its operations. For if there be in reality any arguments of this nature, they surely lie too abstruse for the observation of such imperfect understandings; since it may well employ the utmost care and attention of a philosophic genius to discover and observe them. Animals, therefore, are not guided in these inferences by reasoning: Neither are children: Neither are the generality of mankind, in their ordinary actions and conclusions: Neither are philosophers themselves, who, in all the active parts of life, are, in the main, the same with the vulgar, and are governed by the same maxims. Nature must have provided some other principle, of more ready, and more general use and application; nor can an operation of such immense consequence in life, as that of inferring effects from causes, be trusted to the uncertain process of reasoning and argumentation. Were this doubtful with regard to men, it seems to admit of no question with regard to the brute creation; and the conclusion being once firmly established in the one, we have a strong presumption, from all the rules of analogy, that it ought to be universally admitted, without any exception or reserve. It is custom alone, which engages animals, from every object, that strikes their senses, to infer its usual attendant, and carries their imagination, from the appearance of the one, to conceive the other, in that particular manner, which we denominate *belief.* No other explication can be given of this operation, in all the higher, as well as lower classes of sensitive beings, which fall under our notice and observation.*

But though animals learn many parts of their knowledge from observation, there are also many parts of it, which they derive from the original hand of nature; which much exceed the share of capacity they possess on ordinary occasions; and in which they improve, little or nothing, by the longest practice and experience. These we denominate Instincts, and are so apt to admire as something very extraordinary, and inexplicable by all the disquisitions of human understanding. But our wonder will, perhaps, cease or diminish, when we consider, that the experimental reasoning itself, which we possess in common with beasts, and on which the whole conduct of life depends, is nothing but a species of instinct or mechanical power, that acts in us unknown to ourselves; and in its chief operations, is not directed by any such relations or comparisons of ideas, as are the proper objects of our intellectual faculties. Though the instinct be different, yet still it is an instinct, which teaches a man to avoid the fire; as much as that, which teaches a bird, with such exactness, the art of incubation, and the whole economy and order of its nursery.

SECTION X. OF MIRACLES**

PART I

There is, in Dr. Tillotson's writings, an argument against the *real presence*, which is as concise, and elegant, and strong as any argument can possibly be supposed against a doctrine, so little worthy of a serious refutation. It is acknowledged on all hands, says that learned prelate, that the authority, either of the scripture or of tradition, is founded

---

*Since all reasonings concerning facts or causes is derived merely from custom, it may be asked how it happens, that men so much surpass animals in reasoning, and one man so much surpasses another? Has not the same custom the same influence on all?

We shall here endeavour briefly to explain the great difference in human understandings: After which the reason of the difference between men and animals will easily be comprehended.

**1. When we have lived any time, and have been accustomed to the uniformity of nature we acquire a general habit, by which we always transfer the known to the unknown, and conceive the latter to re-

merely in the testimony of the apostles, who were eye-witnesses to those miracles of our Saviour, by which he proved his divine mission. Our evidence, then, for the truth of the *Christian* religion is less than the evidence for the truth of our senses; because, even in the first authors of our religion, it was no greater; and it is evident it must diminish in passing from them to their disciples; nor can any one rest such confidence in their testimony, as in the immediate object of his senses. But a weaker evidence can never destroy a stronger; and therefore, were the doctrine of the real presence ever so clearly revealed in scripture, it were directly contrary to the rules of just reasoning to give our assent to it. It contradicts sense, though both the scripture and tradition, on which it is supposed to be built, carry not such evidence with them as sense, when they are considered merely as external evidences, and are not brought home to every one's breast, by the immediate operation of the Holy Spirit.

Nothing is so convenient as a decisive argument of this kind, which must at least *silence* the most arrogant bigotry and superstition, and free us from their impertinent solicitations. I flatter myself, that I have discovered an argument of a like nature, which, if just, will, with the wise and learned, be an everlasting check to all kinds of superstitious delusion, and consequently, will be useful as long as the world endures; for so long, I presume, will the accounts of miracles and prodigies be found in all history, sacred and profane.

Though experience be our only guide in reasoning concerning matters of fact; it must be acknowledged, that this guide is not altogether infallible, but in some cases is apt to lead us into errors. One, who in our climate, should expect better weather in any week of June than in one of December, would reason justly, and conformably to experience; but it is certain, that he may happen, in the event, to find himself mistaken. However, we may observe, that, in such a case, he would have no cause to complain of experience; because it commonly informs us beforehand of the uncertainty, by that contrariety of events, which we may learn from a diligent observation. All effects follow not with like certainty from their supposed causes. Some events are found, in all countries and all ages, to have been constantly conjoined together: Others are found to have been more variable, and sometimes to disappoint our expectations; so that, in our

---

semble the former. By means of this general habitual principle, we regard even one experiment as the foundation of reasoning, and expect a similar event with some degree of certainty, where the experiment has been made accurately, and free from all foreign circumstances. It is therefore considered as a matter of great importance to observe the consequences of things; and as one man may very much surpass another in attention and memory and observation, this will make a very great difference in their reasoning.

2. Where there is a complication of causes to produce any effect, one mind may be much larger than another, and better able to comprehend the whole system of objects, and to infer justly their consequences.

3. One man is able to carry on a chain of consequences to a greater length than another.

4. Few men can think long without running into a confusion of ideas, and mistaking one for another; and there are various degrees of this infirmity.

5. The circumstance, on which the effect depends, is frequently involved in other circumstances, which are foreign and extrinsic. The separation of it often requires great attention, accuracy, and subtilty.

6. The forming of general maxims from particular observation is a very nice operation; and nothing is more usual, from haste or narrowness of mind which sees not on all sides than to commit mistakes in this particular.

7. When we reason from analogies, the man, who has the greater experience of the greater promptitude of suggesting analogies, will be the better reasoner.

8. Biases from prejudice, education, passion, party, etc., hang more upon one mind than another.

9. After we have acquired a confidence in human testimony, books and conversation enlarge much more the sphere of one man's experience and thought than those of another.

It would be easy to discover many other circumstances that make a difference in the understandings of men.

reasonings concerning matter of fact, there are all imaginable degrees of assurance, from the highest certainty to the lowest species of moral evidence.

A wise man, therefore, proportions his belief to the evidence. In such conclusions as are founded on an infallible experience, he expects the event with the last degree of assurance, and regards his past experience as a full *proof* of the future existence of that event. In other cases, he proceeds with more caution: He weighs the opposite experiments: He considers which side is supported by the greater number of experiments: to that side he inclines, with doubt and hesitation; and when at last he fixes his judgement, the evidence exceeds not what we properly call *probability*. All probability, then, supposes an opposition of experiments and observations, where the one side is found to overbalance the other, and to produce a degree of evidence, proportioned to the superiority. A hundred instances or experiments on one side, and fifty on another, afford a doubtful expectation of any event; though a hundred uniform experiments, with only one that is contradictory, reasonably begets a pretty strong degree of assurance. In all cases, we must balance the opposite experiments, where they are opposite, and deduct the smaller number from the greater, in order to know the exact force of the superior evidence.

To apply these principles to a particular instance; we may observe, that there is no species of reasoning more common, more useful, and even necessary to human life, than that which is derived from the testimony of men, and the reports of eye-witnesses and spectators. This species of reasoning, perhaps, one may deny to be founded on the relation of cause and effect. I shall not dispute about a word. It will be sufficient to observe that our assurance in any argument of this kind is derived from no other principle than our observation of the veracity of human testimony, and of the usual conformity of facts to the reports of witnesses. It being a general maxim, that no objects have any discoverable connexion together, and that all the inferences, which we can draw from one to another, are founded merely on our experience of their constant and regular conjunction; it is evident, that we ought not to make an exception to this maxim in favour of human testimony, whose connexion with any event seems, in itself, as little necessary as any other. Were not the memory tenacious to a certain degree; had not men commonly an inclination to truth and a principle of probity, were they not sensible to shame, when detected in a falsehood: Were not these, I say, discovered by *experience* to be qualities, inherent in human nature, we should never repose the least confidence in human testimony. A man delirious, or noted for falsehood and villainy, has no manner of authority with us.

And as the evidence, derived from witnesses and human testimony, is founded on past experience, so it varies with the experience, and is regarded either as *proof* or a *probability*, according as the conjunction between any particular kind of report and any kind of object has been found to be constant or variable. There are a number of circumstances to be taken into consideration in all judgements of this kind; and the ultimate standard, by which we determine all disputes, that may arise concerning them, is always derived from experience and observation. Where this experience is not entirely uniform on any side, it is attended with an unavoidable contrariety in our judgements, and with the same opposition and mutual destruction of argument as in every other kind of evidence. We frequently hesitate concerning the reports of others. We balance the opposite circumstances, which cause any doubt or uncertainty; and when we discover a superiority on one side, we incline to it; but still with a diminution of assurance, in proportion to the force of its antagonist.

This contrariety of evidence, in the present case, may be derived from several different causes; from the opposition of contrary testimony; from the character or number of the witnesses; from the manner of their delivering their testimony; or from the union of all these circumstances. We entertain a suspicion concerning any matter of fact, when the witnesses contradict each other; when they are but few, or of a doubtful character; when they have an interest in what they affirm; when they deliver their testimony with hesitation, or on the contrary, with too violent asseverations. There are many other particulars of the same kind, which may diminish or destroy the force of any argument, derived from human testimony.

Suppose, for instance, that the fact, which the testimony endeavours to establish, partakes of the extraordinary and the marvellous; in that case, the evidence, resulting from the testimony, admits of a diminution, greater or less, in proportion as the fact is more or less unusual. The reason why we place any credit in witnesses and historians, is not derived from any *connexion*, which we perceive *a priori*, between testimony and reality, but because we are accustomed to find a conformity between them. But when the fact attested is such a one as has seldom fallen under our observation, here is a contest of two opposite experiences; of which the one destroys the other, as far as its force goes, and the superior can only operate on the mind by the force, which remains. The very same principle of experience, which gives us a certain degree of assurance in the testimony of witnesses, gives us also, in this case, another degree of assurance against the fact, which they endeavour to establish; from which contradiction there necessarily arises a counterpoise, and mutual destruction of belief and authority.

I should not believe such a story were it told me by Cato, was a proverbial saying in Rome, even during the lifetime of that philosophical patriot.* The incredibility of a fact, it was allowed, might invalidate so great an authority.

The Indian prince, who refused to believe the first relations concerning the effects of frost, reasoned justly; and it naturally required very strong testimony to engage his assent to facts, that arose from a state of nature, with which he was unacquainted, and which bore so little analogy to those events, of which he had had constant and uniform experience. Though they were not contrary to his experience, they were not conformable to it.**

But in order to increase the probability against the testimony of witnesses, let us suppose, that the fact, which they affirm, instead of being only marvellous, is really miraculous; and suppose also, that the testimony considered apart and in itself, amounts to an entire proof; in that case, there is proof against proof, of which the strongest must prevail, but still with a diminution of its force, in proportion to that of its antagonist.

A miracle is a violation of the laws of nature; and as a firm and unalterable experience has established these laws, the proof against a miracle, from the very nature of

---

*Plutarch, *Marcus Cato* [*The Life of Cato*].

**No Indian, it is evident, could have experience that water did not freeze in cold climates. This is placing nature in a situation quite unknown to him; and it is impossible for him to tell *a priori* what will result from it. It is making a new experiment, the consequence of which is always uncertain. One may sometimes conjecture from analogy what will follow; but still this is but conjecture. And it must be confessed, that, in the present case of freezing, the event follows contrary to the rules of analogy, and is such as a rational Indian would not look for. The operations of cold upon water are not gradual according to the degrees of cold; but whenever it comes to the freezing point, the water passes in a moment, from the utmost liquidity to perfect hardness. Such an event, therefore, may be denominated *extraordinary*, and requires a pretty strong testimony, to render it credible to people in a warm climate: But still it is not *miraculous*, nor contrary to uniform experience of the course of nature in cases where all the circumstances are the same. The inhabitants of Sumatra have always seen water fluid in their own climate, and the freezing of their rivers ought to be deemed a prodigy: But they never saw water in Muscovy during the winter, and therefore they cannot reasonably be positive what would there be the consequence.

the fact, is as entire as any argument from experience can possibly be imagined. Why is it more than probable, that all men must die; that lead cannot, of itself, remain suspended in the air; that fire consumes wood, and is extinguished by water; unless it be, that these events are found agreeable to the laws of nature, and there is required a violation of these laws, or in other words, a miracle to prevent them? Nothing is esteemed a miracle, if it ever happen in the common course of nature. It is no miracle that a man, seemingly in good health, should die on a sudden: because such a kind of death, though more unusual than any other, has yet been frequently observed to happen. But it is a miracle, that a dead man should come to life; because that has never been observed in any age or country. There must, therefore, be a uniform experience against every miraculous event, otherwise the event would not merit that appellation. And as a uniform experience amounts to a proof, there is here a direct and full *proof*, from the nature of the fact, against the existence of any miracle; nor can such a proof be destroyed, or the miracle rendered credible, but by an opposite proof, which is superior.*

The plain consequence is (and it is a general maxim worthy of our attention), "That no testimony is sufficient to establish a miracle, unless the testimony be of such a kind, that its falsehood would be more miraculous, than the fact, which it endeavours to establish; and even in that case there is a mutual destruction of arguments, and the superior only gives us an assurance suitable to that degree of force, which remains, after deducting the inferior." When anyone tells me, that he saw a dead man restored to life, I immediately consider with myself, whether it be more probable, that this person should either deceive or be deceived, or that the fact, which he relates, should really have happened. I weigh the one miracle against the other; and according to the superiority, which I discover, I pronounce my decision, and always reject the greater miracle. If the falsehood of his testimony would be more miraculous, than the event which he relates; then, and not till then, can he pretend to command my belief or opinion.

PART II

In the foregoing reasoning we have supposed, that the testimony, upon which a miracle is founded, may possibly amount to an entire proof, and that the falsehood of that testimony would be a real prodigy: But it is easy to shew, that we have been a great deal too liberal in our concession, and that there never was a miraculous event established on so full an evidence.

For *first*, there is not to be found, in all history, any miracle attested by a sufficient number of men, of such unquestioned good-sense, education, and learning, as to

---

*Sometimes an event may not, *in itself*, seem to be contrary to the laws of nature, and yet, if it were real, it might, by reason of some circumstances, be denominated a miracle, because, *in fact*, it is contrary to these laws. Thus if a person, claiming a divine authority, should command a sick person to be well, a healthful man to fall down dead, the clouds to pour rain, the winds to blow, in short, should order many natural events, which immediately follow upon his command; these might justly be esteemed miracles, because they are really, in this case, contrary to the laws of nature. For if any suspicion remain, that the event and command concurred by accident, there is no miracle and no transgression of the laws of nature. If this suspicion be removed, there is evidently a miracle, and a transgression of these laws; because nothing can be more contrary to nature than that the voice or command of a man should have such an influence. A miracle may be accurately defined, *a transgression of a law of nature by a particular volition of the Deity, or by the interposition of some invisible agent.* A miracle may either be discovered by men or not. This alters not its nature and essence. The raising of a house or ship into the air is a visible miracle. The raising of a feather, when the wind wants ever so little of a force requisite for that purpose, is as real a miracle, though not so sensible with regard to us.

secure us against all delusion in themselves; of such undoubted integrity, as to place them beyond all suspicion of any design to deceive others; of such credit and reputation in the eyes of mankind, as to have a great deal to lose in case of their being detected in any falsehood; and at the same time, attesting facts performed in such a public manner and in so celebrated a part of the world, as to render the detection unavoidable: All which circumstances are requisite to give us a full assurance in the testimony of men.

Secondly, We may observe in human nature a principle which, if strictly examined, will be found to diminish extremely the assurance, which we might, from human testimony, have, in any kind of prodigy. The maxim, by which we commonly conduct ourselves in our reasonings, is, that the objects, of which we have no experience, resemble those, of which we have; that what we have found to be most usual is always most probable; and that where there is an opposition of arguments, we ought to give the preference to such as are founded on the greatest number of past observations. But though, in proceeding by this rule, we readily reject any fact which is unusual and incredible in an ordinary degree; yet in advancing farther, the mind observes not always the same rule; but when anything is affirmed utterly absurd and miraculous, it rather the more readily admits of such a fact, upon account of that very circumstance, which ought to destroy all its authority. The passion of *surprise* and *wonder*, arising from miracles, being an agreeable emotion, gives a sensible tendency towards the belief of those events, from which it is derived. And this goes so far, that even those who cannot enjoy this pleasure immediately, nor can believe those miraculous events, of which they are informed, yet love to partake of the satisfaction at second-hand or by rebound, and place a pride and delight in exciting the admiration of others.

With what greediness are the miraculous accounts of travellers received, their descriptions of sea and land monsters, their relations of wonderful adventures, strange men, and uncouth manners? But if the spirit of religion join itself to the love of wonder, there is an end of common sense; and human testimony, in these circumstances, loses all pretensions to authority. A religionist may be an enthusiast, and imagine he sees what has no reality: he may know his narrative to be false, and yet persevere in it, with the best intentions in the world, for the sake of promoting so holy a cause: or even where this delusion has no place, vanity, excited by so strong a temptation, operates on him more powerfully than on the rest of mankind in any other circumstances; and self-interest with equal force. His auditors may not have, and commonly have not, sufficient judgement to canvass his evidence: what judgement they have, they renounce by principle, in these sublime and mysterious subjects: or if they were ever so willing to employ it, passion and a heated imagination disturb the regularity of its operations. Their credulity increases his impudence: and his impudence overpowers their credulity.

Eloquence, when at its highest pitch, leaves little room for reason or reflection; but addressing itself entirely to the fancy or the affections, captivates the willing hearers, and subdues their understanding. Happily, this pitch it seldom attains. But what a Tully or a Demosthenes could scarcely effect over a Roman or Athenian audience, every *Capuchin*, every itinerant or stationary teacher can perform over the generality of mankind, and in a higher degree, by touching such gross and vulgar passions.

The many instances of forged miracles, and prophecies, and supernatural events, which, in all ages, have either been detected by contrary evidence, or which detect themselves by their absurdity, prove sufficiently the strong propensity of mankind to the extraordinary and the marvellous, and ought reasonably to beget a suspicion against all relations of this kind. This is our natural way of thinking, even with regard to the most common and most credible events. For instance: There is no kind of report which rises so easily, and spreads so quickly, especially in country places and provincial towns, as those concerning marriages; insomuch that two young persons of equal condition never see each other twice, but the whole neighbourhood immediately join them together. The pleasure of telling a piece of news so interesting, of propagating it, and of being the first reporters of it, spreads the intelligence. And this is so well known, that no man of sense gives attention to these reports, till he find them confirmed by some greater evidence. Do not the same passions, and others still stronger, incline the generality of mankind to believe and report, with the greatest vehemence and assurance, all religious miracles?

Thirdly. It forms a strong presumption against all supernatural and miraculous relations, that they are observed chiefly to abound among ignorant and barbarous nations; or if a civilized people has ever given admission to any of them, that people will be found to have received them from ignorant and barbarous ancestors, who transmitted them with that inviolable sanction and authority, which always attend received opinions. When we peruse the first histories of all nations, we are apt to imagine ourselves transported into some new world; where the whole frame of nature is disjointed, and every element performs its operations in a different manner, from what it does at present. Battles, revolutions, pestilence, famine and death, are never the effect of those natural causes, which we experience. Prodigies, omens, oracles, judgements, quite obscure the few natural events, that are intermingled with them. But as the former grow thinner every page, in proportion as we advance nearer the enlightened ages, we soon learn, that there is nothing mysterious or super-natural in the case, but that all proceeds from the usual propensity of mankind towards the marvellous, and that, though this inclination may at intervals receive a check from sense and learning, it can never be thoroughly extirpated from human nature.

It is strange, a judicious reader is apt to say, upon the perusal of these wonderful historians, *that such prodigious events never happen in our days*. But it is nothing strange, I hope, that men should lie in all ages. You must surely have seen instances enough of that frailty. You have yourself heard many such marvellous relations started, which, being treated with scorn by all the wise and judicious, have at last been abandoned even by the vulgar. Be assured, that those renowned lies, which have spread and flourished to such a monstrous height, arose from like beginnings; but being sown in a more proper soil, shot up at last into prodigies almost equal to those which they relate.

It was a wise policy in that false prophet, Alexander, who though now forgotten, was once so famous, to lay the first scene of his impostures in Paphlagonia, where, as Lucian tells us, the people were extremely ignorant and stupid, and ready to swallow even the grossest delusion. People at a distance, who are weak enough to think the matter at all worth enquiry, have no opportunity of receiving better information. The stories come magnified to them by a hundred circumstances. Fools are industrious in propagating the imposture; while the wise and learned are contented, in general, to deride its absurdity, without informing themselves of the particular facts, by which it may be distinctly refuted. And thus the impostor above mentioned was enabled to proceed, from his ignorant Paphlagonians, to the enlisting of votaries, even among the Grecian philosophers, and men of the most eminent rank and distinction in Rome: nay, could engage the attention of that sage emperor Marcus Aurelius; so far as to make him trust the success of a military expedition to his delusive prophecies.

The advantages are so great, of starting an imposture among an ignorant people, that, even though the delusion should be too gross to impose on the generality of them (*which, though seldom, is sometimes the case*) it has a much better chance for succeeding in remote countries, than if the first scene had been laid in a city renowned for arts and knowledge. The most ignorant and barbarous of these barbarians carry the report abroad. None of their countrymen have a large correspondence, or sufficient credit and authority to contradict and beat down the delusion. Men's inclination to the marvellous has full opportunity to display itself. And thus a story, which is universally exploded in the place where it was first started, shall pass for certain at a thousand miles distance. But had Alexander fixed his residence at Athens, the philosophers of that renowned mart of learning had immediately spread, throughout the whole Roman empire, their sense of the matter; which, being supported by so great authority, and displayed by all the force of reason and eloquence, had entirely opened the eyes of mankind. It is true; Lucian, passing by chance through Paphlagonia, had an opportunity of performing this good office. But, though much to be wished, it does not always happen, that every Alexander meets with a Lucian, ready to expose and detect his impostures.

I may add as a *fourth* reason, which diminishes the authority of prodigies, that there is no testimony for any, even those which have not been expressly detected, that is not opposed by an infinite number of witnesses; so that not only the miracle destroys the credit of testimony, but the testimony destroys itself. To make this the better understood, let us consider, that, in matters of religion, whatever is different is contrary; and that it is impossible the religions of ancient Rome, of Turkey, of Siam, and of China should, all of them, be established on any solid foundation. Every miracle, therefore, pretended to have been wrought in any of these religions (and all of them abound in miracles), as its direct scope is to establish the particular system to which it is attributed; so has it the same force, though more indirectly, to overthrow every other system. In destroying a rival system, it likewise destroys the credit of those miracles, on which that system was established; so that all the prodigies of different religions are to be regarded as contrary facts, and the evidences of these prodigies, whether weak or strong, as opposite to each other. According to this method of reasoning, when we believe any miracle of Mahomet or his successors, we have for our warrant the testimony of a few barbarous Arabians: And on the other hand, we are to regard the authority of Titus Livius, Plutarch, Tacitus, and, in short, of all the authors and witnesses, Grecian, Chinese, and Roman Catholic, who have related any miracle in their particular religion; I say, we are to regard their testimony in the same light as if they had mentioned that Mahometan miracle, and had in express terms contradicted it, with the same certainty as they have for the miracle they relate. This argument may appear over subtile and refined; but is not in reality different from the reasoning of a judge, who supposes, that the credit of two witnesses, maintaining a crime against any one, is destroyed by the testimony of two others, who affirm him to have been two hundred leagues distant, at the same instant when the crime is said to have been committed.

One of the best attested miracles in all profane history, is that which Tacitus reports of Vespasian, who cured a blind man in Alexandria, by means of his spittle, and a lame man by the mere touch of his foot; in obedience to a vision of the god Serapis, who had enjoined them to have recourse to the Emperor, for these miraculous cures. The story may be seen in that fine historian;* where every circumstance seems to add weight to the testimony, and might be displayed at large with all the force of argument and eloquence, if any one were now concerned to enforce the evidence of that exploded and idolatrous superstition. The gravity, solidity, age, and probity of so great an emperor, who, through the whole course of his life, conversed in a familiar manner with his friends and courtiers, and never affected those extraordinary airs of divinity assumed by Alexander and Demetrius. The historian, a contemporary writer, noted for candour and veracity, and withal, the greatest and most penetrating genius, perhaps, of

*Histories, iv. 81. Suetonius gives nearly the same account, *Lives of the Caesars* (Vespasian).

all antiquity; and so free from any tendency to credulity, that he even lies under the contrary imputation, of atheism and profaneness: The persons, from whose authority he related the miracle, of established character for judgement and veracity, as we may well presume; eye-witnesses of the fact, and confirming their testimony, after the Flavian family was despoiled of the empire, and could no longer give any reward, as the price of a lie. *Utrumque, qui interfuere, nunc quoque memorant, postquam nullum mendacio pretium.** To which if we add the public nature of the facts, as related, it will appear, that no evidence can well be supposed stronger for so gross and so palpable a falsehood.

There is also a memorable story related by Cardinal de Retz, which may well deserve our consideration. When that intriguing politician fled into Spain, to avoid the persecution of his enemies, he passed through Saragossa, the capital of Arragon, where he was shown, in the cathedral, a man, who had served seven years as a doorkeeper, and was well known to every body in town, that had ever paid his devotions at that church. He had been seen, for so long a time, wanting a leg; but recovered that limb by the rubbing of holy oil upon the stump; and the cardinal assures us that he saw him with two legs. This miracle was vouched by all the canons of the church; and the whole company in town were appealed to for a confirmation of the fact; whom the cardinal found, by their zealous devotion, to be thorough believers of the miracle. Here the relater was also contemporary to the supposed prodigy, of an incredulous and libertine character, as well as of great genius; the miracle of so *singular* a nature as could scarcely admit of a counterfeit, and the witnesses very numerous, and all of them, in a manner, spectators of the fact, to which they gave their testimony. And what adds mightily to the force of the evidence, and may double our surprise on this occasion, is, that the cardinal himself, who relates the story, seems not to give any credit to it, and consequently cannot be suspected of any concurrence in the holy fraud. He considered justly, that it was not requisite, in order to reject a fact of this nature, to be able accurately to disprove the testimony, and to trace its falsehood, through all the circumstances of knavery and credulity which produced it. He knew, that, as this was commonly altogether impossible at any small distance of time and place; so was it extremely difficult, even where one was immediately present, by reason of the bigotry, ignorance, cunning, and roguery of a great part of mankind. He therefore concluded, like a just reasoner, that such an evidence carried falsehood upon the very face of it, and that a miracle, supported by any human testimony, was more properly a subject of derision than of argument.

There surely never was a greater number of miracles ascribed to one person, than those, which were lately said to have been wrought in France upon the tomb of Abbe Paris, the famous Jansenist, with whose sanctity the people were so long deluded. The curing of the sick, giving hearing to the deaf, and sight to the blind, were every where talked of as the usual effects of that holy sepulchre. But what is more extraordinary; many of the miracles were immediately proved upon the spot, before judges of unquestioned integrity, attested by witnesses of credit and distinction, in a learned age, and on the most eminent theatre that is now in the world. Nor is this all: a relation of them was published and dispersed everywhere; nor were the *Jesuits,* though a learned body, supported by the civil magistrate, and determined enemies to those opinions, in whose favour the miracles were said to have been wrought, ever able distinctly to refute or detect them. Where shall we find such a number of circumstances, agreeing to the corroboration of one fact? And what have we to oppose to

---

*[Those who were present recount both even now that a lie is no longer rewarded.]

such a cloud of witnesses, but the absolute impossibility or miraculous nature of the events, which they relate? And this surely, in the eyes of all reasonable people, will alone be regarded as a sufficient refutation.

Is the consequence just, because some human testimony has the utmost force and authority in some cases, when it relates the battle of Philippi or Pharsalia for instance; that therefore all kinds of testimony must, in all cases, have equal force and authority? Suppose that the Caesarean and Pompeian factions had, each of them, claimed the victory in these battles, and that the historians of each party had uniformly ascribed the advantage to their own side; how could mankind, at this distance, have been able to determine between them? The contrariety is equally strong between the miracles related by Herodotus or Plutarch, and those delivered by Mariana, Bede, or any monkish historian.

The wise lend a very academic faith to every report which favours the passion of the reporter; whether it magnifies his country, his family, or himself, or in any other way strikes in with his natural inclinations and propensities. But what greater temptation than to appear a missionary, a prophet, an ambassador from heaven? Who would not encounter many dangers and difficulties, in order to attain so sublime a character? Or if, by the help of vanity and a heated imagination, a man has first made a convert of himself, and entered seriously into the delusion; who ever scruples to make use of pious frauds, in support of so holy and meritorious a cause?

The smallest spark may here kindle into the greatest flame; because the materials are always prepared for it. The *avidum genus auricularum*,* the gazing populace, receive greedily, without examination, whatever soothes superstition, and promotes wonder.

How many stories of this nature have, in all ages, been detected and exploded in their infancy? How many more have been celebrated for a time, and have afterwards sunk into neglect and oblivion? Where such reports, therefore, fly about, the solution of the phenomenon is obvious; and we judge in conformity to regular experience and observation, when we account for it by the known and natural principles of credulity and delusion. And shall we, rather than have a recourse to so natural a solution, allow of a miraculous violation of the most established laws of nature?

I need not mention the difficulty of detecting, a falsehood in any private or even public history, at the place, where it is said to happen; much more when the scene is removed to ever so small a distance. Even a court of judicature, with all the authority, accuracy, and judgement, which they can employ, find themselves often at a loss to distinguish between truth and falsehood in the most recent actions. But the matter never comes to any issue, if trusted to the common method of altercations and debate and flying rumours; especially when men's passions have taken part on either side.

In the infancy of new religions, the wise and learned commonly esteem the matter too inconsiderable to deserve their attention or regard. And when afterwards they would willingly detect the cheat, in order to undeceive the deluded multitude, the season is now past, and the records and witnesses, which might clear up the matter, have perished beyond recovery.

No means of detection remain, but those which must be drawn from the very testimony itself of the reporters: and these, though always sufficient with the judicious and knowing, are commonly too fine to fall under the comprehension of the vulgar.

Upon the whole, then, it appears, that no testimony for any kind of miracle has ever amounted to a probability, much less to a proof; and that, even supposing it amounted to a proof, it would be opposed by another proof; derived from the very na-

---

*[a genus hungry for gossip] Lucretius, De Rerum Natura, iv.

ture of the fact, which it would endeavour to establish. It is experience only, which gives authority to human testimony; and it is the same experience, which assures us of the laws of nature. When, therefore, these two kinds of experience are contrary, we have nothing to do but subtract the one from the other, and embrace an opinion, either on one side or the other, with that assurance which arises from the remainder. But according to the principle here explained, this substraction, with regard to all popular religions, amounts to an entire annihilation; and therefore we may establish it as a maxim, that no human testimony can have such force as to prove a miracle, and make it a just foundation for any such system of religion.

I beg the limitations here made may be remarked, when I say, that a miracle can never be proved, so as to be the foundation of a system of religion. For I own, that otherwise, there may possibly be miracles, or violations of the usual course of nature, of such a kind as to admit of proof from human testimony; though, perhaps, it will be impossible to find any such in all the records of history. Thus, suppose, all authors, in all languages, agree, that, from the first of January 1600, there was a total darkness over the whole earth for eight days: suppose that the tradition of this extraordinary event is still strong and lively among the people: that all travellers, who return from foreign countries, bring us accounts of the same tradition, without the least variation or contradiction: it is evident, that our present philosophers, instead of doubting the fact, ought to receive it as certain, and ought to search for the causes whence it might be derived. The decay, corruption, and dissolution of nature, is an event rendered probable by so many analogies, that any phenomenon, which seems to have a tendency towards that catastrophe, comes within the reach of human testimony, if that testimony be very extensive and uniform.

But suppose, that all the historians who treat of England, should agree, that, on the first of January 1600, Queen Elizabeth died; that both before and after her death she was seen by her physicians and the whole court, as is usual with persons of her rank; that her successor was acknowledged and proclaimed by the parliament; and that, after being interred a month, she again appeared, resumed the throne, and governed England for three years: I must confess that I should be surprised at the concurrence of so many odd circumstances, but should not have the least inclination to believe so miraculous an event. I should not doubt of her pretended death, and of those other public circumstances that followed it: I should only assert it to have been pretended, and that it neither was, nor possibly could be real. You would in vain object to me the difficulty, and almost impossibility of deceiving the world in an affair of such consequence; the wisdom and solid judgement of that renowned queen; with the little or no advantage which she could reap from so poor an artifice: All this might astonish me; but I would still reply, that the knavery and folly of men are such common phenomena, that I should rather believe the most extraordinary events to arise from their concurrence, then admit of so signal a violation of the laws of nature.

But should this miracle be ascribed to any new system of religion; men, in all ages, have been so much imposed on by ridiculous stories of that kind, that this very circumstance would be a full proof of a cheat, and sufficient, with all men of sense, not only to make them reject the fact, but even reject it without farther examination. Though the Being to whom the miracle is ascribed, be, in this case, Almighty, it does not, upon that account, become a whit more probable; since it is impossible for us to know the attributes or actions of such a Being, otherwise than from the experience which we have of his productions, in the usual course of nature. This still reduces us to past observation, and obliges us to compare the instances of the violation of truth in the testimony of men, with those of the violation of the laws of nature by miracles, in order to judge which of them is most likely and probable. As the violations of truth are more common in the testimony concerning religious miracles, than in that concerning any other matter of fact; this must diminish very much the authority of the former testimony, and make us form a general resolution, never to lend any attention to it, with whatever specious pretence it may be covered.

Lord Bacon seems to have embraced the same principles of reasoning. "We ought," says he, "to make a collection or particular history of all monsters and prodigious births or productions, and in a word of every thing new, rare, and extraordinary in nature. But this must be done with the most severe scrutiny, lest we depart from truth. Above all, every relation must be considered as suspicious, which depends in any degree upon religion, as the prodigies of Livy: And no less so, every thing that is to be found in the writers of natural magic or alchemy, or such authors, who seem, all of them, to have an unconquerable appetite for falsehood and fable.*

I am the better pleased with the method of reasoning here delivered, as I think it may serve to confound those dangerous friends or disguised enemies to the *Christian Religion*, who have undertaken to defend it by the principles of human reason. Our most holy religion is founded on *Faith*, not on reason; and it is a sure method of exposing it to put it to such a trial as it is, by no means, fitted to endure. To make this more evident, let us examine those miracles, related in scripture; and not to lose ourselves in too wide a field, let us confine ourselves to such as we find in the *Pentateuch*, which we shall examine, according to the principles of these pretended Christians, not as the word or testimony of God himself, but as the production of a mere human writer and historian. Here then we are first to consider a book, presented to us by a barbarous and ignorant people, written in an age when they were still more barbarous, and in all probability long after the facts which it relates, corroborated by no concurring testimony, and resembling those fabulous accounts, which every nation gives of its origin. Upon reading this book, we find it full of prodigies and miracles. It gives an account of a state of the world and of human nature entirely different from the present: Of our fall from that state: Of the age of man, extended to near a thousand years: Of the destruction of the world by a deluge: Of the arbitrary choice of one people, as the favourites of heaven; and that people the countrymen of the author: Of their deliverance from bondage by prodigies the most astonishing imaginable: I desire any one to lay his hand upon his heart, and after a serious consideration declare, whether he thinks that the falsehood of such a book, supported by such a testimony, would be more extraordinary and miraculous than all the miracles it relates; which is, however, necessary to make it be received, according to the measures of probability above established.

What we have said of miracles may be applied, without any variation, to prophecies; and indeed, all prophecies are real miracles, and as such only, can be admitted as proofs of any revelation. If it did not exceed the capacity of human nature to foretell future events, it would be absurd to employ any prophecy as an argument for a divine mission or authority from heaven. So that, upon the whole, we may conclude, that the *Christian Religion* not only was at first attended with miracles, but even at this day cannot be believed by any reasonable person without one. Mere reason is insufficient to convince us of its veracity: And whoever is moved by *Faith* to assent to it, is conscious of a continued miracle in his own person, which subverts all the principles of his understanding, and gives him a determination to believe what is most contrary to custom and experience.

Novum Organum, II, aphorism 29.

Section XI. Of a Particular Providence
and of a Future State

I was lately engaged in conversation with a friend who loves sceptical paradoxes; where, though he advanced many principles, of which I can by no means approve, yet as they seem to be curious, and to bear some relation to the chain of reasoning carried on throughout this enquiry, I shall here copy them from my memory as accurately as I can, in order to submit them to the judgement of the reader.

Our conversation began with my admiring the singular good fortune of philosophy, which, as it requires entire liberty above all other privileges, and chiefly flourishes from the free opposition of sentiments and argumentation, received its first birth in an age and country of freedom and toleration, and was never cramped, even in its most extravagant principles, by any creeds, concessions, or penal statutes. For, except the banishment of Protagoras, and the death of Socrates, which last event proceeded partly from other motives, there are scarcely any instances to be met with, in ancient history, of this bigoted jealousy, with which the present age is so much infested. Epicurus lived at Athens to an advanced age, in peace and tranquillity: Epicureans were even admitted to receive the sacerdotal character, and to officiate at the altar, in the most sacred rites of the established religion: And the public encouragement of pensions and salaries was afforded equally, by the wisest of all the Roman emperors, to the professors of every sect of philosophy. How requisite such kind of treatment was to philosophy, in her early youth, will easily be conceived, if we reflect, that, even at present, when she may be supposed more hardy and robust, she bears with much difficulty the inclemency of the seasons, and those harsh winds of calumny and persecution, which blow upon her.

You admire, says my friend, as the singular good fortune of philosophy, what seems to result from the natural course of things, and to be unavoidable in every age and nation. This pertinacious bigotry, of which you complain, as so fatal to philosophy, is really her offspring, who, after allying with superstition, separates himself entirely from the interest of his parent, and becomes her most inveterate enemy and persecutor. Speculative dogmas of religion, the present occasions of such furious dispute, could not possibly be conceived or admitted in the early ages of the world; when mankind, being wholly illiterate, formed an idea of religion more suitable to their weak apprehension, and composed their sacred tenets of such tales chiefly as were the objects of traditional belief, more than of argument or disputation. After the first alarm, therefore, was over, which arose from the new paradoxes and principles of the philosophers; these teachers seem ever after, during the ages of antiquity, to have lived in great harmony with the established superstition, and to have made a fair partition of mankind between them; the former claiming all the learned and wise, the latter possessing all the vulgar and illiterate.

It seems then, say I, that you leave politics entirely out of the question, and never suppose, that a wise magistrate can justly be jealous of certain tenets of philosophy, such as those of Epicurus, which, denying a divine existence, and consequently a providence and a future state, seem to loosen, in a great measure, the ties of morality, and may be supposed, for that reason, pernicious to the peace of civil society.

I know, replied he, that in fact these persecutions never, in any age, proceeded from calm reason, or from experience of the pernicious consequences of philosophy; but arose entirely from passion and prejudice. But what if I should advance farther, and assert, that if Epicurus had been accused before the people, by any of the *sycophants* or informers of those days, he could easily have defended his cause, and proved his principles of philosophy to be as salutary as those of his adversaries, who endeavoured, with such zeal, to expose him to the public hatred and jealousy?

I wish, said I, you would try your eloquence upon so extraordinary a topic, and make a speech for Epicurus, which might satisfy, not the mob of Athens, if you will allow that ancient and polite city to have contained any mob, but the more philosophical part of his audience, such as might be supposed capable of comprehending his arguments.

The matter would not be difficult, upon such conditions, replied he: And if you please, I shall suppose myself Epicurus for a moment, and make you stand for the Athenian people, and shall deliver you such an harangue as will fill all the urn with white beans, and leave not a black one to gratify the malice of my adversaries.

Very well: Pray proceed upon these suppositions.

I come hither, O ye Athenians, to justify in your assembly what I maintained in my school, and I find myself impeached by furious antagonists, instead of reasoning with calm and dispassionate enquirers. Your deliberations, which of right should be directed to questions of public good, and the interest of the commonwealth, are diverted to the disquisitions of speculative philosophy; and these magnificent, but perhaps fruitless enquiries, take place of your more familiar but more useful occupations. But so far as in me lies, I will prevent this abuse. We shall not here dispute concerning the origin and government of worlds. We shall only enquire how far such questions concern the public interest. And if I can persuade you, that they are entirely indifferent to the peace of society and security of government, I hope that you will presently send us back to our schools, there to examine, at leisure, the question the most sublime, but at the same time, the most speculative of all philosophy.

The religious philosophers, not satisfied with the tradition of your forefathers, and doctrine of your priests (in which I willingly acquiesce), indulge a rash curiosity, in trying how far they can establish religion upon the principles of reason; and they thereby excite, instead of satisfying, the doubts, which naturally arise from a diligent and scrutinous enquiry. They paint, in the most magnificent colours, the order, beauty, and wise arrangement of the universe; and then ask, if such a glorious display of intelligence could proceed from the fortuitous concourse of atoms, or if chance could produce what the greatest genius can never sufficiently admire. I shall not examine the justness of this argument. I shall allow it to be as solid as my antagonists and accusers can desire. It is sufficient, if I can prove, from this very reasoning, that the question is entirely speculative, and that, when, in my philosophical disquisitions, I deny a providence and a future state, I undermine not the foundations of society, but advance principles, which they themselves, upon their own topics, if they argue consistently, must allow to be solid and satisfactory.

You then, who are my accusers, have acknowledged, that the chief or sole argument for a divine existence (which I never questioned) is derived from the order of nature; where there appear such marks of intelligence and design, that you think it extravagant to assign for its cause, either chance, or the blind and unguided force of matter. You allow, that this is an argument drawn from effects to causes. From the order of the work, you infer, that there must have been project and forethought in the workman. If you cannot make out this point, you allow, that your conclusion fails; and you pretend not to establish the conclusion in a greater latitude than the phenomena of nature will justify. These are your concessions. I desire you to mark the consequences.

When we infer any particular cause from an effect, we must proportion the one to the other, and can never be allowed to ascribe to the cause any qualities, but what are exactly sufficient to produce the effect. A body of ten ounces raised in any scale may serve as a proof, that the counterbalancing weight exceeds ten ounces; but can never afford a reason that it exceeds a hundred. If the cause, assigned for any effect, be not sufficient to produce it, we must either reject that cause, or add to it such qualities as will give it a just proportion to the effect. But if we ascribe to it further qualities, or affirm it capable of producing other effects, we can only indulge the licence of conjecture, and arbitrarily suppose the existence of qualities and energies, without reason or authority.

The same rule holds, whether the cause assigned be brute unconscious matter, or a rational intelligent being. If the cause be known only by the effect, we never ought to ascribe to it any qualities, beyond what are precisely requisite to produce the effect: Nor can we, by any rules of just reasoning, return back from the cause, and infer other effects from it, beyond those by which alone it is known to us. No one, merely from the sight of one of Zeuxis's pictures, could know, that he was also a statuary or architect, and was an artist no less skilful in stone and marble than in colours. The talents and taste, displayed in the particular work before us; these we may safely conclude the workmen to be possessed of. The cause must be proportioned to the effect; and if we exactly and precisely proportion it, we shall never find in it any qualities, that point farther, or afford an inference concerning any other design or performance. Such qualities must be somewhat beyond what is merely requisite for producing the effect, which we examine.

Allowing, therefore, the gods to be the authors of the existence or order of the universe; it follows, that they possess that precise degree of power, intelligence, and benevolence, which appears in their workmanship; but nothing farther can ever be proved, except we call in the assistance of exaggeration and flattery to supply the defects of argument and reasoning. So far as the traces of any attributes, at present, appear, so far may we conclude these attributes to exist. The supposition of farther attributes is mere hypothesis; much more the supposition, that, in distant regions of space or periods of time, there has been, or will be, a more magnificent display of these attributes, and a scheme of administration more suitable to such imaginary virtues. We can never be allowed to mount up from the universe, the effect, to Jupiter, the cause; and then descend downwards, to infer any new effect from that cause; as if the present effects alone were not entirely worthy of the glorious attributes, which we ascribe to that deity. The knowledge of the cause being derived solely from the effect, they must be exactly adjusted to each other; and the one can never refer to anything farther, or be the foundation of any new inference and conclusion.

You find certain phenomena in nature. You seek a cause or author. You imagine that you have found him. You afterwards become so enamoured of this offspring of your brain, that you imagine it impossible, but he must produce something greater and more perfect than the present scene of things, which is so full of ill and disorder. You forget, that this superlative intelligence and benevolence are entirely imaginary, or, at least, without any foundation in reason; and that you have no ground to ascribe to him any qualities, but what you see he has actually exerted and displayed in his productions. Let your gods, therefore, O philosophers, be suited to the present appearances of nature: and presume not to alter these appearances by arbitrary suppositions, in order to suit them to the attributes, which you so fondly ascribe to your deities.

When priests and poets, supported by your authority, O Athenians, talk of a golden or silver age, which preceded the present state of vice and misery, I hear them with attention and with reverence. But when philosophers, who pretend to neglect authority, and to cultivate reason, hold the same discourse, I pay them not, I own, the same obsequious submission and pious deference. I ask, who carried them into the celestial regions, who admitted them into the councils of the gods, who opened to them the book of fate, that they thus rashly affirm, that their deities have executed, or will execute, any purpose beyond what has actually appeared? If they tell me, that they have mounted on the steps or by the gradual ascent of reason, and by drawing inferences from effects to causes, I still insist, that they have aided the ascent of reason by the wings of imagination; otherwise they could not thus change their manner of inference, and argue from causes to effects; presuming, that a more perfect production than the present world would be more suitable to such perfect beings as the gods, and forgetting that they have no reason to ascribe to these celestial beings any perfection or any attribute, but what can be found in the present world.

Hence all the fruitless industry to account for the ill appearance of nature, and save the honour of the gods; while we must acknowledge the reality of that evil and disorder, with which the world so much abounds. The obstinate and intractable qualities of matter, we are told, or the observance of general laws, or some such reason, is the sole cause, which controlled the power and benevolence of Jupiter, and obliged him to create mankind and every sensible creature so imperfect and so unhappy. These attributes then, are, it seems, beforehand, taken for granted, in their greatest latitude. And upon that supposition, I own that such conjectures may, perhaps, be admitted as plausible solutions of the ill phenomena. But still I ask, Why take these attributes for granted, or why ascribe to the cause any qualities but what actually appear in the effect? Why torture your brain to justify the course of nature upon suppositions, which, for aught you know, may be entirely imaginary, and of which there are to be found no traces in the course of nature?

The religious hypothesis, therefore, must be considered only as a particular method of accounting for the visible phenomena of the universe: but no just reasoner will ever presume to infer from it any single fact, and alter or add to the phenomena, in any single particular. If you think, that the appearances of things prove such causes, it is allowable for you to draw an inference concerning the existence of these causes. In such complicated and sublime subjects, every one should be indulged in the liberty of conjecture and argument. But here you ought to rest. If you come backward, and arguing from your inferred causes, conclude, that any other fact has existed, or will exist, in the course of nature, which may serve as a fuller display of particular attributes; I must admonish you, that you have departed from the method of reasoning, attached to the present subject, and have certainly added something to the attributes of the cause, beyond what appears in the effect; otherwise you could never, with tolerable sense or propriety, add anything to the effect, in order to render it more worthy of the cause.

Where, then, is the odiousness of that doctrine, which I teach in my school, or rather, which I examine in my gardens? Or what do you find in this whole question, wherein the security of good morals, or the peace and order of society, is in the least concerned?

I deny a providence, you say, and supreme governor of the world, who guides the course of events, and punishes the vicious with infamy and disappointment, and rewards the virtuous with honour and success, in all their undertakings. But surely, I deny not the course itself of events, which lies open to every one's inquiry and examination. I acknowledge, that, in the present order of things, virtue is attended with more peace of mind than vice, and meets with a more favour able reception from the world. I am sensible, that, according to the past experience of mankind, friendship is the chief joy of human life, and moderation the only source of tranquillity and happiness. I never balance between the virtuous and the vicious course of life; but am sensible, that, to a well-disposed mind, every advantage is on the side of the former. And what can you say more, allowing all your suppositions and reasonings? You tell me, indeed, that this disposition of things proceeds from intelligence and design. But whatever it proceeds from, the disposition itself, on which depends our happiness or misery, and consequently our conduct and deportment in life is still the same. It is still open for me, as well as you, to regulate my behaviour, by my experience of past events. And if you affirm, that, while a divine providence is allowed, and a supreme distributive justice in the universe, I ought to expect some more particular reward of the good, and punishment of the bad, beyond the ordinary course of events; I here find the same fallacy, which I have before endeavoured to detect. You persist in imagining, that, if we grant that divine existence, for which you so earnestly contend, you may safely infer consequences from it, and add something to the experienced order of nature, by arguing from the attributes which you ascribe to your gods. You seem not to remember, that all your reasonings on this subject can only be drawn from effects to causes; and that every argument, deducted from causes to effects, must of necessity be a gross sophism; since it is impossible for you to know anything of the cause, but what you have antecedently, not inferred, but discovered to the full, in the effect.

But what must a philosopher think of those vain reasoners, who, instead of regarding the present scene of things as the sole object of their contemplation, so far reverse the whole course of nature, as to render this life merely a passage to something farther; a porch, which leads to a greater, and vastly different building; a prologue, which serves only to introduce the piece, and give it more grace and propriety? Whence, do you think, can such philosophers derive their idea of the gods? From their own conceit and imagination surely. For if they derived it from the present phenomena, it would never point to anything farther, but must be exactly adjusted to them. That the divinity may *possibly* be endowed with attributes, which we have never seen exerted, may be governed by principles of action, which we cannot discover to be satisfied: all this will freely be allowed. But still this is mere *possibility* and hypothesis. We never can have reason to *infer* any attributes, or any principles of action in him, but so far as we know them to have been exerted and satisfied.

Are there *any marks of a distributive justice in the world?* If you answer in the affirmative, I conclude, that, since justice here exerts itself, it is satisfied. If you reply in the negative, I conclude, that you have then no reason to ascribe justice, in our sense of it, to the gods. If you hold a medium between affirmation and negation, by saying, that the justice of the gods, at present, exerts itself in part, but not in its full extent; I answer, that you have no reason to give it any particular extent, but only so far as you see it, *at present,* exert itself.

Thus I bring the dispute, O Athenians, to a short issue with my antagonists. The course of nature lies open to my contemplation as well as to theirs. The experienced train of events is the great standard, by which we all regulate our conduct. Nothing else can be appealed to in the field, or in the senate. Nothing else ought ever to be heard of in the schools, or in the closet. In vain would our limited understanding break through those boundaries, which are too narrow for our fond imagination. While we argue from the course of nature, and infer a particular intelligent cause, which first bestowed, and still preserves order in the universe, we embrace a principle, which is both uncertain and useless. It is uncertain; because the subject lies entirely beyond the reach of human experience. It is useless; because our knowledge of this cause being derived entirely from the course of nature, we can never, according to the rules of just reasoning, return back from the cause with any new inference, or making additions to the common and experienced course of nature, establish any new principles of conduct and behaviour.

I observe (said I, finding he had finished his harangue) that you neglect not the artifice of the demagogues of old; and as you were pleased to make me stand for the people, you insinuate yourself into my favour by embracing those principles, to which, you know, I have always expressed a particular attachment. But allowing you to make experience (as indeed I think you ought) the only standard of our judgement concerning this, and all other questions of fact; I doubt not but, from the very same experience, to which you appeal, it may be possible to refute this reasoning, which you have put into the mouth of Epicurus. If you saw, for instance, a half-finished building, surrounded with heaps of brick and stone and mortar, and all the instruments of masonry; could you not *infer* from the effect, that it was a work of design and contrivance? And could you not return again, from this inferred cause, to infer new additions to the effect, and conclude, that the building would soon be finished, and receive all the further improvements, which art could bestow upon it? If you saw upon the sea-shore the print of one human foot, you would conclude, that a man had passed that way, and that he had also left the traces of the other foot, though effaced by the rolling of the sands or inundation of the waters. Why then do you refuse to admit the same method of reasoning with regard to the order of nature? Consider the world and the present life only as an imperfect building, from which you can infer a superior intelligence; and arguing from that superior intelligence, which can leave nothing imperfect; why may you not infer a more finished scheme or plan, which will receive its completion in some distant point of space or time? Are not these methods of reasoning exactly similar? And under what pretence can you embrace the one, while you reject the other?

The infinite difference of the subjects, replied he, is a sufficient foundation for this difference in my conclusions. In works of *human* art and contrivance, it is allowable to advance from the effect to the cause, and returning back from the cause, to form new inferences concerning the effect, and examine the alterations, which it has probably undergone, or may still undergo. But what is the foundation of this method of reasoning? Plainly this: that man is a being, whom we know by experience, whose motives and designs we are acquainted with, and whose projects and inclinations have a certain connexion and coherence, according to the laws which nature has established for the government of such a creature. When, therefore, we find, that any work has proceeded from the skill and industry of man; as we are otherwise acquainted with the nature of the animal, we can draw a hundred inferences concerning what may be expected from him; and these inferences will all be founded in experience and observation. But did we know man only from the single work or production which we examine, it were impossible for us to argue in this manner; because our knowledge of all the qualities, which we ascribe to him, being in that case derived from the production, it is impossible they could point to anything further, or be the foundation of any new inference. The print of a foot in the sand can only prove, when considered alone, that there was some figure adapted to it, by which it was produced: but the print of a human foot proves likewise, from our other experience, that there was probably another foot, which also left its impression, though effaced by time or other accidents. Here we mount from the effect to the cause; and descending again from the cause, infer alterations in the effect; but this is not a continuation of the same simple chain of reasoning. We comprehend in this case a hundred other experiences and observations, concerning the *usual* figure and members of that species of animal, without which this method of argument must be considered as fallacious and sophistical.

The case is not the same with our reasonings from the works of nature. The Deity is known to us only by his productions, and is a single being in the universe, not comprehended under any species or genus, from whose experienced attributes or qualities, we can, by analogy, infer any attribute or quality in him. As the universe shows wisdom and goodness, we infer wisdom and goodness. As it shows a particular degree of these perfections, we infer a particular degree of them, precisely adapted to the effect which we examine. But further attributes or further degrees of the same attributes, we can never be authorized to infer or suppose, by any rules of just reasoning. Now, without some such license of supposition, it is impossible for us to argue from the cause, or infer any alteration in the effect, beyond what has immediately fallen under our observation. Greater good produced by this Being must still prove a greater degree of goodness: a more impartial distribution of rewards and punishments must proceed from a greater regard to justice and equity. Every supposed addition to the works of nature makes an addition to the attributes of the Author of nature; and consequently, being entirely unsupported by any reason or argument, can never be admitted but as mere conjecture and hypothesis.*

The great source of our mistake in this subject, and of the unbounded licence of conjecture, which we indulge, is, that we tacitly consider ourselves, as in the place of the Supreme Being, and conclude, that he will, on every occasion, observe the same conduct, which we ourselves, in his situation, would have embraced as reasonable and eligible. But, besides that the ordinary course of nature may convince us, that almost everything is regulated by principles and maxims very different from ours; besides, this, I say, it must evidently appear contrary to all rules of analogy to reason, from the intentions and projects of men, to those of a Being so different, and so much superior. In human nature, there is a certain experienced coherence of designs and inclinations; so that when, from any fact, we have discovered one intention of any man, it may often be reasonable, from experience, to infer another, and draw a long chain of conclusions concerning his past or future conduct. But this method of reasoning can never have place with regard to a Being, so remote and incomprehensible, who bears much less analogy to any other being in the universe than the sun to a waxen taper, and who discovers himself only by some faint traces or outlines, beyond which we have no authority to ascribe to him any attribute or perfection. What we imagine to be a superior perfection, may really be a defect. Or were it ever so much a perfection, the ascribing of it to the Supreme Being, where it appears not to have been really exerted, to the full, in his works, savours more of flattery and panegyric, than of just reasoning and sound philosophy. All the philosophy, therefore, in the world, and all the religion, which is nothing but a species of philosophy, will never be able to carry us beyond the usual course of experience, or give us measures of conduct and behaviour different from those which are furnished by reflections on common life. No new fact can ever be inferred from the religious hypothesis; no event foreseen or foretold: no reward or punishment expected or dreaded, beyond what is already known by practice and observation. So that my apology for Epicurus will still appear solid and satisfactory; nor have the political interests of society any connexion with the philosophical disputes concerning metaphysics and religion.

There is still one circumstance, replied I, which you seem to have overlooked. Though I should allow your premises, I must deny your conclusion. You conclude, that religious doctrines and reasonings *can* have no influence on life, because they *ought* to

---

*In general, it may, I think, be established as a maxim, that where any cause is known only by its particular effects, it must be impossible to infer any new effects from that cause; since the qualities, which are requisite to produce these new effects along with the former, must either be different, or superior, or of more extensive operation, than those which simply produced the effect, whence alone the cause is supposed to be known to us. We can never, therefore, have any reason to suppose the existence of these qualities. To say, that the new effects proceed only from a continuation of the same energy, which is already known from the first effects, will not remove the difficulty. For even granting this to be the case (which can seldom be supposed), the very continuation and exertion of a like energy (for it is impossible it can be absolutely the same), I say, this exertion of a like energy, in a different period of space and time, is a very arbitrary supposition, and what there cannot possibly be any traces of in the effects, from which all our knowledge of the cause is originally derived. Let the *inferred* cause be exactly proportioned (as it should be) to the known effect; and it is impossible that it can possess any qualities, from which new or different effects can be *inferred*.

have no influence; never considering, that men reason not in the same manner you do, but draw many consequences from the belief of a divine Existence, and suppose that the Deity will inflict punishments on vice, and bestow rewards on virtue, beyond what appear in the ordinary course of nature. Whether this reasoning of theirs be just or not, is no matter. Its influence on their life and conduct must still be the same. And, those, who attempt to disabuse them of such prejudices, may, for aught I know, be good reasoners, but I cannot allow them to be good citizens and politicians; since they free men from one restraint upon their passions, and make the infringement of the laws of society, in one respect, more easy and secure.

After all, I may, perhaps, agree to your general conclusion in favour of liberty, though upon different premises from those, on which you endeavour to found it. I think, that the state ought to tolerate every principle of philosophy; nor is there an instance, that any government has suffered in its political interests by such indulgence. There is no enthusiasm among philosophers; their doctrines are not very alluring to the people; and no restraint can be put upon their reasonings, but what must be of dangerous consequences to the sciences, and even to the state, by paving the way for persecution and oppression in points, where the generality of mankind are more deeply interested and concerned.

But there occurs to me (continued I) with regard to your main topic, a difficulty, which I shall just propose to you without insisting on it; lest it lead into reasonings of too nice and delicate a nature. In a word, I much doubt whether it be possible for a cause to be known only by its effect (as you have all along supposed) or to be of so singular and particular a nature as to have no parallel and no similarity with any other cause or object, that has ever fallen under our observation. It is only when two *species* of objects are found to be constantly conjoined, that we can infer the one from the other; and were an effect presented, which was entirely singular, and could not be comprehended under any known species, I do not see, that we could form any conjecture or inference at all concerning its cause. If experience and observation and analogy be, indeed, the only guides which we can reasonably follow in inferences of this nature; both the effect and cause must bear a similarity and resemblance to other effects and causes, which we know, and which we have found, in many instances, to be conjoined with each other. I leave it to your own reflection to pursue the consequences of this principle. I shall just observe, that, as the antagonists of Epicurus always suppose the universe, an effect quite singular and unparalleled, to be the proof of a Deity, a cause no less singular and unparalleled; your reasonings, upon that supposition, seem, at least, to merit our attention. There is, I own, some difficulty, how we can ever return from the cause to the effect, and, reasoning from our ideas of the former, infer any alteration on the latter, or any addition to it.

SECTION XII. OF THE ACADEMICAL OR SCEPTICAL PHILOSOPHY

PART I

There is not a greater number of philosophical reasonings, displayed upon any subject, than those, which prove the existence of a Deity, and refute the fallacies of *Atheists;* and yet the most religious philosophers still dispute whether any man can be so blinded as to be a speculative atheist. How shall we reconcile these contradictions? The knightserrant, who wandered about to clear the world of dragons and giants, never entertained the least doubt with regard to the existence of these monsters.

The *Sceptic* is another enemy of religion, who naturally provokes the indignation of all divines and graver philosophers; though it is certain, that no man ever met with any such absurd creature, or conversed with a man, who had no opinion or principle concerning any subject, either of action or speculation. This begets a very natural question; What is meant by a sceptic? And how far is it possible to push these philosophical principles of doubt and uncertainty?

There is a species of scepticism, *antecedent* to all study and philosophy, which is much inculcated by Des Cartes and others, as a sovereign preservative against error and precipitate judgement. It recommends an universal doubt, not only of all our former opinions and principles, but also of our very faculties; of whose veracity, say they, we must assure ourselves, by a chain of reasoning, deduced from some original principle, which cannot possibly be fallacious or deceitful. But neither is there any such original principle, which has a prerogative above others, that are self-evident and convincing: or if there were, could we advance a step beyond it, but by the use of those very faculties, of which we are supposed to be already diffident. The Cartesian doubt, therefore, were it ever possible to be attained by any human creature (as it plainly is not) would be entirely incurable; and no reasoning could ever bring us to a state of assurance and conviction upon any subject.

It must, however, be confessed, that this species of scepticism, when more moderate, may be understood in a very reasonable sense, and is a necessary preparative to the study of philosophy, by preserving a proper impartiality in our judgements, and weaning our mind from all those prejudices, which we may have imbibed from education or rash opinion. To begin with clear and self-evident principles, to advance by timorous and sure steps, to review frequently our conclusions, and examine accurately all their consequences; though by these means we shall make both a slow and a short progress in our systems; are the only methods, by which we can ever hope to reach truth, and attain a proper stability and certainty in our determinations.

There is another species of scepticism, *consequent* to science and enquiry, when men are supposed to have discovered either the absolute fallaciousness of their mental faculties, or their unfitness to reach any fixed determination in all those curious subjects of speculation, about which they are commonly employed. Even our very senses are brought into dispute, by a certain species of philosophers; and the maxims of common life are subjected to the same doubt as the most profound principles or conclusions of metaphysics and theology. As these paradoxical tenets (if they may be called tenets) are to be met with in some philosophers, and the refutation of them in several, they naturally excite our curiosity, and make us enquire into the arguments, on which they may be founded.

I need not insist upon the more trite topics, employed by the sceptics in all ages, against the evidence of *sense*; such as those which are derived from the imperfection and fallaciousness of our organs, on numberless occasions; the crooked appearance of an oar in water; the various aspects of objects, according to their different distances; the double images which arise from the pressing one eye; with many other appearances of a like nature. These sceptical topics, indeed, are only sufficient to prove, that the senses alone are not implicitly to be depended on; but that we must correct their evidence by reason, and by considerations, derived from the nature of the medium, the distance of the object, and the disposition of the organ, in order to render them, without their sphere, the proper *criteria* of truth and falsehood. There are other more profound arguments against the senses, which admit not of so easy a solution.

It seems evident, that men are carried, by a natural instinct or prepossession, to repose faith in their senses; and that, without any reasoning, or even almost before the use of reason, we always suppose an external universe, which depends not on our perception, but would exist, though we and every sensible creature were absent or annihilated. Even the animal creations are governed by a like opinion, and preserve this belief of external objects, in all their thoughts, designs, and actions.

It seems also evident, that, when men follow this blind and powerful instinct of nature, they always suppose the very images, presented by the senses, to be the external objects, and never entertain any suspicion, that the one are nothing but representations of the other. This very table, which we see white, and which we feel hard, is believed to exist, independent of our perception, and to be something external to our mind, which perceives it. Our presence bestows not being on it: our absence does not annihilate it. It preserves its existence uniform and entire, independent of the situation of intelligent beings, who perceive or contemplate it.

But this universal and primary opinion of all men is soon destroyed by the slightest philosophy, which teaches us, that nothing can ever be present to the mind but an image or perception, and that the senses are only the inlets, through which these images are conveyed, without being able to produce any immediate intercourse between the mind and the object. The table, which we see, seems to diminish, as we remove farther from it: but the real table, which exists independent of us, suffers no alteration: it was, therefore, nothing but its image, which was present to the mind. These are the obvious dictates of reason; and no man, who reflects, ever doubted, that the existences, which we consider, when we say, *this house* and *that tree*, are nothing but perceptions in the mind, and fleeting copies or representations of other existences, which remain uniform and independent.

So far, then, are we necessitated by reasoning to contradict or depart from the primary instincts of nature, and to embrace a new system with regard to the evidence of our senses. But here philosophy finds herself extremely embarrassed, when she would justify this new system, and obviate the cavils and objections of the sceptics. She can no longer plead the infallible and irresistible instinct of nature: for that led us to a quite different system, which is acknowledged fallible and even erroneous. And to justify this pretended philosophical system, by a chain of clear and convincing argument, or even any appearance of argument, exceeds the power of all human capacity.

By what argument can it be proved, that the perceptions of the mind must be caused by external objects, entirely different from them, though resembling them (if that be possible) and could not arise either from the energy of the mind itself, or from the suggestion of some invisible and unknown spirit, or from some other cause still more unknown to us? It is acknowledged, that, in fact, many of these perceptions arise not from anything external, as in dreams, madness, and other diseases. And nothing can be more inexplicable than the manner, in which body should so operate upon mind as ever to convey an image of itself to a substance, supposed of so different, and even contrary a nature.

It is a question of fact, whether the perceptions of the senses be produced by external objects, resembling them: how shall this question be determined? By experience surely; as all other questions of a like nature. But here experience is, and must be entirely silent. The mind has never anything present to it but the perceptions, and cannot possibly reach any experience of their connexion with objects. The supposition of such a connexion is, therefore, without any foundation in reasoning.

To have recourse to the veracity of the Supreme Being, in order to prove the veracity of our senses, is surely making a very unexpected circuit. If his veracity were at all concerned in this matter, our senses would be entirely infallible; because it is not possible that he can ever deceive. Not to mention, that, if the external world be once called in question, we shall be at a loss to find arguments, by which we may prove the existence of that Being or any of his attributes.

This is a topic, therefore, in which the profounder and more philosophical sceptics will always triumph, when they endeavour to introduce an universal doubt into all subjects of human knowledge and enquiry. Do you follow the instincts and propensities of nature, may they say, in assenting to the veracity of sense? But these lead you to believe that the very perception or sensible image is the external object. Do you disclaim this principle, in order to embrace a more rational opinion, that the perceptions are only representations of something external? You here depart from your natural propensities and more obvious sentiments; and yet are not able to satisfy your reason, which can never find any convincing argument from experience to prove, that the perceptions are connected with any external objects.

There is another sceptical topic of a like nature, derived from the most profound philosophy, which might merit our attention, were it requisite to dive so deep, in order to discover arguments and reasonings, which can so little serve to any serious purpose. It is universally allowed by modern enquirers, that all the sensible qualities of objects, such as hard, soft, hot, cold, white, black, etc. are merely secondary, and exist not in the objects themselves, but are perceptions of the mind, without any external archetype or model, which they represent. If this be allowed, with regard to secondary qualities, it must also follow, with regard to the supposed primary qualities of extension and solidity; nor can the latter be any more entitled to that denomination than the former. The idea of extension is entirely acquired from the senses of sight and feeling; and if all the qualities, perceived by the senses, be in the mind, not in the object, the same conclusion must reach the idea of extension, which is wholly dependent on the sensible ideas or the ideas of secondary qualities. Nothing can save us from this conclusion, but the asserting, that the ideas of those primary qualities are attained by *Abstraction,* an opinion, which, if we examine it accurately, we shall find to be unintelligible, and even absurd. An extension, that is neither tangible nor visible, cannot possibly be conceived: and a tangible or visible extension, which is neither hard nor soft, black or white, is equally beyond the reach of human conception. Let any man try to conceive a triangle in general, which is neither *Isosceles* nor *Scalenum,* nor has any particular length or proportion of sides; and he will soon perceive the absurdity of all the scholastic notions with regard to abstraction and general ideas.*

Thus the first philosophical objection to the evidence of sense or to the opinion of external existence consists in this, that such an opinion, if rested on natural instinct, is contrary to reason, and if referred to reason, is contrary to natural instinct, and at the same time carries no rational evidence with it, to convince an impartial enquirer. The second objection goes farther, and represents this opinion as contrary to reason: at least, if it be a principle of reason, that all sensible qualities are in the mind, not in the object. Bereave matter of all its intelligible qualities, both primary and secondary, you in a manner annihilate it, and leave only a certain unknown, inexplicable *something*, as the cause of our perceptions; a notion so imperfect, that no sceptic will think it worth while to contend against it.

*This argument is drawn from Dr. Berkeley; and indeed most of the writings of that very ingenious author form the best lessons of scepticism, which are to be found either among the ancient or modern philosophers. Bayle not excepted. He professes, however, in his title-page (and undoubtedly with great truth) to have composed his book against the sceptics as well as against the atheists and freethinkers. But that all his arguments, though otherwise intended, are, in reality, merely sceptical, appears from this, that *they admit of no answer and produce no conviction.* Their only effect is to cause that momentary amazement and irresolution and confusion, which is the result of scepticism.

PART II

It may seem a very extravagant attempt of the sceptics to *destroy* reason by argument and ratiocination; yet is this the grand scope of all their enquiries and disputes. They endeavour to find objections, both to our abstract reasonings, and to those which regard matter of fact and existence.

The chief objection against all *abstract* reasonings is derived from the ideas of space and time; ideas, which, in common life and to a careless view, are very clear and intelligible, but when they pass through the scrutiny of the profound sciences (and they are the chief object of these sciences) afford principles, which seem full of absurdity and contradiction. No priestly *dogmas,* invented on purpose to tame and subdue the rebellious reason of mankind, ever shocked common sense more than the doctrine of the infinite divisibility of extension, with its consequences; as they are pompously displayed by all geometricians and metaphysicians, with a kind of triumph and exultation. A real quantity, infinitely less than any finite quantity, containing quantities infinitely less than itself, and so on *in infinitum*; this is an edifice so bold and prodigious, that it is too weighty for any pretended demonstration to support, because it shocks the clearest and most natural principles of human reason.* But what renders the matter more extraordinary, is, that these seemingly absurd opinions are supported by a chain of reasoning, the clearest and most natural; nor is it possible for us to allow the premises without admitting the consequences. Nothing can be more convincing and satisfactory than all the conclusions concerning the properties of circles and triangles; and yet, when these are once received, how can we deny, that the angle of contact between a circle and its tangent is infinitely less than any rectilineal angle, that as you may increase the diameter of the circle *in infinitum,* this angle of contact becomes still less, even *in infinitum,* and that the angle of contact between other curves and their tangents may be infinitely less than those between any circle and its tangent, and so on, *in infinitum?* The demonstration of these principles seems as unexceptionable as that which proves the three angles of a triangle to be equal to two right ones, though the latter opinion be natural and easy, and the former big with contradiction and absurdity. Reason here seems to be thrown into a kind of amazement and suspense, which, without the suggestions of any sceptic, gives her a diffidence of herself, and of the ground on which she treads. She sees a full light, which illuminates certain places; but that light borders upon the most profound darkness. And between these she is so dazzled and confounded, that she scarcely can pronounce with certainty and assurance concerning any one object.

The absurdity of these bold determinations of the abstract sciences seems to become, if possible, still more palpable with regard to time than extension. An infinite number of real parts of time, passing in succession, and exhausted one after another, appears so evident a contradiction, that no man, one should think, whose judgment is not corrupted, instead of being improved, by the sciences, would ever be able to admit of it.

Yet still reason must remain restless, and unquiet, even with regard to that scepticism, to which she is driven by these seeming absurdities and contradictions. How any clear, distinct idea can contain circumstances, contradictory to itself, or to any other clear, distinct idea, is absolutely incomprehensible; and is, perhaps, as absurd as

---

*Whatever disputes there may be about mathematical points, we must allow that there are physical points; that is, parts of extension which cannot be divided or lessened, either by the eye or imagination. These images, then, which are present to the fancy or senses, are absolutely indivisible, and consequently must be allowed by mathematicians to be infinitely less than any real part of extension; and yet nothing appears more certain to reason, than that an infinite number of them composes an infinite extension. How much more an infinite number of those infinitely small parts of extension, which are still supposed infinitely divisible.

any proposition, which can be formed. So that nothing can be more sceptical, or more full of doubt and hesitation, than this scepticism itself, which arises from some of the paradoxical conclusions of geometry or the science of quantity.*

The sceptical objections to *moral* evidence, or to the reasonings concerning matter of fact, are either *popular* or *philosophical*. The popular objections are derived from the natural weakness of human understanding; the contradictory opinions, which have been entertained in different ages and nations; the variations of our judgement in sickness and health, youth and old age, prosperity and adversity; the perpetual contradiction of each particular man's opinions and sentiments; with many other topics of that kind. It is needless to insist farther on this head. These objections are but weak. For as, in common life, we reason every moment concerning fact and existence, and cannot possibly subsist, without continually employing this species of argument, any popular objections, derived from thence, must be insufficient to destroy that evidence. The great subverter of *Pyrrhonism* or the excessive principles of scepticism is action, and employment, and the occupations of common life. These principles may flourish and triumph in the schools; where it is, indeed, difficult, if not impossible, to refute them. But as soon as they leave the shade, and by the presence of the real objects, which actuate our passions and sentiments, are put in opposition to the more powerful principles of our nature, they vanish like smoke, and leave the most determined sceptic in the same condition as other mortals.

The sceptic, therefore, had better keep within his proper sphere, and display those *philosophical* objections, which arise from more profound researches. Here he seems to have ample matter of triumph; while he justly insists, that all our evidence for any matter of fact, which lies beyond the testimony of sense or memory, is derived entirely from the relation of cause and effect; that we have no other idea of this relation than that of two objects, which have been frequently *conjoined* together; that we have no argument to convince us, that objects, which have, in our experience, been frequently conjoined, will likewise, in other instances, be conjoined in the same manner; and that nothing leads us to this inference but custom or a certain instinct of our nature; which it is indeed difficult to resist, but which, like other instincts, may be fallacious and deceitful. While the sceptic insists upon these topics, he shows his force, or rather, indeed, his own and our weakness; and seems, for the time at least, to destroy all assurance and conviction. These arguments might be displayed at greater length, if any durable good or benefit to society could ever be expected to result from them.

For here is the chief and most confounding objection to *excessive* scepticism, that no durable good can ever result from it; while it remains in its full force and vigour. We need only ask a sceptic, *What his meaning is? And what he proposes by all these curious researches?* He is immediately at a loss, and knows not what to answer. A Copernican or Ptolemaic, who supports each his different system of astronomy, may hope to produce a conviction, which will remain constant and durable, with his audi-

---

*It seems to me not impossible to avoid these absurdities and contradictions, if it be admitted, that there is no such thing as abstract or general ideas, properly speaking; but that all general ideas are, in reality, particular ones, attached to a general term, which recalls, upon occasion, other particular ones that resemble, in certain circumstances, the idea, present to the mind. Thus when the term Horse is pronounced, we immediately figure to ourselves the idea of a black or a white animal, of a particular size or figure: But as that term is also usually applied to animals of other colours, figures and sizes these ideas, though not actually present to the imagination, are easily recalled, and our reasoning and conclusion proceed in the same way, as if they were actually present. If this be admitted (as seems reasonable) it follows that all the ideas of quantity, upon which mathematicians reason, are nothing but particular, and such as are suggested by the senses and imagination, and consequently, cannot be infinitely divisible. It is sufficient to have dropped this hint at present, without prosecuting it any farther. It certainly concerns all lovers of science not to expose themselves to the ridicule and contempt of the ignorant by their conclusions; and this seems the readiest solution of these difficulties.

ence. A Stoic or Epicurean displays principles, which may not be durable, but which have an effect on conduct and behaviour. But a Pyrrhonian cannot expect, that his philosophy will have any constant influence on the mind: or if it had, that its influence would be beneficial to society. On the contrary, he must acknowledge, if he will acknowledge anything, that all human life must perish, were his principles universally and steadily to prevail. All discourse, all action would immediately cease; and men remain in a total lethargy, till the necessities of nature, unsatisfied, put an end to their miserable existence. It is true; so fatal an event is very little to be dreaded. Nature is always too strong for principle. And though a Pyrrhonian may throw himself or others into a momentary amazement and confusion by his profound reasonings; the first and most trivial event in life will put to flight all his doubts and scruples, and leave him the same, in every point of action and speculation, with the philosophers of every other sect, or with those who never concerned themselves in any philosophical researches. When he awakes from his dream, he will be the first to join in the laugh against himself, and to confess, that all his objections are mere amusement, and can have no other tendency than to show the whimsical condition of mankind, who must act and reason and believe; though they are not able, by their most diligent enquiry, to satisfy themselves concerning the foundation of these operations, or to remove the objections, which may be raised against them.

Part III

There is, indeed, a more *mitigated* scepticism or *academical* philosophy, which may be both durable and useful, and which may, in part, be the result of this Pyrrhonism, or excessive scepticism, when its undistinguished doubts are, in some measure, corrected by common sense and reflection. The greater part of mankind are naturally apt to be affirmative and dogmatical in their opinions; and while they see objects only on one side, and have no idea of any counterpoising argument, they throw themselves precipitately into the principles, to which they are inclined; nor have they any indulgence for those who entertain opposite sentiments. To hesitate or balance perplexes their understanding, checks their passion, and suspends their action. They are, therefore, impatient till they escape from a state, which to them is so uneasy: and they think, that they could never remove themselves far enough from it, by the violence of their affirmations and obstinacy of their belief. But could such dogmatical reasoners become sensible of the strange infirmities of human understanding, even in its most perfect state, and when most accurate and cautious in its determination; such a reflection would naturally inspire them with more modesty and reserve, and diminish their fond opinion of themselves, and their prejudice against antagonists. The illiterate may reflect on the disposition of the learned, who, amidst all the advantages of study and reflection, are commonly still diffident in their determinations: and if any of the learned be inclined, from their natural temper, to haughtiness and obstinacy, a small tincture of Pyrrhonism might abate their pride, by showing them, that the few advantages, which they may have attained over their fellows, are but inconsiderable, if compared with the universal perplexity and confusion, which is inherent in human nature. In general, there is a degree of doubt, and caution, and modesty, which, in all kinds of scrutiny and decision, ought for ever to accompany a just reasoner.

Another species of *mitigated* scepticism which may be of advantage to man-kind, and which may be the natural result of the Pyrrhonian doubts and scruples, is the limitation of our enquiries to such subjects as are best adapted to the narrow capacity of human understanding. The *imagination* of man is naturally sublime, delighted with whatever is remote and extraordinary, and running, without control, into the most distant parts of space and time in order to avoid the objects, which custom has rendered too familiar to it. A correct *judgement* observes a contrary method, and avoiding all distant and high enquiries, confines itself to common life, and to such subjects as fall under daily practice and experience; leaving the more sublime topics to the embellishment of poets and orators, or to the arts of priests and politicians. To bring us to so salutary a determination, nothing can be more serviceable, than to be once thoroughly convinced of the force of the Pyrrhonian doubt, and of the impossibility, that anything, but the strong power of natural instinct, could free us from it. Those who have a propensity to philosophy, will still continue their researches; because they reflect, that, besides the immediate pleasure, attending such an occupation, philosophical decisions are nothing but the reflections of common life, methodized and corrected. But they will never be tempted to go beyond common life, so long as they consider the imperfection of those faculties which they employ, their narrow reach, and their inaccurate operations. While we cannot give a satisfactory reason, why we believe, after a thousand experiments, that a stone will fall, or fire burn; can we ever satisfy ourselves concerning any determination, which we may form, with regard to the origin of worlds, and the situation of nature, from, and to eternity?

This narrow limitation, indeed, of our enquiries, is, in every respect, so reasonable, that it suffices to make the slightest examination into the natural powers of the human mind and to compare them with their objects, in order to recommend it to us. We shall then find what are the proper subjects of science and enquiry.

It seems to me, that the only objects of the abstract science or of demonstration are quantity and number, and that all attempts to extend this more perfect species of knowledge beyond these bounds are mere sophistry and illusion. As the component parts of quantity and number are entirely similar, their relations become intricate and involved; and nothing can be more curious, as well as useful, than to trace, by a variety of mediums their equality or inequality, through their different appearances. But as all other ideas are clearly distinct and different from each other, we can never advance farther, by our utmost scrutiny, than to observe this diversity, and, by an obvious reflection, pronounce one thing not to be another. Or if there be any difficulty in these decisions, it proceeds entirely from the undeterminate meaning of words, which is corrected by juster definitions. That *the square of the hypothenuse is equal to the square of the other two sides*, cannot be known, let the terms be ever so exactly defined, without a train of reasoning and enquiry. But to convince us of this proposition, *that where there is no property, there can be no injustice*, it is only necessary to define the terms, and explain injustice to be a violation of property. This proposition is, indeed, nothing but a more imperfect definition. It is the same case with all those pretended syllogistical reasonings, which may be found in every other branch of learning, except the sciences of quantity and number and these may safely, I think, be pronounced the only proper objects of knowledge and demonstration.

All other enquiries of men regard only matter of fact and existence; and these are evidently incapable of demonstration. Whatever *is* may *not be*. No negation of a fact can involve a contradiction. The non-existence of any being, without exception, is as clear and distinct an idea as its existence. The proposition, which affirms it not to be, however false, is no less conceivable and intelligible, than that which affirms it to be. The case is different with the sciences, properly so called. Every proposition, which is not true, is there confused and unintelligible. That the cube root of 64 is equal to the half of 10, is a false proposition, and can never be distinctly conceived. But that Caesar, or the angel Gabriel, or any being never existed, may be a false proposition, but still is perfectly conceivable, and implies no contradiction.

The existence, therefore, of any being can only be proved by arguments from its cause or its effect; and these arguments are founded entirely on experience. If we reason *a priori,* anything may appear able to produce anything. The falling of a pebble may, for aught we know, extinguish the sun; or the wish of a man control the planets in their orbits. It is only experience, which teaches us the nature and bounds of cause and effect, and enables us to infer the existence of one object from that of another.* Such is the foundation of moral reasoning, which forms the greater part of human knowledge, and is the source of all human action and behaviour.

Moral reasonings are either concerning particular or general facts. All deliberations in life regard the former; as also all disquisitions in history, chronology, geography, and astronomy.

The sciences, which treat of general facts, are politics, natural philosophy, physic, chemistry, etc. where the qualities, causes and effects of a whole species of objects are enquired into.

Divinity or Theology, as it proves the existence of a Deity, and the immortality of souls, is composed partly of reasonings concerning particular, partly concerning general facts. It has a foundation in *reason,* so far as it is supported by experience. But its best and most solid foundation is *faith* and divine revelation.

Morals and criticism are not so properly objects of the understanding as of taste and sentiment. Beauty, whether moral or natural, is felt, more properly than perceived. Or if we reason concerning it, and endeavour to fix its standard, we regard a new fact, to wit, the general tastes of mankind, or some such fact, which may be the object of reasoning and enquiry.

When we run over libraries, persuaded of these principles, what havoc must we make? If we take in our hand any volume; of divinity or school metaphysics, for instance; let us ask, *Does it contain any abstract reasoning concerning quantity or number?* No. *Does it contain any experimental reasoning concerning matter of fact and existence?* No. Commit it then to the flames: for it can contain nothing but sophistry and illusion.

IMMANUEL KANT
1724–1804

Whereas most modern philosophers (such as Descartes, Berkeley, and Hume) arrived at their basic philosophical positions early in life, Immanuel Kant did not work out his views until well into middle age. Whereas the earlier thinkers wrote major works when still young, Kant's important pieces were written between the ages of fifty-seven and sixty-seven. Whereas the others' works were written for a broad general audience and are relatively accessible to educated readers, Kant wrote in an academic style that is notoriously difficult to follow. Whereas most of the earlier philosophers traveled widely, Kant never left the provincial city in which he was born. Unlike his predecessors, who held many different positions and practiced philosophy on the side, Kant earned his living as a professor of philosophy. Yet Kant is the most important and influential of all modern philosophers.

Kant was born, raised, lived, and died in the town of Königsberg in East Prussia. His parents were lower middle-class, hard-working, simple folk. They belonged to the Lutheran Pietist movement, which cultivated high moral standards and personal devotion to God in Christ. Like Hume, who had a similar religious upbringing (Calvinist Presbyterian), Kant was later critical of his background. But unlike Hume, he remained a deeply religious man.

Through the intervention of his mother's favorite preacher, who was also a professor at the University of Königsberg, young Immanuel gained admittance to a local high school. There he received a solid Pietist education and a firm grounding in the classics. At sixteen, Kant was admitted to the university, where he planned to study the classics. But under the influence of a strong teacher, Martin Knutzen, Kant moved into philosophy and was attracted to the comprehensive scholasticism of Christian Wolff (1679–1754), who had developed Leibniz's philosophy into a rationalistic system.

Following his university studies, Kant worked as a private tutor to wealthy families. By 1755, he was back in the university, where he was employed as an unsalaried lecturer for the next fifteen years. (Given the difficulty of his writing, it is worth noting that his lectures were very popular.) His early lectures focused on the external world, dealing with issues in physics and physical geography. He published an important early work, *Universal History of Nature and Theory of the Heavens* (1755), which explained the structure of the universe in terms of Newtonian physics, without reference to God. During this period, Kant's focus began to shift to the inner world of the mind and the nature of morality. At this time, he also encountered the writings of Hume, which challenged the rationalism he had imbibed from Wolff. He later said that Hume "interrupted my dogmatic slumber, and gave my investigations in the field of speculative philosophy quite a new direction."

In 1770, Kant was given what he had long desired—the chair of logic and metaphysics at the University of Königsberg. In his inaugural address, *Dissertation on the Form and Principles of Sensible and Intelligible Worlds,* Kant declared his intention to reconstruct philosophy. Over the next ten years, he carefully and quietly thought through all his ideas. Finally he wrote his major work, *Critique of Pure Reason.* He wrote it, as he later told a friend, "within four or five months, with the utmost attention to the contents, but with less concern for the presentation or for making things easy for the reader." Unfortunately, when the book appeared, his indifference to readers left most people lost. In 1783, he restated his main points in a work "for the benefit of teachers," the *Prolegomena to Any Future Metaphysics,* and in 1787 he rewrote the *Critique* itself.

Kant's first major work on ethics, *Foundation for the Metaphysics of Morals,* was published in 1785. A further development of his moral views, *Critique of Practical Reason,* appeared in 1788. In 1790, Kant published his third and last critique, the *Critique of Judgment,* which deals with aesthetic judgments and the question of purpose in nature. Kant's other important works include *Metaphysical Foundations of Natural Science* (1786), *Religion Within the Limits of Reason Alone* (1793), *Toward Eternal Peace* (1795), and *Metaphysics of Morals* (1797).

Whereas Kant's writings revolutionized the philosophical world, his personal life was quiet, almost boring. With one minor exception late in life, he was never involved in any scandals or controversies. He never traveled more than a few miles outside Königsberg. A lifelong bachelor, he is said to have awakened and gone to bed at exactly the same time each day. His daily walks were reportedly so regular that people could set their clocks by his approach. A rather frail man, he so carefully guarded his health that he lived a long, productive life. Yet he was also a delightful conversationalist and host, and he had many friends and admirers. At his death in 1804, he was the best-known philosopher in Germany, read, if not understood, throughout Europe.

*   *   *

Responding to the skeptical empiricism of Hume, Kant argued that the mind is not simply a repository of impressions and ideas but it is actively involved in knowing the objects it experiences. Prior to Kant, most thinkers believed that the mind, in knowing, conformed to objects: that the ideas of the mind took on the "shape" of the world outside the mind. Kant argued instead that objects conform to the mind: that how one experiences the world is a result of the way the mind operates. Knowledge is a result of human understanding applied to sense experience.

Space and time are two ways the mind operates. They are not "objects" in the world, derived from sense experience; rather, they are the precondition for our having sense-experience at all: They are the *a priori* (meaning "known independently of sense perceptions," "indubitable") foundations of sensibility. Space and time must be presupposed in order to have experience at all.

Kant goes on to consider the *a priori* foundations of human understanding. He argues that there must be categories of the mind, such as causality and substance, that unify our perceptions. These categories are not found in sense experience; they are innate structures of the mind and the necessary conditions for having any knowledge at all. Without these categories, the world of experience would be utterly chaotic and unknowable.

Of course this knowledge is only a knowledge of things as we experience them in the "phenomenal world." The way things really are, apart from our experience of them, the "noumenal world" of the "things-in-themselves," is not available to us by pure reason. This, according to Kant, means that we cannot have knowledge of God, the world, or even the substantial self. But rather than letting this end in Humean skepticism, Kant suggests that these three "ideas of reason" (God, world, self) stimulate and unify knowledge. They point beyond themselves to possibilities in the noumenai world that pure reason cannot reach. As long as we do not think that we have real knowledge of their objects, these three ideas of reason serve a useful purpose.

Turning to moral theory, Kant develops a "deontological," or "duty-based," theory of morality. An action is good not because it produces consequences such as pleasure or happiness, but because it is done out of duty by a good will. To establish what a person's duty is, Kant develops the "categorical imperative." In the *Foundation for the Metaphysics of Morals*, Kant discusses several versions of this imperative, the most important of which is this: "Act only on that maxim whereby you can at the same time will that it should become a universal law."

Although Kant is best known for his work in epistemology and ethics, he wrote on many topics. His earlier essay "Idea for a Universal History with Cosmopolitan Intent" (1784) is an example of Kant at his nontechnical best. Here the Königsberg recluse shows himself as a brilliant citizen of the world when he introduces the idea of a League of Nations:

> By means of wars and the high tension of never relaxed armaments for these wars, and by means of the distress which every nation must thus suffer, even during times of peace, [Nature] drives man at first to imperfect attempts, but finally, after many devastations and disturbances and even exhaustion of all powers, she drives toward a situation which reason might have anticipated without so many sad experiences: Men leave the lawless state of savages and enter a League of Nations. Thus every state, including the smallest, can find a guarantee for its security and its rights, not in its own power or in its own views of what is just, but in this great League of Nations. . . .

*   *   *

Kant's condensation of the *Critique,* the *Prolegomena to Any Future Metaphysics*, and his *Foundation for the Metaphysics of Morals* are both given here (complete) in the Lewis White Beck translations.

Among the many available books on Kant, Stephen Körner, *Kant* (Baltimore, MD: Penguin Books, 1955) is almost universally accepted as the best introduction. John Kemp, *The Philosophy of Kant* (Oxford: Oxford University Press, 1968); Ralph C.S. Walker, *Kant: The Arguments of the Philosophers* (London: Routledge & Kegan Paul, 1978); C.D. Broad, *Kant: An Introduction* (Cambridge: Cambridge University Press, 1978); Ernst Cassirer, *Kant's Life and Thought*, translated by James Haden (New Haven, CT: Yale University Press, 1982); Ermanno Bencivenga, *Kant's Copernican Revolution* (Oxford: Oxford University Press, 1987); and Otfried Höffe, *Immanuel Kant*, translated by Marshall Farrier (Albany, NY: SUNY Press, 1994) are also helpful. A.C. Ewing, *A Short Commentary on Kant's Critique of Pure Reason* (London: Methuen, 1950) provides an accessible commentary to this difficult work, while Norman Kemp Smith, *A Commentary to Kant's Critique of Pure Reason* (London: Macmillan, 1930) is standard. H.J. Paton, *Kant's Metaphysic of Experience*, two volumes (New York: Humanities Press, 1936) is an alternative interpretation to the N.K. Smith study. T.D. Weldon, *Kant's Critique of Pure Reason* (Oxford: Oxford University Press, 1945, 2nd edition, 1958); Henry E. Allison, *Kant's Transcendental Idealism: An Interpretation and Defense* (New Haven, CT: Yale University Press, 1983); and Lorne Falkenstein, *Kant's Intuitionism: A Commentary on the Transcendental Aesthetic* (Toronto: University of Toronto Press, 1995) are also useful. For works on Kant's moral theory, see W.D. Ross, *Kant's Ethical Theory: A Commentary on the Grundlegung zur Metaphysik der Sitten [Foundation for the Metaphysic of Morals]* (Oxford: Clarendon Press, 1954); Lewis White Beck, *A Commentary on Kant's Critique of Practical Reason* (Chicago: University of Chicago Press, 1960); H.J. Paton, *The Categorical Imperative* (London: 1947; reprinted, New York: Harper & Row, 1967); Roger Sullivan, *An Introduction to Kant's Ethics* (Cambridge: Cambridge University Press, 1994); and Paul Guyer, ed., *Kant's Groundwork of the Metaphysics of Morals* (Lanham, MD: Rowan & Littlefield, 1997). Howard Caygill, *A Kant Dictionary* (Oxford: Basil Blackwell, 1995) provides a useful reference work. For collections of essays, see Lewis White Beck, ed., *Studies in the Philosophy of Kant* (Indianapolis, IN: Bobbs-Merrill, 1965); R.P. Wolff, *Kant* (Garden City, NY: Doubleday, 1967); Ralph C.S. Walker, ed., *Kant on Pure Reason* (Oxford: Oxford University Press, 1982); Beryl Logan, ed., *Immanuel Kant's Prolegomena to Any Future Metaphysics in Focus* (Oxford: Routledge, 1996); and Robin May Schott, ed., *Feminist Interpretations of Kant* (College Park, PA: Pennsylvania State University Press, 1997).

PROLEGOMENA TO ANY FUTURE METAPHYSICS

INTRODUCTION

These *Prolegomena* are for the use, not of mere learners, but of future teachers, and even the latter should not expect that they will be serviceable for the systematic exposition of a ready-made science, but merely for the discovery of the science itself.

There are scholarly men to whom the history of philosophy (both ancient and modern) is philosophy itself; for these the present *Prolegomena* are not written. They must wait till those who endeavor to draw from the fountain of reason itself have completed their work; it will then be the turn of these scholars to inform the world of what has been done. Unfortunately, nothing can be said which, in their opinion, has not been said before, and truly the same prophecy applies to all future time; for since the human reason has for many centuries speculated upon innumerable objects in various ways, it is hardly to be expected that we should not be able to discover analogies for every new idea among the old sayings of past ages.

My purpose is to persuade all those who think metaphysics worth studying that it is absolutely necessary to pause a moment and, regarding all that has been done as though undone, to propose first the preliminary question, "Whether such a thing as metaphysics be even possible at all?"

If it be science, how is it that it cannot, like other sciences, obtain universal and lasting recognition? If not, how can it maintain its pretensions and keep the human mind in suspense with hopes never ceasing, yet never fulfilled? Whether then we demonstrate our knowledge or our ignorance in this field, we must come once for all to a definite conclusion respecting the nature of this so-called science, which cannot possibly remain on its present footing. It seems almost ridiculous, while every other science is continually advancing, that in this, which pretends to be wisdom incarnate, for whose oracle everyone inquires, we should constantly move round the same spot, without gaining a single step. And so its votaries having melted away, we do not find men confident of their ability to shine in other sciences venturing their reputation here, where everybody, however ignorant in other matters, presumes to deliver a final verdict, because in this domain there is actually as yet no standard weight and measure to distinguish sound knowledge from shallow talk.

After all it is nothing extraordinary in the elaboration of a science that, when men begin to wonder how far it has advanced, the question should at last occur whether and how such a science is possible at all. Human reason so delights building that it has several times built up a tower and then razed it to see how the foundation was laid. It is never too late to become reasonable and wise; but if the knowledge comes late, there is always more difficulty in starting a reform.

The question whether a science be possible presupposes a doubt as to its actuality. But such a doubt offends the men whose whole fortune consists of this supposed jewel; hence he who raises the doubt must expect opposition from all sides. Some, in the proud consciousness of their possessions, which are ancient and therefore considered legitimate, will take their metaphysical compendia in their hands and look down on him with

Immanuel Kant, *Prolegomena to Any Future Metaphysics,* a revision of the Paul Carus translation with an introduction by Lewis White Beck (New York: Macmillan/Library of the Liberal Arts, 1950).

contempt; others, who never see anything except it be identical with what they have elsewhere seen before, will not understand him, and everything will remain for a time as if nothing had happened to excite the concern or the hope for an impending change.

Nevertheless, I venture to predict that the independent reader of these *Prolegomena* will not only doubt his previous science, but ultimately be fully persuaded that it cannot exist unless the demands here stated on which its possibility depends be satisfied; and, as this has never been done, that there is, as yet, no such thing as metaphysics. But as it can never cease to be in demand*—since the interest of common sense are so intimately interwoven with it—he must confess that a radical reform, or rather a new birth of the science, after a new plan, is unavoidable, however men may struggle against it for a while.

Since the *Essays* of Locke and Leibniz, or rather since the origin of metaphysics so far as we know its history, nothing has ever happened which could have been more decisive to its fate than the attack made upon it by David Hume. He threw no light on this species of knowledge, but he certainly struck a spark by which light might have been kindled had it caught some inflammable substance and had its smouldering fire been carefully nursed and developed.

Hume started chiefly from a single but important concept in metaphysics, namely, that of the connection of cause and effect (including its derivatives force and action, and so on). He challenged reason, which pretends to have given birth to this concept of herself, to answer him by what right she thinks anything could be so constituted that if that thing be posited, something else also must necessarily be posited; for this is the meaning of the concept of cause. He demonstrated irrefutably that it was perfectly impossible for reason to think *a priori* and by means of concepts such a combination, for it implies necessity. We cannot at all see why, in consequence of the existence of one thing, another must necessarily exist or how the concept of such a combination can arise *a priori*. Hence he inferred that reason was altogether deluded with reference to this concept, which she erroneously considered as one of her own children, whereas in reality it was nothing but a bastard of imagination, impregnated by experience, which subsumed certain representations under the law of association and mistook a subjective necessity (habit) for an objective necessity arising from insight. Hence he inferred that reason had no power to think such combinations, even in general, because her concepts would then be purely fictitious and all her pretended *a priori* cognitions nothing but common experiences marked with a false stamp. In plain language, this means that there is not and cannot be any such thing as metaphysics at all.**

---

*Says Horace:
Rusticus expectat, dum defluat amnis, at ille
Labitur et labetur in omne volubilis aevum.

["A rustic fellow waiteth on the shore
For the river to flow away,
But the river flows, and flows on as before,
And it flows forever and aye."]

Epistle I, 2, 42f.

**Nevertheless Hume called this destructive science metaphysics and attached to it great value. "Metaphysics and morals," he declares, "are the most considerable branches of science. Mathematics and natural philosophy are not half so valuable" ["Of the Rise and Progress of the Arts and Sciences," *Essays Moral, Political, and Literary,* XIV (edited by Green and Grose, I, 187)]. But the acute man merely regarded the negative use arising from the moderation of extravagant claims of speculative reason, and the complete settlement of the many endless and troublesome controversies that mislead mankind. He overlooked the positive injury which results if reason be deprived of its most important prospects, which can alone supply to the will the highest aim for all its endeavors.

However hasty and mistaken Hume's inference may appear, it was at least founded upon investigation, and this investigation deserved the concentrated attention of the brighter spirits of his day as well as determined efforts on their part to discover, if possible, a happier solution of the problem in the sense proposed by him, all of which would have speedily resulted in a complete reform of the science.

But Hume suffered the usual misfortune of metaphysicians, of not being understood. It is positively painful to see how utterly his opponents, Reid, Oswald, Beattie, and lastly Priestley, missed the point of the problem; for while they were ever taking for granted that which he doubted, and demonstrating with zeal and often with impudence that which he never thought of doubting, they so misconstrued his valuable suggestion that everything remained in its old condition, as if nothing had happened. The question was not whether the concept of cause was right, useful, and even indispensable for our knowledge of nature, for this Hume had never doubted; but whether that concept could be thought by reason *a priori,* and consequently whether it possessed an inner truth, independent of all experience, implying a perhaps more extended use not restricted merely to objects of experience. This was Hume's problem. It was solely a question concerning the *origin,* not concerning the *indispensable* need of using the concept. Were the former decided, the conditions of the use and the sphere of its valid application would have been determined as a matter of course.

But to satisfy the conditions of the problem, the opponents of the great thinker should have penetrated very deeply into the nature of reason, so far as it is concerned with pure thinking—a task which did not suit them. They found a more convenient method of being defiant without any insight, namely, the appeal to *common sense.* It is indeed a great gift of God to possess right or (as they now call it) plain common sense. But this common sense must be shown in action by well-considered and reasonable thoughts and words, not by appealing to it as an oracle when no rational justification for one's position can be advanced. To appeal to common sense when insight and science fail, and no sooner—this is one of the subtle discoveries of modern times, by means of which the most superficial ranter can safely enter the lists with the most thorough thinker and hold his own. But as long as a particle of insight remains, no one would think of having recourse to this subterfuge. Seen clearly, it is but an appeal to the opinion of the multitude, of whose applause the philosopher is ashamed, while the popular charlatan glories and boasts in it. I should think that Hume might fairly have laid as much claim to common sense as Beattie and, in addition, to a critical reason (such as the latter did not possess), which keeps common sense in check and prevents it from speculating, or, if speculations are under discussion, restrains the desire to decide because it cannot satisfy itself concerning its own premises. By this means alone can common sense remain sound. Chisels and hammers may suffice to work a piece of wood, but for etching we require an etcher's needle. Thus common sense and speculative understanding are each serviceable, but each in its own way: the former in judgments which apply immediately to experience; the latter when we judge universally from mere concepts, as in metaphysics, where that which calls itself, in spite of the inappropriateness of the name, sound common sense, has no right to judge at all.

I openly confess my recollection* of David Hume was the very thing which many years ago first interrupted my dogmatic slumber and gave my investigations in the field of speculative philosophy a quite new direction. I was far from following him in the

---

*[*Erinnerung.* Kant had probably read Hume before 1760, but only much later (1772?) did he begin to follow "a new direction" under Hume's influence—L.W.B.]

View of Königsberg Castle, Kant's house in foreground. (*British Museum*)

conclusions at which he arrived by regarding, not the whole of his problem, but a part, which by itself can give us no information. If we start from a well-founded, but undeveloped, thought which another has bequeathed to us, we may well hope by continued reflection to advance farther than the acute man to whom we owe the first spark of light.

I therefore first tried whether Hume's objection could not be put into a general form, and soon found that the concept of the connection of cause and effect was by no means the only concept by which the understanding thinks the connection of things *a priori,* but rather that metaphysics consists altogether of such concepts. I sought to ascertain their number; and when I had satisfactorily succeeded in this by starting from a single principle, I proceeded to the deduction of these concepts, which I was now certain were not derived from experience, as Hume had attempted to derive them, but sprang from the pure understanding. This deduction (which seemed impossible to my acute predecessor, which had never even occurred to anyone else, though no one had hesitated to use the concepts without investigating the basis of their objective validity) was the most difficult task which ever could have been undertaken in the service of metaphysics; and the worst was that metaphysics, such as it is, could not assist me in the least because this deduction alone can render metaphysics possible. But as soon as I had succeeded in solving Hume's problem, not merely in a particular case, but with respect to the whole faculty of pure reason, I could proceed safely, though slowly, to determine the whole sphere of pure reason completely and from universal principles, in its boundaries as well as in its contents. This was required for metaphysics in order to construct its system according to a safe plan.

But I fear that the execution of Hume's problem in its widest extent (namely, my *Critique of Pure Reason*) will fare as the problem itself fared when first proposed. It will be misjudged because it is misunderstood, and misunderstood because men choose to skim through the book and not to think through it—a disagreeable task, because the work is dry, obscure, opposed to all ordinary notions, and moreover long-winded. I confess, however, I did not expect to hear from philosophers complaints of want of popularity, entertainment, and facility when the existence of highly prized and indispensable knowledge is at stake, which cannot be established otherwise than by the strictest rules of a scholastic precision. Popularity may follow, but is inadmissible at the beginning. Yet as regards a certain obscurity, arising partly from the diffuseness of the plan, owing to which the principal points of the investigation are easily lost sight of, the complaint is just, and I intend to remove it by the present *Prolegomena.*

The first-mentioned work, which discusses the pure faculty of reason in its whole compass and bounds, will remain the foundation, to which the *Prolegomena,* as a preliminary exercise, refer; for critique as a science must first be established as complete and perfect before we can think of letting metaphysics appear on the scene or even have the most distant hope of attaining it.

We have been long accustomed to seeing antiquated knowledge produced as new by taking it out of its former context and fitting it into a systematic garment of any fancy pattern with new titles. Most readers will set out by expecting nothing else from the *Critique;* but these *Prolegomena* may persuade him that it is a perfectly new science, of which no one has ever even thought, the very idea of which was unknown, and for which nothing hitherto accomplished can be of the smallest use, except it be the suggestion of Hume's doubts. Yet even he did not suspect such a formal science, but ran his ship ashore, for safety's sake, landing on scepticism, there to let it lie and rot; whereas my object is rather to give it a pilot, who, by means of safe principles of navigation drawn from a knowledge of the globe, and provided with a complete chart and compass, may steer the ship safely whither he listeth.

If in a new science which is wholly isolated and unique in its kind, we started with the prejudice that we can judge of things by means of alleged knowledge previously acquired—though this is precisely what has first to be called in question—we should only fancy we saw everywhere what we had already known, because the expressions have a similar sound. But everything would appear utterly metamorphosed, senseless, and unintelligible, because we should have as a foundation our own thoughts, made by long habit a second nature, instead of the author's. But the longwindedness of the work, so far as it depends on the subject and not on the exposition, its consequent unavoidable dryness and its scholastic precision, are qualities which can only benefit the science, though they may discredit the book.

Few writers are gifted with the subtlety and, at the same time, with the grace of David Hume, or with the depth, as well as the elegance, of Moses Mendelssohn. Yet I flatter myself I might have made my own exposition popular had my object been merely to sketch out a plan and leave its completion to others, instead of having my heart in the welfare of the science to which I had devoted myself so long; in truth, it required no little constancy, and even self-denial, to postpone the sweets of an immediate success to the prospect of a slower, but more lasting, reputation.

Making plans is often the occupation of an opulent and boastful mind, which thus obtains the reputation of a creative genius by demanding what it cannot itself supply, by censuring what it cannot improve, and by proposing what it knows not where to find. And yet something more should belong to a sound plan of a general critique of pure reason than mere conjectures if this plan is to be other than the usual declamations of pious aspirations. But pure reason is a sphere so separate and self-contained that we cannot touch a part without affecting all the rest. We can do nothing without first determining the position of each part and its relation to the rest; for, as our judgment within this sphere cannot be corrected by anything without, the validity and use of every part depends upon the relation in which it stands to all the rest within the domain of reason. As in the structure of an organized body, the end of each member can only be deduced from the full conception of the whole. It may, then, be said of such a critique that it is never trustworthy except it be perfectly complete, down to the most minute elements of pure reason. In the sphere of this faculty you can determine and define either everything or nothing.

But although a mere sketch preceding the *Critique of Pure Reason* would be unintelligible, unreliable, and useless, it is all the more useful as a sequel. It enables us to grasp the whole, to examine in detail the chief points of importance in the science, and to improve in many respects our exposition, as compared with the first execution of the work.

With that work complete, I offer here a sketch based on an *analytical* method, while the *Critique* itself had to be executed in the *synthetical* style, in order that the science may present all its articulations, as the structure of a peculiar cognitive faculty, in their natural combination. But should any reader find this sketch, which I publish as the *Prolegomena to Any Future Metaphysics,* still obscure, let him consider that not everyone is bound to study metaphysics; that many minds will succeed very well in the exact and even in deep sciences more closely allied to the empirical, while they cannot succeed in investigations dealing exclusively with abstract concepts. In such cases men should apply their talents to other subjects. But he who undertakes to judge or, still more, to construct a system of metaphysics must satisfy the demands here made, either by adopting my solution or by thoroughly refuting it and substituting another. To evade it is impossible.

In conclusion, let it be remembered that this much abused obscurity (frequently serving as a mere pretext under which people hide their own indolence or dullness) has its uses, since all who in other sciences observe a judicious silence speak authoritatively in metaphysics and make bold decisions, because their ignorance is not here contrasted with the knowledge of others. Yet it does contrast with sound critical principles, which we may therefore commend in the words of Virgil:

> *Ignavum, fucos, pecus a praesepibus arcent.**

PROLEGOMENA

PREAMBLE ON THE PECULIARITIES OF ALL METAPHYSICAL KNOWLEDGE

§ I. Of the Sources of Metaphysics

If it becomes desirable to organize any knowledge as science, it will be necessary first to determine accurately those peculiar features which no other science has in common with it, constituting its peculiarity; otherwise the boundaries of all sciences become confused, and none of them can be treated thoroughly according to its nature.

The peculiar characteristic of a science may consist of a simple difference of object, or of the sources of knowledge, or of the kind of knowledge, or perhaps of all three conjointly. On these, therefore, depends the idea of a possible science and its territory.

First, as concerns the sources of metaphysical knowledge, its very concept implies that they cannot be empirical. Its principles (including not only its maxims but its basic notions) must never be derived from experience. It must not be physical but metaphysical knowledge, namely, knowledge lying beyond experience. It can

---

*["They defend the hives against drones, those indolent creatures"—Georgics IV 168.]

therefore have for its basis neither external experience, which is the source of physics proper, nor internal, which is the basis of empirical psychology. It is therefore *a priori* knowledge, coming from pure understanding and pure reason.

But so far metaphysics would not be distinguishable from pure mathematics; it must therefore be called *pure philosophical* knowledge; and for the meaning of this term I refer to the *Critique of the Pure Reason,** where the distinction between these two employments of reason is sufficiently explained. So far concerning the sources of metaphysical knowledge.

§ 2. Concerning the Kind of Knowledge Which Can Alone Be Called Metaphysical

*a. On the Distinction between Analytical and Synthetical Judgments in General.—*The peculiarity of its sources demands that metaphysical knowledge must consist of nothing but *a priori* judgments. But whatever be their origin or their logical form, there is a distinction in judgments, as to their content, according to which they are either merely *explicative,* adding nothing to the content of knowledge, or *expansive,* increasing the given knowledge. The former may be called *analytical,* the latter *synthetical,* judgments.

Analytical judgments express nothing in the predicate but what has been already actually thought in the concept of the subject, though not so distinctly or with the same (full) consciousness. When I say: "All bodies are extended," I have not amplified in the least my concept of body, but have only analyzed it, as extension was really thought to belong to that concept before the judgment was made, though it was not expressed. This judgment is therefore analytical. On the contrary, this judgment, "All bodies have weight," contains in its predicate something not actually thought in the universal concept of body; it amplifies my knowledge by adding something to my concept, and must therefore be called synthetical.

*b. The Common Principle of All Analytical Judgments Is the Law of Contradiction.—*All analytical judgments depend wholly on the law of contradiction, and are in their nature *a priori* cognitions, whether the concepts that supply them with matter be empirical or not. For the predicate of an affirmative analytical judgment is already contained in the concept of the subject, of which it cannot be denied without contradiction. In the same way its opposite is necessarily denied of the subject in an analytical, but negative, judgment, by the same law of contradiction. Such is the nature of the judgments: "All bodies are extended," and "No bodies are unextended (that is, simple)."

For this very reason all analytical judgments are *a priori* even when the concepts are empirical, as, for example, "Gold is a yellow metal"; for to know this I require no experience beyond my concept of gold as a yellow metal. It is, in fact, the very concept, and I need only analyze it without looking beyond it.

*c. Synthetical Judgments Require a Different Principle from the Law of Contradiction.—*There are synthetical *a posteriori* judgments of empirical origin; but there are also others which are certain *a priori,* and which spring from pure understanding and reason. Yet they both agree in this, that they cannot possibly spring from the principle of analysis, namely, the law of contradiction, alone. They require a quite different principle from which they may be deduced, subject, of course, always to the law of contra-

*Critique of Pure Reason, "Methodology," Ch. I, Sec. 2.

diction, which must never be violated, even though everything cannot be deduced from it. I shall first classify synthetical judgments.

1. *Judgments of Experience* are always synthetical. For it would be absurd to base an analytical judgment on experience, as our concept suffices for the purpose without requiring any testimony from experience. That body is extended is a judgment established *a priori,* and not an empirical judgment. For before appealing to experience, we already have all the conditions of the judgment in the concept, from which we have but to elicit the predicate according to the law of contradiction, and thereby to become conscious of the necessity of the judgment, which experience could not in the least teach us.

2. *Mathematical Judgments* are all synthetical. This fact seems hitherto to have altogether escaped the observation of those who have analyzed human reason: it even seems directly opposed to all their conjectures, though it is incontestably certain and most important in its consequences. For as it was found that the conclusions of mathematicians all proceed according to the law of contradiction (as is demanded by all apodictic certainty), men persuaded themselves that the fundamental principles were known from the same law. This was a great mistake, for a synthetical proposition can indeed be established by the law of contradiction, but only by presupposing another synthetical proposition from which it follows, but never by that law alone.

First of all, we must observe that all strictly mathematical judgments are *a priori,* and not empirical, because they carry with them necessity, which cannot be obtained from experience. But if this be not conceded to me, very good; I shall confine my assertion to *pure mathematics,* the very notion of which implies that it contains pure *a priori* and not empirical knowledge.

It must at first be thought that the proposition $7 + 5 = 12$ is a mere analytical judgment, following from the concept of the sum of seven and five, according to the law of contradiction. But on closer examination it appears that the concept of the sum of $7 + 5$ contains merely their union in a single number, without its being at all thought what the particular number is that unites them. The concept of twelve is by no means thought by merely thinking of the combination of seven and five; and, analyze this possible sum as we may, we shall not discover twelve in the concept. We must go beyond these concepts, by calling to our aid some intuition which corresponds to one of the concepts—that is, either our five fingers or five points (as Segner has it in his *Arithmetic*)—and we must add successively the units of the five given in the intuition to the concept of seven. Hence our concept is really amplified by the proposition $7 + 5 = 12$, and we add to the first concept a second concept not thought in it. Arithmetical judgments are therefore synthetical, and the more plainly according as we take larger numbers; for in such cases it is clear that, however closely we analyze our concepts without calling intuition to our aid, we can never find the sum by such mere dissection.

Just as little is any principle of geometry analytical. That a straight line is the shortest path between two points is a synthetical proposition. For my concept of straight contains nothing of quantity, but only a quality. The concept "shortest" is therefore altogether additional and cannot be obtained by any analysis of the concept "straight line." Here, too, intuition must come to aid us. It alone makes the synthesis possible. What usually makes us believe that the predicate of such apodictic judgments is already contained in our concept, and that the judgment is therefore analytical, is the duplicity of the expression. We must think a certain predicate as attached to a given concept, and necessity indeed belongs to the concepts. But the question is not what we must join in thought *to* the given concept, but what we actually think together with and in it, though obscurely; and so it appears that the predicate belongs to this concept necessarily indeed, yet not directly but indirectly by means of an intuition which must be present.

Some other principles, assumed by geometers, are indeed actually analytical, and depend on the law of contradiction; but they only serve, as identical propositions, as a method of concatenation, and not as principles—for example $a = a$, the whole is equal to itself, or $a + b > a$, the whole is greater than its part. And yet even these, though they are recognized as valid from mere concepts, are admitted in mathematics only because they can be represented in some intuition.

The essential and distinguishing feature of pure mathematical knowledge among all other *a priori* knowledge is that it cannot at all proceed from concepts, but only by means of the construction of concepts.* As therefore in its propositions it must proceed beyond the concept to that which its corresponding intuition contains, these propositions neither can, nor ought to, arise analytically, by dissection of the concept, but are all synthetical.

I cannot refrain from pointing out the disadvantage resulting to philosophy from the neglect of this easy and apparently insignificant observation. Hume being prompted to cast his eye over the whole field of *a priori* cognitions in which human understanding claims such mighty possessions (a calling he felt worthy of a philosopher) heedlessly severed from it a whole, and indeed its most valuable, province, namely, pure mathematics; for he imagined its nature or, so to speak, the state constitution of this empire depended on totally different principles, namely, on the law of contradiction alone; and although he did not divide judgments in this manner formally and universally as I have done here, what he said was equivalent to this: that mathematics contains only analytical, but metaphysics synthetical, *a priori* propositions. In this, however, he was greatly mistaken, and the mistake had a decidedly injurious effect upon his whole conception. But for this, he would have extended his question concerning the origin of our synthetical judgments far beyond the metaphysical concept of causality and included in it the possibility of mathematics *a priori* also, for this latter he must have assumed to be equally synthetical. And then he could not have based his metaphysical propositions on mere experience without subjecting the axioms of mathematics equally to experience, a thing which he was far too acute to do. The good company into which metaphysics would thus have been brought would have saved it from the danger of a contemptuous ill-treatment, for the thrust intended for it must have reached mathematics, which was not and could not have been Hume's intention. Thus that acute man would have been led into considerations which must needs be similar to those that now occupy us, but which would have gained inestimably by his inimitably elegant style.

[3.] *Metaphysical Judgments,* properly so called, are all synthetical. We must distinguish judgments pertaining to metaphysics from metaphysical judgments properly so called. Many of the former are analytical, but they only afford the means for metaphysical judgments, which are the whole end of the science and which are always synthetical. For if there be concepts pertaining to metaphysics (as, for example, that of substance), the judgments springing from simple analysis of them also pertain to metaphysics, as, for example, substance is that which only exists as subject, etc.; and by means of several such analytical judgments we seek to approach the definition of the concepts. But as the analysis of a pure concept of the understanding (the kind of concept pertaining to metaphysics) does not proceed in any different manner from the dis-

---

Critique of Pure Reason, "Methodology," Ch. I, Sec. 1.

section of any other, even empirical, concepts, not belonging to metaphysics (such as, air is an elastic fluid, the elasticity of which is not destroyed by any known degree of cold), it follows that the concept indeed, but not the analytical judgment, is properly metaphysical. This science has something peculiar in the production of its *a priori* cognitions, which must therefore be distinguished from the features it has in common with other rational knowledge. Thus the judgment that all the substance in things is permanent is a synthetical and properly metaphysical judgment.

If the *a priori* concepts which constitute the materials and tools of metaphysics have first been collected according to fixed principles, then their analysis will be of great value; it might be taught as a particular part (as a *philosophia definitiva*), containing nothing but analytical judgments pertaining to metaphysics, and could be treated separately from the synthetical which constitute metaphysics proper. For indeed these analyses are not of much value except in metaphysics, that is, as regards the synthetical judgments which are to be generated by these previously analyzed concepts.

The conclusion drawn in this section then is that metaphysics is properly concerned with synthetical propositions *a priori,* and these alone constitute its end, for which it indeed requires various dissections of its concepts, namely, analytical judgments, but wherein the procedure is not different from that in every other kind of knowledge, in which we merely seek to render our concepts distinct by analysis. But the generation of *a priori* knowledge by intuition as well as by concepts, in fine, of synthetical propositions *a priori,* especially in philosophical knowledge, constitutes the essential subject of metaphysics.

§ 3. A Remark on the General Division of Judgment into Analytical and Synthetical

This division is indispensable, as concerns the critique of human understanding, and therefore deserves to be called classical in such critical investigation, though otherwise it is of little use. But this is the reason why dogmatic philosophers, who always seek the sources of metaphysical judgments in metaphysics itself, and not apart from it in the pure laws of reason generally, altogether neglected this apparently obvious distinction. Thus the celebrated Wolff and his acute follower Baumgarten came to seek the proof of the principle of sufficient reason, which is clearly synthetical, in the principle of contradiction. In Locke's *Essay,* however, I find an indication of my division. For in the fourth book (Chapter III, § 9, seq.), having discussed the various connections of representations in judgments, and their sources, one of which he makes "identity or contradiction" (analytical judgments) and another the coexistence of ideas in a subject (synthetical judgments), he confesses (§ 10) that our (*a priori*) knowledge of the latter is very narrow and almost nothing. But in his remarks on this species of knowledge, there is so little of what is definite and reduced to rules that we cannot wonder if no one, not even Hume, was led to make investigations concerning this sort of proposition. For such general and yet definite principles are not easily learned from other men, who have had them only obscurely in their minds. One must hit on them first by one's own reflection; then one finds them elsewhere, where one could not possibly have found them at first because the authors themselves did not know that such an idea lay at the basis of their observations. Men who never think independently have nevertheless the acuteness to discover everything, after it has been once shown them, in what was said long since, though no one was ever able to see it there before.

§ 4. The General Question of the Prolegomena: Is Metaphysics at All Possible?

Were a metaphysics which could maintain its place as a science really in existence, could we say: "Here is metaphysics; learn it and it will convince you irresistibly and irrevocably of its truth"? This question would then be useless, and there would only remain that other question (which would rather be a test of our acuteness than a proof of the existence of the thing itself): "How is the science possible, and how does reason come to attain it?" But human reason has not been so fortunate in this case. There is no single book to which you can point as you do to Euclid, and say: "This is metaphysics; here you may find the noblest objects of this science, the knowledge of a highest being and of a future existence, proved from principles of pure reason." We can be shown indeed many propositions, demonstrably certain and never questioned; but these are all analytical, and rather concern the materials and the scaffolding for metaphysics than the extension of knowledge, which is our proper object in studying it (§ 2). Even supposing you produce synthetical judgments (such as the law of sufficient reason, which you have never proved, as you ought to, from pure reason *a priori,* though we gladly concede its truth), you lapse, when you try to employ them for your principal purpose, into such doubtful assertions that in all ages one metaphysics has contradicted another, either in its assertions or their proofs, and thus has itself destroyed its own claim to lasting assent. Nay, the very attempts to set up such a science are the main cause of the early appearance of skepticism, a mental attitude in which reason treats itself with such violence that it could never have arisen save from complete despair of ever satisfying its most important aspirations. For long before men began to inquire into nature methodically, they consulted abstract reason, which had to some extent been exercised by means of ordinary experience; for reason is ever present, while laws of nature must usually be discovered with labor. So metaphysics floated to the surface, like foam, which dissolved the moment it was scooped off. But immediately there appeared a new supply on the surface, to be ever eagerly gathered up by some; while others, instead of seeking in the depths the cause of the phenomenon, thought they showed their wisdom by ridiculing the idle labor of their neighbors.

Weary therefore of dogmatism, which teaches us nothing, and of skepticism, which does not even promise us anything—even the quiet state of a contented ignorance—disquieted by the importance of knowledge so much needed, and rendered suspicious by long experience of all knowledge which we believe we possess or which offers itself in the name of pure reason, there remains but one critical question on the answer to which our future procedure depends, namely, "Is metaphysics at all possible?" But this question must be answered, not by sceptical objections to the asseverations of some actual system of metaphysics (for we do not as yet admit such a thing to exist), but from the conception, as yet only problematical, of a science of this sort.

In the *Critique of Pure Reason* I have treated this question synthetically, by making inquiries into pure reason itself and endeavoring in this source to determine the elements as well as the laws of its pure use according to principles. The task is difficult and requires a resolute reader to penetrate by degrees into a system based on no data except reason itself, and which therefore seeks, without resting upon any fact, to unfold knowledge from its original germs. The *Prolegomena,* however, are designed for preparatory exercises; they are intended to point out what we have to do in order to make a science actual if it is possible, rather than to propound it. The *Prolegomena* must therefore rest upon something already known as trustworthy, from which we can set out with confidence and ascend to sources as yet unknown, the discovery of which will not only explain to us what we knew but exhibit a sphere of many cognitions which all spring from the same sources. The method of prolegomena, especially of those designed as a preparation for future metaphysics, is consequently analytical.

But it happens, fortunately, that though we cannot assume metaphysics to be an actual science, we can say with confidence that there is actually given certain pure *a priori* synthetical cognitions, pure mathematics and pure physics; for both contain propositions which are unanimously recognized, partly apodictically certain by mere reason, partly by general consent arising from experience and yet as independent of experience. We have therefore at least some uncontested synthetical knowledge *a priori* and need not ask *whether* it be possible, for it is actual, but *how* it is possible, in order that we may deduce from the principle which makes the given knowledge possible the possibility of all the rest.

§ 5. The General Problem: How Is Knowledge from Pure Reason Possible?

We have already learned the significant distinction between analytical and synthetical judgments. The possibility of analytical propositions was easily comprehended, being entirely founded on the law of contradiction. The possibility of synthetical *a posteriori* judgments, of those which are gathered from experience, also requires no particular explanations, for experience is nothing but a continued synthesis of perceptions. There remain therefore only synthetical propositions *a priori,* of which the possibility must be sought or investigated, because they must depend upon other principles than the law of contradiction.

But here we need not first establish the possibility of such propositions so as to ask whether they are possible. For there are enough of them which indeed are of undoubted certainty; and, as our present method is analytical, we shall start from the fact that such synthetical but purely rational knowledge actually exists; but we must now inquire into the ground of this possibility and ask *how* such knowledge is possible, in order that we may, from the principles of its possibility, be enabled to determine the conditions of its use, its sphere and its limits. The real problem upon which all depends, when expressed with scholastic precision, is therefore: "How are synthetic propositions *a priori* possible?"

For the sake of popular understanding I have above expressed this problem somewhat differently, as an inquiry into purely rational knowledge, which I could do for once without detriment to the desired insight, because, as we have only to do here with metaphysics and its sources, the reader will, I hope, after the foregoing reminders, keep in mind that when we speak of knowing by pure reason we do not mean analytical but synthetical knowledge.*

---

*It is unavoidable that, as knowledge advances, certain expressions which have become classical after having been used since the infancy of science will be found inadequate and unsuitable, and a newer and more appropriate application of the terms will give rise to confusion. [This is the case with the term "analytical."] The analytical method, so far as it is opposed to the synthetical, is very different from one that consists of analytical propositions; it signifies only that we start from what is sought, as if it were given, and ascend to the only conditions under which it is possible. In this method we often use nothing but synthetical propositions, as in mathematical analysis, and it were better to term it the *regressive* method, in contradistinction to the *synthetic* or *progressive.* A principal part of logic too is distinguished by the name of analytic, which here signifies the logic of truth in contrast to dialectic, without considering whether the cognitions belonging to it are analytical or synthetical.

Metaphysics stands or falls with the solution of this problem; its very existence depends upon it. Let anyone make metaphysical assertions with ever so much plausibility, let him overwhelm us with conclusions; but if he has not previously proved able to answer this question satisfactorily, I have a right to say: This is all vain, baseless philosophy and false wisdom. You speak through pure reason and claim, as it were, to create cognitions *a priori* not only by dissecting given concepts, but also by asserting connections which do not rest upon the law of contradiction, and which you claim to conceive quite independently of all experience; how do you arrive at this, and how will you justify such pretensions? An appeal to the consent of the common sense of mankind cannot be allowed, for that is a witness whose authority depends merely upon rumor. Says Horace:

Quodcunque ostendis mihi sic, incredulus odi.*

The answer to this question is as indispensable as it is difficult; and although the principal reason that it was not sought long ago is that the possibility of the question never occurred to anybody, there is yet another reason, namely, that a satisfactory answer to this one question requires a much more persistent, profound, and painstaking reflection than the most diffuse work on metaphysics, which on its first appearance promised immortal fame to its author. And every intelligent reader, when he carefully reflects what this problem requires, must at first be struck with its difficulty, and would regard it as insoluble and even impossible did there not actually exist pure synthetical cognitions *a priori*. This actually happened to David Hume, though he did not conceive the question in its entire universality as is done here and as must be done if the answer is to be decisive for all metaphysics. For how is it possible, says that acute man, that when a concept is given me I can go beyond it and connect with it another which is not contained in it, in such a manner as if the latter *necessarily* belonged to the former? Nothing but experience can furnish us with such connections (thus he concluded from the difficulty which he took to be impossibility), and all that vaunted necessity or, what is the same thing, knowledge assumed to be *a priori* is nothing but a long habit of accepting something as true, and hence of mistaking subjective necessity for objective.

Should my reader complain of the difficulty and the trouble which I shall occasion him in the solution of this problem, he is at liberty to solve it himself in an easier way. Perhaps he will then feel under obligation to the person who has undertaken for him a labor of so profound research and will rather feel some surprise at the facility with which, considering the nature of the subject, the solution has been attained. Yet it has cost years of work to solve the problem in its whole universality (using the term in the mathematical sense, namely, for that which is sufficient for all cases), and finally to exhibit it in the analytical form, as the reader will find it here.

All metaphysicians are therefore solemnly and legally suspended from their occupations till they shall have adequately answered the question, "How are synthetic cognitions *a priori* possible?" For the answer contains the only credentials which they must show when they have anything to offer us in the name of pure reason. But if they do not possess these credentials, they can expect nothing else of reasonable people, who have been deceived so often, than to be dismissed without further inquiry.

If they, on the other hand, desire to carry on their business, not as a science, but as an art of wholesome persuasion suitable to the common sense of man, this calling cannot in justice be denied them. They will then speak the modest language of a ratio-

---

*["To all that which thou provest me thus, I refuse to give credence, and hate"—*Epistle* II, 3, 188.]

nal belief; they will grant that they are not allowed even to conjecture, far less to know, anything which lies beyond the bounds of all possible experience, but only to assume (not for speculative use, which they must abandon, but for practical use only) the existence of something possible and even indispensable for the guidance of the understanding and of the will in life. In this manner alone can they be called useful and wise men, and the more so as they renounce the title of metaphysicians. For the latter profess to be speculative philosophers; and since, when judgments *a priori* are under discussion, poor probabilities cannot be admitted (for what is declared to be known *a priori* is thereby announced as necessary), such men cannot be permitted to play with conjectures, but their assertion must be either science or nothing at all.

It may be said that the entire transcendental philosophy, which necessarily precedes all metaphysics, is nothing but the complete solution of the problem here propounded, in systematic order and completeness, and hence we have hitherto never had any transcendental philosophy. For what goes by its name is properly a part of metaphysics, whereas the former science is intended only to constitute the possibility of the latter and must therefore precede all metaphysics. And it is not surprising that when a whole science, deprived of all help from other sciences and consequently in itself quite new, is required to answer a single question satisfactorily, we should find the answer troublesome and difficult, nay, even shrouded in obscurity.

As we now proceed to this solution according to the analytical method, in which we assume that such cognitions from pure reason actually exist, we can only appeal to two sciences of theoretical knowledge (which alone is under consideration here), namely, pure mathematics and pure natural science. For these alone can exhibit to us objects in intuition, and consequently (if there should occur in them a cognition *a priori*) can show the truth or conformity of the cognition to the object *in concreto,* that is, its actuality, from which we could proceed to the ground of its possibility by the analytical method. This facilitates our work greatly for here universal considerations are not only applied to facts, but even start from them, while in a synthetic procedure they must strictly be derived *in abstracto* from concepts.

But in order to rise from these actual and, at the same time, well-grounded pure cognitions *a priori* to a possible knowledge of the kind as we are seeking, namely, to metaphysics as a science, we must comprehend that which occasions it—I mean the mere natural, though in spite of its truth still suspect, cognition *a priori* which lies at the basis of that science, the elaboration of which without any critical investigation of its possibility is commonly called metaphysics. In a word, we must comprehend the natural conditions of such a science as a part of our inquiry, and thus the transcendental problem will be gradually answered by a division into four questions:

1. How is pure mathematics possible?
2. How is pure natural science possible?
3. How is metaphysics in general possible?
4. How is metaphysics as a science possible?

It may be seen that the solution of these problems, though chiefly designed to exhibit the essential matter of the *Critique,* has yet something peculiar, which for itself alone deserves attention. This is the search for the sources of given sciences in reason itself, so that its faculty of knowing something *a priori* may by its own deeds be investigated and measured. By this procedure these sciences gain, if not with regard to their contents, yet as to their proper use; and while they throw light on the higher question concerning their common origin, they give, at the same time, an occasion better to explain their own nature.

FIRST PART OF THE MAIN TRANSCENDENTAL PROBLEM

How Is Pure Mathematics Possible?

§ 6. Here is a great and established branch of knowledge, encompassing even now a wonderfully large domain and promising an unlimited extension in the future, yet carrying with it thoroughly apodictic certainty, that is, absolute necessity, and therefore resting upon no empirical grounds. Consequently it is a pure product of reason; and, moreover, it is thoroughly synthetical. [Hence the question arises:] "How then is it possible for human reason to produce such knowledge entirely *a priori?*"

Does not this faculty [which produces mathematics], as it neither is nor can be based upon experience, presuppose some ground of knowledge *a priori,* which lies deeply hidden but which might reveal itself by these its effects if their first beginnings were but diligently ferreted out?

§ 7. But we find that all mathematical cognition has this peculiarity: it must first exhibit its concept in intuition and indeed *a priori;* therefore in an intuition which is not empirical but pure. Without this mathematics cannot take a single step; hence its judgments are always *intuitive;* whereas philosophy must be satisfied with *discursive* judgments from mere concepts, and though it may illustrate its doctrines through an intuition, can never derive them from it. This observation on the nature of mathematics gives us a clue to the first and highest condition of its possibility, which is that some pure intuition must form its basis, in which all its concepts can be exhibited or constructed, *in concreto* and yet *a priori.* If we can uncover this pure intuition and its possibility, we may thence easily explain how synthetical propositions *a priori* are possible in pure mathematics, and consequently how this science itself is possible. For just as empirical intuition [namely, sense-perception] enables us without difficulty to enlarge the concept which we frame of an object of intuition by new predicates which intuition itself presents synthetically in experience, so also pure intuition does likewise, only with this difference, that in the latter case the synthetical judgment is *a priori* certain and apodictic, in the former only *a posteriori* and empirically certain; because this latter contains only that which occurs in contingent empirical intuition, but the former that which must necessarily be discovered in pure intuition. Here intuition, being an intuition *a priori,* is inseparably joined with the concept *prior to all experience* or particular perception.

§ 8. But with this step our perplexity seems rather to increase than to lessen. For the question now is, "How is it possible to intuit anything *a priori?*" An intuition is such a representation as would immediately depend upon the presence of the object. Hence it seems impossible to intuit spontaneously *a priori,* because intuition would in that event have to take place without either a former or a present object to refer to, and in consequence could not be intuition. Concepts indeed are such that we can easily form some of them *a priori,* namely, such as contain nothing but the thought of an object in general; and we need not find ourselves in an immediate relation to the object. Take, for instance, the concepts of quantity, of cause, etc. But even these require, in order to be meaningful and significant, a certain concrete use—that is, an application to some intuition by which an object of them is given us. But how can the intuition of the object precede the object itself?

§ 9. If our intuition were of such a nature as to represent things as they are in themselves, there would not be any intuition *a priori,* but intuition would be always empirical. For I can only know what is contained in the object in itself if it is present and given to me. It is indeed even then incomprehensible how the intuition of a present thing should make me know this thing as it is in itself, as its properties cannot migrate into my faculty of representation. But even granting this possibility, an intuition of that sort would not take place *a priori,* that is, before the object were presented to me; for without this latter fact no ground of a relation between my representation and the object can be imagined, unless it depend upon a direct implantation.

Therefore in one way only can my intuition anticipate the actuality of the object, and be a cognition *a priori,* namely: *if my intuition contains nothing but the form of sensibility, antedating in my mind all the actual impressions through which I am affected by objects.*

For that objects of sense can only be intuited according to this form of sensibility I can know *a priori.* Hence it follows that propositions which concern this form of sensuous intuition only are possible and valid for objects of the senses; as also, conversely, that intuitions which are possible *a priori* can never concern any other things than objects of our senses.

§ 10. Accordingly, it is only the form of sensuous intuition by which we can intuit things *a priori,* but by which we can know objects only as they *appear* to us (to our senses), not as they are in themselves; and this assumption is absolutely necessary if synthetical propositions *a priori* be granted as possible or if, in case they actually occur, their possibility is to be comprehended and determined beforehand.

Now, the intuitions which pure mathematics lays at the foundation of all its cognitions and judgments which appear at once apodictic and necessary are space and time. For mathematics must first present all its concepts in intuition, and pure mathematics in pure intuition; that is, it must construct them. If it proceeded in any other way, it would be impossible to take a single step; for mathematics proceeds, not analytically by dissection of concepts, but synthetically, and if pure intuition be wanting there is nothing in which the matter for synthetical judgments *a priori* can be given. Geometry is based upon the pure intuition of space. Arithmetic achieves its concept of number by the successive addition of units in time, and pure mechanics cannot attain its concepts of motion without employing the representation of time. Both representations, however, are only intuitions; for if we omit from the empirical intuitions of bodies and their alterations (motion) everything empirical, that is, belonging to sensation, space and time still remain, which are therefore pure intuitions that lie *a priori* at the basis of the empirical. Hence they can never be omitted; but at the same time, by their being pure intuitions *a priori,* they prove that they are mere forms of our sensibility, which must precede all empirical intuition, that is, perception of actual objects, and conformably to which objects can be known *a priori,* but only as they appear to us.

§ 11. The problem of the present section is therefore solved. Pure mathematics, as synthetical cognition *a priori,* is possible only by referring to no other objects than those of the senses. At the basis of their empirical intuition lies a pure intuition (of space and of time) which is *a priori,* because the latter intuition is nothing but the mere form of sensibility, which precedes the actual appearance of the objects, since in fact it makes them possible. Yet this faculty of intuiting *a priori* affects not the matter of the phenomenon (that is, the sensation in it, for this constitutes that which is empirical), but its form, namely, space and time. Should any man venture to doubt that these are determinations adhering not to things in themselves, but to their relation to our sensibility, I should be glad to know how he can find it possible to know *a priori* how their intuition will be characterized before we have any acquaintance with them and before they are presented to us. Such, however, is the case with space and time. But this is quite comprehensible as soon as both count for nothing more than formal conditions of our sensibility, while the objects count merely as phenomena; for then the form of the phenomenon, that is, pure intuition, can by all means be represented as proceeding from ourselves, that is, *a priori.*

§ 12. In order to add something by way of illustration and confirmation, we need only watch the ordinary and unavoidable procedure of geometers. All proofs of the complete congruence of two given figures (where the one can in every respect be substituted for the other) come ultimately to this, that they may be made to coincide, which is evidently nothing else than a synthetical proposition resting upon immediate intuition; and this intuition must be pure or given *a priori,* otherwise the proposition could not rank as apodictically certain, but would have empirical certainty only. In that case, it could only be said that it is always found to be so and holds good only as far as our perception reaches. That everywhere space (which [in its entirety] is itself no longer the boundary of another space) has three dimensions and that space cannot in any way have more is based on the proposition that not more than three lines can intersect at right angles in one point; but this proposition cannot by any means be shown from concepts, but rests immediately on intuition, and indeed on pure and *a priori* intuition because it is apodictically certain. That we can require a line to be drawn to infinity (*in indefinitum*) or that a series of changes (for example, spaces traversed by motion) shall be infinitely continued presupposes a representation of space and time, which can only attach to intuition—namely, so far as it in itself is bounded by nothing—for from concepts it could never be inferred. Consequently, the basis of mathematics actually is pure intuitions, which make its synthetical and apodictically valid propositions possible. Hence our transcendental deduction of the notions of space and of time explains at the same time the possibility of pure mathematics. Without such a deduction and the assumption "that everything which can be given to our senses (to the external senses in space, to the internal one in time) is intuited by us as it appears to us, not as it is in itself," the truth of pure mathematics may be granted, but its existence could by no means be understood.

§ 13. Those who cannot yet rid themselves of the notion that space and time are actual qualities inherent in things in themselves may exercise their acumen on the following paradox. When they have in vain attempted its solution and are free from prejudices at least for a few moments, they will suspect that the degradation of space and time to mere forms of our sensuous intuition may perhaps be well founded.

If two things are quite equal in all respects as much as can be ascertained by all means possible, quantitatively and qualitatively, it must follow that the one can in all cases and under all circumstances replace the other, and this substitution would not occasion the least perceptible difference. This in fact is true of plane figures in geometry; but some spherical figures exhibit, notwithstanding a complete internal agreement, such a difference in their external relation that the one figure cannot possibly be put in the place of the other. For instance, two spherical triangles on opposite hemispheres, which have an arc of the equator as their common base, may be quite equal, both as regards sides and angles, so that nothing is to be found in either, if it be described for itself alone and completed, that would not equally be applicable to both; and yet the one cannot be put in the place of the other (that is, upon the opposite hemisphere). Here, then, is an internal difference between the two triangles, which difference our understanding cannot describe as internal and which only manifests itself by external relations in space. But I shall adduce examples, taken from common life, that are more obvious still.

What can be more similar in every respect and in every part more alike to my hand and to my ear than their images in a mirror? And yet I cannot put such a hand as is seen in the glass in the place of its original; for if this is a right hand, that in the glass is a left one, and the image or reflection of the right ear is a left one, which never can take the place of the other. There are in this case no internal differences which our understanding could determine by thinking alone. Yet the differences are internal as the senses teach, for, notwithstanding their complete equality and similarity, the left hand cannot be enclosed in the same bounds as the right one (they are not congruent); the glove of one hand cannot be used for the other. What is the solution? These objects are not representations of things as they are in themselves and as some mere* understanding would know them, but sensuous intuitions, that is, appearances whose possibility rests upon the relation of certain things unknown in themselves to something else, namely, to our sensibility. Space is the form of the external intuition of this sensibility, and the internal determination of every space is possible only by the determination of its external relation to the whole of space, of which it is a part (in other words, by its relation to the outer sense). That is to say, the part is possible only through the whole, which is never the case with things in themselves, as objects of the mere understanding, but which may well be the case with mere appearances. Hence the difference between similar and equal things which are not congruent (for instance, two symmetric helices) cannot be made intelligible by any concept, but only by the relation to the right and the left hands which immediately refers to intuition.

Remark I

Pure mathematics, and especially pure geometry, can have objective reality only on condition that they refer merely to objects of sense. But in regard to the latter the principle holds good that our sense representation is not a representation of things in themselves, but of the way in which they appear to us. Hence it follows that the propositions of geometry are not the results of a mere creation of our poetic imagination, and that therefore they cannot be referred with assurance to actual objects; but rather that they are necessarily valid of space, and consequently of all that may be found in space, because space is nothing else than the form of all external appearances, and it is this form alone in which objects of sense can be given to us. Sensibility, the form of which is the basis of geometry, is that upon which the possibility of external appearance depends. Therefore these appearances can never contain anything but what geometry prescribes to them.

It would be quite otherwise if the senses were so constituted as to represent objects as they are in themselves. For then it would not by any means follow from the representation of space, which, with all its properties, serves to the geometer as an *a priori* foundation, that this foundation and everything which is thence inferred must be so in nature. The space of the geometer would be considered a mere fiction, and it would not be credited with objective validity because we cannot see how things must of necessity agree with an image of them which we make spontaneously and previous to our acquaintance with them. But if this image, or rather this formal intuition, is the essential property of our sensibility by means of which alone objects are given to us, and if this sensibility represents not things in themselves but their appearances, then we shall easily comprehend, and at the same time indisputably prove, that all external objects of our world of sense must necessarily coincide in the most rigorous way with the propositions of geometry; because sensibility, by means of its form of external intuition, namely, by space, with which the geometer is occupied, makes those objects possible as mere appearances.

*[In German, *pure.* The clause is meant ironically.—L.W.B.]

It will always remain a remarkable phenomenon in the history of philosophy that there was a time when even mathematicians who at the same time were philosophers began to doubt, not of the accuracy of their geometrical propositions so far as they concerned space, but of their objective validity and the applicability of this concept itself, and of all its corollaries, to nature. They showed much concern whether a line in nature might not consist of physical points, and consequently that true space in the object might consist of simple parts, while the space which the geometer has in his mind cannot be such. They did not recognize that this thought space renders possible the physical space, that is, the extension of matter itself; that this pure space is not at all a quality of things in themselves, but a form of our sensuous faculty of representation; and that all objects in space are mere appearances, that is, not things in themselves but representations of our sensuous intuition. But such is the case, for the space of the geometer is exactly the form of sensuous intuition which we find *a priori* in us, and contains the ground of the possibility of all external appearances (according to their form); and the latter must necessarily and most rigorously agree with the propositions of the geometer, which he draws, not from any fictitious concept, but from the subjective basis of all external appearances which is sensibility itself. In this and no other way can geometry be made secure as to the undoubted objective reality of its propositions against all the intrigues of a shallow metaphysics, which is surprised at them [the geometrical propositions] because it has not traced them to the sources of their concepts.

Remark II

Whatever is given us as object must be given us in intuition. All our intuition, however, takes place by means of the senses only; the understanding intuits nothing but only reflects. And as we have just shown that the senses never and in no manner enable us to know things in themselves, but only their appearances, which are mere representations of the sensibility, we conclude that "all bodies, together with the space in which they are, must be considered nothing but mere representations in us, and exist nowhere but in our thoughts." Is not this manifest idealism?

Idealism consists in the assertion that there are none but thinking beings, all other things which we think are perceived in intuition, being nothing but representations in the thinking beings, to which no object external to them in fact corresponds. I, on the contrary, say that things as objects of our senses existing outside us are given, but we know nothing of what they may be in themselves, knowing only their appearances, that is, the representations which they cause in us by affecting our senses. Consequently I grant by all means that there are bodies without us, that is, things which, though quite unknown to us as to what they are in themselves, we yet know by the representations which their influence on our sensibility procures us. These representations we call "bodies," a term signifying merely the appearance of the thing which is unknown to us, but not therefore less actual. Can this be termed idealism? It is the very contrary.

Long before Locke's time, but assuredly since him, it has been generally assumed and granted without detriment to the actual existence of external things that many of their predicates may be said to belong, not to the things in themselves, but to their appearances, and to have no proper existence outside our representation. Heat, color, and taste, for instance, are of this kind. Now, if I go farther and, for weighty reasons, rank as mere appearances the remaining qualities of bodies also, which are called primary—such as extension, place, and, in general, space, with all that which belongs to it (impenetrability or materiality, shape, etc.)—no one in the least can adduce the reason of its being inadmissible. As little as the man who admits colors not to be properties of the object in itself, but only as modifications of the sense of sight, should on that account be called an idealist, so little can my thesis be named idealistic merely because I find that more, nay, *all the properties which constitute the intuition of a body belong merely to its appearance.*

The existence of the thing that appears is thereby not destroyed, as in genuine idealism, but it is only shown that we cannot possibly know it by the senses as it is in itself.

I should be glad to know what my assertions must be in order to avoid all idealism. Undoubtedly, I should say that the representation of space is not only perfectly conformable to the relation which our sensibility has to objects—that I have said—but that it is quite similar to the object—an assertion in which I can find as little meaning as if I said that the sensation of red has a similarity to the property of cinnabar which excites this sensation in me.

Remark III

Hence we may at once dismiss an easily foreseen but futile objection, "that by admitting the ideality of space and of time the whole sensible world would be turned into mere sham." After all philosophical insight into the nature of sensuous cognition was spoiled by making the sensibility merely a confused mode of representation, according to which we still know things as they are, but without being able to reduce everything in this our representation to a clear consciousness, I proved that sensibility consists, not in this logical distinction of clearness and obscurity, but in the genetic one of the origin of knowledge itself. For sensuous perception represents things not at all as they are, but only the mode in which they affect our senses; and consequently by sensuous perception appearances only, and not things themselves, are given to the understanding for reflection. After this necessary correction an objection rises from an unpardonable and almost intentional misconception, as if my doctrine turned all the things of the world of sense into mere illusion.

When an appearance is given us, we are still quite free as to how we should judge the matter. The appearance depends upon the senses, but the judgment upon the understanding; and the only question is whether in the determination of the object there is truth or not. But the difference between truth and dreaming is not ascertained by the nature of the representations which are referred to objects (for they are the same in both cases), but by their connection according to those rules which determine the coherence of the representations in the concept of an object, and by ascertaining whether they can subsist together in experience or not. And it is not the fault of the appearances if our cognition takes illusion for truth, that is, if the intuition, by which an object is given us, is considered a concept of the thing or even of its existence which the understanding can only think. The senses represent to us the course of the planets as now progressive, now retrogressive; and herein is neither falsehood nor truth, because as long as we hold this to be nothing but appearance we do not judge of the objective character of their motion. But as a false judgment may easily arise when the understanding is not on its guard against this subjective mode of representation being considered objective, we say they appear to move backward; it is not the senses however which must be charged with the illusion, but the understanding, whose province alone it is to make an objective judgment from appearances.

Thus, even if we did not at all reflect on the origin of our representations, whenever we connect our intuitions of sense (whatever they may contain) in space and in time, according to the rules of the coherence of all knowledge in experience, illusion or truth will arise according as we are negligent or careful. It is merely a question of the use of sensuous representations in the understanding, and not of their origin. In the same way, if I consider all the representations of the senses, together with their form, space and time, to be nothing but appearances, and space and time to be a mere form of the sensibility, which is not to be met with in objects out of it, and if I make use of these representations in reference to possible experience only, there is nothing in my regarding them as appearances that can lead astray or cause illusion. For all that they can correctly cohere according to rules of truth in experience. Thus all the propositions of geometry hold good of space as well as of all the objects of the senses, consequently, of all possible experience, whether I consider space as a mere form of the sensibility or as something cleaving to the things themselves. In the former case, however, I comprehend how I can know *a priori* these propositions concerning all the objects of external intuition. Otherwise, everything else as regards all possible experience remains just as if I had not departed from the common view.

But if I venture to go beyond all possible experience with my concepts of space and time, which I cannot refrain from doing if I proclaim them characters inherent in things in themselves (for what should prevent me from letting them hold good of the same things, even though my senses might be different, and unsuited to them?), then a grave error may arise owing to an illusion, in which I proclaim to be universally valid what is merely a subjective condition of the intuition of things and certain only for all objects of senses—namely, for all possible experience; I would refer this condition to things in themselves, and not limit it to conditions of experience.

My doctrine of the ideality of space and of time, therefore, far from reducing the whole sensible world to mere illusion, is the only means of securing the application of one of the most important kinds of knowledge (that which mathematics propounds *a priori*) to actual objects and of preventing its being regarded as mere illusion. For without this observation it would be quite impossible to make out whether the intuitions of space and time, which we borrow from no experience and which yet lie in our representation *a priori,* are not mere phantasms of our brain to which objects do not correspond, at least not adequately; and, consequently, whether we have been able to show its unquestionable validity with regard to all the objects of the sensible world just because they are mere appearances.

Secondly, though these my principles make appearances of the representations of the senses, they are so far from turning the truth of experience into mere illusion that they are rather the only means of preventing the transcendental illusion, by which metaphysics has hitherto been deceived and led to the childish endeavor of catching at bubbles, because appearances, which are mere representations, were taken for things in themselves. Here originated the remarkable occurrence of the antinomy of reason which I shall mention later and which is solved by the single observation that appearance, as long as it is employed in experience, produces truth; but the moment it transgresses the bounds of experience, and consequently becomes transcendent, produces nothing but illusion.

Inasmuch, therefore, as I leave to things as we obtain them by the senses their actuality and only limit our sensuous intuition of these things to this: that it represents in no respect, not even in the pure intuitions of space and of time, anything more than mere appearance of those things, but never their constitution in themselves, this is not a sweeping illusion invented for nature by me. My protestation, too, against all charges of idealism is so valid and clear as even to seem superfluous, were there not incompetent judges who, while they would have an old name for every deviation from their perverse though common opinion and never judge of the spirit of philosophic nomenclature, but cling to the letter only, are ready to put their own conceits in the place of well-defined notions, and thereby deform and distort them. I have myself given this my theory the name of transcendental idealism, but that cannot authorize anyone to confound it either with the empirical idealism of Descartes (indeed, his was only an insoluble problem, owing to which he thought everyone at liberty to deny the existence of the corporeal world because it could never be proved satisfactorily), or with the mystical and visionary idealism of Berkeley, against which and other similar phantasms our *Critique* contains the proper antidote. My idealism concerns not the existence of things (the doubting of which, however, constitutes idealism in the ordinary sense), since it never came into my head to doubt it, but it concerns the sensuous representation of things to which space and time especially belong. Of these [namely, space and time], consequently of all appearances in general, I have only shown that they are neither things (but mere modes of representation) nor determinations belonging to things in themselves. But the word "transcendental," which with me never means a reference of our knowledge to things, but only to the cognitive faculty, was meant to obviate this misconception. Yet rather than give further occasion to it by this word, I now retract it and desire this idealism of mine to be called "critical." But if it be really an objectionable idealism to convert actual things (not appearances) into mere representations, by what name shall we call him who conversely changes mere representations to things? It may, I think, be called "dreaming idealism," in contradistinction to the former, which may be called "visionary," both of which are to be refuted by my transcendental or, better, *critical* idealism.

SECOND PART OF THE MAIN TRANSCENDENTAL PROBLEM

How Is Pure Science of Nature Possible?

§ 14. Nature is the existence of things, so far as it is determined according to universal laws. Should nature signify the existence of things in themselves, we could never know it either *a priori* or *a posteriori.* Not *a priori,* for how can we know what belongs to things in themselves, since this never can be done by the dissection of our concepts (in analytical propositions)? For I do not want to know what is contained in my concept of a thing (for that belongs to its logical essence), but what in the actuality of the thing is superadded to my concept and by which the thing itself is determined in its existence apart from the concept. My understanding and the conditions on which alone it can connect the determination of things in their existence do not prescribe any rule to things [in] themselves; these do not conform to my understanding, but it would have to conform itself to them; they would therefore have to be first given me in order to gather these determinations from them, wherefore they would not be known *a priori.*

But knowledge of the nature of things in themselves *a posteriori* would be equally impossible. For, if experience is to teach us laws to which the existence of things is subject, these laws, if they have reference to things in themselves, would have to hold them of necessity even outside our experience. But experience teaches us what exists and how it exists, but never that it must necessarily exist so and not otherwise. Experience therefore can never teach us the nature of things in themselves.

§ 15. We nevertheless actually possess a pure science of nature in which are propounded, *a priori* and with all the necessity requisite to apodictical propositions, laws to which nature is subject. I need only call to witness that propaedeutic of natural science which, under the title of the universal science of nature, precedes all physics (which is founded upon empirical principles). In it we have mathematics applied to appearances, and also merely discursive principles (or those derived from concepts), which constitute the philosophical part of the pure knowledge of nature. But there are several things in it which are not quite pure and independent of empirical sources, such as the concept of *motion,* that of *impenetrability* (upon which the empirical concept of matter rests), that of *inertia,* and many others, which prevent its being called a perfectly pure science of nature. Besides, it only refers to objects of the outer sense, and therefore does not give an example of a universal science of nature, in the strict sense, for such a science must bring nature in general, whether it regards the object of the outer or that of the inner sense (the object of physics as well as psychology), under universal laws. But among the principles of this universal physics there are a few which actually have the required universality; for instance, the propositions that "substance is permanent," that "every event is determined by a cause according to constant laws," etc. These are actually universal laws of nature, which hold completely *a priori.* There is then in fact a pure science of nature, and the question arises, *How is it possible?*

§ 16. The word *nature* assumes yet another meaning which defines the object, whereas in the former sense it only denotes the conformity to law of the determinations of the existence of things generally. If we consider it *materialiter,* "nature is the complex of all the objects of experience." And with this only are we now concerned, for anyhow things which can never be objects of experience, if they had to be known as to their nature, would oblige us to have recourse to concepts whose meaning could never be given *in concreto* (by any example of possible experience). Consequently we would have to form for ourselves a list of concepts of their nature, the reality whereof could never be determined. That is, we could never learn whether they actually referred to objects or were mere creations of thought. The knowledge of what cannot be an object of experience would be hyperphysical, and with things hyperphysical we are here not concerned, but only with the knowledge of nature, the actuality of which can be confirmed by experience, though this knowledge is possible *a priori* and precedes all experience.

§ 17. The formal aspect of nature in this narrower sense is therefore the conformity to law of all the objects of experience and, so far as it is known *a priori,* their *necessary* conformity. But it has just been shown that the laws of nature can never be known *a priori* in objects so far as they are considered, not in reference to possible experience, but as things in themselves. And our inquiry here extends, not to things in themselves (the properties of which we pass by), but to things as objects of possible experience, and the complex of these is what we here properly designate as nature. And now I ask, when the possibility of knowledge of nature *a priori* is in question, whether it is better to arrange the problem thus: "How can we know *a priori* that things as objects of experience necessarily conform to law?" or thus: "How is it possible to know *a priori* the necessary conformity to law of experience itself as regards all its objects generally?"

Closely considered, the solution of the problem represented in either way amounts, with regard to the pure knowledge of nature (which is the point of the question at issue), entirely to the same thing. For the subjective laws, under which alone an empirical knowledge of things is possible, hold good of these things as objects of possible experience (not as things in themselves, which are not considered here). It is all the same whether I say: "A judgment of perception can never rank as experience without the law that, whenever an event is observed, it is always referred to some antecedent, which it follows according to a universal rule," or: "Everything of which experience teaches that it happens must have a cause."

It is, however, more suitable to choose the first formula. For we can *a priori* and prior to all given objects have a knowledge of those conditions on which alone experience of them is possible, but never of the laws to which things may in themselves be subject, without reference to possible experience. We cannot, therefore, study the nature of things *a priori* otherwise than by investigating the conditions and the universal (though subjective) laws, under which alone such a cognition as experience (as to mere form) is possible, and we determine accordingly the possibility of things as objects of experience. For if I should choose the second formula and seek the *a priori* conditions under which nature as an object of experience is possible, I might easily fall into error and fancy that I was speaking of nature as a thing in itself, and then move round in endless circles, in a vain search for laws concerning things of which nothing is given me.

Accordingly, we shall here be concerned with experience only and the universal conditions of its possibility, which are given *a priori*. Thence we shall define nature as the whole object of all possible experience. I think it will be understood that I here do not mean the rules of the observation of a nature that is already given, for these already presuppose experience. Thus I do not mean how (through experience) we can study the laws of nature, for these would not then be laws *a priori* and would yield us no pure science of nature; but [I mean to ask] how the conditions *a priori* of the possibility of experience are at the same time the sources from which all universal laws of nature must be derived.

§ 18. In the first place we must state that, while all judgments of experience are empirical (that is, have their ground in immediate sense-perception), all empirical judgments are not judgments of experience; but, besides the empirical, and in general besides what is given to the sensuous intuition, special concepts must yet be super-added—concepts which have their origin wholly *a priori* in the pure understanding, and under which every perception must be first of all subsumed and then by their means changed into experience.

Empirical judgments, so far as they have objective validity, are *judgments of experience,* but those which are only subjectively valid I name mere *judgments of perception.* The latter require no pure concept of the understanding, but only the logical connection of perception in a thinking subject. But the former always require, besides the representation of the sensuous intuition, special *concepts originally begotten in the understanding,* which make possible the objective validity of the judgment of experience.

All our judgments are at first merely judgments of perception; they hold good only for us (that is, for our subject), and we do not till afterward give them a new reference (to an object) and desire that they shall always hold good for us and in the same way for everybody else; for when a judgment agrees with an object, all judgments concerning the same object must likewise agree among themselves, and thus the objective validity of the judgment of experience signifies nothing else than its necessary universal validity. And conversely when we have ground for considering a judgment as necessarily having universal validity (which never depends upon perception, but upon the pure concept of the understanding under which the perception is subsumed), we must consider that it is objective also—that is, that it expresses not merely a reference of our perception to a subject, but a characteristic of the object. For there would be no reason for the judgments of other men necessarily agreeing with mine if it were not the unity of the object to which they all refer and with which they accord; hence they must all agree with one another.

§ 19. Therefore objective validity and necessary universality (for everybody) are equivalent terms, and though we do not know the object in itself, yet when we consider a judgment as universal, and hence necessary, we thereby understand it to have objective validity. By this judgment we know the object (though it remains unknown as it is in itself) by the universal and necessary connection of the given perceptions. As this is the case with all objects of sense, judgments of experience take their objective validity, not from the immediate knowledge of the object (which is impossible), but from the condition of universal validity of empirical judgments, which, as already said, never rests upon empirical or, in short, sensuous conditions, but upon a pure concept of the understanding. The object in itself always remains unknown; but when by the concept of the understanding the connection of the representations of the object, which it gives to our sensibility, is determined as universally valid, the object is determined by this relation, and the judgment is objective.

To illustrate the matter: when we say, "The room is warm, sugar sweet, and wormwood bitter,"* we have only subjectively valid judgments. I do not at all expect that I or any other person shall always find it as I now do; each of these sentences only expresses a relation of two sensations to the same subject, that is, myself, and that only in my present state of perception; consequently they are not valid of the object. Such are judgments of perception. Judgments of experience are of quite a different nature. What experience teaches me under certain circumstances, it must always teach me and everybody; and its validity is not limited to the subject nor to its state at a particular time. Hence I pronounce all such judgments objectively valid. For instance, when I say the air is elastic, this judgment is as yet a judgment of perception only; I do nothing but refer two of my sensations to each other. But if I would have it called a judgment of experience, I require this connection to stand under a condition which makes it universally valid. I desire therefore that I and everybody else should always connect necessarily the same perceptions under the same circumstances.

§ 20. We must consequently analyze experience in general in order to see what is contained in this product of the senses and of the understanding, and how the judgment of experience itself is possible. The foundation is the intuition of which I become conscious, that is, perception (*perceptio*), which pertains merely to the senses. But in the next place, there is judging (which belongs only to the understanding). But this judging may be twofold: first, I may merely compare perceptions and connect them in a consciousness of my particular state; or, secondly, I may connect them in consciousness in general. The former judgment is merely a judgment of perception, and hence is of subjective validity only; it is merely a connection of perceptions in my mental state, without reference to the object. Hence it does not, as is commonly imagined, suffice for experience that perceptions are compared and connected in consciousness through judgment; thence arises no universal validity and necessity by virtue of which alone consciousness can be objectively valid, that is, can be called experience.

Quite another judgment therefore is required before perception can become experience. The given intuition must be subsumed under a concept which determines the form of judging in general relatively to the intuition, connects empirical consciousness of intuition in consciousness in general, and thereby procures universal validity for empirical judgments. A concept of this nature is a pure *a priori* concept of the understanding, which does nothing but determine for an intuition the general way in which it can be used for judgments. Let the concept be that of cause; then it determines the intuition which is subsumed under it, for example, that of air, relative to judging in general—

---

*I freely grant that these examples do not represent such judgments of perception as ever could become judgments of experience, even though a concept of the understanding were superadded, because they refer merely to feeling, which everybody knows to be merely subjective and which of course can never be attributed to the object, and consequently never become objective. I only wished to give here an example of a judgment that is merely subjectively valid, containing no ground for necessary universal validity and thereby for a relation to the object. An example of the judgments of perception which become judgments of experience by superadded concepts of the understanding will be given in the next note.

namely, the concept of air in respect to its expansion serves in the relation of antecedent to consequent in a hypothetical judgment. The concept of cause accordingly is a pure concept of the understanding, which is totally disparate from all possible perception and only serves to determine the representation subsumed under it, with respect to judging in general, and so to make a universally valid judgment possible.

Before, therefore, a judgment of perception can become a judgment of experience, it is requisite that the perception should be subsumed under some such concept of the understanding; for instance, air belongs under the concept of cause, which determines our judgment about it in respect to its expansion as hypothetical.* Thereby the expansion of the air is represented, not as merely belonging to the perception of the air in my present state or in several states of mine, or in the perceptual state of others, but as belonging to it necessarily. The judgment, "Air is elastic," becomes universally valid and a judgment of experience only because certain judgments precede it which subsume the intuition of air under the concept of cause and effect; and they thereby determine the perceptions, not merely with respect to one another in me, but with respect to the form of judging in general (which is here hypothetical), and in this way they render the empirical judgment universally valid.

If all our synthetical judgments are analyzed so far as they are objectively valid, it will be found that they never consist of mere intuitions connected only (as is commonly believed) by comparison into a judgment; but that they would be impossible were not a pure concept of the understanding superadded to the concepts abstracted from intuition, under which concept these latter are subsumed and in this manner only combined into an objectively valid judgment. Even the judgments of pure mathematics in their simplest axioms are not exempt from this condition. The principle, "A straight line is the shortest distance between two points," presupposes that the line is subsumed under the concept of magnitude, which certainly is no mere intuition, but has its seat in the understanding alone and serves to determine the intuition (of the line) with regard to the judgments which may be made about it, in respect to their quantity, that is, to plurality (as *judicia plurativa*).* For under them it is understood that in a given intuition there is contained a plurality of homogeneous parts.

§ 21. To prove, then, the possibility of experience so far as it rests upon pure concepts of the understanding *a priori,* we must first represent what belongs to judging in general and the various functions of the understanding in a complete table. For the pure concepts of the understanding must run parallel to these functions, as such concepts are nothing more than concepts of intuitions in general, so far as these are determined by one or other of these functions of judging, in themselves, that is, necessarily and universally. Hereby also the *a priori* principles of the possibility of all experience, as objectively valid empirical knowledge, will be precisely determined. For they are nothing but propositions which subsume all perception (under certain universal conditions of intuition) under those pure concepts of the understanding.

---

*As an easier example, we may take the following: "When the sun shines on the stone, it grows warm." This judgment, however often I and others may have perceived it, is a mere judgment of perception and contains no necessity; perceptions are only usually conjoined in this manner. But if I say, "The sun warms the stone," I add to the perception a concept of the understanding, namely, that of cause, which necessarily connects with the concept of sunshine that of heat, and the synthetical judgment becomes of necessity universally valid, namely, objective, and is converted from a perception into experience.

**This name seems preferable to the term *particularia,* which is used for these judgments in logic. For the latter implies the idea that they are not universal. But when I start from unity (in singular judgments) and so proceed to totality, I must not [even indirectly and negatively] imply any reference to totality. I think plurality merely without totality, and not the exception from totality. This is necessary if logical distinctions are to form the basis of the pure concepts of the understanding. However, logical usage need not be changed.

LOGICAL TABLE OF JUDGMENTS

1 *As to Quantity*	2 *As to Quality*
Universal	Affirmative
Particular	Negative
Singular	Infinite

3 *As to Relation*	4 *As to Modality*
Categorical	Problematic
Hypothetical	Assertoric
Disjunctive	Apodeictic

TRANSCENDENTAL TABLE OF THE CONCEPTS OF THE UNDERSTANDING

1 *As to Quantity*	2 *As to Quality*
Unity (Measure)	Reality
Plurality (Magnitude)	Negation
Totality (Whole)	Limitation

3 *As to Relation*	4 *As to Modality*
Substance	Possibility
Cause	Existence
Community	Necessity

PURE PHYSICAL TABLE OF THE UNIVERSAL PRINCIPLES OF THE SCIENCE OF NATURE

1 Axioms of Intuition	2 Anticipations of Perception
3 Analogies of Experience	4 Postulates of Empirical Thinking Generally

§ 21a. In order to comprise the whole matter in one idea, it is first necessary to remind the reader that we are discussing, not the origin of experience, but that which lies in experience. The former pertains to empirical psychology and would even then never be adequately explained without the latter, which belongs to the critique of knowledge, and particularly of the understanding.

Experience consists of intuitions, which belong to the sensibility, and of judgments, which are entirely a work of the understanding. But the judgments which the understanding forms solely from sensuous intuitions are far from being judgments of experience. For in the one case the judgment connects only the perceptions as they are given in sensuous intuition, while in the other the judgments must express what experience in general and not what the mere perception (which possesses only subjective validity) contains. The judgment of experience must therefore add to the sensuous intuition and its logical connection in a judgment (after it has been rendered universal by comparison) something that determines the synthetical judgment as necessary and therefore as universally valid. This can be nothing else than that concept which represents the intuition as determined in itself with regard to one form of judgment rather than another, namely, a concept of that synthetical unity of intuitions which can only be represented by a given logical function of judgments.

§ 22. The sum of the matter is this: the business of the senses is to intuit, that of the understanding is to think. But thinking is uniting representations in one consciousness. This union originates either merely relative to the subject and is accidental and subjective, or takes place absolutely and is necessary or objective. The union of representations in one consciousness is judgment. Thinking, therefore, is the same as judging or referring representations to judgments in general. Hence judgments are either merely subjective, when representations are referred to a consciousness in one subject only and united in it, or objective, when they are united in consciousness in general, that is, necessarily. The logical functions of all judgments are but various modes of uniting representations in consciousness. But if they serve for concepts, they are concepts of the necessary union of representations in [any] consciousness, and so are principles of objectively valid judgments. This union in consciousness is either analytical, by identity, or synthetical, by the combination and addition of various representations one to another. Experience consists in the synthetical connection of phenomena (perceptions) in consciousness, so far as this connection is necessary. Hence the pure concepts of the understanding are those under which all perceptions must be subsumed ere they can serve for judgments of experience, in which the synthetical unity of the perceptions is represented as necessary and universally valid.*

§ 23. Judgments, when considered merely as the condition of the union of given representations in a consciousness, are rules. These rules, so far as they represent the union as necessary, are rules *a priori,* and, insofar as they cannot be deduced from higher rules, are principles. But in regard to the possibility of all experience, merely in relation to the form of thinking in it, no conditions of judgments of experience are higher than those which bring the appearances, according to the various form of their intuition, under pure concepts of the understanding, which render the empirical judgment objectively valid. These are therefore the *a priori* principles of possible experience.

The principles of possible experience are then at the same time universal laws of nature, which can be known *a priori.* And thus the problem of our second question, "How is the pure science of nature possible?" is solved. For the system which is required for the form of a science is to be met with in perfection here, because, beyond the above-mentioned formal conditions of all judgments in general (and hence of all rules in general) offered in logic, no others are possible, and these constitute a logical system. The concepts grounded thereupon, which contain the *a priori* conditions of all synthetical and necessary judgments, accordingly constitute a transcendental system. Finally the principles, by means of which all phenomena are subsumed under these

---

*But how does the proposition that judgments of experience contain necessity in the synthesis of perceptions agree with my statement so often before inculcated that experience as cognition *a posteriori* can afford contingent judgments only? When I say that experience teaches me something, I mean only the perception that lies in experience—for example, that heat always follows the shining of the sun on a stone; consequently the proposition of experience is always so far accidental. That this heat necessarily follows the shining of the sun is contained indeed in the judgment of experience (by means of the concept of cause), yet is a fact not learned by experience; for conversely, experience is first of all generated by this addition of the concept of the understanding (of cause) to perception. How perception attains this addition may be seen by referring in the *Critique* itself to the [first] section of the "Transcendental Faculty of Judgment."

concepts, constitute a physical system, that is, a system of nature, which precedes all empirical knowledge of nature, and makes it possible. It may in strictness be denominated the universal and pure science of nature.

§ 24. The first of the physical principles subsumes all phenomena, as intuitions in space and time, under the concept of quantity, and is thus a principle of the application of mathematics to experience. The second one subsumes the strictly empirical element, namely, sensation, which denotes the real in intuitions, not indeed directly under the concept of quantity, because sensation is not an intuition that *contains* either space or time, though it places the respective object corresponding to it in both. But still there is between reality (sense-representation) and the zero, or total void of intuition in time, a difference which has a quantity. For between every given degree of light and of darkness, between every degree of heat and of absolute cold, between every degree of weight and of absolute lightness, between every degree of occupancy space and of totally void space, diminishing degrees can be conceived, in the same manner as between consciousness and total unconsciousness (psychological darkness) ever-diminishing degrees obtain. Hence there is no perception that can prove an absolute absence; for instance, no psychological darkness that cannot be considered as consciousness which is only outbalanced by a stronger consciousness. This occurs in all cases of sensation, and so the understanding can anticipate even sensations, which constitute the peculiar quality of empirical representations (appearances), by means of the principle that they all have degree (and consequently that what is real in all appearance has degree). Here is the second application of mathematics (*mathesis intensorum*) to the science of nature.

§ 25. Anent the relation of appearances merely with a view to their existence, the determination of the relation is not mathematical but dynamical, and can never be objectively valid, consequently never fit for experience, if it does not come under *a priori* principles by which the empirical knowledge relative to appearances first becomes possible. Hence appearances must be subsumed under the concept of substance, which as a concept of a thing is the foundation of all determination of existence; or, secondly—so far as a succession is found among appearances, that is, an event—under the concept of an effect with reference to cause; or lastly—so far as coexistence is to be known objectively, that is, by a judgment of experience—under the concept of community (action and reaction). Thus *a priori* principles form the basis of objectively valid, though empirical, judgments—that is, of the possibility of experience so far as it must connect objects as existing in nature. These principles are the real laws of nature, which may be termed "dynamical."

Finally knowledge of the agreement and connection, not only of appearances among themselves in experience, but of their relation to experience in general, belongs to the judgments of experience. This relation contains either their agreement with the formal conditions, which the understanding recognizes, or their coherence with the materials of the senses and of perception, or combines both into one concept. Consequently, their relation to experience in general entails possibility, actuality, and necessity, according to universal laws of nature. This would constitute the physical doctrine of method for distinguishing truth from hypotheses and for determining the limits of certainty of the latter.

§ 26. The third table of principles drawn by the critical method from the nature of the understanding itself shows an inherent perfection, which raises it far above every other table which has hitherto, though in vain, been tried or may yet be tried by analyzing the objects themselves dogmatically. It exhibits all synthetical *a priori* principles completely and according to one principle, namely, the faculty of judging in general, constituting the essence of experience as regards the understanding; so that we can be certain that there are no more such principles. This affords a satisfaction which can never be attained by the dogmatic method. Yet this is not all; there is a still greater merit in it.

We must carefully bear in mind the premise which shows the possibility of this cognition *a priori* and, at the same time, limits all such principles to a condition which must never be lost sight of if we desire it not to be misunderstood and extended in use beyond the original sense which the understanding attaches to it. This limit is that they contain nothing but the conditions of possible experience in general so far as it is subjected to laws *a priori*. Consequently, I do not say that things *in themselves* possess a magnitude; that their reality possesses a degree, their existence a connection of accidents in a substance, etc. This nobody can prove, because such a synthetical connection from mere concepts, without any reference to sensuous intuition on the one side or connection of it in a possible experience on the other, is absolutely impossible. The essential limitation of the concepts in these principles then is that all things *as objects of experience only* stand necessarily *a priori* under the aforementioned conditions.

Hence there follows, secondly, a specifically peculiar mode of proof of these principles; they are not directly referred to appearances and to their relation, but to the possibility of experience, of which appearances constitute the matter only, not the form. Thus they are referred to objectively and universally valid synthetical propositions, in which we distinguish judgments of experience from those of perception. This takes place because appearances, as mere intuitions *occupying a part of space and time,* come under the concept of quantity, which synthetically unites their multiplicity *a priori* according to rules. Again, insofar as the perception contains, besides intuition, sensation, and between the latter and nothing (that is, the total disappearance of sensation), there is an ever-decreasing transition, it is apparent that the real within appearances must have a degree, so far as it (namely, the sensation) *does not itself occupy any part of space or of time.** Still the transition to this real from empty time or empty space is possible only in time. Consequently, although sensation, as the quality of empirical intuition specifically differentiating it from other sensations, can never be known *a priori*, yet it can, in a possible experience in general, as quantity of perception be intensively distinguished from every other similar perception. Hence the application of mathematics to nature, as regards the sensuous intuition by which nature is given to us, thus becomes possible and definite.

Above all, the reader must pay attention to the mode of proof of the principles which occur under the title of "analogies of experience." For these do not refer to the genesis of intuitions, as do the principles of applying mathematics to natural science in general, but to the connection of their existence in an experience; and this can be nothing but the determination of their existence in time according to necessary laws, under which alone the connection is objectively valid and thus becomes experience. The proof, therefore, does not turn on the synthetical unity in the connection of things in themselves, but merely of perceptions; and of these, not in regard to their matter, but to the determination of time and of the relation of their existence in it according to uni-

---

*Heat and light are in a small space just as large, as to degree, as in a large one; in like manner the internal representations, pain, consciousness generally, whether they last a short or a long time, need not vary as to the degree. Hence the quantity is here in a point and in a moment just as great as in any space or time, however great. Degrees are quantities not in intuition, but in mere sensation (or the quantity of the content [*Grundes*] of an intuition). Hence they can only be estimated quantitatively by the relation of 1 to 0, namely, by their capability of decreasing by infinite intermediate degrees to disappearance, or of increasing from naught through infinite gradations to a determinate sensation in a certain time. *Quantitas qualitatis est gradus.* "The quantity of quality is degree."

versal laws. If the empirical determination in relative time is indeed to be objectively valid (that is, to be experience), these universal laws must contain the necessary determination of existence in time generally (namely, according to a rule of the understanding *a priori*).

As these are prolegomena I cannot here further descant on the subject, but my reader (who has probably been long accustomed to consider experience a mere empirical synthesis of perceptions, and hence has not considered that it goes much beyond them since it imparts to empirical judgments universal validity, and for that purpose requires a pure and *a priori* unity of the understanding) is recommended to pay special attention to this distinction of experience from a mere aggregate of perceptions and to judge the mode of proof from this point of view.

§ 27. Now we are prepared to remove Hume's doubt. He justly maintains that we cannot comprehend by reason the possibility of causality, that is, of the reference of the existence of one thing to the existence of another which is necessitated by the former. I add that we comprehend just as little the concept of subsistence, that is, the necessity that at the foundation of the existence of things there lies a subject which cannot itself be a predicate of any other thing; nay, we cannot even form a notion of the possibility of such a thing (though we can point out examples of its use in experience). The very same incomprehensibility affects the community of things, as we cannot comprehend how from the state of one thing an inference to the state of quite another thing beyond it, and *vice versa,* can be drawn, and how substances which have each their own separate existence should depend upon one another necessarily. But I am very far from holding these concepts to be derived merely from experience, and the necessity represented in them to be imaginary and a mere illusion produced in us by long habit. On the contrary, I have amply shown that they and the principles derived from them are firmly established *a priori* before all experience and have their undoubted objective value, though only with regard to experience.

§ 28. Although I have no notion of such a connection of things in themselves, how they can either exist as substances, or act as causes, or stand in community with others (as parts of a real whole), and I can just as little conceive such properties in appearances as such (because those concepts contain nothing that lies in the appearances, but only what the understanding alone must think), we have yet a concept of such a connection of representations in our understanding and in judgments generally. This concept is: that representations appear, in one sort of judgments, as subject in relation to predicates; in another, as ground in relation to consequent; and, in a third, as parts which constitute together a total possible cognition. Furthermore, we know *a priori* that without considering the representation of an object as determined in one or the other of these respects, we can have no valid knowledge of the object; and, if we should occupy ourselves about the object in itself, there is not a single possible attribute by which I could know that it is determined under any of these aspects, that is, under the concept either of substance, or of cause, or (in relation to other substances) of community, for I have no concept of the possibility of such a connection of existence. But the question is not how things in themselves but how the empirical knowledge of things is determined, as regards the above aspects of judgments in general; that is, how things, as objects of experience, can and must be subsumed under these concepts of the understanding. And then it is clear that I completely comprehend, not only the possibility, but also the necessity, of subsuming all appearances under these concepts—that is, of using them for principles of the possibility of experience.

§ 29. In order to test Hume's problematical concept (his *crux metaphysicorum*), the concept of cause, we are first given *a priori,* by means of logic, the form of a conditional judgment in general; that is, we have one cognition given as antecedent and another as consequent. But it is possible that in perception we may meet with a rule of relation which runs thus: that a certain appearance is constantly followed by another (though not conversely); and this is a case for me to use the hypothetical judgment and, for instance, to say if the sun shines long enough upon a body it grows warm. Here there is indeed as yet no necessity of connection or concept of cause. But I proceed and say that, if this proposition, which is merely a subjective connection of perceptions, is to be a proposition of experience, it must be seen as necessary and universally valid. Such a proposition would be that the sun is by its light the cause of heat. The empirical rule is now considered as a law, and as valid, not merely of appearances but valid of them for the purposes of a possible experience which requires universal and therefore necessarily valid rules. I therefore easily comprehend the concept of cause, as a concept necessarily belonging to the mere form of experience, and its possibility as a synthetical union of perceptions in consciousness in general; but I do not at all comprehend the possibility of a thing in general as a cause, because the concept of cause denotes a condition not at all belonging to things, but to experience. For experience can be nothing but objectively valid knowledge of appearances and of their succession, only so far as the earlier can be conjoined with the later according to the rule of hypothetical judgments.

§ 30. Hence if even the pure concepts of the understanding are thought to go beyond objects of experience to things in themselves (*noumena*), they have no meaning whatever. They serve, as it were, only to decipher appearances, that we may be able to read them as experience. The principles which arise from their reference to the sensible world only serve our understanding for empirical use. Beyond this they are arbitrary combinations without objective reality, and we can neither know their possibility *a priori* nor verify—or even render intelligible by any example—their reference to objects; because examples can only be borrowed from some possible experience, and consequently the objects of these concepts can be found nowhere but in a possible experience.

This complete (though to its originator unexpected) solution of Hume's problem rescues for the pure concepts of the understanding their *a priori* origin and for the universal laws of nature their validity as laws of the understanding, yet in such a way as to limit their use to experience, because their possibility depends solely on the reference of the understanding to experience, but with a completely reversed mode of connection which never occurred to Hume—they do not derive from experience, but experience derives from them.

This is, therefore, the result of all our foregoing inquiries: "All synthetical principles *a priori* are nothing more than principles of possible experience" and can never be referred to things in themselves, but to appearances as objects of experience. And hence pure mathematics as well as a pure science of nature can never be referred to anything more than mere appearances, and can only represent either that which makes experience in general possible, or else that which, as it is derived from these principles, must always be capable of being represented in some possible experience.

§ 31. And thus we have at last something definite upon which to depend in all metaphysical enterprises, which have hitherto, boldly enough but always blindly, attempted everything without discrimination. That the aim of their exertions should be so near struck neither the dogmatic thinkers nor those who, confident in their supposed sound common sense, started with concepts and principles of pure reason (which were legitimate and natural, but destined for mere empirical use) in quest of insights to which they neither knew nor could know any definite bounds, because they had never reflected nor were able to reflect on the nature or even on the possibility of such a pure understanding.

Many a naturalist of pure reason (by which I mean the man who believes he can decide in matters of metaphysics without any science) may pretend that he, long ago, by the prophetic spirit of his sound sense, not only suspected but knew and comprehended what is here propounded with so much ado, or, if he likes, with prolix and pedantic pomp: "that with all our reason we can never reach beyond the field of experience." But when he is questioned about his rational principles individually, he must grant that there are many of them which he has not taken from experience and which are therefore independent of it and valid *a priori*. How then and on what grounds will he restrain both himself and the dogmatist, who makes use of these concepts and principles beyond all possible experience because they are recognized to be independent of it? And even he, this adept in sound sense, in spite of all his assumed and cheaply acquired wisdom, is not exempt from wandering inadvertently beyond objects of experience into the field of chimeras. He is often deeply enough involved in them; though, in announcing everything as mere probability, rational conjecture, or analogy, he gives by his popular language a color to his groundless pretensions.

§ 32. Since the oldest days of philosophy, inquirers into pure reason have conceived, besides the things of sense, or appearances (*phenomena*), which make up the sensible world, certain beings of the understanding (*noumena*), which should constitute an intelligible world. And as appearance and illusion were by those men identified (a thing which we may well excuse in an undeveloped epoch), actuality was only conceded to the beings of the understanding.

And we indeed, rightly considering objects of sense as mere appearances, confess thereby that they are based upon a thing in itself, though we know not this thing as it is in itself but only know its appearances, namely, the way in which our senses are affected by this unknown something. The understanding, therefore, by assuming appearances, grants the existence of things in themselves also; and to this extent we may say that the representation of such things as are the basis of appearances, consequently of mere beings of the understanding, is not only admissible but unavoidable.

Our critical deduction by no means excludes things of that sort (*noumena*), but rather limits the principles of the Aesthetic* to this, that they shall not extend to all things—as everything would then be turned into mere appearance—but that they shall hold good only of objects of possible experience. Hereby, then, beings of the understanding are granted, but with the inculcation of this rule which admits of no exception: that we neither know nor can know anything at all definite of these pure beings of the understanding, because our pure concepts of the understanding as well as our pure intuitions extend to nothing but objects of possible experience, consequently to mere things of sense; and as soon as we leave this sphere, these concepts retain no meaning whatever.

§ 33. There is indeed something seductive in our pure concepts of the understanding which tempts us to a transcendent use—a use which transcends all possible experience. Not only are our concepts of substance, of power, of action, of reality, and others, quite independent of experience, containing nothing of sense appearance, and so apparently applicable to things in themselves (*noumena*), but, what strengthens this conjecture, they contain a necessity of determination in themselves, which experience never attains. The concept of cause implies a rule according to which one state follows another necessarily; but experience can only show us that one state of things often or, at most, commonly follows another, and therefore affords neither strict universality nor necessity.

*[That is, the first part of the *Critique of Pure Reason,* establishing space and time as pure intuitions.—L.W.B.]

Hence the concepts of the understanding seem to have a deeper meaning and import than can be exhausted by their merely empirical use, and so the understanding inadvertently adds for itself to the house of experience a much more extensive wing, which it fills with nothing but beings of thought, without ever observing that it has transgressed with its otherwise legitimate concepts the bounds of their use.

§ 34. Two important and even indispensable, though very dry, investigations therefore became indispensable in the *Critique of Pure Reason* [namely, the chapters "The Schematism of the Pure Concepts of the Understanding" and "On the Ground of the Distinction of All Objects as Phenomena and Noumena."] In the former it is shown that the senses furnish, not the pure concepts of the understanding *in concreto,* but only the schema for their use, and that the object conformable to it occurs only in experience (as the product of the understanding from materials of the sensibility). In the latter it is shown that, although our pure concepts of the understanding and our principles are independent of experience, and despite the apparently greater sphere of their use, still nothing whatever can be thought by them beyond the field of experience, because they can do nothing but merely determine the logical form of the judgment relatively to given intuitions. But as there is no intuition at all beyond the field of the sensibility, these pure concepts, as they cannot possibly be exhibited *in concreto,* are void of all meaning; consequently all these *noumena,* together with their complex, the intelligible world,* are nothing but representation of a problem, of which the object in itself is possible but the solution, from the nature of our understanding, totally impossible. For our understanding is not a faculty of intuition, but of the connection of given intuitions in one experience. Experience must therefore contain all the objects for our concepts; but beyond it no concepts have any significance, as there is no intuition that might offer them a foundation.

§ 35. The imagination may perhaps be forgiven for occasional vagaries and for not keeping carefully within the limits of experience, since it gains life and vigor by such flights and since it is always easier to moderate its boldness than to stimulate its languor. But the understanding which ought to *think* can never be forgiven for indulging in vagaries; for we depend upon it alone for assistance to set bounds, when necessary, to the vagaries of the imagination.

But the understanding begins its aberrations very innocently and modestly. It first brings to light the elementary cognitions which inhere in it prior to all experience, but which yet must always have their application in experience. It gradually drops these limits—and what is there to prevent it, as it has quite freely derived its principles from itself? It then proceeds first to newly imagined powers in nature, then to beings outside nature—in short, to a world for whose construction the materials cannot be wanting, because fertile fiction furnishes them abundantly, and though not confirmed it is never refuted by experience. This is the reason that young thinkers are so partial to metaphysics constructed in a truly dogmatic manner, and often sacrifice to it their time and their talents, which might be otherwise better employed.

But there is no use in trying to moderate these fruitless endeavors of pure reason by all manner of cautions as to the difficulties of solving questions so occult, by complaints of the limits of our reason, and by degrading our assertions into mere conjec-

---

*We speak of the "intelligible world," not (as the usual expression is) "intellectual world." For cognitions are intellectual through the understanding and refer to our world of sense also; but objects, in so far as they can be represented merely by the understanding, and to which none of our sensible intuitions can refer, are termed "intelligible." But as some possible intuition must correspond to every object, we would have to assume an understanding that intuits things immediately; but of such we have not the least notion, nor have we any notion of the *beings of the understanding* to which it should be applied.

tures. For if their impossibility is not distinctly shown, and reason's knowledge of it-self does not become a true science, in which the field of its right use is distinguished, so to say, with geometrical certainty from that of its worthless and idle use, these fruit-less efforts will never be wholly abandoned.

§ 36. How is nature itself possible? This question—the highest point that tran-scendental philosophy can ever reach, and to which, as its boundary and completion, it must proceed—really contains two questions.

First: How is nature in the material sense, that is, as to intuition, or considered as the totality of appearances, possible; how are space, time, and that which fills both—the object of sensation—possible generally? The answer is: By means of the constitu-tion of our sensibility, according to which it is in its own way affected by objects which are in themselves unknown to it and totally distinct from those appearances. This answer is given in the *Critique* itself in the "Transcendental Aesthetic," and in these *Prolegomena* by the solution of the first general problem.

Secondly: How is nature possible in the formal sense, as the totality of the rules under which all appearances must come in order to be thought as connected in experi-ence? The answer must be this: It is only possible by means of the constitution of our understanding, according to which all the above representations of the sensibility are necessarily referred to a consciousness, and by which the peculiar way in which we think (namely, by rules) and hence experience also are possible, but must be clearly distinguished from an insight into the objects in themselves. This answer is given in the *Critique* itself in the "Transcendental Logic" and in these *Prolegomena,* in the course of the solution of the second main problem.

But how this peculiar property of our sensibility itself is possible, or that of our understanding and of the apperception which is necessarily its basis and that of all thinking, cannot be further analyzed or answered, because it is of them that we are in need for all our answers and for all our thinking about objects.

There are many laws of nature which we can know only by means of experience; but conformity to law in the connection of appearances, that is, in nature in general, we cannot discover by any experience, because experience itself requires laws which are *a priori* at the basis of its possibility.

The possibility of experience in general is therefore at the same time the univer-sal law of nature, and the principles of experience are the very laws of nature. For we know nature only as the totality of appearances, that is, of representations in us; and hence we can only derive the laws of their connection from the principles of their con-nection in us, that is, from the conditions of their necessary union in one consciousness which constitutes the possibility of experience.

Even the main proposition expounded throughout this section—that universal laws of nature can be known *a priori*—leads naturally to the proposition that the high-est legislation of nature must lie in ourselves, that is, in our understanding; and that we must not seek the universal laws of nature in nature by means of experience, but con-versely must seek nature, as to its universal conformity to law, in the conditions of the possibility of experience which lie in our sensibility and in our understanding. For how were it otherwise possible to know *a priori* these laws, as they are not rules of analyti-cal knowledge but truly synthetical extensions of it?

Such a necessary agreement of the principles of possible experience with the laws of the possibility of nature can only proceed from one of two causes: either these laws are drawn from nature by means of experience, or conversely nature is derived from the laws of the possibility of experience in general and is quite the same as the mere universal conformity to law of the latter. The former is self-contradictory, for the universal laws of nature can and must be known *a priori* (that is, independently of all experience) and be the foundation of all empirical use of the understanding; the latter alternative therefore alone remains.*

But we must distinguish the empirical laws of nature, which always presuppose particular perceptions, from the pure or universal laws of nature, which, without being based on particular perceptions, contain merely the conditions of their necessary union in experience. In relation to the latter, nature and possible experience are quite the same; and as the conformity to law in the latter depends upon the necessary connection of appearances in experience (without which we cannot know any object whatever in the sensible world), consequently upon the original laws of the understanding, it seems at first strange, but is not the less certain, to say: *The understanding does not derive its laws* (a priori) *from, but prescribes them to, nature.*

§ 37. We shall illustrate this seemingly bold proposition by an example, which will show that laws which we discover in objects of sensuous intuition (especially when these laws are known as necessary) are commonly held by us to be such as have been placed there by the understanding, in spite of their being similar in all points to the laws of nature which we ascribe to experience.

§ 38. If we consider the properties of the circle, by which this figure combines in itself so many arbitrary determinations of space in a universal rule, we cannot avoid attributing a constitution to this geometrical thing. Two straight lines, for example, which intersect each other and the circle, howsoever they may be drawn, are always divided so that the rectangle constructed with the segments of the one is equal to that constructed with the segments of the other. The question now is: Does this law lie in the circle or in the understanding? That is, does this figure, independently of the understanding, contain in itself the ground of the law; or does the understanding, having constructed according to its concepts (of the equality of the radii) the figure itself, introduce into it this law of the chords intersecting in geometrical proportion? When we follow the proofs of this law, we soon perceive that it can only be derived from the condition on which the understanding founds the construction of this figure, namely, the concept of the equality of the radii. But if we enlarge this concept to pursue further the unity of various properties of geometrical figures under common laws and consider the circle as a conic section, which of course is subject to the same fundamental conditions of construction as other conic sections, we shall find that all the chords which intersect within the ellipse, parabola, and hyperbola always intersect so that the rectangles of their segments are not indeed equal but always bear a constant ratio to one another. If we proceed still farther to the fundamental teachings of physical astronomy, we find a physical law of reciprocal attraction applicable to all material nature, the rule of which is that it decreases inversely as the square of the distance from each attracting point, that is, as the spherical surfaces increase over which this force spreads, which law seems to be necessarily inherent in the very nature of things, and hence is usually propounded as knowable *a priori.* Simple as the sources of this law are, merely resting upon the relation of spherical surfaces of different radii, its consequences are so valuable with regard to the variety and simplicity of their agreement that not only are all possible orbits of the celestial bodies conic sections, but such a relation of these orbits to one another results that no other law of attraction than that of the inverse square of the distance can be imagined as fit for a cosmical system.

---

*Crusius alone thought of a compromise: that a spirit, who can neither err nor deceive, implanted these laws in us originally. But since false principles often intrude themselves, as indeed the very system of this man shows in not a few instances, we are involved in difficulties as to the use of such a principle in the absence of sure criteria to distinguish the genuine origin from the spurious, since we never can know certainly what the spirit of truth or the father of lies may have instilled into us.

A drawing from Andreas Cellarius's *Harmonia Macrocosmica* (1661) with some of the greatest names of astronomy and cosmology, including (from left to right): Tycho Brahe (1546–1601), Ptolemy (fl. A.D. 130), St. Augustine (A.D. 354–430), Nicholas Copernicus (1473–1543), Galileo Galilei (with pointer) (1564–1642), and Andreas Cellarius (seated at right). (*Library of Congress*)

Here accordingly is nature, which rests upon laws that the understanding knows *a priori*, and chiefly from the universal principles of the determination of space. Now I ask: Do the laws of nature lie in space, and does the understanding learn them by merely endeavoring to find out the enormous wealth of meaning that lies in space; or do they inhere in the understanding and in the way in which it determines space according to the conditions of the synthetical unity in which its concepts are all centered?

Space is something so uniform and as to all particular properties so indeterminate that we should certainly not seek a store of laws of nature in it. Whereas that which determines space to assume the form of a circle, or the figures of a cone and a sphere, is the understanding, so far as it contains the ground of the unity of their constructions.

The mere universal form of intuition, called space, must therefore be the substratum of all intuitions determinable to particular objects; and in it, of course, the condition of the possibility and of the variety of these intuitions lies. But the unity of the objects is entirely determined by the understanding and on conditions which lie in its own nature; and thus the understanding is the origin of the universal order of nature, in that it comprehends all appearances under its own laws and thereby produces, in an *a priori* manner, experience (as to its form), by means of which whatever is to be known only by experience is necessarily subjected to its laws. For we are not concerned with the nature of things in themselves, which is independent of the conditions both of our sensibility and our understanding, but with nature as an object of possible experience; and in this case the understanding, since it makes experience possible, thereby insists that the sensuous world is either not an object of experience at all or that it is nature [namely, the existence of things determined according to universal laws].

Appendix to the Pure Science of Nature

§ 39. *Of the System of the Categories.* There can be nothing more desirable to a philosopher than to be able to derive the scattered multiplicity of the concepts or principles which had occurred to him in concrete use from a principle *a priori,* and to unite everything in this way in one cognition. He formerly only believed that those things which remained after a certain abstraction, and seemed by comparison among one another to constitute a particular kind of cognitions, were completely collected; but this was only an *aggregate.* Now he knows that just so many, neither more nor less, can constitute the kind of cognition, and perceives the necessity of his division. This constitutes comprehension; and only then has he attained a *system.*

To search in our common knowledge for the concepts which do not rest upon particular experience and yet occur in all knowledge from experience, of which they as it were constitute the mere form of connection, presupposes neither greater reflection nor deeper insight than to detect in a language the rules of the actual use of words generally and thus to collect elements for a grammar (in fact both researches are very nearly related), even though we are not able to give a reason why each language has just this and no other formal constitution, and still less why any precise number of such formal determinations in general, neither more nor less, can be found in it.

Aristotle collected ten pure elementary concepts under the name of *categories.** To these, which are also called "predicaments," he found himself obliged afterward to add five post-predicaments,** some of which however (*prius, simul,* and *motus*) are contained in the former; but this rhapsody must be considered (and commended) as a mere hint for future inquirers, not as an idea developed according to rule; and hence it has, in the present more advanced state of philosophy, been rejected as quite useless.

After long reflection on the pure elements of human knowledge (those which contain nothing empirical), I at last succeeded in distinguishing with certainty and in separating the pure elementary notions of the sensibility (space and time) from those of the understanding. Thus the seventh, eighth, and ninth categories had to be excluded from the old list. And the others were of no service to me because there was no principle on which the understanding could be exhaustively investigated, and all the functions, whence its pure concepts arise, determined exhaustively and precisely.

But in order to discover such a principle, I looked about for an act of the understanding which comprises all the rest and is distinguished only by various modifications or phases, in reducing the multiplicity of representation to the unity of thinking in general. I found this act of the understanding to consist in judging. Here, then, the labors of the logicians were ready at hand, though not yet quite free from defects; and with this help I was enabled to exhibit a complete table of the pure functions of the understanding, which are however undetermined with respect to any object. I finally referred these functions of judging to objects in general, or rather to the condition of de-

---

*1. *Substantia.* 2. *Qualitas.* 3. *Quantitas.* 4. *Relatio.* 5. *Actio.* 6. *Passio.* 7. *Quando.* 8. *Ubi.* 9. *Situs.* 10. *Habitus.*

***Oppositum. Prius. Simul. Motus. Habere.*

termining judgments as objectively valid; and so there arose the pure concepts of the understanding, concerning which I could make certain that these, and this exact number only, constitute our whole knowledge of things by pure understanding. I was justified in calling them by their old name "categories," while I reserved for myself the liberty of adding, under the title of "predicables," a complete list of all the concepts deducible from them by combinations, whether among themselves, or with the pure form of the appearance, that is, space or time, or with its matter, so far as it is not yet empirically determined (namely, the object of sensation in general), as soon as a system of transcendental philosophy should be completed, with the construction of which I was engaged in the *Critique of Pure Reason* itself.

Now the essential point in this system of categories, which distinguishes it from the old rhapsody which proceeded without any principle and for which alone it deserves to be considered as philosophy, consists in this: that, by means of it, the true significance of the pure concepts of the understanding and the condition of their use could be precisely determined. For here it became obvious that they are themselves nothing but logical functions, and as such do not produce the least concept of an object, but require sensuous intuition as a basis. These concepts, therefore, only serve to determine empirical judgments (which are otherwise undetermined and indifferent as regards all functions of judging) with respect to the functions of judging, thereby procuring them universal validity and, by means of them, making judgments of experience in general possible.

Such an insight into the nature of the categories, which limits them at the same time to use merely in experience, never occurred either to their first author or to any of his successors; but without this insight (which immediately depends upon their derivation or deduction), they are quite useless and only a miserable list of names, without explanation or rule for their use. Had the ancients ever conceived such a notion, doubtless the whole study of pure rational knowledge, which under the name of metaphysics has for centuries spoiled many a sound mind, would have reached us in quite another shape and would have enlightened the human understanding, instead of actually exhausting it in obscure and vain speculations and rendering it unfit for true science.

This system of categories makes all treatment of every object of pure reason itself systematic, and affords a direction or clue how and through what points of inquiry every metaphysical consideration must proceed in order to be complete; for it exhausts all the possible functions of the understanding, among which every concept must be classed. In like manner the table of principles has been formulated, the completeness of which we can only vouch for by the system of the categories. Even in the division of the concepts,* which must go beyond the physical application of the understanding, it is always the very same clue, which, as it must always be determined *a priori* by the same fixed points of the human understanding, always forms a closed circle. There is no doubt that the object of a pure concept, either of the understanding or of reason, so far as it is to be estimated philosophically and on *a priori* principles, can in this way be completely known. I could not therefore omit to make use of this clue with regard to one of the most abstract ontological divisions, namely, the various distinctions of the concepts of something and of nothing, and to construct accordingly** a systematic and necessary table of their divisions.***

*Cf. the tables in the *Critique of Pure Reason* in the chapters on "The Paralogisms of Pure Reason" and the "System of Cosmological Ideas."

**In the chapter on "The Amphiboly of the Concepts of Reflection," in the *Critique of Pure Reason.*

***On the table of the categories many neat observations may be made, for instance: (1) that the third arises from the first and the second, joined in one concept; (2) that in those of quantity and of quality

And this system, like every other true one founded on a universal principle, shows its inestimable value in that it excludes all foreign concepts which might otherwise intrude among the pure concepts of the understanding, and determines the place of every cognition. Those concepts, which under the name of "concepts of reflection" have been likewise arranged in a table according to the clue of the categories, intrude into ontology without any privilege or just claim to be among the pure concepts of the understanding. The latter are concepts of connection, and thereby of the objects themselves, whereas the former are only concepts of mere comparison of concepts already given, and hence are of quite another nature and use. By my systematic division* they are saved from this confusion. But the value of the special table of the categories will be still more obvious when we separate—as we are about to do—the table of the transcendental concepts of reason from the concepts of the understanding. As the transcendental concepts of reason are of an entirely different nature and origin, the table of them must have quite another form than the table of categories. This so necessary separation has never yet been made in any system of metaphysics, where, as a rule, these Ideas of reason are all mixed up with the concepts of the understanding, as if they were children of the same family—a confusion which was unavoidable in the absence of a definite system of categories.

THIRD PART OF THE MAIN TRANSCENDENTAL PROBLEM

How Is Metaphysics in General Possible?

§ 40. Pure mathematics and pure science of nature had, for their own safety and certainty, no need for such a deduction as we have made of both. For the former rests upon its own evidence, and the latter (though sprung from pure sources of the understanding) upon experience and its thorough confirmation. The pure science of nature cannot altogether refuse and dispense with the testimony of experience; because with all its certainty it can never, as philosophy, rival mathematics. Both sciences, therefore, stood in need of this inquiry, not for themselves, but for the sake of another science: metaphysics.

Metaphysics has to do not only with concepts of nature, which always find their application in experience, but also with pure rational concepts, which never can be given in any possible experience whatever. Consequently it deals with concepts whose objective reality (namely, that they are not mere chimeras) and with assertions whose

---

there is merely a progress from unity to totality or from something to nothing (for this purpose the categories of quality must stand thus: reality, limitation, total negation), without *correlata* or *opposita,* whereas those of relation and of modality have them; (3) that, as in logic categorical judgments are the basis of all others, so the category of substance is the basis of all concepts of actual things; (4) that, as modality in the judgment is not a particular predicate, so by the modal concepts a determination is not superadded to things, etc. Such observations are of great use. If we enumerate all the predicables, which we can find pretty completely in any good ontology (for example, Baumgarten's), and arrange them in classes under the categories, in which operation we must not neglect to add as complete a dissection of all these concepts as possible, there will then arise a merely analytical part of metaphysics which does not contain a single synthetical proposition, which might precede the second (the synthetical) and would, by its precision and completeness, be not only useful but, in virtue of its system, be even to some extent elegant.

*See *Critique of Pure Reason,* "The Amphiboly of the Concepts of Reflection."

truth or falsity cannot be discovered or confirmed by any experience. This part of metaphysics, however, is precisely what constitutes its essential end, to which the rest is only a means, and thus this science is in need of such a deduction for its own sake. The third question now proposed relates therefore as it were to the root and peculiarity of metaphysics, that is, the occupation of reason merely with itself and the supposed knowledge of objects arising immediately from this brooding over its own concepts, without requiring, or indeed being able to reach that knowledge through, experience.*

Without solving this problem, reason can never satisfy itself. The empirical use to which reason limits the pure understanding does not fully satisfy the proper calling of reason. Every single experience is only a part of the whole sphere of its domain, but the absolute totality of all possible experience is itself not experience. Yet it is a necessary problem for reason, the mere representation of which requires concepts quite different from the pure concepts of the understanding, whose use is only *immanent,* or refers to experience, so far as it can be given. Whereas the concepts of reason aim at the completeness, that is, the collective unity of all possible experience, and thereby transcend every given experience. Thus they become *transcendent.*

As the understanding stands in need of categories for experience, reason contains in itself the source of Ideas, by which I mean necessary concepts whose object *cannot* be given in any experience. The latter are inherent in the nature of reason, as the former are in that of the understanding. While the former carry with them an illusion likely to mislead, the illusion of the latter is inevitable, though it certainly can be kept from misleading us.

Since all illusion consists in holding the subjective ground of our judgments to be objective, a self-knowledge of pure reason in its transcendent (presumptuous) use is the sole preservative from the aberrations into which reason falls when it mistakes its calling and transcendently refers to the object that which concerns only its own subject and its guidance in all immanent use.

§ 41. The distinction of Ideas—that is, of pure concepts of reason—from categories, or pure concepts of the understanding, as cognitions of a quite distinct species, origin, and use, is so important a point in founding a science which is to contain the system of all these *a priori* cognitions that, without this distinction, metaphysics is absolutely impossible or is at best a random, bungling attempt to build a castle in the air without a knowledge of the materials or of their fitness for this or any purpose. Had the *Critique of Pure Reason* done nothing but first point out this distinction, it would thereby have contributed more to clear up our conception of, and to guide our inquiry in, the field of metaphysics than all the vain efforts which had hitherto been made to satisfy the transcendent problems of pure reason, but which had never surmised that we were in quite another field than that of the understanding, and hence classed concepts of the understanding and those of reason together as if they were of the same kind.

§ 42. All pure cognitions of the understanding have this feature that their concepts present themselves in experience, and their principles can be confirmed by it; whereas the transcendent cognitions of reason cannot either, as Ideas, appear in experience or, as propositions, ever be confirmed or refuted by it. Hence whatever errors may slip in unawares can only be discovered by pure reason itself—a discovery of much difficulty, because this very reason naturally becomes dialectical by means of its Ideas; and this unavoidable illusion cannot be limited by any objective and dogmatic researches into things, but only by a subjective investigation of reason itself as a source of ideas.

*If we can say that a science is actual, at least in the idea of all men, as soon as it appears that the problems which lead to it are proposed to everybody by the nature of human reason, and that therefore many (though faulty) endeavors are unavoidably made in its behalf, then we are bound to say that metaphysics is subjectively (and indeed necessarily) actual, and therefore, we justly ask, how is it (objectively) possible.

§ 43. In the *Critique of Pure Reason* it was always my greatest care to endeavor, not only carefully to distinguish the several species of knowledge, but to derive concepts belonging to each one of them from their common source. I did this in order that, by knowing whence they originated, I might determine their use with safety and also have the unanticipated but invaluable advantage of knowing, according to principles, the completeness of my enumeration, classification, and specification of concepts *a priori*. Without this, metaphysics is mere rhapsody, in which no one knows whether he has enough or whether and where something is still wanting. We can indeed have this advantage only in pure philosophy, but of this philosophy it constitutes the very essence.

As I had found the origin of the categories in the four logical forms of all the judgments of the understanding, it was quite natural to seek the origin of the Ideas in the three forms of syllogisms. For as soon as these pure concepts of reason (the transcendental Ideas) are given, they could hardly, except they be held innate, be found anywhere else than in the same activity of reason, which, so far as it regards mere form, constitutes the logical element of syllogisms; but, so far as it represents judgments of the understanding as determined *a priori* with respect to one or another form, constitutes transcendental concepts of pure reason.

The formal distinction of syllogisms renders necessary their division into categorical, hypothetical, and disjunctive. The concepts of reason founded on them contain therefore, first, the Idea of the complete subject (the substantial); secondly, the Idea of the complete series of conditions; thirdly, the determination of all concepts in the Idea of a complete complex of that which is possible.* The first idea is psychological, the second cosmological, the third theological; and, as all three give occasion to dialectic, yet each in its own way, the division of the whole dialectic of pure reason into its paralogism, its antinomy, and its Ideal was arranged accordingly. Through this deduction we may feel assured that all the claims of pure reason are completely represented and that none can be wanting, because the faculty of reason itself, whence they all take their origin, is thereby completely surveyed.

§ 44. In these general considerations it is also remarkable that the Ideas of reason, unlike the categories, are of no service to the use of our understanding in experience, but quite dispensable, and become even an impediment to the maxims of a rational knowledge of nature. Yet in another aspect still to be determined they are necessary. Whether the soul is or is not a simple substance is of no consequence to us in the explanation of its phenomena. For we cannot render the concept of a simple being sensuous and thus concretely intelligible by any possible experience. The concept is therefore quite void as regards all hoped-for insight into the cause of appearances and cannot at all serve as a principle of the explanation of that which inner or outer experience supplies. Similarly, the cosmological Ideas of the beginning of the world or of its eternity (*a parte ante*) cannot be of any service to us for the explanation of any event in the world itself. And finally we must, according to a right maxim of the philosophy of nature, refrain from explaining the design of nature as drawn from the will of a Supreme Being, because this would not be natural philosophy but a confession that we have come to the end of it. The use of these Ideas, therefore, is quite dif-

---

*In disjunctive judgments, we consider all possibility as divided in respect to a particular concept. By the ontological principle of the universal determination of a thing in general, I understand the principle that either the one or the other of all possible contradictory predicates must be assigned to any object. This is, at the same time, the principle of all disjunctive judgments, constituting the foundation of a complete whole of possibility, and in it the possibility of every object in general is considered as determined. This may serve as a slight explanation of the above propositions: that the activity of reason in disjunctive syllogisms is formally the same as that by which it fashions the idea of a complete whole of all reality, containing in itself that which is positive in all pairs of contradictory predicates.

ferent from that of those categories by which (and by the principles built upon which) experience itself first becomes possible. But our laborious Analytic of the understanding would be superfluous if we had nothing else in view than the mere knowledge of nature as it can be given in experience; for reason does its work, both in mathematics and in the science of nature, quite safely and well without any of this subtle deduction. Therefore our critical examination of the understanding combines with the Ideas of pure reason for a purpose which lies beyond the empirical use of the understanding; but such an extended use of the understanding we have above declared to be totally inadmissible and without any object or meaning. Yet there must be a harmony between the nature of reason and that of the understanding, and the former must contribute to the perfection of the latter and cannot possibly upset it.

The solution of this question is as follows: Pure reason does not in its Ideas point to particular objects which lie beyond the field of experience, but only requires completeness of the use of the understanding in the system of experience. But this completeness can be a completeness of principles only, not of intuitions and of objects. In order, however, to represent the Ideas definitely, reason conceives them after the fashion of the knowledge of an object. This knowledge is, as far as these rules are concerned, completely determined; but the object is only an Idea [invented for the purpose of] bringing the knowledge of the understanding as near as possible to the completeness indicated by that Idea.

PREFATORY REMARK TO THE DIALECTIC OF PURE REASON

§ 45. We have shown in §§ 33 and 34 that the purity of the categories from all admixture of sensuous restrictions may mislead reason into extending their use beyond all experience to things in themselves; for though these categories themselves find no intuition which can give them meaning or sense *in concreto,* they, as mere logical functions, can represent a thing in general, but not give by themselves alone a determinate concept of anything. Such hyperbolical objects are distinguished by the appellation of *noumena,* or pure beings of the understanding (or better, beings of thought)—such as, for example, "substance"—but conceived without permanence in time, or "cause," but not acting in time, etc. Here predicates that only serve to make the conformity-to-law of experience possible are applied to these concepts, and yet they are deprived of all the conditions of intuition on which alone experience is possible, and so these concepts lose all significance.

There is no danger, however, of the understanding spontaneously making an excursion so very wantonly beyond its own bounds into the field of the mere beings of thought unless it is impelled by foreign laws. But when reason, which cannot be fully satisfied with any empirical use of the rules of the understanding, as being always conditioned, requires a completion of this chain of conditions, then the understanding is forced out of its sphere. And then it partly represents objects of experience in a series so extended that no experience can grasp it; partly even (with a view to complete the series) it seeks entirely beyond it *noumena,* to which it can attach that chain; and so, having at last escaped from the conditions of experience, it makes its stand as it were final. These are then the transcendental Ideas, which, in accord with the true but hidden ends of the natural destiny of our reason, aim, not at extravagant concepts, but at an unbounded extension of their empirical use, yet seduce the understanding by an unavoidable illusion to a transcendent use, which, though deceitful, cannot be restrained within the bounds of experience by any resolution, but only by scientific instruction and with much difficulty.

I. The Psychological Ideas*

§ 46. People have long since observed that in all substances the subject proper, that which remains after all the accidents (as predicates) are abstracted, consequently the *substantial,* remains unknown, and various complaints have been made concerning these limits to our knowledge. But it will be well to consider that the human understanding is not to be blamed for its inability to know the substance of things—that is, to determine it by itself—but rather for demanding definitely to know substance, which is a mere Idea, as though it were a given object. Pure reason requires us to seek for every predicate of a thing its own subject, and for this subject, which is itself necessarily nothing but a predicate, its subject, and so on indefinitely (or as far as we can reach). But hence it follows that we must not hold anything at which we can arrive to be an ultimate subject, and that substance itself never can be thought by our understanding, however deep we may penetrate, even if all nature were unveiled to us. For the specific nature of our understanding consists in thinking everything discursively, that is, by concepts, and so by mere predicates, to which, therefore, the absolute subject must always be wanting. Hence all the real properties by which we know bodies are mere accidents—not excepting even impenetrability, which we can only represent to ourselves as the effect of a power of which the subject is unknown to us.

Now we appear to have this substance in the consciousness of ourselves (in the thinking subject), and indeed in an immediate intuition; for all the predicates of an internal sense refer to the *ego,* as a subject, and I cannot conceive myself as the predicate of any other subject. Hence completeness in the reference of the given concepts as predicates to a subject—not merely an Idea, but an object—that is, the absolute subject itself, seems to be given in experience. But this expectation is disappointed. For the ego is not a concept,** but only the indication of the object of the inner sense, so far as we know it by no further predicate. Consequently it cannot indeed be itself a predicate of any other thing; but just as little can it be a definite concept of an absolute subject, but is, as in all other cases, only the reference of the inner phenomena to their unknown subject. Yet this idea (which serves very well as a regulative principle totally to destroy all materialistic explanations of the internal phenomena of the soul) occasions by a very natural misunderstanding a very specious argument, which infers its nature from this supposed knowledge of the substance of our thinking being. This is specious so far as the knowledge of it falls quite without the complex of experience.

§ 47. But though we may call this thinking self (the soul) "substance," as being the ultimate subject of thinking which cannot be further represented as the predicate of another thing, it remains quite empty and without significance if permanence—the quality which renders the concept of substances in experience fruitful—cannot be proved of it.

But permanence can never be proved of the concept of a substance as a thing in itself, but for the purposes of experience only. This is sufficiently shown by the first Analogy of Experience,*** and whoever will not yield to this proof may try for himself whether he can succeed in proving, from the concept of a subject which does not exist itself as the predicate of another thing, that its existence is absolutely permanent and that it cannot either in itself or by any natural cause originate or be annihilated.

*See *Critique of Pure Reason,* "The Paralogisms of Pure Reason."
**Were the representation of the apperception (the Ego) a concept, by which anything whatever could be thought, it could be used as a predicate of other things or contain predicates in itself. But it is nothing more than the feeling of an existence without the least concept and is only the representation of that to which all thinking stands in relation (*relatione accidentis*).
***In the *Critique of Pure Reason.*

These synthetical *a priori* propositions can never be proved in themselves, but only in reference to things as objects of possible experience.

§ 48. If, therefore, from the concept of the soul as a substance we would infer its permanence, this can hold good as regards possible experience only, not of the soul as a thing in itself and beyond all possible experience. Life is the subjective condition of all our possible experience; consequently we can only infer the permanence of the soul in life, for the death of a man is the end of all experience which concerns the soul as an object of experience, except the contrary be proved—which is the very question in hand. The permanence of the soul can therefore only be proved (and no one cares to do that) during the life of man, but not, as we desire to do, after death. The reason for this is that the concept of substance, so far as it is to be considered necessarily combined with the concept of permanence, can be so combined only according to the principles of possible experience, and therefore for the purposes of experience only.*

§ 49. That there is something real outside us which not only corresponds but must correspond to our outer perceptions can likewise be proved to be, not a connection of things in themselves, but for the sake of experience. This means that there is something empirical, that is, some appearance in space without us, that admits of a satisfactory proof; for we have nothing to do with other objects than those which belong to possible experience, because objects which cannot be given us in any experience are nothing for us. Empirically outside me is that which is intuited in space; and space, together with all the appearances it contains, belongs to the representations whose connection, according to laws of experience, proves their objective truth, just as the connection of the appearances of the inner sense proves the actuality of my soul (as an object of the inner sense). By means of outer experience I am conscious of the actuality of bodies as external appearances in space, in the same manner as by means of the inner experience I am conscious of the existence of my soul in time; but this soul is known only as an object of the inner sense by appearances that constitute an inner state and of which the being in itself, which forms the basis of these appearances, is unknown. Cartesian idealism therefore does nothing but distinguish outer experience from a dream and the conformity to law (as a criterion of its truth) of the former from the irregularity and false illusion of the latter. In both it presupposes space and time as conditions of the existence of objects, and it only inquires whether the objects of the outer senses which we, when awake, put in space, are as actually to be found in it as the object of the internal sense, the soul, is in time; that is, whether experience carries with it sure criteria to distinguish it from imagination. This doubt, however, may easily be disposed of, and we always do so in common life by investigating the connection of

---

*It is indeed very remarkable how carelessly metaphysicians have always passed over the principle of the permanence of substances without ever attempting a proof of it; doubtless because they found themselves abandoned by all proofs as soon as they began to deal with the concept of substance. Common sense, which felt distinctly that without this presupposition no union of perceptions in experience is possible, supplied the want by a postulate. From experience itself it never could derive such a principle, partly because material things (substances) cannot be so traced in all their alterations and dissolutions that the matter can always be found undiminished, partly because the principle contains *necessity,* which is always the sign of an *a priori* principle. People then boldly applied this postulate to the concept of soul as a *substance,* and concluded a necessary continuance of the soul after the death of man (especially as the simplicity of this substance, which is inferred from the indivisibility of consciousness, secured it from destruction by dissolution). Had they found the genuine source of this principle—a discovery which requires deeper researches than they were ever inclined to make—they would have seen that the law of the permanence of substances arises for the purposes of experience only, and hence can hold good of things so far as they are to be known and conjoined with others in experience, but never independently of all possible experience, and consequently cannot hold good of the soul after death.

appearances in both space and time according to universal laws of experience, and we cannot doubt, when the representation of external things throughout agrees therewith that they constitute truthful experience. Material idealism, in which appearances are considered as such only according to their connection in experience may accordingly be very easily refuted; and it is just as sure an experience that bodies exist outside us (in space) as that I myself exist according to the representation of the inner sense (in time), for the concept "outside us" only signifies existence in space. However, as the Ego in the proposition "I am" means not only the object of inner intuition (in time) but the subject of consciousness, just as body means not only outer intuition (in space) but the thing in itself which is the basis of this appearance, then the question whether bodies (as appearances of the outer sense) exist as bodies in nature apart from my thoughts may without any hesitation be denied. But the question whether I myself as an appearance of the inner sense (the soul according to empirical psychology) exist apart from my faculty of representation in time is an exactly similar one and must likewise be answered in the negative. And in this manner everything, when it is reduced to its true meaning, is decided and certain. The formal (which I have also called "transcendental") actually abolishes the material, or Cartesian, idealism. For if space be nothing but a form of my sensibility, it is as a representation in me just as actual as I myself am, and nothing but the empirical truth of the appearances in it remains for consideration. But if this is not the case, if space and the appearances in it are something existing outside us, then all the criteria of experience besides our perception can never prove the actuality of these objects outside us.

II. The Cosmological Ideas*

§ 50. This product of pure reason in its transcendent use is its most remarkable phenomenon. It serves as a very powerful agent to rouse philosophy from its dogmatic slumber and to stimulate it to the arduous task of undertaking a critical examination of reason itself.

I term this Idea cosmological because it always takes its object only in the sensible world and does not need any other world than one whose object is given to sense; consequently it remains in this respect in its native home, does not become transcendent, and is therefore so far not an Idea; whereas to conceive the soul as a simple substance, on the contrary, means to conceive such an object (the simple) as cannot be presented to the senses. Yet, in spite of this, the cosmological idea extends the connection of the conditioned with its condition (whether this is mathematical or dynamical) so far that experience never can keep up with it. It is therefore with regard to this point always an Idea, whose object never can be adequately given in any experience.

§ 51. In the first place, the use of a system of categories becomes here so obvious and unmistakable that, even if there were not several other proofs of it, this alone would sufficiently prove it indispensable in the system of pure reason. There are only four such transcendent Ideas, as many as there are classes of categories; in each of which, however, they refer only to the absolute completeness of the series of the conditions for a given conditioned. In accordance with these cosmological Ideas, there are only four kinds of dialectical assertions of pure reason, which, being dialectical, prove that to each of them, on equally specious principles of pure reason, a contradictory assertion stands opposed. As all the metaphysical art of the most subtle distinction cannot prevent this opposition, it compels the philosopher to recur to the first sources of

*Cf. *Critique of Pure Reason,* "The Antinomy of Pure Reason."

pure reason itself. This antinomy, not arbitrarily invented but founded in the nature of human reason, and hence unavoidable and never ceasing, contains the following four theses together with their antitheses:

1
Thesis
The world has, as to time and space, a beginning (limit).

Antithesis
The world is, as to time and space, infinite.

2
Thesis
Everything in the world consists of [elements that are] simple.

Antithesis
There is nothing simple, but everything is composite.

3
Thesis
There are in the world causes through freedom.

Antithesis
There is no freedom, but all is nature.

4
Thesis
In the series of the world-causes there is some necessary being.

Antithesis
There is nothing necessary in the world, but in this series all is contingent.

§ 52*a*. Here is the most singular phenomenon of human reason, no other instance of which can be shown in any other use of reason. If we, as is commonly done, represent to ourselves the appearances of the sensible world as things in themselves, if we assume the principles of their combination as principles universally valid of things in themselves and not merely of experience, as is usually, nay, without our *Critique* unavoidably, done, there arises an unexpected conflict which never can be removed in the common dogmatic way; because the thesis, as well as the antithesis, can be shown by equally clear, evident, and irresistible proofs—for I pledge myself as to the correctness of all these proofs—and reason therefore perceives that it is divided against itself, a state at which the skeptic rejoices, but which must make the critical philosopher pause and feel ill at ease.

§ 52*b*. We may blunder in various ways in metaphysics without any fear of being detected in falsehood. If we but avoid self-contradiction, which in synthetical though purely fictitious propositions is quite possible, then whenever the concepts which we connect are mere Ideas that cannot be given (with respect to their whole content) in experience, we cannot be refuted by experience. For how can we make out by experience whether the world is from eternity or had a beginning, whether matter is infinitely divisible or consists of simple parts? Such concepts cannot be given in any experience, however extensive, and consequently the falsehood either of the affirmative or the negative proposition cannot be discovered by this touchstone.

The only possible way in which reason could have revealed unintentionally its secret dialectic, falsely announced as its dogmatics, would be when it were made to ground an assertion upon a universally admitted principle and to deduce the exact contrary with the greatest accuracy of inference from another which is equally granted. This is actually here the case with regard to four natural Ideas of reason, whence four assertions on the one side and as many counterassertions on the other arise, each consistently following from universally acknowledged principles. Thus they reveal, by the use of these principles, the dialectical illusion of pure reason, which would otherwise forever remain concealed.

This is therefore a decisive experiment, which must necessarily expose any error lying hidden in the assumptions of reason.* Contradictory propositions cannot both be false, except the concept on which each is founded is self-contradictory; for example, the propositions, "A square circle is round," and "A square circle is not round," are both false. For, as to the former, it is false that the circle is round because it is quadrangular; and it is likewise false that it is not round, that is, angular, because it is a circle. For the logical criterion of the impossibility of a concept consists in this that, if we presuppose it, two contradictory propositions both become false; consequently, as no middle between them is conceivable, nothing at all is thought by that concept.

§ 52c. The first two antinomies, which I call mathematical because they are concerned with the addition or division of the homogeneous, are founded on such a contradictory concept; and hence I explain how it happens that both the thesis and antithesis of the two are false.

When I speak of objects in time and in space, it is not of things in themselves, of which I know nothing, but of things in appearance, that is, of experience, as the particular way of knowing objects which is afforded to man. I must not say of what I think in time or in space, that in itself, and independent of these my thoughts, it exists in space and in time, for in that case I should contradict myself; because space and time, together with the appearances in them, are nothing existing in themselves and outside of my representations, but are nothing only modes of representation, and it is palpably contradictory to say that a mere mode of representation exists without our representation. Objects of the senses therefore exist only in experience, whereas to give them a self-subsisting existence apart from experience or before it is merely to represent to ourselves that experience actually exists apart from experience or before it.

Now if I inquire into the magnitude of the world, as to space and time, it is equally impossible, as regards all my concepts, to declare it infinite or to declare it finite. For neither assertion can be contained in experience, because experience either of an infinite space or of an infinite elapsed time, or again, of the boundary of the world by a void space or by an antecedent void time, is impossible; these are mere Ideas. The magnitude of the world, decided either way, would therefore have to exist in the world itself apart from all experience. But this contradicts the concept of a world of sense, which is merely a complex of the appearances whose existence and connection occur only in our representations, that is, in experience; since this latter is not an object in itself but a mere mode of representation. Hence it follows that, as the concept of an ab-

---

*I therefore would be pleased to have the critical reader to devote to this antinomy of pure reason his chief attention, because nature itself seems to have established it with a view to stagger reason in its daring pretensions and to force it to self-examination. For every proof which I have given of both thesis and antithesis I undertake to be responsible, and thereby to show the certainty of the inevitable antinomy of reason. When the reader is brought by this curious phenomenon to fall back upon the proof of the presumption upon which it rests, he will feel himself obliged to investigate the ultimate foundation of all knowledge by pure reason with me more thoroughly.

solutely existing world of sense is self-contradictory, the solution of the problem concerning its magnitude, whether attempted affirmatively or negatively, is always false.

The same holds of the second antinomy, which relates to the division of appearances. For these are mere representations; and the parts exist merely in their representation, consequently in the division—that is, in a possible experience in which they are given—and the division reaches only as far as the possible experience reaches. To assume that an appearance, for example, that of body, contains in itself before all experience all the parts which any possible experience can ever reach is to impute to a mere appearance, which can exist only in experience, an existence previous to experience. In other words, it would mean that mere representations exist before they can be found in our faculty of representation. Such an assertion is self-contradictory, as also every solution of our misunderstood problem, whether we maintain that bodies in themselves consist of an infinite number of parts or of a finite number of simple parts.

§ 53. In the first (the mathematical) class of antinomies the falsehood of the presupposition consists in representing in one concept something self-contradictory as if it were compatible (that is, an appearance as a thing in itself). But, as to the second (the dynamical) class of antinomies, the falsehood of the presupposition consists in representing as contradictory what is compatible; so that while in the former case the opposed assertions were both false, in this case, on the other hand, where they are opposed to one another by mere misunderstanding, they may both be true.

Any mathematical connection necessarily presupposes homogeneity of what is connected (in the concept of magnitude), while the dynamical one by no means requires this. When we have to deal with extended magnitudes all the parts must be homogeneous with one another and with the whole, whereas in the connection of cause and effect homogeneity may indeed likewise be found but is not necessary; for the concept of causality (by means of which something is posited through something else quite different from it) does not in the least require it.

If the objects of the world of sense are taken for things in themselves and the above laws of nature for laws of things in themselves, the contradiction would be unavoidable. So also, if the subject of freedom were, like other objects, represented as mere appearance, the contradiction would be just as unavoidable; for the same predicate would at once be affirmed and denied of the same kind of object in the same sense. But if natural necessity is referred merely to appearances and freedom merely to things in themselves, no contradiction arises if we at the same time assume or admit both kinds of causality, however difficult or impossible it may be to make the latter kind conceivable.

In appearance every effect is an event, or something that happens in time; it must, according to the universal law of nature, be preceded by a determination of the causal act of its cause—this determination being a state of the cause—which it follows according to a constant law. But this determination of the cause to a causal act must likewise be something that takes place or happens; the cause must have begun to act, otherwise no succession between it and the effect could be conceived. Otherwise the effect, as well as the causal act of the cause, would have always existed. Therefore the determination of the cause to act must also have originated among appearances and must consequently, like its effect, be an event, which must again have its cause, and so on; hence natural necessity must be the condition on which efficient causes are determined. Whereas if freedom is to be a property of certain causes of appearances, it must, as regards these, which are events, be a faculty of starting them spontaneously. That is, it would not require that the causal act of the cause should itself begin [in time], and hence it would not require any other ground to determine its start. But then the cause, as to its causal act, could not rank under time-determinations of its state; that is, it could not be an appearance, but would have to be considered a thing in itself, while only its effects would be appearances.* If without contradiction we can think of the beings of understanding as exercising such an influence on appearances, then natural necessity will attach to all connections of cause and effect in the sensuous world; though, on the other hand, freedom can be granted to the cause which is itself not an appearance (but the foundation of appearance). Nature and freedom therefore can without contradiction be attributed to the very same thing, but in different relations—on one side as an appearance, on the other as a thing in itself.

We have in us a faculty which not only stands in connection with its subjective determining grounds [motives] which are the natural causes of its actions and is so far the faculty of a being that itself belongs to appearances, but is also related to objective grounds which are only Ideas so far as they can determine this faculty. This connection is expressed by the word *ought*. This faculty is called "reason," and, so far as we consider a being (man) entirely according to this objectively determinable reason, he cannot be considered as a being of sense; this property is a property of a thing in itself, a property whose possibility we cannot comprehend. I mean we cannot comprehend how the *ought* should determine (even if it never has actually determined) its activity and could become the cause of actions whose effect is an appearance in the sensible world. Yet the causality of reason would be freedom with regard to the effects in the sensuous world, so far as we can consider *objective grounds,* which are themselves Ideas, as their determinants. For its action in that case would not depend upon subjective conditions, consequently not upon those of time, and of course not upon the law of nature which serves to determine them, because grounds of reason give the rule universally to actions, according to principles, without influence of the circumstances of either time or place.

What I adduce here is merely meant as an example to make the thing intelligible and does not necessarily belong to our problem, which must be decided from mere concepts independently of the properties which we meet in the actual world.

Now I may say without contradiction that all the actions of rational beings, so far as they are appearances (met with in any experience), are subject to the necessity of nature, but the very same actions, as regards merely the rational subject and its faculty of acting according to mere reason, are free. For what is required for the necessity of nature? Nothing more than the determinability of every event in the world of sense according to constant laws, that is, a reference to cause in the [world of] appearance; in this process the thing in itself at its foundation and its causality remain unknown. But, I say, the law of nature remains, whether the rational being is the cause of the effects in the sensuous world from reason—that is, through freedom—or whether it does not determine them on grounds of reason. For if the former is the case, the action is performed according to maxims, the effect of which as appearance is always conformable to constant laws; if the latter is the case, and the action not performed on principles of reason, it is subjected to the empirical laws of the sensibility, and in both cases the effects are connected according to constant laws; more than this we do not require or know concerning natural necessity. But in the former case reason is the cause of these

---

*The Idea of freedom occurs only in the relation of the intellectual, as cause, to the appearance, as effect. Hence we cannot attribute freedom to matter in regard to the incessant action by which it fills its space, though this action takes place from an internal principle. We can likewise find no notion of freedom suitable to purely rational beings, for instance, to God, so far as his action is immanent. For his action, though independent of external determining causes, is determined in his eternal reason, that is, in the divine *nature*. It is only if *something is to start* by an action, and so the effect occurs in the sequence of time, or in the world of sense (for example, the beginning of the world), that we can put the question whether the causal act of the cause must in its turn have been started or whether the cause can originate an effect without its causal act itself beginning. In the former case, the concept of this activity is a concept of natural necessity; in the latter, that of freedom. From this the reader will see that as I explained freedom to be the faculty of starting an event spontaneously, I have exactly hit the concept which is the problem of metaphysics.

laws of nature, and therefore free; in the latter, the effects follow according to mere natural laws of sensibility, because reason does not influence it. But reason itself is not determined on that account by the sensibility (which is impossible) and is therefore free in this case too. Freedom is therefore no hindrance to natural law in appearances; neither does this law abrogate the freedom of the practical use of reason, which is connected with things in themselves, as determining grounds.

Thus practical freedom, namely, the freedom in which reason possesses causality according to objectively determining grounds, is rescued; and yet natural necessity is not in the least curtailed with regard to the very same effects, as appearances. The same remarks will serve to explain what we had to say concerning transcendental freedom and its compatibility with natural necessity in the same subject, but not taken in the same context. For, as to this, every beginning of the action of a being from objective causes regarded as determining grounds is always a *first beginning,* though the same action is in the series of appearances only a *subordinate beginning,* which must be preceded by a state of the cause which determines it and is itself determined in the same manner by another immediately preceding. Thus we are able, in rational beings, or in beings generally so far as their causality is determined in them as things in themselves, to think of a faculty of beginning from themselves a series of states without falling into contradiction with the laws of nature. For the relation of the action to objective grounds of reason is not a time relation; in this case that which determines the causality does not precede in time the action, because such determining grounds represent, not a reference to objects of sense, for example, to causes in the appearances, but to determining causes as things in themselves, which do not fall under conditions of time. And in this way the action, with regard to the causality of reason, can be considered as a first beginning, while in respect to the series of appearances as merely a subordinate beginning. We may therefore without contradiction consider it in the former aspect as free, but in the latter (as it is merely appearance) as subject to natural necessity.

As to the fourth antinomy, it is solved in the same way as the conflict of reason with itself in the third. For, provided the cause *in* the appearance is distinguished from the cause *of* the appearances (so far as it can be thought as a thing in itself), both propositions are perfectly reconcilable: the one, that there is nowhere in the sensuous world a cause (according to similar laws of causality) whose existence is absolutely necessary; the other, that this world is nevertheless connected with a necessary being as its cause (but of another kind and according to another law). The incompatibility of these propositions rests entirely upon the mistake of extending what is valid merely of appearances to things in themselves and in confusing both in one concept.

§ 54. This, then, is the exposition, and this the solution of the whole antinomy in which reason finds itself involved in the application of its principles to the sensible world. The former alone (the mere exposition) would be a considerable service in the cause of our knowledge of human reason, even though the solution might fail fully to satisfy the reader, who has here to combat a natural illusion which has been but recently exposed to him and which he had hitherto always regarded as genuine. For one result at least is unavoidable. As it is quite impossible to prevent this conflict of reason with itself—so long as the objects of the sensible world are taken for things in themselves and not for mere appearances, which they are in fact—the reader is thereby compelled to examine over again the deduction of all our *a priori* knowledge and the proof which I have given of my deduction in order to come to a decision on the question. This is all I require at present; for when in this occupation he shall have thought himself deep enough into the nature of pure reason, those concepts by which alone the solution of the conflict of reason is possible will become sufficiently familiar to him. Without this preparation, I cannot expect an unreserved assent even from the most attentive reader.

III. The Theological Idea*

§ 55. The third transcendental Idea, which affords matter for the most important but (if pursued only speculatively) transcendent and thereby dialectical use of reason, is the Ideal of pure reason. Reason in this case does not, as with the psychological and the cosmological Ideas, begin from experience and err by exaggerating its grounds in striving to attain, if possible, the absolute completeness of their series. Rather, it totally breaks with experience and from mere concepts of what constitutes the absolute completeness of a thing in general; and thus, by means of the Idea of a most perfect primal Being, it proceeds to determine the possibility and therefore the actuality of all other things. And so the mere presupposition of a Being conceived, not in the series of experience yet for the purposes of experience, for the sake of comprehending its connection, order, and unity—in a word, the Idea—is more easily distinguished from the concept of the understanding here than in the former cases. Hence we can easily expose the dialectical illusion which arises from our making the subjective conditions of our thinking objective conditions of objects themselves, and from making an hypothesis necessary for the satisfaction of our reason into a dogma. As the observations of the *Critique* on the pretensions of transcendental theology are intelligible, clear, and decisive, I have nothing more to add on the subject.

General Remark on the Transcendental Ideas

§ 56. The objects which are given us by experience are in many respects incomprehensible, and many questions to which the law of nature leads us when carried beyond a certain point (though still quite conformably to the laws of nature) admit of no answer. An example is the question: Why do material things attract one another? But if we entirely quit nature or, in pursuing its combinations, exceed all possible experience, and so enter the realm of mere Ideas, we cannot then say that the object is incomprehensible and that the nature of things proposes to us insoluble problems. For we are not then concerned with nature or even with given objects, but with mere concepts which have their origin solely in our reason, and with mere beings of thought; and all the problems that arise from our concepts of them must be solved, because of course reason can and must give a full account of its own procedure.** As the psychological, cosmological, and theological Ideas are nothing but pure concepts of reason which cannot be given in any experience, the questions which reason asks us about them are put to us, not by the objects, but by mere maxims of our reason for the sake of its own satisfaction. They must all be capable of satisfactory answers, which are given by showing that they are principles which bring our use of the understanding into thorough agreement, completeness, and synthetical unity, and that they thus hold good of experience only, but of experience as a whole.

Although an absolute whole of experience is impossible, the Idea of a whole of knowledge according to principles must impart to our knowledge a peculiar kind of

---

*Cf. *Critique of Pure Reason,* "The Transcendental Ideal."

**Herr Platner, in his *Aphorismen,* acutely says (§§ 728, 729), "If reason be a criterion, no concept which is incomprehensible to human reason can be possible. Incomprehensibility has place in what is actual only. Here incomprehensibility arises from the insufficiency of the acquired ideas." It sounds paradoxical, but is otherwise not strange to say that in nature there is much that is incomprehensible (for example, the faculty of reproduction); but if we mount still higher and go even beyond nature, everything again becomes comprehensible. For we then quit entirely the objects which can be given us and occupy ourselves merely about Ideas, in which occupation we can easily comprehend the law that reason prescribes by them to the understanding for its use in experience, because the law is the reason's own production.

unity, that of a system, without which it is nothing but piecework and cannot be used for proving the existence of a highest purpose (which can only be the general system of all purposes). I do not here refer only to the practical, but also to the highest purpose of the speculative use of reason.

The transcendental Ideas therefore express the peculiar vocation of reason as a principle of systematic unity in the use of the understanding. Yet if we assume this unity of the mode of knowledge to pertain to the object of knowledge, if we regard that which is merely *regulative* to be *constitutive,* and if we persuade ourselves that we can by means of these Ideas widen our knowledge transcendently or far beyond all possible experience, while it only serves to render experience within itself as nearly complete as possible, that is, to limit its progress by nothing that cannot belong to experience—if we do this, I say—we suffer from a mere misunderstanding in our estimate of the proper role of our reason and of its principles, and a dialectic arises which both confuses the empirical use of reason and sets reason at variance with itself.

CONCLUSION

On the Determination of the Bounds of Pure Reason

§ 57. Having adduced the clearest arguments, it would be absurd for us to hope that we can know more of any object than belongs to the possible experience of it or lay claim to the least knowledge of anything not assumed to be an object of possible experience which would determine it according to the constitution it has in itself. For how could we determine anything in this way, since time, space, and all the concepts of the understanding, and still more all the concepts formed by empirical intuition (perception) in the sensible world, have and can have no other use than to make experience possible? And if this condition is omitted from the pure concepts of the understanding, they do not determine any object and have no meaning whatever.

But it would be, on the other hand, a still greater absurdity if we conceded no things in themselves or set up our experience as the only possible mode of knowing things, our intuition of them in space and in time for the only possible intuition and our discursive understanding for the archetype of every possible understanding; for this would be to wish to have the principles of the possibility of experience considered universal conditions of things in themselves.

Our principles, which limit the use of reason to possible experience, might in this way become transcendent and the limits of our reason be set up as limits of the possibility of things in themselves (as Hume's *Dialogues* may illustrate) if a careful critique did not guard the bounds of our reason with respect to its empirical use and set a limit to its pretensions. Skepticism originally arose from metaphysics and its anarchic dialectic. At first it might, merely to favor the empirical use of reason, announce everything that transcends this use as worthless and deceitful; but by and by, when it was perceived that the very same principles that are used in experience insensibly and apparently with the same right led still further than experience extends, then men began to doubt even the principles of experience. But here there is no danger, for common sense will doubtless always assert its rights. A certain confusion, however, arose in science, which cannot determine how far reason is to be trusted, and why only so far and no farther; and this confusion can only be cleared up and all future relapses obviated by a formal determination, on principle, of the boundary of the use of our reason.

We cannot indeed, beyond all possible experience, form a definite concept of what things in themselves may be. Yet we are not at liberty to abstain entirely from inquiring into them; for experience never satisfies reason fully but, in answering questions, refers us further and further back and leaves us dissatisfied with regard to their complete solution. This anyone may gather from the dialectic of pure reason, which therefore has its good subjective grounds. Having acquired, as regards the nature of our soul, a clear conception of the subject, and having come to the conviction that its manifestations cannot be explained materialistically, who can refrain from asking what the soul really is and, if no concept of experience suffices for the purpose, from accounting for it by a concept of reason (that of a simple immaterial being), though we cannot by any means prove its objective reality? Who can satisfy himself with mere empirical knowledge in all the cosmological questions of the duration and of the magnitude of the world, of freedom or of natural necessity, since every answer given on principles of experience begets a fresh question, which likewise requires its answer and thereby clearly shows the insufficiency of all physical modes of explanation to satisfy reason? Finally, who does not see in the thoroughgoing contingency and dependence of all his thoughts and assumptions on mere principles of experience the impossibility of stopping there? And who does not feel himself compelled, notwithstanding all interdictions against losing himself in transcendent Ideas, to seek rest and contentment, beyond all the concepts which he can vindicate by experience, in the concept of a Being the possibility of the Idea of which cannot be conceived but at the same time cannot be refuted, because it relates to a mere being of the understanding and without it reason must needs remain forever dissatisfied?

Bounds (in extended beings) always presuppose a space existing outside a certain definite place and inclosing it; limits do not require this, but are mere negations which affect a quantity so far as it is not absolutely complete. But our reason, as it were, sees in its surroundings a space for knowledge of things in themselves, though we can never have definite concepts of them and are limited to appearances only.

As long as the knowledge of reason is homogeneous, definite bounds to it are inconceivable. In mathematics and in natural philosophy, human reason admits of limits but not of bounds, namely, it admits that something indeed lies without it, at which it can never arrive, but not that it will at any point find completion in its internal progress. The enlarging of our views in mathematics and the possibility of new discoveries are infinite; and the same is the case with the discovery of new properties of nature, of new powers and laws, by continued experience and its rational combination. But limits cannot be mistaken here, for mathematics refers to appearances only, and what cannot be an object of sensuous intuition, such as the concepts of metaphysics and of morals, lies entirely without its sphere; it can never lead to them, but neither does it require them. There is, therefore, not a continual progress and approximation towards these sciences, and there is not, as it were, any point or line of contact. Natural science will never reveal to us the internal constitution of things, which, though not appearance, yet can serve as the ultimate ground for explaining appearances. Nor does that science require this for its physical explanations. Nay, even if such grounds should be offered from other sources (for instance, the influence of immaterial beings), they must be rejected and not used in the progress of its explanations. For these explanations must only be grounded upon that which as an object of sense can belong to experience, and be brought into connection with our actual perceptions and empirical laws.

But metaphysics leads us towards bounds in the dialectical attempts of pure reason (not undertaken arbitrarily or wantonly, but stimulated thereto by the nature of reason itself). And the transcendental Ideas, as they do not admit of evasion but are never capable of realization, serve to point out to us actually not only the bounds of the pure use of reason, but also the way to determine them. Such is the end and the use of this natural predisposition of our reason, which has brought forth metaphysics as its favorite child, whose generation, like every other in the world, is not to be ascribed to blind chance but to an original germ, wisely organized for great ends. For metaphysics, in its fundamental features, perhaps more than any other science, is placed in us by nature itself and cannot be considered the production of an arbitrary choice or a casual enlargement in the progress of experience from which it is quite disparate.

Reason through all its concepts and laws of the understanding which are sufficient to it for empirical use, that is, within the sensible world, finds in it no satisfaction, because ever-recurring questions deprive us of all hope of their complete solution. The transcendental Ideas which have that completion in view are such problems of reason. But it sees clearly that the sensuous world cannot contain this completion; neither, consequently, can all the concepts which serve merely for understanding the world of sense, for example, space and time, and what we have adduced under the name of pure concepts of the understanding. The sensuous world is nothing but a chain of appearances connected according to universal laws; it has therefore no subsistence by itself; it is not the thing in itself, and consequently must point to that which contains the basis of this appearance, to beings which cannot be known merely as appearances, but as things in themselves. In the knowledge of them alone can reason hope to satisfy its desire for completeness in proceeding from the conditioned to its conditions.

We have above (§§ 33 and 34) indicated the limits of reason with regard to all knowledge of mere beings of thought. Now, since the transcendental Ideas have made it necessary to approach them and thus have led us, as it were, to the spot where the occupied space (namely, experience) touches the void (that of which we can know nothing, namely, *noumena*), we can determine the bounds of pure reason. For in all bounds there is something positive (for example, a surface is the boundary of corporeal space, and is therefore itself a space; a line is a space, which is the boundary of the surface, a point the boundary of the line, but yet always a place in space), but limits contain mere negations. The limits pointed out in those paragraphs are not enough after we have discovered that beyond them there still lies something (though we can never know what it is in itself). For the question now is, What is the attitude of our reason in this connection of what we know with what we do not, and never shall, know? This is an actual connection of a known thing with one quite unknown (and which will always remain so), and though what is unknown should not become in the least more known—which we cannot even hope—yet the concept of this connection must be definite and capable of being rendered distinct.

We must therefore think an immaterial being, a world of understanding, and a Supreme Being (all mere *noumena*), because in them only, as things in themselves, reason finds that completion and satisfaction which it can never hope for in the derivation of appearances from their homogeneous grounds, and because these actually have reference to something distinct from them (and totally heterogeneous), as appearances always presuppose an object in itself and therefore suggest its existence whether we can know more of it or not.

But as we can never know these beings of understanding as they are in themselves, that is, as definite, yet must assume them as regards the sensible world and connect them with it by reason, we are at least able to think this connection by means of such concepts as express their relation to the world of sense. If we represent to ourselves a being of the understanding by nothing but pure concepts of the understanding, we then indeed represent nothing definite to ourselves, and consequently our concept has no significance; but if we think of it by properties borrowed from the sensuous world, it is no longer a being of understanding, but is conceived phenomenally and belongs to the sensible world. Let us take an instance from the notion of the Supreme Being.

The deistic conception is a quite pure concept of reason, but represents only a thing containing all reality, without being able to determine any one reality [in it]; because for that purpose an example must be taken from the world of sense, in which case I should have an object of sense only, not something quite heterogeneous which can never be an object of sense. Suppose I attribute to the Supreme Being understanding, for instance; I have no concept of an understanding other than my own, one that must receive its intuitions by the senses and which is occupied in bringing them under rules of the unity of consciousness. Then the elements of my concept would always lie in the appearance; I should, however, by the insufficiency of the appearance have to go beyond them to the concept of a being which neither depends upon appearances nor is bound up with them as conditions of its determination. But if I separate understanding from sensibility to obtain a pure understanding, then nothing remains but the mere form of thinking without intuition, by which form alone I can know nothing definite and consequently no object. For that purpose I should finally have to conceive another understanding, such as would intuit its objects but of which I have not the least concept, because the human understanding is discursive and can know only by means of general concepts. And the very same difficulties arise if we attribute a will to the Supreme Being, for I have this concept only by drawing it from my inner experience, and therefore from my dependence for satisfaction upon objects whose existence I require; and so the concept rests upon sensibility, which is absolutely incompatible with the pure concept of the Supreme Being.

Hume's objections to deism are weak, and affect only the proofs and not the deistic assertion itself. But as regards theism, which depends on a stricter determination of the concept of the Supreme Being, which in deism is merely transcendent, they are very strong and, as this concept is formed, in certain (in fact in all common) cases irrefutable. Hume always insists that by the mere concept of an original being to which we apply only ontological predicates (eternity, omnipresence, omnipotence) we think nothing definite, and that properties which could yield a concept *in concreto* would have to be superadded. He further insists that it is not enough to say it is cause, but we must explain the nature of its causality, for example, that it is that of an understanding and of a will. He then begins his attacks on the essential point itself, that is, theism, as he had previously directed his battery only against the proofs of deism, an attack which is not very dangerous to it in its consequences. All his dangerous arguments refer to anthropomorphism, which he holds to be inseparable from theism and to make it contradictory in itself; but if the former be abandoned, the latter must vanish with it and nothing remain but deism, of which nothing can come, which is of no value and which cannot serve as any foundation to religion or morals. If this anthropomorphism were really unavoidable, no proofs whatever of the existence of a Supreme Being, even were they all granted, could determine for us the concept of this Being without involving us in contradictions.

If we connect with the command to avoid all transcendent judgments of pure reason the command (which apparently conflicts with it) to proceed to concepts that lie beyond the field of its immanent (empirical) use, we discover that both can subsist together, but only at the boundary of all permitted use of reason. For this boundary belongs to the field of experience as well as to that of the beings of thought, and we are thereby taught how these so remarkable Ideas serve merely for marking the bounds of human reason. On the one hand, they give warning not boundlessly to extend knowledge of experience, as if nothing but world remained for us to know, and yet, on the other hand, not to transgress the bounds of experience and to think of judging about things beyond them as things in themselves.

But we stop at this boundary if we limit our judgment merely to the relation which the world may have to a Being whose very concept lies beyond all the knowledge which we can attain within the world. For we then do not attribute to the Supreme Being any of the properties in themselves by which we represent objects of experience, and thereby avoid *dogmatic* anthropomorphism; but we attribute them to the relation of this Being to the world and allow ourselves a *symbolical* anthropomorphism, which in fact concerns language only and not the object itself.

If I say that we are compelled to consider the world *as if* it were the work of a Supreme Understanding and Will, I really say nothing more than that a watch, a ship, a regiment, bears the same relation to the watchmaker, the shipbuilder, the commanding officer as the world of sense (or whatever constitutes the substratum of this complex of appearances) does to the unknown, which I do not hereby know as it is in itself but as it is for me, that is, in relation to the world of which I am a part.

§ 58. Such a cognition is one of analogy and does not signify (as is commonly understood) an imperfect similarity of two things, but a perfect similarity of relations between two quite dissimilar things.* By means of this analogy, however, there remains a concept of the Supreme Being sufficiently determined *for us,* though we have left out everything that could determine it absolutely or *in itself;* for we determine it as regards the world and hence as regards ourselves, and more do we not require. The attacks which Hume makes upon those who would determine this concept absolutely, by taking the materials for so doing from themselves and the world, do not affect us; and he cannot object to us that we have nothing left if we give up the objective anthropomorphism of the concept of the Supreme Being.

For let us assume at the outset (as Hume in his *Dialogues* makes Philo grant Cleanthes), as a necessary hypothesis, the deistic concept of the First Being, in which this Being is thought by the mere ontological predicates of substance, of cause, and so on. This must be done because reason, actuated in the sensible world by mere conditions which are themselves always conditional, cannot otherwise have any satisfaction; and it therefore can be done without falling into anthropomorphism (which transfers predicates from the world of sense to a Being quite distinct from the world) because those predicates are mere categories which, though they do not give a determinate concept of that Being, yet give a concept not limited to any conditions of sensibility. Thus nothing can prevent our predicating of this Being a causality through reason with regard to the world, and thus passing to theism, without being obliged to attribute to this Being itself this kind of reason, as a property inherent in it. For as to the former, the only possible way of prosecuting the use of reason (as regards all possible experience in complete harmony with itself) in the world of sense to the highest point is to assume a supreme reason as a cause of all the connections in the world. Such a principle must

*There is, for example, an analogy between the juridical relation of human actions and the mechanical relation of moving forces. I never can do anything to another man without giving him a right to do the same to me on the same conditions; just as no mass can act with its moving forces on another mass without thereby occasioning the other to react equally against it. Here right and moving force are quite dissimilar things, but in their relation there is complete similarity. By means of such an analogy, I can obtain a notion of the relation of things which absolutely are unknown to me. For instance, as the promotion of the welfare of children (= a) is to the love of parents (= b), so the welfare of the human species (= c) is to that unknown character in God (= x), which we call love; not as if it had the least similarity to any human inclination, but because we can suppose its relation to the world to be similar to that which things of the world bear one another. But the concept of relation in this case is a mere category, namely, the concept of cause, which has nothing to do with sensibility.

be quite advantageous to reason and can hurt it nowhere in its application to nature. As to the latter, reason is thereby not transferred as a property to the First Being in itself, but only to its relation to the world of sense, and so anthropomorphism is entirely avoided. For nothing is considered here but the cause of the form of reason which is perceived everywhere in the world, and reason is indeed attributed to the Supreme Being so far as it contains the ground of this form of reason in the world, but according to analogy only—that is, so far as this expression shows merely the relation which the Supreme Cause, unknown to us, has to the world in order to determine everything in it conformably to reason in the highest degree. We are thereby kept from using reason as an attribute for the purpose of conceiving God, but not from conceiving the world in such a manner as is necessary to have the greatest possible use of reason within it according to principle. We thereby acknowledge that the Supreme Being is quite inscrutable and even unthinkable in any definite way as to what it is in itself. We are thereby kept, on the one hand, from making a transcendent use of the concepts which we have of reason as an efficient cause (by means of the will), in order to determine the Divine Nature by properties which are only borrowed from human nature, and from losing ourselves in gross and extravagant notions; and, on the other hand, from deluging the contemplation of the world with hyperphysical modes of explanation according to our notions of human reason which we transfer to God, and so from losing for this contemplation its proper rôle, according to which it should be a rational study of mere nature and not a presumptuous derivation of its appearances from a Supreme Reason. The expression suited to our feeble notions is: we conceive the world *as if* it came, in its existence and internal plan, from a Supreme Reason. By this, on the one hand, we know the constitution which belongs to the world itself without pretending to determine the nature of its cause in itself; and, on the other hand, we transfer the ground of this constitution (of the form of reason in the world) upon the *relation* of the Supreme Cause to the world, without finding the world sufficient by itself for that purpose.*

Thus the difficulties which seem to oppose theism disappear by combining with Hume's principle, "not to carry the use of reason dogmatically beyond the field of all possible experience," this other principle, which he quite overlooked, "not to consider the field of experience as one which bounds itself in the eyes of our reason." The *Critique of Pure Reason* here points out the true mean between dogmatism, which Hume combats, and skepticism, which he would substitute for it—a mean which is not like others that we find advisable to determine for ourselves, as it were mechanically (by adopting something from one side and something from the other), and by which nobody is taught a better way, but such a one as can be precisely determined on principles.

§ 59. At the beginning of this note I made use of the metaphor of a boundary, in order to establish the limits of reason in regard to its suitable use. The world of sense contains merely appearances, which are not things in themselves; but the understanding, because it recognizes that the objects of experience are mere appearances, must assume that there are things in themselves, namely, *noumena*. In our reason both are comprehended, and the question is, How does reason proceed to set boundaries to the understanding as regards both these fields? Experience, which contains all that belongs to the sensible world, does not bound itself; it only proceeds in every case from the

---

*I may say that the causality of the Supreme Cause holds the same place with regard to the world that human reason does with regard to its works of art. Here the nature of the Supreme Cause itself remains unknown to me; I only compare its effects (the order of the world), which I know, and their conformity to reason to the effects of human reason, which I also know; and hence I term the former "reason," without attributing to it on that account what I understand in man by this term, or attaching to it anything else known to me as its property.

conditioned to some other equally conditioned object. That which bounds it must lie quite without it, and this is the field of the pure beings of the understanding. But this field, so far as the *determination* of the nature of these beings is concerned, is an empty space for us; and apart from dogmatically defined concepts, we cannot pass beyond the field of possible experience. But as a boundary itself is something positive, which belongs to that which lies within as well as to the space that lies without the given content, it is still an actual positive cognition which reason only acquires by enlarging itself to this boundary, yet without attempting to pass it because it there finds itself in the presence of an empty space in which it can conceive forms of things, but not things themselves. But the setting of a boundary to the field of the understanding by something which is otherwise unknown to it is still a cognition which belongs to reason even at this point, and by which it is neither confined within the sensible nor strays beyond it, but only limits itself, as befits the knowledge of a boundary, to the relation between that which lies beyond it and that which is contained within it.

Natural theology is such a concept at the boundary of human reason, being constrained to look beyond this boundary to the Idea of a Supreme Being (and, for practical purposes, to that of an intelligible world also), not in order to determine anything relatively to this pure being of the understanding, and thus to determine something that lies beyond the world of sense, but in order to guide the use of reason within it according to principles of the greatest possible (theoretical as well as practical) unity. For this purpose, it makes use of the reference of the world of sense to an independent reason as the cause of all its connections. Thereby it does not just *invent* a being, but, as beyond the sensible world there must be something that can be thought only by the pure understanding, it determines that something in this particular way, though only of course by analogy.

And thus there remains our original proposition, which is the *résumé* of the whole *Critique:* "Reason by all its *a priori* principles never teaches us anything more than objects of possible experience, and even of these nothing more than can be known in experience." But this limitation does not prevent reason from leading us to the objective boundary of experience, namely, to the relation to something which is not itself an object of experience but is the ground of all experience. Reason does not, however, teach us anything concerning the thing in itself; it only instructs us as regards its own complete and highest use in the field of possible experience. But this is all that can be reasonably desired in the present case, and with it we have cause to be satisfied.

§ 60. Thus we have fully exhibited metaphysics, in its subjective possibility, as it is actually given in the natural predisposition of human reason and in that which constitutes the essential end of its pursuit. Though we have found that this merely natural use of such a predisposition of our reason, if no discipline arising only from a scientific critique bridles and sets limits to it, involves it in transcendent and specious inferences and really conflicting dialectical inferences, and this fallacious metaphysics is not only unnecessary as regards the promotion of our knowledge of nature but even disadvantageous to it, there yet remains a problem worthy of investigation, which is to find out the natural ends intended by this disposition to transcendent concepts in our nature, because everything that lies in nature must be originally intended for some useful purpose.

Such an inquiry is of a doubtful nature, and I acknowledge that what I can say about it is conjecture only, like every speculation about the ultimate ends of nature. Such conjecture may be allowed me here, for the question does not concern the objective validity of metaphysical judgments but our natural predisposition to them, and therefore does not belong to the system of metaphysics but to anthropology.

When I compare all the transcendental Ideas, the totality of which constitutes the proper problem of natural pure reason, compelling it to quit the mere contemplation of nature, to transcend all possible experience, and in this endeavor to produce the thing (be it knowledge or fiction) called metaphysics, I think I perceive that the aim of this natural tendency is to free our concepts from the fetters of experience and from the limits of the mere contemplation of nature so far as at least to open to us a field containing mere objects for the pure understanding which no sensibility can reach, not indeed for the purpose of speculatively occupying ourselves with them (for there we can find no ground to stand on), but in order that practical principles [may be assumed as at least possible]; for practical principles, unless they find scope for their necessary expectation and hope, could not expand to the universality which reason unavoidably requires from a moral point of view.

So I find that the psychological Idea (however little it may reveal to me the nature of the human soul, which is elevated above all concepts of experience), shows the insufficiency of these concepts plainly enough and thereby deters me from materialism, a psychological concept which is unfit for any explanation of nature and which moreover confines reason in practical respects. The cosmological Ideas, by the obvious insufficiency of all possible knowledge of nature to satisfy reason in its legitimate inquiry, serve in the same manner to keep us from naturalism, which asserts nature to be sufficient for itself. Finally, all natural necessity in the sensible world is conditional, as it always presupposes the dependence of things upon others, and unconditional necessity must be sought only in the unity of a cause different from the world of sense. But as the causality of this cause, in its turn, were it merely nature, could never render the existence of the contingent (as its consequent) comprehensible, reason frees itself by means of the theological Idea from fatalism (both as a blind natural necessity in the coherence of nature itself, without a first principle, and as a blind causality of this principle itself) and leads to the concept of a cause possessing freedom or of a Supreme Intelligence. Thus the transcendental Ideas serve, if not to instruct us positively, at least to destroy the narrowing assertions of materialism, of naturalism, and of fatalism, and thus to afford scope for the moral Ideas beyond the field of speculation. These considerations, I should think, explain in some measure the natural predisposition of which I spoke.

The practical value, which a merely speculative science may have, lies without the bounds of this science, and can therefore be considered as a scholium merely, and like all scholia does not form part of the science itself. This application, however, surely lies within the bounds of philosophy, especially of philosophy drawn from the pure sources of reason, where its speculative use in metaphysics must necessarily be at one with its practical use in morals. Hence the unavoidable dialectic of pure reason, considered in metaphysics as a natural tendency, deserves to be explained not as a mere illusion, which is to be removed, but also, if possible, as a natural provision as regards its end, though this task, a work of supererogation, cannot justly be assigned to metaphysics proper.

The solutions of these questions which are treated in the *Critique** should be considered a second scholium, which, however, has a greater affinity with the subject of metaphysics. For there certain rational principles are expounded which determine *a priori* the order of nature or rather of the understanding, which seeks nature's laws through experience. They seem to be constitutive and legislative with regard to experience, though they spring from pure reason, which cannot be considered, like the understanding, as a principle of possible experience. Now whether or not this harmony rests

Critique of Pure Reason, "Regulative Use of the Ideas of Pure Reason."

upon the fact that, just as nature does not inhere in appearances or in their source (the sensibility) itself, but only in the relation of the latter to the understanding, a thorough unity in applying the understanding to bring about an entirety of all possible experience (in a system) can only belong to the understanding when in relation to reason, with the consequence that experience is in this way mediately subordinate to the legislation of reason—this question may be discussed by those who desire to trace the nature of reason even beyond its use in metaphysics, into the general principles, which will make a history of nature in general systematic. I have presented this task as important, but not attempted its solution in the book itself.*

And thus I conclude the analytical solution of the main question which I had proposed: "How is metaphysics in general possible?" by ascending from the data of its actual use, as shown in its consequences, to the grounds of its possibility.

SOLUTION OF THE GENERAL QUESTION OF THE *PROLEGOMENA*

How Is Metaphysics Possible as Science?

Metaphysics, as a natural disposition of reason, is actual; but if considered by itself alone (as the analytical solution of the third principal question showed), dialectical and illusory. If we think of taking principles from it, and in using them follow the natural, but on that account not less false, illusion, we can never produce science, but only a vain dialectical art, in which one school may outdo another but none can ever acquire a just and lasting approbation.

In order that as a science metaphysics may be entitled to claim, not mere fallacious plausibility, but insight and conviction, a critique of reason itself must exhibit the whole stock of *a priori* concepts, their division according to their various sources (sensibility, understanding, and reason), together with a complete table of them, the analysis of all these concepts, with all their consequences, and especially the possibility of synthetical knowledge *a priori* by means of a deduction of these concepts, the principles and the bounds of their application, all in a complete system. Critique, therefore, and critique alone contains in itself the whole well-proved and well-tested plan, and even all the means, required to establish metaphysics as a science; by other ways and means it is impossible. The question here, therefore, is not so much how this performance is possible as how to set it going and to induce men of clear heads to quit their hitherto perverted and fruitless cultivation for one that will not deceive, and how such a union for the common end may best be directed.

This much is certain, that whoever has once tasted critique will be ever after disgusted with all dogmatic twaddle which he formerly had to put up with because his reason had to have something and could find nothing better for its support.

Critique stands in the same relation to the common metaphysics of the schools as chemistry does to alchemy, or as astronomy to the astrology of the fortune teller. I pledge myself that nobody who has thought through and grasped the principles of critique, even in these *Prolegomena* only, will ever return to that old and sophistical

---

*Throughout in the *Critique* I never lost sight of the plan not to neglect anything, were it ever so recondite, that could render the inquiry into the nature of pure reason complete. Everybody may afterward carry his research as far as he pleases, when he has been merely shown what yet remains to be done. This can reasonably be expected of him who has made it his business to survey the whole field, in order to consign it to others for future cultivation and allotment. And to this branch both the scholia belong, which will hardly recommend themselves because of their dryness to amateurs, and hence are added here for connoisseurs only.

pseudo-science; but will rather with a certain delight look forward to metaphysics, which is now indeed in his power, requiring no more preparatory discoveries and affording permanent satisfaction to reason at last. For here is an advantage upon which, of all possible sciences, metaphysics alone can with certainty reckon: that it can be brought to such completion and fixity as to be in need of no further change or be subject to any augmentation by new discoveries; because here reason has the sources of its knowledge in itself, not in objects and their observation, by which its stock of knowledge could be further increased. When, therefore, it has exhibited the fundamental laws of its faculty completely and so definitely as to avoid all misunderstanding, there remains nothing further which pure reason could know *a priori;* nay, there is no ground even to raise further questions. The sure prospect of knowledge so definite and so compact has a peculiar charm, even though we should set aside all its advantages, of which I shall hereafter speak.

All false art, all vain wisdom, lasts its time but finally destroys itself, and its highest culture is also the epoch of its decay. That this time is come for metaphysics appears from the state into which it has fallen among all learned nations, despite all the zeal with which other sciences of every kind are prosecuted. The old arrangement of our university studies still preserves its shadow. Now and then an academy of science tempts men by offering prizes to write some essay on it, but it is no longer numbered among the rigorous sciences; and let anyone judge for himself how a sophisticated man, if he were called a great metaphysician, would receive the compliment, which may be well meant but is scarcely envied by anybody.

Yet, though the period of the downfall of all dogmatic metaphysics has undoubtedly arrived, we are yet far from being able to say that the period of its regeneration is come by means of a thorough and complete critique of reason. All transitions from a tendency to its contrary pass through the stage of indifference, and this moment is the most dangerous for an author but, in my opinion, the most favorable for the science. For when party spirit has died out by a total dissolution of former connections, minds are in the best state to listen to several proposals for an organization according to a new plan.

When I say that I hope these *Prolegomena* will excite investigation in the field of critique and afford a new and promising object to sustain the general spirit of philosophy, which seems on its speculative side to want sustenance, I can imagine beforehand that everyone whom the thorny paths of my *Critique* have tired and put out of humor will ask me upon what I found this hope. My answer is: upon the irresistible law of necessity.

That the human mind will ever give up metaphysical researches is as little to be expected as that we, to avoid inhaling impure air, should prefer to give up breathing altogether. There will, therefore, always be metaphysics in the world; nay, everyone, especially every reflective man, will have it and, for want of a recognized standard, will shape it for himself after his own pattern. What has hitherto been called metaphysics cannot satisfy any critical mind, but to forego it entirely is impossible; therefore a *Critique of Pure Reason* itself must now be attempted or, if one exists, investigated and brought to the full test, because there is no other means of supplying this pressing want which is something more than mere thirst for knowledge.

Ever since I have come to know critique, whenever I finish reading a book of metaphysical contents which, by the preciseness of its notions, by variety, order, and an easy style, was not only entertaining but also helpful, I cannot help asking, "Has this author indeed advanced metaphysics a single step?" The learned men whose works have been useful to me in other respects and always contributed to the culture of my mental powers will, I hope, forgive me for saying that I have never been able to find either their essays or my own less important ones (though self-love may recommend them to me) to have advanced the science of metaphysics in the least.

There is a very obvious reason for this: metaphysics did not then exist as a science, nor can it be gathered piecemeal; but its germ must be fully preformed in critique. But, in order to prevent all misconception, we must remember what has been already said—that, by the analytical treatment of our concepts, the understanding gains indeed a great deal; but the science of metaphysics is thereby not in the least advanced, because these dissections of concepts are nothing but the materials from which the intention is to carpenter our science. Let the concepts of substance and of accident be ever so well dissected and determined; all this is very well as a preparation for some future use. But if we cannot prove that in all which exists the substance endures and only the accidents vary, our science is not the least advanced by all our analyses.

Metaphysics has hitherto never been able to prove *a priori* either this proposition or that of sufficient reason, still less any more complex theorem such as belongs to psychology or cosmology, or indeed any synthetical proposition. By all its analyzing, therefore, nothing is affected, nothing obtained or forwarded; and the science, after all this bustle and noise, still remains as it was in the days of Aristotle, though there were far better preparations for it than of old if only the clue to synthetical cognitions had been discovered.

If anyone thinks himself offended, he is at liberty to refute my charge by producing a single synthetical proposition belonging to metaphysics which he would prove dogmatically *a priori;* for until he has actually performed this feat I shall not grant that he has truly advanced the science, even if this proposition should be sufficiently confirmed by common experience. No demand can be more moderate or more equitable and, in the (inevitably certain) event of its nonperformance, no assertion more just than that hitherto metaphysics has never existed as a science.

But there are two things which, in case the challenge be accepted, I must deprecate: first, trifling about probability and conjecture, which are suited as little to metaphysics as to geometry; and secondly, a decision by means of the magic wand of so-called common sense, which does not convince everyone but accommodates itself to personal peculiarities.

For as to the former, nothing can be more absurd than in metaphysics, a philosophy from pure reason, to think of grounding our judgments upon probability and conjecture. Everything that is to be known *a priori* is thereby announced as apodictically certain, and must therefore be proved in this way. We might as well think of grounding geometry or arithmetic upon conjectures. As to the calculus of probabilities in the latter, it does not contain probable but perfectly certain judgments concerning the degree of the possibility of certain cases under given uniform conditions, which, in the sum of all possible cases, must infallibly happen according to the rule, though the rule is not sufficiently definite with respect to every single instance. Conjectures (by means of induction and of analogy) can be suffered in an empirical science of nature only, yet even there at least the possibility of what we assume must be quite certain.

The appeal to common sense is even more absurd—if anything more absurd can be imagined—when it is a question of concept and principles claimed as valid, not in so far as they hold with regard to experience, but beyond the conditions of experience. For what is common sense? It is normal good sense, so far it judges right. But what is normal good sense? It is the faculty of the knowledge and use of rules *in concreto,* as distinguished from the speculative understanding, which is a faculty of knowing rules *in abstracto.* Common sense can hardly understand the rule that every event is determined by means of its cause and can never comprehend it in its generality. It therefore demands an example from experience; and when it hears that this rule means nothing but what it always thought when a pane was broken or a kitchen utensil missing, it then understands the principle and grants it. Common sense, therefore, is only of use so far as it can see its rules (though they actually are *a priori*) confirmed by experience; consequently to comprehend them *a priori,* or independently of experience, belongs to the speculative understanding and lies quite beyond the horizon of common sense. But the province of metaphysics is entirely confined to the latter kind of knowledge, and it is certainly a bad sign of common sense to appeal to it as a witness, for it cannot here form any opinion whatever, and men look down upon it with contempt until they are in straits and can find in their speculation neither advice nor help.

It is a common subterfuge of those false friends of common sense (who occasionally prize it highly, but usually despise it) to say that there must surely be at all events some propositions which are immediately certain and of which there is no occasion to give any proof, or even any account at all, because we otherwise could never stop inquiring into the grounds of our judgments. But if we except the principle of contradiction, which is not sufficient to show the truth of synthetical judgments, they can never adduce, in proof of this privilege, anything else indubitable which they can immediately ascribe to common sense, except mathematical propositions, such as twice two make four, between two points there is but one straight line, etc. But these judgments are radically different from those of metaphysics. For in mathematics I can by thinking itself construct whatever I represent to myself as possible by a concept: I add to the first two the other two, one by one, and myself make the number four, or I draw in thought from one point to another all manner of lines, equal as well as unequal; yet I can draw one only which is like itself in all its parts. But I cannot, by all my power of thinking, extract from the concept of a thing the concept of something else whose existence is necessarily connected with the former; for this I must call in experience. And though my understanding furnishes me *a priori* (yet only in reference to possible experience) with the concept of such a connection (that is causation), I cannot exhibit it, like the concepts of mathematics, by intuiting it *a priori,* and so show its possibility *a priori.* This concept, together with the principles of its application, always requires, if it shall hold *a priori*—as is requisite in metaphysics—a justification and deduction of its possibility, because we cannot otherwise know how far it holds good and whether it can be used in experience only or beyond it also.

Therefore in metaphysics, as a speculative science of pure reason, we can never appeal to common sense, but may do so only when we are forced to surrender it and to renounce all pure speculative knowledge which must always be theoretical cognition, and thereby under some circumstances to forego metaphysics itself and its instruction for the sake of adopting a rational faith which alone may be possible for us, sufficient to our wants, and perhaps even more salutary than knowledge itself. For in this case the state of affairs is quite altered. Metaphysics must be science, not only as a whole, but in all its parts; otherwise it is nothing at all; because, as speculation of pure reason, it finds a hold only on common convictions. Beyond its field, however, probability and common sense may be used justly and with advantage, but on quite special principles, the importance of which always depends on their reference to practical life.

This is what I hold myself justified in requiring for the possibility of metaphysics as a science.

APPENDIX

ON WHAT CAN BE DONE TO MAKE METAPHYSICS AS A SCIENCE ACTUAL

Since all the ways heretofore taken have failed to attain the goal, and since without a preceding critique of pure reason it is not likely ever to be attained, the present attempt has a right to an accurate and careful examination, unless it be thought more advisable to give up all pretensions to metaphysics, to which, if men but would consistently adhere to their purpose, no objection can be made.

If we take the course of things as it is, not as it ought to be, there are two sorts of judgments: (1) one a judgment which precedes investigation (in our case one in which the reader from his own metaphysics pronounces judgment on the *Critique of Pure Reason,* which was intended to discuss the very possibility of metaphysics); (2) the other a judgment subsequent to investigation. In the latter, the reader is enabled to ignore for a while the consequences of the critical researches that may be repugnant to his formerly adopted metaphysics, and first examines the grounds whence those consequences are derived. If what common metaphysics propounds were demonstrably certain, as is the case with the theorems of geometry, the former way of judging would hold good. For if the consequences of certain principles are repugnant to established truths, these principles are false and without further inquiry to be repudiated. But if metaphysics does not possess a stock of indisputably certain (synthetical) propositions, and should it even be the case that there are a number of them, which, though among the most plausible, are by their consequences in mutual conflict, and if no sure criterion of the truth of peculiarly metaphysical (synthetical) propositions is to be met with in it, then the former way of judging is not admissible, but the investigation of the principles of the *Critique* must precede all judgments as to its value.

A SPECIMEN OF A JUDGMENT OF THE CRITIQUE PRIOR TO ITS EXAMINATION

Such a judgment is to be found in the *Göttingische gelehrte Anzeigen,* in the supplement to the third part, of January 19, 1782, pages 40 *et seq.*

When an author who is familiar with the subject of his work and endeavors to present his independent reflections in its elaboration falls into the hands of a reviewer who, in his turn, is keen enough to discern the points on which the worth or worthlessness of the book rests, who does not cling to words but goes to the heart of the subject, sifting and testing the principles which the author takes as his point of departure, the severity of the judgment may indeed displease the author, but the public does not care, as it gains thereby. And the author himself may be contented, as an opportunity of correcting or explaining his positions is afforded to him at an early date by the examination of a competent judge, in such a manner that if he believes himself fundamentally right, he can remove in time any stumbling block that might hurt the success of his work.

I find myself, with my reviewer, in quite another position. He seems not to see at all the real matter of the investigation with which (successfully or unsuccessfully) I have been occupied. It is either impatience at thinking out a lengthy work, or vexation at a threatened reform of a science in which he believed he had brought everything to perfection long ago, or, what I am reluctant to suspect, real narrow-mindedness that prevents him from ever carrying his thoughts beyond his school metaphysics. In short, he passes impatiently in review a long series of propositions, of which, without knowing their premises, one can understand nothing, intersperses here and there his censure, the reason of which the reader understands just as little as the propositions against which it is directed; and hence [his report] can neither serve the public nor damage me in the judgment of experts. I should, for these reasons, have passed over this judgment altogether, were it not that it may afford me occasion for some explanations which may in some cases save the readers of these *Prolegomena* from a misconception.

In order to take a position from which my reviewer could most easily set the whole work in a most unfavorable light, without venturing to trouble himself with any special investigation, he begins and ends by saying: "This work is a system of transcendental (or, as he translates it, of higher*) idealism."

A glance at this line soon showed me the sort of criticism that I had to expect, much as though the reviewer were one who had never seen or heard of geometry, having found a Euclid and coming upon various figures in turning over its leaves, were to say, on being asked his opinion of it: "The work is a textbook of drawing; the author introduces a peculiar terminology, in order to give dark, incomprehensible directions, which in the end teach nothing more than what everyone can effect by a fair natural accuracy of eye, etc."

Let us see, in the meantime, what sort of an idealism it is that goes through my whole work, although it does not by a long way constitute the soul of the system.

The dictum of all genuine idealists, from the Eleatic school to Bishop Berkeley, is contained in this formula: "All knowledge through the senses and experience is nothing but sheer illusion, and only in the ideas of the pure understanding and reason is there truth."

The principle that throughout dominates and determines my idealism, is on the contrary: "All knowledge of things merely from pure understanding or pure reason is nothing but sheer illusion, and only in experience is there truth."

But this is directly contrary to idealism proper. How came I then to use this expression for quite an opposite purpose, and how came my reviewer to see it everywhere?

The solution of this difficulty rests on something that could have been very easily understood from the general bearing of the work if the reader had only desired to understand it. Space and time, together with all that they contain, are not things in themselves or their qualities, but belong merely to the appearances of the things in themselves. Up to this point I am one in confession with the above idealists. But these, and among them more particularly Berkeley, regarded space as a mere empirical representation that, like the appearances it contains, is, together with its determinations, known to us only by means of experience or perception. I, on the contrary, prove in the first place that space (and also time, which Berkeley did not consider) and all its

---

*By no means "higher." High towers and metaphysically great men resembling them, round both of which there is commonly much wind, are not for me. My place is the fruitful bathos of experience; and the word "transcendental," the meaning of which is so often explained by me but not once grasped by my reviewer (so carelessly has he regarded everything), does not signify something passing beyond all experience but something that indeed precedes it *a priori,* but that is intended simply to make knowledge of experience possible. If these conceptions overstep experience, their employment is termed "transcendent," which must be distinguished from the immanent use, that is, use restricted to experience. All misunderstandings of this kind have been sufficiently guarded against in the work itself, but my reviewer found his advantage in misunderstanding me.

a priori determinations can be known by us, because, no less than time, it inheres in us as a pure form of our sensibility before all perception or experience and makes all intuition of the form, and therefore all appearances, possible. It follows from this that, as truth rests on universal and necessary laws as its criteria, experience, according to Berkeley, can have no criteria of truth because its phenomena* (according to him) have nothing *a priori* at their foundation, whence it follows that experience is nothing but sheer illusion; whereas with us, space and time (in conjunction with the pure concept of the understanding) prescribe their law to all possible experience *a priori* and, at the same time, afford the certain criterion for distinguishing truth from illusion therein.

My so-called (properly critical) idealism is of quite a special character, in that it subverts the ordinary idealism and in that only through it all *a priori* knowledge, even that of geometry, receives objective reality, which, without my demonstrated ideality of space and time, could not be maintained by the most zealous realists. This being the state of the case, I could wish, in order to avoid all misunderstanding, to have named this conception of mine otherwise, but to alter it altogether is probably impossible. It may be permitted me however, in future, as has been above intimated, to term it "formal" or, better still, "critical" idealism, to distinguish it from the dogmatic idealism of Berkeley and from the skeptical idealism of Descartes.

Beyond this, I find nothing remarkable in the judgment of my book. The reviewer makes sweeping criticisms, a mode prudently chosen, since it does not betray one's own knowledge or ignorance; a single thorough criticism in detail, had it touched the main question, as is only fair, would have exposed either my error or my reviewer's measure of insight into this species of research. It was, moreover, not a badly conceived plan, in order at once to take from readers (who are accustomed to form their conceptions of books from newspaper reports) the desire to read the book itself, to pour out in one breath a number of passages in succession which, torn from their connection with their premises and explanations, must necessarily sound senseless, especially considering how antipathetic they are to all school-metaphysics; to exhaust the reader's patience *ad nauseam,* and then, having made me acquainted with the lucid proposition that persistent illusion is truth, to conclude with the crude paternal moralization: to what end, then, the quarrel with accepted language; to what end, and whence, the idealistic distinction? A judgment which seeks all that is characteristic of my book, first supposed to be metaphysically heterodox, in a mere innovation of the nomenclature proves clearly that my would-be judge has understood nothing of the subject and, in addition, has not understood himself.**

My reviewer speaks like a man who is conscious of important and superior insight which he keeps hidden, for I am aware of nothing recent with respect to meta-

---

*Idealism proper always has a mystical tendency, and can have no other, but mine is solely designed for the purpose of comprehending the possibility of our *a priori* knowledge of objects of experience, which is a problem never hitherto solved or even suggested. In this way all mystical idealism falls to the ground, for (as may be seen in Plato) it inferred from our cognitions *a priori* (even from those of geometry) another intuition different from that of the senses (namely, an intellectual intuition), because it never occurred to anyone that the senses themselves might intuit *a priori*.

**The reviewer often fights with his own shadow. When I oppose the truth of experience to dream, he never thinks that I am here speaking simply of the well-known *somnio objective sumto* of the Wolffian philosophy, which is merely formal, and with which the distinction between sleeping and waking is in no way concerned—a distinction which can indeed have no place in a transcendental philosophy. For the rest, he calls my deduction of the categories and table of the principles of the understanding "common well-known axioms of logic and ontology, expressed in an idealistic manner." The reader need only consult these *Prolegomena* upon this point to convince himself that a more miserable and historically incorrect judgment could hardly be made.

physics that could justify his tone. But he should not withhold his discoveries from the world, for there are doubtless many who, like myself, have not been able to find in all the fine things that have for long past been written in this department anything that has advanced the science by so much as a finger's breadth; we find indeed the giving a new point to definitions, the supplying of lame proofs with new crutches, the adding to the crazy-quilt of metaphysics fresh patches or changing its pattern. But all this is not what the world requires. The world is tired of metaphysical assertions; it wants [to know] the possibility of this science, the sources from which certainty therein can be derived, and certain criteria by which it may distinguish the dialectical illusion of pure reason from truth. To this the critic seems to possess a key, otherwise he would never have spoken out in such a high tone.

But I am inclined to suspect that no such requirement of the science has ever entered his thoughts, for in that case he would have directed his judgment to this point, and even a mistaken attempt in such an important matter would have won his respect. If that be the case, we are once more good friends. He may penetrate as deeply as he likes into his metaphysics, without any one hindering him; only as concerns that which lies outside metaphysics, its sources, which are to be found in reason, he cannot form a judgment. That my suspicion is not without foundation is proved by the fact that he does not mention a word about the possibility of synthetic knowledge *a priori,* the special problem upon the solution of which the fate of metaphysics wholly rests and upon which my *Critique* (as well as the present *Prolegomena*) entirely hinges. The idealism he encountered and which he hung upon was only taken up in the doctrine as the sole means of solving the above problem (although it received its confirmation on other grounds), and hence he must have shown either that the above problem does not possess the importance I attribute to it (even in these *Prolegomena*) or that, by my conception of appearances, it is either not solved at all or can be better solved in another way; but I do not find a word of this in the criticism. The reviewer, then, understands nothing of my work and possibly also nothing of the spirit and essential nature of metaphysics itself; and it is not, what I would rather assume, the hurry of a reviewer to finish his review, incensed at the labor of plodding through so many obstacles, that threw an unfavorable shadow over the work lying before him and made its fundamental features unrecognizable.

There is a good deal to be done before a learned journal, it matters not with what care its writers may be selected, can maintain its otherwise well-merited reputation in the field of metaphysics as elsewhere. Other sciences and branches of knowledge have their standard. Mathematics has it in itself, history and theology in profane or sacred books, natural science and the art of medicine in mathematics and experience, jurisprudence in law books, and even matters of taste in the examples of the ancients. But for the judgment of the thing called metaphysics, the standard has yet to be found. I have made an attempt to determine it, as well as its use. What is to be done, then, until it be found when works of this kind have to be judged of? If they are of a dogmatic character, one may do what one likes; no one will play the master over others here for long before someone else appears to deal with him in the same manner. If, however, they are critical in character, not indeed with reference to other works but to reason itself, so that the standard of judgment cannot be assumed but has first of all to be sought for, then, though objection and blame may indeed be permitted, yet a certain degree of leniency is indispensable, since the need is common to us all and the lack of the necessary insight makes the high-handed attitude of judge unwarranted.

In order, however, to connect my defense with the interest of the philosophical commonwealth, I propose a test, which must be decisive as to the mode whereby all metaphysical investigations may be directed to their common purpose. This is nothing more than what mathematicians have done in establishing the advantage of their methods by competition. I challenge my critic to demonstrate, as is only just, on *a priori* grounds, in his own way, any single really metaphysical proposition asserted by him. Being metaphysical, it must be synthetical and known *a priori* from concepts, but it may also be any one of the most indispensable propositions, as, for instance, the principle of the persistence of substance or of the necessary determination of events in the world by their causes. If he cannot do this (silence however is confession), he must admit that, since metaphysics without apodictic certainty of propositions of this kind is nothing at all, its possibility or impossibility must before all things be established in a critique of pure reason. Thus he is bound either to confess that my principles in the *Critique* are correct, or he must prove their invalidity. But as I can already foresee that, confidently as he has hitherto relied on the certainty of his principles, when it comes to a strict test he will not find a single one in the whole range of metaphysics he can boldly bring forward, I will concede to him an advantageous condition, which can only be expected in such a competition, and will relieve him of the *onus probandi* by laying it on myself.

He finds in these *Prolegomena* and in my *Critique** eight propositions, of which one in each pair contradicts the other, but each of which necessarily belongs to metaphysics, by which it must either be accepted or rejected (although there is not one that has not in its time been assumed by some philosopher). Now he has the liberty of selecting any one of these eight propositions at his pleasure and accepting it without any proof, of which I shall make him a present, but only one (for waste of time will be just as little serviceable to him as to me), and then of attacking my proof of the opposite proposition. If I can save this one and at the same time show that, according to principles which every dogmatic metaphysics must necessarily recognize, the opposite of the proposition adopted by him can be just as clearly proved, it is thereby established that metaphysics has an hereditary failing not to be explained, much less set aside, until we ascend to its birthplace, pure reason itself. And thus my *Critique* must either be accepted or a better one take its place; at least it must be studied, which is the only thing I now require. If, on the other hand, I cannot save my demonstration, then a synthetic proposition *a priori* from dogmatic principles is to be reckoned to the score of my opponent, and I shall deem my impeachment of ordinary metaphysics unjust and pledge myself to recognize his stricture on my *Critique* as justified (although this would not be the consequence by a long way). To this end it would be necessary, it seems to me, that he should step out of his incognito. Otherwise I do not see how it could be avoided that, instead of dealing with one, I should be honored or besieged by several challenges coming from anonymous and unqualified opponents.

PROPOSALS AS TO AN INVESTIGATION OF THE "CRITIQUE"
UPON WHICH A JUDGMENT MAY FOLLOW

I feel obliged to the learned public even for the silence with which it for a long time honored my *Critique,* for this proves at least a postponement of judgment and some supposition that, in a work leaving all beaten tracks and striking out on a new path, in which one cannot at once perhaps so easily find one's way, something may perchance

---

*[The reference is to the theses and antitheses of the antinomies.—L.W.B.]

lie from which an important but at present dead branch of human knowledge may derive new life and productiveness. Hence may have originated a solicitude for the as yet tender shoot, lest it be destroyed by a hasty judgment. A specimen of a judgment, delayed for the above reasons, is now before my eye in the *Gothaische gelehrte Zeitung,* the thoroughness of which—disregarding my praise, which might be suspicious—every reader will himself perceive from the clear and unperverted presentation of a fragment of one of the first principles of my work.

Since an extensive structure cannot be judged of as a whole from a hurried glance, I suggest that it be tested piece by piece from the ground up, and in this, the present *Prolegomena* may fitly be used as a general outline with which the work itself may occasionally be compared. This notion, if it were founded on nothing more than my conceit of importance, such as vanity commonly attributes to all of one's own productions, would be immodest and would deserve to be repudiated with indignation. But now the interests of speculative philosophy have arrived at the point of total extinction, while human reason hangs upon them with inextinguishable affection; and only after having been ceaselessly deceived, does it vainly attempt to change this into indifference.

In our thinking age, it is not to be supposed but that many deserving men would use any good opportunity of working for the common interest of the more and more enlightened reason, if there were only some hope of attaining the goal. Mathematics, natural science, laws, arts, even morality, etc., do not completely fill the soul; there is always a space left over reserved for pure and speculative reason, the emptiness of which prompts us to seek in vagaries, buffooneries, and mysticism for what seems to be employment and entertainment, but what actually is mere pastime undertaken in order to deaden the troublesome voice of reason, which, in accordance with its nature, requires something that can satisfy it and does not merely subserve other ends or the interests of our inclinations. A consideration, therefore, which is concerned only with reason as it exists for it itself has, as I may reasonably suppose, a great fascination for everyone who has attempted thus to extend his conceptions, and I may even say a greater fascination than any other theoretical branch of knowledge, for which he would not willingly exchange it because here all other branches of knowledge and even purposes must meet and unite themselves in a whole.

I offer, therefore, these *Prolegomena* as a sketch and textbook for this investigation, and not the work itself. Although I am even now perfectly satisfied with the latter as far as contents, order, and mode of presentation, and the care that I have expended in weighing and testing every sentence before writing it down are concerned (for it has taken me years to satisfy myself fully, not only as regards the whole, but in some cases even as to the sources of one particular proposition); yet I am not quite satisfied with my exposition in some sections of the Doctrine of Elements,* as for instance in the deduction of the concepts of the understanding or in the chapter on the paralogisms of pure reason, because a certain diffuseness takes away from their clearness, and in place of them what is here said in the *Prolegomena* respecting these sections may be made the basis of the test.**

It is the boast of the Germans that, where steady and continuous industry are requisite, they can carry things farther than other nations. If this opinion be well founded,

---

*[The first part of the *Critique of Pure Reason,* the other being the Methodology.—L.W.B.]

**[These sections were almost completely rewritten in the second edition of the *Critique* (1787), though the new deduction of the categories does not follow the argument of the *Prolegomena.*—L.W.B.]

an opportunity, a task, presents itself the successful issue of which we can scarcely doubt and in which all thinking men can equally take part, though they have hitherto been unsuccessful in accomplishing it and in thus confirming the above good opinion. This is chiefly because the science in question is of so peculiar a kind that it can all at once be brought to completion and to that enduring state beyond which it can never be developed, in the least degree enlarged by later discoveries, or changed if we leave out of account adornment by greater clearness in some places or additional uses. This is an advantage no other science has or can have, because there is none so fully isolated and independent of others and so exclusively concerned with the faculty of cognition pure and simple. And the present moment seems not to be unfavorable to my expectation, for just now, in Germany, no one seems to know wherewith to occupy himself, apart from the so-called useful sciences, so as to pursue not mere play but a business possessing an enduring purpose.

To discover how the endeavors of the learned may be united in such a purpose I must leave to others. In the meantime, it is not my intention to persuade anyone merely to follow my propositions or even to flatter me with the hope that he will do so; but attacks, repetitions, limitations, or confirmation, completion, and extension, as the case may be, should be appended. If the matter be but investigated from its foundation, it cannot fail that a system, albeit not my own, shall be erected that shall be a possession for future generations for which they may have reason to be grateful.

It would lead us too far here to show what kind of metaphysics may be expected when the principles of criticism have been perfected and how, though the old false feathers have been pulled out, it need by no means appear poor and reduced to an insignificant figure but may be in other respects richly and respectably adorned. But other and great uses which would result from such a reform strike one immediately. The ordinary metaphysics had its uses, in that it sought out the elementary concepts of the pure understanding in order to make them clear through analysis and definite through definitions. In this way it was a training for reason, in whatever direction it might be turned. But this was all the good it did. The service was subsequently effaced when it favored conceit by venturesome assertions, sophistry by subtle distinctions and adornment, and shallowness by the ease with which it decided the most difficult problems by means of a little school wisdom, which is only the more seductive the more it has the choice, on the one hand, of taking something from the language of science and, on the other, from that of popular discourse—thus being everything to everybody but in reality nothing at all. By criticism, however, a standard is given to our judgment whereby knowledge may be with certainty distinguished from pseudo-science and firmly founded, being brought into full operation in metaphysics—a mode of thought extending by degrees its beneficial influence over every other use of reason, at once infusing into it the true philosophical spirit. But the service that metaphysics performs also for theology, by making it independent of the judgment of dogmatic speculation and thereby assuring it completely against the attacks of all such opponents, is certainly not to be valued lightly. For ordinary metaphysics, although it promised theology much advantage, could not keep this promise, and by summoning speculative dogmatics to its assistance did nothing but arm enemies against itself. Mysticism, which can prosper in a rationalistic age only when it hides itself behind a system of school metaphysics, under the protection of which it may venture to rave with a semblance of rationality, is driven from theology, its last hiding place, by critical philosophy. Last, but not least, it cannot be otherwise than important to a teacher of metaphysics to be able to say with universal assent that what he expounds is *science,* and that by it genuine services will be rendered to the commonweal.

FOUNDATION FOR THE METAPHYSICS OF MORALS

Preface

Ancient Greek philosophy was divided into three sciences: physics, ethics, and logic. This division conforms perfectly to the nature of the subject, and one need improve on it perhaps only by supplying its principle in order both to insure its exhaustiveness and to define correctly the necessary subdivisions.

All rational knowledge is either material, and concerns some object, or formal, and is occupied only with the form of understanding and reason itself and with the universal rules of thinking, without regard to distinctions among objects. Formal philosophy is called logic. Material philosophy, however, which has to do with definite objects and the laws to which they are subject, is divided into two parts. This is because these laws are either laws of nature or laws of freedom. The science of the former is called physics, and that of the latter ethics. The former is also called theory of nature and the latter theory of morals.

Logic can have no empirical part—a part in which universal and necessary laws of thinking would rest upon grounds taken from experience. For in that case it would not be logic (i.e., a canon for understanding or reason which is valid for all thinking and which must be demonstrated). Natural and moral philosophy, on the other hand, can each have its empirical part. The former must do so, for it must determine the laws of nature as an object of experience, and the latter must do so because it must determine the human will so far as it is affected by nature. The laws of the former are laws according to which everything happens; those of the latter are laws according to which everything ought to happen, but allow for conditions under which what ought to happen often does not.

All philosophy, so far as it is based on experience, may be called empirical; but, so far as it presents its doctrines solely on the basis of *a priori* principles, it may be called pure philosophy. Pure philosophy, when formal only, is logic; when limited to definite objects of the understanding, it is metaphysics.

In this way there arises the idea of a two-fold metaphysics—a metaphysics of nature and a metaphysics of morals. Physics, therefore, will have an empirical part and also a rational part, and ethics likewise. In ethics, however, the empirical part may be called more specifically practical anthropology; the rational part, morals proper.

All crafts, handiworks, and arts have gained by the division of labor, for when one person does not do everything but each limits himself to a particular job which is distinguished from all the others by the treatment it requires, he can do it with greater perfection and more facility. Where work is not thus differentiated and divided, where everyone is a jack-of-all-trades, the crafts remain at a primitive level. It might be worth considering whether pure philosophy in each of its parts does not require a man particularly devoted to it, and whether it would not be better for the learned profession as a whole to warn those who are in the habit of catering to the taste of the public by mixing up the empirical with the rational in all sorts of proportions which they themselves

Immanuel Kant, *Foundation for the Metaphysics of Morals,* 2nd edition, translated by Lewis White Beck (New York: Macmillan/Library of the Liberal Arts, 1990).

do not know—a warning to those who call themselves independent thinkers and who give the name of speculator to those who apply themselves exclusively to the rational part of philosophy. This warning would be that they should not, at one and the same time, carry on two employments which differ widely in the treatment they require, and for each of which perhaps a special talent is required, since the combination of these talents in one person produces only bunglers. I only ask whether the nature of the science does not require that a careful separation of the empirical from the rational part be made, with a metaphysics of nature put before real (empirical) physics and a metaphysics of morals before practical anthropology. Each branch of metaphysics must be carefully purified of everything empirical so that we can know how much pure reason can accomplish in each case and from what sources it creates its *a priori* teaching, whether the latter inquiry be conducted by all moralists (whose name is legion) or only by some who feel a calling to it.

Since my purpose here is directed to moral philosophy, I narrow my proposed question to this: Is it not of the utmost necessity to construct a pure moral philosophy which is completely freed from everything which may be only empirical and thus belong to anthropology? That there must be such a philosophy is self-evident from the common idea of duty and moral laws. Everyone must admit that a law, if it is to hold morally (i.e., as a ground of obligation), must imply absolute necessity; he must admit that the command: Thou shalt not lie, does not apply to men only as if other rational beings had no need to observe it. The same is true for all other moral laws properly so called. He must concede that the ground of obligation here must not be sought in the nature of man or in the circumstances in which he is placed but *a priori* solely in the concepts of pure reason, and that every precept which rests on principles of mere experience, even a precept which is in certain respects universal, so far as it leans in the least on empirical grounds (perhaps only in regard to the motive involved) may be called a practical rule but never a moral law.

Thus not only are moral laws together with their principles essentially different from all practical knowledge in which there is anything empirical, but all moral philosophy rests solely on its pure part. Applied to man, it borrows nothing from knowledge of him (anthropology) but gives man, as a rational being, *a priori* laws. No doubt these laws require a power of judgment sharpened by experience partly in order to decide in which cases they apply and partly to procure for them access to man's will and to provide an impetus to their practice. For man is affected by so many inclinations that, though he is capable of the Idea of a practical pure reason, he is not so easily able to make it concretely effective in the conduct of his life.

A metaphysics of morals is therefore indispensable, not merely because of motives to speculation on the source of the *a priori* practical principles which lie in our reason, but also because morals themselves remain subject to all kinds of corruption so long as the guide and supreme norm for their correct estimation is lacking. For it is not sufficient to that which should be morally good that it conform to the law; it must be done for the sake of the law. Otherwise its conformity is merely contingent and spurious because, though the unmoral ground may indeed now and then produce lawful actions, more often it brings forth unlawful ones. But the moral law can be found in its purity and genuineness (which is the central concern in the practical) nowhere else than in a pure philosophy; therefore metaphysics must lead the way, and without it there can be no moral philosophy. Philosophy which mixes pure principles with empirical ones does not deserve the name, for what distinguishes philosophy from common sense knowledge is its treatment in separate sciences of what is confusedly apprehended in such knowledge. Much less does it deserve the name of moral philosophy, since by this confusion it spoils the purity of morals themselves, and works contrary to its own end.

It should not be thought that what is here required is already present in the celebrated Wolff's propaedeutic to his moral philosophy (i.e., in what he calls *Universal Practical Philosophy*) and that it is not an entirely new field which is to be opened. Precisely because his work was to be universal practical philosophy, it contained no will of any particular kind, such as one determined without any empirical motives by *a priori* principles; in a word, it had nothing which could be called a pure will, since it considered only volition in general with all the actions and conditions which pertain to it in this general sense. Thus his propaedeutic differs from a metaphysic of morals in the same way that general logic is distinguished from transcendental philosophy, the former expounding the actions and rules of thinking in general, and the latter presenting the actions and rules of pure thinking (thinking by which objects are known completely *a priori*). For the metaphysics of morals is meant to investigate the Idea and principles of a possible pure will and not the actions and conditions of human volition as such, which for the most part are drawn from psychology.

That universal practical philosophy discussed (though improperly) laws and duty is no objection to my assertion. For the authors of this science remain even here true to their idea of it. They do not distinguish the motives which are presented completely *a priori* by reason alone and which are thus moral in the proper sense of the world, from empirical motives which the understanding raises to universal concepts by comparing experiences. Rather, they consider motives without regard to the difference in their source but only with reference to their larger or smaller number (as they are considered to be all of the same kind); they thus formulate their concept of obligation, which is anything but moral, but which is all that can be desired in a philosophy which does not decide whether the origin of all possible practical concepts is *a priori* or *a posteriori*.

As a preliminary to a *Metaphysics of Morals* which I intend to publish someday, I issue these *Foundations*. There is, to be sure, no other foundation for such a metaphysics than a critical examination of pure practical reason, just as there is no other foundation for metaphysics than the already published critical examination of pure speculative reason. But, in the first place, a critical examination of pure practical reason is not of such extreme importance as that of the speculative reason, because human reason, even in the commonest mind, can easily be brought to a high degree of correctness and completeness in moral matters while, on the other hand, in its theoretical but pure use it is wholly dialectical. In the second place, I require of a critical examination of pure practical reason, if it is to be complete, that its unity with the speculative be subject to presentation under a common principle, because in the final analysis there can be but one and the same reason which must be different only in application. But I could not bring this to such a completeness without bringing in observations of an altogether different kind and without thereby confusing the reader. For these reasons I have employed the title, *Foundations of the Metaphysics of Morals,* instead of *Critique of Pure Practical Reason.*

Because, in the third place, a *Metaphysics of Morals,* in spite of its forbidding title, is capable of a high degree of popular adaptation to common understanding, I find it useful to separate this preliminary work of laying the foundation, in order not to have to introduce unavoidable subtleties into the latter, more comprehensible work.

The present foundations, however, are nothing more than the search for and establishment of the supreme principle of morality. This constitutes a task altogether complete in design and one which should be kept separate from all other moral inquiry. My conclusions concerning this important question, which has not yet been discussed nearly enough, would, of course, be clarified by application of the principle to the whole system of morality, and it would receive much confirmation by the adequacy which it would everywhere show. But I must forego this advantage which would be, in the final analysis, more personally gratifying than commonly useful, because ease of use and apparent adequacy of a principle are not any sure proof of correctness, but rather awaken a certain partiality which prevents a rigorous investigation and evaluation of it for itself without regard to consequences.

I have adopted in this writing the method which is, I think, most suitable if one wishes to proceed analytically from common knowledge to the determination of its supreme principle, and then synthetically from the examination of this principle and its sources back to common knowledge where it finds its application. The division is therefore as follows:

1. First Section. Transition from Common Sense Knowledge of Morals to the Philosophical
2. Second Section. Transition from Popular Moral Philosophy to the Metaphysics of Morals
3. Third Section. Final Step from the Metaphysics of Morals to the Critical Examination of Pure Practical Reason

FIRST SECTION

TRANSITION FROM COMMON SENSE* KNOWLEDGE OF MORALS TO THE PHILOSOPHICAL

Nothing in the world—indeed nothing even beyond the world—can possibly be conceived which could be called good without qualification except a GOOD WILL. Intelligence, wit, judgment, and other talents of the mind however they may be named, or courage, resoluteness, and perseverence as qualities of temperament, are doubtless in many respects good and desirable; but they can become extremely bad and harmful if the will, which is to make use of these gifts of nature and which in its special constitution is called character, is not good. It is the same with gifts of fortune. Power, riches, honor, even health, general well-being and the contentment with one's condition which is called happiness make for pride and even arrogance if there is not a good will to correct their influence on the mind and on its principle of action, so as to make it generally fitting to its entire end. It need hardly be mentioned that the sight of a being adorned with no feature of a pure and good will yet enjoying lasting good fortune can never give pleasure to an impartial rational observer. Thus the good will seems to constitute the indispensable condition even of worthiness to be happy.

---

*[*gemeine Vernunfterkenntnis* ("common rational knowledge") is one of several expressions Kant uses which may sometimes best be translated as "common sense." Kant is very strict in his censure of those who appeal to common sense as an arbiter in philosophical disputes, yet he accepts it as a starting point, especially in ethics, where he says that the man of common sense has at least as much chance to be right as the philosopher. In this title "common sense" is not being used as a technical term; it just means "what everyone knows" about morality.]

Some qualities seem to be conducive to this good will and can facilitate its action, but in spite of that they have no intrinsic unconditional worth. They rather presuppose a good will, which limits the high esteem which one otherwise rightly has for them and prevents their being held to be absolutely good. Moderation in emotions and passions, self-control, and calm deliberation not only are good in many respects but seem even to constitute part of the inner worth of the person. But however unconditionally they were esteemed by the ancients, they are far from being good without qualification, for without the principles of a good will they can become extremely bad, and the coolness of a villain makes him not only far more dangerous but also more directly abominable in our eyes than he would have seemed without it.

The good will is not good because of what it effects or accomplishes or because of its competence to achieve some intended end; it is good only because of its willing (i.e., it is good in itself). And, regarded for itself, it is to be esteemed as incomparably higher than anything which could be brought about by it in favor of any inclination or even of the sum total of all inclinations. Even if it should happen that, by a particularly unfortunate fate or by the niggardly provision of a step-motherly nature, this will should be wholly lacking in power to accomplish its purpose, and if even the greatest effort should not avail it to achieve anything of its end, and if there remained only the good will—not as a mere wish, but as the summoning of all the means in our power—it would sparkle like a jewel all by itself, as something that had its full worth in itself. Usefulness or fruitlessness can neither diminish nor augment this worth. Its usefulness would be only its setting, as it were, so as to enable us to handle it more conveniently in commerce or to attract the attention of those who are not yet connoisseurs, but not to recommend it to those who are experts or to determine its worth.

But there is something so strange in this idea of the absolute worth of the will alone, in which no account is taken of any use, that, notwithstanding the agreement even of common sense, the suspicion must arise that perhaps only high-flown fancy is its hidden basis, and that we may have misunderstood the purpose of nature in appointing reason as the ruler of our will. We shall therefore examine this idea from this point of view.

In the natural constitution of an organized being (i.e., one suitably adapted to life), we assume as an axiom that no organ will be found for any purpose which is not the fittest and best adapted to that purpose. Now if its preservation, its welfare, in a word its happiness, were the real end of nature in a being having reason and will, then nature would have hit upon a very poor arrangement in appointing the reason of the creature to be the executor of this purpose. For all the actions which the creature has to perform with this intention of nature, and the entire rule of his conduct, would be dictated much more exactly by instinct, and the end would be far more certainly attained by instinct than it ever could be by reason. And if, over and above this, reason should have been granted to the favored creature, it would have served only to let him contemplate the happy constitution of his nature, to admire it, to rejoice in it, and to be grateful for it to its beneficent cause. But reason would not have been given in order that the being should subject his faculty of desire to that weak and delusive guidance and to meddle with the purpose of nature. In a word, nature would have taken care that reason did not break forth into practical use nor have the presumption, with its weak insight, to think out for itself the plan of happiness and the means of attaining it. Nature would have taken over the choice not only of ends but also of the means, and with wise foresight she would have entrusted both to instinct alone.

And, in fact, we find that the more a cultivated reason deliberately devotes itself to the enjoyment of life and happiness, the more the man falls short of true contentment. From this fact there arises in many persons, if only they are candid enough to admit it, a certain degree of misology, hatred of reason. This is particularly the case with those who are most experienced in its use. After counting all the advantages which they draw—I will not say from the invention of the arts of common luxury—from the sciences (which in the end seem to them to be also a luxury of the understanding), they nevertheless find that they have actually brought more trouble on their shoulders instead of gaining in happiness; they finally envy, rather than despise, the common run of men who are better guided by merely natural instinct and who do not permit their reason much influence on their conduct. And we must at least admit that a morose attitude or ingratitude to the goodness with which the world is governed is by no means found always among those who temper or refute the boasting eulogies which are given of the advantages of happiness and contentment with which reason is supposed to supply us. Rather, their judgment is based on the Idea of another and far more worthy purpose of their existence for which, instead of happiness, their reason is properly intended; this purpose, therefore, being the supreme condition to which the private purposes of men must, for the most part, defer.

Since reason is not competent to guide the will safely with regard to its objects and the satisfaction of all our needs (which it in part multiplies), to this end an innate instinct would have led with far more certainty. But reason is given to us as a practical faculty (i.e., one which is meant to have an influence on the will). As nature has elsewhere distributed capacities suitable to the functions they are to perform, reason's proper function must be to produce a will good in itself and not one good merely as a means, since for the former, reason is absolutely essential. This will need not be the sole and complete good, yet it must be the condition of all others, even of the desire for happiness. In this case it is entirely compatible with the wisdom of nature that the cultivation of reason, which is required for the former unconditional purpose, at least in this life restricts in many ways—indeed, can reduce to nothing—the achievement of the latter unconditional purpose, happiness. For one perceives that nature here does not proceed unsuitably to its purpose, because reason, which recognizes its highest practical vocation in the establishment of a good will, is capable of a contentment of its own kind (i.e., one that springs from the attainment of a purpose determined by reason), even though this injures the ends of inclination.

We have, then, to develop the concept of a will which is to be esteemed as good in itself without regard to anything else. It dwells already in the natural and sound understanding and does not need so much to be taught as only to be brought to light. In the estimation of the total worth of our actions it always takes first place and is the condition of everything else. In order to show this, we shall take the concept of duty. It contains the concept of a good will, though with certain subjective restrictions and hindrances, but these are far from concealing it and making it unrecognizable, for they rather bring it out by contrast and make it shine forth all the more brightly.

I here omit all actions which are recognized as opposed to duty, even though they may be useful in one respect or another, for with these the question does not arise as to whether they may be done from duty, since they conflict with it. I also pass over actions which are really in accord with duty and to which one has no direct inclination, rather doing them because impelled to do so by another inclination. For it is easily decided whether an action in accord with duty is done from duty or for some selfish purpose. It is far more difficult to note this difference when the action is in accord with duty and, in addition, the subject has a direct inclination to do it. For example, it is in accord with duty that a dealer should not overcharge an inexperienced customer, and wherever there is much trade the prudent merchant does not do so, but has a fixed price for everyone so that a child may buy from him as cheaply as any other. Thus the customer is honestly served, but this is far from sufficient to warrant the belief that the merchant has behaved in this way from duty and principles of honesty. His own advantage required this behavior, but it cannot be assumed that over and above that he had a direct inclination to his customers and that, out of love, as it were, he gave none an advantage in price over another. The action was done neither from duty nor from direct inclination but only for a selfish purpose.

On the other hand, it is a duty to preserve one's life, and moreover everyone has a direct inclination to do so. But for that reason, the often anxious care which most men take of it has no intrinsic worth, and the maxim of doing so has no moral import. They preserve their lives according to duty, but not from duty. But if adversities and hopeless sorrow completely take away the relish for life; if an unfortunate man, strong in soul, is indignant rather than despondent or dejected over his fate and wishes for death, and yet preserves his life without loving it and from neither inclination nor fear but from duty—then his maxim has moral merit.

To be kind where one can is a duty, and there are, moreover, many persons so sympathetically constituted that without any motive of vanity or selfishness they find an inner satisfaction in spreading joy and rejoice in the contentment of others which they have made possible. But I say that, however dutiful and however amiable it may be, that kind of action has no true moral worth. It is on a level with [actions done from] other inclinations, such as the inclination to honor, which, if fortunately directed to what in fact accords with duty and is generally useful and thus honorable, deserve praise and encouragement, but no esteem. For the maxim lacks the moral import of an action done not from inclination but from duty. But assume that the mind of that friend to mankind was clouded by a sorrow of his own which extinguished all sympathy with the lot of others, and though he still had the power to benefit others in distress their need left him untouched because he was preoccupied with his own. Now suppose him to tear himself, unsolicited by inclination, out of his dead insensibility and to do this action only from duty and without any inclination—then for the first time his action has genuine moral worth. Furthermore, if nature has put little sympathy into the heart of a man, and if he, though an honest man, is by temperament cold and indifferent to the sufferings of others perhaps because he is provided with special gifts of patience and fortitude and expects and even requires that others should have them too—and such a man would certainly not be the meanest product of nature—would not he find in himself a source from which to give himself a far higher worth than he could have got by having a good-natured temperament? This is unquestionably true even though nature did not make him philanthropic, for it is just here that the worth of character is brought out, which is morally the incomparably highest of all: he is beneficent not from inclination, but from duty.

To secure one's own happiness is at least indirectly a duty, for discontent with one's condition under pressure from many cares and amid unsatisfied wants could easily become a great temptation to transgress against duties. But, without any view to duty, all men have the strongest and deepest inclination to happiness, because in this Idea all inclinations are summed up. But the precept of happiness is often so formulated that it definitely thwarts some inclinations, and men can make no definite and certain concept of the sum of satisfaction of all inclinations, which goes under the name of happiness. It is not to be wondered at, therefore, that a single inclination, definite as to what it promises and as to the time at which it can be satisfied, can outweigh a fluctuating idea and that, for example, a man with the gout can choose to enjoy what he likes and to suffer what he may, because according to his calculations at least on this occasion he has not sacrificed the enjoyment of the present moment to a perhaps groundless expectation of a happiness supposed to lie in health. But even in this case if the universal inclination to happiness did not determine his will, and if health were not at least for him a necessary factor in these calculations, there would still remain, as in all other cases, a law that he ought to promote his happiness not from inclination but from duty. Only from this law could his conduct have true moral worth.

It is in this way, undoubtedly, that we should understand those passages of Scripture which command us to love our neighbor and even our enemy, for love as an inclination cannot be commanded. But beneficence from duty, even when no inclination impels it and even when it is opposed by a natural and unconquerable aversion, is practical love, not pathological* love; it resides in the will and not in the propensities of feeling, in principles of action and not in tender sympathy; and it alone can be commanded.

[Thus the first proposition of morality is that to have genuine moral worth, an action must be done from duty.] The second proposition is: An action done from duty does not have its moral worth in the purpose which is to be achieved through it but in the maxim whereby it is determined. Its moral value, therefore, does not depend upon the realization of the object of the action but merely on the principle of the volition by which the action is done irrespective of the objects of the faculty of desire. From the preceding discussion it is clear that the purposes we may have for our actions and their effects as ends and incentives of the will cannot give the actions any unconditional and moral worth. Wherein, then, can this worth lie, if it is not in the will in its relation to its hoped-for effect? It can lie nowhere else than in the principle of the will irrespective of the ends which can be realized by such action. For the will stands, as it were, at the crossroads halfway between its *a priori* principle which is formal and its posteriori incentive which is material. Since it must be determined by something, if it is done from duty it must be determined by the formal principle of volition as such, since every material principle has been withdrawn from it.

The third principle, as a consequence of the two preceding, I would express as follows: Duty is the necessity to do an action from respect for law. I can certainly have an inclination to an object as an effect of the proposed action, but I can never have respect for it precisely because it is a mere effect and not an activity of a will. Similarly, I can have no respect for any inclination whatsoever, whether my own or that of another; in the former case I can at most approve of it and in the latter I can even love it (i.e., see it as favorable to my own advantage). But that which is connected with my will merely as ground and not as consequence, that which does not serve my inclination but overpowers it or at least excludes it from being considered in making a choice—in a word, law itself—can be an object of respect and thus a command. Now as an act from duty wholly excludes the influence of inclination and therewith every object of the will, nothing remains which can determine the will objectively except law and subjectively except pure respect for this practical law. This subjective element is the maxim** that I should follow such a law even if it thwarts all my inclinations.

---

*[Here as elsewhere Kant uses the word pathological to describe motives and actions arising from feeling or bodily impulses, with no suggestion of abnormality or disease.]

**A maxim is the subjective principle of volition. The objective principle (i.e., that which would serve all rational beings also subjectively as a practical principle if reason had full power over the faculty of desire) is the practical law.

Thus the moral worth of an action does not lie in the effect which is expected from it or in any principle of action which has to borrow its motive from this expected effect. For all these effects (agreeableness of my own condition, indeed even the promotion of the happiness of others) could be brought about through other causes and would not require the will of a rational being, while the highest and unconditional good can be found only in such a will. Therefore the preeminent good can consist only in the conception of law in itself (which can be present only in a rational being) so far as this conception and not the hoped-for effect is the determining ground of the will. This preeminent good, which we call moral, is already present in the person who acts according to this conception, and we do not have to look for it first in the result.*

But what kind of law can that be, the conception of which must determine the will without reference to the expected result? Under this condition alone can the will be called absolutely good without qualification. Since I have robbed the will of all impulses which could come to it from obedience to any law, nothing remains to serve as a principle of the will except universal conformity to law as such. That is, I ought never to act in such a way that I could not also will that my maxim should be a universal law. Strict conformity to law as such (without assuming any particular law applicable to certain actions) serves as the principle of the will, and it must serve as such a principle if duty is not to be a vain delusion and chimerical concept. The common sense of mankind (*gemeine Menschenvernunft*) in its practical judgments is in perfect agreement with this and has this principle constantly in view.

Let the question, for example, be: May I, when in distress, make a promise with the intention not to keep it? I easily distinguish the two meanings which the question can have, viz., whether it is prudent to make a false promise, or whether it conforms to duty. The former can undoubtedly be often the case, though I do see clearly that it is not sufficient merely to escape from the present difficulty by this expedient, but that I must consider whether inconveniences much greater than the present one may not later spring from this lie. Even with all my supposed cunning, the consequences cannot be so easily foreseen. Loss of credit might be far more disadvantageous than the misfortune I am now seeking to avoid, and it is hard to tell whether it might not be more prudent to act according to a universal maxim and to make it a habit not to promise anything without intending to fulfill it. But it is soon clear to me that such a maxim is based only on an apprehensive concern with consequences.

To be truthful from duty, however, is an entirely different thing from being truthful out of fear of untoward consequences, for in the former case the concept of the

---

*It might be objected that I seek to take refuge in an obscure feeling behind the word "respect," instead of clearly resolving the question with a concept of reason. But though respect is a feeling, it is not one received through any [outer] influence but is self-wrought by a rational concept; thus it differs specifically from all feelings of the former kind which may be referred to inclination or fear. What I recognize directly as a law for myself I recognize with respect, which means merely the consciousness of the submission of my will to a law without the intervention of other influences on my mind. The direct determination of the will by law and the consciousness of this determination is respect; thus respect can be regarded as the effect of the law on the subject and not as the cause of the law. Respect is properly the conception of a worth which thwarts my self-love. Thus it is regarded as an object neither of inclination nor of fear, though it has something analogous to both. The only object of respect is law, and indeed only the law which we impose on ourselves and yet recognize as necessary in itself. As a law we are subject to it without consulting self-love; as imposed on us by ourselves, it is a consequence of our will. In the former respect it is analogous to fear and in the latter to inclination. All respect for a person is only respect for the law (of righteousness, etc.) of which the person provides an example. Because we see the improvement of our talents as a duty, we think of a person of talent as the example of a law, as it were (the law that we should by practice become like him in his talents), and that constitutes our respect. All so-called moral interest consists solely in respect for the law.

action itself contains a law for me, while in the latter I must first look about to see what results for me may be connected with it. To deviate from the principle of duty is certainly bad, but to be unfaithful to my maxim of prudence can sometimes be very advantageous to me, though it is certainly safer to abide by it. The shortest but most infallible way to find the answer to the question as to whether a deceitful promise is consistent with duty is to ask myself: Would I be content that my maxim of extricating myself from difficulty by a false promise should hold as a universal law for myself as well as for others? And could I say to myself that everyone may make a false promise when he is in a difficulty from which he otherwise cannot escape? Immediately I see that I could will the lie but not a universal law to lie. For with such a law there would be no promises at all, inasmuch as it would be futile to make a pretense of my intention in regard to future actions to those who would not believe this pretense or—if they overhastily did so—would pay me back in my own coin. Thus my maxim would necessarily destroy itself as soon as it was made a universal law.

I do not, therefore, need any penetrating acuteness to discern what I have to do in order that my volition may be morally good. Inexperienced in the course of the world, incapable of being prepared for all its contingencies, I only ask myself: Can I will that my maxim become a universal law? If not, it must be rejected, not because of any disadvantage accruing to myself or even to others, but because it cannot enter as a principle into a possible enactment of universal law, and reason extorts from me an immediate respect for such legislation. I do not as yet discern on what it is grounded (this is a question the philosopher may investigate), but I at least understand that it is an estimation of a worth which far outweighs all the worth of whatever is recommended by the inclinations, and that the necessity that I act from pure respect for the practical law constitutes my duty. To duty every other motive must give place, because duty is the condition of a will good in itself, whose worth transcends everything.

Thus within the moral knowledge of ordinary human reason (*gemeine Menschenvernunft*) we have attained its principle. To be sure, ordinary human reason does not think this principle abstractly in such a universal form, but it always has the principle in view and uses it as the standard for its judgments. It would be easy to show how ordinary human reason, with this compass, knows well how to distinguish what is good, what is bad, and what is consistent or inconsistent with duty. Without in the least teaching common reason anything new, we need only to draw its attention to its own principle (in the manner of Socrates), thus showing that neither science nor philosophy is needed in order to know what one has to do in order to be honest and good, and even wise and virtuous. We might have conjectured beforehand that the knowledge of what everyone is obliged to do and thus also to know would be within the reach of everyone, even of the most ordinary man. Here we cannot but admire the great advantages which the practical faculty of judgment has over the theoretical in ordinary human understanding. In the theoretical, if ordinary reason ventures to go beyond the laws of experience and perceptions of the senses, it falls into sheer inconceivabilities and self-contradictions, or at least into a chaos of uncertainty, obscurity, and instability. In the practical, on the other hand, the power of judgment first shows itself to advantage when common understanding excludes all sensuous incentives from practical laws. It then even becomes subtle, quibbling with its own conscience or with other claims to what should be called right, or wishing to determine accurately, for its own instruction, the worth of certain actions. But the most remarkable thing about ordinary human understanding in its practical concern is that it may have as much hope as any philosopher of hitting the mark. In fact, it is almost more certain to do so that the philosopher, for while he has no principle which common understanding lacks, his judgment is easily confused by a mass of irrelevant considerations so that it easily turns aside from the correct way. Would it not, therefore, be wiser in moral matters to acquiesce in ordinary reasonable judgment and at most to call in philosophy in order to make the system of morals more complete and comprehensible and its rules more convenient for use (especially in disputation), than to steer the ordinary understanding from its happy simplicity in practical matters and to lead it through philosophy into a new path of inquiry and instruction?

Innocence is indeed a glorious thing, but it is very sad that it cannot well maintain itself, being easily led astray. For this reason, even wisdom—which consists more in acting than in knowing—needs science, not so as to learn from it but to secure admission and permanence to its precepts. Man feels in himself a powerful counterpoise against all commands of duty which reason presents to him as so deserving of respect. This counterpoise is his needs and inclinations, the complete satisfaction of which he sums up under the name of happiness. Now reason issues inexorable commands without promising anything to the inclinations. It disregards, as it were, and holds in contempt those claims which are so impetuous and yet so plausible, and which refuse to be suppressed by any command. From this a natural dialectic arises, i.e., a propensity to argue against the stern laws of duty and their validity, or at least to place their purity and strictness in doubt and, where possible, to make them more accordant with our wishes and inclinations. This is equivalent to corrupting them in their very foundations and destroying their dignity—a thing which even ordinary practical reason cannot finally call good.

In this way ordinary human reason is impelled to go outside its sphere and to take a step into the field of practical philosophy. But it is forced to do so not by any speculative need, which never occurs to it so long as it is satisfied to remain merely healthy reason; rather, it is impelled on practical grounds to obtain information and clear instruction respecting the source of its principle and the correct definition of this principle in its opposition to the maxims based on need and inclination. It seeks this information in order to escape from the perplexity of opposing claims and to avoid the danger of losing all genuine moral principles through the equivocation in which it is easily involved. Thus when ordinary practical reason cultivates itself, a dialectic surreptitiously ensues which forces it to seek aid in philosophy, just as the same thing happens in the theoretical use of reason. Ordinary practical reason, like theoretical reason, will find rest only in a complete critical examination of our reason.

SECOND SECTION

TRANSITION FROM POPULAR MORAL PHILOSOPHY TO THE METAPHYSICS OF MORALS

Although we have derived our earlier concept of duty from the ordinary use of our practical reason, it is by no means to be inferred that we have treated it as an empirical concept. On the contrary, if we attend to our experience of the way men act, we meet frequent and, as we must confess, justified complaints that we cannot cite a single sure example of the disposition to act from pure duty. There are also justified complaints that, though much may be done that accords with what duty commands, it is nevertheless always doubtful whether it is done from duty and thus whether it has moral worth.

There have always been philosophers who for this reason have absolutely denied the reality of this disposition in human actions, attributing everything to more or less refined self-love. They have done so without questioning the correctness of the concept of morality. Rather they spoke with sincere regret of the frailty and corruption of human nature, which is noble enough to take as its precept an Idea so worthy of respect but which at the same time is too weak to follow it, employing reason, which should give laws for human nature, only to provide for the interest of the inclinations either singly or, at best, in their greatest possible harmony with one another.

It is, in fact, absolutely impossible by experience to discern with complete certainty a single case in which the maxim of an action, however much it might conform to duty, rested solely on moral grounds and on the conception of one's duty. It sometimes happens that in the most searching self-examination we can find nothing except the moral ground of duty which could have been powerful enough to move us to this or that good action and to such great sacrifice. But from this we cannot by any means conclude with certainty that a secret impulse of self-love, falsely appearing as the Idea of duty, was not actually the true determining cause of the will. For we like to flatter ourselves with a pretended nobler motive, while in fact even the strictest examination can never lead us entirely behind the secret incentives, for when moral worth is in question it is not a matter of actions which one sees but of their inner principles which one does not see.

Moreover, one cannot better serve the wishes of those who ridicule all morality as a mere phantom of human imagination overreaching itself through self-conceit than by conceding that the concepts of duty must be derived only from experience (for they are ready, from indolence, to believe that this is true of all other concepts too). For, by this concession, a sure triumph is prepared for them. Out of love for humanity I am willing to admit that most of our actions are in accord with duty; but if we look more closely at our thoughts and aspirations, we come everywhere upon the dear self, which is always turning up, and it is this instead of the stern command of duty (which would often require self-denial) which supports our plans. One need not be an enemy of virtue, but only a cool observer who does not confuse even the liveliest aspiration for the good with its actuality, to be sometimes doubtful whether true virtue can really be found anywhere in the world. This is especially true as one's years increase and the power of judgment is made wiser by experience and more acute in observation. This being so, nothing can secure us against the complete abandonment of our ideas of duty and preserve in us a well-founded respect for its law except the conviction that, even if there never were actions springing from such pure sources, our concern is not whether this or that was done, but that reason of itself and independently of all appearances commanded what ought to be done. Our concern is with actions of which perhaps the world has never had an example, with actions whose feasibility might be seriously doubted by those who base everything on experience, and yet with actions inexorably commanded by reason. For example, pure sincerity in friendship can be demanded of every man, and this demand is not in the least diminished if a sincere friend has never existed, because this duty, as duty in general, prior to all experience lies in the Idea of reason which determines the will on *a priori* grounds.

No experience, it is clear, can give occasion for inferring the possibility of such apodictic laws. This is especially clear when we add that, unless we wish to deny all truth to the concept of morality and renounce its application to any possible object, we cannot refuse to admit that the law is of such broad significance that it holds not merely for men but for all rational beings as such; we must grant that it must be valid with absolute necessity, and not merely under contingent conditions and with exceptions. For

Immanuel Kant and Luncheon Guests, 1893, by E. Doestling. While Kant led a simple, routine-filled life, he was known as a delightful conversationalist and host who had many friends and admirers. (*The Bettmann Archive*)

with what right could we bring into unlimited respect something that might be valid only under contingent human conditions? And how could laws of the determination of our will be held to be laws of the determination of the will of any rational being whatever and of ourselves in so far as we are rational beings, if they were merely empirical and did not have their origin completely *a priori* in pure, but practical, reason?

Nor could one given poorer counsel to morality than to attempt to derive it from examples. For each example of morality which is exhibited must itself have been previously judged according to principles of morality to see whether it was worthy to serve as an original example or model. By no means could it authoritatively furnish the concept of morality. Even the Holy One of the Gospel must be compared with our ideal of moral perfection before He is recognized as such; even He says of Himself, "Why call ye Me (Whom you see) good? None is good (the archetype of the good) except God only (Whom you do not see)." But whence do we have the concept of God as the highest good? Solely from the Idea of moral perfection which reason formulates *a priori* and which it inseparably connects with the concept of a free will. Imitation has no place in moral matters, and examples serve only for encouragement. That is, they put beyond question the possibility of performing what the law commands, and they make visible that which the practical rule expresses more generally. But they can never justify our guiding ourselves by examples and our setting aside their true original, which lies in reason.

If there is thus no genuine supreme principle of morality which does not rest on pure reason alone independent of all possible experience, I do not believe it is necessary even to ask whether it is well to exhibit these concepts generally (in abstracto), which, together with the principles belonging to them, are established *a priori*. At any rate, the question need not be asked if knowledge of them is to be distinguished from ordinary knowledge and called philosophical. But in our times this question may be necessary. For if we collected votes as to whether pure rational knowledge separated from all experience (i.e., a metaphysics of morals) or popular practical philosophy is to be preferred, it is easily guessed on which side the majority would stand.

This condescension to popular notions is certainly very commendable once the ascent to the principles of pure reason has been satisfactorily accomplished. That would mean the prior establishment of the doctrine of morals on metaphysics and then, when it is established, procuring a hearing for it through popularization. But it is extremely absurd to want to achieve popular appeal in the first investigation, where everything depends on the correctness of the fundamental principles. Not only can this procedure never make claim to that rarest merit of true philosophical popularity, since there is really no art in being generally comprehensible if one thereby renounces all basic insight; but it produces a disgusting jumble of patched-up observations and half-reasoned principles. Shallow pates enjoy this, for it is very useful in everyday chitchat, while the more sensible feel confused and dissatisfied and avert their eyes without being able to help themselves. But philosophers, who see through this delusion, get little hearing when they call people away from this would-be popularity so that they may have genuine popular appeal once they have gained a definite understanding.

One need only look at the essays on morality favored by popular taste. One will sometimes meet with the particular vocation of human nature (but occasionally with the Idea of a rational nature in general), sometimes perfection and sometimes happiness, here moral feeling, there fear of God, a little of this and a little of that in a marvelous mixture. It never occurs to the authors, however, to ask whether the principles of morality are, after all, to be sought anywhere in knowledge of human nature (which we can derive only from experience). And if this is not the case, if the principles are *a priori*, free from everything empirical, and found exclusively in pure rational concepts and not at all in any other place, they never ask whether they should undertake this investigation as a separate inquiry (i.e., as pure practical philosophy) or (if one may use a name so decried) a metaphysics* of morals. They never think of dealing with it alone and bringing it by itself to completeness and of requiring the public, which desires popularization, to await the outcome of this undertaking.

But a completely isolated metaphysics of morals, mixed with no anthropology, no theology, no physics or hyperphysics, and even less with occult qualities (which

---

*If one wishes, the pure philosophy (metaphysics) of morals can be distinguished from the applied (i.e., applied to human nature), just as pure mathematics and pure logic are distinguished from applied mathematics and applied logic. By this designation one is immediately reminded that moral principles are not founded on the peculiarities of human nature but must stand of themselves *a priori*, and that from such principles practical rules for every rational nature, and accordingly for man, must be derivable.

might be called hypophysical), is not only an indispensable substrate of all theoretically sound and definite knowledge of duties; it is also a desideratum of the highest importance to the actual fulfillment of its precepts. For the thought of duty and of the moral law generally, with no admixture of empirical inducements, has an influence on the human heart so much more powerful than all other incentives* which may be derived from the empirical field that reason, in the consciousness of its dignity, despises them and gradually becomes master over them. It has this influence only through reason alone, which thereby first realizes that it can of itself be practical. A mixed theory of morals which is put together from incentives of feelings and inclinations and from rational concepts must, on the other hand, make the mind vacillate between motives which cannot be brought together under any principle and which can lead only accidentally to the good, and frequently lead to the bad.

From what has been said it is clear that all moral concepts have their seat and origin entirely *a priori* in reason. This is just as much the case in the most ordinary reason as in the reason which is speculative to the highest degree. It is obvious that they can be abstracted from no empirical and hence merely contingent cognitions. In the purity of origin lies their worthiness to serve us as supreme practical principles, and to the extent that something empirical is added to them, just this much is subtracted from their genuine influence and from the unqualified worth of actions. Furthermore, it is evident that it is not only of the greatest necessity from a theoretical point of view when it is a question of speculation but also of the utmost practical importance to derive the concepts and laws of morals from pure reason and to present them pure and unmixed, and to determine the scope of this entire practical but pure rational knowledge (the entire faculty of pure practical reason) without making the principles depend upon the particular nature of human reason, as speculative philosophy may permit and even find necessary. But since moral laws should hold for every rational being as such, the principles must be derived from the universal concept of a rational being in general. In this manner all morals, which need anthropology for their application to men, must be completely developed first as pure philosophy (i.e., metaphysics), independently of anthropology (a thing feasibly done in such distinct fields of knowledge). For we know well that if we are not in possession of such a metaphysics, it is not merely futile [to try to] define accurately for the purposes of speculative judgment the moral element of duty in all actions which accord with duty, but impossible to base morals on legitimate principles for even ordinary practical use, especially in moral instruction; and it is only in this manner that pure moral dispositions can be produced and engrafted on men's minds for the purpose of the highest good in the world.

In this study we do not advance merely from the common moral judgment (which here is very worthy of respect) to the philosophical, as this has already been done; but we advance by natural stages from popular philosophy (which goes no farther than it can grope by means of examples) to metaphysics (which is not held back

---

*I have a letter from the late excellent Sulzer in which he asks me why the theories of virtue accomplish so little even though they contain so much that is convincing to reason. My answer was delayed in order that I might make it complete. The answer is only that the teachers themselves have not completely clarified their concepts, and when they wish to make up for this by hunting in every quarter for motives to the morally good so as to make their physic right strong, they spoil it. For the commonest observation shows that if we imagine an act of honesty performed with a steadfast soul and sundered from all view to any advantage in this or another world and even under the greatest temptations of need or allurement, it far surpasses and eclipses any similar action which was affected in the least by any foreign incentive; it elevates the soul and arouses the wish to be able to act in this way. Even moderately young children feel this impression, and one should never represent duties to them in any other way.

by anything empirical and which, as it must measure out the entire scope of rational knowledge of this kind, reaches even Ideas, where examples fail us). In order to make this advance, we must follow and clearly present the practical faculty of reason from its universal rules of determination to the point where the concept of duty arises from it.

Everything in nature works according to laws. Only a rational being has the capacity of acting according to the *conception* of laws (i.e., according to principles). This capacity is the will. Since reason is required for the derivation of actions from laws, will is nothing less than practical reason. If reason infallibly determines the will, the actions which such a being recognizes as objectively necessary are also subjectively necessary. That is, the will is a faculty of choosing only that which reason, independently of inclination, recognizes as practically necessary (i.e., as good). But if reason of itself does not sufficiently determine the will, and if the will is subjugated to subjective conditions (certain incentives) which do not always agree with the objective conditions—in a word, if the will is not of itself in complete accord with reason (which is the actual case with men), then the actions which are recognized as objectively necessary are subjectively contingent, and the determination of such a will according to objective laws is a constraint. That is, the relation of objective laws to a will which is not completely good is conceived as the determination of the will of a rational being by principles of reason to which this will is not by its nature necessarily obedient.

The conception of an objective principle, so far as it constrains a will, is a command (of reason), and the formula of this command is called an *imperative*.

All imperatives are expressed by an "ought" and thereby indicate the relation of an objective law of reason to a will which is not in its subjective constitution necessarily determined by this law. This relation is that of constraint. Imperatives say that it would be good to do or to refrain from doing something, but they say it to a will which does not always do something simply because the thing is presented to it as good to do. Practical good is what determines the will by means of the conception of reason and hence not by subjective causes but objectively, on grounds which are valid for every rational being as such. It is distinguished from the pleasant, as that which has an influence on the will only by means of a sensation from purely subjective causes, which hold for the senses only of this or that person and not as a principle of reason which holds for everyone.*

A perfectly good will, therefore, would be equally subject to objective laws of the good, but it could not be conceived as constrained by them to accord with them, because it can be determined to act by its own subjective constitution only through the conception of the good. Thus no imperatives hold for the divine will or, more generally, for a holy will. The "ought" here is out of place, for the volition of itself is neces-

---

*The dependence of the faculty of desire on sensations is called inclination, and inclination always indicates a need. The dependence of a contingently determinable will on principles of reason, however, is called interest. An interest is present only in a dependent will which is not of itself always in accord with reason; in the divine will we cannot conceive of an interest. But even the human will can take an interest in something without thereby acting from interest. The former means the practical interest in the action; the latter, the pathological interest in the object of the action. The former indicates only the dependence of the will on principles of reason in themselves, while the latter indicates dependence on the principles of reason for the purpose of inclination, since reason gives only the practical rule by which the needs of inclination are to be aided. In the former case the action interests me, and in the latter the object of the action (so far as it is pleasant for me) interests me. In the First Section we have seen that, in the case of an action done from duty, no regard must be given to the interest in the object, but merely to the action itself and its principle in reason (i.e., the law).

sarily in unison with the law. Therefore imperatives are only formulas expressing the relation of objective laws of volition in general to the subjective imperfection of the will of this or that rational being, for example, the human will.

All imperatives command either *hypothetically* or *categorically*. The former present the practical necessity of a possible action as a means to achieving something else which one desires (or which one may possibly desire). The categorical imperative would be one which presented an action as of itself objectively necessary, without regard to any other end.

Since every practical law presents a possible action as good and thus as necessary for a subject practically determinable by reason, all imperatives are formulas of the determination of action which is necessary by the principle of a will which is in any way good. If the action is good only as a means to something else, the imperative is hypothetical; but if it is thought of as good in itself, and hence as necessary in a will which of itself conforms to reason as the principle of this will, the imperative is categorical.

The imperative thus says what action possible for me would be good, and it presents the practical rule in relation to a will which does not forthwith perform an action simply because it is good, in part because the subject does not always know that the action is good, and in part (when he does know it) because his maxims can still be opposed to the objective principles of a practical reason.

The hypothetical imperative, therefore, says only that the action is good to some purpose, possible or actual. In the former case, it is a problematical, in the latter an assertorical, practical principle. The categorical imperative, which declares the action to be of itself objectively necessary without making any reference to any end in view (i.e., without having any other purpose), holds as an apodictical practical principle.

We can think of what is possible only through the powers of some rational being as a possible end in view of any will. As a consequence, the principles of action thought of as necessary to attain a possible end in view which can be achieved by them, are in reality infinitely numerous. All sciences have some practical part consisting of problems which presuppose some purpose as well as imperatives directing how it can be reached. These imperatives can therefore be called, generally, imperatives of skill. Whether the purpose is reasonable and good is not in question at all, for the questions concerns only what must be done in order to attain it. The precepts to be followed by a physician in order to cure his patient and by a poisoner to bring about certain death are of equal value in so far as each does that which will perfectly accomplish his purpose. Since in early youth we do not know what purposes we may have in the course of our life, parents seek to let their children learn a great many things and provide for skill in the use of means to all sorts of ends which they might choose, among which they cannot determine whether any one of them will become their child's actual purpose, though it may be that someday he may have it as his actual purpose. And this anxiety is so great that they commonly neglect to form and correct their children's judgment on the worth of the things which they may make their ends.

There is one end, however, which we may presuppose as actual in all rational beings so far as imperatives apply to them, that is, so far as they are dependent beings. There is one purpose which they not only can have but which we can presuppose that they all *do* have by a necessity of nature. This purpose is happiness. The hypothetical imperative which represents the practical necessity of an action as means to the promotion of happiness is an assertorical imperative. We may not expound it as necessary to a merely uncertain and merely possible purpose, but as necessary to a purpose which we can *a priori* and with assurance assume for everyone because it belongs to his essence. Skill in the choice of means to one's own highest well-being can be called prudence* in the narrowest sense. Thus the imperative which refers to the choice of means to one's own happiness (i.e., the precept of prudence) is still only hypothetical, and the action is not commanded absolutely but commanded only as a means to another end in view.

Finally, there is one imperative which directly commands certain conduct without making its condition some purpose to be reached by it. This imperative is categorical. It concerns not the material of the action and its intended result, but the form and principle from which it originates. What is essentially good in it consists in the mental disposition, the result being what it may. This imperative may be called the imperative of morality.

Volition according to these three principles is plainly distinguished by the dissimilarity in the constraints by which they subject the will. In order to clarify this dissimilarity, I believe that they are most suitably named if one says that they are either rules of skill, counsels of prudence, or commands (laws) of morality, respectively. For law alone implies the concept of an unconditional and objective and hence universally valid necessity, and commands are laws which must be obeyed even against inclination. Counsels do indeed involve necessity, but a necessity that can hold only under a subjectively contingent condition (i.e., whether this or that man counts this or that as part of his happiness). The categorical imperative, on the other hand, is restricted by no condition. As absolutely, though practically, necessary it can be called a command in the strict sense. We could also call the first imperatives technical (belonging to art), the second *pragmatic*** (belonging to well-being), and the third moral (belonging to free conduct as such, i.e., to morals).

The question now arises: How are all these imperatives possible? This question does not require an answer as to how the action which the imperative commands can be performed, but only an answer as to how the constraint of the will, which the imperative expresses in setting the problem, can be conceived. How an imperative of skill is possible requires no particular discussion. Whoever wills the end, so far as reason has decisive influence on his action, wills also the indispensably necessary steps to it that he can take. This proposition, in what concerns the will, is analytical; for, in the willing of an object as an effect, my causality, as an acting cause of this effect shown in my use of the means to it, is already thought, and the imperative derives the concept of actions necessary to this purpose from the concept of willing this purpose. Synthetical propositions undoubtedly are necessary for determining the means to a proposed end, but they do not concern the ground, the act of the will, but only the way to achieve the object. Mathematics teaches, by synthetical propositions only, that in order to bisect a line according to an infallible principle, I must make two intersecting arcs from each of its extremities; but if I know the proposed result can be obtained only by such an ac-

---

*The word "prudence" may be taken in two senses, and it may bear the names of prudence with reference to things of the world and private prudence. The former sense means the skill of a man in having an influence on others so as to use them for his own purposes. The latter is the ability to unite all these purposes to his own lasting advantage. The worth of the first is finally reduced to the latter, and of one who is prudent in the former sense but not in the latter we might better say that he is clever and cunning yet, on the whole, imprudent.

**It seems to me that the proper meaning of the word "pragmatic" could be most accurately defined in this way. For sanctions which properly flow not from the law of states as necessary statutes but from provision for the general welfare are called pragmatic. A history is pragmatically composed when it teaches prudence (i.e., instructs the world how it could provide for its interest better than, or at least as well as, has been done in the past).

tion, then it is an analytical proposition that, if I fully will the effect, I must also will the action necessary to produce it. For it is one and the same thing to conceive of something as an effect which is in a certain way possible through me, and to conceive of myself as acting in this way.

If it were only easy to give a definite concept of happiness, the imperatives of prudence would perfectly correspond to those of skill and would likewise be analytical. For it could then be said in this case as well as in the former that whoever wills the end wills also (necessarily according to reason) the only means to it which are in his power. But it is a misfortune that the concept of happiness is so indefinite that, although each person wishes to attain it, he can never definitely and self-consistently state what it is that he really wishes and wills. The reason for this is that all elements which belong to the concept of happiness are empirical (i.e., they must be taken from experience), while for the Idea of happiness an absolute whole, a maximum, of well-being is needed in my present and in every future condition. Now it is impossible for even a most clear-sighted and most capable but finite being to form here a definite concept of that which he really wills. If he wills riches, how much anxiety, envy, and intrigues might he not thereby draw upon his shoulders! If he wills much knowledge and vision, perhaps it might become only an eye that much sharper to show him as more dreadful the evils which are now hidden from him and which are yet unavoidable; or it might be to burden his desires—which already sufficiently engage him—with even more needs! If he wills long life, who guarantees that it will not be long misery! If he wills at least health, how often has not the discomfort of his body restrained him from excesses into which perfect health would have led him? In short, he is not capable, on any principle and with complete certainty, of ascertaining what would make him truly happy; omniscience would be needed for this. He cannot, therefore, act according to definite principles so as to be happy, but only according to empirical counsels (e.g., those of diet, economy, courtesy, restraint, etc.) which are shown by experience best to promote well-being on the average. Hence the imperatives of prudence cannot, in the strict sense, command (i.e., present actions objectively as practically necessary); thus they are to be taken as counsels (*consilia*) rather than as commands (*praecepta*) of reason, and the task of determining infallibly and universally what action will promote the happiness of a rational being is completely unsolvable. There can be no imperative which would, in the strict sense, command us to do what makes for happiness, because happiness is an ideal not of reason but of imagination, depending only on empirical grounds which one would expect in vain to determine an action through which the totality of consequences—which in fact is infinite—could be achieved. Assuming that the means to happiness could be infallibly stated, this imperative of prudence would be an analytically practical proposition for it differs from the imperative of skill only in that its purpose is given, while in the imperative of skill it is merely a possible purpose. Since both, however, command the means to that which one presupposes as a willed purpose, the imperative which commands the willing of the means to him who wills the end is in both cases analytical. There is, consequently, no difficulty in seeing the possibility of such an imperative.

To see how the imperative of morality is possible, then, is without doubt the only question needing an answer. It is not hypothetical, and thus the objectively conceived necessity cannot be supported by any presupposed purpose, as was the case with the hypothetical imperatives. But it must not be overlooked that it cannot be shown by any example (i.e., it cannot be empirically shown) that there is such an imperative. Rather, it is to be suspected that all imperatives which appear to be categorical are tacitly hypothetical. For instance, when it is said, "Thou shalt not make a false promise," we assume that the necessity of this prohibition is not a mere counsel for the sake of escaping some other evil, so that it would read: "Thou shalt not make a false promise, lest, if it comes to light, thou ruinest thy credit." [In so doing] we assume that an action of this kind must be regarded as in itself bad and that the imperative prohibiting it is categorical, but we cannot show with certainty by any example that the will is here determined by the law alone without any other incentives, although it appears to be so. For it is always possible that secretly fear of disgrace, and perhaps also obscure apprehension of other dangers, may have had an influence on the will. Who can prove by experience the nonexistence of a cause when experience shows us only that we do not perceive the cause? In such a case the so-called moral imperative, which as such appears to be categorical and unconditional, would be actually only a pragmatic precept which makes us attentive to our own advantage and teaches us to consider it.

Thus we shall have to investigate purely *a priori* the possibility of a categorical imperative, for we do not have the advantage that experience would show us the reality of this imperative so that the [demonstration of its] possibility would be necessary only for its explanation, and not for its establishment. In the meantime, this much at least may be seen: the categorical imperative alone can be taken as a practical law, while all other imperatives may be called principles of the will but not laws. This is because what is necessary merely for the attainment of some chosen end can be regarded as itself contingent and we get rid of the precept once we give up the end in view, whereas the unconditional command leaves the will no freedom to choose the opposite. Thus it alone implies the necessity which we require of a law.

Secondly, in the case of the categorical imperative or law of morality, the cause of the difficulty in discerning its possibility is very weighty. This imperative is an *a priori* synthetical practical proposition* and since to discern the possibility of propositions of this sort is so difficult in theoretical knowledge it may well be gathered that it will be no less difficult in practical knowledge.

In attacking this problem, we will first inquire whether the mere concept of a categorical imperative does not also furnish the formula containing the proposition which alone can be a categorical imperative. For even when we know the formula of the imperative, to learn how such an absolute command is possible will require difficult and special labors which we shall postpone to the last Section.

If I think of a hypothetical imperative as such, I do not know what it will contain until the condition is stated [under which it is an imperative]. But if I think of a categorical imperative, I know immediately what it will contain. For since the imperative contains, besides the law, only the necessity of the maxim** of acting in accordance with the law, while the law contains no condition to which it is restricted, nothing remains except the universality of law as such to which the maxim of the action should conform; and this conformity alone is what is represented as necessary by the imperative.

---

*I connect *a priori*, and hence necessarily, the action with the will without supposing as a condition that there is any inclination [to the action] (though I do so only objectively, i.e., under the Idea of a reason which would have complete power over all subjective motives). This is, therefore, a practical proposition which does not analytically derive the willing of an action from some other volition already presupposed (for we do not have such a perfect will); it rather connects it directly with the concept of the will of a rational being as something which is not contained within it.

**A maxim is the subjective principle of acting and must be distinguished from the objective principle (i.e., the practical law). The former contains the practical rule which reason determines according to the conditions of the subject (often his ignorance or inclinations) and is thus the principle according to which the subject acts. The law, on the other hand, is the objective principle valid for every rational being, and the principle by which it ought to act, i.e., an imperative.

There is, therefore, only one categorical imperative. It is: Act only according to that maxim by which you can at the same time will that it should become a universal law.

Now if all imperatives of duty can be derived from this one imperative as a principle, we can at least show what we understand by the concept of duty and what it means, even though it remain undecided whether that which is called duty is an empty concept or not.

The universality of law according to which effects are produced constitutes what is properly called nature in the most general sense (as to form) (i.e., the existence of things so far as it is determined by universal laws). [By analogy], then, the universal imperative of duty can be expressed as follows: Act as though the maxim of your action were by your will to become a universal law of nature.

We shall now enumerate some duties, adopting the usual division of them into duties to ourselves and to others and into perfect and imperfect duties.*

1. A man who is reduced to despair by a series of evils feels a weariness with life but is still in possession of his reason sufficiently to ask whether it would not be contrary to his duty to himself to take his own life. Now he asks whether the maxim of his action could become a universal law of nature. His maxim, however is: For love of myself, I make it my principle to shorten my life when by a longer duration it threatens more evil than satisfaction. But it is questionable whether this principle of self-love could become a universal law of nature. One immediately sees a contradiction in a system of nature whose law would be to destroy life by the feeling whose special office is to impel the improvement of life. In this case it would not exist as nature; hence that maxim cannot obtain as a law of nature, and thus it wholly contradicts the supreme principle of all duty.

2. Another man finds himself forced by need to borrow money. He well knows that he will not be able to repay it, but he also sees that nothing will be lent him if he does not firmly promise to repay it at a certain time. He desires to make such a promise, but he has enough conscience to ask himself whether it is not improper and opposed to duty to relieve his distress in such a way. Now, assuming he does decide to do so, the maxim of his action would be as follows: When I believe myself to be in need of money, I will borrow money and promise to repay it, although I know I shall never be able to do so. Now this principle of self-love or of his own benefit may very well be compatible with his whole future welfare, but the question is whether it is right. He changes the pretension of self-love into a universal law and then puts the question: How would it be if my maxim became a universal law? He immediately sees that it could never hold as a universal law of nature and be consistent with itself; rather it must necessarily contradict itself. For the universality of a law which says that anyone who believes himself to be in need could promise what he pleased with the intention of not fulfilling it would make the promise itself and the end to be accomplished by it impossible; no one would believe what was promised to him but would only laugh at any such assertion as vain pretense.

3. A third finds in himself a talent which could, by means of some cultivation, make him in many respects a useful man. But he finds himself in comfortable circum-

---

*It must be noted here that I reserve the division of duties for a future *Metaphysics of Morals* and that the division here stands as only an arbitrary one (chosen in order to arrange my examples). For the rest, by a perfect duty I here understand a duty which permits no exception in the interest of inclination; thus I have not merely outer but also inner perfect duties. This runs contrary to the usage adopted in the schools, but I am not disposed to defend it here because it is all one to my purpose whether this is conceded or not.

stances and prefers indulgence in pleasure to troubling himself with broadening and improving his fortunate natural gifts. Now, however, let him ask whether his maxim of neglecting his gifts, besides agreeing with his propensity to idle amusement, agrees also with what is called duty. He sees that a system of nature could indeed exist in accordance with such a law, even though man (like the inhabitants of the South Sea Islands) should let his talents rust and resolve to devote his life merely to idleness, indulgence, and propagation—in a word, to pleasure. But he cannot possibly will that this should become a universal law of nature or that it should be implanted in us by a natural instinct. For, as a rational being, he necessarily wills that all his faculties should be developed, inasmuch as they are given him and serve him for all sorts of purposes.

4. A fourth man, for whom things are going well, sees that others (whom he could help) have to struggle with great hardships, and he asks, "What concern of mine is it? Let each one be as happy as heaven wills, or as he can make himself; I will not take anything from him or even envy him; but to his welfare or to his assistance in time of need I have no desire to contribute." If such a way of thinking were a universal law of nature, certainly the human race could exist, and without doubt even better than in a state where everyone talks of sympathy and good will or even exerts himself occasionally to practice them while, on the other hand, he cheats when he can and betrays or otherwise violates the right of man. Now although it is possible that a universal law of nature according to that maxim could exist, it is nevertheless impossible to will that such a principle should hold everywhere as a law of nature. For a will which resolved this would conflict with itself, since instances can often arise in which he would need the love and sympathy of others, and in which he would have robbed himself, by such a law of nature springing from his own will, of all hope of the aid he desires.

The foregoing are a few of the many actual duties, or at least of duties we hold to be actual, whose derivation from the one stated principle is clear. We must be able to will that a maxim of our action become a universal law; this is the canon of the moral estimation of our action generally. Some actions are of such a nature that their maxim cannot even be *thought* as a universal law of nature without contradiction, far from it being possible that one could will that it should be such. In others this internal impossibility is not found, though it is still impossible to *will* that that maxim should be raised to the universality of a law of nature, because such a will would contradict itself. We easily see that a maxim of the first kind conflicts with stricter or narrower (imprescriptable) duty, that of the latter with broader (meritorious) duty. Thus all duties, so far as the kind of obligation (not the object of their action) is concerned, have been completely exhibited by these examples in their dependence upon the same principle.

When we observe ourselves in any transgression of a duty, we find that we do not actually will that our maxim should become a universal law. That is impossible for us; rather, the contrary of this maxim should remain as a law generally, and we only take the liberty of making an exception to it for ourselves or for the sake of our inclination, and for this one occasion. Consequently, if we weighed everything from one and the same standpoint, namely, reason, we would come upon a contradiction in our own will, viz., that a certain principle is objectively necessary as a universal law and yet subjectively does not hold universally but rather admits exceptions. However, since we regard our action at one time from the point of view of a will wholly conformable to reason and then from that of a will affected by inclinations, there is actually no contradiction, but rather an opposition of inclination to the precept of reason (*antagonismus*). In this the universality of the principle (*universalitas*) is changed into mere generality (*generalitas*), whereby the practical principle of reason meets the maxim halfway. Although this cannot be justified in our own impartial judgment, it does show that we actually acknowledge the validity of the categorical imperative and allow ourselves (with all respect to it) only a few exceptions which seem to us to be unimportant and forced upon us.

We have thus at least established that if duty is a concept which is to have significance and actual law-giving authority for our actions, it can be expressed only in categorical imperatives and not at all in hypothetical ones. For every application of it we have also clearly exhibited the content of the categorical imperative which must contain the principle of all duty (if there is such). This is itself very much. But we are not yet advanced far enough to prove *a priori* that that kind of imperative really exists, that there is a practical law which of itself commands absolutely and without any incentives, and that obedience to this law is duty.

With a view to attaining this, it is extremely important to remember that we must not let ourselves think that the reality of this principle can be derived from the particular constitution of human nature. For duty is practical unconditional necessity of action; it must, therefore, hold for all rational beings (to which alone an imperative can apply), and only for that reason can it be a law for all human wills. Whatever is derived from the particular natural situation of man as such, or from certain feelings and propensities, or even from a particular tendency of the human reason which might not hold necessarily for the will of every rational being (if such a tendency is possible), can give a maxim valid for us but not a law; that is, it can give a subjective principle by which we might act if only we have the propensity and inclination, but not an objective principle by which we would be directed to act even if all our propensity, inclination, and natural tendency were opposed to it. This is so far the case that the sublimity and intrinsic worth of the command is the better shown in a duty the fewer subjective causes there are for it and the more they are against it; the latter do not weaken the constraint of the law or diminish its validity.

Here we see philosophy brought to what is, in fact, a precarious position, which should be made fast even though it is supported by nothing in either heaven or earth. Here philosophy must show its purity, as the absolute sustainer of its laws, and not as the herald of laws which an implanted sense or who knows what tutelary nature whispers to it. Those may be better than nothing at all, but they can never afford fundamental principles, which reason alone dictates. These fundamental principles must originate entirely *a priori* and thereby obtain their commanding authority; they can expect nothing from the inclination of men but everything from the supremacy of the law and due respect for it. Otherwise they condemn man to self-contempt and inner abhorrence.

Thus everything empirical is not only wholly unworthy to be an ingredient in the principle of morality but is even highly prejudicial to the purity of moral practices themselves. For, in morals, the proper and inestimable worth of an absolutely good will consists precisely in the freedom of the principle of action from all influences from contingent grounds which only experience can furnish. We cannot too much or too often warn against the lax or even base manner of thought which seeks its principles among empirical motives and laws, for human reason in its weariness is glad to rest on this pillow. In a dream of sweet illusions (in which it embraces not Juno but a cloud), it substitutes for morality a bastard patched up from limbs of very different parentage, which looks like anything one wishes to see in it, but not like virtue to anyone who has ever beheld her in her true form.*

---

*To behold virtue in her proper form is nothing else than to exhibit morality stripped of all admixture of sensuous things and of every spurious adornment of reward or self-love. How much she then eclipses everything which appears charming to the senses can easily be seen by everyone with the least effort of his reason, if it be not spoiled for all abstraction.

The question then is: Is it a necessary law for all rational beings that they should always judge their actions by such maxims as they themselves could will to serve as universal laws? If there is such a law, it must be connected wholly *a priori* with the concept of the will of a rational being as such. But in order to discover this connection, we must, however reluctantly, take a step into metaphysics, although in a region of it different from speculative philosophy, namely into the metaphysics of morals. In a practical philosophy it is not a question of assuming grounds for what happens but of assuming laws of what ought to happen even though it may never happen (that is to say, we assume objective practical laws). Hence in practical philosophy we need not inquire into the reasons why something pleases or displeases, how the pleasure of mere feeling differs from taste, and whether this is distinct from a general satisfaction of reason. Nor need we ask on what the feeling of pleasure or displeasure rests, how desires and inclinations arise, and how, finally, maxims arise from desires and inclination under the co-operation of reason. For all these matters belong to empirical psychology, which would be the second part of physics if we consider it as philosophy of nature so far as it rests on empirical laws. But here it is a question of objectively practical laws and thus of the relation of a will to itself so far as it determines itself only by reason, for everything which has a relation to the empirical automatically falls away, because if reason of itself alone determines conduct, it must necessarily do so *a priori*. The possibility of reason's thus determining conduct must now be investigated.

The will is thought of as a faculty of determining itself to action in accordance with the conception of certain laws. Such a faculty can be found only in rational beings. That which serves the will as the objective ground of its self-determination is a purpose, and if it is given by reason alone it must hold alike for all rational beings. On the other hand, that which contains the ground of the possibility of the action, whose result is an end, is called the means. The subjective ground of desire is the incentive (Triebfeder) while the objective ground of volition is the motive (Bewegungsgrund). Thus arises the distinction between subjective purposes, which rest on incentives, and objective purposes, which depend on motives valid for every rational being. Practical principles are formal when they disregard all subjective purposes; they are material when they have subjective purposes and thus certain incentives as their basis. The purposes that a rational being holds before himself by choice as consequences of his action are material purposes and are without exception only relative, for only their relation to a particularly constituted faculty of desire in the subject gives them their worth. And this worth cannot afford any universal principles for all rational beings or any principles valid and necessary for every volition. That is, they cannot give rise to any practical laws. All these relative purposes, therefore, are grounds for hypothetical imperatives only.

But suppose that there were something the existence of which in itself had absolute worth, something which, as an end in itself, could be a ground of definite laws. In it and only in it could lie the ground of a possible categorical imperative (i.e., of a practical law).

Now, I say, man and, in general, every rational being exists as an end in himself and not merely as a means to be arbitrarily used by this or that will. In all his actions, whether they are directed toward himself or toward other rational beings, he must always be regarded at the same time as an end. All objects of inclination have only conditional worth, for if the inclinations and needs founded on them did not exist, their object would be worthless. The inclinations themselves as the sources of needs, however, are so lacking in absolute worth that the universal wish of every rational being must be indeed to free himself completely from them. Therefore, the worth of any objects to be obtained by our actions is at times conditional. Beings whose existence does not depend on our will but on nature, if they are not rational beings, have only relative worth as means, and are therefore called "things"; rational beings, on the other hand, are designated "persons" because their nature indicates that they are ends in themselves (i.e., things which may not be used merely as means). Such a being is thus an object of respect, and as such restricts all [arbitrary] choice. Such beings are not merely subjective ends whose existence as a result of our action has a worth for us, but are objective ends (i.e., beings whose existence is an end in itself). Such an end is one in the place of which no other end, to which these beings should serve merely as means, can be put. Without them, nothing of absolute worth could be found, and if all worth is conditional and thus contingent, no supreme practical principle for reason could be found anywhere.

Thus if there is to be a supreme practical principle and a categorical imperative for the human will, it must be one that forms an objective principle of the will from the conception of that which is necessarily an end for everyone because it is an end in itself. Hence this objective principle can serve as a universal law. The ground of this principle is: rational nature exists as an end in itself. Man necessarily thinks of his own existence in this way, and thus far it is a subjective principle of human actions. Also every other rational being thinks of his existence on the same rational ground which holds also for myself;* thus it is at the same time an objective principle from which, as a supreme practical ground, it must be possible to derive all laws of the will. The practical imperative, therefore, is the following: Act so that you treat humanity, whether in your own person or in that of another, always as an end and never as a means only. Let us now see whether this can be achieved. To return to our previous examples:

First, according to the concept of necessary duty to oneself, he who contemplates suicide will ask himself whether his action can be consistent with the idea of humanity as an end in itself. If in order to escape from burdensome circumstances he destroys himself, he uses a person merely as a means to maintain a tolerable condition up to the end of life. Man, however, is not a thing, and thus not something to be used merely as a means; he must always be regarded in all his actions as an end in himself. Therefore I cannot dispose of man in my own person so as to mutilate, corrupt, or kill him. (It belongs to ethics proper to define more accurately this basic principle so as to avoid all misunderstanding, e.g., as to amputating limbs in order to preserve myself, or to exposing my life to danger in order to save it; I must therefore omit them here.)

Second, as concerns necessary or obligatory duties to others, he who intends a deceitful promise to others sees immediately that he intends to use another man merely as a means, without the latter at the same time containing the end in himself. For he whom I want to use for my own purposes by means of such a promise cannot possibly assent to my mode of acting against him and thus share in the purpose of this action. This conflict with the principle of other men is even clearer if we cite examples of attacks on their freedom and property, for then it is clear that he who violates the rights of men intends to make use of the person of others merely as means, without considering that, as rational beings, they must always be esteemed at the same time as ends (i.e., only as beings who must be able to embody in themselves the purpose of the very same action).**

*Here I present this proposition as a postulate, but in the last Section grounds for it will be found.

**Let it not be thought that the banal "what you do not wish to be done to you . . ." could here serve as guide or principle, for it is only derived from the principle and is restricted by various limitations. It cannot be a universal law, because it contains the ground neither of duties to one's self nor of the benevolent duties to others (for many a man would gladly consent that others should not benefit him, provided only that he might be excused from showing benevolence to them). Nor does it contain the ground of obligatory duties to another, for the criminal would argue on this ground against the judge who sentences him. And so on.

Third, with regard to contingent (meritorious) duty to oneself, it is not sufficient that the action not conflict with humanity in our person as an end in itself; it must also harmonize with it. In humanity there are capacities for greater perfection which belong to the purpose of nature with respect to humanity in our own person, and to neglect these might perhaps be consistent with the preservation of humanity as an end in itself, but not with the furtherance of that end.

Fourth, with regard to meritorious duty to others, the natural purpose that all men have is their own happiness. Humanity might indeed exist if no one contributed to the happiness of others, provided he did not intentionally detract from it, but this harmony with humanity as an end in itself is only negative, not positive, if everyone does not also endeavor, as far as he can, to further the purposes of others. For the ends of any person, who is an end in himself, must as far as possible be also my ends, if that conception of an end in itself is to have its full effect on me.

This principle of humanity, and in general of every rational creature an end in itself, is the supreme limiting condition on the freedom of action of each man. It is not borrowed from experience, first, because of its universality, since it applies to all rational beings generally, and experience does not suffice to determine anything about them; and secondly, because in experience humanity is not thought of (subjectively) as the purpose of men (i.e., as an object which we of ourselves really make our purpose). Rather it is thought of as the objective end which ought to constitute the supreme limiting condition of all subjective ends whatever they may be. Thus this principle must arise from pure reason. Objectively the ground of all practical legislation lies (according to the first principle) in the rule and form of universality, which makes it capable of being a law (at least a natural law); subjectively it lies in the end. But the subject of all ends is every rational being as an end in itself (by the second principle); from this there follows the third practical principle of the will as the supreme condition of its harmony with universal practical reason, viz, the Idea of the will of every rational being as making universal law.

By this principle all maxims are rejected which are not consistent with the will's giving universal law. The will is not only subject to the law, but subject in such a way that it must be conceived also as itself prescribing the law, of which reason can hold itself to be the author; it is on this ground alone that the will is regarded as subject to the law.

By the very fact that the imperatives are thought of as categorical, either way of conceiving them—as imperatives demanding the lawfulness of actions, resembling the lawfulness of the natural order; or as imperatives of the universal prerogative of the purposes of rational beings as such—excludes from their sovereign authority all admixture of any interest as an incentive to obedience. But we have been assuming the imperatives to be categorical, for that was necessary if we wished to explain the concept of duty; that there are practical propositions which command categorically could not of itself be proved independently, just as little as it can be proved anywhere in this section. One thing, however could have been done: to indicate in the imperative itself, by some determination inherent in it, that in willing from duty the renunciation of all interest is the specific mark of the categorical imperative, distinguishing it from the hypothetical. And this is now done in the third formulation of the principle, viz., in the Idea of the will of every rational being as a will giving universal law. A will which is subject to laws can be bound to them by an interest, but a will giving the supreme law cannot possibly depend upon any interest, for such a dependent will would itself need still another law which would restrict the interest of its self-love to the condition that its [maxim] should be valid as a universal law.

Thus the principle of every human will as a will giving universal law in all its maxims* is very well adapted to being a categorical imperative, provided it is otherwise correct. Because of the Idea of giving universal law, it is based on no interest; and thus of all possible imperatives, it alone can be unconditional. Or, better, converting the proposition: if there is a categorical imperative (a law for the will of every rational being), it can command only that everything be done from the maxim of its will as one which could have as its object only itself considered as giving universal law. For only in this case are the practical principle and the imperative which the will obeys unconditional, because the will can have no interest as its foundation.

If now we look back upon all previous attempts which have ever been undertaken to discover the principle of morality, it is not to be wondered at that they all had to fail. Man was seen to be bound to laws by his duty, but it was not seen that he is subject to his own, but still universal, legislation, and that he is bound to act only in accordance with his own will, which is, however, designed by nature to be a will giving universal law. For if one thought of him as only subject to a law (whatever it may be), this necessarily implied some interest as a stimulus or compulsion to obedience because the law did not arise from his will. Rather, his will had to be constrained by something else to act in a certain way. By this strictly necessary consequence, however, all the labor of finding a supreme ground for duty was irrevocably lost, and one never arrived at duty but only at the necessity of acting from a certain interest. This might be his own interest or that of another, but in either case the imperative always had to be conditional, and could not at all serve as a moral command. The moral principle I will call the principle of *autonomy* of the will in contrast to all other principles which I accordingly count under *heteronomy*.

The concept of any rational being as a being that must regard itself as giving universal law through all the maxims of its will, so that it may judge itself and its actions from this standpoint, leads to a very fruitful concept, namely that of a *realm of ends*.

By *realm* I understand the systematic union of different rational beings through common laws. Because laws determine which ends have universal validity, if we abstract from personal differences of rational beings, and thus from all content of their private purposes, we can think of a whole of all ends in systematic connection, a whole of rational beings as ends in themselves as well as a whole of particular purposes which each may set for himself. This is a realm of ends, which is possible on the principles stated above. For all rational beings stand under the law that each of them should treat himself and all others never merely as means, but in every case at the same time as an end in himself. Thus there arises a systematic union of rational beings through common objective laws. This is a realm which may be called a realm of ends (certainly only an ideal) because what these laws have in view is just the relation of these beings to each other as ends and means.

A rational being belongs to the realm of ends as a member when he gives universal laws in it while also himself subject to these laws. He belongs to it as sovereign when, as legislating, he is subject to the will of no other. The rational being must regard himself always as legislative in a realm of ends possible through the freedom of the will whether he belongs to it as member or as sovereign. He cannot maintain his position as sovereign merely through the maxims of his will, but only when he is a completely independent being without need and with unlimited power adequate to his will.

---

*I may be excused from citing examples to elucidate this principle, for those that have already illustrated the categorical imperative and its formula can here serve the same purpose.

Morality, therefore, consists in the relation of every action to the legislation through which alone a realm of ends is possible. This legislation must be found in every rational being. It must be able to arise from his will, whose principle then is to do no action according to any maxim which would be inconsistent with its being a universal law, and thus to act only so that the will through its maxims could regard itself at the same time as giving universal law. If the maxims do not by their nature already necessarily conform to this objective principle of rational beings as giving universal law, the necessity of acting according to that principle is called practical constraint, which is to say: duty. Duty pertains not to the sovereign of the realm of ends, but rather to each member and to each in the same degree.

The practical necessity of acting according to this principle (duty) does not rest at all on feelings, impulses, and inclinations; it rests solely on the relation of rational beings to one another, in which the will of a rational being must always be regarded as legislative, for otherwise it could not be thought of as an end in itself. Reason, therefore, relates every maxim of the will as giving universal laws to every other will and also to every action towards itself; it does not do so for the sake of any other practical motive or future advantage but rather from the Idea of the dignity of a rational being who obeys no law except one which he himself also gives.

In the realm of ends everything has either a *price* or a *dignity*. Whatever has a price can be replaced by something else as its equivalent; on the other hand, whatever is above all price and therefore admits of no equivalent, has dignity.

That which is related to general human inclinations and needs has a *market price*. That which, without presupposing any need, accords with a certain taste (i.e., with pleasure in the purposeless play of our faculties) has a *fancy price*. But that which constitutes the condition under which alone something can be an end in itself does not have mere relative worth (price) but an intrinsic worth (*dignity*).

Morality is the condition under which alone a rational being can be an end in himself, because only through it is it possible to be a lawgiving member in the realm of ends. Thus morality, and humanity so far as it is capable of morality, alone have dignity. Skill and diligence in work have a market value; wit, lively imagination, and humor have a fancy price; but fidelity in promises and benevolence on principle (not benevolence from instinct) have intrinsic worth. Nature and likewise art contain nothing which could make up for their lack, for their worth consists not in the effects which flow from them nor in any advantage and utility which they procure; it consists only in mental dispositions, maxims of the will, which are ready to reveal themselves in this manner through actions even though success does not favor them. These actions need no recommendation from my subjective disposition or taste in order that they may be looked upon with immediate favor and satisfaction, nor do they have need of any direct propensity or feeling directed to them. They exhibit the will which performs them as the object of an immediate respect, since nothing but reason is required in order to impose them upon the will. The will is not to be cajoled into them, for this, in the case of duties, would be a contradiction. This esteem lets the worth of such a turn of mind be recognized as dignity and puts it infinitely beyond any price; with things of price it cannot in the least be brought into any competition or comparison without, as it were, violating its holiness.

And what is it that justifies the morally good disposition or virtue in making such lofty claims? It is nothing less that the participation it affords the rational being in giving universal laws. He is thus fitted to be a member in a possible realm of ends, to which his own nature already destined him. For, as an end in himself, he is destined to be a lawgiver in the realm of ends, free from all laws of nature and obedient only to those laws which he himself gives. Accordingly, his maxims can belong to a universal legislation to which he is at the same time subject. A thing has no worth other than that determined for it by the law. The lawgiving which determines all worth must therefore have a dignity (i.e., an unconditional and incomparable worth). For the esteem which a rational being must have for it, only the word "respect" is suitable. Autonomy is thus the basis of the dignity of both human nature and every rational nature.

The three aforementioned ways of presenting the principle of morality are fundamentally only so many formulas of the very same law, and each of them unites the others in itself. There is, nevertheless, a difference between them, but the difference is more subjectively than objectively practical, for the difference is intended to bring an Idea of reason closer to intuition (by means of a certain analogy) and thus nearer to feeling. All maxims have:

1. A form, which consists in universality, and in this respect the formula of the moral imperative requires that maxims be chosen as though they should hold as universal laws of nature.
2. A material (i.e., an end), and in this respect the formula says that the rational being, as by its nature an end and thus as an end in itself, must serve in every maxim as the condition restricting all merely relative and arbitrary ends.
3. A complete determination of all maxims by the formula that all maxims which stem from autonomous legislation ought to harmonize with a possible realm of ends as with a realm of nature.*

There is a progression here like that through the categories of the unity of the form of the will (its universality), the plurality of material (the objects, ends), to the all-comprehensiveness or totality of the system of ends. But it is better in moral valuation to follow the rigorous method and to make the universal formula of the categorical imperative the basis: Act according to the maxim which can at the same time make itself a universal law. But if one wishes to gain a hearing for the moral law, it is very useful to bring one and the same action under the three stated principles and thus, so far as possible, bring it nearer to intuition.

We can now end where we started, with the concept of an unconditionally good will. That will is absolutely good which cannot be bad, and thus it is a will whose maxim, when made universal law, can never conflict with itself. Thus this principle is also its supreme law: Always act according to that maxim whose universality as law you can at the same time will. This is the only condition under which a will can never come into conflict with itself, and such an imperative is categorical. Because the validity of the will as a universal law for possible actions has an analogy with the universal connection of the existence of things under universal laws, which is the formal element of nature in general, the categorical imperative can be expressed also as follows: Act on those maxims which can at the same time have themselves as universal laws of nature as their object. Such, then, is the formula of an absolutely good will.

Rational nature is distinguished from others in that it proposes an end to itself. This end would be the material of every good will. Since, however, in the Idea of an absolutely good will without the limiting condition that this or that end be achieved, we must abstract from every end to be actually effected (as any particular end would

*Teleology considers nature as a realm of ends; morals regards a possible realm of ends as a realm of nature. In the former the realm of ends is a theoretical Idea for the explanation of what actually is. In the latter it is a practical Idea for bringing about that which does not exist but which can become actual through our conduct and for making it conform with this Idea.

make each will only relatively good), we must conceive the end here not as one to be brought about, but as a self-existent end, and thus merely negatively, as that which must never be acted against and which consequently must never be valued merely as a means but in every volition also as an end. Now this end can never be other than the subject of all possible ends themselves, because this is at the same time the subject of a possible will which is absolutely good, for the latter cannot without contradiction be made secondary to any other object. The principle: Act with reference to every rational being (whether yourself or another) so that in your maxim it is an end in itself, is thus basically identical with the principle: Act by a maxim which involves its own universal validity for every rational being.

That in the use of means to any end I should restrict my maxim to the condition of its universal validity as a law for every subject is tantamount to saying that the subject of ends (i.e., the rational being itself) must be made the basis of all maxims of actions and thus be treated never as a mere means but as the supreme limiting condition in the use of all means (i.e., as at the same time an end).

It follows incontestably that every rational being must be able to regard himself as an end in himself with reference to all laws to which he may be subject whatever they may be, and thus see himself as giving universal laws. For it is just the fitness of his maxims to universal legislation that indicates that he is an end in himself. It also follows that his dignity (his prerogative) over all merely natural beings entails that he must take his maxims from the point of view that regards himself, and hence also every other rational being, as legislative. Rational beings are, on this account, called persons. In this way, a world of rational beings (*mundus intelligibilis*) is possible as a realm of ends, because of the legislation belonging to all persons as members. Consequently every rational being must act as if by his maxims he were at all times a legislative member of the universal realm of ends. The formal principle of these maxims is: So act as if your maxims should serve at the same time as universal law (for all rational beings).

A realm of ends is thus possible only by analogy with a realm of nature. The former is possible only by maxims (i.e., self-imposed rules), while the latter is possible by laws of efficient causes of things externally necessitated. Regardless of this difference, by analogy we call the natural whole a realm of nature so far as it is related to rational beings as its end; we do so even though the natural whole is looked upon as a machine. Such a realm of ends would actually be realized through maxims whose rule is prescribed to all rational beings by the categorical imperative, if they were universally obeyed. But a rational being, though he scrupulously follow this maxim, cannot for that reason expect every other rational being to be true to it, nor can he expect the realm of nature and its orderly design to harmonize with him as a fitting member of a realm of ends which is possible through himself. That is, he cannot count on its favoring his expectation of happiness. Still the law: Act according to the maxim of a member of a merely potential realm of ends who gives universal law, remains in full force because it commands categorically. And just in this lies the paradox that simply the dignity of humanity as rational nature without any end or advantage to be gained by it, and thus respect for a mere Idea, should serve as the inflexible precept of the will. [There is the further paradox that] the sublimity of the maxims and the worthiness of every rational subject to be a law-giving member in the realm of ends consist precisely in the independence of his maxims from all such incentives. Otherwise he would have to be viewed as subject to only the natural law of his needs. Although the realm of nature as well as that of ends would be thought of as united under a sovereign, so that the latter would no longer remain a mere Idea but would receive true reality, the realm of ends would undoubtedly gain a strong urge in its favor though its intrinsic worth would not be augmented. Regardless of this, even the one and only absolute legislator would still have to be conceived as judging the worth of rational beings only by the disinterested conduct which they prescribe to themselves merely from the Idea. The essence of things is not changed by their external relations, and without reference to these relations a man must be judged only by what constitutes his absolute worth, and this is true whoever his judge may be, even if it be the Supreme Being. Morality is thus the relation of actions to the autonomy of the will (i.e., to the possible giving of universal law by the maxims of the will). The action which can be compatible with the autonomy of the will is permitted; that which does not agree with it is prohibited. The will whose maxims are necessarily in harmony with the laws of autonomy is a holy will or an absolutely good will. The dependence of a will not absolutely good on the principle of autonomy (moral constraint) is *obligation*. Hence obligation cannot be predicated of a holy will. The objective necessity of an action from obligation is called *duty*.

From what has just been said, it can easily be explained how it happens that, although in the concept of duty we think of subjection to law, we do nevertheless at the same time ascribe a certain sublimity and dignity to the person who fulfills all his duties. For though there is no sublimity in him in so far as he is subject to the moral law, yet he is sublime in so far as he is the giver of the law and subject to it for this reason only. We have also shown above how neither fear of nor inclination to the law is the incentive which can give moral worth to action; only respect for it can do so. Our own will, so far as it would act only under the condition of a universal legislation rendered possible by its maxims—this will ideally possible for us—is the proper object of respect, and the dignity of humanity consists just in its capacity to give universal laws under the condition that it is itself subject to this same legislation.

The Autonomy of the Will as the Supreme Principle of Morality

Autonomy of the will is that property of it by which it is a law to itself independent of any property of the objects of its volition. Hence the principle of autonomy is: Never choose except in such a way that the maxims of the choice are comprehended as universal law in the same volition. That this practical rule is an imperative, that is, that the will of every rational being is necessarily bound to it as a condition, cannot be proved by a mere analysis of the concepts occurring in it, because it is a synthetical proposition. To prove it, we would have to go beyond the knowledge of objects to a critical examination of the subject (i.e., to a critique of pure practical reason), for this synthetical proposition which commands apodictically must be susceptible of being known *a priori*. This matter, however, does not belong in the present section. But that the principle of autonomy, which is now in question, is the sole principle of morals can be readily shown by mere analysis of the concepts of morality; for by this analysis we find that its principle must be a categorical imperative and that the imperative commands neither more nor less than this very autonomy.

The Heteronomy of the Will as the Source of All Spurious Principles of Morality

If the will seeks the law which is to determine it elsewhere than in the fitness of its maxims to be given as universal law, and if thus it goes outside and seeks the law in the property of any of its objects, heteronomy always results. For then the will does not give itself the law, but the object through its relation to the will gives the law to it. This relation, whether it rests on inclination or on conceptions of reason, admits of only hypothetical imperatives: I should do something for the reason that I will something else. The moral (categorical) imperative, on the other hand, says that I should act in this or that way even though I have not willed anything else. For example, the former says that I should not lie if I wish to keep my good name. The latter says that I should not lie even though it would not cause me the least injury. The latter, therefore, must disregard every object to such an extent that it has absolutely no influence on the will; it must so disregard it that practical reason (will) may not just minister to any interest not its own but rather show its commanding authority as the supreme legislation. Thus, for instance, I should seek to further the happiness of others, not as though its realization were of consequence to me (because of a direct inclination or some satisfaction related to it indirectly through reason); I should do so solely because the maxim which excludes it from my duty cannot be comprehended as a universal law in one and the same volition.

*Classification of All Possible Principles
of Morality Following from the Assumed
Principle of Heteronomy*

Here as everywhere in the pure use of reason so long as a critical examination of it is lacking, human reason tries all possible wrong ways before it succeeds in finding the one true way.

All principles which can be taken from this point of view are either empirical or rational. The former, drawn from the principles of happiness, are based on physical or moral feeling; the latter, drawn from the principle of perfection, are based either on the rational concept of perfection as a possible result or on the concept of an independent perfection (the will of God) as the determining ground of the will.

Empirical principles are not at all suited to serve as the basis of moral laws. For if the basis of the universality by which they should be valid for all rational beings without distinction (the unconditional practical necessity which is thereby imposed upon them) is derived from a particular tendency of human nature or the accidental circumstance in which it is found, that universality is lost. But the principle of one's own happiness is the most objectionable of the empirical principles. This is not merely because it is false and because experience contradicts the supposition that well-being is always proportional to good conduct, nor yet because this principle contributes nothing to the establishment of morality inasmuch as it is a very different thing to make a man happy from making him good, and to make him prudent and farsighted for his own advantage is far from making him virtuous. Rather, it is because this principle supports morality with incentives which undermine it and destroy all its sublimity, for it puts the motives to virtue and those to vice in the same class, teaching us only to make a better calculation while obliterating the specific difference between them. On the other hand, there is the alleged special sense,* the moral feeling. The appeal to it is superficial, since those who cannot think expect help from feeling, even with respect to that which concerns universal laws; they do so even though feelings naturally differ so infinitely

---

*I count the principle of moral feeling under that of happiness, because every empirical interest promises to contribute to our well-being by the agreeableness that a thing affords, either directly and without a view to future advantage or with a view to it. We must likewise, with Hutcheson, count the principle of sympathy with the happiness of others under the moral sense which he assumed.

in degree that they are incapable of furnishing a uniform standard of the good and bad, and also in spite of the fact that one cannot validly judge for others by means of one's own feeling. Nevertheless, the moral feeling is nearer to morality and its dignity, inasmuch as it pays virtue the honor of ascribing the satisfaction and esteem for her directly to morality, and does not, as it were, say to her face that it is not her beauty but only our advantage which attaches us to her.

Among the rational principles of morality, there is the ontological concept of perfection. It is empty, indefinite, and consequently useless for finding in the immeasurable field of possible reality the greatest possible sum which is suitable to us; and, in specifically distinguishing the reality which is here in question from all other reality, it inevitably tends to move in a circle and cannot avoid tacitly presupposing the morality which it ought to explain. Nevertheless, it is better than the theological concept, which derives morality from a most perfect divine will. It is better not merely because we cannot intuit the perfection of the divine will, having rather to derive it only from our own concepts of which morality itself is foremost, but also because if we do not so derive it (and to do so would involve a most flagrant circle in explanation), the only remaining concept of the divine will is made up of the attributes of desire for glory and dominion combined with the awful conceptions of might and vengeance, and any system of ethics based on them would be directly opposed to morality.

But if I had to choose between the concept of the moral sense and that of perfection in general (neither of which at any rate weakens morality, though neither is capable of serving as its foundation), I would decide for the latter, because it preserves the indefinite Idea of a will good in itself free from corruption until it can be more narrowly defined. It at least withdraws the decision on the question from the realm of sensibility and brings it to the court of pure reason, although it does not even there decide the question.

For the rest, I think I may be excused from a lengthy refutation of all these doctrines. It is so easy, and presumably so well understood even by those whose office requires them to decide for one of these theories (since their students would not tolerate suspension of judgment), that such a refutation would be superfluous. What interests us more, however, is to know that all these principles set up nothing other than heteronomy of the will as the first ground of morality, and thus they necessarily miss their goal.

In every case in which the object of the will must be assumed as prescribing the rule which is to determine the will, the rule is nothing else than heteronomy. The imperative in this case is conditional, stating that if or because one wills such and such an object, one ought to act thus or so. Therefore the imperative can never command morally, that is, categorically. The object may determine the will by means of inclination, as in the principle of one's own happiness, or by means of reason directed to objects of our possible volition in general, as in the principle of perfection; but the will in these cases never determines itself directly by the conception of the action itself but only by the incentive which the foreseen result of the action incites in the will—that is: I ought to do something because I will something else. And here still another law must be assumed in me as the basis for this imperative; it would be a law by which I would necessarily will that other thing; but this law would in its turn require an imperative to restrict this maxim. Since the conception of a result to be obtained by one's own powers incites in the will an impulse which depends upon the natural characteristic of the subject, either of his sensibility (inclination and taste) or understanding and reason; and since these faculties according to the particular constitution of their nature find satisfaction in exercising themselves on the result of the voluntary action, it follows that it would really be nature which would give the law [to the action]. This law, as a law of nature, would have to be known and proved by experience, and as in itself contingent it would be unfit to be an apodictical practical rule such as the moral rule must be. Such a law always represents heteronomy of the will: the will does not give itself the law, but an external impulse gives the law to the will according to nature of the subject which is susceptible to receive it.

The absolutely good will, the principle of which must be a categorical imperative, is thus undetermined with reference to any object. It contains only the form of volition in general, and this form is autonomy. That is, the capability of the maxims of every good will to make themselves universal laws is itself the sole law which the will of every rational being imposes on himself, and it does not need to support this by any incentive or interest.

How such a synthetical practical *a priori* proposition is possible and why it is necessary is a problem whose solution does not lie within the boundaries of the metaphysics of morals. Moreover, we have not here affirmed its truth, and even less professed to command a proof of it. We showed only through the development of the generally received concept of morals that autonomy of the will is unavoidably connected with it, or rather that it is its foundation. Whoever, therefore, holds morality to be something real and not a chimerical idea without truth must also concede its principle which has been derived here. Consequently, this section, like the first, was merely analytical. To prove that morality is not a mere phantom of the mind—and if the categorical imperative, and with it the autonomy of the will, is true and absolutely necessary as an *a priori* proposition, it follows that it is no phantom—requires that a synthetical use of pure practical reason be possible. But we must not venture on this use without first making a critical examination of this faculty of reason. In the last section we shall give the principal features of such an examination that will be sufficient for our purpose.

THIRD SECTION

TRANSITION FROM THE METAPHYSICS OF MORALS TO THE CRITICAL EXAMINATION OF PURE PRACTICAL REASON

The Concept of Freedom Is the Key
to the Explanation of the Autonomy
of the Will

As will is a kind of causality of living beings so far as they are rational, freedom would be that property of this causality by which it can be effective independent of foreign causes determining it, just as natural necessity is the property of the causality of all irrational beings by which they are determined to activity by the influence of foreign causes.

The preceding definition of freedom is negative and therefore affords no insight into its essence. But a positive concept of freedom flows from it which is so much the richer and more fruitful. Since the concept of a causality entails that of laws according to which something (i.e., the effect) must be established through something else which we call cause, it follows that freedom is by no means lawless even though it is not a property of the will according to laws of nature. Rather, it must be a causality of a peculiar kind according to immutable laws. Otherwise a free will would be an absurdity. Natural necessity is, as we have seen, a heteronomy of efficient causes, for every effect is possible only according to the law that something else determines the efficient cause to its causality. What else, then, can the freedom of the will be but autonomy (i.e., the property of the will to be law to itself)? The proposition that the will is a law to itself in all its actions, however, only expresses the principle that we should act according to no other maxim than that which can also have itself as a universal law for its object. And this is just the formula of the categorical imperative and the principle of morality. Therefore a free will and a will under moral laws are identical.

Thus if freedom of the will is presupposed, morality together with its principle follows from it by the mere analysis of its concepts. But the principle: An absolutely good will is one whose maxim can always include itself as a universal law, is nevertheless a synthetical proposition. It is synthetical because by analysis of the concept of an absolutely good will that property of the maxim cannot be found in it. Such synthetical propositions, however, are made possible only by the fact that the two cognitions are connected with each other through their union with a third in which both are to be found. The positive concept of freedom furnishes this third cognition, which cannot be, as in the case of physical causes, the sensible world of nature, in the concept of which we find conjoined the concepts of something as cause in relation to something else as effect. We cannot yet show directly what this third cognition is to which freedom directs us and of which we have an *a priori* Idea, nor can we yet explain the deduction of the concept of freedom from pure practical reason, and therewith the possibility of a categorical imperative. For this, some further preparation is needed.

Freedom Must be Presupposed as the Property of the Will of All Rational Beings

It is not enough to ascribe freedom to our will, on whatever grounds, if we do not also have sufficient grounds for attributing it to all rational beings. For since morality serves as a law for us only as rational beings, it must hold for all rational beings, and since it must be derived exclusively from the property of freedom, freedom as a property of the will of all rational beings must be demonstrated. And it does not suffice to prove it from certain alleged experiences of human nature (which is indeed impossible, as it can be proved only *a priori*), but we must prove it as belonging universally to the activity of rational beings endowed with a will. Now I say that every being which cannot act otherwise than under the Idea of freedom is thereby really free in a practical respect. That is to say, all laws which are inseparably bound with freedom hold for it just as if its wills were proved free in itself by theoretical philosophy.* Now I affirm that we must necessarily grant that every rational being who has a will also has the Idea of freedom and that it acts only under this Idea. For in such a being we think of a reason which is practical (i.e., a reason which has causality with respect to its object). Now we cannot conceive of a reason which, in making its judgments, consciously responds to a bidding from the outside, for then the subject would attribute the determination of its

---

*I propose this argument as sufficient to our purpose: Freedom as an Idea is posited by all rational beings as the basis for their actions. I do so in order to avoid having to prove freedom also in its theoretical aspect. For even if the latter is left unproved, the laws which would obligate a being who was really free would hold for a being who cannot act except under the Idea of his own freedom. Thus we escape the onus which has been pressed on theory.

power of judgment not to reason but to an impulse. Reason must regard itself as the author of its principles, independently of alien influences; consequently as practical reason or as the will of a rational being it must regard itself as free. That is to say, the will of a rational being can be a will of its own only under the Idea of freedom, and therefore from a practical point of view such a will must be ascribed to all rational beings.

Of the Interest Attaching to the Ideas of Morality

We have finally reduced the definite concept of morality to the Idea of freedom, but we could not prove freedom to be actual in ourselves and in human nature. We saw only that we must presuppose it if we would think of a being as rational and conscious of its causality with respect to actions, that is, as endowed with a will; and so we find that on the very same grounds we must ascribe to each being endowed with reason and will the property of determining itself to action under the Idea of its freedom.

From presupposing this Idea [of freedom] there followed also the consciousness of a law of action: that the subjective principles of actions (i.e., maxims) must in every instance be so chosen that they can hold also as objective (i.e., universal) principles, and can thus serve as principles for our giving universal laws. But why should I, as a rational being, and why should all other beings endowed with reason, subject ourselves to this law? I will admit that no interest impels me to do so, for that would then give no categorical imperative. But I must nevertheless take an interest in it and see how it comes about, for this *ought* is properly a *would* that is valid for every rational being provided reason were practical for it without hindrance [i.e., exclusively determined its action]. For beings who, like ourselves, are affected by the senses as incentives different from reason, and who do not always do that which reason by itself alone would have done, that necessity of action is expressed as only an *ought*. The subjective necessity is thus distinguished from the objective.

It therefore seems that we have only presupposed the moral law, the principle of the autonomy of the will in the Idea of freedom, as if we could not prove its reality and objective necessity by itself. Even if that were so, we would still have gained something because we would at least have defined the genuine principle more accurately than had been done before; but with regard to its validity and the practical necessity of subjection to it, we would not have advanced a single step, for we could give no satisfactory answer to anyone who asked us why the universal validity of our maxim as a law had to be the restricting condition of our action. We could not tell on what is based the worth which we ascribe to actions of this kind—a worth so great that there can be no higher interest—nor could we tell how it happens that man believes that it is only through this that he feels his own personal worth, in contrast to which the worth of a pleasant or unpleasant state is to be regarded as nothing.

We do find sometimes that we can take an interest in a personal quality which involves no [personal] interest in any [external] condition, provided only that the [possession of] this quality makes us fit to participate in the [desired] condition in case reason were to effect the allotment of this condition. That is, being worthy of happiness, even without the motive of partaking in happiness, can interest of itself. But this judgment is in fact only the effect of the importance already ascribed to moral laws (if by the Idea of freedom we detach ourselves from every empirical interest). But that we ought so to detach ourselves from every empirical interest, to regard ourselves as free in acting and yet as subject to certain laws, in order to find a worth wholly in our person which would compensate for the loss of everything which could make our situation desirable—how this is possible and hence on what grounds the moral law obligates us still cannot be seen in this way.

We must openly confess that there is a kind of circle here from which it seems that there is no escape. We assume that we are free in the order of efficient causes so that we can conceive of ourselves as subject to moral laws in the order of ends. And then we think of ourselves subject to these laws because we have ascribed freedom of the will to ourselves. This is circular because freedom and self-legislation of the will are both autonomy and thus are reciprocal concepts, and for that reason one of them cannot be used to explain the other and to furnish a ground for it. At most they can be used for the logical purpose of bringing apparently different conceptions of the same object under a single concept (as we reduce different fractions of the same value to the lowest common terms).

One recourse, however, remains open to us, namely, to inquire whether we do not assume a different standpoint when we think of ourselves as causes a priori efficient through freedom from that which we occupy when we conceive of ourselves in the light of our actions as effects which we see before our eyes.

The following remark requires no subtle reflection, and we may suppose that even the commonest understanding can make it, though it does so, after its fashion, by an obscure discernment of judgment which it calls feeling: all conceptions, like those of the senses, which come to us without our choice enable us to know objects only as they affect us, while what they are in themselves remains unknown to us; therefore, as regards this kind of conception, even with the closest attention and clearness which understanding may ever bring to them we can attain only a knowledge of appearances and never a knowledge of things as they are in themselves. When this distinction is once made (perhaps merely because of a difference noticed between conceptions which are given to us from somewhere else and to which we are passive, and those which we produce from ourselves only and in which we show our own activity), it follows of itself that we must admit and assume behind the appearances something else which is not appearance, i.e., things as they are in themselves, although we must admit that we cannot approach them more closely and can never know what they are in themselves, since they can never be known by us except as they affect us. This must furnish a distinction, though a crude one, between a world of sense and a world of understanding. The former, by differences in our sensible faculties, can be very different to various observers, while the latter, which is its foundation, remains always the same. A man may not presume to know even himself as he really is by knowing himself through inner sensation. For since he does not, as it were, produce himself or derive his concept of himself a priori but only empirically, it is natural that he obtain his knowledge of himself through inner sense and consequently only through the appearance of his nature and the way in which his consciousness is affected. But beyond the characteristic of his own subject which is compounded of these mere appearances, he necessarily assumes something else as its basis, namely, his ego as it is in itself. Thus in respect to mere perception and receptivity to sensations he must count himself as belonging to the world of sense; but in respect to that which may be pure activity in himself (i.e., in respect to that which reaches consciousness directly and not by affecting the senses) he must reckon himself as belonging to the intellectual world. But he has no further knowledge of that world.

To such a conclusion the thinking man must come with respect to all things which may present themselves to him. Presumably it is to be met with in the commonest understanding which, as is well known, is very much inclined to expect behind the objects of the senses something else invisible and acting of itself. But common understanding soon spoils it by trying to make the invisible again sensible (i.e., to make it an object of intuition). Thus the common understanding becomes not in the least wiser.

Now man really finds in himself a faculty by which he distinguishes himself from all other things, even from himself so far as he is affected by objects. This faculty is reason. As a pure, spontaneous activity it is elevated even above understanding. For though the latter is also a spontaneous activity and does not, like sense, which is passive, merely contain representations which arise only when one is affected by things, it cannot produce by its activity any other concepts than those which serve to bring the sensible representations under rules and thereby to unite them in one consciousness. Without this use of sensibility it would think nothing at all; on the other hand, reason shows such a pure spontaneity in the case of Ideas that it far transcends anything that sensibility can give to consciousness, and shows its chief occupation in distinguishing the world of sense from the world of understanding, thereby prescribing limits to the understanding itself.

For this reason a rational being must regard itself qua intelligence (and not from the side of his lower faculties) as belonging to the world of understanding and not to that of the senses. Thus it has two standpoints from which it can consider itself and recognize the laws [governing] the employment of its powers and all its actions: first, as belonging to the world of sense, under the laws of nature (heteronomy), and, second, as belonging to the intelligible world under laws which, independent of nature, are not empirical but founded on reason alone.

As a rational being and thus as belonging to the intelligible world, man cannot think of the causality of his own will except under the Idea of freedom, for independence from the determining causes of the world of sense (an independence which reason must always ascribe to itself) is freedom. The concept of autonomy is inseparably connected with the Idea of freedom, and with the former there is inseparably bound the universal principle of morality, which is the ground in Idea of all actions of rational beings, just as natural law is the ground of all appearances.

We have now removed the suspicion which we raised that there might be a hidden circle in our reasoning from freedom to autonomy and from the latter to the moral law. This suspicion was that we laid down the Idea of freedom for the sake of the moral law in order later to derive the law from freedom, and that we were thus unable to give any basis for the law, presenting it only as a *petitio principii* [begging the question] which well-disposed minds might gladly allow us, but which we could never advance as a demonstrable proposition. But we now see that, if we think of ourselves as free, we transport ourselves into the intelligible world as members of it and know the autonomy of the will together with its consequence, morality; whereas if we think of ourselves as obligated, we consider ourselves as belonging both to the world of sense and at the same time to the intelligible world.

How Is a Categorical Imperative Possible?

The rational being counts himself, *qua* intelligence, as belonging to the intelligible world, and only as an efficient cause belonging to it does he call his causality will. On the other side, however, he is conscious of himself as a part of the world of sense in which his actions are found as mere appearances of that causality. But we do not discern how they are possible on the basis of that causality which we do not know; rather, those actions must be regarded as determined by other appearances, namely, desires and inclinations belonging to the world of sense. As a member of the intelligible world only, all my actions would completely accord with the principle of the autonomy of the pure will, and as a part only of the world of sense would they have to be assumed to conform wholly to the natural law of desires and inclinations and thus to the heteronomy of nature. (The former actions would rest on the supreme principle of morality, and the latter on that of happiness.) But since the intelligible world contains the ground of the world of sense and hence of its laws, the intelligible world is (and must be conceived as) directly legislative for my will, which belongs wholly to the intelligible world. Therefore I recognize myself *qua* intelligence as subject to the law of the world of understanding and to the autonomy of the will. That is, I recognize myself as subject to the law of reason which contains in the Idea of freedom the law of the intelligible world, while at the same time I must acknowledge that I am a being which belongs to the world of sense. Therefore I must regard the laws of the intelligible world as imperatives for me, and actions in accord with this principle as duties.

Thus categorical imperatives are possible because the Idea of freedom makes me a member of an intelligible world. Consequently, if I were a member of that world only, all my actions *would* always be in accordance with the autonomy of the will. But since I intuit myself at the same time as a member of the world of sense, my actions *ought* to conform to it, and this categorical "ought" presents a synthetic *a priori* proposition, since besides my will affected by my sensuous desires there is added the Idea of exactly the same will as pure, practical of itself, and belonging to the intelligible world, which according to reason contains the supreme condition of the sensuously affected will. It is similar to the manner in which concepts of the understanding, which of themselves mean nothing but lawful form in general, are added to the intuitions of the sensible world, thus rendering possible *a priori* synthetic propositions on which all knowledge of a system of nature rests.

The practical use of ordinary human reason confirms the correctness of this deduction. When we present examples of honesty of purpose, of steadfastness in following good maxims, and of sympathy and general benevolence even with great sacrifices of advantage and comfort, there is no man, not even the most malicious villain (provided he is otherwise accustomed to using his reason), who does not wish that he also might have these qualities, but because of his inclinations and impulses cannot bring this about, yet at the same time wishes to be free from such inclinations which are burdensome even to him. He thus proves that with a will free from all impulses of sensibility, he in thought transfers himself into an order of things altogether different from that of his desires in the field of sensibility. He cannot expect to obtain by that wish any gratification of desires or any state which would satisfy his actual or even imagined inclinations, for the Idea itself, which elicits this wish from him, would lose its preeminence if he had any such expectation. He imagines himself to be this better person when he transfers himself to the standpoint of a member of the intelligible world to which he is involuntarily impelled by the Idea of freedom (i.e., of independence from the determining causes in the world of sense); and from this standpoint he is conscious of a good will, which on his own confession constitutes the law for his bad will as a member of the world of sense. He acknowledges the authority of the law even while he transgresses it. The moral "ought" is therefore his own volition as a member of the intelligible world, and it is conceived by him as an "ought" only insofar as he regards himself at the same time as a member of the world of sense.

On the Extreme Boundary of All Practical Philosophy

In respect to their will, all men think of themselves as free. Hence arise all judgments of acts as being such as ought to have been done, although they were not done.

But this freedom is not an empirical concept and cannot be such, for it continues to hold even though experience shows the contrary of the demands which are necessarily conceived to be consequences of the supposition of freedom. On the other hand it is equally necessary that everything that happens should be inexorably determined by natural laws, and this natural necessity is likewise no empirical concept because it implies the concept of necessity and thus of *a priori* knowledge. But this concept of a system of nature is confirmed by experience, and it is inevitably presupposed if experience, which is knowledge of the objects of the sense interconnected by universal laws, is to be possible. Therefore freedom is only an Idea of reason whose objective reality in itself is doubtful, while nature is a concept of the understanding which shows and must necessarily show its reality by examples of experience.

There now arises a dialectic of reason, since the freedom ascribed to the will seems to stand in contradiction to natural necessity. At this parting of the ways reason in its speculative aspect finds the path of natural necessity more well-beaten and usable than that of freedom, but in its practical aspect the path of freedom is the only one on which it is possible to make use of reason in our conduct. Hence it is as impossible for the subtlest philosophy as for the commonest reasoning to argue freedom away. Philosophy must therefore assume that no true contradiction will be found between freedom and natural necessity in the same human actions, for it cannot give up the concept of nature any more than that of freedom.

Hence if we should never be able to conceive how freedom is possible, at least this apparent contradiction must be convincingly eradicated. For if even the thought of freedom contradicted itself or nature, it would have to be surrendered in competition with natural necessity.

But it would be impossible to escape this contradiction if the subject, who seems to himself to be free, thought of himself in the same sense or in the same relationship when he calls himself free as when he assumes that in the same action he is subject to natural law. Therefore it is an inescapable task of speculative philosophy to show at least that its illusion of contradiction rests on the fact that we [do not] think of man in a different sense and relationship when we call him free from that in which we consider him as part of nature and subject to its laws. It must show not only that they can very well coexist but also that they must be thought of as necessarily united in one and the same subject; for otherwise no ground could be given as to why we should burden reason with an Idea which, though it may without contradiction be united with another that is sufficiently established, nevertheless involves us in a perplexity which sorely embarrasses reason in its theoretical use. This duty is imposed only on theoretical philosophy, so that it may clear the way for practical philosophy. Thus the philosopher has no choice as to whether he will remove the apparent contradiction or leave it untouched, for in the latter case the theory of it would be unoccupied land, into the possession of which the fatalist could rightly enter and drive all morality from its alleged property as occupying it without title.

Yet we cannot say here that we have reached the boundary of practical philosophy. For the settlement of the controversy does not belong to practical philosophy, as the latter only demands from theoretical reason that it put an end to the discord in which it entangles itself in theoretical questions, so that practical reason may have rest and security from outward attacks which could dispute it the ground on which it desires to erect its edifice.

The title to freedom of the will claimed by ordinary reason is based on the consciousness and the conceded presupposition of the independence of reason from merely subjectively determining causes which together constitute what belongs only to sensation and is included under the general name of sensibility. Man, who in this way regards himself as intelligence, puts himself in a different order of things and in a relationship to determining grounds of an altogether different kind when he thinks of himself as intelligence with a will and thus as endowed with causality, compared with that other order of things and that other set of determining grounds which become relevant when he perceives himself as a phenomenon in the world of sense (as he really is also) and submits his causality to external determination according to natural laws. Now he soon realizes that both can subsist together—indeed, that they must. For there is not the least contradiction between a thing in appearance (as belonging to the world of sense) being subject to certain laws from which, as a thing or being regarded as it is in itself, it is independent. That he must think of himself in this twofold manner rests, with regard to the first, on the consciousness of himself as an object affected through the senses, and, with regard to what is required by the second, on the consciousness of himself as intelligence (i.e., as independent of sensible impressions in the use of reason), and thus as belonging to the intelligible world.

This is why man claims to possess a will which does not make him accountable for what belongs only to his desires and inclinations, but thinks of actions which can be done only by disregarding all his desires and sensuous attractions as possible and indeed as necessary for him. The causality of these actions lies in him as an intelligence and in effects and actions in accordance with principles of an intelligible world, of which he knows only that reason alone, and indeed pure reason independent of sensibility, gives the law in it. Moreover, since it is only as intelligence that he is his proper self (as man he is only appearance of himself), he knows that those laws apply to him directly and categorically, so that that to which inclinations and impulses and hence the entire nature of the world of sense incite him cannot in the least impair the laws of his volition as an intelligence. He does not even hold himself responsible for these inclinations and impulses or attribute them to his proper self (i.e., his will), though he does impute to his will the indulgence which he may grant to them when he permits them to influence his maxims to the detriment of the rational laws of his will.

When practical reason thinks itself into an intelligible world, it does in no way transcend its boundaries. It would do so, however, if it tried to intuit or feel itself into it. The intelligible world is only a negative thought with respect to the world of sense, which does not give reason any laws for determining the will. It is positive only in the single point that freedom as negative determination is at the same time connected with a positive power and even a causality of reason. This causality we call a will to act so that the principle of actions will accord with the essential characteristic of a rational cause (i.e., with the condition of universal validity of a maxim as law). But if it were to borrow an object of the will (i.e., a motive) from the intelligible world, it would overstep its boundaries and pretend to be acquainted with something of which it knows nothing. The concept of a world of understanding is therefore only a standpoint from which reason sees itself forced to take outside appearances, in order to think of itself as practical. If the influences of sensibility were determining for man, this would not be possible; but it is necessary unless he is to be denied the consciousness of himself as an intelligence, and thus as a rational and rationally active cause (i.e., a cause acting in freedom). This thought certainly implies the Idea of an order and legislation different from that of natural mechanism, which applies to the world of sense; and it makes necessary the concept of an intelligible world, the whole of rational beings as things regarded as they are in themselves. But it does not give us the least occasion to think of it otherwise than according to its formal condition only (i.e., the universality of the maxim of the will as law and thus the autonomy of the will), which alone is consistent with freedom. All laws, on the other hand, which are directed to an object make for heteronomy, which belongs only to natural laws and which can apply only to the world of sense.

But reason would overstep its bounds if it undertook to explain how pure reason can be practical, which is the same problem as explaining how freedom is possible.

We can explain nothing but what we can reduce to laws whose object can be given in some possible experience. But freedom is only an Idea, the objective reality which can in no way be shown to accord with natural laws or to be in any possible experience. Since no example in accordance with any analogy can support it, it can never be comprehended or even imagined. It holds only as the necessary presupposition of reason in a being who believes himself conscious of a will (i.e., of a faculty different from the mere faculty of desire, or a faculty of determining himself to act as an intelligence and thus according to laws of reason independently of natural instincts. But where determination according to natural laws comes to an end, there too all explanation ceases, and nothing remains but defense (i.e., refutation of the objections from those who pretend to have seen more deeply into the essence of things and who boldly declare freedom to be impossible). We can show them only that the supposed contradiction they have discovered lies nowhere else than in their necessarily regarding man [only] as appearance in order to make natural law valid with respect to human actions, and now when we require them to think of man *qua* intelligence as a thing regarded as it is in itself, they still persist in considering him as appearance [only]. Obviously, then, the detachment of his causality (his will) from all natural laws of the world of sense in one and the same subject is a contradiction, but this disappears when they reconsider and confess, as is reasonable, that behind the appearances things regarded as they are in themselves must stand as their hidden ground, and that we cannot expect the laws of the activity of these grounds to be the same as those under which their appearances stand.

The subjective impossibility of explaining the freedom of the will is the same as the impossibility of discovering and explaining an interest* which man can take in moral laws. Nevertheless, he does actually take an interest in them, and the foundation of this interest in us we will call the moral feeling. This moral feeling has been erroneously construed by some as the standard for our moral judgment, whereas it must be regarded rather as the subjective effect which the law has upon the will to which reason alone gives objective grounds.

In order to will an action which reason alone prescribes to the sensuously affected rational being as the action which he ought to will, there is certainly required a power of will to instill a feeling of pleasure of satisfaction in the fulfilment of duty, and hence there must be a causality of reason to determine sensibility in accordance with its own principles. But it is wholly impossible to discern, i.e., to make *a priori* conceivable, how a mere thought containing nothing sensuous is able to produce a sensation of pleasure or displeasure. For that is a particular kind of causality of which, as of

---

*Interest is that by which reason becomes practical (i.e., a cause determining the will). We therefore say only of a rational being that he takes an interest in something; irrational creatures feel only sensuous impulses. A direct interest in the action is taken by reason only if the universal validity of its maxim is a sufficient determining ground of the will. Only such an interest is pure. But if reason can determine the will only by means of another object of desire or under the presupposition of a particular feeling of the subject, reason takes merely an indirect interest in the action, and since reason for itself alone without experience can discover neither objects of the will nor a particular feeling which lies at its root, that indirect interest would be only empirical and not a pure interest of reason. The logical interest of reason in advancing its insights is never direct but rather presupposes purposes for which they are to be used.

all causality, we cannot determine anything *a priori* but must consult experience only. But since experience can exemplify the relation of cause to effect only as subsisting between two objects of experience, while here pure reason by mere Ideas (which furnish no object for experience) is to be the cause of an effect which does lie within experience, an explanation of how and why the universality of the maxim as law (and hence morality) interests us is completely impossible for us men. Only this much is certain: that it is valid for us not because it interests us (for that is heteronomy and dependence of practical reason on sensibility, i.e., on a basic feeling; and thus it could never be morally legislating); but that it interests us because it is valid for us as men, inasmuch as it has arisen from our will as intelligence and hence from our proper self; but what belongs to mere appearance is necessarily subordinated to the character of the thing regarded as it is in itself.

Thus the question *How is a categorical imperative possible?* can be answered to this extent: We can cite the only presupposition under which it is possible. This is the Idea of freedom, and we can have insight into the necessity of this presupposition which is sufficient to the practical use of reason (i.e., to the conviction of the validity of this imperative and hence also of the moral law). But how this presupposition itself is possible can never be discerned by any human reason. However, on the presupposition of freedom of the will as an intelligence, its autonomy as the formal condition under which alone it can be determined is a necessary consequence. To presuppose the freedom of the will is not only quite possible, as speculative philosophy itself can prove, for it does not involve itself in a contradiction with the principle of natural necessity in the interconnection of appearances in the world of sense. But it is also unconditionally necessary that a rational being conscious of its causality through reason, and thus conscious of a will different from desires, should practically presuppose freedom (i.e., presuppose it in the Idea as the fundamental condition of all his voluntary acts). Yet how pure reason, without any other incentives whencesoever derived, can by itself be practical (i.e., how the simple principle of the universal validity of its maxims as laws—which would certainly be the form of a pure practical reason—without any material (object) of the will in which we might in advance take some interest), and can itself furnish an incentive and produce an interest which would be called purely moral; or, in other words, *how pure reason can be practical*—to explain this, all human reason is wholly incompetent, and all the pain and work of seeking an explanation of it are wasted.

It is just the same as if I sought to find out how freedom itself as the causality of a will is possible, for in so doing I would leave the philosophical basis of explanation behind, and I have no other. Certainly I could revel in the intelligible world, the world of intelligences, which still remains to me; but although I have a well-founded Idea of it, still I do not have the least knowledge of it, nor can I ever attain knowledge of it by all the exertions of my natural faculty of reason. This intelligible world signifies only a something which remains when I have excluded from the determining grounds of my will everything belonging to the world of sense, in order to isolate the principle of motives from the field of sensibility. I do so by limiting it and showing that it does not contain absolutely everything in itself but that outside it there is still more; but this more I do not know. After banishing all material (i.e., knowledge of objects) from pure reason which formulates this ideal, there remain to me only the form, the practical law of the universal validity of maxims, and, in accordance with this, reason in relation to a pure intelligible world as a possible efficient cause determining the will. Any incentive must here be totally absent unless this Idea of an intelligible world or that in which reason directly takes an interest be the incentive. But to make this conceivable is precisely the problem we cannot solve.

Here, then, is the outermost boundary of all moral inquiry. To define it is very important, both in order that reason may not seek around, on the one hand, in the world of sense, in a way harmful to morals, for the supreme motive and for a comprehensible but empirical interest; and so that it will not, on the other hand, impotently flap its wings in the space (for it, an empty space) of transcendent concepts which we call the intelligible world, without being able to move from its starting point and so losing itself amid phantoms. Furthermore, the Idea of a pure intelligible world as a whole of all intelligences to which we ourselves belong as rational beings (though on the other side we are at the same time members of the world of sense) is always a useful and permissible Idea for the purpose of a rational faith. This is so even though all knowledge terminates at its boundary, for the glorious ideal of a universal realm of ends regarded as they are in themselves (rational beings) can awaken in us a lively interest in the moral law. To that realm we can belong as members only when we scrupulously conduct ourselves by maxims of freedom as if they were laws of nature.

Concluding Remark

The speculative use of reason with respect to nature leads to the absolute necessity of some supreme cause of the world. The practical use of reason with respect to freedom leads also to an absolute necessity, but to the necessity only of laws of actions of a rational being as such. Now it is an essential principle of all use of reason to push its knowledge to an awareness of its necessity, for otherwise it would not be rational knowledge. But it is also an equally essential restriction of this very same reason that it cannot discern the necessity of what is or of what occurs or of what ought to be done unless a condition under which it is or occurs or ought to be done is presupposed. In this way, however, the satisfaction of reason is only postponed further and further by the unceasing search for the condition. Reason, therefore, restlessly seeking the unconditionally necessary, sees itself compelled to assume it though it has no means by which to make it comprehensible; it is happy enough if it can discover only the concept which is compatible with this presupposition. It is, therefore, no objection to our deduction of the supreme principle of morality, but a reproach that we must make to human reason generally, that it cannot render comprehensible the absolute necessity of an unconditional practical law (such as the categorical imperative must be). Reason cannot be blamed for being unwilling to explain it by a condition (i.e., by making some interest its basis), for then the law would cease to be moral and would no longer be the supreme law of freedom. And so we do not indeed comprehend the unconditional practical necessity of the moral imperative; yet we do comprehend its incomprehensibility, which is all that can fairly be demanded of a philosophy which in its principles strives to reach the boundary of human reason.

NINETEENTH-CENTURY PHILOSOPHY

◄○►

The nineteenth century has often been described as the Age of Progress. The scientific discoveries of the seventeenth and eighteenth centuries led to numerous technological advances in Europe and America. These advances, in turn, made possible the Industrial Revolution and the incredible outpouring of goods it produced. Millions left the hard life of the farm, moving to cities and working in factories. In England, for example, in 1800 only 21 percent of the population lived in cities with a population more than ten thousand. By 1890, city-dwellers had become 62 percent of the population. Life in the city seemed full of promise, and the good life seemed within reach of all.

The early ninetheenth-century philosophies of Hegel and Mill epitomized this optimism about the future. Hegel claimed that "Idea" (or "Spirit" or "Mind") was guiding all of history. Contradictions in thought and practice would be overcome as history progressed. For his part, Mill wrote in his major work, *Utilitarianism,* of the "progress of science [which] holds out a promise for the future." Mill argued that free individuals representing the "wisdom of society" could overcome the social problems of the nineteenth century.

Yet by the middle of the century, doubts began to emerge among some thinkers. Kierkegaard questioned the optimistic assumptions of Hegel and expressed skepticism about the inevitability of progress. More fundamentally, Kierkegaard claimed that Hegel's entire system was flawed, because it assumed an objectivity that is unavailable and a finality that does not exist within history. For his part, Marx noted the effect of the Industrial Revolution on the factory worker and called for a change in the social and economic order. Marx also raised questions about Hegel, focusing his attack on Hegel's concept of "Idea."

Towards the end of the century, Nietzsche added his voice to those of the skeptics about nineteenth-century progress. Nietzsche decried the lack of passion brought on by the comforts of the Industrial Revolution. He called on thinking persons to recognize that there are no standards, that "God is dead," and he wished them to assert their "will to power" in overcoming the comfortable mediocrity of his age.

Though Nietzsche died in 1900, the nineteenth century really did not come to an end, in terms of ideas, until 1914. In that year, all the impressive technology that had been developed over the previous century was brought to bear in World War I with the goal of killing people. A system of alliances that had been established in the mid-nineteenth century on the basis of rational, pragmatic considerations ensured that virtually the entire world was involved in the struggle. By the time the war ended, the nineteenth-century optimistic assumption of progress had died.

*   *   *

There are a number of general introductions to nineteenth-century philosophy. Among the classics in this area are Étienne Gilson, *Recent Philosophy: Hegel to the Present* (New York: Random House, 1966); the appropriate works from Frederick Copleston's series, *A History of Philosophy: Volume VII, Fichte to Nietzsche; Volume VIII, Bentham to Russell;* and *Volume IX, Maine de Biran to Sartre* (New York: Image Doubleday, 1963, 1966, 1974); and from Emile Brehier's series, *The History of Philosophy: Volume 6, The Nineteenth Century: Period of Systems, 1800–1850; Volume 7, Contemporary Philosophy, Since 1850,* translated by Joseph Thomas (Chicago: University of Chicago Press, 1969); Karl Löwith, *From Hegel to Nietzsche: The Revolution in Nineteenth-Century Thought,* translated by David E. Green (1964; reprinted New York: Columbia University Press, 1991); and W.T. Jones, *Kant and the Nineteenth Century,* 2nd edition, revised (New York: Harcourt, Brace & World, 1975). More recent general surveys include Roger Scruton, *A Short History of Modern Philosophy: From Descartes to Wittgenstein* (London: Routledge, 1984); Wallace I. Matson, *A New History of Philosophy: Volume II, Modern* (San Diego, CA: Harcourt Brace Jovanovich, 1987); and C.L. Ten, ed., *Routledge History of Philosophy, Volume 7: The Nineteenth Century* (London: Routledge, 1994). The following is a sampling of the many books on specific topics from this era: William Barrett, *Irrational Man* (New York: Doubleday, 1958); David Knight, T*he Age of Science: The Scientific World-View in the Nineteenth Century* (Oxford: Blackwell, 1986); Robert C. Solomon, *Hegel to Existentialism* (Oxford: Oxford University Press, 1987); David Jasper and T.R. Wright, eds., *The Critical Spirit and the Will to Believe: Essays in Nineteenth-Century Literature and Religion* (London: Macmillan, 1989); Mary Ellen Waithe, *A History of Women Philosophers: Volume III, Modern Women Philosophers, 1600–1900* (Dordrecht, Netherlands: Kluwer Academic, 1991); and Mark Francis and John Morrow, *A History of English Political Thought in the Nineteenth Century* (London: Duckworth, 1994).

G.W.F. HEGEL
1770–1831

Georg Wilhelm Friedrich Hegel was born in Stuttgart, in southern Germany. Hegel and his father, a minor government official; his mother, a loving hausfrau (housewife); and his sister and brother were all close, affectionate, and loving. It is easy to see why Hegel would later describe the family as the "immediate Ethical Substance." Following grade school in Stuttgart, at age eighteen, Hegel won a scholarship to Tübingen University, where he studied theology. While there, he met and befriended the poet Johann Christian Friedrich Hölderlin and the philosopher Friedrich Wilhelm Joseph Schelling. The work Hegel submitted to his professors at the university gave no indication of the brilliant philosophical career that was to follow. In fact, his diploma from the university recorded that his knowledge of theology was fair, but his knowledge of philosophy was inadequate. Nevertheless, Hegel was already beginning to write insightful essays, not for classroom assignments, but to clarify his own thoughts.

After graduating from the university in 1793, Hegel spent seven years as a tutor for wealthy families in Bern and Frankfurt. During this time he continued to write essays—mostly on religious topics—that indicated he had moved far away from orthodox Christianity. For example, one early essay compared Jesus and Socrates, and Socrates' ethical teaching was seen as superior.

Following his father's death in 1799, Hegel inherited a modest sum of money, quit tutoring, and joined his friend Schelling at the University of Jena. There Hegel became a *Privatdozent* (an unsalaried lecturer) and coedited a philosophic journal with Schelling. While at Jena, Hegel wrote his first great work, *The Phenomenology of Spirit* (1807), which laid out the major themes of his philosophy. This work included a critique of Schelling's ideas, which ended the friendship.

Before this important work could be published, Napoleon's war with Prussia closed the University of Jena, and so Hegel, whose inheritance had now been exhausted, was forced to find other employment.

After a stint as a newspaper editor, Hegel served eight years in Nürnberg as the rector of a *Gymnasium* (high school). There he published his second major work, *Science of Logic* (1812–1816). He also met and married a young woman from a distinguished family who was half his age, and they had two sons. In 1816, Hegel accepted a chair of philosophy at the University of Heidelberg. He continued his practice of producing a major book at each place he worked by publishing the *Encyclopedia of the Philosophical Sciences in Outline* in 1817. In 1818, Hegel moved to his final institution, the University of Berlin. There he published his *Philosophy of Right* (1821)—and became famous throughout Europe. He remained in Berlin until his death from cholera in 1831.

Following his death, a group of his friends published an eighteen-volume collection of his works, including his early essays and his lectures on aesthetics, the history of philosophy, the philosophy of history, and the philosophy of religion.

*   *   *

Like all philosophers of his age, Hegel was greatly influenced by Kant. Kant had managed to synthesize two previously disparate realities—the rational world of ideas (emphasized by rationalists) with the phenomenal world of perception (emphasized by empiricists). But in so doing, Kant separated the noumenal world of "things-in-themselves" from the phenomenal world of experience and declared the noumenal world unknowable. In a sense, he had reconciled two competing epistemologies—Continental Rationalism and British Empiricism—at the expense of abandoning metaphysics. Hegel sought to go one step further than Kant and effect a complete synthesis that would not only draw together competing epistemologies but would also show the connection between epistemology and metaphysics. The key to this synthesis is the recognition that consciousness is the ultimate reality, or, to use his famous phrase, "What is real is rational—what is rational is real." That is, metaphysical reality (the real) *is* Idea or Spirit or Mind (that which knows). The resulting philosophy is called "Absolute Idealism" because all things that exist are essentially related to absolute Idea or Spirit or Mind.

According to Hegel, traditional rationalism (what he calls *raisonnement*) tends to classify all experience formally into abstract, lifeless universals. Taken to its logical extreme, rationalists end up with the abstraction "Being": "But this mere Being, as it is mere abstraction, is therefore the absolutely negative: which, in a similarly immediate aspect, is just NOTHING." By abstracting away the concreteness or particularity of actual experience, one is left with Being which is Nothing. The short article "Who Thinks Abstractly?" (1807–1808?), reprinted here in Walter Kaufmann's translation, clearly conveys Hegel's contempt for the process of abstraction.

Whereas Being and Nothing are both identical and yet contradictory, according to Hegel, "the truth of Being and Nothing is . . . the unity of the two: and this unity is BECOMING." The unity of Becoming does not obliterate Being and Nothing but holds both in tension in a higher truth. The two parts of the contradiction, together with that which unites or overcomes them, make up a triad. This method of overcoming contradictions by moving to a higher level of truth is known as the "dialectic." Hegel proposed to develop a complete dialectical system of reality based on the three foundational triads of "Being—Nothing—Becoming," "Being—Essence—Notion," and "Idea—Nature—Mind." Though he developed several proposals for this system, Hegel never completed any of them.

Although Hegel never developed a complete system, he did use the dialectical method to explain consciousness. In the section entitled "Relations of Master and Servant" from *The Phenomenology of Spirit* (1807), reprinted here in the J.L.H. Thomas translation, Hegel explains one stage in the dialectical development of consciousness. He begins by pointing out that only by acknowledging an "other" is self-consciousness possible. But if there is an other, then the original self-consciousness feels threatened and asserts its freedom by trying to dominate that other and force acknowledgment of its dominance. The ensuing struggle results in a master who dominates and a servant who is dominated. The master then forces the servant to produce material goods for the enjoyment of the master.

But at this point, the master now depends upon the servant he has dominated. In the first place, his self-consciousness as master is subject to his recognition as master by the servant. But more important, while the master has been consuming or destroying what the servant makes, the servant has been learning to create—to bend nature to his will—and so has established his own self-consciousness in relation to what he has created. Furthermore, the labor of the servant has a permanent quality whereas the master's consumption again depends on the servant's production. So by dominating the servant, the master is dominated.

The solution to this contradiction is to acknowledge that neither master nor servant is free and that freedom is not possible in relationships of domination. The next stage in the dialectic is for the mind to seek freedom within itself.

Hegel's ideas have been both lauded and attacked. His insights on the master-servant relationship made a powerful impression on Marx and Nietzsche. Indeed, Hegel's understanding of dialectical development became a central feature of Marx's thought—though Marx rejected the notion of Absolute Spirit. Phenomenology developed Hegel's insights about the different types of consciousness. The sociology of knowledge developed his notions about the connection between consciousness and the culture of a particular epoch. Chief among Hegel's critics was Kierkegaard, who objected strenuously to the devaluing of the individual, questioned the implicit optimism of the dialectic, and mocked the incompleteness of Hegel's "System." Perhaps Hegel's greatest legacy was not any specific idea, but the vision of a complete historical development of thought.

*   *   *

For a selection of primary source readings for Hegel, see *Hegel, The Essential Writings,* edited by Frederick G. Weiss (New York: Harper & Row, 1974). Many secondary books about Hegel are difficult for beginning students. Two accessible classics are W.T. Stace, *The Philosophy of Hegel* (1924; reprinted New York: Dover, 1955) and G.R.G. Mure, *An Introduction to Hegel* (Oxford: Clarendon Press, 1940). Recent helpful studies include J.N. Findlay, *Hegel: A Re-examination* (New York: Macmillan, 1958); Walter Kaufmann, *Hegel: Reinterpretation, Texts and Commentary* (Garden City, NY: Doubleday, 1965); and, especially, Peter Singer, *Hegel* (Oxford: Oxford University Press, 1983). Charles Taylor's massive *Hegel* (Cambridge: Cambridge University Press, 1975) can be consulted for particular topics. For specialized topics, see H.A. Reyburn, *Ethical Theory of Hegel*

(Oxford: Oxford University Press, 1965); Ivan Soll, *An Introduction to Hegel's Metaphysics* (Chicago: University of Chicago Press, 1969); Walter Kaufmann, ed., *Hegel's Political Philosophy* (New York: Atherton Press, 1970); Quentin Lauer, *Hegel's Idea of Philosophy* (New York: Fordham University Press, 1971); Quentin Lauer, *A Reading of Hegel's "Phenomenology of Spirit"* (New York: Fordham University Press, 1976); Robert C. Solomon, *From Hegel to Existentialism* (New York: Oxford University Press, 1987); Michael N. Forster, *Hegel and Skepticism* (Cambridge, MA: Harvard University Press, 1989); Merold Westphal, *History and Truth in Hegel's "Phenomenology"* (Atlantic Highlands, NJ: Humanities Press, 1990); H. S. Harris, *Hegel: Phenomenology and System* (Cambridge, MA: Hackett, 1995); John Russon, *The Self and Its Body in Hegel's Phenomenology of Spirit* (Toronto: University of Toronto Press, 1997); and Justus Hartnack, *An Introduction to Hegel's Logic,* translated by Lars Aagaard-Mogensen (Cambridge, MA: Hackett, 1998). Karl Marx, *Critique of Hegel's "Philosophy of Right,"* edited by Joseph O'Malley (Cambridge: Cambridge University Press, 1970) is both a critical review of Hegel's work and a major work in its own right. Michael Inwood, *A Hegel Dictionary* (Oxford: Basil Blackwell, 1992) provides a useful reference work. General collections of critical essays include W.E. Steinkraus, ed., *New Studies in Hegel's Philosophy* (New York: Holt, Rinehart & Winston, 1971); Alasdair MacIntyre, ed., *Hegel: A Collection of Critical Essays* (Notre Dame, IN: University of Notre Dame Press, 1972); Michael Inwood, ed., *Hegel* (Oxford: Oxford University Press, 1985); Frederick C. Beiser, ed., *The Cambridge Companion to Hegel* (Cambridge: Cambridge University Press, 1993); the multi-volume Robert Stern, ed., *G.W.F. Hegel: Critical Assessments* (London: Routledge, 1993); Patricia Jagentowicz Mills, ed., *Feminist Interpretations of Hegel* (College Park, PA: Pennsylvania State University Press, 1996); and Micahel Baur and John Russon, eds., *Hegel and the Tradition* (Toronto: University of Toronto Press, 1998).

PHENOMENOLOGY OF SPIRIT

Independence and Dependence of Self-Consciousness: Relations of Master and Servant

Self-consciousness is *in* and *for itself* in and through being in and for itself for another self-consciousness; that is, it is only as something acknowledged, or recognized. The concept of this unity of self-consciousness in its duplication, of the infinitude realising itself in self-consciousness, is a many-sided and many-sensed complex, so that the moments of this complex must both be held carefully apart, and at the same time taken and understood in this differentiation as not distinct, or always also in their opposed

Hegel, *Phenomenology of Spirit,* (B, IV, A: "Independence and Dependence of Self-Consciousness: Relations of Master and Servant"). Translated by J.L.H. Thomas. Reprinted from *Hegel: Selections,* edited by M.J. Inwood, *The Great Philosophers* series, Paul Edwards, general editor (New York: Macmillan, 1989).

sense. The double-sensedness of what is distinguished lies in the essence of self-consciousness, of being infinite, or boundless, that is, immediately the contrary of the determination in which it is established. The laying-apart of the concept of this spiritual unity in its duplication presents to us the movement of *acknowledging.*

There is for self-consciousness another self-consciousness; it has come *outside itself.* This has a twofold significance: *first,* self-consciousness has lost itself, for it finds itself as *another* being; *second,* it has thereby done away with the other, for it does not see the other either as the essential being, but *it itself* in the *other.*

Self-consciousness must do away with this *otherness it* has; this is the doing away with of the first double-sense, and hence itself a second double-sense: *first,* it must set out to do away with *the other* independent being in order thereby to become certain of *itself* as the essential being; *second,* in so doing it sets out to do away with *itself,* for this other being is itself.

This double-sensed doing away with its double-sensed otherness is equally a double-sensed return *into itself;* for, *first,* through doing away it gets itself back, for it becomes once more equal to itself through doing away with *its* otherness; *second,* however, it no less gives back the other self-consciousness to the latter again, for it had itself in the other, it does away with this being *it* has in the other, thus letting the other go free again.

This movement of self-consciousness in its relation to another self-consciousness has been presented in this way now, as *the doing of the one;* but this doing of the one has itself the two-fold significance of being as much *its doing* as *the doing of the other;* for the other is no less independent, shut up within itself, and there is nothing in it that is not owing to itself. The first self-consciousness does not have the object before it as the latter to begin with is merely for desire, but an independent object existing for itself, over which therefore it has of itself no power, unless the object does with itself what self-consciousness does with it. The movement is thus in all respects the double movement of both self-consciousnesses. Each sees the *other one* do the same as it does; each does itself what it demands of the other, and so does what it does only inasmuch as the other does the same; a one-sided doing would be unavailing, because what it is intended should occur can come about only through both.

The doing is therefore double-sensed not only inasmuch as it is a doing as much *to itself* as *to the other,* but also inasmuch as it is undividedly as much the *doing of the one* as *of the other.*

In this movement we see the process repeat itself which presented itself as the play of forces, but in consciousness. What in the earlier process was for us, is here for the extremes themselves. The centre is self-consciousness, which puts itself apart into the extremes; and each extreme is this exchanging of its determination and absolute going over into the opposed extreme. But though, as consciousness, it does indeed come *out of itself,* yet it is in its being-out-of-itself at the same time held back within itself, is *for itself,* and its "outside-itself" is *for it.* It is for consciousness that it immediately *is* and *is not* another consciousness; and, equally, that this other is only for itself in doing away with itself as something being for itself, and only in the being-for-itself of the other is for itself. Each is to the other the centre through which each brings into relation and connects itself with itself, and each is to itself and to the other an immediate entity existing for itself, which at the same time is thus for itself only through this relating, or mediation. They *acknowledge* one another as *mutually acknowledging one other.*

This pure concept of acknowledgement, the duplication of self-consciousness in its unity, will now be studied in the way in which its process appears for self-consciousness. This process will first present the facet of the *inequality* of the two, or the coming out of the centre into the extremes, which, being extremes, are opposed to one another, the one acknowledged only, the other acknowledging only.

Self-consciousness is to begin with simple being-for-itself, equal-with-itself through the exclusion of everything *other from itself;* its essence and absolute object is to it "*I*"; and it is in this *immediacy,* or in this *being* of its being-for-itself, an *individual.* Whatever else there is for it, is as an inessential object, one marked with the character of the negative. But the other is also a self-consciousness: an individual comes on opposite an individual. Thus *immediately* coming on, they are for each other in the way of common objects: *independent* forms, consciousnesses immersed in the *existence* of *life*—for it is as life that the existent object has here determined itself—which have not yet carried out *for each other* the movement of absolute abstraction, of expunging all immediate existence and of being merely the purely negative existence of consciousness equal-with-itself, or which have not yet presented themselves to each other as pure *being-for-self,* that is, as *self*-consciousness. Each is indeed certain of itself, but not of the other, and consequently each's own certainty of itself has as yet no truth; for its truth could only be that its own being-for-itself had presented itself to it as an independent object or, what amounts to the same thing, that the object had presented itself as this pure certainty of itself. This, however, on the concept of acknowledgement is not possible, save that as the other does for the one, so the one does for the other, each with itself through its own activity, and again through the activity of the other, carrying out this pure abstraction of being-for-itself.

The *presentation* of oneself as the pure abstraction of self-consciousness, however, consists in showing oneself to be the pure negation of one's objective way of being, that is, in showing oneself not to be attached to a particular *concrete existence,* nor to the universal individuality of concrete existence in general, nor even to life. This presentation is a *double* doing: doing of the other, and doing through oneself. Inasmuch as it is the doing *of the other,* each then is set upon the death of the other. But in this there is present also the second doing, *the doing through oneself;* for the former contains within itself the staking of one's own life. The relation of the two self-consciousnesses is hence determined in such a way that through the combat for life and death they *prove* themselves and each other.—They must enter this combat, for they must raise the certainty of themselves, *of being for themselves,* to truth in the other and in themselves. And it is solely through the staking of life that freedom arises, that it is confirmed to self-consciousness that it is not *being,* not the *immediate* way in which it comes on, not its being immersed in the expanse of life which is its essence—but that there is nothing present in it which is not for it a vanishing moment, that it is just pure *being-for-itself.* The individual that has not risked life can indeed be acknowledged as a *person;* but it has not attained the truth of this state of acknowledgement as that of an independent self-consciousness. Likewise, each must as much aim at the death of the other as it stakes its own life; for the other means no more to it than it itself does; the individual's essence presents itself to it as another, it is outside itself, it must do away with its being-outside-itself; the other is a consciousness engaged and existing in manifold ways; it must view its otherness as pure being-for-self, or as absolute negation.

This proving through death does away, however, with the truth that was to result from it, just as much as it thereby also does away with the certainty of oneself altogether; for just as life was the *natural* position of consciousness, independence without absolute negativity, so death is the *natural* negation of consciousness, negation without independence, which therefore remains without the required sense of acknowledgement. Through death the certainty has indeed arisen that both risked their life and despised it in themselves and in the other; though not for those who underwent this combat. They do away with their consciousness set in this alien essentiality that is natural concrete existence, or they do away with themselves, and are done away with as the *extremes* which would be for themselves. There thereby vanishes, however, from the play of exchange the essential moment of setting oneself apart into extremes of opposed determinations; and the centre collapses into a dead unity, which is set apart into dead, merely existent, not opposed, extremes; and the two do not mutually give back and receive back themselves from each other through consciousness, but let each other free merely indifferently, as things. Their deed is abstract negation, not the negation of consciousness, which *does away* in such a manner that it *puts by* and *preserves* what is done away, and consequently survives its being-done-away.

In this experience self-consciousness comes to realise that life is as essential to it as pure self-consciousness is. In immediate self-consciousness the simple "I" is the absolute object, which however, for us or in itself, is absolute mediation and has existent independence as an essential moment. The dissolution of that simple unity is the result of the first experience; through it there is established a pure self-consciousness, and a consciousness which is not purely for itself, but is for another consciousness, that is, is as *existent,* or is consciousness in the form of *thinghood*. Both moments are essential;—but as they are to begin with unequal and opposed, and their reflexion into unity is not yet a reality, they are as two opposed forms of consciousness: one, the independent consciousness, to which being-for-self is the essence; the other, the dependent consciousness, to which life or being for another is the essence: the former is the *master,* the latter the *servant.*

The master is the consciousness existing *for itself,* though no longer merely the concept of the latter, but a consciousness existing for itself which is in mediate relation with itself through *another* consciousness, namely through one to whose essence it pertains to be synthesised with independent *being* or thinghood in general. The master relates himself to both these moments, to a *thing* as such, the object of desire, and to the consciousness to whom thinghood is what is essential; and since he (a), *qua* concept of self-consciousness, is immediate relation of *being-for-himself,* but (b) now is also as mediation, or as a being-for-self which is for itself only through another, so he relates himself (a) immediately to both and (b) mediately to each through the other. The master relates himself *to the servant mediately through independent being;* for it is precisely to this that the servant is kept; it is his chain, from which in the combat he could not abstract, and consequently showed himself to be dependent, to have his independence in thinghood. The master, however, is the power over the being in question, for he showed in the combat that it meant merely something negative to him; since he is the power over this being, while this being is the power over the other, the master thus has in this conjunction the other under himself. Likewise the master relates himself *mediately through the servant to the thing,* the servant relates himself, *qua* self-consciousness as such, to the thing negatively also, and does away with it; but the thing is at the same time independent for him, and hence he cannot through his negating dispose of it so far as to destroy it, or he *works* it merely. The master on the other hand *gains* through this mediation the *immediate* relation as the pure negation of the thing, or the *enjoyment;* where desire did not succeed, he succeeds, namely in disposing of the thing and in satisfying himself in the enjoyment of it. Desire did not succeed in this on account of the independence of the thing; the master, however, who has interposed the servant between the thing and himself, thereby connects himself only with the non-independence of the thing, and enjoys it in its purity; the facet of independence, on the other hand, he leaves to the servant, who works it.

In these two moments the master has his acknowledgement, or recognition, by another consciousness granted him; for the other consciousness establishes itself in these moments as something inessential, first, in the working of the thing, second, in the dependence upon a particular existence; in both it cannot achieve mastery over being and attain absolute negation. There is therefore present here the following moment of recognition, that the other consciousness does away with itself as being-for-itself, and so itself does what the other does to it. Likewise the other moment is present, that this doing of the second consciousness is the first's own doing for what the servant does is really the doing of the master; to the latter, solely being-for-himself is the essence; he is the pure negative power to which the thing is nothing, and hence the pure essential doing in this situation; while the servant is not a pure doing, but an inessential one. But for true recognition there is lacking the moment that what the master does to the other he also does to himself, and what the servant does to himself he also does to the other. Thus there has arisen a one-sided and unequal recognizing.

The inessential consciousness is here for the master the object which constitutes the *truth* of the certainty of oneself. But it is evident that this object does not match its concept, and that there where the master has fulfilled himself, he has instead had something quite other than an independent consciousness come to be. It is not such a consciousness that is for him, but a dependent one rather; he is consequently not certain of *being-for-himself* as the truth, and his truth is rather the inessential consciousness, and the inessential doing of the latter.

The *truth* of independent consciousness is accordingly the servile or *subject consciousness*. The latter admittedly appears at first *outside* itself, and not as the truth of self-consciousness. But just as masterhood or dominion, showed that its essence is the converse of what it itself would be, so too, as we shall see, subjection will in its fulfillment turn rather into the contrary of what it is immediately; it will, *qua* consciousness *driven back* into itself, go into itself and turn about to true independence.

We have seen only what subjection is in the context of dominion. But the former is self-consciousness, and accordingly we shall now see what it is in and for itself. First of all, for subjection the master is the essence; hence the *independent consciousness existing for itself* is to subjection *the truth,* which however *for subjection* is not yet *in subjection.* But it has this truth of pure negativity and of *being-for-itself in the event in itself;* for subjection has *experienced* this essence within itself. This consciousness was, namely, not afraid for this or that, or for this instant or that, but for its whole being; for it has felt the fear of death, the absolute lord, or master. In this fear it has been internally broken up, it has been thoroughly shaken in itself, and everything fixed has trembled within it. This pure universal movement, the absolute becoming fluid of all that is permanent, is however the simple essence of self-consciousness, absolute negativity, *pure being-for-itself,* which is consequently *in* this consciousness. This moment of pure being-for-itself is also *for it,* for in the master it has it as its *object.* It is further not merely this universal dissolution in *general,* but in serving it *actually* brings it about; in serving it does away in all *particular* moments with its dependency on natural existence, and works that existence off.

But the feeling of absolute power, in general and in the particulars of service, is only the dissolution *in itself,* and although "the fear of the Lord is the beginning of wisdom," consciousness in this fear is *for its self,* not *being-for-itself.* Through work, however, it comes to itself. In the moment which corresponds to desire in the consciousness of the master, the facet of the inessential relation to the thing seemed to have fallen to the consciousness that serves, inasmuch as in this relation the thing retains its independence. Desire has reserved to itself the pure negating of the object and thereby the unmixed feeling-of-self. This satisfaction is on that account, however, itself just a vanishing, for it lacks the facet of the *object,* or *permanency.* Work by contrast is *contained* desire, *arrested* vanishing, or work *improves.* The negative relation to the object turns into the *form* of the object and into something *enduring,* precisely because to the worker the object has independence. This *negative* centre, or the *activity* that forms, or fashions, is at the same time *the particularity,* or the pure being-for-self of consciousness, which now in work steps out of consciousness into the element of permanency; the consciousness that works therefore attains as a consequence a view of independent being *as itself.*

The fashioning has not only this positive significance, however, that in it the consciousness that serves has itself as pure *being-for-itself* become something *existent;* but also a negative significance as against its first moment, the fear. For, in the improving of the thing, the consciousness which serves has its own negativity, its being-for-itself, become object only by doing away with the opposed existent *form.* But this objective, *negative* thing is precisely the alien being before which it trembled. Now, however, it destroys this alien negative thing, sets *itself* as something negative into the element of permanency, and thereby comes to be *for itself,* something *existing-for-itself.* In the master it has being-for-self as *an other,* or as merely *for it;* in the fear being-for-self is *in the consciousness itself that serves;* in the improving being-for-self comes to be for the consciousness that serves as *its own,* and the latter becomes conscious that it itself is in and for itself. Through being *set outside,* the form does not become to the consciousness that serves something other than the consciousness itself; for it is precisely the form that is its pure being-for-itself, which thereby to consciousness becomes the truth. Through this refinding of itself by itself, then, the consciousness that serves becomes a mind or *sense of its own,* and in the very work in which it seemed to be only *another's sense.*—For this reflexion both moments, that of fear and service in general, as well as that of improving, are necessary, and at the same time both in a general way. Without the discipline of service and obedience, fear remains at the formal stage, and does not spread itself upon the known reality of concrete existence. Without the improving, fear remains inward and silent, and consciousness does not become for itself. If consciousness fashions, or forms, without the initial absolute fear, it is merely a vain sense of self; for its form or negativity is not negativity *in itself,* and its fashioning cannot therefore give it the consciousness of itself as the essence. If it has not endured absolute fear, but only some anxiety, then it has the negative essence remain something external, its substance has not been infected through and through by the negative essence. Inasmuch as not all aspects of its natural consciousness have become insecure, it still *in itself* belongs to some particular existence; its self-sense is *self-will,* a freedom which as yet remains within subjection. No more than it can have the pure form become essence, no more is the form, regarded as something spread over individual things, a universal cultivating, an absolute concept, but is instead a dexterity which has power over merely some things, not over universal power and the whole objective realm of being.

WHO THINKS ABSTRACTLY?

Think? Abstractly?—*Sauve qui peut!* Let those who can save themselves! Even now I can hear a traitor, bought by the enemy, exclaim these words, denouncing this essay because it will plainly deal with metaphysics. For *metaphysics* is a word, no less than *abstract,* and almost *thinking* as well, from which everybody more or less runs away as from a man who has caught the plague.

But the intention here really is not so wicked, as if the meaning of thinking and of abstract were to be explained here. There is nothing the beautiful world finds as intolerable as explanations. I, too, find it terrible when somebody begins to explain, for when worst comes to worst I understand everything myself. Here the explanation of thinking and abstract would in any case be entirely superfluous; for it is only because the beautiful world knows what it means to be abstract that it runs away. Just as one does not desire what one does not know, one also cannot hate it. Nor is it my intent to try craftily to reconcile the beautiful world with thinking or with the abstract as if, under the semblance of small talk, thinking and the abstract were to be put over till in the end they had found their way into society incognito, without having aroused any disgust; even as if they were to be adopted imperceptibly by society, or, as the Swabians say, *hereingezäunselt,* before the author of this complication suddenly exposed this strange guest, namely the abstract, whom the whole party had long treated and recognized under a different title as if he were a good old acquaintance. Such scenes of recognition which are meant to instruct the world against its will have the inexcusable fault that they simultaneously humiliate, and the wirepuller tries with his artifice to gain a little fame; but this humiliation and this vanity destroy the effect, for they push away again an instruction gained at such a price.

In any case, such a plan would be ruined from the start, for it would require that the crucial word of the riddle is not spoken at the outset. But this has already happened in the title. If this essay toyed with such craftiness, these words should not have been allowed to enter right in the beginning; but like the cabinet member in a comedy, they should have been required to walk around during the entire play in their overcoat, unbuttoning it only in the last scene, disclosing the flashing star of wisdom. The unbuttoning of the metaphysical overcoat would be less effective, to be sure, than the unbuttoning of the minister's: it would bring to light no more than a couple of words, and the best part of the joke ought to be that it is shown that society has long been in possession of the matter itself, so what they would gain in the end would be the mere name, while the minister's star signifies something real—a bag of money.

That everybody present should know what thinking is and what is abstract is presupposed in good society, and we certainly are in good society. The question is merely *who* thinks abstractly. The intent, as already mentioned, is not to reconcile society with these things, to expect it to deal with something difficult, to appeal to its conscience not frivolously to neglect such a matter that befits the rank and status of beings gifted with reason. Rather it is my intent to reconcile the beautiful world with itself, although it does not seem to have a bad conscience about this neglect, still, at least deep down, it has a certain respect for abstract thinking as something exalted, and it looks the other way not because it seems too lowly but because it appears too exalted, not because it seems too mean but rather too noble, or conversely because it seems an *Espèce,* some-

Translated by Walter Kaufmann.

thing special; it seems something that does not lend one distinction in general society, like new clothes, but rather something that—like wretched clothes, or rich ones if they are decorated with precious stones in ancient mounts or embroidery that, be it ever so rich, has long become quasi–Chinese—excludes one from society or makes one ridiculous in it.

Who thinks abstractly? The uneducated, not the educated. Good society does not think abstractly because it is too easy, because it is too lowly (not referring to the external status)—not from an empty affectation of nobility that would place itself above that of which it is not capable, but on account of the inward inferiority of the matter.

The prejudice and respect for abstract thinking are so great that sensitive nostrils will begin to smell some satire or irony at this point; but since they read the morning paper they know that there is a prize to be had for satires and that I should therefore sooner earn it by competing for it than give up here without further ado.

I have only to adduce examples for my proposition: everybody will grant that they confirm it. A murderer is led to the place of execution. For the common populace he is nothing but a murderer. Ladies perhaps remark that he is a strong, handsome, interesting man. The populace finds this remark terrible: What? A murderer handsome? How can one think so wickedly and call a murderer handsome; no doubt, you yourselves are something not much better! This is the corruption of morals that is prevalent in the upper classes, a priest may add, knowing the bottom of things and human hearts.

One who knows men traces the development of the criminal's mind: he finds in his history, in his education, a bad family relationship between his father and mother, some tremendous harshness after this human being had done some minor wrong, so he became embittered against the social order—a first reaction to this that in effect expelled him and henceforth did not make it possible for him to preserve himself except through crime.—There may be people who will say when they hear such things: he wants to excuse this murderer! After all I remember how in my youth I heard a mayor lament that writers of books were going too far and sought to extirpate Christianity and righteousness altogether; somebody had written a defense of suicide; terrible, really too terrible!—Further questions revealed that *The Sufferings of Werther* [by Goethe, 1774] were meant.

This is abstract thinking: to see nothing in the murderer except the abstract fact that he is a murderer, and to annul all other human essence in him with this simple quality.

It is quite different in refined, sentimental circles—in Leipzig. There they strewed and bound flowers on the wheel and on the criminal who was tied to it.—But this again is the opposite abstraction. The Christians may indeed trifle with Rosicrucianism, or rather cross-rosism, and wreathe roses around the cross. The cross is the gallows and wheel that have long been hallowed. It has lost its one-sided significance of being the instrument of dishonorable punishment and, on the contrary, suggests the notion of the highest pain and the deepest rejection together with the most joyous rapture and divine honor. The wheel in Leipzig, on the other hand, wreathed with violets and poppies, is a reconciliation à la Kotzebue, a kind of slovenly sociability between sentimentality and badness.

In quite a different manner I once heard a common old woman who worked in a hospital kill the abstraction of the murderer and bring him to life for honor. The severed head had been placed on the scaffold, and the sun was shining. How beautifully, she said, the sun of God's grace shines on Binder's head!—You are not worthy of having the sun shine on you, one says to a rascal with whom one is angry. This woman saw that the murderer's head was struck by the sunshine and thus was still worthy of it.

She raised it from the punishment of the scaffold into the sunny grace of God, and instead of accomplishing the reconciliation with violets and sentimental vanity, saw him accepted in grace in the higher sun.

Old woman, your eggs are rotten! the maid says to the market woman. What? she replies, my eggs rotten? You may be rotten! You say that about my eggs? You? Did not lice eat your father on the highways? Didn't your mother run away with the French, and didn't your grandmother die in a public hospital? Let her get a whole shirt instead of that flimsy scarf; we know well where she got that scarf and her hats: if it were not for those officers, many wouldn't be decked out like that these days, and if their ladyships paid more attention to their households, many would be in jail right now. Let her mend the holes in her stockings!—In brief, she does not leave one whole thread on her. She thinks abstractly and subsumes the other woman—scarf, hat, shirt, etc., as well as her fingers and other parts of her, and her father and whole family, too—solely under the crime that she has found the eggs rotten. Everything about her is colored through and through by these rotten eggs, while those officers of which the market woman spoke—if, as one may seriously doubt, there is anything to that—may have got to see very different things.

To move from the maid to a servant, no servant is worse off than one who works for a man of low class and low income; and he is better off the nobler his master is. The common man again thinks more abstractly, he gives himself noble airs vis-à-vis the servant and relates himself to the other man merely as to a servant; he clings to this one predicate. The servant is best off among the French. The nobleman is familiar with his servant, the Frenchman is his friend. When they are alone, the servant does the talking: see Diderot's *Jacques et son maître;* the master does nothing but take snuff and see what time it is and lets the servant take care of everything else. The nobleman knows that the servant is not merely a servant, but also knows the latest city news, the girls, and harbors good suggestions; he asks him about these matters, and the servant may say what he knows about these questions. With a French master, the servant may not only do this; he may also broach a subject, have his own opinions and insist on them; and when the master wants something, it is not done with an order but he has to argue and convince the servant of his opinion and add a good word to make sure that this opinion retains the upper hand.

In the army we encounter the same difference. Among the Austrians a soldier may be beaten, he is canaille; for whatever has the passive right to be beaten is canaille. Thus the common soldier is for the officer this *abstractum* of a beatable subject with whom a gentleman who has a uniform and port *d'epée* must trouble himself—and that could drive one to make a pact with the devil.

JOHN STUART MILL
1806–1873

John Stuart Mill was born in London, the eldest of James and Harriet Burrow Mill's nine children. His father, a well-known philosopher and follower of Jeremy Bentham, educated young John at home. Beginning with Greek at age three and Latin at age eight, the younger Mill had read six of Plato's dialogues by the age of ten. John spent most of the day in the study with his father, who was writing a history of India. Each morning, they would go on a walk and James would quiz his son on what he had learned the previous day. During these walks, James would often discourse on various topics and then expect his son to prepare a summary of his points for the following day. Given the severity of this schooling—and the fact that his father showed no "signs of feeling"—it is not surprising that John later concluded, "I never was a boy."

The publication of the elder Mill's work on India in 1818 resulted in his receiving a government post as an Assistant Examiner at the East India House. Five years later, James managed to arrange a similar position for his seventeen-year-old son. John worked for the East India House for the next thirty-four years, eventually becoming chief of his department. In his early years as a clerk, John was, like his father, a disciple of Bentham's utilitarianism. John established the Utilitarian Society, contributed articles to the *Westminster Review,* and was active in the London Debating Society. He was developing a reputation as a polemicist for the "philosophic radicals"—those who sought social changes along the lines of Bentham's theories.

But in 1826, at age twenty, Mill suffered a breakdown and went through a period of severe depression. He discovered to his horror that even if all the social changes he advocated were enacted and all the ideas he was taught about happiness were proven correct, it would not make *him* happy. As he later wrote in his *Autobiography,* "All my happiness was to have been found in the continual pursuit of this end. The end had ceased to charm, and how could there ever again be any interest in the means? I seemed to have nothing left to live for." He eventually came to the conclusion that his rigorous intellectual training had weakened his ability to feel emotion. Reading such writers as Wordsworth and Coleridge, he began to teach himself to feel as his father had taught him to think. During this period, he encountered divergent philosophies, such as those of socialist philosopher Claude-Henry Saint-Simon and positivist thinker Auguste Comte, and he began to see some of the inadequacies of the strict quantificational method of Bentham.

In 1831, Mill was introduced to Harriet Taylor, the wife of a successful merchant. They quickly developed a strong friendship and collaborated on a number of works, including *Principles of Political Economy, On Liberty,* and *The Subjection of Women.* Mill attributed to Taylor a number of his most important ideas, including his liberal feminism, and claimed that next to his father, she was the chief intellectual influence on his life. He even claimed she was the inspiration for his major epistemological work, *A System of Logic* (1843). Following her husband's death in 1849, they were finally married in 1851.

John and Harriet Mill moved to Avignon, France, in 1858, with neither of them in good health. Shortly after arriving, Harriet Taylor Mill died, and her daughter came to take care of her stepfather. Over the next seven years, Mill published *On Liberty* (1859), *Utilitarianism* (1861), *Considerations on Representative Government* (1861), *Auguste Comte and Positivism* (1865), and *The Subjection of Women* (written 1861, published 1869). In 1865, Mill was surprised by an offer to run for Parliament. Without campaigning, he was elected and spent two years working on behalf of women's suffrage, Irish land reform, and the rights of blacks in Jamaica. Returning once again to the south of France, he wrote his *Autobiography* just before dying in 1873.

*   *   *

Although Mill wrote on a variety of topics and his work in induction is still used today, he is best known for his modification of Bentham's utilitarianism and his defense of individual liberty. Bentham had taught that ethics should be grounded on maximizing pleasure and minimizing pain, rather than on such abstractions as Kant's "duty" or conscience. Accordingly, Bentham developed a "hedonistic calculus," a mathematical method of determining which actions would most likely provide a greater quantity of pleasure over pain and hence yield happiness. Whereas this system might seem egoistic and individualistic, Bentham claimed that it would be to each individual person's advantage to seek the "greatest happiness of the greatest number."

In his *Utilitarianism,* given here (complete), Mill accepts Bentham's quantitative hedonism and argues that happiness, or pleasure, is the one thing that all people seek. But whereas Bentham's system merely measured quantities of pleasure and pain, Mill maintains that the *quality* of a given pleasure or pain has to be considered as well. Even though a pig might gain a great *quantity* of pleasure from wallowing in the mud, it would be a very low *quality* pleasure; and "It is better to be a human being dissatisfied than a pig satisfied; better to be Socrates dissatisfied than a fool satisfied." According to Mill, the person best able to make a qualitative determination between rival pleasures is the one who has experienced both. Presumably anyone who has both wallowed in the mud *and* studied philosophy would prefer the difficult but fulfilling pleasures of the latter.

Mill's contemporary critics pointed out discrepancies between the philosophy of *Utilitarianism* and that of Mill's other works which advocated induvidual freedom. For example, following the greatest happiness principle of *Utilitarianism,* wouldn't it make sense for society to increase general happiness by intruding on an individual's liberty? Mill countered this objection by arguing that on balance *laissez-faire* individualism will ultimately benefit society, that the diversity of individual choices is more conducive to general happiness than any socially imposed standard. More recent critics have questioned Mill's distinction between private and public—for example, what you choose to do to yourself in the privacy of your home may cost the public money if you end up in a tax-supported hospital. Feminist critics have pointed out the potential oppression of the private/public distinction, questioned the possibility of "perfect equality" if paternalistic structures continue, and assailed Mill's "equal opportunity until marriage" doctrine. But there is no question that as a reforming impulse, Mill's beliefs—about the rights of the individual, the rights of women and minorities, freedom from societal intrusion into personal affairs, and utility rather than tradition—have had an enormous influence.

*   *   *

There are several good overviews of Mill's life and thought, including R.P. Anschutz, *The Philosophy of John Stuart Mill* (Oxford: Oxford University Press, 1953); Karl Britton, *John Stuart Mill* (1953; reprinted New York: Dover, 1969); Alan Ryan, *J.S. Mill* (London: Routledge & Kegan Paul, 1974); and William Thomas, *Mill* (Oxford: Oxford University Press, 1985). F.A. Hayek, *John Stuart Mill and Harriet Taylor* (Chicago: University of Chicago Press, 1951) presents a study of Mill's relationship with Harriet Taylor. For a critical evaluation of his work, see H.J. McCloskey, *John Stuart Mill: A Critical Study* (London: Macmillan, 1971). For more specialized studies, see Dennis F. Thompson, *John Stuart Mill and Representative Government* (Princeton, NJ: Princeton University Press, 1976); Gertrude Himmelfarb, *On Liberty and Liberalism: The Case of John Stuart Mill* (New York: Knopf, 1974); Andrew Pyle's pair of books, *Liberty: Contemporary Responses to John Stuart Mill* and *The Subjection of Women: Contemporary Responses to John Stuart Mill* (both Bristol, UK: Thoemmes Press, 1994 and 1995) and Roger Crisp, *Routledge Philosophy Guidebook to Mill's Utilitarianism* (London: Routledge, 1997). For collections of essays, see J.B. Schneewind, ed., *Mill: A Collection of Critical Essays* (Garden City, NY: Anchor Doubleday, 1968), J.M. Smith and E. Sosa, eds., *Mill's Utilitarianism* (Belmont, CA: Wadsworth, 1969); John Skorupski, ed., *The Cambridge Companion to Mill* (Cambridge: Cambridge University Press, 1997) and G. W. Smith, ed., *John Stuart Mill's Social and Political Thought: Critical Assessments;* four volumes (London: Routledge, 1998).

UTILITARIANISM

CHAPTER 1: GENERAL REMARKS

There are few circumstances among those which make up the present condition of human knowledge, more unlike what might have been expected, or more significant of the backward state in which speculation on the most important subjects still lingers, than the little progress which has been made in the decision of the controversy respecting the criterion of right and wrong. From the dawn of philosophy, the question concerning the *summum bonum,* or, what is the same thing, concerning the foundation of morality, has been accounted the main problem in speculative thought, has occupied the most gifted intellects, and divided them into sects and schools, carrying on a vigorous warfare against one another. And after more than two thousand years the same discussions continue, philosophers are still ranged under the same contending banners, and neither thinkers nor mankind at large seem nearer to being unanimous on the subject, than when the youth Socrates listened to the old Protagoras, and asserted (if Plato's dialogue be grounded on a real conversation) the theory of utilitarianism against the popular morality of the so-called sophist.

It is true that similar confusion and uncertainty, and in some cases similar discordance, exist respecting the first principles of all the sciences, not excepting that which is deemed the most certain of them, mathematics; without much impairing, generally indeed without impairing at all, the trustworthiness of the conclusions of those sciences. An apparent anomaly, the explanation of which is, that the detailed doctrines of a science are not usually deduced from, nor depend for their evidence upon, what are called its first principles. Were it not so, there would be no science more precarious, or whose conclusions were more insufficiently made out, than algebra; which derives none of its certainty from what are commonly taught to learners as its elements, since these, as laid down by some of its most eminent teachers, are as full of fictions as English law, and of mysteries as theology. The truths which are ultimately accepted as the first principles of a science, are really the last results of metaphysical analysis, practised on the elementary notions with which the science is conversant; and their relation to the science is not that of foundations to an edifice, but of roots to a tree, which may perform their office equally well though they be never dug down to and exposed to light. But though in science the particular truths precede the general theory, the contrary might be expected to be the case with a practical art, such as morals or legislation. All action is for the sake of some end, and rules of action, it seems natural to suppose, must take their whole character and colour from the end to which they are subservient. When we engage in a pursuit, a clear and precise conception of what we are pursuing would seem to be the first thing we need, instead of the last we are to look forward to. A test of right and wrong must be the means, one would think, of ascertaining what is right or wrong, and not a consequence of having already ascertained it.

The difficulty is not avoided by having recourse to the popular theory of a natural faculty, a sense or instinct, informing us of right and wrong. For—besides that the existence of such a moral instinct is itself one of the matters in dispute—those believers in it who have any pretensions to philosophy, have been obliged to abandon the idea that it discerns what is right or wrong in the particular case in hand, as our other senses discern the sight or sound actually present. Our moral faculty, according to all those of its interpreters who are entitled to the name of thinkers, supplies us only with the general principles of moral judgments; it is a branch of our reason, not of our sensitive faculty; and must be looked to for the abstract doctrines of morality, not for perception of it in the concrete. The intuitive, no less than what may be termed the inductive, school of ethics, insists on the necessity of general laws. They both agree that the morality of an individual action is not a question of direct perception, but of the application of a law to an individual case. They recognise also, to a great extent, the same moral laws; but differ as to their evidence, and the source from which they derive their authority. According to the one opinion, the principles of morals are evident *a priori,* requiring nothing to command assent, except that the meaning of the terms be understood. According to the other doctrine, right and wrong, as well as truth and falsehood, are questions of observation and experience. But both hold equally that morality must be deduced from principles; and the intuitive school affirm as strongly as the inductive, that there is a science of morals. Yet they seldom attempt to make out a list of the *a priori* principles which are to serve as the premises of the science; still more rarely do they make any effort to reduce those various principles to one first principle, or common ground of obligation. They either assume the ordinary precepts of morals as of *a priori* authority, or they lay down as the common groundwork of those maxims, some generality much less obviously authoritative than the maxims themselves, and which has never succeeded in gaining popular acceptance. Yet to support their pretensions there ought either to be some one fundamental principle or law, at the root of all morality, or if there be several, there should be a determinate order of precedence among them; and the one principle, or the rule for deciding between the various principles when they conflict, ought to be self-evident.

To inquire how far the bad effects of this deficiency have been mitigated in practice, or to what extent the moral beliefs of mankind have been vitiated or made uncertain by the absence of any distinct recognition of an ultimate standard, would imply a complete survey and criticism of past and present ethical doctrine. It would, however, be easy to show that whatever steadiness or consistency these moral beliefs have attained, has been mainly due to the tacit influence of a standard not recognised. Although the non-existence of an acknowledged first principle has made ethics not so much a guide as a consecration of men's actual sentiments, still, as men's sentiments, both of favour and of aversion, are greatly influenced by what they suppose to be the effects of things upon their happiness, the principle of utility, or as Bentham latterly called it, the Greatest Happiness Principle, has had a large share in forming the moral doctrines even of those who most scornfully reject its authority. Nor is there any school of thought which refuses to admit that the influence of actions on happiness is a most material and even predominant consideration in many of the details of morals, however unwilling to acknowledge it as the fundamental principle of morality, and the source of moral obligation. I might go much further, and say that to all those *a priori* moralists who deem it necessary to argue at all, utilitarian arguments are indispensable. It is not my present purpose to criticise these thinkers; but I cannot help referring, for illustration, to a systematic treatise by one of the most illustrious of them, the *Metaphysics of Ethics* by Kant. This remarkable man, whose system of thought will long remain one of the landmarks in the history of philosophical speculation, does, in the treatise in question, lay down a universal first principle as the origin and ground of moral obligation; it is this:—"So act, that the rule on which thou actest would admit of being adopted as a law by all rational beings." But when he begins to deduce from this precept any of the actual duties of morality, he fails, almost grotesquely, to show that there would be any contradiction, any logical (not to say physical) impossibility, in the adoption by all rational beings of the most outrageously immoral rules of conduct. All he shows is that the *consequences* of their universal adoption would be such as no one would choose to incur.

On the present occasion, I shall, without further discussion of the other theories, attempt to contribute something towards the understanding and appreciation of the Utilitarian or Happiness theory, and towards such proof as it is susceptible of. It is evident that this cannot be proof in the ordinary and popular meaning of the term. Questions of ultimate ends are not amenable to direct proof. Whatever can be proved to be good, must be so by being shown to be a means to something admitted to be good without proof. The medical art is proved to be good by its conducing to health; but how is it possible to prove that health is good? The art of music is good, for the reason, among others, that it produces pleasure; but what proof is it possible to give that pleasure is good? If, then, it is asserted that there is a comprehensive formula, including all things which are in themselves good, and that whatever else is good, is not so as an end, but as a mean, the formula may be accepted or rejected, but is not a subject of what is commonly understood by proof. We are not, however, to infer that its acceptance or rejection must depend on blind impulse, or arbitrary choice. There is a larger meaning of the word proof, in which this question is as amenable to it as any other of the disputed questions of philosophy. The subject is within the cognisance of the rational faculty; and neither does that faculty deal with it solely in the way of intuition. Considerations may be presented capable of determining the intellect either to give or withhold its assent to the doctrine; and this is equivalent to proof.

We shall examine presently of what nature are these considerations; in what manner they apply to the case, and what rational grounds, therefore, can be given for accepting or rejecting the utilitarian formula. But it is a preliminary condition of rational acceptance or rejection, that the formula should be correctly understood. I believe that the very imperfect notion ordinarily formed of its meaning, is the chief obstacle which impedes its reception; and that could it be cleared, even from only the grosser misconceptions, the question would be greatly simplified, and a large proportion of its difficulties removed. Before, therefore, I attempt to enter into the philosophical grounds which can be given for assenting to the utilitarian standard, I shall offer some illustrations of the doctrine itself; with the view of showing more clearly what it is, distinguishing it from what it is not, and disposing of such of the practical objections to it as either originate in, or are closely connected with, mistaken interpretations of its meaning. Having thus prepared the ground, I shall afterwards endeavour to throw such light as I can upon the question, considered as one of philosophical theory.

Chapter 2: What Utilitarianism Is

A passing remark is all that needs be given to the ignorant blunder of supposing that those who stand up for utility as the test of right and wrong, use the term in that restricted and merely colloquial sense in which utility is opposed to pleasure. An apology is due to the philosophical opponents of utilitarianism, for even the momentary appearance of confounding them with any one capable of so absurd a misconception; which is the more extraordinary, inasmuch as the contrary accusation, of referring everything to pleasure, and that too in its grossest form, is another of the common charges against utilitarianism: and, as has been pointedly remarked by an able writer, the same sort of persons, and often the very same persons, denounce the theory "as impracticably dry when the word 'utility' precedes the word 'pleasure,' and as too practicably voluptuous when the word 'pleasure' precedes the word 'utility.'" Those who know anything about the matter are aware that every writer, from Epicurus to Bentham, who maintained the theory of utility, meant by it, not something to be contradistinguished from pleasure, but pleasure itself, together with exemption from pain; and instead of opposing the useful to the agreeable or the ornamental, have always declared that the useful means these, among other things. Yet the common herd, including the herd of writers, not only in newspapers and periodicals, but in books of weight and pretension, are perpetually falling into this shallow mistake. Having caught up the word Utilitarian, while knowing nothing whatever about it but its sound, they habitually express by it the rejection, or the neglect, of pleasure in some of its forms; of beauty, of ornament, or of amusement. Nor is the term thus ignorantly misapplied solely in disparagement, but occasionally in compliment; as though it implied superiority to frivolity and the mere pleasures of the moment. And this perverted use is the only one in which the word is popularly known, and the one from which the new generation are acquiring their sole notion of its meaning. Those who introduced the word, but who had for many years discontinued it as a distinctive appellation, may well feel themselves called upon to resume it, if by doing so they can hope to contribute anything towards rescuing it from this utter degradation.*

The creed which accepts as the foundation of morals Utility or the Greatest Happiness Principle holds that actions are right in proportion as they tend to promote happiness, wrong as they tend to produce the reverse of happiness. By happiness is intended pleasure, and the absence of pain; by unhappiness, pain, and the privation of pleasure. To give a clear view of the moral standard set up by the theory, much more requires to be said; in particular, what things it includes in the ideas of pain and pleasure; and to what extent this is left an open question. But these supplementary explanations do not affect the theory of life on which this theory of morality is grounded—namely, that pleasure, and freedom from pain, are the only things desirable as ends; and that all desirable things (which are as numerous in the utilitarian as in any other scheme) are desirable either for the pleasure inherent in themselves, or as means to the promotion of pleasure and the prevention of pain.

Now, such a theory of life excites in many minds, and among them in some of the most estimable in feeling and purpose, inveterate dislike. To suppose that life has (as they express it) no higher end than pleasure—no better and nobler object of desire and pursuit—they designate as utterly mean and grovelling; as a doctrine worthy only of swine, to whom the followers of Epicurus were, at a very early period, contemptuously likened; and modern holders of the doctrine are occasionally made the subject of equally polite comparisons by its German, French, and English assailants.

When thus attacked, the Epicureans have always answered, that it is not they; but their accusers, who represent human nature in a degrading light; since the accusation supposes human beings to be capable of no pleasures except those of which swine are capable. If this supposition were true, the charge could not be gainsaid, but would then be no longer an imputation; for if the sources of pleasure were precisely the same to human beings and to swine, the rule of life which is good enough for the one would be good enough for the other. The comparison of the Epicurean life to that of beasts is felt as degrading, precisely because a beast's pleasures do not

---

*The author of this essay has reason for believing himself to be the first person who brought the word "utilitarian" into use. He did not Invent it, but adopted It from a passing expression in Mr. Galt's *Annals of the Parish*. After using it as a designation for several years, he and others abandoned it from a growing dislike to anything resembling a badge or watchword of sectarian distinction. But as a name for one single opinion, not a set of opinions—to denote the recognition of utility as a standard not any particular way of applying it—the term supplies a want in the language, and offers, in many cases, a convenient mode of avoiding tiresome circumlocution.

satisfy a human being's conceptions of happiness. Human beings have faculties more elevated than the animal appetites, and when once made conscious of them, do not regard anything as happiness which does not include their gratification. I do not, indeed, consider the Epicureans to have been by any means faultless in drawing out their scheme of consequences from the utilitarian principle. To do this in any sufficient manner, many Stoic, as well as Christian elements require to be included. But there is no known Epicurean theory of life which does not assign to the pleasures of the intellect, of the feelings and imagination, and of the moral sentiments, a much higher value as pleasures than to those of mere sensation. It must be admitted, however, that utilitarian writers in general have placed the superiority of mental over bodily pleasures chiefly in the greater permanency, safety, uncostliness, etc., of the former—that is, in their circumstantial advantages rather than in their intrinsic nature. And on all these points utilitarians have fully proved their case; but they might have taken the other, and, as it may be called, higher ground, with entire consistency. It is quite compatible with the principle of utility to recognise the fact, that some kinds of pleasure are more desirable and more valuable than others. It would be absurd that while, in estimating all other things, quality is considered as well as quantity, the estimation of pleasures should be supposed to depend on quantity alone.

If I am asked, what I mean by difference of quality in pleasures, or what makes one pleasure more valuable than another, merely as a pleasure, except its being greater in amount, there is but one possible answer. Of two pleasures, if there be one to which all or almost all who have experience of both give a decided preference, irrespective of any feeling of moral obligation to prefer it, that is the more desirable pleasure. If one of the two is, by those who are competently acquainted with both, placed so far above the other that they prefer it, even though knowing it to be attended with a greater amount of discontent, and would not resign it for any quantity of the other pleasure which their nature is capable of, we are justified in ascribing to the preferred enjoyment a superiority in quality, so far outweighing quantity as to render it, in comparison, of small account.

Now it is an unquestionable fact that those who are equally acquainted with, and equally capable of appreciating and enjoying, both, do give almost marked preference to the manner of existence which employs their higher faculties. Few human creatures would consent to be changed into any of the lower animals, for a promise of the fullest allowance of a beast's pleasures; no intelligent human being would consent to be a fool, no instructed person would be an ignoramus, no person of feeling and conscience would be selfish and base, even though they should be persuaded that the fool, the dunce, or the rascal is better satisfied with his lot than they are with theirs. They would not resign what they possess more than he for the most complete satisfaction of all the desires which they have in common with him. If they ever fancy they would, it is only in cases of unhappiness so extreme, that to escape from it they would exchange their lot for almost any other, however undesirable in their own eyes. A being of higher faculties requires more to make him happy, is capable probably of more acute suffering, and certainly accessible to it at more points, than one of an inferior type; but in spite of these liabilities, he can never really wish to sink into what he feels to be a lower grade of existence. We may give what explanation we please of this unwillingness; we may attribute it to pride, a name which is given indiscriminately to some of the most and to some of the least estimable feelings of which mankind are capable: we may refer it to the love of liberty and personal independence, an appeal to which was with the Stoics one of the most effective means for the inculcation of it; to the love of power, or to the love of excitement, both of which do really enter into and contribute to it: but its most appropriate appellation is a sense of dignity, which all human beings possess in one form or other, and in some, though by no means in exact, proportion to their higher faculties, and which is so essential a part of the happiness of those in whom it is strong, that nothing which conflicts with it could be, otherwise than momentarily, an object of desire to them. Whoever supposes that this preference takes place at a sacrifice of happiness—that the superior being, in anything like equal circumstances, is not happier than the inferior—confounds the two very different ideas, of happiness, and content. It is indisputable that the being whose capacities of enjoyment are low, has the greatest chance of having them fully satisfied; and a highly endowed being will always feel that any happiness which he can look for, as the world is constituted, is imperfect. But he can learn to bear its imperfections, if they are at all bearable; and they will not make him envy the being who is indeed unconscious of the imperfections, but only because he feels not at all the good which those imperfections qualify. It is better to be a human being dissatisfied than a pig satisfied; better to be Socrates dissatisfied than a fool satisfied. And if the fool, or the pig, are of a different opinion, it is because they only know their own side of the question. The other party to the comparison knows both sides.

It may be objected, that many who are capable of the higher pleasures, occasionally, under the influence of temptation, postpone them to the lower. But this is quite compatible with a full appreciation of the intrinsic superiority of the higher. Men often, from infirmity of character, make their election for the nearer good, though they know it to be the less valuable; and this no less when the choice is between two bodily pleasures, than when it is between bodily and mental. They pursue sensual indulgences to the injury of health, though perfectly aware that health is the greater good. It may be further objected, that many who begin with youthful enthusiasm for everything noble, as they advance in years sink into indolence and selfishness. But I do not believe that those who undergo this very common change, voluntarily choose the lower description of pleasures in preference to the higher. I believe that before they devote themselves exclusively to the one, they have already become incapable of the other. Capacity for the nobler feelings is in most natures a very tender plant, easily killed, not only by hostile influences, but by mere want of sustenance; and in the majority of young persons it speedily dies away if the occupations to which their position in life has devoted them, and the society into which it has thrown them, are not favourable to keeping that higher capacity in exercise. Men lose their high aspirations as they lose their intellectual tastes, because they have not time or opportunity for indulging them; and they addict themselves to inferior pleasures, not because they deliberately prefer them, but because they are either the only ones to which they have access, or the only ones which they are any longer capable of enjoying. It may be questioned whether any one who has remained equally susceptible to both classes of pleasures, ever knowingly and calmly preferred the lower; though many, in all ages, have broken down in an ineffectual attempt to combine both.

From this verdict of the only competent judges, I apprehend there can be no appeal. On a question which is the best worth having of two pleasures, or which of two modes of existence is the most grateful to the feelings, apart from its moral attributes and from its consequences, the judgment of those who are qualified by knowledge of both, or, if they differ, that of the majority among them, must be admitted as final. And there needs be the less hesitation to accept this judgment respecting the quality of pleasures, since there is no other tribunal to be referred to even on the question of quantity. What means are there of determining which is the acutest of two pains, or the intensest of two pleasurable sensations, except the general suffrage of those who are familiar with both? Neither pains nor pleasures are homogeneous, and pain is always heterogeneous with pleasure. What is there to decide whether a particular pleasure is worth purchasing at the cost of a particular pain, except the feelings and judgment of the experienced? When, therefore, those feelings and judgment declare the pleasures derived from the higher faculties to be preferable in kind, apart from the question of intensity, to those of which the animal nature, disjoined from the higher faculties, is suspectible, they are entitled on this subject to the same regard.

I have dwelt on this point, as being a necessary part of a perfectly just conception of Utility or Happiness, considered as the directive rule of human conduct. But it is by no means an indispensable condition to the acceptance of the utilitarian standard; for that standard is not the agent's own greatest happiness, but the greatest amount of happiness altogether; and if it may possibly be doubted whether a noble character is always the happier for its nobleness, there can be no doubt that it makes other people happier, and that the world in general is immensely a gainer by it. Utilitarianism, therefore, could only attain its end by the general cultivation of nobleness of character, even if each individual were only benefited by the nobleness of others, and his own, so far as happiness is concerned, were a sheer deduction from the benefit. But the bare enunciation of such an absurdity as this last, renders refutation superfluous.

According to the Greatest Happiness Principle, as above explained, the ultimate end, with reference to and for the sake of which all other things are desirable (whether we are considering our own good or that of other people), is an existence exempt as far as possible from pain, and as rich as possible in enjoyments, both in point of quantity and quality; the test of quality, and the rule for measuring it against quantity, being the preference felt by those who in their opportunities of experience, to which must be added their habits of self-consciousness and self-observation, are best furnished with the means of comparison. This, being, according to the utilitarian opinion, the end of human action, is necessarily also the standard of morality; which may accordingly be defined "the rules and precepts for human conduct" by the observance of which an existence such as has been described might be, to the greatest extent possible, secured to all mankind; and not to them only, but, so far as the nature of things admits, to the whole sentient creation.

Against this doctrine, however, arises another class of objectors, who say that happiness, in any form, cannot be the rational purpose of human life and action; because, in the first place, it is unattainable: and they contemptuously ask, what right hast thou to be happy? a question which Mr. Carlyle clenches by the addition, What right, a short time ago, hadst thou even to be? Next, they say, that men can do without happiness; that all noble human beings have felt this, and could not have become noble but by learning the lesson of Entsagen, or renunciation; which lesson, thoroughly learnt and submitted to, they affirm to be the beginning and necessary condition of all virtue.

The first of these objections would go to the root of the matter were it well founded; for if no happiness is to be had at all by human beings, the attainment of it cannot be the end of morality, or of any rational conduct. Though, even in that case, something might still be said for the utilitarian theory; since utility includes not solely the pursuit of happiness, but the prevention or mitigation of unhappiness; and if the former aim be chimerical, there will be all the greater scope and more imperative need for the latter, so long at least as mankind think fit to live, and do not take refuge in the simultaneous act of suicide recommended under certain conditions by Novalis.* When, however, it is thus positively asserted to be impossible that human life should be happy, the assertion, if not something like a verbal quibble, is at least an exaggeration. If by happiness be meant a continuity of highly pleasurable excitement, it is evi-

*[The German poet Friedrich Leopold Freiherr von Hardenberg (1772–1801).]

dent enough that this is impossible. A state of exalted pleasure lasts only moments, or in some cases, and with some intermissions, hours or days, and is the occasional brilliant flash of enjoyment, not its permanent and steady flame. Of this the philosophers who have taught that happiness is the end of life were as fully aware as those who taunt them. The happiness which they meant was not a life of rapture; but moments of such, in an existence made up of few and transitory pains, many and various pleasures, with a decided predominance of the active over the passive, and having as the foundation of the whole, not to expect more from life than it is capable of bestowing. A life thus composed, to those who have been fortunate enough to obtain it, has always appeared worthy of the name of happiness. And such an existence is even now the lot of many, during some considerable portion of their lives. The present wretched education, and wretched social arrangements, are the only real hindrance to its being attainable by almost all.

The objectors perhaps may doubt whether human beings, if taught to consider happiness as the end of life, would be satisfied with such a moderate share of it. But great numbers of mankind have been satisfied with much less. The main constituents of a satisfied life appear to be two, either of which by itself is often found sufficient for the purpose: tranquillity, and excitement. With much tranquillity, many find that they can be content with very little pleasure: with much excitement, many can reconcile themselves to a considerable quantity of pain. There is assuredly no inherent impossibility in enabling even the mass of mankind to unite both; since the two are so far from being incompatible that they are in natural alliance, the prolongation of either being a preparation for, and exciting a wish for, the other. It is only those in whom indolence amounts to a vice, that do not desire excitement after an interval of repose: it is only those in whom the need of excitement is a disease, that feel the tranquillity which follows excitement dull and insipid, instead of pleasurable in direct proportion to the excitement which preceded it. When people who are tolerably fortunate in their outward lot do not find in life sufficient enjoyment to make it valuable to them, the cause generally is, caring for nobody but themselves. To those who have neither public nor private affections, the excitements of life are much curtailed, and in any case dwindle in value as the time approaches when all selfish interests must be terminated by death: while those who leave after them objects of personal affection, and especially those who have also cultivated a fellow-feeling with the collective interests of mankind, retain as lively an interest in life on the eve of death as in the vigour of youth and health. Next to selfishness, the principal cause which makes life unsatisfactory is want of mental cultivation. A cultivated mind—I do not mean that of a philosopher, but any mind to which the fountains of knowledge have been opened, and which has been taught, in any tolerable degree, to exercise its faculties—finds sources of inexhaustible interest in all that surrounds it; in the objects of nature, the achievements of art, the imaginations of poetry, the incidents of history, the ways of mankind, past and present, and their prospects in the future. It is possible, indeed, to become indifferent to all this, and that too without having exhausted a thousandth part of it; but only when one has had from the beginning no moral or human interest in these things, and has sought in them only the gratification of curiosity.

Now there is absolutely no reason in the nature of things why an amount of mental culture sufficient to give an intelligent interest in these objects of contemplation, should not be the inheritance of every one born in a civilised country. As little is there an inherent necessity that any human being should be a selfish egotist, devoid of every feeling or care but those which centre in his own miserable individuality. Something far superior to this is sufficiently common even now, to give ample earnest of what the human species may be made. Genuine private affections, and a sincere interest in the public good, are possible, though in unequal degrees, to every rightly brought up human being. In a world in which there is so much to interest, so much to enjoy, and so much also to correct and improve, every one who has this moderate amount of moral and intellectual requisites is capable of an existence which may be called enviable; and unless such a person, through bad laws, or subjection to the will of others, is denied the liberty to use the sources of happiness within his reach, he will not fail to find this enviable existence, if he escape the positive evils of life, the great sources of physical and mental suffering—such as indigence, disease, and the unkindness, worthlessness, or premature loss of objects of affection. The main stress of the problem lies, therefore, in the contest with these calamities, from which it is a rare good fortune entirely to escape; which, as things now are, cannot be obviated, and often cannot be in any material degree mitigated. Yet no one whose opinion deserves a moment's consideration can doubt that most of the great positive evils of the world are in themselves removable, and will, if human affairs continue to improve, be in the end reduced within narrow limits. Poverty, in any sense implying suffering, may be completely extinguished by the wisdom of society, combined with the good sense and providence of individuals. Even that most intractable of enemies, disease, may be indefinitely reduced in dimensions by good physical and moral education, and proper control of noxious influences; while the progress of science holds out a promise for the future of still more direct conquests over this detestable foe. And every advance in that direction relieves us from some, not only of the chances which cut short our own lives, but, what concerns us still more, which deprive us of those in whom our happiness is wrapt up. As for vicissitudes of fortune, and other disappointments connected with worldly circumstances, these are principally the effect either of gross imprudence, of ill-regulated desires, or of bad or imperfect social institutions. All the grand sources, in short, of human suffering are in a great degree, many of them almost entirely, conquerable by human care and effort; and though their removal is grievously slow—though a long succession of generations will perish in the breach before the conquest is completed, and this world becomes all that, if will and knowledge were not wanting, it might easily be made—yet every mind sufficiently intelligent and generous to bear a part, however small and unconspicuous, in the endeavour, will draw a noble enjoyment from the contest itself, which he would not for any bribe in the form of selfish indulgence consent to be without.

And this leads to the true estimation of what is said by the objectors concerning the possibility, and the obligation, of learning to do without happiness. Unquestionably it is possible to do without happiness; it is done involuntarily by nineteen-twentieths of mankind, even in those parts of our present world which are least deep in barbarism; and it often has to be done voluntarily by the hero or the martyr, for the sake of something which he prizes more than his individual happiness. But this something, what is it, unless the happiness of others, or some of the requisites of happiness? It is noble to be capable of resigning entirely one's own portion of happiness, or chances of it: but, after all, this self-sacrifice must be for some end; it is not its own end; and if we are told that its end is not happiness, but virtue, which is better than happiness, I ask, would the sacrifice be made if the hero or martyr did not believe that it would earn for others immunity from similar sacrifices? Would it be made if he thought that his renunciation of happiness for himself would produce no fruit for any of his fellow creatures, but to make their lot like his, and place them also in the condition of persons who have renounced happiness? All honour to those who can abnegate for themselves the personal enjoyment of life, when by such renunciation they contribute worthily to

Crystal Palace, London, 1851, designed by Joseph Paxton (1801–1865). Built for the Works of Industry of All Nations exhibit, the building covered nineteen acres and enclosed over thirty million cubic feet. *(The Bettman Archive)*

increase the amount of happiness in the world; but he who does it, or professes to do it, for any other purpose, is no more deserving of admiration than the ascetic mounted on his pillar. He may be an inspiriting proof of what men *can* do, but assuredly not an example of what they *should*.

Though it is only in a very imperfect state of the world's arrangements that any one can best serve the happiness of others by the absolute sacrifice of his own, yet so long as the world is in that imperfect state, I fully acknowledge that the readiness to make such a sacrifice is the highest virtue which can be found in man. I will add, that in this condition of the world, paradoxical as the assertion may be, the conscious ability to do without happiness gives the best prospect of realising such happiness as is attainable. For nothing except that consciousness can raise a person above the chances of life, by making him feel that, let fate and fortune do their worst, they have not power to subdue him: which, once felt, frees him from excess of anxiety concerning the evils of life, and enables him, like many a Stoic in the worst times of the Roman Empire, to cultivate in tranquillity the sources of satisfaction accessible to him, without concerning himself about the uncertainty of their duration, any more than about their inevitable end.

Meanwhile, let utilitarians never cease to claim the morality of self devotion as a possession which belongs by as good a right to them, as either to the Stoic or to the Transcendentalist. The utilitarian morality does recognise in human beings the power of sacrificing their own greatest good for the good of others. It only refuses to admit that the sacrifice is itself a good. A sacrifice which does not increase, or tend to

Interior, Crystal Palace. The palace was a shrine to science, industrialization, and progress. This architectural marvel represented in concrete form Mill's optimism when he spoke of the "wisdom of society" and the "progress of science [which] holds out a promise for the future." (*Victoria and Albert Museum, London*)

increase, the sum total of happiness, it considers as wasted. The only self-renunciation which it applauds, is devotion to the happiness, or to some of the means of happiness, of others; either of mankind collectively, or of individuals within the limits imposed by the collective interests of mankind.

I must again repeat, what the assailants of utilitarianism seldom have the justice to acknowledge, that the happiness which forms the utilitarian standard of what is right in conduct, is not the agent's own happiness, but that of all concerned. As between his own happiness and that of others, utilitarianism requires him to be as strictly impartial as a disinterested and benevolent spectator. In the golden rule of Jesus of Nazareth, we read the complete spirit of the ethics of utility. "To do as you would be done by," and "to love your neighbour as yourself," constitute the ideal perfection of utilitarian morality. As the means of making the nearest approach to this ideal, utility would enjoin, first, that laws and social arrangements should place the happiness, or (as speaking practically it may be called) the interest, of every individual, as nearly as possible in harmony with the interest of the whole; and secondly, that education and opinion, which have so vast a power over human character, should so use that power as to establish in the mind of every individual an indissoluble association between his own happiness and the good of the whole; especially between his own happiness and the practice of such modes of conduct, negative and positive, as regard for the universal happiness prescribes; so that not only he may be unable to conceive the possibility of happiness to himself, consistently with conduct opposed to the general good, but also that a direct impulse to promote the general good may be in every individual one of the habitual motives of action, and the sentiments connected therewith may fill a large and prominent place in every human being's sentient existence. If the impugners of the utilitarian morality represented it to their own minds in this its true character, I know not what recommendation possessed by any other morality they could possibly affirm to be wanting to it; what more beautiful or more exalted developments of human nature any other ethical system can be supposed to foster, or what springs of action, not accessible to the utilitarian, such systems rely on for giving effect to their mandates.

The objectors to utilitarianism cannot always be charged with representing it in a discreditable light. On the contrary, those among them who entertain anything like a just idea of its disinterested character, sometimes find fault with its standard as being too high for humanity. They say it is exacting too much to require that people shall always act from the inducement of promoting the general interests of society. But this is to mistake the very meaning of a standard of morals, and confound the rule of action with the motive of it. It is the business of ethics to tell us what are our duties, or by what test we may know them; but no system of ethics requires that the sole motive of all we do shall be a feeling of duty; on the contrary, ninety-nine hundredths of all our actions are done from other motives, and rightly so done, if the rule of duty does not condemn them. It is the more unjust to utilitarianism that this particular misapprehension should be made a ground of objection to it, inasmuch as utilitarian moralists have gone beyond almost all others in affirming that the motive has nothing to do with the morality of the action, though much with the worth of the agent. He who saves a fellow creature from drowning does what is morally right, whether his motive be duty, or the hope of being paid for his trouble; he who betrays the friend that trusts him, is guilty of a crime, even if his object be to serve another friend to whom he is under greater obligations. But to speak only of actions done from the motive of duty, and in direct obedience to principle: it is a misapprehension of the utilitarian mode of thought, to conceive it as implying that people should fix their minds upon so wide a generality as the world, or society at large. The great majority of good actions are intended not for the benefit of the world, but for that of individuals, of which the good of the world is made up; and the thoughts of the most virtuous man need not on these occasions travel beyond the particular persons concerned, except so far as is necessary to assure himself that in benefiting them he is not violating the rights, that is, the legitimate and authorised expectations, of any one else. The multiplication of happiness is, according to the utilitarian ethics, the object of virtue: the occasions on which any person (except one in a thousand) has it in his power to do this on an extended scale, in other words to be a public benefactor, are but exceptional; and on these occasions alone is he called on to consider public utility; in every other case, private utility, the interest or happiness of some few persons, is all he has to attend to. Those alone the influence of whose actions extends to society in general, need concern themselves habitually about so large an object. In the case of abstinences indeed—of things which people forbear to do from moral considerations, though the consequences in the particular case might be beneficial—it would be unworthy of an intelligent agent not to be consciously aware that the action is of a class which, if practised generally, would be generally injurious, and that this is the ground of the obligation to abstain from it. The amount of regard for the public interest implied in this recognition, is no greater than is demanded by every system of morals, for they all enjoin to abstain from whatever is manifestly pernicious to society.

The same considerations dispose of another reproach against the doctrine of utility, founded on a still grosser misconception of the purpose of a standard of morality, and of the very meaning of the words "right" and "wrong." It is often affirmed that utilitarianism renders men cold and unsympathising; that it chills their moral feelings towards individuals; that it makes them regard only the dry and hard consideration of the consequences of actions, not taking into their moral estimate the qualities from which those actions emanate. If the assertion means that they do not allow their judgment respecting the rightness or wrongness of an action to be influenced by their opinion of the qualities of the person who does it, this is a complaint not against utilitarianism, but against having any standard of morality at all; for certainly no known ethical standard decides an action to be good or bad because it is done by a good or a bad man, still less because done by an amiable, a brave, or a benevolent man, or the contrary. These considerations are relevant, not to the estimation of actions, but of persons; and there is nothing in the utilitarian theory inconsistent with the fact that there are other things which interest us in persons besides the rightness and wrongness of their actions. The Stoics, indeed, with the paradoxical misuse of language which was part of their system, and by which they strove to raise themselves above all concern about anything but virtue, were fond of saying that he who has that has everything; that he, and only he, is rich, is beautiful, is a king. But no claim of this description is made for the virtuous man by the utilitarian doctrine. Utilitarians are quite aware that there are other desirable possessions and qualities besides virtue, and are perfectly willing to allow to all of them their full worth. They are also aware that a right action does not necessarily indicate a virtuous character, and that actions which are blamable, often proceed from qualities entitled to praise. When this is apparent in any particular case, it modifies their estimation, not certainly of the act, but of the agent. I grant that they are, notwithstanding, of opinion, that in the long run the best proof of a good character is good actions; and resolutely refuse to consider any mental disposition as good, of which the predominant tendency is to produce bad conduct. This makes them unpopular with many people; but it is an unpopularity which they must share with every one who regards the distinction between right and wrong in a serious light; and the reproach is not one which a conscientious utilitarian need be anxious to repel.

If no more be meant by the objection than that many utilitarians look on the morality of actions, as measured by the utilitarian standard, with too exclusive a regard, and do not lay sufficient stress upon the other beauties of character which go towards making a human being lovable or admirable, this may be admitted. Utilitarians who have cultivated their moral feelings, but not their sympathies nor their artistic perceptions, do fall into this mistake; and so do all other moralists under the same conditions. What can be said in excuse for other moralists is equally available for them, namely, that, if there is to be any error, it is better that it should be on that side. As a matter of fact, we may affirm that among utilitarians as among adherents of other systems, there is every imaginable degree of rigidity and of laxity in the application of their standard: some are even puritanically rigorous, while others are as indulgent as can possibly be desired by sinner or by sentimentalist. But on the whole, a doctrine which brings prominently forward the interest that mankind have in the repression and prevention of conduct which violates the moral law, is likely to be inferior to no other in turning the sanctions of opinion again such violations. It is true, the question, "What does violate the moral law?" is one on which those who recognise different standards of morality are likely now and then to differ. But difference of opinion on moral questions was not first introduced into the world by utilitarianism, while that doctrine does supply, if not always an easy, at all events a tangible and intelligible mode of deciding such differences.

It may not be superfluous to notice a few more of the common misapprehensions of utilitarian ethics, even those which are so obvious and gross that it might appear impossible for any person of candour and intelligence to fall into them; since persons, even of considerable mental endowments, often give themselves so little trouble to understand the bearings of any opinion against which they entertain a prejudice, and men are in general so little conscious of this voluntary ignorance as a defect, that the vulgarest misunderstandings of ethical doctrines are continually met with in the deliberate writings of persons of the greatest pretensions both to high principle and to philosophy. We not uncommonly hear the doctrine of utility inveighed against as a godless doctrine. If it be necessary to say anything at all against so mere an assumption, we may say that the question depends upon what idea we have formed of the moral character of the Deity. If it be a true belief that God desires, above all things, the happiness of his creatures, and that this was his purpose in their creation, utility is not only not a godless doctrine, but more profoundly religious than any other. If it be meant that utilitarianism does not recognise the revealed will of God as the supreme law of morals, I answer, that a utilitarian who believes in the perfect goodness and wisdom of God, necessarily believes that whatever God has thought fit to reveal on the subject of morals, must fulfil the requirements of utility in a supreme degree. But others besides utilitarians have been of opinion that the Christian revelation was intended, and is fitted, to inform the hearts and minds of mankind with a spirit which should enable them to find for themselves what is right, and incline them to do it when found, rather than to tell them, except in a very general way, what it is; and that we need a doctrine of ethics, carefully followed out, to *interpret* to us the will of God. Whether this opinion is correct or not, it is superfluous here to discuss; since whatever aid religion, either natural or revealed, can afford to ethical investigation, is as open to the utilitarian moralist as to any other. He can use it as the testimony of God to the usefulness or hurtfulness of any given course of action, by as good a right as others can use it for the indication of a transcendental law, having no connection with usefulness or with happiness.

Again, Utility is often summarily stigmatised as an immoral doctrine by giving it the name of "expediency," and taking advantage of the popular use of that term to contrast it with Principle. But the Expedient, in the sense in which it is opposed to the Right, generally means that which is expedient for the particular interest of the agent himself; as when a minister sacrifices the interests of his country to keep himself in place. When it means anything better than this, it means that which is expedient for some immediate object, some temporary purpose, but which violates a rule whose observance is expedient in a much higher degree. The Expedient, in this sense, instead of being the same thing with the useful, is a branch of the hurtful. Thus, it would often be expedient, for the purpose of getting over some momentary embarrassment, or attaining some object immediately useful to ourselves or others, to tell a lie. But inasmuch as the cultivation in ourselves of a sensitive feeling on the subject of veracity, is one of the most useful, and the enfeeblement of that feeling one of the most hurtful, things to which our conduct can be instrumental; and inasmuch as any, even unintentional, deviation from truth, does that much towards weakening the trustworthiness of human assertion, which is not only the principal support of all present social well-being, but the insufficiency of which does more than any one thing that can be named to keep back civilisation, virtue, everything on which human happiness on the largest scale depends; we feel that the violation, for a present advantage, of a rule of such transcendant expediency, is not expedient, and that he who, for the sake of a convenience to himself or to some other individual, does what depends on him to deprive mankind of the good, and inflict upon them the evil, involved in the greater or less reliance which they can place in each other's word, acts the part of one of their worst enemies. Yet that even this rule, sacred as it is, admits of possible exceptions, is acknowledged by all moralists; the chief of which is when the withholding of some fact (as of information from a malefactor, or of bad news from a person dangerously ill) would save an individual (especially an individual other than oneself) from great and unmerited evil, and when the withholding can only be effected by denial. But in order that the exception may not extend itself beyond the need, and may have the least possible effect in weakening reliance on veracity, it ought to be recognised, and, if possible, its limits defined; and if the principle of utility is good for anything, it must be good for weighing these conflicting utilities against one another, and marking out the region within which one or the other preponderates.

Again, defenders of utility often find themselves called upon to reply to such objections as this—that there is not time, previous to action, for calculating and weighing the effects of any line of conduct on the general happiness. This is exactly as if any one were to say that it is impossible to guide our conduct by Christianity, because there is not time, on every occasion on which anything has to be done, to read through the Old and New Testaments. The answer to the objection is, that there has been ample time, namely, the whole past duration of the human species. During all that time, mankind have been learning by experience the tendencies of actions; on which experience all the prudence, as well as all the morality of life, are dependent. People talk as if the commencement of this course of experience had hitherto been put off, and as if, at the moment when some man feels tempted to meddle with the property or life of another, he had to begin considering for the first time whether murder and theft are injurious to human happiness. Even then I do not think that he would find the question very puzzling; but, at all events, the matter is now done to his hand. It is truly a whimsical supposition that, if mankind were agreed in considering utility to be the test of morality, they would remain without any agreement as to what is useful, and would take no measures for having their notions on the subject taught to the young, and enforced by law and opinion. There is no difficulty in proving any ethical standard whatever to work ill, if we suppose universal idiocy to be conjoined with it; but on any hypothesis short of that, mankind must by this time have acquired positive beliefs as to the effects of some actions on their happiness; and the beliefs which have thus come down are the rules of morality for the multitude, and for the philosopher until he has succeeded in finding better. That philosophers might easily do this, even now, on many subjects; that the received code of ethics is by no means of divine right; and that mankind have still much to learn as to the effects of actions on the general happiness, I admit, or rather, earnestly maintain. The corollaries from the principle of utility, like the precepts of every practical art, admit of indefinite improvement, and, in a progressive state of the human mind, their improvement is perpetually going on. But to consider the rules of morality as improvable, is one thing; to pass over the intermediate generalisations entirely, and endeavour to test each individual action directly by the first principle, is another. It is a strange notion that the acknowledgment of a first principle is inconsistent with the admission of secondary ones. To inform a traveller respecting the place of his ultimate destination, is not to forbid the use of landmarks and direction-posts on the way. The proposition that happiness is the end and aim of morality, does not mean that no road ought to be laid down to that goal, or that persons going thither should not be advised to take one direction rather than another. Men really ought to leave off talking a kind of nonsense on this subject, which they would neither talk nor listen to on other matters of practical concernment. Nobody argues that the art of navigation is not founded on astronomy, because sailors cannot wait to calculate the *Nautical Almanac*. Being rational creatures, they go to sea with it ready calculated; and all rational creatures go out upon the sea of life with their minds made up on the common questions of right and wrong, as well as on many of the far more difficult questions of wise and foolish. And this, as long as foresight is a human quality, it is to be presumed they will continue to do. Whatever we adopt as the fundamental principle of morality, we require subordinate principles to apply it by; the impossibility of doing without them, being common to all systems, can afford no argument against any one in particular; but gravely to argue as if no such secondary principles could be had, and as if mankind had remained till no, and always must remain, without drawing any general conclusions from the experience of human life, is as high a pitch, I think, as absurdity has ever reached in philosophical controversy.

The remainder of the stock arguments against utilitarianism mostly consist in laying to its charge the common infirmities of human nature, and the general difficulties which embarrass conscientious persons in shaping their course through life. We are told that a utilitarian will be apt to make his own particular case an exception to moral rules, and, when under temptation, will see a utility in the breach of a rule, greater than he will see in its observance. But is utility the only creed which is able to furnish us with excuses for evil doing, and means of cheating our own conscience? They are afforded in abundance by all doctrines which recognise as a fact in morals the existence of conflicting considerations; which all doctrines do, that have been believed by sane persons. It is not the fault of any creed, but of the complicated nature of human affairs, that rules of conduct cannot be so framed as to require no exceptions, and that hardly any kind of action can safely be laid down as either always obligatory or always condemnable. There is no ethical creed which does not temper the rigidity of its laws, by giving a certain latitude, under the moral responsibility of the agent, for accommodation to peculiarities of circumstances; and under every creed, at the opening thus made, self-deception and dishonest casuistry get in. There exists no moral system under which there do not arise unequivocal cases of conflicting obligation. These are the real difficulties, the knotty points both in the theory of ethics, and in the conscientious guidance of personal conduct. They are overcome practically, with greater or with less success, according to the intellect and virtue of the individual; but it can hardly be pretended that any one will be the less qualified for dealing with them, from possessing an ultimate standard to which conflicting rights and duties can be referred. If utility is the ultimate source of moral obligations, utility may be invoked to decide between them when their demands are incompatible. Though the application of the standard may be difficult, it is better than none at all: while in other systems, the moral laws all claiming independent authority, there is no common umpire entitled to interfere between them; their claims to precedence one over another rest on little better than sophistry, and unless determined, as they generally are, by the unacknowledged influence of considerations of utility, afford a free scope for the action of personal desires and partialities. We must remember that only in these cases of conflict between secondary principles is it requisite that first principles should be appealed to. There is no case of moral obligation in which some secondary principle is not involved; and if only one, there can seldom be any real doubt which one it is, in the mind of any person by whom the principle itself is recognised.

CHAPTER 3: OF THE ULTIMATE
SANCTION OF THE PRINCIPLE OF UTILITY

The question is often asked, and properly so, in regard to any supposed moral standard—What is its sanction? what are the motives to obey it? or more specifically, what is the source of its obligation? whence does it derive its binding force? It is a necessary part of moral philosophy to provide the answer to this question; which, though frequently assuming the shape of an objection to the utilitarian morality, as if it had some special applicability to that above others, really arises in regard to all standards. It arises, in fact, whenever a person is called on to *adopt* a standard, or refer morality to any basis on which he has not been accustomed to rest it. For the customary morality, that which education and opinion have consecrated, is the only one which presents itself to the mind with the feeling of being *in itself* obligatory; and when a person is asked to believe that this morality *derives* its obligation from some general principle round which custom has not thrown the same halo, the assertion is to him a paradox; the supposed corollaries seem to have a more binding force than the original theorem; the superstructure seems to stand better without, than with, what is represented as its foundation. He says to himself, I feel that I am bound not to rob or murder, betray or deceive; but why am I bound to promote the general happiness? If my own happiness lies in something else, why may I not give that the preference?

If the view adopted by the utilitarian philosophy of the nature of the moral sense be correct, this difficulty will always present itself, until the influences which form moral character have taken the same hold of the principle which they have taken of some of the consequences—until, by the improvement of education, the feeling of unity with our fellow-creatures shall be (what it cannot be denied that Christ intended it to be) as deeply rooted in our character, and to our own consciousness as completely a part of our nature, as the horror of crime is in an ordinarily well brought up young person. In the meantime, however, the difficulty has no peculiar application to the doctrine of utility, but is inherent in every attempt to analyse morality and reduce it to principles; which, unless the principle is already in men's minds invested with as much sacredness as any of its applications, always seems to divest them of a part of their sanctity.

The principle of utility either has, or there is no reason why it might not have, all the sanctions which belong to any other system of morals. Those sanctions are either external or internal. Of the external sanctions it is not necessary to speak at any length. They are, the hope of favour and the fear of displeasure, from our fellow-creatures or from the Ruler of the Universe, along with whatever we may have of sympathy or affection for them, or of love and awe of Him, inclining us to do his will independently of selfish consequences. There is evidently no reason why all these motives for observance should not attach themselves to the utilitarian morality, as completely and as powerfully as to any other. Indeed, those of them which refer to our fellow-creatures are sure to do so, in proportion to the amount of general intelligence; for whether there be any other ground of moral obligation than the general happiness or not, men do desire happiness; and however imperfect may be their own practice, they desire and commend all conduct in others towards themselves, by which they think their happiness is promoted. With regard to the religious motive, if men believe, as most profess to do, in the goodness of God, those who think that conduciveness to the general happiness is the essence, or even only the criterion of good, must necessarily believe that it is also that which God approves. The whole force therefore of external reward and punishment, whether physical or moral, and whether proceeding from God or from our fellow men, together with all that the capacities of human nature admit of disinterested devotion to either, become available to enforce the utilitarian morality, in proportion as that morality is recognised; and the more powerfully, the more the appliances of education and general cultivation are bent to the purpose.

So far as to external sanctions. The internal sanction of duty, whatever our standard of duty may be, is one and the same—a feeling in our own mind; a pain, more or less intense, attendant on violation of duty, which in properly cultivated moral natures rises, in the more serious cases, into shrinking from it as an impossibility. This feeling, when disinterested, and connecting itself with the pure idea of duty, and not with some particular form of it, or with any of the merely accessory circumstances, is the essence of Conscience; though in that complex phenomenon as it actually exists, the simple fact is in general all encrusted over with collateral associations, derived from sympathy, from love, and still more from fear; from all the forms of religious feeling; from the recollections of childhood and of all our past life; from self-esteem, desire of the esteem of others, and occasionally even self-abasement. This extreme complication is, I apprehend, the origin of the sort of mystical character which, by a tendency of the human mind of which there are many other examples, is apt to be attributed to the idea of moral obligation, and which leads people to believe that the idea cannot possibly attach itself to any other objects than those which, by a supposed mysterious law, are found in our present experience to excite it. Its binding force, however, consists in the existence of a mass of feeling which must be broken through in order to do what violates our standard of right, and which, if we do nevertheless violate that standard, will probably have to be encountered afterwards in the form of remorse. Whatever theory we have of the nature or origin of conscience, this is what essentially constitutes it.

The ultimate sanction, therefore, of all morality (external motives apart) being a subjective feeling in our own minds, I see nothing embarrassing to those whose standard is utility, in the question, "What is the sanction of that particular standard?" We may answer, the same as of all other moral standards—the conscientious feelings of mankind. Undoubtedly this sanction has no binding efficacy on those who do not possess the feelings it appeals to; but neither will these persons be more obedient to any other moral principle than to the utilitarian one. On them morality of any kind has no hold but through the external sanctions. Meanwhile the feelings exist, a fact in human nature, the reality of which, and the great power with which they are capable of acting on those in whom they have been duly cultivated, are proved by experience. No reason has ever been shown why they may not be cultivated to as great intensity in connection with the utilitarian, as with any other rule of morals.

There is, I am aware, a disposition to believe that a person who sees in moral obligation a transcendental fact, an objective reality belonging to the province of "things in themselves," is likely to be more obedient to it than one who believes it to be entirely subjective, having its seat in human consciousness only. But whatever a person's opinion may be on this point of Ontology, the force he is really urged by is his own subjective feeling, and is exactly measured by its strength. No one's belief that duty is an objective reality is stronger than the belief that God is so; yet the belief in God, apart from the expectation of actual reward and punishment, only operates on conduct through, and in proportion to, the subjective religious feeling. The sanction, so far as it is disinterested, is always in the mind itself; and the notion therefore of the transcendental moralists must be, that this sanction will not exist *in* the mind unless it is believed to have its root out of the mind; and that if a person is able to say to himself, "This which is restraining me, and which is called my conscience, is only a feeling in my own mind," he may possibly draw the conclusion that when the feeling ceases the obligation ceases, and that if he find the feeling inconvenient, he may disregard it, and endeavour to get rid of it. But is this danger confined to the utilitarian morality? Does the belief that moral obligation has its seat outside the mind make the feeling of it too strong to be got rid of? The fact is so far otherwise, that all moralists admit and lament the ease with which, in the generality of minds, conscience can be silenced or stifled. The question, "Need I obey my conscience?" is quite as often put to themselves by persons who never heard of the principle of utility, as by its adherents. Those whose conscientious feelings are so weak as to allow of their asking this question, if they answer it affirmatively, will not do so because they believe in the transcendental theory, but because of the external sanctions.

It is not necessary, for the present purpose, to decide whether the feeling of duty is innate or implanted. Assuming it to be innate, it is an open question to what objects it naturally attaches itself; for the philosophic supporters of that theory are now agreed that the intuitive perception is of principles of morality and not of the details. If there be anything innate in the matter, I see no reason why the feeling which is innate should not be that of regard to the pleasures and pains of others. If there is any principle of morals which is intuitively obligatory, I should say it must be that. If so, the intuitive ethics would coincide with the utilitarian, and there would be no further quarrel between them. Even as it is, the intuitive moralists, though they believe that there are other intuitive moral obligations, do already believe this to be one; for they unanimously hold that a large *portion* of morality turns upon the consideration due to the interests of our fellow-creatures. Therefore, if the belief in the transcendental origin of moral obligation gives any additional efficacy to the internal sanction, it appears to me that the utilitarian principle has already the benefit of it.

On the other hand, if, as is my own belief, the moral feelings are not innate, but acquired, they are not for that reason the less natural. It is natural to man to speak, to reason, to build cities, to cultivate the ground, though these are acquired faculties. The moral feelings are not indeed a part of our nature, in the sense of being in any perceptible degree present in all of us; but this, unhappily, is a fact admitted by those who believe the most strenuously in their transcendental origin. Like the other acquired capacities above referred to, the moral faculty, if not a part of our nature, is a natural outgrowth from it; capable, like them, in a certain small degree, of springing up spontaneously; and susceptible of being brought by cultivation to a high degree of development. Unhappily it is also susceptible, by a sufficient use of the external sanctions and of the force of early impressions, of being cultivated in almost any direction: so that there is hardly anything so absurd or so mischievous that it may not, by means of these influences, be made to act on the human mind with all the authority of conscience. To doubt that the same potency might be given by the same means to the principle of utility, even if it had no foundation in human nature, would be flying in the face of all experience.

But moral associations which are wholly of artificial creation, when intellectual culture goes on, yield by degrees to the dissolving force of analysis: and if the feeling of duty, when associated with utility, would appear equally arbitrary; if there were no leading department of our nature, no powerful class of sentiments, with which that association would harmonise, which would make us feel it congenial, and incline us not only to foster it in others (for which we have abundant interested motives), but also to cherish it in ourselves; if there were not, in short, a natural basis of sentiment for utilitarian morality, it might well happen that this association also, even after it had been implanted by education, might be analysed away.

But there *is* this basis of powerful natural sentiment; and this it is which, when once the general happiness is recognised as the ethical standard, will constitute the strength of the utilitarian morality. This firm foundation is that of the social feelings of mankind; the desire to be in unity with our fellow creatures, which is already a powerful principle in human nature, and happily one of those which tend to become stronger, even without express inculcation, from the influences of advancing civilisation. The social state is at once so natural, so necessary, and so habitual to man, that, except in some unusual circumstances or by an effort of voluntary abstraction, he never conceives himself otherwise than as a member of a body; and this association is riveted more and more, as mankind are further removed from the state of savage independence. Any condition, therefore, which is essential to a state of society, becomes more and more an inseparable part of every person's conception of the state of things which he is born into, and which is the destiny of a human being. Now, society between human beings, except in the relation of master and slave, is manifestly impossible on any other footing than that the interests of all are to be consulted. Society between equals can only exist on the understanding that the interests of all are to be regarded equally. And since in all states of civilisation, every person, except an absolute monarch, has equals, every one is obliged to live on these terms with somebody; and in every age some advance is made towards a state in which it will be impossible to live permanently on other terms with anybody. In this way people grow up unable to conceive as possible to them a state of total disregard of other people's interests. They are under a necessity of conceiving themselves as at least abstaining from all the grosser injuries, and (if only for their own protection) living in a state of constant protest against them. They are also familiar with the fact of cooperating with others and proposing to themselves a collective, not an individual interest as the aim (at least for the time being) of their actions. So long as they are cooperating, their ends are identified with those of others; there is at least a temporary feeling that the interests of others are their own interests. Not only does all strengthening of social ties, and all healthy growth of society, give to each individual a stronger personal interest in practically consulting the welfare of others; it also leads him to identify his *feelings* more and more with their good, or at least with an even greater degree of practical consideration for it. He comes, as though instinctively, to be conscious of himself as a being who *of course* pays regard to others. The good of others becomes to him a thing naturally and necessarily to be attended to, like any of the physical conditions of our existence. Now, whatever amount of this feeling a person has, he is urged by the strongest motives both of interest and of sympathy to demonstrate it, and to the utmost of his power encourage it in others; and even if he has none of it himself, he is as greatly interested as any one else that others should have it. Consequently the smallest germs of the feeling are laid hold of and nourished by the contagion of sympathy and the influences of education; and a complete web of corroborative association is woven round it, by the powerful agency of the external sanctions. This mode of conceiving ourselves and human life, as civilisation goes on, is felt to be more and more natural. Every step in political improvement renders it more so, by removing the sources of opposition of interest, and levelling those inequalities of legal privilege between individuals or classes, owing to which there are large portions of mankind whose happiness it is still practicable to disregard. In an improving state of the human mind, the influences are constantly on the increase, which tend to generate in each individual a feeling of unity with all the rest; which, if perfect, would make him never think of, or desire, any beneficial condition for himself, in the benefits of which they are not included. If we now suppose this feeling of unity to be taught as a religion, and the whole force of education, of institutions, and of opinion, directed, as it once was in the case of religion, to make every person grow up from infancy surrounded on all sides both by the profession and the practice of it, I think that no one, who can realise this conception, will feel any misgiving about the sufficiency of the ultimate sanction for the Happiness morality. To any ethical student who finds the realisation difficult, I recommend, as a means of facilitating it, the second of M. Comte's two principal works, the *Traité de Politique Positive*. I entertain the strongest objections to the system of politics and morals set forth in that treatise; but I think it has superabundantly shown the possibility of giving to the service of humanity, even without the aid of belief in a Providence, both the psychological power and the social efficacy of a religion; making it take hold of human life, and colour all thought, feeling, and action, in a manner of which the greatest ascendancy ever exercised by any religion may be but a type and foretaste; and of which the danger is, not that it should be insufficient, but that it should be so excessive as to interfere unduly with human freedom and individuality.

Neither is it necessary to the feeling which constitutes the binding force of the utilitarian morality on those who recognise it, to wait for those social influences which would make its obligation felt by mankind at large. In the comparatively early state of human advancement in which we now live, a person cannot indeed feel that entireness of sympathy with all others, which would make any real discordance in the general direction of their conduct in life impossible; but already a person in whom the social feeling is at all developed, cannot bring himself to think of the rest of his fellow-creatures as struggling rivals with him for the means of happiness, whom he must desire to see defeated in their object in order that he may succeed in his. The deeply rooted conception which every individual even now has of himself as a social being, tends to make him feel it one of his natural wants that there should be harmony between his feelings and aims and those of his fellow-creatures. If differences of opinion and of mental culture make it impossible for him to share many of their actual feelings—perhaps make him denounce and defy those feelings—he still needs to be conscious that his real aim and theirs do not conflict; that he is not opposing himself to what they really wish for, namely their own good, but is, on the contrary, promoting it. This feeling in most individuals is much inferior in strength to their selfish feelings, and is often wanting altogether. But to those who have it, it possesses all the characters of a natural feeling. It does not present itself to their minds as a superstition of education, or a law despotically imposed by the power of society, but as an attribute which it would not be well for them to be without. This conviction is the ultimate sanction of the greatest happiness morality. This it is which makes any mind, of well-developed feelings, work with, and not against, the outward motives to care for others, afforded by what I have called the external sanctions; and when those sanctions are wanting, or act in an opposite direction, constitutes in itself a powerful internal binding force, in proportion to the sensitiveness and thoughtfulness of the character; since few but those whose mind is a moral blank, could bear to lay out their course of life on the plan of paying no regard to others except so far as their own private interest compels.

CHAPTER 4: OF WHAT SORT OF
PROOF THE PRINCIPLE OF UTILITY IS SUSCEPTIBLE

It has already been remarked, that questions of ultimate ends do not admit of proof, in the ordinary acceptation of the term. To be incapable of proof by reasoning is common to all first principles; to the first premises of our knowledge, as well as to those of our conduct. But the former, being matters of fact, may be the subject of a direct appeal to the faculties which judge of fact—namely, our senses, and our internal consciousness. Can an appeal be made to the same faculties on questions of practical ends? Or by what other faculty is cognisance taken of them?

Questions about ends are, in other words, questions what things are desirable. The utilitarian doctrine is, that happiness is desirable, and the only thing desirable, as an end; all other things being only desirable as means to that end. What ought to be required of this doctrine—what conditions is it requisite that the doctrine should fulfil—to make good its claim to be believed?

The only proof capable of being given that an object is visible, is that people actually see it. The only proof that a sound is audible, is that people hear it: and so of the other sources of our experience. In like manner, I apprehend, the sole evidence it is possible to produce that anything is desirable, is that people do actually desire it. If the end which the utilitarian doctrine proposes to itself were not, in theory and in practice, acknowledged to be an end, nothing could ever convince any person that it was so. No reason can be given why the general happiness is desirable, except that each person, so far as he believes it to be attainable, desires his own happiness. This, however, being a fact, we have not only all the proof which the case admits of, but all which it is possible to require, that happiness is a good: that each person's happiness is a good to that person, and the general happiness, therefore, a good to the aggregate of all persons. Happiness has made out its title as one of the ends of conduct, and consequently one of the criteria of morality.

But it has not, by this alone, proved itself to be the sole criterion. To do that, it would seem, by the same rule, necessary to show, not only that people desire happiness, but that they never desire anything else. Now it is palpable that they do desire things which, in common language, are decidedly distinguished from happiness. They desire, for example, virtue, and the absence of vice, no less really than pleasure and the absence of pain. The desire of virtue is not as universal, but it is as authentic a fact, as the desire of happiness. And hence the opponents of the utilitarian standard deem that they have a right to infer that there are other ends of human action besides happiness, and that happiness is not the standard of approbation and disapprobation.

But does the utilitarian doctrine deny that people desire virtue, or maintain that virtue is not a thing to be desired? The very reverse. It maintains not only that virtue is to be desired, but that it is to be desired disinterestedly, for itself. Whatever may be the opinion of utilitarian moralists as to the original conditions by which virtue is made virtue; however they may believe (as they do) that actions and dispositions are only virtuous because they promote another end than virtue; yet this being granted, and it having been decided, from considerations of this description, what is virtuous, they not only place virtue at the very head of the things which are good as means to the ultimate end, but they also recognise as a psychological fact the possibility of its being, to the individual, a good in itself, without looking to any end beyond it; and hold, that the mind is not in a right state, not in a state conformable to Utility, not in the state most conducive to the general happiness, unless it does love virtue in this manner—as a thing desirable in itself, even although, in the individual instance, it should not produce those other desirable consequences which it tends to produce, and on account of which it is held to be virtue. This opinion is not, in the smallest degree, a departure from the Happiness principle. The ingredients of happiness are very various, and each of them is desirable in itself, and not merely when considered as swelling an aggregate. The principle of utility does not mean that any given pleasure, as music, for instance, or any given exemption from pain, as for example health, is to be looked upon as means to a collective something termed happiness, and to be desired on that account. They are de-sired and desirable in and for themselves; besides being means, they are a part of the end. Virtue, according to the utilitarian doctrine, is not naturally and originally part of the end, but it is capable of becoming so; and in those who love it disinterestedly it has become so, and is desired and cherished, not as a means to happiness, but as a part of their happiness.

To illustrate this farther, we may remember that virtue is not the only thing, orig-inally a means, and which if it were not a means to anything else, would be and remain indifferent, but which by association with what it is a means to, comes to be desired for itself, and that too with the utmost intensity. What, for example, shall we say of the love of money? There is nothing originally more desirable about money than about any heap of glittering pebbles. Its worth is solely that of the things which it will buy; the desires for other things than itself, which it is a means of gratifying. Yet the love of money is not only one of the strongest moving forces of human life, but money is, in many cases, desired in and for itself; the desire to possess it is often stronger than the desire to use it, and goes on increasing when all the desires which point to ends beyond it, to be compassed by it, are falling off. It may, then, be said truly, that money is de-sired not for the sake of an end, but as part of the end. From being a means to happi-ness, it has come to be itself a principal ingredient of the individual's conception of happiness. The same may be said of the majority of the great objects of human life—power, for example, or fame; except that to each of these there is a certain amount of immediate pleasure annexed, which has at least the semblance of being naturally inher-ent in them; a thing which cannot be said of money. Still, however, the strongest nat-ural attraction, both of power and of fame, is the immense aid they give to the attain-ment of our other wishes; and it is the strong association thus generated between them and all our objects of desire, which gives to the direct desire of them the intensity it often assumes, so as in some characters to surpass in strength all other desires. In these cases the means have become a part of the end, and a more important part of it than any of the things which they are means to. What was once desired as an instrument for the attainment of happiness, has come to be desired for its own sake. In being desired for its own sake it is, however, desired as *part* of happiness. The person is made, or thinks he would be made, happy by its mere possession; and is made unhappy by fail-ure to obtain it. The desire of it is not a different thing from the desire of happiness, any more than the love of music, or the desire of health. They are included in happi-ness. They are some of the elements of which the desire of happiness is made up. Hap-piness is not an abstract idea, but a concrete whole; and these are some of its parts. And the utilitarian standard sanctions and approves their being so. Life would be a poor thing, very ill provided with sources of happiness, if there were not this provision of nature, by which things originally indifferent, but conducive to, or otherwise associ-ated with, the satisfaction of our primitive desires, become in themselves sources of pleasure more valuable than the primitive pleasures, both in permanency, in the space of human existence that they are capable of covering, and even in intensity.

Virtue, according to the utilitarian conception, is a good of this description. There was no original desire of it, or motive to it, save its conduciveness to pleasure, and especially to protection from pain. But through the association thus formed, it may be felt a good in itself, and desired as such with as great intensity as any other good; and with this difference between it and the love of money, of power, or of fame, that all of these may, and often do, render the individual noxious to the other members of the society to which he belongs, whereas there is nothing which makes him so much a blessing to them as the cultivation of the disinterested love of virtue. And consequently, the utilitarian standard, while it tolerates and approves those other acquired desires, up to the point beyond which they would be more injurious to the general happiness than promotive of it, enjoins and requires the cultivation of the love of virtue up to the greatest strength possible, as being above all things important to the general happiness.

It results from the preceding considerations, that there is in reality nothing desired except happiness. Whatever is desired otherwise than as a means to some end beyond itself, and ultimately to happiness, is desired as itself a part of happiness, and is not desired for itself until it has become so. Those who desire virtue for its own sake, desire it either because the consciousness of it is a pleasure, or because the consciousness of being without it is a pain, or for both reasons united; as in truth the pleasure and pain seldom exist separately, but almost always together, the same person feeling pleasure in the degree of virtue attained, and pain in not having attained more. If one of these gave him no pleasure, and the other no pain, he would not love or desire virtue, or would desire it only for the other benefits which it might produce to himself or to persons whom he cared for.

We have now, then, an answer to the question, of what sort of proof the principle of utility is susceptible. If the opinion which I have now stated is psychologically true—if human nature is so constituted as to desire nothing which is not either a part of happiness or a means of happiness—we can have no other proof, and we require no other, that these are the only things desirable. If so, happiness is the sole end of human action, and the promotion of it the test by which to judge of all human conduct; from whence it necessarily follows that it must be the criterion of morality, since a part is included in the whole.

And now to decide whether this is really so; whether mankind do desire nothing for itself but that which is a pleasure to them, or of which the absence is a pain; we have evidently arrived at a question of fact and experience, dependent, like all similar questions, upon evidence. It can only be determined by practised self-consciousness and self-observation, assisted by observation of others. I believe that these sources of evidence, impartially consulted, will declare that desiring a thing and finding it pleasant, aversion to it and thinking of it as painful, are phenomena entirely inseparable, or rather two parts of the same phenomenon—in strictness of language, two different modes of naming the same psychological fact: that to think of an object as desirable (unless for the sake of its consequences), and to think of it as pleasant, are one and the same thing; and that to desire anything, except in proportion as the idea of it is pleasant, is a physical and metaphysical impossibility.

So obvious does this appear to me, that I expect it will hardly be disputed: and the objection made will be, not that desire can possibly be directed to anything ultimately except pleasure and exemption from pain, but that the will is a different thing from desire; that a person of confirmed virtue, or any other person whose purposes are fixed, carries out his purposes without any thought of the pleasure he has in contemplating them, or expects to derive from their fulfilment; and persists in acting on them, even though these pleasures are much diminished, by changes in his character or decay of his passive sensibilities, or are out weighed by the pains which the pursuit of the purposes may bring upon him. All this I fully admit, and have stated it elsewhere, as positively and emphatically as any one. Will, the active phenomenon, is a different thing from desire, the state of passive sensibility, and though originally an offshoot from it, may in time take root and detach itself from the parent stock; so much so, that in the case of an habitual purpose, instead of willing the thing because we desire it, we often desire it only because we will it. This, however, is but an instance of that familiar fact, the power of habit, and is no wise confined to the case of virtuous actions. Many indifferent things, which men originally did from a motive of some sort, they continue to do from habit. Sometimes this is done unconsciously, the consciousness coming only after the action: at other times with conscious volition, but volition which has become habitual, and is put in operation by the force of habit, in opposition perhaps to the deliberate preference, as often happens with those who have contracted habits of vicious or hurtful indulgence. Third and last comes the case in which the habitual act of will in the individual instance is not in contradiction to the general intention prevailing at other times, but in fulfilment of it; as in the case of the person of confirmed virtue, and of all who pursue deliberately and consistently any determinate end. The distinction between will and desire thus understood is an authentic and highly important psychological fact; but the fact consists solely in this—that will, like all other parts of our constitution, is amenable to habit, and that we may will from habit what we no longer desire for itself, or desire only because we will it. It is not the less true that will, in the beginning, is entirely produced by desire; including in that term the repelling influence of pain as well as the attractive one of pleasure. Let us take into consideration, no longer the person who has a confirmed will to do right, but him in whom that virtuous will is still feeble, conquerable by temptation, and not to be fully relied on; by what means can it be strengthened? How can the will to be virtuous, where it does not exist in sufficient force, be implanted or awakened? Only by making the person *desire* virtue—by making him think of it in a pleasurable light, or of its absence in a painful one. It is by associating the doing right with pleasure, or the doing wrong with pain, or by eliciting and impressing and bringing home to the person's experience the pleasure naturally involved in the one or the pain in the other, that it is possible to call forth that will to be virtuous, which, when confirmed, acts without any thought of either pleasure or pain. Will is the child of desire, and passes out of the dominion of its parent only to come under that of habit. That which is the result of habit affords no presumption of being intrinsically good; and there would be no reason for wishing that the purpose of virtue should become independent of pleasure and pain, were it not that the influence of the pleasurable and painful associations which prompt to virtue is not sufficiently to be depended on for unerring constancy of action until it has acquired the support of habit. Both in feeling and in conduct, habit is the only thing which imparts certainty; and it is because of the importance to others of being able to rely absolutely on one's feelings and conduct, and to oneself of being able to rely on one's own, that the will to do right ought to be cultivated into this habitual independence. In other words, this state of the will is a means to good, not intrinsically a good; and does not contradict the doctrine that nothing is a good to human beings but in so far as it is either itself pleasurable, or a means of attaining pleasure or averting pain.

But if this doctrine be true, the principle of utility is proved. Whether it is so or not, must now be left to the consideration of the thoughtful reader.

CHAPTER 5: ON THE CONNECTION BETWEEN JUSTICE AND UTILITY

In all ages of speculation, one of the strongest obstacles to the reception of the doctrine that Utility or Happiness is the criterion of right and wrong, has been drawn from the idea of Justice. The powerful sentiment, and apparently clear perception, which that word recalls with a rapidity and certainty resembling an instinct, have seemed to the majority of thinkers to point to an inherent quality in things; to show that the Just must have an existence in Nature as something absolute, generically distinct from every variety of the Expedient, and, in idea, opposed to it, though (as is commonly acknowledged) never, in the long run, disjoined from it in fact.

In the case of this, as of our other moral sentiments, there is no necessary connection between the question of its origin, and that of its binding force. That a feeling is bestowed on us by Nature, does not necessarily legitimate all its promptings. The feeling of justice might be a peculiar instinct, and might yet require, like our other instincts, to be controlled and enlightened by a higher reason. If we have intellectual instincts, leading us to judge in a particular way, as well as animal instincts that prompt us to act in a particular way, there is no necessity that the former should be more infallible in their sphere than the latter in theirs: it may as well happen that wrong judgments are occasionally suggested by those, as wrong actions by these. But though it is one thing to believe that we have natural feelings of justice, and another to acknowledge them as an ultimate criterion of conduct, these two opinions are very closely connected in point of fact. Mankind are always predisposed to believe that any subjective feeling, not otherwise accounted for, is a revelation of some objective reality. Our present object is to determine whether the reality, to which the feeling of justice corresponds, is one which needs any such special revelation; whether the justice or injustice of an action is a thing intrinsically peculiar, and distinct from all its other qualities, or only a combination of certain of those qualities, presented under a peculiar aspect. For the purpose of this inquiry it is practically important to consider whether the feeling itself, of justice and injustice, is *sui generis* like our sensations of colour and taste, or a derivative feeling, formed by a combination of others. And this it is the more essential to examine, as people are in general willing enough to allow, that objectively the dictates of Justice coincide with a part of the field of General Expediency; but inasmuch as the subjective mental feeling of Justice is different from that which commonly attaches to simple expediency, and, except in the extreme cases of the latter, is far more imperative in its demands, people find it difficult to see, in Justice, only a particular kind or branch of general utility, and think that its superior binding force requires a totally different origin.

To throw light upon this question, it is necessary to attempt to ascertain what is the distinguishing character of justice, or of injustice: what is the quality, or whether there is any quality, attributed in common to all modes of conduct designated as unjust (for justice, like many other moral attributes, is best defined by its opposite), and distinguishing them from such modes of conduct as are disapproved, but without having that particular epithet of disapprobation applied to them. If in everything which men are accustomed to characterise as just or unjust, some one common attribute or collection of attributes is always present, we may judge whether this particular attribute or combination of attributes would be capable of gathering round it a sentiment of that peculiar character and intensity by virtue of the general laws of our emotional constitution, or whether the sentiment is inexplicable, and requires to be regarded as a special provision of Nature. If we find the former to be the case, we shall, in resolving this question, have resolved also the main problem: if the latter, we shall have to seek for some other mode of investigating it.

To find the common attributes of a variety of objects, it is necessary to begin by surveying the objects themselves in the concrete. Let us therefore advert successively to the various modes of action, and arrangements of human affairs, which are classed, by universal or widely spread opinion, as Just or as Unjust. The things well known to excite the sentiments associated with those names are of a very multifarious character. I shall pass them rapidly in review, without studying any particular arrangement.

In the first place, it is mostly considered unjust to deprive any one of his personal liberty, his property, or any other thing which belongs to him by law. Here, therefore, is one instance of the application of the terms "just" and "unjust" in a perfectly definite sense, namely, that it is just to respect, unjust to violate, the *legal rights* of any one. But this judgment admits of several exceptions, arising from the other forms in which the notions of justice and injustice present themselves. For example, the person who suffers the deprivation may (as the phrase is) have *forfeited* the rights which he is so deprived of: a case to which we shall return presently. But also—

Secondly; the legal rights of which he is deprived, may be rights which *ought* not to have belonged to him; in other words, the law which confers on him these rights, may be a bad law. When it is so, or when (which is the same thing for our purpose) it is supposed to be so, opinions will differ as to the justice or injustice of infringing it. Some maintain that no law, however bad, ought to be disobeyed by an individual citizen; that his opposition to it, if shown at all, should only be shown in endeavouring to get it altered by competent authority. This opinion (which condemns many of the most illustrious benefactors of mankind, and would often protect pernicious institutions against the only weapons which, in the state of things existing at the time, have any chance of succeeding against them) is defended, by those who hold it, on grounds of expediency; principally on that of the importance, to the common interest of mankind, of maintaining inviolate the sentiment of submission to law. Other persons, again, hold the directly contrary opinion, that any law, judged to be bad, may blamelessly be disobeyed, even though it be not judged to be unjust, but only inexpedient; while others would confine the licence of disobedience to the case of unjust laws: but again, some say, that all laws which are inexpedient are unjust; since every law imposes some restriction on the natural liberty of mankind, which restriction is an injustice, unless legitimated by tending to their good. Among these diversities of opinion, it seems to be universally admitted that there may be unjust laws, and that law, consequently, is not the ultimate criterion of justice, but may give to one person a benefit, or impose on another an evil, which justice condemns. When, however, a law is thought to be unjust, it seems always to be regarded as being so in the same way in which a breach of law is unjust, namely, by infringing somebody's right; which, as it cannot in this case be a legal right, receives a different appellation, and is called a moral right. We may say, therefore, that a second case of injustice consists in taking or withholding from any person that to which he has a *moral right*.

Thirdly, it is universally considered just that each person should obtain that (whether good or evil) which he *deserves* and unjust that he should obtain a good, or be made to undergo an evil, which he does not deserve. This is, perhaps, the clearest and most emphatic form in which the idea of justice is conceived by the general mind. As it involves the notion of desert, the question arises, what constitutes desert? Speaking in a general way, a person is understood to deserve good if he does right, evil if he does wrong; and in a more particular sense, to deserve good from those to whom he does or has done good, and evil from those to whom he does or has done evil. The precept of returning good for evil has never been regarded as a case of the fulfilment of justice, but as one in which the claims of justice are waived, in obedience to other considerations.

Fourthly, it is confessedly unjust to *break faith* with any one: to violate an engagement, either express or implied, or disappoint expectations raised by our own conduct, at least if we have raised those expectations knowingly and voluntarily. Like the other obligations of justice already spoken of, this one is not regarded as absolute, but as capable of being overruled by a stronger obligation of justice on the other side; or by such conduct on the part of the person concerned as is deemed to absolve us from our obligation to him, and to constitute a *forfeiture* of the benefit which he has been led to expect.

Fifthly, it is, by universal admission, inconsistent with justice to be *partial*—to show favour or preference to one person over another, in matters to which favour and preference do not properly apply. Impartiality, however, does not seem to be regarded as a duty in itself, but rather as instrumental to some other duty; for it is admitted that favour and preference are not always censurable, and indeed the cases in which they are condemned are rather the exception than the rule. A person would be more likely to be blamed than applauded for giving his family or friends no superiority in good offices over strangers, when he could do so without violating any other duty; and no one thinks it unjust to seek one person in preference to another as a friend, connection, or companion. Impartiality where rights are concerned is of course obligatory, but this is involved in the more general obligation of giving to every one his right. A tribunal, for example, must be impartial, because it is bound to award, without regard to any other consideration, a disputed object to the one of two parties who has the right to it. There are other cases in which impartiality means, being solely influenced by desert; as with those who, in the capacity of judges, preceptors, or parents, administer reward and punishment as such. There are cases, again, in which it means, being solely influenced by consideration for the public interest; as in making a selection among candidates for a government employment. Impartiality, in short, as an obligation of justice, may be said to mean, being exclusively influenced by the considerations which it is supposed ought to influence the particular case in hand; and resisting the solicitation of any motives which prompt to conduct different from what those considerations would dictate.

Nearly allied to the idea of impartiality is that of *equality,* which often enters as a component part both into the conception of justice and into the practice of it, and, in the eyes of many persons, constitutes its essence. But in this, still more than in any other case, the notion of justice varies in different persons, and always conforms in its variations to their notion of utility. Each person maintains that equality is the dictate of justice, except where he thinks that expediency requires inequality. The justice of giving equal protection to the rights of all, is maintained by those who support the most outrageous inequality in the rights themselves. Even in slave countries it is theoretically admitted that the rights of the slave, such as they are, ought to be as sacred as those of the master; and that a tribunal which fails to enforce them with equal strictness is wanting in justice; while, at the same time, institutions which leave to the slave scarcely any rights to enforce, are not deemed unjust, because they are not deemed inexpedient. Those who think that utility requires distinctions of rank, do not consider it unjust that riches and social privileges should be unequally dispensed; but those who think this inequality inexpedient, think it unjust also. Whoever thinks that government is necessary, sees no injustice in as much inequality as is constituted by giving to the magistrate powers not granted to other people. Even among those who hold levelling doctrines, there are as many questions of justice as there are differences of opinion about expediency. Some Communists consider it unjust that the produce of the labour of the community should be shared on any other principle than that of exact equality; others think it just that those should receive most whose wants are greatest; while others hold that those who work harder, or who produce more, or whose services are more valuable to the community, may justly claim a larger quota in the division of the produce. And the sense of natural justice may be plausibly appealed to in behalf of every one of these opinions.

Among so many diverse applications of the term "justice," which yet is not regarded as ambiguous, it is a matter of some difficulty to seize the mental link which holds them together, and on which the moral sentiment adhering to the term essentially depends. Perhaps, in this embarrassment, some help may be derived from the history of the word, as indicated by its etymology.

In most, if not in all, languages, the etymology of the word which corresponds to "just" points distinctly to an origin connected with the ordinances of law. *Justum* is a form of *jussum,* that which has been ordered. ⟨*Dikaion*⟩ comes directly from ⟨*dike*⟩, a suit at law. *Recht,* from which came *right* and *righteous,* is synonymous with law. The courts of justice, the administration of justice, are the courts and the administration of law. *La justice,* in French, is the established term for judicature. I am not committing the fallacy imputed with some show of truth to Horne Tooke,* of assuming that a word must still continue to mean what it originally meant. Etymology is slight evidence of what the idea now signified is, but the very best evidence of how it sprang up. There can, I think, be no doubt that the *idée mère,* the primitive element, in the formation of the notion of justice, was conformity to law. It constituted the entire idea among the Hebrews, up to the birth of Christianity; as might be expected in the case of a people whose laws attempted to embrace all subjects on which precepts were required, and who believed those laws to be a direct emanation from the Supreme Being. But other nations, and in particular the Greeks and Romans, who knew that their laws had been made originally, and still continued to be made, by men, were not afraid to admit that those men might make bad laws; might do, by law, the same things, and from the same motives, which if done by individuals without the sanction of law, would be called unjust. And hence the sentiment of injustice came to be attached, not to all violations of law, but only to violations of such laws as *ought* to exist, including such as ought to exist, but do not; and to laws themselves, if supposed to be contrary to what ought to be law. In this manner the idea of law and of its injunctions was still predominant in the notion of justice, even when the laws actually in force ceased to be accepted as the standard of it.

It is true that mankind consider the idea of justice and its obligations as applicable to many things which neither are, nor is it desired that they should be, regulated by law. Nobody desires that laws should interfere with the whole detail of private life; yet every one allows that in all daily conduct a person may and does show himself to be either just or unjust. But even here, the idea of the breach of what ought to be law, still lingers in a modified shape. It would always give us pleasure, and chime in with our feelings of fitness, that acts which we deem unjust should be punished, though we do not always think it expedient that this should be done by the tribunals. We forego that gratification on account of incidental inconveniences. We should be glad to see just conduct enforced and injustice repressed, even in the minutest details, if we were not, with reason, afraid of trusting the magistrate with so unlimited an amount of power over individuals. When we think that a person is bound in justice to do a thing, it is an ordinary form of language to say, that he ought to be compelled to do it. We should be gratified to see the obligation enforced by anybody who had the power. If we see that its enforcement by law would be inexpedient, we lament the impossibility, we consider the impunity given to injustice as an evil, and strive to make amends for it by bringing a strong expression of our own and the public disapprobation to bear upon the offender. Thus the idea of legal constraint is still the generating idea of the notion of justice, though undergoing several transformations before that notion, as it exists in an advanced state of society, becomes complete.

The above is, I think, a true account, as far as it goes, of the origin and progressive growth of the idea of justice. But we must observe, that it contains, as yet, nothing to distinguish that obligation from moral obligation in general. For the truth is, that the idea of penal sanction, which is the essence of law, enters not only into the conception of injustice, but into that of any kind of wrong. We do not call anything wrong, unless

---

*[John Tooke (1736–1812), a radical writer and close friend of Bentham.]

we mean to imply that a person ought to be punished in some way or other for doing it; if not by law, by the opinion of his fellow-creatures; if not by opinion, by the reproaches of his own conscience. This seems the real turning point of the distinction between morality and simple expediency. It is a part of the notion of Duty in every one of its forms, that a person may rightfully be compelled to fulfil it. Duty is a thing which may be *exacted* from a person, as one exacts a debt. Unless we think that it may be exacted from him, we do not call it his duty. Reasons of prudence, or the interest of other people, may militate against actually exacting it; but the person himself, it is clearly understood, would not be entitled to complain. There are other things, on the contrary, which we wish that people should do, which we like or admire them for doing, perhaps dislike or despise them for not doing, but yet admit that they are not bound to do; it is not a case of moral obligation; we do not blame them, that is, we do not think that they are proper objects of punishment. How we come by these ideas of deserving and not deserving punishment, will appear, perhaps, in the sequel; but I think there is no doubt that this distinction lies at the bottom of the notions of right and wrong; that we call any conduct wrong, or employ, instead, some other term of dislike or disparagement, according as we think that the person ought, or ought not, to be punished for it; and we say, it would be right to do so and so, or merely that it would be desirable or laudable, according as we would wish to see the person whom it concerns, compelled, or only persuaded and exhorted, to act in that manner.*

This, therefore, being the characteristic difference which marks off, not justice, but morality in general, from the remaining provinces of Expediency and Worthiness; the character is still to be sought which distinguishes justice from other branches of morality. Now it is known that ethical writers divide moral duties into two classes, denoted by the ill-chosen expressions, duties of perfect and of imperfect obligation; the latter being those in which, though the act is obligatory, the particular occasions of performing it are left to our choice; as in the case of charity or beneficence, which we are indeed bound to practise, but not towards any definite person, nor at any prescribed time. In the more precise language of philosophic jurists, duties of perfect obligation are those duties in virtue of which a correlative *right* resides in some person or persons; duties of imperfect obligation are those moral obligations which do not give birth to any right. I think it will be found that this distinction exactly coincides with that which exists between justice and the other obligations of morality. In our survey of the various popular acceptations of justice, the term appeared generally to involve the idea of a personal right—a claim on the part of one or more individuals, like that which the law gives when it confers a proprietary or other legal right. Whether the injustice consists in depriving a person of a possession, or in breaking faith with him, or in treating him worse than he deserves, or worse than other people who have no greater claims, in each case the supposition implies two things—a wrong done, and some assignable person who is wronged. Injustice may also be done by treating a person better than others; but the wrong in this case is to his competitors, who are also assignable persons. It seems to me that this feature in the case—a right in some person, correlative to the moral obligation—constitutes the specific difference between justice, and generosity or beneficence. Justice implies something which it is not only right to do, and wrong not to do, but which some individual person can claim from us as his moral right. No one has a moral right to our generosity or beneficence, because we are not morally bound to practise those virtues towards any given individual.

---

*I see this point enforced and illustrated by Professor Bain, in an admirable chapter (entitled "The Ethical Emotions, or the Moral Sense"), of the second of the two treatises composing his elaborate and profound work on the Mind.

And it will be found with respect to this as to every correct definition, that the instances which seem to conflict with it are those which most confirm it. For if a moralist attempts, as some have done, to make out that mankind generally, though not any given individual, have a right to all the good we can do them, he at once, by that thesis, includes generosity and beneficence within the category of justice. He is obliged to say, that our utmost exertions are due to our fellow-creatures, thus assimilating them to a debt; or that nothing less can be a sufficient return for what society does for us, thus classing the case as one of gratitude; both of which are acknowledged cases of justice. Wherever there is a right, the case is one of justice, and not of the virtue of beneficence: and whoever does not place the distinction between justice and morality in general, where we have now placed it, will be found to make no distinction between them at all, but to merge all morality in justice.

Having thus endeavoured to determine the distinctive elements which enter into the composition of the idea of justice, we are ready to enter on the inquiry, whether the feeling, which accompanies the idea, is attached to it by a special dispensation of nature, or whether it could have grown up, by any known laws, out of the idea itself; and in particular, whether it can have originated in considerations of general expediency.

I conceive that the sentiment itself does not arise from anything which would commonly, or correctly, be termed an idea of expediency; but that though the sentiment does not, whatever is moral in it does.

We have seen that the two essential ingredients in the sentiment of justice are, the desire to punish a person who has done harm and the knowledge or belief that there is some definite individual or individuals to whom harm has been done.

Now it appears to me, that the desire to punish a person who has done harm to some individual is a spontaneous outgrowth from two sentiments, both in the highest degree natural, and which either are or resemble instincts; the impulse of self-defence, and the feeling of sympathy.

It is natural to resent, and to repel or retaliate, any harm done or attempted against ourselves, or against those with whom we sympathise. The origin of this sentiment it is not necessary here to discuss. Whether it be an instinct or a result of intelligence, it is, we know, common to all animal nature; for every animal tries to hurt those who have hurt, or who it thinks are about to hurt, itself or its young. Human beings, on this point, only differ from other animals in two particulars. First, in being capable of sympathising, not solely with their offspring, or, like some of the more noble animals, with some superior animal who is kind to them, but with all human, and even with all sentient, beings. Secondly, in having a more developed intelligence, which gives a wider range to the whole of their sentiments, whether self-regarding or sympathetic. By virtue of his superior intelligence, even apart from his superior range of sympathy, a human being is capable of apprehending a community of interest between himself and the human society of which he forms a part, such that any conduct which threatens the security of the society generally, is threatening to his own, and calls forth his instinct (if instinct it be) of self-defence. The same superiority of intelligence, joined to the power of sympathising with human beings generally, enables him to attach himself to the collective idea of his tribe, his country, or mankind, in such a manner that any act hurtful to them, raises his instinct of sympathy, and urges him to resistance.

The sentiment of justice, in that one of its elements which consists of the desire to punish, is thus, I conceive, the natural feeling of retaliation or vengeance, rendered by intellect and sympathy applicable to those injuries, that is, to those hurts, which wound us through, or in common with, society at large. This sentiment, in itself, has nothing moral in it; what is moral is, the exclusive subordination of it to the social sympathies, so as to wait on and obey their call. For the natural feeling would make us resent indiscriminately whatever any one does that is disagreeable to us; but when moralised by the social feeling, it only acts in the directions conformable to the general good: just persons resenting a hurt to society, though not otherwise a hurt to themselves, and not resenting a hurt to themselves, however painful, unless it be of the kind which society has a common interest with them in the repression of.

It is no objection against this doctrine to say, that when we feel our sentiment of justice outraged, we are not thinking of society at large, or of any collective interest, but only of the individual case. It is common enough certainly, though the reverse of commendable, to feel resentment merely because we have suffered pain; but a person whose resentment is really a moral feeling, that is, who considers whether an act is blamable before he allows himself to resent it—such a person, though he may not say expressly to himself that he is standing up for the interest of society, certainly does feel that he is asserting a rule which is for the benefit of others as well as for his own. If he is not feeling this—if he is regarding the act solely as it affects him individually—he is not consciously just; he is not concerning himself about the justice of his actions. This is admitted even by anti-utilitarian moralists. When Kant (as before remarked) propounds as the fundamental principle of morals, "So act, that thy rule of conduct might be adopted as a law by all rational beings," he virtually acknowledges that the interest of mankind collectively, or at least of mankind indiscriminately, must be in the mind of the agent when conscientiously deciding on the morality of the act. Otherwise he uses words without a meaning: for, that a rule even of utter selfishness could not *possibly* be adopted by all rational beings—that there is any insuperable obstacle in the nature of things to its adoption—cannot be even plausibly maintained. To give any meaning to Kant's principle, the sense put upon it must be, that we ought to shape our conduct by a rule which all rational beings might adopt *with benefit to their collective interest*.

To recapitulate: the idea of justice supposes two things—a rule of conduct, and a sentiment which sanctions the rule. The first must be supposed common to all mankind, and intended for their good. The other (the sentiment) is a desire that punishment may be suffered by those who infringe the rule. There is involved, in addition, the conception of some definite person who suffers by the infringement; whose rights (to use the expression appropriated to the case) are violated by it. And the sentiment of justice appears to me to be, the animal desire to repel or retaliate a hurt or damage to oneself, or to those with whom one sympathises, widened so as to include all persons, by the human capacity of enlarged sympathy, and the human conception of intelligent self-interest. From the latter elements, the feeling derives its morality; from the former, its peculiar impressiveness, and energy of self-assertion.

I have, throughout, treated the idea of a *right* residing in the injured person, and violated by the injury, not as a separate element in the composition of the idea and sentiment, but as one of the forms in which the other two elements clothe themselves. These elements are, a hurt to some assignable person or persons on the one hand, and a demand for punishment on the other. An examination of our own minds, I think, will show, that these two things include all that we mean when we speak of violation of a right. When we call anything a person's right, we mean that he has a valid claim on society to protect him in the possession of it, either by the force of law, or by that of education and opinion. If he has what we consider a sufficient claim, on whatever account, to have something guaranteed to him by society, we say that he has a right to it. If we desire to prove that anything does not belong to him by right, we think this done as soon as it is admitted that society ought not to take measures for securing it to him, but should leave him to chance, or to his own exertions. Thus, a person is said to have a right to what he can earn in fair professional competition; because society ought not to allow any other person to hinder him from endeavouring to earn in that manner as much as he can. But he has not a right to three hundred a year, though he may happen to be earning it; because society is not called on to provide that he shall earn that sum. On the contrary, if he owns ten thousand pounds three percent stock, he *has* a right to three hundred a year because society has come under an obligation to provide him with an income of that amount.

To have a right, then, is, I conceive, to have something which society ought to defend me in the possession of. If the objector goes on to ask, why it ought? I can give him no other reason than general utility. If that expression does not seem to convey a sufficient feeling of the strength of the obligation, nor to account for the peculiar energy of the feeling, it is because there goes to the composition of the sentiment, not a rational only, but also an animal element, the thirst for retaliation; and this thirst derives its intensity, as well as its moral justification, from the extraordinarily important and impressive kind of utility which is concerned. The interest involved is that of security, to every one's feelings the most vital of all interests. All other earthly benefits are needed by one person, not needed by another; and many of them can, if necessary, be cheerfully foregone, or replaced by something else; but security no human being can possibly do without; on it we depend for all our immunity from evil, and for the whole value of all and every good, beyond the passing moment; since nothing but the gratification of the instant could be of any worth to us, if we could be deprived of anything the next instant by whoever was momentarily stronger than ourselves. Now this most indispensable of all necessaries, after physical nutriment, cannot be had, unless the machinery for providing it is kept unintermittedly in active play. Our notion, therefore, of the claim we have on our fellow-creatures to join in making safe for us the very groundwork of our existence, gathers feelings around it so much more intense than those concerned in any of the more common cases of utility, that the difference in degree (as is often the case in psychology) becomes a real difference in kind. The claim assumes that character of absoluteness, that apparent infinity, and incommensurability with all other considerations, which constitute the distinction between the feeling of right and wrong and that of ordinary expediency and inexpediency. The feelings concerned are so powerful, and we count so positively on finding a responsive feeling in others (all being alike interested), that *ought* and *should* grow into *must*, and recognised indispensability becomes a moral necessity, analogous to physical, and often not inferior to it in binding force.

If the preceding analysis, or something resembling it, be not the correct account of the notion of justice; if justice be totally independent of utility, and be a standard per se, which the mind can recognise by simple introspection of itself; it is hard to understand why that internal oracle is so ambiguous, and why so many things appear either just or unjust, according to the light in which they are regarded.

We are continually informed that Utility is an uncertain standard, which every different person interprets differently, and that there is no safety but in the immutable, ineffaceable, and unmistakable dictates of Justice, which carry their evidence in themselves, and are independent of the fluctuations of opinion. One would suppose from this that on questions of justice there could be no controversy; that if we take that for our rule, its application to any given case could leave us in as little doubt as a mathematical demonstration. So far is this from being the fact, that there is as much difference of opinion, and as much discussion, about what is just, as about what is useful to society. Not only have different nations and individuals different notions of justice, but in the mind of one and the same individual, justice is not some one rule, principle, or maxim, but many, which do not always coincide in their dictates, and in choosing between which, he is guided either by some extraneous standard, or by his own personal predilections.

For instance, there are some who say, that it is unjust to punish any one for the sake of example to others; that punishment is just, only when intended for the good of the sufferer himself. Others maintain the extreme reverse, contending that to punish persons who have attained years of discretion, for their own benefit, is despotism and injustice, since if the matter at issue is solely their own good, no one has a right to control their own judgment of it; but that they may justly be punished to prevent evil to others, this being the exercise of the legitimate right of self-defence. Mr. Owen,* again, affirms that it is unjust to punish at all; for the criminal did not make his own character; his education, and the circumstances which surrounded him, have made him a criminal, and for these he is not responsible. All these opinions are extremely plausible; and so long as the question is argued as one of justice simply, without going down to the principles which lie under justice and are the source of its authority, I am unable to see how any of these reasoners can be refuted. For in truth every one of the three builds upon rules of justice confessedly true. The first appeals to the acknowledged injustice of singling out an individual, and making him a sacrifice, without his consent, for other people's benefit. The second relies on the acknowledged justice of self-defence, and the admitted injustice of forcing one person to conform to another's notions of what constitutes his good. The Owenite invokes the admitted principle, that it is unjust to punish any one for what he cannot help. Each is triumphant so long as he is not compelled to take into consideration any other maxims of justice than the one he has selected; but as soon as their several maxims are brought face to face, each disputant seems to have exactly as much to say for himself as the others. No one of them can carry out his own notion of justice without trampling upon another equally binding. These are difficulties; they have always been felt to be such; and many devices have been invented to turn rather than to overcome them. As a refuge from the last of the three, men imagined what they called the freedom of the will; fancying that they could not justify punishing a man whose will is in a thoroughly hateful state, unless it be supposed to have come into that state through no influence of anterior circumstances. To escape from the other difficulties, a favourite contrivance has been the fiction of a contract, whereby at some unknown period all the members of society engaged to obey the laws, and consented to be punished for any disobedience to them; thereby giving to their legislators the right, which it is assumed they would not otherwise have had, of punishing them, either for their own good or for that of society. This happy thought was considered to get rid of the whole difficulty, and to legitimate the infliction of punishment, in virtue of another received maxim of justice, *volenti non fit injuria;* that is not unjust which is done with the consent of the person who is supposed to be hurt by it. I need hardly remark, that even if the consent were not a mere fiction, this maxim is not superior in authority to the others which it is brought in to supersede. It is, on the contrary, an instructive specimen of the loose and irregular manner in which supposed principles of justice grow up. This particular one evidently came into use as a help to the coarse exigencies of courts of law, which are sometimes obliged to be content with very uncertain presumptions, on account of the greater evils which would often arise from any attempt on their part to cut finer. But even courts of law are not able to adhere consistently to the maxim, for they allow voluntary engagements to be set aside on the ground of fraud, and sometimes on that of mere mistake or misinformation.

Again, when the legitimacy of inflicting punishment is admitted, how many conflicting conceptions of justice come to light in discussing the proper apportionment of punishments to offences. No rule on the subject recommends itself so strongly to the

---

*[Robert Owen (1771–1858), a British reformer who argued for environmental determinism.]

primitive and spontaneous sentiment of justice, as the *lex talionis,* an eye for an eye and a tooth for a tooth. Though this principle of the Jewish and of the Mohammedan law has been generally abandoned in Europe as a practical maxim, there is, I suspect, in most minds, a secret hankering after it; and when retribution accidentally falls on an offender in that precise shape, the general feeling of satisfaction evinced bears witness how natural is the sentiment to which this repayment in kind is acceptable. With many, the test of justice in penal infliction is that the punishment should be proportioned to the offence; meaning that it should be exactly measured by the moral guilt of the culprit (whatever be their standard for measuring moral guilt): the consideration, what amount of punishment is necessary to deter from the offence, having nothing to do with the question of justice, in their estimation: while there are others to whom that consideration is all in all; who maintain that it is not just, at least for man, to inflict on a fellow-creature, whatever may be his offences, any amount of suffering beyond the least that will suffice to prevent him from repeating, and others from imitating, his misconduct.

To take another example from a subject already once referred to. In a co-operative industrial association, is it just or not that talent or skill should give a title to superior remuneration? On the negative side of the question it is argued, that whoever does the best he can, deserves equally well, and ought not in justice to be put in a position of inferiority for no fault of his own; that superior abilities have already advantages more than enough, in the admiration they excite, the personal influence they command, and the internal sources of satisfaction attending them, without adding to these a superior share of the world's goods; and that society is bound in justice rather to make compensation to the less favoured, for this unmerited inequality of advantages, than to aggravate it. On the contrary side it is contended, that society receives more from the more efficient labourer; that his services being more useful, society owes him a larger return for them; that a greater share of the joint result is actually his work, and not to allow his claim to it is a kind of robbery; that if he is only to receive as much as others, he can only be justly required to produce as much, and to give a smaller amount of time and exertion, proportioned to his superior efficiency. Who shall decide between these appeals to conflicting principles of justice? Justice has in this case two sides to it, which it is impossible to bring into harmony, and the two disputants have chosen opposite sides; the one looks to what it is just that the individual should receive, the other to what it is just that the community should give. Each, from his own point of view, is unanswerable; and any choice between them, on grounds of justice, must be perfectly arbitrary. Social utility alone can decide the preference.

How many, again, and how irreconcilable, are the standards of justice to which reference is made in discussing the repartition of taxation. One opinion is, that payment to the State should be in numerical proportion to pecuniary means. Others think that justice dictates what they term graduated taxation; taking a higher percentage from those who have more to spare. In point of natural justice a strong case might be made for disregarding means altogether, and taking the same absolute sum (whenever it could be got) from every one: as the subscribers to a mess, or to a club, all pay the same sum for the same privileges, whether they can all equally afford it or not. Since the protection (it might be said) of law and government is afforded to, and is equally required by all, there is no injustice in making all buy it at the same price. It is reckoned justice, not injustice, that a dealer should charge to all customers the same price for the same article, not a price varying according to their means of payment. This doctrine, as applied to taxation, finds no advocates, because it conflicts so strongly with man's feelings of humanity and of social expediency; but the principle of justice which it invokes is as true and as binding as those which can be appealed to against it. Accordingly it exerts a tacit influence on the line of defence employed for other modes of assessing taxation. People feel obliged to argue that the State does more for the rich than for the poor, as a justification for its taking more from them: though this is in reality not true, for the rich would be far better able to protect themselves, in the absence of law or government, than the poor, and indeed would probably be successful in converting the poor into their slaves. Others, again, so far defer to the same conception of justice, as to maintain that all should pay an equal capitation tax for the protection of their persons (these being of equal value to all), and an unequal tax for the protection of their property, which is unequal. To this others reply, that the all of one man is as valuable to him as the all of another. From these confusions there is no other mode of extrication than the utilitarian.

Is, then, the difference between the Just and the Expedient a merely imaginary distinction? Have mankind been under a delusion in thinking that justice is a more sacred thing than policy, and that the latter ought only to be listened to after the former has been satisfied? By no means. The exposition we have given of the nature and origin of the sentiment, recognises a real distinction; and no one of those who profess the most sublime contempt for the consequences of actions as an element in their morality, attaches more importance to the distinction than I do. While I dispute the pretensions of any theory which sets up an imaginary standard of justice not grounded on utility, I account the justice which is grounded on utility to be the chief part, and incomparably the most sacred and binding part, of all morality. Justice is a name for certain classes of moral rules, which concern the essentials of human well-being more nearly, and are therefore of more absolute obligation, than any other rules for the guidance of life; and the notion which we have found to be of the essence of the idea of justice, that of a right residing in an individual, implies and testifies to this more binding obligation.

The moral rules which forbid mankind to hurt one another (in which we must never forget to include wrongful interference with each other's freedom) are more vital to human well-being than any maxims, however important, which only point out the best mode of managing some department of human affairs. They have also the peculiarity, that they are the main element in determining the whole of the social feelings of mankind. It is their observance which alone preserves peace among human beings: if obedience to them were not the rule, and disobedience the exception, every one would see in every one else an enemy, against whom he must be perpetually guarding himself. What is hardly less important, these are the precepts which mankind have the strongest and the most direct inducements for impressing upon one another. By merely giving to each other prudential instruction or exhortation, they may gain, or think they gain, nothing: in inculcating on each other the duty of positive beneficence they have an unmistakable interest, but far less in degree: a person may possibly not need the benefits of others; but he always needs that they should not do him hurt. Thus the moralities which protect every individual from being harmed by others, either directly or by being hindered in his freedom of pursuing his own good, are at once those which he himself has most at heart, and those which he has the strongest interest in publishing and enforcing by word and deed. It is by a person's observance of these that his fitness to exist as one of the fellowship of human beings is tested and decided; for on that depends his being a nuisance or not to those with whom he is in contact. Now it is these moralities primarily which compose the obligations of justice. The most marked cases of injustice, and those which give the tone to the feeling of repugnance which characterises the sentiment, are acts of wrongful aggression, or wrongful exercise of power over some one; the next are those which consist in wrongfully withholding from him something which is his due; in both cases, inflicting on him a positive hurt, either in the form of direct suffering, or of the privation of some good which he had reasonable ground, either of a physical or of a social kind, for counting upon.

The same powerful motives which command the observance of these primary moralities, enjoin the punishment of those who violate them; and as the impulses of self-defence, of defence of others, and of vengeance, are all called forth against such persons, retribution, or evil for evil, becomes closely connected with the sentiment of justice, and is universally included in the idea. Good for good is also one of the dictates of justice; and this, though its social utility is evident, and though it carries with it a natural human feeling, has not at first sight that obvious connection with hurt or injury, which, existing in the most elementary cases of just and un-just, is the source of the characteristic intensity of the sentiment. But the connection, though less obvious, is not less real. He who accepts benefits, and denies a return of them when needed, inflicts a real hurt, by disappointing one of the most natural and reasonable of expectations, and one which he must at least tacitly have encouraged, otherwise the benefits would seldom have been conferred. The important rank, among human evils and wrongs, of the disappointment of expectation, is shown in the fact that it constitutes the principal criminality of two such highly immoral acts as a breach of friendship and a breach of promise. Few hurts which human beings can sustain are greater, and none wound more, than when that on which they habitually and with full assurance relied, fails them in the hour of need; and few wrongs are greater than this mere withholding of good; none excite more resentment, either in the person suffering, or in a sympathising spectator. The principle, therefore, of giving to each what they deserve, that is, good for good as well as evil for evil, is not only included within the idea of Justice as we have defined it, but is a proper object of that intensity of sentiment, which places the Just, in human estimation, above the simply Expedient.

Most of the maxims of justice current in the world, and commonly appealed to in its transactions, are simply instrumental to carrying into effect the principles of justice which we have now spoken of. That a person is only responsible for what he has done voluntarily, or could voluntarily have avoided; that it is unjust to condemn any person unheard; that the punishment ought to be proportioned to the offence, and the like, are maxims intended to prevent the just principle of evil for evil from being perverted to the infliction of evil without that justification. The greater part of these common maxims have come into use from the practice of courts of justice, which have been naturally led to a more complete recognition and elaboration than was likely to suggest itself to others, of the rules necessary to enable them to fulfil their double function, of inflicting punishment when due, and of awarding to each person his right.

That first of judicial virtues, impartiality, is an obligation of justice, partly for the reason last mentioned; as being a necessary condition of the fulfilment of the other obligations of justice. But this is not the only source of the exalted rank, among human obligations, of those maxims of equality and impartiality, which, both in popular estimation and in that of the most enlightened, are included among the precepts of justice. In one point of view, they may be considered as corollaries from the principles already laid down. If it is a duty to do to each according to his deserts, returning good for good as well as repressing evil by evil, it necessarily follows that we should treat all equally well (when no higher duty forbids) who have deserved equally well of *us,* and that society should treat all equally well who have deserved equally well of *it,* that is, who have deserved equally well absolutely. This is the highest abstract standard of social and distributive justice; towards which all institutions, and the efforts of all virtuous citizens, should be made in the utmost possible degree to converge. But this great moral duty rests upon a still deeper foundation, being a direct emanation from the first principle of morals, and not a mere logical corollary from secondary or derivative doctrines. It is involved in the very meaning of Utility, or the Greatest Happiness Principle. That principle is a mere form of words without rational signification, unless one person's happiness, supposed equal in degree (with the proper allowance made for kind), is counted for exactly as much as another's. Those conditions being supplied, Bentham's dictum, "everybody to count for one, nobody for more than one," might be written under the principle of utility as an explanatory commentary.* The equal claim of everybody to happiness in the estimation of the moralist and of the legislator, involves an equal claim to all the means of happiness, except in so far as the inevitable conditions of human life, and the general interest, in which that of every individual is included, set limits to the maxim; and those limits ought to be strictly construed. As every other maxim of justice, so this is by no means applied or held applicable universally; on the contrary, as I have already remarked, it bends to every person's ideas of social expediency. But in whatever case it is deemed applicable at all, it is held to be the dictate of justice. All persons are deemed to have a *right* to equality of treatment, except when some recognised social expediency requires the reverse. And hence all social inequalities which have ceased to be considered expedient, assume the character not of simple inexpediency, but of injustice, and appear so tyrannical, that people are apt to wonder how they ever could have been tolerated; forgetful that they themselves perhaps tolerate other inequalities under an equally mistaken notion of expediency, the correction of which would make that which they approve seem quite as monstrous as what they have at last learnt to condemn. The entire history of social improvement has been a series of transitions, by which one custom or institution after another, from being a supposed primary necessity of social existence, has passed into the rank of a universally stigmatised injustice and tyranny. So it has been with the distinctions of slaves and freemen, nobles and serfs, patricians and plebeians; and so it will be, and in part already is, with the aristocracies of colour, race, and sex.

---

*This implication, in the first principle of the utilitarian scheme, of perfect impartiality between persons, is regarded by Mr. Herbert Spencer (in his *Social Statics*) as a disproof of the pretensions of utility to be a sufficient guide to right, since (he says) the principle of utility presupposes the anterior principle that everybody has an equal right to happiness. It may be more correctly described as supposing that equal amounts of happiness are equally desirable whether felt by the same or by different persons. This, however, is not a pre-supposition; not a premise needful to support the principle of utility, but the very principle itself; for what is the principle of utility, if it be not that "happiness" and "desirable" are synonymous terms? If there Is any anterior principle Implied, it can be no other than this, that the truths of arithmetic are applicable to the valuation of happiness, as of all other measurable quantities.

(Mr. Herbert Spencer in a private communication on the subject of the preceding note, objects to being considered an opponent of utilitarianism, and states that he regards happiness as the ultimate end of morality; but deems that end only partially attainable by empirical generalisations from the observed results of conduct, and completely attainable only by deducing, from the laws of life and the conditions of existence, what kinds of action necessarily tend to produce happiness, and what kinds to produce unhappiness. With the exception of the word "necessarily," I have no dissent to express from this doctrine; and (omitting that word) I am not aware that any modern advocate of utilitarianism is of a different opinion. Bentham, certainly, to whom in the *Social Statics* Mr. Spencer particularly referred, is, least of all writers, chargeable with unwillingness to deduce the effect of actions on happiness from the laws of human nature and the universal conditions of human life. The common charge against him is of relying too exclusively upon such deductions, and declining altogether to be bound by the generalisations from specific experience which Mr. Spencer thinks that utilitarians generally confine themselves to. My own opinion (and, as I collect, Mr. Spencer's) is, that in ethics, as in all other branches of scientific study, the consilience of the results of both these processes, each corroborating and verifying the other, is requisite to give to any general proposition the kind and degree of evidence which constitutes scientific proof.)

It appears from what has been said, that justice is a name for certain moral requirements, which, regarded collectively, stand higher in the scale of social utility, and are therefore of more paramount obligation, than any others; though particular cases may occur in which some other social duty is so important, as to overrule any one of the general maxims of justice. Thus, to save a life, it may not only be allowable, but a duty, to steal, or take by force, the necessary food or medicine, or to kidnap, and compel to officiate, the only qualified medical practitioner. In such cases, as we do not call anything justice which is not a virtue, we usually say, not that justice must give way to some other moral principle, but that what is just in ordinary cases is, by reason of that other principle, not just in the particular case. By this useful accommodation of language, the character of indefeasibility attributed to justice is kept up, and we are saved from the necessity of maintaining that there can be laudable injustice.

The considerations which have now been adduced resolve, I conceive, the only real difficulty in the utilitarian theory of morals. It has always been evident that all cases of justice are also cases of expediency: the difference is in the peculiar sentiment which attaches to the former, as contradistinguished from the latter. If this characteristic sentiment has been sufficiently accounted for; if there is no necessity to assume for it any peculiarity of origin; if it is simply the natural feeling of resentment, moralised by being made coextensive with the demands of social good; and if this feeling not only does but ought to exist in all the classes of cases to which the idea of justice corresponds; that idea no longer presents itself as a stumbling-block to the utilitarian ethics. Justice remains the appropriate name for certain social utilities which are vastly more important, and therefore more absolute and imperative, than any others are as a class (though not more so than others may be in particular cases); and which, therefore, ought to be, as well as naturally are, guarded by a sentiment not only different in degree, but also in kind; distinguished from the milder feeling which attaches to the mere idea of promoting human pleasure or convenience, at once by the more definite nature of its commands, and by the sterner character of its sanctions.

SØREN KIERKEGAARD
1813–1855

Søren Aabye Kierkegaard was born in Copenhagen, Denmark, the youngest child of middle-aged parents. His father, Michael, had been an impoverished serf in a bleak area of northern Denmark. While still a boy, Michael had cursed God for the dreariness of his life and from that point on considered himself and his descendants to be under God's condemnation. The external events of Michael's life gave little indication of such a curse, however, as he worked his way to great wealth as a merchant in Copenhagen. Following the death of his first wife, and before the period of mourning was over, Michael was forced to marry his first wife's maid, Anne Lund, and five months later she bore the first of their five children.

Michael was already fifty-six and retired from business when Søren was born in 1813. Like James Mill, Michael educated Søren at home and also put his son through rigorous intellectual endeavors. But unlike his predecessor, Michael also communicated to his son a strong religious sentiment and deep, though perhaps warped, emotional feelings. Michael often took Søren on "trips of fantasy" while conversing in the family library.

In 1830, at his father's urging, Kierkegaard entered the University of Copenhagen to study theology. While there, he encountered the work of Hegel and reacted strongly against it. Kierkegaard objected to the implicit optimism and the "swallowing up" of contradictions in Hegel's dialectic. But more important, Kierkegaard claimed that even though Hegel's "System" was an impressive philosophical *tour de force,* it did not relate to the lived existence of the individual—it did not give any guidance as to what a person should *do*. A famous entry from Kierkegaard's journal at this time is worth quoting at length:

What I really lack is to be clear in my mind *what I am to do,* not what I am to know, except in so far as a certain understanding must precede every action. The thing is to understand myself, to see what God really wishes *me* to do; the thing is to find a truth which is true *for me,* to find *the idea for which I can live and die.* What would be the use of discovering so-called objective truth, of working through all the systems of philosophy and of being able, if required, to review them all and show up the inconsistencies within each system;—what good would it do me to be able to develop a theory of the state and combine all the details into a single whole, and so construct a world in which I did not live, but only held up to the view of others;—what good would it do me to be able to explain the meaning of Christianity if it had *no* deeper significance *for me and for my life;*—what good would it do me if truth stood before me, cold and naked, not caring whether I recognised her or not, and producing in me a shudder of fear rather than a trusting devotion? I certainly do not deny that I still recognise an *imperative of understanding* and that through it one can work upon men, *but it must be taken up into my life, and that is what I now recognise as the most important thing.**

Kierkegaard did not find the answer for "what to do" in his studies in theology and soon began living what he would later call an "aesthetic" life as a rich merchant's son. He spent large sums of money on food, drink, and clothing. He frequented parties and appeared to be having a great time. But hedonistic indulgence did not really give an answer for "what to do" either, and he plunged into despair. Another entry from his journals makes this clear:

I have just returned from a party of which I was the life and soul; wit poured from my lips, everyone laughed and admired me—but I went away—and the dash should be as long as the earth's orbit ————————————————

and wanted to shoot myself.****

On his son's twenty-fifth birthday, May 15, 1838, Michael revealed to Søren his own sexual sins as well as his understanding of God's condemnation of their family. Four days later, Søren Kierkegaard underwent a religious conversion and was reconciled to his father, who died shortly afterward. Kierkegaard now had an answer for "what to do"—he would live as a penitent seeking to "become a Christian." Kierkegaard finished his theological studies, prepared to become a Lutheran pastor, and became engaged to marry seventeen-year-old Regine Olsen.

But by 1841, Kierkegaard realized that he could never live the life of a Lutheran pastor and devoted husband. He came to believe that the Danish Lutheran church had made religion a matter of intellectual assent to certain objective truths and no longer deserved to be called "Christian." For the rest of his life, Kierkegaard opposed institutional Christianity. The decision to break his engagement to Regine Olsen was a torturous one, but one he believed he had to make. He decided that a "divine veto" had been cast against this marriage, that his role as penitent was incompatible with that of husband.

---

*Søren Kierkegaard, *The Journals of Søren Kierkegaard,* edited and translated by Alexander Dru (London: Oxford University Press, 1938), p. 15 [entry from August 1, 1835].
**Ibid.,* p. 27 [entry from early spring, 1836].

Kierkegaard spent the rest of his short life as a writer, publishing a number of books including *Either/Or* (1843), *Fear and Trembling* (1843), *Philosophical Fragments* (1844), *Stages on Life's Way* (1845), *Concluding Unscientific Post-script* (1846), *The Sickness unto Death* (1849), *Training in Christianity* (1850), and *The Attack upon "Christendom"* (1854–1855). All but the last of these works were written under various pseudonyms, and virtually all of them included attacks on the prevailing Hegelian philosophy of his time. In 1855, while returning from the bank with the last of his considerable inheritance, Kierkegaard collapsed on the street and died soon thereafter.

*   *   *

Kierkegaard's biography is reflected in his philosophical quest to establish what it means to be an individual. In such works as *Either/Or, Stages on Life's Way,* and *Fear and Trembling,* he describes a process of self-actualization through three stages in life: the aesthetic, the ethical, and the religious. At the aesthetic stage, an individual's life centers on either hedonistic pleasure or abstract philosophical speculation. The hedonist lives for the immediate pleasures of the moment without concern for the future. The abstract intellectual (Hegel being the prime example) lives in a theoretical world removed from concrete existence. The hedonist reduces existence to immediate pleasure whereas the abstract speculator reduces existence to thought; but in both cases the aesthete has avoided the either/or decisions of real life, and authentic selfhood has not been achieved. The result, says Kierkegaard, is a life of boredom—and the pointless pursuit of diversions to alleviate such boredom. This was the life Kierkegaard himself lived in his early years at the university.

Those who move beyond the aesthetic to the ethical level choose to accept moral standards and attempt to do their duty. By choosing decisively and accepting responsibility for that choice, an individual's life becomes centralized and unified. For example, the seducing man operates on the aesthetic level where every woman he meets is merely a general source of momentary pleasure. He has no past, no future, only the present desire for fulfillment. He is not really a complete person because he is living life as a series of disconnected "nows." On the other hand, the man who has chosen to fulfill the duties of a faithful husband operates on the ethical level. He has a memory of the past and a hope for the future based on his commitments, which give an integrated wholeness to his present.

But even though universal moral standards can become personal when chosen by an individual, the ethical stage is not sufficient to bring a person to complete self-actualization. The ethical stage leads to a point at which one realizes that one cannot entirely fulfill the moral law, that one is sinful in the presence of God. Only in the religious stage, where one "leaps" to passionate commitment to God, is one totally free from meaninglessness and dread. In the religious stage, a person must be willing to give up everything—even abstract ethical universals—to God. In the selection reprinted here from *Fear and Trembling,* in the Howard and Edna Hong translation, Kierkegaard illustrates this movement from the ethical to the religious stage by contrasting the stories of Agamemnon and Abraham. Although both were called upon by a divinity to sacrifice a child, Agamemnon's sacrifice would serve a higher ethical purpose whereas Abraham's would not. In fact, Abraham was in the odd position of being *tempted* to do the ethical: to not murder/sacrifice Isaac. Yet Abraham had faith in God, rather than Agamemnon's resignation to the gods, and continued to believe that God would return his son to him. Abraham performed a "teleological [i.e., considering the end or goal] suspension of the ethical," giving up what was most dear to him, and by virtue of the absurd, God gave it all back. It is interesting to note that Kierkegaard wrote this work right after he had given up to God what was most dear to him: Regine Olsen. Apparently believing that God would give her back to him, Kierkegaard was shocked when she became engaged to another man.

In the selection from *Concluding Unscientific Postscript,* reprinted here in the Howard and Edna Hong translation, Kierkegaard argues that whereas a logical system is possible, an existential system is not. Hegel's entire systematic enterprise is misguided because it assumes a finality that lived existence never has. When it comes to the important issues of life, such as knowledge of God, no system, no set of objective truths will give any real guidance. According to Kierkegaard, only subjective truth, "An objective uncertainty, held fast through appropriation with the most passionate inwardness," can be the truth for an existing person. Whereas one can never have objective certainty that God exists, one can make it true in one's own life by committing oneself completely and living as if it were true.

Written in Danish and presenting a pessimistic view of objective reason that was out of touch with the spirit of his time, it is not surprising that Kierkegaard's works were ignored for decades. The horror of World War I, together with the work done by Martin Heidegger in philosophy and Karl Barth in theology, brought Kierkegaard's pessimistic assessment of objectivism to prominence. Today Kierkegaard is acknowledged as the "father of existentialism" and is studied widely.

*   *   *

For representative collections of Kierkegaard's writings, see *A Kierkegaard Anthology,* edited by Robert Bretall (New York: Modern Library, 1936) and Walter A. Kaufmann, ed., *Existentialism from Dostoevsky to Sartre* (New York: Meridian Books, 1956). For biographies of Kierkegaard, see Walter Lowrie, *Kierkegaard* (Oxford: Oxford University Press, 1938) for comprehensive coverage, Walter Lowrie, *A Short Life of Kierkegaard* (Princeton, NJ: Princeton University Press, 1942) for a more succinct study, and Bruce H. Kirmmse, ed., *Encounters with Kierkegaard,* (Princeton, NJ: Princeton University Press, 1996) for descriptions of Kierkegaard by his contemporaries. There are a number of general overviews of Kierkegaard's thought, including H. Diem, *Kierkegaard: An Introduction,* translated by David Green (Richmond, VA: John Knox Press, 1966); Josiah Thompson, *Kierkegaard* (New York: Knopf, 1973); Alastair Hannay, *Kierkegaard* (London: Routledge & Kegan Paul, 1982); Diogenes Allen, *Three Outsiders: Pascal, Kierkegaard, Simone Weil* (Cambridge, MA: Cowley, 1983); and Patrick Gardiner, *Kierkegaard* (Oxford: Oxford University Press, 1988). For studies of specific aspects of Kierkegaard's thought, see Louis K. Dupre, *Kierkegaard as Theologian* (New York: Sheed and Ward, 1964); Niels Thulstrup, *Kierkegaard's Relation to Hegel,* translated by George L. Stengren (Princeton, NJ: Princeton University Press, 1980); John W. Elrod, *Kierkegaard and Christendom* (Princeton, NJ: Princeton University Press, 1981); C. Stephen

Evans, *Kierkegaard's "Fragments" and "Postscript": The Religious Philosophy of Johannes Climacus* (Atlantic Highlands, NJ: Humanities Press, 1983); Merold Westphal, *Kierkegaard's Critique of Reason and Society* (Macon, GA: Mercer University Press, 1987); and C. Stephen Evans, *Passionate Reason: Making Sense of Kierkegaard's Philosophical Fragments* (Bloomington: Indiana University Press, 1992). For collections of essays, see H.A. Johnson and N. Thulstrup, eds., *A Kierkegaard Critique* (Chicago: Henry Regnery, 1967); Jerry H. Gill, ed., *Essays on Kierkegaard* (Minneapolis, MN: Burgess, 1969); Josiah Thompson, ed., *Kierkegaard: A Collection of Critical Essays* (Garden City, NY: Anchor Books, 1972); Harold Bloom, ed., *Søren Kierkegaard* (New York: Chelsea House, 1989); Célline Léon and Sylvia Walsh, eds., *Feminist Interpretations of Søren Kierkegaard* (College Park, PA: Pennsylvania State University Press, 1997); Alistair Hannay and Gordon Marino, eds., *The Cambridge Companion to Kierkegaard* (Cambridge: Cambridge University Press, 1997); and Jonathan Rée and Jane Chamberlain, eds., *Kierkegaard: A Critical Reader* (Oxford: Basil Blackwell, 1997).

FEAR AND TREMBLING (in part)

Is There a Teleological Suspension of the Ethical?

The ethical as such is the universal, and as the universal it applies to everyone, which from another angle means that it applies at all times. It rests immanent in itself, has nothing outside itself that is its ⟨*telos*⟩ [end, purpose] but is itself the ⟨*telos*⟩ for everything outside itself, and when the ethical has absorbed this into itself, it goes not further. The single individual, sensately and psychically qualified in immediacy, is the individual who has his ⟨*telos*⟩ in the universal, and it is his ethical task continually to express himself in this, to annul his singularity in order to become the universal. As soon as the single individual asserts himself in his singularity before the universal, he sins, and only by acknowledging this can he be reconciled again with the universal. Every time the single individual, after having entered the universal, feels an impulse to assert himself as the single individual, he is in a spiritual trial [*Anfægtelse*], from which he can work himself only by repentantly surrendering as the single individual in the universal. If this is the highest that can be said of man and his existence, then the ethical is of the same nature as a person's eternal salvation, which is his ⟨*telos*⟩ forevermore and at all times, since it would be a contradiction for this to be capable of being surrendered (that is, teleologically suspended), because as soon as this is suspended it is relinquished, whereas that which is suspended is not relinquished but is preserved in the higher, which is its ⟨*telos*⟩.

If this is the case, then Hegel is right in "The Good and Conscience," where he qualifies man only as the individual and considers this qualification as a "moral form of evil" (see especially *The Philosophy of Right*), which must be annulled [*ophævet*] in the teleology of the moral in such a way that the single individual who remains in that stage either sins or is immersed in spiritual trial. But Hegel is wrong in speaking about faith; he is wrong in not protesting loudly and clearly against Abraham's enjoying honor and glory as a father of faith when he ought to be sent back to a lower court and shown up as a murderer.

Faith is namely this paradox that the single individual is higher than the universal—yet, please note, in such a way that the movement repeats itself, so that after having been in the universal he as the single individual isolates himself as higher than the universal. If this is not faith, then Abraham is lost, then faith has never existed in the world precisely because it has always existed. For if the ethical—that is, social morality—is the highest and if there is in a person no residual incommensurability in some way such that this incommensurability is not evil (i.e., the single individual, who is to be expressed in the universal), then no categories are needed other than what Greek philosophy had or what can be deduced from them by consistent thought. Hegel should not have concealed this, for, after all, he had studied Greek philosophy.

People who are profoundly lacking in learning and are given to clichés are frequently heard to say that a light shines over the Christian world, whereas a darkness enshrouds paganism. This kind of talk has always struck me as strange, inasmuch as every more thorough thinker, every more earnest artist still regenerates himself in the eternal youth of the Greeks. The explanation for such a statement is that one does not know what one should say but only that one must say something. It is quite right to say that paganism did not have faith, but if something is supposed to have been said thereby, then one must have a clearer understanding of what faith is, for otherwise one falls into such clichés. It is easy to explain all existence, faith along with it, without having a conception of what faith is, and the one who counts on being admired for such an explanation is not such a bad calculator, for it is as Boileau says: *Un sot trouve toujours un plus sot, qui l'admire* [One fool always finds a bigger fool, who admires him].

Faith is precisely the paradox that the single individual as the single individual is higher than the universal, is justified before it, not as inferior to it but as superior—yet in such a way, please note, that it is the single individual who, after being subordinate as the single individual to the universal, now by means of the universal becomes the single individual who as the single individual is superior, that the single individual as the single individual stands in an absolute relation to the absolute. This position cannot be mediated, for all mediation takes place only by virtue of the universal; it is and remains for all eternity a paradox, impervious to thought. And yet faith is this paradox, or else (and I ask the reader to bear these consequences *in mente* [in mind] even though it would be too prolix for me to write them all down) or else faith has never existed simply because it has always existed, or else Abraham is lost.

It is certainly true that the single individual can easily confuse this paradox with spiritual trial [*Anfægtelse*], but it ought not to be concealed for that reason. It is certainly true that many persons may be so constituted that they are repulsed by it, but faith ought not therefore to be made into something else to enable one to have it, but one ought rather to admit to not having it, while those who have faith ought to be prepared to set forth some characteristics whereby the paradox can be distinguished from a spiritual trial.

The story of Abraham contains just such a teleological suspension of the ethical. There is no dearth of keen minds and careful scholars who have found analogies to it.

Wanderer Above the Mist, 1817–1818, by Caspar David Friedrich
(1774–1840). "Faith is precisely the paradox that the single
individual as the single individual is higher than the universal. . . .
This position cannot be mediated . . . it is and remains for all
eternity a paradox, impervious to thought." Kierkegaard, *Fear and
Trembling. (Marburg / Art Resource)*

What their wisdom amounts to is the beautiful proposition that basically everything is
the same. If one looks more closely, I doubt very much that anyone in the whole wide
world will find one single analogy, except for a later one, which proves nothing if it is
certain that Abraham represents faith and that it is manifested normatively in him,
whose life not only is the most paradoxical that can be thought but is also so paradoxical that it simply cannot be thought. He acts by virtue of the absurd, for it is precisely
the absurd that he as the single individual is higher than the universal. This paradox
cannot be mediated, for as soon as Abraham begins to do so, he has to confess that he
was in a spiritual trial, and if that is the case, he will never sacrifice Isaac, or if he did
sacrifice Isaac, then in repentance he must come back to the universal. He gets Isaac
back again by virtue of the absurd. Therefore, Abraham is at no time a tragic hero but
is something entirely different, either a murderer or a man of faith. Abraham does not
have the middle term that saves the tragic hero. This is why I can understand a tragic
hero but cannot understand Abraham, even though in a certain demented sense I admire him more than all others.

In ethical terms, Abraham's relation to Isaac is quite simply this: the father shall
love the son more than himself. But within its own confines the ethical has various

gradations. We shall see whether this story contains any higher expression for the ethical that can ethically explain his behavior, can ethically justify his suspending the ethical obligation to the son, but without moving beyond the teleology of the ethical.

When an enterprise of concern to a whole nation is impeded, when such a project is halted by divine displeasure, when the angry deity sends a dead calm that mocks every effort, when the soothsayer carries out his sad task and announces that the deity demands a young girl as sacrifice—then the father must heroically bring this sacrifice. He must nobly conceal his agony, even though he could wish he were "the lowly man who dares to weep" and not the king who must behave in a kingly manner. Although the lonely agony penetrates his breast and there are only three persons in the whole nation who know his agony, soon the whole nation will be initiated into his agony and also into his deed, that for the welfare of all he will sacrifice her, his daughter, this lovely young girl. O bosom! O fair cheeks, flaxen hair (v. 687). And the daughter's tears will agitate him, and the father will turn away his face, but the hero must raise the knife. And when the news of it reaches the father's house, the beautiful Greek maidens will blush with enthusiasm, and if the daughter was engaged, her betrothed will not be angry but will be proud to share in the father's deed, for the girl belonged more tenderly to him than to the father.

When the valiant judge who in the hour of need saved Israel binds God and himself in one breath by the same promise, he will heroically transform the young maiden's jubilation, the beloved daughter's joy to sorrow, and all Israel will sorrow with her over her virginal youth. But every freeborn man will understand, every resolute woman will admire Jephthah, and every virgin in Israel will wish to behave as his daughter did, because what good would it be for Jephthah to win the victory by means of a promise if he did not keep it—would not the victory be taken away from the people again?

When a son forgets his duty, when the state entrusts the sword of judgment to the father, when the laws demand punishment from the father's hand, then the father must heroically forget that the guilty one is his son, he must nobly hide his agony, but no one in the nation, not even the son, will fail to admire the father, and every time the Roman laws are interpreted, it will be remembered that many interpreted them more learnedly but no one more magnificently than Brutus.

But if Agamemnon, while a favorable wind was taking the fleet under full sail to its destination, had dispatched that messenger who fetched Iphigenia to be sacrificed; if Jephthah, without being bound by any promise that decided the fate of the nation, had said to his daughter: Grieve now for two months over your brief youth, and then I will sacrifice you; if Brutus had had a righteous son and yet had summoned the lictors to put him to death—who would have understood them? If, on being asked why they did this, these three men had answered: It is an ordeal in which we are being tried [*forsøges*]—would they have been better understood?

When in the crucial moment Agamemnon, Jephthah, and Brutus heroically have overcome the agony, heroically have lost the beloved, and have only to complete the task externally, there will never be a noble soul in the world without tears of compassion for their agony, of admiration for their deed. But if in the crucial moment these three men were to append to the heroic courage with which they bore the agony the little phrase: But it will not happen anyway—who then would understand them? If they went on to explain: This we believe by virtue of the absurd—who would understand them any better, for who would not readily understand that it was absurd, but who would understand that one could then believe it?

The difference between the tragic hero and Abraham is very obvious. The tragic hero is still within the ethical. He allows an expression of the ethical to have its ⟨*telos*⟩

in a higher expression of the ethical; he scales down the ethical relation between father and son or daughter and father to a feeling that has its dialectic in its relation to the idea of moral conduct. Here there can be no question of a teleological suspension of the ethical itself.

Abraham's situation is different. By his act he transgressed the ethical altogether and had a higher ⟨*telos*⟩ outside it, in relation to which he suspended it. For I certainly would like to know how Abraham's act can be related to the universal, whether any point of contact between what Abraham did and the universal can be found other than that Abraham transgressed it. It is not to save a nation, not to uphold the idea of the state that Abraham does it; it is not to appease the angry gods. If it were a matter of the deity's being angry, then he was, after all, angry only with Abraham, and Abraham's act is totally unrelated to the universal, is a purely private endeavor. Therefore, while the tragic hero is great because of his moral virtue, Abraham is great because of a purely personal virtue. There is no higher expression for the ethical in Abraham's life than that the father shall love the son. The ethical in the sense of the moral is entirely beside the point. Insofar as the universal was present, it was cryptically in Isaac, hidden, so to speak, in Isaac's loins, and must cry out with Isaac's mouth: Do not do this, you are destroying everything.

Why, then, does Abraham do it? For God's sake and—the two are wholly identical—for his own sake. He does it for God's sake because God demands this proof of his faith; he does it for his own sake so that he can prove it. The unity of the two is altogether correctly expressed in the word already used to describe this relationship. It is an ordeal, a temptation. A temptation—but what does that mean? As a rule, what tempts a person is something that will hold him back from doing his duty, but here the temptation is the ethical itself, which would hold him back from doing God's will. But what is duty? Duty is simply the expression for God's will.

Here the necessity of a new category for the understanding of Abraham becomes apparent. Paganism does not know such a relationship to the divine. The tragic hero does not enter into any private relationship to the divine, but the ethical is the divine, and thus the paradox therein can be mediated in the universal.

Abraham cannot be mediated; in other words, he cannot speak. As soon as I speak, I express the universal, and if I do not do so, no one can understand me. As soon as Abraham wants to express himself in the universal, he must declare that his situation is a spiritual trial [*Anfægtelse*], for he has no higher expression of the universal that ranks above the universal he violates.

Therefore, although Abraham arouses my admiration, he also appalls me. The person who denies himself and sacrifices himself because of duty gives up the finite in order to grasp the infinite and is adequately assured; the tragic hero gives up the certain for the even more certain, and the observer's eye views him with confidence. But the person who gives up the universal in order to grasp something even higher that is not the universal—what does he do? Is it possible that this can be anything other than a spiritual trial? And if it is possible, but the individual makes a mistake, what salvation is there for him? He suffers all the agony of the tragic hero, he shatters his joy in the world, he renounces everything, and perhaps at the same time he barricades himself from the sublime joy that was so precious to him that he would buy it at any price. The observer cannot understand him at all; neither can his eye rest upon him with confidence. Perhaps the believer's intention cannot be carried out at all, because it is inconceivable. Or if it could be done but the individual has misunderstood the deity—what salvation would there be for him? The tragic hero needs and demands tears, and where is the envious eye so arid that it could not weep with Agamemnon, but where is the soul so gone astray that it has the audacity to weep for Abraham? The tragic hero finishes his task at a specific moment in time, but as time passes he does what is no less significant: he visits the person encompassed by sorrow, who cannot breathe because of his anguished sighs, whose thoughts oppress him, heavy with tears. He appears to him, breaks the witchcraft of sorrow, loosens the bonds, evokes the tears, and the suffering one forgets his own sufferings in those of the tragic hero. One cannot weep over Abraham. One approaches him with a *horror religiosus,* as Israel approached Mount Sinai. What if he himself is distraught, what if he had made a mistake, this lonely man who climbs Mount Moriah, whose peak towers sky-high over the flatlands of Aulis, what if he is not a sleepwalker safely crossing the abyss while the one standing at the foot of the mountain looks up, shakes with anxiety, and then in his deference and horror does not even dare to call to him?—Thanks, once again thanks, to a man who, to a person overwhelmed by life's sorrows and left behind naked, reaches out the words, the leafage of language by which he can conceal his misery. Thanks to you, great Shakespeare, you who can say everything, everything, everything just as it is—and yet, why did you never articulate this torment? Did you perhaps reserve it for yourself, like the beloved's name that one cannot bear to have the world utter, for with his little secret that he cannot divulge the poet buys this power of the word to tell everybody else's dark secrets. A poet is not an apostle; he drives out devils only by the power of the devil.

But if the ethical is teleologically suspended in this manner, how does the single individual in whom it is suspended exist? He exists as the single individual in contrast to the universal. Does he sin, then, for from the point of view of the idea, this is the form of sin. Thus, even though the child does not sin, because it is not conscious of its existence as such, its existence, from the point of view of the idea, is nevertheless sin, and the ethical makes its claim upon it at all times. If it is denied that this form can be repeated in such a way that it is not sin, then judgment has fallen upon Abraham. How did Abraham exist? He had faith. This is the paradox by which he remains at the apex, the paradox that he cannot explain to anyone else, for the paradox is that he as the single individual places himself in an absolute relation to the absolute. Is he justified? Again, his justification is the paradoxical, for if he is, then he is justified not by virtue of being something universal but by virtue of being the single individual.

How does the single individual reassure himself that he is legitimate? It is a simple matter to level all existence to the idea of the state or the idea of a society. If this is done, it is also simple to mediate, for one never comes to the paradox that the single individual as the single individual is higher than the universal, something I can also express symbolically in a statement by Pythagoras to the effect that the odd number is more perfect than the even number. If occasionally there is any response at all these days with regard to the paradox, it is likely to be: One judges it by the result. Aware that he is a paradox who cannot be understood, a hero who has become a ⟨*skandalon*⟩ [offense] to his age will shout confidently to his contemporaries: The result will indeed prove that I was justified. This cry is rarely heard in our age, inasmuch as it does not produce heroes—this is its defect—and it likewise has the advantage that it produces few caricatures. When in our age we hear these words: It will be judged by the result— then we know at once with whom we have the honor of speaking. Those who talk this way are a numerous type whom I shall designate under the common name of assistant professors. With security in life, they live in their thoughts: they have a *permanent* position and a *secure* future in a well-organized state. They have hundreds, yes, even thousands of years between them and the earthquakes of existence; they are not afraid that such things can be repeated, for then what would the police and the newspapers say? Their life task is to judge the great men, judge them according to the result. Such behavior toward greatness betrays a strange mixture of arrogance and wretchedness— arrogance because they feel called to pass judgment, wretchedness because they feel that their lives are in no way allied with the lives of the great. Anyone with even a smattering *erectioris ingenii* [of nobility of nature] never becomes an utterly cold and clammy worm, and when he approaches greatness, he is never devoid of the thought that since the creation of the world it has been customary for the result to come last and that if one is truly going to learn something from greatness one must be particularly aware of the beginning. If the one who is to act wants to judge himself by the result, he will never begin. Although the result may give joy to the entire world, it cannot help the hero, for he would not know the result until the whole thing was over, and he would not become a hero by that but by making a beginning.

Moreover, in its dialectic the result (insofar as it is finitude's response to the infinite question) is altogether incongruous with the hero's existence. Or should Abraham's receiving Isaac by a *marvel* be able to prove that Abraham was justified in relating himself as the single individual to the universal? If Abraham actually had sacrificed Isaac, would he therefore have been less justified?

But we are curious about the result, just as we are curious about the way a book turns out. We do not want to know anything about the anxiety, the distress, the paradox. We carry on an esthetic flirtation with the result. It arrives just as unexpectedly but also just as effortlessly as a prize in a lottery, and when we have heard the result, we have built ourselves up. And yet no manacled robber of churches is so despicable a criminal as the one who plunders holiness in this way, and not even Judas, who sold his Lord for thirty pieces of silver, is more contemptible than someone who peddles greatness in this way.

It is against my very being to speak inhumanly about greatness, to make it a dim and nebulous far-distant shape or to let it be great but devoid of the emergence of the humanness without which it ceases to be great, for it is not what happens to me that makes me great but what I do, and certainly there is no one who believes that someone became great by winning the big lottery prize. A person might have been born in lowly circumstances, but I would still require him not to be so inhuman toward himself that he could imagine the king's castle only at a distance and ambiguously dream of its greatness, and destroy it at the same time he elevates it because he elevated it so basely. I require him to be man enough to tread confidently and with dignity there as well. He must not be so inhuman that he insolently violates everything by barging right off the street into the king's hall—he loses more thereby than the king. On the contrary, he should find a joy in observing every bidding of propriety with a happy and confident enthusiasm, which is precisely what makes him a free spirit. This is merely a metaphor, for that distinction is only a very imperfect expression of the distance of spirit. I require every person not to think so inhumanly of himself that he does not dare to enter those palaces where the memory of the chosen ones lives or even those where they themselves live. He is not to enter rudely and foist his affinity upon them. He is to be happy for every time he bows before them, but he is to be confident, free of spirit, and always more than a charwoman, for if he wants to be no more than that, he will never get in. And the very thing that is going to help him is the anxiety and distress in which the great were tried, for otherwise, if he has any backbone, they will only arouse his righteous envy. And anything that can be great only at a distance, that someone wants to make great with empty and hollow phrases—is destroyed by that very person.

Who was as great in the world as that favored woman, the mother of God, the Virgin Mary? And yet how do we speak of her? That she was the favored one among women does not make her great, and if it would not be so very odd for those who listen to be able to think just as inhumanly as those who speak, then every young girl might ask: Why am I not so favored? And if I had nothing else to say, I certainly would not dismiss such a question as stupid, because, viewed abstractly, vis-à-vis a favor, every person is just as entitled to it as the other. We leave out the distress, the anxiety, the paradox. My thoughts are as pure as anybody's, and he who can think this way surely has pure thoughts, and, if not, he can expect something horrible, for anyone who has once experienced these images cannot get rid of them again, and if he sins against them, they take a terrible revenge in a silent rage, which is more terrifying than the stridency of ten ravenous critics. To be sure, Mary bore the child wondrously, but she nevertheless did it "after the manner of women," and such a time is one of anxiety, distress, and paradox. The angel was indeed a ministering spirit, but he was not a meddlesome spirit who went to the other young maidens in Israel and said: Do not scorn Mary, the extraordinary is happening to her. The angel went only to Mary, and no one could understand her. Has any woman been as infringed upon as was Mary, and is it not true here also that the one whom God blesses he curses in the same breath? This is the spirit's view of Mary, and she is by no means—it is revolting to me to say it but even more so that people have inanely and unctuously made her out to be thus— she is by no means a lady idling in her finery and playing with a divine child. When, despite this, she said: Behold, I am the handmaid of the Lord—then she is great, and I believe it should not be difficult to explain why she became the mother of God. She needs worldly admiration as little as Abraham needs tears, for she was no heroine and he was no hero, but both of them became greater than these, not by being exempted in any way from the distress and the agony and the paradox, but became greater by means of these.

It is great when the poet in presenting his tragic hero for public admiration dares to say: Weep for him, for he deserves it. It is great to deserve the tears of those who deserve to shed tears. It is great that the poet dares to keep the crowd under restraint, dares to discipline men to examine themselves individually to see if they are worthy to weep for the hero, for the slop water of the snivellers is a debasement of the sacred.— But even greater than all this is the knight of faith's daring to say to the noble one who wants to weep for him: Do not weep for me, but weep for yourself.

We are touched, we look back to those beautiful times. Sweet sentimental longing leads us to the goal of our desire, to see Christ walking about in the promised land. We forget the anxiety, the distress, the paradox. Was it such a simple matter not to make a mistake? Was it not terrifying that this man walking around among the others was God? Was it not terrifying to sit down to eat with him? Was it such an easy matter to become an apostle? But the result, the eighteen centuries—that helps, that contributes to this mean deception whereby we deceive ourselves and others. I do not feel brave enough to wish to be contemporary with events like that, but I do not for that reason severely condemn those who made a mistake, nor do I depreciate those who saw what was right.

But I come back to Abraham. During the time before the result, either Abraham was a murderer every minute or we stand before a paradox that is higher than all mediations.

The story of Abraham contains, then, a teleological suspension of the ethical. As the single individual he became higher than the universal. This is the paradox, which cannot be mediated. How he entered into it is just as inexplicable as how he remains in it. If this is not Abraham's situation, then Abraham is not even a tragic hero but a murderer. It is thoughtless to want to go on calling him the father of faith, to speak of it to men who have an interest only in words. A person can become a tragic hero through his own strength—but not the knight of faith. When a person walks what is in one sense the hard road of the tragic hero, there are many who can give him advice, but he who walks the narrow road of faith has no one to advise him—no one understands him. Faith is a marvel, and yet no human being is excluded from it; for that which unites all human life is passion, and faith is a passion.

CONCLUDING UNSCIENTIFIC POSTSCRIPT (in part)

SECTION II, CHAPTER 2: SUBJECTIVE TRUTH, INWARDNESS; TRUTH IS SUBJECTIVITY

*   *   *

When the question about truth is asked objectively, truth is reflected upon objectively as an object to which the knower relates himself. What is reflected upon is not the relation but that what he relates himself to is the truth, the true. If only that to which he relates himself is the truth, the true, then the subject is in the truth. When the question about truth is asked subjectively, the individual's relation is reflected upon subjectively. If only the how of this relation is in truth, the individual is in truth, even if he in this way were to relate himself to untruth.*

Let us take the knowledge of God as an example. Objectively, what is reflected upon is that this is the true God; subjectively, that the individual relates himself to a something in *such a way* that his relation is in truth a God-relation. Now, on which side is the truth? Alas, must we not at this point resort to mediation and say: It is on neither side; it is in the mediation? Superbly stated, if only someone could say how an existing person goes about being in mediation, because to be in mediation is to be finished; to exist is to become. An existing person cannot be in two places at the same time, cannot be subject-object. When he is closest to being in two places at the same time, he is in passion; but passion is only momentary, and passion is the highest pitch of subjectivity.

The existing person who chooses the objective way now enters upon all approximating deliberation intended to bring forth God objectively, which is not achieved in all eternity, because God is a subject and hence only for subjectivity in inwardness.

---

*The reader will note that what is being discussed here is essential truth, or the truth that is related essentially to existence, and that it is specifically in order to clarify it as inwardness or as subjectivity that the contrast is pointed out.

Søren Kierkegaard, *Concluding Unscientific Postscript,* Section I, Chapter 2, "Possible and Actual Theses by Lessing"; Section II, Chapter 2, "Subjective Truth, Inwardness; Truth is Subjectivity," edited and translated by Howard V. Hong and Edna H. Hong (Princeton, NJ: Princeton University Press). Copyright © 1992 by Princeton University Press. Reprinted by permission of Princeton University Press.

The existing person who chooses the subjective way instantly comprehends the whole dialectical difficulty because he must use some time, perhaps a long time, to find God objectively. He comprehends this dialectical difficulty in all its pain, because he must resort to God at that very moment, because every moment in which he does not have God is wasted.* At that very moment he has God, not by virtue of any objective deliberation but by virtue of the infinite passion of inwardness. The objective person is not bothered by dialectical difficulties such as what it means to put a whole research period into finding God, since it is indeed possible that the researcher would die tomorrow, and if he goes on living, he cannot very well regard God as something to be taken along at his convenience, since God is something one takes along a *tout prix* [at any price], which, in passion's understanding, is the true relationship of inwardness with God.

It is at this point, dialectically so very difficult, that the road swings off for the person who knows what it means to think dialectically and, existing, to think dialectically, which is quite different from sitting as a fantastical being at a desk and writing about something one has never done oneself, quite different from writing *de omnibus dubitandum* and then as an existing person being just as credulous as the most sensate human being. It is here that the road swings off, and the change is this: whereas objective knowledge goes along leisurely on the long road of approximation, itself not actuated by passion, to subjective knowledge every delay is a deadly peril and the decision so infinitely important that it is immediately urgent, as if the opportunity had already passed by unused.

Now, if the problem is to calculate where there is more truth (and, as stated, simultaneously to be on both sides equally is not granted to an existing person but is only a beatifying delusion for a deluded *I–I*), whether on the side of the person who only objectively seeks the true God and the approximating truth of the God-idea or on the side of the person who is infinitely concerned that he in truth relate himself to God with the infinite passion of need—then there can be no doubt about the answer for anyone who is not totally botched by scholarship and science. If someone who lives in the midst of Christianity enters, with knowledge of the true idea of God, the house of God, the house of the true God, and prays, but prays in untruth, and if someone lives in an idolatrous land but prays with all the passion of infinity, although his eyes are resting upon the image of an idol—where, then, is there more truth? The one prays in truth to God although he is worshiping an idol; the other prays in untruth to the true God and is therefore in truth worshiping an idol.

If someone objectively inquires into immortality, and someone else stakes the passion of the infinite on the uncertainty—where, then, is there more truth, and who has more certainty? The one has once and for all entered upon an approximation that never ends, because the certainty of immortality is rooted in subjectivity; the other is immortal and therefore struggles by contending with the uncertainty.

Let us consider Socrates. These days everyone is dabbling in a few proofs or demonstrations—one has many, another fewer. But Socrates! He poses the question

---

*In this way God is indeed a postulate, but not in the loose sense in which it is ordinarily taken. Instead, it becomes clear that this is the only way an existing person enters into a relationship with God: when the dialectical contradiction brings passion to despair and assists him in grasping God with "the category of despair" (faith), so that the postulate, far from being the arbitrary, is in fact *necessary* defense [*Nødværge*], self defense; in this way God is not a postulate, but the existing person's postulating of God is—a necessity [*Nødvendighed*].

objectively, problematically: if there is an immortality. So, compared with one of the modern thinkers with the three demonstrations, was he a doubter? Not at all. He stakes his whole life on this "if"; he dares to die, and with the passion of the infinite he has so ordered his whole life that it might be acceptable—if there is an immortality. Is there any better demonstration for the immortality of the soul? But those who have the three demonstrations do not order their lives accordingly. If there is an immortality, it must be nauseated by their way of living—is there any better counter-demonstration to the three demonstrations? The "fragment" of uncertainty helped Socrates, because he himself helped with the passion of infinity. The three demonstrations are of no benefit whatever to those others, because they are and remain slugs and, failing to demonstrate anything else, have demonstrated it by their three demonstrations.

In the same way a girl has perhaps possessed all the sweetness of being in love through a weak hope of being loved by the beloved, because she herself staked everything on this weak hope; on the other hand, many a wedded matron, who more than once has submitted to the strongest expression of erotic love, has certainly had demonstrations and yet, strangely enough, has not possessed *quod erat demonstrandum* [that which was to be demonstrated]. The Socratic ignorance was thus the expression, firmly maintained with all the passion of inwardness, of the relation of the eternal truth to an existing person, and therefore it must remain for him a paradox as long as he exists. Yet it is possible that in the Socratic ignorance there was more truth in Socrates than in the objective truth of the entire system that flirts with the demands of the times and adapts itself to assistant professors.

Objectively the emphasis is on what is said; subjectively the emphasis is on how it is said. This distinction applies even esthetically and is specifically expressed when we say that in the mouth of this or that person something that is truth can become untruth. Particular attention should be paid to this distinction in our day, for if one were to express in a single sentence the difference between ancient times and our time, one would no doubt have to say: In ancient times there were only a few individuals who knew the truth; now everyone knows it, but inwardness has an inverse relation to it. Viewed esthetically, the contradiction that emerges when truth becomes untruth in this and that person's mouth is best interpreted comically. Ethically-religiously, the emphasis is again on: *how*. But this is not to be understood as manner, modulation of voice, oral delivery, etc., but it is to be understood as the relation of the existing person, in his very existence, to what is said. Objectively, the question is only about categories of thought; subjectively, about inwardness. At its maximum, this "how" is the passion of the infinite, and the passion of the infinite is the very truth. But the passion of the infinite is precisely subjectivity, and thus subjectivity is truth. From the objective point of view, there is no infinite decision, and thus it is objectively correct that the distinction between good and evil is canceled, along with the principle of contradiction, and thereby also the infinite distinction between truth and falsehood. Only in subjectivity is there decision, whereas wanting to become objective is untruth. The passion of the infinite, not its content, is the deciding factor, for its content is precisely itself. In this way the subjective "how" and subjectivity are the truth.

But precisely because the subject is existing, the "how" that is subjectively emphasized is dialectical also with regard to time. In the moment of the decision of passion, where the road swings off from objective knowledge, it looks as if the infinite decision were thereby finished. But at the same moment, the existing person is in the temporal realm, and the subjective "how" is transformed into a striving that is motivated and repeatedly refreshed by the decisive passion of the infinite, but it is nevertheless a striving.

When subjectivity is truth, the definition of truth must also contain in itself an expression of the antithesis to objectivity, a memento of that fork in the road, and this expression will at the same time indicate the resilience of the inwardness. Here is such a definition of truth: *An objective uncertainty, held fast through appropriation with the most passionate inwardness, is the truth,* the highest truth there is for an existing person. At the point where the road swings off (and where that is cannot be stated objectively, since it is precisely subjectivity), objective knowledge is suspended. Objectively he then has only uncertainty, but this is precisely what intensifies the infinite passion of inwardness, and truth is precisely the daring venture of choosing the objective uncertainty with the passion of the infinite. I observe nature in order to find God, and I do indeed see omnipotence and wisdom, but I also see much that troubles and disturbs. The *summa summarum* [sum total] of this is an objective uncertainty, but the inwardness is so very great, precisely because it grasps this objective uncertainty with all the passion of the infinite. In a mathematical proposition, for example, the objectivity is given, but therefore its truth is also an indifferent truth.

But the definition of truth stated above is a paraphrasing of faith. Without risk, no faith. Faith is the contradiction between the infinite passion of inwardness and the objective uncertainty. If I am able to apprehend God objectively, I do not have faith; but because I cannot do this, I must have faith. If I want to keep myself in faith, I must continually see to it that I hold fast the objective uncertainty, see to it that in the objective uncertainty I am "out on 70,000 fathoms of water" and still have faith.

The thesis that subjectivity, inwardness, is truth contains the Socratic wisdom, the undying merit of which is to have paid attention to the essential meaning of existing, of the knower's being an existing person. That is why, in his ignorance, Socrates was in the truth in the highest sense within paganism. To comprehend this, that the misfortune of speculative thought is simply that it forgets again and again that the knower is an existing person, can already be rather difficult in our objective age. "But to go beyond Socrates when one has not even comprehended the Socratic—that, at least, is not Socratic." See "The Moral" in *Fragments*.

Just as in *Fragments,* let us from this point try a category of thought that actually does go beyond. Whether it is true or false is of no concern to me, since I am only imaginatively constructing, but this much is required, that it be clear that the Socratic is presupposed in it, so that I at least do not end up behind Socrates again.

When subjectivity, inwardness, is truth, then truth, objectively defined, is a paradox; and that truth is objectively a paradox shows precisely that subjectivity is truth, since the objectivity does indeed thrust away, and the objectivity's repulsion, or the expression for the objectivity's repulsion, is the resilience and dynamometer of inwardness. The paradox is the objective uncertainty that is the expression for the passion of inwardness that is truth. So much for the Socratic. The eternal, essential truth, that is, the truth that is related essentially to the existing person by pertaining essentially to what it means to exist (viewed Socratically, all other knowledge is accidental, its degree and scope indifferent), is a paradox. Nevertheless the eternal, essential truth is itself not at all a paradox, but it is a paradox by being related to an existing person. Socratic ignorance is an expression of the objective uncertainty; the inwardness of the existing person is truth. In anticipation of what will be discussed later, the following comment is made here: Socratic ignorance is an analogue to the category of the absurd, except that there is even less objective certainty in the repulsion exerted by the absurd, since there is only the certainty that it is absurd, and for that very reason there is infinitely greater resilience in the inwardness. The Socratic inwardness in existing is an analogue to faith, except that the inwardness of faith, corresponding not to the repulsion exerted by igno-rance but to the repulsion exerted by the absurd, is infinitely deeper.

Viewed Socratically, the eternal essential truth is not at all paradoxical in itself, but only by being related to an existing person. This is expressed in another Socratic thesis: that all knowing is a recollecting. This thesis is an intimation of the beginning of speculative thought, but for that very reason Socrates did not pursue it; essentially it became Platonic. This is where the road swings off, and Socrates essentially empha-sizes existing, whereas Plato, forgetting this, loses himself in speculative thought. Socrates' infinite merit is precisely that of being an *existing* thinker, not a speculative thinker who forgets what it means to exist. To Socrates, therefore, the thesis that all knowing is a recollecting has, at the moment of parting and as a continually annulled possibility of speculating, a double significance: (1) that the knower is essentially *inte-ger* [uncorrupted] and that for him there is no other dubiousness with regard to knowl-edge of the eternal truth than this, that he exists, a dubiousness so essential and deci-sive to him that it signifies that existing, the inward deepening in and through existing, is truth; (2) that existence in temporality has no decisive significance, because there is continually the possibility of taking oneself back into eternity by recollecting, even though this possibility is continually annulled because the inward deepening in exist-ing fills up time.*

The great merit of the Socratic was precisely to emphasize that the knower is an existing person and that to exist is the essential. To go beyond Socrates by failing to

---

*This may be the proper place to elucidate a dubiousness in the design of *Fragments,* a dubiousness that was due to my not wanting immediately to make the matter as dialectically difficult as it is, because in our day terminologies and the like are so muddled that it is almost impossible to safeguard oneself against confusion. In order, if possible, to elucidate properly the difference between the Socratic (which was sup-posed to be the philosophical, the pagan philosophical position) and the category of imaginatively con-structed thought, which actually goes beyond the Socratic, I carried the Socratic back to the thesis that all knowing is a recollecting. It is commonly accepted as such, and only for the person who with a very special interest devotes himself to the Socratic, always returning to the sources, only for him will it be important to distinguish between Socrates and Plato on this point. The thesis certainly belongs to both of them, but Socrates continually parts with it because he wants to exist. By holding Socrates to the thesis that all know-ing is recollecting, one turns him into a speculative philosopher instead of what he was, an existing thinker who understood existing as the essential. The thesis that all knowing is recollecting belongs to speculative thought, and recollecting is immanence, and from the point of view of speculation and the eternal there is no paradox. The difficulty, however, is that no human being is speculation, but the speculating person is an ex-isting human being, subject to the claims of existence. To forget this is no merit, but to hold this fast is in-deed a merit and that is precisely what Socrates did. To emphasize existence, which contains within it the-qualification of inwardness, is the Socratic, whereas the Platonic is to purse recollection and immanence. Basically Socrates is thereby beyond all speculation, because he does not have a fantastical beginning where the speculating person changes clothes and then goes on and on and speculates, forgetting the most impor-tant thing, to exist. But precisely because Socrates is in this way beyond speculative thought, he acquires, when rightly depicted, a certain analogous likeness to what the imaginary construction set forth as that which truly goes beyond the Socratic: truth as paradox is an analog to the paradox *sensu eminetiori* [in the more eminent sense]; the passion of inwardness in existing is then an analog to faith *sensu eminentiori.* That the difference is infinite nevertheless, that the designations in *Fragments* of that which truly goes be-yond the Socratic are unchanged, I can easily show, but I was afraid to make complications by promptly using what seem to be the same designations, at least the same words, about the different things when the imaginary construction was to be presented as different from these. Now, I think there would be no objec-tion to speaking of the paradox in connection with Socrates and faith, since it is quite correct to do so, pro-vided that it is understood correctly. Besides, the ancient Greeks also use the word ⟨pistis⟩ [Faith], although by no means in the sense of the imaginary construction, and use it so as to make possible some very illumi-nating observations bearing upon its dissimilarity to faith *sensu eminentiori,* especially with reference to one of Aristotle's works where the term is employed.

understand this is nothing but a mediocre merit. This we must keep *in mente* [in mind] and then see whether the formula cannot be changed in such a way that one actually does go beyond the Socratic.

So, then, subjectivity, inwardness, is truth. Is there a *more inward* expression for it? Yes, if the discussion about "Subjectivity, inwardness, is truth" begins in this way: "Subjectivity is untruth." But let us not be in a hurry. Speculative thought also says that subjectivity is untruth but says it in the very opposite direction, namely, that objectivity is truth. Speculative thought defines subjectivity negatively in the direction of objectivity. The other definition, however, puts barriers in its own way at the very moment it wants to begin, which makes the inwardness so much more inward. Viewed Socratically, subjectivity is untruth if it refuses to comprehend that subjectivity is truth but wants, for example, to be objective. Here, on the other hand, in wanting to begin to become truth by becoming subjective, subjectivity is in the predicament of being untruth. Thus the work goes backward, that is, backward in inwardness. The way is so far from being in the direction of the objective that the beginning only lies even deeper in subjectivity.

But the subject cannot be untruth eternally or be presupposed to have been untruth eternally; he must have become that in time or he becomes that in time. The Socratic paradox consisted in this, that the eternal truth was related to an existing person. But now existence has accentuated the existing person a second time; a change so essential has taken place in him that he in no way can take himself back into eternity by Socratically recollecting. To do this is to speculate; to be able to do this but, by grasping the inward deepening in existence, to annul the possibility of doing it is the Socratic. But now the difficulty is that what accompanied Socrates as an annulled possibility has become an impossibility. If speculating was already of dubious merit in connection with the Socratic, it is now only confusion.

The paradox emerges when the eternal truth and existing are placed together, but each time existing is accentuated, the paradox becomes clearer and clearer. Viewed Socratically, the knower was an existing person, but now the existing person is accentuated in such a way that existence has made an essential change in him.

Let us now call the individual's untruth *sin*. Viewed eternally, he cannot be in sin or be presupposed to have been eternally in sin. Therefore, by coming into existence (for the beginning was that subjectivity is untruth), he becomes a sinner. He is not born as a sinner in the sense that he is presupposed to be a sinner before he is born, but he is born in sin and as a sinner. Indeed, we could call this *hereditary sin*. But if existence has in this way obtained power over him, he is prevented from taking himself back into eternity through recollection. If it is already paradoxical that the eternal truth is related to an existing person, now it is absolutely paradoxical that it is related to such an existing person. But the more difficult it is made for him, recollecting, to take himself out of existence, the more inward his existing can become in existence; and when it is made impossible for him, when he is lodged in existence in such a way that the back door of recollection is forever closed, then the inwardness becomes the deepest. But let us never forget that the Socratic merit was precisely to emphasize that the knower is existing, because the more difficult the matter becomes, the more one is tempted to rush along the easy road of speculative thought, away from terrors and decisions, to fame, honor, a life of ease, etc. If even Socrates comprehended the dubiousness of taking himself speculatively out of existence back into eternity, when there was no dubiousness for the existing person except that he existed and, of course, that existing was the essential—now it is impossible. He must go forward; to go backward is impossible.

Subjectivity is truth. The paradox came into existence through the relating of the eternal, essential truth to the existing person. Let us now go further; let us assume that the eternal, essential truth is itself the paradox. How does the paradox emerge? By placing the eternal, essential truth together with existing. Consequently, if we place it together in the truth itself, the truth becomes a paradox. The eternal truth has come into existence in time. That is the paradox. If the subject just mentioned was prevented by sin from taking himself back into eternity, now he is not to concern himself with this, because now the eternal, essential truth is not behind him but has come in front of him by existing itself or by having existed, so that if the individual, existing, does not lay hold of the truth in existence, he will never have it.

Existence can never be accentuated more sharply than it has been here. The fraud of speculative thought in wanting to recollect itself out of existence has been made impossible. This is the only point to be comprehended here, and every speculation that insists on being speculation shows *eo ipso* [precisely thereby] that it has not comprehended this. The individual can thrust all this away and resort to speculation, but to accept it and then want to cancel it through speculation is impossible, because it is specifically designed to prevent speculation.

When the eternal truth relates itself to an existing person, it becomes the paradox. Through the objective uncertainty and ignorance, the paradox thrusts away in the inwardness of the existing person. But since the paradox is not in itself the paradox, it does not thrust away intensely enough, for without risk, no faith; the more risk, the more faith; the more objective reliability, the less inwardness (since inwardness is subjectivity); the less objective reliability, the deeper is the possible inwardness. When the paradox itself is the paradox, it thrusts away by virtue of the absurd, and the corresponding passion of inwardness is faith.

But subjectivity, inwardness, is truth; if not, we have forgotten the Socratic merit. But when the retreat out of existence into eternity by way of recollection has been made impossible, then, with the truth facing one as the paradox, in the anxiety of sin and its pain, with the tremendous risk of objectivity, there is no stronger expression for inwardness than—to have faith. But without risk, no faith, not even the Socratic faith, to say nothing of the kind we are discussing here.

When Socrates believed that God is, he held fast the objective uncertainty with the entire passion of inwardness, and faith is precisely in this contradiction, in this risk. Now it is otherwise. Instead of the objective uncertainty, there is here the certainty that, viewed objectively, it is the absurd, and this absurdity, held fast in the passion of inwardness, is faith. Compared with the earnestness of the absurd, the Socratic ignorance is like a witty jest, and compared with the strenuousness of faith, the Socratic existential inwardness resembles Greek nonchalance.

What, then, is the absurd? The absurd is that the eternal truth has come into existence in time, that God has come into existence, has been born, has grown up, etc., has come into existence exactly as an individual human being, indistinguishable from any other human being, inasmuch as all immediate recognizability is pre-Socratic paganism and from the Jewish point of view is idolatry. Every qualification of that which actually goes beyond the Socratic must essentially have a mark of standing in relation to the god's having come into existence, because faith, *sensu strictissimo* [in the strictest sense], as explicated in *Fragments*, refers to coming into existence. When Socrates believed that God is [*er til*], he no doubt perceived that where the road swings off there is a road of objective approximation, for example, the observation of nature, world history, etc. His merit was precisely to shun this road, where the quantifying siren song spellbinds and tricks the existing person. In relation to the absurd, the objective approximation resembles the comedy *Misforstaaelse paa Misforstaaelse* [Misunderstanding upon Misunderstanding], which ordinarily is played by assistant professors and speculative thinkers.

It is by way of the objective repulsion that the absurd is the dynamometer of faith in inwardness. So, then, there is a man who wants to have faith; well, let the comedy begin. He wants to have faith, but he wants to assure himself with the aid of objective deliberation and approximation. What happens? With the aid of approximation, the absurd becomes something else; it becomes probable, it becomes more probable, it may become to a high-degree and exceedingly probable. Now he is all set to believe it, and he dares to say of himself that he does not believe as shoemakers and tailors and simple folk do, but only after long deliberation. Now he is all set to believe it, but, lo and behold, now it has indeed become impossible to believe it. The almost probable, the probable, the to-a-high-degree and exceedingly probable—that he can almost know, or as good as know, to a higher degree and exceedingly almost *know*—but *believe* it, that cannot be done, for the absurd is precisely the object of faith and only that can be believed.

Or there is a man who says he has faith, but now he wants to make his faith clear to himself; he wants to understand himself in his faith. Now the comedy begins again. The object of faith becomes almost probable, it becomes as good as probable, it becomes probable, it becomes to a high degree and exceedingly probable. He has finished; he dares to say of himself that he does not believe as shoemakers and tailors or other simple folk do but that he has also understood himself in his believing. What wondrous understanding! On the contrary, he has learned to know something different about faith than he believed and has learned to know that he no longer has faith, since he almost knows, as good as knows, to a high degree and exceedingly almost knows.

Inasmuch as the absurd contains the element of coming into existence, the road of approximation will also be that which confuses the absurd fact of coming into existence, which is the object of faith, with a simple historical fact, and then seeks historical certainty for that which is absurd precisely because it contains the contradiction that something that can become historical only in direct opposition to all human understanding has become historical. This contradiction is the absurd, which can only be believed. If a historical certainty is obtained, one obtains merely the certainty that what is certain is not what is the point in question. A witness can testify that he has believed it and then testify that, far from being a historical certainty, it is in direct opposition to his understanding, but such a witness repels in the same sense as the absurd repels, and a witness who does not repel in this way is *eo ipso* a deceiver or a man who is talking about something altogether different; and such a witness can be of no help except in obtaining certainty about something altogether different. One hundred thousand individual witnesses, who by the special nature of their testimony (that they have believed the absurd) remain individual witnesses, do not become something else en masse so that the absurd becomes less absurd. Why? Because one hundred thousand people individually have believed that it was absurd? Quite the contrary, those one hundred thousand witnesses repel exactly as the absurd does.

But I do not need to develop this further here. In *Fragments* (especially where the difference between the follower at first hand and the follower at second hand is annulled) and in Part One of this book, I have with sufficient care shown that all approximation is futile, since the point is rather to do away with introductory observations, reliabilities, demonstrations from effects, and the whole mob of pawnbrokers and guarantors, in order to get the absurd clear—so that one can believe if one will—I merely say that this must be extremely strenuous.

If speculative thought wants to become involved in this and, as always, say: From the point of view of the eternal, the divine, the theocentric, there is no paradox— I shall not be able to decide whether the speculative thinker is right, because I am only a poor existing human being who neither eternally nor divinely nor theocentrically is able to observe the eternal but must be content with existing. This much, however, is certain, that with speculative thought everything goes backward, back past the Socratic, which at least comprehended that for an existing person existing is the essential; and much less has speculative thought taken the time to comprehend what it means to be *situated* in existence the way the existing person is in the imaginary construction.

The difference between the Socratic position and the position that goes beyond the Socratic is clear enough and is essentially the same as in *Fragments,* for in the latter nothing has changed, and in the former the matter has only been made somewhat more difficult, but nevertheless not more difficult than it is. It has also become somewhat more difficult because, whereas in *Fragments* I set forth the thought-category of the paradox only in an imaginary construction, here I have also latently made an attempt to make clear the necessity of the paradox, and even though the attempt is somewhat weak, it is still something different from speculatively canceling the paradox.

Christianity has itself proclaimed itself to be the eternal, essential truth that has come into existence in time; it has proclaimed itself as *the paradox* and has required the inwardness of faith with regard to what is an offense to the Jews, foolishness to the Greeks—and an absurdity to the understanding. It cannot be expressed more strongly that subjectivity is truth and that objectivity only thrusts away, precisely by virtue of the absurd, and it seems strange that Christianity should have come into the world in order to be explained, alas, as if it were itself puzzled about itself and therefore came into the world to seek out the wise man, the speculative thinker, who can aid with the explanation. It cannot be expressed more inwardly that subjectivity is truth than when subjectivity is at first untruth, and yet subjectivity is truth.

*　*　*

The direct relationship with God is simply paganism, and only when the break has taken place, only then can there be a true God-relationship. But this break is indeed the first act of inwardness oriented to the definition that truth is inwardness. Nature is certainly the work of God, but only the work is directly present, not God. With regard to the individual human being, is this not acting like an illusive author, who nowhere sets forth his result in block letters or provides it beforehand in a preface? And why is God illusive? Precisely because he is truth and in being illusive seeks to keep a person from untruth. The observer does not glide directly to the result but on his own must concern himself with finding it and thereby break the direct relation. But this break is the actual breakthrough of inwardness, an act of self-activity, the first designation of truth as inwardness.

Or is it not the case that God is so unnoticeable, so hidden yet present in his work, that a person might very well live on, marry, be respected and esteemed as husband, father, and captain of the popinjay shooting club, without discovering God in his work, without ever receiving any impression of the infinitude of the ethical, because he managed with an analogy to the speculative confusion of the ethical and the world-historical by managing with custom and tradition in the city where he lived? Just as a mother admonishes her child who is about to attend a party, "Now, mind your manners and watch the other polite children and behave as they do," so he, too, could live on and behave as he saw others behave. He would never do anything first and would never have any opinion unless he first knew that others had it, because "the others" would be his very first. On special occasions he would act like someone who does not know how to eat a course that is served at a banquet; he would reconnoiter until he saw how the others did it etc. Such a person could perhaps know ever so much, perhaps even know the system by rote; he could perhaps live in a Christian country, know how to bow his head every time God's name was mentioned, perhaps also see God in nature if he was in the company of others who saw God; in short, well, he could be a congenial party goer—and yet he would be deceived by the direct relation to truth, to the ethical, to God.

If one were to portray such a person in an imaginary construction, he would be a satire on what it is to be a human being. It is really the God-relationship that makes a human being a human being, but this is what he would lack. Yet no one would hesitate to consider him an actual human being (for the absence of inwardness is not seen directly), although he would be more like a puppet character that very deceptively imitates all the human externalities—would even have children with his wife. At the end of his life, one would have to say that one thing had escaped him: he had not become aware of God. If God could have permitted a direct relationship, he would certainly have become aware. If God had taken the form, for example, of a rare, enormously large green bird, with a red beak, that perched in a tree on the embankment and perhaps even whistled in an unprecedented manner—then our party going man would surely have had his eyes opened; for the first time in his life he would have been able to be the first.

All paganism consists in this, that God is related directly to a human being, as the remarkably striking to the amazed. But the spiritual relationship with God in truth, that is, inwardness, is first conditioned by the actual breakthrough of inward deepening that corresponds to the divine cunning that God has nothing remarkable, nothing at all remarkable, about him—indeed, he is so far from being remarkable that he is invisible, and thus one does not suspect that he is there [er til], although his invisibility is in turn his omnipresence. But an omnipresent being is the very one who is seen everywhere, for example, as a police officer is—how illusive, then, that an omnipresent being is cognizable precisely by his being invisible,* simply and solely by this, because his very visibility would annul his omnipresence. This relation between omnipresence and invisibility is like the relation between mystery and revelation, that the mystery expresses that the revelation is revelation in the stricter sense, that the mystery is the one and only mark by which it can be known, since otherwise a revelation becomes something like a police officer's omnipresence.

If God [Gud] wants to reveal himself in human form and provide a direct relation by taking, for example, the form of a man who is twelve feet tall, then that imaginatively constructed party goer and captain of the popinjay shooting club will surely become aware. But since God is unwilling to deceive, the spiritual relation in truth specifically requires that there be nothing at all remarkable about his form; then the party goer must say: There is nothing to see, not the slightest. If the god [Guden] has

---

*In order to indicate how illusive the rhetorical can be, I shall show here how one could perhaps produce an effect upon a listener rhetorically, even though what was said would be a dialectical retrogression. Suppose a pagan religious orator says that here on earth the god's temple is actually empty, but (and here the rhetorical begins) in heaven, where everything is more perfect, where water is air, and air is ether, there are also temples and shrines for the gods, but the difference is that the gods actually dwell in these temples—that the god actually dwells in the temple is dialectical retrogression, because his not dwelling in the temple is an expression for the spiritual relation to the invisible. But rhetorically it produces the effect.—Incidentally, I had in mind a specific passage by a Greek author, but I shall not quote him.

nothing whatever that is remarkable about him, the party goer is perhaps deceived in not becoming aware at all. But the god is without blame in this, and the actuality of this deception is continually also the possibility of the truth. But if the god has something remarkable about him, he deceives, inasmuch as a human being thus becomes aware of the untruth, and this awareness is also the impossibility of the truth.

In paganism, the direct relation is idolatry; in Christianity, everyone indeed knows that God cannot manifest himself in this way. But this knowledge is not inwardness at all, and in Christianity it can certainly happen with a rote knower that he becomes utterly "without God in the world," which was not the case in paganism, where there was still the untrue relation of idolatry. Idolatry is certainly a dismal substitute, but that the rubric "God" disappears completely is even more mistaken.

Accordingly, not even God relates himself directly to a derived spirit (and this is the wondrousness of creation: not to produce something that is nothing in relation to the Creator, but to produce something that is something and that in the true worship of God can use this something to become by itself nothing before God); even less can one human being relate himself in this way to another *in truth*. Nature, the totality of creation, is God's work, and yet God is not there, but within the individual human being there is a possibility (he is spirit according to his possibility) that in inwardness is awakened to a God-relationship, and then it is possible to see God everywhere. Compared with the spiritual relationship in inwardness, the sensate distinctions of the great, the amazing, the most crying-to-heaven superlatives of a southern nation are a retrogression to idolatry. Is it not as if an author wrote 166 folio volumes and the reader read and read, just as when someone observes and observes nature but does not discover that the meaning of this enormous work lies in the reader himself, because amazement at the many volumes and the five hundred lines to the page, which is similar to amazement at how immense nature is and how innumerable the animal species are, is not understanding.

With regard to the essential truth, a direct relation between spirit and spirit is unthinkable. If such a relation is assumed, it actually means that one party has ceased to be spirit, something that is not borne in mind by many a genius who both assists people *en masse* into the truth and is good-natured enough to think that applause, willingness to listen, signatures, etc. mean accepting the truth. Just as important as the truth, and of the two the even more important one, is the mode in which the truth is accepted, and it is of slight help if one gets millions to accept the truth if by the very mode of their acceptance they are transposed into untruth. And therefore all good-naturedness, all persuasion, all bargaining, all direct attraction with the aid of one's own person in consideration of one's suffering so much for the cause, of one's weeping over humankind, of one's being so enthusiastic, etc.—all such things are a misunderstanding, in relation to the truth a forgery by which, according to one's ability, one helps any number of people to acquire a semblance of truth.

KARL MARX
1818–1883

It is hard to think of a more influential—or more controversial—nineteenth-century thinker than Karl Marx. Not content simply to develop a theory, Marx sought fundamental change in social, economic, and political structures. As he put it, "The philosophers have only *interpreted* the world in various ways; the point is, to *change it*."

Marx was the third of nine children born to Heinrich and Henrietta Marx in the Rhineland town of Trier. His parents were of Jewish ancestry but had converted to Protestant Christianity to protect Heinrich's job as a government lawyer. In 1835, Karl went to the University of Bonn to study law. Hardly the model student, he spent much of his time drinking or writing love letters to his childhood sweetheart and then fiancée, Jenny von Westphalen. At his father's insistence, Marx transferred to the University of Berlin and began to focus on his studies. While there, he abandoned his legal training and began preparing for an academic career as a philosophy professor. He wrote a dissertation contrasting Democritus and Epicurus that was accepted by the University of Jena, and in 1841 Marx received his doctorate in philosophy.

But the leftist politics Marx had adopted while in Berlin made it impossible for him to obtain a university post, so in 1842 he took a position as editor of the *Rheinische Zeitung (Rhenish Gazette)*, a liberal middle-class newspaper in Cologne. Marx was a successful editor—too successful for the government censors who suppressed the paper after an article by Marx on the poverty of the Mosel winemakers. Marx moved to Paris where he became coeditor of the new journal, the *Deutsch-Französische Jahrbücher (German-French Annals)*. With his future seeming secure, Marx finally felt free to marry Jenny in 1843. But the

Jahrbücher closed almost immediately and once again he was unemployed. Fortunately, at about the same time, Marx received a sizable settlement from the shareholders of the *Rheinishe Zeitung,* and he and his new bride were able to live comfortably. Freed from his editing duties, Marx wrote extensively on economic and political matters. He also met the man who was to be his lifelong friend, collaborator, and financial backer: Friedrich Engels (1820–1895). Engels came from a family of wealthy textile industrialists and was, himself, the manager of his family's Manchester, England, branch. Together Marx and Engels produced *The Holy Family* (1845), Marx's first published book, which criticized a number of their fellow leftists.

While pursuing his writing projects, Marx was politically active among German communists living in Paris—activity that led to his expulsion from France in 1845. Living for a time in Brussels, Marx produced *The German Ideology* (1846) and *The Poverty of Philosophy* (1847) while continuing his political involvement. In 1847, he attended the congress of the newly formed Communist League in London. He and Engels were commissioned to produce an easy-to-read pamphlet outlining the league's doctrines. The result was the immensely influential *Manifesto of the Communist Party* (1848).

Following another attempt at editing an opposition newspaper in Cologne—and another expulsion by the government—Marx eventually settled in London. The next two decades were a time of poverty and hardship for the Marx family due as much to financial mismanagement as to lack of income. (Marx reflected often on the irony of his extensive work on capital when he had so little talent for managing it personally.) Marx received some income as a correspondent for the *New York Tribune;* but for the rest of his life, his primary source of income was Engels's gifts. In London, Marx became a fixture in the reading room of the British Museum, where he pored over government records, histories, and the writings of other economists, gathering data to document his thought. There he wrote *Critique of Political Economy* (1859) and began his *magnum opus, Das Kapital (Capital;* 1867). He also continued his political involvement, becoming the leader of the International Working Men's Association. He worked with the International until factional strife, particularly conflict with the anarchist Mikhail Aleksandrovich Bakunin (1814–1876), led Marx to dismantle the organization in 1872.

It wasn't until Marx's final years that he managed to gain some financial stability and to live the life of a bourgeois Victorian gentleman. But these years also brought tragedy and hardship of a different kind. Marx developed boils over his entire body and used creosote, opium, and arsenic, among other remedies, in a futile attempt to effect a cure. His beloved Jenny died in 1881 and his eldest daughter two years later. Shortly thereafter, Marx himself developed bronchitis and also died in 1883.

*   *   *

While a student in Berlin, Marx was influenced by Hegelian philosophy. Hegel had understood *history* as a progressive actualization of the Absolute, but he was somewhat ambiguous about the future. One group of followers, the Old Hegelians, argued in a reactionary way that this progressive actualization was now complete and that Christianity was the Absolute Religion, Hegelianism the Absolute Philosophy, and Prussia the Absolute State. Another group, the Young

Hegelians, led by Bruno Bauer (1809–1882), argued that the dialectical movement of history was continuing. To move to the next stage in this historical dialectic, they sought to expose the contradictions of the existing order.

Although Marx accepted Hegel's dialectical understanding of history, he became convinced that Hegel's philosophy (and that of the Young Hegelians) devalued humanity by its emphasis on the Absolute. Marx then drew on the materialism espoused in Ludwig Feuerbach's work, *The Essence of Christianity* (1841). Feuerbach had argued that Hegel's philosophy was nothing more than rationalized religion, asserting that humans were merely the "self-alienation," or loss of identity, of God. Instead, Feuerbach advocated an atheistic materialism that claimed that "God" was simply the self-alienation of humans. That is, all the divine characteristics were nothing more than idealized human characteristics objectified and projected onto an imagined deity.

Marx used Feuerbach's work to critique Hegel. Marx expressed appreciation for Hegel's dialectical understanding of the "self-creation of man as a process" and points out that Hegel conceives of "objective man" as the result of "his own labor." But Hegel understood labor as being "abstract mental" labor, not the natural, embodied interaction with real objects that concerned Marx. On the other hand, although he appreciated Feuerbach's materialism, Marx held that his predecessor did not tie his criticism to historical development. "As far as Feuerbach is a materialist he does not deal with history, and as far as he considers history he is not a materialist," wrote Marx. Synthesizing the historical development of Hegel and the materialism of Feuerbach, Marx's theory has often been called "dialectical materialism" (though Marx himself did not use that term).

Marx also adapted Feuerbach's concept of alienation, applying it to political, social, and economic interactions. In the section on "Alienated Labor" from the *Economic and Philosophical Manuscripts of 1844,* given here, Marx explains how a capitalist system results in alienation for the worker. The worker's labor is alien to the worker because it belongs to the capitalist. In return for the worker's labor, the capitalist pays the worker a wage—a wage that competition keeps at a subsistence level. Yet the worker must continue to labor in order to survive. This means the worker is now self-alienated since the life activity, the essence of the worker, becomes "only a means for his existence." But alienation is not limited to individuals. Because they have different interests, workers, as an economic class, are alienated from those who own the means of production. This, in turn, gives rise to class struggle because the interests of one class are always in opposition to the interests of other economic classes. Only by having communal ownership of the means of production, that is, by abolishing private property, will such conflict be overcome. Only then will those who work control both the process and the product of their labor. The selection from *Manifesto of the Communist Party,* given here in the Samuel Moore translation, calls on the workers of the world to bring about such a revolutionary change in the modes of production.

Throughout his analysis of the human situation, Marx continually returned to these material forces of production, distribution, exchange, and consumption. In the Preface to *A Contribution to the Critique of Political Economy,* reprinted here in the N.I. Stone translation, Marx explains how the real foundations of society are the productive forces and the relations of production. His brief overview of these forces serves as a helpful introduction to his method and program.

*   *   *

Isaiah Berlin's *Karl Marx: His Life and Environment* (1963; reprinted Oxford: Oxford University Press, 1996) is still considered by many to be the best general introduction to Marx's life and philosophy, whereas more recent studies include David McLellan, *Karl Marx: His Life and Thought* (New York: Harper & Row, 1973); David McLellan, *Karl Marx* (New York: Penguin Books, 1975); Peter Singer, *Marx* (Oxford: Oxford University Press, 1980); Allen W. Wood, *Karl Marx* (London: Routledge & Kegan Paul, 1981); and Jon Elster, *An Introduction to Karl Marx* (Cambridge: Cambridge University Press, 1986). The following are samples of the many more recent studies in particular areas of Marx's thought: Nicholas Lash, *A Matter of Hope: A Theologian's Reflections on the Thought of Karl Marx* (Notre Dame, IN: University of Notre Dame Press, 1982); Nancy Sue Love, *Marx, Nietzsche, and Modernity* (New York: Columbia University Press, 1986); Harold Mah, *The End of Philosophy, The Origin of "Ideology": Karl Marx and the Crisis of the Young Hegelians* (Berkeley: University of California Press, 1987); and Robert Meister, *Political Identity: Thinking Through Marx* (Cambridge, MA: Basil Blackwell, 1990). For an interesting criticism of Marx by one of his contemporaries, see M.A. Bakunin, *Bakunin on Anarchy: Selected Works by the Activist-Founder of World Anarchism,* edited and translated by Sam Dolgoff (New York: Knopf, 1972). For collections of critical essays, see Tom Bottomore, ed., *Modern Interpretations of Marx* (Oxford: Basil Blackwell, 1981); David McLellan, ed., *Marx: The First Hundred Years* (New York: St. Martin's Press, 1983); Terence Ball and James Farr, eds., *After Marx* (Cambridge: Cambridge University Press, 1984); and Terrell Carver, ed., *The Cambridge Companion to Marx* (Cambridge: Cambridge University Press, 1991).

ECONOMIC AND PHILOSOPHICAL MANUSCRIPTS OF 1844 (in part)

ALIENATED LABOUR

[XXII] We have begun from the presuppositions of political economy. We have accepted its terminology and its laws. We presupposed private property; the separation of labour, capital and land, as also of wages, profit and rent; the division of labour; competition; the concept of exchange value, etc. From political economy itself, in its own words, we have shown that the worker sinks to the level of a commodity, and to a most miserable commodity; that the misery of the worker increases with the power and volume of his production; that the necessary result of competition is the accumulation of capital in a few hands, and thus a restoration of monopoly in a more terrible form; and

Economic and Philosophical Manuscripts (1844), from *Karl Marx: Early Writings,* edited and translated by T.B. Bottomore (New York: McGraw-Hill, 1964). Reprinted by permission of McGraw-Hill.

finally that the distinction between capitalist and landlord, and between agricultural labourer and industrial worker, must disappear, and the whole of society divide into the two classes of property *owners* and *propertyless* workers.

Political economy begins with the fact of private property; it does not explain it. It conceives the *material* process of private property, as this occurs in reality, in general and abstract formulas which then serve it as laws. It does not *comprehend* these laws; that is, it does not show how they arise out of the nature of private property. Political economy provides no explanation of the basis for the distinction of labour from capital, of capital from land. When, for example, the relation of wages to profits is defined, this is explained in terms of the interests of capitalists; in other words, what should be explained is assumed. Similarly, competition is referred to at every point and is explained in terms of external conditions. Political economy tells us nothing about the extent to which these external and apparently accidental conditions are simply the expression of a necessary development. We have seen how exchange itself seems an accidental fact. The only motive forces which political economy recognizes are *avarice* and the *war between the avaricious, competition.*

Just because political economy fails to understand the interconnexions within this movement it was possible to oppose the doctrine of competition to that of monopoly, the doctrine of freedom of the crafts to that of the guilds, the doctrine of the division of landed property to that of the great estates; for competition, freedom of crafts, and the division of landed property were conceived only as accidental consequences brought about by will and force, rather than as necessary, inevitable and natural consequences of monopoly, the guild system and feudal property.

Thus we have now to grasp the real connexion between this whole system of alienation—private property, acquisitiveness, the separation of labour, capital and land, exchange and competition, value and the devaluation of man, monopoly and competition—and the system of *money.*

Let us not begin our explanation, as does the economist, from a legendary primordial condition. Such a primordial condition does not explain anything; it merely removes the question into a grey and nebulous distance. It asserts as a fact or event what it should deduce, namely, the necessary relation between two things; for example, between the division of labour and exchange. In the same way theology explains the origin of evil by the fall of man; that is, it asserts as a historical fact what it should explain.

We shall begin from a *contemporary* economic fact. The worker becomes poorer the more wealth he produces and the more his production increases in power and extent. The worker becomes an ever cheaper commodity the more goods he creates. The *devaluation* of the human world increases in direct relation with the *increase in value* of the world of things. Labour does not only create goods; it also produces itself and the worker as a *commodity*, and indeed in the same proportion as it produces goods.

This fact simply implies that the object produced by labour, its product, now stands opposed to it as an *alien being*, as a *power independent* of the producer. The product of labour is labour which has been embodied in an object and turned into a physical thing; this product is an *objectification* of labour. The performance of work is at the same time its objectification. The performance of work appears in the sphere of political economy as a *vitiation* of the worker, objectification as a *loss* and as *servitude to the object,* and appropriation as *alienation.*

So much does the performance of work appear as vitiation that the worker is vitiated to the point of starvation. So much does objectification appear as loss of the object that the worker is deprived of the most essential things not only of life but also of work. Labour itself becomes an object which he can acquire only by the greatest effort and with unpredictable interruptions. So much does the appropriation of the object appear as alienation that the more objects the worker produces the fewer he can possess and the more he falls under the domination of his product, of capital.

All these consequences follow from the fact that the worker is related to the *product of his labour* as to an *alien* object. For it is clear on this presupposition that the more the worker expends himself in work the more powerful becomes the world of objects which he creates in face of himself, the poorer he becomes in his inner life, and the less he belongs to himself. It is just the same as in religion. The more of himself man attributes to God the less he has left in himself. The worker puts his life into the object, and his life then belongs no longer to himself but to the object. The greater his activity, therefore, the less he possesses. What is embodied in the product of his labour is no longer his own. The greater this product is, therefore, the more he is diminished. The *alienation* of the worker in his product means not only that his labour becomes an object, assumes an *external* existence, but that it exists independently, *outside himself,* and alien to him, and that it stands opposed to him as an autonomous power. The life which he has given to the object sets itself against him as an alien and hostile force.

[XXIII] Let us now examine more closely the phenomenon of *objectification;* the worker's production and the *alienation* and *loss* of the object it produces, which is involved in it. The worker can create nothing without *nature,* without the *sensuous external world.* The latter is the material in which his labour is realized, in which it is active, out of which and through which it produces things.

But just as nature affords the *means of existence* of labour, in the sense that labour cannot *live* without objects upon which it can be exercised, so also it provides the *means of existence* in a narrower sense; namely the means of physical existence for the *worker* himself. Thus, the more the worker *appropriates* the external world of sensuous nature by his labour the more he deprives himself of *means of existence,* in two respects: first, that the sensuous external world becomes progressively less an object belonging to his labour or a means of existence of his labour, and secondly, that it becomes progressively less a means of existence in the direct sense, a means for the physical subsistence of the worker.

In both respects, therefore, the worker becomes a slave of the object; first, in that he receives an *object of work,* i.e. receives *work,* and secondly, in that he receives *means of subsistence.* Thus the object enables him to exist, first as a worker and secondly, as a *physical subject.* The culmination of this enslavement is that he can only maintain himself as a *physical subject* so far as he is a *worker,* and that it is only as a *physical subject* that he is a worker.

(The alienation of the worker in his object is expressed as follows in the laws of political economy: the more the worker produces the less he has to consume; the more value he creates the more worthless he becomes; the more refined his product the more crude and misshapen the worker; the more civilized the product the more barbarous the worker; the more powerful the work the more feeble the worker; the more the work manifests intelligence the more the worker declines in intelligence and becomes a slave of nature.)

Political economy conceals the alienation in the nature of labour in so far as it does not examine the direct relationship between the worker (work) and production. Labour certainly produces marvels for the rich but it produces privation for the worker. It produces palaces, but hovels for the worker. It produces beauty, but deformity for the worker. It replaces labour by machinery, but it casts some of the workers back into a barbarous kind of work and turns the others into machines. It produces intelligence, but also stupidity and cretinism for the workers.

The direct relationship of labour to its products is the relationship of the worker to the objects of his production. The relationship of property owners to the objects of production and to production itself is merely a *consequence* of this first relationship and confirms it. We shall consider this second aspect later.

Thus, when we ask what is the important relationship of labour, we are concerned with the relationship of the *worker* to production.

So far we have considered the alienation of the worker only from one aspect; namely, *his relationship with the products of his labour.* However, alienation appears not merely in the result but also in the *process* of *production,* within *productive activity* itself. How could the worker stand in an alien relationship to the product of his activity if he did not alienate himself in the act of production itself? The product is indeed only the *résumé* of activity, of production. Consequently, if the product of labour is alienation, production itself must be active alienation—the alienation of activity and the activity of alienation. The alienation of the object of labour merely summarizes the alienation in the work activity itself.

What constitutes the alienation of labour? First, that the work is *external* to the worker, that it is not part of his nature; and that, consequently, he does not fulfil himself in his work but denies himself, has a feeling of misery rather than well-being, does not develop freely his mental and physical energies but is physically exhausted and mentally debased. The worker, therefore, feels himself at home only during his leisure time, whereas at work he feels homeless. His work is not voluntary but imposed, *forced labour.* It is not the satisfaction of a need, but only a *means* for satisfying other needs. Its alien character is clearly shown by the fact that as soon as there is no physical or other compulsion it is avoided like the plague. External labour, labour in which man alienates himself, is a labour of self-sacrifice, of mortification. Finally, the external character of work for the worker is shown by the fact that it is not his own work but work for someone else, that in work he does not belong to himself but to another person.

Just as in religion the spontaneous activity of human fantasy, of the human brain and heart, reacts independently as an alien activity of gods or devils upon the individual, so the activity of the worker is not his own spontaneous activity. It is another's activity and a loss of his own spontaneity.

We arrive at the result that man (the worker) feels himself to be freely active only in his animal functions—eating, drinking and procreating, or at most also in his dwelling and in personal adornment—while in his human functions he is reduced to an animal. The animal becomes human and the human becomes animal.

Eating, drinking and procreating are of course also genuine human functions. But abstractly considered, apart from the environment of human activities, and turned into final and sole ends, they are animal functions.

We have now considered the act of alienation of practical human activity, labour, from two aspects: (1) the relationship of the worker to the *product of labour* as an alien object which dominates him. This relationship is at the same time the relationship to the sensuous external world, to natural objects, as an alien and hostile world; (2) the relationship of labour to the *act of production* within *labour.* This is the relationship of the worker to his own activity as something alien and not belonging to him, activity as suffering (passivity), strength as powerlessness, creation as emasculation, the *personal* physical and mental energy of the worker, his personal life (for what is life but activity?), as an activity which is directed against himself, independent of him and not belonging to him. This is *self-alienation* as against the above mentioned alienation of the *thing*.

[XXIV] We have now to infer a third characteristic of *alienated labour* from the two we have considered.

Man is a species-being not only in the sense that he makes the community (his own as well as those of other things) his object both practically and theoretically, but also (and this is simply another expression for the same thing) in the sense that he treats himself as the present, living species, as a *universal* and consequently free being.

Species-life, for man as for animals, has its physical basis in the fact that man (like animals) lives from inorganic nature, and since man is more universal than an animal so the range of inorganic nature from which he lives is more universal. Plants, animals, minerals, air, light, etc. constitute, from the theoretical aspect, a part of human consciousness as objects of natural science and art; they are man's spiritual inorganic nature, his intellectual means of life, which he must first prepare for enjoyment and perpetuation. So also, from the practical aspect, they form a part of human life and activity. In practice man lives only from these natural products, whether in the form of food, heating, clothing, housing, etc. The universality of man appears in practice in the universality which makes the whole of nature into his inorganic body: (1) as a direct means of life; and equally (2) as the material object and instrument of his life activity. Nature is the inorganic body of man; that is to say nature, excluding the human body itself. To say that man *lives* from nature means that nature is his *body* with which he must remain in a continuous interchange in order not to die. The statement that the physical and mental life of man, and nature, are interdependent means simply that nature is interdependent with itself, for man is a part of nature.

Since alienated labour: (1) alienates nature from man; and (2) alienates man from himself, from his own active function, his life activity; so it alienates him from the species. It makes *species-life* into a means of individual life. In the first place it alienates species-life and individual life, and secondly, it turns the latter, as an abstraction, into the purpose of the former, also in its abstract and alienated form.

For labour, *life activity, productive life,* now appear to man only as *means* for the satisfaction of a need, the need to maintain his physical existence. Productive life is, however, species-life. It is life creating life. In the type of life activity resides the whole character of a species, its species character; and free, conscious activity is the species character of human beings. Life itself appears only as a *means of life.*

The animal is one with its life activity. It does not distinguish the activity from itself. It is *its activity.* But man makes his life activity itself an object of his will and consciousness. He has a conscious life activity. It is not a determination with which he is completely identified. Conscious life activity distinguishes man from the life activity of animals. Only for this reason is he a species-being. Or rather, he is only a self-conscious being, i.e. his own life is an object for him, because he is a species-being. Only for this reason is his activity free activity. Alienated labour reverses the relationship, in that man because he is a self conscious being makes his life activity, his *being,* only a means for his *existence.*

The practical construction of an *objective world,* the *manipulation* of inorganic nature, is the confirmation of man as a conscious species-being, i.e. a being who treats the species as his own being or himself as a species-being. Of course, animals also produce. They construct nests, dwellings, as in the case of bees, beavers, ants, etc. But they only produce what is strictly necessary for themselves or their young. They produce only in a single direction, while man produces universally. They produce only under the compulsion of direct physical needs, while man produces when he is free from physical need and only truly produces in freedom from such need. Animals produce only themselves, while man reproduces the whole of nature. The products of animal production belong directly to their physical bodies, while man is free in face of his product. Animals construct only in accordance with the standards and needs of the species to which they belong, while man knows how to produce in accordance with the standards of every species and knows how to apply the appropriate standard to the object. Thus man constructs also in accordance with the laws of beauty.

It is just in his work upon the objective world that man really proves himself as a *species-being*. This production is his active species-life. By means of it nature appears as his work and his reality. The object of labour is, therefore, the *objectification of man's species-life;* for he no longer reproduces himself merely intellectually, as in consciousness, but actively and in a real sense, and he sees his own reflection in a world which he has constructed. While, therefore, alienated labour takes away the object of production from man, it also takes away his *species-life,* his real objectivity as a species being, and changes his advantage over animals into a disadvantage in so far as his inorganic body, nature, is taken from him.

Just as alienated labour transforms free and self-directed activity into a means, so it transforms the species-life of man into a means of physical existence.

Consciousness, which man has from his species, is transformed through alienation so that species-life becomes only a means for him. (3) Thus alienated labour turns the *species life of man,* and also nature as his mental species-property, into an *alien* being and into a *means* for his *individual existence.* It alienates from man his own body, external nature, his mental life and his *human* life. (4) A direct consequence of the alienation of man from the product of his labour, from his life activity and from his species-life, is that *man* is *alienated* from other *men.* When man confronts himself he also confronts *other* men. What is true of man's relationship to his work, to the product of his work and to himself, is also true of his relationship to other men, to their labour and to the objects of their labour.

In general, the statement that man is alienated from his species-life means that each man is alienated from others, and that each of the others is likewise alienated from human life.

Human alienation, and above all the relation of man to himself, is first realized and expressed in the relationship between each man and other men. Thus in the relationship of alienated labour every man regards other men according to the standards and relationships in which he finds himself placed as a worker.

[XXV] We began with an economic fact, the alienation of the worker and his production. We have expressed this fact in conceptual terms as *alienated labour,* and in analysing the concept we have merely analysed an economic fact.

Let us now examine further how this concept of alienated labour must express and reveal itself in reality. If the product of labour is alien to me and confronts me as an alien power, to whom does it belong? If my own activity does not belong to me but is an alien, forced activity, to whom does it belong? To a being *other* than myself. And who is this being? The *gods?* It is apparent in the earliest stages of advanced production, e.g. temple building, etc. in Egypt, India, Mexico, and in the service rendered to gods, that the product belonged to the gods. But the gods alone were never the lords of labour. And no more was *nature.* What a contradiction it would be if the more man subjugates nature by his labour, and the more the marvels of the gods are rendered superfluous by the marvels of industry, the more he should abstain from his joy in producing and his enjoyment of the product for love of these powers.

The *alien* being to whom labour and the product of labour belong, to whose service labour is devoted, and to whose enjoyment the product of labour goes, can only be *man* himself. If the product of labour does not belong to the worker, but confronts him as an alien power, this can only be because it belongs to *a man other than the worker.* If his activity is a torment to him it must be a source of enjoyment and pleasure to another. Not the gods, nor nature, but only man himself can be this alien power over men.

Consider the earlier statement that the relation of man to himself is first *realized, objectified,* through his relation to other men. If he is related to the product of his labour, his objectified labour, as to an *alien,* hostile, powerful and independent object, he is related in such a way that another alien, hostile, powerful and independent man is the lord of this object. If he is related to his own activity as to unfree activity, then he is related to it as activity in the service, and under the domination, coercion and yoke, of another man.

Every self-alienation of man, from himself and from nature, appears in the relation which he postulates between other men and himself and nature. Thus religious self-alienation is necessarily exemplified in the relation between laity and priest, or, since it is here a question of the spiritual world, between the laity and a mediator. In the real world of practice this self-alienation can only be expressed in the real, practical relation of man to his fellow men. The medium through which alienation occurs is itself a *practical* one. Through alienated labour, therefore, man not only produces his relation to the object and to the process of production as to alien and hostile men; he also produces the relation of other men to his production and his product, and the relation between himself and other men. Just as he creates his own production as a vitiation, a punishment, and his own product as a loss, as a product which does not belong to him, so he creates the domination of the non-producer over production and its product. As he alienates his own activity, so he bestows upon the stranger an activity which is not his own.

We have so far considered this relation only from the side of the worker, and later on we shall consider it also from the side of the non-worker.

Thus, through alienated labour the worker creates the relation of another man, who does not work and is outside the work process, to this labour. The relation of the worker to work also produces the relation of the capitalist (or whatever one likes to call the lord of labour) to work. *Private property* is, therefore, the product, the necessary result, of *alienated labour,* of the external relation of the worker to nature and to himself.

Private property is thus derived from the analysis of the concept of *alienated labour;* that is, alienated man, alienated labour, alienated life, and estranged man.

We have, of course, derived the concept of *alienated labour (alienated life)* from political economy, from an analysis of the *movement of private property.* But the analysis of this concept shows that although private property appears to be the basis and cause of alienated labour, it is rather a consequence of the latter, just as the gods are *fundamentally* not the cause but the product of confusions of human reason. At a later stage, however, there is a reciprocal influence.

Only in the final stage of the development of private property is its secret revealed, namely, that it is on one hand the *product* of alienated labour, and on the other hand the *means* by which labour is alienated, *the realization of this alienation.*

This elucidation throws light upon several unresolved controversies—

1. Political economy begins with labour as the real soul of production and then goes on to attribute nothing to labour and everything to private property. Proudhon, faced by this contradiction, has decided in favour of labour against private property.

We perceive, however, that this apparent contradiction is the contradiction of *alienated labour* with itself and that political economy has merely formulated the laws of alienated labour.

We also observe, therefore, that *wages* and *private property* are identical, for wages, like the product or object of labour, labour itself remunerated, are only a necessary consequence of the alienation of labour. In the wage system labour appears not as an end in itself but as the servant of wages. We shall develop this point later on and here only bring out some of the [XXVI] consequences.

An enforced *increase in wages* (disregarding the other difficulties, and especially that such an anomaly could only be maintained by force) would be nothing more than a *better remuneration of slaves,* and would not restore, either to the worker or to the work, their human significance and worth.

Even the *equality of incomes* which Proudhon demands would only change the relation of the present-day worker to his work into a relation of all men to work. Society would then be conceived as an abstract capitalist.

2. From the relation of alienated labour to private property it also follows that the emancipation of society from private property, from servitude, takes the political form of the *emancipation of the workers;* not in the sense that only the latter's emancipation is involved, but because this emancipation includes the emancipation of humanity as a whole. For all human servitude is involved in the relation of the worker to production, and all the types of servitude are only modifications or consequences of this relation.

As we have discovered the concept of *private property* by an *analysis* of the concept of *alienated labour,* so with the aid of these two factors we can evolve all the *categories* of political economy, and in every category, e.g. trade, competition, capital, money, we shall discover only a particular and developed expression of these fundamental elements.

However, before considering this structure let us attempt to solve two problems.

1. To determine the general nature of *private property* as it has resulted from alienated labour, in its relation to *genuine human and social property.*

2. We have taken as a fact and analysed the *alienation of labour.* How does it happen, we may ask, that *man alienates his labour?* How is this alienation founded in the nature of human development? We have already done much to solve the problem in so far as we have *transformed* the question concerning the *origin of private property* into a question about the relation between *alienated labour* and the process of development of mankind. For in speaking of private property one believes oneself to be dealing with something external to mankind. But in speaking of labour one deals directly with mankind itself. This new formulation of the problem already contains its solution.

ad (1) *The general nature of private property and its relation to genuine human property.*

We have resolved alienated labour into two parts, which mutually determine each other, or rather, which constitute two different expressions of one and the same relation. *Appropriation* appears as *alienation* and *alienation* as *appropriation,* alienation as genuine acceptance in the community.

We have considered one aspect, *alienated* labour, in its bearing upon the *worker* himself, i.e. *the relation of alienated labour to itself.* And we have found as the necessary consequence of this relation the *property relation* of the *non-worker* to the *worker* and to labour. *Private property* as the material, summarized expression of alienated labour includes both relations; *the relation of the worker to labour, to the product of his labour and to the non-worker,* and the relation of the *non-worker to the worker and to the product of the latter's labour.*

We have already seen that in relation to the worker, who *appropriates* nature by his labour, appropriation appears as alienation, self-activity as activity for another and of another, living as the sacrifice of life, and production of the object as loss of the object to an alien power, an alien man. Let us now consider the relation of this *alien* man to the worker, to labour, and to the object of labour.

It should be noted first that everything which appears to the worker as an *activity of alienation,* appears to the non-worker as a *condition of alienation.* Secondly, the *real, practical* attitude (as a state of mind) of the worker in production and to the product appears to the non-worker who confronts him as a *theoretical* attitude.

[XXVII] Thirdly, the non-worker does everything against the worker which the latter does against himself, but he does not do against himself what he does against the worker.

Let us examine these three relationships more closely.*

MANIFESTO OF THE COMMUNIST PARTY (in part)

A spectre is haunting Europe—the spectre of Communism. All the powers of old Europe have entered into a holy alliance to exorcise this spectre: Pope and Czar, Metternich and Guizot, French Radicals and German police spies.

Where is the party in opposition that has not been decried as communistic by its opponents in power? Where the opposition that has not hurled back the branding reproach of Communism against the more advanced opposition parties, as well as against its reactionary adversaries?

Two things result from this fact:

I. Communism is already acknowledged by all European powers to be itself a power.

II. It is high time that Communists should openly, in the face of the whole world, publish their views, their aims, their tendencies, and meet this nursery tale of the spectre of Communism with a manifesto of the party itself.

To this end, Communists of various nationalities have assembled in London and sketched the following manifesto, to be published in the English, French, German, Italian, Flemish, and Danish languages.

*[The manuscript breaks off unfinished at this point.]

CHAPTER I: BOURGEOIS AND PROLETARIANS*

The History of all hitherto existing society** is the history of class struggles.

Freeman and slave, patrician and plebeian, lord and serf, guild-master*** and journeyman, in a word, oppressor and oppressed stood in constant opposition to one another, carried on an uninterrupted, now hidden, now open fight, a fight that each time ended either in a revolutionary reconstitution of society at large, or in the common ruin of the contending classes.

In the earlier epochs of history we find almost everywhere a complicated arrangement of society into various orders, a manifold gradation of social rank. In ancient Rome we have patricians, knights, plebeians, slaves; in the Middle Ages, feudal lords, vassals, guild-masters, journeymen, apprentices, serfs; in almost all of these classes, again, subordinate gradations.

The modern bourgeois society that has sprouted from the ruins of feudal society has not done away with class antagonisms. It has but established new classes, new conditions of oppression, new forms of struggle in place of the old ones.

Our epoch, the epoch of the bourgeoisie, possesses, however, this distinctive feature: it has simplified the class antagonisms. Society as a whole is more and more splitting up into two great hostile camps, into two great classes directly facing each other—bourgeoisie and proletariat.

From the serfs of the Middle Ages sprang the chartered burghers of the earliest towns. From these burgesses the first elements of the bourgeoisie were developed.

The discovery of America, the rounding of the Cape, opened up fresh ground for the rising bourgeoisie. The East Indian and Chinese markets, the colonization of America, trade with the colonies, the increase in the means of exchange and in commodities generally, gave to commerce, to navigation, to industry, an impulse never before known, and thereby, to the revolutionary element in the tottering feudal society, a rapid development.

The feudal system of industry, in which industrial production was monopolized by closed guilds, now no longer sufficed for the growing wants of the new markets. The manufacturing system took its place. The guild-masters were pushed aside by the manufacturing middle class; division of labor between the different corporate guilds vanished in the face of division of labor in each single workshop.

Meantime the markets kept ever growing, the demand ever rising. Even manufacture no longer sufficed. Thereupon, steam and machinery revolutionized industrial

---

*By *bourgeoisie* is meant the class of modern capitalists, owners of the means of social production, and employers of wage labor; by *proletariat,* the class of modern wage laborers who, having no means of production of their own, are reduced to selling their labor power in order to live.

**That is, all *written* history. In 1837, the pre-history of society, the social organization existing previous to recorded history, was all but unknown. Since then Haxthausen discovered common ownership of land in Russia; Maurer proved it to be the social foundation from which all Teutonic races started in history, and, by and by, village communities were found to be, or to have been, the primitive form of society everywhere from India to Ireland. The inner organization of this primitive communistic society was laid bare, in its typical form, by Morgan's crowning discovery of the true nature of the *gens* and its relation to the *tribe.* With the dissolution of these primeval communities society begins to be differentiated into separate and finally antagonistic classes. I have attempted to retrace this process of dissolution in *The Origin of the Family, Private Property and the State.*

***[Guild-master, that is, a full member of a guild, a master within, not a head of a guild.]

production. The place of manufacture was taken by the giant, modern industry, the place of the industrial middle class, by industrial millionaires—the leaders of whole industrial armies, the modern bourgeois.

Modern industry has established the world market, for which the discovery of America paved the way. This market has given an immense development to commerce, to navigation, to communication by land. This development has, in its turn, reacted on the extension of industry; and in proportion as industry, commerce, navigation, railways extended, in the same proportion the bourgeoisie developed, increased its capital, and pushed into the background every class handed down from the Middle Ages.

We see, therefore, how the modern bourgeoisie is itself the product of a long course of development, of a series of revolutions in the modes of production and of exchange.

Each step in the development of the bourgeoisie was accompanied by a corresponding political advance of that class. An oppressed class under the sway of the feudal nobility, it became an armed and self-governing association in the medieval commune:* here independent urban republic (as in Italy and Germany); there, taxable "third estate" of the monarchy (as in France); afterwards, in the period of manufacture proper, serving either the semi-feudal or the absolute monarchy as a counterpoise against the nobility, and, in fact, cornerstone of the great monarchies in general. The bourgeoisie has at last, since the establishment of modern industry and of the world market, conquered for itself, in the modern representative state, exclusive political sway. The executive of the modern state is but a committee for managing the common affairs of the whole bourgeoisie.

The bourgeoisie has played a most revolutionary role in history.

The bourgeoisie, wherever it has got the upper hand, has put an end to all feudal, patriarchal, idyllic relations. It has pitilessly torn asunder the motley feudal ties that bound man to his "natural superiors," and has left no other bond between man and man than naked self-interest, than callous "cash payment." It has drowned the most heavenly ecstasies of religious fervor, of chivalrous enthusiasm, of philistine sentimentalism, in the icy water of egotistical calculation. It has resolved personal worth into exchange value, and in place of the numberless indefeasible chartered freedoms has set up that single, unconscionable freedom—Free Trade. In one word, for exploitation, veiled by religious and political illusions, it has substituted naked, shameless, direct, brutal exploitation.

The bourgeoisie has stripped of its halo every occupation hitherto honored and looked up to with reverent awe. It has converted the physician, the lawyer, the priest, the poet, the man of science, into its paid wage laborers.

The bourgeoisie has torn away from the family its sentimental veil, and has reduced the family relation to a mere money relation.

The bourgeoisie has disclosed how it came to pass that the brutal display of vigor in the Middle Ages which reactionaries so much admire found its fitting complement in the most slothful indolence. It has been the first to show what man's activity can bring about. It has accomplished wonders far surpassing Egyptian pyramids, Roman

---

*"Commune" was the name taken in France by the nascent towns even before they had conquered from their feudal lords and masters local self-government and political rights as the "Third Estate." Generally speaking, for the economic development of the bourgeoisie, England is here taken as the typical country; for its political development, France.

aqueducts, and Gothic cathedrals; it has conducted expeditions that put in the shade all former migrations of nations and crusades.

The bourgeoisie cannot exist without constantly revolutionizing the instruments of production, and thereby the relations of production, and with them the whole relations of society. Conservation of the old modes of production in unaltered form was, on the contrary, the first condition of existence for all earlier industrial classes. Constant revolutionizing of production, uninterrupted disturbance of all social conditions, everlasting uncertainty and agitation distinguish the bourgeois epoch from all earlier ones. All fixed, fast-frozen relations with their train of ancient and venerable prejudices and opinions are swept away; all new-formed ones become antiquated before they can ossify. All that is solid melts in air, all that is holy is profaned, and man is at last compelled to face with sober senses his real conditions of life and his relations with his kind.

The need of a constantly expanding market for its products chases the bourgeoisie over the whole surface of the globe. It must nestle everywhere, settle everywhere, establish connections everywhere.

The bourgeoisie has through its exploitation of the world market given a cosmopolitan character to production and consumption in every country. To the great chagrin of reactionaries it has drawn from under the feet of industry the national ground on which it stood. All old-established national industries have been destroyed or are daily being destroyed. They are dislodged by new industries whose introduction becomes a life and death question for all civilized nations; by industries that no longer work up indigenous raw material, but raw material drawn from the remotest zones; industries whose products are consumed, not only at home, but in every quarter of the globe. In place of the old wants, satisfied by the production of the country, we find new wants, requiring for their satisfaction the products of distant lands and climes. In place of the old local and national seclusion and self-sufficiency we have intercourse in every direction, universal inter-dependence of nations. And as in material, so also in intellectual production. The intellectual creations of individual nations become common property. National one-sidedness and narrow-mindedness become more and more impossible, and from the numerous national and local literatures there arises a world literature.

The bourgeoisie, by the rapid improvement of all instruments of production, by the immensely facilitated means of communication, draws all nations, even the most barbarian, into civilization. The cheap prices of its commodities are the heavy artillery with which it batters down all Chinese walls, with which it forces the barbarians' intensely obstinate hatred of foreigners to capitulate. It compels all nations, on pain of extinction, to adopt the bourgeois mode of production; it compels them to introduce what it calls civilization into their midst, i.e., to become bourgeois themselves. In a word, it creates a world after its own image.

The bourgeoisie has subjected the country to the rule of the towns. It has created enormous cities, has greatly increased the urban population as compared with the rural, and has thus rescued a considerable part of the population from the idiocy of rural life. Just as it has made the country dependent on the towns, so it has made barbarian and semi-barbarian countries dependent on the civilized ones, nations of peasants on nations of bourgeois, the East on the West.

More and more the bourgeoisie keeps doing away with the scattered state of the population, of the means of production, and of property. It has agglomerated population, centralized means of production, and has concentrated property in a few hands. The necessary consequence of this was political centralization. Independent, or but loosely connected provinces, with separate interests, laws, governments and systems of taxation, became lumped together into one nation, with one government, one code of laws, one national class interest, one frontier and one customs tariff.

The bourgeoisie during its rule of scarce one hundred years has created more massive and more colossal productive forces than have all preceding generations together. Subjection of nature's forces to man, machinery, application of chemistry to industry and agriculture, steam-navigation, railways, electric telegraphs, clearing of whole continents for cultivation, canalization of rivers, whole populations conjured out of the ground—what earlier century had even a presentiment that such productive forces slumbered in the lap of social labor?

We see, then, that the means of production and of exchange which served as the foundation for the growth of the bourgeoisie were generated in feudal society. At a certain stage in the development of these means of production and of exchange, the conditions under which feudal society produced and exchanged, the feudal organization of agriculture and manufacturing industry, in a word, the feudal relations of property became no longer compatible with the already developed productive forces; they became so many fetters. They had to be burst asunder; they were burst asunder.

Into their place stepped free competition, accompanied by a social and political constitution adapted to it, and by the economic and political sway of the bourgeois class.

A similar movement is going on before our own eyes. Modern bourgeois society with its relations of production, of exchange and of property, a society that has conjured up such gigantic means of production and of exchange, is like the sorcerer who is no longer able to control the powers of the nether world whom he has called up by his spells. For many a decade past the history of industry and commerce is but the history of the revolt of modern productive forces against modern conditions of production, against the property relations that are the conditions for the existence of the bourgeoisie and of its rule. It is enough to mention the commercial crises that by their periodical return put the existence of the entire bourgeois society on trial, each time more threateningly. In these crises a great part not only of the existing products, but also of the previously created productive forces, are periodically destroyed. In these crises there breaks out an epidemic that, in all earlier epochs, would have seemed an absurdity—the epidemic of over-production. Society suddenly finds itself put back into a state of momentary barbarism; it appears as if a famine, a universal war of devastation had cut off the supply of every means of subsistence; industry and commerce seem to be destroyed. And why? Because there is too much civilization, too much means of subsistence, too much industry, too much commerce. The productive forces at the disposal of society no longer tend to further the development of the conditions of bourgeois property; on the contrary, they have become too powerful for these conditions, by which they are fettered, and no sooner do they overcome these fetters than they bring disorder into the whole of bourgeois society, endanger the existence of bourgeois property. The conditions of bourgeois society are too narrow to comprise the wealth created by them. And how does the bourgeoisie get over these crises? On the one hand by enforced destruction of a mass of productive forces; on the other, by the conquest of new markets and by the more thorough exploitation of the old ones. That is to say, by paving the way for more extensive and more destructive crises, and by diminishing the means whereby crises are prevented.

The weapons with which the bourgeoisie felled feudalism to the ground are now turned against the bourgeoisie itself.

But not only has the bourgeoisie forged the weapons that bring death to itself; it has also called into existence the men who are to wield those weapons—the modern working class, the proletarians.

In proportion as the bourgeoisie, i.e., capital, is developed, in the same proportion is the proletariat, the modern working class, developed—a class of laborers, who live only so long as they find work, and who find work only so long as their labor increases capital. These laborers, who must sell themselves piecemeal, are a commodity like every other article of commerce, and are consequently exposed to all the vicissitudes of competition, to all the fluctuations of the market.

Owing to the extensive use of machinery and to division of labor, the work of the proletarians has lost all individual character, and, consequently all charm for the workman. He becomes an appendage of the machine, and it is only the most simple, most monotonous, and most easily acquired knack that is required of him. Hence, the cost of production of a workman is restricted almost entirely to the means of subsistence that he requires for his maintenance and for the propagation of his race. But the price of a commodity, and therefore also of labor, is equal to its cost of production. In proportion, therefore, as the repulsiveness of the work increases, the wage decreases. Nay more, in proportion the burden of toil also increases, whether by prolongation of the working hours, by increase of the work exacted in a given time, or by increased speed of the machinery, etc.

Modern industry has converted the little workshop of the patriarchal master into the great factory of the industrial capitalist. Masses of laborers, crowded into the factory, are organized like soldiers. As privates of the industrial army they are placed under the command of a perfect hierarchy of officers and sergeants. Not only are they slaves of the bourgeois class and of the bourgeois state; they are daily and hourly enslaved by the machine, by the overseer, and, above all, by the individual bourgeois manufacturer himself. The more openly this despotism proclaims gain to be its end and aim, the more petty, the more hateful, and the more embittering it is.

The less the skill and exertion of strength implied in manual labor—in other words, the more modern industry develops—the more is the labor of men superseded by that of women. Differences of age and sex have no longer any distinctive social validity for the working class. All are instruments of labor, more or less expensive to use, according to their age and sex.

No sooner has the laborer received his wages in cash, for the moment escaping exploitation by the manufacturer, than he is set upon by the other portions of the bourgeoisie—the landlord, the shopkeeper, the pawnbroker, etc.

The lower strata of the middle class—the small tradespeople, shopkeepers, and retired tradesmen generally, the handicraftsmen and peasants—all these sink gradually into the proletariat, partly because their diminutive capital does not suffice for the scale on which modern industry is carried on and is swamped in the competition with the large capitalists, partly because their specialized skill is rendered worthless by new methods of production. Thus the proletariat is recruited from all classes of the population.

The proletariat goes through various stages of development. With its birth begins its struggle with the bourgeoisie. At first the contest is carried on by individual laborers, then by the workpeople of a factory, then by the operatives of one trade, in one locality, against the individual bourgeois who directly exploits them. They direct their attacks not against the bourgeois conditions of production, but against the instruments of production themselves; they destroy imported wares that compete with their labor, they smash machinery to pieces, they set factories ablaze, they seek to restore by force the vanished status of the workman of the Middle Ages.

At this stage the laborers still form an incoherent mass scattered over the whole country, and broken up by their mutual competition. If anywhere they unite to form more compact bodies, this is not yet the consequence of their own active union, but of the union of the bourgeoisie, which class, in order to attain its own political ends, is compelled to set the whole proletariat in motion, and is, moreover, still able to do so for a time. At this stage, therefore, the proletarians do not fight their enemies, but the enemies of their enemies, the remnants of absolute monarchy, the landowners, the non-industrial bourgeois, the petty bourgeoisie. Thus the whole historical movement is concentrated in the hands of the bourgeoisie; every victory so obtained is a victory for the bourgeoisie.

But with the development of industry the proletariat not only increases in number; it becomes concentrated in greater masses, its strength grows, and it feels that strength more. The various interests and conditions of life within the ranks of the proletariat are more and more equalized, in proportion as machinery obliterates all distinctions of labor and nearly everywhere reduces wages to the same low level. The growing competition among the bourgeois and the resulting commercial crises make the wages of the workers ever more fluctuating. The unceasing improvement of machinery, ever more rapidly developing, makes their livelihood more and more precarious; the collisions between individual workmen and individual bourgeois take more and more the character of collisions between two classes. Thereupon the workers begin to form combinations (trade unions) against the bourgeoisie; they club together in order to keep up the rate of wages; they found permanent associations in order to make provision beforehand for these occasional revolts. Here and there the contest breaks out into riots.

Now and then the workers are victorious, but only for a time. The real fruit of their battles lies not in the immediate result but in the ever expanding union of the workers. This union is furthered by the improved means of communication which are created by modern industry, and which place the workers of different localities in contact with one another. It was just this contact that was needed to centralize the numerous local struggles, all of the same character, into one national struggle between classes. But every class struggle is a political struggle. And that union, which the burghers of the Middle Ages, with their miserable highways, required centuries to attain, the modern proletarians, thanks to railways achieve in a few years.

This organization of the proletarians into a class, and consequently into a political party, is continually being upset again by the competition between the workers themselves. But it ever rises up again, stronger, firmer, mightier. It compels legislative recognition of particular interests of the workers by taking advantage of the divisions among the bourgeoisie itself. Thus the Ten Hour bill in England was carried.

Altogether, collisions between the classes of the old society further the course of development of the proletariat in many ways. The bourgeoisie finds itself involved in a constant battle—at first with the aristocracy; later on, with those portions of the bourgeoisie itself whose interests have become antagonistic to the progress of industry; at all times with the bourgeoisie of foreign countries. In all these battles it sees itself compelled to appeal to the proletariat, to ask for its help, and thus to drag it into the political arena. The bourgeoisie itself, therefore, supplies the proletariat with its own elements of political and general education; in other words, it furnishes the proletariat with weapons for fighting the bourgeoisie.

Further, as we have already seen, entire sections of the ruling classes are, by the advance of industry, precipitated into the proletariat, or are at least threatened in their conditions of existence. These also supply the proletariat with fresh elements of enlightenment and progress.

Finally, in times when the class struggle nears the decisive hour, the process of dissolution going on within the ruling class, in fact within the whole range of old society, assumes such a violent, glaring character that a small section of the ruling class cuts itself adrift and joins the revolutionary class, the class that holds the future in its hands. Just as, therefore, at an earlier period a section of the nobility went over to the bourgeoisie, so now a portion of the bourgeoisie goes over to the proletariat, and in particular, a portion of the bourgeois ideologists who have raised themselves to the level of comprehending theoretically the historical movement as a whole.

Of all the classes that stand face to face with the bourgeoisie today, the proletariat alone is a really revolutionary class. The other classes decay and finally disappear in the face of modern industry; the proletariat is its special and essential product.

The lower middle class, the small manufacturer, the shopkeeper, the artisan, the peasant—all these fight against the bourgeoisie, to save from extinction their existence as fractions of the middle class. They are, therefore, not revolutionary but conservative. Nay more, they are reactionary, for they try to roll back the wheel of history. If by chance they are revolutionary they are so only in view of their impending transfer into the proletariat; they thus defend not their present but their future interests; they desert their own standpoint to adopt that of the proletariat.

The "dangerous class," the social scum (*Lumpenproletariat*), that passively rotting mass thrown off by the lowest layers of old society, may here and there be swept into the movement by a proletarian revolution; its conditions of life, however, prepare it far more for the part of a bribed tool of reactionary intrigue.

The social conditions of the old society no longer exist for the proletariat. The proletarian is without property; his relation to his wife and children has no longer anything in common with bourgeois family relations; modern industrial labor, modern subjection to capital, the same in England as in France, in America as in Germany, has stripped him of every trace of national character. Law, morality, religion are to him so many bourgeois prejudices, behind which lurk in ambush just as many bourgeois interests.

All the preceding classes that got the upper hand sought to fortify their already acquired status by subjecting society at large to their conditions of appropriation. The proletarians cannot become masters of the productive forces of society except by abolishing their own previous mode of appropriation, and thereby also every other previous mode of appropriation. They have nothing of their own to secure and to fortify; their mission is to destroy all previous securities for, and insurances of, individual property.

All previous historical movements were movements of minorities, or in the interest of minorities. The proletarian movement is the self-conscious, independent movement of the immense majority, in the interest of the immense majority. The proletariat, the lowest stratum of our present society, cannot stir, cannot raise itself up, without the whole superincumbent strata of official society being sprung into the air.

Though not in substance, yet in form, the struggle of the proletariat with the bourgeoisie is at first a national struggle. The proletariat of each country must, of course, first of all settle matters with its own bourgeoisie.

In depicting the most general phases of the development of the proletariat we traced the more or less veiled civil war raging within existing society, up to the point where that war breaks out into open revolution, and where the violent overthrow of the bourgeoisie lays the foundation for the sway of the proletariat.

Hitherto, every form of society has been based, as we have already seen, on the antagonism of oppressing and oppressed classes. But in order to oppress a class certain conditions must be assured to it under which it can, at least, continue its slavish existence. The serf, in the period of serfdom, raised himself to membership in the commune, just as the petty bourgeois, under the yoke of feudal absolutism, managed to develop into a bourgeois. The modern laborer, on the contrary, instead of rising with the progress of industry, sinks deeper and deeper below the conditions of existence of his own class. He becomes a pauper, and pauperism develops more rapidly than population and wealth. And here it becomes evident that the bourgeoisie is unfit any longer to be the ruling class in society and to impose its conditions of existence upon society as an overriding law. It is unfit to rule because it is incompetent to assure an existence to its slave within his slavery, because it cannot help letting him sink into such a state that it has to feed him, instead of being fed by him. Society can no longer live under this bourgeoisie, in other words, its existence is no longer compatible with society.

The essential condition for the existence and sway of the bourgeois class is the formation and augmentation of capital; the condition for capital is wage labor. Wage labor rests exclusively on competition between the laborers. The advance of industry, whose involuntary promoter is the bourgeoisie, replaces the isolation of the laborers, due to competition, by their revolutionary combination, due to association. The development of modern industry, therefore, cuts from under its feet the very foundation on which the bourgeoisie produces and appropriates products. What the bourgeoisie, therefore, produces above all are its own grave-diggers. Its fall and the victory of the proletariat are equally inevitable.

*   *   *

[The specific measures called for by the Communist Party] will, of course, be different in different countries.

Nevertheless, in the most advanced countries the following will be pretty generally applicable:

1. Abolition of property in land and application of all rents of land to public purposes.
2. A heavy progressive or graduated income tax.
3. Abolition of all right of inheritance.
4. Confiscation of the property of all emigrants and rebels.
5. Centralization of credit in the hands of the state by means of a national bank with state capital and an exclusive monopoly.
6. Centralization of the means of communication and transport in the hands of the state.
7. Extension of factories and instruments of production owned by the state; the bringing into cultivation of waste lands, and the improvement of the soil generally in accordance with a common plan.
8. Equal obligation of all to work. Establishment of industrial armies, especially for agriculture.
9. Combination of agriculture with manufacturing industries; gradual abolition of the distinction between town and country by a more equable distribution of the population over the country.
10. Free education for all children in public schools. Abolition of child factory labor in its present form. Combination of education with industrial production, etc.

*   *   *

CHAPTER IV: POSITION OF THE COMMUNISTS IN RELATION TO THE VARIOUS EXISTING OPPOSITION PARTIES

Section II has made clear the relations of the Communists to the existing working class parties, such as the Chartists in England and the Agrarian Reformers in America.

The Communists fight for the attainment of the immediate aims, for the enforcement of the momentary interests of the working class; but in the movement of the present they also represent and take care of the future of that movement. In France the Communists ally themselves with the Social-Democrats* against the conservative and radical bourgeoisie, reserving, however, the right to take up a critical position in regard to phrases and illusions traditionally handed down from the great Revolution.

In Switzerland they support the Radicals without losing sight of the fact that this party consists of antagonistic elements, partly of Democratic Socialists, in the French sense, partly of radical bourgeois.

Capital and Labour, cartoon from *Punch* magazine, 1843. The cartoon shows the suffering of the workers and their families that makes possible the bourgeois capitalists' high life. It was in response to conditions such as this that Marx and Engels wrote in *The Communist Manifesto* (1848), "The proletarians have nothing to lose but their chains. They have a world to win. Workingmen of all countries, unite!" *(Library of Congress)*

*The party then represented in Parliament by Ledru-Rollin, in literature by Louis Blanc, in the daily press by the *Réforme*. The name of Social-Democracy signifies, with these its inventors, a section of the Democratic or Republican Party more or less tinged with Socialism.

In Poland they support the party that insists on an agrarian revolution as the prime condition for national emancipation, that party which fomented the insurrection of Cracow in 1846.

In Germany they fight with the bourgeoisie whenever it acts in a revolutionary way, against the absolute monarchy, the feudal squirearchy, and the petty bourgeoisie.

But they never cease for a single instant to instil into the working class the clearest possible recognition of the hostile antagonism between bourgeoisie and proletariat, in order that the German workers may straightway use, as so many weapons against the bourgeoisie, the social and political conditions that the bourgeoisie must necessarily introduce along with its supremacy, and in order that, after the fall of the reactionary classes in Germany, the fight against the bourgeoisie itself may immediately begin.

The Communists turn their attention chiefly to Germany because that country is on the eve of a bourgeois revolution that is bound to be carried out under more advanced conditions of European civilization and with a much more developed proletariat than what existed in England in the 17th and in France in the 18th century, and because the bourgeois revolution in Germany will be but the prelude to an immediately following proletarian revolution.

In short, the Communists everywhere support every revolutionary movement against the existing social and political order of things.

In all these movements they bring to the front as the leading question in each case the property question, no matter what its degree of development at the time.

Finally, they labor everywhere for the union and agreement of the democratic parties of all countries.

The Communists disdain to conceal their views and aims. They openly declare that their ends can be attained only by the forcible overthrow of all existing social conditions. Let the ruling classes tremble at a Communist revolution. The proletarians have nothing to lose but their chains. They have a world to win.

Workingmen of all countries, unite!

A CONTRIBUTION TO THE CRITIQUE
OF POLITICAL ECONOMY (in part)

Author's Preface

* * *

In the social production which men carry on they enter into definite relations that are indispensable and independent of their will; these relations of production correspond to a definite stage of development of their material powers of production. The sum total of these relations of production constitutes the economic structure of society—the real foundation, on which rise legal and political superstructures and to which correspond definite forms of social consciousness. The mode of production in material life determines the general character of the social, political and spiritual processes of life. It is not the consciousness of men that determines their existence, but, on the contrary, their social existence determines their consciousness. At a certain stage of their development, the material forces of production in society come in conflict with the existing relations of production, or—what is but a legal expression for the same thing—with the property relations within which they had been at work before. From forms of development of the forces of production these relations turn into their fetters. Then comes the period of social revolution. With the change of the economic foundation the entire immense superstructure is more or less rapidly transformed. In considering such transformations the distinction should always be made between the material transformation of the economic conditions of production which can be determined with the precision of natural science, and the legal, political, religious, aesthetic or philosophic—in short ideological forms in which men become conscious of this conflict and fight it out. Just as our opinion of an individual is not based on what he thinks of himself, so can we not judge of such a period of transformation by its own consciousness; on the contrary, this consciousness must rather be explained from the contradictions of material life, from the existing conflict between the social forces of production and the relations of production. No social order ever disappears before all the productive forces, for which there is room in it, have been developed; and new higher relations of production never appear before the material conditions of their existence have matured in the womb of the old society. Therefore, mankind always takes up only such problems as it can solve; since, looking at the matter more closely, we will always find that the problem itself arises only when the material conditions necessary for its solution already exist or are at least in the process of formation. In broad outlines we can designate the Asiatic, the ancient, the feudal, and the modern bourgeois methods of production as so many epochs in the progress of the economic formation of society. The bourgeois relations of production are the last antagonistic form of the social process of production—antagonistic not in the sense of individual antagonism, but of one arising from conditions surrounding the life of individuals in society; at the same time the productive forces developing in the womb of bourgeois society create the material conditions for the solution of that antagonism. This social formation constitutes, therefore, the closing chapter of the prehistoric stage of human society.

FRIEDRICH NIETZSCHE
1844–1900

Friedrich Wilhelm Nietzsche was born in Röcken, Prussia, in 1844. He was named in honor of the Prussian king, Friedrich Wilhelm IV, whose birthday, October 15, he shared. Nietzsche's father, Ludwig Nietzsche, was a Lutheran minister and his mother, Franziska Oehler Nietzsche, was the daughter of a Lutheran minister. When Nietzsche was only five years old, his father died from what was called "softening of the brain," after a year of mental instability. The rest of Nietzsche's childhood was spent in a household of women, including his widowed mother, his sister, his anxiety-prone paternal grandmother, and two maiden aunts.

Following grade school, Nietzsche attended a famous boarding school at Pforta, where he did outstanding work. However, while there, Nietzsche suffered migraine headaches, which continued to afflict him until he experienced a mental breakdown in 1889. The medicine he took to relieve the headaches upset his stomach and left him nauseous. For much of his adult life, he alternated between the extremes of headaches and nausea with only short periods of health in between.

In 1864, he enrolled at the University of Bonn to study theology and classical philology (linguistics), but he left within a year. By this time, he had given up whatever religious faith he had and was no longer interested in theology. He then moved to the University of Leipzig to continue his studies in philology. His professor at Leipzig, Friedrich Ritschl, was so impressed with Nietzsche's work that he published some of his papers and later recommended him for a chair of classical philology at the University of Basel. In 1869, at the unusual age of only twenty-four, Nietzsche was given the chair as an associate professor. He had produced neither a doctoral dissertation nor the additional book normally required of an associate professor, but Leipzig immediately awarded him a doctorate without examination or thesis, and within a year he was promoted to full professor at Basel.

In 1872, Nietzsche published his first book, *The Birth of Tragedy*, which included a laudatory section on Richard Wagner's music. Over the next four years, Nietzsche wrote four meditations (published collectively in English as *Thoughts Out of Season*), the last of which was another tribute to Wagner. During this period, Nietzsche and Wagner were close friends; and Nietzsche often visited Wagner's villa on Lake Lucerne. But by 1878, they had broken relations over Wagner's nationalism and anti-Semitism.

Nietzsche's health began to deteriorate, and he was forced to resign from the university in 1879. Over the next ten years, Nietzsche traveled and devoted all his remaining energy to writing, publishing such books as *The Gay Science* (1882), *Thus Spoke Zarathustra* (1883–1885), *Beyond Good and Evil* (1886), *On the Genealogy of Morality* (1887), and his final denunciation of his former friend, *The Case of Wagner* (1888).

By the end of 1888, Nietzsche showed signs of oncoming madness, and in January 1889 he collapsed in the street in Turin, Italy, while hugging the neck of a horse. For the next eleven years until his death in 1900, he lived in the care of his mother and sister. Works that he had written in 1888, including *The Will to Power, Twilight of the Idols, The Anti-Christ,* and his outrageous autobiography *Ecco Homo* (which includes chapter headings such as "Why I Am So Clever"), were published after distorted editing by his sister. Only in the twentieth century have unedited versions of these works become available.

The cause of Nietzsche's insanity has been vigorously debated. Critics have held that his ideas caused it and claim to have found evidence of insanity in many of his writings. His sister romanticized that he went mad because Germany spurned him. More likely explanations are that he contracted syphilis during a rare sexual escapade while a young man or that he simply inherited a brain disease from his father.

* * *

Nietzsche's style of writing in epigrams, aphorisms, stories, poetry, and essays virtually defies an editor to systematically summarize his thought. Even though Nietzsche never sought to build a system, there are recurring, interwoven themes represented by the selections given here.

In *The Birth of Tragedy,* translated by Francis Golffing, Nietzsche presents a distinction between Apollonian and Dionysian tendencies in art. The Apollonian tendency (named for the Greek god of the sun, Apollo) represents the harmony and restraint exemplified by Greek sculpture and architecture. The Dionysian tendency (named for the Greek god of wine and revelry, Dionysos) represents wild abandonment as exemplified by the drunken sexual frenzies of the Dionysian cult festivals or the music of Beethoven's Ninth Symphony. Greek tragedy arises as a synthesis of Apollonian form and Dionysian urges. But Greek tragedy is in turn superseded by Greek rationalism as exemplified by Socrates: the theoretical man who optimistically sees knowledge as the panacea to the problems of life. What is needed now, Nietzsche argues, is a new synthesis of these Dionysian and Apollonian tendencies by an "artistic" Socrates. Such a

Socratic figure would be a creative genius who would honestly face the harshness of life without losing a clear rational analytic perspective.

In order to face life honestly and clearly, the creative genius must begin by proclaiming the death of God. With the death of God, all values dependent on some external law-giver collapses and the individual is free to create self-defined values. By the "death of God," Nietzsche does not mean that there once was a diety who got old and passed away, nor that people no longer should live holy lives. Rather, Nietzsche claims that all *absolutes* have collapsed and there is no transcendent basis in any area—whether religion, philosophy, science, or politics—for making meaning out of life. The brief selection here from *Thus Spoke Zarathustra,* translated by Walter Kaufmann, is one of several passages in which Nietzsche announces the death of God.

In our selection from *Twilight of the Idols,* also translated by Walter Kaufmann, Nietzsche examines how philosophers have tried to find something transcendent, something permanent. Beginning with the Pre-Socratic thinker Parmenides, philosophers have been unwilling to accept the actual transitory world of "becoming." Instead they have denigrated this world, labeling it "apparent," and have in its place invented an immutable world of "being." But, as Nietzsche explains, "Any distinction between a 'true' and an 'apparent' world—whether in the Christian manner or in the manner of Kant . . . is only a suggestion of decadence, a symptom of the *decline of life.*"

The genius who can embrace "becoming," who acknowledges the death of all external values, could become an *Übermensch* ("overman" or "superman"). Such an overman would be a this-world antithesis to God and would affirm life without any resentment. The overman would be to humans as humans are to apes. But, most important, the overman would be one who acknowledges and celebrates the *will to power.*

According to Nietzsche, all human behavior can be understood in terms of the will to power and every relationship between persons is a power relationship. Those who affirm their power and define themselves on their own terms represent "master morality." In this morality, the hero asserts the will to power by taking direct action. On the other hand "slave morality" denies the will to power by claiming to find values "out there," ordained by God or some other transcendent law-giver. In slave morality, as explained in our final selection from Walter Kaufmann's translation of *The Anti-Christ,* the will to power is perverted into resentment in order to gain the imaginary powers of revenge and pity. Beginning with the Jews, and completed by the Christians, this slave morality has infected all of Europe with its life-denying poison, claims Nietzsche. What is now needed is a "revaluation of all values," which would affirm our will to power and move us "beyond good and evil."

This will to power need not mean oppressing others; it can also be expressed *within* the person. That is, more than gaining power over others, the will to power can lead to power over the self. The overman will be the one who uses power in this way to "overcome his animal nature, organize the chaos of his passions, sublimate his impulses, and give style to his character,"* becoming completely free and self-created.

Ironically, despite his distaste for anti-Semitism and his emphasis on the *self-*overcoming aspects of the will to power, Nietzsche was hailed as a hero by the Nazis. They used his emphases on the master morality and the will to power as a justification for their atrocities. Nietzsche's sister, Elisabeth, married a German anti-Semite and in her old age eagerly received Adolph Hitler at the Nietzsche Archives. However, despite its unfortunate association with the Nazis, Nietzsche's thought has continued to be influential, as his insights have been developed by existentialists, phenomenologists, psychoanalysts, poststructuralists, and deconstructionists, as well as poets and novelists.

*   *   *

A representative sampling of Neitzsche's thought can be found in *The Portable Nietzsche,* edited by Walter A. Kaufmann (New York: Viking Press, 1968). The best general introduction to Nietzsche's thought remains Walter A. Kaufmann, *Nietzsche: Philosopher, Psychologist, Antichrist* (Princeton, NJ: Princeton University Press, 1968). Recent overviews include Richard Schacht, *Nietzsche* (London: Routledge, 1983); Alexander Nehamas, *Nietzsche: Life as Literature* (Cambridge, MA: Harvard University Press, 1985); Graham Parke, *Composing the Soul* (Chicago: University of Chicago Press, 1994); John Richardson, *Nietzsche's System* (Oxford: Oxford University Press, 1995); and Michael Tanner, *Nietzsche* (Oxford: Oxford University Press, 1995). Ivo Frenzel, *Friedrich Nietzsche: An Illustrated Biography,* translated by Joachim Neugroschel (New York: Pegasus, 1967); and Sander L. Gilman, ed., *Conversations with Nietzsche: A Life in the Words of His Contemporaries,* translated by David J. Parent (New York: Oxford University Press, 1987), provide general biographies, whereas H.F. Peters, *Zarathustra's Sister: The Case of Elisabeth and Friedrich Nietzsche* (New York: Crown, 1977), presents a fascinating history of the expropriation of Nietzsche's thought in the service of German anti-Semitism. Walter A. Kaufmann, *Nietzsche, Heidegger, and Buber* (New York: McGraw-Hill, 1980); Allan Megill, *Prophets of Extremity: Nietzsche, Heidegger, Foucault, Derrida* (Berkeley: University of California Press, 1985); and Paul S. Miklowitz, *Metaphysics to Metafictions: Hegel, Nietzsche, and the End of Philosophy* (Albany, NY: SUNY Press, 1999) show the connections between Nietzsche and other important thinkers. For collections of critical essays, see Robert C. Solomon, ed., *Nietzsche: A Collection of Critical Essays* (Garden City, NY: Anchor Doubleday, 1973); Harold Bloom, ed., *Friedrich Nietzsche* (New York: Chelsea House, 1987); Richard Schacht, ed., *Nietzsche, Genealogy, Morality: Essays on Nietzsche's On the Genealogy of Morals* (Berkeley: University of California Press, 1994); Peter Sedgwick, ed., *Nietzsche: A Critical Reader* (Oxford: Basil Blackwell, 1995); Bernd Magnus and Kathleen Higgins, *The Cambridge Companion to Nietzsche* (Cambridge: Cambridge University Press, 1996); Kelly Oliver and Marilyn Pearsall, eds., *Feminist Interpretations of Nietzsche* (College Park, PA: Pennsylvania State University Press, 1998); and Daniel W. Conway, Nietzsche: Critical Assessments, four volumes (London: Routledge, 1998). Finally, Robert C. Solomon and Kathleen M. Higgins, eds., *Reading Nietzsche* (New York: Oxford University Press, 1988) provide helpful introductory essays on several of Nietzsche's works, while Daniel W. Conway, *Nietzsche's Dangerous Game: Philosophy in the Twilight of the Idols* (Cambridge: Cambridge University Press, 1997) focuses on Nietzsche's later work.

---

*Walter Kaufmann, *Nietzsche: Philosopher, Psychologist, Antichrist* (Princeton, NJ: Princeton University Press, 1950), p. 316.

THE BIRTH OF TRAGEDY (in part)

I. Much will have been gained for esthetics once we have succeeded in apprehending directly—rather than merely *ascertaining*—that art owes its continuous evolution to the Apollonian-Dionysiac duality, even as the propagation of the species depends on the duality of the sexes, their constant conflicts and periodic acts of reconciliation. I have borrowed my adjectives from the Greeks, who developed their mystical doctrines of art through plausible *embodiments,* not through purely conceptual means. It is by those two art-sponsoring deities, Apollo and Dionysos, that we are made to recognize the tremendous split, as regards both origins and objectives, between the plastic, Apollonian arts and the non-visual art of music inspired by Dionysos. The two creative tendencies developed alongside one another, usually in fierce opposition, each by its taunts forcing the other to more energetic production, both perpetuating in a discordant concord that agon which the term art but feebly denominates: until at last, by the thaumaturgy of an Hellenic act of will, the pair accepted the yoke of marriage and, in this condition, begot Attic tragedy, which exhibits the salient features of both parents.

To reach a closer understanding of both these tendencies, let us begin by viewing them as the separate art realms of *dream* and *intoxication,* two physiological phenomena standing toward one another in much the same relationship as the Apollonian and Dionysiac. It was in a dream, according to Lucretius, that the marvelous gods and goddesses first presented themselves to the minds of men. That great sculptor, Phidias, beheld in a dream the entrancing bodies of more-than-human beings, and likewise, if anyone had asked the Greek poets about the mystery of poetic creation, they too would have referred him to dreams and instructed him much as Hans Sachs instructs us in *Die Meistersinger:*

> My friend, it is the poet's work
> Dreams to interpret and to mark.
> Believe me that man's true conceit
> In a dream becomes complete:
> All poetry we ever read
> Is but true dreams interpreted.

The fair illusion of the dream sphere, in the production of which every man proves himself an accomplished artist, is a precondition not only of all plastic art, but even, as we shall see presently, of a wide range of poetry. Here we enjoy an immediate apprehension of form, all shapes speak to us directly, nothing seems indifferent or redundant. Despite the high intensity with which these dream realities exist for us, we still have a residual sensation that they are illusions; at least such has been my experience—and the frequency, not to say normality, of the experience is borne out in many passages of the poets. Men of philosophical disposition are known for their constant premonition that our everyday reality, too, is an illusion, hiding another, totally different kind of reality. It was Schopenhauer who considered the ability to view at certain

The Birth of Tragedy, translated by Francis Golffing from *The Birth of Tragedy and The Genealogy of Morals,* by Friedrich Nietzsche. Copyright © 1956 by Doubleday, a division of Bantam Doubleday Dell Publishing Group, Inc. Used by permission of Doubleday, a division of Bantam Doubleday Dell Publishing Group, Inc.

times all men and things as mere phantoms or dream images to be the true mark of philosophic talent. The person who is responsive to the stimuli of art behaves toward the reality of dream much the way the philosopher behaves toward the reality of existence: he observes exactly and enjoys his observations, for it is by these images that he interprets life, by these processes that he rehearses it. Nor is it by pleasant images only that such plausible connections are made: the whole divine comedy of life, including its somber aspects, its sudden balkings, impish accidents, anxious expectations, moves past him, not quite like a shadow play—for it is he himself, after all, who lives and suffers through these scenes—yet never without giving a fleeting sense of illusion; and I imagine that many persons have reassured themselves amidst the perils of dream by calling out, "It is a dream! I want it to go on." I have even heard of people spinning out the causality of one and the same dream over three or more successive nights. All these facts clearly bear witness that our innermost being, the common substratum of humanity, experiences dreams with deep delight and a sense of real necessity. This deep and happy sense of the necessity of dream experiences was expressed by the Greeks in the image of Apollo. Apollo is at once the god of all plastic powers and the soothsaying god. He who is etymologically the "lucent" one, the god of light, reigns also over the fair illusion of our inner world of fantasy. The perfection of these conditions in contrast to our imperfectly understood waking reality, as well as our profound awareness of nature's healing powers during the interval of sleep and dream, furnishes a symbolic analogue to the soothsaying faculty and quite generally to the arts, which make life possible and worth living. But the image of Apollo must incorporate that thin line which the dream image may not cross, under penalty of becoming pathological, of imposing itself on us as crass reality: a discreet limitation, a freedom from all extravagant urges, the sapient tranquillity of the plastic god. His eye must be sunlike, in keeping with his origin. Even at those moments when he is angry and ill-tempered there lies upon him the consecration of fair illusion. In an eccentric way one might say of Apollo what Schopenhauer says, in the first part of *The World as Will and Idea,* of man caught in the veil of Maya: "Even as on an immense, raging sea, assailed by huge wave crests, a man sits in a little rowboat trusting his frail craft, so, amidst the furious torments of this world, the individual sits tranquilly, supported by the *principium individuationis* and relying on it." One might say that the unshakable confidence in that principle has received its most magnificent expression in Apollo, and that Apollo himself may be regarded as the marvelous divine image of the *principium individuationis,* whose looks and gestures radiate the full delight, wisdom, and beauty of "illusion."

In the same context Schopenhauer has described for us the tremendous awe which seizes man when he suddenly begins to doubt the cognitive modes of experience, in other words, when in a given instance the law of causation seems to suspend itself. If we add to this awe the glorious transport which arises in man, even from the very depths of nature, at the shattering of the *principium individuationis,* then we are in a position to apprehend the essence of Dionysiac rapture, whose closest analogy is furnished by physical intoxication. Dionysiac stirrings arise either through the influence of those narcotic potions of which all primitive races speak in their hymns, or through the powerful approach of spring, which penetrates with joy the whole frame of nature. So stirred, the individual forgets himself completely. It is the Same Dionysiac power which in medieval Germany drove ever increasing crowds of people singing and dancing from place to place; we recognize in these St. John's and St. Vitus' dancers the bacchic choruses of the Greeks, who had their precursors in Asia Minor and as far back as Babylon and the orgiastic Sacaea. There are people who, either from lack of experience or out of sheer stupidity, turn away from such phenomena, and, strong in the sense of their own sanity, label them either mockingly or pityingly "endemic diseases." These benighted souls have no idea how cadaverous and ghostly their "sanity" appears as the intense throng of Dionysiac revelers sweeps past them.

Not only does the bond between man and man come to be forged once more by the magic of the Dionysiac rite, but nature itself, long alienated or subjugated, rises again to celebrate the reconciliation with her prodigal son, man. The earth offers its gifts voluntarily, and the savage beasts of mountain and desert approach in peace. The chariot of Dionysos is bedecked with flowers and garlands; panthers and tigers stride beneath his yoke. If one were to convert Beethoven's "Paean to Joy" into a painting, and refuse to curb the imagination when that multitude prostrates itself reverently in the dust, one might form some apprehension of Dionysiac ritual. Now the slave emerges as a freeman; all the rigid, hostile walls which either necessity or despotism has erected between men are shattered. Now that the gospel of universal harmony is sounded, each individual becomes not only reconciled to his fellow but actually at one with him—as though the veil of Maya had been torn apart and there remained only shreds floating before the vision of mystical Oneness. Man now expresses himself

Starry Night, 1889, by Vincent van Gogh (1853–1890). It is hard not to think of the paintings of Nietzsche's contemporary Vincent van Gogh when reading Nietzsche's words: "If one were to convert Beethoven's 'Paean to Joy' into a painting, and refuse to curb the imagination when that multitude prostrates itself reverently in the dust, one might form some apprehension of Dionysiac ritual." *(©The Museum of Modern Art, New York. Acquired through the Lillie P. Bliss Bequest.)*

through song and dance as the member of a higher community; he has forgotten how to walk, how to speak, and is on the brink of taking wing as he dances. Each of his gestures betokens enchantment; through him sounds a supernatural power, the same power which makes the animals speak and the earth render up milk and honey. He feels himself to be godlike and strides with the same elation and ecstasy as the gods he has seen in his dreams. No longer the *artist,* he has himself become a *work of art: the productive power of the whole universe is now manifest in his transport, to the glorious satisfaction of the primordial One. The finest clay, the most precious marble— man—is here kneaded and hewn, and the chisel blows of the Dionysiac world artist* are accompanied by the cry of the Eleusinian mystagogues: "Do you fall on your knees, multitudes, do you divine your creator?"

II. So far we have examined the Apollonian and Dionysiac states as the product of formative forces arising directly from nature without the mediation of the human artist. At this stage artistic urges are satisfied directly, on the one hand through the imagery of dreams, whose perfection is quite independent of the intellectual rank, the artistic development of the individual; on the other hand, through an ecstatic reality which once again takes no account of the individual and may even destroy him, or else redeem him through a mystical experience of the collective. In relation to these immediate creative conditions of nature every artist must appear as "imitator," either as the Apollonian dream artist or the Dionysiac ecstatic artist, or, finally (as in Greek tragedy, for example) as dream and ecstatic artist in one. We might picture to ourselves how the last of these, in a state of Dionysiac intoxication and mystical self-abrogation, wandering apart from the reveling throng, sinks upon the ground, and how there is then revealed to him his own condition—complete oneness with the essence of the universe—in a dream similitude.

Having set down these general premises and distinctions, we now turn to the Greeks in order to realize to what degree the formative forces of nature were developed in them. Such an inquiry will enable us to assess properly the relation of the Greek artist to his prototypes or, to use Aristotle's expression, his "imitation of nature." Of the dreams the Greeks dreamed it is not possible to speak with any certainty, despite the extant dream literature and the large number of dream anecdotes. But considering the incredible accuracy of their eyes, their keen and unabashed delight in colors, one can hardly be wrong in assuming that their dreams too showed a strict consequence of lines and contours, hues and groupings, a progression of scenes similar to their best bas-reliefs. The perfection of these dream scenes might almost tempt us to consider the dreaming Greek as a Homer and Homer as a dreaming Greek; which would be as though the modern man were to compare himself in his dreaming to Shakespeare.

Yet there is another point about which we do not have to conjecture at all: I mean the profound gap separating the Dionysiac Greeks from the Dionysiac barbarians. Throughout the range of ancient civilization (leaving the newer civilizations out of account for the moment) we find evidence of Dionysiac celebrations which stand to the Greek type in much the same relation as the bearded satyr, whose name and attributes are derived from the he-goat, stands to the god Dionysos. The central concern of such celebrations was, almost universally, a complete sexual promiscuity overriding every form of established tribal law; all the savage urges of the mind were unleashed on those occasions until they reached that paroxysm of lust and cruelty which has always struck me as the "witches' cauldron" *par excellence.* It would appear that the Greeks were for a while quite immune from these feverish excesses which must have reached them by every known land or sea route. What kept Greece safe was the proud, imposing image of Apollo, who in holding up the head of the Gorgon to those brutal and grotesque Dionysiac forces subdued them. Doric art has immortalized Apollo's majestic rejection of all license. But resistance became difficult, even impossible, as soon as similar urges began to break forth from the deep substratum of Hellenism itself. Soon the function of the Delphic god developed into something quite different and much more limited: all he could hope to accomplish now was to wrest the destructive weapon, by a timely gesture of pacification, from his opponent's hand. That act of pacification represents the most important event in the history of Greek ritual; every department of life now shows symptoms of a revolutionary change. The two great antagonists have been reconciled. Each feels obliged henceforth to keep to his bounds, each will honor the other by the bestowal of periodic gifts, while the cleavage remains fundamentally the same. And yet, if we examine what happened to the Dionysiac powers under the pressure of that treaty we notice a great difference: in the place of the Babylonian Sacaea, with their throwback of men to the condition of apes and tigers, we now see entirely new rites celebrated: rites of universal redemption, of glorious transfiguration. Only now has it become possible to speak of nature's celebrating an aesthetic triumph; only now has the abrogation of the *principium individuationis* become an aesthetic event. That terrible witches' brew concocted of lust and cruelty has lost all power under the new conditions. Yet the peculiar blending of emotions in the heart of the Dionysiac reveler—his ambiguity if you will—seems still to hark back (as the medicinal drug harks back to the deadly poison) to the days when the infliction of pain was experienced as joy while a sense of supreme triumph elicited cries of anguish from the heart. For now in every exuberant joy there is heard an undertone of terror, or else a wistful lament over an irrecoverable loss. It is as though in these Greek festivals a sentimental trait of nature were coming to the fore, as though nature were bemoaning the fact of her fragmentation, her decomposition into separate individuals. The chants and gestures of these revelers, so ambiguous in their motivation, represented an absolute *novum* in the world of the Homeric Greeks; their Dionysiac music, in especial, spread abroad terror and a deep shudder. It is true: music had long been familiar to the Greeks as an Apollonian art, as a regular beat like that of waves lapping the shore, a plastic rhythm expressly developed for the portrayal of Apollonian conditions. Apollo's music was a Doric architecture of sound—of barely hinted sounds such as are proper to the cithara. Those very elements which characterize Dionysiac music and, after it, music quite generally: the heart-shaking power of tone, the uniform stream of melody, the incomparable resources of harmony—all those elements had been carefully kept at a distance as being inconsonant with the Apollonian norm. In the Dionysiac dithyramb man is incited to strain his symbolic faculties to the utmost; something quite unheard of is now clamoring to be heard: the desire to tear asunder the veil of Maya, to sink back into the original oneness of nature; the desire to express the very essence of nature symbolically. Thus an entirely new set of symbols springs into being. First all the symbols pertaining to physical features: mouth, face, the spoken word, the dance movement which coordinates the limbs and bends them to its rhythm. Then suddenly all the rest of the symbolic forces—music and rhythm as such, dynamics, harmony—assert themselves with great energy. In order to comprehend this total emancipation of all the symbolic powers one must have reached the same measure of inner freedom those powers themselves were making manifest; which is to say that the votary of Dionysos could not be understood except by his own kind. It is not difficult to imagine the awed surprise with which the Apollonian Greek must have looked on him. And that surprise would be further increased as the latter realized, with a shudder, that all this was not so alien to him after all, that his Apollonian consciousness was but a thin veil hiding from him the whole Dionysiac realm.

III. In order to comprehend this we must take down the elaborate edifice of Apollonian culture stone by stone until we discover its foundations. At first the eye is struck by the marvelous shapes of the Olympian gods who stand upon its pediments, and whose exploits, in shining bas-relief, adorn its friezes. The fact that among them we find Apollo as one god among many, making no claim to a privileged position, should not mislead us. The same drive that found its most complete representation in Apollo generated the whole Olympian world, and in this sense we may consider Apollo the father of that world. But what was the radical need out of which that illustrious society of Olympian beings sprang?

Whoever approaches the Olympians with a different religion in his heart, seeking moral elevation, sanctity, spirituality, loving-kindness, will presently be forced to turn away from them in ill-humored disappointment. Nothing in these deities reminds us of asceticism, high intellect, or duty: we are confronted by luxuriant, triumphant *existence,* which deifies the good and the bad indifferently. And the beholder may find himself dismayed in the presence of such overflowing life and ask himself what potion these heady people must have drunk in order to behold, in whatever direction they looked, Helen laughing back at them, the beguiling image of their own existence. But we shall call out to this beholder, who has already turned his back: Don't go! Listen first to what the Greeks themselves have to say of this life, which spreads itself before you with such puzzling serenity. An old legend has it that King Midas hunted a long time in the woods for the wise Silenus, companion of Dionysos, without being able to catch him. When he had finally caught him the king asked him what he considered man's greatest good. The daemon remained sullen and uncommunicative until finally, forced by the king, he broke into a shrill laugh and spoke: "Ephemeral wretch, begotten by accident and toil, why do you force me to tell you what it would be your greatest boon not to hear? What would be best for you is quite beyond your reach: not to have been born, not to be, to be *nothing.* But the second best is to die soon."

What is the relation of the Olympian gods to this popular wisdom? It is that of the entranced vision of the martyr to his torment.

Now the Olympian magic mountain opens itself before us, showing us its very roots. The Greeks were keenly aware of the terrors and horrors of existence; in order to be able to live at all they had to place before them the shining fantasy of the Olympians. Their tremendous distrust of the titanic forces of nature: *Moira,* mercilessly enthroned beyond the knowable world; the vulture which fed upon the great philanthropist Prometheus; the terrible lot drawn by wise Oedipus; the curse on the house of Atreus which brought Orestes to the murder of his mother: that whole Panic philosophy, in short, with its mythic examples, by which the gloomy Etruscans perished, the Greeks conquered—or at least hid from view—again and again by means of this artificial Olympus. In order to live at all the Greeks had to construct these deities. The Apollonian need for beauty had to develop the Olympian hierarchy of joy by slow degrees from the original titanic hierarchy of terror, as roses are seen to break from a thorny thicket. How else could life have been borne by a race so hypersensitive, so emotionally intense, so equipped for suffering? The same drive which called art into being as a completion and consummation of existence, and as a guarantee of further existence, gave rise also to that Olympian realm which acted as a transfiguring mirror to the Hellenic will. The gods justified human life by living it themselves—the only satisfactory theodicy ever invented. To exist in the clear sunlight of such deities was now felt to be the highest good, and the only real grief suffered by Homeric man was inspired by the thought of leaving that sunlight, especially when the departure seemed imminent. Now it became possible to stand the wisdom of Silenus on its head and proclaim that it was the worst evil for man to die soon, and second worst for him to die at all. Such laments as arise now arise over short-lived Achilles, over the generations ephemeral as leaves, the decline of the heroic age. It is not unbecoming to even the greatest hero to yearn for an afterlife, though it be as a day laborer. So impetuously, during the Apollonian phase, does man's will desire to remain on earth, so identified does he become with existence, that even his lament turns to a song of praise.

It should have become apparent by now that the harmony with nature which we late-comers regard with such nostalgia, and for which Schiller has coined the cant term naive, is by no means a simple and inevitable condition to be found at the gateway to every culture, a kind of paradise. Such a belief could have been endorsed only by a period for which Rousseau's Emile was an artist and Homer just such an artist nurtured in the bosom of nature. Whenever we encounter "naïveté" in art, we are face to face with the ripest fruit of Apollonian culture—which must always triumph first over titans, kill monsters, and overcome the somber contemplation of actuality, the intense susceptibility to suffering, by means of illusions strenuously and zestfully entertained. But how rare are the instances of true naïveté, of that complete identification with the beauty of appearance! It is this achievement which makes Homer so magnificent— Homer, who, as a single individual, stood to Apollonian popular culture in the same relation as the individual dream artist to the oneiric capacity of a race and of nature generally. The naïveté of Homer must be viewed as a complete victory of Apollonian illusion. Nature often uses illusions of this sort in order to accomplish its secret purposes. The true goal is covered over by a phantasm. We stretch out our hands to the latter, while nature, aided by our deception, attains the former. In the case of the Greeks it was the will wishing to behold itself in the work of art, in the transcendence of genius; but in order so to behold itself its creatures had first to view themselves as glorious, to transpose themselves to a higher sphere, without having that sphere of pure contemplation either challenge them or upbraid them with insufficiency. It was in that sphere of beauty that the Greeks saw the Olympians as their mirror images; it was by means of that aesthetic mirror that the Greek will opposed suffering and the somber wisdom of suffering which always accompanies artisic talent. As a monument to its victory stands Homer, the naive artist.

THUS SPOKE ZARATHUSTRA (in part)

Zarathustra's Prologue

[1] When Zarathustra was thirty years old he left his home and the lake of his home and went into the mountains. Here he enjoyed his spirit and his solitude, and for ten years did not tire of it. But at last a change came over his heart, and one morning he rose with the dawn, stepped before the sun, and spoke to it thus:

"You great star, what would your happiness be had you not those for whom you shine?

"For ten years you have climbed to my cave: you would have tired of your light and of the journey had it not been for me and my eagle and my serpent.

"But we waited for you every morning, took your overflow from you, and blessed you for it.

"Behold, I am weary of my wisdom, like a bee that has gathered too much honey; I need hands outstretched to receive it.

"I would give away and distribute, until the wise among men find joy once again in their folly, and the poor in their riches.

"For that I must descend to the depths, as you do in the evening when you go behind the sea and still bring light to the underworld, you over rich star.

"Like you, I must go *under*—go down, as is said by man, to whom I want to descend.

"So bless me then, you quiet eye that can look even upon an all-too-great happiness without envy!

"Bless the cup that wants to overflow, that the water may flow from it golden and carry everywhere the reflection of your delight.

"Behold, this cup wants to become empty again, and Zarathustra wants to become man again."

Thus Zarathustra began to go under.

[2] Zarathustra descended alone from the mountains, encountering no one. But when he came into the forest, all at once there stood before him an old man who had left his holy cottage to look for roots in the woods. And thus spoke the old man to Zarathustra:

"No stranger to me is this wanderer: many years ago he passed this way. Zarathustra he was called, but he has changed. At that time you carried your ashes to the mountains; would you now carry your fire into the valleys? Do you not fear to be punished as an arsonist?

"Yes, I recognize Zarathustra. His eyes are pure, and around his mouth there hides no disgust. Does he not walk like a dancer?

"Zarathustra has changed, Zarathustra has become a child, Zarathustra is an awakened one; what do you now want among the sleepers? You lived in your solitude as in the sea, and the sea carried you. Alas, would you now climb ashore? Alas, would you again drag your own body?"

Zarathustra answered: "I love man."

"Why," asked the saint, "did I go into the forest and the desert? Was it not because I loved man all-too-much? Now I love God; man I love not. Man is for me too imperfect a thing. Love of man would kill me."

Zarathustra answered: "Did I speak of love? I bring men a gift."

"Give them nothing!" said the saint. "Rather, take part of their load and help them to bear it—that will be best for them, if only it does you good! And if you want to give them something, give no more than alms, and let them beg for that!"

"No," answered Zarathustra. "I give no alms. For that I am not poor enough."

The saint laughed at Zarathustra and spoke thus: "Then see to it that they accept your treasures. They are suspicious of hermits and do not believe that we come with gifts. Our steps sound too lonely through the streets. And what if at night, in their beds, they hear a man walk by long before the sun has risen—they probably ask themselves, Where is the thief going?

"Do not go to man. Stay in the forest! Go rather even to the animals! Why do you not want to be as I am—a bear among bears, a bird among birds?"

"And what is the saint doing in the forest?" asked Zarathustra.

The saint answered: "I make songs and sing them; and when I make songs, I laugh, cry, and hum: thus I praise God. With singing, crying, laughing, and humming, I praise the god who is my god. But what do you bring us as a gift?"

When Zarathustra had heard these words he bade the saint farewell and said: "What could I have to give you? But let me go quickly lest I take something from you!" And thus they separated, the old one and the man, laughing as two boys laugh.

But when Zarathustra was alone he spoke thus to his heart: "Could it be possible? This old saint in the forest has not yet heard anything of this, that God is *dead!*"

[3] When Zarathustra came into the next town, which lies on the edge of the forest, he found many people gathered together in the market place; for it had been promised that there would be a tightrope walker. And Zarathustra spoke thus to the people:

"I teach you the overman. Man is something that shall be overcome. What have you done to overcome him?

"All beings so far have created something beyond themselves; and do you want to be the ebb of this great flood and even go back to the beasts rather than overcome man? What is the ape to man? A laughingstock or a painful embarrassment. And man shall be just that for the overman: a laughingstock or a painful embarrassment. You have made your way from worm to man, and much in you is still worm. Once you were apes, and even now, too, man is more ape than any ape.

"Whoever is the wisest among you is also a mere conflict and cross between plant and ghost. But do I bid you become ghosts or plants?

"Behold, I teach you the overman. The overman is the meaning of the earth. Let your will say: the overman *shall be* the meaning of the earth! I beseech you, my brothers, *remain faithful to the earth,* and do not believe those who speak to you of otherworldly hopes! Poison-mixers are they, whether they know it or not. Despisers of life are they, decaying and poisoned themselves, of whom the earth is weary: so let them go.

"Once the sin against God was the greatest sin; but God died, and these sinners died with him. To sin against the earth is now the most dreadful thing, and to esteem the entrails of the unknowable higher than the meaning of the earth.

"Once the soul looked contemptuously upon the body, and then this contempt was the highest: she wanted the body meager, ghastly, and starved. Thus she hoped to escape it and the earth. Oh, this soul herself was still meager, ghastly, and starved: and cruelty was the lust of this soul. But you, too, my brothers, tell me: what does your body proclaim of your soul? Is not your soul poverty and filth and wretched contentment?

"Verily, a polluted stream is man. One must be a sea to be able to receive a polluted stream without becoming unclean. Behold, I teach you the overman: he is this sea; in him your great contempt can go under.

"What is the greatest experience you can have? It is the hour of the great contempt. The hour in which your happiness, too, arouses your disgust, and even your reason and your virtue.

"The hour when you say, 'What matters my happiness? It is poverty and filth and wretched contentment. But my happiness ought to justify existence itself.'

"The hour when you say, 'What matters my reason? Does it crave knowledge as the lion his food? It is poverty and filth and wretched contentment.'

"The hour when you say, 'What matters my virtue? As yet it has not made me rage. How weary I am of my good and my evil! All that is poverty and filth and wretched contentment.'

"The hour when you say, 'What matters my justice? I do not see that I am flames and fuel. But the just are flames and fuel.'

"The hour when you say, 'What matters my pity? Is not pity the cross on which he is nailed who loves man? But my pity is no crucifixion.'

"Have you yet spoken thus? Have you yet cried thus? Oh, that I might have heard you cry thus!

"Not your sin but your thrift cries to heaven; your meanness even in your sin cries to heaven.

"Where is the lightning to lick you with its tongue? Where is the frenzy with which you should be inoculated?

"Behold, I teach you the overman: he is this lightning, he is this frenzy."

When Zarathustra had spoken thus, one of the people cried: "Now we have heard enough about the tightrope walker; now let us see him tool." And all the people laughed at Zarathustra. But the tightrope walker, believing that the word concerned him, began his performance.

TWILIGHT OF THE IDOLS (in part)

MAXIMS AND ARROWS

1. Idleness is the beginning of all psychology. What? Should psychology be a vice?*

2. Even the most courageous among us only rarely has the courage for that which he really knows.

3. To live alone one must be a beast or a god, says Aristotle. Leaving out the third case: one must be both—a philosopher.

4. "All truth is simple." Is that not doubly a lie?

5. I want, once and for all, *not* to know many things. Wisdom sets limits to knowledge too.

6. In our own wild nature we find the best recreation from our un-nature, from our spirituality.

7. What? Is man merely a mistake of God's? Or God merely a mistake of man's?

8. *Out of life's school of war:* What does not destroy me, makes me stronger.

9. Help yourself, then everyone will help you. Principle of neighbor-love.

10. Not to perpetrate cowardice against one's own acts! Not to leave them in the lurch afterward! The bite of conscience is indecent.

11. Can an ass be tragic? To perish under a burden one can neither bear nor throw off? The case of the philosopher.

12. If we have our own *why* of life, we shall get along with almost any *how*. Man does *not* strive for pleasure; only the Englishman does.

13. Man has created woman—out of what? Out of a rib of his god—of his "ideal."

14. What? You search? You would multiply yourself by ten, by a hundred? You seek followers? Seek zeros!

15. Posthumous men—*I*, for example—are understood worse than timely ones, but *heard* better. More precisely: we are never understood—*hence* our authority.

*There is a German proverb: "Idleness is the beginning of all vices."

16. *Among women:* "Truth? Oh, you don't know truth. Is it not an attempt to assassinate all our *pudeurs?*"

17. That is an artist as I love artists, modest in his needs—. he really wants only two things, his bread and his art—*panem et Circen.**

18. Whoever does not know how to lay his will into things, at least lays some *meaning* into them: that means, he has the faith that they already obey a will. (Principle of "faith.")

19. What? You elected virtue and the swelled bosom and yet you leer enviously at the advantages of those without qualms? But virtue involves *renouncing* "advantages." (Inscription for an anti-Semite's door.)

20. The perfect woman perpetrates literature as she perpetrates a small sin: as an experiment, in passing, looking around to see if anybody notices it—and to make sure that somebody does.

21. To venture into all sorts of situations in which one may not have any sham virtues, where, like the tightrope walker on his rope, one either stands or falls—or gets away.

22. "Evil men have no songs." How is it, then, that the Russians have songs?

23. "German spirit": for the past eighteen years a contradiction in terms.

24. By searching out origins, one becomes a crab, The historian looks backward; eventually he also *believes* backward.

25. Contentment protects even against colds. Has a woman who knew herself to be well dressed ever caught cold? I am assuming that she was barely dressed.

26. I mistrust all systematizers and I avoid them. The *will* to a system is a lack of integrity.

27. Women are considered profound. Why? Because one never fathoms their depths. Women aren't even shallow.

28. If a woman has manly virtues, one feels like running away; and if she has no manly virtues, she herself runs away.

29. "How much conscience has had to chew on in the past! And what excellent teeth it had! And today—what is lacking?" A dentist's question.

30. One rarely rushes into a single error. Rushing into the first one, one always does too much. So one usually perpetrates another one—and now one does too little.

---

panem et circenses, "bread and circuses"—here changed by Nietzsche into "bread and Circe," art being compared to the Homeric sorceress.

31. When stepped on, a worm doubles up. That is clever. In that way he lessens the probability of being stepped on again. In the language of morality: *humility*.

32. There is a hatred of lies and simulation, stemming from an easily provoked sense of honor. There is another such hatred, from cowardice, since lies are for*bidden* by a divine commandment. Too cowardly to lie.

33. How little is required for pleasure! The sound of a bagpipe. Without music, life would be an error. The German imagines even God singing songs.

34. *On ne peut penser et écrire qu'assis** (G. Flaubert). There I have caught you, nihilist! The sedentary life is the very sin against the Holy Spirit. Only thoughts reached by walking have value.

35. There are cases in which we are like horses, we psychologists, and become restless: we see our own shadow wavering up and down before us. A psychologist must turn his eyes from himself to eye anything at all.

36. Whether we immoralists are *harming* virtue? just as little as anarchists harm princes. Only since the latter are shot at do they again sit securely on their thrones. Moral: *morality must be shot at.*

37. You run *ahead?* Are you doing it as a shepherd? Or as an exception? A third case would be the fugitive. *First* question of conscience.

38. Are you genuine? Or merely an actor? A representative? Or that which is represented? In the end, perhaps you are merely a copy of an actor. *Second* question of conscience.

39. *The disappointed one speaks.* I searched for great human beings; I always found only the *apes* of their ideals.

40. Are you one who looks on? Or one who lends a hand? Or one who looks away and walks off? *Third* question of conscience.

41. Do you want to walk along? Or walk ahead? Or walk by yourself? One must know *what* one wants and *that* one wants. *Fourth* question of conscience.

42. Those were steps for me, and I have climbed up over them: to that end I had to pass over them. Yet they thought that I wanted to retire on them.

43. What does it matter if *I* remain right. I am much too right. And he who laughs best today will also laugh last.

44. The formula of my happiness: a Yes, a No, a straight line, a *goal.*

---

*"One can think and write, except sitting."

THE PROBLEM OF SOCRATES

[1] Concerning life, the wisest men of all ages have judged alike: *it is no good.* Always and everywhere one has heard the same sound from their mouths—a sound full of doubt, full of melancholy, full of weariness of life, full of resistance to life. Even Socrates said, as He died; "To live—that means to be sick a long time: I owe Asclepius the Savior a rooster." Even Socrates was tired of it. What does that evidence? What does it evince? Formerly one would have said (—oh, it has been said, and loud enough, and especially by our pessimists): "At least something of all this must be true! The consensus of the sages evidences the truth." Shall we still talk like that today? *May* we? "At least something must be *sick* here," *we* retort. These wisest men of all ages—they should first be scrutinized closely. Were they all perhaps shaky on their legs? late? tottery? decadents? Could it be that wisdom appears on earth as a raven, inspired by a little whiff of carrion?

[2] This irreverent thought that the great sages are *types of decline* first occurred to me precisely in a case where it is most strongly opposed by both scholarly and unscholarly prejudice: I recognized Socrates and Plato to be symptoms of degeneration, tools of the Greek dissolution, pseudo-Greek, anti-Greek *(Birth of Tragedy*, 1872). The consensus of the sages—I comprehended this ever more clearly—proves least of all that they were right in what they agreed on: it shows rather that they themselves, these wisest men, agreed in some *physiological* respect, and hence adopted the same negative attitude to life—*had to* adopt it. Judgments, judgments of value, concerning life, for it or against it, can, in the end, never be true: they have value only as symptoms, they are worthy of consideration only as symptoms; in themselves such judgments are stupidities. One must by all means stretch out one's fingers and make the attempt to grasp this amazing finesse, *that the value of life cannot be estimated*. Not by the living, for they are an interested party, even a bone of contention, and not judges; not by the dead, for a different reason. For a philosopher to see a problem in the value of life is thus an objection to him, a question mark concerning his wisdom, an un-wisdom. Indeed? All these great wise men—they were not only decadents but not wise at all? But I return to the problem of Socrates.

[3] In origin, Socrates belonged to the lowest class: Socrates was plebs. We know, we can still see for ourselves, how ugly he was. But ugliness, in itself an objection, is among the Greeks almost a refutation. Was Socrates a Greek at all? Ugliness is often enough the expression of a development that has been crossed, *thwarted* by crossing. Or it appears as declining development. The anthropologists among the criminologists tell us that the typical criminal is ugly: *monstrum in fronte, monstrum in animo.* But the criminal is a decadent. Was Socrates a typical criminal? At least that would not be contradicted by the famous judgment of the physiognomist which sounded so offensive to the friends of Socrates. A foreigner who knew about faces once passed through Athens and told Socrates to his face that he *was a monstrum*— that he harbored in himself all the bad vices and appetites. And Socrates merely answered: "You know me, sir!"

[4] Socrates' decadence is suggested not only by the admitted wantonness and anarchy of his instincts, but also by the hypertrophy of the logical faculty and that *sarcasm of the rachitic* which distinguishes him. Nor should we forget those auditory hallucinations which, as "the *daimonion* of Socrates," have been interpreted religiously. Everything in him is exaggerated, *buffo,* a caricature, everything is at the same time concealed, ulterior, subterranean. I seek to comprehend what idiosyncrasy begot that

Socratic equation of reason, virtue, and happiness: that most bizarre of all equations, which. moreover, is opposed to all the instincts of the earlier Greeks.

[5] With Socrates, Greek taste changes in favor of dialectics. What really happened there? Above all, a *noble* taste is thus vanquished; with dialectics the plebs come to the top. Before Socrates, dialectic manners were repudiated in good society: they were considered bad manners, they were compromising. The young were warned against them. Furthermore, all such presentations of one's reasons were distrusted. Honest things, like honest men, do not carry their reasons in their hands like that. It is indecent to show all five fingers. What must first be proved is worth little. Wherever authority still forms part of good bearing, where one does not give reasons but commands, the dialectician is a kind of buffoon: one laughs at him, one does not take him seriously. Socrates was the buffoon who *got himself taken seriously:* what really happened there?

[6] One chooses dialectic only when one has no other means. One knows that one arouses mistrust with it, that it is not very persuasive. Nothing is easier to erase than a dialectical effect: the experience of every meeting at which there are speeches proves this. It can only be *self-defense* for those who no longer have other weapons. One must have to *enforce* one's right: until one reaches that point, one makes no use of it. The Jews were dialecticians for that reason; Reynard the Fox was one—and Socrates too?

[7] Is the irony of Socrates an expression of revolt? Of plebeian *ressentiment?* Does he, as one oppressed, enjoy his own ferocity in the knife-thrusts of his syllogisms? Does he *avenge* himself on the noble people whom he fascinates? As a dialectician, one holds a merciless tool in one's hand; one can become a tyrant by means of it; one compromises those one conquers. The dialectician leaves it to his opponent to prove that he is no idiot: be makes one furious and helpless at the same time. The dialectician renders the intellect of his opponent powerless. Indeed? Is dialectic only, a form of *revenge* in Socrates?

[8] I have given to understand how it was that Socrates could repel: it is therefore all the more necessary to explain his fascination. That he discovered a new kind of *agon* ["contest"], that he became its first fencing master for the noble circles of Athens, is one point. He fascinated by appealing to the agonistic impulse of the Greeks-he introduced a variation into the wrestling match between young men and youths. Socrates was also a great *erotic*.

[9] But Socrates guessed even more. He saw *through* his noble Athenians; he comprehended that his own case, his idiosyncrasy, was no longer exceptional. The same kind of degeneration was quietly developing everywhere: old Athens was coming to an end. And Socrates understood that all the world *needed* him—his means, his cure, his personal artifice of self-preservation. Everywhere the instincts were in anarchy; everywhere one was within five paces of excess: *monstrum in animo* was the general danger. "The impulses want to play the tyrant; one must invent a *counter-tyrant* who is stronger." When the physiognomist had revealed to Socrates who he was—a cave of bad appetites—the great master of irony let slip another word which is the key to Ms character. "This is true," he said, "but I mastered them all." *How* did Socrates become master over *himself?* His case was, at bottom, merely the extreme case only the most striking instance of what was then beginning to be a universal distress: no one was any longer master over himself, the instincts turned *against* each other. He fascinated, being this extreme case; his awe-inspiring ugliness proclaimed him as such to all who could see; he fascinated, of course, even more as an answer, a solution, an apparent *cure* of this case.

[10] When one finds it necessary to turn *reason* into a tyrant, as Socrates did, the danger cannot be slight that something else will play the tyrant. Rationality was then hit upon as the savior; neither Socrates nor his "patients" had any choice about being rational: it was *de rigeur,* it was their last resort. The fanaticism with which all Greek reflection throws itself upon rationality betrays a desperate situation; there was danger, there was but one choice: either to perish or—to be *absurdly rational.* The moralism of the Greek philosophers from Plato on is pathologically conditioned; so is their esteem of dialectics. Reason-virtue-happiness, that means merely that one must imitate Socrates and counter the dark appetites with a permanent daylight—the daylight of reason. One must be clever, clear, bright at any price: any concession to the instincts, to the unconscious, leads *downward.*

[11] I have given to understand how it was that Socrates fascinated he seemed to be a physician, a savior. Is it necessary to go on to demonstrate the error in his faith in "rationality at any price"? It is a self-deception on the part of philosophers and moralists if they believe that they are extricating themselves from decadence when they merely wage war against it. Extrication lies beyond their strength: what they choose as a means, as salvation, is itself but another expression of decadence; they change its expression, but they do not get rid of decadence itself. Socrates was a misunderstanding; *the whole improvement—morality, including the Christian, was a misunderstanding.* The most blinding daylight; rationality at any price; life, bright, cold, cautious, conscious, without instinct, in opposition to the instincts—all this too was a mere disease, another disease, and by no means a return to "virtue," to "health," to happiness. To *have* to fight the instincts—that is the formula of decadence: as long as life *is ascending,* happiness equals instinct.

[12] Did he himself still comprehend this, this most brilliant of all self-outwitters? Was this what he said to himself in the end, in the *wisdom* of his courage to die? Socrates *wanted* to die: not Athens, but he himself chose the hemlock; he forced Athens to sentence him. "Socrates is no physician," he said softly to himself; "here death alone is the physician. Socrates himself has merely been sick a long time."

"REASON" IN PHILOSOPHY

[1] You ask me which of the philosophers' traits are really idiosyncrasies? For example, their lack of historical sense, their hatred of the very idea of becoming, their Egypticism. They think that they show their *respect* for a subject when they de-historicize it, *sub specie aeterni*—when they turn it into a mummy. All that philosophers have handled for thousands of years have been concept-mummies; nothing real escaped their grasp alive. When these honorable idolaters of concepts worship something, they kill it and stuff it; they threaten the life of everything they worship. Death, change, old age, as well as procreation and growth, are to their minds objections—even refutations. Whatever has being does not become; whatever becomes does not have being. Now they all believe, desperately even, in what has being. But since they never grasp it, they seek for reasons why it is kept from them. "There must be mere appearance, there must be some deception which prevents us from perceiving that which has being: where is the deceiver?"

"We have found him," they cry ecstatically; "it is the senses! These senses, which are so immoral in other ways too, deceive us concerning the *true* world. Moral: let us free ourselves from the deception of the senses, from becoming, from history, from lies; history is nothing but faith in the senses, faith in lies. Moral: let us say No to all who have faith in the senses, to all the rest of mankind; they are all 'mob.' Let us be philosophers! Let us be mummies! Let us represent monotono-theism by adopting the expression of a gravedigger! And above all, away with the body, this wretched *idée fixe* of the senses, disfigured by all the fallacies of logic, refuted, even impossible, although it is impudent enough to behave as if it were real!"

[2] With the highest respect, I except the name of *Heraclitus.* When the rest of the philosophic folk rejected the testimony of the senses because they showed multiplicity and change, he rejected their testimony because they showed things as if they had permanence and unity. Heraclitus too did the senses an injustice. They lie neither in the way the Eleatics believed, nor as he believed—they do not lie at all. What we *make* of their testimony, that alone introduces lies; for example, the lie of unity, the lie of thinghood, of substance, of permanence. "Reason" is the cause of our falsification of the testimony of the senses. Insofar as the senses show becoming, passing away, and change, they do not lie. But Heraclitus will remain eternally right with his assertion that being is an empty fiction. The "apparent" world is the only one: the "true" world is merely added by a lie.

[3] And what magnificent instruments of observation we possess in our senses! This nose, for example, of which no philosopher has yet spoken with reverence and gratitude, is actually the most delicate instrument so far at our disposal: it is able to detect minimal differences of motion which even a spectroscope cannot detect. Today we possess science precisely to the extent to which we have decided to *accept* the testimony of the senses—to the extent to which we sharpen them further, arm them, and have learned to think them through. The rest is miscarriage and not-yet-science-in other words, metaphysics, theology, psychology, epistemology—or formal science, a doctrine of signs, such as logic and that applied logic which is called mathematics. In them reality is not encountered at all, not even as a problem—no more than the question of the value of such a sign-convention as logic.

[4] The other idiosyncrasy of the philosophers is no less dangerous; it consists in confusing the last and the first. They place that which comes at the end—unfortunately! for it ought not to come at all!—namely, the "highest concepts," which means the most general, the emptiest concepts, the last smoke of evaporating reality, in the beginning, *as* the beginning. This again is nothing but their way of showing reverence: the higher *may* not grow out of the lower, may not have grown at all. Moral: whatever is of the first rank must be *causa sui* [self-caused]. Origin out of something else is considered an objection, a questioning of value. All the highest values are of the first rank; all the highest concepts, that which has being, the unconditional, the good, the true, the perfect—all these cannot have become and must therefore be *causa sui.* All these, moreover, cannot be unlike each other or in contradiction to each other. Thus they arrive at their stupendous concept, "God." That which is last, thinnest, and emptiest is put first, as *the* cause, as *ens realissimum* [the most real being]. Why did mankind have to take seriously the brain afflictions of sick web-spinners? They have paid dearly for it!

[5] At long last, let us contrast the very different manner in which we conceive the problem of error and appearance. (I say "we" for politeness' sake.) Formerly, alteration, change, any becoming at all, were taken as proof of mere appearance, as an indication that there must be something which led us astray. Today, conversely, precisely

insofar as the prejudice of reason forces us to posit unity, identity, permanence, substance, cause, thinghood, being, we see ourselves somehow caught in error, compelled into error. So certain are we, on the basis of rigorous examination, that this is where the error lies.

It is no different in this case than with the movement of the sun: there our eye is the constant advocate of error, here it is our language. In its origin language belongs in the age of the most rudimentary form of psychology. We enter a realm of crude fetishism when we summon before consciousness the basic presuppositions of the metaphysics of language, in plain talk, the presuppositions of reason. Everywhere it sees a doer and doing; it believes in will as *the* cause; it believes in the ego, in the ego as being, in the ego as substance, and it projects this faith in the ego-substance upon all things—only thereby does it first *create* the concept of "thing." Everywhere "being" is projected by thought, pushed underneath, as the cause; the concept of being follows, and is a derivative of, the concept of ego. In the beginning there is that great calamity of an error that the will is something which is effective, that will is a capacity. Today we know that it is only a word.

Very much later, in a world which was in a thousand ways more enlightened, philosophers, to their great surprise, became aware of the sureness, the subjective certainty, in our handling of the categories of reason: they concluded that these categories could not be derived from anything empirical—for everything empirical plainly contradicted them. Whence, then, were they derived?

And in India, as in Greece, the same mistake was made: "We must once have been at home in a higher world (instead of a very much lower one, which would have been the truth); we must have been divine, for we have reason!" Indeed, nothing has yet possessed a more naive power of persuasion than the error concerning being, as it has been formulated by the Eleatics, for example. After all, every word we say and every sentence speak in its favor. Even the opponents of the Eleatics still succumbed to the seduction of their concept of being: Democritus, among others, when he invented his atom. "Reason" in language—oh, what an old deceptive female she is! I am afraid we are not rid of God because we still have faith in grammar.

[6] It will be appreciated if I condense so essential and so new an insight into four theses. In that way I facilitate comprehension; in that way I provoke contradiction.

First proposition. The reasons for which "this" world has been characterized as "apparent" are the very reasons which indicate its reality; any other kind of reality is absolutely indemonstrable.

Second proposition. The criteria which have been bestowed on the "true being" of things are the criteria of not-being, of *naught;* the "true world" has been constructed out of contradiction to the actual world: indeed an apparent world, insofar as it is merely a moral-optical illusion.

Third proposition. To invent fables about a world "other" than this one has no meaning at all, unless an instinct of slander, detraction, and suspicion against life has gained the upper hand in us: in that case, we avenge ourselves against life with a phantasmagoria of "another," a "better" life.

Fourth proposition. Any distinction between a "true" and an "apparent" world—whether in the Christian manner or in the manner of Kant (in the end, an underhanded Christian)—is only a suggestion of decadence, a symptom of the *decline of life.* That the artist esteems appearance higher than reality is no objection to this proposition. For "appearance" in this case means reality *once more,* only by way of selection, reinforcement, and correction. The tragic artist is no pessimist: he is precisely the one who says Yes to everything questionable, even to the terrible—he is *Dionysian.*

How the "True World" Finally Became a Fable

The History of an Error

1. The true world—attainable for the sage, the pious, the virtuous man; he lives in it, *he is it.*

(The oldest form of the idea, relatively sensible, simple, and persuasive. A circumlocution for the sentence, "I, Plato, *am* the truth.")

2. The true world—unattainable for now, but promised for the sage, the pious, the virtuous man ("for the sinner who repents")

(Progress of the idea: it becomes more subtle, insidious, incomprehensible—*it becomes female,* it becomes Christian.)

3. The true world—unattainable, indemonstrable, unpromisable; but the very thought of it—a consolation, an obligation, an imperative.

(At bottom, the old sun, but seen through mist and skepticism. The idea has become elusive, pale, Nordic, Königsbergian [i.e., Kantian].)

4. The true world—unattainable? At any rate, unattained. And being unattained, also *unknown.* Consequently, not *consoling,* redeeming, or obligating: how could something unknown obligate us?

(Gray morning. The first yawn of reason. The cockcrow of positivism.)

5. The "true" world—an idea which is no longer good for anything, not even obligating—an idea which has become useless and superfluous—*consequently,* a refuted idea: let us abolish it!

(Bright day; breakfast; return of *bon sens* and cheerfulness; Plato's embarrassed blush; pandemonium of all free spirits.)

6. The true world—we have abolished. What world has remained? The apparent one perhaps? But no! *With the true world we have also abolished the apparent one.*

(Noon; moment of the briefest shadow; end of the longest error; high point of humanity; INCIPIT ZARATHUSTRA.)

Morality as Anti-Nature

[1] All passions have a phase when they are merely disastrous, when they drag down their victim with the weight of stupidity—and a later, very much later phase when they wed the spirit, when they "spiritualize" themselves. Formerly, in view of the element of stupidity in passion, war was declared on passion itself, its destruction was plotted; all the old moral monsters are agreed on this: *il faut tuer les passions* [one must kill the passions]. The most famous formula for this is to be found in the New Testament, in that Sermon on the Mount, where, incidentally, things are by no means looked at from a height. There it is said, for example, with particular reference to sexuality: "If thy eye offend thee, pluck it out." Fortunately, no Christian acts in accordance with this precept. *Destroying* the passions and cravings, merely as a preventive measure against their stupidity and the unpleasant consequences of this stupidity—today this itself strikes us as merely another acute form of stupidity. We no longer admire dentists who "pluck out" teeth so that they will not hurt any more.

To be fair, it should be admitted, however, that on the ground out of which Christianity grew, the concept of the *"spiritualization* of passion" could never have been formed. After all the first church, as is well known, fought against the "intelligent" in favor of the "poor in spirit." How could one expect from it an intelligent war against passion? The church fights passion with excision in every sense: its practice, its "cure," is *castratism.* It never asks: "How can one spiritualize, beautify, deify a craving?" It has at all times laid the stress of discipline on extirpation (of sensuality, of pride, of the lust to rule, of avarice, of vengefulness). But an attack on the roots of passion means an attack on the roots of life: the practice of the church *is hostile to life.*

[2] The same means in the fight against a craving—castration, extirpation—is instinctively chosen by those who are too weak-willed, too degenerate, to be able to impose moderation on themselves; by those who are so constituted that they require *La Trappe,* [The Trappist Order] to use a figure of speech, or (without any figure of speech) some kind of definitive declaration of hostility, a *cleft* between themselves and the passion. Radical means are indispensable only for the degenerate; the weakness of the will—or, to speak more definitely, the inability not to respond to a stimulus—is itself merely another form of degeneration. The radical hostility, the deadly hostility against sensuality, is always a symptom to reflect on: it entitles us to suppositions concerning the total state of one who is excessive in this manner.

This hostility, this hatred, by the way, reaches its climax only when such types lack even the firmness for this radical cure, for this renunciation of their "devil." One should survey the whole history of the priests and philosophers, including the artists: the most poisonous things against the senses have been said not by the impotent, nor by ascetics, but by the impossible ascetics, by those who really were in dire need of being ascetics.

[3] The spiritualization of sensuality is called *love:* it represents a great triumph over Christianity. Another triumph is our spiritualization of *hostility.* It consists in a profound appreciation of the value of having enemies: in short, it means acting and thinking in the opposite way from that which has been the rule. The church always wanted the destruction of its enemies; we, we immoralists and Antichristians, find our advantage in this, that the church exists. In the political realm too, hostility has now become more spiritual—much more sensible, much more thoughtful, much more *considerate.* Almost every party understands how it is in the interest of its own self-preservation that the opposition should not lose all strength; the same is true of power politics. A new creation in particular—the new *Reich,* for example—needs enemies more than friends: in opposition alone does it *feel* itself necessary, in opposition alone does it *become* necessary.

Our attitude to the "internal enemy" is no different: here too we have spiritualized hostility; here too we have come to appreciate its value. The price of fruitfulness is to be rich in internal opposition; one remains young only as long as the soul does not stretch itself and desire peace. Nothing has become more alien to us than that desideratum of former times, "peace of soul," the *Christian* desideratum; there is nothing we envy less than the moralistic cow and the fat happiness of the good conscience. One has renounced the *great* life when one renounces war.

In many cases, to be sure, "peace of soul" is merely a misunderstanding—something else, which lacks only a more honest name. Without further ado or prejudice, a few examples. "Peace of soul" can be, for one, the gentle radiation of a rich animality into the moral (or religious) sphere. Or the beginning of weariness, the first shadow of evening, of any kind of evening. Or a sign that the air is humid, that south winds are approaching. Or unrecognized gratitude for a good digestion (sometimes called "love of man"). Or the attainment of calm by a convalescent who feels a new relish in all things and waits. Or the state which follows a thorough satisfaction of our dominant passion, the well-being of a rare repletion. Or the senile weakness of our will, our cravings, our vices. Or laziness, persuaded by vanity to give itself moral airs. Or the emergence of certainty, even a dreadful certainty, after long tension and torture by uncertainty. Or the expression of maturity and mastery in the midst of doing, creating, working, and willing—calm breathing, *attained* "freedom of the will." *Twilight of the Idols*—who knows? perhaps also only a kind of "peace of soul."

[4] I reduce a principle to a formula. Every naturalism in morality—that is, every healthy morality—is dominated by an instinct of life; some commandment of life is fulfilled by a determinate canon of "shalt" and "shalt not"; some inhibition and hostile element on the path of life is thus removed. *Anti-natural* morality—that is, almost every morality which has so far been taught, revered, and preached—turns, conversely, *against* the instincts of life: it is *condemnation* of these instincts, now secret, now outspoken and impudent. When it says, "God looks at the heart," it says No to both the lowest and the highest desires of life, and posits God as the *enemy* of *life*. The saint in whom God delights is the ideal eunuch. Life has come to an end where the "kingdom of God" begins.

[5] Once one has comprehended the outrage of such a revolt against life as has become almost sacrosanct in Christian morality, one has, fortunately, also comprehended something else: the futility, apparentness, absurdity, and *mendaciousness* of such a revolt. A condemnation of life by the living remains in the end a mere symptom of a certain kind of life: the question whether it is justified or unjustified is not even raised thereby. One would require a position *outside* of life, and yet have to know it as well as one, as many, as all who have lived it, in order to be permitted even to touch the problem of the *value* of life: reasons enough to comprehend that this problem is for us an unapproachable problem. When we speak of values, we speak with the inspiration, with the way of looking at things, which is part of life: life itself forces us to posit values; life itself values through us when we posit values. From this it follows that even that anti-natural morality which conceives of God as the counter-concept and condemnation of life is only a value judgment of life—but of what life? of what kind of life? I have already given the answer: of declining, weakened, weary, condemned life. Morality, as it has so far been understood—as it has in the end been formulated once more by Schopenhauer, as "negation of the will to life"—is; the very *instinct of decadence,* which makes an imperative of itself. It says: *"Perish!"* It is a condemnation pronounced by the condemned.

[6] Let us finally consider how naive it is altogether to say: "Man *ought* to be such and such!" Reality shows us an enchanting wealth of types, the abundance of a lavish play and change of forms—and some wretched loafer of a moralist comments: "No! Man ought to be different." He even knows what man should be like, this wretched bigot and prig: he paints himself on the wall and comments, *"Ecce homo!"* But even when the moralist addresses himself only to the single human being and says to him, "You ought to be such and such!" he does not cease to make himself ridiculous. The single human being is a piece of *fatum* from the front and from the rear, one law more, one necessity more for all that is yet to come and to be. To say to him, "Change yourself!" is to demand that everything be changed, even retroactively. And indeed there have been consistent moralists who wanted man to be different, that is, virtuous—they wanted him remade in their own image as a prig: to that end, they *negated* the world! No small madness! No modest kind of immodesty!

Morality, insofar as it *condemns* for its own sake, and not out of regard for the concerns, considerations, and contrivances of life, is a specific error with which one ought to have no pity—an *idiosyncrasy of degenerates* which has caused immeasurable harm.

We others, we immoralists, have, conversely, made room in our hearts for every kind of understanding, comprehending, and *approving.* We do not easily negate; we make it a point of honor to be *affirmers.* More and more, our eyes have opened to that economy which needs and knows how to utilize all that the holy witlessness of the priest, of the *diseased* reason in the priest, rejects—that economy in the law of life which finds an advantage even in the disgusting species of the prigs, the priests, the virtuous. *What* advantage? But we ourselves, we immoralists, are the answer.

THE FOUR GREAT ERRORS

[1] *The error of confusing cause and effect.* There is no more dangerous error than that of mistaking the effect for the cause-. I call it the real corruption of reason. Yet this error belongs among the most ancient and recent habits of mankind. It is even hallowed among us and goes by the name of "religion" or "morality." Every single sentence which religion and morality formulate contains it; priests and legislators of moral codes are the originators of this corruption of reason.

I give an example. Everybody knows the book of the famous Cornaro in which he recommends his slender diet as a recipe for a long and happy life—a virtuous one too. Few books have been read so much; even now thousands of copies are sold in England every year. I do not doubt that scarcely any book (except the Bible, as is meet) has done as much harm, has *shortened* as many lives, as this well-intentioned *curiosum.* The reason: the mistaking of the effect for the cause. The worthy Italian thought his diet was the *cause* of his long life, whereas the precondition for a long life, the extraordinary slowness of his metabolism, the consumption of so little, was the cause of his slender diet. He was not free to eat little *or* much; his frugality was not a matter of "free will": he became sick when he ate more. But whoever is no carp not only does well to eat properly, but needs to. A scholar in our time, with his rapid consumption of nervous energy, would simply destroy himself with Cornaro's diet. *Crede experto* ["Believe him who has tried!"]

[2] The most general formula on which every religion and morality is founded is: "Do this and that, refrain from this and that—then you will be happy! Otherwise. . . ." Every morality, every religion, is this imperative; I call it the great original sin of reason, the *immortal unreason.* In my mouth, this formula is changed into its opposite—first example of my "revaluation of all values": a well-turned-out human being, a "happy one," *must* perform certain actions and shrinks instinctively from other actions; he carries the order, which he represents physiologically, into his relations with other human beings and things. In a formula: his virtue is the *effect* of his happiness. A long life, many descendants—this is not the wages of virtue; rather virtue itself is that slowing down of the metabolism which leads, among other things, also to a long life, many descendants—in short, to *Cornarism.*

The church and morality say: "A generation, a people, are destroyed by license and luxury." My *recovered* reason says: when a people approaches destruction, when it degenerates physiologically, then license and luxury *follow* from this (namely, the craving for ever stronger and more frequent stimulation, as every exhausted nature knows it). This young man turns pale early and wilts; his friends say; that is due to this or that disease. I say: that he became diseased, that he did not resist the disease, was already the effect of art impoverished life or hereditary exhaustion. The newspaper reader says: this party destroys itself by making such a mistake. My *higher* politics says: a party which makes such mistakes has reached its end; it has lost its sureness of instinct. Every mistake in every sense is the effect of the degeneration of instinct, of the disintegration of the will: one could almost define what is bad in this way. All that is good is instinct—and hence easy, necessary, free. Laboriousness is an objection; the god is typically different from the hero. (In my language light feet are the first attribute of divinity.)

[3] *The error of a false causality.* People have believed at all times that they knew what a cause is; but whence did we take our knowledge—or more precisely, our faith that we had such knowledge? From the realm of the famous "inner facts," of which not a single one has so far proved to be factual. We believed ourselves to be causal in the act of willing: we thought that here at least we caught causality in the act. Nor did one doubt that all the antecedents of an act, its causes, were to be sought in consciousness and would be found there once sought—as "motives": else one would not have been free and responsible for it. Finally, who would have denied that a thought is caused? that the ego causes the thought?

Of these three "inward facts" which seem to guarantee causality, the first and most persuasive is that of the will as cause. The conception of a consciousness ("spirit") as a cause, and later also that of the ego as cause (the "subject"), are only afterbirths: first the causality of the will was firmly accepted as given, as *empirical.*

Meanwhile we have thought better of it. Today we no longer believe a word of all this. The "inner world" is full of phantoms and will-o'-the-wisps: the will is one of them. The will no longer moves anything, hence does not explain anything either—it merely accompanies vents; it can also be absent. The so-called *motive:* another error. Merely a surface phenomenon of consciousness, something alongside the deed that is more likely to cover up the antecedents of the deeds than to represent them. And as for the *ego!* That has become a fable, a fiction, a play on words: it has altogether ceased to think, feel, or will!

What follows from this? There are no mental causes at all. The whole of the allegedly empirical evidence for that has gone to the devil. That is what follows! And what a fine abuse we had perpetrated with this "empirical, evidence"; we *created* the world on this basis as a world of causes, a world of will, a world of spirits. The most ancient and enduring psychology was at work here and did not do anything else: all that happened was considered a doing, all doing the effect of a will; the world became to it a multiplicity of doers; a doer (a "subject") was slipped under all that happened. It was out of himself that man projected his three "inner facts"—that in which he believed most firmly, the will, the spirit, the ego. He even took the concept of being from, the concept of the ego; he posited "things" as "being," in his image, in accordance with his concept of the ego as a cause. Small wonder that later he always found in things only that *which he had put into them.* The thing itself, to say it once more, the concept of thing is a mere reflex of the faith in the ego as cause. And even your atom, my dear mechanists and physicists—how much error, how much rudimentary psychology is still residual in your atom! Not to mention the "thing-in-itself," the *horrendum pudendum* of the metaphysicians! The error of the spirit as cause mistaken for reality! And made the very measure of reality! And called God!

[4] *The error of Imaginary causes.* To begin with dreams: *ex post facto*, a cause is slipped under a particular sensation (for example, one following a far-off cannon shot)—often a whole little novel in which the dreamer turns up as the protagonist. The sensation endures meanwhile in a kind of resonance: it waits, as it were, until the causal instinct permits it to step into the foreground now no longer as a chance occurrence, but as "meaning." The cannon shot appears in a *causal* mode, in an apparent reversal of time. What is really later, the motivation, is experienced first—often with a hundred details which pass like lightning—and the shot *follows*. What has happened? The representations which were *produced* by a certain state have been misunderstood as its causes.

In fact, we do the same thing when awake. Most of our general feeling—every kind of inhibition, pressure, tension, and explosion in the play and counterplay of our organs, and particularly the state of the *nervus sympathicus*—excite our causal instinct: we want to have a reason for feeling this way or that—for feeling bad or for feeling good. We are never satisfied merely to state the fact that we feel this way or that; we admit this fact only—become conscious of it only—when we have furnished some kind of motivation. Memory, which swings into action in such cases, unknown to us, brings up earlier states of the same kind, together with the causal interpretations associated with them—not their real causes. The faith, to be sure, that such representations, such accompanying conscious processes, are the causes, is also brought forth by memory. Thus originates a habitual acceptance of a particular causal interpretation, which, as a matter of fact, inhibits any investigation into the real cause—even precludes it.

[5] *The psychological explanation of this.* To derive something unknown from something familiar relieves, comforts, and satisfies, besides giving a feeling of power. With the unknown, one is confronted with danger, discomfort, and care; the first instinct is to abolish these painful states. First principle: any explanation is better than none. Since at bottom it is merely a matter of wishing to be rid of oppressive representations, one is not too particular about the means of getting rid of them: the first representation that explains the unknown as familiar feels so good that one "considers it true." The proof of pleasure ("of strength") as a criterion of truth.

The causal instinct is thus conditional upon, and excited by, the feeling of fear. The "why?" shall, if at all possible, not give the cause for its own sake so much as for a *particular kind of cause*—a cause that is comforting, liberating, and relieving. That it is something already familiar, experienced, and inscribed in the memory, which is posited as a cause, that is the first consequence of this need. That which is new and strange and has not been experienced before, is excluded as a cause. Thus one searches not only for some kind of explanation to serve as a cause, but for a particularly selected and preferred kind of explanation—that which has most quickly and most frequently abolished the feeling of the strange, new, and hitherto unexperienced: the *most habitual* explanations. Consequence: one kind of positing of causes predominates more and more, is concentrated into a system, and finally emerges as *dominant*, that is, as simply precluding other causes and explanations. The banker immediately thinks of "business," the Christian of "sin," and the girl of her love.

[6] *The whole realm of morality and religion belongs under this concept of imaginary causes.* The "explanation" of *disagreeable* general feelings. They are produced by beings that are hostile to us (evil spirits: the most famous case—the misun-

derstanding of the hysterical as witches). They are produced by acts which cannot be approved (the feeling of "sin," of "sinfulness," is slipped under a physiological discomfort; one always finds reasons for being dissatisfied with oneself). They are produced as punishments, as payment for something we should not have done, for what we should not have *been* (impudently generalized by Schopenhauer into a principle in which morality appears as what it really is—as the very poisoner and slanderer of life: "Every great pain, whether physical or spiritual, declares what we deserve; for it could not come to us if we did not deserve it." (*World as Will and Representation* II, 666). They are produced as effects of ill-considered actions that turn out badly. (Here the affects, the senses, are posited as causes, as "guilty"; and physiological calamities are interpreted with the help of other calamities as "deserved.")

The "explanation" of *agreeable* general feelings. They are produced by trust in God. They are produced by the consciousness of good deeds (the so-called "good conscience"—a physiological state which at times looks so much like good digestion that it is hard to tell them apart). They are produced by the successful termination of some enterprise (a naïve fallacy: the successful termination of some enterprise does not by any means give a hypochondriac or a Pascal agreeable general feelings). They are produced by faith, charity, and hope—the Christian virtues.

In truth, all these supposed explanations are resultant states and, as it were, translations of pleasurable or unpleasurable feelings into a false dialect: one is in a state of hope *because* the basic physiological feeling is once again strong and rich; one trusts in God *because* the feeling of fullness and strength gives a sense of rest. Morality and religion belong altogether to the *psychology of error:* in every single case, cause and effect are confused; or truth is confused with the effects of *believing* something to be true; or a state of consciousness is confused with its causes.

[7] *The error of free will.* Today we no longer have any pity for the concept of "free will": we know only too well what it really is—the foulest of all theologians' artifices, aimed at making mankind "responsible" in their sense, that is, *dependent upon them.* Here I simply supply the psychology of all "making responsible."

Wherever responsibilities are sought, it is usually the instinct of wanting to judge and punish which is at work. Becoming has been deprived of its innocence when any being-such-and-such is traced back to will, to purposes, to acts of responsibility: the doctrine of the will has been invented essentially for the purpose of punishment, that is, because one wanted to impute guilt. The entire old psychology, the psychology of will, was conditioned by the fact that its originators, the priests at the head of ancient communities, wanted to create for themselves the right to punish—or wanted to create this right for God. Men were considered "free" so that they might be judged and punished—so that they might become *guilty:* consequently, every act had to be considered as willed, and the origin of every act had to be considered as lying within the consciousness (and thus the most fundamental counterfeit in *psychologicis* was made the principle of psychology itself).

Today, as we have entered into the reverse movement and we immoralists are trying with all our strength to take the concept of guilt and the concept of punishment out of the world again, and to cleanse psychology, history, nature, and social institutions and sanctions of them, there is in our eyes no more radical opposition than that of the theologians, who continue with the concept of a "moral world-order" to infect the innocence of becoming by means of "punishment" and "guilt." Christianity is a metaphysics of the hangman.

[8] What alone can be *our* doctrine? That no one *gives* man his qualities—neither God, nor society, nor his parents and ancestors, nor he himself. (The nonsense of the last idea was taught as "intelligible freedom" by Kant—perhaps by Plato already.) No one is responsible for man's being there at all, for his being such-and-such, or for his being in these circumstances or in this environment. The fatality of his essence is not to be disentangled from the fatality of all that has been and will be. Man is not the effect of some special purpose, of a will, and end; nor is he the object of an attempt to attain an "ideal of humanity" or an "ideal of happiness" or an "ideal of morality." It is absurd to wish to devolve one's essence on some end or other. We have invented the concept of "end": in reality there is no end.

One is necessary, one is a piece of fatefulness, one belongs to the whole, one is in the whole; there is nothing which could judge, measure, compare, or sentence our being, for that would mean judging, measuring, comparing, or sentencing the whole. But there nothing besides the whole. That nobody is held responsible any longer, that the mode of being may not be traced back to a *causa prima,* that the world does not form a unity either as a sensorium or as "spirit"— alone is the great liberation; with this alone is the innocence of becoming restored. The concept of "God" was until now the greatest objection to existence. We deny God, we deny the responsibility in God: only thereby do we redeem the world.

THE ANTI-CHRIST (in part)

FIRST BOOK: ATTEMPT AT A CRITIQUE OF CHRISTIANITY

*   *   *

2. What is good? Everything that heightens the feeling of power in man, the will to power, power itself.

What is bad? Everything that is born of weakness.

What is happiness? The feeling that power is *growing,* that resistance is overcome.

Not contentedness but more power; not peace but war; not virtue but fitness (Renaissance virtue, *virtù,* virtue that is moraline*-free).

The weak and the failures shall perish: first principle of our love of man. And they shall even be given every possible assistance.

---

*The coinage of a man who neither smoked nor drank coffee.

What is more harmful than any vice? Active pity for all the failures and all the weak: Christianity.

3. The problem I thus pose is not what shall succeed mankind in the sequence of living beings (man is an *end*), but what type of man shall be *bred,* shall be *willed,* for being higher in value, worthier of life, more certain of a future.

Even in the past this higher type has appeared often—but as a fortunate accident, as an exception, never as something *willed.* In fact, this has been the type most dreaded—almost *the* dreadful—and from dread the opposite type was willed, bred, and *attained:* the domestic animal, the herd animal, the sick human animal—the Christian.

4. Mankind does *not* represent a development toward something better or stronger or higher in the sense accepted today. "Progress" is merely a modern idea, that is, a false idea. The European of today is vastly inferior in value to the European of the Renaissance: further development is altogether *not* according to any necessity in the direction of elevation, enhancement, or strength.

In another sense, success in individual cases is constantly encountered in the most widely different places and cultures: here we really do find a *higher type,* which is, in relation to mankind as a whole, a kind of overman. Such fortunate accidents of great success have always been possible and will perhaps always be possible. And even whole families, tribes, or peoples may occasionally represent such a *bull's-eye.*

5. Christianity should not be beautified and embellished: it has waged deadly war against this higher type of man; it has placed all the basic instincts of this type under the ban; and out of these instincts it has distilled evil and the Evil One: the strong man as the typically reprehensible man, the "reprobate." Christianity has sided with all that is weak and base, with all failures; it has made an ideal of whatever *contradicts* the instinct of the strong life to preserve itself; it has corrupted the reason even of those strongest in spirit by teaching men to consider the supreme values of the spirit as something sinful, as something that leads into error—as temptations. The most pitiful example: the corruption of Pascal, who believed in the corruption of his reason through original sin when it had in fact been corrupted only by his Christianity.

6. It is a painful, horrible spectacle that has dawned on me: I have drawn back the curtain from the *corruption* of man. In my mouth, this word is at least free from one suspicion: that it might involve a moral accusation of man. It is meant—let me emphasize this once more—*moraline-free.* So much so that I experience this corruption most strongly precisely where men have so far aspired most deliberately to "virtue" and "godliness." I understand corruption, as you will guess, in the sense of decadence: it is my contention that all the values in which mankind now sums up its supreme desiderata are *decadence-values.*

I call an animal, a species, or an individual corrupt when it loses its instincts, when it chooses, when it prefers, what is disadvantageous for it. A history of "lofty sentiments," of the "ideals of mankind"—and it is possible that I shall have to write it—would almost explain too *why* man is so corrupt. Life itself is to my mind the instinct for growth, for durability, for an accumulation of forces, for *power:* where the will to power is lacking there is decline. It is my contention that all the supreme values of mankind *lack* this will—that the values which are symptomatic of decline, *nihilistic* values, are lording it under the holiest name.

7. Christianity is called the religion of *pity.* Pity stands opposed to the tonic emotions which heighten our vitality: it has a depressing effect. We are deprived of strength when we feel pity. That loss of strength which suffering as such inflicts on life is still further increased and multiplied by pity. Pity makes suffering contagious. Under certain circumstances, it may engender a total loss of life and vitality out of all

proportion to the magnitude of the cause (as in the case of the death of the Nazarene). That is the first consideration, but there is a more important one.

Suppose we measure pity by the value of the reactions it usually produces; then its perilous nature appears in an even brighter light. Quite in general, pity crosses the law of development, which is the law of *selection.* It preserves what is ripe for destruction; it defends those who have been disinherited and condemned by life; and by the abundance of the failures of all kinds which it keeps alive, it gives life itself a gloomy and questionable aspect.

Some have dared to call pity a virtue (in every *noble* ethic it is considered a weakness); and as if this were not enough, it has been made *the* virtue, the basis and source of all virtues. To be sure—one should always keep this in mind—this was done by a philosophy that was nihilistic and had inscribed the *negation of life* upon its shield. Schopenhauer was consistent enough: pity negates life and renders it *more deserving of negation.*

Pity is the *practice* of nihilism. To repeat: this depressive and contagious instinct crosses those instincts which aim at the preservation of life and at the enhancement of its value. It multiplies misery and conserves all that is miserable, and is thus a prime instrument of the advancement of decadence: pity persuades men to *nothingness!* Of course, one does not say "nothingness" but "beyond" or "God," or "*true* life," or Nirvana, salvation, blessedness.

This innocent rhetoric from the realm of the religious-moral idiosyncrasy appears much less innocent as soon as we realize which tendency it is that here shrouds itself in sublime words: *hostility against life.* Schopenhauer was hostile to life; therefore pity became a virtue for him.

Aristotle, as is well known, considered pity a pathological and dangerous condition, which one would be well advised to attack now and then with a purge: he understood tragedy as a purge. From the standpoint of the instinct of life, a remedy certainly seems necessary for such a pathological and dangerous accumulation of pity as it is represented by the case of Schopenhauer (and unfortunately by our entire literary and artistic decadence from St. Petersburg to Paris, from Tolstoy to Wagner)—to puncture it and make it *burst.*

In our whole unhealthy modernity there is nothing more unhealthy than Christian pity. To be physicians *here,* to be inexorable here, to wield the scalpel *here*—that is *our* part, that is *our* love of man, that is how we are philosophers, we *Hyperboreans.*

*　　*　　*

62. With this I am at the end and I pronounce my judgment. I *condemn* Christianity. I raise against the Christian church the most terrible of all accusations that any accuser ever uttered. It is to me the highest of all conceivable corruptions. It has had the will to the last corruption that is even possible. The Christian church has left nothing untouched by its corruption; it has turned every value into an un-value, every truth into a lie, every integrity into a vileness of the soul. Let anyone dare to speak to me of its "humanitarian" blessings! To *abolish* any distress ran counter to its deepest advantages: it lived on distress, it *created* distress to eternalize *itself.*

The worm of sin, for example: with this distress the church first enriched mankind. The "equality of souls before God," this falsehood, this *pretext* for the rancor of all the base-minded, this explosive of a concept which eventually became revolution, modern idea, and the principle of decline of the whole order of society—is *Christian* dynamite. "Humanitarian" blessings of Christianity! To breed out of *humanitas* a self-contradiction, an art of self-violation, a will to lie at any price, a repugnance, a contempt for all good and honest instincts! Those are some of the blessings of Christianity!

Parasitism as the *only* practice of the church; with its ideal of anemia, of "holiness," draining all blood, all love, all hope for life; the beyond as the will to negate every reality; the cross as the mark of recognition for the most subterranean conspiracy that ever existed—against health, beauty, whatever has turned out well, courage, spirit, *graciousness* of the soul, *against life itself.*

This eternal indictment of Christianity I will write on all walls, wherever there are walls—I have letters to make even the blind see.

I call Christianity the one great curse, the one great innermost corruption, the one great instinct of revenge, for which no means is poisonous, stealthy, subterranean, *small* enough—I call it the one immortal blemish of mankind.

And time is reckoned from the *dies nefastus* with which this calamity began— after the *first* day of Christianity! *Why not rather after its last day? After today?* Revaluation of all values!

TWENTIETH-CENTURY PHILOSOPHY

————◄O►————

by Hans Bynagle

The major twentieth-century philosophical traditions are notoriously difficult to characterize in a nutshell. Generalizations, especially, are perilous and apt to be misleading. Fortunately, one can begin to sketch a philosophical map, albeit a *very* rough one, in terms that are largely geographical. One of the major lines that can be drawn on our map divides the philosophical tradition that dominates most of the European continent, known accordingly as Continental philosophy, from the dominant philosophical tradition of England, the United States, and some other countries subject to strong British or American influence (such as Canada and Australia) known as Anglo-American philosophy.

I can offer here only the most rudimentary characterizations of a few of the main strands of Continental philosophy beginning with Phenomenology. Founded around the turn of this century by Edmund Husserl, and developed by Martin Heidegger, Phenomenology is essentially a philosophical method, one that focuses on careful inspection and description of phenomena or appearances, defined as any object of conscious experience, i.e., that which we are conscious *of*. The inspection and description are supposed to be effected without any presuppositions, and that includes any presuppositions as to whether such objects of consciousness are "real" or correspond to something "external," or as to what their causes or consequences may be. It is believed that by this method the essential structures of experience and its objects can be uncovered. The sorts of

Adapted from Hans Bynagle, "A Map of Twentieth-Century Philosophy," *Philosophy: A Guide to the Reference Literature,* 2nd edition (Littleton, CO: Libraries Unlimited, 1997). Reprinted by permission of the author.

experiences and phenomena that Phenomenologists have sought to describe are highly varied, including, for instance, time consciousness, mathematics and logic, perception, experience of the social world, our experience of our own bodies, and moral, aesthetic, and religious experience.

Existentialism, unlike Phenomenology, is not primarily a philosophical method. Neither is it exactly a set of doctrines (at least not any *one* set) but more an outlook or attitude supported by diverse doctrines centered about certain common themes. These themes include the human condition, or the relation of the individual to the world; the human response to that condition (described often in strongly affective and preponderantly negative terms such as "despair," "dread," "anxiety," "guilt," "bad faith," "nausea"); being, especially the difference between the being of persons (which is "existence") and the being of other kinds of things; human freedom; the significance (and unavoidability) of choice and decision in the absence of certainty; and the concreteness and subjectivity of life as lived, over against abstractions and false objectifications.

Existentialism is often thought to be anti-religious (and is, in some of its versions), but there has in fact been a strong current of Christian Existentialism, beginning with the figure often credited with originating Existentialism, the nineteenth-century Danish philosopher Kierkegaard. Existentialism's relationship to Phenomenology is a matter of some controversy, but at least one can say that many of the later Existentialist thinkers, Sartre among them, have employed Phenomenological methods to arrive at or support their specific variations on Existial themes. While Existentialism has been on the wane since the 1960s, it has enjoyed exceptional prominence, even popularity, for a philosophical movement, in part because of its literary expressions by writers such as Sartre, Albert Camus, de Beauvoir, and Marcel.

Structuralism is an interdisciplinary movement united by the principle that social and cultural phenomena, including belief systems and every kind of discourse (literary, political, scientific, etc.), are best understood by analogy with language, itself best understood as a structure of relations among its component parts. Just as in language the crucial determinant of meaning (according to the early structural linguist Ferdinand de Saussure) is neither individual words nor their reference to things outside language but their interrelationships within the linguistic structure, so the crucial element in all social and cultural phenomena is the underlying structure that determines the functions of the various parts. A good deal of Structuralist analysis has been concerned with a kind of unmasking, that is, with revealing political, social, or psychological phenomena as (allegedly) not what they seem or what participants believe them to be but as determined by structures often concealed from view.

This unmasking impulse persists with the group of thinkers sometimes designated Post-structuralists, who both rejected certain presuppositions of Structuralism and added their own more radical ideas about the fundamental role of language in constructing all human perceptions and conceptions of reality. A particular form of this unmasking tendency is Deconstruction, introduced in the work of Jacques Derrida, who is generally counted among Post-structuralists. Any attempt to define Deconstruction must labor in the shadow of Derrida's apparent rejection in advance of all such attempts. Nonetheless, it has seemed fair to many interpreters to characterize it as a form of textual criticism or interpretation whose aim is to unmask and overcome hidden "privileging" that occurs in texts of all kinds. This privileging, for example the privileging of reason, the masculine, the sacred, the literal, or the objective, etc., entails the exclusion, suppression, or marginalization of their opposites—passion, the feminine, the profane, the metaphorical, the subjective, etc.—while at the same time it must presuppose these opposites to sustain or even to make sense of the privileged concept. In this way, it is maintained, texts regularly undermine their own assumptions. As a reading technique uncovering alleged hidden agendas behind the ostensible meaning of a text, Deconstruction takes the further step of denying that the text has a definite meaning. This has become a key thesis for the currents of literary theorizing and criticism that followed in Derrida's wake.

$$* \quad * \quad *$$

Turning the the other dominant twentieth-century philosophical tradition, it is not uncommon to equate Anglo-American philosophy with what is called Analytic or Analytical philosophy. But the term is also used in a broader sense to encompass other movements that have flourished chiefly on British and American soil, for instance Pragmatism, Naturalism, and Process Philosophy. There is much to be said for the wider meaning, which avoids the suggestion that philosophy in England and America is more monolithic than it really is. The equation of Anglo-American with Analytic is also unfortunate from another point of view, in that Analytic philosophy has become the dominant mode of philosophizing in some other areas as well, notably the Scandinavian countries, to say nothing of the inroads it has made in areas where other approaches still dominate the field (the other side of the blurring and bridging of the Continental/Anglo-American boundary), e.g., in Germany. However, given all those qualifications and others, there is no question that Analytic philosophy is the most important philosophical current within the Anglo-American sphere. It is also the one most often contrasted with (and actively opposed to) the Continental movements described above.

What Analytic philosophy is is not so easy to say. I believe it is possible to distinguish at least three variants, though they probably represent points on a spectrum rather than discrete alternatives. In the widest and loosest sense, Analytic philosophy is hardly more than a philosophical style, one that takes extreme care with the meanings of words (sometimes with precise definitions of terms and consistency in their use, sometimes with the nuances of ordinary language), that tends to present arguments in meticulous step-by-step fashion (often endeavoring to leave nothing implicit), and that pays close, sometimes minute, attention to logical relations (often using logical symbolism or specialized logical terminology to render such relations transparent). In a narrower sense, "Analytic philosophy" designates a philosophical outlook that holds that the primary task or even (in its more extreme version) the only proper task of philosophy—the primary or proper method for attacking philosophical problems—is analysis of one sort or another: of meanings, of concepts, of logical relations, or all of these. We can call this the methodological version. Finally, one may occasionally encounter the term "Analytic philosophy" in contexts where it is reserved for one or more specific doctrines regarding the outcome of correct philosophical analysis. While the Analytic tradition (in either of the two wider senses) owes a great deal to certain specific doctrinal versions—and to major figures who propounded them, such as Bertrand Russell, Ludwig Wittgenstein, and Logical Positivists such as A.J. Ayer—it would be incorrect to say that Analytic philosophy is the dominant orientation among British and American philosophers if one has in mind this narrower meaning. In fact, it is not clear that this is true under any but the widest meaning distinguished above.

Common to those who subscribe to the Analytic approach, whether in the broadest sense or a narrower one, is the conviction that to some significant degree, philosophical problems, puzzles, and errors are rooted in language and can be solved or avoided, as the case may be, by a sound understanding of language and careful attention to its workings. (Willard Van Orman Quine, for example, exhibits this strategy in his careful examination of the analytic-synthetic distinction.) This method has tended to focus much attention on language and on its close relative, logic, as objects of study for their own sake. (The relationship between language and logic is itself a question subjected to considerable inquiry and debate.) Detractors are apt to point to this concern—they might say this obsession—with language and logic as one aspect of the trivialization of philosophy with which they charge the Analytic movement. Many who are generally loyal or sympathetic to Analytic philosophy may agree that it tended to draw philosophy away from "deep" questions. In any case, the last two to three decades have seen, on the one hand, increased self-searching as to the limitations of the Analytic approach, and on the other, more efforts to apply it to such deeper questions—about the meaning of life, for instance, or the nature of the moral life—in a way that takes them seriously.

*   *   *

For secondary works on twentieth-century philosophy, consult the appropriate works from Frederick Copleston's series *A History of Philosophy, Volumes VIII: Bentham to Russell* and *Volume IX: Maine de Brian to Sartre* (New York: Image Doubleday, 1966 and 1974). For the history of specific movements in twentieth-century Western philosophy, see Michael Corrado, *The Analytic Tradition in Philosophy: Background and Issues* (Chicago: American Library Association, 1975); Robert C. Solomon, *From Hegel to Existentialism* (Oxford: Oxford University Press, 1987); Richard Kearney, ed., *Twentieth-Century Continental Philosophy* (London: Routledge, 1994); Giovanna Borradori, *The American Philosopher,* translated by Rosanna Crocitto (Chicago: University of Chicago Press, 1994); D.S. Clarke, *Philosophy's Second Revolution: Early and Recent Analytic Philosophy* (La Salle, IL: Open Court, 1997); and Simon Critchley and William Schroeder, eds., *A Companion to Continental Philosophy* (Oxford: Basil Blackwell, 1997). Surveys that focus exclusively on recent philosophy include John Passmore, *Recent Philosophers* (La Salle, IL: Open Court, 1985); Hugh J. Silverman, ed., *Philosophy and Non-Philosophy since Merleau-Ponty* (London: Routledge, 1988); and John Lechte, *Fifty Key Contemporary Thinkers: From Structuralism to Postmodernity* (London: Routledge, 1994). Robert Audi, ed., *The Cambridge Dictionary of Philosophy* (Cambridge: Cambridge University Press, 1995); Stuart Brown et al., *Biographical Dictionary of Twentieth-Century Philosophers* (London: Routledge, 1996); and Hans Bynagle, *Philosophy: A Guide to the Reference Literature,* 2nd edition (Littleton, CO: Libraries Unlimited, 1997) provide helpful reference works.

EDMUND HUSSERL
1859–1938

Edmund Husserl was born in Prostějov (Prossnitz), Moravia, in what is now the Czech Republic; at that time, it was part of the Austrian Empire. After attending elementary school in Prostějov, Husserl went to *gymnasia* (high schools) in Vienna and Olmütz before enrolling at the University of Leipzig in 1876. For two years, he studied mathematics, physics, and astronomy, attending philosophy lectures only in his spare time. In 1878, he transferred to the Friedrich-Wilhelm University of Berlin, where he continued his study of mathematics (under the renowned Karl Weierstrass) as well as his hobby of philosophy. After three years, he moved to the University of Vienna, where he received a Ph.D. in mathematics in 1883.

Husserl was offered a teaching position in mathematics at Berlin, but he decided to remain in Vienna so that he could continue studying philosophy. He worked with the philosophical psychologist Franz Brentano (1838–1917) during the next two years. Following Brentano's advice, Husserl then moved to the University of Halle, where he published his first book, *Philosophy of Arithmetic* (1891). In 1901, he moved to the University of Göttingen, where he spent the next sixteen years and published a number of important works, including *Ideas: General Introduction to Pure Phenomenology* (1913). His last post was at the University of Freiburg, where he taught until his retirement in 1928. Among his Freiburg associates was Martin Heidegger. Following retirement, Husserl wrote voluminously—though little was published during his lifetime. Toward the end of his life, the Nazis barred him from formal academic activities because of his Jewish ancestry.

After his death in 1938, the Husserl Archive was established in Louvain, Belgium. The Archive has preserved, transcribed, and, over the decades, published

Husserl's shorthand notes as the *Husserliana series.* The Archive has also hosted congresses on, and published essays in, phenomenology.

*   *   *

Franz Brentano, Husserl's teacher, criticized British empiricism for its tendency to present consciousness in terms of ideas or representations. Brentano argued that the key constituent of mental states is intentionality—thought's correlation rather than its immobile state. In order to have consciousness, one must be conscious of something. One cannot just think, one must think *about* something; one cannot just desire, one must have desire *for* something; one cannot just be aware, one must be aware *of* something. In each case, the "something" is the "intentional object" of consciousness. Contrary to Kant, Brentano held that consciousness does not *construct* these objects, it only *points to* them.

The end of the nineteenth century brought two quite different responses to Brentano. The analytic tradition, which tended to dominate English-speaking philosophy, focused almost exclusively on objects of consciousness, ignoring consciousness itself. The phenomenological tradition, dominant on the European continent, examined the nature of consciousness itself.

Husserl is the acknowledged founder of this phenomenological response. Like Descartes, Husserl considered consciousness the main topic for philosophy. In examining the form of this consciousness, Husserl discovered what he called "the natural standpoint":

> I am aware of a world, spread out in space endlessly, and in time becoming and become, without end. I am aware of it, that means, first of all, I discover it immediately, intuitively, I experience it. Through sight, touch, hearing, etc., . . . corporeal things somehow spatially distributed are *for me simply there,* . . . "present," whether or not I pay them special attention by busying myself with them, considering, thinking, feeling, willing.*

This is the world as it is actually lived by an individual. Although we can develop "worlds" of arithmetic or science by our knowledge of things from a particular standpoint, the natural standpoint—the world as actually lived by individuals—is always prior to, and conditioning of, any particular knowledge possible.

Yet according to Husserl, it is possible to get behind this natural standpoint to identify an invariant intentional structure. Husserl developed a method of "bracketing," which he called ⟨*epoché*⟩ (from the Greek word for noncommitment or suspended judgment). For example, I may look with pleasure at a blossoming apple tree. From the natural standpoint, I can see that the tree exists outside of me in space and time and that I am enjoying my psychical state of pleasure. From this standpoint, moreover, there is an assumed relation between me and the apple tree. But Descartes had shown that this perception could be mistaken—I could be hallucinating. As a result, my knowledge of the tree is uncertain. But I can suspend my judgments about the tree and perform an ⟨*epoché*⟩. This "bracketing" moves me from a natural to a phenomenological standpoint,

---

*Edmund Husserl, *Ideas: General Introduction to Pure Phenomenology,* translated by W.R. Boyce Gibson (Atlantic Highlands, NJ: Humanities Press, 1931), Section 2, Chapter 1, ¶27. (Emphasis in original.)

from which I now recognize "a nexus of exotic experiences of perception and pleasure valuation." Of this nexus of intending tree-experiences I *am* certain. By no longer referring to objective existence, by applying the phenomenological ⟨*epochē*⟩ instead, I have arrived at the pure datum of intending experience.

In the latter part of *Ideas* and in several other works, Husserl developed this method further, showing how to use the newly acquired phenomenological data. For example, in examining the experience of time, Husserl found that "lived time" is not the time of clocks and calendars but is always experienced as now. Similarly, in the experience of "lived space" one always finds oneself *here,* and everything else at different degrees of *there.* In his article on "Phenomenology" for the *Encyclopædia Brittanica,* given here (complete), Husserl explained that it is possible to apply the phenomenological method not only to the *objects* of consciousness but to consciousness itself. When we perform such an ⟨*epochē*⟩ on consciousness, we discover an invariant structure: the transcendental ego. "The 'I' and the 'we,' which we apprehend, presuppose the hidden 'I' and 'we' to whom they are 'present.'"

Husserl's thought continues to be influential. Martin Heidegger used the phenomenological method to develop his ontology, and Jean-Paul Sartre used the method to develop his own "existential" interpretation of consciousness. Maurice Merleau-Ponty refined and further applied the phenomenological method. Husserl has lived on through his followers.

*   *   *

For works on phenomenology in general, see Herbert Speigelberg, *The Phenomenological Movement,* two volumes (The Hague, The Netherlands: Martinus Nijhoff, 1960); Joseph J. Kockelmans, ed., *Phenomenology* (Garden City, NY: Anchor Doubleday, 1967); and Christopher Macann, *Four Phenomenological Philosophers: Husserl, Heidegger, Sartre, Merleau-Ponty* (London: Routledge, 1993). For a clear and concise comparison of phenomenology and the analytic tradition, see W.T. Jones, *The Twentieth Century to Wittgenstein and Sartre,* 2nd edition (New York: Harcourt Brace Jovanovich, 1975), Chapters 7 and 8.

Marvin Farber, *The Foundations of Phenomenology* (Albany, NY: SUNY Press, 1943) provides a standard study of Husserl's thought, whereas Joseph J. Kockelmans, *A First Introduction to Husserl's Phenomenology* (Pittsburgh, PA: Duquesne University Press, 1967); David Bell, *Husserl* (New York: Routledge, 1990); and Rudolf Bernet, Iso Kern, and Eduard Marbach, *An Introduction to Husserlian Phenomenology* (Evanston, IL: Northwestern University Press, 1993) provide introductions. Paul Ricoeur, *Husserl: An Analysis of His Phenomenology,* translated by Edward G. Ballard and Lester E. Embree (Evanston, IL: Northwestern University Press, 1967), and Hans-Georg Gadamer, *Philosophical Hermeneutics,* translated by David E. Linge (Berkeley: University of California Press, 1976) have written studies of Husserl as well as important works of philosophy themselves. Among the many studies of particular areas of Husserl's thought, see David Carr, *Phenomenology and the Problem of History: A Study of Husserl's Transcendental Philosophy* (Evanston, IL: Northwestern University Press, 1974); Erazim V. Kohák, *Idea and Experience: Edmund Husserl's Project of Phenomenology in "Ideas I"* (Chicago: University of Chicago Press, 1978); Timothy J. Stapleton, Husserl and Heidegger: *The Question of a Phenomenological Beginning* (Albany, NY: SUNY Press, 1983); and James M. Edie, *Edmund Husserl's Phenomenology: A Critical Commentary* (Bloomington: Indiana University Press, 1987). For collections of essays, see R.O. Elveton, ed., *The Phenomenology of Husserl* (Chicago: Quadrangle Books, 1970); Frederick Elliston and Peter McCormick, eds., *Husserl: Expositions and Appraisals* (Notre Dame, IN: University of Notre Dame Press, 1977)—especially David Carr's article, "Husserl's Problematic Concept of the Life-World"; Robert Sokolowski, ed., *Edmund Husserl and the Phenomenological Tradition* (Washington, DC: Catholic University of America Press, 1988); Barry Smith and David Woodruff Smith, eds., *The Cambridge Companion to Husserl* (Cambridge: Cambridge University Press, 1995); and the *Husserl Studies,* an ongoing journal published by Kluwer Academic Publishers, Hingham, MA.

PHENOMENOLOGY

Phenomenology denotes a new, descriptive, philosophical method, which, since the concluding years of the last century, has established (1) an *a priori* psychological discipline, able to provide the only secure basis on which a strong empirical psychology can be built, and (2) a universal philosophy, which can supply an organum for the methodical revision of all the sciences.

I. PHENOMENOLOGICAL PSYCHOLOGY

Present-day psychology, as the science of the "psychical" in its concrete connection with spatio-temporal reality, regards as its material whatever is present in the world as "egoistic"; i.e., "living," perceiving, thinking, willing, etc., actual, potential and habitual. And as the psychical is known as a certain stratum of existence, proper to men and beasts, psychology may be considered as a branch of anthropology and zoology. But animal nature is a part of physical reality, and that which is concerned with physical reality is natural science. Is it, then, possible to separate the psychical cleanly enough from the physical to establish a pure psychology parallel to natural science? That a purely psychological investigation is practicable within limits is shown by our obligation to it for our fundamental conceptions of the psychical, and most of those of the psycho-physical.

But before determining the question of an unlimited psychology, we must be sure of the characteristics of psychological experience and the psychical data it provides. We turn naturally to our immediate experiences. But we cannot discover the psychical in any experience, except by a "reflection," or perversion of the ordinary attitude. We are accustomed to concentrate upon the matters, thoughts, and values of the moment, and not upon the psychical "act of experience" in which these are apprehended. This "act" is revealed by a "reflection"; and a reflection can be practised on every experience. Instead of the matters themselves, the values, goals, utilities, etc., we regard the subjective experiences in which these "appear." These "appearances" are phenomena, whose nature is to be a "consciousness-of" their object, real or unreal as it be. Common language catches this sense of "relativity," saying, I was thinking *of* something, I was frightened *of* something, etc. Phenomenological psychology takes its name from the "phenomena," with the psychological aspect of which it is concerned: and the word "intentional" has been borrowed from the scholastic to denote the essential "reference" character of the phenomena. All consciousness is "intentional."

In unreflective consciousness we are "directed" upon objects, we "intend" them, and reflection reveals this to be an immanent process characteristic of all experience, though infinitely varied in form. To be conscious of something is no empty having of that something in consciousness. Each phenomenon has its own intentional structure, which analysis shows to be an ever-widening system of individually intentional and intentionally related components. The perception of a cube, for example, reveals a multiple and synthesized intention: a continuous variety in the "appearance" of the cube, according to differences in the points of view from which it is seen, and corresponding differences in "perspective," and all the difference between the "front side" actually seen at the moment and the "backside" which is not seen, and which remains, therefore, relatively "indeterminate," and yet is supposed equally to be existent. Observation of this "stream" of "appearance-aspects" and of the manner of their synthesis, shows that every phase and interval is already in itself a "consciousness-of" something, yet in such a way that with the constant entry of new phases the total consciousness, at any moment, lacks not synthetic unity, and is, in fact, a consciousness of one and the same object. The intentional structure of the train of a perception must conform to a certain type, if any physical object is to be perceived as there! And if the same object be intuited in other modes, if it be imagined, or remembered, or copied, all its intentional forms recur, though modified in character from what they were in the perception, to correspond to their new modes. The same is true of every kind of psychical experience. Judgment, valuation, pursuit, these also are no empty experiences having in consciousness of judgments, values, goals and means, but are likewise experiences compounded of an intentional stream, each conforming to its own fast type.

Phenomenological psychology's comprehensive task is the systematic examination of the types and forms of intentional experience, and the reduction of their structures to the prime intentions, learning thus what is the nature of the psychical, and comprehending the being of the soul.

The validity of these investigations will obviously extend beyond the particularity of the psychologist's own soul. For psychical life may be revealed to us not only in self-consciousness but equally in our consciousness of other selves, and this latter source of experience offers us more than a reduplication of what we find in our self-consciousness, for it establishes the differences between "own" and "other" which we experience, and presents us with the characteristics of the "social-life." And hence the further task accrues to psychology of revealing the intentions of which the "social life" consists.

PHENOMENOLOGICAL-PSYCHOLOGICAL AND EIDETIC REDUCTIONS.

The Phenomenological psychology must examine the self's experience of itself and its derivative experience of other selves and of society, but whether, in so doing, it can be free of all psycho-physical admixture, is not yet clear. Can one reach a really pure self-experience and purely psychical data? This difficulty, even since Brentano's discovery of intentionality, as the fundamental character of the psychical, has blinded psychologists to the possibilities of phenomenological psychology. The psychologist finds his

Nude Descending a Staircase, Number 2, 1912, by Marcel Duchamp (1887–1968).
Duchamp's shattered and reassembled nude figure descending the staircase in robotic
rhythm purposely challenges the viewer to derive a personal interpretation of the
image—to move beyond the natural standpoint with its judgments concerning spacio-
temporal existence. *(Philadelphia Museum of Art: Louise and Walter Arensberg
Collection)*

self-consciousness mixed everywhere with "external" experience, and non-psychical realities. For what is experienced as external belongs not to the intentional "internal," though our experience of it belongs there as an experience of the external. The phenomenologist, who will only notice phenomena, and know purely his own "life," must practice an ⟨epochē⟩. He must inhibit every ordinary objective "position," and partake in no judgement concerning the objective world. The experience itself will remain what it was, an experience of this house, of this body, of this world in general, in its particular mode. For one cannot describe any intentional experience, even though it be "illusory," a self-contradicting judgment and the like, without describing what in the experience is, as such, the object of consciousness.

Our comprehensive ⟨epochē⟩ puts, as we say, the world between brackets, excludes the world which is simply there! from the subject's field, presenting in its stead the so-and-so-experienced-perceived-remembered-judged-thought-valued-etc., world, as such, the "bracketed" world. Not the world or any part of it appears, but the "sense" of the world. To enjoy phenomenological experience we must retreat from the objects posited in the natural attitude to the multiple modes of their "appearance," to the "bracketed" objects.

The phenomenological reduction to phenomena, to the purely psychical, advances by two steps: (1) systematic and radical ⟨epochē⟩ of every objectifying "position" in an experience, practised both upon the regard of particular objects and upon the entire attitude of mind, and (2) expert recognition, comprehension and description of the manifold "appearances" of what are no longer "objects" but "unities" of "sense." So that the phenomenological description will comprise two parts, description of the "noetic" (⟨neo⟩) or "experiencing" and description of the "noematic" (⟨noema⟩) or the "experienced." Phenomenological experience, is the only experience which may properly be called "internal" and there is no limit to its practice. And as a similar "bracketing" of objective, and description of what then "appears" (⟨"noema"⟩ in ⟨"noesis"⟩)), can be performed upon the "life" of another self which we represent to ourselves, the "reductive" method can be extended from one's own self-experience to one's experience of other selves. And, further, that society, which we experience in a common consciousness, may be reduced not only to the intentional fields of the individual consciousness, but also by the means of an inter-subjective reduction, to that which unites these, namely the phenomenological unity of the social life. Thus enlarged, the psychological concept of internal experience reaches its full extent.

But it takes more than the unity of a manifold "intentional life," with its inseparable complement of "sense-unities," to make a "soul." For from the individual life that "ego-subject" cannot be disjoined, which persists as an identical ego or "pole," to the particular intentions, and the "habits" growing out of these. Thus the "inter-subjective," phenomenologically reduced and concretely apprehended, is seen to be a "society" of "persons," who share a conscious life.

Phenomenological psychology can be purged of every empirical and psychophysical element, but, being so purged, it cannot deal with "matters of fact." Any closed field may be considered as regards its "essence," its ⟨eidos⟩, and we may disregard the factual side of our phenomena, and use them as "examples" merely. We shall ignore individual souls and societies, to learn their a priori, their "possible" forms. Our thesis will be "theoretical," observing the invariable through variation, disclosing a typical realm of a priori. There will be no psychical existence whose "style" we shall not know. Psychological phenomenology must rest upon eidetic phenomenology.

The phenomenology of the perception of bodies, for example, will not be an account of actually occurring perceptions, or those which may be expected to occur, but of that invariable "structure," apart from which no perception of a body, single or prolonged, can be conceived. The phenomenological reduction reveals the phenomena of actual internal experience; the eidetic reduction, the essential forms constraining psychical existence.

Men now demand that empirical psychology shall conform to the exactness required by modern natural science. Natural science, which was once a vague, inductive empiric, owes its modern character to the *a priori* system of forms, nature as it is "conceivable," which its separate disciplines, pure geometry, laws of motion, time, etc., have contributed. The methods of natural science and psychology are quite distinct, but the latter, like the former, can only reach "exactness" by a rationalization of the "essential."

The psycho-physical has an *a priori* which must be learned by any complete psychology, this *a priori* is not phenomenological, for it depends no less upon the essence of physical, or more particularly organic nature.

II. TRANSCENDENTAL PHENOMENOLOGY

Transcendental philosophy may be said to have originated in Descartes, and phenomenological psychology in Locke, Berkeley and Hume, although the latter did not grow up primarily as a method or discipline to serve psychology, but to contribute to the solution of the transcendental problematic which Descartes had posed. The theme propounded in the *Meditations* was still dominant in a philosophy which it had initiated. All reality, so it ran, and the whole of the world which we perceive as existent, may be said to exist only as the content of our own representations, judged in our judgments, or, at best, proved by our own knowing. There lay impulse enough to rouse all the legitimate and illegitimate problems of transcendence, which we know. Descartes' "Doubting" first disclosed "transcendental subjectivity," and his "Ego Cogito" was its first conceptual handling. But the Cartesian transcendental "Mens" became the "Human Mind," which Locke undertook to explore; and Locke's exploration turned into a psychology of the internal experience. And since Locke thought his psychology could embrace the transcendental problems, in whose interest he had begun his work, he became the founder of a false psychologistical philosophy which has persisted because men have not analysed their concept of "subjective" into its twofold significance. Once the transcendental problem is fairly stated, the ambiguity of the sense of the "subjective" becomes apparent, and establishes the phenomenological psychology to deal with its one meaning, and the transcendental phenomenology with its other.

Phenomenological psychology has been given the priority in this article, partly because it forms a convenient stepping-stone to the philosophy and partly because it is nearer to the common attitude than is the transcendental. Psychology, both in its eiditic and empirical disciplines, is a "positive" science, promoted in the "natural attitude" with the world before it for the ground of all its themes, while transcendental experience is difficult to realize because it is "supreme" and entirely "unworldly." Phenomenological psychology, although comparatively new, and completely new as far as it uses intentional analysis, can be approached from the gates of any of the positive sciences: and, being once reached, demands only a reemployment, in a more stringent mode, of its formal mechanism of reduction and analysis, to disclose the transcendental phenomena.

But it is not to be doubted that transcendental phenomenology could be developed independently of all psychology. The discovery of the double relativity of consciousness suggests the practice of both reductions. The psychological reduction does not reach beyond the psychical in animal realities, for psychology subserves real existence, and even its eidetic is confined to the possibilities of real worlds. But the transcendental problem will include the entire world and all its sciences, to "doubt" the whole. The world "originates" in us, as Descartes led men to recognize and within us acquires its habitual influence. The general significance of the world, and the definite sense of its particulars, is something of which we are conscious within our perceiving, representing, thinking, valuing life, and therefore something "constituted" in some subjective genesis.

The world and its property, "in and for itself," exists as it exists, whether I, or we, happen, or not, to be conscious of it. But let once this general world, make its "appearance" in consciousness as "the" world. It is thenceforth related to the subjective, and all its existence and the manner of it, assumes a new dimension, becoming "incompletely intelligible," "questionable." Here, then, is the transcendental problem; this "making its appearance," this "being for us" of the world, which can only gain its significance "subjectively," what is it? We may call the world "internal" because it is related to consciousness, but how can this quite "general" world, whose "immanent" being is as shadowy as the consciousness wherein it "exists," contrive to appear before us in a variety of "particular" aspects, which experience assures us are the aspects of an independent, self-existent world? The problem also touches every "ideal" world, the world of pure number, for example, and the world of "truths in themselves." And no existence, or manner of existence, is less wholly intelligible than ourselves. Each by himself, and in society, we, in whose consciousness the world is valid, being men, belong ourselves to the world. Must we, then, refer ourselves to ourselves to gain a worldly sense, a worldly being? Are we both psychologically to be called men, subjects of a psychical life, and yet be transcendental to ourselves and the whole world, being subjects of a transcendental world-constituting life? Psychical subjectivity, the "I" and "we" of everyday intent, may be experienced as it is in itself under the phenomenological-psychological reduction, and being eidetically treated, may establish a phenomenological psychology. But the transcendental subjectivity, which for want of language we can only call again, "I myself," "we ourselves," cannot be found under the attitude of psychological or natural science, being no part at all of the objective world, but that subjective conscious life itself, wherein the world and all its content is made for "us," for "me." We that are, indeed, men, spiritual and bodily, existing in the world, are, therefore, "appearances" unto ourselves, parcel of what "we" have constituted, pieces of the significance "we" have made. The "I" and "we," which we apprehend, presuppose a hidden "I" and "we" to whom they are "present."

To this transcendental subjectivity transcendental experience gives us direct approach. As the psychical experience was purified, so is the transcendental, by a reduction. The transcendental reduction may be regarded as a certain further purification of the psychological interest. The universal is carried to a further stage. Henceforth the "bracketing" includes not the world only but its "souls" as well. The psychologist reduces the ordinarily valid world to a subjectivity of "souls," which are a part of the world which they inhabit. The transcendental phenomenologist reduces the already psychologically purified to the transcendental, that most general, subjectivity, which makes the world and its "souls," and confirms them.

I no longer survey my perception experiences, imagination-experiences, the psychological data which my psychological experience reveals: I learn to survey transcendental experience. I am no longer interested in my own existence. I am interested in the pure intentional life, wherein my psychically real experiences have occurred. This step raises the transcendental problem (the transcendental being defined as the quality of that which is consciousness) to its true level. We have to recognize that relativity to consciousness is not only an actual quality of our world, but, from eidetic necessity, the quality of every conceivable world. We may, in a free fancy, vary our actual world, and transmute it to any other which we can imagine, but we are obliged with the world to vary ourselves also, and ourselves we cannot vary except within the limits prescribed to us by the nature of subjectivity. Change worlds as we may, each must ever be a world such as we could experience, prove upon the evidence of our theories and inhabit with our practice. The transcendental problem is eidetic. My psychological experiences, perceptions, imaginations and the like remain in form and content what they were, but I see them as "structures" now, for I am face to face at last with the ultimate structure of consciousness.

It is obvious that, like every other intelligible problem, the transcendental problem derives the means of its solution from an existence-stratum, which it presupposes and sets beyond the reach of its enquiry. This realm is no other than the bare subjectivity of consciousness in general, while the realm of its investigation remains not less than every sphere which can be called "objective," which considered in its totality, and at its root, is the conscious life. No one, then, can justly propose to solve the transcendental problem by psychology either empirical or eidetic-phenomenological, without *petitio principii* [begging the question], for psychology's "subjectivity" and "consciousness" are not that subjectivity and consciousness, which our philosophy will investigate. The transcendental reduction has supplanted the psychological reduction. In the place of the psychological "I" and "we," the transcendental "I" and "we" are comprehended in the concreteness of transcendental consciousness. But though the transcendental "I" is not my psychological "I," it must not be considered as if it were a second "I," for it is no more separated from my psychological "I" in the conventional sense of separation, than it is joined to it in the conventional sense of being joined.

Transcendental self-experience may, at any moment, merely by a change of attitude, be turned back into psychological self-experience. Passing, thus, from the one to the other attitude, we notice a certain "identity" about the ego. What I saw under the psychological reflection as "my" objectification, I see under the transcendental reflection as self-objectifying, or, as we may also say, as objectified by the transcendental "I." We have only to recognize that what makes the psychological and transcendental spheres of experience parallel is an "identity" in their significance, and that what differentiates them is merely a change of attitude, to realize that the psychological and transcendental phenomenologies will also be parallel. Under the more stringent ⟨*epochē*⟩ the psychological subjectivity is transformed into the transcendental subjectivity, and the psychological inter-subjectivity into the transcendental inter-subjectivity. It is this last which is the concrete, ultimate ground, whence all that transcends consciousness, including all that is real in the world, derives the sense of its existence. For all objective existence is essentially "relative," and owes its nature to a unity of intention, which being established according to transcendental laws, produces consciousness with its habit of belief and its conviction.

PHENOMENOLOGY, THE UNIVERSAL SCIENCE.

Thus, as phenomenology is developed, the Leibnitzian foreshadowing of a universal ontology, the unification of all conceivable *a priori* sciences, is improved, and realized upon the new and non-dogmatic basis of phenomenological method. For phenomenology as the science of all concrete phenomena proper to subjectivity and inter-subjectivity, is *eo ipso* an *a priori* science of all possible existence and existences. Phenomenology is universal in its scope, because there is no *a priori* which does not depend upon its intentional constitution, and derive from this its power of engendering habits in the consciousness that knows it, so that the establishment of any *a priori* must reveal the subjective process by which it is established.

Once the *a priori* disciplines, such as the mathematical sciences, are incorporated within phenomenology, they cannot thereafter be beset by "paradoxes" or disputes concerning principles: and those sciences which have become *a priori* independently of phenomenology, can only hope to set their methods and premises beyond criticism, by founding themselves upon it. For their very claim to be positive, dogmatic sciences bears witness to their dependency, as branches, merely, of that universal, eidetic ontology, which is phenomenology.

The endless task, this exposition of the universum of the *a priori,* by referring all objectives to their transcendental "origin," may be considered as one function in the construction of a universal science of fact, where every department, including the positive, will be settled on its *a priori.* So that our last division of the complete phenomenology is thus: eidetic phenomenology, or the universal ontology, for a first philosophy; and second philosophy as the science of the transcendental inter-subjectivity or universum of fact.

Thus the antique conception of philosophy as the universal science, philosophy in the Platonic, philosophy in the Cartesian, sense, that shall embrace all knowledge, is once more justly restored. All rational problems, and all those problems, which for one reason or another, have come to be known as "philosophical," have their place within phenomenology, finding from the ultimate source of transcendental experience or eidetic intuition, their proper form and the means of their solution. Phenomenology itself learns its proper function of transcendental human "living" from an entire relationship to "self." It can intuite life's absolute norms and learn life's original teleological structure. Phenomenology is not less than man's whole occupation with himself in the service of the universal reason. Revealing life's norms, he does in fact, set free a stream of new consciousness intent upon the infinite idea of entire humanity, humanity in fact and truth.

Metaphysical, teleological, ethical problems, and problems of the history of philosophy, the problem of judgment, all significant problems in general, and the transcendental bonds uniting them, lie within phenomenology's capability.

Phenomenological philosophy is but developing the mainsprings of old Greek philosophy, and the supreme motive of Descartes. These have not died. They split into rationalism and empiricism. They stretch over Kant and German idealism, and reach the present, confused day. They must be reassumed, subjected to methodical and concrete treatment. They can inspire a science without bounds.

Phenomenology demands of phenomenalists that they shall forgo particular closed systems of philosophy, and share decisive work with others toward persistent philosophy.

BERTRAND RUSSELL
1872–1970

Bertrand Arthur William Russell was born into a prestigious family in Trelleck, Wales. His parents, Lord and Lady Amberley, were close friends with John Stuart Mill, and Russell's grandfather, Lord John Russell, had been prime minister to Queen Victoria. Both of Russell's parents died by the time he was three, and so, with his brother, he was sent to live with his grandparents, Lord and Lady Russell. When his grandfather died a few years later, his grandmother took responsibility for his education. Unlike most privileged English boys, Russell did not attend a boarding school—Lady Russell did not approve of them. Instead, she arranged for a series of Swiss and German governesses, followed by English tutors, to educate her grandsons. Although Russell thus enjoyed virtually every privilege, he later reported that his adolescent life seemed so bleak that he would have committed suicide had he not been "restrained by the desire to know more mathematics."

In 1890, Russell entered Cambridge University, where he was finally able to study his beloved mathematics on his own. His years at the university were the happiest of his life. He quickly established himself as one of the brightest students, and he formed several close friendships, including a lifelong one with G.E. Moore (1873–1958). Following graduation, Russell served briefly with the British ambassador to France before moving to Berlin to study economics and political theory. In 1895, Russell was elected a fellow of Trinity College, Cambridge, and worked extensively on the foundations of mathematics. He published *Principles of Mathematics* (1903) and, together with Alfred North Whitehead, the epoch-making *Principia Mathematica* (1910–1913). During this time, Russell also made the first of three unsuccessful runs for Parliament.

Russell was appointed lecturer in philosophy at Cambridge in 1910—a position he held until 1916, when he was dismissed for his opposition to the continued fighting of World War I. He also spent six months in jail for alleging that U.S. troops were used for strikebreaking in America. He was reinstated in his Cambridge position in 1919 but soon resigned and never again assumed permanent teaching duties. During his years as a lecturer, Russell also produced some of his most important works of philosophy and logic, including *The Problems of Philosophy* (1912), *Our Knowledge of the External World* (1914), and *Introduction to Mathematical Philosophy* (written while in prison and published in 1919).

In his post-teaching period, Russell wrote and lectured widely—often taking controversial positions on social and political issues. For example, he alienated many of his socialist friends when, after a visit to the Soviet Union in 1920, he published his observations in *The Theory and Practice of Bolshevism:*

> [Russia is] one vast prison in which the jailors were cruel bigots. When I found my friends applauding these men as liberators and regarding the regime that they were creating as a paradise, I wondered . . . whether it was my friends or I that were mad.

His book *Marriage and Morals* (1929) caused a stir by minimizing the seriousness of extramarital affairs and by advocating informal trial marriages. His works on religion, *What I Believe* (1925), *Religion and Science* (1935), and *Why I Am Not a Christian* (1957), made Russell's atheism explicit. Russell also tried his hand at practical social reform. With his second wife Dora, he started a school in 1927 to implement the educational theories of his books *On Education: Especially Early Childhood* (1926) and *Education and the Social Order* (1932).

In 1938, Russell accepted a visiting professorship at the University of Chicago and later at the University of California at Los Angeles. He declined a permanent offer from UCLA in order to accept an invitation from the College of the City of New York; however, before he could begin teaching a judge ruled him unfit, claiming, among other things, that Russell's appointment would constitute "a chair of indecency." Russell mocked the decision on the title page of his *An Inquiry into Meaning and Truth,* published the next year, by listing his many honors and then adding "Judicially pronounced unworthy to be Professor of Philosophy at the College of the City of New York (1940)." To that long list of honors, he would be able to add the Nobel Prize for literature in 1950.

In his later years, Russell continued to write on a variety of topics—and to get into trouble with authorities. At age eighty-nine, he served another jail sentence—this time for his part in a nuclear-disarmament rally in London. By the time of his death, in 1970, Russell was acknowledged as the leading British philosopher of the century.

* * *

It is difficult to summarize Russell's thought, partly because he developed and abandoned several philosophical theories during his long lifetime. Philosopher C.D. Broad once commented, "As we all know, Mr. Russell produces a different system of philosophy every few years." Even though the specifics of Russell's philosophic enterprise evolved, reflecting his fertile and inventive mind, at least two basic assumptions remained within his mature philosophy.

First, Russell believed philosophy should be scientific and analytical. As he wrote in "Logical Atomism" (1924):

> Although . . . comprehensive construction is part of the business of philosophy, I do not believe it is the most important part. The most important part, to my mind, consists in criticizing and clarifying notions which are apt to be regarded as funda- mental and accepted uncritically. As instances I might mention: mind, matter, con- sciousness, knowledge, experience, causality, will, time. I believe all these notions to be inexact and approximate, essentially infected with vagueness, incapable of forming part of any exact science.

Second, in "criticizing and clarifying notions," Russell was committed to the principle of parsimony known as "Ockham's Razor" (after the medieval thinker, William of Ockham). Ockham's injunction asserted that "entities are not to be multiplied beyond necessity," meaning one should always seek the simplest ex- planation. Russell's version of this principle, articulated in several of his works, states that "Whenever possible, substitute constructions out of known entities for inferences to unknown entities."

In the selection from *The Problems of Philosophy* reprinted here, Russell wields this razor in an analysis of the common objects of our sensory perception and our language about such objects. Russell points out that sense-data are the only "known entities" actually given in experience:

> What the senses *immediately* tell us is not the truth about the object as it is apart from us, but only the truth about certain sense-data which, so far as we can see, de- pend upon the relations between us and the object. [Emphasis in original.]

Rather than inferring some "unknown entity" (such as "being" or "sub- stance") as the cause of our sense-data, we can consider a given object to be the class or collection of all sense-data we normally associate with that object. Our knowledge of physical objects is not direct but is gained by "acquaintance" with the sense-data that make up the appearance of an object.

The language used to make propositions about such objects also depends on ac- quaintance. To use language in a meaningful manner, "the meaning we attach to our words must be something with which we are acquainted" either in terms of a thing or a description. Using Russell's example, a statement about Julius Caesar can be meaningful because, although we have no acquaintance with the "thing" (i.e., we have not met Caesar), we do have in mind some description of Caesar.

While this selection includes some of Russell's major themes and gives some sense of his style, his contributions to philosophy go beyond what has been in- cluded. His work in mathematics and logic changed both of those disciplines; his theory of logical atomism represented an important step in the philosophy of lan- guage; his theories of descriptions and of types helped clear up a number of logi- cal puzzles; and in addition there are his writings on education, sociology, poli- tics, and religion. In short, Russell touched on virtually all areas of human existence, and even those who differ with his conclusions cannot help but be im- pressed with the breadth and depth of his thought.

*   *   *

For biographical information, see Ronald William Clark, *The Life of Bertrand Russell* (New York: Knopf, 1976); Katharine Tait, *My Father, Bertrand Russell* (Bristol, UK: Thoemmes, 1996); or Russell's autobiography, *The Autobiography of Bertrand Russell* (Boston: Little, Brown, 1967). A.J. Ayer, *Russell and Moore: The Analytic Heritage* (Cambridge, MA: Harvard University Press, 1971) puts Russell's thought in the context of analytic philosophy, whereas J. Watling, *Bertrand Russell* (New York: British Book Center, 1971); A.J. Ayer, *Bertrand Russell* (Chicago: University of Chicago Press, 1988); and John Slater, *Bertrand Russell* (Bristol, Gloucester: Thoemmes, 1994) provide general introductions. Studies on specific areas of Russell's thought include Lillian Woodworth Aiken, *Bertrand Russell's Philosophy of Morals* (New York: Humanities Press, 1963); Robert J. Clack, *Bertrand Russell's Philosophy of Language* (The Hague, The Netherlands: Martinus Nijhoff, 1969); and Elizabeth R. Eames, *Bertrand Russell's Theory of Knowledge* (New York: George Braziller, 1969). For collections of essays, see Paul A. Schilpp, ed., *The Philosophy of Bertrand Russell* (New York: Tudor, 1951)—part of the Library of Living Philosophers; Ralph Schoenman, ed., *Bertrand Russell: Philosopher of the Century* (Boston: Little, Brown, 1967); E.D. Klernke, ed., *Essays on Bertrand Russell* (Urbana: University of Illinois Press, 1970); D.F. Pears, ed., *Bertrand Russell* (Garden City, NY: Anchor Doubleday, 1972); A.D. Irvine and G.A. Wedeking, eds., *Russell and Analytic Philosophy* (Toronto:University of Toronto Press, 1993); Ray Monk and Anthony Palmer, eds., *Bertrand Russell and the Origins of Analytical Philosophy* (Bristol, UK: Thoemmes, 1996).

THE PROBLEMS OF PHILOSOPHY
(in part)

CHAPTER 1: APPEARANCE AND REALITY

Is there any knowledge in the world which is so certain that no reasonable man could doubt it? This question, which at first sight might not seem difficult, is really one of the most difficult that can be asked. When we have realized the obstacles in the way of a straightforward and confident answer, we shall be well launched on the study of philosophy—for philosophy is merely the attempt to answer such ultimate questions, not carelessly and dogmatically, as we do in ordinary life and even in the sciences, but critically, after exploring all that makes such questions puzzling, and after realizing all the vagueness and confusion that underlie our ordinary ideas.

In daily life, we assume as certain many things which, on a closer scrutiny, are found to be so full of apparent contradictions that only a great amount of thought enables us to know what it is that we really may believe. In the search for certainty, it is natural to begin with our present experiences, and in some sense, no doubt, knowledge

Bertrand Russell, *The Problems of Philosophy* (Oxford: Oxford University Press, 1912). Reprinted by permission of Oxford University Press.

is to be derived from them. But any statement as to what it is that our immediate experiences make us know is very likely to be wrong. It seems to me that I am now sitting in a chair, at a table of a certain shape, on which I see sheets of paper with writing or print. By turning my head I see out of the window buildings and clouds and the sun. I believe that the sun is about ninety-three million miles from the earth; that it is a hot globe many times bigger than the earth; that, owing to the earth's rotation, it rises every morning, and will continue to do so for an indefinite time in the future. I believe that, if any other normal person comes into my room, he will see the same chairs and tables and books and papers as I see, and that the table which I see is the same as the table which I feel pressing against my arm. All this seems to be so evident as to be hardly worth stating, except in answer to a man who doubts whether I know anything. Yet all this may be reasonably doubted, and all of it requires much careful discussion before we can be sure that we have stated it in a form that is wholly true.

To make our difficulties plain, let us concentrate attention on the table. To the eye it is oblong, brown, and shiny, to the touch it is smooth and cool and hard; when I tap it, it gives out a wooden sound. Any one else who sees and feels and hears the table will agree with this description, so that it might seem as if no difficulty would arise; but as soon as we try to be more precise our troubles begin. Although I believe that the table is "really" of the same colour all over, the parts that reflect the light look much brighter than the other parts, and some parts look white because of reflected light. I know that, if I move, the parts that reflect the light will be different, so that the apparent distribution of colours on the table will change. It follows that if several people are looking at the table at the same moment, no two of them will see exactly the same distribution of colours, because no two can see it from exactly the same point of view, and any change in the point of view makes some change in the way the light is reflected.

For most practical purposes these differences are unimportant, but to the painter they are all-important: the painter has to unlearn the habit of thinking that things seem to have the colour which common sense says they "really" have, and to learn the habit of seeing things as they appear. Here we have already the beginning of one of the distinctions that cause most trouble in philosophy—the distinction between "appearance" and "reality," between what things seem to be and what they are. The painter wants to know what things seem to be, the practical man and the philosopher want to know what they are; but the philosopher's wish to know this is stronger than the practical man's, and is more troubled by knowledge as to the difficulties of answering the question.

To return to the table. It is evident from what we have found, that there is no colour which preeminently appears to be *the* colour of the table, or even of any one particular part of the table—it appears to be of different colours from different points of view, and there is no reason for regarding some of these as more really its colour than others. And we know that even from a given point of view the colour will seem different by artificial light, or to a colour-blind man, or to a man wearing blue spectacles, while in the dark there will be no colour at all, though to touch and hearing the table will be unchanged. This colour is not something which is inherent in the table, but something depending upon the table and the spectator and the way the light falls on the table. When, in ordinary life, we speak of *the* colour of the table, we only mean the sort of colour which it will seem to have to a normal spectator from an ordinary point of view under usual conditions of light. But the other colours which appear under other conditions have just as good a right to be considered real; and therefore, to avoid favouritism, we are compelled to deny that, in itself, the table has any one particular colour.

The same thing applies to the texture. With the naked eye one can see the grain, but otherwise the table looks smooth and even. If we looked at it through a microscope, we should see roughnesses and hills and valleys, and all sorts of differences that are imperceptible to the naked eye. Which of these is the "real" table? We are naturally tempted to say that what we see through the microscope is more real, but that in turn would be changed by a still more powerful microscope. If, then, we cannot trust what we see with the naked eye, why should we trust what we see through a microscope? Thus, again, the confidence in our senses with which we began deserts us.

The *shape* of the table is no better. We are all in the habit of judging as to the "real" shapes of things, and we do this so unreflectingly that we come to think we actually see the real shapes. But, in fact, as we all have to learn if we try to draw, a given thing looks different in shape from every different point of view. If our table is "really" rectangular, it will look, from almost all points of view, as if it had two acute angles and two obtuse angles. If opposite sides are parallel, they will look as if they converged to a point away from the spectator; if they are of equal length, they will look as if the nearer side were longer. All these things are not commonly noticed in looking at a table, because experience has taught us to construct the "real" shape from the apparent shape, and the "real" shape is what interests us as practical men. But the "real" shape is not what we see, it is something inferred from what we see. And what we see is constantly changing in shape as we move about the room; so that here again the senses seem not to give us the truth about the table itself, but only about the appearance of the table.

Similar difficulties arise when we consider the sense of touch. It is true that the table always gives us a sensation of hardness, and we feel that it resists pressure. But the sensation we obtain depends upon how hard we press the table and also upon what part of the body we press with; thus the various sensations due to various pressures or various parts of the body cannot be supposed to reveal *directly* any definite property of the table, but at most to be *signs* of some property which perhaps *causes* all the sensations, but is not actually apparent in any of them. And the same applies still more obviously to the sounds which can be elicited by rapping the table.

Thus it becomes evident that the real table, if there is one, is not the same as what we immediately experience by sight or touch or hearing. The real table, if there is one, is not *immediately* known to us all, but must be an inference from what is immediately known. Hence, two very difficult questions at once arise; namely, (1) Is there a real table at all? (2) If so, what sort of object can it be?

It will help us in considering these questions to have a few simple terms of which the meaning is definite and clear. Let us give the name of "sense-data" to the things that are immediately known in sensation: such things as colours, sounds, smells, hardnesses, roughnesses, and so on. We shall give the name "sensation" to the experience of being immediately aware of these things. Thus, whenever we see a colour, we have a sensation of the colour, but the colour itself is a sense-datum, not a sensation. The colour is that *of* which we are immediately aware, and the awareness itself is the sensation. It is plain that if we are to know anything about the table, it must be by means of the sense-data—brown colour, oblong shape, smoothness, etc.—which we associate with the table; but, for the reasons which have been given, we cannot say that the table *is* the sense-data, or even that the sense-data are directly properties of the table. Thus a problem arises as to the relation of the sense-data to the real table, supposing there is such a thing.

The real table, if it exists, we will call a "physical object." Thus we have to consider the relation of sense-data to physical objects. The collection of all physical objects is called "matter." Thus our two questions may be re-stated as follows: (1) Is there any such thing as matter? (2) If so, what is its nature?

The philosopher who first brought prominently forward the reasons for regarding the immediate objects of our senses as not existing independently of us was Bishop

Berkeley (1685–1753). His *Three Dialogues between Hylas and Philonous, in Opposition to Sceptics and Atheists,* undertake to prove that there is no such thing as matter at all, and that the world consists of nothing but minds and their ideas. Hylas has hitherto believed in matter, but he is no match for Philonous, who mercilessly drives him into contradictions and paradoxes, and makes his own denial of matter seem, in the end, as if it were almost common sense. The arguments employed are of very different value: some are important and sound, others are confused or quibbling. But Berkeley retains the merit of having shown that the existence of matter is capable of being denied without absurdity, and that if there are any things that exist independently of us they cannot be the immediate objects of our sensations.

There are two different questions involved when we ask whether matter exists, and it is important to keep them clear. We commonly mean by "matter" something which is opposed to "mind," something which we think of as occupying space and as radically incapable of any sort of thought or consciousness. It is chiefly in this sense that Berkeley denies matter; that is to say, he does not deny that the sense-data which we commonly take as signs of the existence of the table are really signs of the existence *of* something independent of us, but he does deny that this something is, non-mental, that it is neither mind nor ideas entertained by some mind. He admits that there must be something which continues to exist when we go out of the room or shut our eyes, and that what we call seeing the table does really give us reason for believing in something which persists even when we are not seeing it. But he thinks that this something cannot be radically different in nature from what we see, and cannot be independent of seeing altogether, though it must be independent of *our* seeing. He is thus led to regard the "real" table as an idea in the mind of God. Such an idea has the required permanence and independence of ourselves, without being—as matter would otherwise be—something quite unknowable, in the sense that we can only infer it, and can never be directly and immediately aware of it.

Other philosophers since Berkeley have also held that, although the table does not depend for its existence upon being seen by me, it does depend upon being seen (or otherwise apprehended in sensation) by *some* mind—not necessarily the mind of God, but more often the whole collective mind of the universe. This they hold, as Berkeley does, chiefly because they think there can be nothing real—or at any rate nothing known to be real—except minds and their thoughts and feelings. We might state the argument by which they support their view in some such way as this: "Whatever can be thought of is an idea in the mind of the person thinking of it; therefore nothing can be thought of except ideas in minds; therefore anything else is inconceivable, and what is inconceivable cannot exist."

Such an argument, in my opinion, is fallacious; and of course those who advance it do not put it so shortly or so crudely. But whether valid or not, the argument has been very widely advanced in one form or another; and very many philosophers, perhaps a majority, have held that there is nothing real except minds and their ideas. Such philosophers are called "idealists." When they come to explaining matter, they either say, like Berkeley, that matter is really nothing but a collection of ideas, or they say, like Leibniz (1646–1716), that what appears as matter is really a collection of more or less rudimentary minds.

But these philosophers, though they deny matter as opposed to mind, nevertheless, in another sense, admit matter. It will be remembered that we asked two questions; namely, (1) Is there a real table at all? (2) If so, what sort of object can it be? Now both Berkeley and Leibniz admit that there is a real table, but Berkeley says it is certain ideas in the mind of God, and Leibniz says it is a colony of souls. Thus both of them answer our first question in the affirmative, and only diverge from the views of ordinary mortals in their answer to our second question. In fact, almost all philosophers seem to be agreed that there is a real table: they almost all agree that, however much our sense-data—colour, shape, smoothness, etc.—may depend upon us, yet their occurrence is a sign of something existing independently of us, something differing, perhaps, completely from our sense-data, and yet to be regarded as causing those sense-data whenever we are in a suitable relation to the real table.

Now obviously this point in which the philosophers are agreed—the view that there *is* a real table, whatever its nature may be—is vitally important, and it will be worth while to consider what reasons there are for accepting this view before we go on to the further question as to the nature of the real table. Our next chapter, therefore, will be concerned with the reasons for supposing that there is a real table at all.

Before we go farther it will be well to consider for a moment what it is that we have discovered so far. It has appeared that, if we take any common object of the sort that is supposed to be known by the senses, what the senses *immediately* tell us is not the truth about the object as it is apart from us, but only the truth about certain sense-data which, so far as we can see, depend upon the relations between us and the object. Thus what we directly see and feel is merely "appearance," which we believe to be a sign of some "reality" behind. But if the reality is not what appears, have we any means of knowing whether there is any reality at all? And if so, have we any means of finding out what it is like?

Such questions are bewildering, and it is difficult to know that even the strangest hypotheses may not be true. Thus our familiar table, which has roused but the slightest thoughts in us hitherto, has become a problem full of surprising possibilities. The one thing we know about it is that it is not what it seems. Beyond this modest result, so far, we have the most complete liberty of conjecture. Leibniz tells us it is a community of souls; Berkeley tells us it is an idea in the mind of God; sober science, scarcely less wonderful, tells us it is a vast collection of electric charges in violent motion.

Among these surprising possibilities, doubt suggests that perhaps there is no table at all. Philosophy, if it cannot *answer* so many questions as we could wish, has at least the power of *asking* questions which increase the interest of the world, and show the strangeness and wonder lying just below the surface even in the commonest things of daily life.

*   *   *

CHAPTER 5: KNOWLEDGE BY ACQUAINTANCE AND KNOWLEDGE BY DESCRIPTION

In the preceding chapter [on "Idealism"] we saw that there are two sorts of knowledge: knowledge of things, and knowledge of truths. In this chapter we shall be concerned exclusively with knowledge of things, of which in turn we shall have to distinguish two kinds. Knowledge of things, when it is of the kind we call knowledge by *acquaintance,* is essentially simpler than any knowledge of truths, and logically independent of knowledge of truths, though it would be rash to assume that human beings ever, in fact, have acquaintance with things without at the same time knowing some truth about them. Knowledge of things by *description,* on the contrary, always involves, as we shall find in the course of the present chapter, some knowledge of truths as its source and ground. But first of all we must make clear what we mean by "acquaintance" and what we mean by "description."

We shall say that we have *acquaintance* with anything of which we are directly aware, without the intermediary of any process of inference or any knowledge of truths. Thus in the presence of my table I am acquainted with the sense-data that make up the appearance of my table—its colour, shape, hardness, smoothness, etc.; all these are things of which I am immediately conscious when I am seeing and touching my table. The particular shade of colour that I am seeing may have many things said about it—I may say that it is brown, that it is rather dark, and so on. But such statements, though they make me know truths *about* the colour, do not make me know the colour itself any better than I did before: so far as concerns knowledge of the colour itself, as opposed to knowledge of truths about it, I know the colour perfectly and completely when I see it, and no further knowledge of it itself is even theoretically possible. Thus the sense-data which make up the appearance of my table are things with which I have acquaintance, things immediately known to me just as they are.

My knowledge of the table as a physical object, on the contrary, is not direct knowledge. Such as it is, it is obtained through acquaintance with the sense-data that make up the appearance of the table. We have seen that it is possible, without absurdity, to doubt whether there is a table at all, whereas it is not possible to doubt the sense-data. My knowledge of the table is of the kind which we shall call "knowledge by description." The table is "the physical object which causes such-and-such sense-data." This *describes* the table by means of the sense-data. In order to know anything at all about the table, we must know truths connecting it with things with which we have acquaintance: we must know that "such-and-such sense-data are caused by a physical object." There is no state of mind in which we are directly aware of the table; all our knowledge of the table is really knowledge of *truths,* and the actual thing which is the table is not, strictly speaking, known to us at all. We know a description, and we know that there is just one object to which this description applies, though the object itself is not directly known to us. In such a case, we say that our knowledge of the object is knowledge by description.

All our knowledge, both knowledge of things and knowledge of truths, rests upon acquaintance as its foundation. It is therefore important to consider what kinds of things there are with which we have acquaintance.

Sense-data, as we have already seen, are among the things with which we are acquainted; in fact, they supply the most obvious and striking example of knowledge by acquaintance. But if they were the sole example, our knowledge would be very much more restricted than it is. We should only know what is now present to our senses: we could not know anything about the past—not even that there was a past—nor could we know any truths about our sense-data, for all knowledge of truths, as we shall show, demands acquaintance with things which are of an essentially different character from sense-data, the things which are sometimes called "abstract ideas," but which we shall call "universals." We have therefore to consider acquaintance with other things besides sense-data if we are to obtain any tolerably adequate analysis of our knowledge.

The first extension beyond sense-data to be considered is acquaintance by memory. It is obvious that we often remember what we have seen or heard or had otherwise present to our senses, and that in such cases we are still immediately aware of what we remember, in spite of the fact that it appears as past and not as present. This immediate knowledge by memory is the source of all our knowledge concerning the past: without it, there could be no knowledge of the past by inference, since we should never know that there was anything past to be inferred.

The next extension to be considered is acquaintance by *introspection.* We are not only aware of things, but we are often aware of being aware of them. When I see the sun, I am often aware of my seeing the sun; thus "my seeing the sun" is an object with which I have acquaintance. When I desire food, I may be aware of my desire for food; thus "my desiring food" is an object with which I am acquainted. Similarly we may be aware of our feeling pleasure or pain, and generally of the events which happen in our minds. This kind of acquaintance, which may be called self-consciousness, is the source of all our knowledge of mental things. It is obvious that it is only what goes on in our own minds that can be thus known immediately. What goes on in the minds of others is known to us through our perception of their bodies, that is, through the sense-data in us which are associated with their bodies. But for our acquaintance with the contents of our own minds, we should be unable to imagine the minds of others, and therefore we could never arrive at the knowledge that they have minds. It seems natural to suppose that self-consciousness is one of the things that distinguish men from animals: animals, we may suppose, though they have acquaintance with sense-data, never become aware of this acquaintance. I do not mean that they *doubt* whether they exist, but that they have never become conscious of the fact that they have sensations and feelings, nor therefore of the fact that they, the subjects of their sensations and feelings, exist.

We have spoken of acquaintance with the contents of our minds as *self-consciousness*, but it is not, of course, consciousness of our *self:* it is consciousness of particular thoughts and feelings. The question whether we are also acquainted with our bare selves, as opposed to particular thoughts and feelings, is a very difficult one, upon which it would be rash to speak positively. When we try to look into ourselves we always seem to come upon some particular thought or feeling, and not upon the "I" which has the thought or feeling. Nevertheless there are some reasons for thinking that we are acquainted with the "I," though the acquaintance is hard to disentangle from other things. To make clear what sort of reason there is, let us consider for a moment what our acquaintance with particular thoughts really involves.

When I am acquainted with "my seeing the sun," it seems plain that I am acquainted with two different things in relation to each other. On the one hand there is the sense-datum which represents the sun to me, on the other hand there is that which sees this sense-datum. All acquaintance, such as my acquaintance with the sense-datum which represents the sun, seems obviously a relation between the person acquainted and the object with which the person is acquainted. When a case of acquaintance is one with which I can be acquainted (as I am acquainted with my acquaintance with the sense-datum representing the sun), it is plain that the person acquainted is myself. Thus, when I am acquainted with my seeing the sun, the whole fact with which I am acquainted is "Self-acquainted-with-sense-datum."

Further, we know the truth "I am acquainted with this sense-datum." It is hard to see how we could know this truth, or even understand what is meant by it, unless we were acquainted with something which we call "I." It does not seem necessary to suppose that we are acquainted with a more or less permanent person, the same today as yesterday, but it does seem as though we must be acquainted with that thing, whatever its nature, which sees the sun and has acquaintance with sense-data. Thus, in some sense it would seem we must be acquainted with our Selves as opposed to our particular experiences. But the question is difficult, and complicated arguments can be adduced on either side. Hence, although acquaintance with ourselves seems *probably* to occur, it is not wise to assert that it undoubtedly does occur.

We may therefore sum up as follows what has been said concerning acquaintance with things that exist. We have acquaintance in sensation with the data of the outer senses, and in introspection with the data of what may be called the inner sense— thoughts, feelings, desires, etc.; we have acquaintance in memory with things which have been data either of the outer senses or of the inner sense. Further, it is probable, though not certain, that we have acquaintance with Self, as that which is aware of things or has desires towards things.

In addition to our acquaintance with particular existing things, we also have acquaintance with what we shall call universals, that is to say, general ideas, such as *whiteness, diversity, brotherhood,* and so on. Every complete sentence must contain at least one word which stands for a universal, since all verbs have a meaning which is universal. . . . It is only necessary [at this point] to guard against the supposition that whatever we can be acquainted with must be something particular and existent. Awareness of universals is called conceiving, and a universal of which we are aware is called a *concept.*

It will be seen that among the objects with which we are acquainted are not included physical objects (as opposed to sense-data), nor other people's minds. These things are known to us by what I call "knowledge by description," which we must now consider.

By a "description" I mean any phrase of the form "a so-and-so" or "the so-and-so." A phrase of the form "a so-and-so" I shall call an "ambiguous" description; a phrase of the form "the so-and-so" (in the singular) I shall call a "definite" description. Thus "a man" is an ambiguous description, and "the man with the iron mask" is a definite description. There are various problems connected with ambiguous descriptions, but I pass them by, since they do not directly concern the matter we are discussing, which is the nature of our knowledge concerning objects in cases where we know that there is an object answering to a definite description, though we are not *acquainted* with any such object. This is a matter which is concerned exclusively with *definite* descriptions. I shall therefore, in the sequel, speak simply of "descriptions" when I mean "definite descriptions." Thus a description will mean any phrase of the form "the so-and-so" in the singular.

We shall say that an object is "known by description" when we know that it is "the so-and-so," i.e. when we know that there is one object, and no more, having a certain property; and it will generally be implied that we do not have knowledge of the same object by acquaintance. We know that the man with the iron mask existed, and many propositions are known about him; but we do not know who he was. We know that the candidate who gets the most votes will be elected, and in this case we are very likely also acquainted (in the only sense in which one can be acquainted with some one else) with the man who is, in fact, the candidate who will get the most votes; but we do not know which of the candidates he is, i.e. we do not know any proposition of the form "A is the candidate who will get most votes" where A is one of the candidates by name. We shall say that we have "merely descriptive knowledge" of the so-and-so when, although we know that the so-and-so exists, and although we may possibly be acquainted with the object which is, in fact, the so-and-so, yet we do not know any proposition "*a* is the so-and-so," where *a* is something with which we are acquainted.

When we say "the so-and-so exists," we mean that there is just one object which is the so-and-so. The proposition "*a* is the so-and-so" means that *a* has the property so-

and-so, and nothing else has. "Mr. A. is the Unionist candidate for this constituency" means "Mr. A. is a Unionist candidate for this constituency, and no one else is." "The Unionist candidate for this constituency exists" means "some one is a Unionist candidate for this constituency, and no one else is." Thus, when we are acquainted with an object which is the so-and-so, we know that the so-and-so exists; but we may know that the so-and-so exists when we are not acquainted with any object which we know to be the so-and-so, and even when we are not acquainted with any object which, in fact, is the so-and-so.

Common words, even proper names, are usually really descriptions. That is to say, the thought in the mind of a person using a proper name correctly can generally only be expressed explicitly if we replace the proper name by a description. Moreover, the description required to express the thought will vary for different people, or for the same person at different times. The only thing constant (so long as the name is rightly used) is the object to which the name applies. But so long as this remains constant, the particular description involved usually makes no difference to the truth or falsehood of the proposition in which the name appears.

Let us take some illustrations. Suppose some statement made about Bismarck. Assuming that there is such a thing as direct acquaintance with oneself, Bismarck himself might have used his name directly to designate the particular person with whom he was acquainted. In this case, if he made a judgement about himself, he himself might be a constituent of the judgement. Here the proper name has the direct use which it always wishes to have, as simply standing for a certain object, and not for a description of the object. But if a person who knew Bismarck made a judgement about him, the case is different. What this person was acquainted with were certain sense-data which he connected (rightly, we will suppose) with Bismarck's body. His body, as a physical object, and still more his mind, were only known as the body and the mind connected with these sense-data. That is, they were known by description. It is, of course, very much a matter of chance which characteristics of a man's appearance will come into a friend's mind when he thinks of him; thus the description actually in the friend's mind is accidental. The essential point is that he knows that the various descriptions all apply to the same entity, in spite of not being acquainted with the entity in question.

When we, who did not know Bismarck, make a judgement about him, the description in our minds will probably be some more or less vague mass of historical knowledge—far more, in most cases, than is required to identify him. But, for the sake of illustration, let us assume that we think of him as "the first Chancellor of the German Empire." Here all the words are abstract except "German." The word "German" will, again, have different meanings for different people. To some it will recall travels in Germany, to some the look of Germany on the map, and so on. But if we are to obtain a description which we know to be applicable, we shall be compelled, at some point, to bring in a reference to a particular with which we are acquainted. Such reference is involved in any mention of past, present, and future (as opposed to definite dates), or of here and there, or of what others have told us. Thus it would seem that, in some way or other, a description known to be applicable to a particular must involve some reference to a particular with which we are acquainted, if our knowledge about the thing described is not to be merely what follows *logically* from the description. For example, "the most long-lived of men" is a description involving only universals, which must apply to some man, but we can make no judgements concerning this man which involve knowledge about him beyond what the description gives. If, however, we say, "The first Chancellor of the German Empire was an astute diplomatist," we can only be assured of the truth of our judgement in virtue of something with which we are acquainted—usually a testimony heard or read. Apart from the information we convey to others, apart from the fact about the actual Bismarck, which gives importance to our judgement, the thought we really have contains the one or more particulars involved, and otherwise consists wholly of concepts.

All names of places—London, England, Europe, the Earth, the Solar System—similarly involve, when used, descriptions which start from some one or more particulars with which we are acquainted. I suspect that even the Universe, as considered by metaphysics, involves such a connexion with particulars. In logic, on the contrary, where we are concerned not merely with what does exist, but with whatever might or could exist or be, no reference to actual particulars is involved.

It would seem that, when we make a statement about something only known by description, we often *intend* to make our statement, not in the form involving the description, but about the actual thing described. That is to say, when we say anything about Bismarck, we should like, if we could, to make the judgement which Bismarck alone can make, namely, the judgement of which he himself is a constituent. In this we are necessarily defeated, since the actual Bismarck is unknown to us. But we know that there is an object B, called Bismarck, and that B was an astute diplomatist. We can thus *describe* the proposition we should like to affirm, namely, "B was an astute diplomatist," where B is the object which was Bismarck. If we are describing Bismarck as "the first Chancellor of the German Empire," the proposition we should like to affirm may be described as "the proposition asserting, concerning the actual object which was the first Chancellor of the German Empire, that this object was an astute diplomatist." What enables us to communicate in spite of the varying descriptions we employ is that we know there is a true proposition concerning the actual Bismarck, and that however we may vary the description (so long as the description is correct) the proposition described is still the same. This proposition, which is described and is known to be true, is what interests us; but we are not acquainted with the proposition itself, and do not know it, though we know it is true.

It will be seen that there are various stages in the removal from acquaintance with particulars: there is Bismarck to people who knew him; Bismarck to those who only know of him through history; the man with the iron mask; the longest-lived of men. These are progressively further removed from acquaintance with particulars; the first comes as near to acquaintance as is possible in regard to another person; in the second, we shall still be said to know "who Bismarck was"; in the third, we do not know who was the man with the iron mask, though we can know many propositions about him which are not logically deducible from the fact that he wore an iron mask; in the fourth, finally, we know nothing beyond what is logically deducible from the definition of the man. There is a similar hierarchy in the region of universals. Many universals, like many particulars, are only known to us by description. But here, as in the case of particulars, knowledge concerning what is known by description is ultimately reducible to knowledge concerning what is known by acquaintance.

The fundamental principle in the analysis of prepositions containing descriptions is this: *Every proposition which we can understand must be composed wholly of constituents with which we are acquainted.*

We shall not at this stage attempt to answer all the objections which may be urged against this fundamental principle. For the present, we shall merely point out that, in some way or other, it must be possible to meet these objections, for it is scarcely conceivable that we can make a judgement or entertain a supposition without knowing what it is that we are judging or supposing about. We must attach *some* meaning to the words we use, if we are to speak significantly and not utter mere noise; and the meaning we attach to our words must be something with which we are acquainted. Thus when, for example, we make a statement about Julius Caesar, it is plain that Julius Caesar himself is not before our minds, since we are not acquainted with him. We have in mind some *description* of Julius Caesar: "the man who was assassinated on the Ides of March," "the founder of the Roman Empire," or, perhaps, merely "the man whose name was *Julius Caesar.*" (In this last description, *Julius Caesar* is a noise or shape with which we are acquainted.) Thus our statement does not mean quite what it seems to mean, but means something involving, instead of Julius Caesar, some description of him which is composed wholly of particulars and universals with which we are acquainted.

The chief importance of knowledge by description is that it enables us to pass beyond the limits of our private experience. In spite of the fact that we can only know truths which are wholly composed of terms which we have experienced in acquaintance, we can yet have knowledge by description of things which we have never experienced. In view of the very narrow range of our immediate experience, this result is vital, and until it is understood, much of our knowledge must remain mysterious and therefore doubtful.

*   *   *

CHAPTER 15: THE VALUE OF PHILOSOPHY

Having now come to the end of our brief and very incomplete review of the problems of philosophy, it will be well to consider, in conclusion, what is the value of philosophy and why it ought to be studied. It is the more necessary to consider this question, in view of the fact that many men, under the influence of science or of practical affairs, are inclined to doubt whether philosophy is anything better than innocent but useless trifling, hair-splitting distinctions, and controversies on matters concerning which knowledge is impossible.

This view of philosophy appears to result, partly from a wrong conception of the ends of life, partly from a wrong conception of the kind of goods which philosophy strives to achieve. Physical science, through the medium of inventions, is useful to innumerable people who are wholly ignorant of it; thus the study of physical science is to be recommended, not only, or primarily, because of the effect on the student, but rather because of the effect on mankind in general. Thus utility does not belong to philosophy. If the study of philosophy has any value at all for others than students of philosophy, it must be only indirectly, through its effects upon the lives of those who study it. It is in these effects, therefore, if anywhere, that the value of philosophy must be primarily sought.

But further, if we are not to fail in our endeavour to determine the value of philosophy, we must first free our minds from the prejudices of what are wrongly called "practical" men. The "practical" man, as this word is often used, is one who recognizes only material needs, who realizes that men must have food for the body, but is oblivious of the necessity of providing food for the mind. If all men were well off, if poverty and disease had been reduced to their lowest possible point, there would still remain much to be done to produce a valuable society; and even in the existing world the goods of the mind are at least as important as the goods of the body. It is exclusively among the goods of the mind that the value of philosophy is to be found; and only those who are not indifferent to these goods can be persuaded that the study of philosophy is not a waste of time.

Philosophy, like all other studies, aims primarily at knowledge. The knowledge it aims at is the kind of knowledge which gives unity and system to the body of sciences, and the kind which results from a critical examination of the grounds of our convictions, prejudices, and beliefs. But it cannot be maintained that philosophy has had any very great measure of success in its attempts to provide definite answers to its questions. If you ask a mathematician, a mineralogist, a historian, or any other man of learning, what definite body of truths has been ascertained by his science, his answer will last as long as you are willing to listen. But if you put the same question to a philosopher, he will, if he is candid, have to confess that his study has not achieved positive results such as have been achieved by other sciences. It is true that this is partly accounted for by the fact that, as soon as definite knowledge concerning any subject becomes possible, this subject ceases to be called philosophy, and now becomes a separate science. The whole study of the heavens, which now belongs to astronomy, was once included in philosophy; Newton's great work was called "the mathematical principles of natural philosophy." Similarly, the study of the human mind, which was a part of philosophy, has now been separated from philosophy and has become the science of psychology. Thus, to a great extent, the uncertainty of philosophy is more apparent than real: those questions which are already capable of definite answers are placed in the sciences, while those only to which, at present, no definite answer can be given, remain to form the residue which is called philosophy.

This is, however, only a part of the truth concerning the uncertainty of philosophy. There are many questions—and among them those that are of the profoundest interest to our spiritual life—which, so far as we can see, must remain insoluble to the human intellect unless its powers become of quite a different order from what they are now. Has the universe any unity of plan or purpose, or is it a fortuitous concourse of atoms? Is consciousness a permanent part of the universe, giving hope of indefinite growth in wisdom, or is it a transitory accident on a small planet on which life must ultimately become impossible? Are good and evil of importance to the universe or only to man? Such questions are asked by philosophy, and variously answered by various philosophers. But it would seem that, whether answers be otherwise discoverable or not, the answers suggested by philosophy are none of them demonstrably true. Yet, however slight may be the hope of discovering an answer, it is part of the business of philosophy to continue the consideration of such questions, to make us aware of their importance, to examine all the approaches to them, and to keep alive that speculative interest in the universe which is apt to be killed by confining ourselves to definitely ascertainable knowledge.

Many philosophers, it is true, have held that philosophy could establish the truth of certain answers to such fundamental questions. They have supposed that what is of most importance in religious beliefs could be proved by strict demonstration to be true. In order to judge of such attempts, it is necessary to take a survey of human knowledge, and to form an opinion as to its methods and its limitations. On such a subject it would be unwise to pronounce dogmatically; but if the investigations of our previous chapters have not led us astray, we shall be compelled to renounce the hope of finding philosophical proofs of religious beliefs. We cannot, therefore, include as part of the value of philosophy any definite set of answers to such questions. Hence, once more, the value of philosophy must not depend upon any supposed body of definitely ascertainable knowledge to be acquired by those who study it.

The value of philosophy is, in fact, to be sought largely in its very uncertainty. The man who has not tincture of philosophy goes through life imprisoned in the prejudices derived from common sense, from the habitual beliefs of his age or his nation, and from convictions which have grown up in his mind without the co-operation or consent of his deliberate reason. To such a man the world tends to become definite, finite, obvious; common objects rouse no questions, and unfamiliar possibilities are contemptuously rejected. As soon as we begin to philosophize, on the contrary, we find, as we saw in our opening chapters, that even the most everyday things lead to problems to which only very incomplete answers can be given. Philosophy, though unable to tell us with certainty what is the true answer to the doubts which it raises, is able to suggest many possibilities which enlarge our thoughts and free them from the tyranny of custom. Thus, while diminishing our feeling of certainty as to what things are, it greatly increases our knowledge as to what they may be; it removes the somewhat arrogant dogmatism of those who have never travelled into the region of liberating doubt, and it keeps alive our sense of wonder by showing familiar things in an unfamiliar aspect.

Apart from its utility in showing unsuspected possibilities, philosophy has a value—perhaps its chief value—through the greatness of the objects which it contemplates, and the freedom from narrow and personal aims resulting from this contemplation. The life of the instinctive man is shut up within the circle of his private interests: family and friends may be included, but the outer world is not regarded except as it may help or hinder what comes within the circle of instinctive wishes. In such a life there is something feverish and confined, in comparison with which the philosophic life is calm and free. The private world of instinctive interests is a small one, set in the midst of a great and powerful world which must, sooner or later, lay our private world in ruins. Unless we can so enlarge our interests as to include the whole outer world, we remain like a garrison in a beleaguered fortress, knowing that the enemy prevents escape and that ultimate surrender is inevitable. In such a life there is no peace, but a constant strife between the insistence of desire and the powerlessness of will. In one way or another, if our life is to be great and free, we must escape this prison and this strife.

One way of escape is by philosophic contemplation. Philosophic contemplation does not, in its widest survey, divide the universe into two hostile camps—friends and foes, helpful and hostile, good and bad—it views the whole impartially. Philosophic contemplation, when it is unalloyed, does not aim at proving that the rest of the universe is akin to man. All acquisition of knowledge is an enlargement of the Self, but this enlargement is best attained when it is not directly sought. It is obtained when the desire for knowledge is alone operative, by a study which does not wish in advance that its objects should have this or that character, but adapts the Self to the characters which it finds in its objects. This enlargement of Self is not obtained when, taking the Self as it is, we try to show that the world is so similar to this Self that knowledge of it is possible without any admission of what seems alien. The desire to prove this is a form of self-assertion and, like all self-assertion, it is an obstacle to the growth of Self which it desires, and of which the Self knows that it is capable. Self-assertion, in philosophic speculation as elsewhere, views the world as a means to its own ends; thus it makes the world of less account than Self, and the Self sets bounds to the greatness of its goods. In contemplation, on the contrary, we start from the not-Self, and through its greatness the boundaries of Self are enlarged; through the infinity of the universe the mind which contemplates it achieves some share in infinity.

For this reason greatness of soul is not fostered by those philosophies which assimilate the universe to Man. Knowledge is a form of union of Self and not-Self; like all union, it is impaired by dominion, and therefore by any attempt to force the universe into conformity with what we find in ourselves. There is a widespread philosophical tendency towards the view which tells us that Man is the measure of all things, that truth is man-made, that space and time and the world of universals are properties of the mind, and that, if there be anything not created by the mind, it is unknowable and of no account for us. This view, if our previous discussions were correct, is untrue; but in addition to being untrue, it has the effect of robbing philosophic contemplation of all that gives it value, since it fetters contemplation to Self. What it calls knowledge is not a union with the not-Self, but a set of prejudices, habits, and desires, making an impenetrable veil between us and the world beyond. The man who finds pleasure in such a theory of knowledge is like the man who never leaves the domestic circle for fear his word might not be law.

The true philosophic contemplation, on the contrary, finds its satisfaction in every enlargement of the not-Self, in everything that magnifies the objects contemplated, and thereby the subject contemplating. Everything, in contemplation, that is personal or private, everything that depends upon habit, self-interest, or desire, distorts the object, and hence impairs the union which the intellect seeks. By thus making a barrier between subject and object, such personal and private things become a prison to the intellect. The free intellect will see as God might see, without a *here* and *now,* without hopes and fears, without the trammels of customary beliefs and traditional prejudices, calmly, dispassionately, in the sole and exclusive desire of knowledge— knowledge as impersonal, as purely contemplative, as it is possible for man to attain. Hence also the free intellect will value more the abstract and universal knowledge into which the accidents of private history do not enter, than the knowledge brought by the senses, and dependent, as such knowledge must be, upon an exclusive and personal point of view and a body whose sense-organs distort as much as they reveal.

The mind which has become accustomed to the freedom and impartiality of philosophic contemplation will preserve something of the same freedom and impartiality in the world of action and emotion. It will view its purposes and desires as parts of the whole, with the absence of insistence that results from seeing them as infinitesimal fragments in a world of which all the rest is unaffected by any one man's deeds. The impartiality which, in contemplation, is the unalloyed desire for truth, is the very same quality of mind which, in action, is justice, and in emotion is that universal love which can be given to all, and not only to those who are judged useful or admirable. Thus contemplation enlarges not only the objects of our thoughts, but also the objects of our actions and our affections: it makes us citizens of the universe, not only of one walled city at war with all the rest. In this citizenship of the universe consists man's true freedom, and his liberation from the thraldom of narrow hopes and fears.

Thus, to sum up our discussion of the value of philosophy; philosophy is to be studied, not for the sake of any definite answers to its questions, since no definite answers can, as a rule, be known to be true, but rather for the sake of the questions themselves; because these questions enlarge our conception of what is possible, enrich our intellectual imagination and diminish the dogmatic assurance which closes the mind against speculation; but above all because, through the greatness of the universe which philosophy contemplates, the mind also is rendered great, and becomes capable of that union with the universe which constitutes its highest good.

MARTIN HEIDEGGER
1889–1976

Martin Heidegger was born and died in the small German town of Messkirch in the Black Forest region of Baden-Württemberg. His father was the caretaker of the local Catholic church. Heidegger was reared as a Catholic and attended local secondary schools, where he was particularly interested in the ancient Greeks and the classics; this classical heritage remained the bedrock of his intellectual life. As a teenager in a Jesuit seminary, he was captivated by Franz Brentano's work on Aristotle's understanding of "Being." He made the study of Being his life's work and never wavered from that goal.

After a brief period as a Jesuit novice, Heidegger studied philosophy at the University of Freiburg. Excused from World War I for health reasons, he finished his studies in 1916 with a thesis on the medieval thinker John Duns Scotus. For the next seven years, he taught at the university, the last three years as the assistant to Edmund Husserl. During this period of time, Heidegger apprenticed himself to Husserl's phenomenological method, using it on his own special study of Being. In 1923, Heidegger moved to the University of Marburg where, in 1927, he published *Being and Time,* which proved to be his *magnum opus.* This work was dedicated to his teacher and friend Husserl. When Husserl retired in 1928, Heidegger assumed Husserl's chair of philosophy at the University of Freiburg.

What followed is one of the most controversial episodes in recent philosophy. When the Nazis came to power in 1933, the rector of the University of Freiburg was ousted and Heidegger was elected to replace him. In the course of his inaugural lecture as rector, Heidegger made the following remarks:

"Academic Freedom," celebrated so often, is banished from the German university; . . . this freedom was not genuine because it was only negative. . . . The concept of freedom [for] the German student is now brought back to its truth. From this truth the bond and service of the German student will unfold in [the] future.*

Later that same year Heidegger wrote in the student newspaper:

Doctrine and "ideas" shall no longer govern your existence. The Führer himself, and only he, is the current and future reality of Germany, and his word is your law. Learn to know ever more deeply within you: "From now on every matter demands determination and every action demands responsibility."
  Heil Hitler!
  MARTIN HEIDEGGER**

Critics claim that Heidegger had always been sympathetic to the Nazi cause and that he apparently disowned his teacher Husserl (who was Jewish). As late as 1953, Heidegger affirmed the "inner truth and greatness" of the Nazi movement. He once said that philosophy could be done properly only in either the German or the Greek language and that among the moderns, the Germans alone, as a people placed by history between the barbarians of America to the west and Russia to the east, could save Western thought.

Heidegger's supporters point to his refusal to endorse the firing of two anti-Nazi deans, which led to his resignation as rector within a year. Furthermore, say some, it is unfair to judge Heidegger's early support for the Nazis from a post–Second World War point of view. Heidegger in 1933 could not be expected to know the unspeakable horrors of 1939 to 1945. Finally, supporters ask philosophers especially to avoid the *argumentum ad hominem:* Even if Heidegger were partially compromised, that is not sufficient reason to dismiss a whole body of thought.

Whatever the truth in this debate, Allied occupation powers considered the evidence of Nazi collaboration sufficient to bar Heidegger from teaching between 1945 and 1951. Hence, after the war, Heidegger spent much of his time in his simple hut at Todtnauberg in the Black Forest. He retired permanently from teaching in 1959. Late in life he visited Greece and France but lived his final years largely in quiet seclusion.

*   *   *

In his major work, *Being and Time (Sein und Zeit),* Heidegger announced the interest that would dominate his writings throughout his life: "The question of the meaning of Being." According to Heidegger, the Pre-Socratics had understood Being, but subsequent Western thinkers had forgotten Being itself by focusing too intently on individual beings. As a result, contemporary metaphysics no longer recalled the seminal question of Being.

---

*Die Selbstbehauptung der Deutschen Universität (The Self-Affirmation of the German University, 1933) as quoted in Walter Kaufmann, *Discovering the Mind, Volume II: Nietzsche, Heidegger, and Buber* (New York: McGraw-Hill, 1980), p. 221.

**Freiburger Studentenzeitung, November 3, 1933, p. 1, quoted in Martin Heidegger, *German Existentialism,* translated with an introduction by Dagobert D. Runes (New York: Philosophical Library, 1965), pp. 27–28.

Nazi Party Congress at Nuremberg, 1934 (Hitler is standing in the center). The lives of an entire generation of philosophers were directly influenced by Hitler's rise to power in 1934. Husserl died as an outcast because of his Jewish ancestry; Heidegger was an early Nazi sympathizer (though there is a great deal of debate about his later feelings toward and involvement with the party); Sartre was a German prisoner-of-war and later a member of the resistance; Wittgenstein volunteered as a hospital orderly in England; and Ayer and Quine served in the Allied war effort. *(National Archive)*

In order to gain some understanding of Being, Heidegger suggests we examine the one being with which we are intimately acquainted: the human being. The phenomenological method (Husserl), which "unconceals" the data of experience by allowing these data to "show themselves," provides the way to such an examination. Using this method to examine the self, one discovers one's self as a "being-in-the-world" or *Dasein* ("being-there").

Dasein is different from other realities. First, "in its very Being, that Being is an issue for it"; that is, *Dasein* is aware of Being. Second, the kind of Being of which *Dasein* is aware is called "existence." Human existence is not to be grasped the way one understands the existence of rocks or planets, but in the special ways of anticipation of, and decision for, possibilities. As the self confronts its choices, it especially recognizes that with death, "being-in-the-world" eventually becomes "no-longer-being-there." This awareness of *Dasein* as "being-toward-death" is filled with *Angst* (dread). Borrowing Kierkegaard's analysis of dread, Heidegger says that the self can try to avoid this *Angst* by losing the "I" in the "they"—that is, by ignoring its individuality and becoming part of the crowd. But a "they" existence is "inauthentic" and removed from Being. Instead, authentic being—"being-toward-death"—can reveal to *Dasein* a "freedom" that releases it from the "Illusions of the 'they'" and allows it to embrace Angst.

In our selection from *An Introduction to Metaphysics* (1953), given here in the Ralph Manheim translation, Heidegger puts the question of Being in stark terms: "Why is there anything at all, rather than nothing?" This might seem an odd question to us, but it is odd (asserts Heidegger) only because we have lost our original amazement in the very presence of Being itself. Following a lengthy discussion of this issue, Heidegger asks the further question, "How is it with being?" Not well at all, he concludes. Heidegger argues that modern "technological frenzy" has led us to the brink of disaster because it induces the awful forgetfulness of Being. But Heidegger does not end with pessimism. It is possible, he concludes,

> to recapture, to repeat, the beginning of our historical spiritual existence, in order to transform it into a new beginning . . . to restore man's historical being-there (*Dasein*) . . . to the domain of being, which it was originally incumbent on man to open up for himself.

Heidegger has had more than his share of critics. Analytic philosophers have particularly criticized his use of language. One such philosopher concluded that "Heidegger's account of human life, where it is not vacuous, is transparently false."* However, despite the criticisms of his life and thought, Heidegger has profoundly affected philosophy—especially in the field he originated: philosophical hermeneutics. Further, his insights have been developed in psychoanalysis and literary theory and in phenomenology and theology, and they continue to shape contemporary views.

*   *   *

General introductions to Heidegger's thought include Marjorie Grene, *Martin Heidegger* (New York: Hillary House, 1957); W.J. Richardson, *Heidegger: Through Phenomenology to Thought* (New York: Humanities Press, 1963); J.A. Kockelman, *Heidegger: A First Introduction to His Philosophy,* translated by T. Schrynemakers (Pittsburgh, PA: Duquesne University Press, 1965); J.L. Mehta, *Martin Heidegger: The Way and the Vision* (Honolulu: University Press of Hawaii, 1976); George Steiner, *Martin Heidegger* (New York: Viking Press, 1978); Michael Inwood, *Heidegger* (Oxford: Oxford University Press, 1997); and Herman Philipse, *Heidegger's Philosophy of Being: A Critical Interpretation* (Princeton: Princeton University Press, 1999). For criticism of Heidegger's thought, see Walter Kaufmann, *Discovering the Mind, Volume II: Nietzsche, Heidegger, and Buber* (New York: McGraw-Hill, 1980); Hans-Georg Gadamer, *Heidegger's Ways,* translated by John W. Stanley (Albany, NY: SUNY Press, 1994); and Joanna Hodge, *Heidegger and Ethics* (Oxford: Routledge, 1995). Michael Gelven, *A Commentary on Heidegger's "Being and Time"* (New York: Harper & Row, 1970); E.F. Kaelin, *Heidegger's "Being and Time": A Reading for Readers* (Tallahassee: University Presses of Florida, 1988); and Stephen

*Alasdair MacIntyre, "Existentialism," in D.J. O'Connor, *A Critical History of Western Philosophy* (New York: The Free Press, 1964), p. 518.

Mulhall, *Heidegger and Being and Time* (Oxford: Routledge, 1996) provide guides to Heidegger's major work. For comparative studies, see Arne Naess, *Four Modern Philosophers: Carnap, Wittgenstein, Heidegger, Sartre,* translated by Alastair Hannay (Chicago: University of Chicago Press, 1968); Timothy J. Stapleton, *Husserl and Heidegger* (Albany, NY: SUNY Press, 1983); Allan Megill, *Prophets of Extremity: Nietzsche, Heidegger, Foucault, Derrida* (Berkeley: University of California Press, 1985); and Ron L. Cooper, *Heidegger and Whitehead: A Phenomenological Examination into the Intelligibility of Experience* (Athens: Ohio University Press, 1993). Collections of essays include Thomas Sheehan, ed., *Heidegger: The Man and the Thinker* (Chicago: Precedent, 1981); Hubert L. Dreyfus and Harrison Hall, eds., *Heidegger: A Critical Reader* (Oxford: Basil Blackwell, 1992); John Sallis, ed., *Reading Heidegger* (Bloomington: Indiana University Press, 1993); Charles Guignon, ed., *The Cambridge Companion to Heidegger* (Cambridge: Cambridge University Press, 1993); and the multivolume Christopher Macann, ed., *Martin Heidegger: Critical Assessments* (Oxford: Routledge, 1993). For advanced studies on Heidegger, see titles in the series "Northwestern University Studies in Phenomenology & Existential Philosophy."

Finally, out of the large number of recent books on the controversy surrounding Heidegger's Nazi ties, one may consult Victor Farías, *Heidegger and Nazism,* edited by Joseph Margolis and Tom Rockmore (Philadelphia: Temple University Press, 1989); Joseph Margolis and Tom Rockmore, eds., *The Heidegger Case* (Philadelphia: Temple University Press, 1992); Tom Rockmore, *On Heidegger's Nazism and Philosophy* (Berkeley: University of California Press, 1992); Heinrich Wiegrand Petzet, *Encounters and Dialogues with Martin Heidegger 1929–1976,* translated by Parvis Emad and Kenneth Malz (Chicago: University of Chicago Press, 1993); Richard Wolin, ed., *The Heidegger Controversy* (Cambridge, MA: MIT Press, 1993); Leslie Paul Thiele, *Timely Meditations: Martin Heidegger and Postmodern Politics* (Princeton, NJ: Princeton University Press, 1995); Berel Lang, *Heidegger's Silence* (Ithaca, NY: Cornell University Press, 1996); and Julian Young, *Heidegger, Philosophy, and Nazism* (Cambridge: Cambridge University Press, 1997).

AN INTRODUCTION TO METAPHYSICS
(in part)

CHAPTER 1: THE FUNDAMENTAL QUESTION
OF METAPHYSICS

Why are there essents* rather than nothing? That is the question. Clearly it is no ordinary question. "Why are there essents, why is there anything at all, rather than nothing?"—obviously this is the first of all questions, though not in a chronological sense. Individuals and peoples ask a good many questions in the course of their historical passage through time. They examine, explore, and test a good many things before they run into the question "Why are there essents rather than nothing?" Many men never encounter this question, if by encounter we mean not merely to hear and read about it as an interrogative formulation but to ask the question, that is, to bring it about, to raise it, to feel its inevitability.

And yet each of us is grazed at least once, perhaps more than once, by the hidden power of this question, even if he is not aware of what is happening to him. The question looms in moments of great despair, when things tend to lose all their weight and all meaning becomes obscured. Perhaps it will strike but once like a muffled bell that rings into our life and gradually dies away. It is present in moments of rejoicing, when all the things around us are transfigured and seem to be there for the first time, as if it might be easier to think they are not than to understand that they are and are as they are. The question is upon us in boredom, when we are equally removed from despair and joy, and everything about us seems so hopelessly commonplace that we no longer care whether anything is or is not—and with this the question "Why are there essents rather than nothing?" is evoked in a particular form.

But this question may be asked expressly, or, unrecognized as a question, it may merely pass through our lives like a brief gust of wind; it may press hard upon us, or, under one pretext or another, we may thrust it away from us and silence it. In any case it is never the question that we ask first in point of time.

But it is the first question in another sense—in regard to rank. This may be clarified in three ways. The question "Why are there essents rather than nothing?" is first in rank for us first because it is the most far reaching, second because it is the deepest, and finally because it is the most fundamental of all questions.

It is the widest of all questions. It confines itself to no particular essent of whatever kind. The question takes in everything, and this means not only everything that is present in the broadest sense but also everything that ever was or will be. The range of this question finds its limit only in nothing, in that which simply is not and never was. Everything that is not nothing is covered by this question, and ultimately even nothing itself; not because it is *something*, since after all we speak of it, but because it is nothing. Our question reaches out so far that we can never go further. We do not inquire into this and that, or into each essent in turn, but from the very outset into the essent as

---

*Essents" = "existents," "things that are."

Martin Heidegger, *An Introduction to Metaphysics,* translated by Ralph Manheim, Chapter 1 (New Haven, CT: Yale University Press, 1959), pp. 1–51. Reprinted by permission.

a whole, or, as we say for reasons to be discussed below: into the essent as such in its entirety.

This broadest of questions is also the deepest: Why are there essents . . . ? Why, that is to say, on what ground? from what source does the essent derive? on what ground does it stand? The question is not concerned with particulars, with what essents are and of what nature at any time, here and there, with how they can be changed, what they can be used for, and so on. The question aims at the ground of what is insofar as it is. To seek the ground is to try to get to the bottom; what is put in question is thus related to the ground. However, since the question is a question, it remains to be seen whether the grounds arrived at is really a ground, that is, whether it provides a foundation; whether it is a primal ground *[Ur-grund];* or whether it fails to provide a foundation and is an abyss *[Ab-grund];* or whether the ground is neither one nor the other but presents only a perhaps necessary appearance of foundation—in other words, it is a non-ground *[Ungrund].* Be that as it may, the ground in question must account for the being of the essent as such. This question "why" does not look for causes that are of the same kind and on the same level as the essent itself. This "why" does not move on any one plane but penetrates to the "underlying" *["zu-grunde" liegend]* realms and indeed to the very last of them, to the limit; turning away from the surface, from all shallowness, it strives toward the depths; this broadest of all questions is also the deepest.

Finally, this broadest and deepest question is also the most fundamental. What do we mean by this? If we take the question in its full scope, namely the essent as such in its entirety, it readily follows that in asking this question we keep our distance from every particular and individual essent, from every this and that. For we mean the essent as a whole, without any special preference. Still, it is noteworthy that in this questioning *one* kind of essent persists in coming to the fore, namely the men who ask the question. But the question should not concern itself with any particular essent. In the spirit of its unrestricted scope, all essents are of equal value. An elephant in an Indian jungle "is" just as much as some chemical combustion process at work on the planet Mars, and so on.

Accordingly, if our question "Why are there essents rather than nothing?" is taken in its fullest sense, we must avoid singling out any special, particular essent, including man. For what indeed is man? Consider the earth within the endless darkness of space in the universe. By way of comparison it is a tiny grain of sand; between it and the next grain of its own size there extends a mile or more of emptiness; on the surface of this grain of sand there lives a crawling, bewildered swarm of supposedly intelligent animals, who for a moment have discovered knowledge.* And what is the temporal extension of a human life amid all the millions of years? Scarcely a move of the second hand, a breath. Within the essent as a whole there is no legitimate ground for singling out this essent which is called mankind and to which we ourselves happen to belong.

But whenever the essent as a whole enters into this question, a privileged, unique relation arises between it and the act of questioning. For through this questioning the essent as a whole is for the first time opened up *as such* with a view to its possible ground, and in the act of questioning it is kept open. In relation to the essent as such in its entirety the asking of the question is not just any occurrence within the realm of the essent, like the falling of raindrops for example. The question "why" may be said to confront the essent as a whole, to break out of it, though never completely. But that is exactly why the act of questioning is privileged. Because it confronts the essent as a

---

*Cf. Nietzsche, *Über Wahreit und Lüge im aussermoralischen Sinne.* 1873 Nachlass.

whole, but does not break loose from it, the content of the question reacts upon the questioning itself. Why the why? What is the ground of this question "why" which presumes to ask after the ground of the essent as a whole? Is the ground asked for in this why not merely a foreground—which would imply that the sought-for ground is again an essent? Does not the "first" question nevertheless come first in view of the intrinsic rank of the question of being and its modulations?

To be sure, the things in the world, the essents, are in no way affected by our asking of the question "Why are there essents rather than nothing?" Whether we ask it or not, the planets move in their orbits, the sap of life flows through plant and animal.

But *if* this question is asked and if the act of questioning is really carried out, the content and the object of the question react inevitably on the act of questioning. Accordingly this questioning is not just any occurrence but a privileged happening that we call an event.

This question and all the questions immediately rooted in it, the questions in which this one question unfolds—this question "why" is incommensurable with any other. It encounters the search for its own why. At first sight the question "Why the why?" looks like a frivolous repetition ad infinitum of the same interrogative formulation, like an empty and unwarranted brooding over words. Yes, beyond a doubt, that is how it looks. The question is only whether we wish to be taken in by this superficial look and so regard the whole matter as settled, or whether we are capable of finding a significant event in this recoil of the question "why" upon itself.

But if we decline to be taken in by surface appearances we shall see that this question "why," this question as to the essents as such in its entirety, goes beyond any mere playing with words, provided we possess sufficient intellectual energy to make the question actually recoil into its "why"—for it will not do so of its own accord. In so doing we find out that this privileged question "why" has its ground in a leap through which man thrusts away all the previous security, whether real or imagined, of his life. The question is asked only in this leap; it is the leap; without it there is no asking. What "leap" means here will be elucidated later. Our questioning is not yet the leap; for this it must undergo a transformation; it still stands perplexed in the face of the essent. Here it may suffice to say that the leap in this questioning opens up its own source—with this leap the question arrives at its own ground. We call such a leap, which opens up its own source, the original source or origin *[Ur-sprung],* the findings of one's own ground. It is because the question "Why are there essents rather than nothing?" breaks open the ground for all authentic questions and is thus at the origin *[Ur-sprung]* of them all that we must recognize it as the most fundamental of all questions.

It is the most fundamental of questions because it is the broadest and deepest, and conversely.

In this threefold sense the question is the first in rank—first, that is, in the order of questioning within the domain which this first question opens, defining its scope and thus founding it. Our question is the *question* of all authentic questions, i.e. of all self-questioning questions, and whether consciously or not it is necessarily implicit in every question. No questioning and accordingly no single scientific "problem" can be fully intelligible if it does not include, i.e. ask, the question of all questions. Let us be clear about this from the start: it can never be objectively determined whether anyone, whether we, really ask this question, that is whether we make the leap, or never get beyond a verbal formula. In a historical setting that does not recognize questioning as a fundamental human force, the question immediately loses its rank.

Anyone for whom the Bible is divine revelation and truth has the answer to the question "Why are there essents rather than nothing?" even before it is asked: everything that is, except God himself, has been created by Him. God himself, the increate creator, "is." One who holds to such faith can in a way participate in the asking of our question, but he cannot really question without ceasing to be a believer and taking all the consequences of such a step. He will only be able to act "as if" . . . On the other hand a faith that does not perpetually expose itself to the possibility of unfaith is no faith but merely a convenience: the believer simply makes up his mind to adhere to the traditional doctrine. This is neither faith nor questioning, but the indifference of those who can busy themselves with everything, sometimes even displaying a keen interest in faith as well as questioning.

What we have said about security in faith as one position in regard to the truth does not imply that the biblical "In the beginning God created heaven and earth" is an answer to our question. Quite aside from whether these words from the Bible are true or false for faith, they can supply no answer to our question because they are in no way related to it. Indeed, they cannot even be brought into relation with our question. From the standpoint of faith our question is "foolishness."

Philosophy is this very foolishness. A "Christian philosophy" is a round square and a misunderstanding. There is, to be sure, a thinking and questioning elaboration of the world of Christian experience, i.e. of faith. That is theology. Only epochs which no longer fully believe in the true greatness of the task of theology arrive at the disastrous notion that philosophy can help to provide a refurbished theology if not a substitute for theology, which will satisfy the needs and tastes of the time. For the original Christian faith philosophy is foolishness. To philosophize is to ask "Why are there essents rather than nothing?" Really to ask the question signifies: a daring attempt to fathom this unfathomable question by disclosing what it summons us to ask, to push our questioning to the very end. Where such an attempt occurs there is philosophy.

It would not serve our purpose to begin our discussion with a detailed report on philosophy. But there are a few things that all must know who wish to concern themselves with philosophy. They can be briefly stated.

All essential philosophical questioning is necessarily untimely. This is so because philosophy is always projected far in advance of its time, or because it connects the present with its antecedent, with what *initially* was. Philosophy always remains a knowledge which not only cannot be adjusted to a given epoch but on the contrary imposes its measure upon its epoch.

Philosophy is essentially untimely because it is one of those few things that can never find an immediate echo in the present. When such an echo seems to occur, when a philosophy becomes fashionable, either it is no real philosophy or it has been misinterpreted and misused for ephemeral and extraneous purposes.

Accordingly, philosophy cannot be directly learned like manual and technical skills; it cannot be directly applied, or judged by its usefulness in the manner of economic or other professional knowledge.

But what is useless can still be a force, perhaps the only real force that has no immediate echo in everyday life can be intimately bound up with a nation's profound historical development, and can even anticipate it. What is untimely will have its own times. This is true of philosophy. Consequently there is no way of determining once and for all what the task of philosophy is, and accordingly what must be expected of it. Every stage and every beginning of its development bears within it its own law. All that can be said is what philosophy cannot be and cannot accomplish.

A question has been stated: "Why are there essents rather than nothing?" We have claimed first place for this question and explained in what sense it is regarded as first.

We have not even begun to ask the question itself, but have digressed into a discussion about it. Such a digression is indispensable. For this question has nothing in common with our habitual concerns. There is no way of familiarizing ourselves with this question by a gradual transition from the things to which we are accustomed. Hence it must, as it were, be singled out in advance, presented. Yet in introducing the question and speaking of it, we must not postpone, let alone forget, the questioning itself.

Here then let us conclude our preliminary remarks.

Every essential form of spiritual life is marked by ambiguity. The less commensurate it is with other forms, the more it is misinterpreted.

Philosophy is one of the few autonomous creative possibilities and at times necessities of man's historical being-there.* The current misinterpretations of philosophy, all of which have some truth about them, are legion. Here we shall mention only two, which are important because of the light they throw on the present and future situation of philosophy. The first misinterpretation asks too much of philosophy. The second distorts its function.

Roughly speaking, philosophy always aims at the first and last grounds of the essent, with particular emphasis on man himself and on the meaning and goals of human being-there. This might suggest that philosophy can and must provide a foundation on which a nation will build its historical life and culture. But this is beyond the power of philosophy. As a rule such excessive demands take the form of a belittling of philosophy. It is said, for example: Because metaphysics did nothing to pave the way for the revolution it should be rejected. This is no cleverer than saying that because the carpenter's bench is useless for flying it should be abolished. Philosophy can never *directly* supply the energies and create the opportunities and methods that bring about a historical change; for one thing, because philosophy is always the concern of the few. Which few? The creators, those who initiate profound transformations. It spreads only indirectly, by devious paths that can never be laid out in advance, until at last, at some future date, it sinks to the level of a commonplace; but by then it has long been forgotten as original philosophy.

What philosophy essentially can and must be is this: a thinking that breaks the paths and opens the perspectives of the knowledge that sets the norms and hierarchies, of the knowledge in which and by which a people fulfills itself historically and culturally, the knowledge that kindles and necessitates all inquiries and thereby threatens all values.

The second misinterpretation involves a distortion of the function of philosophy. Even if philosophy can provide no foundation for a culture, the argument goes, it is nevertheless a cultural force, whether because it gives us an over-all, systematic view of what is, supplying a useful chart by which we may find our way amid the various possible things and realms of things, or because it relieves the sciences of their work by reflecting on their premises, basic concepts, and principles. Philosophy is expected to promote and even to accelerate—to make easier as it were—the practical and technical business of culture.

---

*[The word *Dasein* is ordinarily translated as "existence." It is used in "normal," popular discourse. But Heidegger breaks it into its components *Da,* "there" and *Sein,* "being," and puts his own definition on it. In general he means man's conscious, historical existence in the world, which is always projected into a there beyond its here. The German word *Dasein* has often been carried over into translations; the English strikes me as preferable]

But—it is in the very nature of philosophy never to make things easier but only more difficult. And this not merely because its language strikes the everyday understanding as strange if not insane. Rather, it is the authentic function of philosophy to challenge historical being there and hence, in the last analysis, being pure and simple. It restores to things, to the essents, their weight (being). How so? Because the challenge is one of the essential prerequisites for the birth of all greatness, and in speaking of greatness we are referring primarily to the works and destinies of nations. We can speak of historical destiny only where an authentic knowledge of things dominates man's being-there. And it is philosophy that opens up the paths and perspectives of such knowledge.

The misinterpretations with which philosophy is perpetually beset are promoted most of all by people of our kind, that is, by professors of philosophy. It is our customary business—which may be said to be justified and even useful—to transmit a certain knowledge of the philosophy of the past, as part of a general education. Many people suppose that this is philosophy itself, whereas at best it is the technique of philosophy.

In correcting these two misinterpretations I cannot hope to give you at one stroke a clear conception of philosophy. But I do hope that you will be on your guard when the most current judgments and even supposed observations assail you unawares. Such judgments are often disarming, precisely because they seem so natural. You hear remarks such as "Philosophy leads to nothing," "You can't do anything with philosophy," and readily imagine that they confirm an experience of your own. There is no denying the soundness of these two phrases, particularly common among scientists and teachers of science. Any attempt to refute them by proving that after all it does "lead to something" merely strengthens the prevailing misinterpretation to the effect that the everyday standards by which we judge bicycles or sulphur baths are applicable to philosophy.

It is absolutely correct and proper to say that "You can't do anything with philosophy." It is only wrong to suppose that this is the last word on philosophy. For the rejoinder imposes itself: granted that we cannot do anything with philosophy, might not philosophy, if we concern ourselves with it, do something *with* us? So much for what philosophy is not.

At the outset we stated a question: "Why are there essents rather than nothing?" We have maintained that to ask this question is to philosophize. When in our thinking we open our minds to this question, we first of all cease to dwell in any of the familiar realms. We set aside everything that is on the order of the day. Our question goes beyond the familiar and the things that have their place in everyday life. Nietzsche once said (*Werke* 7, 269): "A philosopher is a man who never ceases to experience, see, hear, suspect, hope, and dream extraordinary things . . ."

To philosophize is to inquire into the extra-ordinary. But because, as we have just suggested, this questioning recoils upon itself, not only what is asked after is extraordinary but also the asking itself. In other words: this questioning does not lie along the way so that we bump into it one day unexpectedly. Nor is it part of everyday life: there is no requirement or regulation that forces us into it; it gratifies no urgent or prevailing need. The questioning itself is "out of order." It is entirely voluntary, based wholly and uniquely on the mystery of freedom, on what we have called the leap. The same Nietzsche said: "Philosophy . . . is a voluntary living amid ice and mountain heights" (*Werke,* 15, 2). To philosophize, we may now say, is an extra-ordinary inquiry into the extra-ordinary.

In the age of the earliest and crucial unfolding of Western philosophy among the Greeks, who first raised the authentic question of the essent as such in its entirety, the essent was called ⟨*physis*⟩. This basic Greek word for the essent is customarily translated as "nature." This derives from the Latin translation, *natura,* which properly means "to be born," "birth." But with this Latin translation the original meaning of the Greek word ⟨*physis*⟩ is thrust aside, the actual philosophical force of the Greek word is destroyed. This is true not only of the Latin translation of *this* word but of all other Roman translations of the Greek philosophical language. What happened in this translation from the Greek into the Latin is not accidental and harmless; it marks the first stage in the process by which we cut ourselves off and alienated ourselves from the original essence of Greek philosophy. The Roman translation was later taken over by Christianity and the Christian Middle Ages. And the Christian Middle Ages were prolonged in modern philosophy, which, moving in the conceptual world of the Middle Ages, coined those representations and terms by means of which we still try to understand the beginnings of Western philosophy. These beginnings are regarded as something that present-day philosophers have supposedly transcended and long since left behind them.

But now let us skip over this whole process of deformation and decay and attempt to regain the unimpaired strength of language and words; for words and language are not wrappings in which things are packed for the commerce of those who write and speak. It is in words and language that things first come into being and are. For this reason the misuse of language in idle talk, in slogans and phrases, destroys our authentic relation to things. What does the word ⟨*physis*⟩ denote? It denotes self-blossoming emergence (e.g. the blossoming of a rose), opening up, unfolding, that which manifests itself in such unfolding and perseveres and endures in it; in short, the realm of things that emerge and linger on. According to the dictionary ⟨*phyein*⟩ means to grow or make to grow. But what does growing mean? Does it imply only to increase quantitatively, to become more and larger?

⟨*Physis*⟩ as emergence can be observed everywhere, e.g. in celestial phenomena (the rising of the sun), in the rolling of the sea, in the growth of plants, in the coming forth of man and animal from the womb. But ⟨*physis*⟩, the realm of that which arises, is not synonymous with these phenomena, which today we regard as part of "nature." This opening up and inward-jutting-beyond-itself [*in-sich-aus-sich-hinausstehen*] must not be taken as a process among other processes that we observe in the realm of the essent. ⟨*Physis*⟩ is being itself, by virtue of which essents become and remain observable.

The Greeks did not learn what ⟨*physis*⟩ is through natural phenomena, but the other way around: it was through a fundamental poetic and intellectual experience of being that they discovered what they had to call ⟨*physis*⟩. It was this discovery that enabled them to gain a glimpse into nature in the restricted sense. Hence ⟨*physis*⟩ originally encompassed heaven as well as earth, the stone as well as the plant, the animal as well as man, and it encompassed human history as a work of men and the gods; and ultimately and first of all, it meant the gods themselves as subordinated to destiny. ⟨*Physis*⟩ means the power that emerges and the enduring realm under its sway. This power of emerging and enduring includes "becoming" as well as "being" in the restricted sense of inert duration. ⟨*Physis*⟩ is the process of a-rising, of emerging from the hidden, whereby the hidden is first made to stand.

But if, as is usually done, ⟨*physis*⟩ is taken not in the original sense of the power to emerge and endure, but in the later and present signification of nature; and if moreover the motion of material things, of the atoms and electrons, of what modern physics investigates as ⟨*physis*⟩, is taken to be the fundamental manifestation of nature, then the first philosophy of the Greeks becomes a nature philosophy, in which all things are held to be of a material nature. In this case the beginning of Greek philosophy, as is perfectly proper for a beginning according to the common-sense view, gives the impression of what we, once again in Latin, designate as primitive. Thus the Greeks become essentially a higher type of Hottentot, whom modern science has left far behind. Disregarding the lesser absurdities involved in this view of the beginning of Western philosophy as something primitive, we need only say this: those who put forward such an interpretation forget that what is under discussion is philosophy, one of man's few great achievements. But what is great can only begin great. Its beginning is in fact the greatest thing of all. A small beginning belongs only to the small, whose dubious greatness it is to diminish all things; small are the beginnings of decay, though it may later become great in the sense of the enormity of total annihilation.

The great begins great, maintains itself only through the free recurrence of greatness within it, and if it is great ends also in greatness. So it is with the philosophy of the Greeks. It ended in greatness with Aristotle. Only prosaic common sense and the little man imagine that the great must endure forever, and equate this duration with eternity.

The Greeks called the essent as a whole ⟨*physis*⟩. But it should be said in passing that even within Greek philosophy a narrowing of the word set in forthwith, although the original meaning did not vanish from the experience, knowledge, and orientation of Greek philosophy. Knowledge of its original meaning still lives on in Aristotle, when he speaks of the grounds of the essent as such (see *Metaphysics,* I, 1003a27).

But this narrowing of ⟨*physis*⟩ in the direction of "physics" did not occur in the way that we imagine today. We oppose the psychic, the animated, the living, to the "physical." But for the Greeks all this belonged to ⟨*physis*⟩ and continued to do so even after Aristotle. They contrasted it with what they called ⟨*thesis*⟩, thesis, ordinance, or ⟨*nomos*⟩, law, rule in the sense of ⟨*ethos*⟩. This, however, denotes not mere norms but mores, based on freely accepted obligations and traditions; it is that which concerns free behavior and attitudes, the shaping of man's historical being, the ⟨*ethos*⟩ which under the influence of morality was later degraded to the ethical.

The meaning of ⟨*physis*⟩ is further restricted by contrast with ⟨*technē*⟩—which denotes neither art nor technology but a knowledge, the ability to plan and organize freely, to master institutions (cf. Plato's *Phaedrus*). ⟨*Technē*⟩ is creating, building in the sense of a deliberate producing. (It would require a special study to explain what is essentially the same in ⟨*physis*⟩ and ⟨*technē*⟩.) The physical was opposed to the historical, a domain which for the Greeks was part of the originally broader concept of ⟨*physis*⟩. But this has nothing whatever to do with a naturalistic interpretation of history. The realm of being as such and as a whole is ⟨*physis*⟩—i.e. its essence and character are defined as that which emerges and endures. It is experienced primarily through what in a way imposes itself most immediately on our attention, and this was the later, narrower sense of ⟨*physis*⟩: ⟨*ta physei onta, ta physika*⟩, nature. If the question concerning ⟨*physis*⟩ in general was asked at all, i.e. if it was asked: What is the realm of being as such? it was primarily ⟨*ta physei onta*⟩ that gave the point of departure. Yet from the very outset the question could not dwell in this or that realm of nature, inanimate bodies, plants, animals, but had to reach out beyond ⟨*ta physika*⟩.

In Greek, "beyond something" is expressed by the word ⟨*meta*⟩. Philosophical inquiry into the realm of being as such is ⟨*meta ta physika*⟩; this inquiry goes beyond the essent, it is metaphysics. Here it is not important to follow the genesis and history of this term in detail.

Accordingly, the question to which we have given first rank, "Why are there essents rather than nothing?" is the fundamental question of metaphysics. Metaphysics is a name for the pivotal point and core of all philosophy.

[In this introduction our treatment of the entire subject has been intentionally superficial and hence essentially vague. According to our explanation of the word ⟨*physis*⟩, it signifies the being of the essent. If the questioning is ⟨*peri physeōs*⟩, if it concerns the being of the essent, then the discussion has gone beyond ⟨*physis*⟩, beyond "physics" in the ancient sense, and essentially beyond ⟨*ta physika*⟩, beyond essents, and deals with being. From the very first "physics" has determined the essence and history of metaphysics. Even in the doctrines of being as pure act (Thomas Aquinas), as absolute concept (Hegel), as eternal recurrence of the identical will to power (Nietzsche), metaphysics has remained unalterably "physics."

But the inquiry into being as such is of a different nature and origin.

Within the purview of metaphysics and thinking on its level, we can, to be sure, consider the question about being as such as merely a mechanical repetition of the question about the essent as such. In this case the question about being as such is just another transcendental question, though one of a higher order. But this reinterpretation of the question about being as such bars the road to its appropriate unfolding.

However, this new interpretation comes readily to mind; it is bound to suggest itself, particularly as we have spoken in *Sein und Zeit* of a "transcendental horizon." But the "transcendental" there intended is not that of the subjective consciousness; rather, it defines itself in terms of the existential-ecstatic temporality of human being-there. Yet the reinterpretation of the question of being as such tends to take the same form as the question of the essent as such, chiefly because the essential origin of the question of the existent as such and with it the essence of metaphysics remain obscure. And this draws all questions that are in any way concerned with being into the indeterminate.

In the present attempt at an "introduction to metaphysics" I shall keep this confused state of affairs in mind.

In the current interpretation the "question of being" signifies the inquiry into the essent as such (metaphysics). But from the standpoint of *Sein und Zeit,* the "question of being" means the inquiry into being as such. This signification of the title is also the appropriate one from the standpoint of the subject matter and of linguistics; for the "question of being" in the sense of the metaphysical question regarding the essent as such does *not inquire* thematically into being. In this way of asking, being remains forgotten.

But just as ambiguous as the "question of being" referred to in the title is what is said about "forgetfulness of being." It is pointed out—quite correctly—that metaphysics inquires into the being of the essent and that it is therefore an obvious absurdity to impute a forgetfulness of being to metaphysics.

But if we consider the question of being in the sense of an inquiry into being as such, it becomes clear to anyone who follows our thinking that being as such is precisely hidden from metaphysics, and remains forgotten—and so radically that the forgetfulness of being, which itself falls into forgetfulness, is the unknown but enduring impetus to metaphysical questioning.

If for the treatment of the "question of being" in the indeterminate sense we choose the name "metaphysics," then the title of the present work is ambiguous. For at first sight the questioning seems to remain within the sphere of the essent as such, yet at the very first sentence it strives to depart from this sphere in order to consider and inquire into another realm. Actually the title of the work is deliberately ambiguous.

The fundamental question of this work is of a different kind from the leading question of metaphysics. Taking what was said in *Sein und Zeit* (pp. 21f. and 37f.) as a starting point, we inquired into the *"disclosure of being."* "Disclosure of being" means the unlocking of what forgetfulness of being closes and hides. And it is through this questioning that a light first falls on the essence of metaphysics that had hitherto also been hidden.]

"Introduction to metaphysics" means accordingly: an introduction to the asking of the fundamental question. But questions and particularly fundamental questions do not just occur like stones and water. Questions are not found ready-made like shoes and clothes and books. Questions are, and are only as they are actually asked. A leading into the asking of the fundamental questions is consequently not a going to something that lies and stands somewhere; no, this leading-to must first awaken and create the questioning. The leading is itself a questioning advance, a preliminary questioning. It is a leading for which in the very nature of things there can be no following. When we hear of disciples, "followers," as in a school of philosophy for example, it means that the nature of questioning is misunderstood. Such schools can exist only in the domain of scientific and technical work. Here everything has its definite hierarchical order. This work is also an indispensable part of philosophy and has today been lost. But the best technical ability can never replace the actual power of seeing and inquiring and speaking.

"Why are there essents rather than nothing?" That is the question. To state the interrogative sentence, even in a tone of questioning, is not yet to question. To repeat the interrogative sentence several times in succession does not necessarily breathe life into the questioning; on the contrary, saying the sentence over and over may well dull the questioning.

But even though the interrogative sentence is not the question and not the questioning, it must not be taken as a mere linguistic form of communication, as though, for example, the interrogative sentence were only a statement "about" a question. When I say to you "Why are there essents rather than nothing?" the purpose of my speaking and questioning is not to communicate to you the fact that a process of questioning is now at work within me. The spoken interrogative sentence can of course be interpreted in this way, but this means precisely that the questioning has not been heard. In this case you do not join me in questioning, nor do you question yourself. No sign of a questioning attitude or state of mind is awakened. Such a state of mind consists in a *willing* to know. Willing—that is no mere wishing or striving. Those who wish to know also seem to question; but they do not go beyond the stating of the question; they stop precisely where the question begins. To question is to will to know. He who wills, he who puts his whole existence into a will, is resolved. Resolve does not shift about; it does not shirk, but acts from out of the moment and never stops. Resolve is no mere decision to act, but the crucial beginning of action that anticipates and reaches through all action. To will is to be resolved. (The essence of willing is here carried back to determination *[Ent-schlossenheit, "unclosedness"]*. But the essence of resolve lies in the opening, the coming-out-of-cover *[Ent-borgenheit]* of human being-there into the clearing of being, and not in a storing up of energy for "action." See *Sein und Zeit,* §44 and §60. But its relation to being is one of letting-be. The idea that all willing should be grounded in letting-be offends the understanding. See my lecture *Vom Wesen der Wahrheit,* 1930.)

But to know means: to be able to stand in the truth. Truth is the manifestness of the essent. To know is accordingly the ability to stand *[stehen]* in the manifestness of the essent, to endure *[bestehen]* it. Merely to have information, however abundant, is not to know. Even if curricula and examination requirements concentrate this information into what is of the greatest practical importance, it still does not amount to knowledge. Even if this information, pruned down to the most indispensable needs, is "close to life," its possession is not knowledge. The man who possesses such information and has learned a few practical tricks, will still be perplexed in the presence of real reality, which is always different from what the philistine means by down-to-earth; he will always be a bungler. Why? Because he has no knowledge, for to know means *to be able to learn.*

In the common-sense view, to be sure, knowledge belongs to the man who has no further need to learn because he has finished learning. No, only that man is knowing who understands that he must keep learning over and over again and who above all, on the basis of this understanding, has attained to the point where he is always *able to learn.* This is much more difficult than to possess information.

Ability to learn presupposes ability to inquire. Inquiry is the willing to-know analyzed above: the resolve to be able to stand in the openness of the essent. Since we are concerned with the asking of the question that is first in rank, clearly the willing as well as the knowing is of a very special kind. So much the less will the interrogative sentence, even if it is uttered in an authentically questioning tone and even if the listener joins in the questioning, exhaustively reproduce the question. The questioning, which indeed is sounded in the interrogative sentence but which is still enclosed, wrapped up in the words, remains to be unwrapped. The questioning attitude must clarify and secure itself in this process, it must be consolidated by training.

Our next task lies in the development of the question "Why are there essents rather than nothing?" In what direction can it be asked? First of all the question is accessible in the interrogative sentence, which gives a kind of approximation of it. Hence its linguistic formulation must be correspondingly broad and loose. Let us consider our sentence in this respect. "Why are there essents rather than nothing?" The sentence has a caesura. "Why are there essents?" With these words the question is actually asked. The formulation of the question includes: 1) a definite indication of what is put into question, of what is *questioned;* 2) an indication of what the question is about, of what is asked. For it is clearly indicated what the question is about, namely the essent. What is asked after, that which is asked, is the why, i.e. the ground. What follows in the interrogative sentence, "rather than nothing," is only an appendage, which may be said to turn up of its own accord if for purposes of introduction we permit ourselves to speak loosely, a turn of phrase that says nothing further about the question or the object of questioning, an ornamental flourish. Actually the question is far more unambiguous and definite without such an appendage, which springs only from the prolixity of loose discourse. "Why are there essents?" The addition "rather than nothing" is dropped not only because we are striving for a strict formulation of the question but even more because it says nothing. For why should we go on to ask about nothing? Nothing is simply nothing. Here there is nothing more to inquire about. And above all, in talking about nothing or nothingness, we are not making the slightest advance toward the knowledge of the essent.

He who speaks of nothing does not know what he is doing. In speaking of nothing he makes it into a something. In speaking he speaks against what he intended. He contradicts himself. But discourse that contradicts itself offends against the fundamental rule of discourse (⟨*logos*⟩), against "logic." To speak of nothing is illogical. He who speaks and thinks illogically is unscientific. But he who goes so far as to speak of nothing in the realm of philosophy, where logic has its very home, exposes himself most particularly to the accusation of offending against the fundamental rule of all thinking. Such a speaking about nothing consists entirely of meaningless propositions. Moreover: he who takes the nothing seriously is allying himself with nothingness. He is patently promoting the spirit of negation and serving the cause of disintegration. Not only is speaking of nothing utterly repellent to thought; it also undermines all culture and all faith. What disregards the fundamental law of thought and also destroys faith and the will to build is pure nihilism.

On the basis of such considerations we shall do well, in our interrogative sentence, to cross out the superfluous words "rather than nothing" and limit the sentence to the simple and strict form: "Why are there essents?"

To this there would be no objection if . . . if in formulating our question, if altogether, in the asking of this question, we were as free as it may have seemed to us up to this point. But in asking this question we stand in a tradition. For philosophy has always, from time immemorial, asked about the ground of what is. With this question it began and with this question it will end, provided that it ends in greatness and not in an impotent decline. Ever since the question about the essent began, the question about the nonessent, about nothing, has gone side by side with it. And not only outwardly, in the manner of a by-product. Rather, the question about nothing has been asked with the same breadth, depth, and originality as the question about the essent. The manner of asking about nothing may be regarded as a gauge and hallmark for the manner of asking about the essent.

If we bear this in mind, the interrogative sentence uttered in the beginning, "Why are there essents rather than nothing?" seems to express the question about the essent far more adequately than the abbreviated version. It is not looseness of speech or prolixity that leads us to mention nothing. Nor is it an invention of ours; no, it is only strict observance of the original tradition regarding the meaning of the fundamental question.

Still, this speaking of nothing remains in general repellent to thought and in particular demoralizing. But what if both our concern for the fundamental rules of thought and our fear of nihilism, which both seem to counsel against speaking of nothing, should be based on a misunderstanding? And this indeed is the case. True, this misunderstanding is not accidental. It is rooted in long years of failure to understand the question about the essent. And this failure to understand arises from an increasingly hardened forgetfulness of being.

For it cannot be decided out of hand whether logic and its fundamental rules can, altogether, provide a standard for dealing with the question about the essent as such. It might be the other way around. Perhaps the whole body of logic as it is known to us, perhaps all the logic that we treat as a gift from heaven, is grounded in a very definite answer to the question about the essent; perhaps, in consequence, all thinking which solely follows the laws of thought prescribed by traditional logic is incapable from the very start of even understanding the question about the essent by its own resources, let alone actually unfolding the question and guiding it toward an answer. Actually it is only an appearance of strict, scientific method when we invoke the principle of contradiction and logic in general, in order to prove that all thinking and speaking about nothing are contradictory and therefore meaningless. In such a contention "logic" is regarded as a court of justice, established for all eternity, whose rights as first and last authority no rational man will impugn. Anyone who speaks against logic is therefore tacitly or explicitly accused of irresponsibility. And the mere accusation is taken as a proof and an argument relieving one of the need for any further, genuine reflection.

It is perfectly true that we cannot talk about nothing, as though it were a thing like the rain outside or a mountain or any object whatsoever. In principle, nothingness remains inaccessible to science. The man who wishes truly to speak about nothing must of necessity become unscientific. But this is a misfortune only so long as one supposes that scientific thinking is the only authentic rigorous thought, and that it alone can and must be made into the standard of philosophical thinking. But the reverse is true. All scientific thought is merely a derived form of philosophical thinking, which proceeded to freeze into its scientific cast. Philosophy never arises out of science or through science and it can never be accorded equal rank with the sciences. No, it is prior in rank, and not only "logically" or in a table representing the system of the sciences. Philosophy stands in a totally different realm and order. Only poetry stands in the same order as philosophy and its thinking, though poetry and thought are not the same thing. To speak of nothing will always remain a horror and an absurdity for science. But aside from the philosopher, the poet can do so—and not because, as common sense supposes, poetry is without strict rules, but because the spirit of poetry (only authentic and great poetry is meant) is essentially superior to the spirit that prevails in all mere science. By virtue of this superiority the poet always speaks as though the essent were being expressed and invoked for the first time. Poetry, like the thinking of the philosopher, has always so much world space to spare that in it each thing—a tree, a mountain, a house, the cry of a bird—loses all indifference and commonplaceness.

Authentic speaking about nothing always remains extraordinary. It cannot be vulgarized. It dissolves if it is placed in the cheap acid of a merely logical intelligence. Consequently true discourse about nothing can never be immediate like the description of a picture for example. Here I should like to cite a passage from one of Knut Hamsun's last works, *The Road Leads On*. The work forms a whole with *Vagabonds* and *August*. It describes the last years and end of this August, who embodies the uprooted modern man who can do everything equally well yet who cannot lose his ties with the extraordinary, because even in his weakness and despair he remains authentic and superior. In his last days August is alone in the high mountains. And the poet says: "Here he sits between his ears and all he hears is emptiness. An amusing conception, indeed. On the sea there were both motion and sound, something for the ear to feed upon, a chorus of waters. Here nothingness meets nothingness and the result is zero, not even a hole. Enough to make one shake one's head, utterly at a loss."*

We see that there is something very interesting about nothing. Let us then go back to our interrogative sentence; let us ask it through, and see whether this "rather than nothing" is merely a meaningless appendage or whether it does not have an essential meaning even in our provisional statement of the question.

Let us begin with the abbreviated, seemingly simpler, and ostensibly stricter form of the question: "Why are there essents?" When we inquire in this way, we start from the essent. The essent *is*. It is given, it confronts us; accordingly, it is to be found at any time, and it is, in certain realms, known to us. Now this essent, from which we start, is immediately questioned as to its ground. The questioning advances immediately toward a ground. Such a method is only an extension and enlargement, so to speak, of a method practiced in everyday life. Somewhere in the vineyard, for example, the vine-disease occurs; something incontestably present. We ask: where does it come from, where and what is the reason for it, the ground? Similarly the essent as a whole is present. We ask: where and what is the ground? This manner of questioning is represented in the simple formula: Why are there essents? Where and what is their ground? Tacitly we are asking after another and higher kind of essent. But here the question is not by any means concerned with the essent as such and as a whole.

But if we put the question in the form of our original interrogative sentence: "Why are there essents rather than nothing?" this addition prevents us in our questioning from beginning directly with an unquestionably given essent and, having scarcely

---

*Knut Hamsun, *The Road Leads On* (Coward-McCann, 1934), p. 508. Translated by Eugene Gay-Tifft.

begun, from continuing on to another expected essent as a ground. Instead this essent, through questioning, is held out into the possibility of nonbeing. Thereby the why takes on a very different power and penetration. Why is the essent torn away from the possibility of nonbeing? Why does it not simply keep falling back into nonbeing? Now the essent is no longer that which just happens to be present; it begins to waver and os- cillate, regardless of whether or not we recognize the essent in all certainty, regardless of whether or not we apprehend it in its full scope. Henceforth the essent as such oscil- lates, insofar as we draw it into the question. The swing of the pendulum extends to the extreme and sharpest contrary possibility, to nonbeing and nothingness. And the search for the why undergoes a parallel change. It does not aim simply at providing an also present ground and explanation for what is present; now a ground is sought which will explain the emergence of the essent as an overcoming of nothingness. The ground that is now asked after is the ground of the decision for the essent over against nothingness, or more precisely, the ground for the oscillation of the essent, which sustains and un- binds us, half being, half not being, which is also why we can belong entirely to no thing, not even to ourselves; yet being-there *[Dasein]* is in every case mine.

[The qualification "in every case mine" means that being-there is allotted to me in order that my self should be being-there. But being there signifies: care of the ecstat- ically manifested being of the essent as such, not only of human being. Being-there is "in every case mine"; this means neither "posited through me" nor "apportioned to an individual ego." Being-there is *itself* by virtue of its essential relation to being in gen- eral. That is the meaning of the sentence that occurs frequently in *Sein und Zeit:* Being- there implies awareness of being.]

It is already becoming clearer that this "rather than nothing" is no superfluous appendage to the real question, but is an essential component of the whole interroga- tive sentence, which as a whole states an entirely different question from that intended in the question "Why are there essents?" With our question we place ourselves in the essent in such a way that it loses its self-evident character *as the essent.* The essent be- gins to waver between the broadest and most drastic extremes: "either essents—or nothing"—and thereby the questioning itself loses all solid foundation. Our question- ing being-there is suspended, and in this suspense is nevertheless self-sustained.

But the essent is not changed by our questioning. It remains what it is and as it is. Our questioning is after all only a psycho-spiritual process in us which, whatever course it may take, cannot in any way affect the essent itself. True, the essent remains as it is manifested to us. But it cannot slough off the problematic fact that it might also not be what it is and as it is. We do not experience this possibility as something that we add to the essent by thinking; rather, the essent itself elicits this possibility, and in this possibility reveals itself. Our questioning only opens up the horizon, in order that the essent may dawn in such questionableness.

We still know far too little about the process of such questioning, and what we do know is far too crude. In this questioning we seem to belong entirely to ourselves. Yet it is this questioning that moves us into the open, provided that in questioning it transform itself (which all true questioning does), and cast a new space over everything and into everything.

The main thing is not to let ourselves be led astray by overhasty theories, but to ex- perience things as they are on the basis of the first thing that comes to hand. This piece of chalk has extension; it is a relatively solid, grayish white thing with a definite shape, and apart from all that, it is a thing to write with. This particular thing has the attribute of lying here; but just as surely, it has the attribute of potentially not lying here and not being so large. The possibility of being guided along the blackboard and of being used up is not something that we add to the thing by thought. Itself, as this essent, is in this possibility; otherwise it would not be chalk as a writing material. Correspondingly, every essent has in it this potentiality in a different way. This potentiality belongs to the chalk. It has in it-self a definite aptitude for a definite use. True, we are accustomed and inclined, in seek-ing this potentiality in the chalk, to say that we cannot see or touch it. But that is a preju-dice, the elimination of which is part of the unfolding of our question. For the present our question is only to open up the essent in its wavering between nonbeing and being. Inso-far as the essent resists the extreme possibility of nonbeing, it stands in being, but it has never caught up with or overcome the possibility of nonbeing.

We suddenly find ourselves speaking of the nonbeing and being of the essent, without saying how this being or nonbeing is related to the essent. Are the two terms the same? The essent and its being? What, for example, is "the essent" in this piece of chalk? The very question is ambiguous, because the word "the essent" can be under-stood in two respects, like the Greek ⟨to on⟩. The essent means first *that* which is at any time, in particular this grayish white, so-and-so-shaped, light, brittle mass. But "the es-sent" also means that which "brings it about," so to speak, that this thing is an essent rather than a nonessent, that which constitutes its being if it *is*. In accordance with this twofold meaning of the word "the essent," the Greek ⟨to on⟩ often has the second sig-nificance, not the essent itself, not that which is, but "is-ness," essentness, being. Over against this, "the essent" in the first sense signifies all or particular essent things them-selves, in respect to themselves and not to their is-ness, their ⟨ousia⟩.

The first meaning of ⟨to on⟩ refers to ⟨ta onta⟩ (⟨entia⟩), the second to ⟨to einai⟩ (*esse*). We have listed what the essent is in the piece of chalk. This was relatively easy to do. It was also easy to see that the object named can also *not* be, that this chalk need ultimately not be here and not be. What then is being in distinction to what can stand in being or fall back into nonbeing—what is being in distinction to the essent? Is it the same as the essent? We ask the question once again. But in the foregoing we did not list being; we listed only material mass, grayish-white light, so-and-so-shaped, brittle. But where is the being situated? It must belong to the chalk, for this chalk *is*.

We encounter the essent everywhere; it sustains and drives us, enchants and fills us, elevates and disappoints us; but with all this, where is, and wherein consists, the being of the essent? One might reply: this distinction between the essent and its being may occa-sionally have an importance from the standpoint of language and even of meaning; this distinction can be effected in mere thought, i.e. in ideas and opinions, but is it certain that anything essent in the essent corresponds to the distinction? And even this merely cogi-tated distinction is questionable; for it remains unclear what is to be thought under the name of "being." Meanwhile it suffices to know the essent and secure our mastery over it. To go further and introduce being as distinct from it is artificial and leads to nothing.

We have already said a certain amount about this frequent question: What comes of such distinctions? Here we are going to concentrate on our undertaking. We ask: "Why are there essents rather than nothing?" And in this question we seemingly stick to the essent and avoid all empty brooding about being. But what really are we asking? Why the essent as such is. We are asking for the ground of the essent: that it is and is what it is, and that there is not rather nothing. Fundamentally we are asking about being. But how? We are asking about the being of the essent. We are questioning the essent in regard to its being.

But if we persevere in our questioning we shall actually be questioning forward, asking about being in respect to its ground, even if this question remains undeveloped and it remains undecided whether being itself is not in itself a ground and a sufficient ground. If we regard this question of being as the first question in order of rank, should we ask it without knowing how it stands with being and how being stands in its distinction to the essent? How shall we inquire into, not to say find, the ground for the being of the essent, if we have not adequately considered and understood being itself? This undertaking would be just as hopeless as if someone were to try to bring out the cause and ground of a fire, and yet claim that he need not worry about the actual course of the fire or examine the scene of it.

Thus it transpires that the question "Why are there essents rather than nothing?" compels us to ask the preliminary question: "How does it stand with being?"

Here we are asking about something which we barely grasp, which is scarcely more than the sound of a word for us, and which puts us in danger of serving a mere word idol when we proceed with our questioning. Hence it is all the more indispensable that we make it clear from the very outset how it stands at present with being and with our understanding of being. And in this connection the main thing is to impress it on our experience that we cannot immediately grasp the being of the essent itself, either through the essent or in the essent—or anywhere else.

A few examples may be helpful. Over there, across the street, stands the high school building. An essent. We can look over the building from all sides, we can go in and explore it from cellar to attic, and note everything we encounter in that building: corridors, staircases, schoolrooms, and their equipment. Everywhere we find essents and we even find them in a very definite arrangement. Now where is the being of this high school? For after all it is. The building is. If anything belongs to this essent, it is its being; yet we do not find the being inside it.

Nor does the being consist in the fact that we look at the essent. The building stands there even if we do not look at it. We can find it only because it already is. Moreover, this building's being does not by any means seem to be the same for everyone. For us, who look at it or ride by, it is different than for the pupils who sit in it; not because they see it only from within but because for them this building really is what it is and as it is. You can, as it were, smell the being of this building in your nostrils. The smell communicates the being of this essent far more immediately and truly than any description or inspection could ever do. But on the other hand the building's being is not based on this odor that is somewhere in the air.

How does it stand with being? Can you see being? We see essents; this chalk for example. But do we see being as we see color and light and shade? Or do we hear, smell, taste, feel being? We hear the motorcycle racing through the street. We hear the grouse gliding through the forest. But actually we hear only the whirring of the motor, the sound the grouse makes. As a matter of fact it is difficult to describe even the pure sound, and we do not ordinarily do so, because it is *not* what we commonly hear. [From the standpoint of sheer sound] we always hear *more*. We hear the flying bird, even though strictly speaking we should say: a grouse is nothing audible, it is no manner of tone that fits into a scale. And so it is with the other senses. We touch velvet, silk; we see them directly as this and that kind of essent, the one different from the other. Wherein lies and wherein consists being?

But we must take a wider look around us and consider the lesser and greater circle within which we spend our days and hours, wittingly and unwittingly, a circle whose limits shift continuously and which is suddenly broken through.

A heavy storm coming up in the mountains "is," or what here amounts to the same thing, "was" during the night. Wherein consists its being?

A distant mountain range under a broad sky . . . It "is." Wherein consists the being? When and to whom does it reveal itself? To the traveler who enjoys the landscape, or to the peasant who makes his living in it and from it, or to the meteorologist who is preparing a weather report? Who of these apprehends being? All and none. Or is what these men apprehend of the mountain range under the great sky only certain aspects of it, not the mountain range itself as it "is" as such, not that wherein its actual being consists? Who may be expected to apprehend this being? Or is it a non-sense, contrary to the sense of being, to inquire after what is in itself, behind those aspects? Does the being lie in the aspects?

The door of an early Romanesque church is an essent. How and to whom is its being revealed? To the connoisseur of art, who examines it and photographs it on an excursion, or to the abbot who on a holiday passes through this door with his monks, or to the children who play in its shadow on a summer's day? How does it stand with the being of this essent?

A state—*is*. By virtue of the fact that the state police arrest a suspect, or that so-and-so-many typewriters are clattering in a government building, taking down the words of ministers and state secretaries? Or "is" the state in a conversation between the chancellor and the British foreign minister? The state is. But where is being situated? Is it situated anywhere at all?

A painting by Van Gogh. A pair of rough peasant shoes, nothing else. Actually the painting represents nothing. But as to what *is* in that picture, you are immediately alone with it as though you yourself were making your way wearily homeward with your hoe on an evening in late fall after the last potato fires have died down. What is here? The canvas? The brush strokes? The spots of color?

What in all these things we have just mentioned is the being of the essent? We run (or stand) around in the world with our silly subtleties and conceit. But where in all this is being?

All the things we have named *are* and yet—when we wish to apprehend being, it is always as though we were reaching into the void. The being after which we inquire is almost like nothing, and yet we have always rejected the contention that the essent in its entirety *is not*.

But being remains unfindable, almost like nothing, or ultimately *quite* so. Then, in the end, the word "being" is no more than an empty word. It means nothing real, tangible, material. Its meaning is an unreal vapor. Thus in the last analysis Nietzsche was perfectly right in calling such "highest concepts" as being "the last cloudy streak of evaporating reality." Who would want to chase after such a vapor, when the very term is merely a name for a great fallacy! "Nothing indeed has exercised a more simple power of persuasion hitherto than the error of Being . . ."*

"Being"—a vapor and a fallacy? What Nietzsche says here of being is no random remark thrown out in the frenzy of preparation for his central, never finished work. No, this was his guiding view of being from the earliest days of his philosophical effort. It is the fundamental support and determinant of his philosophy. Yet even now this philosophy holds its ground against all the crude importunities of the scribblers who cluster round him more numerous with each passing day. And so far there seems to be no end in sight to this abuse of Nietzsche's work. In speaking here of Nietzsche, we mean to have nothing to do with all that—or with blind hero worship for that matter. The task in hand is too crucial and at the same time too sobering. It consists first of all, if we are to gain a true grasp of Nietzsche, in bringing his accomplishment to a full unfolding. Being a vapor, a fallacy? If this were so, the only possible consequence would be to abandon the question "Why are there essents as such and as a

The Twilight of Idols, Nietzsche's Complete Works, Edinburgh and London, 16 (1911), 19, 22.

whole, rather than nothing?" For what good is the question if what it inquires into is only a vapor and a fallacy?

Does Nietzsche speak the truth? Or was he himself only the last victim of a long process of error and neglect, but as such the unrecognized witness to a new necessity?

Is it the fault of being that it is so involved? is it the fault of the word that it remains so empty? or are we to blame that with all our effort, with all our chasing after the essent, we have fallen out of being? And should we not say that the fault did not begin with us, or with our immediate or more remote ancestors, but lies in something that runs through Western history from the very beginning, a happening which the eyes of all the historians in the world will never perceive, but which nevertheless happens, which happened in the past and will happen in the future? What if it were possible that man, that nations in their greatest movements and traditions, are linked to being and yet had long fallen out of being, without knowing it, and that this was the most powerful and most central cause of their decline? (See *Sein und Zeit,* §38, in particular pp. 179f.)

We do not ask these questions incidentally, and still less do they spring from any particular outlook or state of mind; no, they are questions to which we are driven by that preliminary question which sprang necessarily from our main question "How does it stand with being?"—a sober question perhaps, but assuredly a very useless one. And yet a *question,* the question: is "being" a mere word and its meaning a vapor or is it the spiritual destiny of the Western world?

This Europe, in its ruinous blindness forever on the point of cutting its own throat, lies today in a great pincers, squeezed between Russia on one side and America on the other. From a metaphysical point of view, Russia and America are the same; the same dreary technological frenzy, the same unrestricted organization of the average man. At a time when the farthermost corner of the globe has been conquered by technology and opened to economic exploitation; when any incident whatever, regardless of where or when it occurs, can be communicated to the rest of the world at any desired speed; when the assassination of a king in France and a symphony concert in Tokyo can be "experienced" simultaneously; when time has ceased to be anything other than velocity, instantaneousness, and simultaneity, and time as history has vanished from the lives of all peoples; when a boxer is regarded as a nation's great man; when mass meetings attended by millions are looked on as a triumph—then, yes then, through all this turmoil a question still haunts us like a specter: What for?— Whither?—And what then?

The spiritual decline of the earth is so far advanced that the nations are in danger of losing the last bit of spiritual energy that makes it possible to see the decline (taken in relation to the history of "being"), and to appraise it as such. This simple observation has nothing to do with *Kulturpessimismus,* and of course it has nothing to do with any sort of optimism either; for the darkening of the world, the flight of the gods, the destruction of the earth, the transformation of men into a mass, the hatred and suspicion of everything free and creative, have assumed such proportions throughout the earth that such childish categories as pessimism and optimism have long since become absurd.

We are caught in a pincers. Situated in the center, our nation incurs the severest pressure. It is the nation with the most neighbors and hence the most endangered. With all this, it is the most metaphysical of nations. We are certain of this vocation, but our people will only be able to wrest a destiny from it if *within itself* it creates a resonance, a possibility of resonance for this vocation, and takes a creative view of its tradition. All this implies that this nation, as a historical nation, must move itself and thereby the history of the West beyond the center of their future "happening" and into the primordial realm of the powers of being. If the great decision regarding Europe is not to bring annihilation, that decision must be made in terms of new spiritual energies unfolding historically from out of the center.

To ask "How does it stand with being?" means nothing less than to recapture, to repeat *[wieder-holen],* the beginning of our historical spiritual existence, in order to transform it into a new beginning. This is possible. It is indeed the crucial form of history, because it begins in the fundamental event. But we do not repeat a beginning by reducing it to something past and now known, which need merely be imitated; no, the beginning must be begun again, more radically, with all the strangeness, darkness, insecurity that attend a true beginning. Repetition as we understand it is anything but an improved continuation with the old methods of what has been up to now.

The question "How is it with being?" is included as a preliminary question in our central question "Why are there essents rather than nothing?" If we now begin to look into that which is questioned in our preliminary question, namely being, the full truth of Nietzsche's dictum is at once apparent. For if we look closely, what more is "being" to us than a mere word, an indeterminate meaning, intangible as a vapor? Nietzsche's judgment, to be sure, was meant in a purely disparaging sense. For him "being" is a delusion that should never have come about. Is "being," then, indeterminate, vague as a vapor? It is indeed. But we do not mean to sidestep this fact. On the contrary, we must see how much of a fact it is if we are to perceive its full implication.

Our questioning brings us into the landscape we must inhabit as a basic prerequisite, if we are to win back our roots in history. We shall have to ask why this fact, that for us "being" is no more than a word and a vapor, should have arisen precisely today, or whether and why it has existed for a long time. We must learn to see that this fact is not as harmless as it seems at first sight. For ultimately what matters is not that the word "being" remains a mere sound and its meaning a vapor, but that we have fallen away from what this word says and for the moment cannot find our way back; that it is for this and no other reason that the word "being" no longer applies to anything, that everything, if we merely take hold of it, dissolves like a tatter of cloud in the sunlight. Because this is so—that is why we ask about being. And we ask because we know that truths have never fallen into any nation's lap. The fact that people still cannot and do not wish to understand this question, even if it is asked in a still more fundamental form, deprives the question of none of its cogency.

Of course we can, seemingly with great astuteness and perspicacity, revive the old familiar argument to the effect that "being" is the most universal of concepts, that it covers anything and everything, even the nothing which also, in the sense that it is thought or spoken, "is" something. Beyond the domain of this most universal concept "being," there is, in the strictest sense of the word, nothing more, on the basis of which being itself could be more closely determined. The concept of being is an ultimate. Moreover, there is a law of logic that says: the more comprehensive a concept is—and what could be more comprehensive than the concept of "being"?—the more indeterminate and empty is its content.

For every normally thinking man—and we all should like to be normal men—this reasoning is immediately and wholly convincing. But the question now arises: does the designation of being as the most universal concept strike the essence of being, or is it not from the very outset such a misinterpretation that all questioning becomes hopeless? This then is the question: can being be regarded only as the most universal concept which inevitably occurs in all special concepts, or is being of an entirely different essence, and hence anything but an object of "ontology," provided we take this word in its traditional sense?

The word "ontology" was first coined in the seventeenth century. It marks the development of the traditional doctrine of the essent into a discipline of philosophy and a branch of the philosophical system. But the traditional doctrine was an academic classification and ordering of what for Plato and Aristotle and again for Kant was a question, though no longer to be sure a primordial one. And it is in this sense that the word "ontology" is used today. Under this title each school of philosophy has set up and described a branch within its system. But we can also take the word "ontology" in the "broadest sense," "without reference to ontological directions and tendencies" (cf. *Sein und Zeit,* p. 11, top). In this case "ontology" signifies the endeavor to make being manifest itself, and to do so by way of the question "how does it stand with being?" (and not only with the essent as such). But since thus far this question has not even been heard, let alone echoed; since it has been expressly rejected by the various schools of academic philosophy, which strive for an "ontology" in the traditional sense, it may be preferable to dispense in the future with the terms "ontology" and "ontological." Two modes of questioning which, as we now see clearly, are worlds apart, should not bear the same name.

We ask the questions "How does it stand with being?" "What is the meaning of being?" *not* in order to set up an ontology on the traditional style, much less to criticize the past mistakes of ontology. We are concerned with something totally different: to restore man's historical being-there—and that always includes our own future being-there in the totality of the history allotted to us—to the domain of being, which it was originally incumbent on man to open up for himself. All this, to be sure, in the limits within which philosophy can accomplish anything.

Out of the fundamental question of metaphysics, "Why are there essents rather than nothing?" we have separated the preliminary question, "How does it stand with being?" The relation between the two questions requires clarification, for it is of a special kind. Ordinarily a preliminary question is dealt with before and outside the main question, though in reference to it. But, in principle, philosophical questions are never dealt with as though we might some day cast them aside. Here the preliminary question is not by any means outside of the main question; rather, it is the flame which burns as it were in the asking of the fundamental question; it is the flaming center of all questioning. That is to say: it is crucial for the first asking of the fundamental question that in asking its *preliminary* question we derive the decisive fundamental attitude that is here essential. That is why we have related the question of being to the destiny of Europe, where the destiny of the earth is being decided—while our own historic being-there proves to be the center for Europe itself.

The question is:

Is being a mere word and its meaning a vapor, or does what is designated by the word "being" hold within it the historical destiny of the West?

To many ears the question may sound violent and exaggerated: for one might in a pinch suppose that a discussion of the question of being might be related in some very remote and indirect way to the decisive historical question of the earth, but assuredly not that the basic position and attitude of our questioning might be directly determined by the history of the human spirit on earth. And yet this relationship exists. Since our purpose is to set in motion the asking of the preliminary question, we must now show that, and to what extent, the asking of this question is an immediate and fundamental factor in the crucial historical question. For this demonstration it is necessary to anticipate an essential insight in the form of an assertion.

We maintain that this preliminary question and with it the fundamental question of metaphysics are historical questions through and through. But do not metaphysics and philosophy thereby become a historical science? Historical science after all investigates the temporal, while philosophy investigates the timeless. Philosophy is historical only insofar as it—like every work of the spirit—realizes itself in time. But in this sense the designation of metaphysical questioning as historical cannot characterize metaphysics, but merely expresses something obvious. Accordingly, the assertion is either meaningless and superfluous or else impossible, because it creates an amalgam of two fundamentally different kinds of science: philosophy and historical science.

In answer to this it must be said:

1. Metaphysics and philosophy are not sciences at all, and the fact that their questioning is basically historical cannot make them so.

2. Historical science does not determine a fundamental relation to history, but always presupposes such a relation. It is only for this reason that historical science can distort men's relation to history, which itself is always historical; or misinterpret it and degrade it to a mere knowledge of antiquities; or else deal with crucial fields in the light of this once established relation to history, and so produce cogent history. A historical relation between our historical being-there and history may become an object of knowledge and mark an advanced state of knowledge; but it need not. Moreover, all relations to history cannot be scientifically objectified and given a place in science, and it is precisely the essential ones that cannot. Historical science can never produce the historical relation to history. It can only illuminate a relation once supplied, ground it in knowledge, which is indeed an absolute necessity for the historical being-there of a wise people, and not either an "advantage" or a "disadvantage." Because it is only in philosophy—as *distinguished from all science*—that essential relations to the realm of what is take shape, this relation can, indeed must, for us today be a fundamentally historical one.

But for an understanding of our assertion that the "metaphysical" asking of the preliminary question is historical through and through, it is above all necessary to consider this: for us history is not synonymous with the past; for the past is precisely what is no longer happening. And much less is history the merely contemporary, which never happens but merely "passes," comes and goes by. History as happening is an acting and being acted upon which pass through the *present,* which are determined from out of the future, and which take over the past. It is precisely the present that vanishes in happening.

Our asking of the fundamental question of metaphysics is historical because it opens up the process of human being-there in its essential relations—i.e. its relations to the essent as such and as a whole—opens it up to unasked possibilities, futures, and at the same time binds it back to its past beginning, so sharpening it and giving it weight in its present. In this questioning our being-there is summoned to its history in the full sense of the word, called to history and to a decision in history. And this not after the fact, in the sense that we draw ethical, ideological lessons from it. No, the basic attitude of the questioning is in itself historical; it stands and maintains itself in happening, in giving out of happening for the sake of happening.

But we have not yet come to the essential reason why this inherently historical asking of the question about being is actually an integral part of history on earth. We have said that the world is darkening. The essential episodes of this darkening are: the flight of the gods, the destruction of the earth, the standardization of man, the preeminence of the mediocre.

What do we mean by world when we speak of a darkening of the world? World is always world of the *spirit*. The animal has no world nor any environment *[Umwelt]*. Darkening of the world means emasculation of the spirit, the disintegration, wasting away, repression, and misinterpretation of the spirit. We shall attempt to explain the emasculation of the spirit in one respect, that of misinterpretation. We have said: Europe lies in a pincers between Russia and America, which are metaphysically the same, namely in regard to their world character and their relation to the spirit. What makes the situation of Europe all the more catastrophic is that this enfeeblement of the spirit originated in Europe itself and—though prepared by earlier factors—was definitively determined by its own spiritual situation in the first half of the nineteenth century. It was then that occurred what is popularly and succinctly called the "collapse of German idealism." This formula is a kind of shield behind which the already dawning spirit-lessness, the dissolution of the spiritual energies, the rejection of all original inquiry into grounds and men's bond with the grounds, are hidden and masked. It was not German idealism that collapsed; rather, the age was no longer strong enough to stand up to the greatness, breadth, and originality of that spiritual world, i.e. truly to realize it, for to realize a philosophy means something very different from applying theorems and insights. The lives of men began to slide into a world which lacked that depth from out of which the essential always comes to man and comes back to man, so compelling him to become superior and making him act in conformity to a rank. All things sank to the same level, a surface resembling a blind mirror that no longer reflects, that casts nothing back. The prevailing dimension became that of extension and number. Intelligence no longer meant a wealth of talent, lavishly spent, and the command of energies, but only what could be learned by everyone, the practice of a routine, always associated with a certain amount of sweat and a certain amount of show. In America and in Russia this development grew into a boundless etcetera of indifference and always-the-sameness—so much so that the quantity took on a quality of its own. Since then the domination in those countries of a cross section of the indifferent mass has become something more than a dreary accident. It has become an active onslaught that destroys all rank and every world-creating impulse of the spirit, and calls it a lie. This is the onslaught of what we call the demonic (in the sense of destructive evil). There are many indications of the emergence of this demonism, identical with the increasing helplessness and uncertainty of Europe against it and within itself. One of these signs is the emasculation of the spirit through misinterpretation; we are still in the midst of this process. This misinterpretation of the spirit may be described briefly in four aspects.

1. The crux of the matter is the reinterpretation of the spirit as *intelligence,* or mere cleverness in examining and calculating given things and the possibility of changing them and complementing them to make new things. This cleverness is a matter of mere talent and practice and mass division of labor. The cleverness itself is subject to the possibility of organization, which is never true of the spirit. The attitude of the litterateur and esthete is merely a late consequence and variation of the spirit falsified into intelligence. Mere intelligence is a semblance of spirit, masking its absence.

2. The spirit falsified into intelligence thus falls to the level of a tool in the service of others, a tool the manipulation of which can be taught and learned. Whether this use of intelligence relates to the regulation and domination of the material conditions of production (as in Marxism) or in general to the intelligent ordering and explanation of everything that is present and already posited at any time (as in positivism), or whether it is applied to the organization and regulation of a nation's vital resources and race—in any case the spirit as intelligence becomes the impotent superstructure of something else, which, because it is without spirit or even opposed to the spirit, is taken for the actual reality. If the spirit is taken as intelligence, as is done in the most extreme form of Marxism, then it is perfectly correct to say, in defense against it, that in the order of the effective forces of human being-there, the spirit, i.e.

intelligence, must always be ranked below healthy physical activity and character. But this order becomes false once we understand the true essence of the spirit. For all true power and beauty of the body, all sureness and boldness in combat, all authenticity and inventiveness of the understanding, are grounded in the spirit and rise or fall only through the power or impotence of the spirit. The spirit is the sustaining, dominating principle, the first and the last, not merely an indispensable third factor.

3. As soon as the misinterpretation sets in that degrades the spirit to a tool, the energies of the spiritual process, poetry and art, statesmanship and religion, become subject to *conscious* cultivation and planning. They are split into branches. The spiritual world becomes culture and the individual strives to perfect himself in the creation and preservation of this culture. These branches become fields of free endeavor, which sets its own standards and barely manages to live up to them. These standards of production and consumption are called values. The cultural values preserve their meaning only by restricting themselves to an autonomous field: poetry for the sake of poetry, art for the sake of art, science for the sake of science.

Let us consider the example of science, which is of particular concern to us here at the university. The state of science since the turn of the century—it has remained unchanged despite a certain amount of house cleaning—is easy to see. Though today two seemingly different conceptions of science seem to combat one another—science as technical, practical, professional knowledge and science as cultural value per se— both are moving along the same downgrade of misinterpretation and emasculation of the spirit. They differ only in this: in the present situation the technical, practical conception of science as specialization can at least lay claim to frank and clear consistency, while the reactionary interpretation of science as a cultural value, now making its reappearance, seeks to conceal the impotence of the spirit behind an unconscious lie. The confusion of spiritlessness can even go so far as to lead the upholders of the technical, practical view of science to profess their belief in science as a cultural value; then the two understand each other perfectly in the same spiritlessness. We may choose to call the institution where the specialized sciences are grouped together for purposes of teaching and research a university, but this is no more than a name; the "university" has ceased to be a fundamental force for unity and responsibility. What I said here in 1929, in my inaugural address, is still true of the German university: "The scientific fields are still far apart. Their subjects are treated in fundamentally different ways. Today this hodgepodge of disciplines is held together only by the technical organization of the universities and faculties and preserves what meaning it has only through the practical aims of the different branches. The sciences have lost their roots in their essential ground" (*Was ist Metaphysik?* 1929, p. 8). Science today in all its branches is a technical, practical business of gaining and transmitting information. An awakening of the spirit cannot take its departure from such science. It is itself in need of an awakening.

4. The last misinterpretation of the spirit is based on the above mentioned falsifications which represent the spirit as intelligence, and intelligence as a serviceable tool which, along with its product, is situated in the realm of culture. In the end the spirit as utilitarian intelligence and the spirit as culture become holiday ornaments cultivated along with many other things. They are brought out and exhibited as a proof that there is no intention to combat culture or favor barbarism. In the beginning Russian Communism took a purely negative attitude but soon went over to propagandist tactics of this kind.

In opposition to this multiple misinterpretation of the spirit, we define the essence of the spirit briefly as follows (I shall quote from the address I delivered on the occasion of my appointment as rector, because of its succinct formulation): "Spirit is neither empty cleverness nor the irresponsible play of the wit, nor the boundless work of dismemberment carried on by the practical intelligence; much less is it world reason; no, spirit is a fundamental, knowing resolve toward the essence of being" (*Rektoratsrede,* p. 13). Spirit is the mobilization of the powers of the essent as such and as a whole. Where spirit prevails, the essent as such becomes always and at all times more essent. Thus the inquiry into the essent as such and as a whole, the asking of the question of being, is one of the essential and fundamental conditions for an awakening of the spirit and hence for an original world of historical being-there. It is indispensable if the peril of world darkening is to be forestalled and if our nation in the center of the Western world is to take on its historical mission. Here we can explain only in these broad outlines why the asking of the question of being is in itself through and through historical, and why, accordingly, our question as to whether being will remain a mere vapor for us or become the destiny of the West is anything but an exaggeration and a rhetorical figure.

But if our question about being has this essential and decisive character, we must above all take an absolutely serious view of *the fact* that gives the question its immediate necessity, the fact that for us being has become little more than a mere word and its meaning an evanescent vapor. This is not the kind of fact which merely confronts us as something alien and other, which we need merely note as an occurrence. It is a fact in which we stand. It is a state of our being-there. And by state, of course, I do not mean a quality that can be demonstrated only psychologically. Here state means our entire constitution, the way in which we ourselves are constituted in regard to being. Here we are not concerned with psychology but with our history in an essential respect. When we call it a "fact" that being for us is a mere word and vapor, we are speaking very provisionally. We are merely holding fast, establishing something which has not yet been thought through, for which we still have no locus, even if it looks as though this something were an occurrence among us, here and now, or "in" us, as we like to say.

One would like to integrate the individual fact that for us being remains no more than an empty word and an evanescent vapor with the more general fact that many words, and precisely the essential ones, are in the same situation; that the language in general is worn out and used up—an indispensable but masterless means of communication that may be used as one pleases, as indifferent as a means of public transport, as a street car which everyone rides in. Everyone speaks and writes away in the language, without hindrance and above all *without danger.* That is certainly true. And only a very few are capable of thinking through the full implications of this misrelation and unrelation of present-day being-there to language.

But the emptiness of the word "being," the total disappearance of its appellative force, is not merely a particular instance of the general exhaustion of language; rather, the destroyed relation to being as such is the actual reason for the general misrelation to language.

The organizations for the purification of the language and defense against its progressive barbarization are deserving of respect. But such efforts merely demonstrate all the more clearly that we no longer know what is at stake in language. Because the destiny of language is grounded in a nation's *relation to being,* the question of being will involve us deeply in the question of language. It is more than an outward accident that now, as we prepare to set forth, in all its implication, the fact of the evaporation of being, we find ourselves compelled to take linguistic considerations as our starting point.

LUDWIG WITTGENSTEIN
1889–1951

Ludwig Wittgenstein was born into one of Vienna's leading families. His father, Karl, was a wealthy steel industrialist and his mother, Leopoldine, a concert pianist. Johannes Brahams, Gustaf Mahler, and Pablo Casals were frequent houseguests of the Wittgensteins. Educated at home by tutors, Wittgenstein showed great promise in mathematics and engineering. According to one report, he built a working sewing machine from matchsticks at age ten.

Wittgenstein remained home until age fifteen, when he enrolled at the *Linz Realschule,* where he studied engineering for two years before transferring to Berlin. In 1908, Wittgenstein enrolled at the University of Manchester, England, for studies in aerodynamics. While designing a propeller, Wittgenstein developed an interest in mathematics, which led him to Cambridge. There, from 1912 to 1913, he studied with Bertrand Russell. Russell later recalled one of his first encounters with Wittgenstein:

> At the end of his first term at Cambridge he came to me and said, "Will you please tell me whether I am a complete idiot or not?" I replied, "My dear fellow, I don't know. Why are you asking me?" He said, "Because if I am a complete idiot, I shall become an aeronaut; but, if not, I shall become a philosopher." I told him to write me something during the vacation on some philosophical subject and I would then tell him whether he was a complete idiot or not. At the beginning of the following term he brought me the fulfillment of this suggestion. After reading only one sentence, I said to him, "No, you must not become an aeronaut."*

*Bertrand Russell, *Portraits from Memory* (London: George Allen & Unwin, 1957), pp. 26–27.

Wittgenstein immersed himself in philosophical studies, filling notebooks with ideas. When World War I began in 1914, he enlisted as a machine-gunner in the Austrian army. While in the army, he continued his philosophical work, writing a short treatise in 1918 based on his notebooks. That same year, he was captured by the Italian army. In captivity, he managed to send a copy of this treatise to Russell, who considered it a work of genius and arranged for its publication as the *Tractatus Logico-Philosophicus* (1921). This was the only philosophical book Wittgenstein published during his lifetime.

Wittgenstein believed his *Tractatus* gave the definitive answer to all philosophical problems. Following the war, therefore, he left philosophy completely. After a course at a teacher's training college, he spent the next six years as a schoolteacher in remote Austrian villages. But teaching did not suit his temperament, and he was desperately unhappy. He resigned in 1926 and worked as a monastery gardener before moving back to Vienna to design a house for his sister. While in Vienna, Wittgenstein began talking philosophy again with Moritz Schlick, professor of philosophy at the University of Vienna, and with other professors who admired his *Tractatus.*

Philosophically revived, Wittgenstein returned to Cambridge in 1929, and, after submitting his now famous *Tractatus* as a doctoral dissertation, he became a research fellow of Trinity College. Again, Wittgenstein filled notebooks with philosophical reflections and prepared them for publication. But, with the exception of one paper, Wittgenstein never saw any of his new ideas in print; he always considered his newest thoughts incomplete or not yet adequately formulated.

For the rest of his life, Wittgenstein continued his association with Cambridge—though he never felt completely comfortable with academic life. On several occasions, he left the university, sometimes living in isolation in his hut in Norway. In 1939, he was appointed professor of philosophy at Cambridge, succeeding G.E. Moore. But before he could take the chair, World War II began, and he volunteered as a hospital orderly in London. He returned to Cambridge following the war, but he found his job so dreadful he resigned after two years. Living alone in Ireland, he completed his second major work, *Philosophical Investigations,* though again he could not bring himself to publish it. (It appeared posthumously in 1953.)

During a visit to the United States in 1949, his health began to deteriorate. On his return to Cambridge, doctors discovered prostate cancer, and he died eighteen months later, in 1951. Since his death, his literary executors have published over a dozen books of uncompleted manuscripts, notes, lectures, and letters.

* * *

Throughout his adult life, Wittgenstein was interested in philosophy as an activity rather than as a set of theories. He believed that the goal of philosophy is to remove or "dissolve" problems, and the primary means for doing this is analysis of language. According to Wittgenstein, most philosophical problems can be traced to a misuse of language. In one of his early notebooks he wrote:

> Philosophy gives no pictures of reality and can neither confirm nor confute scientific investigations. Philosophy teaches us the logical form of propositions: that is its fundamental task.*

*Ludwig Wittgenstein, *Notebooks 1914–1916* (London: Basil Blackwell, 1961), p. 93.

Thirty-five years later, he still maintained this philosophical position: "Philosophy is a battle against the bewitchment of our intelligence by means of language."*

But despite this theme, Wittgenstein developed two different ways to understand language. The early Wittgenstein created a "picture theory of meaning" that held that language consists of statements or propositions that picture the world. Just as a picture has something in common with that which it pictures, so language has a logical form in common with the world it pictures. This logical form is usually obscured by ordinary language, so the philosopher's job is to clear up ordinary language by crafting a language that more perfectly pictures the world. This perfected language will have to exclude many propositions (such as those in ethics, metaphysics, or religion), consigning them to silence. Our selection from the *Tractatus,* translated by D.F. Pears and B.F. McGuiness, presents this early theory.

Wittgenstein's early theory was adopted and modified by Moritz Schlick and his "Vienna Circle." This group developed a philosophy that came to be called "logical positivism." Like Wittgenstein, they worked on an ideal language, free from the ambiguities of ordinary discourse, that would clearly exhibit its logical form. They also held that such a language would exclude the propositions of ethics, metaphysics, and religion. (For more on logical positivism, see the introduction to A.J. Ayer, pages 1123–1126.)

The early Wittgenstein, and the logical positivism that adapted many of his ideas, profoundly impacted the philosophy of the mid-twentieth century. But Wittgenstein himself moved to a different understanding of language: a "language game" theory. This theory found the earlier picture theory too narrow; a perfected language is neither possible nor desirable. As he explains in our selection from the *Investigations,* given here in the G.E.M. Anscombe translation, there are many kinds of meaningful sentences that share certain characteristics, but not others. Just as there is no one characteristic common to all games, so there is no one theory to explain all language uses. The proper way to understand a sentence is not to break it down into its constituent parts and analyze its logical form. Instead, we should examine the "forms of life" out of which the sentence arises, to see what "game" it is playing. "The meaning of a word," Wittgenstein wrote, "is its use in the language."

The later Wittgenstein was not interested in creating a perfect language. He sought rather to expose the underlying assumptions of language and the forms of life out of which our sentences arise. By understanding language in terms of the social environment that gives it birth, the later Wittgenstein encouraged a sociological understanding of language. Accordingly, Wittgenstein argued against the idea of a private language—a language apart from communal interactions.

The influence of Wittgenstein's early work peaked in the 1950s. But his later understanding of philosophy and his lifelong conception of philosophy as activity are still influential, particularly in the English-speaking world. For example, feminist philosophers have used Wittgenstein's insights to show how patriarchal language both influences and is influenced by social structures, and theologians have tried to understand the language of sacred texts by exploring their historical contexts. Wittgenstein's belief that the aim of philosophy is to dissolve problems—"To shew the fly the way out of the fly-bottle"—has continued to impress, or, as critics would say, to depress, philosophy.

---

*Ludwig Wittgenstein, *Philosophical Investigations* (New York: Macmillan, 1958), no. 109, p. 47.

* * *

Among the many general introductions to Wittgenstein's life and thought, Anthony Kenney, *Wittgenstein* (Cambridge, MA: Harvard University Press, 1973) still provides one of the best. Also helpful are George Pitcher, *The Philosophy of Wittgenstein* (Englewood Cliffs, NJ: Prentice Hall, 1964); David Pears, *Ludwig Wittgenstein* (New York: Viking Press, 1970); A.J. Ayer, *Wittgenstein* (Chicago: University of Chicago Press, 1985); Joachim Schulte, *Wittgenstein: An Introduction,* translated by William H. Brenner and John F. Holley (Albany, NY: SUNY Press, 1992); P.M.S. Hacker, *Wittgenstein's Place in Twentieth-Century Analytic Philosophy* (Oxford: Basil Blackwell, 1996); and the more specialized David G. Stern, *Wittgenstein on Mind and Language* (Oxford: Oxford University Press, 1995). Norman Malcolm, *Ludwig Wittgenstein: A Memoir* (London: Oxford University Press, 1958); K.T. Fann, ed., *Wittgenstein: The Man and His Philosophy* (New York: Delta, 1967); and O.K. Bouwsma, *Wittgenstein: Conversations, 1949–1951* (Indianapolis, IN: Hackett, 1986) all provide personal memoirs, whereas Allan Janik and Stephen Toulmin, *Wittgenstein's Vienna* (New York: Simon & Schuster, 1973) and Ray Monk, *Ludwig Wittgenstein: The Duty of Genius* (New York: Penguin Books, 1992) give biographies. For guides to Wittgenstein's two major works, see G.E.M. Anscombe, *An Introduction to Wittgenstein's "Tractatus"* (London: Hillary House, 1959); H.O. Mounce, *Wittgenstein's "Tractatus"* (Chicago: University of Chicago Press, 1981); Garth Hallett, *A Companion to Wittgenstein's "Philosophical Investigations"* (Ithaca, NY: Cornell University Press, 1977); G.P. Baker and P.M.S. Hacker, *Wittgenstein: Understanding and Meaning* (Chicago: University of Chicago Press, 1979); Marie McGinn, *Routledge Philosophy Guidebook to Wittgenstein and the Philosophical Investigations* (Oxford: Routledge, 1997); and William H. Brenner, *Wittgenstein's Philosophical Investigations* (Albany, NY: SUNY Press, 1999). Hans-Johann Glock, *A Wittgenstein Dictionary* (Oxford: Basil Blackwell, 1995) provides a useful reference work. Collections of essays include Irving Copi, ed., *Essays on Wittgenstein's "Tractatus"* (New York: Macmillan, 1966); George Pitcher, ed., *Wittgenstein's "Investigations"* (Garden City, NY: Anchor Doubleday, 1966); Peter A. French, Theodore E. Uehling, Jr., and Howard K. Wettstein, eds., *The Wittgenstein Legacy* (Notre Dame, IN: University of Notre Dame Press, 1992); Robert L. Arrington and Johann Glock, eds., *Wittgenstein and Quine* (Oxford: Routledge, 1996); and Hans Sluga and David G. Stern, eds., *The Cambridge Companion to Wittgenstein* (Cambridge: Cambridge University Press, 1996).

TRACTATUS LOGICO-PHILOSOPHICUS (in part)

Preface

Perhaps this book will be understood only by someone who has himself already had the thoughts that are expressed in it—or at least similar thoughts.—So it is not a textbook.—Its purpose would be achieved if it gave pleasure to one person who read and understood it.

Ludwig Wittgenstein, *Tractatus Logico-Philosophicus,* Translated by D.F. Pears and B.F. McGuiness (London: Routledge & Kegan Paul PLC, 1972). Reprinted by permission of Routledge & Kegan Paul.

The book deals with the problems of philosophy, and shows, I believe, that the reason why these problems are posed is that the logic of our language is misunderstood. The whole sense of the book might be summed up in the following words: what can be said at all can be said clearly, and what we cannot talk about we must consign to silence.

Thus the aim of the book is to set a limit to thought, or rather—not to thought, but to the expression of thoughts: for in order to be able to set a limit to thought, we should have to find both sides of the limit thinkable (i.e. we should have to be able to think what cannot be thought).

It will therefore only be in language that the limit can be set, and what lies on the other side of the limit will simply be nonsense.

I do not wish to judge how far my efforts coincide with those of other philosophers. Indeed, what I have written here makes no claim to novelty in detail, and the reason why I give no sources is that it is a matter of indifference to me whether the thoughts that I have had have been anticipated by someone else.

I will only mention that I am indebted to Frege's great works and to the writings of my friend Mr. Bertrand Russell for much of the stimulation of my thoughts.

If this work has any value, it consists in two things: the first is that thoughts are expressed in it, and on this score the better the thoughts are expressed—the more the nail has been hit on the head—the greater will be its value.—Here I am conscious of having fallen a long way short of what is possible. Simply because my powers are too slight for the accomplishment of the task.—May others come and do it better.

On the other hand the *truth* of the thoughts that are here set forth seems to me unassailable and definitive. I therefore believe myself to have found, on all essential points, the final solution of the problems. And if I am not mistaken in this belief, then the second thing in which the value of this work consists is that it shows how little is achieved when these problems are solved.

TRACTATUS LOGICO-PHILOSOPHICUS

1*	The world is all that is the case.
1.1	The world is the totality of facts, not of things.
1.11	The world is determined by the facts, and by their being *all* the facts.
1.12	For the totality of facts determines what is the case, and also whatever is not the case.
1.13	The facts in logical space are the world.
1.2	The world divides into facts.
1.21	Each item can be the case or not the case while everything else remains the same.
2	What is the case—a fact—is the existence of states of affairs.
2.01	A state of affairs (a state of things) is a combination of objects (things).
2.011	It is essential to things that they should be possible constituents of states of affairs.
2.012	In logic nothing is accidental: if a thing *can* occur in a state of affairs, the possibility of the state of affairs must be written into the thing itself.

*[The decimal numbers assigned to the individual propositions indicate the logical importance of the propositions, the stress laid on them in my exposition. The propositions *n*.1, *n*.2, *n*.3, etc. are comments on proposition no. *n;* the propositions *n.m*1, *n.m*2, etc. are comments on proposition no. *n.m;* and so on.]

2.0121   It would seem to be a sort of accident, if it turned out that a situation would fit a thing that could already exist entirely on its own.

   If things can occur in states of affairs, this possibility must be in them from the beginning.

   (Nothing in the province of logic can be merely possible. Logic deals with every possibility and all possibilities are its facts.)

   Just as we are quite unable to imagine spatial objects outside space or temporal objects outside time, so too there is *no* object that we can imagine excluded from the possibility of combining with others.

   If I can imagine objects combined in states of affairs, I cannot imagine them excluded from the *possibility* of such combinations.

2.0122   Things are independent in so far as they can occur in all *possible* situations, but this form of independence is a form of connexion with states of affairs, a form of dependence. (It is impossible for words to appear in two different roles: by themselves, and in propositions.)

2.0123   If I know an object I also know all its possible occurrences in states of affairs. (Every one of these possibilities must be part of the nature of the object.)

   A new possibility cannot be discovered later.

2.01231   If I am to know an object, though I need not know its external properties, I must know all its internal properties.

2.0124   If all objects are given, then at the same time all *possible* states of affairs are also given.

2.013   Each thing is, as it were, in a space of possible states of affairs. This space I can imagine empty, but I cannot imagine the thing without the space.

2.0131   A spatial object must be situated in infinite space. (A spatial point is an argument-place.)

   A speck in the visual field, though it need not be red, must have some colour: it is, so to speak, surrounded by colour-space. Tones must have some pitch, objects of the sense of touch *some* degree of hardness, and so on.

2.014   Objects contain the possibility of all situations.

2.0141   The possibility of its occurring in states of affairs is the form of an object.

2.02   Objects are simple.

2.0201   Every statement about complexes can be resolved into a statement about their constituents and into the propositions that describe the complexes completely.

2.021   Objects make up the substance of the world. That is why they cannot be composite.

2.0211   If the world had no substance, then whether a proposition had sense would depend on whether another proposition was true.

2.0212   In that case we could not sketch out any picture of the world (true or false).

2.022   It is obvious that an imagined world, however different it may be from the real one, must have *something*—a form—in common with it.

2.023   Objects are just what constitute this unalterable form.

2.0231   The substance of the world *can* only determine a form, and not any material properties. For it is only by means of propositions that material properties are represented—only by the configuration of objects that they are produced.

2.0232   In a manner of speaking, objects are colourless.

2.0233   If two objects have the same logical form, the only distinction between them, apart from their external properties, is that they are different.

2.02331   Either a thing has properties that nothing else has, in which case we can immediately use a description to distinguish it from the others and refer to it; or, on the other hand, there are several things that have the whole set of their properties in common, in which case it is quite impossible to indicate one of them.

For if there is nothing to distinguish a thing, I cannot distinguish it, since if I do it will be distinguished after all.

2.024   Substance is what subsists independently of what is the case.

2.025   It is form and content.

2.0251   Space, time, and colour (being coloured) are forms of objects.

2.026   There must be objects, if the world is to have an unalterable form.

2.027   Objects, the unalterable, and the subsistent are one and the same.

2.0271   Objects are what is unalterable and subsistent; their configuration is what is changing and unstable.

2.0272   The configuration of objects produces states of affairs.

2.03   In a state of affairs objects fit into one another like the links of a chain.

2.031   In a state of affairs objects stand in a determinate relation to one another.

2.032   The determinate way in which objects are connected in a state of affairs is the structure of the state of affairs.

2.033   Its form is the possibility of its structure.

2.034   The structure of a fact consists of the structures of states of affairs.

2.04   The totality of existing states of affairs is the world.

2.05   The totality of existing states of affairs also determines which states of affairs do not exist.

2.06   The existence and non-existence of states of affairs is reality.

(We also call the existence of states of affairs a positive fact, and their non-existence a negative fact.)

2.061   States of affairs are independent of one another.

2.062   From the existence or non-existence of one state of affairs it is impossible to infer the existence or non-existence of another.

2.063   The sum-total of reality is the world.

2.1   We picture facts to ourselves.

2.11   A picture presents a situation in logical space, the existence and non-existence of states of affairs.

2.12   A picture is a model of reality.

2.13   In a picture objects have the elements of the picture corresponding to them.

2.131   In a picture the elements of the picture are the representatives of objects.

2.14   What constitutes a picture is that its elements are related to one another in a determinate way.

2.141   A picture is a fact.

2.15   The fact that the elements of a picture are related to one another in a determinate way represents that things are related to one another in the same way.

Let us call this connexion of its elements the structure of the picture, and let us call the possibility of this structure the pictorial form of the picture.

2.151   Pictorial form is the possibility that things are related to one another in the same way as the elements of the picture.

2.1511   *That* is how a picture is attached to reality; it reaches right out to it.

2.1512   It is laid against reality like a ruler.

2.15121   Only the end-points of the graduating lines actually *touch* the object that is to be measured.

2.1513   So a picture, conceived in this way, also includes the pictorial relationship, which makes it into a picture.

Composition in Yellow, Red, Blue and Black, 1921, by Piet Mondrian (1872–1944). The painter/draftsman Mondrian constructed nonobjective paintings with mathematical precision. The clarity of form and structure, together with the lack of any ornamentation, provides a visual metaphor for the precision and austerity of Wittgenstein's *Tractatus*. *(Giraudon/Art Resource, NY)*

2.1514   The pictorial relationship consists of the correlations of the picture's elements with things.

2.1515   These correlations are, as it were, the feelers of the picture's elements, with which the picture touches reality.

2.16   If a fact is to be a picture, it must have something in common with what it depicts.

2.161   There must be something identical in a picture and what it depicts, to enable the one to be a picture of the other at all.

2.17   What a picture must have in common with reality, in order to be able to depict it—correctly or incorrectly—in the way it does, is its pictorial form.

2.171   A picture can depict any reality whose form it has.

A spatial picture can depict anything spatial, a coloured one anything coloured, etc.

2.172   A picture cannot, however, depict its pictorial form: it displays it.

2.173   A picture represents its subject from a position outside it. (Its standpoint is its representational form.) That is why a picture represents its subject correctly or incorrectly.

2.174   A picture cannot, however, place itself outside its representational form.

2.18   What any picture, of whatever form, must have in common with reality, in order to be able to depict it—correctly or incorrectly—in any way at all, is logical form, i.e. the form of reality.

2.181   A picture whose pictorial form is logical form is called a logical picture.

2.182   Every picture is *at the same time* a logical one. (On the other hand, not every picture is, for example, a spatial one.)

2.19   Logical pictures can depict the world.

2.2   A picture has logico-pictorial form in common with what it depicts.

2.201   A picture depicts reality by representing a possibility of existence and non-existence of states of affairs.

2.202   A picture represents a possible situation in logical space.

2.203   A picture contains the possibility of the situation that it represents.

2.21   A picture agrees with reality or fails to agree; it is correct or incorrect, true or false.

2.22   What a picture represents it represents independently of its truth or falsity, by means of its pictorial form.

2.221   What a picture represents is its sense.

2.222   The agreement or disagreement of its sense with reality constitutes its truth or falsity.

2.223   In order to tell whether a picture is true or false we must compare it with reality.

2.224   It is impossible to tell from the picture alone whether it is true or false.

2.225   There are no pictures that are true *a priori*.

3   A logical picture of facts is a thought.

3.001   "A state of affairs is thinkable"—this means that we can picture it to ourselves.

3.01   The totality of true thoughts is a picture of the world.

3.02   A thought contains the possibility of the situation of which it is the thought. What is thinkable is possible too.

3.03   Thought can never be of anything illogical, since, if it were, we should have to think illogically.

3.031   It used to be said that God could create anything except what would be contrary to the laws of logic.—The reason being that we could not say what an "illogical" world would look like.

3.032   It is as impossible to represent in language anything that "contradicts logic" as it is in geometry to represent by its co-ordinates a figure that contradicts the laws of space, or to give the co-ordinates of a point that does not exist.

3.0321   Though a state of affairs that would contravene the laws of physics can be represented by us spatially, one that would contravene the laws of geometry cannot.

3.04   If a thought were correct , it would be a thought whose possibility ensured its truth.

3.05   *A priori* knowledge that a thought was true would be possible only if its truth were recognizable from the thought itself (without anything to compare it with).

3.1   In a proposition a thought finds an expression that can be perceived by the senses.

3.11   We use the perceptible sign of a proposition (spoken or written, etc.) as a projection of a possible situation.

The method of projection is to think out the sense of the proposition.

3.12   I call the sign with which we express a thought a propositional sign.—And a proposition is a propositional sign in its projective relation to the world.

3.13   A proposition includes all that the projection includes, but not what is projected.

Therefore, though what is projected is not itself included, its possibility is.

A proposition does not actually contain its sense, but does contain the possibility of expressing it.

("The content of a proposition" means the content of a proposition that has sense.)

A proposition contains the form, but not the content, of its sense.

3.14   What constitutes a propositional sign is that in it its elements (the words) stand in a determinate relation to one another.

A propositional sign is a fact.

3.141   A proposition is not a medley of words.—(Just as a theme in music is not a medley of notes.)

A proposition is articulated.

3.142   Only facts can express a sense, a set of names cannot.

3.143   Although a propositional sign is a fact, this is obscured by the usual form of expression in writing or print.

For in a printed proposition, for example, no essential difference is apparent between a propositional sign and a word.

(That is what made it possible for Frege to call a proposition a composite name.)

3.1431   The essence of a propositional sign is very clearly seen if we imagine one composed of spatial objects (such as tables, chairs, and books) instead of written signs.

Then the spatial arrangement of these things will express the sense of the proposition.

*   *   *

6.4   All propositions are of equal value.

6.41   The sense of the world must lie outside the world. In the world everything is as it is, and everything happens as it does happen: in it no value exists—and if it did, it would have no value.

If there is any value that does have value, it must lie outside the whole sphere of what happens and is the case. For all that happens and is the case is accidental.

What makes it non-accidental cannot lie *within* the world, since if it did it would itself be accidental.

It must lie outside the world.

6.42   And so it is impossible for there to be propositions of ethics.

Propositions can express nothing of what is higher.

6.421   It is clear that ethics cannot be put into words. Ethics is transcendental.

(Ethics and aesthetics are one and the same.)

6.422   When an ethical law of the form, "Thou shalt . . .," is laid down, one's first thought is, "And what if I do not do it?" It is clear, however, that ethics has nothing to do with punishment and reward in the usual sense of the terms. So our question about the consequences of an action must be unimportant.—At least those consequences should not be events. For there must be something right about the question we posed. There must indeed be some kind of ethical reward and ethical punishment, but they must reside in the action itself.

(And it is also clear that the reward must be something pleasant and the punishment something unpleasant.)

6.423   It is impossible to speak about the will in so far as it is the subject of ethical attributes.

And the will as a phenomenon is of interest only to psychology.

6.43   If good or bad acts of will do alter the world, it can only be the limits of the world that they alter, not the facts, not what can be expressed by means of language.

In short their effect must be that it becomes an altogether different world. It must, so to speak, wax and wane as a whole.

The world of the happy man is a different one from that of the unhappy man.

6.431   So too at death the world does not alter, but comes to an end.

6.4311 Death is not an event in life: we do not live to experience death.

If we take eternity to mean not infinite temporal duration but timelessness, then eternal life belongs to those who live in the present.

Our life has no end in just the way in which our visual field has no limits.

6.4312 Not only is there no guarantee of the temporal immortality of the human soul, that is to say of its eternal survival after death; but, in any case, this assumption completely fails to accomplish the purpose for which it has always been intended. Or is some riddle solved by my surviving for ever? Is not this eternal life itself as much of a riddle as our present life? The solution of the riddle of life in space and time lies *outside* space and time.

(It is certainly not the solution of any problems of natural science that is required.)

6.432   *How* things are in the world is a matter of complete indifference for what is higher. God does not reveal himself *in* the world.

6.4321 The facts all contribute only to setting the problem, not to its solution.

6.44   It is not *how* things are in the world that is mystical, but *that* it exists.

6.45   To view the world *sub specie aeterni* is to view it as a whole—a limited whole.

Feeling the world as a limited whole—it is this that is mystical.

6.5   When the answer cannot be put into words, neither can the question be put into words.

The riddle does not exist.

If a question can be framed at all, it is also *possible* to answer it.

6.51   Scepticism is *not* irrefutable, but obviously nonsensical, when it tries to raise doubts where no questions can be asked.

For doubt can exist only where a question exists, a question only where an answer exists, and an answer only where something *can be said.*

6.52   We feel that even when *all possible* scientific questions have been answered, the problems of life remain completely untouched. Of course there are then no questions left, and this itself is the answer.

6.521   The solution of the problem of life is seen in the vanishing of the problem.

(Is not this the reason why those who have found after a long period of doubt that the sense of life became clear to them have then been unable to say what constituted that sense?)

6.522   There are, indeed, things that cannot be put into words. They *make themselves manifest.* They are what is mystical.

6.53   The correct method in philosophy would really be the following: to say nothing except what can be said, i.e. propositions of natural science—i.e. something that has nothing to do with philosophy—and then, whenever someone else wanted to say something metaphysical, to demonstrate to him that he had failed to give a meaning to certain signs in his propositions. Although it would not be satisfying to the other person—he would not have the feeling that we were teaching him philosophy—*this* method would be the only strictly correct one.

6.54   My propositions serve as elucidations in the following way: anyone who understands me eventually recognizes them as nonsensical, when he has used them—as steps—to climb up beyond them. (He must, so to speak, throw away the ladder after he has climbed up it.)

He must transcend these propositions, and then he will see the world aright.

7   What we cannot speak about we must consign to silence.

PHILOSOPHICAL INVESTIGATIONS
(in part)

1. "When they (my elders) named some object, and accordingly moved towards something, I saw this and I grasped that the thing was called by the sound they uttered when they meant to point it out. Their intention was shewn by their bodily movements, as it were the natural language of all peoples: the expression of the face, the play of the

Reprinted with permission of Blackwell Publisher from Ludwig Wittgenstein: *Philosophical Investigations,* 3rd edition, 1–47, 65–71, 241, 257–258, 305, 309, translated by G.E.M. Anscombe.

eyes, the movement of other parts of the body, and the tone of voice which expresses our state of mind in seeking, having, rejecting, or avoiding something. Thus, as I heard words repeatedly used in their proper places in various sentences, I gradually learnt to understand what objects they signifed; and after I had trained my mouth to form these signs, I used them to express my own desires" (Augustine, *Confessions,* I. 8).

These words, it seems to me, give us a particular picture of the essence of human language. It is this: the individual words in language name objects—sentences are combinations of such names. In this picture of language we find the roots of the following idea: Every word has a meaning. This meaning is correlated with the word. It is the object for which the word stands.

Augustine does not speak of there being any difference between kinds of word. If you describe the learning of language in this way you are, I believe, thinking primarily of nouns like "table," "chair," "bread," and of people's names, and only secondarily of the names of certain actions and properties; and of the remaining kinds of word as something that will take care of itself.

Now think of the following use of language: I send someone shopping. I give him a slip marked "five red apples." He takes the slip to the shopkeeper, who opens the drawer marked "apples"; then he looks up the word "red" in a table and finds a colour sample opposite it; then he says the series of cardinal numbers—I assume that he knows them by heart—up to the word "five" and for each number he takes an apple of the same colour as the sample out of the drawer. It is in this and similar ways that one operates with words. "But how does he know where and how he is to look up the word 'red' and what he is to do with the word 'five'?" Well, I assume that he acts as I have described. Explanations come to an end somewhere.—But what is the meaning of the word "five"?—No such thing was in question here, only how the word "five" is used.

2. That philosophical concept of meaning has its place in a primitive idea of the way language functions. But one can also say that it is the idea of a language more primitive than ours.

Let us imagine a language for which the description given by Augustine is right. The language is meant to serve for communication between a builder A and an assistant B. A is building with building-stones: there are blocks, pillars, slabs and beams. B has to pass the stones, and that in the order in which A needs them. For this purpose they use a language consisting of the words "block," "pillar," "slab," "beam." A calls them out;—B brings the stone which he has learnt to bring at such-and-such a call.— Conceive this as a complete primitive language.

3. Augustine, we might say, does describe a system of communication; only not everything that we call language is this system. And one has to say this in many cases where the question arises "Is this an appropriate description or not?" The answer is: "Yes, it is appropriate, but only for this narrowly circumscribed region, not for the whole of what you were claiming to describe."

It is as if someone were to say: "A game consists in moving objects about on a surface according to certain rules . . ."—and we replied: You seem to be thinking of board games, but there are others. You can make your definition correct by expressly restricting it to those games.

4. Imagine a script in which the letters were used to stand for sounds, and also as signs of emphasis and punctuation. (A script can be conceived as a language for describing sound-patterns.) Now imagine someone interpreting that script as if there were simply a correspondence of letters to sounds and as if the letters had not also completely different functions. Augustine's conception of language is like such an oversimple conception of the script.

5. If we look at the example in ¶1, we may perhaps get an inkling how much this general notion of the meaning of a word surrounds the working of language with a haze which makes clear vision impossible. It disperses the fog to study the phenomena of language in primitive kinds of application in which one can command a clear view of the aim and functioning of the words.

A child uses such primitive forms of language when it learns to talk. Here the teaching of language is not explanation, but training.

6. We could imagine that the language of ¶2 was the *whole* language of A and B; even the whole language of a tribe. The children are brought up to perform *these* actions, to use these words as they do so, and to react in *this* way to the words of others.

An important part of the training will consist in the teacher's pointing to the objects, directing the child's attention to them, and at the same time uttering a word; for instance, the word "slab" as he points to that shape. (I do not want to call this "ostensive definition," because the child cannot as yet ask what the name is. I will call it "ostensive teaching of words." I say that it will form an important part of the training, because it is so with human beings; not because it could not be imagined otherwise.) This ostensive teaching of words can be said to establish an association between the word and the thing. But what does this mean? Well, it may mean various things; but one very likely thinks first of all that a picture of the object comes before the child's mind when it hears the word. But now, if this does happen—is it the purpose of the word?— Yes, it *may* be the purpose.—I can imagine such a use of words (of series of sounds). (Uttering a word is like striking a note on the keyboard of the imagination.) But in the language of ¶2 it is *not* the purpose of the words to evoke images. (It may, of course, be discovered that that helps to attain the actual purpose.)

But if the ostensive teaching has this effect,—am I to say that it effects an understanding of the word? Don't you understand the call "Slab!" if you act upon it in such-and-such a way?—Doubtless the ostensive teaching helped to bring this about; but only together with a particular training. With different training the same ostensive teaching of these words would have effected a quite different understanding.

"I set the brake up by connecting up rod and lever."—Yes, given the whole of the rest of the mechanism. Only in conjunction with that is it a brake-lever, and separated from its support it is not even a lever; it may be anything, or nothing.

7. In the practice of the use of language (2) one party calls out the words, the other acts on them. In instruction in the language the following process will occur: the learner *names* the objects; that is, he utters the word when the teacher points to the stone.—And there will be this still simpler exercise: the pupil repeats the words after the teacher— both of these being processes resembling language.

We can also think of the whole process of using words in (2) as one of those games by means of which children learn their native language. I will call these games "language-games" and will sometimes speak of a primitive language as a language-game.

And the processes of naming the stones and of repeating words after someone might also be called language-games. Think of much of the use of words in games like ring-a-ring-a-roses.

I shall also call the whole, consisting of language and the actions into which it is woven, the "language-game."

8. Let us now look at an expansion of language (2). Besides the four words "block," "pillar," etc., let it contain a series of words used as the shopkeeper in (I) used the numerals (it can be the series of letters of the alphabet); further, let there be two words, which may as well be "there" and "this" (because this roughly indicates their purpose),

that are used in connexion with a pointing gesture; and finally a number of colour samples. A gives an order like: "d—slab—there." At the same time he shews the assistant a colour sample, and when he says "there" he points to a place on the building site. From the stock of slabs B takes one for each letter of the alphabet up to "d," of the same colour as the sample, and brings them to the place indicated by A.—On other occasions A gives the order "this—there." At "this" he points to a building stone. And so on.

9. When a child learns this language, it has to learn the series of 'numerals' a, b, c, ... by heart. And it has to learn their use.—Will this training include ostensive teaching of the words?—Well, people will, for example, point to slabs and count: "a, b, c slabs."—Something more like the ostensive teaching of the words "block," "pillar," etc. would be the ostensive teaching of numerals that serve not to count but to refer to groups of objects that can be taken in at a glance. Children do learn the use of the first five or six cardinal numerals in this way.

Are "there" and "this" also taught ostensively?—Imagine how one might perhaps teach their use. One will point to places and things—but in this case the pointing occurs in the *use* of the words too and not merely in learning the use.—

10. Now what do the words of this language *signify?*—What is supposed to shew what they signify, if not the kind of use they have? And we have already described that. So we are asking for the expression "This word signifies this" to be made a part of the description. In other words the description ought to take the form: "The word ... signifies ..."

Of course, one can reduce the description of the use of the word "slab" to the statement that this word signifies this object. This will be done when, for example, it is merely a matter of removing the mistaken idea that the word "slab" refers to the shape of building-stone that we in fact call a "block"— but the kind of '*referring*' this is, that is to say the use of these words for the rest, is already known.

Equally one can say that the signs "a," "b," etc. signify numbers; when for example this removes the mistaken idea that "a," "b," "c," play the part actually played in language by "block," "slab," "pillar." And one can also say that "c" means this number and not that one; when for example this serves to explain that the letters are to be used in the order a, b, c, d, etc. and not in the order a, b, d, c.

But assimilating the descriptions of the uses of words in this way cannot make the uses themselves any more like one another. For, as we see, they are absolutely unlike.

11. Think of the tools in a toolbox: there is a hammer, pliers, a saw, a screwdriver, a rule, a glue-pot, glue, nails and screws.—The functions of words are as diverse as the functions of these objects. (And in both cases there are similarities.)

Of course, what confuses us is the uniform appearance of words when we hear them spoken or meet them in script and print. For their *application* is not presented to us so clearly. Especially when we are doing philosophy!

12. It is like looking into the cabin of a locomotive. We see handles all looking more or less alike. (Naturally, since they are all supposed to be handled.) But one is the handle of a crank which can be moved continuously (it regulates the opening of a valve); another is the handle of a switch, which has only two effective positions, it is either off or on; a third is the handle of a brake-lever, the harder one pulls on it, the harder it brakes; a fourth, the handle of a pump: it has an effect only so long as it is moved to and fro.

13. When we say: "Every word in language signifies something" we have so far said *nothing whatever;* unless we have explained exactly what distinction we wish to make. (It might be, of course, that we wanted to distinguish the words of language [8]

from words 'without meaning' such as occur in Lewis Carroll's poems, or words like "Lilliburlero" in songs.)

14. Imagine someone's saying: "*All* tools serve to modify something. Thus the hammer modifies the position of the nail, the saw the shape of the board, and so on."—And what is modified by the rule, the glue-pot, the nails?—"Our knowledge of a thing's length, the temperature of the glue, and the solidity of the box." Would anything be gained by this assimilation of expressions?—

15. The word "to signify" is perhaps used in the most straightforward way when the object signified is marked with the sign. Suppose that the tools A uses in building bear certain marks. When A shews his assistant such a mark, he brings the tool that has that mark on it.

It is in this and more or less similar ways that a name means and is given to a thing.—It will often prove useful in philosophy to say to ourselves: naming something is like attaching a label to a thing.

16. What about the colour samples that A shews to B: are they part of the *language*? Well, it is as you please. They do not belong among the words; yet when I say to someone: "Pronounce the word 'the'," you will count the second "the" as part of the sentence. Yet it has a role just like that of a colour-sample in language-game (8); that is, it is a sample of what the other is meant to say.

It is most natural, and causes least confusion, to reckon the samples among the instruments of the language.

((Remark on the reflexive pronoun "*this* sentence."))

17. It will be possible to say: In language (8) we have different kinds *of word*. For the functions of the word "slab" and the word "block" are more alike than those of "slab" and "d." But how we group words into kinds will depend on the aim of the classification,—and on our own inclination.

Think of the different points of view from which one can classify tools or chessmen.

18. Do not be troubled by the fact that languages (2) and (8) consist only of orders. If you want to say that this shews them to be incomplete, ask yourself whether our language is complete;—whether it was so before the symbolism of chemistry and the notation of the infinitesimal calculus were incorporated in it; for these are, so to speak, suburbs of our language. (And how many houses or streets does it take before a town begins to be a town?) Our language can be seen as an ancient city: a maze of little streets and squares, of old and new houses, and of houses with additions from various periods; and this surrounded by a multitude of new boroughs with straight regular streets and uniform houses.

19. It is easy to imagine a language consisting only of orders and reports in battle.—Or a language consisting only of questions and expressions for answering yes and no. And innumerable others.—And to imagine a language means to imagine a form of life.

But what about this: is the call "Slab!" in example (2) a sentence or a word?—If a word, surely it has not the same meaning as the like-sounding word of our ordinary language, for in ¶2 it is a call. But if a sentence, it is surely not the elliptical sentence: "Slab!" of our language. As far as the first question goes you can call "Slab!" a word and also a sentence; perhaps it could be appropriately called a 'degenerate sentence' (as one speaks of a degenerate hyperbola); in fact it is our 'elliptical' sentence.—But that is surely only a shortened form of the sentence "Bring me a slab," and there is no such sentence in example (2).—But why should I not on the contrary have called the sentence "Bring me a slab" a *lengthening* of the sentence "Slab!"?—Because if you shout "Slab!" you really mean: "Bring me a slab."—But how do you do this: how do you mean that while you say "Slab!"? Do you say the unshortened sentence to yourself? And why should I translate the call "Slab!" into a different expression in order to say what someone means by it? And if they mean the same thing—why should I not say: "When he says 'Slab!' he means 'Slab!' "? Again, if you can mean "Bring me the slab," why should you not be able to mean "Slab!"? But when I call "Slab!" then what I want is, *that he should bring me a slab!*—Certainly, but does 'wanting this' consist in thinking in some form or other a different sentence from the one you utter?—

20. But now it looks as if when someone says "Bring me a slab" he could mean this expression as *one* long word corresponding to the single word "Slab!" Then can one mean it sometimes as one word and sometimes as four? And how does one usually mean it? I think we shall be inclined to say: we mean the sentence as four words when we use it in contrast with other sentences such as "*Hand* me a slab," "Bring *him* a slab," "Bring *two* slabs," etc.; that is, in contrast with sentences containing the separate words of our command in other combinations.—But what does using one sentence in contrast with others consist in? Do the others, perhaps, hover before one's mind? *All* of them? And *while* one is saying the one sentence, or before, or afterwards?—No. Even if such an explanation rather tempts us, we need only think for a moment of what actually happens in order to see that we are going astray here. We say that we use the command in contrast with other sentences because *our language* contains the possibility of those other sentences. Someone who did not understand our language, a foreigner, who had fairly often heard someone giving the order: "Bring me a slab!" might believe that this whole series of sounds was one word corresponding perhaps to the word for "building-stone" in his language. If he himself had then given this order perhaps he would have pronounced it differently, and we should say: he pronounces it so oddly because he takes it for a *single* word.—But then, is there not also something different going on in him when he pronounces it,—something corresponding to the fact that he conceives the sentence as a single word?—Either the same thing may go on in him, or something different. For what goes on in you when you give such an order? Are you conscious of its consisting of four words *while* you are uttering it? Of course you have a mastery of this language—which contains those other sentences as well—but is this having a mastery something that *happens* while you are uttering the sentence?—And I have admitted that the foreigner will probably pronounce a sentence differently if he conceives it differently; but what we call his wrong conception *need* not lie in anything that accompanies the utterance of the command.

The sentence is 'elliptical,' not because it leaves out something that we think when we utter it, but because it is shortened—in comparison with a particular paradigm of our grammar.—Of course one might object here: "You grant that the shortened and the unshortened sentence have the same sense.—What is this sense, then? Isn't there a verbal expression for this sense?" But doesn't the fact that sentences have the same sense consist in their having the same *use?*—(In Russian one says "stone red" instead of "the stone is red"; do they feel the copula to be missing in the sense, or attach it in *thought?*)

21. Imagine a language-game in which A asks and B reports the number of slabs or blocks in a pile, or the colours and shapes of the building-stones that are stacked in such-and-such a place.—Such a report might run: "Five slabs." Now what is the difference between the report or statement "Five slabs" and the order "Five slabs!"?—Well, it is the part which uttering these words plays in the language-game. No doubt the tone of voice and the look with which they are uttered, and much else besides, will also be different. But we could also imagine the tone's being the same—for an order and a report can be spoken in a *variety* of tones of voice and with various expressions of face—the difference being only in the application. (Of course, we might use the words

"statement" and "command" to stand for grammatical forms of sentence and intonations; we do in fact call "Isn't the weather glorious to-day?" a question, although it is used as a statement.) We could imagine a language in which *all* statements had the form and tone of rhetorical questions; or every command the form of the question "Would you like to . . .?" Perhaps it will then be said: "What he says has the form of a question but is really a command,"—that is, has the function of a command in the technique of using the language. (Similarly one says "You will do this" not as a prophecy but as a command. What makes it the one or the other?)

22. Frege's idea that every assertion contains an assumption, which is the thing that is asserted, really rests on the possibility found in our language of writing every statement in the form: "It is asserted that such-and-such is the case."—But "that such-and-such is the case" is not a sentence in our language—so far it is not a *move* in the language-game. And if I write, not "It is asserted that . . . .," but "It is asserted: such-and-such is the case," the words "It is asserted" simply become superfluous.

We might very well also write every statement in the form of a question followed by a "Yes"; for instance: "Is it raining? Yes!" Would this shew that every statement contained a question?

Of course we have the right to use an assertion sign in contrast with a question-mark, for example, or if we want to distinguish an assertion from a fiction or a supposition. It is only a mistake if one thinks that the assertion consists of two actions, entertaining and asserting (assigning the truth-value, or something of the kind), and that in performing these actions we follow the propositional sign roughly as we sing from the musical score. Reading the written sentence loud or soft is indeed comparable with singing from a musical score, but '*meaning*' (thinking) the sentence that is read is not.

Frege's assertion sign marks the *beginning of the sentence*. Thus its function is like that of the full-stop. It distinguishes the whole period from a clause *within* the period. If I hear someone say "it's raining" but do not know whether I have heard the beginning and end of the period, so far this sentence does not serve to tell me anything.

23. But how many kinds of sentences are there? Say assertion, question, and command?—There are *countless* kinds: countless different kinds of use of what we call "symbols," "words," "sentences." And this multiplicity is not something fixed, given once for all; but new types of language, new language-games, as we may say, come into existence, and others become obsolete and get forgotten. (We can get a *rough picture* of this from the changes in mathematics.)

Here the term "language-*game*" is meant to bring into prominence the fact that the *speaking* of language is part of an activity, or of a form of life.

Review the multiplicity of language-games in the following examples, and in others:

> Giving orders, and obeying them—
> Describing the appearance of an object, or giving its measurements—
> Constructing an object from a description (a drawing)—
> Reporting an event—
> Speculating about an event—
> Forming and testing a hypothesis—
> Presenting the results of an experiment in tables and diagrams—
> Making up a story; and reading it—
> Play-acting—
> Singing catches—
> Guessing riddles—

Making a joke; telling it—
Solving a problem in practical arithmetic—
Translating from one language into another—
Asking, thanking, cursing, greeting, praying.

Imagine a picture representing a boxer in a particular stance. Now, this picture can be used to tell someone how he should stand, should hold himself; or how he should not hold himself; or how a particular man did stand in such-and-such a place; and so on. One might (using the language of chemistry) call this picture a proposition-radical. This will be how Frege thought of the "assumption." [Note added by Wittgenstein.]

—It is interesting to compare the multiplicity of the tools in language and of the ways they are used, the multiplicity of kinds of word and sentence, with what logicians have said about the structure of language. (Including the author of the *Tractatus Logico-Philosophicus.*)

24. If you do not keep the multiplicity of language-games in view you will perhaps be inclined to ask questions like: "What is a question?"—Is it the statement that I do not know such-and-such, or the statement that I wish the other person would tell me . . . ? Or is it the description of my mental state of uncertainty?—And is the cry "Help!" such a description?

Think how many different kinds of thing are called "description": description of a body's position by means of its co-ordinates; description of a facial expression; description of a sensation of touch; of a mood.

Of course it is possible to substitute the form of statement or description for the usual form of question: "I want to know whether . . ." or "I am in doubt whether . . ."— but this does not bring the different language-games any closer together.

The significance of such possibilities of transformation, for example of turning all statements into sentences beginning "I think" or "I believe" (and thus, as it were, into descriptions of my inner life) will become clearer in another place. (Solipsism.)

25. It is sometimes said that animals do not talk because they lack the mental capacity. And this means: "they do not think, and that is why they do not talk." But— they simply do not talk. Or to put it better: they do not use language—if we except the most primitive forms of language.—Commanding, questioning, recounting, chatting, are as much a part of our natural history as walking, eating, drinking, playing.

26. One thinks that learning language consists in giving names to objects. Viz., to human beings, to shapes, to colours, to pains, to moods, to numbers, etc. To repeat—naming is something like attaching a label to a thing. One can say that this is preparatory to the use of a word. But *what* is it a preparation *for?*

27. "We name things and then we can talk about them: can refer to them in talk."—As if what we did next were given with the mere act of naming. As if there were only one thing called "talking about a thing." Whereas in fact we do the most various things with our sentences. Think of exclamations alone, with their completely different functions.

Water!
Away!
Ow!
Help!
Fine!
No!

Are you inclined still to call these words "names of objects"?

In languages (2) and (8) there was no such thing as asking something's name. This, with its correlate, ostensive definition, is, we might say, a language-game on its own. That is really to say: we are brought up, trained, to ask: "What is that called?"—upon which the name is given. And there is also a language-game of inventing a name for something, and hence of saying, "This is . . . ." and then using the new name. (Thus, for example, children give names to their dolls and then talk about them and to them. Think in this connexion how singular is the use of a person's name to *call* him!)

28. Now one can ostensively define a proper name, the name of a colour, the name of a material, a numeral, the name of a point of the compass and so on. The definition of the number two, "That is called 'two'"—pointing to two nuts—is perfectly exact.—But how can two be defined like that? The person one gives the definition to doesn't know what one wants to call "two"; he will suppose that "two" is the name given to *this* group of nuts!—He *may* suppose this; but perhaps he does not. He might make the opposite mistake; when I want to assign a name to this group of nuts, he might understand it as a numeral. And he might equally well take the name of a person, of which I give an ostensive definition, as that of a colour, of a race, or even of a point of the compass. That is to say: an ostensive definition can be variously interpreted in *every* case.

29. Perhaps you say: two can only be ostensively defined in *this* way: "This *number* is called 'two.'" For the word "number" here shews what place in language, in grammar, we assign to the word. But this means that the word "number" must be explained before the ostensive definition can be understood.—The word "number" in the definition does indeed shew this place; does shew the post at which we station the word. And we can prevent misunderstandings by saying: "This *colour* is called so-and-so," "This *length* is called so-and-so," and so on. That is to say: misunderstandings are sometimes averted in this way. But is there only *one* way of taking the word "colour" or "length"?—Well, they just need defining.—Defining, then, by means of other words! And what about the last definition in this chain? (Do not say: "There isn't a 'last' definition." That is just as if you chose to say: "There isn't a last house in this road; one can always build an additional one.")

Whether the word "number" is necessary in the ostensive definition depends on whether without it the other person takes the definition otherwise than I wish. And that will depend on the circumstances under which it is given, and on the person I give it to.

And how he 'takes' the definition is seen in the use that he makes of the word defined.

30. So one might say: the ostensive definition explains the use—the meaning—of the word when the overall role of the word in language is clear. Thus if I know that someone means to explain a colour-word to me the ostensive definition "That is called 'sepia'" will help me to understand the word.—And you can say this, so long as you do not forget that all sorts of problems attach to the words "to know" or "to be clear."

One has already to know (or be able to do) something in order to be capable of asking a thing's name. But what does one have to know?

Could one define the word "red" by pointing to something that was *not red*? That would be as if one were supposed to explain the word "*modest*" to someone whose English was weak, and one pointed to an arrogant man and said "That man is *not* modest." That it is ambiguous is no argument against such a method of definition. Any definition can be misunderstood.

But it might well be asked: are we still to call this "definition"?—For, of course, even if it has the same practical consequences, the same *effect* on the learner, it plays a different part in the calculus from what we ordinarily call "ostensive definition" of the word "red." [Note added by Wittgenstein.]

---

31. When one shews someone the king in chess and says: "This is the king," this does not tell him the use of this piece—unless he already knows the rules of the game up to this last point: the shape of the king. You could imagine his having learnt the rules of the game without ever having been shewn an actual piece. The shape of the chessman corresponds here to the sound or shape of a word.

One can also imagine someone's having learnt the game without ever learning or formulating rules. He might have learnt quite simple board-games first, by watching, and have progressed to more and more complicated ones. He too might be given the explanation "This is the king,"—if, for instance, he were being shewn chessmen of a shape he was not used to. This explanation again only tells him the use of the piece be-cause, as we might say, the place for it was already prepared. Or even: we shall only say that it tells him the use, if the place is already prepared. And in this case it is so, not because the person to whom we give the explanation already knows rules, but because in another sense he is already master of a game.

Consider this further case: I am explaining chess to someone; and I begin by pointing to a chessman and saying: "This is the king; it can move like this, . . . and so on."—In this case we shall say: the words "This is the king" (or "This is called the 'king'") are a definition only if the learner already 'knows what a piece in a game is.' That is, if he has already played other games, or has watched other people playing 'and understood'—*and similar things*. Further, only under these conditions will he be able to ask relevantly in the course of learning the game: "What do you call this?"—that is, this piece in a game.

We may say: only someone who already knows how to do something with it can significantly ask a name.

And we can imagine the person who is asked replying: "Settle the name yourself"—and now the one who asked would have to manage everything for himself.

32. Someone coming into a strange country will sometimes learn the language of the inhabitants from ostensive definitions that they give him; and he will often have to guess the meaning of these definitions; and will guess sometimes right, sometimes wrong.

And now, I think, we can say: Augustine describes the learning of human lan-guage as if the child came into a strange country and did not understand the language of the country; that is, as if it already had a language, only not this one. Or again: as if the child could already *think*, only not yet speak. And "think" would here mean some-thing like "talk to itself."

33. Suppose, however, someone were to object: "It is not true that you must al-ready be master of a language in order to understand an ostensive definition: all you need—of course I—is to know or guess what the person giving the explanation is pointing to. That is, whether for example to the shape of the object, or to its colour, or to its number, and so on." And what does 'pointing to the shape,' 'pointing to the colour' consist in? Point to a piece of paper.—And now point to its shape—now to its colour—now to its number (that sounds queer).—How did you do it?—You will say that you 'meant' a different thing each time you pointed. And if I ask how that is done, you will say you concentrated your attention on the colour, the shape, etc. But I ask again: how is *that* done?

Suppose someone points to a vase and says "Look at that marvelous blue—the shape isn't the point."—Or: "Look at the marvelous shape—the colour doesn't matter." Without doubt you will do something *different* when you act upon these two invitations. But do you always do the *same* thing when you direct your attention to the colour? Imagine various different cases. To indicate a few:

"Is this blue the same as the blue over there? Do you see any difference?"—

You are mixing paint and you say "It's hard to get the blue of this sky."

"It's turning fine, you can already see blue sky again."

"Look what different effects these two blues have."

"Do you see the blue book over there? Bring it here."

"This blue signal-light means. . . ."

"What's this blue called?—Is it 'indigo'?"

You sometimes attend to the colour by putting your hand up to keep the outline from view; or by not looking at the outline of the thing; sometimes by staring at the object and trying to remember where you saw that colour before.

You attend to the shape, sometimes by tracing it, sometimes by screwing up your eyes so as not to see the colour clearly, and in many other ways. I want to say: This is the sort of thing that happens while one 'directs one's attention to this or that.' But it isn't these things by themselves that make us say someone is attending to the shape, the colour, and so on. Just as a move in chess doesn't consist simply in moving a piece in such-and-such a way on the board—nor yet in one's thoughts and feelings as one makes the move: but in the circumstances that we call "playing a game of chess," "solving a chess problem," and so on.

34. But suppose someone said: "I always do the same thing when I attend to the shape: my eye follows the outline and I feel. . . ." And suppose this person to give someone else the ostensive definition "That is called a 'circle,'" pointing to a circular object and having all these experiences cannot his hearer still interpret the definition differently, even though he sees the other's eyes following the outline, and even though he feels what the other feels? That is to say: this 'interpretation' may also consist in how he now makes use of the word; in what he points to, for example, when told: "Point to a circle."—For neither the expression "to intend the definition in such-and-such a way" nor the expression "to interpret the definition in such-and-such a way" stands for a process which accompanies the giving and hearing of the definition.

35. There are, of course, what can be called "characteristic experiences" of pointing to (e.g.) the shape. For example, following the outline with one's finger or with one's eyes as one points.—But *this* does not happen in all cases in which I 'mean the shape,' and no more does any other one characteristic process occur in all these cases.—Besides, even if something of the sort did recur in all cases, it would still depend on the circumstances—that is, on what happened before and after the pointing—whether we should say "He pointed to the shape and not to the colour."

For the words "to point to the shape," "to mean the shape," and so on, are not used in the same way as *these:* "to point to this book (not to that one)," "to point to the chair, not the table," and so on.—Only think how differently we *learn* the use of the words "to point to this thing," "to point to that thing," and on the other hand "to point to the colour, not the shape," "to mean the colour," and so on.

To repeat: in certain cases, especially when one points 'to the shape' or 'to the number' there are characteristic experiences and ways of pointing—'characteristic' because they recur often (not always) when shape or number are 'meant.' But do you also know of an experience characteristic of pointing to a piece in a game *as a piece in a game?* All the same one can say: "I mean that this *piece* is called the 'king,' not this particular bit of wood I am pointing to." (Recognizing, wishing, remembering, etc.)

36. And we do here what we do in a host of similar cases: because we cannot specify any *one* bodily action which we call pointing to the shape (as opposed, for example, to the colour), we say that a *spiritual* [mental, intellectual] activity corresponds to these words.

Where our language suggests a body and there is none: there, we should like to say, is a *spirit.*

37. What is the relation between name and thing named?—Well, what is it? Look at language-game (2) or at another one: there you can see the sort of thing this relation consists in. This relation may also consist, among many other things, in the fact that hearing the name calls before our mind the picture of what is named; and it also consists, among other things, in the name's being written on the thing named or being pronounced when that thing is pointed at.

38. But what, for example, is the word "this" the name of in language-game (8) or the word "that" in the ostensive definition "that is called. . . ."?—If you do not want to produce confusion you will do best not to call these words names at all.—Yet, strange to say, the word "this" has been called the only *genuine* name; so that anything else we call a name was one only in an inexact, approximate sense.

This queer conception springs from a tendency to sublime the logic of our language—as one might put it. The proper answer to it is: we call very different things "names"; the word "name" is used to characterize many different kinds of use of a word, related to one another in many different ways;—but the kind of use that "this" has is not among them.

What is it to mean the words "*That* is blue" at one time as a statement about the object one is pointing to—at another as an explanation of the word "blue"? Well, in the second case one really means "That is called 'blue.'"—Then can one at one time mean the word "is" as "is called" and the word "blue" as "'blue,'" and another time mean "is" really as "is"?

It is also possible for someone to get an explanation of the words out of what was intended as a piece of information. [Marginal note: Here lurks a crucial superstition.]

Can I say "bububu" and mean "If it doesn't rain I shall go for a walk"?—It is only in a language that I can mean something by something. This shews clearly that the grammar of "to mean" is not like that of the expression "to imagine" and the like. [Note added by Wittgenstein.]

It is quite true that, in giving an ostensive definition for instance, we often point to the object named and say the name. And similarly, in giving an ostensive definition for instance, we say the word "this" while pointing to a thing. And also the word "this" and a name often occupy the same position in a sentence. But it is precisely characteristic of a name that it is defined by means of the demonstrative expression "That is N" (or "That is called 'N'"). But do we also give the definitions: "That is called 'this,'" or "This is called 'this'"?

This is connected with the conception of naming as, so to speak, an occult process. Naming appears as a *queer* connexion of a word with an object.—And you really get such a queer connexion when the philosopher tries to bring out *the* relation between name and thing by staring at an object in front of him and repeating a name or even the word "this" innumerable times. For philosophical problems arise when language *goes on holiday*. And *here* we may indeed fancy naming to be some remarkable act of mind, as it were a baptism of an object. And we can also say the word "this" *to* the object, as it were *address* the object as "this"—a queer use of this word, which doubtless only occurs in doing philosophy.

39. But why does it occur to one to want to make precisely this word into a name, when it evidently is *not* a name?—That is just the reason. For one is tempted to make an objection against what is ordinarily called a name. It can be put like this: *a name ought really to signify a simple*. And for this one might perhaps give the following reasons: The word "Excalibur," say, is a proper name in the ordinary sense. The sword Excalibur consists of parts combined in a particular way. If they are combined differently Excalibur does not exist. But it is clear that the sentence "Excalibur has a sharp blade" makes sense whether Excalibur is still whole or is broken up. But if "Excalibur" is the name of an object, this object no longer exists when Excalibur is broken in pieces; and as no object would then correspond to the name it would have no meaning. But then the sentence "Excalibur has a sharp blade" would contain a word that had no meaning, and hence the sentence would be nonsense. But it does make sense; so there must always be something corresponding to the words of which it consists. So the word "Excalibur" must disappear when the sense is analysed and its place be taken by words which name simples. It will be reasonable to call these words the real names.

40. Let us first discuss *this* point of the argument: that a word has no meaning if nothing corresponds to it.—It is important to note that the word "meaning" is being used illicitly if it is used to signify the thing that 'corresponds' to the word. That is to confound the meaning of a name with the *bearer* of the name. When Mr. N. N. dies one says that the bearer of the name dies, not that the meaning dies. And it would be nonsensical to say that, for if the name ceased to have meaning it would make no sense to say "Mr. N. N. is dead."

41. In §15 we introduced proper names into language (8). Now suppose that the tool with the name "N" is broken. Not knowing this, A gives B the sign "N." Has this sign meaning now or not?—What is B to do when he is given it?—We have not settled anything about this. One might ask: what *will* he do? Well, perhaps he will stand there at a loss, or shew A the pieces. Here one *might* say: "N" has become meaningless; and this expression would mean that the sign "N" no longer had a use in our language-game (unless we gave it a new one). "N" might also become meaningless because, for whatever reason, the tool was given another name and the sign "N" no longer used in the language-game.—But we could also imagine a convention whereby B has to shake his head in reply if A gives him the sign belonging to a tool that is broken.—In this way the command "N" might be said to be given a place in the language-game even when the tool no longer exists, and the sign "N" to have meaning even when its bearer ceases to exist.

42. But has for instance a name which has *never* been used for a tool also got a meaning in that game? Let us assume that "X" is such a sign and that A gives this sign to B—well, even such signs could be given a place in the language-game, and B might have, say, to answer them too with a shake of the head. (One could imagine this as a sort of joke between them.)

43. For a *large* class of cases—though not for all—in which we employ the word "meaning" it can be defined thus: the meaning of a word is its use in the language.

And the *meaning* of a name is sometimes explained by pointing to its *bearer*.

44. We said that the sentence "Excalibur has a sharp blade" made sense even when Excalibur was broken in pieces. Now this is so because in this language-game a name is also used in the absence of its bearer. But we can imagine a language-game

with names (that is, with signs which we should certainly include among names) in which they are used only in the presence of the bearer; and so could always be replaced by a demonstrative pronoun and the gesture of pointing.

45. The demonstrative "this" can never be without a bearer. It might be said: "so long as there is a *this*, the word 'this' has a meaning too, whether *this* is simple or complex." But that does not make the word into a name. On the contrary: for a name is not used with, but only explained by means of, the gesture of pointing.

46. What lies behind the idea that names really signify simples?—

Socrates says in the *Theaetetus:* "If I make no mistake, I have heard some people say this: there is no definition of the primary elements—so to speak—out of which we and everything else are composed; for everything that exists in its own right can only be *named*, no other determination is possible, neither that it *is* nor that it *is not.* . . . But what exists in its own right has to be . . . named without any other determination. In consequence it is impossible to give an account of any primary element; for it, nothing is possible but the bare name; its name is all it has. But just as what consists of these primary elements is itself complex, so the names of the elements become descriptive language by being compounded together. For the essence of speech is the composition of names."

Both Russell's 'individuals' and my 'objects' (*Tractatus Logico-Philosophicus*) were such primary elements.

47. But what are the simple constituent parts of which reality is composed?— What are the simple constituent parts of a chair?—The bits of wood of which it is made? Or the molecules, or the atoms?—"Simple" means: not composite. And here the point is: in what sense 'composite'? It makes no sense at all to speak absolutely of the 'simple parts of a chair.'

Again: Does my visual image of this tree, of this chair, consist of parts? And what are its simple component parts? Multi-colouredness is one kind of complexity; another is, for example, that of a broken outline composed of straight bits. And a curve can be said to be composed of an ascending and a descending segment.

If I tell someone without any further explanation: "What I see before me now is composite," he will have the right to ask: "What do you mean by 'composite'? For there are all sorts of things that that can mean!"—The question "Is what you see composite?" makes good sense if it is already established what kind of complexity—that is, which particular use of the word—is in question. If it had been laid down that the visual image of a tree was to be called "composite" if one saw not just a single trunk, but also branches, then the question "Is the visual image of this tree simple or composite?" and the question "What are its simple component parts?" would have a clear sense—a clear use. And of course the answer to the second question is not "The branches" (that would be an answer to the *grammatical* question: "What are here called 'simple component parts'?") but rather a description of the individual branches.

But isn't a chessboard, for instance, obviously, and absolutely, composite?— You are probably thinking of the composition out of thirty-two white and thirty-two black squares. But could we not also say, for instance, that it was composed of the colours black and white and the schema of squares? And if there are quite different ways of looking at it, do you still want to say that the chessboard is absolutely 'composite'?—Asking "Is this object composite?" *outside* a particular language-game is like what a boy once did, who had to say whether the verbs in certain sentences were in the active or passive voice, and who racked his brains over the question whether the verb "to sleep" meant something active or passive.

We use the word "composite" (and therefore the word "simple") in an enormous number of different and differently related ways. (Is the colour of a square on a chessboard simple, or does it consist of pure white and pure yellow? And is white simple, or does it consist of the colours of the rainbow?—Is this length of 2 cm. simple, or does it consist of two parts, each 1 cm. long? But why not of one bit 3 cm. long, and one bit 1 cm. long measured in the opposite direction?)

To the *philosophical* question: "Is the visual image of this tree composite, and what are its component parts?" the correct answer is: "That depends on what you understand by 'composite'." (And that is of course not an answer but a rejection of the question.)

* * *

65. Here we come up against the great question that lies behind all these considerations.—For someone might object against me: "You take the easy way out! You talk about all sorts of language-games, but have nowhere said what the essence of a language-game, and hence of language, is: what is common to all these activities, and what makes them into language or parts of language. So you let yourself off the very part of the investigation that once gave you yourself most headache, the part about the *general form of propositions* and of language."

And this is true.—Instead of producing something common to all that we call language, I am saying that these phenomena have no one thing in common which makes us use the same word for all,—but that they are *related* to one another in many different ways. And it is because of this relationship, or these relationships, that we call them all "language." I will try to explain this.

66. Consider for example the proceedings that we call "games." I mean board-games, card-games, ball-games, Olympic games, and so on. What is common to them all?—Don't say: "There *must* be something common, or they would not be called 'games'"—but *look and see* whether there is anything common to all.—For if you look at them you will not see something that is common to *all,* but similarities, relationships, and a whole series of them at that. To repeat: don't think, but look!—Look for example at board-games, with their multifarious relationships. Now pass to card-games; here you find many correspondences with the first group, but many common features drop out, and others appear. When we pass next to ball-games, much that is common is retained, but much is lost.—Are they all 'amusing'? Compare chess with noughts and crosses. Or is there always winning and losing, or competition between players? Think of patience. In ball-games there is winning and losing; but when a child throws his ball at the wall and catches it again, this feature has disappeared. Look at the parts played by skill and luck; and at the difference between skill in chess and skill in tennis. Think now of games like ring-a-ring-a-roses; here is the element of amusement, but how many other characteristic features have disappeared! And we can go through the many, many other groups of games in the same way; can see how similarities crop up and disappear.

And the result of this examination is: we see a complicated network of similarities overlapping and criss-crossing: sometimes overall similarities, sometimes similarities of detail.

67. I can think of no better expression to characterize these similarities than "family resemblances"; for the various resemblances between members of a family: build, features, colour of eyes, gait, temperament, etc., etc. overlap and criss-cross in the same way.—And I shall say: "games" form a family.

And for instance the kinds of number form a family in the same way. Why do we call something a "number"? Well, perhaps because it has a—direct—relationship with several things that have hitherto been called number; and this can be said to give it an indirect relationship to other things we call the same name. And we extend our concept of number as in spinning a thread we twist fibre on fibre. And the strength of the thread does not reside in the fact that some one fibre runs through its whole length, but in the overlapping of many fibres.

But if someone wished to say: "There is something common to all these constructions—namely the disjunction of all their common properties"—I should reply: Now you are only playing with words. One might as well say: "Something runs through the whole thread—namely the continuous overlapping of those fibres."

68. "All right: the concept of number is defined for you as the logical sum of these individual interrelated concepts: cardinal numbers, rational numbers, real numbers, etc.; and in the same way the concept of a game as the logical sum of a corresponding set of sub-concepts."—It need not be so. For I *can* give the concept 'number' rigid limits in this way, that is, use the word "number" for a rigidly limited concept, but I can also use it so that the extension of the concept is *not* closed by a frontier. And this is how we do use the word "game." For how is the concept of a game bounded? What still counts as a game and what no longer does? Can you give the boundary? No. You can *draw* one; for none has so far been drawn. (But that never troubled you before when you used the word "game.")

"But then the use of the word is unregulated, the 'game' we play with it is unregulated."—It is not everywhere circumscribed by rules; but no more are there any rules for how high one throws the ball in tennis, or how hard; yet tennis is a game for all that and has rules too.

69. How should we explain to someone what a game is? I imagine that we should describe *games* to him, and we might add: "This *and similar things* are called 'games'." And do we know any more about it ourselves? Is it only other people whom we cannot tell exactly what a game is?—But this is not ignorance. We do not know the boundaries because none have been drawn. To repeat, we can draw a boundary—for a special purpose. Does it take that to make the concept usable? Not at all! (Except for that special purpose.) No more than it took the definition: 1 pace = 75 cm to make the measure of length 'one pace' usable. And if you want to say "But still, before that it wasn't an exact measure," then I reply: very well, it was an inexact one.—Though you still owe me a definition of exactness.

70. "But if the concept 'game' is uncircumscribed like that, you don't really know what you mean by a 'game'."—When I give the description: "The ground was quite covered with plants"—do you want to say I don't know what I am talking about until I can give a definition of a plant?

My meaning would be explained by, say, a drawing and the words "The ground looked roughly like this." Perhaps I even say "it looked *exactly* like this."—Then were just *this* grass and *these* leaves there, arranged just like this? No, that is not what it means. And I should not accept any picture as exact in *this* sense.

Someone says to me: "Shew the children a game." I teach them gaming with dice, and the other says "I didn't mean that sort of game." Must the exclusion of the game with dice have come before his mind when he gave me the order? [Note added by Wittgenstein.]

---

71. One might say that the concept 'game' is a concept with blurred edges.—"But is a blurred concept a concept at all?"—Is an indistinct photograph a picture of a

person at all? Is it even always an advantage to replace an indistinct picture by a sharp one? Isn't the indistinct one often exactly what we need?

Frege compares a concept to an area and says that an area with vague boundaries cannot be called an area at all. This presumably means that we cannot do anything with it.—But is it senseless to say: "Stand roughly there"? Suppose that I were standing with someone in a city square and said that. As I say it I do not draw any kind of boundary, but perhaps point with my hand—as if I were indicating a particular *spot*. And this is just how one might explain to someone what a game is. One gives examples and intends them to be taken in a particular way.—I do not, however, mean by this that he is supposed to see in those examples that common thing which I—for some reason—was unable to express; but that he is now to *employ* those examples in a particular way. Here giving examples is not an *indirect* means of explaining—in default of a better. For any general definition can be misunderstood too. The point is that *this* is how we play the game. (I mean the language-game with the word "game.")

*   *   *

241. "So you are saying that human agreement decides what is true and what is false?"—It is what human beings say that is true and false; and they agree in the *language* they use. That is not agreement in opinions but in form of life.

*   *   *

257. "What would it be like if human beings shewed no outward signs of pain (did not groan, grimace, etc.)? Then it would be impossible to teach a child the use of the word 'tooth-ache'."—Well, let's assume the child is a genius and itself invents a name for the sensation!—But then, of course, he couldn't make himself understood when he used the word.—So does he understand the name, without being able to explain its meaning to anyone?—But what does it mean to say that he has 'named his pain'?—How has he done this naming of pain?! And whatever he did, what was its purpose?—When one says "He gave a name to his sensation" one forgets that a great deal of stage-setting in the language is presupposed if the mere act of naming is to make sense. And when we speak of someone's having given a name to pain, what is presupposed is the existence of the grammar of the word "pain"; it shews the post where the new word is stationed.

258. Let us imagine the following case. I want to keep a diary about the recurrence of a certain sensation. To this end I associate it with the sign "S" and write this sign in a calendar for every day on which I have the sensation. I will remark first of all that a definition of the sign cannot be formulated.—But still I can give myself a kind of ostensive definition.—How? Can I point to the sensation? Not in the ordinary sense. But I speak, or write the sign down, and at the same time I concentrate my attention on the sensation—and so, as it were, point to it inwardly.—But what is this ceremony for? for that is all it seems to be! A definition surely serves to establish the meaning of a sign.—Well, that is done precisely by the concentrating of my attention; for in this way I impress on myself the connexion between the sign and the sensation.—But "I impress it on myself" can only mean: this process brings it about that I remember the connexion *right* in the future. But in the present case I have no criterion of correctness. One would like to say: whatever is going to seem right to me is right. And that only means that here we can't talk about 'right.'

*   *   *

305. "But you surely cannot deny that, for example, in remembering, an inner process takes place."—What gives the impression that we want to deny anything? When one says "Still, an inner process does take place here"—one wants to go on: "After all, you *see* it." And it is this inner process that one means by the word "remembering."—The impression that we wanted to deny something arises from our setting our faces against the picture of the 'inner process.' What we deny is that the picture of the inner process gives us the correct idea of the use of the word "to remember." We say that this picture with its ramifications stands in the way of our seeing the use of the word as it is.

*   *   *

309. What is your aim in philosophy?—To shew the fly the way out of the fly-bottle.

A.J. AYER
1910–1989

Alfred Jules Ayer was born in London, the only child of immigrant parents. His father, Jules Ayer, was a Swiss-born businessman, and his mother, Reine Citroen Ayer, was a Dutch Jew whose distant cousin had founded the well-known Citroen automobile company. At age seven, Ayer was sent to boarding school at Eastbourne, and at age twelve he won an academic scholarship to prestigious Eton College. For the next six years, he studied the classics, enjoyed the theater, and participated actively in sports (he was quite good at tennis and fantasized about becoming a professional cricket player). During this time, he also gave up all religious belief.

In 1928, Ayer won a scholarship in classics to Christ Church College, Oxford. There he studied philosophy as well as Greek and Roman history. He was fascinated by the philosophy of the early Wittgenstein and spent time in Cambridge with the philosopher. After graduation, he became a lecturer at Christ Church; but the college had overhired, and he was given a two-term leave. He used this time to visit Austria, where he met Moritz Schlick and became an enthusiastic member of the "Vienna Circle" of logical positivists. Returning to Oxford full of zeal for the new philosophy, he wrote his most famous book, *Language, Truth, and Logic* (1936). The twenty-six-year-old Ayer immediately became the leading apologist for logical positivism in the English-speaking world.

After five years as a research student at Christ Church and after service in the Welsh Guards during World War II, Ayer became Fellow and Dean of Wadham, Oxford. In 1946, he was elected Grote Professor of Philosophy of Mind and Logic at University College, London. During this time he wrote extensively, modifying some of the brasher statements of his earlier writings. His major work from this period was his theory of knowledge, *The Problem of Knowledge* (1956). In addition to writing, Ayer served as editor of the Pelican Philosophy Series and president of the Aristotelian Society, was an activist in liberal political causes, and appeared as a regular guest on the BBC television program "The Brains Trust." In 1960, he returned to Oxford as Wykeham Professor of Logic. While at Oxford, he also lectured throughout the world. Though obliged to retire from his chair at Oxford at age sixty-seven, Ayer continued to write and teach until his death in 1989.

A year before his death, Ayer had a "somewhat agonising but very astonishing experience" when his heart stopped beating for four minutes. In an article entitled "What I Saw When I Was Dead . . . ," Ayer described the incident:

> I was confronted by a red light, exceedingly bright, and also very painful, even when I turned away from it. I was aware that this light was responsible for the government of the universe.*

In the same article, Ayer made it clear that this event in no way shook his atheistic convictions.

*   *   *

Logical positivism has its roots in the empiricism of David Hume and the language theory of the early Wittgenstein. Hume had divided all meaningful ideas into two classes—those concerned with "relations of ideas" and those concerned with "matters of fact." The *a priori* propositions of logic and pure mathematics (known as "analytic" propositions) comprise the former class and propositions that depend on observation and experimentation (known as "synthetic") comprise the latter. But metaphysical ideas did not fit either class and hence were considered vacuous or meaningless. Wittgenstein's early *Tractatus* called for a philosophical language stripped of such meaningless statements:

> The correct method in philosophy would really be the following: to say nothing except what can be said, i.e. propositions of natural science—i.e. something that has nothing to do with philosophy—and then, whenever someone else wanted to say something metaphysical, to demonstrate to him that he had failed to give a meaning to certain signs in his propositions. . . . [T]his method would be the only strictly correct one.

Ayer, together with Moritz Schlick and the rest of the Vienna Circle, sought to develop this "correct" philosophy. The members of the circle called themselves "positivists" because they wanted to eliminate all metaphysical pseudo-propositions and to show that only logic, mathematics, and the natural sciences provide genuine knowledge. They were "logical" positivists because they claimed that the logical analysis of supposed metaphysical assertions will not show them to be *false* but rather *meaningless.*

To determine which propositions were meaningful and which were not, logical positivists such as Ayer developed a verification criterion of meaning. In our

---

*Spectator, 16 July 1988, as quoted in A.J. Ayer, *The Philosophy of A.J. Ayer,* edited by Lewis E. Hahn (LaSalle, IL: Open Court, 1992), p. 48.

selection from *Language, Truth, and Logic,* Ayer gives this version of the criterion for synthetic propositions:

> We say that a sentence is factually significant to any given person, if, and only if, he knows how to verify the proposition which it purports to express—that is, if he knows what observations would lead him, under certain conditions, to accept the proposition as being true, or reject it as being false.

Ayer immediately makes three qualifications to this principle. In the first place, he points out that he is only talking about "verifiability in principle." It might not be practically possible for me at this time, for example, to verify or falsify the existence of Tasmanian Devils on the island of Tasmania, but there is nothing in *principle* to keep me from doing so. Second, he distinguishes between "strong" and "weak" verification. A proposition is verifiable in the strong sense "if, and only if, its truth could be conclusively established in experience." But this "strong" verification would eliminate all general propositions such as "a body tends to expand when it is heated" since such truths cannot be "conclusively" established by a finite number of observations. Instead, Ayer opted for a weaker sense of verification: "Would any observations be relevant to the determination of its truth or falsehood?" Finally, Ayer made it clear that his criterion applies only to *synthetic* propositions. The propositions of philosophy, including the verification criterion itself, are "held to be linguistically necessary, and so analytic."

This last qualification points to a problem that was to vex the logical positivists: How does one verify the verification criterion? What observations would lead one to accept the proposition previously given ("We say that a sentence is factually significant . . .") as true, or reject it as false? In the *Tractatus,* Wittgenstein had noticed this problem with self-reference and concluded that the propositions that made up the *Tractatus* itself were "nonsense"—but that one could still use them to "see the world aright." Ayer sought to avoid the problem by claiming that the verification criterion was analytic, a mere tautology, and so not subject to the criterion. But if the criterion is only a tautology, it would tell us nothing about the world. How could it then function as a test of meaning and what prevents it from being completely arbitrary?

In his later writings Ayer tried different ways of grounding the verification criterion, as did other positivists, but none of these attempts has satisfied contemporary philosophers. Partially as a result of the problems involved in developing a credible verification criterion, logical positivism no longer exists as a movement. But the spirit of hard-nosed positivistic empiricism is still with us.

* * *

For works on logical positivism, see R.W. Ashby, "Logical Positivism," in D.J. O'Connor, ed., *A Critical History of Western Philosophy* (New York: The Free Press, 1964); Peter Achinstein and Stephen F. Barker, *The Legacy of Logical Positivism* (Baltimore: The Johns Hopkins University Press, 1969); Barry R. Gross, *Analytic Philosophy: An Historical Introduction* (New York: Pegasus, 1970); Frederick C. Copleston, *Contemporary Philosophy: Studies of Logical Positivism and Existentialism* (New York: Barnes & Noble, 1979); and Oswald Hanfling, *Logical Positivism* (New York: Columbia University Press, 1981). For a collection of primary source readings, see Oswald Hanfling, ed., *Essential Readings in Logical Positivism* (Oxford: Blackwell, 1981).

A good text for specific aspects of Ayer's thought is A.J. Ayer, *The Philosophy of A.J. Ayer,* edited by Lewis E. Hahn (La Salle, IL: Open Court, 1992), another volume in the outstanding Library of Living Philosophers Series. John Foster, *Ayer* (London: Routledge, 1985), gives a detailed discussion of Ayer's ideas, while Graham Macdonald and Crispin Wright, eds., *Fact, Science, and Morality: Essays on A.J. Ayer's "Language, Truth, and Logic"* (New York: Blackwell, 1987), and Barry Gower, ed., *Logical Positivism in Perspective: Essays on "Language, Truth and Logic"* (London: Croom Helm, 1987), gather essays on Ayer's most important work. A general collection of essays is A. Phillips Griffiths, ed., *A.J. Ayer Memorial Essays* (Cambridge: Cambridge University Press, 1991).

LANGUAGE, TRUTH AND LOGIC
(in part)

PREFACE TO FIRST EDITION

The views which are put forward in this treatise derive from the doctrines of Bertrand Russell and Wittgenstein, which are themselves the logical outcome of the empiricism of Berkeley and David Hume. Like Hume, I divide all genuine propositions into two classes: those which, in his terminology, concern "relations of ideas," and those which concern "matters of fact." The former class comprises the *a priori* propositions of logic and pure mathematics, and these I allow to be necessary and certain only because they are analytic. That is, I maintain that the reason why these propositions cannot be confuted in experience is that they do not make any assertion about the empirical world, but simply record our determination to use symbols in a certain fashion. Propositions concerning empirical matters of fact, on the other hand, I hold to be hypotheses, which can be probable but never certain. And in giving an account of the method of their validation I claim also to have explained the nature of truth.

To test whether a sentence expresses a genuine empirical hypothesis, I adopt what may be called a modified verification principle. For I require of an empirical hypothesis, not indeed that it should be conclusively verifiable, but that some possible sense-experience should be relevant to the determination of its truth or falsehood. If a putative proposition fails to satisfy this principle, and is not a tautology, then I hold that it is metaphysical, and that, being metaphysical, it is neither true nor false but literally senseless. It will be found that much of what ordinarily passes for philosophy is metaphysical according to this criterion, and, in particular, that it can not be significantly asserted that there is a non-empirical world of values, or that men have immortal souls, or that there is a transcendent God.

A.J. Ayer, *Language, Truth and Logic.* New York: Dover Publications, 1936. Reprinted by permission.

As for the propositions of philosophy themselves, they are held to be linguistically necessary, and so analytic. And with regard to the relationship of philosophy and empirical science, it is shown that the philosopher is not in a position to furnish speculative truths, which would, as it were, compete with the hypotheses of science, nor yet to pass *a priori* judgements upon the validity of scientific theories, but that his function is to clarify the propositions of science by exhibiting their logical relationships, and by defining the symbols which occur in them. Consequently I maintain that there is nothing in the nature of philosophy to warrant the existence of conflicting philosophical "schools." And I attempt to substantiate this by providing a definitive solution of the problems which have been the chief sources of controversy between philosophers in the past.

The view that philosophizing is an activity of analysis is associated in England with the work of G.E. Moore and his disciples. But while I have learned a great deal from Professor Moore, I have reason to believe that he and his followers are not prepared to adopt such a thoroughgoing phenomenalism as I do, and that they take a rather different view of the nature of philosophical analysis. The philosophers with whom I am in the closest agreement are those who compose the "Viennese circle," under the leadership of Moritz Schlick, and are commonly known as logical positivists. And of these I owe most to Rudolf Carnap. Further, I wish to acknowledge my indebtedness to Gilbert Ryle, my original tutor in philosophy, and to Isaiah Berlin, who have discussed with me every point in the argument of this treatise, and made many valuable suggestions, although they both disagree with much of what I assert. . . .

CHAPTER 1: THE ELIMINATION OF METAPHYSICS

The traditional disputes of philosophers are, for the most part, as unwarranted as they are unfruitful. The surest way to end them is to establish beyond question what should be the purpose and method of a philosophical enquiry. And this is by no means so difficult a task as the history of philosophy would lead one to suppose. For if there are any questions which science leaves it to philosophy to answer, a straightforward process of elimination must lead to their discovery.

We may begin by criticising the metaphysical thesis that philosophy affords us knowledge of a reality transcending the world of science and common sense. Later on, when we come to define metaphysics and account for its existence, we shall find that it is possible to be a metaphysician without believing in a transcendent reality; for we shall see that many metaphysical utterances are due to the commission of logical errors, rather than to a conscious desire on the part of their authors to go beyond the limits of experience. But it is convenient for us to take the case of those who believe that it is possible to have knowledge of a transcendent reality as a starting-point for our discussion. The arguments which we use to refute them will subsequently be found to apply to the whole of metaphysics.

One way of attacking a metaphysician who claimed to have knowledge of a reality which transcended the phenomenal world would be to enquire from what premises his propositions were deduced. Must he not begin, as other men do, with the evidence of his senses? And if so, what valid process of reasoning can possibly lead him to the conception of a transcendent reality? Surely from empirical premises nothing whatsoever concerning the properties, or even the existence, of anything super-empirical can legitimately be inferred. But this objection would be met by a denial on the part of the metaphysician that his assertions were ultimately based on the evidence of his senses. He would say that he was endowed with a faculty of intellectual intuition which enabled him to know facts that could not be known through sense-experience. And even if it could be shown that he was relying on empirical premises, and that his venture into a non-empirical world was therefore logically unjustified, it would not follow that the assertions which he made concerning this non-empirical world could not be true. For the fact that a conclusion does not follow from its putative premise is not sufficient to show that it is false. Consequently one cannot overthrow a system of transcendent metaphysics merely by criticising the way in which it comes into being. What is required is rather a criticism of the nature of the actual statements which comprise it. And this is the line of argument which we shall, in fact, pursue. For we shall maintain that no statement which refers to a "reality" transcending the limits of all possible sense-experience can possibly have any literal significance; from which it must follow that the labours of those who have striven to describe such a reality have all been devoted to the production of nonsense.

It may be suggested that this is a proposition which has already been proved by Kant. But although Kant also condemned transcendent metaphysics, he did so on different grounds. For he said that the human understanding was so constituted that it lost itself in contradictions when it ventured out beyond the limits of possible experience and attempted to deal with things in themselves. And thus he made the impossibility of a transcendent metaphysic not, as we do, a matter of logic, but a matter of fact. He asserted, not that our minds could not conceivably have had the power of penetrating beyond the phenomenal world, but merely that they were in fact devoid of it. And this leads the critic to ask how, if it is possible to know only what lies within the bounds of sense-experience, the author can be justified in asserting that real things do exist beyond, and how he can tell what are the boundaries beyond which the human understanding may not venture, unless he succeeds in passing them himself. As Wittgenstein says, "in order to draw a limit to thinking, we should have to think both sides of this limit,"* a truth to which Bradley gives a special twist in maintaining that the man who is ready to prove that metaphysics is impossible is a brother metaphysician with a rival theory of his own.**

Whatever force these objections may have against the Kantian doctrine, they have none whatsoever against the thesis that I am about to set forth. It cannot here be said that the author is himself overstepping the barrier he maintains to be impassable. For the fruitlessness of attempting to transcend the limits of possible sense-experience will be deduced, not from a psychological hypothesis concerning the actual constitution of the human mind, but from the rule which determines the literal significance of language. Our charge against the metaphysician is not that he attempts to employ the understanding in a field where it cannot profitably venture, but that he produces sentences which fail to conform to the conditions under which alone a sentence can be literally significant. Nor are we ourselves obliged to talk nonsense in order to show that all sentences of a certain type are necessarily devoid of literal significance. We need only formulate the criterion which enables us to test whether a sentence expresses a genuine proposition about a matter of fact, and then point out that the sentences under consideration fail to satisfy it. And this we shall now proceed to do. We shall first of all

---

*Tractatus Logico-Philosophicus, Preface.
**Bradley, Appearance and Reality, 2nd ed., p. 1.

formulate the criterion in somewhat vague terms, and then give the explanations which are necessary to render it precise.

The criterion which we use to test the genuineness of apparent statements of fact is the criterion of verifiability. We say that a sentence is factually significant to any given person, if, and only if, he knows how to verify the proposition which it purports to express—that is, if he knows what observations would lead him, under certain conditions, to accept the proposition as being true, or reject it as being false. If, on the other hand, the putative proposition is of such a character that the assumption of its truth, or falsehood, is consistent with any assumption whatsoever concerning the nature of his future experience, then, as far as he is concerned, it is, if not a tautology, a mere pseudo-proposition. The sentence expressing it may be emotionally significant to him; but it is not literally significant. And with regard to questions the procedure is the same. We enquire in every case what observations would lead us to answer the question, one way or the other; and, if none can be discovered, we must conclude that the sentence under consideration does not, as far as we are concerned, express a genuine question, however strongly its grammatical appearance may suggest that it does.

As the adoption of this procedure is an essential factor in the argument of this book, it needs to be examined in detail.

In the first place, it is necessary to draw a distinction between practical verifiability, and verifiability in principle. Plainly we all understand, in many cases believe, propositions which we have not in fact taken steps to verify. Many of these are propositions which we could verify if we took enough trouble. But there remain a number of significant propositions, concerning matters of fact, which we could not verify even if we chose; simply because we lack the practical means of placing ourselves in the situation where the relevant observations could be made. A simple and familiar example of such a proposition is the proposition that there are mountains on the farther side of the moon. No rocket has yet been invented which would enable me to go and look at the farther side of the moon, so that I am unable to decide the matter by actual observation. But I do know what observations would decide it for me, if, as is theoretically conceivable, I were once in a position to make them. And therefore I say that the proposition is verifiable in principle, if not in practice, and is accordingly significant. On the other hand, such a metaphysical pseudo-proposition as "the Absolute enters into, but is itself incapable of, evolution and progress," is not even in principle verifiable. For one cannot conceive of an observation which would enable one to determine whether the Absolute did, or did not, enter into evolution and progress. Of course it is possible that the author of such a remark is using English words in a way in which they are not commonly used by English-speaking people, and that he does, in fact, intend to assert something which could be empirically verified. But until he makes us understand how the proposition that he wishes to express would be verified, he fails to communicate anything to us. And if he admits, as I think the author of the remark in question would have admitted, that his words were not intended to express either a tautology or a proposition which was capable, at least in principle, of being verified, then it follows that he has made an utterance which has no literal significance even for himself.

A further distinction which we must make is the distinction between the "strong" and the "weak" sense of the term "verifiable." A proposition is said to be verifiable, in the strong sense of the term, if, and only if, its truth could be conclusively established in experience. But it is verifiable, in the weak sense, if it is possible for experience to render it probable. In which sense are we using the term when we say that a putative proposition is genuine only if it is verifiable?

It seems to me that if we adopt conclusive verifiability as our criterion of significance, as some positivists have proposed, our argument will prove too much. Consider, for example, the case of general propositions of law—such propositions, namely, as "arsenic is poisonous"; "all men are mortal"; "a body tends to expand when it is heated." It is of the very nature of these propositions that their truth cannot be established with certainty by any finite series of observations. But if it is recognised that such general propositions of law are designed to cover an infinite number of cases, then it must be admitted that they cannot, even in principle, be verified conclusively. And then, if we adopt conclusive verifiability as our criterion of significance, we are logically obliged to treat these general propositions of law in the same fashion as we treat the statements of the metaphysician.

In face of this difficulty, some positivists have adopted the heroic course of saying that these general propositions are indeed pieces of nonsense, albeit an essentially important type of nonsense. But here the introduction of the term "important" is simply an attempt to hedge. It serves only to mark the authors' recognition that their view is somewhat too paradoxical, without in any way removing the paradox. Besides, the difficulty is not confined to the case of general propositions of law, though it is there revealed most plainly. It is hardly less obvious in the case of propositions about the remote past. For it must surely be admitted that, however strong the evidence in favour of historical statements may be, their truth can never become more than highly probable. And to maintain that they also constituted an important, or unimportant, type of nonsense would be unplausible, to say the very least. Indeed, it will be our contention that no proposition, other than a tautology, can possibly be anything more than a probable hypothesis. And if this is correct, the principle that a sentence can be factually significant only if it expresses what is conclusively verifiable is self-stultifying as a criterion of significance. For it leads to the conclusion that it is impossible to make a significant statement of fact at all.

Nor can we accept the suggestion that a sentence should be allowed to be factually significant if, and only if, it expresses something which is definitely confutable by experience. Those who adopt this course assume that, although no finite series of observations is ever sufficient to establish the truth of a hypothesis beyond all possibility of doubt, there are crucial cases in which a single observation, or series of observations, can definitely confute it. But, as we shall show later on, this assumption is false. A hypothesis cannot be conclusively confuted any more than it can be conclusively verified. For when we take the occurrence of certain observations as proof that a given hypothesis is false, we presuppose the existence of certain conditions. And though, in any given case, it may be extremely improbable that this assumption is false, it is not logically impossible. We shall see that there need be no self-contradiction in holding that some of the relevant circumstances are other than we have taken them to be, and consequently that the hypothesis has not really broken down. And if it is not the case that any hypothesis can be definitely confuted, we cannot hold that the genuineness of a proposition depends on the possibility of its definite confutation.

Accordingly, we fall back on the weaker sense of verification. We say that the question that must be asked about any putative statement of fact is not, Would any observations make its truth or falsehood logically certain? but simply, Would any observations be relevant to the determination of its truth or falsehood? And it is only if a negative answer is given to this second question that we conclude that the statement under consideration is nonsensical.

To make our position clearer, we may formulate it in another way. Let us call a proposition which records an actual or possible observation an experiential proposition. Then we may say that it is the mark of a genuine factual proposition, not that it should be equivalent to an experiential proposition, or any finite number of experiential propositions, but simply that some experiential propositions can be deduced from it in conjunction with certain other premises without being deducible from those other premises alone.

This criterion seems liberal enough. In contrast to the principle of conclusive verifiability, it clearly does not deny significance to general propositions or to propositions about the past. Let us see what kinds of assertion it rules out.

A good example of the kind of utterance that is condemned by our criterion as being not even false but nonsensical would be the assertion that the world of sense-experience was altogether unreal. It must, of course, be admitted that our senses do sometimes deceive us. We may, as the result of having certain sensations, expect certain other sensations to be obtainable which are, in fact, not obtainable. But, in all such cases, it is further sense-experience that informs us of the mistakes that arise out of sense-experience. We say that the senses sometimes deceive us, just because the expectations to which our sense-experiences give rise do not always accord with what we subsequently experience. That is, we rely on our senses to substantiate or confute the judgements which are based on our sensations. And therefore the fact that our perceptual judgements are sometimes found to be erroneous has not the slightest tendency to show that the world of sense-experience is unreal. And, indeed, it is plain that no conceivable observation, or series of observations, could have any tendency to show that the world revealed to us by sense-experience was unreal. Consequently, anyone who condemns the sensible world as a world of mere appearance, as opposed to reality, is saying something which, according to our criterion of significance, is literally nonsensical.

An example of a controversy which the application of our criterion obliges us to condemn as fictitious is provided by those who dispute concerning the number of substances that there are in the world. For it is admitted both by monists, who maintain that reality is one substance, and by pluralists, who maintain that reality is many, that it is impossible to imagine any empirical situation which would be relevant to the solution of their dispute. But if we are told that no possible observation could give any probability either to the assertion that reality was one substance or to the assertion that it was many, then we must conclude that neither assertion is significant. We shall see later on that there are genuine logical and empirical questions involved in the dispute between monists and pluralists. But the metaphysical question concerning "substance" is ruled out by our criterion as spurious.

A similar treatment must be accorded to the controversy between realists and idealists, in its metaphysical aspect. A simple illustration, which I have made use of in a similar argument elsewhere, will help to demonstrate this. Let us suppose that a picture is discovered and the suggestion made that it was painted by Goya. There is a definite procedure for dealing with such a question. The experts examine the picture to see in what way it resembles the accredited works of Goya, and to see if it bears any marks which are characteristic of a forgery; they look up contemporary records for evidence of the existence of such a picture, and so on. In the end, they may still disagree, but each one knows what empirical evidence would go to confirm or discredit his opinion. Suppose, now, that these men have studied philosophy, and some of them proceed to maintain that this picture is a set of ideas in the perceiver's mind, or in God's mind, others that it is objectively real. What possible experience could any of them have which would be relevant to the solution of this dispute one way or the other? In the ordinary sense of the term "real," in which it is opposed to "illusory," the reality of the picture is not in doubt. The disputants have satisfied themselves that the picture is real, in this sense, by obtaining a correlated series of sensations of sight and sensations of touch. Is there any similar process by which they could discover whether the picture was real, in the sense in which the term "real" is opposed to "ideal"? Clearly there is none. But, if that is so, the problem is fictitious according to our criterion. This does not mean that the realist-idealist controversy may be dismissed without further ado. For it can legitimately be regarded as a dispute concerning the analysis of existential propositions, and so as involving a logical problem which, as we shall see, can be definitively solved. What we have just shown is that the question at issue between idealists and realists becomes fictitious when, as is often the case, it is given a metaphysical interpretation.

There is no need for us to give further examples of the operation of our criterion of significance. For our object is merely to show that philosophy, as a genuine branch of knowledge, must be distinguished from metaphysics. We are not now concerned with the historical question how much of what has traditionally passed for philosophy is actually metaphysical. We shall, however, point out later on that the majority of the "great philosophers" of the past were not essentially metaphysicians, and thus reassure those who would otherwise be prevented from adopting our criterion by considerations of piety.

As to the validity of the verification principle . . . it will be shown that all propositions which have factual content are empirical hypotheses; and that the function of an empirical hypothesis is to provide a rule for the anticipation of experience. And this means that every empirical hypothesis must be relevant to some actual, or possible, experience, so that a statement which is not relevant to any experience is not an empirical hypothesis, and accordingly has no factual content. But this is precisely what the principle of verifiability asserts.

It should be mentioned here that the fact that the utterances of the metaphysician are nonsensical does not follow simply from the fact that they are devoid of factual content. It follows from that fact, together with the fact that they are not *a priori* propositions. . . . *a priori* propositions, which have always been attractive to philosophers on account of their certainty, owe this certainty to the fact that they are tautologies. We may accordingly define a metaphysical sentence as a sentence which purports to express a genuine proposition, but does, in fact, express neither a tautology nor an empirical hypothesis. And as tautologies and empirical hypotheses form the entire class of significant propositions, we are justified in concluding that all metaphysical assertions are nonsensical. Our next task is to show how they come to be made.

The use of the term "substance," to which we have already referred, provides us with a good example of the way in which metaphysics mostly comes to be written. It happens to be the case that we cannot, in our language, refer to the sensible properties of a thing without introducing a word or phrase which appears to stand for the thing itself as opposed to anything which may be said about it. And, as a result of this, those who are infected by the primitive superstition that to every name a single real entity must correspond assume that it is necessary to distinguish logically between the thing itself and any, or all, of its sensible properties. And so they employ the term "substance" to refer to the thing itself. But from the fact that we happen to employ a single word to refer to a thing, and make that word the grammatical subject of the sentences in which we refer to the sensible appearances of the thing, it does not by any means follow that the thing itself is a "simple entity," or that it cannot be defined in terms of the totality of its appearances. It is true that in talking of "its" appearances we appear to distinguish the thing from the appearances, but that is simply an accident of linguistic usage. Logical analysis shows that what makes these "appearances" the "appearances of" the same thing is not their relationship to an entity other than themselves, but their relationship to one another. The metaphysician fails to see this because he is misled by a superficial grammatical feature of his language.

A simpler and clearer instance of the way in which a consideration of grammar leads to metaphysics is the case of the metaphysical concept of Being. The origin of our temptation to raise questions about Being, which no conceivable experience would enable us to answer, lies in the fact that, in our language, sentences which express existential propositions and sentences which express attributive propositions may be of the same grammatical form. For instance, the sentences "Martyrs exist" and "Martyrs suffer" both consist of a noun followed by an intransitive verb, and the fact that they have grammatically the same appearance leads one to assume that they are of the same logical type. It is seen that in the proposition "Martyrs suffer," the members of a certain species are credited with a certain attribute, and it is sometimes assumed that the same thing is true of such a proposition as "Martyrs exist." If this were actually the case, it would, indeed, be as legitimate to speculate about the Being of martyrs as it is to speculate about their suffering. But, as Kant pointed out, existence is not an attribute. For, when we ascribe an attribute to a thing, we covertly assert that it exists: so that if existence were itself an attribute, it would follow that all positive existential propositions were tautologies, and all negative existential propositions self-contradictory; and this is not the case. So that those who raise questions about Being which are based on the assumption that existence is an attribute are guilty of following grammar beyond the boundaries of sense.

A similar mistake has been made in connection with such propositions as "Unicorns are fictitious." Here again the fact that there is a superficial grammatical resemblance between the English sentences "Dogs are faithful" and "Unicorns are fictitious," and between the corresponding sentences in other languages, creates the assumption that they are of the same logical type. Dogs must exist in order to have the property of being faithful, and so it is held that unless unicorns in some way existed they could not have the property of being fictitious. But, as it is plainly self-contradictory to say that fictitious objects exist, the device is adopted of saying that they are real in some non-empirical sense—that they have a mode of real being which is different from the mode of being of existent things. But since there is no way of testing whether an object is real in this sense, as there is for testing whether it is real in the ordinary sense, the assertion that fictitious objects have a special non-empirical mode of real being is devoid of all literal significance. It comes to be made as a result of the assumption that being fictitious is an attribute. And this is a fallacy of the same order as the fallacy of supposing that existence is an attribute, and it can be exposed in the same way.

In general, the postulation of real non-existent entities results from the superstition, just now referred to, that, to every word or phrase that can be the grammatical subject of a sentence, there must somewhere be a real entity corresponding. For as there is no place in the empirical world for many of these "entities," a special non-empirical world is invoked to house them. To this error must be attributed, not only the utterances of a Heidegger, who bases his metaphysics on the assumption that "Nothing" is a name which is used to denote something peculiarly mysterious, but also the prevalence of such problems as those concerning the reality of propositions and universals whose senselessness, though less obvious, is no less complete.

These few examples afford a sufficient indication of the way in which most metaphysical assertions come to be formulated. They show how easy it is to write sentences which are literally nonsensical without seeing that they are nonsensical. And thus we see that the view that a number of the traditional "problems of philosophy" are metaphysical, and consequently fictitious, does not involve any incredible assumptions about the psychology of philosophers.

Among those who recognise that if philosophy is to be accounted a genuine branch of knowledge it must be defined in such a way as to distinguish it from metaphysics, it is fashionable to speak of the metaphysician as a kind of misplaced poet. As his statements have no literal meaning, they are not subject to any criteria of truth or falsehood: but they may still serve to express, or arouse, emotion, and thus be subject to ethical or aesthetic standards. And it is suggested that they may have considerable value, as means of moral inspiration, or even as works of art. In this way, an attempt is made to compensate the metaphysician for his extrusion from philosophy.

I am afraid that this compensation is hardly in accordance with his deserts. The view that the metaphysician is to be reckoned among the poets appears to rest on the assumption that both talk nonsense. But this assumption is false. In the vast majority of cases the sentences which are produced by poets do have literal meaning. The difference between the man who uses language scientifically and the man who uses it emotively is not that the one produces sentences which are incapable of arousing emotion, and the other sentences which have no sense, but that the one is primarily concerned with the expression of true propositions, the other with the creation of a work of art. Thus, if a work of science contains true and important propositions, its value as a work of science will hardly be diminished by the fact that they are inelegantly expressed. And similarly, a work of art is not necessarily the worse for the fact that all the propositions comprising it are literally false. But to say that many literary works are largely composed of falsehoods is not to say that they are composed of pseudo-propositions. It is, in fact, very rare for a literary artist to produce sentences which have no literal meaning. And where this does occur, the sentences are carefully chosen for their rhythm and balance. If the author writes nonsense, it is because he considers it most suitable for bringing about the effects for which his writing is designed.

The metaphysician, on the other hand, does not intend to write nonsense. He lapses into it through being deceived by grammar, or through committing errors of reasoning, such as that which leads to the view that the sensible world is unreal. But it is not the mark of a poet simply to make mistakes of this sort. There are some, indeed, who would see in the fact that the metaphysician's utterances are senseless a reason against the view that they have aesthetic value. And, without going so far as this, we may safely say that it does not constitute a reason for it.

It is true, however, that although the greater part of metaphysics is merely the embodiment of humdrum errors, there remain a number of metaphysical passages which are the work of genuine mystical feeling; and they may more plausibly be held to have moral or aesthetic value. But, as far as we are concerned, the distinction between the kind of metaphysics that is produced by a philosopher who has been duped by grammar, and the kind that is produced by a mystic who is trying to express the inexpressible, is of no great importance: what is important to us is to realise that even the utterances of the metaphysician who is attempting to expound a vision are literally senseless; so that henceforth we may pursue our philosophical researches with as little regard for them as for the more inglorious kind of metaphysics which comes from a failure to understand the workings of our language.

JEAN-PAUL SARTRE
1905–1980

In addition to being one of the leading philosophers of the twentieth century, Jean-Paul Sartre was also an essayist, novelist, playwright, and editor. His name has become synonymous with existentialism, a movement that exploded beyond the boundaries of the academy to enter virtually every area of Western culture. Sartre himself became as famous as the philosophy he taught, and at his death in 1980 almost fifty thousand people accompanied his casket to Paris's Montparnasse Cemetery.

Jean-Paul-Charles-Aymard Sartre was born in Paris in 1905, the only child of naval officer Jean-Baptiste Sartre and his wife Anne-Marie Schweitzer Sartre. Barely a year after his birth, his father died. Jean-Paul and his mother moved in with her parents. Sartre's maternal grandfather, a German-language teacher, had a study filled with books; this room fascinated the young Sartre. He taught himself to read, and by the age of eight he had read such French classics as *Madame Bovary*. While still a boy, his devotion to books overwhelmed all other devotions—including that to religion. From about the age of twelve, Sartre said that he was a confirmed atheist. He did exceptionally well in his studies, exhibiting a clear independence of mind. One of his teachers noted on his report card: "Excellent student: mind already lively, good at discussing questions, but needs to depend a little less on himself."

In 1924, Sartre enrolled at the prestigious École Normale Supérieure. Over the next four years, he studied for the *agrégation* in philosophy (the highest degree except for the doctorate in the French system), but surprisingly he failed the written examination on his first attempt. He retook the examination a year later and placed first.

Guernica, 1937, by Pablo Picasso (1881–1973). In 1937 the city of Guernica was destroyed by German bombers simply for the purpose of testing their new weapons. Sartre's friend Picasso created this painting to memorialize the innocent sacrifice of the Spanish people. This representation of broken, fragmented pieces of humanity wrung by pain and anxiety capture well the reality of death and violence. Sartre insisted that to live fully one must squarely face such suffering. *(Museo del Prador, Madrid)*

The person who took second in that 1929 examination was his study partner, Simone de Beauvoir. That same year, Sartre suggested to her that they take "a two-year lease" on each other. Though neither believed in the bourgeois institution of marriage, and each had a variety of lovers, the two remained "companions" for life.

Over the next ten years, Sartre served briefly in the army, studied in Berlin, taught at a number of lycées, and began writing. Among his early publications were the philosophical novel *Nausea* (1938) and the collection of short stories *The Wall* (1939).

In 1939, Sartre was called up for active duty by the French army. Within the year, he was captured by the Germans. Released a few months later, he seemed to return to a quiet life of teaching and writing. But Sartre was secretly a member of the French resistance. He was never involved in the armed resistance but worked with the intellectual resistance group Socialism and Liberty. Even during the war, Sartre continued his writing, and in 1943 he published his most important philosophical text, *Being and Nothingness.* Three years later, *Existentialism Is a Humanism,* his most widely read philosophical work, was published.

After the war, Sartre retired from teaching and, with Maurice Merleau-Ponty and de Beauvoir, founded the influential journal *Les Temps modernes.* He was awarded the Nobel Prize for literature in 1964 but refused to accept it. Together with de Beauvoir, he spent the rest of his life writing and promoting revolutionary political causes. Frequently joining students or union workers in demonstrations, Sartre even served as president of the International War Crimes Tribunal, which condemned U.S. intervention in Vietnam. He was attracted to Marxist thought—though he frequently criticized the French Communist Party for its inadequacies. The discrepancies between the determinism of Marxist theory and

Sartre's existentialist emphasis on radical freedom have been the subject of many books. (See the suggested readings.)

Throughout his life, Sartre preferred the pleasures of the café over the joys of the hearth. For years he and de Beauvoir were fixtures at La Coupole, a restaurant on the Left Bank of Paris frequented by artists. But eventually his health deteriorated, exacerbated by his frequent use of amphetamines, and he was forced to retire to his apartment. After an agonizingly slow decline, Sartre died in 1980.

* * *

Like Heidegger before him, Sartre was fascinated with "being." According to Sartre, there are two categories of being: "being-in-itself" (*être en-soi*) and "being-for-itself" (*être pour-soi*). *Being-in-itself* is complete in itself, "solid," fixed, and totally given: "Uncreated, without reason for being, without connection with any other being, being-in-itself is superfluous for all eternity." Like Parmenides' One, being-in-itself simply is. This is the being of rocks and trees. This being-in-itself has no sufficient reason for being, no purpose or meaning— it is "absurd."

Being-for-itself, on the other hand, is incomplete and fluid and without a determined structure. Being-for-itself is the being of human consciousness that at every moment is freely choosing its future. This consciousness arises by virtue of its power of negation, based on freedom: "[Consciousness] constitutes itself in its own flesh as the nihilation of a possibility which another human reality projects as its possibility. For that reason it must arise in the world as a Not." Individual consciousness constitutes itself by freely rejecting all roles that others try to force upon it. It is precisely in the act of saying "No" to all attempts to make me into a being-in-itself that I create myself as a being-for-itself.

In creating myself, I do not choose what I will become on the basis of preexisting values. There are no eternal values, no givens for me to use. Dostoevsky's character Ivan Karamazov had claimed, "If there is no God, all things are lawful." Sartre agreed and added that since there was no God, all things are, indeed, lawful. In fact, there is no possible justification for any choice I might make, since justification implies an appeal to given values. I am free to choose my values without any external justification.

Although this freedom is complete, it is not absolute. In the first place, as a free being, I encounter other free beings. My world is interrupted when the "other" gives me "the look." By looking at me, the other objectifies me, makes me a part of his or her world, part of his or her freedom: "Thus being-seen constitutes me as a being without defenses for a freedom which is not my freedom." But I can regain my freedom by looking back and by an act of will transforming the other into an object for me. (This world of people-objects led Sartre to exclaim, "Hell is other people.")

Second, I must acknowledge the "facticity" found in existence. I cannot change the fact that this tree is in front of me or that I cannot walk through it. But even here my freedom still prevails. I freely create the *meaning* of this tree as an object to climb or as a source of lumber or as a thing to be preserved or as a biological specimen. In creating these meanings, I create the world in which I live.

Some people are unwilling to face up to this radical freedom and turn their power of negation inward upon consciousness itself. In our selection from *Being and Nothingness,* translated by Hazel E. Barnes, Sartre calls this negative turn "bad faith." To live in bad faith is to deny oneself as a being-for-itself in order to become a being-in-itself; it is to blame others or circumstances for what one has become. This mode of being is bad faith because it refuses to acknowledge that only the individual determines the meanings of externals. Furthermore, one always has alternatives (for example, no matter the circumstances, one could always commit suicide), and so one's choice is always free.

In *Existentialism Is a Humanism,* translated here by Bernard Frechtman, Sartre expands on this freedom while defending the basic ideas of existentialism. He begins by discussing human artifacts, such as a book or a paper-cutter. An object like a paper-cutter begins as an essence, that is, as an "ensemble of both the production routines and the properties which enable it to be both produced and defined." One conceives of a paper-cutter (essentially) and how to make it and only then does one construct it. The essence of a paper-cutter precedes its existence. According to Sartre, theists believe that God does the same with human beings. First God conceives of humans and then creates them. But Sartre says that there is no God, and hence no preexisting human essence: "There is no human nature, since there is no God to conceive it." Instead, "Man is nothing else but what he makes of himself." For humans, existence precedes essence.

When one realizes the implications of this atheism and the primacy of freedom, one is brought to anguish and forlornness. But Sartre strongly denied that this state necessarily led to despair. Even though all my actions are indeed ultimately futile because of my eventual death, and existence is in fact absurd, I can still choose my actions and so give my life meaning. As Sartre concluded, "In this sense existentialism is optimistic, a doctrine of action."

* * *

There are many studies of existentialism; see especially Gabriel Marcel, *The Philosophy of Existentialism,* translated by Manya Harari (New York: Citadel Press, 1956); Hazel E. Barnes, *An Existentialist Ethic* (Chicago: University of Chicago Press, 1967); and William Barrett's two books, *Irrational Man* (Garden City, NY: Doubleday, 1962) and *What Is Existentialism?* (New York: Grove Press, 1964). For primary source materials, see Walter Kaufmann, ed., *Existentialism from Dostoevsky to Sartre* (New York: Viking Press, 1956) and Charles Guignon and Derk Pereboom, *Existentialism: Basic Texts* (Indianapolis, IN: Hackett, 1994).

For biographies of Sartre, see Annie Cohen-Solal, *Sartre: A Life,* translated by Anna Cancogni (New York: Pantheon Books, 1987); John Gerassi, *Jean-Paul Sartre: Hated Conscience of His Century* (Chicago: University of Chicago Press, 1989); and Simone de Beauvoir's recounting of Sartre's final days, *Adieux: A Farewell to Sartre* (New York: Pantheon, 1984). For general introductions to Sartre's thought, see Mary Warnock, *The Philosophy of Sartre* (London: Hutchinson, 1965); Anthony Manser, *Sartre: A Philosophic Study* (London: Athlone Press, 1966); Arthur C. Danto, *Jean-Paul Sartre* (New York: Viking Press, 1975); and Peter Caws, *Sartre* (London: Routledge & Kegan Paul, 1979). Iris Murdoch, *Sartre: Romantic Rationalist* (New Haven, CT: Yale University Press, 1959) explores the philosophical ideas in Sartre's novels. There are several discussions of Sartre's Marxism, including W. Desan, *The Marxism of Jean-Paul Sartre* (Garden City, NY: Doubleday, 1965); Mark Poster, *Sartre's Marxism* (Cambridge: Cambridge University Press, 1982); and Thomas R. Flynn,

Sartre and Marxist Existentialism: The Test Case of Collective Responsibility (Chicago: University of Chicago Press, 1984). For collections of essays, see Edith Kern, ed., *Sartre: A Collection of Critical Essays* (Englewood Cliffs, NJ: Prentice Hall, 1962); Mary Warnock, ed., *Sartre* (Garden City, NY: Anchor Doubleday, 1971); Hugh J. Silverman and Frederick A. Elliston, eds., *Jean-Paul Sartre: Contemporary Approaches to His Philosophy* (Pittsburgh, PA: Duquesne University Press, 1980); Paul A. Schilpp, ed., *The Philosophy of Jean-Paul Sartre* (La Salle, IL: Open Court, 1981); Christina Howells, ed., *The Cambridge Companion to Sartre* (Cambridge: Cambridge University Press, 1992); and the multi-volume William L. McBride, *Sartre and Existentialism* (Hamden, CT: Garland, 1997).

BEING AND NOTHINGNESS (in part)

CHAPTER 2: BAD FAITH

I. BAD FAITH AND FALSEHOOD

The human being is not only the being by whom *négatités* are disclosed in the world; he is also the one who can take negative attitudes with respect to himself. In our Introduction we defined consciousness as "a being such that in its being, its being is in question in so far as this being implies a being other than itself." But now that we have examined the meaning of "the question," we can at present also write the formula thus: "Consciousness is a being, the nature of which is to be conscious of the nothingness of its being." In a prohibition or a veto, for example, the human being denies a future transcendence. But this negation is not explicative. My consciousness is not restricted to *envisioning a négatité.* It constitutes itself in its own flesh as the nihilation of a possibility which another human reality projects as its possibility. For that reason it must arise in the world as a Not; it is as a Not that the slave first apprehends the master, or that the prisoner who is trying to escape sees the guard who is watching him. There are even men (e.g., caretakers, overseers, gaolers) whose social reality is uniquely that of the Not, who will live and die, having forever been only a Not upon the earth. Others so as to make the Not a part of their very subjectivity establish their human personality as a perpetual negation. This is the meaning and function of what Scheler calls "the man of resentment"—in reality, the Not. But there exist more subtle behaviors, the description of which will lead us further into the inwardness of consciousness. Irony is one of these. In irony a man annihilates what he posits within one and the same act; he leads us to believe in order not to be believed; he affirms to deny and denies to affirm; he creates a positive object but it has no being other than its nothingness. Thus attitudes of negation toward the self permit us to raise a new question: What are we to say

Jean-Paul Sartre, *Being and Nothingness,* translated by Hazel E. Barnes (New York: Philosophical Library, 1956). Reprinted by permission.

is the being of man who has the possibility of denying himself? But it is out of the question to discuss the attitude of "self-negation" in its universality. The kinds of behavior which can be ranked under this heading are too diverse; we risk retaining only the abstract form of them. It is best to choose and to examine one determined attitude which is essential to human reality and which is such that consciousness instead of directing its negation outward turns it toward itself. This attitude, it seems to me, is *bad faith (mauvaise foi)*.

Frequently this is identified with falsehood. We say indifferently of a person that he shows signs of bad faith or that he lies to himself. We shall willingly grant that bad faith is a lie to oneself, on condition that we distinguish the lie to oneself from lying in general. Lying is a negative attitude we will agree to that. But this negation does not bear on consciousness itself, it aims only at the transcendent. The essence of the lie implies in fact that the liar actually is in complete possession of the truth which he is hiding. A man does not lie about what he is ignorant of; he does not lie when he spreads an error of which he himself is the dupe; he does not lie when he is mistaken. The ideal description of the liar would be a cynical consciousness, affirming truth within himself, denying it in his words, and denying that negation as such. Now this doubly negative attitude rests on the transcendent; the fact expressed is transcendent since it does not exist, and the original negation rests on a *truth;* that is, on a particular type of transcendence. As for the inner negation which I effect correlatively with the affirmation for myself of the truth, this rests on words, that is, on an event in the world. Furthermore the inner disposition of the liar is positive; it could be the object of an affirmative judgment. The liar intends to deceive and he does not seek to hide this intention from himself nor to disguise the translucency of consciousness; on the contrary, he has recourse to it when there is a question of deciding secondary behavior. It explicitly exercises a regulatory control over all attitudes. As for his flaunted intention of telling the truth ("I'd never want to deceive you! This is true! I swear it!")—all this, of course, is the object of an inner negation, but also it is not recognized by the liar as his intention. It is played, imitated, it is the intention of the character which he plays in the eyes of his questioner, but this character, precisely because he does not exist, is a transcendent. Thus the lie does not put into the play the inner structure of present consciousness; all the negations which constitute it bear on objects which by this fact are removed from consciousness. The lie then does not require special ontological foundation, and the explanations which the existence of negation in general requires are valid without change in the case of deceit. Of course we have described the ideal lie; doubtless it happens often enough that the liar is more or less the victim of his lie, that he half persuades himself of it. But these common, popular forms of the lie are also degenerate aspects of it; they represent intermediaries between falsehood and bad faith. The lie is a behavior of transcendence.

The lie is also a normal phenomenon of what Heidegger calls the *"Mit-sein"* ["being with" others]. It presupposes my existence, the existence of the *Other,* my existence *for* the Other, and the existence of the Other *for* me. Thus there is no difficulty in holding that the liar must make the project of the lie in entire clarity and that he must possess a complete comprehension of the lie and of the truth which he is altering. It is sufficient that an over-all opacity hide his intentions from the *Other;* it is sufficient that the Other can take the lie for truth. By the lie consciousness affirms that it exists by nature as *hidden from the Other;* it utilizes for its own profit the ontological duality of myself and myself in the eyes of the Other.

The situation can not be the same for bad faith if this, as we have said, is indeed a lie to oneself. To be sure, the one who practices bad faith is hiding a displeasing truth or presenting as truth a pleasing untruth. Bad faith then has in appearance the structure of falsehood. Only what changes everything is the fact that in bad faith it is from myself that I am hiding the truth. Thus the duality of the deceiver and the deceived does not exist here. Bad faith on the contrary implies in essence the unity of a *single* consciousness. This does not mean that it can not be conditioned by the *Mit-sein* like all other phenomena of human reality, but the *Mit-sein* can call forth bad faith only by presenting itself as a *situation* which bad faith permits surpassing; bad faith does not come from outside to human reality. One does not undergo his bad faith; one is not infected with it; it is not a state. But consciousness affects itself with bad faith. There must be an original intention and a project of bad faith; this project implies a comprehension of bad faith as such and a pre-reflective apprehension (of) consciousness as affecting itself with bad faith. It follows first that the one to whom the lie is told and the one who lies are one and the same person, which means that I must know in my capacity as deceiver the truth which is hidden from me in my capacity as the one deceived. Better yet I must know the truth very exactly *in order* to conceal it more carefully—and this not at two different moments, which at a pinch would allow us to reestablish a semblance of duality—but in the unitary structure of a single project. How then can the lie subsist if the duality which conditions it is suppressed?

To this difficulty is added another which is derived from the total translucency of consciousness. That which affects itself with bad faith must be conscious (of) its bad faith since the being of consciousness is consciousness of being. It appears then that I must be in good faith, at least to the extent that I am conscious of my bad faith. But then this whole psychic system is annihilated. We must agree in fact that if I deliberately and cynically attempt to lie to myself, I fail completely in this undertaking; the lie falls back and collapses beneath my look; it is ruined *from behind* by the very consciousness of lying to myself which pitilessly constitutes itself well within my project as its very condition. We have here an evanescent phenomenon which exists only in and through its own differentiation. To be sure, these phenomena are frequent and we shall see that there is in fact an "evanescence" of bad faith, which, it is evident, vacillates continually between good faith and cynicism: Even though the existence of bad faith is very precarious, and though it belongs to the kind of psychic structures which we might call "metastable," [Sartre's word for "subject to sudden changes"] it presents nonetheless an autonomous and durable form. It can even be the normal aspect of life for a very great number of people. A person can *live* in bad faith, which does not mean that he does not have abrupt awakenings to cynicism or to good faith, but which implies a constant and particular style of life. Our embarrassment then appears extreme since we can neither reject nor comprehend bad faith.

* * *

II. Patterns of Bad Faith

If we wish to get out of this difficulty, we should examine more closely the patterns of bad faith and attempt a description of them. This description will permit us perhaps to fix more exactly the conditions for the possibility of bad faith; that is, to reply to the question we raised at the outset: "What must be the being of man if he is to be capable of bad faith?"

Take the example of a woman who has consented to go out with a particular man for the first time. She knows very well the intentions which the man who is speaking to her cherishes regarding her. She knows also that it will be necessary sooner or later for her to make a decision. But she does not want to realize the urgency; she concerns herself only with what is respectful and discreet in the attitude of her companion. She does not apprehend this conduct as an attempt to achieve what we call "the first approach"; that is, she does not want to see possibilities of temporal development which his conduct presents. She restricts this behavior to what is in the present; she does not wish to read in the phrases which he addresses to her anything other than their explicit meaning. If he says to her, "I find you so attractive!" she disarms this phrase of its sexual background; she attaches to the conversation and to the behavior of the speaker, the immediate meanings, which she imagines as objective qualities. The man who is speaking to her appears to her sincere and respectful as the table is round or square, as the wall coloring is blue or gray. The qualities thus attached to the person she is listening to are in this way fixed in a permanence like that of things, which is no other than the projection of the strict present of the qualities into the temporal flux. This is because she does not quite know what she wants. She is profoundly aware of the desire which she inspires, but the desire cruel and naked would humiliate and horrify her. Yet she would find no charm in a respect which would be only respect. In order to satisfy her, there must be a feeling which is addressed wholly to her *personality*—i.e., to her full freedom—and which would be a recognition of her freedom. But at the same time this feeling must be wholly desire; that is, it must address itself to her body as object. This time then she refuses to apprehend the desire for what it is; she does not even give it a name; she recognizes it only to the extent that it transcends itself toward admiration, esteem, respect and that it is wholly absorbed in the more refined forms which it produces, to the extent of no longer figuring anymore as a sort of warmth and density. But then suppose he takes her hand. This act of her companion risks changing the situation by calling for an immediate decision. To leave the hand there is to consent in herself to flirt, to engage herself. To withdraw it is to break the troubled and unstable harmony which gives the hour its charm. The aim is to postpone the moment of decision as long as possible. We know what happens next; the young woman leaves her hand there, but she *does not notice* that she is leaving it. She does not notice because it happens by chance that she is at this moment all intellect. She draws her companion up to the most lofty regions of sentimental speculation; she speaks of Life, of her life, she shows herself in her essential aspect—a personality, a consciousness. And during this time the divorce of the body from the soul is accomplished; the hand rests inert between the warm hands of her companion—neither consenting nor resisting—a thing.

We shall say that this woman is in bad faith. But we see immediately that she uses various procedures in order to maintain herself in this bad faith. She has disarmed the actions of her companion by reducing them to being only what they are; that is, to existing in the mode of the in-itself. But she permits herself to enjoy his desire, to the extent that she will apprehend it as not being what it is, will recognize its transcendence. Finally, while sensing profoundly the presence of her own body—to the degree of being disturbed perhaps—she realizes herself as *not being* her own body, and she contemplates it as though from above as a passive object to which events can *happen* but which can neither provoke them nor avoid them because all its possibilities are outside of it. What unity do we find in these various aspects of bad faith? It is a certain art of forming contradictory concepts which unite in themselves both an idea and the negation of that idea. The basic concept which is thus engendered utilizes the double property of the human being, who is at once a *facticity* and a *transcendence.* These two aspects of human reality are and ought to be capable of a valid coordination. But bad faith does not wish either to coordinate them nor to surmount them in a synthesis. Bad faith seeks to affirm their identity while preserving their differences. It must affirm facticity as *being* transcendence and transcendence as *being* facticity, in such a way that at the instant when a person apprehends the one, he can find himself abruptly faced with the other.

We can find the prototype of formulae of bad faith in certain famous expressions which have been rightly conceived to produce their whole effect in a spirit of bad faith. Take for example the title of a work by Jacques Chardonne, *Love Is Much More than Love.** We see here how unity is established between present love in its facticity—"the contact of two skins," sensuality, egoism, Proust's mechanism of jealousy, Adler's battle of the sexes, *etc.*—and love as transcendence—Mauriac's "river of fire," the longing for the infinite, Plato's *eros,* Lawrence's deep cosmic intuition, etc. Here we leave facticity to find ourselves suddenly beyond the present and the factual condition of man, beyond the psychological, in the heart of metaphysics. On the other hand, the title of a play by Sarment, *I Am Too Great for Myself,*** which also presents characters in bad faith, throws us first into full transcendence in order suddenly to imprison us within the narrow limits of our factual essence. We will discover this structure again in the famous sentence: "He has become what he was" or in its no less famous opposite: "Eternity at last changes each man into himself." It is well understood that these various formulae have only the appearance of bad faith; they have been conceived in this paradoxical form explicitly to shock the mind and discountenance it by an enigma. But it is precisely this appearance which is of concern to us. What counts here is that the formulae do not constitute new, solidly structured ideas; on the contrary, they are formed so as to remain in perpetual disintegration and so that we may slide at any time from naturalistic present to transcendence and vice versa.

We can see the use which bad faith can make of these judgments which all aim at establishing that I am not what I am. If I were only what I am, I could, for example, seriously consider an adverse criticism which someone makes of me, question myself scrupulously, and perhaps be compelled to recognize the truth in it. But thanks to transcendence, I am not subject to all that I am. I do not even have to discuss the justice of the reproach. As Suzanne says to Figaro, "To prove that I am right would be to recognize that I can be wrong." I am on a plane where no reproach can touch me since what I really am is my transcendence. I flee from myself, I escape myself, I leave my tattered garment in the hands of the fault-finder. But the ambiguity necessary for bad faith comes from the fact that I affirm here that I am my transcendence in the mode of being of a thing. It is only thus, in fact, that I can feel that I escape all reproaches. It is in the sense that our young woman purifies the desire of anything humiliating by being willing to consider it only as pure transcendence, which she avoids even naming. But inversely "I Am Too Great for Myself," while showing our transcendence changed into facticity, is the source of an infinity of excuses for our failures or our weaknesses. Similarly the young coquette maintains transcendence to the extent that the respect, the esteem manifested by the actions of her admirer are already on the plane of the transcendent. But she arrests this transcendence, she glues it down with all the facticity of the present; respect is nothing other than respect, it is an arrested surpassing which no longer surpasses itself toward anything.

But although this *metastable* concept of "transcendence-facticity" is one of the most basic instruments of bad faith, it is not the only one of its kind. We can equally

---

L'amour, c'est beaucoup plus que l'amour.
**Je suis trop grand pour moi.*

well use another kind of duplicity derived from human reality which we will express roughly by saying that its being-for-itself implies complementarily a being-for-others. Upon any one of my conducts it is always possible to converge two looks, mine and that of the Other. The conduct will not present exactly the same structure in each case. But as we shall see later, as each look perceives it, there is between these two aspects of my being, no difference between appearance and being—as if I were to myself the truth of myself and as if the Other possessed only a deformed image of me. The equal dignity of being, possessed by my being-for-others and by my being-for-myself permits a perpetually disintegrating synthesis and a perpetual game of escape from the for-itself to the for-others and from the for-others to the for-itself. We have seen also the use which our young lady made of our being-in-the-midst-of-the-world—*i.e.,* of our inert presence as a passive object among other objects—in order to relieve herself suddenly from the functions of her being-in-the-world—that is, from the being which causes there to be a world by projecting itself beyond the world toward its own possibilities. Let us note finally the confusing syntheses which play on the nihilating ambiguity of these temporal ⟨*ekstases*⟩, affirming at once that I am what I have been (the man who deliberately arrests *himself* at one period in his life and refuses to take into consideration the later changes) and that I am not what I have been (the man who in the face of reproaches or rancor dissociates himself from his past by insisting on his freedom and on his perpetual re-creation). In all these concepts, which have only a transitive role in the reasoning and which are eliminated from the conclusion (like hypochondriacs in the calculations of physicians), we find again the same structure. We have to deal with human reality as a being which is what it is not and which is not what it is.

But what exactly is necessary in order for these concepts of disintegration to be able to receive even a pretence of existence, in order for them to be able to appear for an instant to consciousness, even in a process of evanescence? A quick examination of the idea of sincerity, the antithesis of bad faith, will be very instructive in this connection. Actually sincerity presents itself as a demand and consequently is not a state. Now what is the ideal to be attained in this case? It is necessary that a man be *for himself* only what he is. But is this not precisely the definition of the in-itself—or if you prefer—the principle of identity? To posit as an ideal the being of things, is this not to assert by the same stroke that this being does not belong to human reality and that the principle of identity, far from being a universal axiom universally applied, is only a synthetic principle enjoying a merely regional universality? Thus in order that the concepts of bad faith can put us under illusion at least for an instant, in order that the candor of "pure hearts" (cf. Gide, Kessel) can have validity for human reality as an ideal, the principle of identity must not represent a constitutive principle of human reality and human reality must not be necessarily what it is but must be able to be what it is not. What does this mean?

If man is what he is, bad faith is for ever impossible and candor ceases to be his ideal and becomes instead his being. But is man what he is? And more generally, how can he be what he is when he exists as consciousness of being? If candor or sincerity is a universal value, it is evident that the maxim "one must be what one is" does not serve solely as a regulating principle for judgments and concepts by which I express what I am. It posits not merely an ideal of knowing but an ideal of being; it proposes for us an absolute equivalence of being with itself as a prototype of being. In this sense it is necessary that we *make ourselves* what we are. But what are we then if we have the constant obligation to make ourselves what we are, if our mode of being is having the obligation to be what we are?

Let us consider this waiter in the café. His movement is quick and forward, a little too precise, a little too rapid. He comes toward the patrons with a step a little too quick. He bends forward a little too eagerly; his voice, his eyes express an interest a little too solicitous for the order of the customer. Finally there he returns, trying to imitate in his walk the inflexible stiffness of some kind of automaton while carrying his tray with the recklessness of a tight-rope-walker by putting it in a perpetually unstable, perpetually broken equilibrium which he perpetually reestablishes by a light movement of the arm and hand. All his behavior seems to us a game. He applies himself to chaining his movements as if they were mechanisms, the one regulating the other; his gestures and even his voice seem to be mechanisms; he gives himself the quickness and pitiless rapidity of things. He is playing, he is amusing himself. But what is he playing? We need not watch long before we can explain it: he is playing *at being* a waiter in a café. There is nothing there to surprise us. The game is a kind of marking out and investigation. The child plays with his body in order to explore it, to take inventory of it; the waiter in the café plays with his condition in order to *realize* it. This obligation is not different from that which is imposed on all tradesmen. Their condition is wholly one of ceremony. The public demands of them that they realize it as a ceremony; there is the dance of the grocer, of the tailor, of the auctioneer, by which they endeavour to persuade their clientele that they are nothing but a grocer, an auctioneer, a tailor. A grocer who dreams is offensive to the buyer, because such a grocer is not wholly a grocer. Society demands that he limit himself to his function as a grocer, just as the soldier at attention makes himself into a soldier-thing with a direct regard which does not see at all, which is no longer meant to see, since it is the rule and not the interest of the moment which determines the point he must fix his eyes on (the sight "fixed at ten paces"). There are indeed many precautions to imprison a man in what he is, as if we lived in perpetual fear that he might escape from it, that he might break away and suddenly elude his condition.

In a parallel situation, from within, the waiter in the café can not be immediately a café waiter in the sense that this inkwell *is* an inkwell, or the glass is a glass. It is by no means that he can not form reflective judgments or concepts concerning his condition. He knows well what it "means": the obligation of getting up at five o'clock, of sweeping the floor of the shop before the restaurant opens, of starting the coffee pot going, etc. He knows the rights which it allows: the right to the tips, the right to belong to a union, etc. But all these concepts, all these judgments refer to the transcendent. It is a matter of abstract possibilities, of rights and duties conferred on a "person possessing rights." And it is precisely this person *who I have to be* (if I am the waiter in question) and who I am not. It is not that I do not wish to be this person or that I want this person to be different. But rather there is no common measure between his being and mine. It is a "representation" for others and for myself, which means that I can be he only in *representation.* But if I represent myself as him, I am not he; I am separated from him as the object from the subject, separated by *nothing,* but this nothing isolates me from him. I can not be he, I can only play *at being* him; that is, imagine to myself that I am he. And thereby I affect him with nothingness. In vain do I fulfill the functions of a café waiter. I can be he only in the neutralized mode, as the actor is Hamlet, by mechanically making the *typical gestures* of my state and by aiming at myself as an imaginary café waiter through those gestures taken as an "analogue." What I attempt to realize is a being-in-itself of the café waiter, as if it were not just in my power to confer their value and their urgency upon my duties and the rights of my position, as if it were not my free choice to get up each morning at five o'clock or to remain in bed, even though it meant getting fired. As if from the very fact that I sustain this role in existence I did not transcend it on every side, as if I did not constitute myself as one *beyond* my condition. Yet there is no doubt that I am in a sense a café waiter—otherwise could I not just as well call myself a diplomat or a reporter? But if I am one, this can not be in the mode of being-in-itself. I am a waiter in the mode of *being what I am not*.

Furthermore we are dealing with more than mere social positions; I am never any one of my attitudes, any one of my actions. The good speaker is the one who plays at speaking, because he can not *be speaking*. The attentive pupil who wishes to be attentive, his eyes riveted on the teacher, his ears open wide, so exhausts himself in playing the attentive role that he ends up by no longer hearing anything. Perpetually absent to my body, to my acts, I am despite myself that "divine absence" of which Valéry speaks. I can not say either that I *am* here or that I *am* not here, in the sense that we say "that box of matches *is* on the table"; this would be to confuse my "being-in-the-world" with a "being-in-the-midst-of-the-world." Nor that I *am* standing, nor that I *am* seated; this would be to confuse my body with the idiosyncratic totality of which it is only one of the structures. On all sides I escape being and yet—I am.

But take a mode of being which concerns only myself: I am sad. One might think that surely I am the sadness in the mode of being what I am. What is the sadness, however, if not the intentional unity which comes to reassemble and animate the totality of my *conduct*? It is the meaning of this dull look with which I view the world, of my bowed shoulders, of my lowered head, of the listlessness in my whole body. But at the very moment when I adopt each of these attitudes, do I not know that I shall not be able to hold on to it? Let a stranger suddenly appear and I will lift up my head, I will assume a lively cheerfulness. What will remain of my sadness except that I obligingly promise it an appointment for later after the departure of the visitor? Moreover is not this sadness itself a conduct? Is it not consciousness which affects itself with sadness as a magical recourse against a situation too urgent? And in this case even, should we not say that being sad means first to make oneself sad? That may be, someone will say, but after all doesn't giving oneself the being of sadness mean to receive this being? It makes no difference from where I receive it. The fact is that a consciousness which affects itself with sadness is sad precisely for this reason. But it is difficult to comprehend the nature of consciousness; the being-sad is not a ready-made being which I give to myself as I can give this book to my friend. I do not possess the property of *affecting myself with being*. If I make myself sad, I must continue to make myself sad from beginning to end. I can not treat my sadness as an impulse finally achieved and put it on file without recreating it, nor can I carry it in the manner of an inert body which continues its movement after the initial shock. There is no inertia in consciousness. If I make myself sad, it is because I *am* not sad—the being of the sadness escapes me by and in the very act by which I affect myself with it. The being-in-itself of sadness perpetually haunts my consciousness (of) being sad, but it is as a value which I can not realize; it stands as a regulative meaning of my sadness, not as its constitutive modality.

Someone may say that my consciousness at least is, whatever may be the object or the state of which it makes itself consciousness. But how do we distinguish my consciousness (of) being sad from sadness? Is it not all one? It is true in a way that my consciousness is, if one means by this that for another it is a part of the totality of being on which judgments can be brought to bear. But it should be noted, as Husserl clearly understood, that my consciousness appears originally to the Other as an absence. It is the object always present as the *meaning* of all my attitudes and all my conduct—and always absent, for it gives itself to the intuition of another as a perpetual question—still better, as a perpetual freedom. When Pierre looks at me, I know of course that he is looking at me. His eyes, things in the world, are fixed on my body, a thing in the world—that is the objective fact of which I can say: it *is*. But it is also a fact *in the world*. The meaning of this look is not a fact in the world, and this is what makes me uncomfortable. Although I make smiles, promises, threats, nothing can get hold of the approbation, the free judgment which I seek; I know that it is always beyond. I sense it in my very attitude, which is no longer like that of the worker toward the things he uses as instruments. My reactions, to the extent that I project myself toward the Other, are no longer for myself but are rather mere *presentations;* they await being constituted as graceful or uncouth, sincere or insincere, etc., by an apprehension which is always beyond my efforts to provoke, an apprehension which will be provoked by my efforts only if of itself it lends them force (that is, only in so far as it causes itself to be provoked from the outside), *which is its own mediator with the transcendent.* Thus the objective fact of the being-in-itself of the consciousness of the Other is posited in order to disappear in negativity and in freedom: consciousness of the Other is as not-being; its being-in-itself "here and now" is not-to-be.

CONSCIOUSNESS OF THE *OTHER IS WHAT IT IS NOT.*

Furthermore the being of my own consciousness does not appear to me as the consciousness of the Other. It is because it makes itself, since its being is consciousness of being. But this means that making sustains being; consciousness has to be its own being, it is never sustained by being; it sustains being in the heart of subjectivity, which means once again that it is inhabited by being but that it is not being: *consciousness is not what it is.*

Under these conditions what can be the significance of the ideal of sincerity except as a task impossible to achieve, of which the very meaning is in contradiction with the structure of my consciousness. To be sincere, we said, is to be what one is. That supposes that I am not originally what I am. But here naturally Kant's "You ought, therefore you can" is implicitly understood. I can *become* sincere; this is what my duty and my effort to achieve sincerity imply. But we definitely establish that the original structure of "not being what one is" renders impossible in advance all movement toward being in itself or "being what one is." And this impossibility is not hidden from consciousness; on the contrary, it is the very stuff of consciousness; it is the embarrassing constraint which we constantly experience; it is our very incapacity to recognize ourselves, to constitute ourselves as being what we are. It is this necessity which means that, as soon as we posit ourselves as a certain being, by a legitimate judgment, based on inner experience or correctly deduced from *a priori* or empirical premises, then by that very positing we surpass this being—and that not toward another being but toward emptiness, toward nothing.

How then can we blame another for not being sincere or rejoice in our own sincerity since this sincerity appears to us at the same time to be impossible? How can we in conversation, in confession, in introspection, even attempt sincerity since the effort will by its very nature be doomed to failure and since at the very time when we announce it we have a prejudicative comprehension of its futility? In introspection I try to determine exactly what I am, to make up my mind to be my true self without delay—even though it means consequently to set about searching for ways to change myself. But what does this mean if not that I am constituting myself as a thing? Shall I determine the ensemble of purposes and motivations which have pushed me to do this or that action? But this is already to postulate a causal determinism which constitutes the flow of my states of consciousness as a succession of physical states. Shall I uncover in myself "drives," even though it be to affirm them in shame? But is this not deliberately to forget that these drives are realized with my consent, that they are not forces of nature but that I lend them their efficacy by a perpetually renewed decision concerning their value. Shall I pass judgment on my character, on my nature? Is this not to veil from myself at that moment what I know only too well, that I thus judge a past to which by definition my present is not subject? The proof of this is that the same man who in sincerity posits that he is what in actuality he was, is indignant at the reproach of another and tries to disarm it by asserting that he can no longer be what he was. We are readily astonished and upset when the penalties of the court affect a man who in his new freedom is no longer the guilty person he was. But at the same time we require of this man that he recognize himself as being this guilty one. What then is sincerity except precisely a phenomenon of bad faith? Have we not shown indeed that in bad faith human reality is constituted as a being which is what it is not and which is not what it is?

Let us take an example: A homosexual frequently has an intolerable feeling of guilt, and his whole existence is determined in relation to this feeling. One will readily foresee that he is in bad faith. In fact it frequently happens that this man, while recognizing his homosexual inclination, while avowing each and every particular misdeed which he has committed, refuses with all his strength to consider himself "*a paederast.*" His case is always "different," peculiar; there enters into it something of a game, of chance, of bad luck; the mistakes are all in the past; they are explained by a certain conception of the beautiful which women can not satisfy; we should see in them the results of a restless search, rather than the manifestations of a deeply rooted tendency, etc., etc. Here is assuredly a man in bad faith who borders on the comic since, acknowledging all the facts which are imputed to him, he refuses to draw from them the conclusion which they impose. His friend, who is his most severe critic, becomes irritated with this duplicity. The critic asks only one thing—and perhaps then he will show himself indulgent: that the guilty one recognize himself as guilty, that the homosexual declare frankly—whether humbly or boastfully matters little—"I am a paederast." We ask here: Who is in bad faith? The homosexual or the champion of sincerity?

The homosexual recognizes his faults, but he struggles with all his strength against the crushing view that his mistakes constitute for him a destiny. He does not wish to let himself be considered as a thing. He has an obscure but strong feeling that an homosexual is not an homosexual as this table is a table or as this red-haired man is red-haired. It seems to him that he has escaped from each mistake as soon as he has posited it and recognized it; he even feels that the psychic duration by itself cleanses him from each misdeed, constitutes for him an undetermined future, causes him to be born anew. Is he wrong? Does he not recognize in himself the peculiar, irreducible character of human reality? His attitude includes then an undeniable comprehension of truth. But at the same time he needs this perpetual rebirth, this constant escape in order to live; he must constantly put himself beyond reach in order to avoid the terrible judgment of collectivity. Thus he plays on the word *being*. He would be right actually if he understood the phrase, "I am not a paederast" in the sense of "I am not what I am." That is, if he declared to himself, "To the extent that a pattern of conduct is defined as the conduct of a paederast and to the extent that I have adopted this conduct, I am a paederast. But to the extent that human reality can not be finally defined by patterns of conduct, I am not one." But instead he slides surreptitiously towards a different connotation of the word "being." He understands "not being" in the sense of "not-being-in-itself." He lays claim to "not being a paederast" in the sense in which this table is not an inkwell. He is in bad faith.

But the champion of sincerity is not ignorant of the transcendence of human reality, and he knows how at need to appeal to it for his own advantage. He makes use of it even and brings it up in the present argument. Does he not wish, first in the name of sincerity, then of freedom, that the homosexual reflect on himself and acknowledge himself as an homosexual? Does he not let the other understand that such a confession will win indulgence for him? What does this mean if not that the man who will acknowledge himself as an homosexual will no longer be the same as the homosexual whom he acknowledges being and that he will escape into the region of freedom and of good will? The critic asks the man then to be what he is in order no longer to be what he is. It is the profound meaning of the saying, "A sin confessed is half pardoned." The critic demands of the guilty one that he constitute himself as a thing, precisely in order no longer to treat him as a thing. And this contradiction is constitutive of the demand of sincerity. Who can not see how offensive to the Other and how reassuring for me is a statement such as, "He's just a paederast," which removes a disturbing freedom from a trait and which aims at henceforth constituting all the acts of the Other as consequences following strictly from his essence. That is actually what the critic is demanding of his victim—that he constitute himself as a thing, that he should entrust his freedom to his friend as a fief, in order that the friend should return it to him subsequently—like a suzerain to his vassal. The champion of sincerity is in bad faith to the degree that in order to reassure himself, he pretends to judge, to the extent that he demands that freedom as freedom constitute itself as a thing. We have here only one episode in that battle to the death of consciousnesses which Hegel calls "the relation of the master and the slave." A person appeals to another and demands that in the name of his nature as consciousness he should radically destroy himself as consciousness, but while making this appeal he leads the other to hope for a rebirth beyond this destruction.

Very well, someone will say, but our man is abusing sincerity, playing one side against the other. We should not look for sincerity in the relation of the *Mit-sein* but rather where it is pure—in the relations of a person with himself. But who can not see that objective sincerity is constituted in the same way? Who can not see that the sincere man constitutes himself as a thing in order to escape the condition of a thing by the same act of sincerity? The man who confesses that he is evil has exchanged his disturbing "freedom-for-evil" for an inanimate character of evil; he *is* evil, he clings to himself, he is what he is. But by the same stroke, he escapes from that *thing,* since it is he who contemplates it, since it depends on him to maintain it under his glance or to let it collapse in an infinity of particular acts. He derives a *merit* from his sincerity, and the deserving man is not the evil man as he is evil but as he is beyond his evilness. At the same time the evil is disarmed since it is nothing, save on the plane of determinism, and since in confessing it, I posit my freedom in respect to it; my future is virgin; everything is allowed to me.

Thus the essential structure of sincerity does not differ from that of bad faith since the sincere man constitutes himself as what he is *in order not to be it.* This explains the truth recognized by all that one can fall into bad faith through being sincere. As Valéry pointed out, this is the case with Stendhal. Total, constant sincerity as a constant effort to adhere to oneself is by nature a constant effort to dissociate oneself from oneself. A person frees himself from himself by the very act by which he makes himself an object for himself. To draw up a perpetual inventory of what one is means constantly to re-deny oneself and to take refuge in a sphere where one is no longer anything but a pure, free regard. The goal of bad faith, as we said, is to put oneself out of reach; it is an escape. Now we see that we must use the same terms to define sincerity. What does this mean?

In the final analysis the goal of sincerity and the goal of bad faith are not so different. To be sure, there is a sincerity which bears on the past and which does not concern us here; I am sincere if I confess *having had* this pleasure or that intention. We shall see that if this sincerity is possible, it is because in his fall into the past, the being of man is constituted as a being-in-itself. But here our concern is only with the sincerity which aims at itself in present immanence. What is its goal? To bring me to confess to myself what I am in order that I may finally coincide with my being; in a word, to cause myself to be, in the mode of the in-itself, what I am in the mode of "not being what I am." Its assumption is that fundamentally I am already, in the mode of the in-itself, what I have to be. Thus we find at the base of sincerity a continual game of mirror and reflection, a perpetual passage from the being which is what it is, to the being which is not what it is and inversely from the being which is not what it is to the being which is what it is. And what is the goal of bad faith? To cause me to be what I am, in the mode of "not-being-what-one-is," or not to be what I am in the mode of "being-what-one-is." We find here the same game of mirrors. In fact in order for me to have an intention of sincerity, I must at the outset simultaneously be and not be what I am. Sincerity does not assign to me a mode of being or a particular quality, but in relation to that quality it aims at making me pass from one mode of being to another mode of being. This second mode of being, the ideal of sincerity, I am prevented by nature from attaining; and at the very moment when I struggle to attain it, I have a vague prejudicative comprehension that I shall not attain it. But all the same, in order for me to be able to conceive an intention in bad faith, I must have such a nature that within my being I escape from my being. If I were sad or cowardly in the way in which this inkwell is an inkwell, the possibility of bad faith could not even be conceived. Not only should I be unable to escape from my being; I could not even imagine that I could escape from it. But if bad faith is possible by virtue of a simple project, it is because so far as my being is concerned, there is no difference between being and non-being if I am cut off from my project.

Bad faith is possible only because sincerity is conscious of missing its goal inevitably, due to its very nature. I can try to apprehend myself as "*not being cowardly*," when I *am* so, only on condition that the "being cowardly" is itself "in question" at the very moment when it exists, on condition that it is itself *one* question, that at the very moment when I wish to apprehend it, it escapes me on all sides and annihilates itself. The condition under which I can attempt an effort in bad faith is that in one sense, I *am not* this coward which I do not wish to be. But if I were not cowardly in the simple mode of not-being-what-one-is-not, I would be "in good faith" by declaring that I am not cowardly. Thus this inapprehensible coward is evanescent; in order for me not to be cowardly, I must in some way also be cowardly. That does not mean that I must be "a little" cowardly, in the sense that "a little" signifies "to a certain degree cowardly— and not cowardly to a certain degree." No. I must at once both be and not be totally and in all respects a coward. Thus in this case bad faith requires that I should not be what I am; that is, that there be an imponderable difference separating being from non-being in the mode of being of human reality.

But bad faith is not restricted to denying the qualities which I possess, to not seeing the being which I am. It attempts also to constitute myself as being what I am not. It apprehends me positively as courageous when I am not so. And that is possible, once again, only if I am what I am not; that is, if non-being in me does not have being even as non-being. Of course necessarily I am not courageous; otherwise bad faith would not be bad faith. But in addition my effort in bad faith must include the ontological comprehension that even in my usual being what I am, I am not it really and that there is no such difference between the being of "being-sad," for example—which I am in the mode of not being what I am—and the "non-being" of not-being-courageous which I wish to hide from myself. Moreover it is particularly requisite that the very negation of being should be itself the object of a perpetual nihilation, that the very meaning of "non-being" be perpetually in question in human reality. If I were not courageous in the way in which this inkwell is not a table; that is, if I were isolated in my cowardice, propped firmly against it, incapable of putting it in relation to its opposite, if I were not capable of *determining* myself as cowardly—that is, to deny courage to myself and thereby to escape my cowardice in the very moment that I posit it—if it were not on principle *impossible* for me to coincide with my *not-being-courageous* as well as with my being—courageous—then any project of bad faith would be prohibited me. Thus in order for bad faith to be possible, sincerity itself must be in bad faith. The condition of the possibility for bad faith is that human reality, in its most immediate being, in the intrastructure of the pre-reflective *cogito,* must be what it is not and not be what it is.

III. THE "FAITH" OF BAD FAITH

We have indicated for the moment only those conditions which render bad faith conceivable, the structures of being which permit us to form concepts of bad faith. We can not limit ourselves to these considerations; we have not yet distinguished bad faith from falsehood. The two-faced concepts which we have described would without a doubt be utilized by a liar to discountenance his questioner, although their two-faced quality being established on the being of man and not on some empirical circumstance can and ought to be evident to all. The true problem of bad faith stems evidently from the fact that bad faith is *faith.* It can not be either a cynical lie or certainty—if certainty is the intuitive possession of the object. But if we take belief as meaning the adherence of being to its object when the object is not given or is given indistinctly, then bad faith is belief; and the essential problem of bad faith is a problem of belief.

How can we believe by bad faith in the concepts which we forge expressly to persuade ourselves? We must note in fact that the project of bad faith must be itself in bad faith. I am not only in bad faith at the end of my effort when I have constructed my two-faced concepts and when I have persuaded myself. In truth, I have not persuaded myself; to the extent that I could be so persuaded, I have always been so. And at the very moment when I was disposed to put myself in bad faith, I of necessity was in bad faith with respect to this same disposition. For me to have represented it to myself as bad faith would have been cynicism; to believe it sincerely innocent would have been in good faith. The decision to be in bad faith does not dare to speak its name; it believes itself and does not believe itself in bad faith; it believes itself and does not believe itself in good faith. It is this which from the upsurge of bad faith, determines the later attitude and, as it were, the *Weltanschauung* of bad faith.

Bad faith does not hold the norms and criteria of truth as they are accepted by the critical thought of good faith. What it decides first, in fact, is the nature of truth. With bad faith a truth appears, a method of thinking, a type of being which is like that of objects; the ontological characteristic of the world of bad faith with which the subject suddenly surrounds himself is this: that here being is what it is not, and is not what it is. Consequently a peculiar type of evidence appears: *non-persuasive* evidence. Bad faith apprehends evidence but it is resigned in advance to not being fulfilled by this evidence, to not being persuaded and transformed into good faith. It makes itself humble and modest; it is not ignorant, it says, that faith is decision and that after each intuition, it must decide and will what it is. Thus bad faith in its primitive project and in its coming into the world decides on the exact nature of its requirements. It stands forth in the firm resolution *not to demand too much,* to count itself satisfied when it is barely persuaded, to force itself in decisions to adhere to uncertain truths. This original project of bad faith is a decision in bad faith on the nature of faith. Let us understand clearly that there is no question of a reflective, voluntary decision, but of a spontaneous determination of our being. One *puts oneself* in bad faith as one goes to sleep and one is in bad faith as one dreams. Once this mode of being has been realized, it is as difficult to get out of it as to wake oneself up; bad faith is a type of being in the world, like waking or dreaming, which by itself tends to perpetuate itself, although its structure is of the *metastable* type. But bad faith is conscious of its structure, and it has taken precautions by deciding that the *metastable* structure is the structure of being and that non-persuasion is the structure of all convictions. It follows that if bad faith is faith and if it includes in its original project its own negation (it determines itself to be not quite convinced in order to convince itself that I am what I am not), then to start with, a faith which wishes itself to be not quite convinced must be possible. What are the conditions for the possibility of such a faith?

I believe that my friend Pierre feels friendship for me. I believe it in good *faith.* I believe it but I do not have for it any self-evident intuition, for the nature of the object does not lend itself to intuition. I *believe* it; that is, I allow myself to give in to all impulses to trust it; I decide to believe in it, and to maintain myself in this decision; I conduct myself, finally, as if I were certain of it—and all this in the synthetic unity of one and the same attitude. This which I define as good faith is what Hegel would call the *immediate.* It is simple faith. Hegel would demonstrate at once that the immediate calls for mediation and that belief by becoming *belief for itself,* passes to the state of non-belief. If *I believe* that my friend Pierre likes me, this means that his friendship appears to me as the meaning of all his acts. Belief is a particular consciousness of *the meaning* of Pierre's acts. But if I know that I believe, the belief appears to me as pure subjective determination without external correlative. This is what makes the very word "to believe" a term utilized indifferently to indicate the unwavering firmness of belief ("My God, I believe in you") and its character as disarmed and strictly subjective. ("Is Pierre my friend? I do not know; I believe so.") But the nature of consciousness is such that in it the mediate and the immediate are one and the same being. To believe is to know that one believes, and to know that one believes is no longer to believe. Thus to believe is not to believe any longer because that is only to believe—this in the unity of one and the same non-thetic self-consciousness. To be sure, we have here forced the description of the phenomenon by designating it with the word *to know;* non-thetic consciousness is not to *know.* But it is in its very translucency at the origin of all knowing. Thus the non-thetic consciousness (of) believing is destructive of belief. But at the same time the very law of the pre-reflective *cogito* implies that the being of believing ought to be the consciousness of believing.

Thus belief is a being which questions its own being, which can realize itself only in its destruction, which can manifest itself to itself only by denying itself. It is a being for which to be is to appear and to appear is to deny itself. To believe is not-to-believe. We see the reason for it; the being of consciousness is to exist by itself, then to make itself be and thereby to pass beyond itself. In this sense consciousness is perpetually escaping itself, belief becomes non-belief, the immediate becomes mediation, the absolute becomes relative, and the relative becomes absolute. The ideal of good faith (to believe what one believes) is, like that of sincerity (to be what one is), an ideal of being-in-itself. Every belief is a belief that falls short; one never wholly believes what one believes. Consequently the primitive project of bad faith is only the utilization of this self-destruction of the fact of consciousness. If every belief in good faith is an impossible belief, then there is a place for every impossible belief. My inability to *believe* that I am courageous will not discourage me since every belief involves not quite believing. I shall define this impossible belief as *my* belief. To be sure, I shall not be able to hide from myself that I believe in order not to believe and that I do not believe *in order* to believe. But the subtle, total annihilation of bad faith by itself can not surprise me; it exists at the basis of all faith. What is it then? At the moment when I wish to believe myself courageous I know that I am a coward. And this certainly would come to destroy my belief. But *first,* I am not any more courageous than cowardly, if we are to understand this in the mode of being of the-in-itself. In the second place, I do not *know* that I am courageous; such a view of myself can be accompanied only by *belief,* for it surpasses pure reflective certitude. In the third place, it is very true that bad faith does not succeed in believing what it wishes to believe. But it is precisely as the acceptance of not believing what it believes that it is bad faith. Good faith wishes to flee the "not-believing-what-one-believes" by finding refuge in being. Bad faith flees being by taking refuge in "not-believing-what-one-believes." It has disarmed all beliefs in advance—those which it would like to take hold of and, by the same stroke, the others, those which it wishes to flee. In *willing* this self-destruction of belief, from which science escapes by searching for evidence, it ruins the beliefs which are opposed to it, which reveal themselves as *being only* belief. Thus we can better understand the original phenomenon of bad faith.

In bad faith there is no cynical lie nor knowing preparation for deceitful concepts. But the first act of bad faith is to flee what it can not flee, to flee what it is. The very project of flight reveals to bad faith an inner disintegration in the heart of being, and it is this disintegration which bad faith wishes to be. In truth, the two immediate attitudes which we can take in the face of our being are conditioned by the very nature of this being and its immediate relation with the in-itself. Good faith seeks to flee the inner disintegration of my being in the direction of the in-itself which it should be and is not. Bad faith seeks to flee the in-itself by means of the inner disintegration of my being. But it denies this very disintegration as it denies that it is itself bad faith. Bad faith seeks by means of "not-being-what-one-is" to escape from the in-itself which I am not in the mode of being what one is not. It denies itself as bad faith and aims at the in-itself which I am not in the mode of "not-being-what-one-is-not."* If bad faith is possible, it is because it is an immediate, permanent threat to every project of the human being; it is because consciousness conceals in its being a permanent risk of bad faith. The origin of this risk is the fact that the nature of consciousness simultaneously is to be what it is not and not to be what it is. In the light of these remarks we can now approach the ontological study of consciousness, not as the totality of the human being, but as the instantaneous nucleus of this being.

---

*If it is indifferent whether one is in good or in bad faith, because bad faith reapprehends good faith and slides to the very origin of the project of good faith, that does not mean that we can not radically escape bad faith. But this supposes a self-recovery of being which was previously corrupted. This self-recovery we shall call authenticity, the description of which has no place here.

EXISTENTIALISM IS A HUMANISM

. . . What is meant by the term *existentialism*?

Most people who use the word would be rather embarrassed if they had to explain it, since, now that the word is all the rage, even the work of a musician or painter is being called existentialist. A gossip columnist in *Clartés* signs himself *The Existentialist*, so that by this time the word has been so stretched and has taken on so broad a meaning, that it no longer means anything at all. It seems that for want of an avantgarde doctrine analogous to surrealism, the kind of people who are eager for scandal and flurry turn to this philosophy which in other respects does not at all serve their purposes in this sphere.

Actually, it is the least scandalous, the most austere of doctrines. It is intended strictly for specialists and philosophers. Yet it can be defined easily. What complicates matters is that there are two kinds of existentialist; first, those who are Christian, among whom I would include Jaspers and Gabriel Marcel, both Catholic; and on the other hand the atheistic existentialists, among whom I class Heidegger, and then the French existentialists and myself. What they have in common is that they think that existence precedes essence, or, if you prefer, that subjectivity must be the starting point.

Just what does that mean? Let us consider some object that is manufactured, for example, a book or a paper-cutter: here is an object which has been made by an artisan whose inspiration came from a concept. He referred to the concept of what a paper-cutter is and likewise to a known method of production, which is part of the concept, something which is, by and large, a routine. Thus, the paper-cutter is at once an object produced in a certain way and, on the other hand, one having a specific use; and one cannot postulate a man who produces a paper-cutter but does not know what it is used for. Therefore, let us say that, for the paper-cutter, essence—that is, the ensemble of both the production routines and the properties which enable it to be both produced and defined—precedes existence. Thus, the presence of the paper-cutter or book in front of me is determined. Therefore, we have here a technical view of the world whereby it can be said that production precedes existence.

When we conceive God as the Creator, He is generally thought of as a superior sort of artisan. Whatever doctrine we may be considering, whether one like that of Descartes or that of Leibnitz, we always grant that will more or less follows understanding or, at the very least, accompanies it, and that when God creates He knows exactly what He is creating. Thus, the concept of man in the mind of God is comparable to the concept of paper-cutter in the mind of the manufacturer, and, following certain techniques and a conception, God produces man, just as the artisan, following a definition and a technique, makes a paper-cutter. Thus, the individual man is the realization of a certain concept in the divine intelligence.

In the eighteenth century, the atheism of the *philosophes* discarded the idea of God, but not so much for the notion that essence precedes existence. To a certain extent, this idea is found everywhere; we find it in Diderot, in Voltaire, and even in Kant. Man has a human nature; this human nature, which is the concept of the human, is found in all men, which means that each man is a particular example of a universal concept, man. In Kant, the result of this universality is that the wild-man, the natural

Jean-Paul Sartre, *Existentialism Is a Humanism,* translated by Bernard Frechtman (New York: Philosophical Library, 1947). Reprinted by permission.

man, as well as the bourgeois, are circumscribed by the same definition and have the same basic qualities. Thus, here too the essence of man precedes the historical existence that we find in nature.

Atheistic existentialism, which I represent, is more coherent. It states that if God does not exist, there is at least one being in whom existence precedes essence, a being who exists before he can be defined by any concept, and that this being is man, or, as Heidegger says, human reality. What is meant here by saying that existence precedes essence? It means that, first of all, man exists, turns up, appears on the scene, and, only afterwards, defines himself. If man, as the existentialist conceives him, is indefinable, it is because at first he is nothing. Only afterward will he be something, and he himself will have made what he will be. Thus, there is no human nature, since there is no God to conceive it. Not only is man what he conceives himself to be, but he is also only what he wills himself to be after this thrust toward existence.

Man is nothing else but what he makes of himself. Such is the first principle of existentialism. It is also what is called subjectivity, the name we are labeled with when charges are brought against us. But what do we mean by this, if not that man has a greater dignity than a stone or table? For we mean that man first exists, that is, that man first of all is the being who hurls himself toward a future and who is conscious of imagining himself as being in the future. Man is at the start a plan which is aware of itself, rather than a patch of moss, a piece of garbage, or a cauliflower; nothing exists prior to this plan; there is nothing in heaven; man will be what he will have planned to be. Not what he will want to be. Because by the word "will" we generally mean a conscious decision, which is subsequent to what we have already made of ourselves. I may want to belong to a political party, write a book, get married; but all that is only a manifestation of an earlier, more spontaneous choice that is called "will." But if existence really does precede essence, man is responsible for what he is. Thus, existentialism's first move is to make every man aware of what he is and to make the full responsibility of his existence rest on him. And when we say that a man is responsible for himself, we do not only mean that he is responsible for his own individuality, but that he is responsible for all men.

The word subjectivism has two meanings, and our opponents play on the two. Subjectivism means, on the one hand, that an individual chooses and makes himself; and, on the other, that it is impossible for man to transcend human subjectivity. The second of these is the essential meaning of existentialism. When we say that man chooses his own self, we mean that every one of us does likewise; but we also mean by that that in making this choice he also chooses all men. In fact, in creating the man that we want to be, there is not a single one of our acts which does not at the same time create an image of man as we think he ought to be. To choose to be this or that is to affirm at the same time the value of what we choose, because we can never choose evil. We always choose the good, and nothing can be good for us without being good for all.

If, on the other hand, existence precedes essence, and if we grant that we exist and fashion our image at one and the same time, the image is valid for everybody and for our whole age. Thus, our responsibility is much greater than we might have supposed, because it involves all mankind. If I am a workingman and choose to join a Christian trade-union rather than be a communist, and if by being a member I want to show that the best thing for man is resignation, that the kingdom of man is not of this world, I am not only involving my own case—I want to be resigned for everyone. As a result, my action has involved all humanity. To take a more individual matter, if I want to marry, to have children; even if this marriage depends solely on my own circumstances or passion or wish, I am involving all humanity in monogamy and not merely myself. Therefore, I am responsible for myself and for everyone else. I am creating a certain image of man of my own choosing. In choosing myself, I choose man.

This helps us understand what the actual content is of such rather grandiloquent words as anguish, forlornness, despair. As you will see, it's all quite simple.

First, what is meant by anguish? The existentialists say at once that man is in anguish. What that means is this: the man who involves himself and who realizes that he is not only the person he chooses to be, but also a law-maker who is, at the same time, choosing all mankind as well as himself, can not help escape the feeling of his total and deep responsibility. Of course, there are many people who are not anxious; but we claim that they are hiding their anxiety, that they are fleeing from it. Certainly, many people believe that when they do something, they themselves are the only ones involved, and when someone says to them, "What if everyone acted that way?" they shrug their shoulders and answer, "Everyone doesn't act that way." But really, one should always ask himself, "What would happen if everybody looked at things that way?" There is no escaping this disturbing thought except by a kind of double-dealing. A man who lies and makes excuses for himself by saying "not everybody does that," is someone with an uneasy conscience, because the act of lying implies that a universal value is conferred upon the lie.

Anguish is evident even when it conceals itself. This is the anguish that Kierkegaard called the anguish of Abraham. You know the story: an angel has ordered Abraham to sacrifice his son; if it really were an angel who has come and said, "You are Abraham, you shall sacrifice your son," everything would be all right. But everyone might first wonder, "Is it really an angel, and am I really Abraham? What proof do I have?"

There was a mad woman who had hallucinations; someone used to speak to her on the telephone and give her orders. Her doctor asked her, "Who is it who talks to you?" She answered, "He says it's God." What proof did she really have that it was God? If an angel comes to me, what proof is there that it's an angel? And if I hear voices, what proof is there that they come from heaven and not from hell, or from the subconscious, or a pathological condition? What proves that they are addressed to me? What proof is there that I have been appointed to impose my choice and my conception of man on humanity? I'll never find any proof or sign to convince me of that. If a voice addresses me, it is always for me to decide that this is the angel's voice; if I consider that such an act is a good one, it is I who will choose to say that it is good rather than bad.

Now, I'm not being singled out as an Abraham, and yet at every moment I'm obliged to perform exemplary acts. For every man, everything happens as if all mankind had its eyes fixed on him and were guiding itself by what he does. And every man ought to say to himself, "Am I really the kind of man who has the right to act in such a way that humanity might guide itself by my actions?" And if he does not say that to himself, he is masking his anguish.

There is no question here of the kind of anguish which would lead to quietism, to inaction. It is a matter of a simple sort of anguish that anybody who has had responsibilities is familiar with. For example, when a military officer takes the responsibility for an attack and sends a number of men to death, he chooses to do so, and in the main he alone makes the choice. Doubtless, orders come from above, but they are too broad; he interprets them, and on this interpretation depend the lives of ten or fourteen or twenty men. In making a decision he can not help having a certain anguish. All leaders know this anguish. That doesn't keep them from acting; on the contrary, it is the very condition of their action. For it implies that they envisage a number of possibilities, and when they choose one, they realize that it has value only because it is chosen. We shall see that this kind of anguish, which is the kind that existentialism describes, is explained, in addition, by a direct responsibility to the other men whom it involves. It is not a curtain separating us from action, but is part of action itself.

When we speak of forlornness, a term Heidegger was fond of, we mean only that God does not exist and that we have to face all the consequences of this. The existentialist is strongly opposed to a certain kind of secular ethics which would like to abolish God with the least possible expense. About 1880, some French teachers tried to set up a secular ethic which went something like this: God is a useless and costly hypothesis; we are discarding it; but, meanwhile, in order for there to be an ethics, a society, a civilization, it is essential that certain values be taken seriously and that they be considered as having an *a priori* existence. It must be obligatory, *a priori,* to be honest, not to lie, not to beat your wife, to have children, etc., etc. So we're going to try a little device which will make it possible to show that values exist all the same, inscribed in a heaven of ideas, though otherwise God does not exist. In other words—and this, I believe, is the tendency of everything called reformism in France—nothing will be changed if God does not exist. We shall find ourselves with the same norms of honesty, progress, and humanism, and we shall have made of God an outdated hypothesis which will peacefully die off by itself.

The existentialist, on the contrary, thinks it very distressing that God does not exist, because all possibility of finding values in a heaven of ideas disappears along with Him; there can no longer be an *a priori* Good, since there is no infinite and perfect consciousness to think it. Nowhere is it written that the Good exists, that we must be honest, that we must not lie; because the fact is we are on a plane where there are only men. Dostoevski said, "If God didn't exist, everything would be possible." That is the very starting point of existentialism. Indeed, everything is permissible if God does not exist, and as a result man is forlorn, because neither within him nor without does he find anything to cling to. He can't start making excuses for himself.

If existence really does precede essence, there is no explaining things away by reference to a fixed and given human nature. In other words, there is not determinism, man is free, man is freedom. On the other hand, if God does not exist, we find no values or commands to turn to which legitimize our conduct. So, in the bright realm of values, we have no excuse behind us, nor justification before us. We are alone, with no excuses.

That is the idea I shall try to convey when I say that man is condemned to be free. Condemned, because he did not create himself, yet, in other respects is free; because, once thrown into the world, he is responsible for everything he does. The existentialist does not believe in the power of passion. He will never agree that a sweeping passion is a ravaging torrent which fatally leads a man to certain acts and is therefore an excuse. He thinks that man is responsible for his passion.

The existentialist does not think man is going to help himself by finding in the world some omen by which to orient himself. Because he thinks that man will interpret the omen to suit himself. Therefore, he thinks that man, with no support and no aid, is condemned every moment to invent man. Ponge, in a very fine article, has said, "Man is the future of man." That's exactly it. But if it is taken to mean that this future is recorded in heaven, that God sees it, then it is false, because it would really no longer be a future. If it is taken to mean that, whatever a man may be, there is a future to be forged, a virgin future before him, then this remark is sound. But then we are forlorn.

To give you an example which will enable you to understand forlornness better, I shall cite the case of one of my students who came to see me under the following circumstances: his father was on bad terms with his mother, and, moreover, was inclined to be a collaborationist; his older brother had been killed in the German offensive of 1940, and the young man, with somewhat immature but generous feelings, wanted to avenge him. His mother lived alone with him, very much upset by the half-treason of her husband and the death of her older son; the boy was her only consolation.

The boy was faced with the choice of leaving for England and joining the Free French Forces—that is, leaving his mother behind—or remaining with his mother and helping her to carry on. He was fully aware that the woman lived only for him and that his going-off—and perhaps his death—would plunge her into despair. He was also aware that every act that he did for his mother's sake was a sure thing, in the sense that it was helping her to carry on, whereas every effort he made toward going off and fighting was an uncertain move which might run aground and prove completely useless; for example, on his way to England he might, while passing through Spain, be detained indefinitely in a Spanish camp; he might reach England or Elgiers and be stuck in an office at a desk job. As a result, he was faced with two very different kinds of action: one, concrete, immediate, but concerning only one individual; the other concerned an incomparably vaster group, a national collectivity, but for that very reason was dubious, and might be interrupted en route. And, at the same time, he was wavering between two kinds of ethics. On the one hand, an ethics of sympathy, of personal devotion; on the other, a broader ethics, but one whose efficacy was more dubious. He had to choose between the two.

Who could help him choose? Christian doctrine? No. Christian doctrine says, "Be charitable, love your neighbor, take the more rugged path, etc., etc." But which is the more rugged path? Whom should he love as a brother? The fighting man or his mother? Which does the greater good, the vague act of fighting in a group, or the concrete one of helping a particular human being to go on living? Who can decide *a priori*? Nobody. No book of ethics can tell him. The Kantian ethics says, "Never treat any person as a means, but as an end." Very well, if I stay with my mother, I'll treat her as an end and not as a means; but by virtue of this very fact, I'm running the risk of treating the people around me who are fighting, as means; and, conversely, if I go to join those who are fighting, I'll be treating them as an end, and, by doing that, I run the risk of treating my mother as a means.

If values are vague, and if they are always too broad for the concrete and specific case that we are considering, the only thing left for us is to trust our instincts. That's what this young man tried to do; and when I saw him, he said, "In the end, feeling is what counts. I ought to choose whichever pushes me in one direction. If I feel that I love my mother enough to sacrifice everything else for her—my desire for vengeance, for action, for adventure—then I'll stay with her. If, on the contrary, I feel that my love for my mother isn't enough, I'll leave."

But how is the value of a feeling determined? What gives his feeling for his mother value? Precisely the fact that he remained with her. I may say that I like so-and-so well enough to sacrifice a certain amount of money for him, but I may say so only if I've done it. I may say "I love my mother well enough to remain with her" if I have remained with her. The only way to determine the value of this affection is, precisely, to perform an act which confirms and defines it. But, since I require this affection to justify my act, I find myself caught in a vicious circle.

On the other hand, Gide has well said that a mock feeling and a true feeling are almost indistinguishable; to decide that I love my mother and will remain with her, or to remain with her by putting on an act, amount somewhat to the same thing. In other words, the feeling is formed by the acts one performs; so, I can not refer to it in order to act upon it. Which means that I can neither seek within myself the true condition which will impel me to act, nor apply to a system of ethics for concepts which will permit me to act. You will say, "At least, he did go to a teacher for advice." But if you seek advice from a priest, for example, you have chosen this priest; you already knew, more or less, just about what advice he was going to give you. In other words, choosing your adviser is involving yourself. The proof of this is that if you are a Christian, you will say, "Consult a priest." But some priests are collaborating, some are just marking time, some are resisting. Which to choose? If the young man chooses a priest who is resisting or collaborating, he has already decided on the kind of advice he's going to get. Therefore, in coming to see me he knew the answer I was going to give him, and I had only one answer to give: "You're free, choose, that is, invent." No general ethics can show you what is to be done; there are no omens in the world. The Catholics will reply, "But there are." Granted—but, in any case, I myself choose the meaning they have.

When I was a prisoner, I knew a rather remarkable young man who was a Jesuit. He had entered the Jesuit order in the following way: he had a number of very bad breaks; in childhood, his father died, leaving him in poverty, and he was a scholarship student at a religious institution where he was constantly made to feel that he was being kept out of charity; then, he failed to get any of the honors and distinctions that children like; later on, at about eighteen, he bungled a love affair; finally, at twenty-two, he failed in military training, a childish enough matter, but it was the last straw.

This young fellow might well have felt that he had botched everything. It was a sign of something, but of what? He might have taken refuge in bitterness or despair. But he very wisely looked upon all this as a sign that he was not made for secular triumphs, and that only the triumphs of religion, holiness, and faith were open to him. He saw the hand of God in all this, and so he entered the order. Who can help seeing that he alone decided what the sign meant?

Some other interpretation might have been drawn from this series of setbacks; for example, that he might have done better to turn carpenter or revolutionist. Therefore, he is fully responsible for the interpretation. Forlornness implies that we ourselves choose our being. Forlornness and anguish go together.

As for despair, the term has a very simple meaning. It means that we shall confine ourselves to reckoning only with what depends upon our will, or on the ensemble of probabilities which make our action possible. When we want something, we always have to reckon with probabilities. I may be counting on the arrival of a friend. The friend is coming by rail or street-car; this supposes that the train will arrive on schedule, or that the street-car will not jump the track. I am left in the realm of possibility; but possibilities are to be reckoned with only to the point where my action comports with the ensemble of these possibilities, and no further. The moment the possibilities I am considering are not rigorously involved by my action, I ought to disengage myself from them, because no God, no scheme, can adapt the world and its possibilities to my will. When Descartes said, "Conquer yourself rather than the world," he meant essentially the same thing.

The Marxists to whom I have spoken reply, "You can rely on the support of others in your action, which obviously has certain limits because you're not going to live forever. That means: rely on both what others are doing elsewhere to help you, in China, in Russia, and what they will do later on, after your death, to carry on the action and lead it to its fulfillment, which will be the revolution. You even *have* to rely upon that, otherwise you're immoral." I reply at once that I will always rely on fellow-fighters insofar as these comrades are involved with me in a common struggle, in the unity of a party or a group in which I can more or less make my weight felt; that is, one whose ranks I am in as a fighter and whose movements I am aware of at every moment. In such a situation, relying on the unity and will of the party is exactly like counting on the fact that the train will arrive on time, or that the car won't jump the track. But, given that man is free and that there is no human nature for me to depend on, I can not count on men whom I do not know by relying on human goodness or man's concern for the good of society. I don't know what will become of the Russian revolution; I may make an example of it to the extent that at the present time it is apparent that the proletariat plays a part in Russia that it plays in no other nation. But I can't swear that this will inevitably lead to a triumph of the proletariat. I've got to limit myself to what I see.

Given that men are free and that tomorrow they will freely decide what man will be, I can not be sure that, after my death, fellow-fighters will carry on my work to bring it to its maximum perfection. Tomorrow, after my death, some men may decide to set up Fascism, and the others may be cowardly and muddled enough to let them do it. Fascism will then be the human reality, so much the worse for us.

Actually, things will be as man will have decided they are to be. Does that mean that I should abandon myself to quietism? No. First, I should involve myself; then, act on the old saw, "Nothing ventured, nothing gained." Nor does it mean that I shouldn't belong to a party, but rather that I shall have no illusions and shall do what I can. For example, suppose I ask myself, "Will socialization, as such, ever come about?" I know nothing about it. All I know is that I'm going to do everything in my power to bring it about. Beyond that, I can't count on anything. Quietism is the attitude of people who say, "Let others do what I can't do." The doctrine I am presenting is the very opposite of quietism, since it declares, "There is no reality except in action." Moreover, it goes further, since it adds, "Man is nothing else than his plan; he exists only to the extent that he fulfills himself; he is therefore nothing else than the ensemble of his acts, nothing else than his life."

WILLARD VAN ORMAN QUINE
1908–

Willard Van Orman Quine was the youngest of the sons born to Robert Quine and Harriet Van Orman Quine of Akron, Ohio. His mother was a schoolteacher and his father a worker in heavy industry. As a child, Quine developed a lifelong fascination with travel and maps. On summer vacations, he would draw careful maps of nearby lakes and sell copies to local cabin owners. The young Quine also excelled in mathematics and languages. In 1926, he enrolled at Oberlin College, where he majored in mathematics and studied philosophy. His research led him to mathematical philosophy, logic, and the philosophy of Bertrand Russell. In Russell he found a kindred spirit—they shared a logical approach to philosophical problems and a religious skepticism.

Quine went to Harvard University for graduate studies in 1930. He married his college sweetheart, buried himself in studies with such noted philosophers as C.I. Lewis and Alfred North Whitehead, finished his course work, passed preliminary examinations, and received his master's degree—all in a year. The following year he completed a 290-page dissertation on logic and received his Ph.D. degree at age twenty-three. *A System of Logistic* (1934), a revision of this dissertation, became the first of his fifteen published books.

The year Quine received his doctorate, he was also awarded Harvard's Sheldon Traveling Fellowship. He took the title of the fellowship seriously, and in one year he and his wife visited twenty-seven countries. Quine met several members of the Vienna Circle and studied logic in Warsaw with the great Polish logicians Alfred Tarski, Stanisław Leśniewski, and Jan Łukasiewicz. At the end of the year, he was elected into Harvard's Society of Fellows, which gave him, among other emoluments, three years pay and no duties. Among his five colleagues as junior fellows was the promising young psychologist B.F. Skinner.

Quine taught at Harvard until 1942. During the Second World War, his skill in languages and his gift for logic were put to use translating and analyzing decoded messages from German submarines. In 1946, Quine returned to Harvard and teaching. Except for sabbaticals and visiting professorships (and traveling in over one hundred countries), Quine remained a professor at Harvard until his retirement in 1978. Quine still lives in Boston and uses an office at Harvard—when not traveling.

*   *   *

In his autobiography, Quine explains that he has always despised conceptual constraints and has "been at pains to blur the boundaries between natural science, mathematics, and philosophy." Nowhere is this impatience with divisions more apparent than in Quine's critique of the analytic-synthetic distinction.

Ever since Hume first distinguished between "relations of ideas" and "matters of fact," philosophers have divided all propositions into two categories: analytic and synthetic. Yet in his famous paper "Two Dogmas of Empiricism," reprinted here (complete), Quine argues on the basis of various tests of meaning, synonymity, definition, and semantics that such a division has never been clearly made and that there is no compelling reason for believing such a separation can be made.

For example, the foundational propositions of logic and mathematics have been held to be true by convention independent of any matters of fact. Thus the proposition (1) "No unmarried man is married" is true regardless of the various interpretations of "man" and "married." But there are also semantic propositions, such as (2) "No bachelor is married," which are claimed to be equally analytic. As Quine points out, it is common to believe that this latter (supposed) analytic proposition can be made into a truth of logic by "putting synonyms for synonyms; thus (2) can be turned into (1) by putting 'unmarried man' for its synonym 'bachelor'." But what is our criterion of synonymity and how is it any more clear than our criterion of "analyticity"? We could say that propositions (1) and (2) are synonymous if the term "bachelor" in (2) is *defined* as "unmarried man." But what is the basis for such a definition? Does analyticity depend on the empirical observations of a lexicographer or the authority of a dictionary? We could say that these propositions are synonymous if proposition (2) is "necessarily true." However, this would be begging the question; to say a proposition is "necessary" is to say it is analytic. Quine concludes that analyticity as a clearly distinguished notion is "an unempirical dogma of empiricists, a metaphysical article of faith."

Having critiqued the analytic-synthetic distinction, Quine next turns his attention to another empirical dogma: the verification theory of meaning and the reductionism that it presupposes. According to this theory of meaning, the meaning of any statement is the "method of empirically confirming or inferring it." But such a theory implies that each meaningful statement can be reduced to an equivalent statement that contains only references to immediate experience. Logical positivist such as Ayer sought to develop such a reductionistic language. But according to Quine, Ayer and the others are relying on the nonexistent analytic-synthetic distinction to separate the "linguistic components" from the "factual components" in any individual statement. Furthermore, *no* statement, taken by itself, could be confirmed or discredited by sensory experience because there could always be a further experience that would overturn the original statement.

Quine concludes:

> The totality of our so-called knowledge or beliefs, from the most casual matters of geography and history to the profoundest laws of atomic physics or even of pure mathematics and logic, is a man-made fabric which impinges on experience only along the edges.

Individual experiences "along the edges" may be dismissed as errors or hallucinations if they disturb more central beliefs. But even our core beliefs of mathematics and logic are subject to possible revision. There is no final truth nor even a clear distinction between the truths of logic and the truths of experience, that is, between analytic and synthetic.

*   *   *

Alex Orenstein, *Willard Van Orman Quine* (Boston: Twayne, 1977) provides a good place to begin further study, whereas Roger F. Gibson, *The Philosophy of W.V. Quine: An Expository Essay* (Tampa: University Presses of Florida, 1982); George D. Romanas, *Quine and Analytic Philosophy* (Cambridge: MIT Press, 1983); Ilham Dilman, *Quine on Ontology, Necessity, and Experience: A Philosophical Critique* (Albany, NY: SUNY Press, 1984); and Christopher Hookway, *Quine: Language, Experience, and Reality* (Stanford, CA: Stanford University Press, 1988) have written critical investigations. For information on Quine's life, see his autobiography, *The Time of My Life: An Autobiography* (Cambridge: MIT Press, 1985). For collections of essays, see Donald Davidson and Jaakko Hintikka, eds., *Words and Objections: Essays on the Work of W.V. Quine* (Dordrecht, The Netherlands: D. Reidel, 1969); Robert W. Shahan and Chris Swoyer, eds., *Essays on the Philosophy of W.V. Quine* (Norman: University of Oklahoma Press, 1979); Robert Barrett and Roger Gibson, eds., *Perspectives on Quine* (Oxford: Basil Blackwell, 1993); Paolo Leonardi and Marlo Santambrogio, eds., *On Quine: New Essays* (Cambridge: Cambridge University Press, 1994); Robert L. Arrington and Johann Glock, eds., *Wittgenstein and Quine* (Oxford: Routledge, 1996); and, especially, Lewis Edwin Hahn and Paul Arthur Schilpp, eds., *The Philosophy of W.V. Quine* (La Salle, IL: Open Court, 1986), another volume in the Library of Living Philosophers Series, which includes Quine's responses to critics and a short version of his autobiography.

TWO DOGMAS OF EMPIRICISM

Modern empiricism has been conditioned in large part by two dogmas. One is a belief in some fundamental cleavage between truths which are *analytic,* or grounded in meanings independently of matters of fact, and truths which are *synthetic,* or grounded in fact. The other dogma is *reductionism:* the belief that each meaningful statement is equivalent to some logical construct upon terms which refer to immediate experience. Both dogmas, I shall argue, are ill-founded. One effect of abandoning them is, as we shall see, a blurring of the supposed boundary between speculative metaphysics and natural science. Another effect is a shift toward pragmatism.

1. BACKGROUND FOR ANALYTICITY

Kant's cleavage between analytic and synthetic truths was foreshadowed in Hume's distinction between relations of ideas and matters of fact, and in Leibniz's distinction between truths of reason and truths of fact. Leibniz spoke of the truths of reason as true in all possible worlds. Picturesqueness aside, this is to say that the truths of reason are those which could not possibly be false. In the same vein we hear analytic statements defined as statements whose denials are self-contradictory. But this definition has small explanatory value; for the notion of self-contradictoriness, in the quite broad sense needed for this definition of analyticity, stands in exactly the same need of clarification as does the notion of analyticity itself. The two notions are the two sides of a single dubious coin.

Kant conceived of an analytic statement as one that attributes to its subject no more than is already conceptually contained in the subject. This formulation has two shortcomings: it limits itself to statements of subject-predicate form, and it appeals to a notion of containment which is left at a metaphorical level. But Kant's intent, evident more from the use he makes of the notion of analyticity than from his definition of it, can be restated thus: a statement is analytic when it is true by virtue of meanings and independently of fact. Pursuing this line, let us examine the concept of *meaning* which is presupposed.

Meaning, let us remember, is not to be identified with naming. Frege's example of 'Evening Star' and 'Morning Star,' and Russell's of 'Scott' and 'the author of *Waverley,'* illustrate that terms can name the same thing but differ in meaning. The distinction between meaning and naming is no less important at the level of abstract terms. The terms '9' and 'the number of the planets' name one and the same abstract entity but presumably must be regarded as unlike in meaning; for astronomical observation was needed, and not mere reflection on meanings, to determine the sameness of the entity in question.

From Willard Van Orman Quine, *From a Logical Point of View,* Chapter 2, pp. 20–46. Cambridge: Harvard University Press, 1953. Copyright © 1953 by The President and Fellows of Harvard College. Reprinted by permission of Harvard University Press and *The Philosophical Review.*

The above examples consist of singular terms, concrete and abstract. With general terms, or predicates, the situation is somewhat different but parallel. Whereas a singular term purports to name an entity, abstract or concrete, a general term does not; but a general term is *true of* an entity, or of each of many, or of none. The class of all entities of which a general term is true is called the *extension* of the term. Now paralleling the contrast between the meaning of a singular term and the entity named, we must distinguish equally between the meaning of a general term and its extension. The general terms 'creature with a heart' and 'creature with kidneys,' for example, are perhaps alike in extension but unlike in meaning.

Confusion of meaning with extension, in the case of general terms, is less common than confusion of meaning with naming in the case of singular terms. It is indeed a commonplace in philosophy to oppose intension (or meaning) to extension, or, in a variant vocabulary, connotation to denotation.

The Aristotelian notion of essence was the forerunner, no doubt, of the modern notion of intension or meaning. For Aristotle it was essential in men to be rational, accidental to be two-legged. But there is an important difference between this attitude and the doctrine of meaning. From the latter point of view it may indeed be conceded (if only for the sake of argument) that rationality is involved in the meaning of the word 'man' while two-leggedness is not; but two-leggedness may at the same time be viewed as involved in the meaning of 'biped' while rationality is not. Thus from the point of view of the doctrine of meaning it makes no sense to say of the actual individual, who is at once a man and a biped, that his rationality is essential and his two-leggedness accidental or vice versa. Things had essences for Aristotle, but only linguistic forms have meanings. Meaning is what essence becomes when it is divorced from the object of reference and wedded to the word.

For the theory of meaning a conspicuous question is the nature of its objects: what sort of things are meanings? A felt need for meant entities may derive from an earlier failure to appreciate that meaning and reference are distinct. Once the theory of meaning is sharply separated from the theory of reference, it is a short step to recognizing as the primary business of the theory of meaning simply the synonymy of linguistic forms and the analyticity of statements; meanings themselves, as obscure intermediary entities, may well be abandoned.

The problem of analyticity then confronts us anew. Statements which are analytic by general philosophical acclaim are not, indeed, far to seek. They fall into two classes. Those of the first class, which may be called *logically true,* are typified by:

(1) No unmarried man is married.

The relevant feature of this example is that it not merely is true as it stands, but remains true under any and all reinterpretations of 'man' and 'married.' If we suppose a prior inventory of *logical* particles, comprising 'no,' 'un-,' 'not,' 'if,' 'then,' 'and,' etc., then in general a logical truth is a statement which is true and remains true under all reinterpretations of its components other than the logical particles.

But there is also a second class of analytic statements, typified by:

(2) No bachelor is married.

The characteristic of such a statement is that it can be turned into a logical truth by putting synonyms for synonyms; thus (2) can be turned into (1) by putting 'unmarried man' for its synonym 'bachelor.' We still lack a proper characterization of this second class of analytic statements, and therewith of analyticity generally, inasmuch as we have had in the above description to lean on a notion of "synonymy" which is no less in need of clarification than analyticity itself.

In recent years Carnap has tended to explain analyticity by appeal to what he calls state-descriptions. A state-description is any exhaustive assignment of truth values to the atomic, or noncompound, statements of the language. All other statements of the language are, Carnap assumes, built up of their component clauses by means of the familiar logical devices, in such a way that the truth value of any complex statement is fixed for each state-description by specifiable logical laws. A statement is then explained as analytic when it comes out true under every state description. This account is an adaptation of Leibniz's "true in all possible worlds." But note that this version of analyticity serves its purpose only if the atomic statements of the language are, unlike 'John is a bachelor' and 'John is married,' mutually independent. Otherwise there would be a state-description which assigned truth to 'John is a bachelor' and to 'John is married,' and consequently 'No bachelors are married' would turn out synthetic rather than analytic under the proposed criterion. Thus the criterion of analyticity in terms of state-descriptions serves only for languages devoid of extralogical synonym-pairs, such as 'bachelor' and 'unmarried man'—synonym-pairs of the type which give rise to the "second class" of analytic statements. The criterion in terms of state-descriptions is a reconstruction at best of logical truth, not of analyticity.

I do not mean to suggest that Carnap is under any illusions on this point. His simplified model language with its state-descriptions is aimed primarily not at the general problem of analyticity but at another purpose, the clarification of probability and induction. Our problem, however, is analyticity; and here the major difficulty lies not in the first class of analytic statements, the logical truths, but rather in the second class, which depends on the notion of synonymy.

2. DEFINITION

There are those who find it soothing to say that the analytic statements of the second class reduce to those of the first class, the logical truths, by *definition;* 'bachelor,' for example, is *defined* as 'unmarried man.' But how do we find that 'bachelor' is defined as 'unmarried man'? Who defined it thus, and when? Are we to appeal to the nearest dictionary, and accept the lexicographer's formulation as law? Clearly this would be to put the cart before the horse. The lexicographer is an empirical scientist, whose business is the recording of antecedent facts; and if he glosses 'bachelor' as 'unmarried man' it is because of his belief that there is a relation of synonymy between those forms, implicit in general or preferred usage prior to his own work. The notion of synonymy presupposed here has still to be clarified, presumably in terms relating to linguistic behavior. Certainly the "definition" which is the lexicographer's report of an observed synonymy cannot be taken as the ground of the synonymy.

Definition is not, indeed, an activity exclusively of philologists. Philosophers and scientists frequently have occasion to "define" a recondite term by paraphrasing it into terms of a more familiar vocabulary. But ordinarily such a definition, like the philologist's, is pure lexicography, affirming a relation of synonymy antecedent to the exposition in hand.

Just what it means to affirm synonymy, just what the interconnections may be which are necessary and sufficient in order that two linguistic forms be properly describable as synonymous, is far from clear; but, whatever these interconnections may be, ordinarily they are grounded in usage. Definitions reporting selected instances of synonymy come then as reports upon usage.

There is also, however, a variant type of definitional activity which does not limit itself to the reporting of preexisting synonymies. I have in mind what Carnap calls *explication*—an activity to which philosophers are given, and scientists also in their more philosophical moments. In explication the purpose is not merely to paraphrase the definiendum into an outright synonym, but actually to improve upon the definiendum by refining or supplementing its meaning. But even explication, though not merely reporting a preexisting synonymy between definiendum and definiens, does rest nevertheless on *other* preexisting synonymies. The matter may be viewed as follows. Any word worth explicating has some contexts which, as wholes, are clear and precise enough to be useful; and the purpose of explication is to preserve the usage of these favored contexts while sharpening the usage of other contexts. In order that a given definition be suitable for purposes of explication, therefore, what is required is not that the definiendum in its antecedent usage be synonymous with the definiens, but just that each of these favored contexts of the definiendum, taken as a whole in its antecedent usage, be synonymous with the corresponding context of the definiens.

Two alternative definientia may be equally appropriate for the purposes of a given task of explication and yet not be synonymous with each other; for they may serve interchangeably within the favored contexts but diverge elsewhere. By cleaving to one of these definientia rather than the other, a definition of explicative kind generates, by fiat, a relation of synonymy between definiendum and definiens which did not hold before. But such a definition still owes its explicative function, as seen, to preexisting synonymies.

There does, however, remain still an extreme sort of definition which does not hark back to prior synonymies at all: namely, the explicitly conventional introduction of novel notations for purposes of sheer abbreviation. Here the definiendum becomes synonymous with the definiens simply because it has been created expressly for the purpose of being synonymous with the definiens. Here we have a really transparent case of synonymy created by definition; would that all species of synonymy were as intelligible. For the rest, definition rests on synonymy rather than explaining it.

The word 'definition' has come to have a dangerously reassuring sound, owing no doubt to its frequent occurrence in logical and mathematical writings. We shall do well to digress now into a brief appraisal of the role of definition in formal work.

In logical and mathematical systems either of two mutually antagonistic types of economy may be striven for, and each has its peculiar practical utility. On the one hand we may seek economy of practical expression—ease and brevity in the statement of multifarious relations. This sort of economy calls usually for distinctive concise notations for a wealth of concepts. Second, however, and oppositely, we may seek economy in grammar and vocabulary; we may try to find a minimum of basic concepts such that, once a distinctive notation has been appropriated to each of them, it becomes possible to express any desired further concept by mere combination and iteration of our basic notations. This second sort of economy is impractical in one way, since a poverty in basic idioms tends to a necessary lengthening of discourse. But it is practical in another way: it greatly simplifies theoretical discourse *about* the language, through minimizing the terms and the forms of construction wherein the language consists.

Both sorts of economy, though prima facie incompatible, are valuable in their separate ways. The custom has consequently arisen of combining both sorts of economy by forging in effect two languages, the one a part of the other. The inclusive language, though redundant in grammar and vocabulary, is economical in message lengths, while the part, called primitive notation, is economical in grammar and vocabulary. Whole and part are correlated by rules of translation whereby each idiom not in primitive notation is equated to some complex built up of primitive notation. These rules of translation are the so-called *definitions* which appear in formalized systems. They are best viewed not as adjuncts to one language but as correlations between two languages, the one a part of the other.

But these correlations are not arbitrary. They are supposed to show how the primitive notations can accomplish all purposes, save brevity and convenience, of the redundant language. Hence the definiendum and its definiens may be expected, in each case, to be related in one or another of the three ways lately noted. The definiens may be a faithful paraphrase of the definiendum into the narrower notation, preserving a direct synonymy* as of antecedent usage; or the definiens may, in the spirit of explication, improve upon the antecedent usage of the definiendum; or finally, the definiendum may be a newly created notation, newly endowed with meaning here and now.

In formal and informal work alike, thus, we find that definition—except in the extreme case of the explicitly conventional introduction of new notations—hinges on prior relations of synonymy. Recognizing then that the notion of definition does not hold the key to synonymy and analyticity, let us look further into synonymy and say no more of definition.

3. INTERCHANGEABILITY

A natural suggestion, deserving close examination, is that the synonymy of two linguistic forms consists simply in their interchangeability in all contexts without change of truth value—interchangeability, in Leibniz's phrase, *salva veritate*. Note that synonyms so conceived need not even be free from vagueness, as long as the vaguenesses match.

But it is not quite true that the synonyms 'bachelor' and 'unmarried man' are everywhere interchangeable *salva veritate*. Truths which become false under substitution of 'unmarried man' for 'bachelor' are easily constructed with the help of 'bachelor of arts' or 'bachelor's buttons'; also with the help of quotation, thus:

'Bachelor' has less than ten letters.

Such counterinstances can, however, perhaps be set aside by treating the phrases 'bachelor of arts' and 'bachelor's buttons' and the quotation ''bachelor'' each as a single indivisible word and then stipulating that the interchangeability *salva veritate* which is to be the touchstone of synonymy is not supposed to apply to fragmentary occurrences inside of a word. This account of synonymy, supposing it acceptable on other counts, has indeed the drawback of appealing to a prior conception of "word" which can be counted on to present difficulties of formulation in its turn. Nevertheless some progress might be claimed in having reduced the problem of synonymy to a problem of wordhood. Let us pursue this line a bit, taking "word" for granted.

---

*According to an important variant sense of 'definition,' the relation preserved may be the weaker relation of mere agreement in reference. . . . But definition in this sense is better ignored in the present connection, being irrelevant to the question of synonymy.

The question remains whether interchangeability *salva veritate* (apart from occurrences within words) is a strong enough condition for synonymy, or whether, on the contrary, some heteronymous expressions might be thus interchangeable. Now let us be clear that we are not concerned here with synonymy in the sense of complete identity in psychological associations or poetic quality; indeed no two expressions are synonymous in such a sense. We are concerned only with what may be called *cognitive* synonymy. Just what this is cannot be said without successfully finishing the present study; but we know something about it from the need which arose for it in connection with analyticity in ¶1. The sort of synonymy needed there was merely such that any analytic statement could be turned into a logical truth by putting synonyms for synonyms. Turning the tables and assuming analyticity, indeed, we could explain cognitive synonymy of terms as follows (keeping to the familiar example): to say that 'bachelor' and 'unmarried man' are cognitively synonymous is to say no more nor less than that the statement:

(3) All and only bachelors are unmarried men

is analytic.*

What we need is an account of cognitive synonymy not presupposing analyticity—if we are to explain analyticity conversely with help of cognitive synonymy as undertaken in ¶1. And indeed such an independent account of cognitive synonymy is at present up for consideration, namely, interchangeability *salva veritate* everywhere except within words. The question before us, to resume the thread at last, is whether such interchangeability is a sufficient condition for cognitive synonymy. We can quickly assure ourselves that it is, by examples of the following sort. The statement:

(4) Necessarily all and only bachelors are bachelors

is evidently true, even supposing 'necessarily' so narrowly construed as to be truly applicable only to analytic statements. Then, if 'bachelor' and 'unmarried man' are interchangeable *salva veritate,* the result:

(5) Necessarily all and only bachelors are unmarried men

of putting 'unmarried man' for an occurrence of 'bachelor' in (4) must, like (4), be true. But to say that (5) is true is to say that (3) is analytic, and hence that 'bachelor' and 'unmarried man' are cognitively synonymous.

Let us see what there is about the above argument that gives it its air of hocus-pocus. The condition of interchangeability *salva veritate* varies in its force with variations in the richness of the language at hand. The above argument supposes we are working with a language rich enough to contain the adverb 'necessarily,' this adverb being so construed as to yield truth when and only when applied to an analytic statement. But can we condone a language which contains such an adverb? Does the adverb really make sense? To suppose that it does is to suppose that we have already made satisfactory sense of 'analytic.' Then what are we so hard at work on right now?

---

*This is cognitive synonymy in a primary, broad sense. Carnap and Lewis have suggested how, once this notion is at hand, a narrower sense of cognitive synonymy which is preferable for some purposes can in turn be derived. But this special ramification of concept-building lies aside from the present purposes and must not be confused with the broad sort of cognitive synonymy here concerned.

Our argument is not flatly circular, but something like it. It has the form, figuratively speaking, of a closed curve in space.

Interchangeability *salva veritate* is meaningless until relativized to a language whose extent is specified in relevant respects. Suppose now we consider a language containing just the following materials. There is an indefinitely large stock of one-place predicates (for example, '*F*' where '*Fx*' means that *x* is a man) and many-place predicates (for example, '*G*' where '*Gxy*' means that *x* loves *y*), mostly having to do with extralogical subject matter. The rest of the language is logical. The atomic sentences consist each of a predicate followed by one or more variables '*x*,' '*y*,' etc.; and the complex sentences are built up of the atomic ones by truth functions ('not,' 'and,' 'or,' etc.) and quantification. In effect such a language enjoys the benefits also of descriptions and indeed singular terms generally, these being contextually definable in known ways. Even abstract singular terms naming classes, classes of classes, etc., are contextually definable in case the assumed stock of predicates includes the two-place predicate of class membership. Such a language can be adequate to classical mathematics and indeed to scientific discourse generally, except in so far as the latter involves debatable devices such as contrary-to-fact conditionals or modal adverbs like 'necessarily.' Now a language of this type is extensional, in this sense: any two predicates which agree extensionally (that is, are true of the same objects) are interchangeable *salva veritate*.

In an extensional language, therefore, interchangeability *salva veritate* is no assurance of cognitive synonymy of the desired type. That 'bachelor' and 'unmarried man' are interchangeable *salva veritate* in an extensional language assures us of no more than that (3) is true. There is no assurance here that the extensional agreement of 'bachelor' and 'unmarried man' rests on meaning rather than merely on accidental matters of fact, as does the extensional agreement of 'creature with a heart' and 'creature with kidneys.'

For most purposes extensional agreement is the nearest approximation to synonymy we need care about. But the fact remains that extensional agreement falls far short of cognitive synonymy of the type required for explaining analyticity in the manner of ¶1. The type of cognitive synonymy required there is such as to equate the synonymy of 'bachelor' and 'unmarried man' with the analyticity of (3), not merely with the truth of (3).

So we must recognize that interchangeability *salva veritate,* if construed in relation to an extensional language, is not a sufficient condition of cognitive synonymy in the sense needed for deriving analyticity in the manner of ¶1. If a language contains an intensional adverb 'necessarily' in the sense lately noted, or other particles to the same effect, then interchangeability *salva veritate* in such a language does afford a sufficient condition of cognitive synonymy; but such a language is intelligible only in so far as the notion of analyticity is already understood in advance.

The effort to explain cognitive synonymy first, for the sake of deriving analyticity from it afterward as in ¶1, is perhaps the wrong approach. Instead we might try explaining analyticity somehow without appeal to cognitive synonymy. Afterward we could doubtless derive cognitive synonymy from analyticity satisfactorily enough if desired. We have seen that cognitive synonymy of 'bachelor' and 'unmarried man' can be explained as analyticity of (3). The same explanation works for any pair of one-place predicates, of course, and it can be extended in obvious fashion to many-place predicates. Other syntactical categories can also be accommodated in fairly parallel fashion. Singular terms may be said to be cognitively synonymous when the statement of identity formed by putting '=' between them is analytic. Statements may be said simply to be cognitively synonymous when their biconditional (the result of joining them by 'if and only if') is analytic.* If we care to lump all categories into a single formulation, at the expense of assuming again the notion of "word" which was appealed to early in this section, we can describe any two linguistic forms as cognitively synonymous when the two forms are interchangeable (apart from occurrences within "words") *salva* (no longer *veritate* but) *analyticitate*. Certain technical questions arise, indeed, over cases of ambiguity or homonymy; let us not pause for them, however, for we are already digressing. Let us rather turn our backs on the problem of synonymy and address ourselves anew to that of analyticity.

4. SEMANTICAL RULES

Analyticity at first seemed most naturally definable by appeal to a realm of meanings. On refinement, the appeal to meanings gave way to an appeal to synonymy or definition. But definition turned out to be a will-o'-the-wisp, and synonymy turned out to be best understood only by dint of a prior appeal to analyticity itself. So we are back at the problem of analyticity.

I do not know whether the statement 'Everything green is extended' is analytic. Now does my indecision over this example really betray an incomplete understanding, an incomplete grasp of the "meanings," of 'green' and 'extended'? I think not. The trouble is not with 'green' or 'extended,' but with 'analytic.'

It is often hinted that the difficulty in separating analytic statements from synthetic ones in ordinary language is due to the vagueness of ordinary language and that the distinction is clear when we have a precise artificial language with explicit "semantical rules." This, however, as I shall now attempt to show, is a confusion.

The notion of analyticity about which we are worrying is a purported relation between statements and languages: a statement S is said to be *analytic* for a language L, and the problem is to make sense of this relation generally, that is, for variable 'S' and 'L.' The gravity of this problem is not perceptibly less for artificial languages than for natural ones. The problem of making sense of the idiom 'S is analytic for L,' with variable 'S' and 'L,' retains its stubbornness even if we limit the range of the variable 'L' to artificial languages. Let me now try to make this point evident.

For artificial languages and semantical rules we look naturally to the writings of Carnap. His semantical rules take various forms, and to make my point I shall have to distinguish certain of the forms. Let us suppose, to begin with, an artificial language L_0 whose semantical rules have the form explicitly of a specification, by recursion or otherwise, of all the analytic statements of L_0. The rules tell us that such and such statements, and only those, are the analytic statements of L_0. Now here the difficulty is simply that the rules contain the word 'analytic,' which we do not understand! We understand what expressions the rules attribute analyticity to, but we do not understand what the rules attribute to those expressions. In short, before we can understand a rule which begins 'A statement S is analytic for language L_0 if and only if . . .,' we must understand the general relative term 'analytic for'; we must understand 'S is analytic for L' where 'S' and 'L' are variables.

Alternatively we may, indeed, view the so-called rule as a conventional definition of a new simple symbol 'analytic-for-L_0,' which might better be written untenden-

---

*The 'if and only if' itself is intended in the true functional sense.

tiously as '*K*' so as not to seem to throw light on the interesting word 'analytic.' Obviously any number of classes *K, M, N*, etc. of statements of L_0 can be specified for various purposes or for no purpose; what does it mean to say that *K*, as against *M, N*, etc., is the class of the "analytic" statements of L_0?

By saying what statements are analytic for L_0 we explain 'analytic-for-L_0' but not 'analytic,' not 'analytic for.' We do not begin to explain the idiom '*S* is analytic for *L*' with variable '*S*' and '*L*,' even if we are content to limit the range of '*L*' to the realm of artificial languages.

Actually we do know enough about the intended significance of 'analytic' to know that analytic statements are supposed to be true. Let us then turn to a second form of semantical rule, which says not that such and such statements are analytic but simply that such and such statements are included among the truths. Such a rule is not subject to the criticism of containing the un-understood word 'analytic'; and we may grant for the sake of argument that there is no difficulty over the broader term 'true.' A semantical rule of this second type, a rule of truth, is not supposed to specify all the truths of the language; it merely stipulates, recursively or otherwise, a certain multitude of statements which, along with others unspecified, are to count as true. Such a rule may be conceded to be quite clear. Derivatively, afterward, analyticity can be demarcated thus: a statement is analytic if it is (not merely true but) true according to the semantical rule.

Still there is really no progress. Instead of appealing to an unexplained word 'analytic,' we are now appealing to an unexplained phrase 'semantical rule.' Not every true statement which says that the statements of some class are true can count as a semantical rule—otherwise *all* truths would be "analytic" in the sense of being true according to semantical rules. Semantical rules are distinguishable, apparently, only by the fact of appearing on a page under the heading 'Semantical Rules'; and this heading is itself then meaningless.

We can say indeed that a statement is *analytic-for-L_0* if and only if it is true according to such and such specifically appended "semantical rules," but then we find ourselves back at essentially the same case which was originally discussed: '*S* is *analytic-for-L_0* if and only if. . . .' Once we seek to explain '*S* is analytic for *L*' generally for variable '*L*' (even allowing limitation of '*L*' to artificial languages), the explanation 'true according to the semantical rules of *L*' is unavailing; for the relative term 'semantical rule of' is as much in need of clarification, at least, as 'analytic for.'

It may be instructive to compare the notion of semantical rule with that of postulate. Relative to a given set of postulates, it is easy to say what a postulate is: it is a member of the set. Relative to a given set of semantical rules, it is equally easy to say what a semantical rule is. But given simply a notation, mathematical or otherwise, and indeed as thoroughly understood a notation as you please in point of the translations or truth conditions of its statements, who can say which of its true statements rank as postulates? Obviously the question is meaningless—as meaningless as asking which points in Ohio are starting points. Any finite (or effectively specifiable infinite) selection of statements (preferably true ones, perhaps) is as much a set of postulates as any other. The word 'postulate' is significant only relative to an act of inquiry; we apply the word to a set of statements just in so far as we happen, for the year or the moment, to be thinking of those statements in relation to the statements which can be reached from them by some set of transformations to which we have seen fit to direct our attention. Now the notion of semantical rule is as sensible and meaningful as that of postulate, if conceived in a similarly relative spirit—relative, this time, to one or another particular enterprise of schooling unconversant persons in sufficient conditions for truth of statements of some natural or artificial language *L*. But from this point of view no one signalization of a subclass of the truths of L is intrinsically more a semantical rule than another; and, if 'analytic' means 'true by semantical rules,' no one truth of L is analytic to the exclusion of another.

It might conceivably be protested that an artificial language L (unlike a natural one) is a language in the ordinary sense *plus* a set of explicit semantical rules—the whole constituting, let us say, an ordered pair; and that the semantical rules of L then are specifiable simply as the second component of the pair L. But, by the same token and more simply, we might construe an artificial language L outright as an ordered pair whose second component is the class of its analytic statements; and then the analytic statements of L become specifiable simply as the statements in the second component of L. Or better still, we might just stop tugging at our bootstraps altogether.

Not all the explanations of analyticity known to Carnap and his readers have been covered explicitly in the above considerations, but the extension to other forms is not hard to see. Just one additional factor should be mentioned which sometimes enters: sometimes the semantical rules are in effect rules of translation into ordinary language, in which case the analytic statements of the artificial language are in effect recognized as such from the analyticity of their specified translations in ordinary language. Here certainly there can be no thought of an illumination of the problem of analyticity from the side of the artificial language.

From the point of view of the problem of analyticity the notion of an artificial language with semantical rules is a *feu follet par excellence*. Semantical rules determining the analytic statements of an artificial language are of interest only in so far as we already understand the notion of analyticity; they are of no help in gaining this understanding.

Appeal to hypothetical languages of an artificially simple kind could conceivably be useful in clarifying analyticity, if the mental or behavioral or cultural factors relevant to analyticity—whatever they may be—were somehow sketched into the simplified model. But a model which takes analyticity merely as an irreducible character is unlikely to throw light on the problem of explicating analyticity.

It is obvious that truth in general depends on both language and extralinguistic fact. The statement 'Brutus killed Caesar' would be false if the world had been different in certain ways, but it would also be false if the word 'killed' happened rather to have the sense of 'begat.' Thus one is tempted to suppose in general that the truth of a statement is somehow analyzable into a linguistic component and a factual component. Given this supposition, it next seems reasonable that in some statements the factual component should be null; and these are the analytic statements. But, for all its a priori reasonableness, a boundary between analytic and synthetic statements simply has not been drawn. That there is such a distinction to be drawn at all is an unempirical dogma of empiricists, a metaphysical article of faith.

5. THE VERIFICATION THEORY AND REDUCTIONISM

In the course of these somber reflections we have taken a dim view first of the notion of meaning, then of the notion of cognitive synonymy, and finally of the notion of analyticity. But what, it may be asked, of the verification theory of meaning? This phrase has established itself so firmly as a catchword of empiricism that we should be very unscientific indeed not to look beneath it for a possible key to the problem of meaning and the associated problems.

The verification theory of meaning, which has been conspicuous in the literature from Peirce onward, is that the meaning of a statement is the method of empirically confirming or infirming it. An analytic statement is that limiting case which is confirmed no matter what.

As urged in ¶1, we can as well pass over the question of meanings as entities and move straight to sameness of meaning, or synonymy. Then what the verification theory says is that statements are synonymous if and only if they are alike in point of method of empirical confirmation or infirmation.

This is an account of cognitive synonymy not of linguistic forms generally, but of statements.* However, from the concept of synonymy of statements we could derive the concept of synonymy for other linguistic forms, by considerations somewhat similar to those at the end of ¶3. Assuming the notion of "word," indeed, we could explain any two forms as synonymous when the putting of the one form for an occurrence of the other in any statement (apart from occurrences within "words") yields a synonymous statement. Finally, given the concept of synonymy thus for linguistic forms generally, we could define analyticity in terms of synonymy and logical truth as in ¶1. For that matter, we could define analyticity more simply in terms of just synonymy of statements together with logical truth; it is not necessary to appeal to synonymy of linguistic forms other than statements. For a statement may be described as analytic simply when it is synonymous with a logically true statement.

So, if the verification theory can be accepted as an adequate account of statement synonymy, the notion of analyticity is saved after all. However, let us reflect. Statement synonymy is said to be likeness of method of empirical confirmation or infirmation. Just what are these methods which are to be compared for likeness? What, in other words, is the nature of the relation between a statement and the experiences which contribute to or detract from its confirmation?

The most naive view of the relation is that it is one of direct report. This is *radical reductionism.* Every meaningful statement is held to be translatable into a statement (true or false) about immediate experience. Radical reductionism, in one form or another, well antedates the verification theory of meaning explicitly so called. Thus Locke and Hume held that every idea must either originate directly in sense experience or else be compounded of ideas thus originating; and taking a hint from Tooke we might rephrase this doctrine in semantical jargon by saying that a term, to be significant at all, must be either a name of a sense datum or a compound of such names or an abbreviation of such a compound. So stated, the doctrine remains ambiguous as between sense data as sensory events and sense data as sensory qualities; and it remains vague as to the admissible ways of compounding. Moreover, the doctrine is unnecessarily and intolerably restrictive in the term-by-term critique which it imposes. More reasonably, and without yet exceeding the limits of what I have called radical reductionism, we may take full statements as our significant units—thus demanding that our statements as wholes be translatable into sense-datum language, but not that they be translatable term by term.

This emendation would unquestionably have been welcome to Locke and Hume and Tooke, but historically it had to await an important reorientation in semantics—the reorientation whereby the primary vehicle of meaning came to be seen no longer in the

---

*The doctrine can indeed be formulated with terms rather than statements as the units. Thus Lewis describes the meaning of a term as "*a criterion in mind,* by reference to which one is able to apply or refuse to apply the expression in question in the case of presented, or imagined, things or situations."

term but in the statement. This reorientation, seen in Bentham and Frege, underlies Russell's concept of incomplete symbols defined in use; also it is implicit in the verification theory of meaning, since the objects of verification are statements.

Radical reductionism, conceived now with statements as units, set itself the task of specifying a sense-datum language and showing how to translate the rest of significant discourse, statement by statement, into it. Carnap embarked on this project in the *Aufbau.*

The language which Carnap adopted as his starting point was not a sense-datum language in the narrowest conceivable sense, for it included also the notations of logic, up through higher set theory. In effect it included the whole language of pure mathematics. The ontology implicit in it (that is, the range of values of its variables) embraced not only sensory events but classes, classes of classes, and so on. Empiricists there are who would boggle at such prodigality. Carnap's starting point is very parsimonious, however, in its extralogical or sensory part. In a series of constructions in which he exploits the resources of modern logic with much ingenuity, Carnap succeeds in defining a wide array of important additional sensory concepts which, but for his constructions, one would not have dreamed were definable on so slender a basis. He was the first empiricist who, not content with asserting the reducibility of science to terms of immediate experience, took serious steps toward carrying out the reduction.

If Carnap's starting point is satisfactory, still his constructions were, as he himself stressed, only a fragment of the full program. The construction of even the simplest statements about the physical world was left in a sketchy state. Carnap's suggestions on this subject were, despite their sketchiness, very suggestive. He explained spatio-temporal point-instants as quadruples of real numbers and envisaged assignment of sense qualities to point-instants according to certain canons. Roughly summarized, the plan was that qualities should be assigned to point-instants in such a way as to achieve the laziest world compatible with our experience. The principle of least action was to be our guide in constructing a world from experience.

Carnap did not seem to recognize, however, that his treatment of physical objects fell short of reduction not merely through sketchiness, but in principle. Statements of the form 'Quality q is at point-instant $x;y;z;t$' were, according to his canons, to be apportioned truth values in such a way as to maximize and minimize certain over-all features, and with growth of experience the truth values were to be progressively revised in the same spirit. I think this is a good schematization (deliberately oversimplified, to be sure) of what science really does; but it provides no indication, not even the sketchiest, of how a statement of the form 'Quality q is at $x;y;z;t$' could ever be translated into Carnap's initial language of sense data and logic. The connective 'is at' remains an added undefined connective; the canons counsel us in its use but not in its elimination.

Carnap seems to have appreciated this point afterward; for in his later writings he abandoned all notion of the translatability of statements about the physical world into statements about immediate experience. Reductionism in its radical form has long since ceased to figure in Carnap's philosophy.

But the dogma of reductionism has, in a subtler and more tenuous form, continued to influence the thought of empiricists. The notion lingers that to each statement, or each synthetic statement, there is associated a unique range of possible sensory events such that the occurrence of any of them would add to the likelihood of truth of the statement, and that there is associated also another unique range of possible sensory events whose occurrence would detract from that likelihood. This notion is of course implicit in the verification theory of meaning.

The dogma of reductionism survives in the supposition that each statement, taken in isolation from its fellows, can admit of confirmation or infirmation at all. My countersuggestion, issuing essentially from Carnap's doctrine of the physical world in the *Aufbau,* is that our statements about the external world face the tribunal of sense experience not individually but only as a corporate body.

The dogma of reductionism, even in its attenuated form, is intimately connected with the other dogma—that there is a cleavage between the analytic and the synthetic. We have found ourselves led, indeed, from the latter problem to the former through the verification theory of meaning. More directly, the one dogma clearly supports the other in this way: as long as it is taken to be significant in general to speak of the confirmation and infirmation of a statement, it seems significant to speak also of a limiting kind of statement which is vacuously confirmed, *ipso facto,* come what may; and such a statement is analytic.

The two dogmas are, indeed, at root identical. We lately reflected that in general the truth of statements does obviously depend both upon language and upon extralinguistic fact; and we noted that this obvious circumstance carries in its train, not logically but all too naturally, a feeling that the truth of a statement is somehow analyzable into a linguistic component and a factual component. The factual component must, if we are empiricists, boil down to a range of confirmatory experiences. In the extreme case where the linguistic component is all that matters, a true statement is analytic. But I hope we are now impressed with how stubbornly the distinction between analytic and synthetic has resisted any straightforward drawing. I am impressed also, apart from prefabricated examples of black and white balls in an urn, with how baffling the problem has always been of arriving at any explicit theory of the empirical confirmation of a synthetic statement. My present suggestion is that it is nonsense, and the root of much nonsense, to speak of a linguistic component and a factual component in the truth of any individual statement. Taken collectively, science has its double dependence upon language and experience; but this duality is not significantly traceable into the statements of science taken one by one.

The idea of defining a symbol in use was, as remarked, an advance over the impossible term-by-term empiricism of Locke and Hume. The statement, rather than the term, came with Bentham to be recognized as the unit accountable to an empiricist critique. But what I am now urging is that even in taking the statement as unit we have drawn our grid too finely. The unit of empirical significance is the whole of science.

6. EMPIRICISM WITHOUT THE DOGMAS

The totality of our so-called knowledge or beliefs, from the most casual matters of geography and history to the profoundest laws of atomic physics or even of pure mathematics and logic, is a man-made fabric which impinges on experience only along the edges. Or, to change the figure, total science is like a field of force whose boundary conditions are experience. A conflict with experience at the periphery occasions readjustments in the interior of the field. Truth values have to be redistributed over some of our statements. Reevaluation of some statements entails reevaluation of others, because of their logical interconnections—the logical laws being in turn simply certain further statements of the system, certain further elements of the field. Having reevaluated one statement we must reevaluate some others, which may be statements logically connected with the first or may be the statements of logical connections themselves. But the total field is so underdetermined by its boundary conditions, experience, that there is much latitude of choice as to what statements to reevaluate in the light of any single contrary experience. No particular experiences are linked with any particular statements in the interior of the field, except indirectly through considerations of equilibrium affecting the field as a whole.

If this view is right, it is misleading to speak of the empirical content of an individual statement—especially if it is a statement at all remote from the experiential periphery of the field. Furthermore it becomes folly to seek a boundary between synthetic statements, which hold contingently on experience, and analytic statements, which hold come what may. Any statement can be held true come what may, if we make drastic enough adjustments elsewhere in the system. Even a statement very close to the periphery can be held true in the face of recalcitrant experience by pleading hallucination or by amending certain statements of the kind called logical laws. Conversely, by the same token, no statement is immune to revision. Revision even of the logical law of the excluded middle has been proposed as a means of simplifying quantum mechanics; and what difference is there in principle between such a shift and the shift whereby Kepler superseded Ptolemy, or Einstein Newton, or Darwin Aristotle?

For vividness I have been speaking in terms of varying distances from a sensory periphery. Let me try now to clarify this notion without metaphor. Certain statements, though *about* physical objects and not sense experience, seem peculiarly germane to sense experience—and in a selective way: some statements to some experiences, others to others. Such statements, especially germane to particular experiences, I picture as near the periphery. But in this relation of "germaneness" I envisage nothing more than a loose association reflecting the relative likelihood, in practice, of our choosing one statement rather than another for revision in the event of recalcitrant experience. For example, we can imagine recalcitrant experiences to which we would surely be inclined to accommodate our system by reevaluating just the statement that there are brick houses on Elm Street, together with related statements on the same topic. We can imagine other recalcitrant experiences to which we would be inclined to accommodate our system by reevaluating just the statement that there are no centaurs, along with kindred statements. A recalcitrant experience can, I have urged, be accommodated by any of various alternative reevaluations in various alternative quarters of the total system; but, in the cases which we are now imagining, our natural tendency to disturb the total system as little as possible would lead us to focus our revisions upon these specific statements concerning brick houses or centaurs. These statements are felt, therefore, to have a sharper empirical reference than highly theoretical statements of physics or logic or ontology. The latter statements may be thought of as relatively centrally located within the total network, meaning merely that little preferential connection with any particular sense data obtrudes itself.

As an empiricist I continue to think of the conceptual scheme of science as a tool, ultimately, for predicting future experience in the light of past experience. Physical objects are conceptually imported into the situation as convenient intermediaries—not by definition in terms of experience, but simply as irreducible posits comparable, epistemologically, to the gods of Homer. For my part I do, qua lay physicist, believe in physical objects and not in Homer's gods; and I consider it a scientific error to believe otherwise. But in point of epistemological footing the physical objects and the gods differ only in degree and not in kind. Both sorts of entities enter our conception only as cultural posits. The myth of physical objects is epistemologically superior to most in that it has proved more efficacious than other myths as a device for working a manageable structure into the flux of experience.

Positing does not stop with macroscopic physical objects. Objects at the atomic level are posited to make the laws of macroscopic objects, and ultimately the laws of experience, simpler and more manageable; and we need not expect or demand full definition of atomic and subatomic entities in terms of macroscopic ones, any more than definition of macroscopic things in terms of sense data. Science is a continuation of common sense, and it continues the common-sense expedient of swelling ontology to simplify theory.

Physical objects, small and large, are not the only posits. Forces are another example; and indeed we are told nowadays that the boundary between energy and matter is obsolete. Moreover, the abstract entities which are the substance of mathematics—ultimately classes and classes of classes and so on up—are another posit in the same spirit. Epistemologically these are myths on the same footing with physical objects and gods, neither better nor worse except for differences in the degree to which they expedite our dealings with sense experiences.

The over-all algebra of rational and irrational numbers is underdetermined by the algebra of rational numbers, but is smoother and more convenient; and it includes the algebra of rational numbers as a jagged or gerrymandered part. Total science, mathematical and natural and human, is similarly but more extremely underdetermined by experience. The edge of the system must be kept squared with experience; the rest, with all its elaborate myths or fictions, has as its objective the simplicity of laws.

Ontological questions, under this view, are on a par with questions of natural science. Consider the question whether to countenance classes as entities. This, as I have argued elsewhere, is the question whether to quantify with respect to variables which take classes as values. Now Carnap has maintained that this is a question not of matters of fact but of choosing a convenient language form, a convenient conceptual scheme or framework for science. With this I agree, but only on the proviso that the same be conceded regarding scientific hypotheses generally. Carnap has recognized that he is able to preserve a double standard for ontological questions and scientific hypotheses only by assuming an absolute distinction between the analytic and the synthetic; and I need not say again that this is a distinction which I reject.

The issue over there being classes seems more a question of convenient conceptual scheme; the issue over there being centaurs, or brick houses on Elm Street, seems more a question of fact. But I have been urging that this difference is only one of degree, and that it turns upon our vaguely pragmatic inclination to adjust one strand of the fabric of science rather than another in accommodating some particular recalcitrant experience. Conservatism figures in such choices, and so does the quest for simplicity.

Carnap, Lewis, and others take a pragmatic stand on the question of choosing between language forms, scientific frameworks; but their pragmatism leaves off at the imagined boundary between the analytic and the synthetic. In repudiating such a boundary I espouse a more thorough pragmatism. Each man is given a scientific heritage plus a continuing barrage of sensory stimulation; and the considerations which guide him in warping his scientific heritage to fit his continuing sensory promptings are, where rational, pragmatic.

JACQUES DERRIDA
1930–

In the spirit of his celebrated dictum that "there is nothing outside the text," Jacques Derrida long resisted the publication of information about his life. For seventeen years (1962–1979) he even refused to have a personal photograph accompany his texts. However, his fame as the founder of what came to be called "deconstruction" led him to provide biographical "scraps."

Born in 1930 near Algiers, Jacques Derrida as a Jew was forced to leave school in 1942 until the Free French repealed Vichy racial laws. At nineteen, he moved to Paris to prepare for the École Normale Supérieure, where he subsequently studied and taught philosophy. Though his first published work (1962)—about Husserl's essay on geometry—won a philosophical prize, Derrida was not widely known until 1966. At a conference on France's new structuralism at Johns Hopkins University, Derrida gave a paper—"Structure, Sign, and Play in the Discourse of the Human Sciences"—that daringly exposed contradictions in the thought of structuralism's leading figure, Lévi-Strauss. Derrida's critique became one of the important building blocks in what came to be called "poststructuralism."

The following year, Derrida continued his critique, publishing no less than three books showing how structuralist positions refuted their own theses. The books—*Of Grammatology; Writing and Difference;* and *Speech and Phenomena* (as the titles were translated)—created a storm of philosophical debate in France. In these works, Derrida showed how his critique went beyond structuralism and attacked the enterprise of philosophy itself. "Deconstruction," as Derrida's approach in these works was now called, claimed that the very nature of a written text—of every traditional text and not just the structuralist's—undermines itself.

To "deconstruct" a text, then, is to dismantle inherent hierarchical systems of thought, to seek out unregarded details, to find the "margins" of the text, where there are new possibilities of interpretation.

In 1972, Derrida published three additional works, translated as *Dissemination, Margins of Philosophy,* and *Positions,* which continued to influence poststructuralism in the 1970s. As Derrida's fame grew, he accepted a visiting professorship first at Yale University, and then at the University of California in Irvine. In the 1980s, Derrida gave himself to political causes such as the abolition of apartheid. He also became actively interested in architecture, which he regarded as the last bastion of metaphysics. He helped architect Peter Eisenman design a garden in Paris that explores the relationship between center and periphery. Born on the periphery of colonial France, on the margin of Algiers, as a marginalized Jew, Derrida constantly examined the philosophical relation between margin and center (and often employed language that is only marginally understandable). All for a purpose.

*   *   *

Derrida believes that Western philosophy is built upon a "Metaphysics of Presence": upon, that is to say, the idea that there is an origin of knowledge from which "truth" can be made present. Philosophy has always seen itself as the arbiter of reason, the discipline that adjudicates what is and is not. Forms of writing other than philosophical discourse, such as poetic or literary writing, have been judged inferior, and removed from the truth. In *Of Grammatology,* Derrida calls this positing of a center that can situate certainty *logocentrism.* Philosophy thinks it can talk about "meaning" through a language unsullied by the imprecision of metaphors. *Au Contraire!* Philosophical discourse is not privileged in any way, and any attempt to explain what "meaning" *means* will self-destruct. Put more precisely, the signifiers of language systems cannot refer to a transcendental *signified* originating in the mind of the speaker because the "signified" is itself created by the conventional, and hence arbitrary, signifiers of language. Signifiers therefore merely refer to other signifiers (e.g., words refer only to other words). The "meaning" is always deferred and Presence is never actually present. Signifiers attain significance only in their differences from each other (the signifier "cat" is neither "cap" nor "car") or in what they define themselves against ("to be asleep" is understood in contrast to "to be awake").

To highlight the ambiguities of language, Derrida coined the word "*différance.*" In French, this word sounds no different from the French word "*différénce,*" which comes from the verb "*différer,*" meaning both "to differ" and "to defer." Whereas the definition of *différénce* reminds us that signifiers defer meaning as they differ both from their referents and from each other, the written word *différance* calls attention in a striking way to the limitations of the spoken word. The spoken word can establish no aural distinction between *différénce* and *différance.* Derrida thus questions the traditional privileging of speech over writing, which goes back at least as far as Plato. For example, in the *Phaedrus,* Plato had placed writing as one step further removed than speaking from Ideal Form. Derrida shows, however, that even as Plato sought to place speech closer to the source of meaning, he could not keep writing out of his system. At one point in the *Phaedrus,* Plato states that speech "is *written* in the soul of the listener" (emphasis added).

This is just one example of how Derrida repeatedly exposes the repressed figures of speech in even the most systematic of thinkers. According to Derrida, all systems of thought contain "traces" of that which they define themselves against. Thus, whereas many philosophers have thought literature merely sugarcoated philosophy, Derrida has reversed this hierarchy to say that the discourse of philosophy is merely literary medicine—an assumption that is hard for many to swallow. For Derrida, all writing is reduced (or elevated) to the same level, with no privileging of one genre as more "meaning-ful" than another. This may explain why deconstruction—with its close reading of texts to unearth language working against itself—made its greatest impact in literature, rather than in philosophy.

Our selection, "Signature, Event, Context," translated by Samuel Weber and Jeffrey Mehlman, exhibits these deconstructive themes. Derrida begins by deconstructing the signifier "communication," showing how context will not serve to clarify the meaning of this word. Next, he exposes the ways writing has been privileged over speech. Thirdly, he explores Austin's concept of a speech act, finding much with which to agree. But finally, he argues that Austin is still operating within the metaphysics of Presence, requiring a signature or some other continuing presence to secure the speech act.

Derrida concludes our selection by claiming that the inversion of the hierarchy—speech over writing, like that of philosophy over literature—is part of his deconstruction of binaries that have molded the tradition of Western metaphysics. Philosophy has continually worked with pairs in which the first term was seen as the origin or foundation for the second: truth/fiction, reality/appearance, thought/language, signified/signifier, center/margin, male/female, objective/subjective, essential/inessential. Derrida does not want merely to invert these polarities to create a new countersystem. Instead he "destabilizes" these pairings to show that any privileging of one term over the other is an arbitrary construction, usually politically motivated, which must be deconstructed. As he says, "Deconstruction does not consist in passing from one concept to another, but in overturning and displacing a conceptual order, as well as the nonconceptual order with which the conceptual order is articulated."

But what about Derrida's writings themselves—do they not represent a conceptual order, an attempt to communicate "meaning"? Derrida goes to great pains to avoid the systemization of his own thought, constantly inventing new terms to destabilize his readers' sense that they understand his "philosophy." In the meantime, although he works to expose the failures of language to make present meaning, he acknowledges that, since language is all we have, he must situate himself inside a system even as he is breaking it apart. He signals this paradox, or *aporia,* of language by borrowing a technique from Heidegger, who simultaneously included and deleted the word Being in his works by placing an X over it: Be̶i̶n̶g. Derrida crosses out certain metaphysically loaded words, putting them "under erasure." He asserts the inadequacy of a signifier like na̶t̶ure to have a definitive meaning, while also acknowledging that thought cannot operate without the term. Derrida demonstrates that his own writing—like everyone else's—is not innocent, that it cannot become a coherent theoretical system corresponding to reality. Derrida has therefore been called a nihilist. His defenders, however, call this accusation inaccurate. Derrida never denies the existence of an Absolute; he only asserts the impossibility of putting the Absolute into words.

*   *   *

For a general overview of Derrida, see Christopher Norris, *Derrida* (Cambridge, MA: Harvard University Press, 1987). Allan Megill, *Prophets of Extremity: Nietzsche, Heidegger, Foucault, Derrida* (Berkeley: University of California Press, 1985); Diane P. Michelfelder and Richard E. Palmer, eds., *Dialogue and Deconstruction: The Gadamer-Derrida Encounter* (Albany, NY: SUNY Press, 1989); Roy Boyne, *Foucault and Derrida: The Other Side of Reason* (London: Unwin Hyman, 1990); and Simon Critchley, *The Ethics of Deconstruction: Derrida & Levinas* (Oxford: Basil Blackwell, 1992) provide comparative studies. John D. Caputo, *The Prayers and Tears of Jacques Derrida: Religion without Religion* (Bloomington: Indiana University Press, 1997) is a recent specialized study. Gary A. Olson and Irene Gale, eds., *(Inter)view: Cross-Disciplinary Perspectives on Rhetoric and Literacy* (Carbondale: Southern Illinois University Press, 1991); Jacques Derrida, *Points. . . : Interview 1974–1994,* edited by Elisabeth Weber (Stanford, CA: Stanford University Press, 1995); and John Caputo, ed., *Deconstruction in a Nutshell: A Conversation with Jacques Derrida* (New York: Fordham University Press, 1997) include discussions with Derrida. For a treatment of the specific issues raised in our selection, see John R. Searle, *Expression and Meaning: Studies in the Theory of Speech Acts* (Cambridge: Cambridge University Press, 1979); Stanley Cavell, *Philosophical Passages: Wittgenstein, Emerson, Austin, Derrida* (Oxford: Blackwell, 1995); and Graham Ward, *Barth, Derrida and the Language of Theology* (Cambridge: Cambridge University Press, 1995). For a feminist reading of Derrida, see Ellen K. Feder, Mary C. Rawlinson, and Emily Zakin, eds., *Derrida and Feminism* (Oxford: Routledge, 1997). General collections of critical essays include John Sallis, ed., *Deconstruction and Philosophy: The Texts of Jacques Derrida* (Chicago: University of Chicago Press, 1987); David Wood, ed., *Derrida: A Critical Reader* (Oxford: Basil Blackwell, 1992); Harold Coward and Toby Foshay, eds., *Derrida and Negative Theology* (Albany, NY: SUNY Press, 1992); and Gary B. Madison, ed., *Working through Derrida* (Evanston, IL: Northwestern University Press, 1993). Finally, in Geoffrey Bennington and Jacques Derrida, *Jacques Derrida* (Chicago: University of Chicago Press, 1993), the top two-thirds of each page give Bennington's comment on Derrida's thought, whereas Derrida himself writes "in the margin" along the bottom of each page.

"SIGNATURE, EVENT, CONTEXT"

> "Still confining ourselves for simplicity
> to *spoken* utterance."
> —Austin, *How to Do Things with Words*

Is it certain that to the word *communication* corresponds a concept that is unique, univocal, rigorously controllable, and transmittable: in a word, communicable? Thus, in accordance with a strange figure of discourse, one must first of all ask oneself whether or not the word or signifier "communication" communicates a determinate content, an identifiable meaning, or a describable value. However, even to articulate and to propose this question I have had to anticipate the meaning of the word *communication:* I have been constrained to predetermine communication as a vehicle, a means of transport or transitional medium of a *meaning,* and moreover of a *unified* meaning. If *communication* possessed several meanings and if this plurality should prove to be irreducible, it would not be justifiable to define communication *a priori* as the transmission of a *meaning,* even supposing that we could agree on what each of these words (transmission, meaning, etc.) involved. And yet, we have no prior authorization for neglecting *communication* as a word, or for impoverishing its polysemic aspects; indeed, this word opens up a semantic domain that precisely does not limit itself to semantics, semiotics, and even less to linguistics. For one characteristic of the semantic field of the word communication is that it designates nonsemantic movements as well. Here, even a provisional recourse to ordinary language and to the equivocations of natural language instructs us that one can, for instance, *communicate a movement* or that a tremor *[ébranlement],* a shock, a displacement of force can be communicated—that is, propagated, transmitted. We also speak of different or remote places communicating with each other by means of a passage or opening. What takes place, in this sense, what is transmitted, communicated, does not involve phenomena of meaning or signification. In such cases we are dealing neither with a semantic or conceptual content, nor with a semiotic operation, and even less with a linguistic exchange.

We would not, however, assert that this non-semiotic meaning of the word *communication,* as it works in ordinary language, in one or more of the so-called natural languages, constitutes the *literal* or *primary [primitif]* meaning and that consequently the semantic, semiotic, or linguistic meaning corresponds to a derivation, extension, or reduction, a metaphoric displacement. We would not assert, as one might be tempted to do, that semio-linguistic communication acquired its title *more metaphorico,* by analogy with "physical" or "real" communication, inasmuch as it also serves as a passage, transporting and transmitting something, rendering it accessible. We will not assert this for the following reasons:

1. because the value of the notion of *literal meaning [sens propre]* appears more problematical than ever, and

2. because the value of displacement, of transport, etc., is precisely constitutive of the concept of metaphor with which one claims to comprehend the semantic dis-

Jacques Derrida, "Signature, Event, Context," translated by Samuel Weber and Jeffrey Mehlman, from *Glyph* 1, 1977. Reprinted by permission of the Johns Hopkins University Press.

placement that is brought about from communication as a non-semiolinguistic phenomenon to communication as a semio-linguistic phenomenon.

(Let me note parenthetically that this communication is going to concern, indeed already concerns, the problem of polysemy and of communication, of dissemination—which I shall oppose to polysemy—and of communication. In a moment a certain concept of writing cannot fail to arise that may transform itself and perhaps transform the problematic under consideration.)

It seems self-evident that the ambiguous field of the word "communication" can be massively reduced by the limits of what is called a context (and I give notice, again parenthetically, that this particular communication will be concerned with the problem of context and with the question of determining exactly how writing relates to context in general). For example, in a philosophic *colloquium* on philosophy in the *French language,* a conventional context—produced by a kind of consensus that is implicit but structurally vague—seems to prescribe that one propose "communications" concerning communication, communications in a discursive form, colloquial communications, oral communications destined to be listened to, and to engage or to pursue dialogues within the horizon of an intelligibility and truth that is meaningful, such that ultimately general agreement may, in principle, be attained. These communications are supposed to confine themselves to the element of a determinate, "natural" language, here designated as French, which commands certain very particular uses of the word communication. Above all, the object of such communications is supposed, by priority or by privilege, to organize itself around communication qua discourse, or in any case qua signification. Without exhausting all the implications and the entire structure of an "event" such as this one, an effort that would require extended preliminary analysis, the conditions that I have just recalled seem to be evident; and those who doubt it need only consult our program to be convinced.

But are the conditions *[les réquisits]* of a context ever absolutely determinable? This is, fundamentally, the most general question that I shall endeavor to elaborate. Is there a rigorous and scientific concept of *context?* Or does the notion of context not conceal, behind a certain confusion, philosophical presuppositions of a very determinate nature? Stating it in the most summary manner possible, I shall try to demonstrate why a context is never absolutely determinable, or rather, why its determination can never be entirely certain or saturated. This structural non-saturation would have a double effect:

1. it would mark the theoretical inadequacy of the *current concept of context* (linguistic or nonlinguistic), as it is accepted in numerous domains of research, including all the concepts with which it is systematically associated;

2. it would necessitate a certain generalization and a certain displacement of the concept of writing. This concept would no longer be comprehensible in terms of communication, at least in the limited sense of a transmission of meaning. Inversely, it is within the general domain of writing, defined in this way, that the effects of semantic communication can be determined as effects that are particular, secondary, inscribed, and supplementary.

WRITING AND TELECOMMUNICATION

If we take the notion of writing in its currently accepted sense—one which should not—and that is essential—be considered innocent, primitive, or natural, it can only be seen as a *means of communication.* Indeed, one is compelled to regard it as an especially potent means of communication, *extending* enormously, if not infinitely, the domain of oral or gestural communication. This seems obvious, a matter of general agreement. I shall not describe all the *modes* of this extension in time and in space. I shall, however, pause for a moment to consider the import *[valeur]* of *extension* to which I have just referred. To say that writing extends the field and the powers of locutory or gestural communication presupposes, does it not, a sort of *homogeneous* space of communication? Of course the compass of voice or of gesture would encounter therein a factual limit, an empirical boundary of space and of time; while writing, in the same time and in the same space, would be capable of relaxing those limits and of opening the same *field* to a very much larger scope. The meaning or contents of the semantic message would thus be transmitted, *communicated,* by different *means,* by more powerful technical mediations, over a far greater distance, but still within a medium that remains fundamentally continuous and self-identical, a homogeneous element through which the unity and wholeness of meaning would not be affected in its essence. Any alteration would therefore be accidental.

The system of this interpretation (which is also, in a certain manner, *the* system of interpretation, or in any case of all hermeneutical interpretation), however currently accepted it may be, or inasmuch as it is current, like common sense, has been *represented* through the history of philosophy. I would even go so far as to say that it is the interpretation of writing that is peculiar and proper to philosophy. I shall limit myself to a single example, but I do not believe that a single counterexample can be found in the entire history of philosophy as such; I know of no analysis that contradicts, essentially, the one proposed by Condillac, under the direct influence of Warburton, in the *Essay on the Origin of Human Knowledge (Essai sur l'origine des connaissances humaines).* I have chosen this example because it contains an *explicit* reflection on the origin and function of the written text (this explicitness is not to be found in every philosophy, and the particular conditions both of its emergence and of its eclipse must be analyzed) which organizes itself here within a philosophical discourse that, in this case and throughout philosophy, presupposes the simplicity of the origin, the continuity of all derivation, of all production, of all analysis, and the homogeneity of all dimensions [ordres]. Analogy is a major concept in the thought of Condillac. I have also chosen this example because the analysis, "retracing" the origin and function of writing, is placed, in a rather uncritical manner, *under the authority of the category of communication.** If men write it is: (1) because they have to communicate; (2) because what they have to communicate is their "thought," their "ideas," their representations. Thought, as representation, precedes and governs communication, which transports the "idea," the signified content; (3) because men are *already* in a state that allows them to communicate their thought to themselves and to each other when, in a continuous manner, they invent the particular means of communication, writing. Here is a passage from chapter XIII of the Second Part ("On Language and Method"), First Section ("On the Origins and Progress of Language") (Writing is thus a modality of language and marks a continual progression in an essentially linguistic communication), paragraph XIII, "On Writing": "Men in a state of communicating their thoughts by means of sounds, felt the necessity of imagining new signs capable of perpetuating those thoughts and of making them known to persons who are *absent*" (I underscore this

---

*The Rousseauist theory of language and of writing is also introduced under the general title of *communication* ("On the diverse means of communicating our thoughts" is the title of the first chapter of the *Essay on the Origin of Languages).*

value of *absence,* which, if submitted to renewed questioning, will risk introducing a certain break in the homogeneity of the system). Once men are already in the state of "communicating their thoughts," and of doing it by means of sounds (which is, according to Condillac, a second step, when articulated language has come to "supplant" *[suppléer]* the language of action, which is the single and radical principle of all language), the birth and progress of writing will follow in a line that is direct, simple, and continuous. The history of writing will conform to a law of mechanical economy: to gain or save the most space and time possible by means of the most convenient abbreviation; hence writing will never have the slightest effect on either the structure or the contents of the meaning (the ideas) that it is supposed to transmit *[véhiculer].* The same content, formerly communicated by gestures and sounds, will henceforth be transmitted by writing, by successively different modes of notation, from pictographic writing to alphabetic writing, collaterally by the hieroglyphic writing of the Egyptians and the ideographic writing of the Chinese. Condillac continues:

> Thus, the imagination will represent to them only the very *same* images that they had already expressed through actions and words, and which had, from the very beginning, rendered language figural and metaphorical. *The most natural means* was thus to depict *[dessiner]* images of things. *To express the idea* of a man or of a horse, one represented the form of the one or of the other, and the first attempt at writing was nothing but a simple painting. (My emphasis—J.D.)

The representational character of the written communication—writing as picture, reproduction, imitation of its content—will be the invariant trait of all progress to come. The concept of *representation* is here indissociable from those of *communication* and of *expression* that I have emphasized in Condillac's text. Representation, of course, will become more complex, will develop supplementary ramifications and degrees; it will become the representation of a representation in various systems of writing, hieroglyphic, ideographic, or phonetic-alphabetical, but the representative structure which marks the first degree of expressive communication, the relation idea/sign, will never be either annulled or transformed. Describing the history of the types of writing, their continuous derivation from a common root that is never displaced and which establishes a sort of community of analogical participation among all the species of writing, Condillac concludes (in what is virtually a citation of Warburton, as is most of this chapter):

> Thus, the general history of writing proceeds by simple gradation from the state of painting to that of the letter; for letters are the final steps that are left to be taken after the Chinese marks which, on the one hand, participate in the nature of Egyptian hieroglyphics, and on the other, participate in that of letters just as the hieroglyphs participate both in Mexican paintings and Chinese characters. These characters are so close to our writing that an alphabet simply diminishes the inconvenience of their great number and is their succinct abbreviation.

Having thus confirmed the motif of economic reduction in its *homogeneous* and *mechanical* character, let us now return to the notion of *absence* that I underscored, in passing, in the text of Condillac. How is that notion determined there?

1. It is first of all the absence of the addressee. One writes in order to communicate something to those who are absent. The absence of the sender, of the receiver *[destinateur],* from the mark that he abandons, and which cuts itself off from him and continues to produce effects independently of his presence and of the present actuality

of his intentions *[vouloir-dire]*, indeed even after his death, his absence, which more-over belongs to the structure of all writing—and I shall add further on, of all language in general—this absence is not examined by Condillac.

2. The absence of which Condillac speaks is determined in the most classic man-ner as a continuous modification and progressive extenuation of presence. Representa-tion regularly *supplants [supplée]* presence. However, articulating all the moments of experience insofar as it is involved in signification ("to supplant," *suppléer*, is one of the most decisive and most frequent operational concepts in Condillac's *Essay**), this operation of supplementation is not exhibited as a break in presence but rather as a continuous and homogeneous reparation and modification of presence in the represen-tation.

I am not able to analyze, here, everything presupposed in Condillac's philosophy and elsewhere, by this concept of absence as the modification of presence. Let us note only that this concept governs another operational notion (for the sake of convenience I invoke the classical opposition between *operational* and *thematic*) which is no less de-cisive for the *Essay: tracing and retracing*. Like the concept of supplanting *[sup-pléance]*, the concept of trace would permit an interpretation quite different from Condillac's. According to him, tracing means "expressing," "representing," "recall-ing," "rendering present" ("Thus painting probably owes its origin to the necessity of tracing our thoughts in the manner described, and this necessity has doubtless con-tributed to preserving the language of action as that which is most readily depictable" ["On Writing," p. 128]). The sign comes into being at the same time as imagination and memory, the moment it is necessitated by the absence of the object from present perception *[la perception présente]* ("Memory, as we have seen, consists in nothing but the power of recalling the signs of our ideas, or the circumstances that accompa-nied them; and this power only takes place by virtue of the *analogy of the signs* [my emphasis—J.D.: this concept of analogy, which organizes the entire system of Condil-lac, provides the general guarantee of all the continuities and in particular that linking presence to absence] that we have chosen; and by the order that we have instituted among our ideas, the objects that we wish to retrace are bound up with several of our present needs." [1, 11 ch. iv, #39]). This holds true for all the orders of signs distin-guished by Condillac (arbitrary, accidental, and even natural, distinctions that Condil-lac qualifies and, on certain points, even calls into question in his letters to Cramer). The philosophical operation that Condillac also calls "retracing" consists in reversing, by a process of analysis and continuous decomposition, the movement of genetic de-rivation that leads from simple sensation and present perception to the complex edifice of representation: from ordinary presence to the language of the most formal calculus *[calcul]*.

It would be easy to demonstrate that, fundamentally, this type of analysis of writ-ten signification neither begins nor ends with Condillac. If I call this analysis "ideolog-ical," I do so neither to oppose its notions to "scientific" concepts nor to appeal to the dogmatic—one might also say ideological—usage to which the term "ideology" is often put, while seldom subjecting either the various possibilities or the history of the word to serious consideration. If I define notions such as those of Condillac as "ideo-logical" it is because, against the background *[sur le fond]* of a vast, powerful, and

---

*Language supplants action or perception: articulated language supplants the language of action: writing supplants articulated language, etc. [The word, *supplée*, used by Derrida and here by Rousseau, im-plies the double notion of supplanting, replacing, and also supplementing, bringing to completion, remedy-ing—Trans.]

systematic philosophical tradition dominated by the prominence of the *idea (eidos, idea),* they delineate the field of reflection of the French "ideologues," who in the wake of Condillac elaborated a theory of the sign as representation of the idea which itself represented the object perceived. From that point on, communication is that which circulates a representation as an ideal content (meaning); and writing is a species of this general communication. A species: a communication admitting a relative specificity within a genre.

If we now ask ourselves what, in this analysis, is the essential predicate of this *specific difference,* we rediscover *absence.*

I offer here the following two propositions or hypotheses:

1. since every sign, whether in the "language of action" or in articulated language (before even the intervention of writing in the classical sense), presupposes a certain absence (to be determined), the absence within the particular field of writing will have to be of an original type if one intends to grant any specificity whatsoever to the written sign;

2. if perchance the predicate thus introduced to characterize the absence peculiar and proper to writing were to find itself no less appropriate to every species of sign and of communication, the consequence would be a general shift; writing would no longer be one species of communication, and all the concepts to whose generality writing had been subordinated (including the *concept* itself qua meaning, idea or grasp of meaning and of idea, the concept of communication, of the sign, etc.) would appear to be non-critical, ill-formed, or destined, rather, to insure the authority and the force of a certain historical discourse.

Let us attempt, then, while still continuing to take this classical discourse as our point of departure, to characterize the absence that seems to intervene in a specific manner in the functioning of writing.

A written sign is proffered in the absence of the receiver. How to style this absence? One could say that at the moment when I am writing, the receiver may be absent from my field of present perception. But is not this absence merely a distant presence, one which is delayed or which, in one form or another, is idealized in its representation? This does not seem to be the case, or at least this distance, divergence, delay, this deferral *[différance]* must be capable of being carried to a certain absoluteness of absence if the structure of writing, assuming that writing exists, is to constitute itself. It is at that point that the *différance* [difference and deferral, *trans.*] as writing could no longer (be) an (ontological) modification of presence. In order for my "written communication" to retain its function as writing, i.e., its readability, it must remain readable despite the absolute disappearance of any receiver, determined in general. My communication must be repeatable—iterable—in the absolute absence of the receiver or of any empirically determinable collectivity of receivers. Such iterability—(iter, again, probably comes from *itara, other* in Sanskrit, and everything that follows can be read as the working out of the logic that ties repetition to alterity) structures the mark of writing itself, no matter what particular type of writing is involved (whether pictographical, hieroglyphic, ideographic, phonetic, alphabetic, to cite the old categories). A writing that is not structurally readable—iterable—beyond the death of the addressee would not be writing. Although this would seem to be obvious, I do not want it accepted as such, and I shall examine the final objection that could be made to this proposition. Imagine a writing whose code would be so idiomatic as to be established and known, as secret cipher, by only two "subjects." Could we maintain that, following the death of the receiver, or even of both partners, the mark left by one of them is still writing? Yes, to the extent that, organized by a code, even an unknown and nonlinguistic one, it is constituted in its identity as a mark by its iterability, in the absence of such and such a person, and hence ultimately of every empirically determined "subject." This implies that there is no such thing as a code organon of iterability—which could be structurally secret. The possibility of repeating and thus of identifying the marks is implicit in every code, making it into a network *[une grille]* that is communicable, transmittable, decipherable, iterable for a third, and hence for every possible user in general. To be what it is, all writing must, therefore, be capable of functioning in the radical absence of every empirically determined receiver in general. And this absence is not a continuous modification of presence, it is a rupture in presence, the "death" or the possibility of the "death" of the receiver inscribed in the structure of the mark (I note in passing that this is the point where the value or the "effect" of transcendentality is linked necessarily to the possibility of writing and of "death" as analyzed). The perhaps paradoxical consequence of my here having recourse to iteration and to code: the disruption, in the last analysis, of the authority of the code as a finite system of rules; at the same time, the radical destruction of any context as the protocol of code. We will come to this in a moment.

What holds for the receiver holds also, for the same reasons, for the sender or the producer. To write is to produce a mark that will constitute a sort of machine which is productive in turn, and which my future disappearance will not, in principle, hinder in its functioning, offering things and itself to be read and to be rewritten. When I say "my future disappearance" *[disparition:* also, demise, *trans.],* it is in order to render this proposition more immediately acceptable. I ought to be able to say my disappearance, pure and simple, my nonpresence in general, for instance the nonpresence of my intention of saying something meaningful *[mon vouloir-dire, mon intention-designification],* of my wish to communicate, from the emission or production of the mark. For a writing to be a writing it must continue to "act" and to be readable even when what is called the author of the writing no longer answers for what he has written, for what he seems to have signed, be it because of a temporary absence, because he is dead or, more generally, because he has not employed his absolutely actual and present intention or attention, the plenitude of his desire to say what he means, in order to sustain what seems to be written "in his name." One could repeat at this point the analysis outlined above this time with regard to the addressee. The situation of the writer and of the underwriter *[du souscripteur:* the signatory, *trans.]* is, concerning the written text, basically the same as that of the reader. This essential drift *[dérive]* bearing on writing as an iterative structure, cut off from all absolute responsibility, from *consciousness* as the ultimate authority, orphaned and separated at birth from the assistance of its father, is precisely what Plato condemns in the *Phaedrus.* If Plato's gesture is, as I believe, the philosophical movement par excellence, one can measure what is at stake here.

Before elaborating more precisely the inevitable consequences of these nuclear traits of all writing—that is: (1) the break with the horizon of communication as communication of consciousnesses or of presences and as linguistical or semantic transport of the desire to mean what one says *[vouloir-dire];* (2) the disengagement of all writing from the semantic or hermeneutic horizons which, inasmuch as they are horizons of meaning, are riven *[crever]* by writing; (3) the necessity of disengaging from the concept of polysemics what I have elsewhere called *dissemination,* which is also the concept of writing; (4) the disqualification or the limiting of the concept of context, whether "real" or "linguistic," inasmuch as its rigorous theoretical determination as well as its empirical saturation is rendered impossible or insufficient by writing—I would like to demonstrate that the traits that can be recognized in the classical, narrowly defined concept of writing, are generalizable. They are valid not only for all orders of "signs" and for all languages in general but moreover, beyond semio-linguistic communication, for the entire field of what philosophy would call experience, even the experience of being: the above-mentioned "presence."

What are in effect the essential predicates in a minimal determination of the classical concept of writing?

1. A written sign, in the current meaning of this word, is a mark that subsists, one which does not exhaust itself in the moment of its inscription and which can give rise to an iteration in the absence and beyond the presence of the empirically determined subject who, in a given context, has emitted or produced it. This is what has enabled us, at least traditionally, to distinguish a "written" from an "oral" communication.

2. At the same time, a written sign carries with it a force that breaks with its context, that is, with the collectivity of presences organizing the moment of its inscription. This breaking force *[force de rupture]* is not an accidental predicate but the very structure of the written text. In the case of a so-called "real" context, what I have just asserted is all too evident. This allegedly real context includes a certain "present" of the inscription, the presence of the writer to what he has written, the entire environment and the horizon of his experience, and above all the intention, the wanting-to-say-what-he-means, which animates his inscription at a given moment. But the sign possesses the characteristic of being readable even if the moment of its production is irrevocably lost and even if I do not know what its alleged author-scriptor consciously intended to say at the moment he wrote it, i.e. abandoned it to its essential drift. As far as the internal semiotic context is concerned, the force of the rupture is no less important: by virtue of its essential iterability, a written syntagma can always be detached from the chain in which it is inserted or given without causing it to lose all possibility of functioning, if not all possibility of "communicating," precisely. One can perhaps come to recognize other possibilities in it by inscribing it *grafting* it onto other chains. No context can entirely enclose it. Nor any code, the code here being both the possibility and impossibility of writing, of its essential iterability (repetition alterity).

3. This force of rupture is tied to the spacing *[espacement]* that constitutes the written sign: spacing which separates it from other elements of the internal contextual chain (the always open possibility of its disengagement and graft), but also from all forms of present reference (whether past or future in the modified form of the present that is past or to come), objective or subjective. This spacing is not the simple negativity of a lacuna but rather the emergence of the mark. It does not remain, however, as the labor of the negative in the service of meaning, of the living concept, of the *telos,* supersedable and reducible in the *Aufhebung* of a dialectic.

Are these three predicates, together with the entire system they entail, limited, as is often believed, strictly to "written" communication in the narrow sense of this word? Are they not to be found in all language, in spoken language for instance, and ultimately in the totality of "experience" insofar as it is inseparable from this field of the mark, which is to say, from the network of effacement and of difference, of units of iterability, which are separable from their internal and external context and also from themselves, inasmuch as the very iterability which constituted their identity does not permit them ever to be a unity that is identical to itself?

Let us consider any element of spoken language, be it a small or large unit. The first condition of its functioning is its delineation with regard to a certain code; but I prefer not to become too involved here with this concept of code which does not seem very reliable to me; let us say that a certain self-identity of this element (mark, sign, etc.) is required to permit its recognition and repetition. Through empirical variations of tone, voice, etc., possibly of a certain accent, for example, we must be able to recognize the identity, roughly speaking, of a signifying form. Why is this identity paradoxically the division or dissociation of itself, which will make of this phonic sign a grapheme? Because this unity of the signifying form only constitutes itself by virtue of its iterability, by the possibility of its being repeated in the absence not only of its "referent," which is self-evident, but in the absence of a determinate signified or of the intention of actual signification, as well as of all intention of present communication. This structural possibility of being weaned from the referent or from the signified (hence from communication and from its context) seems to me to make every mark, including those which are oral, a grapheme in general; which is to say, as we have seen, the nonpresent *remainder [restance]* of a differential mark cut off from its putative "production" or origin. And I shall even extend this law to all "experience" in general if it is conceded that there is no experience consisting of pure presence but only of chains of differential marks.

Let us dwell for a moment on this point and return to that absence of the referent and even of the signified meaning, and hence of the correlative intention to signify. The absence of referent is a possibility easily enough admitted today. This possibility is not only an empirical eventuality. It constructs the mark; and the potential presence of the referent at the moment it is designated does not modify in the slightest the structure of the mark, which implies that the mark can do without the referent. Husserl, in his *Logical Investigations,* analyzed this possibility very rigorously, and in a two-fold manner:

1. An utterance *[énoncé]* whose object is not impossible but only possible can very well be made and understood without its real object (its referent) being present, either to the person who produced the statement or to the one who receives it. If while looking out the window, I say: "The sky is blue," this utterance will be intelligible (let us say, provisionally if you like, communicable) even if the interlocutor does not see the sky; even if I do not see it myself, if I see it badly, if I am mistaken or if I wish to mislead my interlocutor. Not that this is always the case; but the structure of possibility of this utterance includes the capability to be formed and to function as a reference that is empty or cut off from its referent. Without this possibility, which is also that of iterability in general, "generable," and generative of all marks, there would be no utterance.

2. The absence of the signified. Husserl analyzes this as well. He judges it to be always possible even if, according to the axiology and teleology that governs his analysis, he judges this possibility to be inferior, dangerous, or "critical": it opens the phenomenon of the crisis of meaning. This absence of meaning can take three forms:

A. I can manipulate symbols without animating them, in an active and actual manner, with the attention and intention of signification (crisis of mathematical symbolism, according to Husserl). Husserl insists on the fact that this does not prevent the sign from functioning: the crisis or the emptiness of mathematical meaning does not limit its technical progress (the intervention of writing is decisive here, as Husserl himself remarks in *The Origin of Geometry*).

B. Certain utterances can have a meaning although they are deprived of *objective* signification. "The circle is squared" is a proposition endowed with meaning. It has sufficient meaning at least for me to judge it false or contradictory (*widersinnig* and not *sinnlos,* Husserl says). I place this example under the category of the absence of the signified, although in this case the tripartite division into signifier/signified/referent is not adequate to a discussion of the Husserlian analysis. "Squared circle" marks the absence of a referent, certainly, as well as that of a certain signified, but not the absence of meaning. In these two cases, the crisis of meaning (nonpresence in general, absence as the absence of the referent—of the perception—or of the meaning—of the intention of actual signification) is still bound to the essential possibility of writing; and this crisis is not an accident, a factual and empirical anomaly of spoken language, it is also its positive possibility and its "internal" structure, in the form of a certain outside *[dehors]*.

C. Finally there is what Husserl calls *Sinnlosigkeit* or agrammaticality. For instance, "the green is either" or "abracadabra" *[le vert est ou; the ambiguity of ou or où is noted below, trans.]*. In such cases Husserl considers that there is no language any more, or at least no "logical" language, no cognitive language such as Husserl construes in a teleological manner, no language accorded the possibility of the intuition of objects given in person and signified in *truth*. We are confronted here with a decisive difficulty. Before stopping to deal with it, I note a point that touches our discussion of communication, namely that the primary interest of the Husserlian analysis to which I am referring here (while precisely detaching it up to a certain point, from its context or its teleological and metaphysical horizon, an operation which itself ought to provoke us to ask how and why it is always possible), is its claim rigorously to dissociate (not without a certain degree of success) from every phenomenon of communication the analysis of the sign or the expression *(Ausdruck)* as signifying sign, the seeking to say something *(bedeutsames Zeichen).**

Let us return to the case of agrammatical *Sinnlosigkeit*. What interests Husserl in the *Logical Investigations* is the system of rules of a universal grammar, not from a linguistic point of view but from a logical and epistemological one. In an important note to the second edition,** he specifies that his concern is with a pure *logical* grammar, that is, with the universal conditions of possibility for a morphology of significations in their cognitive relation to a possible object, not with a pure grammar in *general*, considered from a psychological or linguistic point of view. Thus, it is solely in a context determined by a will to know, by an epistemic intention, by a conscious relation to the object as cognitive object within a horizon of truth, solely in this oriented contextual field is "the green is either" unacceptable. But as "the green is either" or "abracadabra" do not constitute their context by themselves, nothing prevents them from functioning in another context as signifying marks (or indices, as Husserl would say). Not only in contingent cases such as a translation from German into French, which would endow "the green is either" with grammaticality, since "either" *[oder]* becomes for the ear "where" *[où]* (a spatial mark). "Where has the green gone (of the lawn: the green is where)," "Where is the glass gone in which I wanted to give you something to drink?" *["Où est passé le verre dans lequel je voulais vous donner à boire?"]* But even "the

---

*"Up to now, we have considered expressions in their communicative function. This derives essentially from the fact that expressions operate as indexes. But a large role is also assigned to expressions in the life of the soul inasmuch as it is not engaged in a relation of communication. It is clear that this modification of the function does not affect what makes expressions expressions. They have, as before, their *Bedeutungen* and the same *Bedeutungen* as in collocution" (*Logical Investigations* I, ch. 1, #8). What I assert here implies the interpretation that I have offered of the Husserlian procedure on this point. I therefore refer the reader to *Speech and Phenomena (La voix et le phénomène)*.

**"In the first edition I spoke of 'pure grammar,' a name that was conceived on the analogy of 'pure science of nature' in Kant, and expressly designated as such. But to the extent that it cannot be affirmed that the pure morphology of *Bedeutungen* englobes all grammatical a prioris in their universality, since for example relations of communication between psychic subjects, which are so important for grammar, entail their own *a prioris*, the expression of *pure logical grammar* deserves priority" (*LI* II, part 2, ch. iv).

green is either" itself still signifies an *example of agrammaticality*. And this is the possibility on which I want to insist: the possibility of disengagement and citational graft which belongs to the structure of every mark, spoken or written, and which constitutes every mark in writing before and outside of every horizon of semio-linguistic communication; in writing, which is to say in the possibility of its functioning being cut off, at a certain point, from its "original" desire-to-say-what-one-means *[vouloir-dire]* and from its participation in a saturable and constraining context. Every sign, linguistic or nonlinguistic, spoken or written (in the current sense of this opposition), in a small or large unit, can be cited, put between quotation marks; in so doing it can break with every given context, engendering an infinity of new contexts in a manner which is absolutely illimitable. This does not imply that the mark is valid outside of a context, but on the contrary that there are only contexts without any center or absolute anchoring *[ancrage]*. This citationality, this duplication or duplicity, this iterability of the mark is neither an accident nor an anomaly, it is that (normal/abnormal) without which a mark could not even have a function called "normal." What would a mark be that could not be cited? Or one whose origins would not get lost along the way?

Parasites. Iter, of Writing: That It Perhaps Does Not Exist

I now propose to elaborate a bit further this question with special attention to but in order, as well, to pass beyond—the problematic of the performative. It concerns us here for several reasons:

1. First of all, Austin, through his emphasis on an analysis of perlocution and above all of illocution, appears to consider speech acts only as acts of communication. The author of the introduction to the French edition of *How To Do Things With Words,* quoting Austin, notes as much: "It is by comparing constative utterances (i.e., classical 'assertions,' generally considered as true or false 'descriptions' of facts) with performative utterances (from the English 'performative,' i.e., allowing to accomplish something through speech itself) that Austin is led to consider every utterance worthy of the name (i.e., intended to communicate—thus excluding, for example, reflex-exclamations) as being primarily and above all a speech act produced in the total situation in which the interlocutors find themselves" (*How To Do Things With Words,* p. 147, G. Lane, Introduction to the French translation, p. 19).

2. This category of communication is relatively new. Austin's notions of illocution and perlocution do not designate the transference or passage of a thought-content, but, in some way, the communication of an original movement (to be defined within a *general theory of action*), an operation and the production of an effect. Communicating, in the case of the performative, if such a thing, in all rigor and in all purity, should exist (for the moment, I am working within that hypothesis and at that stage of the analysis), would be tantamount to communicating a force through the impetus *[impulsion]* of a mark.

3. As opposed to the classical assertion, to the constative utterance, the performative does not have its referent (but here that word is certainly no longer appropriate, and this precisely is the interest of the discovery) outside of itself or, in any event, before and in front of itself. It does not describe something that exists outside of language and prior to it. It produces or transforms a situation, it effects; and even if it can be said that a constative utterance also effectuates something and always transforms a situation, it cannot be maintained that that constitutes its internal structure, its manifest function or destination, as in the case of the performative.

4. Austin was obliged to free the analysis of the performative from the authority of the truth *value,* from the true/false opposition,* at least in its classical form, and to substitute for it at times the value of force, of difference of force (*illocutionary* or *perlocutionary* force). (In this line of thought, which is nothing less than Nietzschean, this in particular strikes me as moving in the direction of Nietzsche himself, who often acknowledged a certain affinity for a vein of English thought.)

For these four reasons, at least, it might seem that Austin has shattered the concept of communication as a purely semiotic, linguistic, or symbolic concept. The performative is a "communication" which is not limited strictly to the transference of a semantic content that is already constituted and dominated by an orientation toward truth (be it the *unveiling* of what is in its being or the *adequation-congruence* between a judicative utterance and the thing itself).

And yet—such at least is what I should like to attempt to indicate now—all the difficulties encountered by Austin in an analysis which is patient, open, aporetical, in constant transformation, often more fruitful in the acknowledgment of its impasses than in its positions, strike me as having a common root. Austin has not taken into account of what—in the structure of *locution* (thus before any illocutory or perlocutory determination)—already entails that system of predicates I call *graphematic in general* and consequently blurs *[brouille]* all the oppositions which follow, oppositions whose pertinence, purity, and rigor Austin has unsuccessfully attempted to establish.

In order to demonstrate this, I shall take for granted the fact that Austin's analyses at all times require a value of *context,* and even of a context exhaustively determined, in theory or teleologically; the long list of "infelicities" which in their variety may affect the performative event always comes back to an element in what Austin calls the total context.** One of those essential elements—and not one among others—remains, classically, consciousness, the conscious presence of the intention of the speaking subject in the totality of his speech act. As a result, performative communication becomes once more the communication of an intentional meaning,*** even if that meaning has no referent in the form of a thing or of a prior or exterior state of things. The conscious presence of speakers or receivers participating in the accomplishment of a performative, their conscious and intentional presence in the totality of the operation, implies teleologically that no *residue [reste]* escapes the present totalization. No residue, either in the definition of the requisite conventions, or in the internal and linguistic context, or in the grammatical form, or in the semantic determination of the words employed; no irreducible polysemy, that is, no "dissemination" escaping the horizon of the unity of meaning. I quote from the first two lectures of *How To Do Things With Words:*

> Speaking generally, it is always necessary that the *circumstances* in which the words are uttered should be in some way, or ways, *appropriate,* and it is very commonly necessary that either the speaker himself or other persons should *also* perform certain *other* actions, whether "physical" or "mental" actions or even acts of uttering further words. Thus, for

---

*Austin names the "two fetishes which I admit to an inclination to play Old Harry with, viz. (1) the true/false fetish, (2) the value/fact fetish" (p. 150).

**He says, for example, that "The total speech act in the total speech situation is the *only actual* phenomenon which, in the last resort, we are engaged in elucidating" (p. 147).

***Which occasionally requires Austin to reintroduce the criterion of truth in his description of performatives. Cf., for example, pp. 50–52 and pp. 89–90.

naming the ship, it is essential that I should be the person appointed to name her, for (Christian) marrying, it is essential that I should not be already married with a wife living, sane and undivorced, and so on; for a bet to have been made, it is generally necessary for the offer of the bet to have been accepted by a taker (who must have done something, such as to say "Done"), and it is hardly a gift if I *say* "I give it you" but never hand it over.

So far, well and good. (pp. 8–9)

In the Second Lecture, after eliminating the grammatical criterion in his customary manner, Austin examines the possibility and the origin of failures or "infelicities" of performative utterance. He then defines the six indispensable—if not sufficient conditions of success. Through the values of "conventional procedure," "correctness," and "completeness," which occur in the definition, we necessarily find once more those of an exhaustively definable context, of a free consciousness present to the totality of the operation, and of absolutely meaningful speech *[vouloir-dire]* master of itself: the teleological jurisdiction of an entire field whose organizing center remains *intention.** Austin's procedure is rather remarkable and typical of that philosophical tradition with which he would like to have so few ties. It consists in recognizing that the possibility of the negative (in this case, of infelicities) is in fact a structural possibility, that failure is an essential risk of the operations under consideration; then, in a move which is almost *immediately simultaneous,* in the name of a kind of ideal regulation, it excludes that risk as accidental, exterior, one which teaches us nothing about the linguistic phenomenon being considered. This is all the more curious—and, strictly speaking, untenable—in view of Austin's ironic denunciation of the "fetishized" opposition: *value/fact.*

Thus, for example, concerning the conventionality without which there is no performative, Austin acknowledges that *all* conventional acts are exposed to failure: "it seems clear in the first place that, although it has excited us (or failed to excite us) in connexion with certain acts which are or are in part acts of *uttering words,* infelicity is an ill to which *all* acts are heir which have the general character of ritual or ceremonial, all *conventional* acts: not indeed that *every* ritual is liable to every form of infelicity (but then nor is every performative utterance)" (pp. 18–19, Austin's emphasis [reprinted p. 316 in this volume]).

In addition to the questions posed by a notion as historically sedimented as "convention," it should be noted at this point:

1. that Austin, at this juncture, appears to consider solely the conventionality constituting the *circumstance* of the utterance *[énoncé],* its contextual surroundings, and not a certain conventionality intrinsic to what constitutes the speech act *[locution]* itself, all that might be summarized rapidly under the problematical rubric of "the arbitrary nature of the sign," which extends, aggravates, and radicalizes the difficulty. "Ritual" is not a possible occurrence *[éventualité],* but rather, as iterability, a structural characteristic of every mark.

2. that the value of risk or exposure to infelicity, even though, as Austin recognizes, it can affect *a priori* the totality of conventional acts, is not interrogated as an essential predicate or as a *law.* Austin does not ponder the consequences issuing from the fact that a possibility—a possible risk—is *always* possible, and is in some sense a necessary possibility. Nor whether—once such a necessary possibility of infelicity is

*Pp. 10–15.

recognized—infelicity still constitutes an accident. What is a success when the possibility of infelicity *[échec]* continues to constitute its structure?

The opposition success/failure *[échec]* in illocution and in perlocution thus seems quite insufficient and extremely secondary *[dérivée]*. It presupposes a general and systematic elaboration of the structure of locution that would avoid an endless alternation of essence and accident. Now it is highly significant that Austin rejects and defers that "general theory" on at least two occasions, specifically in the Second Lecture. I leave aside the first exclusion.

> I am not going into the general doctrine here: in many such cases we may even say the act was "void" (or voidable for duress or undue influence) and so forth. Now I suppose some very general high-level doctrine might embrace both what we have called infelicities *and* these other "unhappy" features of the doing of actions—in our case actions containing a performative utterance—in a single doctrine: but we are not including this kind of unhappiness—we must just remember, though, that features of this sort can and do constantly obtrude into any case we are discussing. Features of this sort would normally come under the heading of "extenuating circumstances" or of "factors reducing or abrogating the agent's responsibility," and so on. (p. 21, my emphasis)

The second case of this exclusion concerns our subject more directly. It involves precisely the possibility for every performative utterance (and *a priori* every other utterance) to be "quoted." Now Austin excludes this possibility (and the general theory which would account for it) with a kind of lateral insistence, all the more significant in its off-handedness. He insists on the fact that this possibility remains *abnormal,* parasitic, that it constitutes a kind of extenuation or agonized succumbing of language that we should strenuously distance ourselves from and resolutely ignore. And the concept of the "ordinary," thus of "ordinary language," to which he has recourse is clearly marked by this exclusion. As a result, the concept becomes all the more problematical, and before demonstrating as much, it would no doubt be best for me simply to read a paragraph from the Second Lecture:

> (ii) Secondly, as *utterances* our performances are *also* heir to certain other kinds of ill, which infect *all* utterances. And these likewise, though again they might be brought into a more general account, we are deliberately at present excluding. I mean, for example, the following: a performative utterance will, for example, be *in a peculiar way* hollow or void if said by an actor on the stage, or if introduced in a poem, or spoken in soliloquy. This applies in a similar manner to any and every utterance—a sea-change in special circumstances. Language in such circumstances is in special ways—intelligibly-used not *seriously* [my emphasis, J.D.], but in many ways *parasitic* upon its normal use—ways which fall under the doctrine of the *etiolations* of language. All this we are *excluding* from consideration. Our performative utterances, felicitous or not, are to be understood as issued in ordinary circumstances. (pp. 21–22 [reprinted pp. 317–318 in this volume].)

Austin thus excludes, along with what he calls a "sea-change," the "non-serious," "parasitism," "etiolation," "the non-ordinary" (along with the whole general theory which, if it succeeded in accounting for them, would no longer be governed by those oppositions), all of which he nevertheless recognizes as the possibility available to every act of utterance. It is as just such a "parasite" that writing has always been treated by the philosophical tradition, and the connection in this case is by no means coincidental.

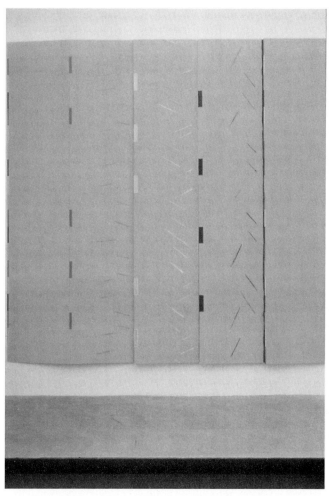

Open Warfare, 1991, by Jeremy Gilbert-Rolfe. Derrida holds that the limits
or frame of a given piece defines an inside and an outside but also "permits,
and even encourages, a complicated movement or passage across it both
from inside-out and outside-in" (from David Carroll, *Paraesthetics:
Foucault, Lyotard, Derrida* (New York: Methuen, 1987), p. 136). Gilbert-
Rolfe's painting exemplifies this deferral of meaning as its pattern suggests
a continuation beyond itself. *(Jeremy Gilbert-Rolfe)*

I would therefore pose the following question: is this general possibility necessarily one of a failure or trap into which language may *fall* or lose itself as in an abyss
situated outside of or in front of itself? What is the status of this *parasitism?* In other
words, does the quality of risk admitted by Austin surround language like a kind of
ditch or external place of perdition which speech *[la locution]* could never hope to
leave, but which it can escape by remaining "at home," by and in itself, in the shelter
of its essence or *telos?* Or, on the contrary, is this risk rather its internal and positive

condition of possibility? Is that outside its inside, the very force and law of its emer-gence? In this last case, what would be meant by an "ordinary" language defined by the exclusion of the very law of language? In excluding the general theory of this struc-tural parasitism, does not Austin, who nevertheless claims to describe the facts and events of ordinary language, pass off as ordinary an ethical and teleological determina-tion (the univocity of the utterance [énoncé]—that he acknowledges elsewhere [pp. 72–73] remains a philosophical "ideal"—the presence to self of a total context, the transparency of intentions, the presence of meaning [vouloir-dire] to the absolutely singular uniqueness of a speech act, etc.)?

For, ultimately, isn't it true that what Austin excludes as anomaly, exception, "nonserious,"* citation (on stage, in a poem, or a soliloquy) is the determined modifi-cation of a general citationality or rather, a general iterability—without which there would not even be a "successful" performative? So that—a paradoxical but unavoid-able conclusion—a successful performative is necessarily an "impure" performative, to adopt the word advanced later on by Austin when he acknowledges that there is no "pure" performative.**

I take things up here from the perspective of positive possibility and not simply as instances of failure or infelicity: would a performative utterance be possible if a ci-tational doubling [doublure] did not come to split and dissociate from itself the pure singularity of the event? I pose the question in this form in order to prevent an objec-tion. For it might be said: you cannot claim to account for the so-called graphematic structure of locution merely on the basis of the occurrence of failures of the performa-tive, however real those failures may be and however effective or general their possi-bility. You cannot deny that there are also performatives that succeed, and one has to account for them: meetings are called to order (Paul Ricoeur did as much yesterday); people say: "I pose a question"; they bet, challenge, christen ships, and sometimes even marry. It would seem that such events have occurred. And even if only one had taken place only once, we would still be obliged to account for it.

I'll answer: "Perhaps." We should first be clear on what constitutes the status of "occurrence" or the eventhood of an event that entails in its allegedly present and sin-gular emergence the intervention of an utterance [énoncé] that in itself can be only repetitive or citational in its structure, or rather, since those two words may lead to confusion: iterable. I return then to a point that strikes me as fundamental and that now concerns the status of events in general, of events of speech or by speech, of the strange logic they entail and that often passes unseen.

Could a performative utterance succeed if its formulation did not repeat a "coded" or iterable utterance, or in other words, if the formula I pronounce in order to open a meeting, launch a ship or a marriage were not identifiable as conforming with an iterable model, if it were not then identifiable in some way as a "citation"? Not that citationality in this case is of the same sort as in a theatrical play, a philosophical refer-ence, or the recitation of a poem. That is why there is a relative specificity, as Austin says, a "relative purity" of performatives. But this relative purity does not emerge in

---

*Austin often refers to the suspicious status of the "non-serious" (cf., for example, pp. 104, 121). This is fundamentally linked to what he says elsewhere about oratio obliqua (pp. 70–71) and mime.

**From this standpoint, one might question the fact, recognized by Austin, that "very commonly the same sentence is used on different occasions of utterance in both ways, performative and constative. The thing seems hopeless from the start, if we are to leave utterances as they stand and seek for a crite-rion." The graphematic root of citationality (iterability) is what creates this embarrassment and makes it impossible, as Austin says, "to lay down even a list of all possible criteria."

opposition to citationality or iterability, but in opposition to other kinds of iteration within a general iterability which constitutes a violation of the allegedly rigorous purity of every event of discourse or every *speech act.* Rather than oppose citation or iteration to the noniteration of an event, one ought to construct a differential typology of forms of iteration, assuming that such a project is tenable and can result in an exhaustive program, a question I hold in abeyance here. In such a typology, the category of intention will not disappear; it will have its place, but from that place it will no longer be able to govern the entire scene and system of utterances *[l'enonciation].* Above all, at that point, we will be dealing with different kinds of marks or chains of iterable marks and not with an opposition between citational utterances, on the one hand, and singular and original event-utterances, on the other. The first consequence of this will be the following: given that structure of iteration, the intention animating the utterance will never be through and through present to itself and to its content. The iteration structuring it *a priori* introduces into it a dehiscence and a cleft *[brisure]* which are essential. The "non-serious," the *oratio obliqua* will no longer be able to be excluded, as Austin wished, from "ordinary" language. And if one maintains that such ordinary language, or the ordinary circumstances of language, excludes a general citationality or iterability, does that not mean that the "ordinariness" in question—the thing and the notion—shelter a lure, the teleological lure of consciousness (whose motivations, indestructible necessity, and systematic effects would be subject to analysis)? Above all, this essential absence of intending the actuality of utterance, this structural unconsciousness, if you like, prohibits any saturation of the context. In order for a context to be exhaustively determinable, in the sense required by Austin, conscious intention would at the very least have to be totally present and immediately transparent to itself and to others, since it is a determining center *[foyer]* of context. The concept of or the search for—the context thus seems to suffer at this point from the same theoretical and "interested" uncertainty as the concept of the "ordinary," from the same metaphysical origins: the ethical and teleological discourse of consciousness. A reading of the connotations, this time, of Austin's text, would confirm the reading of the descriptions; I have just indicated its principle.

Différance, the irreducible absence of intention or attendance to the performative utterance, the most "event-ridden" utterance there is, is what authorizes me, taking account of the predicates just recalled, to posit the general graphematic structure of every "communication." By no means do I draw the conclusion that there is no relative specificity of effects of consciousness, or of effects of speech (as opposed to writing in the traditional sense), that there is no performative effect, no effect of ordinary language, no effect of presence or of discursive event (speech act). It is simply that those effects do not exclude what is generally opposed to them, term by term; on the contrary, they presuppose it, in an asymmetrical way, as the general space of their possibility.

SIGNATURES

That general space is first of all spacing as a disruption of presence in a mark, what I here call writing. That all the difficulties encountered by Austin intersect in the place where both writing and presence are in question is for me indicated in a passage such as that in Lecture V in which the divided instance of the juridic signature *[seing]* emerges.

Is it an accident if Austin is there obliged to note: "I must explain again that we are floundering here. To feel the firm ground of prejudice slipping away is exhilarating, but brings its revenges" (p. 61). Shortly before, an "impasse" had appeared, resulting from the search for "any *single simple* criterion of grammar and vocabulary" in distinguishing between performative or constative utterances. (I should say that it is this critique of linguisticism and of the authority of the code, a critique based on an analysis of language, that most interested and convinced me in Austin's undertaking.) He then attempts to justify, with nonlinguistic reasons, the preference he has shown in the analysis of performatives for the forms of the first person, the present indicative, the active voice. The justification, in the final instance, is the reference made therein to what Austin calls the *source* (p. 60)* of the utterance. This notion of *source*—and what is at stake in it is clear—frequently reappears in what follows and governs the entire analysis in the phase we are examining. Not only does Austin not doubt that the source of an oral utterance in the present indicative active is *present* to the utterance *[énonciation]* and its statement *[énoncé]* (I have attempted to explain why we had reasons not to believe so), but he does not even doubt that the equivalent of this tie to the source utterance is simply evident in and assured by a *signature:*

> Where there is *not,* in the verbal formula of the utterance, a reference to the person doing the uttering, and so the acting, by means of the pronoun "I" (or by his personal name), then in fact he will be "referred to" in one of two ways:
>   (a) In verbal utterances, *by his being the person who does* the uttering—what we may call the utterance-*origin* which is used generally in any system of verbal reference-coordinates.
>   (b) In written utterances (or "inscriptions"), *by his appending his signature* (this has to be done because, of course, written utterances are not tethered to their origin in the way spoken ones are). (pp. 60–61)

An analogous function is attributed by Austin to the formula "hereby" in official documents.

From this point of view, let us attempt to analyze signatures, their relation to the present and to the source. I shall consider it as an implication of the analysis that every predicate established will be equally valid for that oral "signature" constituted—or aspired to—by the presence of the "author" as a "person who utters," as a "source," to the production of the utterance.

By definition, a written signature implies the actual or empirical nonpresence of the signer. But, it will be claimed, the signature also marks and retains his having-been present in a past now or present *[maintenant]* which will remain a future *now* or present *[maintenant]*, thus in a general *maintenant,* in the transcendental form of presentness *[maintenance]*. That general *maintenance* is in some way inscribed, pinpointed in the always evident and singular present punctuality of the form of the signature. Such is the enigmatic originality of every paraph. In order for the tethering to the source to occur, what must be retained is the absolute singularity of a signature-event and a signature-form: the pure reproducibility of a pure event.

---

*[Austin's term is "utterance origin"; Derrida's term (source) is hereafter translated as "source."— Trans.]

Is there such a thing? Does the absolute singularity of signature as event ever occur? Are there signatures?

Yes, of course, every day. Effects of signature are the most common thing in the world. But the condition of possibility of those effects is simultaneously, once again, the condition of their impossibility, of the impossibility of their rigorous purity. In order to function, that is, to be readable, a signature must have a repeatable, iterable, imitable form; it must be able to be detached from the present and singular intention of its production. It is its sameness which, by corrupting its identity and its singularity, divides its seal *[sceau]*. I have already indicated above the principle of this analysis.

To conclude this very *dry** discussion:

1. as writing, communication, if we retain that word, is not the means of transference of meaning, the exchange of intentions and meanings *[vouloir-dire]*, discourse and the "communication of consciousnesses." We are witnessing not an end of writing that would restore, in accord with McLuhan's ideological representation, a transparency or an immediacy to social relations; but rather the increasingly powerful historical expansion of a general writing, of which the system of speech, consciousness, meaning, presence, truth, etc., would be only an effect, and should be analyzed as such. It is the exposure of this effect that I have called elsewhere logocentrism;

2. the semantic horizon that habitually governs the notion of communication is exceeded or split by the intervention of writing, that is, by a dissemination irreducible to *polysemy*. Writing is read; it is not the site, "in the last instance," of a hermeneutic deciphering, the decoding of a meaning or truth;

3. despite the general displacement of the classical, "philosophical," occidental concept of writing, it seems necessary to retain, provisionally and strategically, the old name. This entails an entire logic of *paleonymics* that I cannot develop here.** Very schematically: an opposition of metaphysical concepts (e.g., speech/writing, presence/absence, etc.) is never the confrontation of two terms, but a hierarchy and the order of a subordination. Deconstruction cannot be restricted or immediately pass to a neutralization: it must, through a double gesture, a double science, a double writing— put into practice a reversal of the classical opposition *and* a general *displacement* of the system. It is on that condition alone that deconstruction will provide the means of *intervening* in the field of oppositions it criticizes and that is also a field of nondiscursive forces. Every concept, moreover, belongs to a systematic chain and constitutes in itself a system of predicates. There is no concept that is metaphysical in itself. There is a labor—metaphysical or not—performed on conceptual systems. Deconstruction does not consist in moving from one concept to another, but in reversing and displacing a conceptual order as well as the nonconceptual order with which it is articulated. For example, writing, as a classical concept, entails predicates that have been subordinated, excluded, or held in abeyance by forces and according to necessities to be analyzed. It is those predicates (I have recalled several of them) whose force of generality, generalization, and generativity is liberated, grafted onto a "new" concept of writing that corresponds as well to what has always *resisted* the prior organization of forces, always constituted the *residue* irreducible to the dominant force organizing the hierarchy that we may refer to, in brief, as logocentric. To leave to this new concept the old name of

---

*[The French word for dry here is sec which combines the initial letters of Derrida's three word title: Signature, Event, Context.]

**Cf. La dissémination and Positions.

.s tantamount to maintaining the structure of the *graft,* the transition and indis-
.e adherence to an effective *intervention* in the constituted historical field. It is
: to everything at stake in the operations of deconstruction the chance and the
, the power of *communication.*

But this will have been understood, as a matter of course, especially in a philo-
nical colloquium: a disseminating operation removed from the presence (of being)
:ording to all its modifications; writing, if there is any, perhaps communicates, but
;rtainly does not exist. Or barely, hereby, in the form of the most improbable sig-
ature.

(*Remark:* the—written—text of this—oral—communication was to have been addressed to the *Association of French Speaking Societies of Philosophy* before the meeting. Such a missive therefore had to be
signed. Which I did, and counterfeit here. Where?
There. J.D.)

J. DERRIDA